Praise for *CISSP® All-in-One Exam Guide*

Fernando's latest update to the *CISSP All-In-One Exam Guide* continues the tradition started in past collaborations with Shon Harris of breaking down key concepts and critical skills in a way that prepares the reader for the exam. Once again the material proves to be not only a vital asset to exam preparation but a valued resource reference for use well after the exam has been passed.

Stefanie Keuser, CISSP,
Chief Information Officer,
Military Officers Association of America

The *CISSP All-in-One Exam Guide* is the only book one needs to pass the CISSP exam. Fernando Maymí is not just an author, he is a leader in the cybersecurity industry. His insight, knowledge, and expertise is reflected in the content provided in this book. The book will not only give you what you need to pass the exam, it can also be used to help you further your career in cybersecurity.

Marc Coady, CISSP,
Compliance Analyst,
Costco Wholesale

A must-have reference for any cyber security practitioner, this book provides invaluable practical knowledge on the increasingly complex universe of security concepts, controls, and best practices necessary to do business in today's world.

Steve Zalewski,
Former Chief Information Security Officer,
Levi Strauss & Co.

Shon Harris put the CISSP certification on the map with this golden bible of the CISSP. Fernando Maymí carries that legacy forward beautifully with clarity, accuracy, and balance. I am sure that Shon would be proud.

David R. Miller, CISSP, CCSP, GIAC GISP GSEC GISF,
PCI QSA, LPT, ECSA, CEH, CWNA, CCNA, SME, MCT,
MCIT Pro EA, MCSE: Security, CNE, Security+, etc.

An excellent reference. Written clearly and concisely, this book is invaluable to students, educators, and practitioners alike.

Dr. Joe Adams,
Founder and Executive Director,
Michigan Cyber Range

A lucid, enlightening, and comprehensive tour de force through the breadth of cyber security. Maymí and Harris are masters of the craft.

Dr. Greg Conti,
Founder,
Kopidion LLC

I wish I found this book earlier in my career. It certainly was the single tool I used to pass the CISSP exam, but more importantly it has taught me about security from many aspects I did not even comprehend previously. I think the knowledge that I gained from this book is going to help me in many years to come. Terrific book and resource!

Janet Robinson,
Chief Security Officer

ALL ■ IN ■ ONE

CISSP®

EXAM GUIDE

ABOUT THE AUTHORS

Fernando Maymí, PhD, CISSP, is a security practitioner with over 25 years' experience in the field. He is currently Vice President of Training at IronNet Cybersecurity, where, besides developing cyber talent for the company, its partners, and customers, he has led teams providing strategic consultancy, security assessments, red teaming, and cybersecurity exercises around the world. Previously, he led advanced research and development projects at the intersection of artificial intelligence and cybersecurity, stood up the U.S. Army's think tank for strategic cybersecurity issues, and was a West Point faculty member for over 12 years. Fernando worked closely with Shon Harris, advising her on a multitude of projects, including the sixth edition of the *CISSP All-in-One Exam Guide*.

Shon Harris, CISSP, was the founder and CEO of Shon Harris Security LLC and Logical Security LLC, a security consultant, a former engineer in the Air Force's Information Warfare unit, an instructor, and an author. Shon owned and ran her own training and consulting companies for 13 years prior to her death in 2014. She consulted with Fortune 100 corporations and government agencies on extensive security issues. She authored three best-selling CISSP books, was a contributing author to *Gray Hat Hacking: The Ethical Hacker's Handbook* and *Security Information and Event Management (SIEM) Implementation*, and a technical editor for *Information Security Magazine*.

About the Contributor/Technical Editor

Bobby E. Rogers is an information security engineer working as a contractor for Department of Defense agencies, helping to secure, certify, and accredit their information systems. His duties include information system security engineering, risk management, and certification and accreditation efforts. He retired after 21 years in the U.S. Air Force, serving as a network security engineer and instructor, and has secured networks all over the world. Bobby has a master's degree in information assurance (IA) and is pursuing a doctoral degree in cybersecurity from Capitol Technology University in Maryland. His many certifications include CISSP-ISSEP, CEH, and MCSE: Security, as well as the CompTIA A+, Network+, Security+, and Mobility+ certifications.

ALL ■ IN ■ ONE

CISSP®

EXAM GUIDE

Ninth Edition

Fernando Maymí
Shon Harris

New York Chicago San Francisco
Athens London Madrid Mexico City
Milan New Delhi Singapore Sydney Toronto

McGraw Hill books are available at special quantity discounts to use as premiums and sales promotions, or for use in corporate training programs. To contact a representative, please visit the Contact Us pages at www.mhprofessional.com.

CISSP® All-in-One Exam Guide, Ninth Edition

3 4 5 6 7 8 9 LCR 25 24 23 22

Library of Congress Control Number: 2021945290

ISBN 978-1-260-46737-6
MHID 1-260-46737-6

Sponsoring Editor
Wendy Rinaldi

Editorial Supervisor
Janet Walden

Project Manager
Meeta Singh,
KnowledgeWorks Global Ltd.

Acquisitions Coordinator
Emily Walters

Technical Editor
Bobby E. Rogers

Copy Editor
William McManus

Proofreader
Lisa McCoy

Indexer
Ted Laux

Production Supervisor
Thomas Somers

Composition
KnowledgeWorks Global Ltd.

Illustration
KnowledgeWorks Global Ltd.

Art Director, Cover
Jeff Weeks

We dedicate this book to all those
who have served others selflessly.

CONTENTS AT A GLANCE

CONTENTS

FROM THE AUTHOR

Thank you for investing your resources in this ninth edition of the *CISSP All-in-One Exam Guide*. I am confident you'll find it helpful, not only as you prepare for the CISSP exam, but as a reference in your future professional endeavors. That was one of the overarching goals of Shon Harris when she wrote the first six editions and is something I've strived to uphold in the last three. It is not always easy, but I think you'll be pleased with how we've balanced these two requirements.

(ISC)² does a really good job of grounding the CISSP Common Body of Knowledge (CBK) in real-world applications, but (let's face it) there's always a lot of room for discussion and disagreements. There are very few topics in cybersecurity (or pretty much any other field) on which there is universal agreement. To balance the content of this book between exam preparation and the murkiness of real-world applications, we've included plenty of comments and examples drawn from our experiences.

I say "our experiences" deliberately because the voice of Shon remains vibrant, informative, and entertaining in this edition, years after her passing. I've preserved as many of her insights as possible while ensuring the content is up to date and relevant. I also strove to maintain the conversational tone that was such a hallmark of her work. The result is a book that (I hope) reads more like an essay (or even a story) than a textbook but is grounded in good pedagogy. It should be easy to read but still prepare you for the exam.

Speaking of the exam, the changes that (ISC)² made to the CBK in 2021 are not dramatic but are still significant. Each domain was tweaked in some way, and seven of the eight domains had multiple topics added (domain 1 was the exception here). These changes, coupled with the number of topics that were growing stale in the eighth edition of this book, prompted me to completely restructure this edition. I tore each domain and topic down to atomic particles and then re-engineered the entire book to integrate the new objectives, which are listed in Table 1.

Domain 2: Asset Security	
2.4	Manage data lifecycle
2.4.1	Data roles (i.e., owners, controllers, custodians, processors, users/subjects)
2.4.3	Data location
2.4.4	Data maintenance
2.5	Ensure appropriate asset retention (e.g., End-of-Life (EOL), End-of-Support (EOS))
Domain 3: Security Architecture and Engineering	
(Under 3.7 Understand methods of cryptanalytic attacks)	
3.7.1	Brute force
3.7.4	Frequency analysis

Table 1 CBK 2021: New Objectives (*continued*)

Domain 3: Security Architecture and Engineering	
3.7.6	Implementation attacks
3.7.8	Fault injection
3.7.9	Timing
3.7.10	Man-in-the-Middle (MITM)
3.7.11	Pass the hash
3.7.12	Kerberos exploitation
3.7.13	Ransomware
(Under 3.9 Design site and facility security controls)	
3.9.9	Power (e.g., redundant, backup)
Domain 4: Communication and Network Security	
(Under 4.1 Assess and implement secure design principles in network architectures)	
4.1.3	Secure protocols
4.1.6	Micro-segmentation (e.g., Software Defined Networks (SDN), Virtual eXtensible Local Area Network (VXLAN), Encapsulation, Software-Defined Wide Area Network (SD-WAN))
4.1.8	Cellular networks (e.g., 4G, 5G)
(Under 4.3 Implement secure communication channels according to design)	
4.3.6	Third-party connectivity
Domain 5: Identity and Access Management (IAM)	
(Under 5.1 Control physical and logical access to assets)	
5.1.5	Applications
(Under 5.2 Manage identification and authentication of people, devices, and services)	
5.2.8	Single Sign On (SSO)
5.2.9	Just-In-Time (JIT)
(Under 5.4 Implement and manage authorization mechanisms)	
5.4.6	Risk based access control
(Under 5.5 Manage the identity and access provisioning lifecycle)	
5.5.3	Role definition (e.g., people assigned to new roles)
5.5.4	Privilege escalation (e.g., managed service accounts, use of sudo, minimizing its use)
5.6	Implement authentication systems
5.6.1	OpenID Connect (OIDC)/Open Authorization (OAuth)
5.6.2	Security Assertion Markup Language (SAML)
5.6.3	Kerberos
5.6.4	Remote Authentication Dial-In User Service (RADIUS)/Terminal Access Controller Access Control System Plus (TACACS+)
Domain 6: Security Assessment and Testing	
(Under 6.2 Conduct security control testing)	
6.2.9	Breach attack simulations
6.2.10	Compliance checks

Table 1 CBK 2021: New Objectives

Domain 6: Security Assessment and Testing	
(Under 6.3 Collect security process data (e.g., technical and administrative))	
6.3.6	Disaster Recovery (DR) and Business Continuity (BC)
(Under 6.4 Analyze test output and generate report)	
6.4.1	Remediation
6.4.2	Exception handling
6.4.3	Ethical disclosure
Domain 7: Security Operations	
(Under 7.1 Understand and comply with investigations)	
7.1.5	Artifacts (e.g., computer, network, mobile device)
(Under 7.2 Conduct logging and monitoring activities)	
7.2.5	Log management
7.2.6	Threat intelligence (e.g., threat feeds, threat hunting)
7.2.7	User and Entity Behavior Analytics (UEBA)
(Under 7.7 Operate and maintain detective and preventative measures)	
7.7.8	Machine learning and Artificial Intelligence (AI) based tools
(Under 7.11 Implement Disaster Recovery (DR) processes)	
7.11.7	Lessons learned
Domain 8: Software Development Security	
(Under 8.2 Identify and apply security controls in software development ecosystems)	
8.2.1	Programming languages
8.2.2	Libraries
8.2.3	Tool sets
8.2.5	Runtime
8.2.6	Continuous Integration and Continuous Delivery (CI/CD)
8.2.7	Security Orchestration, Automation, and Response (SOAR)
8.2.10	Application security testing (e.g., Static Application Security Testing (SAST), Dynamic Application Security Testing (DAST))
(Under 8.4 Assess security impact of acquired software)	
8.4.1	Commercial-off-the-shelf (COTS)
8.4.2	Open source
8.4.3	Third-party
8.4.4	Managed services (e.g., Software as a Service (SaaS), Infrastructure as a Service (IaaS), Platform as a Service (PaaS))
(Under 8.5 Define and apply secure coding guidelines and standards)	
8.5.4	Software-defined security

Table 1 CBK 2021: New Objectives (*continued*)

Note that some of these objectives were implicit in the previous (2018) version of the CBK and were therefore covered in the eighth edition of this book. The fact that they are now explicit is an indication of their increased importance both in the exam and in the real world. (Please pay particular attention to these as you prepare for the exam.) All in all, this ninth edition is significantly different (and improved) when compared to the previous one. I think you'll agree. Thank you, again, for investing in this ninth edition.

ACKNOWLEDGMENTS

I would like to thank all the people who work in the information security industry who are driven by their passion, dedication, and a true sense of doing right. These selfless professionals sacrifice their personal time to prevent, block, and respond to the relentless efforts of malicious actors around the world. We all sleep more peacefully at night because you remain at the ready.

In this ninth edition, I would also like to thank the following:

- Ronald C. Dodge, Jr., who introduced me to Shon Harris and, in so doing, started me off on one of the best adventures of my life
- Kathy Conlon, who, more than anyone else, set the conditions that led to nine editions of this book
- Carol Remicci
- David Harris
- The men and women of our armed forces, who selflessly defend our way of life

WHY BECOME A CISSP?

As our world changes, the need for improvements in security and technology continues to grow. Organizations around the globe are desperate to identify and recruit talented and experienced security professionals to help protect their assets and remain competitive. As a Certified Information Systems Security Professional (CISSP), you will be seen as a security professional of proven ability who has successfully met a predefined standard of knowledge and experience that is well understood and respected throughout the industry. By keeping this certification current, you will demonstrate your dedication to staying abreast of security developments.

Consider some of the reasons for attaining a CISSP certification:

- To broaden your current knowledge of security concepts and practices
- To demonstrate your expertise as a seasoned security professional
- To become more marketable in a competitive workforce
- To increase your salary and be eligible for more employment opportunities
- To bring improved security expertise to your current occupation
- To show a dedication to the security discipline

The CISSP certification helps organizations identify which individuals have the ability, knowledge, and experience necessary to implement solid security practices; perform risk analysis; identify necessary countermeasures; and help the organization as a whole protect its facility, network, systems, and information. The CISSP certification also shows potential employers you have achieved a level of proficiency and expertise in skill sets and knowledge required by the security industry. The increasing importance placed on security by organizations of all sizes will only continue in the future, leading to even greater demands for highly skilled security professionals. The CISSP certification shows that a respected third-party organization has recognized an individual's technical and theoretical knowledge and expertise, and distinguishes that individual from those who lack this level of knowledge.

Understanding and implementing security practices is an essential part of being a good network administrator, programmer, or engineer. Job descriptions that do not specifically target security professionals still often require that a potential candidate have a good understanding of security concepts and how to implement them. Due to staff size and budget restraints, many organizations can't afford separate network and security staffs. But they still believe security is vital to their organization. Thus, they often try to combine knowledge of technology and security into a single role. With a CISSP designation, you can put yourself head and shoulders above other individuals in this regard.

The CISSP Exam

Because the CISSP exam covers the eight domains making up the CISSP CBK, it is often described as being "an inch deep and a mile wide," a reference to the fact that many questions on the exam are not very detailed and do not require you to be an expert in every subject. However, the questions do require you to be familiar with many *different* security subjects.

The CISSP exam comes in two versions depending on the language in which the test is written. The English version uses Computerized Adaptive Testing (CAT) in which the number of questions you are asked depends on your measured level of knowledge but ranges from 100 to 150. Of these, 25 questions will not count toward your score, as they are being evaluated for inclusion in future exams (this is why they are sometimes called pre-test questions). Essentially, the easier it is for the test software to determine your level of proficiency, the fewer questions you'll get. Regardless of how many questions you are presented, though, you will have no more than three hours to complete the test. When the system has successfully assessed your level of knowledge, the test will end regardless of how long you've been at it.

EXAM TIP CAT questions are intentionally designed to "feel" hard (based on the system's estimate of your knowledge), so don't be discouraged. Just don't get bogged down because you must answer at least 100 questions in three hours.

The non-English version of the CISSP exam is also computer-based but is linear, fixed-form (not adaptive) and comprises 250 questions, which must be answered in no more than six hours. Like the CAT version, 25 questions are pre-test (unscored), so you will be graded on the other 225 questions. The 25 research questions are integrated into the exam, so you won't know which go toward your final grade.

Regardless of which version of the exam you take, you need a score of 700 points out of a possible 1,000. In both versions, you can expect multiple choice and innovative questions. Innovative questions incorporate drag-and-drop (i.e., take a term or item and drag it to the correct position in the frame) or hotspot (i.e., click the item or term that correctly answers the question) interfaces, but are otherwise weighed and scored just like any other question. The questions are pulled from a much larger question bank to ensure the exam is as unique as possible for each examinee. In addition, the test bank constantly changes and evolves to more accurately reflect the real world of security. The exam questions are continually rotated and replaced in the bank as necessary. Questions are weighted based on their difficulty; not all questions are worth the same number of points. The exam is not product or vendor oriented, meaning no questions will be specific to certain products or vendors (for instance, Windows, Unix, or Cisco). Instead, you will be tested on the security models and methodologies used by these types of systems.

EXAM TIP There is no penalty for guessing. If you can't come up with the right answer in a reasonable amount of time, then you should guess and move on to the next question.

(ISC)², which stands for International Information Systems Security Certification Consortium, also includes scenario-based questions in the CISSP exam. These questions present a short scenario to the test taker rather than asking the test taker to identify terms and/or concepts. The goal of the scenario-based questions is to ensure that test takers not only know and understand the concepts within the CBK but also can apply this knowledge to real-life situations. This is more practical because in the real world you won't be challenged by having someone asking you, "What is the definition of collusion?" You need to know how to detect and prevent collusion from taking place, in addition to knowing the definition of the term.

After passing the exam, you will be asked to supply documentation, supported by a sponsor, proving that you indeed have the type of experience required to obtain CISSP certification. The sponsor must sign a document vouching for the security experience you are submitting. So, make sure you have this sponsor lined up prior to registering for the exam and providing payment. You don't want to pay for and pass the exam, only to find you can't find a sponsor for the final step needed to achieve your certification.

The reason behind the sponsorship requirement is to ensure that those who achieve the certification have real-world experience to offer organizations. Book knowledge is extremely important for understanding theory, concepts, standards, and regulations, but it can never replace hands-on experience. Proving your practical experience supports the relevance of the certification.

A small sample group of individuals selected at random will be audited after passing the exam. The audit consists mainly of individuals from (ISC)^2 calling on the candidates' sponsors and contacts to verify the test taker's related experience.

One of the factors that makes the CISSP exam challenging is that most candidates, although they work in the security field, are not necessarily familiar with all eight CBK domains. If a security professional is considered an expert in vulnerability testing or application security, for example, she may not be familiar with physical security, cryptography, or forensics. Thus, studying for this exam will broaden your knowledge of the security field.

The exam questions address the eight CBK security domains, which are described in Table 2.

Domain	Description
Security and Risk Management	This domain covers many of the foundational concepts of information systems security. Some of the topics covered include • Professional ethics • Security governance and compliance • Legal and regulatory issues • Personnel security policies • Risk management
Asset Security	This domain examines the protection of assets throughout their life cycle. Some of the topics covered include • Identifying and classifying information and assets • Establishing information and asset handling requirements • Provisioning resources securely • Managing the data life cycle • Determining data security controls and compliance requirements

Table 2 Security Domains that Make Up the CISSP CBK (*continued*)

Domain	Description
Security Architecture and Engineering	This domain examines the development of information systems that remain secure in the face of a myriad of threats. Some of the topics covered include • Secure design principles • Security models • Selection of effective controls • Cryptography • Physical security
Communication and Network Security	This domain examines network architectures, communications technologies, and network protocols with the goal of understanding how to secure them. Some of the topics covered include • Secure network architectures • Secure network components • Secure communications channels
Identity and Access Management (IAM)	Identity and access management is one of the most important topics in information security. This domain covers the interactions between users and systems as well as between systems and other systems. Some of the topics covered include • Controlling physical and logical access to assets • Identification and authentication • Authorization mechanisms • Identity and access provisioning life cycle • Implementing authentication systems
Security Assessment and Testing	This domain examines ways to verify the security of our information systems. Some of the topics covered include • Assessment and testing strategies • Testing security controls • Collecting security process data • Analyzing and reporting results • Conducting and facilitating audits
Security Operations	This domain covers the many activities involved in the daily business of maintaining the security of our networks. Some of the topics covered include • Investigations • Logging and monitoring • Change and configuration management • Incident management • Disaster recovery
Software Development Security	This domain examines the application of security principles to the acquisition and development of software systems. Some of the topics covered include • The software development life cycle • Security controls in software development • Assessing software security • Assessing the security implications of acquired software • Secure coding guidelines and standards

Table 2 Security Domains that Make Up the CISSP CBK (*continued*)

What Does This Book Cover?

This book covers everything you need to know to become an (ISC)²-certified CISSP. It teaches you the hows and whys behind organizations' development and implementation of policies, procedures, guidelines, and standards. It covers network, application, and system vulnerabilities; what exploits them; and how to counter these threats. This book explains physical security, operational security, and why systems implement the security mechanisms they do. It also reviews the U.S. and international security criteria and evaluations performed on systems for assurance ratings, what these criteria mean, and why they are used. This book also explains the legal and liability issues that surround computer systems and the data they hold, including such subjects as computer crimes, forensics, and what should be done to properly prepare computer evidence associated with these topics for court.

While this book is mainly intended to be used as a study guide for the CISSP exam, it is also a handy reference guide for use after your certification.

Tips for Taking the CISSP Exam

Many people feel as though the exam questions are tricky. Make sure to read each question and its answer choices thoroughly instead of reading a few words and immediately assuming you know what the question is asking. Some of the answer choices may have only subtle differences, so be patient and devote time to reading through the question more than once.

A common complaint heard about the CISSP exam is that some questions seem a bit subjective. For example, whereas it might be easy to answer a technical question that asks for the exact mechanism used in Transport Layer Security (TLS) that protects against man-in-the-middle attacks, it's not quite as easy to answer a question that asks whether an eight-foot perimeter fence provides low, medium, or high security. Many questions ask the test taker to choose the "best" approach, which some people find confusing and subjective. These complaints are mentioned here not to criticize (ISC)² and the exam writers, but to help you better prepare for the exam. This book covers all the necessary material for the exam and contains many questions and self-practice tests. Most of the questions are formatted in such a way as to better prepare you for what you will encounter on the actual exam. So, make sure to read all the material in the book, and pay close attention to the questions and their formats. Even if you know the subject well, you may still get some answers wrong—it is just part of learning how to take tests.

In answering many questions, it is important to keep in mind that some things are inherently more valuable than others. For example, the protection of human lives and welfare will almost always trump all other responses. Similarly, if all other factors are equal and you are given a choice between an expensive and complex solution and a simpler and cheaper one, the second will win most of the time. Expert advice (e.g., from an attorney) is more valuable than that offered by someone with lesser credentials. If one of the possible responses to a question is to seek or obtain advice from an expert, pay close attention to that question. The correct response may very well be to seek out that expert.

Familiarize yourself with industry standards and expand your technical knowledge and methodologies outside the boundaries of what you use today. We cannot stress enough that being the "top dog" in your particular field doesn't mean you are properly prepared for all eight domains the exam covers.

When you take the CISSP exam at the Pearson VUE test center, other certification exams may be taking place simultaneously in the same room. Don't feel rushed if you see others leaving the room early; they may be taking a shorter exam.

How to Use This Book

Much effort has gone into putting all the necessary information into this book. Now it's up to you to study and understand the material and its various concepts. To best benefit from this book, you might want to use the following study method:

- Study each chapter carefully and make sure you understand each concept presented. Many concepts must be fully understood, and glossing over a couple here and there could be detrimental to your success on the exam. The CISSP CBK contains hundreds of individual topics, so take the time needed to understand them all.
- Make sure to study and answer all of the questions. If any questions confuse you, go back and study the corresponding sections again. Remember, you will encounter questions on the actual exam that do not seem straightforward. Do not ignore the confusing questions, thinking they're not well worded. Instead, pay even closer attention to them because they are included for a reason.
- If you are not familiar with specific topics, such as firewalls, laws, physical security, or protocol functionality, use other sources of information (books, articles, and so on) to attain a more in-depth understanding of those subjects. Don't just rely solely on what you think you need to know to pass the CISSP exam.
- After reading this book, study the questions and answers, and take the practice tests. Then review the (ISC)^2 exam objectives and make sure you are comfortable with each bullet item presented. If you are not comfortable with some items, revisit the chapters in which they are covered.
- If you have taken other certification exams—such as Cisco or Microsoft—you might be used to having to memorize details and configuration parameters. But remember, the CISSP test is "an inch deep and a mile wide," so make sure you understand the concepts of each subject *before* trying to memorize the small, specific details.
- Remember that the exam is looking for the "best" answer. On some questions test takers do not agree with any or many of the answers. You are being asked to choose the best answer out of the four being offered to you.

PART I

Security and Risk Management

CHAPTER 1

Cybersecurity Governance

This chapter presents the following:

- Fundamental cybersecurity concepts
- Security governance principles
- Security policies, standards, procedures, and guidelines
- Personnel security policies and procedures
- Security awareness, education, and training

The only truly secure system is one that is powered off, cast in a block of concrete and sealed in a lead-lined room with armed guards—and even then I have my doubts.

—Eugene H. Spafford

While some of us may revel in thinking about and implementing cybersecurity, the fact is that most organizations would much rather focus on many other things. Businesses exist to generate profits for their shareholders. Most nonprofit organizations are dedicated to furthering particular social causes such as charity, education, or religion. Apart from security service providers, organizations don't exist specifically to deploy and maintain firewalls, intrusion detection systems, identity management technologies, and encryption devices. No corporation really wants to develop hundreds of security policies, deploy antimalware products, maintain vulnerability management systems, constantly update its incident response capabilities, and have to comply with the myriad of security laws, regulations, and standards that exist worldwide. Business owners would like to be able to make their widgets, sell their widgets, and go home with a nice profit in their pockets. But things are not that simple.

Organizations are increasingly faced with attackers who want to steal customer data to carry out identity theft and banking fraud. Company secrets are commonly being stolen by internal and external entities for economic espionage purposes. Systems are being hijacked and used within botnets to attack other organizations, mine cryptocurrencies, or spread spam. Company funds are being secretly siphoned off through complex and hard-to-identify digital methods, commonly by organized criminal rings in different countries. And organizations that find themselves in the crosshairs of attackers may come under constant attack that brings their systems and websites offline for hours or days. Companies are required to practice a wide range of security disciplines today to keep their market share, protect their customers and bottom line, stay out of jail, and still sell their widgets.

As we start our exploration of the Certified Information Systems Security Professional (CISSP) Common Body of Knowledge (CBK) in this chapter, we will define what cybersecurity means and how it must be governed by, well, CISSPs. Each organization must develop an enterprise-wide security program that consists of technologies, procedures, and processes covered throughout this book. As you go along in your security career, you will find that most organizations have some (but rarely all) pieces to the puzzle of an "enterprise-wide security program" in place. Many of the security programs in place today can be thought of as lopsided or lumpy. The security programs excel within the disciplines that the team is most familiar with, and the other disciplines are found lacking. It is your responsibility to become as well rounded in security as possible so that you can identify these deficiencies in security programs and help improve upon them. This is why the CISSP exam covers a wide variety of technologies, methodologies, and processes—you must know and understand them holistically if you are going to help an organization carry out security holistically.

Fundamental Cybersecurity Concepts and Terms

As cybersecurity professionals, our efforts are ultimately focused on the protection of our information systems. These systems consist of people, processes, and technologies designed to operate on information. To protect them means to ensure the confidentiality, integrity, and availability (the CIA triad) of all assets in our information systems as well as the authenticity and nonrepudiation of tasks performed in them. Each asset will require different levels of these types of protection, as we will see in the following sections.

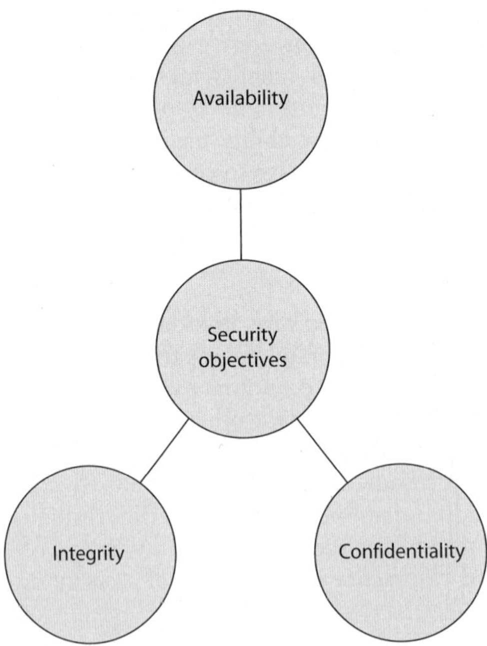

Confidentiality

Confidentiality means keeping unauthorized entities (be they people or processes) from gaining access to information assets. It ensures that the necessary level of secrecy is enforced at each junction of data processing and prevents unauthorized disclosure. This level of secrecy should prevail while data resides on systems and devices within the network, as it is transmitted, and once it reaches its destination. Confidentiality can be provided by encrypting data as it is stored and transmitted, by enforcing strict access control and data classification, and by training personnel on the proper data protection procedures.

Attackers can thwart confidentiality mechanisms by network monitoring, shoulder surfing, stealing credentials, breaking encryption schemes, and social engineering. These topics will be addressed in more depth in later chapters, but briefly, *shoulder surfing* is when a person looks over another person's shoulder and watches their keystrokes or views data as it appears on a computer screen. *Social engineering* is when one person tricks another person into sharing confidential information, for example, by posing as someone authorized to have access to that information. Social engineering can take many forms. Any one-to-one communication medium can be used to perform social engineering attacks.

Users can intentionally or accidentally disclose sensitive information by not encrypting it before sending it to another person, by falling prey to a social engineering attack, by sharing a company's trade secrets, or by not using extra care to protect confidential information when processing it.

Integrity

Integrity means that an asset is free from unauthorized alterations. Only authorized entities should be able to modify an asset, and only in specific authorized ways. For example, if you are reviewing orders placed by customers on your online store, you should not be able to increase the price of any items in those orders after they have been purchased. It is your store, so you can clearly change prices as you wish. You just shouldn't be able to do it after someone agrees to buy an item at a certain price and gives you authorization to charge their credit card.

Environments that enforce and provide this attribute of security ensure that attackers, or mistakes by users, do not compromise the integrity of systems or data. When an attacker inserts malware or a back door into a system, the system's integrity is compromised. This can, in turn, harm the integrity of information held on the system by way of corruption, malicious modification, or the replacement of data with incorrect data. Strict access controls, intrusion detection, and hashing can combat these threats.

Authorized users can also affect a system or its data's integrity by mistake (although internal users may also commit malicious deeds). For example, a user with a full hard drive may unwittingly delete a configuration file under the mistaken assumption that deleting a file must be okay because the user doesn't remember ever using it. Or a user may insert incorrect values into a data-processing application that ends up charging a customer $3,000 instead of $300. Incorrectly modifying data kept in databases is another common way users may accidentally corrupt data—a mistake that can have lasting effects.

Security should streamline users' capabilities and give them only certain choices and functionality, so errors become less common and less devastating. System-critical files should be restricted from viewing and access by users. Applications should provide mechanisms that check for valid and reasonable input values. Databases should let only authorized individuals modify data, and data in transit should be protected by encryption or other mechanisms.

Availability

Availability protection ensures reliable and timely access to data and resources to authorized individuals. Network devices, computers, and applications should provide adequate functionality to perform in a predictable manner with an acceptable level of performance. They should be able to recover from disruptions in a secure and quick fashion, so productivity is not negatively affected. Necessary protection mechanisms must be in place to protect against inside and outside threats that could affect the availability and productivity of all business-processing components.

Like many things in life, ensuring the availability of the necessary resources within an organization sounds easier to accomplish than it really is. Networks have many pieces that must stay up and running (routers, switches, proxies, firewalls, and so on). Software has many components that must be executing in a healthy manner (operating system, applications, antimalware software, and so forth). And an organization's operations can potentially be negatively affected by environmental aspects (such as fire, flood, HVAC issues, or electrical problems), natural disasters, and physical theft or attacks. An organization must fully understand its operational environment and its availability weaknesses so that it can put in place the proper countermeasures.

Authenticity

One of the curious features of the modern Internet is that sometimes we are unsure of who is putting out the things we read and download. Does that patch really come from Microsoft? Did your boss really send you that e-mail asking you to buy $10,000 worth of gift cards? *Authenticity* protections ensure we can trust that something comes from its claimed source. This concept is at the heart of authentication, which establishes that an entity trying to log into a system is really who it claims to be.

Authenticity in information systems is almost always provided through cryptographic means. As an example, when you connect to your bank's website, the connection should be encrypted using Transport Layer Security (TLS), which in turn uses your bank's digital certificate to authenticate to your browser that it truly is that bank on the other end and not an impostor. When you log in, the bank takes a cryptographic hash of the credentials you provide and compares them to the hash the bank has in your records to ensure it really is you on the other end.

Nonrepudiation

While authenticity establishes that an entity is who it claims to be at a particular point in time, it doesn't really provide historical proof of what that entity did or agreed to. For example, suppose Bob logs into his bank and then applies for a loan. He doesn't read the fine print until later, at which point he decides he doesn't like the terms of the transaction, so he calls up the bank to say he never signed the contract and to please make it go away. Although the session was authenticated, Bob could claim that he walked away from his computer while logged into the bank's website, that his cat walked over the keyboard and stepped on ENTER, executing the transaction, and that Bob never intended to sign the loan application. It was the cat. Sadly, his claim could hold up in court.

Nonrepudiation, which is closely related to authenticity, means that someone cannot disavow being the source of a given action. For example, suppose Bob's bank had implemented a procedure for loan applications that required him to "sign" the application by entering his personal identification number (PIN). Now the whole cat defense falls apart unless Bob could prove he trained his cat to enter PINs.

Most commonly, nonrepudiation is provided through the use of digital signatures. Just like your physical signature on a piece of paper certifies that you either authored it or agree to whatever is written on it (e.g., a contract), the digital version attests to your sending an e-mail, writing software, or agreeing to a contract. We'll discuss digital signatures later in this book, but for now it will be helpful to remember that they are cryptographic products that, just like an old-fashioned physical signature, can be used for a variety of purposes.

EXAM TIP A good way to differentiate authenticity and nonrepudiation is that authenticity proves to *you* that you're talking to a given person at a given point in time. Nonrepudiation proves to *anyone* that a given person did or said something in the past.

Balanced Security

In reality, when information security is considered, it is commonly only through the lens of keeping secrets secret (confidentiality). The integrity and availability threats tend to be overlooked and only dealt with after they are properly compromised. Some assets have a critical confidentiality requirement (e.g., company trade secrets), some have critical integrity requirements (e.g., financial transaction values), and some have critical availability requirements (e.g., e-commerce web servers). Many people understand the concepts of the CIA triad, but may not fully appreciate the complexity of implementing the necessary controls to provide all the protection these concepts cover. The following provides a *short* list of some of these controls and how they map to the components of the CIA triad.

Availability:

- Redundant array of independent disks (RAID)
- Clustering
- Load balancing
- Redundant data and power lines
- Software and data backups

- Disk shadowing
- Co-location and offsite facilities
- Rollback functions
- Failover configurations

Integrity:

- Hashing (data integrity)
- Configuration management (system integrity)
- Change control (process integrity)
- Access control (physical and technical)
- Software digital signing
- Transmission cyclic redundancy check (CRC) functions

Confidentiality:

- Encryption for data at rest (whole disk, database encryption)
- Encryption for data in transit (IPSec, TLS, PPTP, SSH, described in Chapter 4)
- Access control (physical and technical)

All of these control types will be covered in this book. What is important to realize at this point is that while the concept of the CIA triad may seem simplistic, meeting its requirements is commonly more challenging.

Other Security Terms

The words "vulnerability," "threat," "risk," and "exposure" are often interchanged, even though they have different meanings. It is important to understand each word's definition and the relationships between the concepts they represent.

A *vulnerability* is a weakness in a system that allows a threat source to compromise its security. It can be a software, hardware, procedural, or human weakness that can be exploited. A vulnerability may be a service running on a server, unpatched applications or operating systems, an unrestricted wireless access point, an open port on a firewall, lax physical security that allows anyone to enter a server room, or unenforced password management on servers and workstations.

A *threat* is any potential danger that is associated with the exploitation of a vulnerability. If the threat is that someone will identify a specific vulnerability and use it against the organization or individual, then the entity that takes advantage of a vulnerability is referred to as a *threat agent* (or *threat actor*). A threat agent could be an intruder accessing the network through a port on the firewall, a process accessing data in a way that violates the security policy, or an employee circumventing controls in order to copy files to a medium that could expose confidential information.

A *risk* is the likelihood of a threat source exploiting a vulnerability and the corresponding business impact. If a firewall has several ports open, there is a higher likelihood that an intruder will use one to access the network in an unauthorized method. If users are not educated on processes and procedures, there is a higher likelihood that an employee will make an unintentional mistake that may destroy data. If an intrusion detection system (IDS) is not implemented on a network, there is a higher likelihood an attack will go unnoticed until it is too late. Risk ties the vulnerability, threat, and likelihood of exploitation to the resulting business impact.

An *exposure* is an instance of being exposed to losses. A vulnerability exposes an organization to possible damages. If password management is lax and password rules are not enforced, the organization is exposed to the possibility of having users' passwords compromised and used in an unauthorized manner. If an organization does not have its wiring inspected and does not put proactive fire prevention steps into place, it exposes itself to potentially devastating fires.

A *control*, or *countermeasure*, is put into place to mitigate (reduce) the potential risk. A countermeasure may be a software configuration, a hardware device, or a procedure that eliminates a vulnerability or that reduces the likelihood a threat agent will be able to exploit a vulnerability. Examples of countermeasures include strong password management, firewalls, a security guard, access control mechanisms, encryption, and security awareness training.

NOTE The terms "control," "countermeasure," and "safeguard" are interchangeable terms. They are mechanisms put into place to reduce risk.

If an organization has antimalware software but does not keep the signatures up to date, this is a vulnerability. The organization is vulnerable to more recent malware attacks. The threat is that a threat agent will insert malware into the environment and disrupt productivity. The risk is the likelihood of a threat agent using malware in the environment and the resulting potential damage. If this happens, then a vulnerability has been exploited and the organization is exposed to loss. The countermeasures in this situation are to update the signatures and install the antimalware software on all computers. The relationships among risks, vulnerabilities, threats, and countermeasures are shown in Figure 1-1.

Applying the right countermeasure can eliminate the vulnerability and exposure, and thus reduce the risk. The organization cannot eliminate the threat agent, but it can protect itself and prevent this threat agent from exploiting vulnerabilities within the environment.

Many people gloss over these basic terms with the idea that they are not as important as the sexier things in information security. But you will find that unless a security team has an agreed-upon language in place, confusion will quickly take over. These terms embrace the core concepts of security, and if they are confused in any manner, then the activities that are rolled out to enforce security are commonly confused.

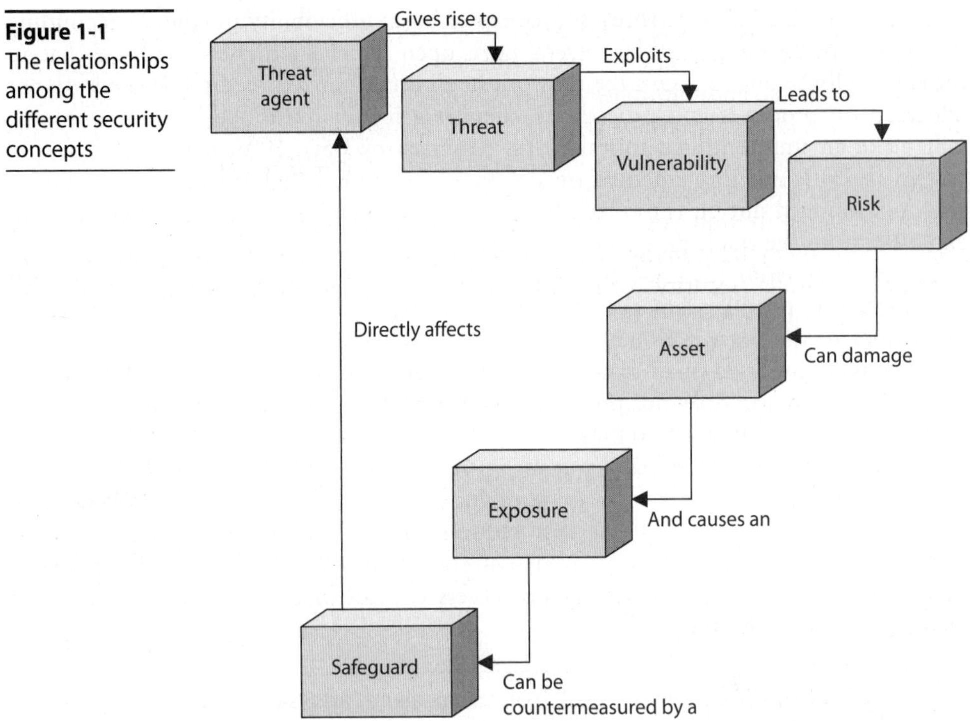

Figure 1-1 The relationships among the different security concepts

Security Governance Principles

Now that we have established a shared vocabulary for the fundamental cybersecurity concepts and understand how they relate to each other, let's turn our attention to how we can prioritize, assess, and continuously improve the security of our organizations. This is where security governance comes into play. *Security governance* is a framework that supports the security goals of an organization being set and expressed by senior management, communicated throughout the different levels of the organization, and consistently applied and assessed. Security governance grants power to the entities who need to implement and enforce security and provides a way to verify the performance of these necessary security activities. Senior management not only needs to set the direction of security but also needs a way to be able to view and understand how their directives are being met or not being met.

If a board of directors and CEO demand that security be integrated properly at all levels of the organization, how do they know it is really happening? Oversight mechanisms must be developed and integrated so that the people who are ultimately responsible for an organization are constantly and consistently updated on the overall health and security posture of the organization. This happens through properly defined communication channels, standardized reporting methods, and performance-based metrics.

Let's compare two companies. Company A has an effective security governance program in place and Company B does not. Now, to the untrained eye it would seem as though Companies A and B are equal in their security practices because they both have security policies, procedures, and standards in place, the same security technology controls (firewalls, endpoint detection, identity management, and so on), defined security roles, and security awareness training. You may think, "These two companies are on the ball and quite evolved in their security programs." But if you look closer, you will see some critical differences (listed in Table 1-1).

Does the organization you work for look like Company A or Company B? Most organizations today have many of the pieces and parts to a security program (policies, standards, firewalls, security team, IDS, and so on), but management may not be

Company A	Company B
Board members understand that information security is critical to the company and demand to be updated quarterly on security performance and breaches.	Board members do not understand that information security is in their realm of responsibility and focus solely on corporate governance and profits.
The chief executive officer (CEO), chief financial officer (CFO), chief information officer (CIO), chief information security officer (CISO), and business unit managers participate in a risk management committee that meets each month, and information security is always one topic on the agenda to review.	The CEO, CFO, and business unit managers feel as though information security is the responsibility of the CIO, CISO, and IT department and do not get involved.
Executive management sets an acceptable risk level that is the basis for the company's security policies and all security activities.	The CISO copied some boilerplate security policies, inserted his company's name, and had the CEO sign them.
Executive management holds business unit managers responsible for carrying out risk management activities for their specific business units.	All security activity takes place within the security department; thus, security works within a silo and is not integrated throughout the organization.
Critical business processes are documented along with the risks that are inherent at the different steps within the business processes.	Business processes are not documented and not analyzed for potential risks that can affect operations, productivity, and profitability.
Employees are held accountable for any security breaches they participate in, either maliciously or accidentally.	Policies and standards are developed, but no enforcement or accountability practices have been envisioned or deployed.
Security products, managed services, and consulting services are purchased and deployed in an informed manner. They are also constantly reviewed to ensure they are cost-effective.	Security products, managed services, and consulting services are purchased and deployed without any real research or performance metrics to determine the return on investment or effectiveness.
The organization is continuing to review its processes, including security, with the goal of continued improvement.	The organization does not analyze its performance for improvement, but continually marches forward and makes similar mistakes over and over again.

Table 1-1 Security Governance Program: A Comparison of Two Companies

truly involved, and security has not permeated throughout the organization. Some organizations rely just on technology and isolate all security responsibilities within the IT group. If security were just a technology issue, then this security team could properly install, configure, and maintain the products, and the company would get a gold star and pass the audit with flying colors. But that is not how information security works. It is much more than just technological solutions. Security must be driven throughout the organization, and having several points of responsibility and accountability is critical.

At this point, you may be asking, "So, what does security governance actually look like in the real world?" Security governance is typically implemented as a formal cybersecurity program or an information security management system (ISMS). Whichever of these names you call it, it is a collection of policies, procedures, baselines, and standards that an organization puts in place to make sure that its security efforts are aligned with business needs, streamlined, and effective, and that no security controls are missing. Figure 1-2 illustrates many of the elements that go into a complete security program.

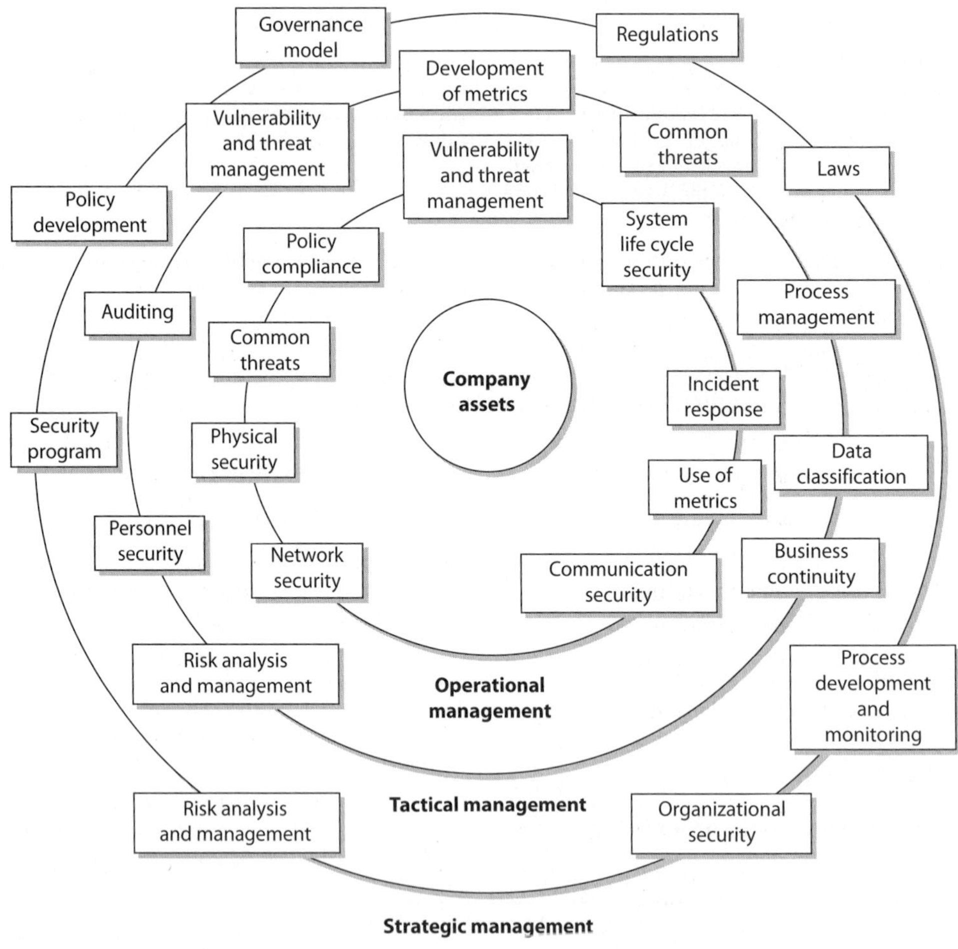

Figure 1-2 A complete security program contains many items.

Aligning Security to Business Strategy

An *enterprise security architecture* is a subset of an enterprise architecture (discussed in depth in Chapter 4) and implements an information security strategy. It consists of layers of solutions, processes, and procedures and the way they are linked across an enterprise strategically, tactically, and operationally. It is a comprehensive and rigorous method for describing the structure and behavior of all the components that make up a holistic ISMS. The main reason to develop an enterprise security architecture is to ensure that security efforts align with business practices in a standardized and cost-effective manner. The architecture works at an abstraction level and provides a frame of reference. Besides security, this type of architecture allows organizations to better achieve interoperability, integration, ease of use, standardization, and governance.

How do you know if an organization does not have an enterprise security architecture in place? If the answer is "yes" to most of the following questions, this type of architecture is not in place:

- Does security take place in silos throughout the organization?
- Is there a continual disconnect between senior management and the security staff?
- Are redundant products purchased for different departments for overlapping security needs?
- Is the security program made up of mainly policies without actual implementation and enforcement?
- When a user's access requirements increase because of business needs, does the network administrator just modify the access controls without the user manager's documented approval?
- When a new product is being rolled out, do unexpected interoperability issues pop up that require more time and money to fix?
- Do many "one-off" efforts take place instead of following standardized procedures when security issues arise?
- Are the business unit managers unaware of their security responsibilities and how their responsibilities map to legal and regulatory requirements?
- Is "sensitive data" defined in a policy, but the necessary controls are not fully implemented and monitored?
- Are stovepipe (point) solutions implemented instead of enterprise-wide solutions?
- Are the same expensive mistakes continuing to take place?
- Is security governance currently unavailable because the enterprise is not viewed or monitored in a standardized and holistic manner?
- Are business decisions being made without taking security into account?
- Are security personnel usually putting out fires with no real time to look at and develop strategic approaches?
- Are some business units engaged in security efforts that other business units know nothing about?

If many of these answers are "yes," no useful architecture is in place. Now, the following is something very interesting the authors have seen over several years. Most organizations have multiple problems in the preceding list and yet they focus on each item as if it is unconnected to the other problems. What the CSO, CISO, and/or security administrator does not always understand is that these are just *symptoms* of a treatable disease. The "treatment" is to put one person in charge of a team that develops a phased-approach enterprise security architecture rollout plan. The goals are to integrate technology-oriented and business-centric security processes; link administrative, technical, and physical controls to properly manage risk; and integrate these processes into the IT infrastructure, business processes, and the organization's culture.

A helpful tool for aligning an organization's security architecture with its business strategy is the *Sherwood Applied Business Security Architecture (SABSA)*, which is shown in Table 1-2. It is a layered framework, with its first layer describing the business context within which the security architecture must exist. Each layer of the framework decreases in abstraction and increases in detail, so it builds upon the others and moves from policy to practical implementation of technology and solutions. The idea is to provide a chain of traceability through the contextual, conceptual, logical, physical, component, and operational levels.

	Assets (What)	**Motivation (Why)**	**Process (How)**	**People (Who)**	**Location (Where)**	**Time (When)**
Contextual	The business	Business risk model	Business process model	Business organization and relationships	Business geography	Business time dependencies
Conceptual	Business attributes profile	Control objectives	Security strategies and architectural layering	Security entity model and trust framework	Security domain model	Security-related lifetimes and deadlines
Logical	Business information model	Security policies	Security services	Entity schema and privilege profiles	Security domain definitions and associations	Security processing cycle
Physical	Business data model	Security rules, practices, and procedures	Security mechanisms	Users, applications, and user interface	Platform and network infrastructure	Control structure execution
Component	Detailed data structures	Security standards	Security products and tools	Identities, functions, actions, and ACLs	Processes, nodes, addresses, and protocols	Security step timing and sequencing
Operational	Assurance of operation continuity	Operation risk management	Security service management and support	Application and user management and support	Security of sites, networks, and platforms	Security operations schedule

Table 1-2 SABSA Architecture Framework

The following outlines the questions that are to be asked and answered at each level of the framework:

- ***What* are you trying to do at this layer?** The assets to be protected by your security architecture.
- ***Why* are you doing it?** The motivation for wanting to apply security, expressed in the terms of this layer.
- ***How* are you trying to do it?** The functions needed to achieve security at this layer.
- ***Who* is involved?** The people and organizational aspects of security at this layer.
- ***Where* are you doing it?** The locations where you apply your security, relevant to this layer.
- ***When* are you doing it?** The time-related aspects of security relevant to this layer.

SABSA is a framework and methodology for enterprise security architecture and service management. Since it is a *framework*, this means it provides a structure for individual architectures to be built from. Since it is a *methodology* also, this means it provides the processes to follow to build and maintain this architecture. SABSA provides a life-cycle model so that the architecture can be constantly monitored and improved upon over time.

EXAM TIP You do not need to memorize the SABSA framework, but you do need to understand how security programs align with business strategies.

For an enterprise security architecture to be successful in its development and implementation, the following items must be understood and followed: strategic alignment, business enablement, process enhancement, and security effectiveness. We'll cover the first three of these in the following sections but will cover security effectiveness in Chapter 18 when we discuss security assessments.

Strategic Alignment

Strategic alignment means the business drivers and the regulatory and legal requirements are being met by the enterprise security architecture. Security efforts must provide and support an environment that allows an organization to not only survive, but thrive. The security industry has grown up from the technical and engineering world, not the business world. In many organizations, while the IT security personnel and business personnel might be located physically close to each other, they are commonly worlds apart in how they see the same organization they work in. Technology is only a tool that supports a business; it is not the business itself. The IT environment is analogous to the circulatory system within a human body; it is there to support the body—the body does not exist to support the circulatory system. And security is analogous to the immune system of the body—it is there to protect the overall environment. If these critical systems (business, IT, security) do not work together in a concerted effort, there will be deficiencies and imbalances. While deficiencies and imbalances lead to disease in the body, deficiencies and imbalances within an organization can lead to risk and security compromises.

Business Enablement

When looking at the *business enablement* requirement of the enterprise security architecture, we need to remind ourselves that each organization exists for one or more specific business purposes. Publicly traded companies are in the business of increasing shareholder value. Nonprofit organizations are in the business of furthering a specific set of causes. Government organizations are in the business of providing services to their citizens. Companies and organizations do not exist for the sole purpose of being secure. Security cannot stand in the way of business processes, but should be implemented to better enable them.

Business enablement means the core business processes are integrated into the security operating model—they are standards based and follow a risk tolerance criteria. What does this mean in the real world? Let's say a company's accountants have figured out that if they allow the customer service and support staff to work from home, the company would save a lot of money on office rent, utilities, and overhead—plus, the company's insurance would be cheaper. The company could move into this new model with the use of virtual private networks (VPNs), firewalls, content filtering, and so on. Security enables the company to move to this different working model by providing the necessary protection mechanisms. If a financial institution wants to enable its customers to view bank account information and carry out money transfers online, it can offer this service if the correct security mechanisms are put in place (access control, authentication, secure connections, etc.). Security should help the organization thrive by providing the mechanisms to do new things safely.

Process Enhancement

Process enhancement can be quite beneficial to an organization if it takes advantage of this capability when it is presented to it. An organization that is serious about securing its environment will have to take a close look at many of the business processes that take place on an ongoing basis. Many times, these processes are viewed through the eyeglasses of security, because that's the reason for the activity, but this is a perfect chance to enhance and improve upon the same processes to increase productivity. When you look at many business processes taking place in all types of organizations, you commonly find a duplication of efforts, manual steps that can be easily automated, or ways to streamline and reduce time and effort that are involved in certain tasks. This is commonly referred to as *process reengineering*.

When an organization is developing its security enterprise components, those components must be integrated into the business processes to be effective. This can allow for process management to be refined and calibrated. This, in turn, allows for security to be integrated in system life cycles and day-to-day operations. So, while business enablement means "we can do new stuff," process enhancement means "we can do stuff better."

Organizational Processes

The processes we just covered are regular day-to-day ones. There are other processes that happen less frequently but may have a much more significant impact on the security posture of the organization. Let's dig a bit deeper into some of these key organizational processes and how our security efforts align with, enable, and enhance them.

Mergers and Acquisitions

As companies grow, they often acquire new capabilities (e.g., markets, products, and intellectual property) by merging with another company or outright acquiring it. *Mergers and acquisitions (M&A)* always take place for business reasons, but they almost always have significant cybersecurity implications. Think of it this way: your company didn't acquire only the business assets of that other company it just purchased; it also acquired its security program and all the baggage that may come with it. Suppose that during the M&A process you discover that the company that your company is acquiring has a significant but previously unknown data breach. This is exactly what happened in 2017 when Verizon acquired Yahoo! and discovered that the latter had experienced two massive security breaches. The acquisition went forward, but at a price that was $350 million lower than originally agreed.

One of the ways in which companies protect themselves during a merger or acquisition is by conducting extensive audits of the company they are about to merge with or acquire. There are many service providers who now offer *compromise assessments*, which are in-depth technical examinations of a company's information systems to determine whether an undocumented compromise is ongoing or has happened in the past. It's sort of like exploratory surgery; let's open up the patient and see what we find. Another approach is to conduct an audit of the ISMS, which is more focused on policies, procedures, and controls.

Divestitures

A *divestiture*, on the other hand, is when your company sells off (or otherwise gets rid of) a part of itself. There are many reasons why a company may want to divest itself of a business asset, such as having a business unit that is not profitable or no longer well aligned with the overarching strategy. If the divestiture involves a sale or transfer of an asset to another company, that company is going to audit that asset. In other words, for us cybersecurity professionals, a divestiture is when we have to answer tough questions from the buyer, and an M&A is when we are the ones asking the tough questions of someone else. They are two sides to the same coin.

If your company is divesting assets for whose security you are responsible, you will probably work closely with the business and legal teams to identify any problem areas that might reduce the value of the assets being sold. For example, if there are any significant vulnerabilities in those assets, you may want to apply controls to mitigate the related risks. If you discover a compromise, you want to eradicate it and recover from it aggressively.

A less obvious cybersecurity implication of divestiture is the need to segment the part or parts of the ISMS that involve the asset(s) in question. If your company is selling a business unit, it undoubtedly has security policies, procedures, and controls that apply to it but may also apply to other business areas. Whoever is acquiring the assets will want to know what those are, and maybe even test them at a technical level. You need to be prepared to be audited without revealing any proprietary or confidential information in the process. Be sure to keep your legal team close to ensure you are responsive to what is required of you, but nothing else.

Governance Committees

The organizational processes we've described so far (M&A and divestitures) are triggered by a business decision to either acquire or get rid of some set of assets. There is another key process that is ongoing in many organizations with mature cybersecurity practices. A *governance committee* is a standing body whose purpose is to review the structures and practices of the organization and report its findings to the board of directors. While it may sound a bit scary to have such a committee watching over everything you do, they can actually be your allies by shining a light on the tough issues that you cannot solve by yourself without help from the board. It is important for you to know who is who in your organization and who can help get what you need to ensure a secure environment.

Organizational Roles and Responsibilities

Senior management and other levels of management understand the vision of the organization, the business goals, and the objectives. The next layer down is the functional management, whose members understand how their individual departments work, what roles individuals play within the organization, and how security affects their department directly. The next layers are operational managers and staff. These layers are closer to the actual operations of the organization. They know detailed information about the technical and procedural requirements, the systems, and how the systems are used. The employees at these layers understand how security mechanisms integrate into systems, how to configure them, and how they affect daily productivity. Every layer offers different insight into what type of role security plays within an organization, and each should have input into the best security practices, procedures, and chosen controls to ensure the agreed-upon security level provides the necessary amount of protection without negatively affecting the company's productivity.

EXAM TIP Senior management always carries the ultimate responsibility for the organization.

Although each layer is important to the overall security of an organization, some specific roles must be clearly defined. Individuals who work in smaller environments (where everyone must wear several hats) may get overwhelmed with the number of roles presented next. Many commercial businesses do not have this level of structure in their security teams, but many large companies, government agencies, and military units do. What you need to understand are the responsibilities that must be assigned and whether they are assigned to just a few people or to a large security team. These roles include the executive management, security officer, data owner, data custodian, system owner, security administrator, supervisor (user manager), change control analyst, data analyst, user, auditor, and the guy who gets everyone coffee.

Executive Management

The individuals designated as executive management typically are those whose titles start with "chief," and collectively they are often referred to as the "C-suite." Executive leaders are ultimately responsible for everything that happens in their organizations, and as such are considered the ultimate business and function owners. This has been evidenced time and again (as we will see shortly) in high-profile cases wherein executives have been fired, sued, or even prosecuted for organizational failures or fraud that occurred under their leadership. Let's start at the top of a corporate entity, the CEO.

Chief Executive Officer The *chief executive officer (CEO)* has the day-to-day management responsibilities of an organization. This person is often the chairperson of the board of directors and is the highest-ranking officer in the company. This role is for the person who oversees the company's finances, strategic planning, and operations from a high level. The CEO is usually seen as the visionary for the company and is responsible for developing and modifying the company's business plan. The CEO sets budgets; forms partnerships; and decides on what markets to enter, what product lines to develop, how the company will differentiate itself, and so on. This role's overall responsibility is to ensure that the company grows and thrives.

NOTE The CEO can delegate tasks, but not necessarily responsibility. More and more regulations dealing with information security are holding the CEO accountable for ensuring the organization practices due care and due diligence with respect to information security, which is why security departments across the land are receiving more funding. Personal liability for the decision makers and purse-string holders has loosened those purse strings, and companies are now able to spend more money on security than before. (Due care and due diligence are described in detail in Chapter 3.)

Chief Financial Officer The *chief financial officer (CFO)* is responsible for the corporation's accounting and financial activities and the overall financial structure of the organization. This person is responsible for determining what the company's financial needs will be and how to finance those needs. The CFO must create and maintain the company's capital structure, which is the proper mix of equity, credit, cash, and debt financing. This person oversees forecasting and budgeting and the processes of submitting financial statements to the regulators and stakeholders.

Chief Information Officer The *chief information officer (CIO)* may report to either the CEO or CFO, depending upon the corporate structure, and is responsible for the strategic use and management of information systems and technology within the organization. Over time, this position has become more strategic and less operational in

Executives and Incarcerations and Fines, Oh My!

The CFO and CEO are responsible for informing stakeholders (creditors, analysts, employees, management, investors) of the firm's financial condition and health. After the corporate debacles at Enron and WorldCom uncovered in 2001–2002, the U.S. government enacted the Sarbanes-Oxley Act (SOX), which prescribes to the CEO and CFO financial reporting responsibilities and includes penalties and potential *personal* liability for failure to comply. SOX gave the Securities Exchange Commission (SEC) more authority to create regulations that ensure these officers cannot simply pass along fines to the corporation for personal financial misconduct. Under SOX, they can personally be fined millions of dollars and/or go to jail. The following list provides a sampling of some of the cases in the past decade in which C-suite executives have been held accountable for cybersecurity issues under various laws:

- **August 2020** Joseph Sullivan, former chief information security officer at Uber, was charged with obstruction of justice and misprision of a felony in connection with the attempted cover-up of the 2016 hack of Uber.
- **July 2019** Facebook agreed to pay $100M in fines for making misleading disclosures concerning the risks to user data after becoming aware that Cambridge Analytica had improperly collected and misused PII on nearly 30M Facebook users in 2014 and 2015. The company neither admitted nor denied the SEC allegations as part of this agreement.
- **March 2019** Jun Ying, a former chief information officer for Equifax, pled guilty and was subsequently convicted to four months in prison on charges of insider trading for allegedly selling his stock in the company after discovering a massive data breach. He suspected (correctly) that the stock would lose value once the breach became known.
- **March 2018** Martin Shkreli, a notorious pharmaceutical executive, was sentenced to seven years in prison after being convicted of securities fraud stemming from his alleged use of funds from new companies to pay down debts previously incurred by financially troubled companies.
- **December 2017** KIT Digital's former CEO Kaleil Isaza Tuzman was found guilty of market manipulation and fraud charges. His former CFO, Robin Smyth, had previously pled guilty and turned government witness against Tuzman. As of this writing, Tuzman is still awaiting sentencing.
- **June 2015** Joe White, the former CFO of Shelby Regional Medical Center, was sentenced to 23 months in federal prison after making false claims to receive payments under the Medicare Electronic Health Record Incentive Program.

These are only some of the big cases that made it into the headlines. Other executives have also received punishments for "creative accounting" and fraudulent activities.

many organizations. CIOs oversee and are responsible for the day-in, day-out technology operations of a company, but because organizations are so dependent upon technology, CIOs are being asked to sit at the corporate table more and more.

CIO responsibilities have extended to working with the CEO (and other management) on business-process management, revenue generation, and how business strategy can be accomplished with the company's underlying technology. This person usually should have one foot in techno-land and one foot in business-land to be effective because she is bridging two very different worlds.

The CIO sets the stage for the protection of company assets and is ultimately responsible for the success of the company's security program. Direction should be coming down from the CEO, and there should be clear lines of communication between the board of directors, the C-level staff, and mid-management.

Chief Privacy Officer The *chief privacy officer (CPO)* is a newer position, created mainly because of the increasing demands on organizations to protect a long laundry list of different types of data. This role is responsible for ensuring that customer, company, and employee data is kept safe, which keeps the company out of criminal and civil courts and hopefully out of the headlines. This person is often an attorney with privacy law experience and is directly involved with setting policies on how data is collected, protected, and given out to third parties. The CPO often reports to the chief security officer.

It is important that the CPO understand the privacy, legal, and regulatory requirements the organization must comply with. With this knowledge, the CPO can then develop the organization's policies, standards, procedures, controls, and contract agreements to ensure that privacy requirements are being properly met. Remember also that organizations are responsible for knowing how their suppliers, partners, and other third parties are protecting this sensitive information. The CPO may be responsible for reviewing the data security and privacy practices of these other parties.

Some companies have carried out risk assessments without considering the penalties and ramifications they would be forced to deal with if they do not properly protect the information they are responsible for. Without considering these liabilities, risk cannot be properly assessed.

Privacy

Privacy is different from security. *Privacy* indicates the amount of control an individual should be able to have and expect to have as it relates to the release of their own sensitive information. *Security* refers to the mechanisms that can be put into place to provide this level of control.

It is becoming more critical (and more difficult) to protect personally identifiable information (PII) because of the increase of identity theft and financial fraud threats. PII is a combination of identification elements (name, address, phone number, account number, etc.). Organizations must have privacy policies and controls in place to protect their employee and customer PII. Chapter 3 discusses PII in depth.

CSO vs. CISO

The CSO and CISO may have similar or very different responsibilities, depending on the individual organization. In fact, an organization may choose to have both, either, or neither of these roles. It is up to an organization that has either or both of these roles to define their responsibilities. By and large, the CSO role usually has a further-reaching list of responsibilities compared to the CISO role. The CISO is usually focused more on technology and has an IT background. The CSO usually is required to understand a wider range of business risks, including physical security, not just technological risks.

The CSO is usually more of a businessperson and typically is present in larger organizations. If a company has both roles, the CISO reports directly to the CSO.

The CSO is commonly responsible for ensuring *convergence*, which is the formal cooperation between previously disjointed security functions. This mainly pertains to physical and IT security working in a more concerted manner instead of working in silos within the organization. Issues such as loss prevention, fraud prevention, business continuity planning, legal/regulatory compliance, and insurance all have physical security and IT security aspects and requirements. So one individual (CSO) overseeing and intertwining these different security disciplines allows for a more holistic and comprehensive security program.

The organization should document how privacy data is collected, used, disclosed, archived, and destroyed. Employees should be held accountable for not following the organization's standards on how to handle this type of information.

Chief Security Officer The *chief security officer (CSO)* is responsible for understanding the risks that the company faces and for mitigating these risks to an acceptable level. This role is responsible for understanding the organization's business drivers and for creating and maintaining a security program that facilitates these drivers, along with providing security, compliance with a long list of regulations and laws, and any customer expectations or contractual obligations.

The creation of this role is a mark in the "win" column for the security industry because it means security is finally being seen as a business issue. Previously, security was relegated to the IT department and was viewed solely as a technology issue. As organizations began to recognize the need to integrate security requirements and business needs, creating a position for security in the executive management team became more of a necessity. The CSO's job is to ensure that business is not disrupted in any way due to security issues. This extends beyond IT and reaches into business processes, legal issues, operational issues, revenue generation, and reputation protection.

Data Owner

The *data owner* (information owner) is usually a member of management who is in charge of a specific business unit and who is ultimately responsible for the protection and use of a specific subset of information. The data owner has due-care responsibilities and thus will be held responsible for any negligent act that results in the corruption or disclosure of the data. The data owner decides upon the classification of the data she is responsible for and alters that classification if the business need arises. This person is also responsible for ensuring that the necessary security controls are in place, defining security requirements per classification and backup requirements, approving any disclosure activities, ensuring that proper access rights are being used, and defining user access criteria. The data owner approves access requests or may choose to delegate this function to business unit managers. And the data owner will deal with security violations pertaining to the data she is responsible for protecting. The data owner, who obviously has enough on her plate, delegates responsibility of the day-to-day maintenance of the data protection mechanisms to the data custodian.

NOTE Data ownership takes on a different meaning when outsourcing data storage requirements. You may want to ensure that the service contract includes a clause to the effect that all data is and shall remain the sole and exclusive property of your organization.

Data Custodian

The *data custodian* (information custodian) is responsible for maintaining and protecting the data. This role is usually filled by the IT or security department, and the duties include implementing and maintaining security controls; performing regular backups of the data; periodically validating the integrity of the data; restoring data from backup media; retaining records of activity; and fulfilling the requirements specified in the company's security policy, standards, and guidelines that pertain to information security and data protection.

System Owner

The *system owner* is responsible for one or more systems, each of which may hold and process data owned by different data owners. A system owner is responsible for integrating security considerations into application and system purchasing decisions and development projects. The system owner is responsible for ensuring that adequate security is being provided by the necessary controls, password management, remote access controls, operating system configurations, and so on. This role must ensure that the systems are

Data Owner Issues

Each business unit should have a data owner who protects the unit's most critical information. The company's policies must give the data owners the necessary authority to carry out their tasks.

This is not a technical role, but rather a business role that must understand the relationship between the unit's success and the protection of this critical asset. Not all businesspeople understand this role, so they should be given the necessary training.

properly assessed for vulnerabilities and must report any that are discovered to the incident response team and data owner.

Security Administrator

The *security administrator* is responsible for implementing and maintaining specific security network devices and software in the enterprise. These controls commonly include firewalls, an intrusion detection system (IDS), intrusion prevention system (IPS), antimalware, security proxies, data loss prevention, etc. It is common for a delineation to exist between the security administrator's responsibilities and the network administrator's responsibilities. The security administrator has the main focus of keeping the network secure, and the network administrator has the focus of keeping things up and running.

A security administrator's tasks commonly also include creating new system user accounts, implementing new security software, testing security patches and components, and issuing new passwords. The security administrator must make sure access rights given to users support the policies and data owner directives.

Supervisor

The *supervisor* role, also called *user manager*, is ultimately responsible for all user activity and any assets created and owned by these users. For example, suppose Kathy is the supervisor of ten employees. Her responsibilities would include ensuring that these employees understand their responsibilities with respect to security; making sure the employees' account information is up to date; and informing the security administrator when an employee is fired, suspended, or transferred. Any change that pertains to an employee's role within the company usually affects what access rights they should and should not have, so the user manager must inform the security administrator of these changes immediately.

Change Control Analyst

Since the only thing that is constant is change, someone must make sure changes happen securely. The *change control analyst* is responsible for approving or rejecting requests to make changes to the network, systems, or software. This role must make certain that the change will not introduce any vulnerabilities, that it has been properly tested, and that it is properly rolled out. The change control analyst needs to understand how various changes can affect security, interoperability, performance, and productivity.

Data Analyst

Having proper data structures, definitions, and organization is very important to a company. The *data analyst* is responsible for ensuring that data is stored in a way that makes the most sense to the company and the individuals who need to access and work with it. For example, payroll information should not be mixed with inventory information; the purchasing department needs to have a lot of its values in monetary terms; and the inventory system must follow a standardized naming scheme. The data analyst may be responsible for architecting a new system that will hold company information or advising in the purchase of a product that will do so. The data analyst works with the data owners to help ensure that the structures set up coincide with and support the company's business objectives.

User

The *user* is any individual who routinely uses the data for work-related tasks. The user must have the necessary level of access to the data to perform the duties within their position and is responsible for following operational security procedures to ensure the data's confidentiality, integrity, and availability to others.

Auditor

The function of the *auditor* is to periodically check that everyone is doing what they are supposed to be doing and to ensure the correct controls are in place and are being maintained securely. The goal of the auditor is to make sure the organization complies with its own policies and the applicable laws and regulations. Organizations can have internal auditors and/or external auditors. The external auditors commonly work on behalf of a regulatory body to make sure compliance is being met.

While many security professionals fear and dread auditors, they can be valuable tools in ensuring the overall security of the organization. Their goal is to find the things you have missed and help you understand how to fix the problems.

Why So Many Roles?

Most organizations will not have all the roles previously listed, but what is important is to build an organizational structure that contains the necessary roles and map the correct security responsibilities to them. This structure includes clear definitions of responsibilities, lines of authority and communication, and enforcement capabilities. A clear-cut structure takes the mystery out of who does what and how things are handled in different situations.

Security Policies, Standards, Procedures, and Guidelines

Computers and the information processed on them usually have a direct relationship with a company's critical missions and objectives. Because of this level of importance, senior management should make protecting these items a high priority and provide the necessary support, funds, time, and resources to ensure that systems, networks, and information are protected in the most logical and cost-effective manner possible. A comprehensive management approach must be developed to accomplish these goals successfully. This is because everyone within an organization may have a different set of personal values and experiences they bring to the environment with regard to security. It is important to make sure everyone is consistent regarding security at a level that meets the needs of the organization.

For a company's security plan to be successful, it must start at the top level and be useful and functional at every single level within the organization. Senior management needs to define the scope of security and identify and decide what must be protected and to what extent. Management must understand the business needs and compliance requirements (regulations, laws, and liability issues) for which it is responsible regarding security and ensure that the company as a whole fulfills its obligations. Senior management also must determine what is expected from employees and what the consequences of noncompliance will be. These decisions should be made by the individuals who will be held ultimately responsible if something goes wrong. But it is a common practice to bring in the expertise of the security officers to collaborate in ensuring that sufficient policies and controls are being implemented to achieve the goals being set and determined by senior management.

A security program contains all the pieces necessary to provide overall protection to an organization and lays out a long-term security strategy. A security program's documentation should be made up of security policies, procedures, standards, guidelines, and baselines. The human resources and legal departments must be involved in the development and enforcement of rules and requirements laid out in these documents.

ISMS vs. Enterprise Security Architecture

What is the difference between an ISMS and an enterprise security architecture? An ISMS outlines the controls that need to be put into place (risk management, vulnerability management, business continuity planning, data protection, auditing, configuration management, physical security, etc.) and provides direction on how those controls should be managed throughout their life cycle. The ISMS specifies the pieces and parts that need to be put into place to provide a holistic security program for the organization overall and how to properly take care of those pieces and parts. The enterprise security architecture illustrates how these components are to be integrated into the different layers of the current business environment. The security components of the ISMS have to be interwoven throughout the business environment and not siloed within individual company departments.

For example, the ISMS will dictate that risk management needs to be put in place, and the enterprise security architecture will chop up the risk management components and illustrate how risk management needs to take place at the strategic, tactical, and operational levels. As another example, the ISMS could dictate that data protection needs to be put into place. The security architecture can show how this happens at the infrastructure, application, component, and business level. At the infrastructure level we can implement data loss protection technology to detect how sensitive data is traversing the network. Applications that maintain sensitive data must have the necessary access controls and cryptographic functionality. The components within the applications can implement the specific cryptographic functions. And protecting sensitive company information can be tied to business drivers, which is illustrated at the business level of the architecture.

The ISO/IEC 27000 series (which outlines the ISMS and is covered in detail in Chapter 4) is very policy oriented and outlines the necessary components of a security program. This means that the ISO standards are general in nature, which is not a defect—they were created that way so that they could be applied to various types of businesses, companies, and organizations. But since these standards are general, it can be difficult to know how to implement them and map them to your company's infrastructure and business needs. This is where the enterprise security architecture comes into play. The architecture is a tool used to ensure that what is outlined in the security standards is implemented throughout the different layers of an organization.

The language, level of detail, formality of the documents, and supporting mechanisms should be examined by the policy developers. Security policies, standards, guidelines, procedures, and baselines must be developed with a realistic view to be most effective. Highly structured organizations usually follow documentation in a more uniform way. Less structured organizations may need more explanation and emphasis to promote compliance. The more detailed the rules are, the easier it is to know when one has been violated. However, overly detailed documentation and rules can prove to be more burdensome than helpful. The business type, its culture, and its goals must be evaluated to make sure the proper language is used when writing security documentation.

There are a lot of legal liability issues surrounding security documentation. If your organization has a policy outlining how it is supposed to be protecting sensitive information and it is found out that your organization is not practicing what it is preaching, criminal charges and civil suits could be filed and successfully executed. It is important that an organization's security does not just look good on paper, but in action also.

Security Policy

A *security policy* is an overall general statement produced by senior management (or a selected policy board or committee) that dictates what role security plays within the organization. A security policy can be an organizational policy, an issue-specific policy, or a system-specific policy. In an *organizational security policy*, management establishes how a security program will be set up, lays out the program's goals, assigns responsibilities, shows the strategic and tactical value of security, and outlines how enforcement should be carried out. This policy must address applicable laws, regulations, and liability issues and how they are to be satisfied. The organizational security policy provides scope and direction for all future security activities within the organization. It also describes the amount of risk senior management is willing to accept.

The organizational security policy has several important characteristics that must be understood and implemented:

- Business objectives should drive the policy's creation, implementation, and enforcement. The policy should not dictate business objectives.
- It should be an easily understood document that is used as a reference point for all employees and management.
- It should be developed and used to integrate security into all business functions and processes.
- It should be derived from and support all legislation and regulations applicable to the company.
- It should be reviewed and modified as a company changes, such as through adoption of a new business model, a merger with another company, or change of ownership.
- Each iteration of the policy should be dated and under version control.
- The units and individuals who are governed by the policy must have easy access to it. Policies are commonly posted on portals on an intranet.

- It should be created with the intention of having the policies in place for several years at a time. This will help ensure policies are forward-thinking enough to deal with potential changes that may arise.
- The level of professionalism in the presentation of the policies reinforces their importance, as well as the need to adhere to them.
- It should not contain language that isn't readily understood by everyone. Use clear and declarative statements that are easy to understand and adopt.
- It should be reviewed on a regular basis and adapted to correct incidents that have occurred since the last review and revision of the policies.

A process for dealing with those who choose not to comply with the security policies must be developed and enforced so there is a structured method of response to noncompliance. This establishes a process that others can understand and thus recognize not only what is expected of them but also what they can expect as a response to their noncompliance.

Organizational security policies are also referred to as master security policies. An organization will have many policies, and they should be set up in a hierarchical manner. The organizational (master) security policy is at the highest level, with policies underneath it that address security issues specifically. These are referred to as issue-specific policies.

An *issue-specific policy*, also called a *functional policy*, addresses specific security issues that management feels need more detailed explanation and attention to make sure a comprehensive structure is built and all employees understand how they are to comply with these security issues. For example, an organization may choose to have an e-mail security policy that outlines what management can and cannot do with employees' e-mail messages for monitoring purposes, that specifies which e-mail functionality employees can or cannot use, and that addresses specific privacy issues.

As a more specific example, an e-mail policy might state that management can read any employee's e-mail messages that reside on the mail server, but not when they reside on the user's workstation. The e-mail policy might also state that employees cannot use e-mail to share confidential information or pass inappropriate material and that they may be subject to monitoring of these actions. Before they use their e-mail clients, employees should be asked to confirm that they have read and understand the e-mail policy, either by signing a confirmation document or clicking Yes in a confirmation dialog box. The policy provides direction and structure for the staff by indicating what they can and cannot do. It informs the users of the expectations of their actions, and it provides liability protection in case an employee cries "foul" for any reason dealing with e-mail use.

EXAM TIP A policy needs to be technology and solution independent. It must outline the goals and missions, but not tie the organization to specific ways of accomplishing them.

A common hierarchy of security policies is outlined here, which illustrates the relationship between the master policy and the issue-specific policies that support it:

Organizational policy:

- Acceptable use policy
- Risk management policy
- Vulnerability management policy
- Data protection policy
- Access control policy
- Business continuity policy
- Log aggregation and auditing policy
- Personnel security policy
- Physical security policy
- Secure application development policy
- Change control policy
- E-mail policy
- Incident response policy

A *system-specific policy* presents the management's decisions that are specific to the actual computers, networks, and applications. An organization may have a system-specific policy outlining how a database containing sensitive information should be protected, who can have access, and how auditing should take place. It may also have a system-specific policy outlining how laptops should be locked down and managed. This policy type is directed to one or a group of similar systems and outlines how they should be protected.

Policies are written in broad terms to cover many subjects in a general fashion. Much more granularity is needed to actually support the policy, and this happens with the use of procedures, standards, guidelines, and baselines. The policy provides the foundation. The procedures, standards, guidelines, and baselines provide the security framework. And the necessary security controls (administrative, technical, and physical) are used to fill in the framework to provide a full security program.

Standards

Standards refer to mandatory activities, actions, or rules. Standards describe specific requirements that allow us to meet our policy goals. They are unambiguous, detailed, and measurable. There should be no question as to whether a specific asset or action complies with a given standard.

Organizational security standards may specify how hardware and software products are to be used. They can also be used to indicate expected user behavior. They provide a

Types of Policies

Policies generally fall into one of the following categories:

- **Regulatory** This type of policy ensures that the organization is following standards set by specific industry regulations (HIPAA, GLBA, SOX, PCI DSS, etc.; see Chapter 3). It is very detailed and specific to a type of industry. It is used in financial institutions, healthcare facilities, public utilities, and other government-regulated industries.
- **Advisory** This type of policy strongly advises employees as to which types of behaviors and activities should and should not take place within the organization. It also outlines possible ramifications if employees do not comply with the established behaviors and activities. This policy type can be used, for example, to describe how to handle medical or financial information.
- **Informative** This type of policy informs employees of certain topics. It is not an enforceable policy, but rather one that teaches individuals about specific issues relevant to the company. It could explain how the company interacts with partners, the company's goals and mission, and a general reporting structure in different situations.

means to ensure that specific technologies, applications, parameters, and procedures are implemented in a uniform (standardized) manner across the organization. Organizational standards may require that all employees use a specific smart card as their access control token, that its certificate expire after 12 months, and that it be locked after three unsuccessful attempts to enter a personal identification number (PIN). These rules are compulsory within a company, and if they are going to be effective, they must be enforced.

An organization may have an issue-specific data classification policy that states "All confidential data must be properly protected." It would need a supporting data protection standard outlining how this protection should be implemented and followed, as in "Confidential information must be protected with AES256 at rest and in transit."

Tactical and strategic goals are different. A strategic goal can be viewed as the ultimate endpoint, while tactical goals are the steps necessary to achieve it. As shown in Figure 1-3, standards, guidelines, and procedures are the tactical tools used to achieve and support the directives in the security policy, which is considered the strategic goal.

EXAM TIP The term *standard* has more than one meaning in our industry. Internal documentation that lays out rules that must be followed is a standard. But sometimes, best practices, as in the ISO/IEC 27000 series, are referred to as standards because they were developed by a standards body. And as we will see later, we have specific technologic standards, as in IEEE 802.11. You need to understand the context of how this term is used. The CISSP exam will not try and trick you on this word; just know that the industry uses it in several different ways.

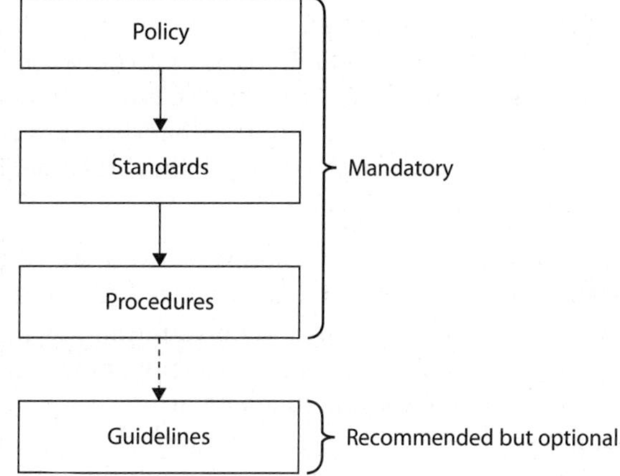

Figure 1-3 Policies are implemented through standards, procedures, and guidelines.

Baselines

The term *baseline* refers to a point in time that is used as a comparison for future changes. Once risks have been mitigated and security put in place, a baseline is formally reviewed and agreed upon, after which all further comparisons and development are measured against it. A baseline results in a consistent reference point.

Let's say that your doctor has told you that you're overweight due to your diet of donuts, pizza, and soda. (This is very frustrating to you because the supplement company's TV commercial said you could eat whatever you wanted and just take their very expensive pills every day and lose weight.) The doctor tells you that you need to exercise each day and elevate your heart rate to double its normal rate for 30 minutes twice a day. How do you know when you are at double your heart rate? You find out your baseline (regular heart rate) by using a heart rate monitor or going old school and manually taking your pulse with a stopwatch. So you start at your baseline and continue to exercise until you have doubled your heart rate or die, whichever comes first.

Baselines are also used to define the minimum level of protection required. In security, specific baselines can be defined per system type, which indicates the necessary settings and the level of protection being provided. For example, a company may stipulate that all accounting systems must meet an Evaluation Assurance Level (EAL) 4 baseline. This means that only systems that have gone through the Common Criteria process and achieved this rating can be used in this department. Once the systems are properly configured, this is the necessary baseline. When new software is installed, when patches or upgrades are applied to existing software, or when other changes to the system take place, there is a good chance the system may no longer be providing its necessary minimum level of protection (its baseline). Security personnel must assess the systems as changes take place and ensure that the baseline level of security is always being met. If a technician installs a patch on a system and does not ensure the baseline is still being met, there could be new vulnerabilities introduced into the system that will allow attackers easy access to the network.

NOTE Baselines that are not technology oriented should be created and enforced within organizations as well. For example, a company can mandate that while in the facility all employees must have a badge with a picture ID in view at all times. It can also state that visitors must sign in at a front desk and be escorted while in the facility. If these rules are followed, then this creates a baseline of protection.

Guidelines

Guidelines are recommended actions and operational guides to users, IT staff, operations staff, and others when a specific standard does not apply. They can also be used as a recommended way to achieve specific standards when those do apply. Guidelines can deal with the methodologies of technology, personnel, or physical security. Life is full of gray areas, and guidelines can be used as a reference during those times. Whereas standards are specific mandatory rules, guidelines are general approaches that provide the necessary flexibility for unforeseen circumstances.

A policy might state that access to confidential data must be audited. A supporting guideline could further explain that audits should contain sufficient information to allow for reconciliation with prior reviews. Supporting procedures would outline the necessary steps to configure, implement, and maintain this type of auditing.

Procedures

Procedures are detailed step-by-step tasks that should be performed to achieve a certain goal. The steps can apply to users, IT staff, operations staff, security members, and others who may need to carry out specific tasks. Many organizations have written procedures on how to install operating systems, configure security mechanisms, implement access control lists, set up new user accounts, assign computer privileges, audit activities, destroy material, report incidents, and much more.

Procedures are considered the lowest level in the documentation chain because they are closest to the computers and users (compared to policies) and provide detailed steps for configuration and installation issues.

Procedures spell out how the policy, standards, and guidelines will actually be implemented in an operating environment. If a policy states that all individuals who access confidential information must be properly authenticated, the supporting procedures will explain the steps for this to happen by defining the access criteria for authorization, how access control mechanisms are implemented and configured, and how access activities are audited. If a policy states that backups should be performed, then the procedures will define the detailed steps necessary to perform the backup, the timelines of backups, the storage of backup media, and so on. Procedures should be detailed enough to be both understandable and useful to a diverse group of individuals.

Implementation

To tie these items together, let's walk through an implementation example. A corporation's security *policy* indicates that confidential information should be properly protected.

It states the issue in very broad and general terms. A supporting *standard* mandates that all customer information held in databases must be encrypted with the Advanced Encryption Standard (AES) algorithm while it is stored and that it cannot be transmitted over the Internet unless IPSec encryption technology is used. The standard indicates what type of protection is required and provides another level of granularity and explanation. The supporting *procedures* explain exactly how to implement the AES and IPSec technologies, and the *guidelines* cover how to handle cases when data is accidentally corrupted or compromised during transmission. Once the software and devices are configured as outlined in the procedures, this is considered the *baseline* that must always be maintained. All of these work together to provide a company with a security structure.

Unfortunately, security policies, standards, procedures, baselines, and guidelines often are written because an auditor instructed a company to document these items, but then they are placed on a file server and are not shared, explained, or used. To be useful, they must be put into action. Employees aren't going to follow the rules if they don't know the rules exist. Security policies and the items that support them not only must be developed but must also be implemented and enforced.

To be effective, employees need to know about security issues within these documents; therefore, the policies and their supporting counterparts need visibility. Awareness training, manuals, presentations, newsletters, and screen banners can achieve this visibility. It must be clear that the directives came from senior management and that the full management staff supports these policies. Employees must understand what is expected of them in their actions, behaviors, accountability, and performance.

Implementing security policies and the items that support them shows due care by the company and its management staff. Informing employees of what is expected of them and the consequences of noncompliance can come down to a liability issue. For example, if a company fires an employee because he was downloading pornographic material to the company's computer, the employee may take the company to court and win if the employee can prove he was not properly informed of what was considered acceptable and unacceptable use of company property and what the consequences were. Security awareness training is covered later in this chapter, but personnel security is much broader than that.

Personnel Security

Although society has evolved to be extremely dependent upon technology in the workplace, people are still the key ingredient to a successful company. But in security circles, people are often the weakest link. Either accidentally through mistakes or lack of training, or intentionally through fraud and malicious intent, personnel cause more serious and hard-to-detect security issues than hacker attacks, outside espionage, or equipment failure. Although the future actions of individuals cannot be predicted, it is possible to minimize the risks by implementing preventive measures. These include hiring the most qualified individuals, performing background checks, using detailed job descriptions, providing necessary training, enforcing strict access controls, and terminating individuals in a way that protects all parties involved.

Several items can be put into place to reduce the possibilities of fraud, sabotage, misuse of information, theft, and other security compromises. *Separation of duties (SoD)* makes sure that one individual cannot complete a critical task by herself. In the movies, when a submarine captain needs to launch a nuclear missile to blow up the enemy and save (or end) civilization as we know it, the launch usually requires two codes to be entered into the launching mechanism by two different senior crewmembers. This is an example of separation of duties, and it ensures that the captain cannot complete such an important and terrifying task all by himself.

Separation of duties is a security control that can reduce the potential for fraud. For example, an employee cannot complete a critical financial transaction by herself. She will need to have her supervisor's approval before the transaction can be completed. There is usually a third person involved who verifies that this procedure was followed.

In an organization that practices separation of duties, collusion must take place for fraud to be committed. *Collusion* means that at least two people are working together to cause some type of destruction or fraud. In our example, the employee and her supervisor must be participating in the fraudulent activity to make it happen. Even if this were to happen, the third person who reviewed the transaction would provide a way to detect this collusion early enough (hopefully) to stop the transaction.

Two variations of separation of duties are *split knowledge* and *dual control.* In both cases, two or more individuals are authorized and required to perform a duty or task. In the case of split knowledge, no one person knows or has all the details to perform a task. For example, two managers might be required to open a bank vault, with each only knowing part of the combination. In the case of dual control, two individuals are again authorized to perform a task, but both must be available and active in their participation to complete the task or mission. For example, two officers must perform an identical key-turn in a nuclear missile submarine, each out of reach of the other, to launch a missile. The control here is that no one person has the capability of launching a missile, because they cannot reach to turn both keys at the same time.

These are examples of what is generally known as an *m of n control,* which is a control that requires a certain number of agents (m) out of a pool of authorized agents (n) to complete an operation. This type of control can also be called *quorum authentication,* because it requires the collaboration of a certain number of individuals (the quorum). In the bank vault example, if there were five managers authorized to open the vault and two were required to actually open it, this would be a 2 of 5 control, since $m = 2$ and $n = 5$. You don't want to make n too big because that increases the odds that two individuals could secretly conspire to do something harmful. On the other hand, you would not want m and n to have the same value, since the loss of any one individual would render the vault unopenable!

Job rotation (rotation of assignments) is an administrative detective control that can be put into place to uncover fraudulent activities. No one person should stay in one position for a long time because they may end up having too much control over a segment of the business. Such total control could result in fraud or the misuse of resources. Employees should be moved into different roles with the idea that they may be able to detect suspicious activity carried out by the previous employee filling that position. This type of control is commonly implemented in financial institutions.

Employees in sensitive areas should be forced to take their vacations, which is known as a *mandatory vacation*. While they are on vacation, other individuals fill their positions and thus can usually detect any fraudulent errors or activities. Two of the many ways to detect fraud or inappropriate activities would be the discovery of activity on someone's user account while they're supposed to be away on vacation, or if a specific problem stopped while someone was away and not active on the network. These anomalies are worthy of investigation. Employees who carry out fraudulent activities commonly do not take vacations because they do not want anyone to figure out what they are doing behind the scenes. This is why they must periodically be required to be away from the organization for a period of time, usually two weeks. Placing someone on administrative leave during an investigation is also a form of mandatory vacation.

Candidate Screening and Hiring

The issues, policies, and procedures discussed in the previous section are important to consider in the daily operations of your organization's staff, but let's not get too far ahead of ourselves. Personnel security starts way before a staff member shows up for work. Hiring the right candidate for a position can have a significant impact on the organization's security.

Depending on the position to be filled, human resources should perform a level of candidate screening to ensure that the company hires the right individual for the right job. Each candidate's skills should be tested and evaluated, and the caliber and character of the individual should be examined. Joe might be the best programmer in the state, but if someone looks into his past and finds out he served prison time because he hacked into a bank, the hiring manager might not be so eager to bring Joe into the organization.

Human resources should contact candidates' references, review their military records, if applicable, verify their educational background, obtain their credit report, check out their publicly viewable social media presence, and, if necessary, require proof of a recently administered negative drug test. Many times, candidates are able to conceal important personal behaviors, which is why hiring practices now include scenario questions, personality tests, and observations of the individual, instead of just looking at a person's work history. When a person is hired, he is bringing his skills and whatever other baggage he carries. A company can reduce its heartache pertaining to personnel by first conducting useful and careful hiring practices.

The goal is to hire the "right person" and not just hire a person for "right now." Employees represent an investment on the part of the organization, and by taking the time and hiring the right people for the jobs, the organization will be able to maximize its investment and achieve a better return. Many organizations place a lot of value on determining whether a candidate is a good "cultural" fit. This means that the person will blend well into the culture that already exists in the company. People who fit in are more likely to follow the existing norms, policies, and procedures.

A detailed background check can reveal some interesting information. Things like unexplained gaps in employment history, the validity and actual status of professional certifications, criminal records, driving records, job titles that have been misrepresented, credit histories, unfriendly terminations, appearances on suspected terrorist watch lists, and even real reasons for having left previous jobs can all be determined through the use of background checks. This has real benefit to the employer and the organization because it serves as the first line of defense for the organization against being attacked from within. Any negative information found in these areas could be indicators of potential problems that the candidate could create for the company at a later date if hired. Take the credit report, for instance. On the surface, the candidate's credit standing may seem to be personal information that the organization doesn't need to know about, but if the report indicates the potential employee has a poor credit standing and a history of financial problems, your organization certainly won't want to place that person in charge of its accounting, or even the petty cash.

Ultimately, the goal of performing background checks is to achieve several different things for the organization at the same time:

- Mitigate risk
- Lower hiring and training costs and the turnover rate for employees
- Protect customers and employees from someone who could potentially conduct malicious and dishonest actions that could harm the organization, its employees, and its customers as well as the general public

In many cases, it is also harder to go back and conduct background checks after the individual has been hired and is working, because there will need to be a specific cause or reason for conducting this kind of investigation. If any employee moves to a position of greater security sensitivity or potential risk, a follow-up investigation should be considered.

Possible background check criteria could include

- National identification number trace
- Criminal check
- Sexual offender registry check
- Employment verification
- Education verification
- Professional reference verification
- Immigration check
- Professional license/certification verification
- Credit report
- Drug screening

Employment Agreements and Policies

Congratulations! Your organization found the right candidate who passed its screening with flying colors and accepted the offer of employment. Now what? Depending on the jurisdiction in which your organization is located, it may be legally required as an employer to enter into a contract or other agreement with the candidate in order for the hiring action to be official. Whether or not this is a requirement for your organization, it is almost always a good idea to put this employment agreement in writing and ensure that it is signed by both parties. If you are a hiring manager, you should always follow the guidance provided by your human resources and legal teams, but it is useful to be aware of how this all works.

One of the key elements of an employment agreement is a reference to the policies that are applicable to employees in their new roles. Again, depending on where you are in the world, some policies (typically those dealing with safety and welfare) may be required to be included or referenced in the agreement. At a minimum, the employment agreement should include language pointing to the employee manual or other repository of policies for your organization. The point is that every new hire should sign an agreement stating that they are aware of the policies with which they must comply as a condition of employment. This becomes particularly helpful if there are any allegations of misconduct later on. For example, absent a signed employment agreement, if an employee deliberately (or even maliciously) accesses a computer or files that she shouldn't, she could claim she was never told it was wrong and get off the hook. According to the Federal Bureau of Investigation (FBI) manual on prosecuting computer crimes, "it is relatively easy to prove that a defendant had only limited authority to access a computer in cases where the defendant's access was limited by restrictions that were memorialized in writing, such as terms of service, a computer access policy, a website notice, or an employment agreement or similar contract."

Another important element of an employment agreement is the establishment of a probationary period. This is a period of time during which it is relatively easy to fire the new employee for misconduct or just failing to live up to expectations. Depending on the laws in your jurisdiction, it could be difficult to get rid of an employee even if it's obvious they are not working out. A probationary period could be helpful should you decide that your new hire is not as good as you thought.

Onboarding, Transfers, and Termination Processes

Onboarding is the process of turning a candidate into a trusted employee who is able to perform all assigned duties. Having a structured and well-documented onboarding process not only will make the new employee feel valued and welcome but will also ensure that your organization doesn't forget any security tasks. Though the specific steps will vary by organization, the following are some that are pretty universal:

- The new employee attends all required security awareness training.
- The new employee must read all security policies, be given an opportunity to have any questions about the policies answered, and sign a statement indicating they understand and will comply with the policies.
- The new employee is issued all appropriate identification badges, keys, and access tokens pursuant to their assigned roles.
- The IT department creates all necessary accounts for the new employee, who signs into the systems and sets their passwords (or changes any temporary passwords).

Organizations should develop *nondisclosure agreements (NDAs)* and require them to be signed by new employees to protect the organization and its sensitive information. NDAs typically specify what is considered sensitive information, how it should be protected, when it can be shared with others, and how long these obligations last after the employee (or the agreement) is terminated.

One of the most overlooked issues in personnel security is what happens when an employee's role within the organization changes. This could be a promotion (or demotion), assumption of new additional roles, loss of old roles, transfer to another business unit, or perhaps the result of a total restructuring of a business unit. Typically, what happens is that whatever old authorizations the employee had are never taken away, but new ones are added. Over time, employees who've been transferred or reassigned could accumulate a very extensive set of authorizations on information systems that they no longer need to access. IT and security staff need to be involved in transfers and role changes so that they can determine what policies apply and which permissions should be added, left in place, or removed. The goal is to ensure that every staff member has the permissions they need to do their jobs, and not a single one more.

Unfortunately, sometimes organizations have to terminate employees. Because terminations can happen for a variety of reasons, and terminated people have different reactions, companies should have a specific set of procedures to follow with every termination to ensure that their security posture isn't undermined in the process. For example:

- The employee must leave the facility immediately under the supervision of a manager or security guard.
- The employee must surrender any identification badges or keys, be asked to complete an exit interview, and return company supplies.
- That user's accounts and passwords must be disabled or changed immediately.

These actions may seem harsh when they actually take place, but too many companies have been hurt by vengeful employees who have retaliated against the companies after their positions were revoked for one reason or another. If an employee is disgruntled in any way or the termination is unfriendly, that employee's accounts must be disabled right away, and all passwords on all systems must be changed.

Practical Tips on Terminations

Without previous arrangement, an employee cannot be compelled to complete an exit interview, despite the huge value to the company of conducting such interviews. Neither can an employee be compelled to return company property, as a practical matter, if he or she simply chooses not to. The best way to motivate departing employees to comply is to ensure that any severance package they may be eligible for is contingent upon completion of these tasks, and that means having them agree to such conditions up-front, as part of their employment agreement.

Vendors, Consultants, and Contractors

Many companies today could not perform their business functions without the services of an assortment of vendors, consultants, and contractors who have different levels of access to the companies' facilities and information systems. From the janitorial staff who have physical access to virtually any area of a facility to the outsourced software developers in a different country who could introduce (willingly or otherwise) vulnerabilities (or even backdoors) to the companies' most sensitive systems, the risks associated with vendors, consultants, and contractors can be significant if left unmitigated.

There are a number of approaches to dealing with third parties in your environment from an information security standpoint. One approach is to enter into service agreements that require contractors to use security controls that are at least as stringent as your organization's security controls, *and* to prove it. The service agreement could include specific requirements for security controls or leverage existing standards such as the International Organization for Standardization (ISO) 27001 certification (which we discuss in Chapter 4). Either way, the agreement must specify a way to verify compliance with the contractual obligations and clearly state the penalties for failing to meet those obligations.

Another approach to dealing with third parties is to assume that vendors, consultants, and contractors are untrusted and place strict controls around every aspect of their performance. For example, you could require that janitors be escorted by designated employees and that outsourced developers work on virtual desktop infrastructure under the control of your organization. You could also require that highly sensitive assets (e.g., proprietary algorithms, trade secrets, and customer data) be off limits to these third parties. This approach will likely reduce certain risks but may not be ideal for building partnerships or engendering mutual trust.

There is no single best way to deal with the security issues inherent in working with third parties. As with every aspect of personnel security, you should work in close coordination with your business units, human resources staff, and legal counsel. Coordinating with legal counsel is particularly critical, because your organization's liability may (and often does) extend to the actions and inactions of your vendors, consultants, and contractors. For example, if your organization's network is breached because one of your contractors violated policies and that breach resulted in customers' PII being stolen and causing them financial losses, your company could be liable for their damages. This is known as *downstream liability*.

Compliance Policies

There are many forms of liability that may pertain to your organization. Your organization may be subject to external regulations that require special attention and compliance from a security standpoint. Examples are healthcare providers in the United States, who fall under the Healthcare Insurance Portability and Accountability Act (HIPAA); companies that handle payment card information, which must follow the Payment Card Industry Data Security Standard (PCI DSS); and organizations that handle personal information of citizens of the European Union, which fall under the General Data Protection Regulation (GDPR). Many more examples exist, but the point is that if your organization is regulated, then your personnel security practices must comply with these regulations. As a security leader, you should know which regulations apply to your organization and how security policies, including personnel security ones, work to ensure regulatory compliance.

Privacy Policies

Even if your organization doesn't fall under GDPR or any of the myriad of similar privacy regulations and laws, there are good reasons for you to ensure that your organization has a privacy policy and that your information security practices are aligned with it. For example, suppose you have a policy that allows employees to privately check personal webmail during their breaks, and you also have a policy of decrypting and inspecting all web traffic on your networks to ensure no adversaries are using encryption to sneak around your security controls. These two policies could be in conflict with each other. Worse yet, an employee could sue for violation of privacy if his e-mail messages are intercepted and read by your security team.

Security Awareness, Education, and Training Programs

Even if you develop security policies that protect organizational assets and are aligned with all relevant laws and regulations, it is all for naught if nobody knows what they are expected to do. For an organization to achieve the desired results of its security program, it must communicate the what, how, and why of security to its employees. Security awareness training should be comprehensive, tailored for specific groups, and organization-wide. It should repeat the most important messages in different formats; be kept up to date; be entertaining, positive, and humorous; be simple to understand; and—most important—be supported by senior management. Management must allocate the resources for this activity and enforce its attendance within the organization.

The goal is for each employee to understand the importance of security to the company as a whole and to each individual. Expected responsibilities and acceptable behaviors must be clarified, and noncompliance repercussions, which could range from a warning to dismissal, must be explained before being invoked. Security awareness training can modify employees' behavior and attitude toward security. This can best be achieved through a formalized process of security awareness training.

Degree or Certification?

Some roles within the organization need hands-on experience and skill, meaning that the hiring manager should be looking for specific industry certifications. Some positions require more of a holistic and foundational understanding of concepts or a business background, and in those cases a degree may be required. Table 1-3 provides more information on the differences between awareness, training, and education.

	Awareness	Training	Education
Attribute	"What"	"How"	"Why"
Level	Information	Knowledge	Insight
Learning objective	Recognition and retention	Skill	Understanding
Example teaching method	**Media:** Videos Newsletters Posters CBT Social engineering testing	**Practical Instruction:** Lecture and/or demo Case study Hands-on practice	**Theoretical Instruction:** Seminar and discussion Reading and study Research
Test measure	True/False, multiple choice (identify learning)	Problem solving—i.e., recognition and resolution (apply learning)	Essay (interpret learning)
Impact timeframe	Short-term	Intermediate	Long-term

Table 1-3 Aspects of Awareness, Training, and Education

Methods and Techniques to Present Awareness and Training

Because security is a topic that can span many different aspects of an organization, it can be difficult to communicate the correct information to the right individuals. By using a formalized process for security awareness training, you can establish a method that will provide you with the best results for making sure security requirements are presented to the right people in an organization. This way you can make sure everyone understands what is outlined in the organization's security program, why it is important, and how it fits into the individual's role in the organization. The higher levels of training typically are more general and deal with broader concepts and goals, and as the training moves down to specific jobs and tasks, it becomes more situation specific as it directly applies to certain positions within the company.

A security awareness program is typically created for at least three types of audiences: management, staff, and technical employees. Each type of awareness training must be geared toward the individual audience to ensure each group understands its particular responsibilities, liabilities, and expectations. If technical security training were given to senior management, their eyes would glaze over as soon as protocols and firewalls were mentioned. On the flip side, if legal ramifications, company liability issues pertaining to protecting data, and shareholders' expectations were discussed with the IT group, they would quickly turn to their smartphone and start tweeting, browsing the Internet, or texting their friends.

Members of senior management would benefit the most from a short, focused security awareness orientation that discusses corporate assets and financial gains and losses pertaining to security. They need to know how stock prices can be negatively affected by compromises, understand possible threats and their outcomes, and know why security must be integrated into the environment the same way as other business processes. Because members of management must lead the rest of the company in support of security, they must gain the right mindset about its importance.

Middle management would benefit from a more detailed explanation of the policies, procedures, standards, and guidelines and how they map to the individual departments for which each middle manager is responsible. Middle managers should be taught why their support for their specific departments is critical and what their level of responsibility is for ensuring that employees practice safe computing activities. They should also be shown how the consequences of noncompliance by individuals who report to them can affect the company as a whole and how they, as managers, may have to answer for such indiscretions.

Staff training, which typically involves the largest portion of an organization, should provide plenty of examples of specific behaviors that are expected, recommended, and forbidden. This is an opportunity to show how alert users can be sensors providing early warning of attacks, which can dramatically improve the security posture of any organization. This can be accomplished by training the staff to recognize and report the sorts of attacks they are likely to face. Conversely, it is important to also show the consequences, organizational and personal, of being careless or violating policies and procedures.

The technical departments must receive a different presentation that aligns more to their daily tasks. They should receive a more in-depth training to discuss technical configurations, incident handling, and how to recognize different types of security compromises.

Perhaps no other topic is more important or better illustrates the need to communicate security issues differently to each of these three audiences than the topic of social engineering. *Social engineering* is the deliberate manipulation of a person or group of persons to persuade them to do something they otherwise wouldn't or shouldn't. In a security context, this typically means getting a member of the organization to violate a security policy or procedure or to help an attacker compromise a system. The most common form of social engineering is *phishing*, which is the use of e-mail messages to perform social engineering. While all employees should know that they should not click on links or open attachments in e-mail messages if they don't recognize the sender, executives, managers, and end users should be presented the problem in a different light.

Regardless of how the training is presented, it is usually best to have each employee sign a document indicating they have heard and understand all the security topics discussed and that they also understand the ramifications of noncompliance. This reinforces the policies' importance to the employee and also provides evidence down the road if the employee claims they were never told of these expectations. Awareness training should happen during the hiring process and at least annually after that. Attendance of training should also be integrated into employment performance reports.

Various methods should be employed to reinforce the concepts of security awareness. Things like screen banners, employee handbooks, and even posters can be used as ways to remind employees about their duties and the necessities of good security practices. But there are other ways to drive employee engagement. For example, *gamification* is the application of elements of game play to other activities such as security awareness training. By some accounts, gamification can improve employees' skill retention by 40 percent. Another approach is to leverage employees who are not formally part of the security program and yet have the skills and aptitudes that make them security advocates within their own business units. These individuals can be identified and deliberately nurtured to act as conduits between business units and the security program. They can become *security champions*, which are members of an organization that, though their job descriptions do not include security, inform and encourage the adoption of security practices within their own teams.

Periodic Content Reviews

The only constant in life is change, so it should come as no surprise that after we develop the curricula and materials for security awareness training, we have to keep them up to date by conducting periodic content reviews. It is essential that this be a deliberate process and not done in an ad hoc manner. One way to do this is to schedule refreshes at specific intervals like semi-annually or yearly and assign the task to an individual owner. This person would work with a team to review and update the plan and materials but is ultimately responsible for keeping the training up to date.

Another approach is to have content reviews be triggered by other events. For example, reviews can be required whenever any of the following occur:

- A security policy is added, changed, or discontinued
- A major incident (or pattern of smaller incidents) occurs that could've been avoided or mitigated through better security awareness
- A major new threat is discovered
- A major change is made to the information systems or security architecture
- An assessment of the training program shows deficiencies

Program Effectiveness Evaluation

Many organizations treat security awareness training as a "check in the box" activity that is done simply to satisfy a requirement. The reality, however, is that effective training has both objectives (why we do it) and outcomes (what people can do after participating in it). The objectives are usually derived from senior-level policies or directives and drive the development of outcomes, which in turn drive the content and methods of delivery. For example, if the objective is reducing the incidence of successful phishing attacks, then it would be appropriate to pursue an outcome of having end users be able to detect a phishing e-mail. Both the objective and the outcome are measurable, which makes it easier to answer the question "is this working?"

We can evaluate whether the security training program is effective in improving an organization's security posture by simply measuring things before the training and then after it. Continuing the earlier example, we could keep track of the number of successful phishing attacks and see what happens to that number after the training has been conducted. This would be an assessment of the objective. We could also take trained and untrained users and test their ability to detect phishing e-mails. We would expect the trained users to fare better at this task, which would test the outcome. If we see that the number of phishing attacks remains unchanged (or worse, grows) or that the users are no better at detecting phishing e-mails after the training, then maybe the program is not effective.

When assessing the effectiveness of a training program, it is very important to analyze the data and not jump to conclusions. In the phishing example, there are many possible explanations for the lack of improvement. Maybe the adversaries are sending more-sophisticated messages that are harder to detect. Similarly, the results could simply show that the users just don't care and will continue to click links and open attachments until the consequences become negative enough for them. The point is to consider the root causes of the measurements when assessing the training.

Professional Ethics

Security awareness and training, of course, build on the notion that there are right ways and wrong ways in which to behave. This is the crux of ethics, which can be based on many different issues and foundations. Ethics can be relative to different situations and interpreted differently from individual to individual. Therefore, they are often a topic of debate. However, some ethics are less controversial than others, and these types of ethics are easier to expect of all people.

An interesting relationship exists between law and ethics. Most often, laws are based on ethics and are put in place to ensure that others act in an ethical way. However, laws do not apply to everything—that is when ethics should kick in. Some things may not be illegal, but that does not necessarily mean they are ethical.

Certain common ethical fallacies are used by many in the computing world to justify unethical acts. They exist because people look at issues differently and interpret (or misinterpret) rules and laws that have been put into place. The following are examples of these ethical fallacies:

- Hackers only want to learn and improve their skills. Many of them are not making a profit off of their deeds; therefore, their activities should not be seen as illegal or unethical.
- The First Amendment protects and provides the right for U.S. citizens to write viruses.
- Information should be shared freely and openly; therefore, sharing confidential information and trade secrets should be legal and ethical.
- Hacking does not actually hurt anyone.

(ISC)² Code of Professional Ethics

(ISC)² requires all certified system security professionals to commit to fully supporting its Code of Ethics. If a CISSP intentionally or knowingly violates this Code of Ethics, he or she may be subject to a peer review panel, which will decide whether the certification should be revoked.

The (ISC)² Code of Ethics for the CISSP is listed on the (ISC)² site at https://www.isc2.org/Ethics. The following list is an overview, but each CISSP candidate should read the full version and understand the Code of Ethics before attempting this exam. The code's preamble makes it clear that "[t]he safety and welfare of society and the common good, duty to our principals, and to each other, requires that we adhere, and be seen to adhere, to the highest ethical standards of behavior." It goes on to provide four canons for CISSPs:

- Protect society, the common good, necessary public trust and confidence, and the infrastructure
- Act honorably, honestly, justly, responsibly, and legally
- Provide diligent and competent service to principals
- Advance and protect the profession

Organizational Code of Ethics

More regulations are requiring organizations to have an ethical statement and potentially an ethical program in place. The ethical program is to serve as the "tone at the top," which means that the executives need to ensure not only that their employees are acting ethically but also that they themselves are following their own rules. The main goal is to ensure that the motto "succeed by any means necessary" is not the spoken or unspoken culture of a work environment. Certain structures can be put into place that provide a breeding ground for unethical behavior. If the CEO gets more in salary based on stock prices, then she may find ways to artificially inflate stock prices, which can directly hurt the investors and shareholders of the company. If managers can only be promoted based on the amount of sales they bring in, these numbers may be fudged and not represent reality. If an employee can only get a bonus if a low budget is maintained, he might be willing to take shortcuts that could hurt company customer service or product development. Although ethics seem like things that float around in the ether and make us feel good to talk about, they have to be actually implemented in the real corporate world through proper business processes and management styles.

The Computer Ethics Institute

The *Computer Ethics Institute* is a nonprofit organization that works to help advance technology by ethical means.

The Computer Ethics Institute has developed its own Ten Commandments of Computer Ethics:

1. Thou shalt not use a computer to harm other people.
2. Thou shalt not interfere with other people's computer work.
3. Thou shalt not snoop around in other people's computer files.
4. Thou shalt not use a computer to steal.
5. Thou shalt not use a computer to bear false witness.
6. Thou shalt not copy or use proprietary software for which you have not paid.

7. Thou shalt not use other people's computer resources without authorization or proper compensation.
8. Thou shalt not appropriate other people's intellectual output.
9. Thou shalt think about the social consequences of the program you are writing or the system you are designing.
10. Thou shalt always use a computer in ways that ensure consideration and respect for your fellow humans.

Chapter Review

This chapter laid out some of the fundamental principles of cybersecurity: the meaning of security, how it is governed, and the means by which it is implemented in an enterprise. It then focused on the most important aspect of security: people. They are the most important asset to any organization and can also be the greatest champions, or underminers, of cybersecurity. The difference lies in who we hire, what roles we assign to them, and how we train them. Bring the right people into the right seats and train them well and you'll have a robust security posture. Do otherwise at your own peril.

Our collective goal in information systems security boils down to ensuring the availability, integrity, and confidentiality of our information in an environment rich in influencers. These include organizational goals, assets, laws, regulations, privacy, threats, and, of course, people. Each of these was discussed in some detail in this chapter. Along the way, we also covered tangible ways in which we can link security to each of the influencers. As CISSPs we must be skilled in creating these linkages, as we are trusted to be able to apply the right solution to any security problem.

Quick Review

- The objectives of security are to provide confidentiality, integrity, availability, authenticity, and nonrepudiation.
- Confidentiality means keeping unauthorized entities (be they people or processes) from gaining access to information assets.
- Integrity means that that an asset is free from unauthorized alterations.
- Availability protection ensures reliability and timely access to data and resources to authorized individuals.
- Authenticity protections ensure we can trust that something comes from its claimed source.
- Nonrepudiation, which is closely related to authenticity, means that someone cannot disavow being the source of a given action.
- A vulnerability is a weakness in a system that allows a threat source to compromise its security.

- A threat is any potential danger that is associated with the exploitation of a vulnerability.
- A threat source (or threat agent, or threat actor) is any entity that can exploit a vulnerability.
- A risk is the likelihood of a threat source exploiting a vulnerability and the corresponding business impact.
- A control, or countermeasure, is put into place to mitigate (reduce) the potential risk.
- Security governance is a framework that provides oversight, accountability, and compliance.
- An information security management system (ISMS) is a collection of policies, procedures, baselines, and standards that an organization puts in place to make sure that its security efforts are aligned with business needs, streamlined, and effective and that no security controls are missing.
- An enterprise security architecture implements an information security strategy and consists of layers of solutions, processes, and procedures and the way they are linked across an enterprise strategically, tactically, and operationally.
- An enterprise security architecture should tie in strategic alignment, business enablement, process enhancement, and security effectiveness.
- Security governance is a framework that supports the security goals of an organization being set and expressed by senior management, communicated throughout the different levels of the organization, and consistently applied and assessed.
- Senior management always carries the ultimate responsibility for the organization.
- A security policy is a statement by management dictating the role security plays in the organization.
- Standards are documents that describe specific requirements that are compulsory in nature and support the organization's security policies.
- A baseline is a minimum level of security.
- Guidelines are recommendations and general approaches that provide advice and flexibility.
- Procedures are detailed step-by-step tasks that should be performed to achieve a certain goal.
- Job rotation and mandatory vacations are administrative security controls that can help detect fraud.
- Separation of duties ensures no single person has total control over a critical activity or task.
- Split knowledge and dual control are two variations of separation of duties.

- Social engineering is an attack carried out to manipulate a person into providing sensitive data to an unauthorized individual.
- Security awareness training should be comprehensive, tailored for specific groups, and organization-wide.
- Gamification is the application of elements of game play to other activities such as security awareness training.
- Security champions, which are members of an organization that, though their job descriptions do not include security, inform and encourage the adoption of security practices within their own teams.
- Professional ethics codify the right ways for a group of people to behave.

Questions

Please remember that these questions are formatted and asked in a certain way for a reason. Keep in mind that the CISSP exam is asking questions at a conceptual level. Questions may not always have the perfect answer, and the candidate is advised against always looking for the perfect answer. Instead, the candidate should look for the best answer in the list.

1. Which factor is the most important item when it comes to ensuring security is successful in an organization?
   A. Senior management support
   B. Effective controls and implementation methods
   C. Updated and relevant security policies and procedures
   D. Security awareness by all employees

Use the following scenario to answer Questions 2–4. Todd is a new security manager and has the responsibility of implementing personnel security controls within the financial institution where he works. Todd knows that many employees do not fully understand how their actions can put the institution at risk; thus, he needs to develop a security awareness program. He has determined that the bank tellers need to get a supervisory override when customers have checks over $3,500 that need to be cashed. He has also uncovered that some employees have stayed in their specific positions within the company for over three years. Todd would like to be able to investigate some of the activities of bank personnel to see if any fraudulent activities have taken place. Todd is already ensuring that two people must use separate keys at the same time to open the bank vault.

2. Todd documents several fraud opportunities that the employees have at the financial institution so that management understands these risks and allocates the funds and resources for his suggested solutions. Which of the following best describes the control Todd should put into place to be able to carry out fraudulent investigation activity?
   A. Separation of duties
   B. Job rotation
   C. Mandatory vacations
   D. Split knowledge
3. If the financial institution wants to ensure that fraud cannot happen successfully unless collusion occurs, what should Todd put into place?
   A. Separation of duties
   B. Job rotation
   C. Social engineering
   D. Split knowledge
4. Todd wants to be able to prevent fraud from taking place, but he knows that some people may get around the types of controls he puts into place. In those situations he wants to be able to identify when an employee is doing something suspicious. Which of the following incorrectly describes what Todd is implementing in this scenario and what those specific controls provide?
   A. Separation of duties, by ensuring that a supervisor must approve the cashing of a check over $3,500. This is an administrative control that provides preventive protection for Todd's organization.
   B. Job rotation, by ensuring that one employee only stays in one position for up to three months at a time. This is an administrative control that provides detective capabilities.
   C. Security awareness training, which can also emphasize enforcement.
   D. Dual control, which is an administrative detective control that can ensure that two employees must carry out a task simultaneously.
5. Which term denotes a potential cause of an unwanted incident, which may result in harm to a system or organization?
   A. Vulnerability
   B. Exploit
   C. Threat
   D. Attacker

6. A CISSP candidate signs an ethics statement prior to taking the CISSP examination. Which of the following would be a violation of the $(ISC)^2$ Code of Ethics that could cause the candidate to lose his or her certification?
   A. E-mailing information or comments about the exam to other CISSP candidates
   B. Submitting comments on the questions of the exam to $(ISC)^2$
   C. Submitting comments to the board of directors regarding the test and content of the class
   D. Conducting a presentation about the CISSP certification and what the certification means
7. You want to ensure that your organization's finance department, and only the finance department, has access to the organization's bank statements. Which of the security properties would be most important?
   A. Confidentiality
   B. Integrity
   C. Availability
   D. Both A and C
8. You want to make use of the OpenOffice productivity software suite mandatory across your organization. In what type of document would you codify this?
   A. Policy
   B. Standard
   C. Guideline
   D. Procedure
9. For an enterprise security architecture to be successful in its development and implementation, which of the following items is not essential?
   A. Strategic alignment
   B. Security guidelines
   C. Business enablement
   D. Process enhancement
10. Which of the following practices is likeliest to mitigate risks when considering a candidate for hiring?
   A. Security awareness training
   B. Nondisclosure agreement (NDA)
   C. Background checks
   D. Organizational ethics

Answers

1. **A.** Without senior management's support, a security program will not receive the necessary attention, funds, resources, and enforcement capabilities.
2. **C.** Mandatory vacation is an administrative detective control that allows for an organization to investigate an employee's daily business activities to uncover any potential fraud that may be taking place. The employee should be forced to be away from the organization for a two-week period, and another person should be put into that role. The idea is that the person who was rotated into that position may be able to detect suspicious activities.
3. **A.** Separation of duties is an administrative control that is put into place to ensure that one person cannot carry out a critical task by himself. If a person were able to carry out a critical task alone, this could put the organization at risk. Collusion is when two or more people come together to carry out fraud. So if a task was split between two people, they would have to carry out collusion (working together) to complete that one task and carry out fraud.
4. **D.** Dual control is an administrative preventive control. It ensures that two people must carry out a task at the same time, as in two people having separate keys when opening the vault. It is not a detective control. Notice that the question asks what Todd is *not* doing. Remember that on the exam you need to choose the *best* answer. In many situations you will not like the question or the corresponding answers on the CISSP exam, so prepare yourself. The questions can be tricky, which is one reason why the exam itself is so difficult.
5. **C.** The question provides the definition of a threat. The term attacker (option D) could be used to describe a threat agent that is, in turn, a threat, but use of this term is much more restrictive. The best answer is a threat.
6. **A.** A CISSP candidate and a CISSP holder should never discuss with others what was on the exam. This degrades the usefulness of the exam to be used as a tool to test someone's true security knowledge. If this type of activity is uncovered, the person could be stripped of their CISSP certification because this would violate the terms of the NDA into which the candidate enters prior to taking the test. Violating an NDA is a violation of the ethics canon that requires CISSPs to act honorably, honestly, justly, responsibly, and legally.
7. **D.** Confidentiality is ensuring that unauthorized parties (i.e., anyone other than finance department employees) cannot access protected assets. Availability is ensuring that authorized entities (i.e., finance) maintain access to assets. In this case, both confidentiality and availability are important to satisfy the requirements as stated.
8. **B.** Standards describe mandatory activities, actions, or rules. A policy is intended to be strategic, so it would not be the right document. A procedure describes the manner in which something must be done, which is much broader than is needed to make using a particular software suite mandatory across your organization. Finally, guidelines are recommended but optional practices.

9. **B.** Security guidelines are optional recommendations on issues that are not covered by mandatory policies, standards, or procedures. A successful enterprise security architecture is aligned with the organization's strategy, enables its business, and enhances (rather than hinders) its business processes.

10. **C.** The best way to reduce risk is to conduct background checks before you offer employment to a candidate. This ensures you are hiring someone whose past has been examined for any obviously disqualifying (or problematic) issues. The next step would be to sign an employment agreement that would include an NDA, followed by onboarding, which would include security awareness training and indoctrination into the organizational code of ethics.

CHAPTER 2

Risk Management

This chapter presents the following:

- Risk management (assessing risks, responding to risks, monitoring risks)
- Supply chain risk management
- Business continuity

A ship in harbor is safe, but that is not what ships are built for.

—William G.T. Shedd

We next turn our attention to the concept that should underlie every decision made when defending our information systems: risk. Risk is so important to understand as a cybersecurity professional that we not only cover it in detail in this chapter (one of the longest in the book) but also return to it time and again in the rest of the book. We start off narrowly by focusing on the vulnerabilities in our organizations and the threats that would exploit them to cause us harm. That sets the stage for an in-depth discussion of the main components of risk management: framing, assessing, responding to, and monitoring risks. We pay particular attention to supply chain risks, since these represent a big problem to which many organizations pay little or no attention. Finally, we'll talk about business continuity because it is so closely linked to risk management. We'll talk about disaster recovery, a closely related concept, in later chapters.

Risk Management Concepts

Risk in the context of security is the likelihood of a threat source exploiting a vulnerability and the corresponding business impact. *Risk management (RM)* is the process of identifying and assessing risk, reducing it to an acceptable level, and ensuring it remains at that level. There is no such thing as a 100-percent-secure environment. Every environment has vulnerabilities and threats. The skill is in identifying these threats, assessing the probability of them actually occurring and the damage they could cause, and then taking the right steps to reduce the overall level of risk in the environment to what the organization identifies as acceptable.

Risks to an organization come in different forms, and they are not all computer related. As we saw in Chapter 1, when a company acquires another company, it takes on a lot of risk in the hope that this move will increase its market base, productivity, and profitability. If a company increases its product line, this can add overhead, increase the need for personnel and storage facilities, require more funding for different materials, and maybe increase insurance premiums and the expense of marketing campaigns. The risk is that this added overhead might not be matched in sales; thus, profitability will be reduced or not accomplished.

When we look at information security, note that an organization needs to be aware of several types of risk and address them properly. The following items touch on the major categories:

- **Physical damage** Fire, water, vandalism, power loss, and natural disasters
- **Human interaction** Accidental or intentional action or inaction that can disrupt productivity
- **Equipment malfunction** Failure of systems and peripheral devices
- **Inside and outside attacks** Hacking, cracking, and attacking
- **Misuse of data** Sharing trade secrets, fraud, espionage, and theft
- **Loss of data** Intentional or unintentional loss of information to unauthorized parties
- **Application error** Computation errors, input errors, and software defects

Threats must be identified, classified by category, and evaluated to calculate their damage potential to the organization. Real risk is hard to measure, but prioritizing the potential risks in the order of which ones must be addressed first is obtainable.

Holistic Risk Management

Who really understands risk management? Unfortunately, the answer to this question is that not enough people inside or outside of the security profession really get it. Even though information security is big business today, the focus all too often is on applications, devices, viruses, and hacking. Although these items all must be considered and weighed in risk management processes, they should be considered pieces of the overall security puzzle, not the main focus of risk management.

Security is a business issue, but businesses operate to make money, not just to be secure. A business is concerned with security only if potential risks threaten its bottom line, which they can in many ways, such as through the loss of reputation and customer base after a database of credit card numbers is compromised; through the loss of thousands of dollars in operational expenses from a new computer worm; through the loss of proprietary information as a result of successful company espionage attempts; through the loss of confidential information from a successful social engineering attack; and so on. It is critical that security professionals understand these individual threats, but it is more important that they understand how to calculate the risk of these threats and map them to business drivers.

To properly manage risk within an organization, you have to look at it holistically. Risk, after all, exists within a context. The U.S. National Institute of Standards and Technology (NIST) Special Publication (SP) 800-39, *Managing Information Security Risk*, defines three tiers to risk management:

- **Organization view (Tier 1)** Concerned with risk to the organization as a whole, which means it frames the rest of the conversation and sets important parameters such as the risk tolerance level.
- **Mission/business process view (Tier 2)** Deals with the risk to the major functions of the organization, such as defining the criticality of the information flows between the organization and its partners or customers.
- **Information systems view (Tier 3)** Addresses risk from an information systems perspective. Though this is where we will focus our discussion, it is important to understand that it exists within the context of (and must be consistent with) other, more encompassing risk management efforts.

These tiers are dependent on each other, as shown in Figure 2-1. Risk management starts with decisions made at the organization tier, which flow down to the other two tiers. Feedback on the effects of these decisions flows back up the hierarchy to inform the next set of decisions to be made. Carrying out risk management properly means that you have a holistic understanding of your organization, the threats it faces, the countermeasures that can be put into place to deal with those threats, and continuous monitoring to ensure the acceptable risk level is being met on an ongoing basis.

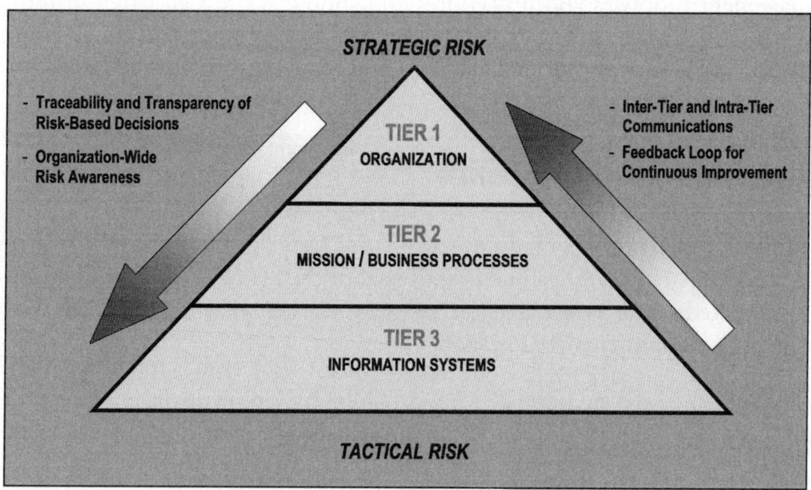

Figure 2-1 The three tiers of risk management (Source: NIST SP 800-39)

Information Systems Risk Management Policy

Proper risk management requires a strong commitment from senior leaders, a documented process that supports the organization's mission, an information systems risk management (ISRM) policy, and a delegated ISRM team. The ISRM policy should be a subset of the organization's overall risk management policy (*risks to an organization include more than just information security issues*) and should be mapped to the organizational security policies. The ISRM policy should address the following items:

- The objectives of the ISRM team
- The level of risk the organization will accept and what is considered an acceptable level of risk
- Formal processes of risk identification
- The connection between the ISRM policy and the organization's strategic planning processes
- Responsibilities that fall under ISRM and the roles to fulfill them
- The mapping of risk to internal controls
- The approach toward changing staff behaviors and resource allocation in response to risk analysis
- The mapping of risks to performance targets and budgets
- Key metrics and performance indicators to monitor the effectiveness of controls

The ISRM policy provides the foundation and direction for the organization's security risk management processes and procedures and should address all issues of information security. It should provide direction on how the ISRM team communicates information on the organization's risks to senior management and how to properly execute management's decisions on risk mitigation tasks.

The Risk Management Team

Each organization is different in its size, security posture, threat profile, and security budget. One organization may have one individual responsible for ISRM or a team that works in a coordinated manner. The overall goal of the team is to ensure that the organization is protected in the most cost-effective manner. This goal can be accomplished only if the following components are in place:

- An established risk acceptance level provided by senior management
- Documented risk assessment processes and procedures
- Procedures for identifying and mitigating risks
- Appropriate resource and fund allocation from senior management
- Security awareness training for all staff members associated with information assets
- The ability to establish improvement (or risk mitigation) teams in specific areas when necessary

- The mapping of legal and regulation compliancy requirements to control and implement requirements
- The development of metrics and performance indicators so as to measure and manage various types of risks
- The ability to identify and assess new risks as the environment and organization change
- The integration of ISRM and the organization's change control process to ensure that changes do not introduce new vulnerabilities

Obviously, this list is a lot more than just buying a new shiny firewall and calling the organization safe.

The ISRM team, in most cases, is not made up of employees with the dedicated task of risk management. It consists of people who already have a full-time job in the organization and are now tasked with something else. Thus, senior management support is necessary so proper resource allocation can take place.

Of course, all teams need a leader, and ISRM is no different. One individual should be singled out to run this rodeo and, in larger organizations, this person should be spending 50 to 70 percent of their time in this role. Management must dedicate funds to making sure this person receives the necessary training and risk analysis tools to ensure it is a successful endeavor.

The Risk Management Process

By now you should believe that risk management is critical to the long-term security (and even success) of your organization. But how do you get this done? NIST SP 800-39 describes four interrelated components that comprise the risk management process. These are shown in Figure 2-2. Let's consider each of these components briefly now, since they will nicely frame the remainder of our discussion of risk management.

- **Frame risk** Risk framing defines the context within which all other risk activities take place. What are our assumptions and constraints? What are the organizational priorities? What is the risk tolerance of senior management?
- **Assess risk** Before we can take any action to mitigate risk, we have to assess it. This is perhaps the most critical aspect of the process, and one that we will discuss at length. If your risk assessment is spot-on, then the rest of the process becomes pretty straightforward.
- **Respond to risk** By now, we've done our homework. We know what we should, must, and can't do (from the framing component), and we know what we're up against in terms of threats, vulnerabilities, and attacks (from the assess component). Responding to the risk becomes a matter of matching our limited resources with our prioritized set of controls. Not only are we mitigating significant risk, but, more importantly, we can tell our bosses what risk we can't do anything about because we're out of resources.

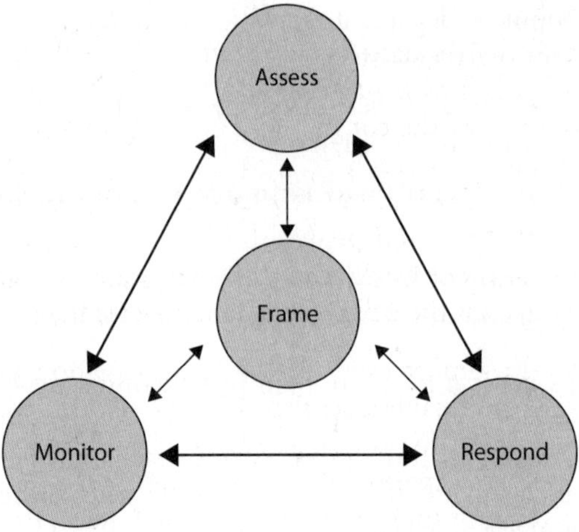

Figure 2-2 The components of the risk management process

- **Monitor risk** No matter how diligent we've been so far, we probably missed something. If not, then the environment likely changed (perhaps a new threat source emerged or a new system brought new vulnerabilities). In order to stay one step ahead of the bad guys, we need to continuously monitor the effectiveness of our controls against the risks for which we designed them.

You will notice that our discussion of risk so far has dealt heavily with the whole framing process. In the preceding sections, we've talked about the organization (top to bottom), the policies, and the team. The next step is to assess the risk, and what better way to start than by understanding threats and the vulnerabilities they might exploit.

Overview of Vulnerabilities and Threats

To focus our efforts on the likely (and push aside the less likely) risks to our organizations, we need to consider what it is that we have that someone (or something) else may be able to take, degrade, disrupt, or destroy. As we will see later (in the section "Assessing Risks"), inventorying and categorizing our information systems is a critical early step in the process. For the purpose of modeling the threat, we are particularly interested in the vulnerabilities inherent in our systems that could lead to the compromise of their confidentiality, integrity, or availability. We then ask the question, "Who would want to exploit this vulnerability, and why?" This leads us to a deliberate study of our potential adversaries, their motivations, and their capabilities. Finally, we determine whether a given threat source has the means to exploit one or more vulnerabilities in order to attack our assets.

NOTE We will discuss threat modeling in detail in Chapter 9.

Vulnerabilities

Everything built by humans is vulnerable to something. Our information systems, in particular, are riddled with vulnerabilities even in the best-defended cases. One need only read news accounts of the compromise of the highly protected and classified systems of defense contractors and even governments to see that this universal principle is true. To properly analyze vulnerabilities, it is useful to recall that information systems consist of information, processes, and people that are typically, but not always, interacting with computer systems. Since we discuss computer system vulnerabilities in detail in Chapter 6, we will briefly discuss the other three components here.

Information In almost every case, the information at the core of our information systems is the most valuable asset to a potential adversary. Information within a computer information system (CIS) is represented as data. This information may be stored (data at rest), transported between parts of our system (data in transit), or actively being used by the system (data in use). In each of its three states, the information exhibits different vulnerabilities, as listed in the following examples:

- **Data at rest** Data is copied to a thumb drive and given to unauthorized parties by an insider, thus compromising its confidentiality.
- **Data in transit** Data is modified by an external actor intercepting it on the network and then relaying the altered version (known as a man-in-the-middle or MitM attack), thus compromising its integrity.
- **Data in use** Data is deleted by a malicious process exploiting a "time-of-check to time-of-use" (TOC/TOU) or "race condition" vulnerability, thus compromising its availability.

Processes Most organizations implement standardized processes to ensure the consistency and efficiency of their services and products. It turns out, however, that efficiency is pretty easy to hack. Consider the case of shipping containers. Someone wants to ship something from point A to point B, say a container of bananas from Brazil to Belgium. Once the shipping order is placed and the destination entered, that information flows from the farm to a truck carrier, to the seaport of origin to the ocean carrier, to the destination seaport, to another truck carrier, and finally to its destination at some distribution center in Antwerp. In most cases, nobody pays a lot of attention to the address once it is entered. But what if an attacker knew this and changed the address while the shipment was at sea? The attacker could have the shipment show up at a different destination and even control the arrival time. This technique has actually been used by drug and weapons smuggling gangs to get their "bananas" to where they need them.

This sort of attack is known as *business process compromise (BPC)* and is commonly targeted at the financial sector, where transaction amounts, deposit accounts, or other parameters are changed to funnel money to the attackers' pockets. Since business processes are almost always instantiated in software as part of a CIS, process vulnerabilities can be thought of as a specific kind of software vulnerability. As security professionals, however, it is important that we take a broader view of the issue and think about the business processes that are implemented in our software systems.

People Many security experts consider humans to be the weakest link in the security chain. Whether or not you agree with this, it is important to consider the specific vulnerabilities that people present in a system. Though there are many ways to exploit the human in the loop, there are three that correspond to the bulk of the attacks, summarized briefly here:

- **Social engineering** This is the process of getting a person to violate a security procedure or policy, and usually involves human interaction or e-mail/text messages.
- **Social networks** The prevalence of social network use provides potential attackers with a wealth of information that can be leveraged directly (e.g., blackmail) or indirectly (e.g., crafting an e-mail with a link that is likely to be clicked) to exploit people.
- **Passwords** Weak passwords can be cracked in milliseconds using rainbow tables and are very susceptible to dictionary or brute-force attacks. Even strong passwords are vulnerable if they are reused across sites and systems.

Threats

As you identify the vulnerabilities that are inherent to your organization and its systems, it is important to also identify the sources that could attack them. The International Organization for Standardization and the International Electrotechnical Commission in their joint ISO/IEC standard 27000 define a *threat* as a "potential cause of an unwanted incident, which can result in harm to a system or organization." While this may sound somewhat vague, it is important to include the full breadth of possibilities. When a threat is one or more humans, we typically use the term *threat actor* or *threat agent*. Let's start with the most obvious: malicious humans.

Cybercriminals Cybercriminals are the most common threat actors encountered by individuals and organizations. Most cybercriminals are motivated by greed, but some just enjoy breaking things. Their skills run the gamut, from so-called *script kiddies* with just a basic grasp of hacking (but access to someone else's scripts or tools) to sophisticated cybercrime gangs who develop and sometimes sell or rent their services and tools to others. Cybercrime is the fastest-growing sector of criminal activity in many countries.

One of the factors that makes cybercrime so pervasive is that every connected device is a target. Some devices are immediately monetizable, such as your personal smartphone or home computer containing credentials, payment card information, and access to your financial institutions. Other targets provide bigger payouts, such as the finance systems in your place of work. Even devices that are not, by themselves, easily monetizable can be hijacked and joined into a botnet to spread malware, conduct distributed denial-of-service (DDoS) attacks, or serve as staging bases from which to attack other targets.

Nation-State Actors Whereas cybercriminals tend to cast a wide net in an effort to maximize their profits, nation-state actors (or simply *state actors*) are very selective in who they target. They use advanced capabilities to compromise systems and establish a persistent presence to allow them to collect intelligence (e.g., sensitive data, intellectual property, etc.) for extended periods. After their presence is established, state actors may use prepositioned assets to trigger devastating effects in response to world events. Though their main motivations tend to be espionage and gaining persistent access to critical infrastructure, some state actors maintain good relations with cybercrime groups in their own country, mostly for the purposes of plausible deniability. By collaborating with these criminals, state actors can make it look as if an attack against another nation was a crime and not an act of war. At least one country is known to use its national offensive cyber capabilities for financial profit, stealing millions of dollars all over the world.

Many security professionals consider state actors a threat mostly to government organizations, critical infrastructure like power plants, and anyone with sophisticated research and development capabilities. In reality, however, these actors can and do target other organizations, typically to use them as a springboard into their ultimate targets. So, even if you work for a small company that seems uninteresting to a foreign nation, you could find your company in a state actor's crosshairs.

Hacktivists Hacktivists use cyberattacks to effect political or social change. The term covers a diverse ecosystem, encompassing individuals and groups of various skillsets and capabilities. Hacktivists' preferred objectives are highly visible to the public or yield information that, when made public, aims to embarrass government entities or undermine public trust in them.

Internal Actors Internal actors are people within the organization, such as employees, former employees, contractors, or business associates, who have inside information concerning the organization's security practices, data, and computer systems. Broadly speaking, there are two types of insider threats: negligent and malicious. A negligent insider is one who fails to exercise due care, which puts their organization at risk. Sometimes, these individuals knowingly violate policies or disregard procedures, but they are not doing so out of malicious intent. For example, an employee could disregard a policy requiring visitors to be escorted at all times because someone shows up wearing the uniform of a telecommunications company and claiming to be on site to fix an outage. This insider trusts the visitor, which puts the organization at risk, particularly if that person is an impostor.

The second type of insider threat is characterized by malicious intent. Malicious insiders use the knowledge they have about their organization either for their own advantage (e.g., to commit fraud) or to directly cause harm (e.g., by deleting sensitive files). While some malicious insiders plan their criminal activity while they are employees in good standing, others are triggered by impending termination actions. Knowing (or suspecting) that they're about to be fired, they may attempt to steal sensitive data (such as customer contacts or design documents) before their access is revoked. Other malicious insiders may be angry and plant malware or destroy assets in an act of revenge. This insider threat highlights the need for the "zero trust" secure design principle (discussed in Chapter 9). It is also a really good reason to practice the termination processes discussed in Chapter 1.

In the wake of the massive leak of classified data attributed to Edward Snowden in 2012, there's been increased emphasis on techniques and procedures for identifying and mitigating the insider threat source. While the deliberate insider dominates the news, it is important to note that the accidental insider can be just as dangerous, particularly if they fall into one of the vulnerability classes described in the preceding section.

Nature Finally, the nonhuman threat source can be just as important as the ones we've previously discussed. Hurricane Katrina in 2005 and the Tohoku earthquake and tsunami in 2011 serve as reminders that natural events can be more destructive than any human attack. They also force the information systems security professional to consider threats that fall way outside the norm. Though it is easier and, in many cases, cheaper to address likelier natural events such as a water main break or a fire in a facility, one should always look for opportunities to leverage countermeasures that protect against both mild and extreme events for small price differentials.

Identifying Threats and Vulnerabilities

Earlier, it was stated that the definition of a risk is the probability of a threat exploiting a vulnerability to cause harm to an asset and the resulting business impact. Many types of threat actors can take advantage of several types of vulnerabilities, resulting in a variety of specific threats, as outlined in Table 2-1, which represents only a sampling of the risks many organizations should address in their risk management programs.

Other types of threats can arise in an environment that are much harder to identify than those listed in Table 2-1. These other threats have to do with application and user errors. If an application uses several complex equations to produce results, the threat can be difficult to discover and isolate if these equations are incorrect or if the application is using inputted data incorrectly. This can result in *illogical processing* and *cascading errors* as invalid results are passed on to another process. These types of problems can lie within application code and are very hard to identify.

Threat Actor	Can Exploit This Vulnerability	To Cause This Effect
Cybercriminal	Lack of antimalware software	Ransomed data
Nation-state actor	Password reuse in privileged accounts	Unauthorized access to confidential information
Negligent user	Misconfigured parameter in the operating system	Loss of availability due to a system malfunction
Fire	Lack of fire extinguishers	Facility and computer loss or damage, and possibly loss of life
Malicious insider	Poor termination procedures	Deletion of business-critical information
Hacktivist	Poorly written web application	Website defacement
Burglar	Lack of security guard	Breaking windows and stealing computers and devices

Table 2-1 Relationship of Threats and Vulnerabilities

User errors, whether intentional or accidental, are easier to identify by monitoring and auditing users' activities. Audits and reviews must be conducted to discover if employees are inputting values incorrectly into programs, misusing technology, or modifying data in an inappropriate manner.

After the ISRM team has identified the vulnerabilities and associated threats, it must investigate the ramifications of any of those vulnerabilities being exploited. Risks have *loss potential*, meaning that the organization could lose assets or revenues if a threat agent actually exploited a vulnerability. The loss may be corrupted data, destruction of systems and/or the facility, unauthorized disclosure of confidential information, a reduction in employee productivity, and so on. When performing a risk assessment, the team also must look at *delayed loss* when assessing the damages that can occur. Delayed loss is secondary in nature and takes place well after a vulnerability is exploited. Delayed loss may include damage to the organization's reputation, loss of market share, accrued late penalties, civil suits, the delayed collection of funds from customers, resources required to reimage other compromised systems, and so forth.

For example, if a company's web servers are attacked and taken offline, the immediate damage (loss potential) could be data corruption, the man-hours necessary to place the servers back online, and the replacement of any code or components required. The company could lose revenue if it usually accepts orders and payments via its website. If getting the web servers fixed and back online takes a full day, the company could lose a lot more sales and profits. If getting the web servers fixed and back online takes a full week, the company could lose enough sales and profits to not be able to pay other bills and expenses. This would be a delayed loss. If the company's customers lose confidence in it because of this activity, the company could lose business for months or years. This is a more extreme case of delayed loss.

These types of issues make the process of properly quantifying losses that specific threats could cause more complex, but they must be taken into consideration to ensure reality is represented in this type of analysis.

Assessing Risks

A *risk assessment*, which is really a tool for risk management, is a method of identifying vulnerabilities and threats and assessing the possible impacts to determine where to implement security controls. After parts of a risk assessment are carried out, the results are analyzed. *Risk analysis* is a detailed examination of the components of risk that is used to ensure that security is cost-effective, relevant, timely, and responsive to threats. It is easy to apply too much security, not enough security, or the wrong security controls and to spend too much money in the process without attaining the necessary objectives. Risk analysis helps organizations prioritize their risks and shows management the amount of resources that should be applied to protecting against those risks in a sensible manner.

EXAM TIP The terms risk assessment and risk analysis, depending on who you ask, can mean the same thing, or one must follow the other, or one is a subpart of the other. Here, we treat risk assessment as the broader effort, which is reinforced by specific risk analysis tasks as needed. This is how you should think of it for the CISSP exam.

Risk analysis has four main goals:

- Identify assets and their value to the organization.
- Determine the likelihood that a threat exploits a vulnerability.
- Determine the business impact of these potential threats.
- Provide an economic balance between the impact of the threat and the cost of the countermeasure.

Risk analysis provides a *cost/benefit comparison*, which compares the annualized cost of controls to the potential cost of loss. A control, in most cases, should not be implemented unless the annualized cost of loss exceeds the annualized cost of the control itself. This means that if a facility is worth $100,000, it does not make sense to spend $150,000 trying to protect it.

It is important to figure out what you are *supposed* to be doing before you dig right in and start working. Anyone who has worked on a project without a properly defined scope can attest to the truth of this statement. Before an assessment is started, the team must carry out *project sizing* to understand what assets and threats should be evaluated. Most assessments are focused on physical security, technology security, or personnel security. Trying to assess all of them at the same time can be quite an undertaking.

One of the risk assessment team's tasks is to create a report that details the asset valuations. Senior management should review and accept the list and use these values to determine the scope of the risk management project. If management determines at this early stage that some assets are not important, the risk assessment team should not spend additional time or resources evaluating those assets. During discussions with management, everyone involved must have a firm understanding of the value of the security CIA triad—confidentiality, integrity, and availability—and how it directly relates to business needs.

Management should outline the scope of the assessment, which most likely will be dictated by organizational compliance requirements as well as budgetary constraints. Many projects have run out of funds, and consequently stopped, because proper project sizing was not conducted at the onset of the project. Don't let this happen to you.

A risk assessment helps integrate the security program objectives with the organization's business objectives and requirements. The more the business and security objectives are in alignment, the more successful both will be. The assessment also helps the organization draft a proper budget for a security program and its constituent security components. Once an organization knows how much its assets are worth and the possible threats those assets are exposed to, it can make intelligent decisions about how much money to spend protecting those assets.

A risk assessment must be supported and directed by senior management if it is to be successful. Management must define the purpose and scope of the effort, appoint a team to carry out the assessment, and allocate the necessary time and funds to conduct it. It is essential for senior management to review the outcome of the risk assessment and to act on its findings. After all, what good is it to go through all the trouble of a risk assessment and *not* react to its findings? Unfortunately, this does happen all too often.

Asset Valuation

To understand possible losses and how much we may want to invest in preventing them, we must understand the value of an asset that could be impacted by a threat. The value placed on information is relative to the parties involved, what work was required to develop it, how much it costs to maintain, what damage would result if it were lost or destroyed, how much money enemies would pay for it, and what liability penalties could be endured. If an organization does not know the value of the information and the other assets it is trying to protect, it does not know how much money and time it should spend on protecting them. If the calculated value of your company's secret formula is *x*, then the total cost of protecting it should be some value less than *x*. Knowing the value of our information allows us to make quantitative cost/benefit comparisons as we manage our risks.

The preceding logic applies not only to assessing the value of *information* and protecting it but also to assessing the value of the organization's other assets, such as facilities, systems, and even intangibles like the value of the brand, and protecting them. The value of the organization's facilities must be assessed, along with all printers, workstations, servers, peripheral devices, supplies, and employees. You do not know how much is in danger of being lost if you don't know what you have and what it is worth in the first place.

The actual value of an asset is determined by the importance it has to the organization as a whole. The value of an asset should reflect all identifiable costs that would arise if the asset were actually impaired. If a server cost $4,000 to purchase, this value should not be input as the value of the asset in a risk assessment. Rather, the cost of replacing or repairing it, the loss of productivity, and the value of any data that may be corrupted or lost must be accounted for to properly capture the amount the organization would lose if the server were to fail for one reason or another.

The following issues should be considered when assigning values to assets:

- Cost to acquire or develop the asset
- Cost to maintain and protect the asset
- Value of the asset to owners and users
- Value of the asset to adversaries
- Price others are willing to pay for the asset
- Cost to replace the asset if lost
- Operational and production activities affected if the asset is unavailable
- Liability issues if the asset is compromised
- Usefulness and role of the asset in the organization
- Impact of the asset's loss on the organization's brand or reputation

Understanding the value of an asset is the first step to understanding what security mechanisms should be put in place and what funds should go toward protecting it. A very important question is how much it could cost the organization to *not* protect the asset.

Determining the value of assets may be useful to an organization for a variety of reasons, including the following:

- To perform effective cost/benefit analyses
- To select specific countermeasures and safeguards
- To determine the level of insurance coverage to purchase
- To understand what exactly is at risk
- To comply with legal and regulatory requirements

Assets may be tangible (computers, facilities, supplies) or intangible (reputation, data, intellectual property). It is usually harder to quantify the values of intangible assets, which may change over time. How do you put a monetary value on a company's reputation? This is not always an easy question to answer, but it is important to be able to do so.

Risk Assessment Teams

Each organization has different departments, and each department has its own functionality, resources, tasks, and quirks. For the most effective risk assessment, an organization must build a risk assessment team that includes individuals from many or all departments to ensure that all of the threats are identified and addressed. The team members may be part of management, application programmers, IT staff, systems integrators, and operational managers—indeed, any key personnel from key areas of the organization. This mix is necessary because if the team comprises only individuals from the IT department, it may not understand, for example, the types of threats the accounting department faces with data integrity issues, or how the organization as a whole would be affected if the accounting department's data files were wiped out by an accidental or intentional act.

Asking the Right Questions

When looking at risk, it's good to keep several questions in mind. Raising these questions helps ensure that the risk assessment team and senior management know what is important. Team members must ask the following:

- What event could occur (threat event)?
- What could be the potential impact (risk)?
- How often could it happen (frequency)?
- What level of confidence do we have in the answers to the first three questions (certainty)?

A lot of this information is gathered through internal surveys, interviews, or workshops. Viewing threats with these questions in mind helps the team focus on the tasks at hand and assists in making the decisions more accurate and relevant.

Or, as another example, the IT staff may not understand all the risks the employees in the warehouse would face if a natural disaster were to hit, or what it would mean to their productivity and how it would affect the organization overall. If the risk assessment team is unable to include members from various departments, it should, at the very least, make sure to interview people in each department so it fully understands and can quantify all threats.

The risk assessment team must also include people who understand the processes that are part of their individual departments, meaning individuals who are at the right levels of each department. This is a difficult task, since managers sometimes delegate any sort of risk assessment task to lower levels within the department. However, the people who work at these lower levels may not have adequate knowledge and understanding of the processes that the risk assessment team may need to deal with.

Methodologies for Risk Assessment

The industry has different standardized methodologies for carrying out risk assessments. Each of the individual methodologies has the same basic core components (identify vulnerabilities, associate threats, calculate risk values), but each has a specific focus. Keep in mind that the methodologies have a lot of overlapping similarities because each one has the specific goal of identifying things that could hurt the organization (vulnerabilities and threats) so that those things can be addressed (risk reduced). What make these methodologies different from each other are their unique approaches and focuses.

If you need to deploy an organization-wide risk management program and integrate it into your security program, you should follow the OCTAVE method. If you need to focus just on IT security risks during your assessment, you can follow NIST SP 800-30. If you have a limited budget and need to carry out a focused assessment on an individual system or process, you can follow the Facilitated Risk Analysis Process. If you really want to dig into the details of how a security flaw within a specific system could cause negative ramifications, you could use Failure Modes and Effect Analysis or fault tree analysis.

NIST SP 800-30

NIST SP 800-30, Revision 1, *Guide for Conducting Risk Assessments*, is specific to information systems threats and how they relate to information security risks. It lays out the following steps:

1. Prepare for the assessment.
2. Conduct the assessment:
    a. Identify threat sources and events.
    b. Identify vulnerabilities and predisposing conditions.
    c. Determine likelihood of occurrence.
    d. Determine magnitude of impact.
    e. Determine risk.
3. Communicate results.
4. Maintain assessment.

The NIST risk management methodology is mainly focused on computer systems and IT security issues. It does not explicitly cover larger organizational threat types, as in succession planning, environmental issues, or how security risks associate to business risks. It is a methodology that focuses on the operational components of an enterprise, not necessarily the higher strategic level.

FRAP

Facilitated Risk Analysis Process (FRAP) is a second type of risk assessment methodology. The crux of this qualitative methodology is to focus only on the systems that really need assessing, to reduce costs and time obligations. FRAP stresses prescreening activities so that the risk assessment steps are only carried out on the item(s) that needs it the most. FRAP is intended to be used to analyze one system, application, or business process at a time. Data is gathered and threats to business operations are prioritized based upon their criticality. The risk assessment team documents the controls that need to be put into place to reduce the identified risks along with action plans for control implementation efforts.

This methodology does not support the idea of calculating exploitation probability numbers or annualized loss expectancy values. The criticalities of the risks are determined by the team members' experience. The author of this methodology (Thomas Peltier) believes that trying to use mathematical formulas for the calculation of risk is too confusing and time consuming. The goal is to keep the scope of the assessment small and the assessment processes simple to allow for efficiency and cost-effectiveness.

OCTAVE

The *Operationally Critical Threat, Asset, and Vulnerability Evaluation (OCTAVE)* methodology was created by Carnegie Mellon University's Software Engineering Institute (SIE). OCTAVE is intended to be used in situations where people manage and direct the risk evaluation for information security within their organization. This places the people who work inside the organization in the power positions of being able to make the decisions regarding what is the best approach for evaluating the security of their organization. OCTAVE relies on the idea that the people working in these environments best understand what is needed and what kind of risks they are facing. The individuals who make up the risk assessment team go through rounds of facilitated workshops. The facilitator helps the team members understand the risk methodology and how to apply it to the vulnerabilities and threats identified within their specific business units. OCTAVE stresses a self-directed team approach.

The scope of an OCTAVE assessment is usually very wide compared to the more focused approach of FRAP. Where FRAP would be used to assess a system or application, OCTAVE would be used to assess all systems, applications, and business processes within the organization.

The OCTAVE methodology consists of the seven processes (or steps) listed here:

1. Identify enterprise knowledge.
2. Identify operational area knowledge.
3. Identify staff knowledge.

4. Establish security requirements.
5. Map high-priority information assets to information infrastructure.
6. Perform infrastructure vulnerability evaluation.
7. Conduct multidimensional risk analysis.
8. Develop protection strategy.

FMEA

Failure Modes and Effect Analysis (FMEA) is a method for determining functions, identifying functional failures, and assessing the causes of failure and their failure effects through a structured process. FMEA is commonly used in product development and operational environments. The goal is to identify where something is most likely going to break and either fix the flaws that could cause this issue or implement controls to reduce the impact of the break. For example, you might choose to carry out an FMEA on your organization's network to identify single points of failure. These single points of failure represent vulnerabilities that could directly affect the productivity of the network as a whole. You would use this structured approach to identify these issues (vulnerabilities), assess their criticality (risk), and identify the necessary controls that should be put into place (reduce risk).

The FMEA methodology uses failure modes (how something can break or fail) and effects analysis (impact of that break or failure). The application of this process to a chronic failure enables the determination of where exactly the failure is most likely to occur. Think of it as being able to look into the future and locate areas that have the potential for failure and then applying corrective measures to them before they do become actual liabilities.

By following a specific order of steps, the best results can be maximized for an FMEA:

1. Start with a block diagram of a system or control.
2. Consider what happens if each block of the diagram fails.
3. Draw up a table in which failures are paired with their effects and an evaluation of the effects.
4. Correct the design of the system, and adjust the table until the system is not known to have unacceptable problems.
5. Have several engineers review the Failure Modes and Effect Analysis.

Table 2-2 is an example of how an FMEA can be carried out and documented. Although most organizations will not have the resources to do this level of detailed work for every system and control, an organization can carry it out on critical functions and systems that can drastically affect the organization.

FMEA was first developed for systems engineering. Its purpose is to examine the potential failures in products and the processes involved with them. This approach proved to be successful and has been more recently adapted for use in evaluating risk management priorities and mitigating known threat vulnerabilities.

Prepared by:							
Approved by:							
Date:							
Revision:							
				Failure Effect on . . .			
Item Identification	**Function**	**Failure Mode**	**Failure Cause**	**Component or Functional Assembly**	**Next Higher Assembly**	**System**	**Failure Detection Method**
IPS application content filter	Inline perimeter protection	Fails to close	Traffic overload	Single point of failure Denial of service	IPS blocks ingress traffic stream	IPS is brought down	Health check status sent to console and e-mail to security administrator
Central antivirus signature update engine	Push updated signatures to all servers and workstations	Fails to provide adequate, timely protection against malware	Central server goes down	Individual node's antivirus software is not updated	Network is infected with malware	Central server can be infected and/or infect other systems	Heartbeat status check sent to central console, and e-mail to network administrator
Fire suppression water pipes	Suppress fire in building 1 in 5 zones	Fails to close	Water in pipes freezes	None	Building 1 has no suppression agent available	Fire suppression system pipes break	Suppression sensors tied directly into fire system central console
Etc.							

Table 2-2 How an FMEA Can Be Carried Out and Documented

FMEA is used in assurance risk management because of the level of detail, variables, and complexity that continues to rise as corporations understand risk at more granular levels. This methodical way of identifying potential pitfalls is coming into play more as the need for risk awareness—down to the tactical and operational levels—continues to expand.

Fault Tree Analysis

While FMEA is most useful as a survey method to identify major failure modes in a given system, the method is not as useful in discovering complex failure modes that may be involved in multiple systems or subsystems. A *fault tree analysis* usually proves to be a more useful approach to identifying failures that can take place within more complex environments and systems. First, an undesired effect is taken as the root or top event of a tree of logic. Then, each situation that has the potential to cause that effect is added to the tree as a series of logic expressions. Fault trees are then labeled with actual numbers pertaining to failure probabilities. This is typically done by using computer programs that can calculate the failure probabilities from a fault tree.

Figure 2-3 shows a simplistic fault tree and the different logic symbols used to represent what must take place for a specific fault event to occur.

When setting up the tree, you must accurately list all the threats or faults that can occur within a system. The branches of the tree can be divided into general categories, such as physical threats, network threats, software threats, Internet threats, and component failure threats. Then, once all possible general categories are in place, you can trim them and effectively prune from the tree the branches that won't apply to the system in question. In general, if a system is not connected to the Internet by any means, remove that general branch from the tree.

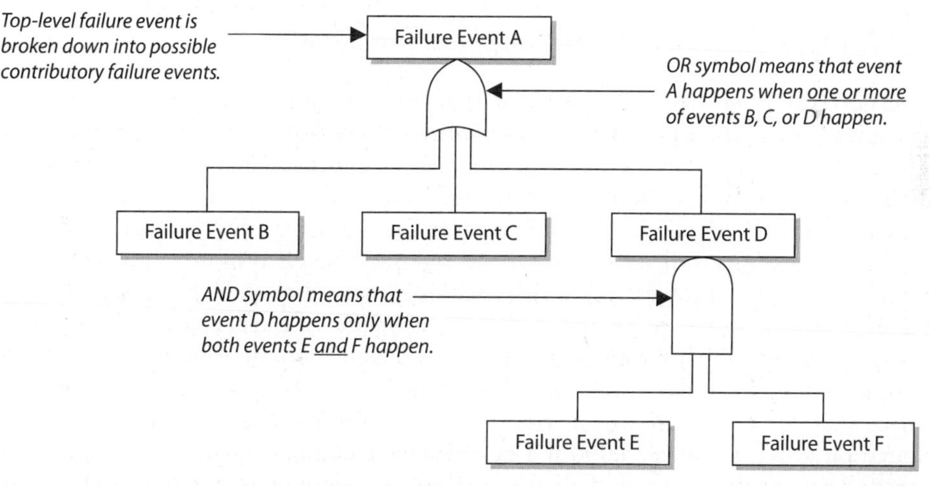

Figure 2-3 Fault tree and logic components

Some of the most common software failure events that can be explored through a fault tree analysis are the following:

- False alarms
- Insufficient error handling
- Sequencing or order
- Incorrect timing outputs
- Valid but unexpected outputs

Of course, because of the complexity of software and heterogeneous environments, this is a very small sample list.

EXAM TIP A risk assessment is used to gather data. A risk analysis examines the gathered data to produce results that can be acted upon.

Risk Analysis Approaches

So up to this point, we have accomplished the following items:

- Developed a risk management policy
- Developed a risk management team
- Identified organizational assets to be assessed
- Calculated the value of each asset
- Identified the vulnerabilities and threats that can affect the identified assets
- Chosen a risk assessment methodology that best fits our needs

The next thing we need to figure out is if our risk analysis approach should be quantitative or qualitative in nature. A *quantitative risk analysis* is used to assign monetary and numeric values to all elements of the risk analysis process. Each element within the analysis (asset value, threat frequency, severity of vulnerability, impact damage, safeguard costs, safeguard effectiveness, uncertainty, and probability items) is quantified and entered into equations to determine total and residual risks. It is more of a scientific or mathematical approach (objective) to risk analysis compared to qualitative. A *qualitative risk analysis* uses a "softer" approach to the data elements of a risk analysis. It does not quantify that data, which means that it does not assign numeric values to the data so that it can be used in equations. As an example, the results of a quantitative risk analysis could be that the organization is at risk of losing $100,000 if a buffer overflow were exploited on a web server, $25,000 if a database were compromised, and $10,000 if a file server were compromised. A qualitative risk analysis would not present these findings in monetary values, but would assign ratings to the risks, as in Red, Yellow, and Green.

A quantitative analysis uses risk calculations that attempt to predict the level of monetary losses and the probability for each type of threat. Qualitative analysis does not use calculations. Instead, it is more opinion and scenario based (subjective) and uses a rating system to relay the risk criticality levels.

Quantitative and qualitative approaches have their own pros and cons, and each applies more appropriately to some situations than others. An organization's management and risk analysis team, and the tools they decide to use, will determine which approach is best.

In the following sections we will dig into the depths of quantitative analysis and then revisit the qualitative approach. We will then compare and contrast their attributes.

Automated Risk Analysis Methods

Collecting all the necessary data that needs to be plugged into risk analysis equations and properly interpreting the results can be overwhelming if done manually. Several automated risk analysis tools on the market can make this task much less painful and, hopefully, more accurate. The gathered data can be reused, greatly reducing the time required to perform subsequent analyses. The risk analysis team can also print reports and comprehensive graphs to present to management.

EXAM TIP Remember that vulnerability assessments are different from risk assessments. A vulnerability assessment just finds the vulnerabilities (the holes). A risk assessment calculates the probability of the vulnerabilities being exploited and the associated business impact.

The objective of these tools is to reduce the manual effort of these tasks, perform calculations quickly, estimate future expected losses, and determine the effectiveness and benefits of the security countermeasures chosen. Most automatic risk analysis products port information into a database and run several types of scenarios with different parameters to give a panoramic view of what the outcome will be if different threats come to bear. For example, after such a tool has all the necessary information inputted, it can be rerun several times with different parameters to compute the potential outcome if a large fire were to take place; the potential losses if a virus were to damage 40 percent of the data on the main file server; how much the organization would lose if an attacker were to steal all the customer credit card information held in three databases; and so on. Running through the different risk possibilities gives an organization a more detailed understanding of which risks are more critical than others, and thus which ones to address first.

Steps of a Quantitative Risk Analysis

If we choose to carry out a quantitative risk analysis, then we are going to use mathematical equations for our data interpretation process. The most common equations used for this purpose are the *single loss expectancy (SLE)* and the *annualized loss expectancy (ALE)*. The SLE is a monetary value that is assigned to a single event that represents the organization's potential loss amount if a specific threat were to take place. The equation is laid out as follows:

Asset Value × Exposure Factor (EF) = SLE

The *exposure factor (EF)* represents the percentage of loss a realized threat could have on a certain asset. For example, if a data warehouse has the asset value of $150,000, it can be estimated that if a fire were to occur, 25 percent of the warehouse would be damaged, in which case the SLE would be $37,500:

Asset Value ($150,000) × Exposure Factor (25%) = $37,500

This tells us that the organization could potentially lose $37,500 if a fire were to take place. But we need to know what our annual potential loss is, since we develop and use our security budgets on an annual basis. This is where the ALE equation comes into play. The ALE equation is as follows:

SLE × Annualized Rate of Occurrence (ARO) = ALE

The *annualized rate of occurrence (ARO)* is the value that represents the estimated frequency of a specific threat taking place within a 12-month timeframe. The range can be from 0.0 (never) to 1.0 (once a year) to greater than 1 (several times a year), and anywhere in between. For example, if the probability of a fire taking place and damaging our data warehouse is once every 10 years, the ARO value is 0.1.

So, if a fire within an organization's data warehouse facility can cause $37,500 in damages, and the frequency (or ARO) of a fire taking place has an ARO value of 0.1 (indicating once in 10 years), then the ALE value is $3,750 ($37,500 × 0.1 = $3,750).

The ALE value tells the organization that if it wants to put in controls to protect the asset (warehouse) from this threat (fire), it can sensibly spend $3,750 or less per year to provide the necessary level of protection. Knowing the real possibility of a threat and how much damage, in monetary terms, the threat can cause is important in determining how much should be spent to try and protect against that threat in the first place. It would not make good business sense for the organization to spend more than $3,750 per year to protect itself from this threat.

Clearly, this example is overly simplistic in focusing strictly on the structural losses. In the real world, we should include other related impacts such as loss of revenue due to the disruption, potential fines if the fire was caused by a violation of local fire codes, and injuries to employees that would require medical care. The number of factors to consider can be pretty large and, to some of us, not obvious. This is why you want to have a diverse risk assessment team that can think of all the myriad impacts that a simple event might have.

Uncertainty

In risk analysis, uncertainty refers to the degree to which you lack confidence in an estimate. This is expressed as a percentage, from 0 to 100 percent. If you have a 30 percent confidence level in something, then it could be said you have a 70 percent uncertainty level. Capturing the degree of uncertainty when carrying out a risk analysis is important, because it indicates the level of confidence the team and management should have in the resulting figures.

Asset	Threat	Single Loss Expectancy (SLE)	Annualized Rate of Occurrence (ARO)	Annualized Loss Expectancy (ALE)
Facility	Fire	$230,000	0.1	$23,000
Trade secret	Stolen	$40,000	0.01	$400
File server	Failed	$11,500	0.1	$1,150
Business data	Ransomware	$283,000	0.1	$28,300
Customer credit card info	Stolen	$300,000	3.0	$900,000

Table 2-3 Breaking Down How SLE and ALE Values Are Used

Now that we have all these numbers, what do we do with them? Let's look at the example in Table 2-3, which shows the outcome of a quantitative risk analysis. With this data, the organization can make intelligent decisions on what threats must be addressed first because of the severity of the threat, the likelihood of it happening, and how much could be lost if the threat were realized. The organization now also knows how much money it should spend to protect against each threat. This will result in good business decisions, instead of just buying protection here and there without a clear understanding of the big picture. Because the organization's risk from a ransomware incident is $28,300, it would be justified in spending up to this amount providing ransomware preventive measures such as offline file backups, phishing awareness training, malware detection and prevention, or insurance.

When carrying out a quantitative analysis, some people mistakenly think that the process is purely objective and scientific because data is being presented in numeric values. But a purely quantitative analysis is hard to achieve because there is still some subjectivity when it comes to the data. How do we know that a fire will only take place once every 10 years? How do we know that the damage from a fire will be 25 percent of the value of the asset? We don't know these values exactly, but instead of just pulling them out of thin air, they should be based upon historical data and industry experience. In quantitative risk analysis, we can do our best to provide all the correct information, and by doing so we will come close to the risk values, but we cannot predict the future and how much future incidents will cost us or the organization.

Results of a Quantitative Risk Analysis

The risk analysis team should have clearly defined goals. The following is a short list of what generally is expected from the results of a risk analysis:

- Monetary values assigned to assets
- Comprehensive list of all significant threats
- Probability of the occurrence rate of each threat
- Loss potential the organization can endure per threat in a 12-month time span
- Recommended controls

Although this list looks short, there is usually an incredible amount of detail under each bullet item. This report will be presented to senior management, which will be concerned with possible monetary losses and the necessary costs to mitigate these risks. Although the report should be as detailed as possible, it should also include an executive summary so that senior management can quickly understand the overall findings of the analysis.

Qualitative Risk Analysis

Another method of risk analysis is *qualitative*, which does not assign numbers and monetary values to components and losses. Instead, qualitative methods walk through different scenarios of risk possibilities and rank the seriousness of the threats and the validity of the different possible countermeasures based on opinions. (A wide-sweeping analysis can include hundreds of scenarios.) Qualitative analysis techniques include judgment, best practices, intuition, and experience. Examples of qualitative techniques to gather data are Delphi, brainstorming, storyboarding, focus groups, surveys, questionnaires, checklists, one-on-one meetings, and interviews. The risk analysis team will determine the best technique for the threats that need to be assessed, as well as the culture of the organization and individuals involved with the analysis.

The team that is performing the risk analysis gathers personnel who have knowledge of the threats being evaluated. When this group is presented with a scenario that describes threats and loss potential, each member responds with their gut feeling and experience on the likelihood of the threat and the extent of damage that may result. This group explores a scenario of each identified vulnerability and how it would be exploited. The "expert" in the group, who is most familiar with this type of threat, should review the scenario to ensure it reflects how an actual threat would be carried out. Safeguards that would diminish the damage of this threat are then evaluated, and the scenario is played out for each safeguard. The exposure possibility and loss possibility can be ranked as high, medium, or low on a scale of 1 to 5 or 1 to 10.

A common qualitative risk matrix is shown in Figure 2-4. Once the selected personnel rank the likelihood of a threat happening, the loss potential, and the advantages of each

Likelihood	Consequences				
	Insignificant	Minor	Moderate	Major	Severe
Almost certain	M	H	H	E	E
Likely	M	M	H	H	E
Possible	L	M	M	H	E
Unlikely	L	M	M	M	H
Rare	L	L	M	M	H

Figure 2-4 Qualitative risk matrix: likelihood vs. consequences (impact)

The Delphi Technique

The Delphi technique is a group decision method used to ensure that each member gives an honest opinion of what he or she thinks the result of a particular threat will be. This avoids a group of individuals feeling pressured to go along with others' thought processes and enables them to participate in an independent and anonymous way. Each member of the group provides his or her opinion of a certain threat and turns it in to the team that is performing the analysis. The results are compiled and distributed to the group members, who then write down their comments anonymously and return them to the analysis group. The comments are compiled and redistributed for more comments until a consensus is formed. This method is used to obtain an agreement on cost, loss values, and probabilities of occurrence without individuals having to agree verbally.

safeguard, this information is compiled into a report and presented to management to help it make better decisions on how best to implement safeguards into the environment. The benefits of this type of analysis are that communication must happen among team members to rank the risks, evaluate the safeguard strengths, and identify weaknesses, and the people who know these subjects the best provide their opinions to management.

Let's look at a *simple* example of a qualitative risk analysis.

The risk analysis team presents a scenario explaining the threat of a hacker accessing confidential information held on the five file servers within the organization. The risk analysis team then distributes the scenario in a written format to a team of five people (the IT manager, database administrator, application programmer, system operator, and operational manager), who are also given a sheet to rank the threat's severity, loss potential, and each safeguard's effectiveness, with a rating of 1 to 5, 1 being the least severe, effective, or probable. Table 2-4 shows the results.

Threat = Hacker Accessing Confidential Information	Severity of Threat	Probability of Threat Taking Place	Potential Loss to the Organization	Effectiveness of Firewall	Effectiveness of Intrusion Detection System	Effectiveness of Honeypot
IT manager	4	2	4	4	3	2
Database administrator	4	4	4	3	4	1
Application programmer	2	3	3	4	2	1
System operator	3	4	3	4	2	1
Operational manager	5	4	4	4	4	2
Results	3.6	3.4	3.6	3.8	3	1.4

Table 2-4 Example of a Qualitative Analysis

This data is compiled and inserted into a report and presented to management. When management is presented with this information, it will see that its staff (or a chosen set) feels that purchasing a firewall will protect the organization from this threat more than purchasing an intrusion detection system (IDS) or setting up a honeypot system.

This is the result of looking at only one threat, and management will view the severity, probability, and loss potential of each threat so it knows which threats cause the greatest risk and should be addressed first.

Quantitative vs. Qualitative

Each method has its advantages and disadvantages, some of which are outlined in Table 2-5 for purposes of comparison.

The risk analysis team, management, risk analysis tools, and culture of the organization will dictate which approach—quantitative or qualitative—should be used. The goal of either method is to estimate an organization's real risk and to rank the severity of the threats so the correct countermeasures can be put into place within a practical budget.

Table 2-5 refers to some of the positive aspects of the quantitative and qualitative approaches. However, not everything is always easy. In deciding to use either a quantitative or qualitative approach, the following points might need to be considered.

Quantitative Cons:

- Calculations can be complex. Can management understand how these values were derived?
- Without automated tools, this process is extremely laborious.
- More preliminary work is needed to gather detailed information about the environment.
- Standards are not available. Each vendor has its own way of interpreting the processes and their results.

Attribute	Quantitative	Qualitative
Requires no calculations		X
Requires more complex calculations	X	
Involves high degree of guesswork		X
Provides general areas and indications of risk		X
Is easier to automate and evaluate	X	
Used in risk management performance tracking	X	
Allows for cost/benefit analysis	X	
Uses independently verifiable and objective metrics	X	
Provides the opinions of the individuals who know the processes best		X
Shows clear-cut losses that can be accrued within one year's time	X	

Table 2-5 Quantitative vs. Qualitative Characteristics

Qualitative Cons:

- The assessments and results are subjective and opinion based.
- Eliminates the opportunity to create a dollar value for cost/benefit discussions.
- Developing a security budget from the results is difficult because monetary values are not used.
- Standards are not available. Each vendor has its own way of interpreting the processes and their results.

NOTE Since a purely quantitative assessment is close to impossible and a purely qualitative process does not provide enough statistical data for financial decisions, these two risk analysis approaches can be used in a hybrid approach. Quantitative evaluation can be used for tangible assets (monetary values), and a qualitative assessment can be used for intangible assets (priority values).

Responding to Risks

Once an organization knows the amount of total and residual risk it is faced with, it must decide how to handle it. Risk can be dealt with in four basic ways: transfer it, avoid it, reduce it, or accept it.

Many types of insurance are available to organizations to protect their assets. If an organization decides the total risk is too high to gamble with, it can purchase insurance, which would *transfer the risk* to the insurance company.

If an organization decides to terminate the activity that is introducing the risk, this is known as *risk avoidance*. For example, if a company allows employees to use instant messaging (IM), there are many risks surrounding this technology. The company could decide not to allow any IM activity by employees because there is not a strong enough business need for its continued use. Discontinuing this service is an example of risk avoidance.

Another approach is *risk mitigation*, where the risk is reduced to a level considered acceptable enough to continue conducting business. The implementation of firewalls, training, and intrusion/detection protection systems or other control types represent types of risk mitigation efforts.

The last approach is to *accept the risk*, which means the organization understands the level of risk it is faced with, as well as the potential cost of damage, and decides to just live with it and not implement the countermeasure. Many organizations will accept risk when the cost/benefit ratio indicates that the cost of the countermeasure outweighs the potential loss value.

A crucial issue with risk acceptance is understanding why this is the best approach for a specific situation. Unfortunately, today many people in organizations are accepting risk and not understanding fully what they are accepting. This usually has to do with the relative newness of risk management in the security field and the lack of education and experience in those personnel who make risk decisions. When business managers are charged with the responsibility of dealing with risk in their department, most of the time they will accept whatever risk is put in front of them because their real goals pertain to getting a project finished and out the door. They don't want to be bogged down by this silly and irritating security stuff.

Risk acceptance should be based on several factors. For example, is the potential loss lower than the countermeasure? Can the organization deal with the "pain" that will come with accepting this risk? This second consideration is not purely a cost decision, but may entail noncost issues surrounding the decision. For example, if we accept this risk, we must add three more steps in our production process. Does that make sense for us? Or if we accept this risk, more security incidents may arise from it, and are we prepared to handle those?

The individual or group accepting risk must also understand the potential visibility of this decision. Let's say a company has determined that it is not legally required to protect customers' first names, but that it does have to protect other items like Social Security numbers, account numbers, and so on. So, the company ensures that its current activities are in compliance with the regulations and laws, but what if its customers find out that it is not protecting their full names and they associate this with identity fraud because of their lack of education on the matter? The company may not be able to handle this potential reputation hit, even if it is doing all it is supposed to be doing. Perceptions of a company's customer base are not always rooted in fact, but the possibility that customers will move their business to another company is a potential fact your company must comprehend.

Figure 2-5 shows how a risk management program can be set up, which ties together many of the concepts covered thus far in this chapter.

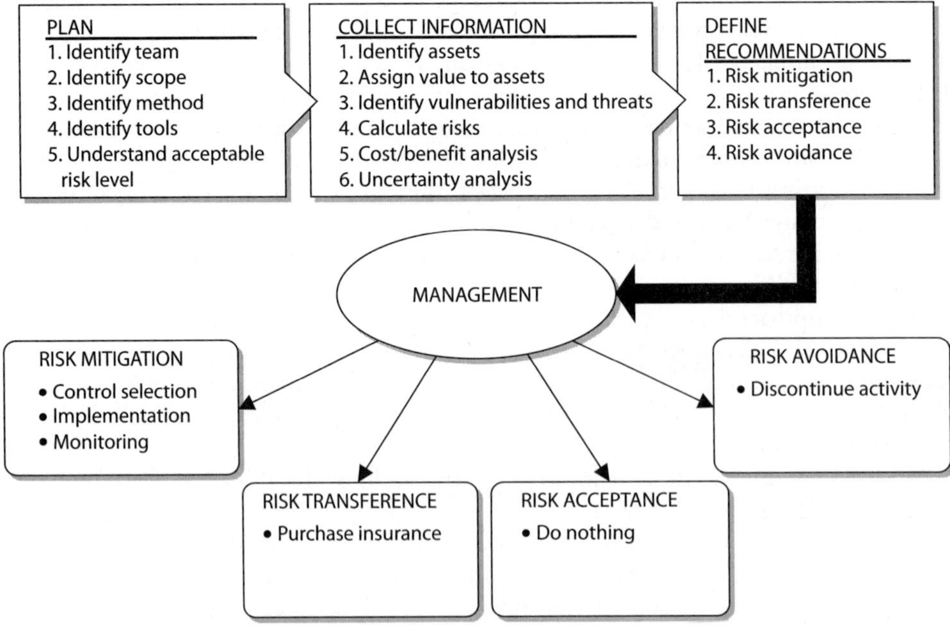

Figure 2-5 How a risk management program can be set up

Total Risk vs. Residual Risk

The reason an organization implements countermeasures is to reduce its overall risk to an acceptable level. As stated earlier, no system or environment is 100 percent secure, which means there is always some risk left over to deal with. This is called *residual risk*.

Residual risk is different from *total risk*, which is the risk an organization faces if it chooses not to implement any type of safeguard. An organization may choose to take on total risk if the cost/benefit analysis results indicate this is the best course of action. For example, if there is a small likelihood that an organization's web servers can be compromised and the necessary safeguards to provide a higher level of protection cost more than the potential loss in the first place, the organization will choose not to implement the safeguard, choosing to deal with the total risk.

There is an important difference between total risk and residual risk and which type of risk an organization is willing to accept. The following are conceptual formulas:

threats × vulnerability × asset value = total risk
(threats × vulnerability × asset value) × controls gap = residual risk

You may also see these concepts illustrated as the following:

total risk – countermeasures = residual risk

NOTE The previous formulas are not constructs you can actually plug numbers into. They are instead used to illustrate the relation of the different items that make up risk in a conceptual manner. This means no multiplication or mathematical functions actually take place. It is a means of understanding what items are involved when defining either total or residual risk.

During a risk assessment, the threats and vulnerabilities are identified. The possibility of a vulnerability being exploited is multiplied by the value of the assets being assessed, which results in the total risk. Once the controls gap (protection the control cannot provide) is factored in, the result is the residual risk. Implementing countermeasures is a way of mitigating risks. Because no organization can remove all threats, there will always be some residual risk. The question is what level of risk the organization is willing to accept.

Countermeasure Selection and Implementation

Countermeasures are the means by which we reduce specific risks to acceptable levels. This section addresses identifying and choosing the right countermeasures for computer systems. It gives the best attributes to look for and the different cost scenarios to investigate when comparing different types of countermeasures. The end product of the analysis of choices should demonstrate why the selected control is the most advantageous to the organization.

NOTE The terms control, countermeasure, safeguard, security mechanism, and protection mechanism are synonymous in the context of information systems security. We use them interchangeably.

Control Selection

A security control must make good business sense, meaning it is cost-effective (its benefit outweighs its cost). This requires another type of analysis: a *cost/benefit analysis*. A commonly used cost/benefit calculation for a given safeguard (control) is

(ALE before implementing safeguard) – (ALE after implementing safeguard) – (annual cost of safeguard) = value of safeguard to the organization

For example, if the ALE of the threat of a hacker bringing down a web server is $12,000 prior to implementing the suggested safeguard, and the ALE is $3,000 after implementing the safeguard, while the annual cost of maintenance and operation of the safeguard is $650, then the value of this safeguard to the organization is $8,350 each year.

Recall that the ALE has two factors, the single loss expectancy and the annual rate of occurrence, so safeguards can decrease either or both. The countermeasure referenced in the previous example could aim to reduce the costs associated with restoring the web server, or make it less likely that it is brought down, or both. All too often, we focus our attention on making the threat less likely, while, in some cases, it might be less expensive to make it easier to recover.

The cost of a countermeasure is more than just the amount filled out on the purchase order. The following items should be considered and evaluated when deriving the full cost of a countermeasure:

- Product costs
- Design/planning costs
- Implementation costs
- Environment modifications (both physical and logical)
- Compatibility with other countermeasures
- Maintenance requirements
- Testing requirements
- Repair, replacement, or update costs
- Operating and support costs
- Effects on productivity
- Subscription costs
- Extra staff-hours for monitoring and responding to alerts

Many organizations have gone through the pain of purchasing new security products without understanding that they will need the staff to maintain those products. Although tools automate tasks, many organizations were not even carrying out these tasks before, so they do not save on staff-hours, but many times require more hours. For example, Company A decides that to protect many of its resources, purchasing an intrusion detection system is warranted. So, the company pays $5,500 for an IDS. Is that the total cost? Nope. This software should be tested in an environment that is segmented from the production environment to uncover any unexpected activity. After this testing is complete and the security group feels it is safe to insert the IDS into its production environment, the security group must install the monitoring management software, install the sensors, and properly direct the communication paths from the sensors to the management console. The security group may also need to reconfigure the routers to redirect traffic flow, and it definitely needs to ensure that users cannot access the IDS management console. Finally, the security group should configure a database to hold all attack signatures and then run simulations.

Costs associated with an IDS alert response should most definitely be considered. Now that Company A has an IDS in place, security administrators may need additional alerting equipment such as smartphones. And then there are the time costs associated with a response to an IDS event.

Anyone who has worked in an IT group knows that some adverse reaction almost always takes place in this type of scenario. Network performance can take an unacceptable hit after installing a product if it is an inline or proactive product. Users may no longer be able to access a server for some mysterious reason. The IDS vendor may not have explained that two more service patches are necessary for the whole thing to work correctly. Staff time will need to be allocated for training and to respond to all of the alerts (true or false) the new IDS sends out.

So, for example, the cost of this countermeasure could be $23,500 for the product and licenses; $2,500 for training; $3,400 for testing; $2,600 for the loss in user productivity once the product is introduced into production; and $4,000 in labor for router reconfiguration, product installation, troubleshooting, and installation of the two service patches. The real cost of this countermeasure is $36,000. If our total potential loss was calculated at $9,000, we went over budget by 300 percent when applying this countermeasure for the identified risk. Some of these costs may be hard or impossible to identify before they are incurred, but an experienced risk analyst would account for many of these possibilities.

Types of Controls

In our examples so far, we've focused on countermeasures like firewalls and IDSs, but there are many more options. Controls come in three main categories: administrative, technical, and physical. *Administrative controls* are commonly referred to as "soft controls" because they are more management oriented. Examples of administrative controls are security documentation, risk management, personnel security, and training. *Technical controls* (also called logical controls) are software or hardware components, as in firewalls, IDS, encryption, and identification and authentication mechanisms. And *physical controls* are items put into place to protect facilities, personnel, and resources. Examples of physical controls are security guards, locks, fencing, and lighting.

These control categories need to be put into place to provide *defense-in-depth*, which is the coordinated use of multiple security controls in a layered approach, as shown in Figure 2-6. A multilayered defense system minimizes the probability of successful penetration and compromise because an attacker would have to get through several different types of protection mechanisms before she gained access to the critical assets. For example, Company A can have the following physical controls in place that work in a layered model:

- Fence
- Locked external doors
- Closed-circuit TV (CCTV)
- Security guard
- Locked internal doors
- Locked server room
- Physically secured computers (cable locks)

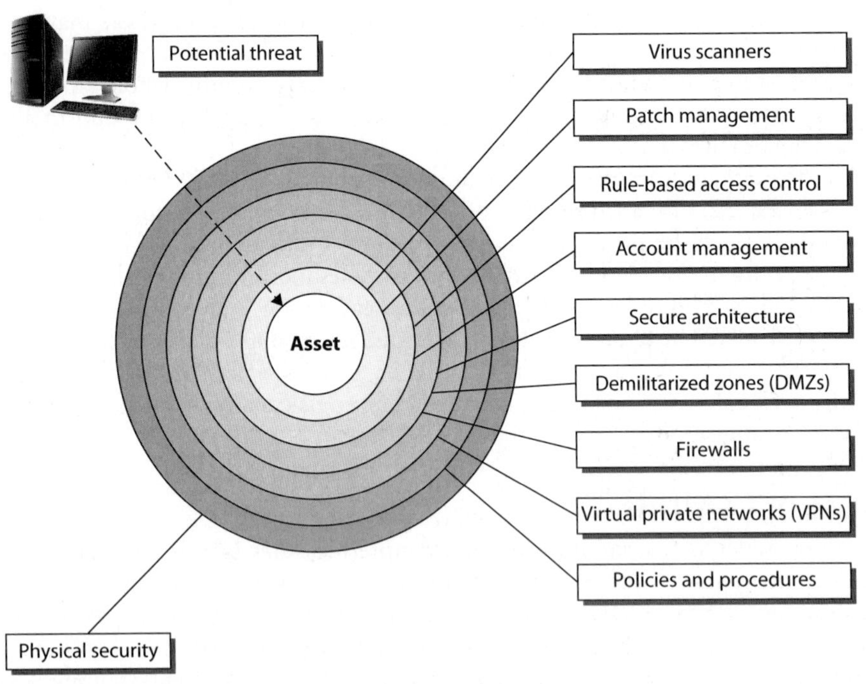

Figure 2-6 Defense-in-depth

Technical controls that are commonly put into place to provide this type of layered approach are

- Firewalls
- Intrusion detection system
- Intrusion prevention system
- Antimalware
- Access control
- Encryption

The types of controls that are actually implemented must map to the threats the organization faces, and the number of layers that are put into place must map to the sensitivity of the asset. The rule of thumb is the more sensitive the asset, the more layers of protection that must be put into place.

So the different *categories* of controls that can be used are administrative, technical, and physical. But what do these controls actually *do* for us? We need to understand what the different control types can provide us in our quest to secure our environments.

The different types of security controls are *preventive*, *detective*, *corrective*, *deterrent*, *recovery*, and *compensating*. By having a better understanding of the different control types, you will be able to make more informed decisions about what controls will be best used in specific situations. The six different control types are as follows:

- **Preventive** Intended to avoid an incident from occurring
- **Detective** Helps identify an incident's activities and potentially an intruder
- **Corrective** Fixes components or systems after an incident has occurred
- **Deterrent** Intended to discourage a potential attacker
- **Recovery** Intended to bring the environment back to regular operations
- **Compensating** Provides an alternative measure of control

Once you understand fully what the different controls do, you can use them in the right locations for specific risks.

When looking at a security structure of an environment, it is most productive to use a preventive model and then use detective, corrective, and recovery mechanisms to help support this model. Basically, you want to stop any trouble before it starts, but you must be able to quickly react and combat trouble if it does find you. It is not feasible to prevent everything; therefore, what you cannot prevent, you should be able to quickly detect. That's why preventive and detective controls should always be implemented together and should complement each other. To take this concept further: what you can't prevent, you should be able to detect, and if you detect something, it means you weren't able to prevent it, and therefore you should take corrective action to make sure it is indeed prevented the next time around. Therefore, all three types work together: preventive, detective, and corrective.

The control types described next (administrative, physical, and technical) are preventive in nature. These are important to understand when developing an enterprise-wide security program. Obviously, these are only provided as illustrative examples. Keep in mind as you go over them that a specific control may fall within multiple classifications. For example, most security cameras could be considered preventive (since they may dissuade criminals from breaking in if they are highly visible), detective (if there is a person monitoring them live), and corrective (if they are used to track a criminal that breached your physical perimeter).

Preventive: Administrative

- Policies and procedures
- Effective hiring practices
- Pre-employment background checks
- Controlled termination processes
- Data classification and labeling
- Security awareness

Preventive: Physical

- Badges, swipe cards
- Guards, dogs
- Fences, locks, mantraps

Preventive: Technical

- Passwords, biometrics, smart cards
- Encryption, secure protocols, call-back systems, database views, constrained user interfaces
- Antimalware software, access control lists, firewalls, IPS

Table 2-6 shows how these types of control mechanisms perform different security functions. Many students get themselves wrapped around the axle when trying to get their mind around which control provides which functionality. This is how this train of thought usually takes place: "A security camera system is a detective control, but if an attacker sees its cameras, it could be a deterrent." Let's stop right here. Do not make this any harder than it has to be. When trying to map the functionality requirement to a control, think of the *main* reason that control would be put into place. A firewall tries to prevent something bad from taking place, so it is a preventive control. Auditing logs is done after an event took place, so it is detective. A data backup system is developed so that data can be recovered; thus, this is a recovery control. Computer images are created so that if software gets corrupted, they can be reloaded; thus, this is a corrective control.

Note that some controls can serve different functions. Security guards can deter would-be attackers, but if they don't deter all of them, they can also stop (prevent)

Control Type:	Preventive	Detective	Corrective	Deterrent	Recovery	Compensating
Controls by Category:						
Physical						
Fences				X		
Locks	X					
Badge system	X					
Security guard	X	X	X	X		
Mantrap doors	X					
Lighting				X		
Motion detectors		X				
Closed-circuit TVs		X				
Offsite facility					X	X
Administrative						
Security policy	X					X
Monitoring and supervising		X				X
Separation of duties	X					
Job rotation		X		X		
Information classification	X					
Investigations		X				
Security awareness training	X					
Technical						
ACLs	X					
Encryption	X					
Audit logs		X				
IDS		X				
Antimalware software	X	X				
Workstation images			X			
Smart cards	X					
Data backup					X	

Table 2-6 Control Categories and Types

the ones that try to get into a facility. Perhaps the attacker was particularly sneaky and he managed to get into an office building, in which case the security guards can be detective controls as they make the rounds and even corrective controls when they find the intruder, call law enforcement, and escort the attacker out of the building and into the backseat of a police car. When taking the CISSP exam, look for clues in the question to determine which functionality is most relevant.

One control functionality that some people struggle with is a compensating control. Let's look at some examples of compensating controls to best explain their function. If your organization needed to implement strong physical security, you might suggest to management that they employ security guards. But after calculating all the costs of security guards, your organization might decide to use a compensating (alternative) control that provides similar protection but is more affordable—as in a fence. In another example, let's say you are a security administrator and you are in charge of maintaining the organization's firewalls. Management tells you that a certain protocol that you know is vulnerable to exploitation has to be allowed through the firewall for business reasons. The network needs to be protected by a compensating (alternative) control pertaining to this protocol, which may be setting up a proxy server for that specific traffic type to ensure that it is properly inspected and controlled. So a compensating control is just an alternative control that provides similar protection as the original control but has to be used because it is more affordable or allows specifically required business functionality.

Several types of security controls exist, and they all need to work together. The complexity of the controls and of the environment they are in can cause the controls to contradict each other or leave gaps in security. This can introduce unforeseen holes in the organization's protection that are not fully understood by the implementers. An organization may have very strict technical access controls in place and all the necessary administrative controls up to snuff, but if any person is allowed to physically access any system in the facility, then clear security dangers are present within the environment. Together, these controls should work in harmony to provide a healthy, safe, and productive environment.

The risk assessment team must evaluate the security controls' functionality and effectiveness. When selecting a security control, some attributes are more favorable than others. Table 2-7 lists and describes attributes that should be considered before purchasing and committing to a security control.

Security controls can provide deterrence attributes if they are highly visible. This tells potential evildoers that adequate protection is in place and that they should move on to an easier target. Although the control may be highly visible, attackers should not be able to discover the way it works, thus enabling them to attempt to modify it, or know how to get around the protection mechanism. If users know how to disable the antimalware program that is taking up CPU cycles or know how to bypass a proxy server to get to the Internet without restrictions, they will do so.

Control Assessments

Once you select the administrative, technical, and physical controls that you think will reduce your risks to acceptable levels, you have to ensure that this is actually the case.

Characteristic	Description
Modular	The control can be installed or removed from an environment without adversely affecting other mechanisms.
Provides uniform protection	A security level is applied in a standardized method to all mechanisms the control is designed to protect.
Provides override functionality	An administrator can override the restriction if necessary.
Defaults to least privilege	When installed, the control defaults to a lack of permissions and rights instead of installing with everyone having full control.
Independence of control and the asset it is protecting	The given control can protect multiple assets, and a given asset can be protected by multiple controls.
Flexibility and security	The more security the control provides, the better. This functionality should come with flexibility, which enables you to choose different functions instead of all or none.
Usability	The control does not needlessly interfere with users' work.
Asset protection	The asset is still protected even if the countermeasure needs to be reset.
Easily upgraded	Software continues to evolve, and updates should be able to happen painlessly.
Auditing functionality	The control includes a mechanism that provides auditing at various levels of verbosity.
Minimizes dependence on other components	The control should be flexible and not have strict requirements about the environment into which it will be installed.
Must produce output in usable and understandable format	The control should present important information in a format easy for humans to understand and use for trend analysis.
Testable	The control should be able to be tested in different environments under different situations.
Does not introduce other compromises	The control should not provide any covert channels or back doors.
System and user performance	System and user performance should not be greatly affected by the control.
Proper alerting	The control should have the capability for thresholds to be set as to when to alert personnel of a security breach, and this type of alert should be acceptable.
Does not affect assets	The assets in the environment should not be adversely affected by the control.

Table 2-7 Characteristics to Consider When Assessing Security Controls

A *control assessment* is an evaluation of one or more controls to determine the extent to which they are implemented correctly, operating as intended, and producing the desired outcome. Let's look at each of those test elements in turn using anonymized examples from the real world.

You may have chosen the right control for a given risk, but you also need *verification* that the manner in which it is implemented is correct too. Let's suppose you decide to upgrade a firewall to mitigate a number of risks you've identified. You invest a ton of money in the latest and greatest firewall and apply a bunch of rules to filter out the good from the bad. And yet, you forget to change the administrator's default password, and an attacker is able to log into your firewall, lock out the security team by changing the password, and then change the rules to allow malicious traffic through. The technical control was good, it just wasn't implemented correctly. You avoid this by developing a thorough set of tests that look at every aspect of the implementation and ensure no steps were skipped or done wrong.

Another aspect of verification is to ensure that the controls are operating as intended. You may have implemented the control correctly, but there are many reasons why it may not work as you expected it would. For example, suppose you implement a policy that all personnel in a facility must wear identification badges. Employees, contractors, and visitors each get their own unique badge design to differentiate them. The policy is implemented, and all staff are trained on it, but after a few weeks people get complacent and stop noticing whether they (or others) are wearing badges. The administrative control was properly implemented but is not working as intended. The control assessment should include operational checks, such as having different people (perhaps some who are well known in the organization and some who are not part of it) walk through the facility with no badges and see whether they are challenged or reported.

Finally, we want *validation* that the controls are producing the desired outcomes. Controls are selected for the purpose of reducing risk…so are they? Suppose you install temperature sensors in your data center that generate alarms whenever they get too hot. You are trying to reduce the risk of hardware failures due to high temperatures. These physical controls are properly installed and work as intended. In fact, they generate alarms every day during peak usage hours. Are they reducing the risk? Unless you upgrade the underpowered air conditioning unit, all these alarms will do nothing to help you avoid outages. Any assessment of your controls must explicitly test whether the risk for which they were selected is actually being reduced.

EXAM TIP An easy way to differentiate verification and validation is that verification answers the question "did we implement the control right?" while validation answers the question "did we implement the right control?"

Security and Privacy

Security effectiveness deals with metrics such as meeting service level agreement (SLA) requirements, achieving returns on investment (ROIs), meeting set baselines, and providing management with a dashboard or balanced scorecard system. These are ways to determine how useful the current security solutions and architecture as a whole are performing.

Another side to assessing security controls is ensuring that they do not violate our privacy policies and regulations. It does us no good to implement the best security controls if they require gross violations of people's right to keep certain information about themselves from being known or used in inappropriate ways. For example, an organization could have a policy that allows employees to use the organization's assets for personal purposes while they are on breaks. The same organization has implemented Transport Layer Security (TLS) proxies that decrypt all network traffic in order to conduct deep packet analysis and mitigate the risk that a threat actor is using encryption to hide her malicious deeds. Normally, the process is fully automated and no other staff members look at the decrypted communications. Periodically, however, security staff manually check the system to ensure everything is working properly. Now, suppose an employee reveals some very private health information to a friend over her personal webmail and that traffic is monitored and observed by a security staffer. That breach of privacy could cause a multitude of ethical, regulatory, and even legal problems for the organization.

When implementing security controls, it is critical to consider their privacy implications. If your organization has a chief privacy officer (or other privacy professional), that person should be part of the process of selecting and implementing security controls to ensure they don't unduly (or even illegally) violate employee privacy.

Monitoring Risks

We really can't just build a risk management program (or any program, for that matter), call it good, and go home. We need a way to assess the effectiveness of our work, identify deficiencies, and prioritize the things that still need work. We need a way to facilitate decision making, performance improvement, and accountability through collection, analysis, and reporting of the necessary information. More importantly, we need to be able to identify changes in the environment and be able to understand their impacts on our risk posture. All this needs to be based on facts and metrics. As the saying goes, "You can't manage something you can't measure."

Risk monitoring is the ongoing process of adding new risks, reevaluating existing ones, removing moot ones, and continuously assessing the effectiveness of our controls at mitigating all risks to tolerable levels. Risk monitoring activities should be focused on three key areas: effectiveness, change, and compliance. The risk management team should continually look for improvement opportunities, periodically analyze the data gathered from each key area, and report its findings to senior management. Let's take a closer look at how we might go about monitoring and measuring each area.

Effectiveness Monitoring

There are many reasons why the effectiveness of our security controls decreases. Technical controls may not adapt quickly to changing threat actor behaviors. Employees may lose awareness of (or interest in) administrative controls. Physical controls may not keep up with changing behaviors as people move in and through our facilities. How do we measure this decline in the effectiveness of our controls and, more importantly, the rising risks to our organizations? This is the crux of effectiveness monitoring.

One approach is to keep track of the number of security incidents by severity. Let's say that we implemented controls to reduce the risk of ransomware attacks. We redesigned our security awareness training, deployed a new endpoint detection and response (EDR) solution, and implemented an automated offline backup system. Subsequently, the number of ransomware-related incidents sharply declined across all severity categories. While we still see a handful of localized cases here and there, no data is lost, nobody is forced offline, and business is humming. However, recently we are noticing that the number of low-severity incidents has started to increase. These are cases where the ransomware makes it onto a workstation but is stopped as it attempts to encrypt files. If we're not paying attention to this trend, we may miss the fact that the malware is evolving and becoming more effective at evading our EDR solution. We'd be giving the adversary a huge advantage by letting them experiment and improve while we do nothing about it. This is why effectiveness monitoring is important, and why it has to be tied to specific metrics that can be quantified and analyzed over time.

In the previous example, the metric was the number of incidents related to ransomware in our environment. There are many other metrics you could use, depending on the control in question. You could use a red team and measure the number of times it is successful at compromising various assets. You could use the number of suspected phishing attacks reported by alert employees. Whatever your approach, you should determine the effectiveness metrics you'll use to monitor controls when you decide to use those controls. Then, you really need to track those metrics over time to identify trends. Failure to do so will result, almost inevitably, in the gradual (or perhaps sudden) increase in risk until, one sad day, it is realized.

NOTE The Center for Internet Security (CIS) publishes a helpful (and free) document titled "CIS Controls Measures and Metrics," currently in its seventh version. It provides specific measures for each control as well as goals for their values in your organization.

A good way to enable effectiveness monitoring is to establish a standing group that periodically checks known threats and the controls that are meant to mitigate them. An example of this is a threat working group (TWG), which consists of members of all major parts of the organization, meeting regularly (say, monthly) to review the list of risks (sometimes called a risk registry) and ensure that threats and controls remain valid. The TWG assigns owners to each risk and ensures those persons or groups are keeping up their responsibilities. The TWG can also be the focal point for scheduling security assessments, be they internal or external, to verify and validate the controls.

Change Monitoring

Even if you keep track of known threats and the risks they pose, it is likely that changes in your organization's environment will introduce new risks. There are two major sources of change that impact your overall risk: information systems and business. The first is perhaps the most obvious to cybersecurity professionals. A new system is introduced, an old one retired, or an existing one updated or reconfigured. Any of these changes can produce new risks or change those you are already tracking. Another source of changes that introduce risks is the business itself. Over time, your organization will embark on new ventures, change internal processes, or perhaps merge with or acquire another organization.

All these changes need to be carefully analyzed to ensure an accurate understanding of their effects on the overall risk posture.

Monitoring changes to your environment and dealing with the risks they could introduce is part of a good change management process. Typically, organizations will have a change advisory board (CAB) or a similarly named standing group that reviews and approves any changes such as the development of new policies, systems, and business processes. The CAB measures changes through a variety of metrics that also are used to monitor risks, such as the following:

- Number of unauthorized changes
- Average time to implement a change
- Number of failed changes
- Number of security incidents attributable to changes

NOTE We will discuss change management in more detail in Chapter 19.

Compliance Monitoring

Something else that could change in your organization and affect your risk are legal, regulatory, and policy requirements. Compliance monitoring is a bit easier than effectiveness monitoring and change monitoring, because compliance tends to change fairly infrequently. Laws and external regulations usually take years to change, while internal regulations and policies should be part of the change management process we discussed previously. Though the frequency of compliance changes is fairly low, these changes can have significant impacts in the organization. A great example of this is the General Data Protection Regulation (GDPR) that came into effect in May 2018. It was years in the making, but it has had huge effects on any organization that stores or processes data belonging to a person from the European Union (EU).

Another aspect of compliance monitoring is responding to audit findings. Whether it is an external or internal audit, any findings dealing with compliance need to be addressed. If the audit reveals risks that are improperly mitigated, the risk team needs to respond to them. Failure to do so could result in significant fines or even criminal charges.

So, what can we measure to monitor our compliance? It varies among organizations, but here are some common metrics to consider:

- Number of audit findings
- Ratio of internal (i.e., self-discovered) to external (i.e., audit) inquiries
- Average time to close an inquiry
- Number of internal disciplinary actions related to compliance

No organization is perfectly compliant all the time, so there is always an element of compliance risk. These risks, however, increase dramatically if there is no formal process for searching for and dealing with issues that violate policies, regulations, or laws.

Risk Reporting

Risk reporting is an essential component of risk management in general and risk monitoring in particular. (Recall that risk management encompasses framing, assessing, responding to, and monitoring the risks.) Reporting enables organizational decision-making, security governance, and day-to-day operations. It is also important for compliance purposes.

So, how *should* we report risks? There is no set formula for reporting, but there are a couple of guiding principles. The first one is to understand the audience. There are at least three groups at which you may target risk reports: executives (and board members), managers, and risk owners. Each requires a different approach.

Executives and Board Members

Senior leaders in an organization are generally not interested in the details, nor should they be. Their role is to set and monitor the strategic direction, not to run day-to-day operations. These leaders want to know whether risks can be properly mitigated or require change to the organizational strategy. They will be interested in the biggest risks to the organization and will want to know what is being done to address them. Executives and board members should also be briefed on risks that have been "accepted" and what their potential impacts could be.

When dealing with senior decision makers, risk heat maps, such as illustrated in Figure 2-7, are typically used rather than verbose descriptions. This is to ensure that these leaders can get the information they need at a glance in order to decide whether strategic adjustments may be needed. In Figure 2-7, board members likely would be interested in

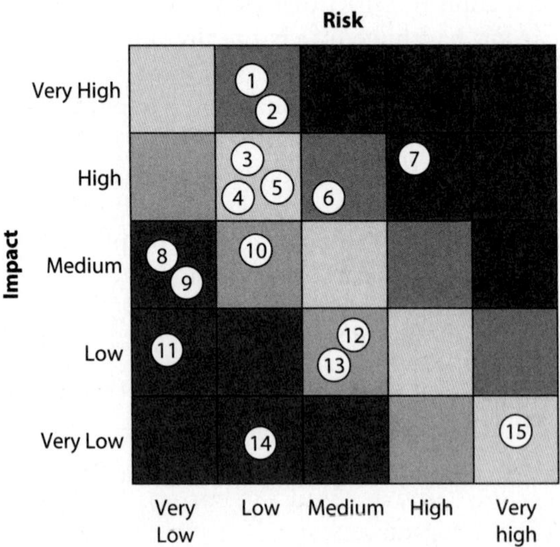

Figure 2-7 Sample risk heat map

discussing risk item #7 first since it is particularly significant. That is the point of a heat map: it allows senior-level audiences to home in on the important topics for discussion.

Managers

Managers across the organization will need much more detailed reports because they are responsible for, well, managing the risks. They will want to know current risks and how they've been trending over time. Are risks decreasing or increasing? Either way, why? Where does progress seem to be stuck? These are some of the questions managers will want the report to answer. They will also want to be able to drill into specific items of interest to get into the details, such as who owns the risk, how we are responding to the risk, and why the current approach may not be working.

Many organizations rely on risk management dashboards for this level of reporting. These dashboards may be part of a risk management tool, in which case they'd be interactive and allow drilling into specific items in the report. Organizations without these automated tools typically use spreadsheets to generate graphs (showing trends over time) or even manually developed slides. Whatever the approach, the idea is to present actionable information allowing business unit managers to track their progress over time with respect to risks.

Risk Owners

This is the internal audience that needs the most detailed reporting, because the risk owners are the staff members responsible for managing individual risks. They take direction from management as they respond to specific risks. For example, if the organization decides to transfer a given risk, the risk owner will be responsible for ensuring the insurance policy is developed and acquired effectively. This will include performance indicators, such as cost, coverage, and responsiveness. Cybersecurity insurance companies often require that certain controls be in place in order to provide coverage, so the risk owner must also ensure that these conditions are met so that the premiums are not being paid in vain.

Continuous Improvement

Only by reassessing the risks on a periodic basis can the risk management team's statements on security control performance be trusted. If the risk has not changed and the safeguards implemented are functioning in good order, then it can be said that the risk is being properly mitigated. Regular risk management monitoring will support the information security risk ratings.

Vulnerability analysis and continued asset identification and valuation are also important tasks of risk management monitoring and performance. The cycle of continued risk analysis is a very important part of determining whether the safeguard controls that have been put in place are appropriate and necessary to safeguard the assets and environment.

Continuous improvement is the practice of identifying opportunities, mitigating threats, improving quality, and reducing waste as an ongoing effort. It is the hallmark of mature and effective organizations.

Level	Maturity	Characteristics
1	Initial	Risk activities are ad hoc, reactive, and poorly controlled.
2	Repeatable	Procedures are documented and (mostly) followed.
3	Defined	Standard procedures, tools, and methods are applied consistently.
4	Managed	Quantitative methods are applied both to risk management and to the program.
5	Optimizing	Data-driven innovation occurs across the entire organization.

Table 2-8 Typical Maturity Model

Risk Maturity Modeling

Maturity models are tools that allow us to determine the ability of our organizations for continuous improvement. We generally assess the maturity of an organization's risk management on a scale of 1 to 5, as shown in Table 2-8. There is actually a level 0, which is where the organization is not managing risk at all.

While it may be tempting to think that we should all strive to achieve the highest level of maturity with regard to risk management, the reality is that we should reach the right level of maturity given our resources, strategies, and business environment. It would make little sense for a very small retail company to strive for level 5, because doing so would require a level of resource investment that is not realistic. Conversely, it would be a very bad idea for a large enterprise in the defense industry to be satisfied with a maturity level 1, because the risks it faces are substantial. Ultimately, the level of maturity that makes sense is a business decision, not a cybersecurity one.

Supply Chain Risk Management

Many organizations fail to consider their supply chain when managing risk, despite the fact that it often presents a convenient and easier back door to an attacker. So what is a supply chain anyway? A supply chain is a sequence of suppliers involved in delivering some product. If your company manufactures laptops, your supply chain will include the vendor that supplies your video cards. It will also include whoever makes the integrated circuits that go on those cards, as well as the supplier of the raw chemicals that are involved in that process. The supply chain also includes suppliers of services, such as the company that maintains the heating, ventilation, and air conditioning (HVAC) systems needed to keep your assembly lines running.

The various organizations that make up your supply chain will have a different outlook on security than you do. For one thing, their threat modeling will include different threats than yours. Why would a criminal looking to steal credit card information target an HVAC service provider? This is exactly what happened in 2013 when Target had over 40 million credit cards compromised. Target had done a reasonable job at securing its perimeter, but not its internal networks. The attacker, unable (or maybe just unwilling) to penetrate Target's outer shell head-on, decided to exploit the vulnerable network of one of Target's HVAC service providers and steal its credentials. Armed with these, the thieves were able to gain access to the point of sale terminals and, from there, the credit card information.

The basic processes you'll need to implement to manage risk in your supply chain are the same ones you use in the rest of your risk management program. The differences are mainly in what you look at (that is, the scope of your assessments) and what you can do about it (legally and contractually). A good resource to help integrate supply chain risk into your risk management program is NIST SP 800-161, *Supply Chain Risk Management Practices for Federal Information Systems and Organizations.*

One of the first things you'll need to do is to create a supply chain map for your organization. This is essentially a network diagram of who supplies what to whom, down to your ultimate customers. Figure 2-8 depicts a simplified systems integrator company ("Your Company"). It has a hardware components manufacturer that supplies it hardware and is, in turn, supplied by a materials producer. Your Company receives software from a developer and receives managed security from an external service provider. The hardware and software components are integrated and configured into Your Company's product, which is then shipped to its distributor and on to its customers. In this example, the company has four suppliers on which to base its supply chain risk assessment. It is also considered a supplier to its distributor.

Now, suppose the software developer in Figure 2-8 is attacked and the threat actors insert malicious code into the developer's software product. Anyone who receives that application from Your Company, or perhaps through an otherwise legitimate software update, also gets a very stealthy piece of malware that "phones home" to these actors, telling them where the malware is and what its host network looks like. These are sophisticated, nation-state spies intent on remaining undetected while they penetrate some very specific targets. If an infected organization is of interest to them, they'll deliver the next stage of malware with which to quietly explore and steal files. Otherwise, they'll

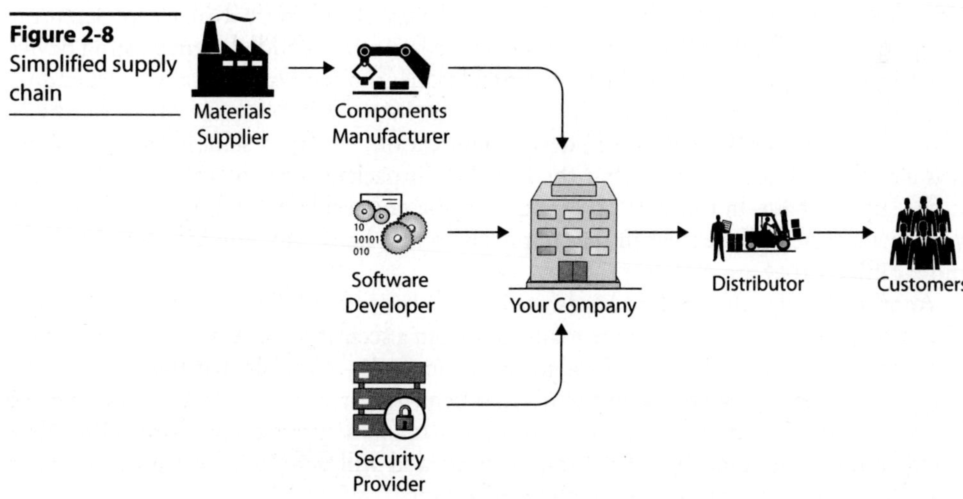

Figure 2-8 Simplified supply chain

tell the malware to go dormant, making their actions extremely difficult to detect. This is a high-level description of a cyber campaign discovered in late 2020 that exploited the Orion software developed by U.S.-based firm SolarWinds. The magnitude of this series of attacks underscores the importance of managing risk introduced by your suppliers.

Upstream and Downstream Suppliers

Suppliers are "upstream" from your company if they supply materials, goods, or services to your company and your company uses those in turn to provide whatever it is that it supplies to others. The core vulnerability that exists in these supply arrangements is that you could allow untrusted hardware, software, or services into your organization or products, where they could cause security problems. The Greeks used this to their advantage against the Trojans.

Conversely, your company may be upstream from others in the same supply chain. These would be your company's downstream suppliers. While it may be tempting to think that you should be concerned only about supply chain security upstream, those who follow your company in the supply chain may have their own set of upstream requirements for your firm. Furthermore, your customers may not care that a security issue was caused by your downstream distributor; your brand name could be damaged all the same.

Risks Associated with Hardware, Software, and Services

While we explore risks inherent in *any* hardware, software, and services later in this book, for now let's consider those risks that are specifically tied to supply chains. That is to say, what risks do you face when you acquire something (or someone's service) and insert it into your information systems?

Hardware

One of the major supply chain risks is the addition of hardware Trojans to electronic components. A hardware Trojan is an electronic circuit that is added to an existing device in order to compromise its security or provide unauthorized functionality. Depending on the attacker's access, these mechanisms can be inserted at any stage of the hardware development process (specification, design, fabrication, testing, assembly, or packaging). It is also possible to add them after the hardware is packaged by intercepting shipments in the supply chain. In this case, the Trojan may be noticeable if the device is opened and visually inspected. The earlier in the supply chain that hardware Trojans are inserted, the more difficult they are to detect.

Another supply chain risk to hardware is the substitution of counterfeit components. The problems with these clones are many, but from a security perspective one of the most important is that they don't go through the same quality controls that the real ones do. This leads to lower reliability and abnormal behavior. It could also lead to undetected hardware Trojans (perhaps inserted by the illicit manufacturers themselves). Obviously, using counterfeits could have legal implications and will definitely be a problem when you need customer support from the manufacturer.

Software

Like hardware, third-party software can be Trojaned by an adversary in your supply chain, particularly if it is custom-made for your organization. This could happen if your supplier reuses components (like libraries) developed elsewhere and to which the attacker has access. It can also be done by a malicious insider working for the supplier or by a remote attacker who has gained access to the supplier's software repositories. Failing all that, the software could be intercepted in transit to you, modified, and then sent on its way. This last approach could be made more difficult for the adversary by using code signing or hashes, but it is still possible.

Services

More organizations are outsourcing services to allow them to focus on their core business functions. Organizations use hosting companies to maintain websites and e-mail servers, service providers for various telecommunication connections, disaster recovery companies for co-location capabilities, cloud computing providers for infrastructure or application services, developers for software creation, and security companies to carry out vulnerability management. It is important to realize that while you can outsource functionality, you cannot outsource risk. When your organization is using these third-party service providers, it can still be ultimately responsible if something like a data breach takes place. The following are some things an organization should do to reduce its risk when outsourcing:

- Review the service provider's security program
- Conduct onsite inspection and interviews
- Review contracts to ensure security and protection levels are agreed upon
- Ensure service level agreements are in place
- Review internal and external audit reports and third-party reviews
- Review references and communicate with former and existing customers
- Review Better Business Bureau reports
- Ensure the service provider has a business continuity plan (BCP) in place
- Implement a nondisclosure agreement (NDA)
- Understand the provider's legal and regulatory requirements

Service outsourcing is prevalent within organizations today but is commonly forgotten about when it comes to security and compliance requirements. It may be economical to outsource certain functionalities, but if this allows security breaches to take place, it can turn out to be a very costly decision.

Other Third-Party Risks

An organization's supply chain is not its only source of third-party risks. There are many other ways in which organizations may be dependent on each other that don't really fit the supplier–consumer model. For example, many companies have a network of channel partners that help them directly or indirectly sell products. Others engage in general or limited partnerships for specific projects, and these relationships require sharing some resources and risks. Most organizations nowadays have a complex web of (sometimes not so obvious) third parties on whom they rely to some extent and who, therefore, introduce risks.

Minimum Security Requirements

The key to effectively mitigating risks to an organization introduced by its suppliers is to clearly state each party's requirements in the contract or agreement that governs their relationship. In terms of cybersecurity, this includes whatever measures are needed to protect sensitive data at rest, in transit, and in use. It also includes the actions the supplier shall perform should the data become compromised, as well as the means through which the purchasing organization may proactively verify compliance. In summary, the critical classes of requirements that should be included in a contractual agreement are as follows.

- **Data protection** Proactive cybersecurity measures
- **Incident response** Reactive cybersecurity measures
- **Verification means** Ways in which the customer may verify the preceding requirements

If any requirements are missing, ambiguously stated, or otherwise vitiated, the supplier agreement can become void, voidable, or unenforceable. So, how do you verify that your supplier is complying with all contractual requirements dealing with risk? Third-party assessments are considered best practice and may be required for compliance (e.g., with PCI DSS). The following are some examples of external evaluations that would indicate a supplier's ability to comply with its contractual obligations:

- ISO 27001 certification
- U.S. Department of Defense Cybersecurity Maturity Model Certification (CMMC)
- Payment Card Industry Digital Security Standard (PCI DSS) certification
- Service Organization Control 1 (SOC1) or 2 (SOC2) report
- U.S. Federal Risk and Authorization Management Program (FedRAMP) authorization

NOTE We will discuss these third-party evaluations in subsequent chapters.

Other third-party evaluations, such as vulnerability assessments and penetration tests, are helpful in establishing a baseline of security in the organization. However, by themselves, these limited-scope tests are insufficient to verify that the supplier is able to fulfill its contractual obligations.

Service Level Agreements

A *service level agreement (SLA)* is a contractual agreement that states that a service provider guarantees a certain level of service. If the service is not delivered at the agreed-upon level (or better), then there are consequences (typically financial) for the service provider. SLAs provide a mechanism to mitigate some of the risk from service providers in the supply chain. For example, an Internet service provider (ISP) may sign an SLA of 99.999 percent (commonly called "five nines") uptime to the Internet backbone. That means that the ISP guarantees less than 26 seconds of downtime per month.

Business Continuity

Though we strive to drive down the risks of negative effects in our organizations, we can be sure that sooner or later an event will slip through and cause negative impacts. Ideally, the losses are contained and won't affect the major business efforts. However, as security professionals we need to have plans in place for when the unthinkable happens. Under those extreme (and sometimes unpredictable) conditions, we need to ensure that our organizations continue to operate at some minimum acceptable threshold capacity and quickly bounce back to full productivity.

Business continuity (BC) is an organization's ability to maintain business functions or quickly resume them in the event that risks are realized and result in disruptions. The events can be pretty mundane, such as a temporary power outage, loss of network connectivity, or a critical employee (such as a systems administrator) suddenly becoming ill. These events could also be major disasters, such as an earthquake, explosion, or energy grid failure. *Disaster recovery (DR)*, by contrast to BC, is the process of minimizing the effects of a disaster or major disruption. It means taking the necessary steps to ensure that the resources, personnel, and business processes are safe and able to resume operation in a timely manner. So, DR is part of BC and the *disaster recovery plan (DRP)* covers a subset of events compared to the broader *business continuity plan (BCP)*.

EXAM TIP A business continuity plan (BCP) and a disaster recovery plan (DRP) are related but different. The DRP is a subset of the BCP and is focused on the immediate aftermath of a disaster. The BCP is much broader and covers any disruption including (but not limited to) disasters.

NOTE We discuss disaster recovery plans in detail in Chapter 23.

A BCP can include getting critical systems to another environment while repair of the original facilities is underway, getting the right people to the right places during this time, and performing business in a different mode until regular conditions are back in place. A BCP also involves dealing with customers, partners, and shareholders through different channels until everything returns to normal. So, disaster recovery deals with,

"Oh my goodness, the sky is falling," and continuity planning deals with, "Okay, the sky fell. Now, how do we stay in business until someone can put the sky back where it belongs?"

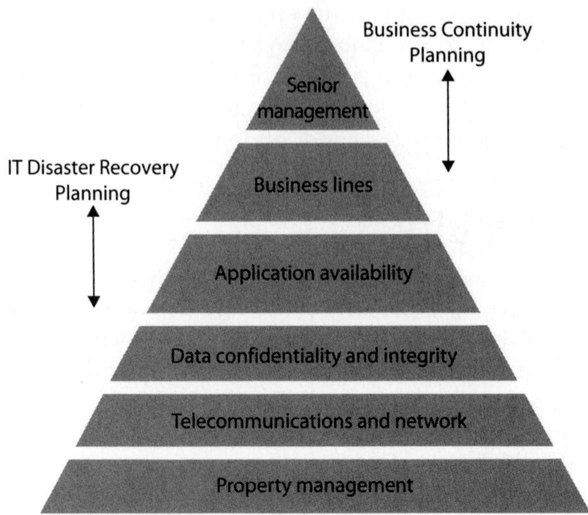

While disaster recovery and business continuity planning are directed at the development of plans, *business continuity management (BCM)* is the holistic management process that should cover both of them. BCM provides a framework for integrating resilience with the capability for effective responses in a manner that protects the interests of an organization's key stakeholders. The main objective of BCM is to allow the organization to continue to perform business operations under various conditions.

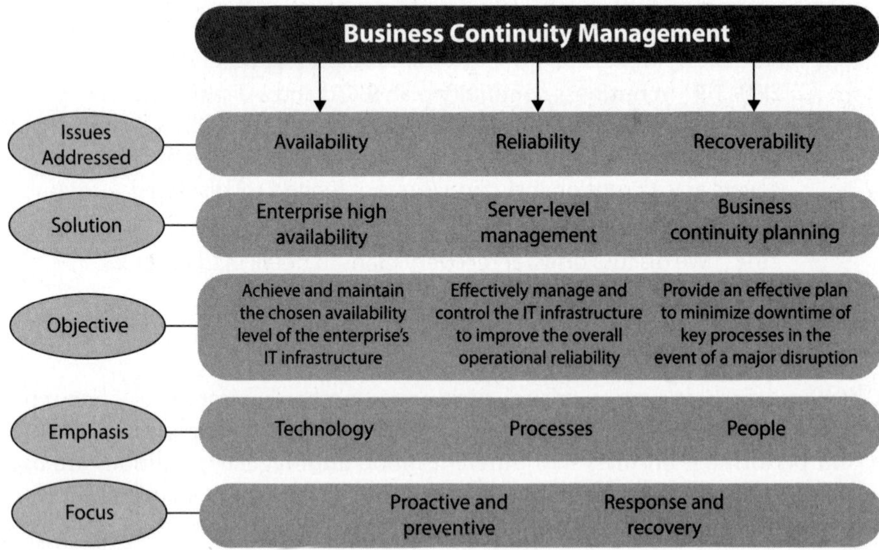

Certain characteristics run through many of the chapters in this book: availability, integrity, and confidentiality. Here, we point out that integrity and confidentiality must be considered not only in everyday procedures but also in those procedures undertaken immediately after a disaster or disruption. For instance, it may not be appropriate to leave a server that holds confidential information in one building while everyone else moves to another building. Equipment that provides secure VPN connections may be destroyed and the team might respond by focusing on enabling remote access functionality while forgetting about the needs of encryption. In most situations the organization is purely focused on getting back up and running, thus focusing on functionality. If security is not integrated and implemented properly, the effects of the physical disaster can be amplified as threat actors come in and steal sensitive information. Many times an organization is much more vulnerable *after* a disaster hits, because the security services used to protect it may be unavailable or operating at a reduced capacity. Therefore, it is important that if the organization has secret stuff, it stays secret.

Availability is one of the main themes behind business continuity planning, in that it ensures that the resources required to keep the business going will continue to be available to the people and systems that rely upon them. This may mean backups need to be done religiously and that redundancy needs to be factored into the architecture of the systems, networks, and operations. If communication lines are disabled or if a service is rendered unusable for any significant period of time, there must be a quick and tested way of establishing alternative communications and services. We will be diving into the many ways organizations can implement availability solutions for continuity and recovery purposes throughout this section.

When looking at business continuity planning, some organizations focus mainly on backing up data and providing redundant hardware. Although these items are extremely important, they are just small pieces of the organization's overall operations pie. Hardware and computers need people to configure and operate them, and data is usually not useful unless it is accessible by other systems and possibly outside entities. Thus, a larger picture

Business Continuity Planning

Preplanned procedures allow an organization to

- Provide an immediate and appropriate response to emergency situations
- Protect lives and ensure safety
- Reduce business impact
- Resume critical business functions
- Work with outside vendors and partners during the recovery period
- Reduce confusion during a crisis
- Ensure survivability of the organization
- Get "up and running" quickly after a disaster

of how the various processes within an organization work together needs to be understood. Planning must include getting the right people to the right places, documenting the necessary configurations, establishing alternative communications channels (voice and data), providing power, and making sure all dependencies are properly understood and taken into account.

It is also important to understand how automated tasks can be carried out manually, if necessary, and how business processes can be safely altered to keep the operation of the organization going. This may be critical in ensuring the organization survives the event with the least impact to its operations. Without this type of vision and planning, when a disaster hits, an organization could have its backup data and redundant servers physically available at the alternative facility, but the people responsible for activating them may be standing around in a daze, not knowing where to start or how to perform in such a different environment.

Standards and Best Practices

Although no specific scientific equation must be followed to create continuity plans, certain best practices have proven themselves over time. The National Institute of Standards and Technology is responsible for developing best practices and standards as they pertain to U.S. government and military environments. It is common for NIST to document the requirements for these types of environments, and then everyone else in the industry uses NIST's documents as guidelines. So these are "musts" for U.S. government organizations and "good to have" for other, nongovernment entities.

NIST outlines the following steps in SP 800-34, Rev. 1, *Contingency Planning Guide for Federal Information Systems*:

1. *Develop the continuity planning policy statement.* Write a policy that provides the guidance necessary to develop a BCP and that assigns authority to the necessary roles to carry out these tasks.
2. *Conduct the business impact analysis (BIA).* Identify critical functions and systems and allow the organization to prioritize them based on necessity. Identify vulnerabilities and threats, and calculate risks.
3. *Identify preventive controls.* Once threats are recognized, identify and implement controls and countermeasures to reduce the organization's risk level in an economical manner.
4. *Create contingency strategies.* Formulate methods to ensure systems and critical functions can be brought online quickly.
5. *Develop an information system contingency plan.* Write procedures and guidelines for how the organization can still stay functional in a crippled state.
6. *Ensure plan testing, training, and exercises.* Test the plan to identify deficiencies in the BCP, and conduct training to properly prepare individuals on their expected tasks.
7. *Ensure plan maintenance.* Put in place steps to ensure the BCP is a living document that is updated regularly.

Although NIST SP 800-34 deals specifically with IT contingency plans, these steps are similar when creating enterprise-wide BCPs and BCM programs.

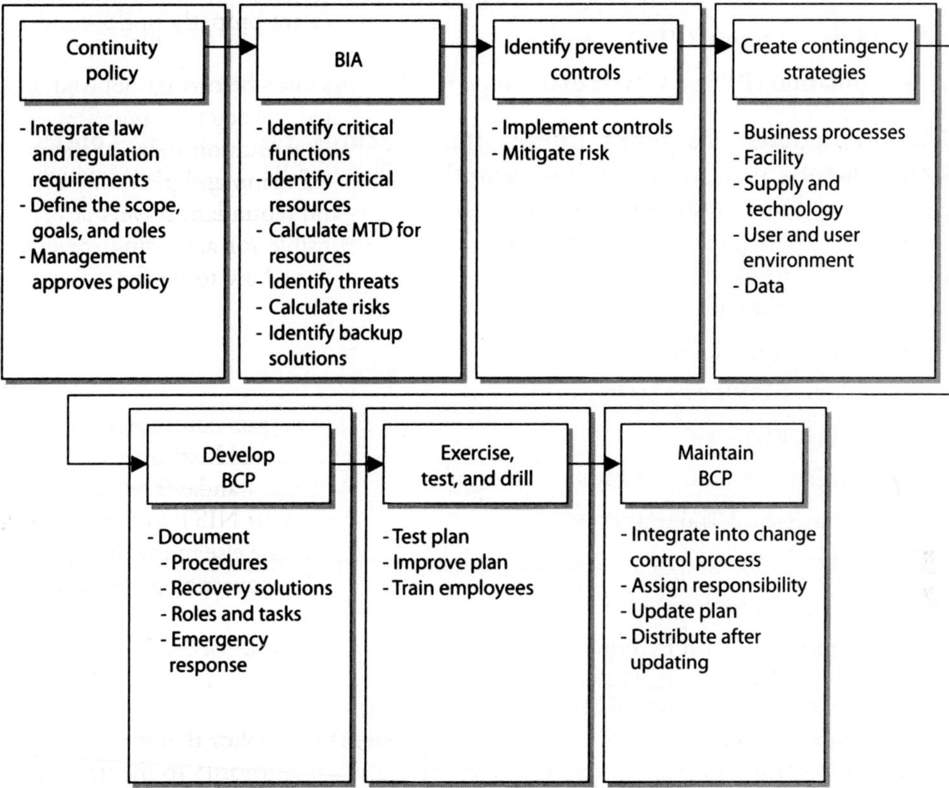

Since BCM is so critical, it is actually addressed by other standards-based organizations, listed here:

ISO/IEC 27031:2011 Guidelines for information and communications technology readiness for business continuity. This ISO/IEC standard is a component of the overall ISO/IEC 27000 series.

ISO 22301:2019 International standard for business continuity management systems. The specification document against which organizations will seek certification.

Business Continuity Institute's Good Practice Guidelines (GPG) Represents the consensus view of an international group of BC practitioners. As of this writing, the latest edition was published in 2018. It is organized around six Professional Practices (PP):

- **Policy and Program Management (PP1)** Focuses on governance
- **Embedding Business Continuity (PP2)** Provides guidance on embedding BCM in the organization's culture, which includes awareness and training

- **Analysis (PP3)** Addresses organizational review, risk assessment, and business impact analysis, among other topics
- **Design (PP4)** Focuses on identifying and selecting the right BC solutions
- **Implementation (PP5)** Addresses what should go into the BC plan
- **Validation (PP6)** Covers exercising, maintaining, and reviewing the program

DRI International Institute's Professional Practices for Business Continuity Management Best practices and framework to allow for BCM processes, which are broken down into the following sections:

- Program Initiation and Management
- Risk Assessment
- Business Impact Analysis
- Business Continuity Strategies
- Incident Response
- Plan Development and Implementation
- Awareness and Training Programs
- Business Continuity Plan Exercise, Assessment, and Maintenance
- Crisis Communications
- Coordination with External Agencies

Why are there so many sets of best practices and which is the best for your organization? If your organization is part of the U.S. government or a government contracting organization, then you need to comply with the NIST standards. If your organization is in Europe or your organization does business with other organizations in Europe, then you might need to follow the European Union Agency for Cybersecurity (ENISA) requirements. While we are not listing all of them here, there are other country-based BCM standards that your organization might need to comply with if it is residing in or does business in one of those specific countries. If your organization needs to get ISO certified, then ISO/IEC 27031 and ISO 22301 could be the standards to follow. While the first of these is focused on IT, the second is broader in scope and addresses the needs of the entire organization.

Making BCM Part of the Enterprise Security Program

As we already explained, every organization should have security policies, procedures, standards, and guidelines. People who are new to information security commonly think that this is one pile of documentation that addresses all issues pertaining to security, but it is more complicated than that—of course.

Business continuity planning ought to be fully integrated into the organization as a regular management process, just like auditing or strategic planning or other "normal"

Understanding the Organization First

An organization has no real hope of rebuilding itself and its processes after a disaster if it does not have a good understanding of how its organization works in the first place. This notion might seem absurd at first. You might think, "Well, of course an organization knows how it works." But you would be surprised at how difficult it is to fully understand an organization down to the level of detail required to rebuild it. Each individual may know and understand his or her little world within the organization, but hardly anyone at any organization can fully explain how each and every business process takes place.

processes. Instead of being considered an outsider, BCP should be "part of the team." Further, final responsibility for BCP should belong not to the BCP team or its leader, but to a high-level executive manager, preferably a member of the executive board. This will reinforce the image and reality of continuity planning as a function seen as vital to the organizational chiefs.

By analyzing and planning for potential disruptions to the organization, the BCP team can assist other business disciplines in their own efforts to effectively plan for and respond effectively and with resilience to emergencies. Given that the ability to respond depends on operations and management personnel throughout the organization, such capability should be developed organization-wide. It should extend throughout every location of the organization and up the employee ranks to top-tier management.

As such, the BCP program needs to be a living entity. As an organization goes through changes, so should the program, thereby ensuring it stays current, usable, and effective. When properly integrated with change management processes, the program stands a much better chance of being continually updated and improved upon. Business continuity is a foundational piece of an effective security program and is critical to ensuring relevance in time of need.

A very important question to ask when first developing a BCP is *why* it is being developed. This may seem silly and the answer may at first appear obvious, but that is not always the case. You might think that the reason to have these plans is to deal with an unexpected disaster and to get people back to their tasks as quickly and as safely as possible, but the full story is often a bit different. Why are most companies in business? To make money and be profitable. If these are usually the main goals of businesses, then any BCP needs to be developed to help achieve and, more importantly, maintain these goals. The main reason to develop these plans in the first place is to reduce the risk of financial loss by improving the company's ability to recover and restore operations. This encompasses the goals of mitigating the effects of the disaster.

Not all organizations are businesses that exist to make profits. Government agencies, military units, nonprofit organizations, and the like exist to provide some type of protection or service to a nation or society. Whereas a company must create its BCP to ensure that revenue continues to come in so that the company can stay in business, other types of organizations must create their BCPs to make sure they can still carry out their critical tasks. Although the focus and business drivers of the organizations and companies may differ, their BCPs often have similar constructs—which is to get their critical processes up and running.

Protecting what is most important to a company is rather difficult if what is most important is not first identified. Senior management is usually involved with this step because it has a point of view that extends beyond each functional manager's focus area of responsibility. Senior management has the visibility needed to establish the scope of the plan. The company's BCP should be focused on the company's critical mission and business functions. And, conversely, the BCP must support the organization's overall strategy. The functions must have priorities set upon them to indicate which is most crucial to a company's survival. The scope of the BCP is defined by which of these functions are considered important enough to warrant the investment of resources required for BC.

As stated previously, for many companies, financial operations are most critical. As an example, an automotive company would be affected far more seriously if its credit and loan services were unavailable for a day than if, say, an assembly line went down for a day, since credit and loan services are where it generates the biggest revenues. For other organizations, customer service might be the most critical area to ensure that order processing is not negatively affected. For example, if a company makes heart pacemakers and its physician services department is unavailable at a time when an operating room surgeon needs to contact it because of a complication, the results could be disastrous for the patient. The surgeon and the company would likely be sued, and the company would likely never again be able to sell another pacemaker to that surgeon, her colleagues, or perhaps even the patient's health maintenance organization (HMO). It would be very difficult to rebuild reputation and sales after something like that happened.

Advanced planning for emergencies covers issues that were thought of and foreseen. Many other problems may arise that are not covered in the BCP; thus, flexibility in the plan is crucial. The plan is a systematic way of providing a checklist of actions that should take place right after a disaster. These actions have been thought through to help the people involved be more efficient and effective in dealing with traumatic situations.

The most critical part of establishing and maintaining a current BCP is management support. Management must be convinced of the necessity of such a plan. Therefore, a business case must be made to obtain this support. The business case may include current vulnerabilities, regulatory and legal obligations, the current status of recovery plans, and recommendations. Management is mostly concerned with cost/benefit issues, so preliminary numbers need to be gathered and potential losses estimated. A cost/benefit analysis should include shareholder, stakeholder, regulatory, and legislative impacts, as well as impacts on products, services, and personnel. The decision of how a company should recover is commonly a business decision and should always be treated as such.

Business Impact Analysis

Business continuity planning deals with uncertainty and chance. What is important to note here is that even though you cannot predict whether or when a disaster will happen, that doesn't mean you can't plan for it. Just because we are not planning for an earthquake to hit us tomorrow morning at 10 A.M. doesn't mean we can't plan the activities required to successfully survive when an earthquake (or a similar disaster) does hit. The point of making these plans is to try to think of all the possible disasters that could take place, estimate the potential damage and loss, categorize and prioritize the potential disasters, and develop viable alternatives in case those events do actually happen.

A *business impact analysis (BIA)* is considered a *functional analysis*, in which a team collects data through interviews and documentary sources; documents business functions, activities, and transactions; develops a hierarchy of business functions; and finally applies a classification scheme to indicate each individual function's criticality level. But how do we determine a classification scheme based on criticality levels?

The BCP committee must identify the threats to the organization and map them to the following characteristics:

- Maximum tolerable downtime and disruption for activities
- Operational disruption and productivity
- Financial considerations
- Regulatory responsibilities
- Reputation

The committee will not truly understand all business processes, the steps that must take place, or the resources and supplies these processes require. So the committee must gather this information from the people who do know—department managers and specific employees throughout the organization. The committee starts by identifying the people who will be part of the BIA data-gathering sessions. The committee needs to identify how it will collect the data from the selected employees, be it through surveys, interviews, or workshops. Next, the team needs to collect the information by actually conducting surveys, interviews, and workshops. Data points obtained as part of the information gathering will be used later during analysis. It is important that the team members ask about how different tasks—whether processes, transactions, or services, along with any relevant dependencies—get accomplished within the organization. The team should build process flow diagrams, which will be used throughout the BIA and plan development stages.

Upon completion of the data collection phase, the BCP committee needs to conduct a BIA to establish which processes, devices, or operational activities are critical. If a system stands on its own, doesn't affect other systems, and is of low criticality, then it can be classified as a tier-two or tier-three recovery step. This means these resources will not be dealt with during the recovery stages until the most critical (tier one) resources are up and running. This analysis can be completed using a standard risk assessment as illustrated in Figure 2-9.

Risk Assessment

To achieve success, the organization should systematically plan and execute a formal BCP-related risk assessment. The assessment fully takes into account the organization's

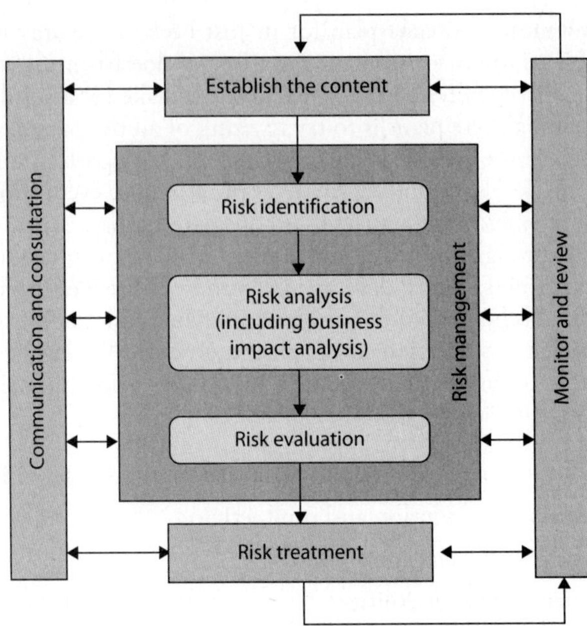

Figure 2-9 Risk assessment process

tolerance for continuity risks. The risk assessment also makes use of the data in the BIA to supply a consistent estimate of exposure.

As indicators of success, the risk assessment should identify, evaluate, and record all relevant items, which may include

- Vulnerabilities for all of the organization's most time-sensitive resources and activities
- Threats and hazards to the organization's most urgent resources and activities
- Measures that cut the possibility, length, or effect of a disruption on critical services and products
- Single points of failure; that is, concentrations of risk that threaten business continuity
- Continuity risks from concentrations of critical skills or critical shortages of skills
- Continuity risks due to outsourced vendors and suppliers
- Continuity risks that the BCP program has accepted, that are handled elsewhere, or that the BCP program does not address

Risk Assessment Evaluation and Process

In a BCP setting, a risk assessment looks at the impact and likelihood of various threats that could trigger a business disruption. The tools, techniques, and methods of risk assessment include determining threats, assessing probabilities, tabulating threats, and analyzing costs and benefits.

PART I

The end goals of a business continuity–focused risk assessment include

- Identifying and documenting single points of failure
- Making a prioritized list of threats to the particular business processes of the organization
- Putting together information for developing a management strategy for risk control and for developing action plans for addressing risks
- Documenting acceptance of identified risks, or documenting acknowledgment of risks that will not be addressed

The risk assessment is assumed to take the form of the equation Risk = Threat × Impact × Probability. However, the BIA adds the dimension of time to this equation. In other words, risk mitigation measures should be geared toward those things that might most rapidly disrupt critical business processes and commercial activities.

The main parts of a risk assessment are

- Review the existing strategies for risk management
- Construct a numerical scoring system for probabilities and impacts
- Make use of a numerical score to gauge the effect of the threat
- Estimate the probability of each threat
- Weigh each threat through the scoring system
- Calculate the risk by combining the scores of likelihood and impact of each threat
- Get the organization's sponsor to sign off on these risk priorities
- Weigh appropriate measures
- Make sure that planned measures that alleviate risk do not heighten other risks
- Present the assessment's findings to executive management

Threats can be man-made, natural, or technical. A man-made threat may be an arsonist, a terrorist, or a simple mistake that can have serious outcomes. Natural threats may be tornadoes, floods, hurricanes, or earthquakes. Technical threats may be data corruption, loss of power, device failure, or loss of a data communications line. It is important to identify all possible threats and estimate the probability of them happening. Some issues may not immediately come to mind when developing these plans, such as an employee strike, vandals, disgruntled employees, or hackers, but they do need to be identified. These issues are often best addressed in a group with scenario-based exercises. This ensures that if a threat becomes reality, the plan includes the ramifications on *all* business tasks, departments, and critical operations. The more issues that are thought of and planned for, the better prepared an organization will be if and when these events take place.

The BCP committee needs to step through scenarios in which the following problems result:

- Equipment malfunction or unavailable equipment
- Unavailable utilities (HVAC, power, communications lines)
- Facility becomes unavailable
- Critical personnel become unavailable
- Vendor and service providers become unavailable
- Software and/or data corruption

The specific scenarios and damage types can vary from organization to organization.

Assigning Values to Assets

Qualitative and quantitative impact information should be gathered and then properly analyzed and interpreted. The goal is to see exactly how an organization will be affected by different threats. The effects can be economical, operational, or both. Upon completion of the data analysis, it should be reviewed with the most knowledgeable people within the organization to ensure that the findings are appropriate and that it describes the real risks and impacts the organization faces. This will help flush out any additional data points not originally obtained and will give a fuller understanding of all the possible business impacts.

Loss criteria must be applied to the individual threats that were identified. The criteria may include the following:

- Loss in reputation and public confidence
- Loss of competitive advantages

BIA Steps

The more detailed and granular steps of a BIA are outlined here:

1. Select individuals to interview for data gathering.
2. Create data-gathering techniques (surveys, questionnaires, qualitative and quantitative approaches).
3. Identify the organization's critical business functions.
4. Identify the resources these functions depend upon.
5. Calculate how long these functions can survive without these resources.
6. Identify vulnerabilities and threats to these functions.
7. Calculate the risk for each different business function.
8. Document findings and report them to management.

We cover each of these steps in this chapter.

- Increase in operational expenses
- Violations of contract agreements
- Violations of legal and regulatory requirements
- Delayed-income costs
- Loss in revenue
- Loss in productivity

These costs can be direct or indirect and must be properly accounted for.

For instance, if the BCP team is looking at the threat of a terrorist bombing, it is important to identify which business function most likely would be targeted, how all business functions could be affected, and how each bulleted item in the loss criteria would be directly or indirectly involved. The timeliness of the recovery can be critical for business processes and the company's survival. For example, it may be acceptable to have the customer-support functionality out of commission for two days, whereas five days may leave the company in financial ruin.

After identifying the critical functions, it is necessary to find out exactly what is required for these individual business processes to take place. The resources that are required for the identified business processes are not necessarily just computer systems, but may include personnel, procedures, tasks, supplies, and vendor support. It must be understood that if one or more of these support mechanisms is not available, the critical function may be doomed. The team must determine what type of effect unavailable resources and systems will have on these critical functions.

The BIA identifies which of the organization's critical systems are needed for survival and estimates the outage time that can be tolerated by the organization as a result of various unfortunate events. The outage time that can be endured by an organization is referred to as the *maximum tolerable downtime (MTD)* or *maximum tolerable period of disruption (MTPD)*, which is illustrated in Figure 2-10.

Figure 2-10 Maximum tolerable downtime

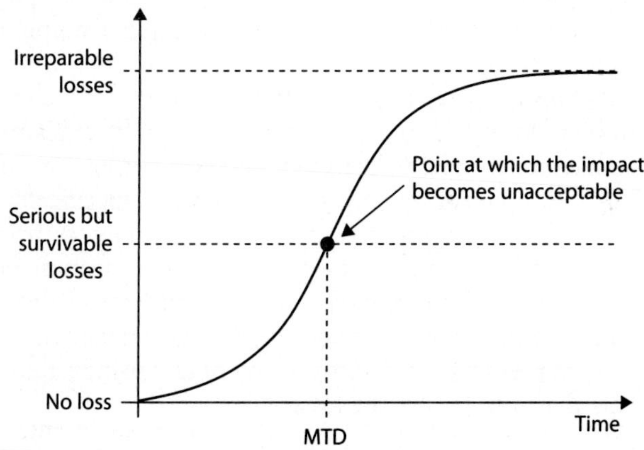

The following are some MTD estimates that an organization may use. Note that these are sample estimates that will vary from organization to organization and from business unit to business unit.

- **Nonessential** 30 days
- **Normal** 7 days
- **Important** 72 hours
- **Urgent** 24 hours
- **Critical** Minutes to hours

Each business function and asset should be placed in one of these categories, depending upon how long the organization can survive without it. These estimates will help the organization determine what backup solutions are necessary to ensure the availability of these resources. The shorter the MTD, the higher priority of recovery for the function in question. Thus, the items classified as Urgent should be addressed before those classified as Normal.

For example, if being without a T1 communication line for three hours would cost the company $130,000, the T1 line could be considered Critical, and thus the company should put in a backup T1 line from a different carrier. If a server going down and being unavailable for ten days will only cost the company $250 in revenue, this would fall into the Normal category, and thus the company may not need to have a fully redundant server waiting to be swapped out. Instead, the company may choose to count on its vendor's SLA, which may promise to have it back online in eight days.

Sometimes the MTD will depend in large measure on the type of organization in question. For instance, a call center—a vital link to current and prospective clients—will have a short MTD, perhaps measured in minutes instead of weeks. A common solution is to split up the calls through multiple call centers placed in differing locales. If one call center is knocked out of service, the other one can temporarily pick up the load. Manufacturing can be handled in various ways. Examples include subcontracting the making of products to an outside vendor, manufacturing at multiple sites, and warehousing an extra supply of products to fill gaps in supply in case of disruptions to normal manufacturing.

The BCP team must try to think of all possible events that might occur that could turn out to be detrimental to an organization. The BCP team also must understand it cannot possibly contemplate all events, and thus protection may not be available for every scenario introduced. Being properly prepared specifically for a flood, earthquake, terrorist attack, or lightning strike is not as important as being properly prepared to respond to *anything* that damages or disrupts critical business functions.

All of the previously mentioned disasters could cause these results, but so could a meteor strike, a tornado, or a wing falling off a plane passing overhead. So the moral of the story is to be prepared for the loss of any or all business resources, instead of focusing on the events that could cause the loss.

EXAM TIP A BIA is performed at the beginning of business continuity planning to identify the areas that would suffer the greatest financial or operational loss in the event of a disaster or disruption. It identifies the organization's critical systems needed for survival and estimates the outage time that can be tolerated by the organization as a result of a disaster or disruption.

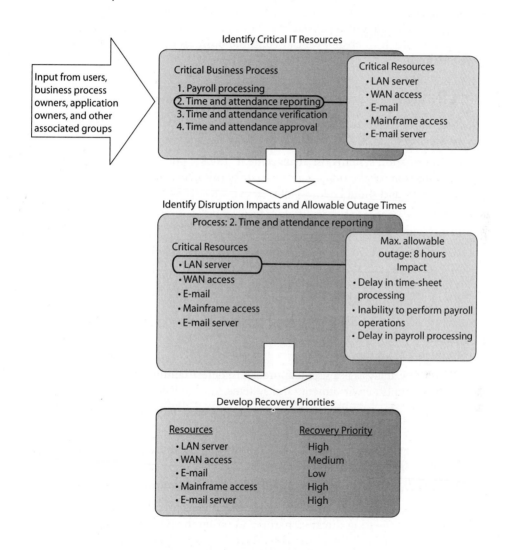

Chapter Review

We took a very detailed look at the way in which we manage risk to our information systems. We know that no system is truly secure, so our job is to find the most likely and the most dangerous threat actions so that we can address them first. The process of quantifying losses and their probabilities of occurring is at the heart of risk assessments. Armed with that information, we are able to make good decisions in terms of controls, processes, and costs. Our approach is focused not solely on the human adversary but also on any source of loss to our organizations. Most importantly, we use this information to devise ways in which to ensure we can continue business operations in the face of any reasonable threat.

Quick Review

- Risk management is the process of identifying and assessing risk, reducing it to an acceptable level, and ensuring it remains at that level.
- An information systems risk management (ISRM) policy provides the foundation and direction for the organization's security risk management processes and procedures and should address all issues of information security.
- A threat is a potential cause of an unwanted incident, which may result in harm to a system or organization.
- Four risk assessment methodologies with which you should be familiar are NIST SP 800-30; Facilitated Risk Analysis Process (FRAP); Operationally Critical Threat, Asset, and Vulnerability Evaluation (OCTAVE); and Failure Modes and Effect Analysis (FMEA).
- Failure Modes and Effect Analysis (FMEA) is a method for determining functions, identifying functional failures, and assessing the causes of failure and their effects through a structured process.
- A fault tree analysis is a useful approach to detect failures that can take place within complex environments and systems.
- A quantitative risk analysis attempts to assign monetary values to components within the analysis.
- A purely quantitative risk analysis is not possible because qualitative items cannot be quantified with precision.
- Qualitative risk analysis uses judgment and intuition instead of numbers.
- Qualitative risk analysis involves people with the requisite experience and education evaluating threat scenarios and rating the probability, potential loss, and severity of each threat based on their personal experience.
- Single loss expectancy × frequency per year = annualized loss expectancy (SLE × ARO = ALE)

- The main goals of risk analysis are the following: identify assets and assign values to them, identify vulnerabilities and threats, quantify the impact of potential threats, and provide an economic balance between the impact of the risk and the cost of the safeguards.
- Capturing the degree of uncertainty when carrying out a risk analysis is important, because it indicates the level of confidence the team and management should have in the resulting figures.
- Automated risk analysis tools reduce the amount of manual work involved in the analysis. They can be used to estimate future expected losses and calculate the benefits of different security measures.
- The risk management team should include individuals from different departments within the organization, not just technical personnel.
- Risk can be transferred, avoided, reduced, or accepted.
- Threats × vulnerability × asset value = total risk.
- (Threats × vulnerability × asset value) × controls gap = residual risk.
- When choosing the right safeguard to reduce a specific risk, the cost, functionality, and effectiveness must be evaluated and a cost/benefit analysis performed.
- There are three main categories of controls: administrative, technical, and physical.
- Controls can also be grouped by types, depending on their intended purpose, as preventive, detective, corrective, deterrent, recovery, and compensating.
- A control assessment is an evaluation of one or more controls to determine the extent to which they are implemented correctly, operating as intended, and producing the desired outcome.
- Security control verification answers the question "did we implement the control right?" while validation answers the question "did we implement the right control?"
- Risk monitoring is the ongoing process of adding new risks, reevaluating existing ones, removing moot ones, and continuously assessing the effectiveness of your controls at mitigating all risks to tolerable levels.
- Change management processes deal with monitoring changes to your environment and dealing with the risks they could introduce.
- Continuous improvement is the practice of identifying opportunities, mitigating threats, improving quality, and reducing waste as an ongoing effort. It is the hallmark of mature and effective organizations.
- A supply chain is a sequence of suppliers involved in delivering some product.
- Business continuity management (BCM) is the overarching approach to managing all aspects of BCP and DRP.
- A business continuity plan (BCP) contains strategy documents that provide detailed procedures that ensure critical business functions are maintained and that help minimize losses of life, operations, and systems.

- A BCP provides procedures for emergency responses, extended backup operations, and post-disaster recovery.
- A BCP should have an enterprise-wide reach, with each individual organizational unit having its own detailed continuity and contingency plans.
- A BCP needs to prioritize critical applications and provide a sequence for efficient recovery.
- A BCP requires senior executive management support for initiating the plan and final approval.
- BCPs can quickly become outdated due to personnel turnover, reorganizations, and undocumented changes.
- Executives may be held liable if proper BCPs are not developed and used.
- Threats can be natural, man-made, or technical.
- The business impact analysis (BIA) is one of the most important first steps in the planning development. Qualitative and quantitative data on the business impact of a disaster need to be gathered, analyzed, interpreted, and presented to management.
- Executive commitment and support are the most critical elements in developing the BCP.
- A business case must be presented to gain executive support. This is done by explaining regulatory and legal requirements, exposing vulnerabilities, and providing solutions.
- Plans should be prepared by the people who will actually carry them out.
- The planning group should comprise representatives from all departments or organizational units.
- The BCP team should identify the individuals who will interact with external players, such as the reporters, shareholders, customers, and civic officials. Response to the disaster should be done quickly and honestly, and should be consistent with any other organizational response.

Questions

Please remember that these questions are formatted and asked in a certain way for a reason. Keep in mind that the CISSP exam is asking questions at a conceptual level. Questions may not always have the perfect answer, and the candidate is advised against always looking for the perfect answer. Instead, the candidate should look for the best answer in the list.

1. When is it acceptable to not take action on an identified risk?
   A. Never. Good security addresses and reduces all risks.
   B. When political issues prevent this type of risk from being addressed.
   C. When the necessary countermeasure is complex.
   D. When the cost of the countermeasure outweighs the value of the asset and potential loss.

2. Which is the most valuable technique when determining if a specific security control should be implemented?
   A. Risk analysis
   B. Cost/benefit analysis
   C. ALE results
   D. Identifying the vulnerabilities and threats causing the risk
3. Which best describes the purpose of the ALE calculation?
   A. Quantifies the security level of the environment
   B. Estimates the loss possible for a countermeasure
   C. Quantifies the cost/benefit result
   D. Estimates the loss potential of a threat in a span of a year
4. How do you calculate residual risk?
   A. Threats × risks × asset value
   B. (Threats × asset value × vulnerability) × risks
   C. SLE × frequency = ALE
   D. (Threats × vulnerability × asset value) × controls gap
5. Why should the team that will perform and review the risk analysis information be made up of people in different departments?
   A. To make sure the process is fair and that no one is left out.
   B. It shouldn't. It should be a small group brought in from outside the organization because otherwise the analysis is biased and unusable.
   C. Because people in different departments understand the risks of their department. Thus, it ensures the data going into the analysis is as close to reality as possible.
   D. Because the people in the different departments are the ones causing the risks, so they should be the ones held accountable.
6. Which best describes a quantitative risk analysis?
   A. A scenario-based analysis to research different security threats
   B. A method used to apply severity levels to potential loss, probability of loss, and risks
   C. A method that assigns monetary values to components in the risk assessment
   D. A method that is based on gut feelings and opinions
7. Why is a truly quantitative risk analysis not possible to achieve?
   A. It is possible, which is why it is used.
   B. It assigns severity levels. Thus, it is hard to translate into monetary values.
   C. It is dealing with purely quantitative elements.
   D. Quantitative measures must be applied to qualitative elements.

Use the following scenario to answer Questions 9–11. A company has an e-commerce website that carries out 60 percent of its annual revenue. Under the current circumstances, the annualized loss expectancy for a website against the threat of attack is $92,000. After implementing a new application-layer firewall, the new ALE would be $30,000. The firewall costs $65,000 per year to implement and maintain.

8. How much does the firewall save the company in loss expenses?

A. $62,000

B. $3,000

C. $65,000

D. $30,000

9. What is the value of the firewall to the company?

A. $62,000

B. $3,000

C. –$62,000

D. –$3,000

10. Which of the following describes the company's approach to risk management?

A. Risk transference

B. Risk avoidance

C. Risk acceptance

D. Risk mitigation

Use the following scenario to answer Questions 11–13. A small remote office for a company is valued at $800,000. It is estimated, based on historical data, that a fire is likely to occur once every ten years at a facility in this area. It is estimated that such a fire would destroy 60 percent of the facility under the current circumstances and with the current detective and preventive controls in place.

11. What is the single loss expectancy (SLE) for the facility suffering from a fire?

A. $80,000

B. $480,000

C. $320,000

D. 60%

12. What is the annualized rate of occurrence (ARO)?

A. 1

B. 10

C. .1

D. .01

13. What is the annualized loss expectancy (ALE)?
    A. $480,000
    B. $32,000
    C. $48,000
    D. .6
14. Which of the following is not one of the three key areas for risk monitoring?
    A. Threat
    B. Effectiveness
    C. Change
    D. Compliance
15. What is one of the first steps in developing a business continuity plan?
    A. Identify a backup solution.
    B. Perform a simulation test.
    C. Perform a business impact analysis.
    D. Develop a business resumption plan.

Answers

1. **D.** Organizations may decide to live with specific risks they are faced with if the cost of trying to protect themselves would be greater than the potential loss if the threat were to become real. Countermeasures are usually complex to a degree, and there are almost always political issues surrounding different risks, but these are not reasons to not implement a countermeasure.
2. **B.** Although the other answers may seem correct, B is the best answer here. This is because a risk analysis is performed to identify risks and come up with suggested countermeasures. The annualized loss expectancy (ALE) tells the organization how much it could lose if a specific threat became real. The ALE value will go into the cost/benefit analysis, but the ALE does not address the cost of the countermeasure and the benefit of a countermeasure. All the data captured in answers A, C, and D is inserted into a cost/benefit analysis.
3. **D.** The ALE calculation estimates the potential loss that can affect one asset from a specific threat within a one-year time span. This value is used to figure out the amount of money that should be earmarked to protect this asset from this threat.
4. **D.** The equation is more conceptual than practical. It is hard to assign a number to an individual vulnerability or threat. This equation enables you to look at the potential loss of a specific asset, as well as the controls gap (what the specific countermeasure cannot protect against). What remains is the residual risk, which is what is left over after a countermeasure is implemented.

5. **C.** An analysis is only as good as the data that goes into it. Data pertaining to risks the organization faces should be extracted from the people who understand best the business functions and environment of the organization. Each department understands its own threats and resources, and may have possible solutions to specific threats that affect its part of the organization.
6. **C.** A quantitative risk analysis assigns monetary values and percentages to the different components within the assessment. A qualitative analysis uses opinions of individuals and a rating system to gauge the severity level of different threats and the benefits of specific countermeasures.
7. **D.** During a risk analysis, the team is trying to properly predict the future and all the risks that future may bring. It is somewhat of a subjective exercise and requires educated guessing. It is very hard to properly predict that a flood will take place once in ten years and cost a company up to $40,000 in damages, but this is what a quantitative analysis tries to accomplish.
8. **A.** $62,000 is the correct answer. The firewall reduced the annualized loss expectancy (ALE) from $92,000 to $30,000 for a savings of $62,000. The formula for ALE is single loss expectancy × annualized rate of occurrence = ALE. Subtracting the ALE value after the firewall is implemented from the value before it was implemented results in the potential loss savings this type of control provides.
9. **D.** –$3,000 is the correct answer. The firewall saves $62,000, but costs $65,000 per year. 62,000 – 65,000 = –3,000. The firewall actually costs the company more than the original expected loss, and thus the value to the company is a negative number. The formula for this calculation is (ALE before the control is implemented) – (ALE after the control is implemented) – (annual cost of control) = value of control.
10. **D.** Risk mitigation involves employing controls in an attempt to reduce either the likelihood or damage associated with an incident, or both. The four ways of dealing with risk are accept, avoid, transfer, and mitigate (reduce). A firewall is a countermeasure installed to reduce the risk of a threat.
11. **B.** $480,000 is the correct answer. The formula for single loss expectancy (SLE) is asset value × exposure factor (EF) = SLE. In this situation the formula would work out as asset value ($800,000) × exposure factor (60%) = $480,000. This means that the company has a potential loss value of $480,000 pertaining to this one asset (facility) and this one threat type (fire).
12. **C.** The annualized rate occurrence (ARO) is the frequency that a threat will most likely occur within a 12-month period. It is a value used in the ALE formula, which is SLE × ARO = ALE.
13. **C.** $48,000 is the correct answer. The annualized loss expectancy formula (SLE × ARO = ALE) is used to calculate the loss potential for one asset experiencing one threat in a 12-month period. The resulting ALE value helps to determine the amount that can reasonably be spent in the protection of that asset. In this situation, the company should not spend over $48,000 on protecting this

asset from the threat of fire. ALE values help organizations rank the severity level of the risks they face so they know which ones to deal with first and how much to spend on each.

14. **A.** Risk monitoring activities should be focused on three key areas: effectiveness, change, and compliance. Changes to the threat landscape should be incorporated directly into the first two, and indirectly into compliance monitoring.

15. **C.** A business impact analysis includes identifying critical systems and functions of an organization and interviewing representatives from each department. Once management's support is solidified, a BIA needs to be performed to identify the threats the company faces and the potential costs of these threats.

CHAPTER 3

Compliance

This chapter presents the following:

- Regulations, laws, and crimes involving computers
- Intellectual property
- Data breaches
- Compliance requirements
- Investigations

If you think compliance is expensive, try noncompliance.

—Paul McNulty

Rules, formal or otherwise, are essential for prosperity in any context. This is particularly true when it comes to cybersecurity. Even if our adversaries don't follow the rules (and clearly they don't), we must understand the rules that apply to us and follow them carefully. In this chapter, we discuss the various laws and regulations that deal with computer information systems. We can't really address each piece of legislation around the world, since that would take multiple books longer than this one. However, we will offer as examples some of the most impactful laws and regulations affecting multinational enterprises. These include laws and regulations applicable to cybercrimes, privacy, and intellectual property, among others. The point of this chapter is not to turn you into a cyberlaw expert, but to make you aware of some of the topics about which you should have conversations with your legal counsel and compliance colleagues as you develop and mature your cybersecurity program.

Laws and Regulations

Before we get into the details of what you, as a cybersecurity leader, are required to do, let's start by reviewing some foundational concepts about what laws and regulations are, exploring how they vary around the world, and then putting them into a holistic context.

Law is a system of rules created by either a government or a society, recognized as binding by that group, and enforced by some specific authority. Laws apply equally to everyone in the country or society. It is important to keep in mind that laws are not always written down and may be customary, as discussed shortly. *Regulations*, by contrast, are written rules dealing with specific details or procedures, issued by an executive body and having the force of law. Regulations apply only to the specific entities that fall under the authority of the agency that issues them. So, while any U.S.-based organization is subject to a U.S. law called the Computer Fraud and Abuse Act (CFAA), only U.S. organizations that deal with data concerning persons in the European Union (EU) would also be subject to the General Data Protection Regulation (GDPR).

Types of Legal Systems

Your organization may be subject to laws and regulations from multiple jurisdictions. As just mentioned, if your organization is based in the United States but handles data of citizens of the EU, your organization is subject to both the CFAA and the GDPR. It is important to keep in mind that different countries can have very different legal systems. Your legal department will figure out jurisdictions and applicability, but you need to be aware of what this disparity of legal systems means to your cybersecurity program. To this end, it is helpful to become familiar with the major legal systems you may come across. In this section, we cover the core components of the various legal systems and what differentiates them.

Civil (Code) Law System

- System of law used in continental European countries such as France and Spain.
- Different legal system from the common law system used in the United Kingdom and United States.
- Civil law system is rule-based law, not precedent-based.
- For the most part, a civil law system is focused on codified law—or written laws.
- The history of the civil law system dates to the sixth century when the Byzantine emperor Justinian codified the laws of Rome.
- Civil *legal systems* should not be confused with the civil (or tort) *laws* found in the United States.
- The civil legal system was established by states or nations for self-regulation; thus, the civil law system can be divided into subdivisions, such as French civil law, German civil law, and so on.
- It is the most widespread legal system in the world and the most common legal system in Europe.
- Under the civil legal system, lower courts are not compelled to follow the decisions made by higher courts.

Common Law System

- Developed in England.
- Based on previous interpretations of laws:
    - In the past, judges would walk throughout the country enforcing laws and settling disputes.

    - The judges did not have a written set of laws, so they based their laws on custom and precedent.
    - In the 12th century, the king of England (Henry II) imposed a unified legal system that was "common" to the entire country.
    - Reflects the community's morals and expectations.
    - Led to the creation of barristers, or lawyers, who actively participate in the litigation process through the presentation of evidence and arguments.
- Today, the common law system uses judges and juries of peers. If the jury trial is waived, the judge decides the facts.
- Typical systems consist of a higher court, several intermediate appellate courts, and many local trial courts. Precedent flows down through this system. Tradition also allows for "magistrate's courts," which address administrative decisions.
- The common law system is broken down into criminal, civil/tort, and administrative.

Criminal Law System

- Based on common law, statutory law, or a combination of both.
- Addresses behavior that is considered harmful to society.
- Punishment usually involves a loss of freedom, such as incarceration, or monetary fines.
- Responsibility is on the prosecution to prove guilt beyond a reasonable doubt (innocent until proven guilty).

Civil/Tort Law System

- Offshoot of criminal law.
- Under civil law, the defendant owes a legal duty to the victim. In other words, the defendant is obligated to conform to a particular standard of conduct, usually set by what a "reasonable person of ordinary prudence" would do to prevent foreseeable injury to the victim.
- The defendant's breach of that duty causes injury to the victim; usually physical or financial.
- Categories of civil law:
    - **Intentional** Examples include assault, intentional infliction of emotional distress, or false imprisonment.
    - **Wrongs against property** An example is nuisance against landowner.
    - **Wrongs against a person** Examples include car accidents, dog bites, and a slip and fall.
    - **Negligence** An example is wrongful death.
    - **Nuisance** An example is trespassing.

- **Dignitary wrongs** Include invasion of privacy and civil rights violations.
- **Economic wrongs** Examples include patent, copyright, and trademark infringement.
- **Strict liability** Examples include a failure to warn of risks and defects in product manufacturing or design.

Administrative (Regulatory) Law System

- Laws and legal principles created by administrative agencies to address a number of areas, including international trade, manufacturing, environment, and immigration.

Customary Law System

- Deals mainly with personal conduct and patterns of behavior.
- Based on traditions and customs of the region.
- Emerged when cooperation of individuals became necessary as communities merged.
- Not many countries work under a purely customary law system, but instead use a mixed system where customary law is an integrated component. (Codified civil law systems emerged from customary law.)
- Mainly used in regions of the world that have mixed legal systems (for example, China and India).
- Restitution is commonly in the form of a monetary fine or service.

Religious Law System

- Based on religious beliefs of the region.
  - In Islamic countries, the law is based on the rules of the Koran.
  - The law, however, is different in every Islamic country.
  - Jurists and clerics have a high degree of authority.
- Covers all aspects of human life, but commonly divided into
  - Responsibilities and obligations to others.
  - Religious duties.
- Knowledge and rules as revealed by God, which define and govern human affairs.
- Rather than create laws, lawmakers and scholars attempt to discover the truth of law.
- Law, in the religious sense, also includes codes of ethics and morality, which are upheld and required by God. For example, Hindu law, Sharia (Islamic law), Halakha (Jewish law), and so on.

Mixed Law System

- Two or more legal systems are used together and apply cumulatively or interactively.

- Most often mixed law systems consist of civil and common law.
- A combination of systems is used as a result of more or less clearly defined fields of application.
- Civil law may apply to certain types of crimes, while religious law may apply to other types within the same region.
- Examples of mixed law systems include those in Holland, Canada, and South Africa.

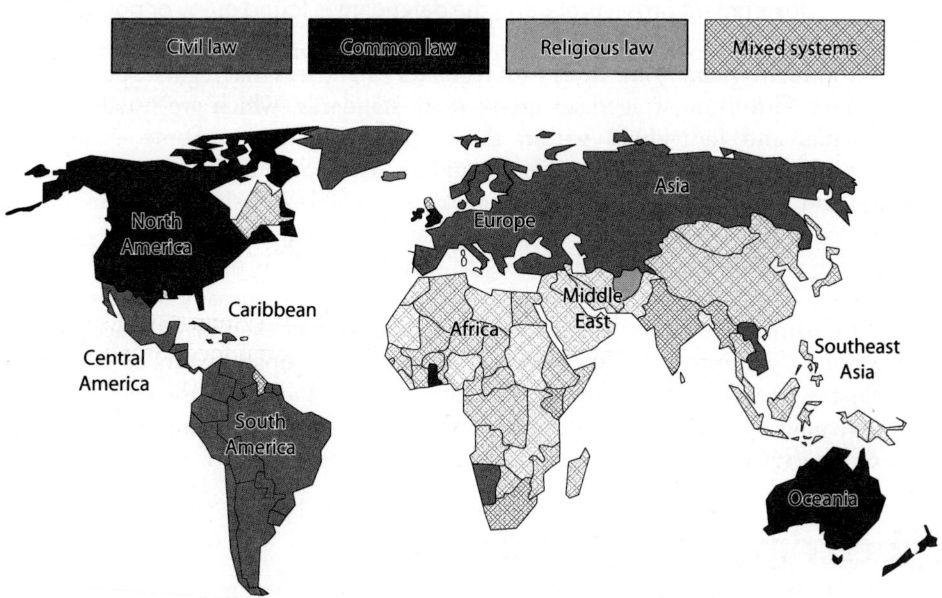

Common Law Revisited

These different legal systems are certainly complex, and while you are not expected to be a lawyer to pass the CISSP exam, having a high-level understanding of the different types (civil, common, customary, religious, mixed) is important. The exam will dig more into the specifics of the common law legal system and its components. Under the common law legal system, *civil law* deals with wrongs against individuals or organizations that result in damages or loss. This is referred to as *tort law*. Examples include trespassing, battery, negligence, and product liability. A successful civil lawsuit against a defendant would result in financial restitution and/or community service instead of a jail sentence. When someone sues another person in civil court, the jury decides upon *liability* instead of innocence or guilt. If the jury determines the defendant is liable for the act, then the jury decides upon the compensatory and/or punitive damages of the case.

Criminal law is used when an individual's conduct violates the government laws, which have been developed to protect the public. Jail sentences are commonly the punishment for criminal law cases that result in conviction, whereas in civil law cases the punishment is usually an amount of money that the liable individual must pay the victim. For example, in the O.J. Simpson case, the defendant was first tried and found not guilty in the criminal law case, but then was found liable in the civil law case. This seeming contradiction can happen because the burden of proof is lower in civil cases than in criminal cases.

EXAM TIP Civil law generally is derived from common law (case law), cases are initiated by private parties, and the defendant is found liable or not liable for damages. Criminal law typically is statutory, cases are initiated by government prosecutors, and the defendant is found guilty or not guilty.

Administrative/regulatory law deals with regulatory standards that regulate performance and conduct. Government agencies create these standards, which are usually applied to companies and individuals within those specific industries. Some examples of administrative laws could be that every building used for business must have a fire detection and suppression system, must have clearly visible exit signs, and cannot have blocked doors, in case of a fire. Companies that produce and package food and drug products are regulated by many standards so that the public is protected and aware of their actions. If an administrative law case determines that a company did not abide by specific regulatory standards, officials in the company could even be held accountable. For example, if a company makes tires that shred after a couple of years of use because the company doesn't comply with manufacturing safety standards, the officers in that company could be liable under administrative, civil, or even criminal law if they were aware of the issue but chose to ignore it to keep profits up.

Cybercrimes and Data Breaches

So far, we've discussed laws and regulations only in a general way to provide a bit of context. Let's now dive into the laws and regulations that are most relevant to our roles as cybersecurity leaders. Computer crime laws (sometimes collectively referred to as *cyberlaw*) around the world deal with some of the core issues: unauthorized access, modification or destruction of assets, disclosure of sensitive information, and the use of malware (malicious software).

Although we usually only think of the victims and their systems that were attacked during a crime, laws have been created to combat three categories of crimes. A *computer-assisted crime* is where a computer was used as a tool to help carry out a crime. A *computer-targeted crime* concerns incidents where a computer was the victim of an attack crafted to harm it (and its owners) specifically. The last type of crime is where a computer is not necessarily the attacker or the target, but just happened to be involved when a crime was carried out. This category is referred to as *computer is incidental*.

Some examples of computer-assisted crimes are

- Exploiting financial systems to conduct fraud
- Stealing military and intelligence material from government computer systems
- Conducting industrial espionage by attacking competitors and gathering confidential business data

- Carrying out information warfare activities by leveraging compromised influential accounts
- Engaging in hacktivism, which is protesting a government's or organization's activities by attacking its systems and/or defacing its website

Some examples of computer-targeted crimes include

- Distributed denial-of-service (DDoS) attacks
- Stealing passwords or other sensitive data from servers
- Installing cryptominers to mine cryptocurrency on someone else's computers
- Conducting a ransomware attack

NOTE The main issues addressed in computer crime laws are unauthorized modification, disclosure, destruction, or access and inserting malicious programming code.

Some confusion typically exists between the two categories—computer-assisted crimes and computer-targeted crimes—because intuitively it would seem any attack would fall into both of these categories. One system is carrying out the attacking, while the other system is being attacked. The difference is that in computer-assisted crimes, the computer is only being used as a tool to carry out a traditional type of crime. Without computers, people still steal, cause destruction, protest against organizations (for example, companies that carry out experiments upon animals), obtain competitor information, and go to war. So these crimes would take place anyway; the computer is simply one of the tools available to the attacker. As such, it helps that threat actor become more efficient at carrying out a crime.

Computer-assisted crimes are usually covered by regular criminal laws in that they are not always considered a "computer crime." One way to look at it is that a computer-*targeted* crime could not take place without a computer, whereas a computer-*assisted* crime could. Thus, a computer-targeted crime is one that did not, and could not, exist before use of computers became common. In other words, in the good old days, you could not carry out a buffer overflow on your neighbor or install malware on your enemy's system. These crimes require that computers be involved.

If a crime falls into the "computer is incidental" category, this means a computer just happened to be involved in some secondary manner, but its involvement is still significant. For example, if you have a friend who works for a company that runs the state lottery and he gives you a printout of the next three winning numbers and you type them into your computer, your computer is just the storage place. You could have just kept the piece of paper and not put the data in a computer. Another example is child pornography. The actual crime is obtaining and sharing child pornography pictures or graphics. The pictures could be stored on a file server or they could be kept in a physical file in someone's desk. So if a crime falls within this category, the computer is not attacking another computer and a computer is not being attacked, but the computer is still used in some significant manner.

Because computing devices are everywhere in modern society, computers are incidental to most crimes today. In a fatal car crash, the police may seize the drivers' mobile devices to look for evidence that either driver was texting at the time of the accident. In a domestic assault case, investigators may seek a court order to obtain the contents of the home's virtual assistant, such as Amazon Alexa, because it may contain recorded evidence of the crime.

You may say, "So what? A crime is a crime. Why break it down into these types of categories?" The reason these types of categories are created is to allow current laws to apply to these types of crimes, even though they are in the digital world. Let's say someone is on your computer just looking around, not causing any damage, but she should not be there. Should legislators have to create a new law stating, "Thou shall not browse around in someone else's computer," or should law enforcement and the courts just apply the already created trespassing law? What if a hacker got into a traffic-control system and made all of the traffic lights turn green at the exact same time? Should legislators go through the hassle of creating a new law for this type of activity, or should law enforcement and the courts use the already created (and understood) manslaughter and murder laws? Remember, a crime is a crime, and a computer is just a new tool to carry out traditional criminal activities.

Now, this in no way means countries can just depend upon the laws on the books and that every computer crime can be countered by an existing law. Many countries have had to come up with new laws that deal specifically with different types of computer crimes. For example, the following are just *some* of the laws that have been created or modified in the United States to cover the various types of computer crimes:

- 18 USC 1029: Fraud and Related Activity in Connection with Access Devices
- 18 USC 1030: Fraud and Related Activity in Connection with Computers
- 18 USC 2510 et seq.: Wire and Electronic Communications Interception and Interception of Oral Communications
- 18 USC 2701 et seq.: Stored Wire and Electronic Communications and Transactional Records Access
- Digital Millennium Copyright Act
- Cyber Security Enhancement Act of 2002

EXAM TIP You do not need to know these laws for the CISSP exam; they are just examples.

Complexities in Cybercrime

Since we have a bunch of laws to get the digital bad guys, this means we have this whole cybercrime thing under control, right? Alas, cybercrimes have only increased over the years and will not stop anytime soon. Several contributing factors explain why these activities have not been properly stopped or even curbed. These include issues related to proper attribution of the attacks, the necessary level of protection for networks, and successful prosecution once an attacker is captured.

Many attackers are never caught because they spoof their addresses and identities and use methods to cover their digital footsteps. Many attackers break into networks, take whatever resources they were after, and clean the logs that tracked their movements and activities. Because of this, many organizations do not even know their systems have been violated. Even if an attacker's activities are detected, it does not usually lead to the true identity of the individual, though it does alert the organization that a specific vulnerability was exploited.

Attackers commonly hop through several systems before attacking their victim so that tracking down the attackers will be more difficult. This is exemplified by a threat actor approach known as an *island-hopping attack*, which is when the attacker compromises an easier target that is somehow connected to the ultimate one. For instance, consider a major corporation like the one depicted on the right side of Figure 3-1. It has robust cybersecurity and relies on a regional supplier for certain widgets. Since logistics are oftentimes automated, these two companies have trusted channels of communication between them so their computers can talk to each other about when more widgets might be needed and where. The supplier, in turn, relies on a small company that produces special screws for the widgets. This screw manufacturer employs just a couple of people working out of the owner's garage and is a trivial target for an attacker. So, rather than target the major corporation directly, a cybercriminal could attack the screw manufacturer's unsecured computers, use them to gain a foothold in the supplier, and then use that company's trusted relationship with the well-defended target to ultimately get into its systems. This particular type of island-hopping attack is also known as a *supply-chain attack* because it exploits trust mechanisms inherent in supply chains.

Many companies that are victims of an attack usually just want to ensure that the vulnerability the attacker exploited is fixed, instead of spending the time and money to go after and prosecute the attacker. This is a huge contributing factor as to why cybercriminals get away with their activities. Some regulated organizations—for instance, financial institutions—by law, must report breaches. However, most organizations do not have to report breaches or computer crimes. No company wants its dirty laundry out in the open for everyone to see. The customer base will lose confidence, as will

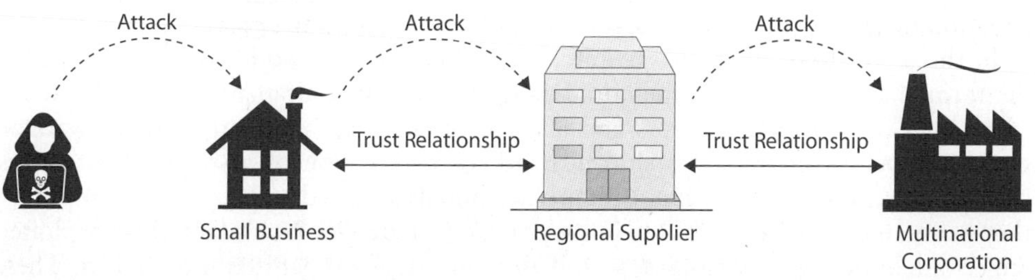

Figure 3-1 A typical island-hopping attack

the shareholders and investors. We do not actually have true computer crime statistics because most are not reported.

Although regulations, laws, and attacks help make senior management more aware of security issues, when their company ends up in the headlines with reports of how they lost control of over 100,000 credit card numbers, security suddenly becomes very important to them.

NOTE Even though some institutions must, by law, report security breaches and crimes, that does not mean they all follow this law. Some of these institutions, just like many other organizations, often simply fix the vulnerability and sweep the details of the attack under the carpet.

The Evolution of Attacks

Perpetrators of cybercrime have evolved from bored teenagers with too much time on their hands to organized crime rings with very defined targets and goals. In the early 1990s, hackers were mainly made up of people who just enjoyed the thrill of hacking. It was seen as a challenging game without any real intent of harm. Hackers used to take down large websites (e.g., Yahoo!, MSN, Excite) so their activities made the headlines and they won bragging rights among their fellow hackers. Back then, virus writers created viruses that simply replicated or carried out some benign activity, instead of the more malicious actions they could have carried out. Unfortunately, today, these trends have taken on more sinister objectives as the Internet has become a place of business. This evolution is what drove the creation of the antivirus (now antimalware) industry.

Three powerful forces converged in the mid to late 1990s to catapult cybercrime forward. First, with the explosive growth in the use of the Internet, computers became much more lucrative targets for criminals. Second, there was an abundance of computer experts who had lost their livelihoods with the end of the Soviet Union. Some of these bright minds turned to cybercrime as a way to survive the tough times in which they found themselves. Finally, with increased demand for computing systems, many software developers were rushing to be first to market, all but ignoring the security (or lack thereof) of their products and creating fertile ground for remote attacks from all over the world. These forces resulted in the emergence of a new breed of cybercriminal possessing knowledge and skills that quickly overwhelmed many defenders. As the impact of the increased threat was realized, organizations around the world started paying more attention to security in a desperate bid to stop their cybercrime losses.

In the early 2000s, there was a shift from cybercriminals working by themselves to the formation of organized cybercrime gangs. This change dramatically improved the capabilities of these threat actors and allowed them to go after targets that, by then, were very well defended. This shift also led to the creation of vast, persistent attack infrastructures on a global scale. After cybercriminals attacked and exploited computers, they maintained a presence for use in support of later attacks. Nowadays, these exploited targets are known as malicious *bots*, and they are usually organized into *botnets*. These botnets can be used to carry out DDoS attacks, transfer spam or pornography, or do whatever the attacker commands the bot software to do. Figure 3-2 shows the many uses cybercriminals have for compromised computers.

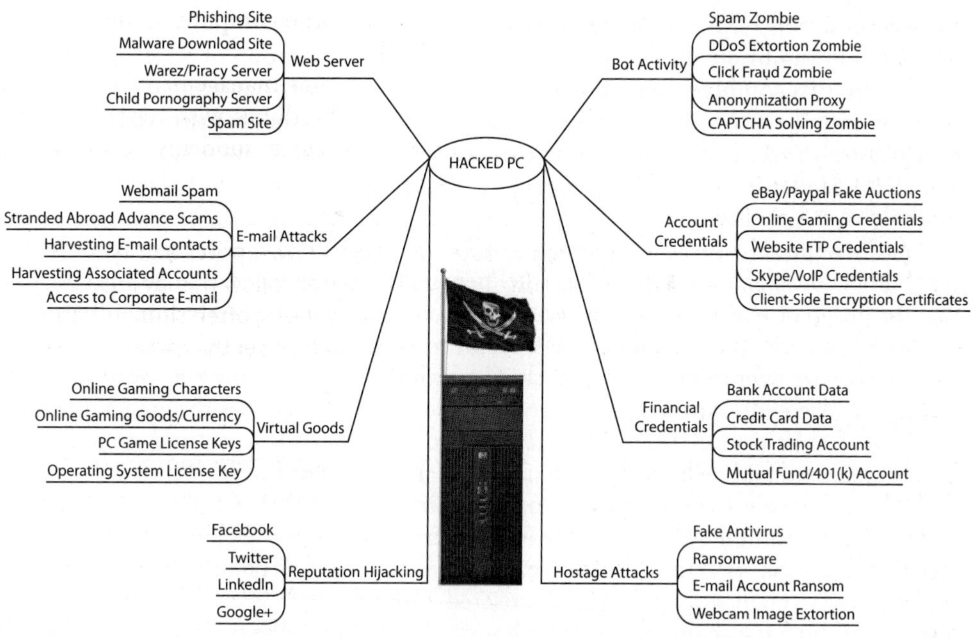

Figure 3-2 Malicious uses for a compromised computer (Source: www.krebsonsecurity.com)

EXAM TIP You may see the term *script kiddies* on the exam (or elsewhere). It refers to hackers who do not have the requisite skills to carry out specific attacks without the tools provided on the Internet or through friends.

A recent development in organized cybercrime is the emergence of so-called Hacking as a Service (HaaS), which is a play on cloud computing services such as Software as a Service (SaaS). HaaS represents the commercialization of hacking skills, providing access to tools, target lists, credentials, hackers for hire, and even customer support. In the last couple of years, there has been a significant increase in the number of marketplaces in which HaaS is available.

Many times hackers are just scanning systems looking for a vulnerable running service or sending out malicious links in e-mails to unsuspecting victims. They are just looking for any way to get into any network. This would be the shotgun approach to network attacks. Another, more dangerous, attacker has you in the proverbial crosshairs and is determined to identify your weakest point and exploit it. As an analogy, the thief that goes around rattling door knobs to find one that is not locked is not half as dangerous as the one who will watch you day in and day out to learn your activity patterns, where you work, what type of car you drive, and who your family is and patiently wait for your most vulnerable moment to ensure a successful and devastating attack.

We call this second type of attacker an *advanced persistent threat (APT)*. This is a military term that has been around for ages, but since the digital world is effectively a battleground, this term is more relevant each and every day. How an APT differs from the plain old vanilla attacker is that the APT is commonly a group of attackers, not just one hacker, that combine their knowledge and abilities to carry out whatever exploit will get them into the environment they are seeking. The APT is very focused and motivated to aggressively and successfully penetrate a network with various different attack methods and then clandestinely hide its presence while achieving a well-developed, multilevel foothold in the environment.

The "advanced" aspect of the term APT pertains to the expansive knowledge, capabilities, and skill base of the APT. The "persistent" component has to do with the fact that the group of attackers is not in a hurry to launch an attack quickly, but will wait for the most beneficial moment and attack vector to ensure that its activities go unnoticed. This is what we refer to as a "low-and-slow" attack. This type of attack is coordinated by human involvement, rather than just a virus type of threat that goes through automated steps to inject its payload. The APT has specific objectives and goals and is commonly highly organized and well funded, which makes it the biggest threat of all.

APTs commonly use custom-developed malicious code that is built specifically for its target, has multiple ways of hiding itself once it infiltrates the environment, may be able to polymorph itself in replication capabilities, and has several different "anchors" to make it hard to eradicate even if it is discovered. Once the code is installed, it commonly sets up a covert back channel (as regular bots do) so that it can be remotely controlled by the group of attackers. The remote control functionality allows the attackers to traverse the network with the goal of gaining continuous access to critical assets.

APT infiltrations are usually very hard to detect with host-based solutions because the attackers put the code through a barrage of tests against the most up-to-date detection applications on the market. A common way to detect these types of threats is through network traffic changes. For example, changes in DNS queries coming out of your network could indicate that an APT has breached your environment and is using DNS tunneling to establish command and control over the compromised hosts. The APT will likely have multiple control servers and techniques to communicate so that if one connection gets detected and removed, the APT still has an active channel to use. The APT may implement encrypted tunnels over HTTPS so that its data that is in transmission cannot be inspected. Figure 3-3 illustrates the common steps and results of APT activity.

The ways of getting into a network are basically endless (exploit a web service, induce users to open e-mail links and attachments, gain access through remote maintenance accounts, exploit operating systems and application vulnerabilities, compromise connections from home users, etc.). Each of these vulnerabilities has its own fixes (patches, proper configuration, awareness, proper credential practices, encryption, etc.). It is not only these fixes that need to be put in place; we need to move to a more effective situational awareness model. We need to have better capabilities of knowing what is happening throughout our network in near to real time so that our defenses can react quickly and precisely.

The landscape continues to evolve, and the lines between threat actors are sometimes blurry. We already mentioned the difficulty in attributing an attack to a specific individual so that criminal charges may be filed. Something that makes this even harder is the practice among some governments of collaborating with criminal groups in their countries.

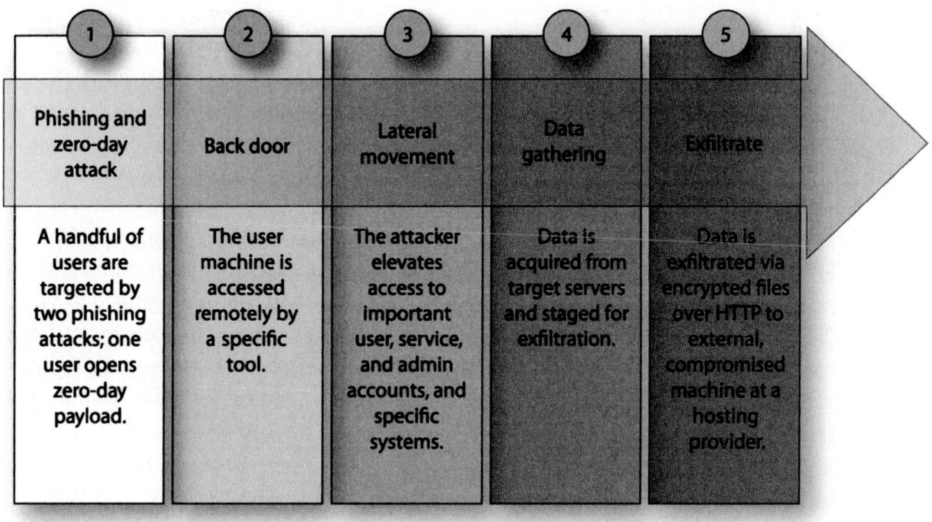
1
2
3
4
5
Phishing and zero-day attack
Back door
Lateral movement
Data gathering
Exfiltrate
A handful of users are targeted by two phishing attacks; one user opens zero-day payload.
The user machine is accessed remotely by a specific tool.
The attacker elevates access to important user, service, and admin accounts, and specific systems.
Data is acquired from target servers and staged for exfiltration.
Data is exfiltrated via encrypted files over HTTP to external, compromised machine at a hosting provider.

Figure 3-3 Gaining access into an environment and extracting sensitive data

Common Internet Crime Schemes

- Business e-mail compromise
- Business fraud
- Charity and disaster fraud
- Counterfeit prescription drugs
- Credit card fraud
- Election crimes and security
- Identity theft
- Illegal sports betting
- Nigerian letter, or "419"
- Ponzi/pyramid
- Ransomware
- Sextortion

Find out how these types of computer crimes are carried out by visiting https://www.fbi.gov/scams-and-safety/common-scams-and-crimes.

> **Do You Trust Your Neighbor?**
>
> Most organizations do not like to think about the fact that the enemy might be inside the organization and working internally. It is more natural to view threats as the faceless unknowns that reside on the outside of our environment. Employees have direct and privileged access to an organization's assets, and they are commonly not as highly monitored compared to traffic that is entering the network from external entities. The combination of too much trust, direct access, and the lack of monitoring allows for a lot of internal fraud and abuse to go unnoticed.
>
> There have been many criminal cases over the years where employees at various organizations have carried out embezzlement or have launched revenge attacks after they were fired or laid off. While it is important to have fortified walls to protect us from the outside forces that want to cause us harm, it is also important to realize that our underbelly is more vulnerable. Employees, contractors, and temporary workers who have direct access to critical resources introduce risks that need to be understood and countermeasured.

The way it works is that the government looks the other way as long as the crimes are committed in other countries. When the government needs a bit of help to obfuscate what it's doing to another government, it enlists the help of the cybercrime gang they've been protecting (or at least tolerating) and tell them what to do and to whom. To the target, it looks like a cybercrime but in reality it had nation-state goals.

So while the sophistication of the attacks continues to increase, so does the danger of these attacks. Isn't that just peachy?

Up until now, we have listed some difficulties of fighting cybercrime: the anonymity the Internet provides the attacker; attackers are organizing and carrying out more sophisticated attacks; the legal system is running to catch up with these types of crimes; and organizations are just now viewing their data as something that must be protected. All these complexities aid the bad guys, but what if we throw in the complexity of attacks taking place between different countries?

International Issues

If a hacker in Ukraine attacks a bank in France, whose legal jurisdiction is that? How do these countries work together to identify the criminal and carry out justice? Which country is required to track down the criminal? And which country should take this person to court? Well, the short answer is: it depends.

When computer crime crosses international boundaries, the complexity of such issues shoots up considerably and the chances of the criminal being brought to any court decreases. This is because different countries have different legal systems, some countries have no laws pertaining to computer crime, jurisdiction disputes may erupt, and some governments may not want to play nice with each other. For example, if someone in Iran attacked a system in Israel, do you think the Iranian government would help Israel track down the attacker? What if someone in North Korea attacked a military system in the

United States? Do you think these two countries would work together to find the hacker? Maybe or maybe not—or perhaps the attack was carried out by a government agency pretending to be a cybercrime gang.

There have been efforts to standardize the different countries' approaches to computer crimes because they happen so easily over international boundaries. Although it is very easy for an attacker in China to send packets through the Internet to a bank in Saudi Arabia, it is very difficult (because of legal systems, cultures, and politics) to motivate these governments to work together.

The *Council of Europe (CoE) Convention on Cybercrime*, also known as the Budapest Convention, is one example of an attempt to create a standard international response to cybercrime. In fact, it is the first international treaty seeking to address computer crimes by coordinating national laws and improving investigative techniques and international cooperation. One of the requirements of the treaty is that signatories develop national legislation outlawing a series of cybercrimes, such as hacking, computer-related fraud, and child pornography. The convention's objectives also include the creation of a framework for establishing jurisdiction and extradition of the accused. For example, extradition can only take place when the event is a crime in both jurisdictions. As of April 2021, 68 countries around the world (not just in Europe) have signed or ratified the treaty, contributing to the global growth in effective cybercrime legislation that is internationally interoperable. According to the United Nations (UN), 79 percent of the world's countries (that's 154) now have cybercrime laws. All these laws vary, of course, but they may impact your own organization depending on where you do business and with whom.

Data Breaches

Among the most common cybercrimes are those relating to the theft of sensitive data. In fact, it is a rare month indeed when one doesn't read or hear about a major data breach. Information is the lifeblood of most major corporations nowadays, and threat actors know this. They have been devoting a lot of effort over the past several years to compromising and exploiting the data stores that, in many ways, are more valuable to organizations than any vault full of cash. This trend continues unabated, which makes data breaches one of the most important issues in cybersecurity today.

In a way, data breaches can be thought of as the opposite of privacy: data owners lose control of who has the ability to access their data. When an organization fails to properly protect the privacy of its customers' data, it increases the likelihood of experiencing a data breach. It should not be surprising, therefore, that some of the same legal and regulatory issues that apply to privacy also apply to data breaches.

It is important to note that data breaches need not involve a violation of personal privacy. Indeed, some of the most publicized data breaches have had nothing to do with personally identifiable information (PII) but with intellectual property (IP). It is worth pausing to properly define the term *data breach* as a security event that results in the actual or potential compromise of the confidentiality or integrity of protected information by unauthorized actors. Protected information can be PII, IP, protected health information (PHI), classified information, or any other information that can cause damage to an individual or organization.

Personally Identifiable Information

Personally identifiable information (PII) is data that can be used to uniquely identify, contact, or locate a single person or can be used with other sources to uniquely identify a single individual. PII needs to be highly protected because it is commonly used in identity theft, financial crimes, and various criminal activities.

While it seems as though defining and identifying PII should be easy and straightforward, what different countries, federal governments, and state governments consider to be PII differs.

The U.S. Office of Management and Budget in its memorandum M-07-16, "Safeguarding Against and Responding to the Breach of Personally Identifiable Information," defines PII as "information that can be used to distinguish or trace an individual's identity, either alone or when combined with other personal or identifying information that is linked or linkable to a specific individual." Determining what constitutes PII, then, depends on a specific risk assessment of the likelihood that the information can be used to uniquely identify an individual. This is all good and well, but doesn't really help us recognize information that might be considered PII. Typical components are listed here:

- Full name (if not common)
- National identification number
- Home address
- IP address (in some cases)
- Vehicle registration plate number
- Driver's license number
- Face, fingerprints, or handwriting
- Credit card numbers
- Digital identity
- Birthday
- Birthplace
- Genetic information

The following items are less often used because they are commonly shared by so many people, but they can fall into the PII classification and may require protection from improper disclosure:

- First or last name, if common
- Country, state, or city of residence
- Age, especially if nonspecific

- Gender or race
- Name of the school they attend or workplace
- Grades, salary, or job position
- Criminal record

As a security professional, it is important to understand which legal and regulatory requirements are triggered by data breaches. To further complicate matters, most U.S. states, as well as many other countries, have enacted distinct laws with subtle but important differences in notification stipulations. As always when dealing with legal issues, it is best to consult with an attorney. This section is simply an overview of some of the legal requirements of which you should be aware.

U.S. Laws Pertaining to Data Breaches

We've already mentioned various U.S. federal statutes dealing with cybercrimes. Despite our best efforts, there will be times when our information systems are compromised and personal information security controls are breached. Let's briefly highlight some of the laws that are most relevant to data breaches:

- California Consumer Privacy Act (CCPA)
- Health Insurance Portability and Accountability Act (HIPAA)
- Health Information Technology for Economic and Clinical Health (HI-TECH) Act
- Gramm-Leach-Bliley Act of 1999
- Economic Espionage Act of 1996

It is worth recalling here that data breaches are not only violations of customer privacy. When a threat actor compromises a target corporation's network and exposes its intellectual property, a breach has occurred. While the other laws we have discussed in this section deal with protecting customers' PII, the Economic Espionage Act protects corporations' IP. When you think of data breaches, it is critical that you consider both PII and IP exposure.

Almost every U.S. state has enacted legislation that requires government and private entities to disclose data breaches involving PII. The most important of these is probably the California Consumer Privacy Act, which went into effect in 2020. The CCPA is perhaps the broadest and most far-reaching of U.S. state laws around PII breaches, but it is certainly not the only one. In almost every case, PII is defined by the states as the combination of first and last name with any of the following:

- Social Security number
- Driver's license number
- Credit or debit card number with the security code or PIN

Unfortunately, that is where the commonalities end. The laws are so different that compliance with all of them is a difficult and costly issue for most corporations. In some states, simple access to files containing PII triggers a notification requirement, while in other states the organization must only notify affected parties if the breach is reasonably likely to result in illegal use of the information. Many experts believe that the CCPA will set an example for other states and may provide a template for other countries.

European Union Laws Pertaining to Data Breaches

Global organizations that move data across other country boundaries must be aware of and follow the Organisation for Economic Co-operation and Development (OECD) *Guidelines on the Protection of Privacy and Transborder Flows of Personal Data.* Since most countries have a different set of laws pertaining to the definition of private data and how it should be protected, international trade and business get more convoluted and can negatively affect the economy of nations. The OECD is an international organization that helps different governments come together and tackle the economic, social, and governance challenges of a globalized economy. Because of this, the OECD came up with guidelines for the various countries to follow so that data is properly protected and everyone follows the same type of rules.

The core principles defined by the OECD are as follows:

- **Collection Limitation Principle** Collection of personal data should be limited, obtained by lawful and fair means, and with the knowledge of the subject.
- **Data Quality Principle** Personal data should be kept complete and current and be relevant to the purposes for which it is being used.
- **Purpose Specification Principle** Subjects should be notified of the reason for the collection of their personal information at the time that it is collected, and organizations should only use it for that stated purpose.
- **Use Limitation Principle** Only with the consent of the subject or by the authority of law should personal data be disclosed, made available, or used for purposes other than those previously stated.
- **Security Safeguards Principle** Reasonable safeguards should be put in place to protect personal data against risks such as loss, unauthorized access, modification, and disclosure.
- **Openness Principle** Developments, practices, and policies regarding personal data should be openly communicated. In addition, subjects should be able to easily establish the existence and nature of personal data, its use, and the identity and usual residence of the organization in possession of that data.
- **Individual Participation Principle** Subjects should be able to find out whether an organization has their personal information and what that information is, to correct erroneous data, and to challenge denied requests to do so.
- **Accountability Principle** Organizations should be accountable for complying with measures that support the previous principles.

NOTE Information on the OECD Guidelines can be found at www.oecd.org/internet/ieconomy/privacy-guidelines.htm.

Although the OECD Guidelines were a great start, they were not enforceable or uniformly applied. The European Union in many cases takes individual privacy much more seriously than most other countries in the world, so in 1995 it enacted the Data Protection Directive (DPD). As a directive, it was not directly enforceable, but EU member states were required to enact laws that were consistent with it. The intent of this was to create a set of laws across the EU that controlled the way in which European organizations had to protect the personal data and privacy of EU citizens. The Safe Harbor Privacy Principles were then developed to outline how U.S.-based organizations could comply with European privacy laws. For a variety of reasons, this system of directives, laws, and principles failed to work well in practice and had to be replaced.

The General Data Protection Regulation (GDPR) was adopted by the EU in April 2016 and became enforceable in May 2018. It protects the personal data and privacy of EU citizens. The GDPR, unlike a directive such as the DPD, has the full weight of a law in all 27 member states of the EU. This means that each state does not have to write its own version, which harmonizes data protection regulations and makes it easier for organizations to know exactly what is expected of them throughout the bloc. The catch is that these requirements are quite stringent, and violating them exposes an organization to a maximum fine of 4 percent of that organization's global turnover. For a company like Google, that would equate to over $4 billion if they were ever shown to not be in compliance. Ouch!

The GDPR defines three relevant entities:

- **Data subject** The individual to whom the data pertains
- **Data controller** Any organization that collects data on EU residents
- **Data processor** Any organization that processes data for a data controller

The regulation applies if any one of the three entities is based in the EU, but it also applies if a data controller or processor has data pertaining to an EU resident. The GDPR impacts every organization that holds or uses European personal data both inside and outside of Europe. In other words, if your organization is a U.S.-based company that has never done business with the EU, but it has an EU citizen working as a summer intern, it probably has to comply with the GDPR or risk facing stiff penalties.

The GDPR set of protected types of privacy data is more inclusive than regulations and laws outside the EU. Among others, protected privacy data includes

- Name
- Address
- ID numbers

- Web data (location, IP address, cookies)
- Health and genetic data
- Biometric data
- Racial or ethnic data
- Political opinions
- Sexual orientation

To ensure this data is protected, the GDPR requires that most data controllers and data processors formally designate a Data Protection Officer (DPO). DPOs are internal compliance officers that act semi-independently to ensure that their organizations follow the letter of the regulation. While DPOs are not ultimately responsible if their organizations are not in compliance (at least according to the GDPR), in practice they are charged with monitoring compliance, advising controllers on when and how to conduct data protection impact assessments, and maintaining all required records.

Key provisions of the GDPR include

- **Consent** Data controllers and data processors cannot use personal data without explicit consent of the data subjects.
- **Right to be informed** Data controllers and data processors must inform data subjects about how their data is, will, or could be used.
- **Right to restrict processing** Data subjects can agree to have their data stored by a collector but disallow it to be processed.
- **Right to be forgotten** Data subjects can request that their personal data be permanently deleted.
- **Data breaches** Data controllers must report a data breach to the supervisory authority of the EU member state involved within 72 hours of becoming aware of it.

Other Nations' Laws Pertaining to Data Breaches

As might be expected, the rest of the world is a hodgepodge of laws with varying data breach notification conditions and requirements. As of this writing, the United Nations lists at least 62 countries that have no legally mandated notification requirements whatsoever. This is concerning because unscrupulous organizations have been known to outsource their data-handling operations to countries with no data breach laws in order to circumvent the difficulties in reconciling the different country and state requirements.

The EU's GDPR, though it has been called too restrictive and costly by some, has served as a model for other countries to implement similar legislation. For example, the two newest data protection laws, which came into full effect in 2020, are Brazil's General Personal Data Protection Law (Lei Geral de Proteção de Dados, or LGPD) and Thailand's Personal Data Protection Act (PDPA). Both apply to all organizations that handle the personal information of these countries' residents, whether they are physically located within the country or not. Thailand's PDPA further provides for jail time in particularly egregious cases.

Again, you do not need to know all these international laws to become a CISSP. However, you need to be aware that they exist and may impact your business and cybersecurity even if you didn't know your organization had interests in those countries. It is best to consult your organization's legal or compliance team to determine which laws apply to your own team.

Import/Export Controls

Another complexity that comes into play when an organization is attempting to work with organizations in other parts of the world is import and export laws. Each country has its own specifications when it comes to what is allowed in its borders and what is allowed out. For example, the *Wassenaar Arrangement* implements export controls for "Conventional Arms and Dual-Use Goods and Technologies." It is currently made up of 42 countries and lays out rules on how the following items can be exported from country to country:

- **Category 1** Special Materials and Related Equipment
- **Category 2** Material Processing
- **Category 3** Electronics
- **Category 4** Computers
- **Category 5** Part 1: Telecommunications
- **Category 5** Part 2: Information Security
- **Category 6** Sensors and Lasers
- **Category 7** Navigation and Avionics
- **Category 8** Marine
- **Category 9** Aerospace and Propulsion

The main goal of the Wassenaar Arrangement is to prevent the buildup of military capabilities that could threaten regional and international security and stability. So, everyone is keeping an eye on each other to make sure no one country's weapons can take everyone else out. The idea is to try and make sure everyone has similar offensive and defensive military capabilities with the hope that we won't end up blowing each other up.

One item the agreement deals with is cryptography, which is considered a *dual-use good* because it can be used for both military and civilian purposes. The agreement recognizes the danger of exporting products with cryptographic functionality to countries that are in the "offensive" column, meaning that they are thought to have friendly ties with terrorist organizations and/or want to take over the world through the use of weapons of mass destruction. If the "good" countries allow the "bad" countries to use cryptography, then the "good" countries cannot snoop and keep tabs on what the "bad" countries are up to.

The specifications of the Wassenaar Arrangement are complex and always changing. Which countries fall within the "good" and "bad" categories changes, and what can be exported to whom and how changes. In some cases, no products that contain cryptographic functions can be exported to a specific country; some countries are allowed to import only products with limited cryptographic functions; some countries require certain licenses to be granted; and other countries (the "good" countries) have no restrictions.

While the Wassenaar Arrangement deals mainly with the exportation of items, some countries (China, Russia, Iran, etc.) have cryptographic *import* restrictions that have to be understood and followed. These countries do not allow their citizens to use cryptography because they believe that the ability to monitor many aspects of a citizen's online activities is essential to effectively governing people. This obviously gets very complex for companies who sell products that use integrated cryptographic functionality. One version of the product may be sold to China if it has no cryptographic functionality. Another version may be sold to Russia if a certain international license is in place. A fully functioning product can be sold to Canada, because who are they ever going to hurt?

It is important to understand the import and export requirements your organization must meet when interacting with entities in other parts of the world. You could inadvertently break a country's law or an international treaty if you do not get the right type of lawyers involved in the beginning and follow the approved processes.

Transborder Data Flow

While import and export controls apply to products, a much more common asset that constantly moves in and out of every country is data, and, as you might imagine at this point, there are laws, regulations, and processes that address what data can be moved where, when, why, how, and by whom. A *transborder data flow (TDF)* is the movement of machine-readable data across a political boundary such a country's border. This data is generated or acquired in one country but may be stored and processed in other countries as a result of TDFs. In a modern, connected world, this happens all the time. For example, just imagine all the places your personal data will go when you make an airline reservation to travel overseas, especially if you have a layover along the way.

NOTE Transborder data flows are sometimes called cross-border data flows.

Some governments control transborder data flows by enacting *data localization* laws that require certain types of data to be stored and processed within the borders of their respective country, sometimes exclusively. There are many reasons for these laws, but they pretty much boil down to protecting their citizens, either by ensuring a higher standard of privacy protection or by allowing easier monitoring of their actions (typically the things citizens try to do overseas). Data localization can increase the cost of doing business in some countries because your organization may have to provision (and protect) information systems in that country that it otherwise wouldn't.

Ironically, the very technology trend that initially fueled data localization concerns, cloud computing services, ultimately became an important tool to address those concerns in a cost-effective manner. At their onset, cloud computing services promised affordable access to resources around the globe, sometimes by shifting loads and storage from one region to another. In recent years, the major cloud service providers have adapted to localization laws by offering an increasing number of regions (sometimes down to individual countries) where the data is guaranteed to remain.

Privacy

Privacy is becoming more threatened as the world increasingly relies on computing technology. There are several approaches to addressing privacy, including the generic approach and regulation by industry. The generic approach is *horizontal enactment*—rules that stretch across all industry boundaries. It affects all industries, including government. Regulation by industry is *vertical enactment.* It defines requirements for specific verticals, such as the financial sector and health care. In both cases, the overall objective is twofold. First, the initiatives seek to protect citizens' personally identifiable information. Second, the initiatives seek to balance the needs of government and businesses to collect and use PII with consideration of security issues.

In response, countries have enacted privacy laws. For example, although the United States already had the Federal Privacy Act of 1974, it has enacted new laws, such as the Gramm-Leach-Bliley Act of 1999 and HIPAA, in response to an increased need to protect personal privacy information. These are examples of a vertical approach to addressing privacy, whereas the EU's GDPR, Canada's Personal Information Protection and Electronic Documents Act, and New Zealand's Privacy Act of 1993 are horizontal approaches. Most countries nowadays have some sort of privacy requirements in their laws and regulations, so we need to be aware of their impact on our information systems and their security to avoid nasty legal surprises.

Licensing and Intellectual Property Requirements

Another way to get into trouble, whether domestically or internationally, is to run afoul of intellectual property laws. As previously introduced, *intellectual property (IP)* is a type of property created by human intellect. It consists of ideas, inventions, and expressions that are uniquely created by a person and can be protected from unauthorized use by others. Examples are song lyrics, inventions, logos, and secret recipes. IP laws do not necessarily look at who is right or wrong, but rather how an organization or individual can protect what it rightfully owns from unauthorized duplication or use and what it can do if these laws are violated.

So who designates what constitutes authorized use? The owner of the IP does this by granting licenses. A *license* is an agreement between an IP owner (the licensor) and somebody else (the licensee), granting that party the right to use the IP in very specific ways. For example, the licensee can only use the IP for a year unless they renew the license (presumably after paying a subscription fee). A license can also be, and frequently is, nontransferable, meaning only the licensees, and not their family members or friends, can use it. Another common provision in the agreement is whether or not the license will be exclusive to the licensee.

Licenses can become moot if the IP is not properly protected by the licensor. An organization must implement safeguards to protect resources that it claims to be intellectual property and must show that it exercised due care (reasonable acts of protection) in its efforts to protect those resources. For example, if an employee sends a file to a friend and the company terminates the employee based on the activity of illegally sharing IP, then in a wrongful termination case brought by the employee, the company must show the court why this file is so important to the company, what type of damage could be or has been caused as a result of the file being shared, and, most important, what the company had done to protect that file. If the company did not secure the file and tell its employees that they were not allowed to copy and share that file, then the company will most likely lose the case. However, if the company implemented safeguards to protect that file and had an acceptable use policy in its employee manual that explained that copying and sharing the information within the file was prohibited and that the punishment for doing so could be termination, then the company could not be found liable of wrongfully terminating the employee.

Intellectual property can be protected by different legal mechanisms, depending upon the type of resource it is. As a CISSP, you should be knowledgeable of four types of IP laws: trade secrets, copyrights, trademarks, and patents. These topics are addressed in depth in the following sections, followed by tips on protecting IP internally and combating software piracy.

Trade Secret

Trade secret law protects certain types of information or resources from unauthorized use or disclosure. For a company to have its resource qualify as a trade secret, the resource must provide the company with some type of competitive value or advantage. A trade secret can be protected by law if developing it requires special skill, ingenuity, and/or expenditure of money and effort. This means that a company cannot say the sky is blue and call it a trade secret.

A *trade secret* is something that is proprietary to a company and important for its survival and profitability. An example of a trade secret is the formula used for a soft drink, such as Coke or Pepsi. The resource that is claimed to be a trade secret must be confidential and protected with certain security precautions and actions. A trade secret could also be a new form of mathematics, the source code of a program, a method of making the perfect jelly bean, or ingredients for a special secret sauce. A trade secret has no expiration date unless the information is no longer secret or no longer provides economic benefit to the company.

Many companies require their employees to sign a nondisclosure agreement (NDA), confirming that they understand its contents and promise not to share the company's trade secrets with competitors or any unauthorized individuals. Companies require an NDA both to inform the employees of the importance of keeping certain information secret and to deter them from sharing this information. Having employees sign the NDA also gives the company the right to fire an employee or bring charges if the employee discloses a trade secret.

A low-level engineer working at Intel took trade secret information that was valued by Intel at $1 billion when he left his position at the company and went to work at his new employer, rival chipmaker Advanced Micro Devices (AMD). Intel discovered that this person still had access to Intel's most confidential information even after starting work at AMD. He even used the laptop that Intel provided to him to download 13 critical documents that contained extensive information about the company's new processor developments and product releases. Unfortunately, these stories are not rare, and companies are constantly dealing with challenges of protecting the very data that keeps them in business.

Copyright

In the United States, *copyright law* protects the right of the creator of an original work to control the public distribution, reproduction, display, and adaptation of that original work. The law covers many categories of work: pictorial, graphic, musical, dramatic, literary, pantomime, motion picture, sculptural, sound recording, and architectural. Copyright law does not cover the specific resource, as does trade secret law. It protects the *expression* of the idea of the resource instead of the resource itself. A copyright is usually used to protect an author's writings, an artist's drawings, a programmer's source code, or specific rhythms and structures of a musician's creation. Computer programs and manuals are just two examples of items protected under the Federal Copyright Act. The program or manual is covered under copyright law once it has been written. Although including a warning and the copyright symbol (©) is not required, doing so is encouraged so others cannot claim innocence after copying another's work.

Copyright protection does not extend to any method of operations, process, concept, or procedure, but it does protect against unauthorized copying and distribution of a protected work. It protects the form of expression rather than the subject matter. A patent deals more with the subject matter of an invention; copyright deals with how that invention is represented. In that respect, copyright is weaker than patent protection, but the duration of copyright protection is longer. Copyright protection exists for the life of the creator plus 70 years. If the work was created jointly by multiple authors, the 70 years start counting after the death of the last surviving one.

Computer programs can be protected under the copyright law as literary works. The law protects both the source code and object code, which can be an operating system, application, or database. In some instances, the law can protect not only the code but also the structure, sequence, and organization. The user interface is part of the definition of a software application structure; therefore, one vendor cannot copy the exact composition of another vendor's user interface.

Copyright infringement cases have exploded in numbers since the rise of "warez" sites that use the common BitTorrent protocol. BitTorrent is a peer-to-peer file sharing protocol and is one of the most common protocols for transferring large files. Warez is a term that refers to copyrighted works distributed or traded without fees or royalties, in general violation of the copyright law. The term generally refers to unauthorized releases by groups, as opposed to file sharing between friends.

Once a warez site posts copyrighted material, it is very difficult to have it removed because law enforcement is commonly overwhelmed with larger criminal cases and does not have the bandwidth to go after these "small fish." Another issue with warez sites is that the actual servers may reside in another country; thus, legal jurisdiction makes things more difficult and the country that the server resides within may not even have a copyright law. Film and music recording companies have had the most success in going after these types of offenders because they have the funds and vested interest to do so.

Trademark

A *trademark* is slightly different from a copyright in that it is used to protect a word, name, symbol, sound, shape, color, or combination of these. The reason a company would trademark one of these, or a combination, is that it represents the company (brand identity) to a group of people or to the world. Companies have marketing departments that work very hard to create something new that will cause the company to be noticed and stand out in a crowd of competitors, and trademarking the result of this work with a government registrar is a way of properly protecting it and ensuring others cannot copy and use it.

Companies cannot trademark a number or common word. This is why companies create new names—for example, Intel's Pentium and Apple's iPhone. However, unique colors can be trademarked, as well as identifiable packaging, which is referred to as "trade dress." Thus, Novell Red and UPS Brown are trademarked, as are some candy wrappers.

Registered trademarks are generally protected for ten years, but can be renewed for another ten years indefinitely. In the United States, you must file paperwork with the U.S. Patent and Trademark Office (USPTO) between the fifth and sixth years showing that you are actually using the trademark. This means that you can't just create a trademark you don't ever use and still keep others from using it. You have to file another "Declaration of Use" between the ninth and tenth year, and then every nine to ten years thereafter.

NOTE In 1883, international harmonization of trademark laws began with the Paris Convention, which in turn prompted the Madrid Agreement of 1891. Today, international trademark law efforts and international registration are overseen by the World Intellectual Property Organization (WIPO), an agency of the United Nations. The United States is a party to this agreement.

There have been many interesting trademark legal battles over the years. In one case a person named Paul Specht started a company named "Android Data" and had his company's trademark approved in 2002. Specht's company failed, and although he attempted to sell it and the trademark, he had no buyers. When Google announced that it was going to release a new mobile operating system called Android, Specht built a new website using his old company's name to try and prove that he was indeed still using this trademark. Specht took Google to court and asked for $94 million in trademark infringement damages. The court ruled in Google's favor and found that Google was not liable for damages.

Patent

Patents are given to individuals or organizations to grant them legal ownership of, and enable them to exclude others from using or copying, the invention covered by the patent. The invention must be novel, useful, and not obvious—which means, for example, that a company could not patent air. Thank goodness. If a company figured out how to patent air, we would have to pay for each and every breath we took!

After the inventor completes an application for a patent and it is approved, the patent grants a limited property right to exclude others from making, using, or selling the invention for a specific period of time. For example, when a pharmaceutical company develops a specific drug and acquires a patent for it, that company is the only one that can manufacture and sell this drug until the stated year in which the patent is up (usually 20 years from the date of approval). After that, the information is in the public domain, enabling all companies to manufacture and sell this product, which is why the price of a drug drops substantially after its patent expires and generic versions hit the market.

The patent process also applies to algorithms. If an inventor of an algorithm acquires a patent, she has full control over who can use the algorithm in their products. If the inventor lets a vendor incorporate the algorithm, she will most likely get a fee and possibly a license fee on each instance of the product that is sold.

Patents are ways of providing economic incentives to individuals and organizations to continue research and development efforts that will most likely benefit society in some fashion. Patent infringement is huge within the technology world today. Large and small product vendors seem to be suing each other constantly with claims of patent infringement. The problem is that many patents are written at a very high level. For example, if Inge developed a technology that accomplishes functionality A, B, and C, you could actually develop your own technology in your own way that also accomplished A, B, and C. You might not even know that Inge's method or patent existed; you just developed this solution on your own. Yet if Inge did this type of work first and obtained the patent, then she could go after you legally for infringement.

EXAM TIP A patent is the strongest form of intellectual property protection.

The amount of patent litigation in the technology world is remarkable. In October 2020, Centripetal Networks won a $1.9 billion award against Cisco Systems involving network threat detection technologies. In April of the same year, Apple and Broadcom were ordered to pay Caltech $1.1 billion because they infringed multiple Caltech patents pertaining to wireless error correction codes. Even though the amounts of these awards are certainly eye-popping, they are not the only notable ones. It turns out that 2020 was a pretty rough year for Apple, because it was also ordered to pay $506 million to PanOptis and another $109 million to WiLAN in two other infringement cases.

This is just a brief list of recent patent litigation. These patent cases are like watching 100 Ping-Pong matches going on all at the same time, each containing its own characters and dramas, and involving millions and billions of dollars.

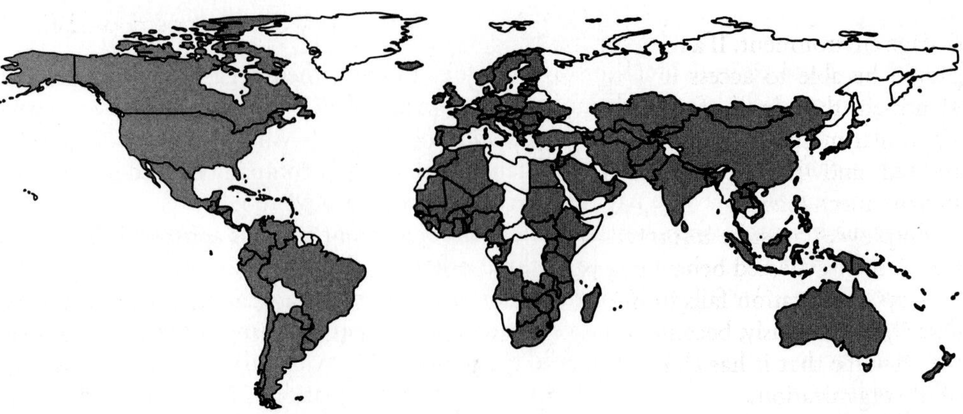

Figure 3-4 Defendants added to litigation campaigns by year (Data provided by RPX Corporation on 12/14/20. © 2020 RPX Corporation)

While the various vendors are fighting for market share in their respective industries, another reason for the increase in patent litigation is the emergence of nonpracticing entities (NPEs), also known as patent trolls. NPE (or patent troll) is a term used to describe a person or company who obtains patents, not to protect their invention, but to aggressively and opportunistically go after another entity that tries to create something based upon them. A patent troll has no intention of manufacturing an item based upon their patent, but wants to get licensing fees from an entity that does manufacture the item. For example, let's say that Donald has ten new ideas for ten different technologies. He puts them through the patent process and gets them approved, but he has no intention of putting in all the money and risk it takes to actually create these technologies and attempt to bring them to market. He is going to wait until you do this and then he is going to sue you for infringing upon his patent. If he wins the court case, you have to pay him licensing fees for the product you developed and brought to market.

It is important to do a patent search before putting effort into developing a new methodology, technology, or business method. As you can see in Figure 3-4, there is a lot of litigation due to patent infringement, and thousands of new defendants are being added to the party each year. These cases are very costly but can oftentimes be avoided with a bit of homework.

Internal Protection of Intellectual Property

Ensuring that specific resources are protected by the previously mentioned laws is very important, but other measures must be taken internally to make sure the resources that are confidential in nature are properly identified and protected.

The resources protected by one of the previously mentioned laws need to be identified and integrated into the organization's data classification scheme. This should be directed by management and carried out by the IT staff. The identified resources should have the necessary level of access control protection, auditing enabled, and a proper storage environment. If a resource is deemed secret, then not everyone in the organization should be able to access it. Once the individuals who are allowed to have access are identified, their level of access and interaction with the resource should be defined in a granular method. Attempts to access and manipulate the resource should be properly audited, and the resource should be stored on a protected system with the necessary security mechanisms.

Employees must be informed of the level of secrecy or confidentiality of the resource and of their expected behavior pertaining to that resource.

If an organization fails in one or all of these steps, it may not be covered by the laws described previously, because it may have failed to practice due care and properly protect the resource that it has claimed to be so important to the survival and competitiveness of the organization.

Software Piracy

Software piracy occurs when the intellectual or creative work of an author is used or duplicated without permission or compensation to the author. It is an act of infringement on ownership rights, and if the pirate is caught, he could be sued civilly for damages, be criminally prosecuted, or both.

When a vendor develops an application, it usually licenses the program rather than sells it outright. The license agreement contains provisions relating to the approved use of the software and the corresponding manuals. If an individual or organization fails to observe and abide by those requirements, the license may be terminated and, depending on the actions, criminal charges may be leveled. The risk to the vendor that develops and licenses the software is the loss of profits it would have earned.

There are four categories of software licensing. *Freeware* is software that is publicly available free of charge and can be used, copied, studied, modified, and redistributed without restriction. *Shareware*, or *trialware*, is used by vendors to market their software. Users obtain a free, trial version of the software. Once the user tries out the program, the user is asked to purchase a copy of it. *Commercial* software is, quite simply, software that is sold for or serves commercial purposes. And, finally, *academic* software is software that is provided for academic purposes at a reduced cost. It can be open source, freeware, or commercial software.

Some software vendors sell bulk licenses, which enable several users to use the product simultaneously. These master agreements define proper use of the software along with restrictions, such as whether corporate software can also be used by employees on their home machines. One other prevalent form of software licensing is the End User License Agreement (EULA). It specifies more granular conditions and restrictions than a master agreement. Other vendors incorporate third-party license-metering software that keeps track of software usability to ensure that the customer stays within the license limit and otherwise complies with the software licensing agreement.

The information security officer should be aware of all these types of contractual commitments required by software companies. This person needs to be educated on the restrictions the organization is under and make sure proper enforcement mechanisms are in place. If an organization is found guilty of illegally copying software or using more copies than its license permits, the security officer in charge of this task may be primarily responsible.

Thanks to easy access to high-speed Internet, employees' ability—if not the temptation—to download and use pirated software has greatly increased. The June 2018 BSA Global Software Survey, a study conducted by the Business Software Alliance (BSA) and International Data Corporation (IDC), found that 37 percent of the software installed on personal computers globally was not properly licensed. This means that for every two dollars' worth of legal software that is purchased, one dollar's worth is pirated. Software developers often use these numbers to calculate losses resulting from pirated copies. The assumption is that if the pirated copy had not been available, then everyone who is using a pirated copy would have instead purchased it legally.

Not every country recognizes software piracy as a crime, but several international organizations have made strides in curbing the practice. The Federation Against Software Theft (FAST) and the Business Software Alliance (author of the Global Software Survey) are organizations that promote the enforcement of proprietary rights of software. This is a huge issue for companies that develop and produce software, because a majority of their revenue comes from licensing fees. The study also estimates that the total economic damage experienced by the industry was $46.3 billion in losses in 2018.

One of the offenses an individual or organization can commit is to decompile vendor object code. This is usually done to figure out how the application works by obtaining the original source code, which is confidential, and perhaps to reverse-engineer it in the hope of understanding the intricate details of its functionality. Another purpose of reverse-engineering products is to detect security flaws within the code that can later be exploited. This is how some buffer overflow vulnerabilities are discovered.

Many times, an individual decompiles the object code into source code and either finds security holes to exploit or alters the source code to produce some type of functionality that the original vendor did not intend. In one example, an individual decompiled a program that protects and displays e-books and publications. The vendor did not want anyone to be able to copy the e-publications its product displayed and thus inserted an encoder within the object code of its product that enforced this limitation. The individual decompiled the object code and figured out how to create a decoder that would overcome this restriction and enable users to make copies of the e-publications, which infringed upon those authors' and publishers' copyrights.

The individual was arrested and prosecuted under the *Digital Millennium Copyright Act (DMCA)*, which makes it illegal to create products that circumvent copyright protection mechanisms. Interestingly enough, many computer-oriented individuals protested this person's arrest, and the company prosecuting (Adobe) quickly decided to drop all charges.

DMCA is a U.S. copyright law that criminalizes the production and dissemination of technology, devices, or services that circumvent access control measures that are put into place to protect copyright material. So if you figure out a way to "unlock" the proprietary way that Barnes & Noble protects its e-books, you can be charged under this act. Even if you don't share the actual copyright-protected books with someone, you still broke this specific law and can be found guilty.

NOTE The European Union passed a similar law called the Copyright Directive.

Compliance Requirements

While it is important to know *which* specific laws and regulations your organization needs to be compliant with, it is also important to know *how* to ensure that compliance is being met and how to properly convey that to the necessary stakeholders. If it hasn't already done so, your organization should develop a compliance program that outlines what needs to be put into place to be compliant with the necessary internal and external drivers. Then, an audit team should periodically assess how well the organization is doing to meet the identified requirements.

The first step is to identify which laws and regulations your organization needs to be compliant with (e.g., GDPR, HIPAA, PCI DSS, etc.). This will give you the specific requirements that the laws and regulations impose on your organization. The requirements, in turn, inform your risk assessment and allow you to select the appropriate controls to ensure compliance. Once this is all done and tested, the auditors have stuff to audit. These auditors can be internal or external to the organization and will have long checklists of items that correspond with the legal, regulatory, and policy requirements the organization must meet.

NOTE Audits and auditors will be covered in detail in Chapter 18.

It is common for organizations to develop *governance, risk, and compliance (GRC)* programs, which allow for the integration and alignment of the activities that take place in each one of these silos of a security program. If the same *key performance indicators (KPIs)* are used in the governance, risk, and compliance auditing activities, then the resulting reports can effectively illustrate the overlap and integration of these different concepts. For example, if a healthcare organization is not compliant with various HIPAA requirements, this is a type of risk that management must be aware of so that it can ensure the right activities and controls are put into place. Also, how does executive management carry out security governance if it does not understand the risks the organization is facing and the outstanding compliance issues? It is important for all of these things to be understood by the decision makers in a holistic manner so that they can make the best decisions pertaining to protecting the organization as a whole. The agreed-upon KPI values are commonly provided to executive management in dashboards or scorecard formats, which allow management to quickly understand the health of the organization from a GRC point of view.

Contractual, Legal, Industry Standards, and Regulatory Requirements

Regulations in computer and information security cover many areas for many different reasons. We've already covered some of these areas, such as data privacy, computer misuse, software copyright, data protection, and controls on cryptography. These regulations can be implemented in various arenas, such as government and private sectors, for reasons dealing with environmental protection, intellectual property, national security, personal privacy, public order, health and safety, and prevention of fraudulent activities.

Security professionals have so much to keep up with these days, from understanding how the latest ransomware attacks work and how to properly protect against them, to inventorying sensitive data and ensuring it only exists in approved places with the right protections. Professionals also need to follow which new security products are released and how they compare to the existing products. This is followed up by keeping track of new technologies, service patches, hotfixes, encryption methods, access control mechanisms, telecommunications security issues, social engineering, and physical security. Laws and regulations have been ascending the list of things that security professionals also need to be aware of. This is because organizations must be compliant with more and more laws and regulations, both domestically and internationally, and noncompliance can result in a fine or a company going out of business, and in some cases certain executive management individuals ending up in jail.

Laws, regulations, and directives developed by governments or appointed agencies do not usually provide detailed instructions to follow to properly protect computers and company assets. Each environment is too diverse in topology, technology, infrastructure, requirements, functionality, and personnel. Because technology changes at such a fast pace, these laws and regulations could never successfully represent reality if they were too detailed. Instead, they state high-level requirements that commonly puzzle organizations about how to be compliant with them. This is where the security professional comes to the rescue.

In the past, security professionals were expected to know how to carry out penetration tests, configure firewalls, and deal only with the technology issues of security. Today, security professionals are being pulled out of the server rooms and asked to be more involved in business-oriented issues. As a security professional, you need to understand the laws and regulations that your organization must comply with and what controls must be put in place to accomplish compliance. This means the security professional now must have a foot in both the technical world and the business world.

But it's not just laws and regulations you need to be aware of. Your organization may also need to be compliant with certain standards in order to be competitive (or even do business) in certain sectors. If your organization processes credit cards, then it has to comply with the Payment Card Industry Data Security Standard (PCI DSS). This is not a law or even a government regulation; instead, it is an example of a mandatory industry standard. If your organization is a financial institution that is considered part of the critical national infrastructure of the United Kingdom, then it may have to comply with the CBEST standard even though any reputable organization in that sector is expected to do so voluntarily. And, finally, if your organization wants to sell cloud services to the U.S. government, it won't even be considered unless it is Federal Risk and Authorization Management Program (FedRAMP) certified. So, compliance is not just about laws and regulations. There are many other standards that may be critical to the success of your organization.

Another compliance requirement that is sometimes missed by cybersecurity professionals is related to contracts and other legally binding agreements. In the course of doing business, your organization may enter into agreements that may have security requirements. For example, your organization may partner with another organization and thereby gain access to its sensitive data. The partnering agreement may have a clause requiring both organizations to ensure that they have certain controls in place to protect that data. If these protections are not already part of your own security architecture and you fail to implement them (or even become aware of them), you would not be in compliance with the contractual obligations, which could make your organization liable in the event of a breach. The point is that we need to have open lines of communication with our legal and business colleagues to ensure we are made aware of any security clauses before we enter into a contract.

If You Are Not a Lawyer, You Are Not a Lawyer

Many times organizations ask their security professionals to help them figure out how to be compliant with the necessary laws and regulations. While you might be aware of and have experience with some of these laws and regulations, there is a high likelihood that you are not aware of all the necessary federal and state laws, regulations, and international requirements your organization must meet. These laws, regulations, and directives morph over time and new ones are added, and while you may think you are interpreting them correctly, you may be wrong. It is critical that an organization get its legal department involved with compliancy issues. Many security professionals have been in this situation over many years. At many organizations, the legal staff does not know enough about all of these issues to ensure the organization is properly protected. In this situation, advise the organization to contact outside counsel to help them with these issues.

Organizations look to security professionals to have all the answers, especially in consulting situations. You will be brought in as the expert. But if you are not a lawyer, you are not a lawyer and should advise your customer properly in obtaining legal help to ensure proper compliance in all matters. The increasing use of cloud computing is adding an incredible amount of legal and regulatory compliance confusion to current situations.

It is a good idea to have a clause in any type of consulting agreement you use that explicitly outlines these issues so that if and when the organization gets hauled to court after a computer breach, your involvement will be understood and previously documented.

Over time, the CISSP exam has become more global in nature and less U.S.-centric. Specific questions on U.S. laws and regulations have been taken out of the test, so you do not need to spend a lot of time learning them and their specifics. Be familiar with why laws are developed and put in place and their overall goals, instead of memorizing specific laws and dates.

Privacy Requirements

Privacy compliance requirements stem from the various data protection laws and regulations we've already covered in this chapter (for example, CCPA, GDPR, and HIPAA). The hard part is ensuring you are aware of all the localities within which your organization gathers, stores, and processes various types of private data. The good news is that, at their core, these laws are not all that different from one another in terms of the security controls they require. In almost every case, the controls are reasonable things we would want to have anyway. So, most of the work you'll require to remain compliant is pretty straightforward.

Where things get a bit murkier is when we consider what data is covered and when we are required to notify someone. For example, the GDPR covers PII on EU persons and HIPAA covers PHI on any patient treated by a U.S. healthcare provider. So, if you suffer a data breach affecting the PHI of a German national who received care in your U.S. facilities, you will most likely have to follow both reporting procedures in these two laws. Under the GDPR, you'd have 72 hours from the time of discovery, while under HIPAA, you could have up to 60 days. The notified parties, in addition to the individual whose information was compromised, vary in each case, which further complicates things.

The best approach is collaborate with your business and legal colleague to develop detailed notification procedures that cover each potential breach. Once you're satisfied that your organization can comply with the notification requirements, you should exercise different scenarios to test the procedures and ensure everyone is trained on how to execute them. A breach will ruin your day all by itself, so there's no sense in adding the need to figure out compliance requirements at the point of crisis to make it worse. Furthermore, having procedures that are periodically exercised can help prove to any investigators that you were doing the right things all along.

Liability and Its Ramifications

Executives may be held responsible and liable under various laws and regulations. They could be sued by stockholders and customers if they do not practice due diligence and due care. *Due diligence* can be defined as doing everything within one's power to prevent a bad thing from happening. Examples of this would be setting appropriate policies, researching the threats and incorporating them into a risk management plan, and ensuring audits happen at the right times. *Due care*, on the other hand, means taking the precautions that a reasonable and competent person would take in the same situation. For example, someone who ignores a security warning and clicks through to a malicious website would fail to exercise due care.

EXAM TIP Due diligence is normally associated with leaders, laws, and regulations. Due care is normally applicable to everyone, and failure to exercise it could be used to show negligence.

Before you can figure out how to properly protect yourself, you need to find out what it is you are protecting yourself against. This is what due diligence is all about—researching and assessing the current level of vulnerabilities so the true risk level is understood. Only after these steps and assessments take place can effective controls and safeguards be identified and implemented.

Due Care vs. Due Diligence

Due diligence is the act of gathering the necessary information so the best decision-making activities can take place. Before a company purchases another company, it should carry out due diligence activities so that the purchasing company does not have any "surprises" down the road. The purchasing company should investigate all relevant aspects of the past, present, and predictable future of the business of the target company. If this does not take place and the purchase of the new company hurts the original company financially or legally, the decision makers could be found liable (responsible) and negligent by the shareholders.

In information security, similar data gathering should take place so that there are no "surprises" down the road and the risks are fully understood before they are accepted. If a financial company is going to provide online banking functionality to its customers, the company needs to fully understand all the risks this service entails for the company. Website hacking attempts will increase, account fraud attempts will increase, database attacks will increase, social engineering attacks will increase, and so forth. While this company is offering its customers a new service, it is also making itself a juicier target for attackers and lawyers. The company needs to carry out due diligence to understand all these risks before offering this new service so that the company can make the best business decisions. If it doesn't implement proper countermeasures, the company opens itself up to potential criminal charges, civil suits, regulatory fines, loss of market share, and more.

Due care pertains to acting responsibly and "doing the right thing." It is a legal term that defines the standards of performance that can be expected, either by contract or by implication, in the execution of a particular task. Due care ensures that a minimal level of protection is in place in accordance with the best practice in the industry.

If an organization does not have sufficient security policies, necessary countermeasures, and proper security awareness training in place, it is not practicing due care and can be found negligent. If a financial institution that offers online banking does not implement TLS for account transactions, for example, it is not practicing due care.

Many times due diligence (data gathering) has to be performed so that proper due care (prudent actions) can take place.

Senior management has an obligation to protect the organization from a long list of activities that can negatively affect it, including protection from malicious code, natural disasters, privacy violations, infractions of the law, and more. The costs and benefits of this protection should be evaluated in monetary and nonmonetary terms to ensure that the cost of security does not outweigh the expected benefits. Security should be proportional to potential loss estimates pertaining to the severity, likelihood, and extent of potential damage.

As Figure 3-5 shows, there are many costs to consider when it comes to security breaches: loss of business, response activities, customer and partner notification, and detection and escalation measures. These types of costs need to be understood so that the organization can practice proper due care by implementing the necessary controls to reduce the risks and these costs. Security mechanisms should be employed to reduce the frequency and severity of security-related losses. A sound security program is a smart business practice.

Senior management needs to decide upon the amount of risk it is willing to take pertaining to computer and information security, and implement security in an economical and responsible manner. These risks do not always stop at the boundaries of the organization. Many organizations work with third parties, with whom they must share sensitive data. The main organization is still liable for the protection of this sensitive data that it owns, even if the data is on another organization's network. This is why more and more regulations are requiring organizations to evaluate their third-party security measures.

If one of the organizations does not provide the necessary level of protection and its negligence affects a partner it is working with, the affected organization can sue the upstream organization. For example, let's say Company A and Company B have constructed an extranet. Company A does not put in controls to detect and deal with viruses. Company A

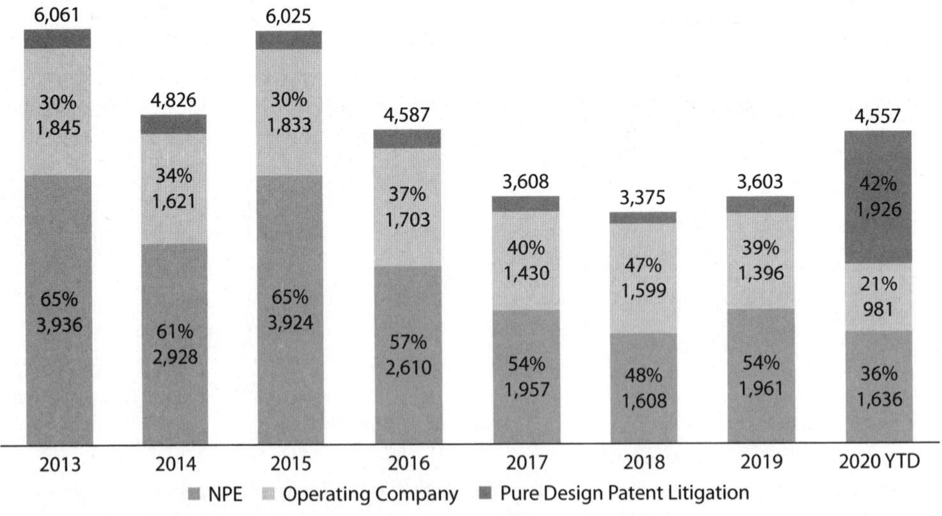

Figure 3-5 Data breach costs (Source: Ponemon Institute and IBM Security)

gets infected with a destructive virus and it is spread to Company B through the extranet. The virus corrupts critical data and causes a massive disruption to Company B's production. Therefore, Company B can sue Company A for being negligent. Both companies need to make sure they are doing their part to ensure that their activities, or the lack of them, will not negatively affect another company, which is referred to as *downstream liability*.

EXAM TIP *Responsibility* generally refers to the obligations and expected actions and behaviors of a particular party. An obligation may have a defined set of specific actions that are required, or a more general and open approach, which enables the party to decide how it will fulfill the particular obligation. *Accountability* refers to the ability to hold a party responsible for certain actions or inaction.

Each company has different requirements when it comes to its list of due care responsibilities. If these steps are not taken, the company may be charged with negligence if damage arises out of its failure to follow these steps. To prove negligence in court, the plaintiff must establish that the defendant had a *legally recognized obligation*, or duty, to protect the plaintiff from unreasonable risks and that the defendant's failure to protect the plaintiff from an unreasonable risk (breach of duty) was the *proximate cause* of the plaintiff's damages. Penalties for negligence can be either civil or criminal, ranging from actions resulting in compensation for the plaintiff to jail time for violation of the law.

EXAM TIP *Proximate cause* is an act or omission that naturally and directly produces a consequence. It is the superficial or obvious cause for an occurrence. It refers to a cause that leads directly, or in an unbroken sequence, to a particular result. It can be seen as an element of negligence in a court of law.

Requirements for Investigations

Investigations are launched for a multitude of specific reasons. Maybe you suspect an employee is using your servers to mine bitcoin after hours, which in most places would be a violation of acceptable use policies. Maybe you think civil litigation is reasonably foreseeable or you uncover evidence of crime on your systems. Sometimes, we are the targets of investigation and not the investigators, such as when a government regulator suspects we are not in compliance. Though the investigative process is similar regardless of the reason, it is important to differentiate the types of investigations you are likely to come across.

Administrative

An *administrative investigation* is one that is focused on policy violations. These represent the least impactful (to the organization) type of investigation and will likely result in administrative action if the investigation supports the allegations. For instance, violations of voluntary industry standards (such as PCI DSS) could result in an administrative investigation, particularly if the violation resulted in some loss or bad press for the organization. In the worst case, someone can get fired. Typically, however, someone is counseled not to do something again and that is that. Either way, you want to keep your human resources (HR) staff involved as you proceed.

Criminal

A seemingly administrative affair, however, can quickly get stickier. Suppose you start investigating someone for a possible policy violation and along the way discover that person was involved in what is likely criminal activity. A *criminal investigation* is one that is aimed at determining whether there is cause to believe beyond a reasonable doubt that someone committed a crime. The most important thing to consider is that we, as information systems security professionals, are not qualified to determine whether or not someone broke the law; that is the job of law enforcement agencies (LEAs). Our job, once we have reason to believe that a crime may have taken place, is to preserve evidence, ensure the designated people in our organizations contact the appropriate LEA, and assist them in any way that is appropriate.

Civil

Not all statutes are criminal, however, so it is possible to have an alleged violation of a law result in something other than a criminal investigation. The two likeliest ways to encounter this is regarding possible violations of civil law or government regulations. A *civil investigation* is typically triggered when a lawsuit is imminent or ongoing. It is similar to a criminal investigation, except that instead of working with an LEA you will probably be working with attorneys from both sides (the plaintiff is the party suing and the defendant is the one being sued). Another key difference in civil (versus criminal) investigations is that the standard of proof is much lower; instead of proving beyond a reasonable doubt, the plaintiff just has to show that the preponderance of the evidence supports the allegation.

Regulatory

Somewhere between the previous three (administrative, criminal, and civil investigations) lies the fourth kind you should know. A *regulatory investigation* is initiated by a government regulator when there is reason to believe that the organization is not in compliance. These vary significantly in scope and could look like any of the other three types of investigation depending on the severity of the allegations. As with criminal investigations, the key thing to remember is that your job is to preserve evidence and assist the regulator's investigators as appropriate.

Chapter Review

The fact that the Internet is a global medium does not negate the power of governments to establish and enforce laws that govern what can be done by whom on networks within each country. This can create challenges for cybersecurity professionals whose organizations have clients, partners, or activities in multiple jurisdictions. The most important thing you can do as a CISSP is develop a good relationship with your legal team and use that to ensure you are aware of all the legal and regulatory requirements that may pertain to cybersecurity. Then, after you implement the necessary controls, check with your lawyer friends again to ensure you've exercised due diligence. Keep checking, because laws and regulations do change over time, particularly if you are operating in multiple countries.

Quick Review

- Law is a system of rules (written or otherwise), created by a government, that apply equally to everyone in the country.
- Regulations are written rules issued by an executive body, covering specific issues, and apply only to the specific entities that fall under the authority of the agency that issues them.
- Civil law system:
    - Uses prewritten rules and is not based on precedent.
    - Is different from civil (tort) laws, which work under a common law system.
- Common law system:
    - Made up of criminal, civil, and administrative laws.
- Customary law system:
    - Addresses mainly personal conduct and uses regional traditions and customs as the foundations of the laws.
    - Is usually mixed with another type of listed legal system rather than being the sole legal system used in a region.
- Religious law system:
    - Laws are derived from religious beliefs and address an individual's religious responsibilities; commonly used in Muslim countries or regions.
- Mixed law system:
    - Uses two or more legal systems.
- Criminal law deals with an individual's conduct that violates government laws developed to protect the public.
- Civil law deals with wrongs committed against individuals or organizations that result in injury or damages. Civil law does not use prison time as a punishment, but usually requires financial restitution.
- Administrative, or regulatory, law covers standards of performance or conduct expected by government agencies from companies, industries, and certain officials.
- Many attacks cross international borders, which make them harder to prosecute because doing so requires deconflicting the laws of the various countries involved; attackers use this to their advantage.

- Island-hopping attacks are those in which an attacker compromises an easier target that has a trusted connection to the ultimate target.
- An advanced persistent threat (APT) is a sophisticated threat actor that has the means and the will to devote extraordinary resources to compromising a specific target and remaining undetected for extended periods of time.
- A data breach is a security event that results in the actual or potential compromise of the confidentiality or integrity of protected information by unauthorized actors.
- Personally identifiable information (PII) is data that can be used to uniquely identify, contact, or locate a single person or can be used with other sources to uniquely identify a single individual.
- Each country has specific rules that control what can be legally imported and exported. This applies particularly to some cryptographic tools and techniques.
- A transborder data flow (TDF) is the movement of machine-readable data across a political boundary such as a country's border.
- Data localization laws require that certain types of data be stored and processed in that country, sometimes exclusively.
- Intellectual property (IP) is a type of property created by human intellect that consists of ideas, inventions, and expressions that are uniquely created by a person and can be protected from unauthorized use by others.
- A license is an agreement between an intellectual property (IP) owner (the licensor) and somebody else (the licensee), granting that party the right to use the IP in very specific ways.
- Trade secrets are deemed proprietary to a company and often include information that provides a competitive edge. The information is protected as long as the owner takes the necessary protective actions.
- Copyright protects the expression of ideas rather than the ideas themselves.
- Trademarks protect words, names, product shapes, symbols, colors, or a combination of these used to identify products or a company. These items are used to distinguish products from the competitors' products.
- A patent grants ownership and enables that owner to legally enforce his rights to exclude others from using the invention covered by the patent.
- Due diligence can be defined as doing everything within one's power to prevent a bad thing from happening. It is normally associated with leaders, laws, and regulations.
- Due care means taking the precautions that a reasonable and competent person would take in the same situation. It is normally applicable to everyone, and its absence could be used to show negligence.
- Administrative investigations are focused on policy violations.

- Criminal investigations are aimed at determining whether there is cause to believe that someone committed a crime.
- A civil investigation is typically triggered when a lawsuit is imminent or ongoing, and is similar to a criminal investigation, except that instead of working with law enforcement agencies you will probably be working with attorneys from both sides.
- A regulatory investigation is initiated by a government regulator when there is reason to believe that the organization is not in compliance.

Questions

Please remember that these questions are formatted and asked in a certain way for a reason. Keep in mind that the CISSP exam is asking questions at a conceptual level. Questions may not always have the perfect answer, and the candidate is advised against always looking for the perfect answer. Instead, the candidate should look for the best answer in the list.

1. When can executives be charged with negligence?
   - **A.** If they follow the transborder laws
   - **B.** If they do not properly report and prosecute attackers
   - **C.** If they properly inform users that they may be monitored
   - **D.** If they do not practice due care when protecting resources
2. To better deal with computer crime, several legislative bodies have taken what steps in their strategy?
   - **A.** Expanded several privacy laws
   - **B.** Broadened the definition of property to include data
   - **C.** Required corporations to have computer crime insurance
   - **D.** Redefined transborder issues
3. Which of the following is true about data breaches?
   - **A.** They are exceptionally rare.
   - **B.** They always involve personally identifiable information (PII).
   - **C.** They may trigger legal or regulatory requirements.
   - **D.** The United States has no laws pertaining to data breaches.

Use the following scenario to answer Questions 4–6. Business is good and your company is expanding operations into Europe. Because your company will be dealing with personal information of European Union (EU) citizens, you know that it will be subject to the EU's General Data Protection Regulation (GDPR). You have a mature security program that is certified by the International Organization for Standardization (ISO), so you are confident you can meet any new requirements.

4. Upon learning of your company's plans to expand into Europe, what should be one of the first things you do?

   A. Consult your legal team

   B. Appoint a Data Protection Officer (DPO)

   C. Label data belonging to EU persons

   D. Nothing, because your ISO certification should cover all new requirements

5. You have determined all the new GDPR requirements and estimate that you will need an additional $250,000 to meet them. How can you best justify this investment to your senior business leaders?

   A. It is the right thing to do.

   B. You are legally required to provide that money.

   C. You'll make way more profits than that in the new market.

   D. The cost of noncompliance could easily exceed the additional budget request.

6. Your Security Operations Center (SOC) chief notifies you of a data breach in which your organization's entire customer list may have been compromised. As the data controller, what are your notification requirements?

   A. No later than 72 hours after you contain the breach

   B. Within 30 days of the breach

   C. As soon as possible, but within 60 days of becoming aware of the breach

   D. No later than 72 hours after becoming aware of the breach

Use the following scenario to answer Questions 7–9. Faced with a lawsuit alleging patent infringement, your CEO stands up a working group to look at licensing and intellectual property (IP) issues across the company. The intent is to ensure that the company is doing everything within its power to enforce IP rights, both its own rights and others' rights. The CEO asks you to lead an effort to look internally and externally for any indication that your company is violating the IP rights of others or that your own IP is being used by unauthorized parties.

7. Which term best describes what the CEO is practicing?

   A. Due care

   B. Due diligence

   C. Compliance

   D. Downstream liability

8. You discover that another organization is publishing some of your company's copyrighted blogs on its website as if they were its own. What is your best course of action?
   A. Do nothing; the blogs are not particularly valuable, and you have bigger problems
   B. Contact the webmasters directly and ask them to take the blogs down
   C. Have the legal team send a cease-and-desist order to the offending organization
   D. Report your findings to the CEO
9. You discover dozens of workstations running unlicensed productivity software in a virtual network that is isolated from the Internet. Why is this a problem?
   A. Users should not be able to install their own applications.
   B. It is not a problem as long as the virtual machines are not connected to the Internet.
   C. Software piracy can have significant financial and even criminal repercussions.
   D. There is no way to register the licenses if the devices cannot access the Internet.
10. Which of the following would you use to control the public distribution, reproduction, display, and adaptation of an original white paper written by your staff?
    A. Copyright
    B. Trademark
    C. Patent
    D. Trade secret
11. Many privacy laws dictate which of the following rules?
    A. Individuals have a right to remove any data they do not want others to know.
    B. Agencies do not need to ensure that the data is accurate.
    C. Agencies need to allow all government agencies access to the data.
    D. Agencies cannot use collected data for a purpose different from what they collected it for.
12. Which of the following has an incorrect definition mapping?
    i. Civil (code) law: Based on previous interpretations of laws
    ii. Common law: Rule-based law, not precedent-based
    iii. Customary law: Deals mainly with personal conduct and patterns of behavior
    iv. Religious law: Based on religious beliefs of the region
    A. i, iii
    B. i, ii, iii
    C. i, ii
    D. iv

Answers

1. **D.** Executives are held to a certain standard and are expected to act responsibly when running and protecting an organization. These standards and expectations equate to the due care concept under the law. Due care means to carry out activities that a reasonable person would be expected to carry out in the same situation. If an executive acts irresponsibly in any way, she can be seen as not practicing due care and be held negligent.
2. **B.** Many times, what is corrupted, compromised, or taken from a computer is data, so current laws have been updated to include the protection of intangible assets, as in data. Over the years, data and information have become many organizations' most valuable asset, which must be protected by the laws.
3. **C.** Organizations experiencing a data breach may be required by laws or regulations to take certain actions. For instance, many countries have disclosure requirements that require notification to affected parties and/or regulatory bodies within a specific timeframe.
4. **A.** Your best bet when facing a new legal or regulatory environment or issue is to consult with your legal team. It is their job to tell you what you're required to do, and your job to get it done. Your will almost certainly need to appoint a Data Protection Officer (DPO), and you will probably need to label or otherwise categorize data belonging to EU persons, but you still need to check with your attorneys first.
5. **D.** Fines for noncompliance with the GDPR can range from up to €20 million (approximately $22.5 million) to 4 percent of a company's annual global revenue—whichever is greater. While it is true that this is the right thing to do, that answer is not as compelling to business leaders whose job is to create value for their shareholders.
6. **D.** The GDPR has the strictest breach notification requirements of any data protection law in the world. Your organization is required to notify the supervisory authority of the EU member state involved within 72 hours of becoming aware of the breach. Examples of supervisory authorities are the Data Protection Commission in Ireland, the Hellenic Data Protection Authority in Greece, and the Agencia Española de Protección de Datos in Spain.
7. **B.** Due diligence is doing everything within one's power to prevent a bad thing from happening and is normally associated with an organization's leaders. Given the CEO's intent, this is the best answer. Compliance could be an answer but is not the best one since the scope of the effort appears to be very broad and there is no mention of specific laws or regulations with which the CEO wants to comply.
8. **C.** A company must protect resources that it claims to be intellectual property such as copyrighted material and must show that it exercised due care (reasonable acts of protection) in its efforts to protect those resources. If you

ignore this apparent violation, it may be much more difficult to enforce your rights later when more valuable IP is involved. You should never attempt to do this on your own. That's why you have a legal team!

9. **C.** Whether or not the computers on which unlicensed software runs can reach the Internet is irrelevant. The fact is that your company is using a software product that it is not authorized to use, which is considered software piracy.

10. **A.** A copyright fits the situation precisely. A patent could be used to protect a novel invention described in the paper, but the question did not imply that this was the case. A trade secret cannot be publicly disseminated, so it does not apply. Finally, a trademark protects only a word, symbol, sound, shape, color, or combination of these.

11. **D.** The Federal Privacy Act of 1974 and the General Data Protection Regulation (GDPR) were created to protect personal data. These acts have many stipulations, including that the information can only be used for the reason for which it was collected.

12. **C.** The following has the proper definition mappings:

    i. Civil (code) law: Rule-based law, not precedent-based

    ii. Common law: Based on previous interpretations of laws

    iii. Customary law: Deals mainly with personal conduct and patterns of behavior

    iv. Religious law: Based on religious beliefs of the region

CHAPTER 4

Frameworks

This chapter presents the following:

- Overview of frameworks
- Risk frameworks
- Information security frameworks
- Enterprise architecture frameworks
- Other frameworks

You can't build a great building on a weak foundation.

—Gordon B. Hinckley

The previous chapters have covered a lot of material dealing with governance, risk, and compliance. By now, you may be asking yourself, "How does this all fit together into an actionable process?" This is where frameworks come to the rescue. You can think of a framework as a strong foundation on which to build whatever it is you're trying to build, whether it's a risk management program or security controls. A framework gives you just enough rigidity to keep your effort from collapsing under its own weight, but still gives you a lot of leeway so that you can customize the framework to your particular situation. While it is possible (though very difficult) to build successful programs all by yourself, why reinvent the wheel when you can leverage the hard-earned lessons of other experts in the field?

In this chapter, we will discuss a variety of frameworks that you are likely to encounter both in your job and when taking the CISSP exam. We divide them into three groups: risk frameworks, information security frameworks, and enterprise architecture frameworks. Risk management enables any successful information security program, so we'll tackle those two groups in that order, followed by enterprise architecture frameworks. We'll then round out our discussion with the other frameworks and concepts that you should know.

Overview of Frameworks

A *framework* is a basic structure underlying a system, concept, or text. So the purpose of frameworks in IT and cybersecurity is to provide structure to the ways in which we manage risks, develop enterprise architectures, and secure all our assets. Think of frameworks as the consensus of many great minds on how we should approach these issues.

As you will see in the following sections, various for-profit and nonprofit organizations have developed their own frameworks for risk management, security programs, security controls, process management, and enterprise development. We will examine their similarities and differences and illustrate where each is used within the industry. The following is a basic breakdown.

Risk:

- **NIST RMF** The Risk Management Framework, developed by the National Institute of Standards and Technology, is composed of three interrelated NIST Special Publications (SPs): 800-39, 800-37, and 800-30.
- **ISO/IEC 27005** Focused on risk treatment, this joint International Organization for Standardization/International Electrotechnical Commission framework is best used in conjunction with ISO/IEC 27000 series standards.
- **OCTAVE** The Operationally Critical Threat, Asset, and Vulnerability Evaluation framework, developed at Carnegie Mellon University, is focused on risk assessment.
- **FAIR** The FAIR Institute's Factor Analysis of Information Risk framework focuses on more precisely measuring the probabilities of incidents and their impacts.

Security Program:

- **ISO/IEC 27000 series** This is a series of international standards on how to develop and maintain an information security management system (ISMS), developed by ISO and IEC.
- **NIST Cybersecurity Framework** Driven by the need to secure government systems, NIST developed this widely used and comprehensive framework for risk-driven information security.

Security Controls:

- **NIST SP 800-53** This NIST publication provides a catalog of controls and a process for selecting them in order to protect U.S. federal systems.
- **CIS Controls** The Center for Internet Security (CIS) Controls framework is one of the simplest approaches for companies of all sizes to select and implement the right controls.
- **COBIT 2019** This is a business framework to allow for IT enterprise management and governance that was developed by ISACA.

Enterprise Architecture:

- **Zachman Framework** This is a model for the development of enterprise architectures, developed by John Zachman.
- **TOGAF** The Open Group Architecture Framework is a model and methodology for the development of enterprise architectures.

- **DoDAF** The U.S. Department of Defense Architecture Framework was developed to ensure interoperability of systems to meet military mission goals.
- **SABSA** The Sherwood Applied Business Security Architecture model and methodology for the development of information security enterprise architectures was developed by the SABSA Institute.

NOTE Chapter 1 already discussed the SABSA model.

Risk Frameworks

By combining the definition of a framework in the previous section with our definition of risk management in Chapter 2, we can define a *risk management framework (RMF)* as a structured process that allows an organization to identify and assess risk, reduce it to an acceptable level, and ensure that it remains at that level. In essence, an RMF is a structured approach to risk management.

As you might imagine, there is no shortage of RMFs out there. What is important to you as a security professional is to ensure your organization has an RMF that works for you. That being said, there are some frameworks that have enjoyed widespread success and acceptance. You should at least be aware of these, and ideally adopt (and perhaps modify) one of them to fit your organization's particular needs. We'll cover the NIST RMF in more detail, mostly to familiarize you with the components of this framework, but also because it is the one you are most likely to encounter in your career.

NIST RMF

The NIST Risk Management Framework (RMF) is described in three core interrelated Special Publications (there are other key publications specific to individual steps of the RMF):

- SP 800-37, Revision 2, *Risk Management Framework for Information Systems and Organizations*
- SP 800-39, *Managing Information Security Risk*
- SP 800-30, Revision 1, *Guide for Conducting Risk Assessments*

This framework incorporates the key elements of risk management that you should know as a security professional. It is important to keep in mind, however, that it is geared toward federal government entities and may have to be modified to fit your own needs.

The NIST RMF outlines the seven-step process shown in Figure 4-1, each of which will be addressed in turn in the following sections. It is important to note that this is a never-ending cycle because our information systems are constantly changing. Each change needs to be analyzed to determine whether it should trigger another trip around the loop.

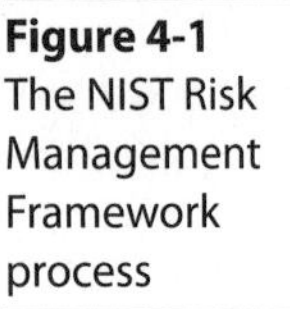

Figure 4-1 The NIST Risk Management Framework process

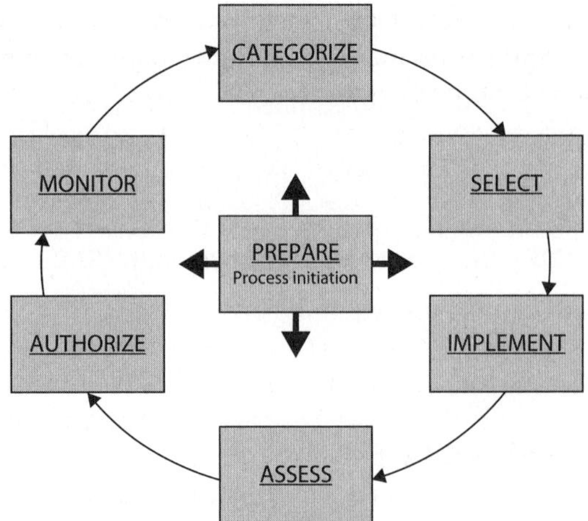

Prepare

The first step is to ensure that the top executives and the senior leaders (at both the strategic and operational levels) are in sync across the organization. This includes agreeing on roles, priorities, constraints, and risk tolerance. Another key activity during the prepare step is to conduct an organizational risk assessment that provides a common point of reference for the entire team to communicate about strategic risks. One of the outcomes of this assessment is the identification of high-value assets, on which the entire effort will be focused.

Categorize

The next step is to categorize your information systems based on criticality and sensitivity of the information to be processed, stored, or transmitted by those systems. The idea is to create categories for your systems based on how important they are so that you can prioritize your defensive resources. All U.S. government agencies are required to use the following NIST SP 800-60 documents for this purpose: *Volume I: Guide for Mapping Types of Information and Information Systems to Security Categories* and *Volume II: Appendices to Guide for Mapping Types of Information and Information Systems to Security Categories.*

NIST SP 800-60 applies sensitivity and criticality to each security objective (confidentiality, integrity, and availability) to determine a system's criticality. For example, suppose you have a customer relationship management (CRM) system. If its confidentiality were to be compromised, this would cause significant harm to your company, particularly if the information fell into the hands of your competitors. The system's integrity and availability, on the other hand, would probably not be as critical to your business, so they would be classified as relatively low. The format for describing the security category (SC) of this CRM would be as follows:

$$SC_{CRM} = \{(\textbf{confidentiality}, \textit{high}),(\textbf{integrity}, \textit{low}),(\textbf{availability}, \textit{low})\}$$

SP 800-60 uses three SCs: low impact, moderate impact, and high impact. A low-impact system is defined as an information system in which all three of the security objectives are low. A moderate-impact system is one in which at least one of the security objectives is moderate and no security objective is greater than moderate. Finally, a high-impact system is an information system in which at least one security objective is high. This method of categorization is referred to as the "high water mark" because it uses the highest security objective category to determine the overall category of the system. In our example, the SC of the CRM system would be high because at least one objective (confidentiality) is rated high.

Select

Once you have categorized your systems, it is time to select, and quite possibly tailor, the controls you will use to protect them. The NIST RMF defines three types of security controls: common, system-specific, and hybrid. A *common control* is one that applies to multiple systems and exists outside of their individual boundaries. Following our CRM example, if you placed a web application firewall (WAF) in front of the CRM (and in front of all your other web applications), that would be an example of a common control. The WAF is outside the system boundary of the CRM and protects it and other systems.

System-specific controls, on the other hand, are implemented within the system boundary and, obviously, protect only that specific system. The system owner, and not the broader organization, is responsible for these. An example would be a login page on the CRM that forces the use of Transport Layer Security (TLS) to encrypt the user credentials. If the authentication subsystem was an integral part of the CRM, then this would be an example of an application-specific control.

Wouldn't it be wonderful if everything was black or white, true or false? Alas, the real world is much messier than that. Oftentimes, controls blur the line between common and system-specific and become something else. A *hybrid control*, according to the NIST RMF, is one that is partly common and partly system-specific. Continuing our CRM example, a hybrid control could be security awareness training. There would be a common aspect to the training (e.g., don't share your password) but also some system-specific content (e.g., don't save your customers' information and e-mail it to your personal account so that you can reach out to them while you're on vacation).

The specific controls required to mitigate risks to acceptable levels are documented in the NIST control catalog, NIST SP 800-53, Revision 5, *Security and Privacy Controls for Information Systems and Organizations*. We'll discuss this publication later in this chapter, but for now it is worth noting that it provides a mapping between the impact categories we assigned to information systems in the categorize step of this RMF and specific controls that mitigate risks to those systems.

Implement

There are two key tasks in this step: implementation and documentation. The first part is very straightforward. For example, if you determined in the previous step that you need to add a rule to your WAF to filter out attacks like Structured Query Language (SQL) injection, you implement that rule. Simple. The part with which many of us struggle is the documentation of this change.

The documentation is important for two obvious reasons. First, it allows everyone to understand what controls exist, where, and why. Have you ever inherited a system that is configured in a seemingly nonsensical way? You try to understand why certain parameters or rules exist but hesitate to change them because the system might fail. Likely, this was the result of either improper documentation or (even worse) a successful attack. The second reason why documentation is important is that it allows us to fully integrate the controls into the overall assessment and monitoring plan. Failing to do this invites having controls that quietly become obsolete and ineffective over time and result in undocumented risks.

Assess

The security controls we implement are useful to our overall risk management effort only insofar as we can assess them. It is absolutely essential to our organizations to have a comprehensive plan that assesses all security controls (common, hybrid, and system-specific) with regard to the risks they are meant to address. This plan must be reviewed and approved by the appropriate official(s), and it must be exercised.

To execute an assessment plan, you will, ideally, identify an assessor who is both competent and independent from the team that implemented the controls. This person must act as an honest broker that not only assesses the effectiveness of the controls but also ensures the documentation is appropriate for the task. For this reason, it is important to include all necessary assessment materials in the plan.

The assessment determines whether or not the controls are effective. If they are, then the results are documented in the report so that they are available as references for the next assessment. If the controls are not effective, then the report documents the results, the remediation actions that were taken to address the shortcomings, and the outcome of the reassessment. Finally, the appropriate security plans are updated to include the findings and recommendations of the assessment.

NOTE An assessment of security controls is also called an audit. We discuss audits in detail in Chapter 18.

Authorize

As we already discussed, no system is ever 100 percent risk-free. At this stage in the RMF, we present the results of both our risk and controls assessments to the appropriate decision-maker in order to get approval to connect our information system into our broader architecture and operate it. This person (or group) is legally responsible and accountable for the system while it is operating, and therefore must make a true risk-based decision to allow the system to operate. This person determines whether the risk exposure is acceptable to the organization. This normally requires a review of a plan of action that addresses how and when the organization will deal with the remaining weaknesses and deficiencies in the information system. In many organizations this authorization is given for a set period of time, which is usually specified in a plan of action and milestones (POAM or POA&M).

Monitor

These milestones we just mentioned are a key component of the monitoring or continuous improvement stage of the RMF. At a minimum, we must periodically look at all our controls and determine whether they are still effective. Has the threat changed its tactics, techniques, and procedures (TTPs)? Have new vulnerabilities been discovered? Has an undocumented or unapproved change to our configuration altered our risk equations? These are only some of the issues that we address through ongoing monitoring and continuous improvement.

ISO/IEC 27005

ISO/IEC 27005, updated in 2018, is another widely used information security risk management framework. Similar to the NIST RMF we just discussed, ISO/IEC 27005 provides guidelines for information security risk management in an organization but does not dictate a specific approach for implementing it. In other words, the framework tells us what sorts of things we ought to do, but not how to do them. Similarly to how the NIST RMF can be paired with the security controls in NIST SP 800-53, ISO/IEC 27005 is best used in conjunction with ISO/IEC 27001, which, as we'll see shortly, provides a lot more structure to information security program development.

The risk management process defined by ISO/IEC 27005 is illustrated in Figure 4-2. It all starts with establishing the context in which the risks exist. This is similar to the

Figure 4-2 ISO/IEC 27005 risk management process

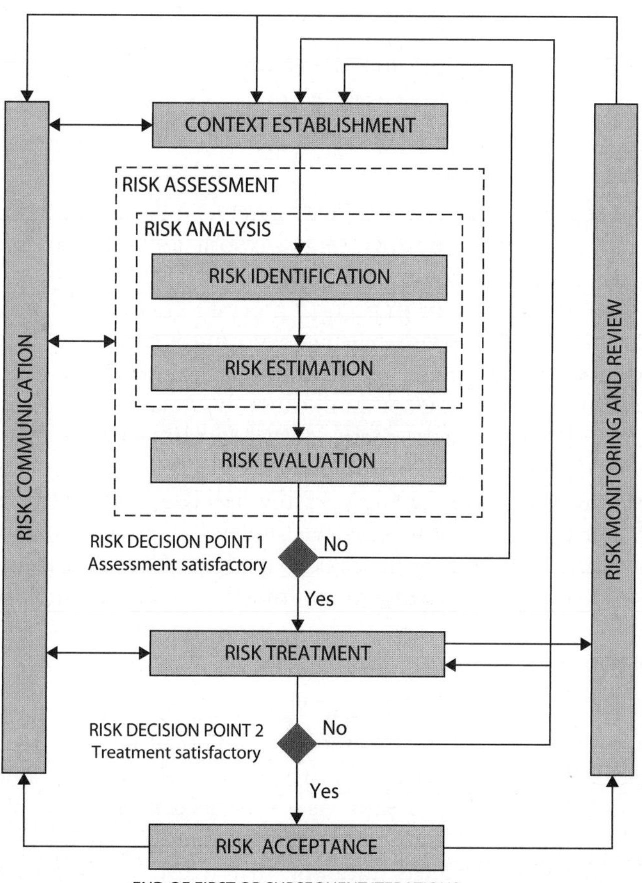

business impact analysis (BIA) we discussed in Chapter 2, but it adds new elements, such as evaluation criteria for risks as well as the organizational risk appetite. The risk assessment box in the middle of the figure should look familiar, since we also discussed this process (albeit with slightly different terms) in Chapter 2.

The risk treatment step is similar to the NIST RMF steps of selecting and implementing controls but is broader in scope. Rather than focusing on controls to mitigate the risks, ISO/IEC 27005 outlines four ways in which the risk can be treated:

- **Mitigate** the risk by implementing controls that bring it to acceptable levels.
- **Accept** the risk and hope it doesn't realize, which assumes that the impact of this risk is less than the cost of treating it.
- **Transfer** the risk to another entity such as an insurance company or a business partner.
- **Avoid** the risk by not implementing the information system that brings it, or by changing business practices so the risk is no longer present or is reduced to acceptable levels.

NOTE The NIST RMF also briefly touches on these treatments in the authorize step of its process.

Risk acceptance in ISO/IEC 27005 is very similar to the authorize step in the NIST RMF, and the risk monitoring steps in both are very similar. A notable difference between these two RMFs, on the other hand, is that ISO/IEC 27005 explicitly identifies risk communication as an important process. This is an essential component of any risk management methodology, since we cannot enlist the help of senior executives, partners, or other stakeholders if we cannot effectively convey our message to a variety of audiences. Just because this communication is not explicitly called out in the NIST RMF or any other RMF, however, doesn't decrease its importance.

As you can see, this framework doesn't really introduce anything new to the risk conversation we've been having over the last two chapters; it just rearranges things a bit. Of course, despite these high-level similarities, the two risk-based frameworks we've discussed differ in how they are implemented. For best results, you should combine ISO/IEC 27005 risk management with an ISO/IEC 27001 security program.

OCTAVE

The Operationally Critical Threat, Asset, and Vulnerability Evaluation (OCTAVE) is not really a framework per se. Rather, it is a methodology for risk assessments developed at Carnegie Mellon University. So, while it falls short of a framework, it is fairly commonly used in the private sector. As a cybersecurity professional, you really should be aware of it and know when it might come in handy.

OCTAVE is self-directed, meaning that it uses a small team of representatives of IT and the business sides of the organization to conduct the analysis. This promotes collaboration on identifying risks and facilitates communication with business leaders on those risks. It also follows the approach of focusing on the most critical assets in risk analysis to prioritize areas of attention. OCTAVE follows the 80/20 Pareto principle, which states that 80 percent of the consequences come from 20 percent of the causes. This highlights one of the key benefits of this methodology, which is its focus on speed based on the fact that, for most businesses, time is money.

This risk assessment methodology is divided into three phases. The first is an organizational view, in which the analysis team defines threat profiles based on assets that are critical to the business. The second phase then looks at the organization's technology infrastructure to identify vulnerabilities that might be exploited by those threats. Finally, in the third phase, the team analyses and classifies individual risks as high, medium, or low and then develops mitigation strategies for each. This classification scheme belies one of the advantages or drawbacks (depending on your perspective) of OCTAVE: it is fundamentally a qualitative approach to assessing risks.

FAIR

If you want to apply a more rigorous, quantitative approach to managing risk, you may want to read up on the Factor Analysis of Information Risk (FAIR), which is a proprietary framework for understanding, analyzing, and measuring information risk. In fact, if you want a quantitative approach, this is pretty much the only international standard framework you can use. Recall that a quantitative approach is one in which risks are reduced to numbers (typically monetary quantities), while a qualitative approach uses categories of risks such as low, medium, and high.

The main premise of FAIR is that we should focus not on possible threats but on probable threats. Thus, its quantitative nature makes a lot of sense. In this framework, risk is defined as the "probable frequency and probable magnitude of future loss," where loss can be quantified as lost productivity, costs of replacement or response, fines, or competitive advantage. Note that each of these can be reduced (perhaps with a bit of work) to monetary quantities. If this approach appeals to you, consider it in conjunction with the discussion of quantitative risk assessment in Chapter 2.

Information Security Frameworks

Armed with the knowledge gained from the risk management frameworks, we are now ready to properly secure our information systems. After all, our main goal is to develop cost-effective defenses that enable our organizations to thrive despite the risks they face. For this reason, most information security frameworks have an explicit tie-in to risk management.

Broadly speaking, information security frameworks can be divided into two categories: those that look holistically at the entire security program, and those that are focused on controls. These are not mutually exclusive, by the way. As we will see, the NIST Cybersecurity Framework is compatible with the NIST SP 800-53 controls. Nor do information security frameworks have to be implemented in a wholesale manner. This is, after all, the beauty of frameworks: we get to pick and choose the parts that make the most sense to us and then tailor those to our specific organizational needs.

Security Program Frameworks

Let's start at the top. A security program is made up of many components: logical, administrative, and physical protection mechanisms (i.e., controls); procedures; business processes; and people. These components all work together to provide a protection level for an environment. Each has an important place in the framework, and if one is missing or incomplete, the whole framework may be affected. The program should work in layers: each layer provides support for the layer above it and protection for the layer below it. Because a security program is a framework, organizations are free to plug in different types of technologies, methods, and procedures to accomplish the necessary protection level for their environment.

A security program based upon a flexible framework sounds great, but how do we build one? Before a fortress is built, the structure is laid out in blueprints by an architect. We need a detailed plan to follow to properly build our security program. Thank goodness industry standards have been developed just for this purpose. Let's take a closer look at two of the most popular information security program frameworks: the ISO/IEC 27000 series and the NIST Cybersecurity Framework.

ISO/IEC 27000 Series

The International Organization for Standardization (ISO) and the International Electrotechnical Commission (IEC) 27000 series serves as industry best practices for the management of security controls in a holistic manner within organizations around the world. The list of standards that makes up this series grows each year. Collectively, these standards describe an information security management system (ISMS), but each standard has a specific focus (such as metrics, governance, auditing, and so on). The currently published ISO/IEC 27000 series of standards (with a bunch of them omitted) include the following:

- **ISO/IEC 27000** Overview and vocabulary
- **ISO/IEC 27001** ISMS requirements
- **ISO/IEC 27002** Code of practice for information security controls
- **ISO/IEC 27003** ISMS implementation guidance
- **ISO/IEC 27004** ISMS monitoring, measurement, analysis, and evaluation
- **ISO/IEC 27005** Information security risk management
- **ISO/IEC 27007** ISMS auditing guidelines
- **ISO/IEC 27014** Information security governance
- **ISO/IEC 27017** Security controls for cloud services
- **ISO/IEC 27019** Security for process control in the energy industry
- **ISO/IEC 27031** Business continuity
- **ISO/IEC 27033** Network security
- **ISO/IEC 27034** Application security
- **ISO/IEC 27035** Incident management

- **ISO/IEC 27037** Digital evidence collection and preservation
- **ISO/IEC 27050** Electronic discovery
- **ISO/IEC 27799** Health organizations

It is common for organizations to seek an ISO/IEC 27001 certification by an accredited third party. The third party assesses the organization against the ISMS requirements laid out in ISO/IEC 27001 and attests to the organization's compliance level. Just as (ISC)² attests to information security professionals' knowledge once they pass the CISSP exam, the third party attests to the security practices within the boundaries of the organization it evaluates.

It is useful to understand the differences between the ISO/IEC 27000 series of standards and how they relate to each other. Figure 4-3 illustrates the differences between general requirements, general guidelines, and sector-specific guidelines.

EXAM TIP You don't have to memorize the entire ISO/IEC 27000 series of standards. You just need to be aware of them.

As you probably realize, ISO 27001 is the most important of these standards for most organizations. It is not enough to simply purchase the document and implement it in your environment; you actually need an external party (called a Certification Body) to audit you and certify that you are in compliance with the standard. This ISO 27001 certification is useful to demonstrate to your customers and partners that you are not a security risk to them, which in some cases can be a contractual obligation. Additionally,

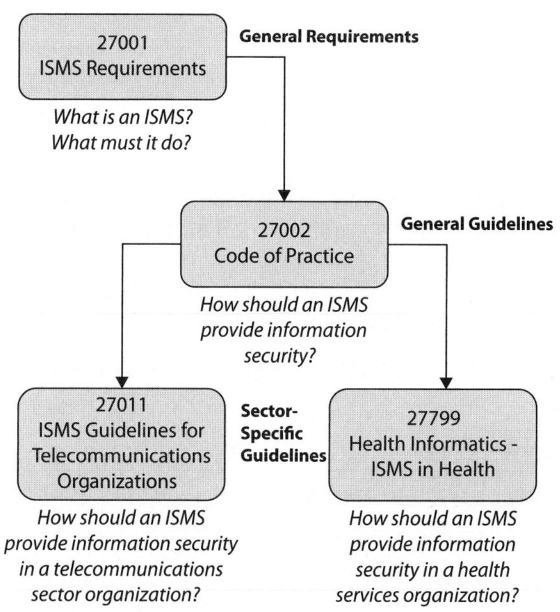

Figure 4-3 How ISO/IEC 27000 standards relate to each other

this certification can help avoid regulatory fines by proving that the organization practices due diligence in protecting its information systems. The certification process can take a year or longer (depending on how mature your security program is), but for many medium and large business, it is worth the investment.

NIST Cybersecurity Framework

On February 12, 2013, U.S. President Barack Obama signed Executive Order 13636, calling for the development of a voluntary cybersecurity framework for organizations that are part of the critical infrastructure. The goal of this construct was for it to be flexible, repeatable, and cost-effective so that it could be prioritized for better alignment with business processes and goals. A year to the day later, NIST published the "Framework for Improving Critical Infrastructure Cybersecurity," commonly called the Cybersecurity Framework, which was the result of a collaborative process with members of the government, industry, and academia. The Cybersecurity Framework is divided into three main components:

- **Framework Core** Consists of the various activities, outcomes, and references common to all organizations. These are broken down into five functions, 22 categories, and 98 subcategories.
- **Implementation Tiers** Categorize the degree of rigor and sophistication of cybersecurity practices, which can be Partial (tier 1), Risk Informed (tier 2), Repeatable (tier 3), or Adaptive (tier 4). The goal is not to force an organization to move to a higher tier, but rather to inform its decisions so that it can do so if it makes business sense.
- **Framework Profile** Describes the state of an organization with regard to the Cybersecurity Framework categories and subcategories. A Framework Profile enables decision-makers to compare the "as-is" situation to one or more "to-be" possibilities, so that they can align cybersecurity and business priorities and processes in ways that make sense to that particular organization. An organization's Framework Profile is tailorable based on the requirements of the industry segment within which it operates and the organization's needs.

The Framework Core practices organize cybersecurity activities into five higher-level functions with which you should be familiar. Everything we do can be aligned with one of these:

- **Identify** Understand your organization's business context, resources, and risks.
- **Protect** Develop appropriate controls to mitigate risk in ways that make sense.
- **Detect** Discover in a timely manner anything that threatens your security.
- **Respond** Quickly contain the effects of anything that threatens your security.
- **Recover** Return to a secure state that enables business activities after an incident.

EXAM TIP For the exam, you should remember the five functions of the NIST Cybersecurity Framework and the fact that it is voluntary.

Security Control Frameworks

Up to now we have reviewed the ISO/IEC 27000 series and the NIST CSF, both of which outline the necessary components of an organizational security program. Now we are going to get more focused and look at the objectives of the controls we are going to put into place to accomplish the goals outlined in our security program and enterprise architecture. This is where security control frameworks come in handy. This section presents three popular frameworks: NIST SP 800-53, CIS Controls, and COBIT.

NIST SP 800-53

One of the standards that NIST has been responsible for developing is SP 800-53, *Security and Privacy Controls for Information Systems and Organizations*, currently in its fifth revision (Rev. 5). It outlines controls that agencies need to put into place to be compliant with the Federal Information Processing Standards (FIPS). It is worth noting that, although this publication is aimed at federal government organizations, many other organizations have voluntarily adopted it to help them better secure their systems.

Basically, SP 800-53 provides specific guidance on how to select security controls. It prescribes a four-step process for applying controls:

1. Select the appropriate security control baselines.
2. Tailor the baselines.
3. Document the security control selection process.
4. Apply the controls.

The first step assumes that you have already determined the security categories (SCs) of your information systems based on criticality and sensitivity of the information to be processed, stored, or transmitted by those systems. SP 800-53 uses three SCs: low impact, moderate impact, and high impact. If this sounds familiar, that's because we discussed this categorization earlier in this chapter when we covered the NIST RMF and SP 800-60.

This exercise in categorizing your information systems is important because it enables you to prioritize your work. It also determines which of the more than 1,000 controls listed in SP 800-53 you need to apply to it. These controls are broken down into 20 families. Table 4-1 outlines the control categories that are addressed in SP 800-53, Rev. 5.

Let's circle back to the example of the customer relationship management system we used when discussing the NIST RMF. Recall that we determined that the CRM's SC was high because the impact of a loss of confidentiality was high. We can go through the entire catalog of controls and see which of them apply to this hypothetical CRM. In the

ID	Family	ID	Family
AC	Access Control	PE	Physical and Environmental Protection
AT	Awareness and Training	PL	Planning
AU	Audit and Accountability	PM	Program Management
CA	Assessment, Authorization, and Monitoring	PS	Personnel Security
CM	Configuration Management	PT	PII Processing and Transparency
CP	Contingency Planning	RA	Risk Assessment
IA	Identification and Authentication	SA	System and Services Acquisition
IR	Incident Response	SC	System and Communications Protection
MA	Maintenance	SI	System and Information Integrity
MP	Media Protection	SR	Supply Chain Risk Management

Table 4-1 NIST SP 800-53 Control Categories

interest of brevity, we will only look at the first three controls (IR-1, IR-2, and IR-3) in the Incident Response, or IR family. You can see in Table 4-2 how these controls apply to the different SCs. Since the CRM is SC high, all three controls are required for it. You can also see that IR-2 and IR-3 have control enhancements listed.

Let's dive into the first control and see how we would use it. Chapter 3 of SP 800-53 is a catalog that describes in detail what each security control is. If we go to the description

Control No.	Control Name *CONTROL ENHANCEMENT NAME*	Control Baselines Low	 Mod.	 High
IR-1	Policy and Procedures	X	X	X
IR-2	Incident Response Training	X	X	X
IR-2(1)	*Simulated Events*			X
IR-2(2)	*Automated Training Environments*			X
IR-2(3)	*Breach*			
IR-3	Incident Response Testing		X	X
IR-3(1)	*Automated Testing*			
IR-3(2)	*Coordination with Related Plans*		X	X

Table 4-2 Sample Mapping of Security Controls to the Three Security Categories in SP 800-53

of the baseline IR-1 (Incident Response Policy and Procedures) control, we see that it requires that the organization do the following:

- **a.** Develop, document, and disseminate to [*Assignment: organization-defined personnel or roles*]:
  - **1.** [*Selection (one or more): Organization-level; Mission/business process-level; System-level*] incident response policy that:
    - **(a.)** Addresses purpose, scope, roles, responsibilities, management commitment, coordination among organizational entities, and compliance; and
    - **(b.)** Is consistent with applicable laws, executive orders, directives, regulations, policies, standards, and guidelines; and
  - **2.** Procedures to facilitate the implementation of the incident response policy and associated incident response controls;
- **b.** Designate an [*Assignment: organization-defined official*] to manage the development, documentation, and dissemination of the incident response policy and procedures; and
- **c.** Review and update the current incident response:
  - **1.** Policy [*Assignment: organization-defined frequency*] and following [*Assignment: organization-defined events*]; and
  - **2.** Procedures [*Assignment: organization-defined frequency*] and following [*Assignment: organization-defined events*].

Notice that there are assignments in square brackets in five of these requirements. These are parameters that enable an organization to tailor the baseline controls to its own unique conditions and needs. For example, in the first assignment (IR-1.a), we could specify who receives the policies and procedures; in the second (IR-1.a.1), we could specify the level(s) at which the incident response policy applies; in the third (IR-1.b), we could identify the individual (by role, not name) responsible for the policy; and in the last two assignments (IR-1.c.1 and IR-1.c.2), we could provide the frequency and triggering events for policy and procedure reviews. This is all a "fill in the blanks" approach to tailoring the controls to meet your organization's unique conditions.

EXAM TIP You do not need to memorize the controls, control enhancements, or assignments of NIST SP 800-53. We provide them here to illustrate how a framework provides structure while still allowing you room to customize it.

CIS Controls

The Center for Internet Security (CIS) is a nonprofit organization that, among other things, maintains a list of 20 critical security controls designed to mitigate the threat of the majority of common cyberattacks. It is another example (together with NIST SP 800-53) of a controls framework. The CIS Controls, currently in Version 7.1, are shown in Figure 4-4.

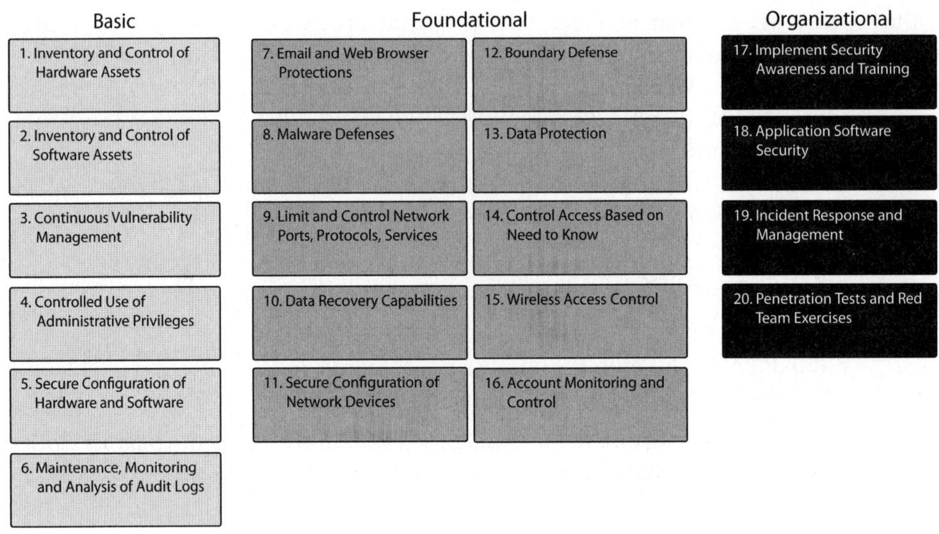

Figure 4-4 CIS Controls

Despite CIS's use of the word "controls," you should really think of these like the 20 families of controls in SP 800-53. Under these 20 controls, there are a total of 171 subcontrols that have similar granularity as those established by the NIST. For example, if we look into control 13 (Data Protection), we can see the nine subcontrols listed in Table 4-3.

Subcontrol	Title	IG1	IG2	IG3
13.1	Maintain an Inventory of Sensitive Information	X	X	X
13.2	Remove Sensitive Data or Systems Not Regularly Accessed by Organization	X	X	X
13.3	Monitor and Block Unauthorized Network Traffic			X
13.4	Only Allow Access to Authorized Cloud Storage or Email Providers		X	X
13.5	Monitor and Detect Any Unauthorized Use of Encryption			X
13.6	Encrypt Mobile Device Data	X	X	X
13.7	Manage USB Devices		X	X
13.8	Manage System's External Removable Media's Read/Write Configurations			X
13.9	Encrypt Data on USB Storage Devices			X

Table 4-3 Data Protection Subcontrols Mapped to Implementation Groups

The CIS recognizes that not every organization will have the resources (or face the risks) necessary to implement all controls. For this reason, they are grouped into three categories, listed next. While every organization should strive for full implementation, this approach provides a way to address the most urgent requirements first and then build on them over time.

- **Basic** These key controls should be implemented by every organization to achieve minimum essential security.
- **Foundational** These controls embody technical best practices to improve an organization's security.
- **Organizational** These controls focus on people and processes to maintain and improve cybersecurity.

A useful tool to help organizations match their implementation of controls to their resource levels are implementation groups (IGs). Version 7.1 of the CIS controls describes the following three IGs:

- **Implementation Group 1** Small to medium-sized organizations with limited IT and cybersecurity expertise whose principal concern is to keep the business operational. The sensitivity of the data that they are trying to protect is low and principally surrounds employee and financial information.
- **Implementation Group 2** Larger organizations with multiple departments, including one responsible for managing and protecting IT infrastructure. Small organizational units. These organizations often store and process sensitive client or company information and may have regulatory compliance burdens. A major concern is loss of public confidence if a breach occurs.
- **Implementation Group 3** Large organizations that employ security experts with different specialty areas. Their systems and data contain sensitive information or functions that are subject to regulatory and compliance oversight. Successful attacks against these organizations can cause significant harm to the public welfare.

You can see in Table 4-3 how subcontrols can be mapped to these implementation groups. This helps ensure that limited resources are focused on the most critical requirements.

COBIT 2019

COBIT 2019 (the name used to be an acronym for Control Objectives for Information Technologies) is a framework for governance and management developed by ISACA (which formerly stood for the Information Systems Audit and Control Association) and the IT Governance Institute (ITGI). It helps organizations optimize the value of their IT by balancing resource utilization, risk levels, and realization of benefits. This is all done by explicitly tying stakeholder drivers to stakeholder needs to organizational goals (to meet those needs) to IT goals (to meet or support the organizational goals). It is a holistic approach based on six key principles of governance systems:

1. Provide stakeholder value
2. Holistic approach

3. Dynamic governance system
4. Governance distinct from management
5. Tailored to enterprise needs
6. End-to-end governance system

Everything in COBIT is ultimately linked to the stakeholders through a series of transforms called cascading goals. The concept is pretty simple. At any point in our IT governance or management processes, we should be able to ask the question "why are we doing this?" and be led to an IT goal that is tied to an enterprise goal, which is in turn tied to a stakeholder need. COBIT specifies 13 enterprise and 13 alignment goals that take the guesswork out of ensuring we consider all dimensions in our decision-making processes.

These two sets of 13 goals are different but related. They ensure that we are aligned with the sixth principle of covering the enterprise end to end by explicitly tying enterprise and IT goals in both the governance and management dimensions, which is the fourth principle. These goals were identified by looking for commonalities (or perhaps universal features) of a large set of organizations. The purpose of this analysis is to enable a holistic approach, which is the second key principle in COBIT.

The COBIT framework includes, but differentiates, enterprise governance and management. The difference between these two is that governance is a set of higher-level processes aimed at balancing the stakeholder value proposition, while management is the set of activities that achieve enterprise objectives. As a simplifying approximation, you can think of governance as the things that the C-suite leaders do and management as the things that the other organizational leaders do. Figure 4-5 illustrates how the

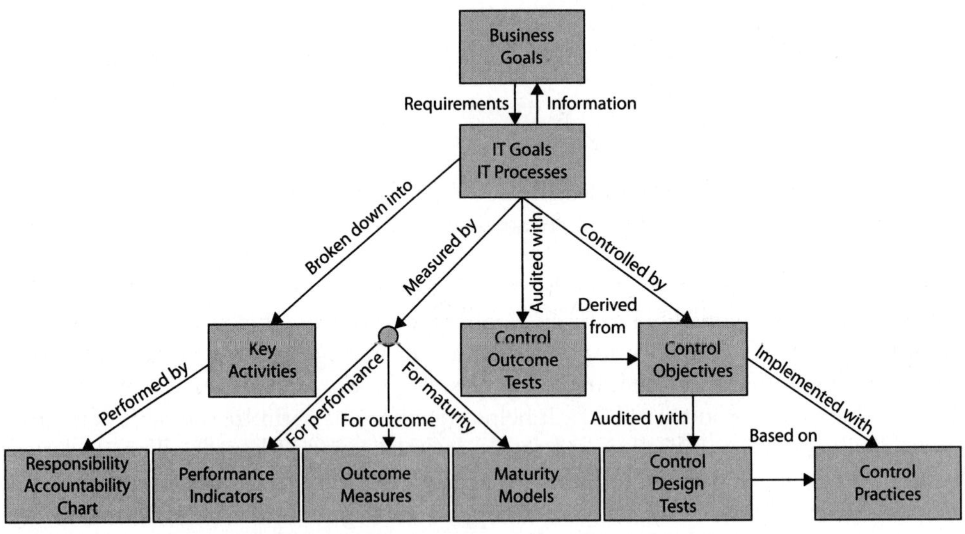

Figure 4-5 COBIT framework

five governance and 35 management objectives defined by COBIT are organized into five domains. Governance objectives all fall within the Evaluate, Direct and Monitor (EDM) domain. Management objectives, on the other hand, fall into four domains: Align, Plan and Organize (APO), Build, Acquire and Implement (BAI), Deliver, Service and Support (DSS), and Monitor, Evaluate and Assess (MEA).

A majority of the security compliance auditing practices used today in the industry are based off of COBIT. So if you want to make your auditors happy and pass your compliance evaluations, you should learn, practice, and implement the control objectives outlined in COBIT, which are considered industry best practices.

TIP Many people in the security industry mistakenly assume that COBIT is purely security focused, when in reality it deals with all aspects of information technology, security being only one component. COBIT is a set of practices that can be followed to carry out IT governance, which requires proper security practices.

Enterprise Architecture Frameworks

Organizations have a choice when attempting to secure their environment as a whole. They can just toss in products here and there, which are referred to as point solutions or stovepipe solutions, and hope the ad hoc approach magically works in a manner that secures the environment evenly and covers all of the organization's vulnerabilities. Most organizations, particularly small and medium businesses, don't start with a secure architecture. Instead, they focus on their core business, get just enough security to survive, and adjust things as they grow. This organic growth model lends itself to short-term measures that result in a "constantly putting out fires" approach. It is usually easier and cheaper for senior management to approve money for a new security tool than to approve the time, money, and business disruption needed to re-architect an information system to properly secure it.

The second approach to securing an organization's environment would be to define an enterprise security architecture, allow it to be the guide when implementing solutions to ensure business needs are met, provide standard protection across the environment, and reduce the number of security surprises the organization will run into. The catch is that if a company has been following the first ad hoc approach for a while, it can be very challenging (and expensive) to rebuild its infrastructure without causing pain to a lot of people. Although implementing an enterprise security architecture does not necessarily promise pure utopia, it does tame the chaos and gets the security staff and organization into a more proactive and mature mindset when dealing with security as a whole.

Developing an architecture from scratch is not an easy task. Sure, it is easy to draw a big box with smaller boxes inside of it, but what do the boxes represent? What are the relationships between the boxes? How does information flow between the boxes? Who needs to view these boxes, and what aspects of the boxes do they need for decision making? An architecture is a conceptual construct. It is a tool to help individuals understand a complex item (such as an enterprise) in digestible chunks. An example of an architecture is the Open Systems Interconnection (OSI) networking model, an abstract model used to illustrate the architecture of a networking stack. A networking stack within a computer is very complex because it has so many protocols, interfaces, services, and hardware specifications. But when we think about it in a modular framework (the OSI seven layers), we can better understand the network stack as a whole and the relationships between the individual components that make it up.

NOTE The OSI network stack will be covered extensively in Chapter 11.

An *enterprise architecture* encompasses the essential and unifying components of an organization. It expresses the enterprise structure (form) and behavior (function). It embodies the enterprise's components, their relationships to each other, and their relationships to the environment.

This section covers several different enterprise architecture frameworks. Each framework has its own specific focus, but they all provide guidance on how to build individual architectures so that they are useful tools to a diverse set of individuals. Notice the difference between an architecture *framework* and an actual architecture. You use the framework as a guideline on how to build an architecture that best fits your company's needs. Each company's architecture will be different because companies have different business drivers, security and regulatory requirements, cultures, and organizational structures—but if each starts with the same architecture *framework*, then their architectures will have similar structures and goals. It is similar to three people starting with a ranch-style house blueprint. One person chooses to have four bedrooms built because they have three children, one person chooses to have a larger living room and three bedrooms, and the other person chooses two bedrooms and two living rooms. Each person started with the same blueprint (framework) and modified it to meet their needs (architecture).

When developing an architecture, first the *stakeholders* need to be identified, the people who will be looking at and using the architecture. Next, the *views* need to be developed, which is how the information that is most important to the different stakeholders will be illustrated in the most useful manner. The NIST developed a framework, illustrated in Figure 4-6, that shows that companies have several different viewpoints. Executives need to understand the company from a business point of view, business process developers need to understand what type of information needs to be collected to support business activities, application developers need to understand system requirements that maintain and process the information, data modelers need to know how to structure data elements, and the technology group needs to understand the network components required to support the layers above it. They are all looking at an architecture of the same company; it is just being presented in views that they understand and that directly relate to their responsibilities within the organization.

An enterprise architecture enables you to not only understand the company from several different views, but also understand how a change that takes place at one level will affect items at other levels. For example, if there is a new business requirement, how is it going to be supported at each level of the enterprise? What type of new information must

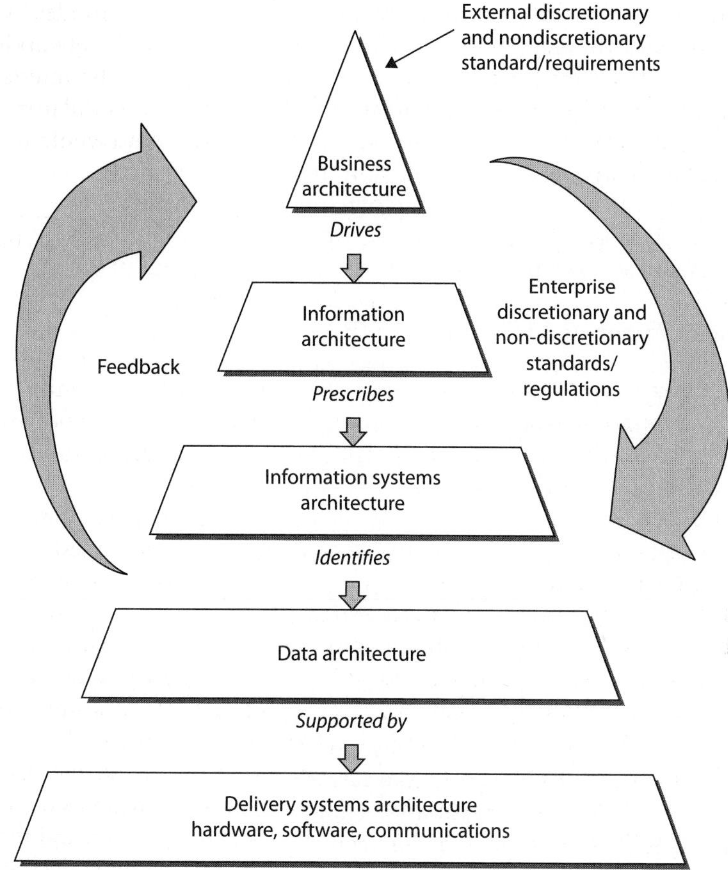

Figure 4-6 NIST enterprise architecture framework

be collected and processed? Do new applications need to be purchased or current ones modified? Are new data elements required? Will new networking devices be required? An architecture enables you to understand all the things that will need to change just to support one new business function.

The architecture can be used in the opposite direction also. If a company is looking to do a technology refresh, will the new systems still support all of the necessary functions in the layers above the technology level? An architecture enables you to understand an organization as one complete organism and identify how changes to one internal component can directly affect another one.

Why Do We Need Enterprise Architecture Frameworks?

As you have probably experienced, business people and technology people sometimes seem like totally different species. Business people use terms like "net profits," "risk universes," "portfolio strategy," "hedging," "commodities," and so on. Technology people use terms like "deep packet inspection," "layer three devices," "cross-site scripting," "load balancing," and so forth. Think about the acronyms techies like us throw around—TCP, APT, ICMP, RAID, UDP, L2TP, PPTP, IPSec, and AES. We can have complete conversations between ourselves without using any real words. And even though business people and technology people use some of the same words, they have totally different meanings to the individual groups. To business people, a protocol is a set of approved processes that must be followed to accomplish a task. To technical people, a protocol is a standardized manner of communication between computers or applications. Business and technical people use the term "risk," but each group is focusing on very different risks a company can face—market share versus security breaches. And even though each group uses the term "data" the same, business people look at data only from a functional point of view and security people look at data from a risk point of view.

This divide between business perspectives and technology perspectives not only can cause confusion and frustration—it commonly costs money. If the business side of the house wants to offer customers a new service, as in paying bills online, there may have to be extensive changes to the current network infrastructure, applications, web servers, software logic, cryptographic functions, authentication methods, database structures, and so on. What seems to be a small change in a business offering can cost a lot of money when it comes to adding up the new technology that needs to be purchased and implemented, programming that needs to be carried out, re-architecting of networks, and the like. It is common for business people to feel as though the IT department is more of an impediment when it comes to business evolution and growth, and in turn the IT department feels as though the business people are constantly coming up with outlandish and unrealistic demands with no supporting budgets.

This type of confusion between business and technology people has caused organizations around the world to implement incorrect solutions because they did not understand the business functionality to technical specifications requirements. This results in having to repurchase new solutions, carry out rework, and waste an amazing amount of time. Not only does this cost the organization more money than it should have in the first place, business opportunities may be lost, which can reduce market share. So we need a tool that both business people and technology people can use to reduce confusion, optimize business functionality, and not waste time and money. This is where business enterprise architectures come into play. They allow both groups (business and technology) to view the same organization in ways that make sense to them.

When you go to the doctor's office, there is a poster of a skeleton system on one wall, a poster of a circulatory system on the other wall, and another poster of the organs that make up a human body. These are all different views of the same thing, the human body. This is the same functionality that enterprise architecture frameworks provide: different views of the same thing. In the medical field we have specialists (podiatrists, brain surgeons, dermatologists, oncologists, ophthalmologists, etc.). Each organization is also made up of its own specialists (HR, marketing, accounting, IT, R&D, management, etc.). But there also has to be an understanding of the entity (whether it is a human body or company) holistically, which is what an enterprise architecture attempts to accomplish.

Zachman Framework

One of the first enterprise architecture frameworks that was created is the *Zachman Framework*, created by John Zachman. This model is generic, and is well suited to frame the work we do in information systems security. A sample (though fairly simplified) representation is depicted in Table 4-4.

Perspective (Audience)	Interrogatives					
	What	How	Where	Who	When	Why
Contextual (Executives)	Assets and Liabilities	Business Lines	Business Locales	Partners, Clients, and Employees	Milestones and Major Events	Business Strategy
Conceptual (Business Mgrs.)	Products	Business Processes	Logistics and Communications	Workflows	Master Calendar	Business Plan
Architectural (System Architects)	Data Models	Systems Architectures	Distributed Systems Architectures	Use Cases	Project Schedules	Business Rule Models
Technological (Engineers)	Data Management	Systems Designs	System Interfaces	Human Interfaces	Process Controls	Process Outputs
Implementation (Technicians)	Data Stores	Programs	Network Nodes and Links	Access Controls	Network/ Security Operations	Performance Metrics
Enterprise	Information	Functions	Networks	Organizations	Schedules	Strategies

Table 4-4 Zachman Framework for Enterprise Architecture

The Zachman Framework is a two-dimensional model that uses six basic communication interrogatives (What, How, Where, Who, When, and Why) intersecting with different perspectives (Executives, Business Managers, System Architects, Engineers, Technicians, and Enterprise-wide) to give a holistic understanding of the enterprise. This framework was developed in the 1980s and is based on the principles of classical business architecture that contain rules that govern an ordered set of relationships. One of these rules is that each row should describe the enterprise completely from that row's perspective. For example, IT personnel's jobs require them to see the organization in terms of data stores, programs, networks, access controls, operations, and metrics. Though they are (or at least should be) aware of other perspectives and items, the performance of their duties in the example organization is focused on these items.

The goal of this framework is to be able to look at the same organization from different viewpoints. Different groups within a company need the same information, but presented in ways that directly relate to their responsibilities. A CEO needs financial statements, scorecards, and balance sheets. A network administrator needs network schematics, a systems engineer needs interface requirements, and the operations department needs configuration requirements. If you have ever carried out a network-based vulnerability test, you know that you cannot tell the CEO that some systems are vulnerable to time-of-check to time-of-use (TOC/TOU) attacks or that the company software allows for client-side browser injections. The CEO needs to know this information, but in a language she can understand. People at each level of the organization need information in a language and format that are most useful to them.

A business enterprise architecture is used to optimize often fragmented processes (both manual and automated) into an integrated environment that is responsive to change and supportive of the business strategy. The Zachman Framework has been around for many years and has been used by many organizations to build or better define their business environment. This framework is not security oriented, but it is a good template to work with because it offers direction on how to understand an actual enterprise in a modular fashion.

The Open Group Architecture Framework

Another enterprise architecture framework is *The Open Group Architecture Framework (TOGAF)*, which has its origins in the U.S. Department of Defense. It provides an approach to design, implement, and govern an enterprise information architecture.

TOGAF is a framework that can be used to develop the following architecture types:

- Business architecture
- Data architecture
- Applications architecture
- Technology architecture

TOGAF can be used to create these individual architecture types through the use of its *Architecture Development Method (ADM)*. This method is an iterative and cyclic process that allows requirements to be continuously reviewed and the individual architectures to be updated as needed. These different architectures can allow a technology architect to understand the enterprise from four different views (business, data, application, and technology) so she can ensure her team develops the necessary technology to work within the environment and all the components that make up that environment and meet business requirements. The technology may need to span many different types of networks, interconnect with various software components, and work within different business units. As an analogy, when a new city is being constructed, people do not just start building houses here and there. Civil engineers lay out roads, bridges, waterways, and zones for commercial and residential development. A large organization that has a distributed and heterogeneous environment that supports many different business functions can be as complex as a city. So before a programmer starts developing code, the architecture of the software needs to be developed in the context of the organization it will work within.

NOTE Many technical people have a negative visceral reaction to models like TOGAF. They feel it's too much work, that it's a lot of fluff, is not directly relevant, and so on. If you handed the same group of people a network schematic with firewalls, IDSs, and virtual private networks (VPNs), they would say, "Now we're talking about security!" Security technology works within the construct of an organization, so the organization must be understood also.

Military-Oriented Architecture Frameworks

It is hard enough to construct enterprise-wide solutions and technologies for one organization—think about an architecture that has to span many different complex government agencies to allow for interoperability and proper hierarchical communication channels. This is where the *Department of Defense Architecture Framework (DoDAF)* comes into play. When the U.S. DoD purchases technology products and weapon systems, enterprise architecture documents must be created based upon DoDAF standards to illustrate how they will properly integrate into the current infrastructures. The focus of the architecture framework is on command, control, communications, computers, intelligence, surveillance, and reconnaissance systems and processes. It is not only important that these different devices communicate using the same protocol types and interoperable software components but also that they use the same data elements. If an image is captured from a spy satellite, downloaded to a centralized data repository, and then loaded into a piece of software to direct an unmanned drone, the military personnel cannot have their operations interrupted because one piece of software cannot read another software's data output. The DoDAF helps ensure that all systems, processes, and personnel work in a concerted effort to accomplish its missions.

NOTE While DoDAF was developed to support mainly military missions, it has been expanded upon and morphed for use in business enterprise environments.

When attempting to figure out which architecture framework is best for your organization, you need to find out who the stakeholders are and what information they need from the architecture. The architecture needs to represent the company in the most useful manner to the people who need to understand it the best. If your company has people (stakeholders) who need to understand the company from a business process perspective, your architecture needs to provide that type of view. If there are people who need to understand the company from an application perspective, your architecture needs a view that illustrates that information. If people need to understand the enterprise from a security point of view, that needs to be illustrated in a specific view. So one main difference between the various enterprise architecture frameworks is what type of information they provide and how they provide it.

Other Frameworks

Along with ensuring that we have the proper controls in place, we also want to have ways to construct and improve our business, IT, and security processes in a structured and controlled manner. The security controls can be considered the "things," and processes are how we use these things. We want to use them properly, effectively, and efficiently.

ITIL

ITIL (formerly the *Information Technology Infrastructure Library)* was developed in the 1980s by the UK's Central Computer and Telecommunications Agency (which was subsumed in the late 1990s by the now defunct Office of Government Commerce). ITIL is now controlled by AXELOS, which is a joint venture between the government of the UK and the private firm Capita. ITIL is the de facto standard of best practices for IT service management. ITIL was created because of the increased dependence on information technology to meet business needs. Unfortunately, as previously discussed, a natural divide exists between business people and IT people in most organizations because they use different terminology and have different focuses within the organization. The lack of a common language and understanding of each other's domain (business versus IT) has caused many companies to ineffectively blend their business objectives and IT functions. This improper blending usually generates confusion, miscommunication, missed deadlines, missed opportunities, increased cost in time and labor, and frustration on both the business and technical sides of the house.

ITIL blends all parts of an organization using a four-dimensional model built around the concept of value for the stakeholders. The dimensions in this model, illustrated in Figure 4-7, are organizations and people, value streams and processes, information and technology, and partners and suppliers. These exist in a broader context that is influenced by factors that can be political, economic, social, technological, legal, or environmental. Effective organizations must consider all four dimensions within their broader context when planning, developing, and offering products and/or services if they are to provide value.

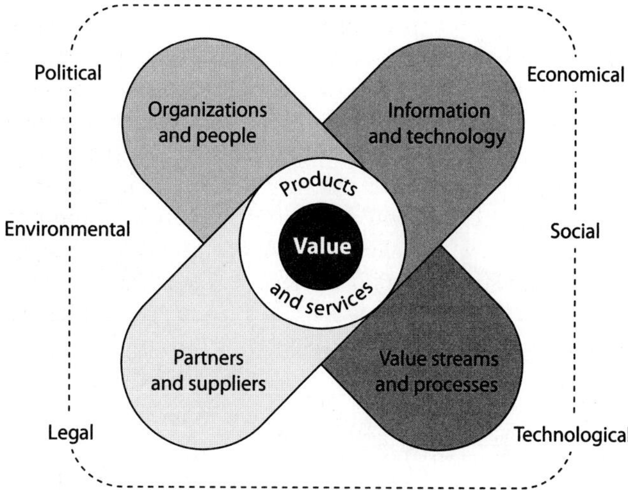

Figure 4-7 ITIL

Six Sigma

Six Sigma is a process improvement methodology. Its goal is to improve process quality by using statistical methods of measuring operation efficiency and reducing variation, defects, and waste. Six Sigma is being used in the security assurance industry in some instances to measure the success factors of different controls and procedures. Six Sigma was developed by Motorola with the goal of identifying and removing defects in its manufacturing processes. The maturity of a process is described by a sigma rating, which indicates the percentage of defects that the process contains. While it started in manufacturing, Six Sigma has been applied to many types of business functions, including information security and assurance.

Capability Maturity Model

While we know that we constantly need to make our security program better, it is not always easy to accomplish because "better" is a vague and nonquantifiable concept. The only way we can really improve is to know where we are starting from, where we need to go, and the steps we need to take in between. Every security program has a maturity level, which could range from nonexistent to highly optimized. In between these two extremes, there are different levels. An example of a Capability Maturity Model (CMM) is illustrated in Figure 4-8. Each maturity level within this model represents an evolutionary stage. Some security programs are chaotic, ad hoc, unpredictable, and usually insecure. Some security programs have documentation created, but the actual processes are not taking place. Some security programs are quite evolved, streamlined, efficient, and effective.

EXAM TIP The CISSP exam puts more emphasis on CMM compared to ITIL and Six Sigma because it is more heavily used in the security industry.

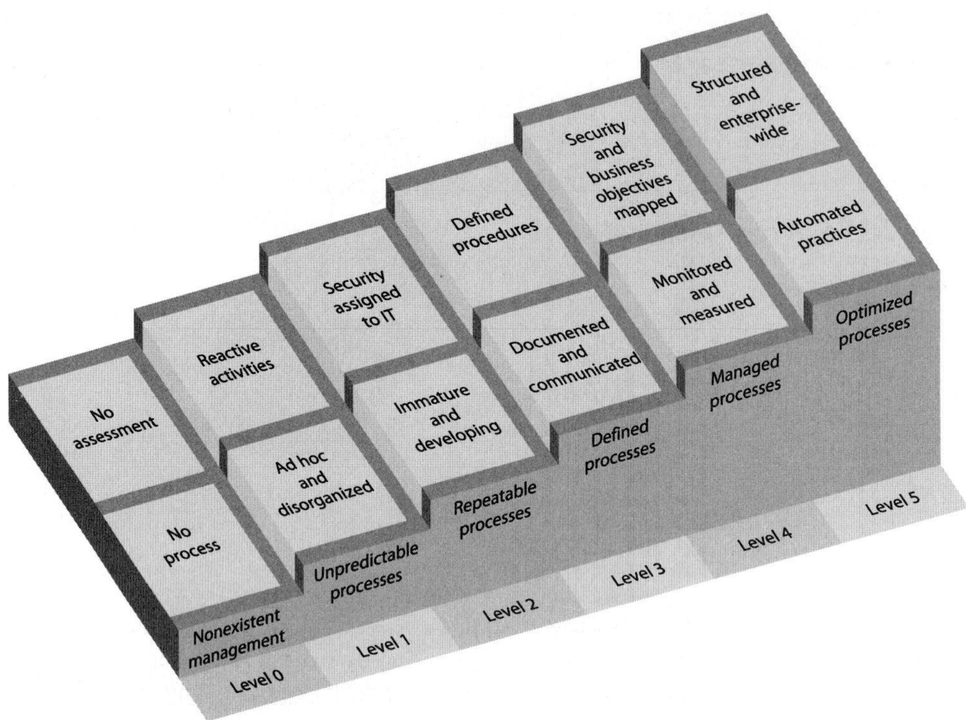

Figure 4-8 Capability Maturity Model for a security program

Security Program Development

No organization is going to put all the previously listed items (NIST RMF, OCTAVE, FAIR, ISO/IEC 27000, NIST CSF, NIST SP 800-53, CIS Controls, COBIT 2019, Zachman Framework, ITIL, Six Sigma, CMM) into place. But it is a good toolbox of things you can pull from, and you will find some fit the organization you work in better than others. You will also find that as your organization's security program matures, you will see more clearly where these various standards, frameworks, and management components come into play. While these items are separate and distinct, there are basic things that need to be built in for any security program and its corresponding controls. This is because the basic tenets of security are universal no matter if they are being deployed in a corporation, government agency, business, school, or nonprofit organization. Each entity is made up of people, processes, data, and technology, and each of these things needs to be protected.

Top-Down Approach

A security program should use a top-down approach, meaning that the initiation, support, and direction come from top management; work their way through middle management; and then reach staff members. In contrast, a bottom-up approach refers to a situation in which staff members (usually IT) try to develop a security program without getting proper management support and direction. A bottom-up approach is commonly less effective, not broad enough to address all security risks, and doomed to fail. A top-down approach makes sure the people actually responsible for protecting the company's assets (senior management) are driving the program. Senior management are not only ultimately responsible for the protection of the organization but also hold the purse strings for the necessary funding, have the authority to assign needed resources, and are the only ones who can ensure true enforcement of the stated security rules and policies. Management's support is one of the most important pieces of a security program. A simple nod and a wink will not provide the amount of support required.

The crux of CMM is to develop structured steps that can be followed so an organization can evolve from one level to the next and constantly improve its processes and security posture. A security program contains a lot of elements, and it is not fair to expect every part to be properly implemented within the first year of its existence. And some components, as in forensics capabilities, really cannot be put into place until some rudimentary pieces are established, as in incident management. So if we really want our baby to be able to run, we have to lay out ways that it can first learn to walk.

Putting It All Together

While the cores of these various security standards and frameworks are similar, it is important to understand that a security program has a life cycle that is always continuing, because it should be constantly evaluated and improved upon. The life cycle of any process can be described in different ways. We will use the following steps:

1. Plan and organize
2. Implement
3. Operate and maintain
4. Monitor and evaluate

Without setting up a life-cycle approach to a security program and the security management that maintains the program, an organization is doomed to treat security as merely another project. Anything treated as a project has a start and stop date, and at the stop date everyone disperses to other projects. Many organizations have had good intentions in their security program kickoffs, but do not implement the proper structure to ensure that security management is an ongoing and continually improving process. The result is a lot of starts and stops over the years and repetitive work that costs more than it should, with diminishing results.

The main components of each phase are provided here.

Plan and Organize:

- Establish management commitment.
- Establish oversight steering committee.
- Assess business drivers.
- Develop a threat profile on the organization.
- Carry out a risk assessment.
- Develop security architectures at business, data, application, and infrastructure levels.
- Identify solutions per architecture level.
- Obtain management approval to move forward.

Implement:

- Assign roles and responsibilities.
- Develop and implement security policies, procedures, standards, baselines, and guidelines.
- Identify sensitive data at rest and in transit.
- Implement the following blueprints:
    - Asset identification and management
    - Risk management
    - Vulnerability management
    - Compliance
    - Identity management and access control
    - Change control
    - Software development life cycle
    - Business continuity planning
    - Awareness and training
    - Physical security
    - Incident response
- Implement solutions (administrative, technical, physical) per blueprint.
- Develop auditing and monitoring solutions per blueprint.
- Establish goals, SLAs, and metrics per blueprint.

Operate and Maintain:

- Follow procedures to ensure all baselines are met in each implemented blueprint.
- Carry out internal and external audits.
- Carry out tasks outlined per blueprint.
- Manage SLAs per blueprint.

Monitor and Evaluate:

- Review logs, audit results, collected metric values, and SLAs per blueprint.
- Assess goal accomplishments per blueprint.
- Carry out quarterly meetings with steering committees.
- Develop improvement steps and integrate into the Plan and Organize phase.

Many of the items mentioned in the previous list are covered throughout this book. This list is provided to show how all of these items can be rolled out in a sequential and controllable manner.

Although the previously covered standards and frameworks are very helpful, they are also very high level. For example, if a standard simply states that an organization must secure its data, a great amount of work will be called for. This is where the security professional really rolls up her sleeves, by developing security blueprints. *Blueprints* are important tools to identify, develop, and design security requirements for specific business needs. These blueprints must be customized to fulfill the organization's security requirements, which are based on its regulatory obligations, business drivers, and legal obligations. For example, let's say Company Y has a data protection policy, and its security team has developed standards and procedures pertaining to the data protection strategy the company should follow. The blueprint will then get more granular and lay out the processes and components necessary to meet requirements outlined in the policy, standards, and requirements. This would include at least a diagram of the company network that illustrates the following:

- Where the sensitive data resides within the network
- The network segments that the sensitive data transverses
- The different security solutions in place (VPN, TLS, PGP) that protect the sensitive data
- Third-party connections where sensitive data is shared
- Security measures in place for third-party connections
- And more…

The blueprints to be developed and followed depend upon the organization's business needs. If Company Y uses identity management, it needs a blueprint outlining roles, registration management, authoritative source, identity repositories, single sign-on solutions, and so on. If Company Y does not use identity management, it does not need to build a blueprint for this.

So the blueprint lays out the security solutions, processes, and components the organization uses to match its security and business needs. These blueprints must be applied to the different business units within the organization. For example, the identity management practiced in each of the different departments should follow the crafted blueprint. Following these blueprints throughout the organization allows for standardization, easier metrics gathering, and governance. Figure 4-9 illustrates where these blueprints come into play when developing a security program.

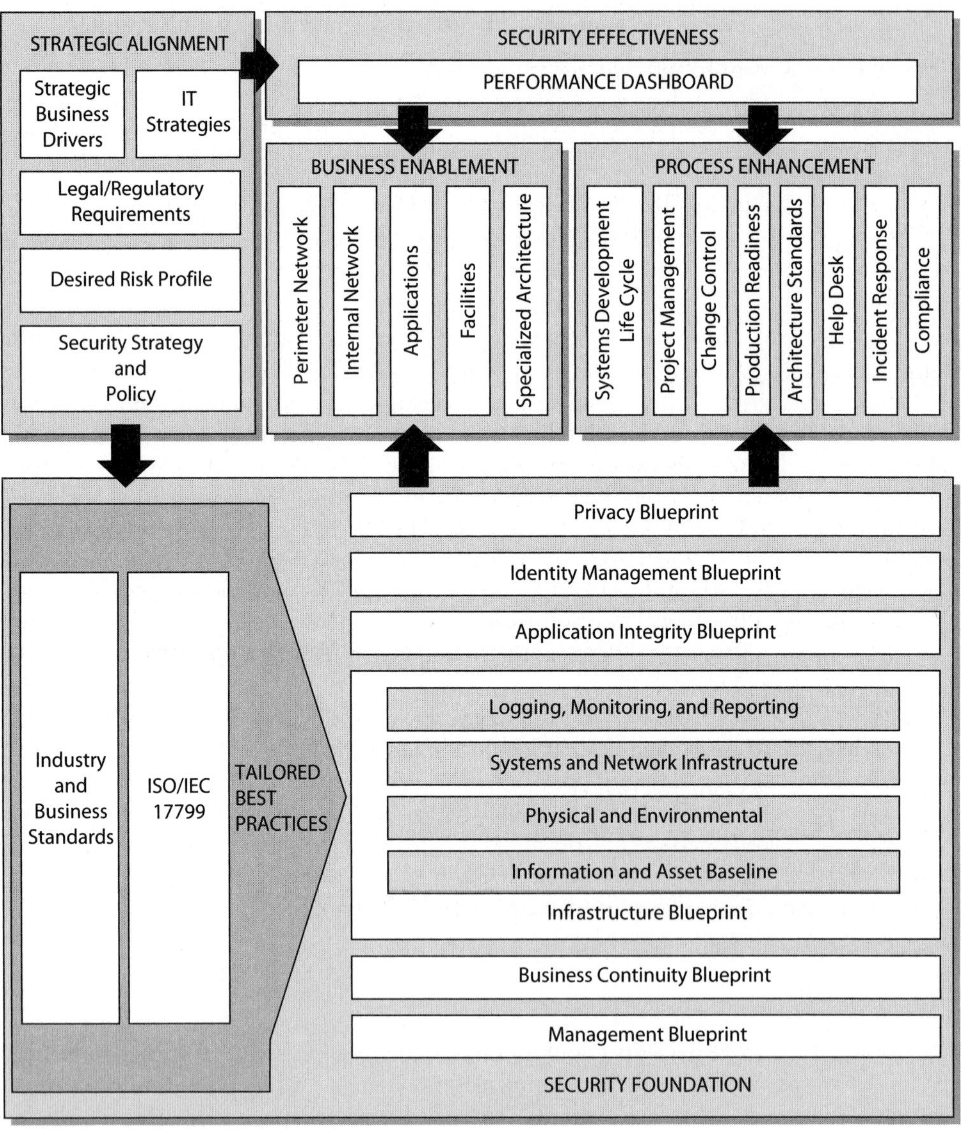

Figure 4-9 Blueprints must map the security and business requirements.

To tie these pieces together, you can think of the NIST Cybersecurity Framework that works mainly at the policy level as a *description* of the type of house you want to build (ranch style, five bedrooms, three baths). The security enterprise framework is the *architecture* layout of the house (foundation, walls, ceilings). The blueprints are the detailed descriptions of specific components of the house (window types, security system, electrical system, plumbing). And the control objectives are the building specifications and codes that need to be met for safety (electrical grounding and wiring, construction material, insulation, and fire protection). A building inspector will use his checklists (building codes) to ensure that you are building your house safely. Which is just like how an auditor will use his checklists (like NIST SP 800-53) to ensure that you are building and maintaining your security program securely.

Once your house is built and your family moves in, you set up schedules and processes for everyday life to happen in a predictable and efficient manner (dad picks up kids from school, mom cooks dinner, teenager does laundry, dad pays the bills, everyone does yard work). This is analogous to ITIL—process management and improvement. If the family is made up of anal overachievers with the goal of optimizing these daily activities to be as efficient as possible, they could integrate a Six Sigma approach where continual process improvement is a focus.

Chapter Review

This chapter should serve at least two purposes for you. First, it familiarizes you with the various frameworks you need to know to pass your CISSP exam. Though some of these frameworks don't fit neatly into one category, we did our best to group them in ways that would help you remember them. So, we have risk management, information security, enterprise architecture, and "other" frameworks. Within information security, we further subdivided the frameworks into those that are focused on program-level issues and those that are primarily concerned with controls. You don't have to know every detail of each framework to pass the exam, but you really should know at least one or two key points about each to differentiate them.

The second purpose of this chapter is to serve as a reference for your professional life. We focused our discussion on the frameworks that are most likely to show up in your work places so that you have a desktop reference to which you can turn when someone asks your opinion about one of these frameworks. While this second purpose of the chapter should apply to the whole book, it is particularly applicable to this chapter because frameworks are tools that don't change very often (especially within an organization), so you may become very familiar with the one(s) you use but a bit rusty on the rest. Grouping them all in this chapter may help you in the future.

Quick Review

- A framework is a guiding document that provides structure to the ways in which we manage risks, develop enterprise architectures, and secure all our assets.
- The most common risk management frameworks (RMFs) are the NIST RMF, ISO/IEC 27005, OCTAVE, and FAIR.

- The seven steps of the NIST RMF are prepare, categorize, select, implement, assess, authorize, and monitor.
- Security controls in the NIST frameworks can be classified as *common* (if they exist outside of a system and apply to multiple systems), *system-specific* (if they exist inside a system boundary and protect only the one system), or *hybrid* (if they are a combination of the other two).
- Risks in a risk management framework can be treated in one of four ways: mitigated, accepted, transferred, or avoided.
- Operationally Critical Threat, Asset, and Vulnerability Evaluation (OCTAVE) is a team-oriented risk management methodology that employs workshops and is commonly used in the commercial sector.
- The Factor Analysis of Information Risk (FAIR) risk management framework is the only internationally recognized quantitative approach to risk management.
- The most common information security program frameworks are ISO/IEC 27001 and the NIST Cybersecurity Framework.
- ISO/IEC 27001 is the standard for the establishment, implementation, control, and improvement of the information security management system.
- The NIST Cybersecurity Framework's official name is the "Framework for Improving Critical Infrastructure Cybersecurity."
- The NIST Cybersecurity Framework organizes cybersecurity activities into five higher-level functions: identify, protect, detect, respond, and recover.
- The most common security controls frameworks are NIST SP 800-53, the CIS Controls, and COBIT.
- NIST SP 800-53, *Security and Privacy Controls for Information Systems and Organizations*, catalogs over 1,000 security controls grouped into 20 families.
- The Center for Internet Security (CIS) Controls is a framework consisting of 20 controls and 171 subcontrols organized in implementation groups to address any organization's security needs from small to enterprise level.
- COBIT is a framework of control objectives and allows for IT governance.
- Enterprise architecture frameworks are used to develop architectures for specific stakeholders and present information in views.
- Blueprints are functional definitions for the integration of technology into business processes.
- Enterprise architecture frameworks are used to build individual architectures that best map to individual organizational needs and business drivers.
- The most common enterprise architecture frameworks are the Zachman and SABSA ones, but you should also be aware of TOGAF and DoDAF.
- Zachman Framework is an enterprise architecture framework, and SABSA is a security enterprise architecture framework.

- ITIL is a set of best practices for IT service management.
- Six Sigma is used to identify defects in processes so that the processes can be improved upon.
- A Capability Maturity Model (CMM) allows for processes to improve in an incremented and standard approach.

Questions

Please remember that these questions are formatted and asked in a certain way for a reason. Keep in mind that the CISSP exam is asking questions at a conceptual level. Questions may not always have the perfect answer, and the candidate is advised against always looking for the perfect answer. Instead, the candidate should look for the best answer in the list.

1. Which of the following standards would be most useful to you in ensuring your information security management system follows industry best practices?
   A. NIST SP 800-53
   B. Six Sigma
   C. ISO/IEC 27000 series
   D. COBIT
2. What is COBIT and where does it fit into the development of information security systems and security programs?
   A. Lists of standards, procedures, and policies for security program development
   B. Current version of ISO 17799
   C. A framework that was developed to deter organizational internal fraud
   D. Open standard for control objectives
3. Which publication provides a catalog of security controls for information systems?
   A. ISO/IEC 27001
   B. ISO/IEC 27005
   C. NIST SP 800-37
   D. NIST SP 800-53
4. ISO/IEC 27001 describes which of the following?
   A. The Risk Management Framework
   B. Information security management system
   C. Work product retention standards
   D. International Electrotechnical Commission standards

5. Which of the following is *not* true about Operationally Critical Threat, Asset and Vulnerability Evaluation (OCTAVE)?
   A. It is the only internationally recognized quantitative risk management framework.
   B. It was developed by Carnegie Mellon University.
   C. It is focused only on risk assessments.
   D. It is a team-oriented risk management methodology that employs workshops.
6. What is a key benefit of using the Zachman Framework?
   A. Ensures that all systems, processes, and personnel are interoperable in a concerted effort to accomplish organizational missions
   B. Use of the iterative and cyclic Architecture Development Method (ADM)
   C. Focus on internal SLAs between the IT department and the "customers" it serves
   D. Allows different groups within the organization to look at it from different viewpoints
7. Which of the following describes the Center for Internet Security (CIS) Controls framework?
   A. Consists of over 1,000 controls, divided into 20 families, that are mapped to the security category of an information system
   B. Balances resource utilization, risk levels, and realization of benefits by explicitly tying stakeholder needs to organizational goals to IT goals
   C. Developed to determine the maturity of an organization's processes
   D. Consists of 20 controls divided into three groups to help organizations incrementally improve their security posture
8. Which of the following is not one of the seven steps in the NIST Risk Management Framework (RMF)?
   A. Monitor security controls
   B. Establish the context
   C. Assess security controls
   D. Authorize information system
9. The information security industry is made up of various best practices, standards, models, and frameworks. Some were not developed first with security in mind, but can be integrated into an organizational security program to help in its effectiveness and efficiency. It is important to know of all of these different approaches so that an organization can choose the ones that best fit its business needs and culture. Which of the following best describes the approach(es) that should be put into place if an organization wants to integrate a way to improve its security processes over a period of time?
   i. ITIL should be integrated because it allows for the mapping of IT service process management, business drivers, and security improvement.

ii. Six Sigma should be integrated because it allows for the defects of security processes to be identified and improved upon.

iii. A Capability Maturity Model should be integrated because it provides distinct maturity levels.

iv. The Open Group Architecture Framework should be integrated because it provides a structure for process improvement.

A. i, iii

B. ii, iii, iv

C. ii, iii

D. ii, iv

Use the following scenario to answer Questions 10–12. You are hired as the chief information security officer (CISO) for a medium-size research and development company. Its research file servers were recently breached, resulting in a significant loss of intellectual property. The company is about to start a critical research project and wants to ensure another breach doesn't happen. The company doesn't have risk management or information security programs, and you've been given a modest budget to hire a small team and get things started.

10. Which of the following risk management frameworks would probably *not* be well suited to your organization?

A. ISO/IEC 27005

B. NIST Risk Management Framework (RMF)

C. Operationally Critical Threat, Asset, and Vulnerability Evaluation (OCTAVE)

D. Factor Analysis of Information Risk (FAIR)

11. You decide to adopt the NIST Risk Management Framework (RMF) and are in the process of categorizing your information systems. How would you determine the security category (SC) of your research file servers (RFS)?

A. SC_{RFS} = (probable frequency) × (probable future loss)

B. SC_{RFS} = {(confidentiality, *high*),(integrity, *medium*),(availability, *low*)} = *high*

C. SC_{RFS} = {(confidentiality, *high*),(integrity, *medium*),(availability, *low*)} = *medium*

D. SC_{RFS} = Threat × Impact × Probability

12. When selecting the controls for the research file servers, which of the following security control frameworks would be best?

A. NIST SP 800-53, *Security and Privacy Controls for Information Systems and Organizations*

B. ISO/IEC 27002 code of practice for information security controls

C. Center for Information Security (CIS) Controls

D. COBIT 2019

Answers

1. **C.** The ISO/IEC 27000 series is the only option that addresses best practices across the breadth of an ISMS. NIST SP 800-53 and COBIT both deal with controls, which are a critical but not the only component of an ISMS.
2. **D.** COBIT is an open framework developed by ISACA and the IT Governance Institute (ITGI). It defines goals for the controls that should be used to properly manage IT and ensure IT maps to business needs.
3. **D.** NIST Special Publication (SP) 800-53, *Security and Privacy Controls for Information Systems and Organizations*, catalogs over 1,000 security controls. ISO/IEC 27005 and NIST SP 800-37 both describe risk management frameworks, while ISO/IEC 27001 is focused on information security management systems (ISMSs).
4. **B.** ISO/IEC 27001 provides best practice recommendations on information security management systems (ISMSs).
5. **A.** OCTAVE is not a quantitative methodology. The only such methodology for risk management we've discussed is FAIR.
6. **D.** One of the key benefits of the Zachman Framework is that it allows organizations to integrate business and IT infrastructure requirements in a manner that is presentable to a variety of audiences by providing different viewpoints. This helps keep business and IT on the same sheet of music. The other answers describe the DoDAF (A), TOGAF (B), and ITIL (C).
7. **D.** There are 20 CIS controls and 171 subcontrols organized so that any organization, regardless of size, can focus on the most critical controls and improve over time as resources become available. The other answers describe NIST SP 800-53 (A), COBIT 2019 (B), and Capability Maturity Model (C).
8. **B.** Establishing the context is a step in ISO/IEC 27005, not in the NIST RMF. While it is similar to the RMF's prepare step, there are differences between the two. All the other responses are clearly steps in the NIST RMF process.
9. **C.** The best process improvement approaches provided in this list are Six Sigma and Capability Maturity Model. The following outlines the definitions for all items in this question:
   - **TOGAF** Model and methodology for the development of enterprise architectures, developed by The Open Group
   - **ITIL** Processes to allow for IT service management, developed by the United Kingdom's Office of Government Commerce
   - **Six Sigma** Business management strategy that can be used to carry out process improvement
   - **Capability Maturity Model (CMM)** Organizational development for process improvement

10. **D.** The Factor Analysis of Information Risk (FAIR) framework uses a quantitative approach to risk assessment. As we discussed in Chapter 2, this approach requires a lot more expertise and resources than quantitative ones. Since your organization is just getting started with risk management and information security and your resources are limited, this would not be a good fit.
11. **B.** The NIST RMF relies on the Federal Information Processing Standard Publication 199 (FIPS 199) categorization standard, which breaks down a system's criticality by security objective (confidentiality, integrity, availability) and then applies the highest security objective category (the "high water mark") to determine the overall category of the system.
12. **A.** Because you're using the NIST RMF, NIST SP 800-53 is the best answer because the two frameworks are tightly integrated. None of the other answers is necessarily wrong; they're just not as well suited as SP 800-53 for the given scenario.

PART II

Asset Security

CHAPTER 5

Assets

This chapter presents the following:

- Identification and classification of information and assets
- Information and asset handling requirements
- Secure resource provisioning
- The data life cycle
- Data compliance requirements

You don't know what you've got till it's gone.

—Joni Mitchell

An asset is, by definition, anything of worth to an organization. This includes people, partners, equipment, facilities, reputation, and information. We already touched on the importance of some of these assets when we addressed risk in Chapter 2. While every asset needs to be protected, our coverage of the second CISSP domain in this chapter and the next one focuses a bit more narrowly on protecting information assets. This is because, apart from people, information is typically the most valuable asset to an organization. It lies at the heart of every information system, so precision focus on its protection makes a lot of sense.

Information, of course, exists in context; it is acquired or created at a particular point in time through a specific process and (usually) for a purpose. It moves through an organization's information systems, sometimes adding value to processes and sometimes waiting to be useful. Eventually, the information outlives its utility (or becomes a liability) and must be disposed of appropriately. We start off our discussion of asset security by addressing two fundamental questions: "What do we have?" and "Why should we care?" The first question is probably rather obvious, since we cannot protect that of which we're not aware. The second question may sound flippant, but it really gets to the heart of how important an asset is to the organization. We've already tackled this (at least with regard to data) in Chapter 4 in our discussion of the categorize step of the NIST Risk Management Framework. Data and asset classification, as we will shortly see, is very similar to the categorization we've already explored. Let's get to it!

EXAM TIP An information asset can be either the data, the device on which it is stored and used, or both. In the exam, when you see the term *asset* by itself, it typically means only the device.

Information and Assets

An *asset* can be defined as anything that is useful or valuable. In the context of products and services, this value is usually considered financially: how much would someone pay for it minus how much does the thing cost. If that value is positive, we call the thing an asset. However, if that value is negative (that is, the thing costs more than what someone would pay for it), then we call the thing a liability. Clearly, assets can be both tangible things like computers and firewalls and intangible things like data or reputation. It is important to narrow down the definition for purposes of the CISSP exam, so in this domain, we consider assets as tangible things and we deal with data separately.

Information is a set of data items, placed in a context, and having some meaning. Data is just an item. It could be the word "yes," the time "9:00," or the name "Fernando's Café" and, by itself, has no meaning. Put this data together in the context of an answer to the question "Would you like to have coffee tomorrow morning?" and now we have information. Namely, that we'll be sharing a beverage tomorrow morning at a particular place. Data processing yields information, and this is why we often use these two terms interchangeably when talking about security issues.

Identification

Whether we are concerned with data security or asset security (or both), we first have to know what we have. Identification is simply establishing what something is. When you look at a computing device occupying a slot in your server rack, you may want to know what it is. You may want to identify it. The most common way of doing this is by placing tags on our assets and data. These tags can be physical (e.g., stickers), electronic (e.g., radio frequency identification [RFID] tags), or logical (e.g., software license keys). Using tags is critically important to establishing and maintaining accurate inventories of our assets.

But what about data? Do we need to identify it and track it like we do with our more tangible assets? The answer is: it depends. Most organizations have at least some data that is so critical that, were it to become lost or corrupted or even made public, the impact would be severe. Think of financial records at a bank, or patient data at a healthcare provider. These organizations would have a very bad day indeed if any of those records were lost, inaccurate, or posted on the dark web. To prevent this, they go to great lengths to identify and track their sensitive information, usually by using metadata embedded in files or records.

While it may not be critical (or even feasible) for many organizations to identify all their information, it is critical to most of us to at least decide how much effort should be put into protecting different types of data (or assets, for that matter). This is where classification comes in handy.

Classification

Classification just means saying that something belongs to a certain class. We could say, for example, that your personnel file belongs to the class named "private" and that your organization's marketing brochure for the latest appliance belongs to the class "public." Right away, we would have a sense that your file has more value to your organization than the brochure. The rationale behind assigning values to different assets and data is that this enables an organization to gauge the amount of funds and resources that should go toward protecting each class, because not all assets and data have the same value to an organization. After identifying all important data, it should be properly classified. An organization copies and creates a lot of data that it must maintain, so classification is an ongoing process and not a one-time effort.

Data Classification

An important metadata item that should be attached to all our information is a classification level. This classification tag, which remains attached (and perhaps updated) throughout the life cycle of the data, is important to determining the protective controls we apply to the data.

Information can be classified by sensitivity, criticality, or both. Either way, the classification aims to quantify how much loss an organization would likely suffer if the information was lost. The *sensitivity* of information is commensurate with the losses to an organization if that information was revealed to unauthorized individuals. This kind of compromise has made headlines in recent years with the losses of information suffered by organizations such as Equifax, Sina Weibo, and Marriott International. In each case, the organizations lost trust and had to undertake expensive responses because sensitive data was compromised.

The *criticality* of information, on the other hand, is an indicator of how the loss of the information would impact the fundamental business processes of the organization. In other words, critical information is that which is essential for the organization to continue operations. For example, Code Spaces, a company that provided code repository services, was forced to shut down in 2014 after an unidentified individual or group deleted its code repositories. This data was critical to the operations of the company and, without it, the corporation had no choice but to go out of business.

Once data is segmented according to its sensitivity or criticality level, the organization can decide what security controls are necessary to protect different types of data. This ensures that information assets receive the appropriate level of protection, and classifications indicate the priority of that security protection. The primary purpose of data classification is to indicate the level of confidentiality, integrity, and availability protection that is required for each type of data set. Many people mistakenly only consider the confidentiality aspects of data protection, but we need to make sure our data is not modified in an unauthorized manner and that it is available when needed.

Data classification helps ensure that data is protected in the most cost-effective manner. Protecting and maintaining data costs money, but spending money for the information that actually requires protection is important. If you were in charge of making sure Russia does not know the encryption algorithms used when transmitting information to and from U.S. spy satellites, you would use more extreme (and expensive) security measures than you would use to protect your peanut butter and banana sandwich recipe from your next-door neighbor.

Each classification should have separate handling requirements and procedures pertaining to how that data is accessed, used, and destroyed. For example, in a corporation, confidential information may be accessed only by senior management and a select few trusted employees throughout the company. Accessing the information may require two or more people to enter their access codes. Auditing could be very detailed and its results monitored daily, and paper copies of the information may be kept in a vault. To properly erase this data from the media, degaussing or overwriting procedures may be required. Other information in this company may be classified as sensitive, allowing a slightly larger group of people to view it. Access control on the information classified as sensitive may require only one set of credentials. Auditing happens but is only reviewed weekly, paper copies are kept in locked file cabinets, and the data can be deleted using regular measures when it is time to do so. Then, the rest of the information is marked public. All employees can access it, and no special auditing or destruction methods are required.

EXAM TIP Each classification level should have its own handling and destruction requirements.

Classification Levels There are no hard and fast rules on the classification levels that an organization should use. Table 5-1 explains the types of classifications available. An organization could choose to use any of the classification levels presented in Table 5-1. One organization may choose to use only two layers of classifications, while another organization may choose to use four. Note that some classifications are more commonly used for commercial businesses, whereas others are military classifications.

The following are the common levels of sensitivity from the highest to the lowest for commercial business:

- Confidential
- Private
- Sensitive
- Public

And here are the levels of sensitivity from the highest to the lowest for military purposes:

- Top secret
- Secret
- Confidential
- Controlled unclassified information
- Unclassified

Classification	Definition	Example	Organizations That Would Use This
Public	• Disclosure is not welcome, but it would not cause an adverse impact to company or personnel.	• How many people are working on a specific project • Upcoming projects	Commercial business
Sensitive	• Requires special precautions to ensure the integrity and confidentiality of the data by protecting it from unauthorized modification or deletion. • Requires higher-than-normal assurance of accuracy and completeness.	• Financial information • Details of projects • Profit earnings and forecasts	Commercial business
Private	• Personal information for use within a company. • Unauthorized disclosure could adversely affect personnel or the company.	• Work history • Human resources information • Medical information	Commercial business
Confidential	• For use within the company only. • Data exempt from disclosure under the Freedom of Information Act or other laws and regulations. • Unauthorized disclosure could seriously affect a company.	• Trade secrets • Healthcare information • Programming code • Information that keeps the company competitive	Commercial business Military
Unclassified	• Data is not sensitive or classified.	• Computer manual and warranty information • Recruiting information	Military
Controlled unclassified information (CUI)	• Sensitive, but not secret. • Information that cannot legally be made public.	• Health records • Answers to test scores	Military
Secret	• If disclosed, it could cause serious damage to national security.	• Deployment plans for troops • Unit readiness information	Military
Top secret	• If disclosed, it could cause grave damage to national security.	• Blueprints of new weapons • Spy satellite information • Espionage data	Military

Table 5-1 Commercial Business and Military Data Classifications

The classifications listed in Table 5-1 are *commonly* used in the industry, but there is a lot of variance. An organization first must decide the number of data classifications that best fit its security needs, then choose the classification naming scheme, and then define what the names in those schemes represent. Company A might use the classification level "confidential," which represents its most sensitive information. Company B might use "top secret," "secret," and "confidential," where confidential represents its least sensitive information. Each organization must develop an information classification scheme that best fits its business and security needs.

EXAM TIP The terms "unclassified," "secret," and "top secret" are usually associated with governmental organizations. The terms "private," "proprietary," and "sensitive" are usually associated with nongovernmental organizations.

It is important to not go overboard and come up with a long list of classifications, which will only cause confusion and frustration for the individuals who will use the system. The classifications should not be too restrictive either, because many types of data may need to be classified. As with every other issue in security, we must balance our business and security needs.

Each classification should be unique and separate from the others and not have any overlapping effects. The classification process should also outline how information is controlled and handled through its life cycle (from creation to termination).

NOTE An organization must make sure that whoever is backing up classified data—and whoever has access to backed-up data—has the necessary clearance level. A large security risk can be introduced if low-level technicians with no security clearance have access to this information during their tasks.

Once the scheme is decided upon, the organization must develop the criteria it will use to decide what information goes into which classification. The following list shows some criteria parameters an organization may use to determine the sensitivity of data:

- The usefulness of data
- The value of data
- The age of data
- The level of damage that could be caused if the data were disclosed
- The level of damage that could be caused if the data were modified or corrupted
- Legal, regulatory, or contractual responsibility to protect the data
- Effects the data has on security
- Who should be able to access the data
- Who should maintain the data
- Who should be able to reproduce the data
- Lost opportunity costs that could be incurred if the data were not available or were corrupted

Applications and sometimes whole systems may need to be classified. The applications that hold and process classified information should be evaluated for the level of protection they provide. You do not want a program filled with security vulnerabilities to process and "protect" your most sensitive information. The application classifications should be based on the assurance (confidence level) the organization has in the software and the type of information it can store and process.

CAUTION The classification rules must apply to data no matter what format it is in: digital, paper, video, fax, audio, and so on.

Asset Classification

Information is not the only thing we should classify. Consider that information must reside somewhere. If a confidential file is stored and processed in the CEO's laptop, then that device (and its hard drive if it is removed) should also be considered worthy of more protection. Typically, the classification of an asset (like a removable drive or a laptop) used to store or process information should be as high as the classification of the most valuable data in it. If an asset has public, sensitive, and confidential information, then that asset should be classified as private (the highest of the three classifications) and protected accordingly.

Classification Procedures

The following outlines the necessary steps for a proper classification program:

1. Define classification levels.
2. Specify the criteria that will determine how data is classified.
3. Identify data owners who will be responsible for classifying data.
4. Identify the data custodian who will be responsible for maintaining data and its security level.
5. Indicate the security controls, or protection mechanisms, required for each classification level.
6. Document any exceptions to the previous classification issues.
7. Indicate the methods that can be used to transfer custody of the information to a different data owner.
8. Create a procedure to periodically review the classification and ownership. Communicate any changes to the data custodian.
9. Indicate procedures for declassifying the data.
10. Integrate these issues into the security awareness program so all employees understand how to handle data at different classification levels.

Physical Security Considerations

We discuss data security in detail in Chapter 10. However, that data lives physically in devices and printed documents, both of which require protection also. The main threats that physical security components combat are theft, interruptions to services, physical damage, compromised system and environment integrity, and unauthorized access. Real loss is determined by the cost to replace the stolen items, the negative effect on productivity, the negative effect on reputation and customer confidence, fees for consultants that may need to be brought in, and the cost to restore lost data and production levels. Many times, organizations just perform an inventory of their hardware and provide value estimates that are plugged into risk analysis to determine what the cost to the organization would be if the equipment were stolen or destroyed. However, the data held within the equipment may be much more valuable than the equipment itself, and proper recovery mechanisms and procedures also need to be plugged into the risk assessment for a more realistic and fair assessment of cost. Let's take a look at some of the controls we can use in order to mitigate risks to our data and to the media on which it resides.

Protecting Mobile Devices

Mobile devices are almost indispensable. For most of us, significant chunks of our personal and work lives are chronicled in our smartphones or tablets. Employees who use these devices as they travel for work may have extremely sensitive company or customer data on their systems that can easily fall into the wrong hands. This problem can be mitigated to a point by ensuring our employees use company devices for their work, so we can implement policies and controls to protect them. Still, many organizations allow their staff members to bring their own devices (BYOD) to the workplace and/or use them for work functions. In these cases, it is not only security but also privacy that should receive serious attention.

There is no one-size-fits-all solution to protecting company, let alone personal, mobile devices. Still, the following list provides some of the mechanisms that can be used to protect these devices and the data they hold:

- Inventory all mobile devices, including serial numbers, so they can be properly identified if they are stolen and then recovered.
- Harden the operating system by applying baseline secure configurations.
- Stay current with the latest security updates and patches.
- Ensure mobile devices have strong authentication.
- Register all devices with their respective vendors, and file a report with the vendor when a device is stolen. If a stolen device is sent in for repairs after it is stolen, it will be flagged by the vendor if you have reported the theft.
- Do not check mobile devices as luggage when flying. Always carry them on with you.
- Never leave a mobile device unattended, and carry it in a nondescript carrying case.

- Engrave the device with a symbol or number for proper identification.
- Back up all data on mobile devices to an organizationally controlled repository.
- Encrypt all data on a mobile device.
- Enable remote wiping of data on the device.

Tracing software can be installed so that your device can "phone home" if it is taken from you. Several products offer this tracing capability. Once installed and configured, the software periodically sends in a signal to a tracking center or allows you to track it through a website or application. If you report that your device has been stolen, the vendor of this software may work with service providers and law enforcement to track down and return your device.

Paper Records

It is easy to forget that many organizations still process information on paper records. The fact that this is relatively rare compared to the volume of their electronic counterparts is little consolation when a printed e-mail with sensitive information finds its way into the wrong hands and potentially causes just as much damage. Here are some principles to consider when protecting paper records:

- Educate your staff on proper handling of paper records.
- Minimize the use of paper records.
- Ensure workspaces are kept tidy so it is easy to tell when sensitive papers are left exposed, and routinely audit workspaces to ensure sensitive documents are not exposed.
- Lock away all sensitive paperwork as soon as you are done with it.
- Prohibit taking sensitive paperwork home.
- Label all paperwork with its classification level. Ideally, also include its owner's name and disposition (e.g., retention) instructions.
- Conduct random searches of employees' bags as they leave the office to ensure sensitive materials are not being taken home.
- Destroy unneeded sensitive papers using a crosscut shredder, or consider contracting a document destruction company.

Safes

An organization may have need for a safe. Safes are commonly used to store backup data tapes, original contracts, or other types of valuables. The safe should be penetration resistant and provide fire protection. The types of safes an organization can choose from are

- **Wall safe** Embedded into the wall and easily hidden
- **Floor safe** Embedded into the floor and easily hidden

- **Chests** Stand-alone safes
- **Depositories** Safes with slots, which allow the valuables to be easily slipped in
- **Vaults** Safes that are large enough to provide walk-in access

If a safe has a combination lock, it should be changed periodically, and only a small subset of people should have access to the combination or key. The safe should be in a visible location, so anyone who is interacting with the safe can be seen. It should also be covered by a video surveillance system that records any activity around it. The goal is to uncover any unauthorized access attempts. Some safes have passive or thermal relocking functionality. If the safe has a *passive relocking* function, it can detect when someone attempts to tamper with it, in which case extra internal bolts will fall into place to ensure it cannot be compromised. If a safe has a *thermal relocking* function, when a certain temperature is met (possibly from drilling), an extra lock is implemented to ensure the valuables are properly protected.

Managing the Life Cycle of Assets

A life-cycle model describes the changes that an entity experiences during its lifetime. While it may seem odd to refer to assets as having a "life," the fact is that their utility for (and presence within) organizations can be described with clear start and end points. That is the lifetime of the asset within that organization (even if it gets refurbished and used elsewhere). After the asset departs, its utility is oftentimes transferred to its replacement even if the new asset is different than the original in meaningful ways. That new asset will, in turn, be replaced by something else, and so on.

The life cycle, which is shown in Figure 5-1, starts with the identification of a new requirement. Whoever identifies the new requirement either becomes its champion or

Figure 5-1 The IT asset life cycle

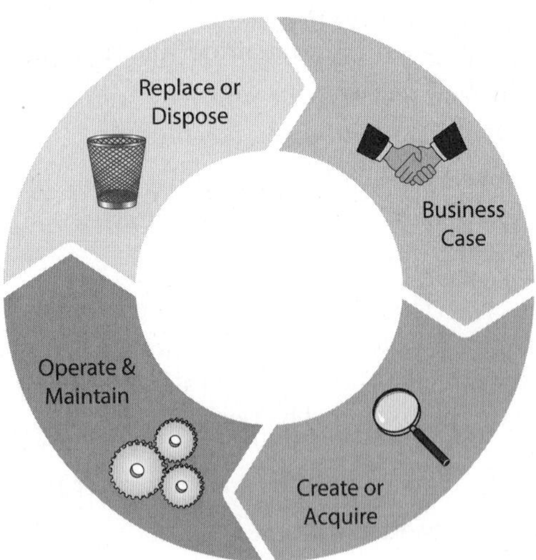

finds someone else to do so. The champion for this requirement then makes a business case for it that shows that the existing assets are unable to satisfy this need. The champion also explains why the organization really should get a new asset, which typically includes a conversation about risks and return on investment (ROI). If the champion is successful, senior management validates the requirement and identifies the needed resources (people, money, time).

The validated requirement then goes to a change management board, giving the different organizational stakeholders a say in what, how, and when the asset will be acquired. This board's goal is to ensure that this new asset doesn't break any processes, introduce undue risks, or derail any ongoing projects. In mature organizations, the change management process also attempts to look over the horizon and see what the long-term ramifications of this asset might be. After the board determines how to proceed, the new asset is either developed in-house or acquired from a vendor.

The third phase of asset management is also the longest one: operation and maintenance (O&M). Before the asset is put into operation, the IT and security operations teams configure it to balance three (sometimes competing) goals: it must be able to do whatever it was acquired to do, it must be able to do it without interfering or breaking anything else, and it must be secure. This configuration will almost certainly need to change over time, which is why we discuss configuration management in Chapter 20.

NOTE This initial part of the O&M phase is usually the most problematic for a new asset and is a major driver for the use of an integrated product team (IPT) such as DevOps, which we discuss in Chapter 24.

Eventually, the asset is no longer effective (in terms of function or cost) or required. At this point, it moves out of O&M and is retired. This move, as you may have already guessed, triggers another review by the change management board, because retiring the asset is likely to have effects on other resources or processes. Once the process of retirement is hashed out, the asset is removed from production. At this point, the organization needs to figure out what to do with the thing. If the asset stored any data, the data probably has to be purged. If the asset has any environmentally hazardous materials, it has to be properly discarded. If it might be useful to someone else, it might be donated or sold. At any rate, the loss of this asset may result in a new requirement being identified, which starts the whole asset management life cycle again, as shown in Figure 5-1.

Ownership

In most cases, whoever makes the business case for an asset ultimately owns it, but this is not always the case. Asset *ownership*, once the asset shows up and as long as it remains in the organization, entails responsibility for the effective management of the asset over its whole life cycle. Ownership in this sense is somewhat different than ownership in a strictly legal sense. The legal owner of a server could be the corporation that buys it, while the life cycle owner would be whatever employee or department is responsible for it on a day-to-day basis.

Inventories

One of the fundamental responsibilities for asset owners is to keep track of their assets. Though the approaches to tracking hardware and software vary, they are both widely recognized as critical controls. At the very least, it is very difficult to defend an asset that you don't know you have. As obvious as this sounds, many organizations lack an accurate and timely inventory of their hardware and software.

Tracking Hardware

Seemingly, maintaining awareness of which devices are in your organization should be an easier task than tracking your software. A hardware device can be seen, touched, and bar-scanned. It can also be sensed electronically once it is connected to the network. If you have the right tools and processes available, tracking hardware should not be all that difficult, right? Not so fast. It turns out that the set of problems ranges from supply chain security to insider threats and everything in between.

Let's start with the basics. How do you ensure that a new device you've ordered is the right one and free of back doors or piracy issues? There have been multiple reports in the news media recently of confirmed or suspected back doors installed in hardware assets by either manufacturers (e.g., pirated hardware) or by third parties (e.g., government spy agencies) before the assets get to the organization that acquired them. In response to these and other threats, the International Organization for Standardization published ISO 28000:2007 as a means for organizations to use a consistent approach to securing their supply chains. In essence, we want to ensure we purchase from trusted sources, use a trusted transportation network, and have effective inspection processes to mitigate the risk of pirated, tampered, or stolen hardware.

But even if we can assure ourselves that all the hardware we acquire is legitimate, how would we know if someone else were to add devices to our networks? Asset monitoring includes not only tracking our known devices but also identifying unknown ones that may occasionally pop up in our enclaves. Examples that come to mind from personal experience include rogue wireless access points, personal mobile devices, and even (believe it or not) telephone modems. Each introduces unknown (and thus unmitigated) risks. The solution is to have a comprehensive monitoring process that actively searches for these devices and ensures compliance with your organization's security policies.

In many cases, monitoring devices on the premises can be as simple as having a member of the security or IT team randomly walk through every space in the organization looking for things that are out of place. This becomes even more effective if this person does this after work hours and also looks for wireless networks as part of these walks. Alternatively, much of this monitoring can be done using device management platforms and a variety of sensors.

Tracking Software

Obviously, we can't just walk around and inventory our software. The unique challenges of tracking software are similar to those of managing hardware, but with a few important differences. Unlike hardware, software assets can be copied or installed multiple times. This could be a problem from a licensing perspective. Commercial applications typically have limits on how many times you can install a single license. The terms of these licensing agreements vary wildly from single-use to enterprise-wide. It bears pointing out that tracking what software is installed on which systems, and for which users, is an important part of software asset management. Otherwise, you risk violating software licenses.

Using unlicensed software not only is unethical but also exposes an organization to financial liability from the legitimate product vendors. This liability can manifest in a number of ways, including having the organization reported to the vendor by a disgruntled employee. It could also come up when certain software packages "phone home" to the vendors' servers or when downloading software patches and updates. Depending on the number and types of licenses, this could end up costing significant amounts of money in retroactive licensing fees.

Pirated software is even more problematic because many forms of it include back doors installed by the pirates or are Trojan horses. Even if this were not the case, it would almost certainly be impossible to update or patch this software, which makes it inherently more insecure. Since no IT staff in their right mind would seriously consider using pirated software as an organizational policy, its presence on a network would suggest that at least some users have privileges that are being abused and to which they may not be entitled.

Another problem created by the fact that you can copy and install software on multiple systems, apart from unlicensed or pirated software, is security. If you lose track of how many copies of which software are on your systems, it is harder to ensure they are all updated and patched. Vulnerability scanners and patch management systems are helpful in this regard, but depending on how these systems operate, you could end up with periods (perhaps indefinitely long) of vulnerability.

The solution to the software tracking problem is multifaceted. It starts with an assessment of the legitimate application requirements of the organization. Perhaps some users need an expensive photo editing software suite, but its provisioning should be carefully controlled and only available to that set of users in order to minimize the licensing costs. Once the requirements are known and broken down by class of user, there are several ways to keep a handle on what software exists on which systems. Here are some of the most widely accepted best practices:

- **Application whitelisting** A whitelist is a list of software that is allowed to execute on a device or set of devices. Implementing this approach not only prevents unlicensed or unauthorized software from being installed but also protects against many classes of malware.
- **Using Gold Masters** A Gold Master is a standard image workstation or server that includes properly configured and authorized software. Organizations may have multiple images representing different sets of users. The use of Gold Masters simplifies new device provisioning and configuration, particularly if the users are not allowed to modify them.
- **Enforcing the principle of least privilege** If the typical users are not able to install any software on their devices, then it becomes a lot harder for rogue applications to show up in our networks. Furthermore, if we apply this approach, we mitigate risks from a very large set of attacks.

- **Device management software** Unified endpoint management (UEM) systems allow you to fully and remotely manage most devices, including smartphones, tablets, laptops, printers, and even Internet of Things (IoT) devices.
- **Automated scanning** Every device on your network should be periodically scanned to ensure it is running only approved software with proper configurations. Deviations from this policy should be logged and investigated by the IT or security team.

Licensing Issues

Companies have the ethical obligation to use only legitimately purchased software applications. Software makers and their industry representation groups such as The Software Alliance (BSA) use aggressive tactics to target companies that use pirated (illegal) copies of software.

Companies are responsible for ensuring that software in the corporate environment is not pirated and that the licenses (that is, license counts) are being abided by. An operations or configuration management department is often where this capability is located in a company. Automated asset management systems, or more general system management systems, may be able to report on the software installed throughout an environment, including a count of installations of each. These counts should be compared regularly (perhaps quarterly) against the inventory of licensed applications and counts of licenses purchased for each application. Applications that are found in the environment and for which no license is known to have been purchased by the company, or applications found in excess of the number of licenses known to have been purchased, should be investigated.

When applications are found in the environment for which the authorized change control and supply chain processes were not followed, they need to be brought under control, and the business area that acquired the application outside of the approved processes must be educated as to the legal and information security risks their actions may pose to the company. Many times, the business unit manager would need to sign a document indicating he understands this risk and is personally accepting it.

An application for which no valid business need can be found should be removed, and the person who installed the application should be educated and warned that future such actions may result in more severe consequences—like termination. This may sound extreme, but installing pirated software is not only an ethical violation but also both a liability risk and a potential vector for introducing malware. Organizations that use or tolerate unlicensed products are sometimes turned in by disgruntled employees as an act of revenge.

Companies should have an acceptable use policy (AUP) that indicates what software users can install and informs users that the environment will be surveyed from time to time to verify compliance. Technical controls should be emplaced to prevent unauthorized users from being able to install unauthorized software in the environment.

A fundamental best practice in software asset management is to prevent users from installing software and requiring them to submit a request for a system administrator to do so instead. This allows the administrator to ensure the software is properly licensed and added to the appropriate management systems. It also enables effective configuration management across the enterprise.

Controlling the existing hardware and software on our networks should be a precondition to provisioning new services and capabilities. To do otherwise risks making an already untenable position even worse.

Secure Provisioning

The term "provisioning" is overloaded in the technology world, which is to say that it means different actions to different people. To a telecommunications service provider, it could mean the process of running wires, installing customer premises equipment, configuring services, and setting up accounts to provide a given service (e.g., DSL). To an IT department, it could mean the acquisition, configuration, and deployment of an information system (e.g., a new server) within a broader enterprise environment. Finally, to a cloud services provider, provisioning could mean automatically spinning up a new instance of that physical server that the IT department delivered to us.

For the purpose of the CISSP exam, *provisioning* is the set of all activities required to provide one or more new information services to a user or group of users ("new" meaning previously not available to that user or group). Though this definition is admittedly broad, it does subsume all that the overloaded term means. As you will see in the following sections, the specific actions included in various types of provisioning vary significantly, while remaining squarely within our given definition.

At the heart of provisioning is the imperative to provide these information services in a secure manner. In other words, we must ensure that both the services and the devices on which they rely are secure. We already discussed supply chain risks in asset acquisition in Chapter 2. So, assuming you have a trusted supply chain, you would want to start with a Gold Master image applied to your devices as soon as you receive them. Ideally, you would then configure them according to the needs defined in the business and adapted to whatever classes of user they will support. Finally, you scan for vulnerabilities (just to be sure) and deploy it on the network. Easy, right?

Well, it gets a bit trickier when you deal with remote employees, which for many organizations are an increasing portion of their workforce. Some of the added concerns to consider are listed here:

- Securely shipping the devices to users
- Securely sending credentials to users
- Requirements for virtual private network (VPN) connectivity
- Remote monitoring of whether or not the device is on the VPN
- Making remote configuration changes
- Multifactor authentication while the device is disconnected

Obviously, the list of issues will very much depend on your particular situation. You may not have any remote users but perhaps you have a data center or hosting provider who owns the physical environment in which your assets reside. That presents its own set of concerns you need to think through in terms of secure provisioning. Finally, and perhaps inescapably, many of us have to consider unique issues when dealing with cloud assets.

Provisioning Cloud Assets

Generally, cloud provisioning is the set of all activities required to provide one or more new cloud assets to a user or group of users. So what exactly are these cloud assets? As we will see in Chapter 7, cloud computing is generally divided into three types of service: Infrastructure as a Service (IaaS), Platform as a Service (PaaS), and Software as a Service (SaaS). The provisioning of each type of service presents its own set of issues.

When we are dealing with provisioning IaaS assets, our user population is limited to the IT department. To see why this is true, we need only consider a noncloud (that is, physical) equivalent: provisioning a new server or router. Because these assets typically impact a large number of users in the organization, we must be very careful in planning and testing their provisioning. Accordingly, these provisioning actions often require the approval of the senior leadership or of the change control committee. Only a very small group of IT personnel should be able to perform such provisioning.

PaaS is similar to IaaS in terms of organizational impact, but oftentimes has a more limited scope. A platform, in this context, is typically a service such as a web or database management service. Though the IT team typically handles the provisioning, in some cases someone else in the organization may handle it. Consider, for example, the case of a development (intranet-only) web service that is being provisioned to test a web application that a team of coders is developing. Depending on the scope, context, and accessibility, this provisioning could be delegated to any one of the developers, though someone in IT would first constrain the platform to ensure it is accessible only to that team.

Finally, SaaS could be provisioned by a larger pool of users within the constraints established by the IT team in accordance with the organizational policy. If a given group of users is authorized to use the customer relationship management (CRM) system, then those users should be able to log into their accounts and self-provision that and any other applications to which they are authorized.

As you can see, the provisioning of cloud assets should be increasingly more controlled depending on the organizational impact and the risk profile of the specific asset. The key to secure provisioning is carefully setting up the cloud computing environment so that properly configured applications, platforms, and infrastructure are rapidly available to authorized users when and where they need them. After all, one of the benefits of cloud computing is the promise of self-service provisioning in near real time.

Asset Retention

Assets typically remain in use until they are no longer required, they become obsolete, or their O&M costs exceed their value to the organization. If they are no longer required, they may still be retained for some time in anticipation of future needs or perhaps for emergency use. Asset retention should be a deliberate decision that is documented and periodically revisited. Ideally, this is done as part of the change management process to ensure the retained (and no longer in use) assets don't pose undue risks.

Suppose your organization has a policy of refreshing laptops for its workforce every three years. After the latest refresh, you end up with a dozen laptops that are no longer required. Someone suggests you keep them around in case of an emergency, so you do. A couple of refresh cycles later, you end up with dozens of laptops (some of them potentially unable to run modern software) clogging up your storage spaces. This is a problem for at least four reasons. Firstly, you've run out of storage space. Secondly, there is a risk of theft since nobody is paying much attention to the laptops in the closet. Thirdly, they may no longer work when that emergency finally happens and you decide to pull them out and use them. Finally, and perhaps most seriously, unless they were properly decommissioned, they could have sensitive data in their disk drives that nobody is aware of.

Your asset retention decision-making should consider the fact that your asset life cycle may differ from its manufacturer's intended one. Original equipment manufacturers (OEMs) sell a particular product only for a specific period of time, typically one to three years. After that, they'll move on to the next version or may stop making it altogether. Either way, the product is no longer sold. OEMs will, however, continue to support their product after this point for some time, usually another three to six years. Replacement parts may still be sold and customer support resources will remain available to registered owners. *End-of-life (EOL)* for an asset is that point in time when its OEM is neither manufacturing nor sustaining it. In other words, you can't send it in for repairs, buy spare parts, or get technical assistance from the OEM. The risk in using assets after their announced EOL is that hardware failures will be much more difficult to address at reasonable costs.

There is a related term, *end-of-support (EOS)*, which is sometimes also called end-of-service-life (EOSL), that means that the manufacturer is no longer patching bugs or vulnerabilities on the product. Typically, manufacturers will continue issuing patches after a product reaches EOL for another few years. Sometimes, however, EOL and EOS coincide. Either way, we face significant risk after the product reaches EOS because whatever vulnerabilities are discovered will remain unpatched, meaning the asset is much more likely to be exploited.

Whether the business needs change or the asset reaches EOL or EOS, eventually it's time to retire it, which may drive a new business case. Before throwing an asset in the recycling bin, however, we need to properly decommission it.

Decommissioning Assets

Once an asset has reached the end of its useful life in your organization, it's important to follow a thorough process to decommission it. *Decommissioning* is the set of all activities required to permanently remove an existing asset from an operational environment. In a way, it is the opposite of provisioning.

The specific tasks required to decommission assets vary greatly depending on what the asset is. However, there are some overarching thoughts to consider before pulling the proverbial plug. These include the following:

- *Decommission only within the change management process.* The only way to minimize the risk of unintended (adverse) consequences when you pull the plug is to ensure that everyone who may have a stake in the asset is part of the decision.

- *Ensure that the asset is no longer in use.* It may seem obvious, but there may be unknown users (or uses) of the asset that were never properly documented. You'd hate to pull the plug, only to find out you killed a critical business process.
- *Review the impact on data retention.* We'll discuss data retention later in this chapter, but you have to ensure that there isn't any data in the asset (and only in that asset) that needs to be preserved.
- *Securely wipe any data on the asset.* It seems like just about every asset has the potential to hold sensitive data in nonvolatile memory or disk. Be sure you understand the persistent data storage capabilities in the asset, and you wipe them.
- *Safely dispose of the hardware.* Many assets have hazardous components such as lithium batteries that require special handling. Don't just toss that old computer into the dumpster before checking for environmental or safety hazards first.

Data Life Cycle

The data life cycle differs from the asset life cycle in some important ways. First, it usually doesn't cost anything to acquire most of the data our organizations use. Sure, there are notable exceptions, but, overall, we don't really have to demonstrate the ROI or get the chief financial officer (CFO) to agree that we need to know what each customer buys on an e-commerce site. (Actually, a CFO should be justifiably worried if that data is *not* being collected.) Another significant difference is that we can share our data with as many others as we'd like without losing it. Finally, data tends to be archived rather than disposed of when it is no longer immediately useful. Sure, we can put a workstation in a storage room in case we need it later, but this is the exception rather than the norm when dealing with tangible assets.

There are a number of data life-cycle models out there. The one we will use for our discussion is fairly simple but still effective when considering the changing nature of data and the security implications of those dynamics. At a macro level, we can divide the life of our data into six phases: acquisition, storage, use, sharing, archival, and destruction, as shown in Figure 5-2.

Data Acquisition

Generally speaking, data is acquired by an organization in one of three ways: collected directly, copied from elsewhere, or created from scratch. Collection is possible when an organization has sensors in an environment of interest. For example, an e-commerce site has a web server that can *collect* the IP address of visitors and what page referred them to the site. The application server can further collect the identity of each customer, which products they explored, and what they eventually bought. All this data can be enhanced by buying customer data from ad agencies and having it *copied* into a local data store. Finally, the marketing department can analyze all that data and *create* reports and forecasts.

Figure 5-2 The data life cycle

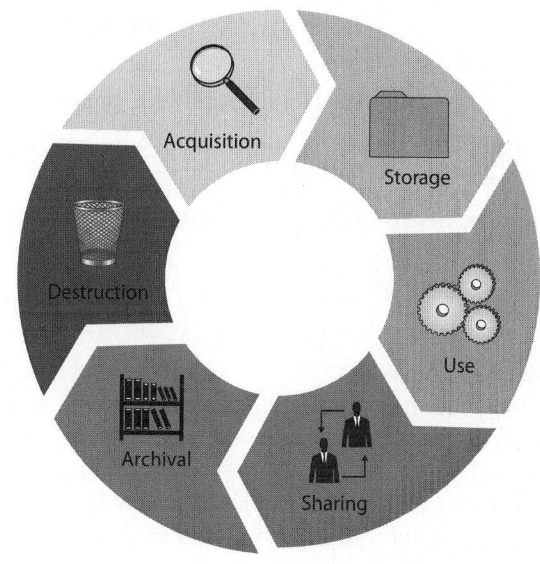

Data Collection

We must ensure that the data we collect, particularly when it is personal in nature, is necessary for our jobs. Generally speaking, organizations should collect the least amount of private personal data required for the performance of their business functions. In many cases, this is not a matter of choice but of law. As of 2020, over 128 countries have enacted privacy protection laws that affect organizations within their jurisdictions. It is important to note that privacy protections vary widely among countries. The European Union is one of the most restrictive regions with respect to privacy, while China effectively has no restrictions, and therefore no real privacy protections. The United States has very few restrictions on the collection of private data by nongovernmental organizations at the national level, but has states such as California with protections similar to those of the EU. The point is that you have to be aware of the specific privacy laws that pertain to the places in which your organization stores or uses its data. This is particularly important when you outsource services (which may require access to your data) to third parties in a different country.

Apart from applicable laws and regulations, the types of personal data that your organization collects, as well as its life-cycle considerations, must be a matter of explicit written policy. Your privacy policy needs to cover your organization's collection, use, disclosure, and protection of employee and client data. Many organizations break their privacy policy into two documents: an internal document that covers employee data, and an external document that covers customer information. At a minimum, you want to answer the following questions when writing your policy:

- What personal data is collected (e.g., name, website visits, e-mail messages, etc.)?
- Why do we collect this data and how do we use it (e.g., to provide a service, for security)?

- With whom do we share this data (e.g., third-party providers, law enforcement agencies)?
- Who owns the collected data (e.g., subject, organization)?
- What rights does the subject of this data have with regard to it (e.g., opt out, restrictions)?
- When do we destroy the data (e.g., after five years, never)?
- What specific laws or regulations exist that pertain to this data (e.g., HIPAA, GDPR)?

Data Storage

After data is acquired, but before it can be used, it must be stored somewhere. There are also other steps we must take to make the information useful. Typically, we attach both system metadata (e.g., author, date/time of creation, and permissions) and business process metadata (e.g., classification, project, and owner) to it. Finally, the data is indexed to facilitate searching and assigned to one or more data stores. In smaller organizations, much of this process is invisible to the user. All that person knows is that when they create a contact in the CRM system, an order in the purchasing system, or a ticket in the workflow system, the entry is magically available to everyone in the organization who needs to access the information. In larger organizations, the process needs to be carefully architected.

Finally, there are policy controls that we have to apply. For instance, we have to encrypt credit card numbers and certain other personally identifiable information (PII) wherever

Where in the World Is My Data?

Data location can be a particularly important issue, especially when dealing with personal, healthcare, or national security data. As we discussed in Chapter 3, some countries have *data localization* laws that require certain types of data to be stored and processed in that country (examples include China and Russia). Other countries have enacted *data sovereignty* laws that stipulate that anyone who stores or processes certain types of data (typically personal data on their citizens), whether or not they do so locally, must comply with those countries' laws. Meeting these requirements can be impossible without data classification. It can also be either enabled or hindered by cloud services. Used properly, cloud service providers can help ensure data localization requirements are met by restricting certain classifications of data to a region or even a specific country. If, on the other hand, data location is not considered when architecting a cloud solution, it is very likely that sensitive data will end up in some random location at some point, potentially causing no shortage of headaches (and perhaps legal and financial liability) to its owners.

we store them. We also have to implement strict controls on who gets to access sensitive information. Additionally, we may have to provide some sort of rollback capability to revert data to a previous state, particularly if users or processes may be able to corrupt it. These and many other important considerations must be deliberately addressed as we store the data and not as an afterthought.

Data Retention

There is no universal agreement on how long an organization should retain data. Legal and regulatory requirements (where they exist) vary among countries and business sectors. What is universal is the need to ensure your organization has and follows a documented data retention policy. Doing otherwise is flirting with disaster, particularly when dealing with pending or ongoing litigation. It is not enough, of course, to simply have a policy; you must ensure it is being followed, and you must document this through regular audits.

NOTE When outsourcing data storage, it is important to specify in the contract language how long the storage provider will retain your data after you stop doing business with them and what process they will use to eradicate your data from their systems.

A very straightforward and perhaps tempting approach would be to look at the lengthiest legal or regulatory retention requirement imposed on your organization and then apply that timeframe to all your data retention. The problem with this approach is that it will probably make your retained data set orders of magnitude greater than it needs to be. Not only does this impose additional storage costs, but it also makes it more difficult to comply with electronic discovery (e-discovery) orders. When you receive an e-discovery order from a court, you are typically required to produce a specific amount of data (usually pretty large) within a given timeframe (usually very short). Obviously, the more data you retain, the more difficult and expensive this process will be.

A better approach is to segregate the specific data sets that have mandated retention requirements and handle those accordingly. Everything else should have a retention period that minimally satisfies the business requirements. Commonly, different business units within medium and large organizations have different retention requirements. For instance, a company may want to keep data from its research and development (R&D) division for a much longer period than it keeps data from its customer service division. R&D projects that are not particularly helpful today may be so at a later date, but audio recordings of customer service calls probably don't have to hang around for several years.

NOTE Be sure to get buy-in from your legal counsel when developing or modifying data retention and privacy policies.

Developing a Retention Policy

At its core, every data retention policy answers three fundamental questions:

- What data do we keep?
- How long do we keep this data?
- Where do we keep this data?

Most security professionals understand the first two questions. After all, many of us are used to keeping tax records for three years in case we get audited. The "what" and the "how long" are easy. The last question, however, surprises more than a few of us. The twist is that the question is not so much about the location per se, but rather the manner in which the data is kept at that location. In order to be useful to us, retained data must be easy to locate and retrieve.

Think about it this way. Suppose your organization had a business transaction with Acme Corporation in which you learned that Acme was involved in the sale of a particular service to a client in another country. Two years later, you receive a third-party subpoena asking for any data you may have regarding that sale. You know you retain all your data for three years, but you have no idea where the relevant data may be. Was it an e-mail, a recording of a phone conversation, the minutes from a meeting, or something else? Where would you go looking for it? Alternatively, how could you make a case to the court that locating and providing the data would be too costly for your organization?

What Data We Retain There are many reasons to retain data. Among the more common ones are data analysis (to plot trends and make predictions), historical knowledge (how did we deal with this in the past?), and regulatory requirements. Again, legal counsel must be involved in this process to ensure all legal obligations are being met. Beyond these obligations, there will be specific information that is important to the business for a variety of reasons. It is also worth considering what data might be valuable in light of business arrangements, partnerships, or third-party dealings.

The decision to retain data must be deliberate, specific, and enforceable. We want to keep only the data that we consciously decide to keep, and then we want to ensure that we can enforce that retention. Importantly, there should be a way for us to ensure that data that should not be retained is promptly and properly disposed of. If this sounds painful, we need only consider the consequences of not getting this process right. Many companies have endured undue hardships because they couldn't develop, implement, and enforce a proper retention policy. Among the biggest challenges in this realm is the balance between business needs and employee or customer privacy.

How Long We Retain Once upon a time, there were two main data retention longevity approaches: the "keep nothing" camp and the "keep everything" camp. As the legal processes caught up with modern computer technology, it became clear that (except in very limited cases) these approaches were not acceptable. For starters, whether they

Data Retention in the Age of Big Data

The term *big data* refers to collections of data that exhibit five characteristics: volume, velocity, variety, veracity, and value. Volume refers to the sheer size of the data collection, which exceeds what can reasonably be stored in traditional systems like a regular data server or a conventional database management system. Velocity describes the high speed with which new data is added, while variety means that the data is not all in the same format or even concerning the same things. Because the data comes from a multitude of sources, its veracity is difficult to establish, but we oftentimes deal with this by looking for trends and clusters rather than individual data points. Finally, there is an expectation that all this data adds value to our organizations, which justifies the costs of storing and processing it in the first place.

This last point is the crux of data retention in the age of big data: just because we *can* keep every data point from every business unit and occasionally get valuable insights is not sufficient reason to keep the data. It is far easier (and way more cost effective) to develop a retention policy that allows us to build big data stores as needed, but does so in a way that balances risks, costs, and value. Are there privacy or confidentiality issues concerning any of the data? Could any data create a legal liability for the organization? Is any of the data likely to be subject to e-discovery? If so, how difficult would it be to comply with an e-discovery order?

Apart from any legal or regulatory concerns, there's also the practical one of deciding what data is useful and what is just taking up storage space. Even if the price tag of storage doesn't seem excessive now, left unchecked, we can get there quicker than expected if we keep pumping data in. And when we get there, how would we go about removing the data we no longer want or need?

This all underscores the importance of being deliberate about building our big data stores and having policies and procedures that support valid organizational requirements, while mitigating risks at a reasonable cost.

retained nothing or everything, organizations following one of these extreme approaches found out it was difficult to defend themselves in lawsuits. The first group had nothing with which to show due diligence, for instance, while those in the second group had too much information that plaintiffs could use against them. So what is the right data retention policy? Ask your legal counsel. Seriously.

There are myriads of statutory and regulatory retention requirements, which vary from jurisdiction to jurisdiction (sometimes even within the same country). There are also best practices and case law to consider, so we won't attempt to get too specific here. Still, Table 5-2 provides some general guidelines sufficient to start the conversation with your attorneys.

Type of Data	General Period of Retention
Business documents (e.g., meeting minutes)	7 years
Invoices	5 years
Accounts payable and receivable	7 years
Human resource files	7 years (for employees who leave) or 3 years (for candidates who were not hired)
Tax records	3 years after taxes were paid
Legal correspondence	Permanently

Table 5-2 Typical Retention Periods for Different Types of Data

How We Retain Data In order for retained data to be useful, it must be accessible in a timely manner. It really does us no good to have data that takes an inordinate (and perhaps prohibitive) amount of effort to query. To ensure this accessibility, we need to consider various issues, including the ones listed here.

- **Taxonomy** A taxonomy is a scheme for classifying data. This classification can be made using a variety of categories, including functional (e.g., human resources, product development), chronological (e.g., 2020), organizational (e.g., executives, union employees), or any combination of these or other categories.
- **Classification** The sensitivity classification of the data determines the controls we place on it both while it is in use and when it gets archived. This is particularly important because many organizations protect sensitive information while in use, but not so much after it goes into the archives.
- **Normalization** Retained data comes in a variety of formats, including word processing documents, database records, flat files, images, PDF files, video, and so on. Simply storing the data in its original format is not sufficient in any but the most trivial cases. Instead, we need to develop tagging schemas that make the data searchable.
- **Indexing** Retained data must be searchable if we are to quickly pull out specific items of interest. The most common approach to making data searchable is to build indexes for it. Many archiving systems implement this feature, but others do not. Either way, the indexing approach must support the likely future queries on the archived data.

Ideally, archiving occurs in a centralized, regimented, and homogenous manner. We all know, however, that this is seldom the case. We may have to compromise in order to arrive at solutions that meet our minimum requirements within our resource constraints. Still, as we plan and execute our retention strategies, we must remain focused on how we will efficiently access archived data many months or years later.

E-Discovery

Discovery of electronically stored information (ESI), or *e-discovery*, is the process of producing for a court or external attorney all ESI pertinent to a legal proceeding. For example, if your company is being sued for damages resulting from a faulty product, the plaintiff's attorney could get an e-discovery order compelling you to produce all e-mail between the QA team and senior executives in which the product's faults are discussed. If your data retention policy and procedures are adequate, e-discovery should not require excessive efforts. If, on the other hand, you have been slack about retention, such an order could cripple the organization.

The Electronic Discovery Reference Model (EDRM) identifies eight steps, though they are not necessarily all required, nor are they performed in a linear manner:

1. **Identification** of data required under the order.
2. **Preservation** of this data to ensure it is not accidentally or routinely destroyed while complying with the order.
3. **Collection** of the data from the various stores in which it may be.
4. **Processing** to ensure the correct format is used for both the data and its metadata.
5. **Review** of the data to ensure it is relevant.
6. **Analysis** of the data for proper context.
7. **Production** of the final data set to those requesting it.
8. **Presentation** of the data to external audiences to prove or disprove a claim.

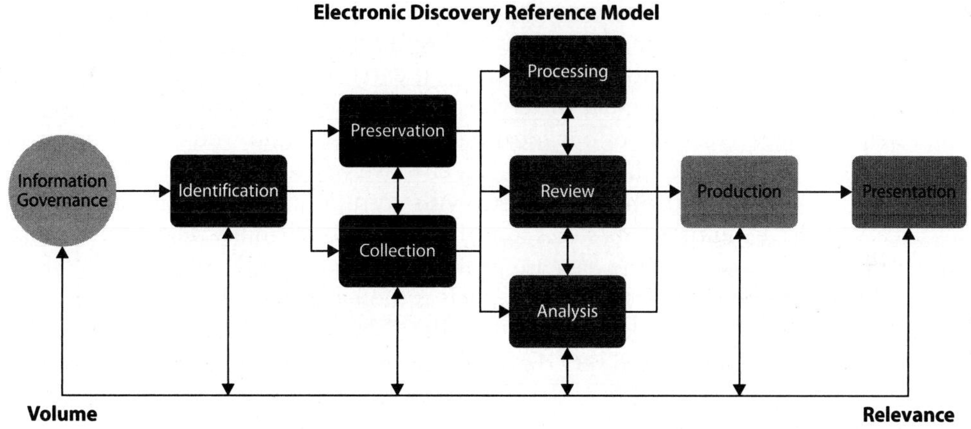

Electronic Discovery Reference Model

(Source: EDRM; www.edrm.net)

Data Use

After data is acquired and stored, it will spend much of its time being used. That is to say it will be read and modified by a variety of users with the necessary access level. From a security perspective, this stage in the data life cycle presents the most challenges in terms of ensuring confidentiality, integrity, and availability. You want the information available, but only to the right people who should then be able to modify it in authorized ways.

Consistency is also an issue with regard to policy and regulatory compliance. As the information is used and aggregated, it may trigger requirements that must be automatically enforced. For example, a document that refers to a project using a code word or name may be unclassified and freely available, but if that word/name is used in conjunction with other details (a place, purpose, or team members' names), then it would make the entire document classified. Changes in the information as it is in use must be mapped to the appropriate internal policies, and perhaps to regulations or laws.

Data Maintenance

As data is being used, we have to ensure that it remains accurate and internally consistent. Suppose that Sally is a salesperson in our organization. She meets a prospective customer named Charlie and enters his contact information and other details into a CRM system. E-mails are exchanged, meetings are scheduled, and documents are filed with Charlie's data. One day, Charlie gets a promotion and moves to corporate headquarters. Just like that, his title, phone number, and address all change. How do we ensure that we update this data and that we do it across the entire organization? Sure, the CRM piece is easy, but what about the myriad of other places in which the now obsolete data exists? We need to have a plan for maintaining the accuracy of data that is being used and may be critical to our business processes.

We must also consider what happens when the data is incorrect when it is first acquired. There was a recent story in the news about a police clerk who incorrectly entered the personal information of a convicted murderer who had just been transferred to his station. The information was actually that of an innocent citizen who had, earlier that day, applied for a permit. The erroneous information was shared across the country with local, national, and even private organizations. By the time the error was discovered, there was no way to globally correct the entry. To this day, that innocent man is periodically denied employment or services because some system shows that he is a convicted murderer. For most of our organizations, this scenario would likely result in hefty fines or a major lawsuit unless we had an effective way to maintain our data.

Another case for data maintenance deals with corruption and inconsistencies. For instance, if we have multiple data stores for performance or reliability purposes, we must ensure that modifications to the data are replicated. We also need to have mechanisms for automatically resolving inconsistencies, such as those that would occur from a server having a power outage after data has been modified but before it has been replicated. This is particularly important in very dynamic systems that have rollback capabilities.

Data Sharing

Gone are the days when any of us could accomplish anything significant solely on our own. Virtually every organization in the world, particularly those with information systems, is part of a supply chain. Information sharing is a key enabler of modern supply chains. Without it, we wouldn't be able to log into our systems (especially if you have a third-party identity management service like Google or Facebook), send or receive e-mail, or sell widgets online (it's hard to sell something without sharing payment card information with a payment processor).

While we all have some data sharing requirements imposed by our IT infrastructure, we also willingly share data with others for specific business reasons. For example, an e-commerce site will almost certainly partner with a digital advertising firm to drum up business and with a logistics company to deliver tangible goods. It may also partner with other companies that offer complementary goods or services and collect referral fees from each other. There are many other reasons to share data, but the important concept here is that this sharing needs to be deliberate. If you share the wrong data, or do so in the wrong way, you could lose competitive advantage or even break the law.

To avoid data sharing nightmares, be sure to involve all the necessary staff (business, IT, security, legal) in the conversation early. Discuss the business need to share data and restrict that data to the minimum essential to satisfy that need. Document the agreement in a legally binding contract that's been approved by your legal counsel. This agreement needs to specify the obligations of each party with regard to the entire shared data life cycle. For example, what data will be shared, how it will be stored and used by each party, with whom it may be shared, how it will be archived and for how long, and, finally, when and how it will be destroyed.

Data Archival

The data in our systems will likely stop being used regularly (or at all) at some point. When this happens, but before we get rid of it, we probably want to retain it for a variety of reasons. Maybe we anticipate that it will again be useful at a later time, or maybe we are required to keep it around for a certain period of time, as is the case with certain financial information. Whatever the reason for moving this data off to the side, the fact that it is no longer regularly used could mean that unauthorized or accidental access and changes to it could go undetected for a long time if we don't implement appropriate controls. Of course, the same lack of use could make it easier to detect this threat if we do have the right controls.

Another driver for retention is the need for backups. Whether we're talking about user or back-end backups, it is important to consider our risk assessment when deciding which backups are protected and how. To the extent that end-user backups are performed to removable disk drives, it is difficult to imagine a scenario in which these backups should not be encrypted. Every major operating system provides a means to perform automatic backups as well as encrypt those backups. Let's take advantage of this.

This all leads us to the question of how long we need to retain data. If we discard it too soon, we risk not being able to recover from a failure or an attack. We also risk not being able to comply with e-discovery requests or subpoenas. If we keep the data for too long,

Backup vs. Archive

The terms backup and archive are sometimes used interchangeably. In reality, they have different meanings that are best illustrated using the life-cycle model described in this section. A data *backup* is a copy of a data set currently in use that is made for the purpose of recovering from the loss of the original data. Backup data normally becomes less useful as it gets older.

A data *archive* is a copy of a data set that is no longer in use, but is kept in case it is needed at some future point. When data is archived, it is usually removed from its original location so that the storage space is available for data in use.

we risk excessive costs as well as increased liabilities. The answer, once again, is that this is all part of our risk management process and needs to be codified in policies.

Data Destruction

Sooner or later, every organization will have to dispose of data. This usually, but not always, means data destruction. Old mailboxes, former employee records, and past financial transactions are all examples of data sets that must, at some point, be destroyed. When this time comes, there are two important issues to consider: that the data does in fact get destroyed, and that it is destroyed correctly. When we discuss roles and responsibilities later in this chapter, we'll see who is responsible for ensuring that both of these issues are taken care of.

A twist on the data destruction issue is when we need to transfer the data to another party and then destroy it on our data stores. For instance, organizations hosting services for their clients typically have to deal with requests to do a bulk export of their data when they migrate to another provider. Companies sometimes sell accounts (e.g., home mortgages) to each other, in which case the data is transferred and eventually (after the mandatory retention period) destroyed on the original company's systems.

No matter the reason, we have to ensure that the data is properly destroyed. How this is done is, again, tied to our risk management. The bottom line is that the data must be rendered sufficiently difficult for an adversary to recover so that the risk of such recovery is acceptable to our organization. This is not hard to do when we are dealing with physical devices such as hard disk drives that can be wiped, degaussed, or shredded (or all of these in particularly risk-adverse organizations such as certain government entities). Data destruction can be a bit more complicated when we deal with individual files (or parts thereof) or database records (such as many e-mail systems use for mailbox storage). Further complicating matters, it is very common for multiple copies of each data item to exist across our information systems. How can you ensure that all versions are gone? The point is that the technical details of how and where the data is stored are critical to ensuring its proper destruction.

Data Remanence

Even when policies exist (and are enforced and audited) to ensure the protection of privacy, it is possible for technical issues to threaten this privacy. It is a well-known fact that most data deletion operations do not, in fact, erase anything; normally, they simply mark the memory as available for other data, without wiping (or even erasing) the original data. This is true not only of file systems but also of databases. Since it is difficult to imagine a data store that would not fit in either of these two constructs, it should be clear that simply "deleting" data will likely result in data remanence issues.

NOTE NIST Special Publication 800-88, Revision 1, *Guidelines for Media Sanitization* (December 2014), describes the best practices for combating data remanence.

Let's consider what happens when we create a text file using the File Allocation Table (FAT) file system. Though this original form of FAT is antiquated, its core constructs

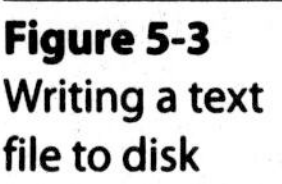

Figure 5-3 Writing a text file to disk

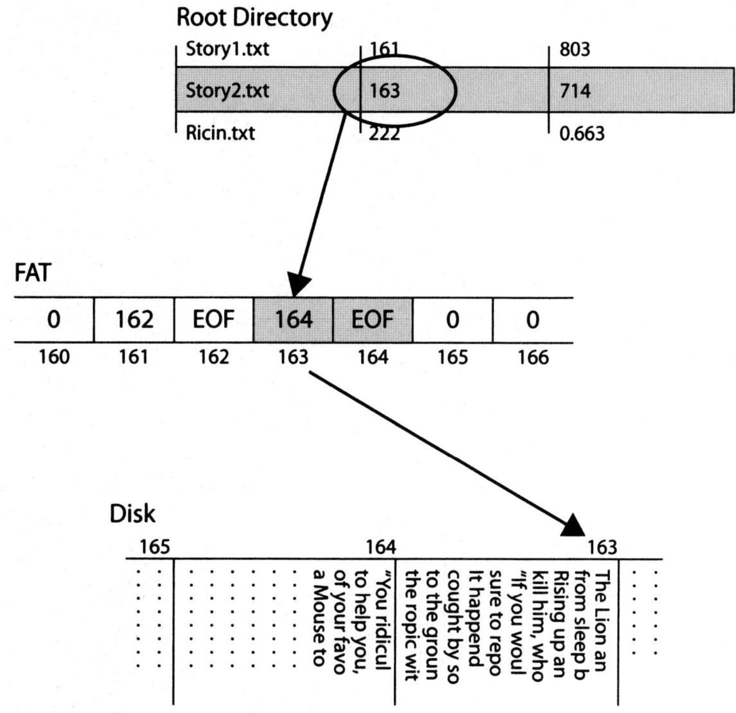

(e.g., disk blocks, free block list/table, file metadata table) are also found at the heart of all other modern file systems. Its simplicity makes it a wonderful training tool for the purpose of explaining file creation and deletion.

Suppose we type up the famous Aesop fable titled "The Lion and the Mouse" in a text editor and save it to disk. The operating system will ask us for a filename, which will be Story2.txt for this example. The system will then check the File Allocation Table for available blocks on which to store the text file. As shown in Figure 5-3, the system creates a directory entry for the file containing the name (Story2.txt), location of the first block (163), and the file size in bytes (714). In our simplistic example, each block is 512 bytes in size, so we'll need two of them. Fortunately, block 164 is right next to the start block and is also free. The system will use the entry for block 163 (the first block of the file) to point to the next block containing it (164). This allows files to occupy discontinuous blocks if the disk is heavily fragmented. That chain of blocks could be quite long if the file was big enough and we didn't run out of disk space first. In our simple example, however, we just need two blocks, so block 164 is the final one in use and gets a special label of EOF to denote the end of the file.

Suppose we decide to delete the file. Instead of cleaning up the table, the FAT file system will simply replace the first character of the filename in the directory table with a reserved character (shown in Figure 5-4 as a question mark) to indicate that the file was deleted. The starting block will be preserved in the directory, but the corresponding entries in the File Allocation Table are zeroed out to show that those blocks are available

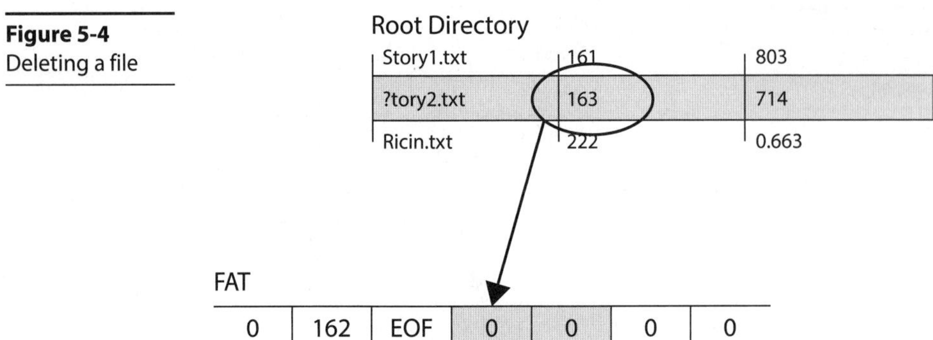

Figure 5-4 Deleting a file

for other files. As you can see in Figure 5-4, the contents of the file on the disk remain intact. This is why data remanence is such a big problem: because file systems almost never securely wipe data when deleting files.

At some point, however, users will create new files and save them to disk, which could result in our original data being partly or completely overwritten. This is shown in Figure 5-5. In this case, the new file requires only one block of disk space because it only contains the text "Hello World!" Suppose the user calls this file "hello.txt" and the system stores it in block 163, which used to be the start block for the previous Story2.txt file. That block will be overwritten with the new file's content and almost certainly padded with empty characters to fill out the block. The next block, however, contains the remainder of the deleted file, so partial contents are still available to anyone with the right recovery tools. Note also that the original file's metadata is preserved in the directory table until that block is needed for another file.

This example, though simplistic, illustrates the process used by almost every file system when creating and deleting files. The data structures may be named differently in modern versions of Windows, Linux, and macOS, but their purpose and behavior remain essentially the same. In fact, many databases use a similar approach to "deleting" entries by simply marking them as deleted without wiping the original data.

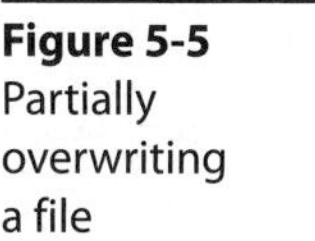

Figure 5-5 Partially overwriting a file

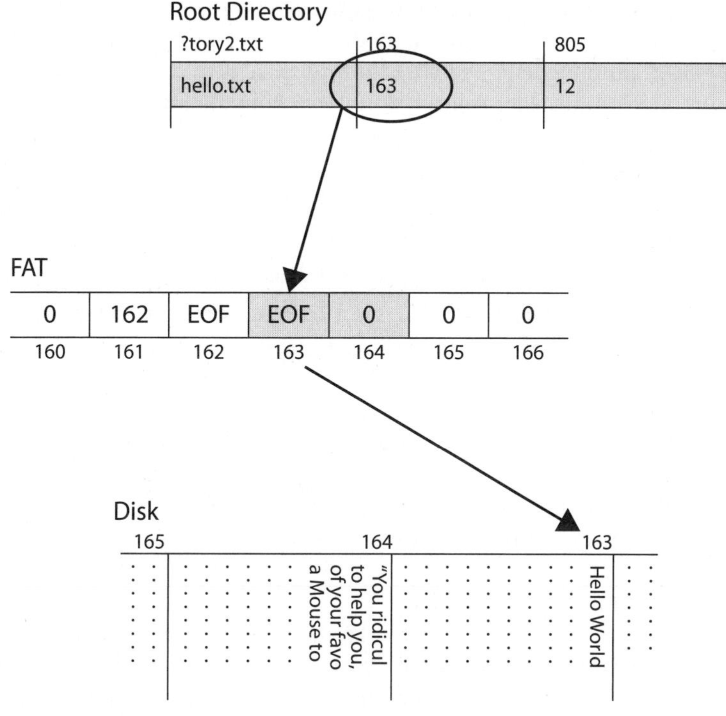

To counter data remanence, it is important to identify procedures for ensuring that private data is properly removed. Generally speaking, there are four approaches to eliminating data remanence:

- **Overwriting** Overwriting data entails replacing the 1's and 0's that represent it on storage media with random or fixed patterns of 1's and 0's in order to render the original data unrecoverable. This should be done at least once (e.g., overwriting the medium with 1's, 0's, or a pattern of these), but may have to be done more than that. For many years the U.S. Department of Defense (DoD) standard 5220.22-M required that media be overwritten seven times. This standard has since been superseded. DoD systems with sensitive information must now be degaussed.
- **Degaussing** This is the process of removing or reducing the magnetic field patterns on conventional disk drives or tapes. In essence, a powerful magnetic force is applied to the media, which results in the wiping of the data and sometimes the destruction of the motors that drive the platters. While it may still be possible to recover the data, it is typically cost prohibitive to do so.
- **Encryption** Many mobile devices take this approach to quickly and securely render data unusable. The premise is that the data is stored on the medium in encrypted format using a strong key. To render the data unrecoverable, the system simply needs to securely delete the encryption key, which is many times faster than deleting the encrypted data. Recovering the data in this scenario is typically computationally infeasible.

- **Physical destruction** Perhaps the best way to combat data remanence is to simply destroy the physical media. The two most commonly used approaches to destroying media are to shred it or expose it to caustic or corrosive chemicals that render it unusable. Another approach is incineration.

Data Roles

The data life cycle and, just as importantly, its protection, is driven by responsible and accountable individuals within each organization. We've already seen how data breaches can wreak havoc on otherwise successful companies and even drive them (or their key leaders) out of business. While this is not an exhaustive list, the following sections describe some of the key responsibilities by role when it comes to protecting data.

Data Controllers

Data controllers decide why and how different types of data will be processed. These are the senior managers that set policies with regard to the management of the data life cycle, particularly with regard to sensitive data such as personal data. Once these controllers set the policy, it is up to the rest of the organization to abide by it.

Data Owners

Data owners are responsible for the life cycle management of a set of data. Among the responsibilities of the data owners are data classification and the approval of disclosure requests. The data owners, therefore, indirectly or directly decide who gets access to specific data. This is particularly important given that these individuals typically are senior managers within the organization. In reality, the majority of these decisions should be codified in formal written policies. Any exceptions to policy should be just that—exceptions—and must be properly documented.

Data Custodians

It is good and well to have policies addressing the life cycle of your data, but someone needs to implement them at the technical level. These individuals are the data custodians, who are responsible for controlling access to the data, implementing the required security controls, and ensuring that both the data and manner in which it is used can be audited. Data custodians also participate in the change management process for all matters pertaining to the data life cycle.

Data Processors

The group of users best positioned to protect (or compromise) data consists of those who deal with that data on a routine basis: *data processors*. These individuals can be found in a variety of places within the organization depending on what particular data is of concern. The critical issue here is that these individuals understand the boundaries of what acceptable behavior is and (just as importantly) know what to do when data is accidentally or intentionally handled in a manner that does not conform to applicable policies. The best ways to address this issue are through training and auditing. On the one hand, data processors must be properly trained to handle their duties and responsibilities. On the other hand, there must be routine inspections to ensure their behavior complies with all applicable laws, regulations, and policies.

Data Subjects

All personal data concerns a real individual. The person about whom the data is concerned is the data subject. While data subjects are seldom involved in the organizational data life cycle, we all have a solemn duty to protect them and their privacy as we use their data for our own purposes. Respect for the data subjects is foundational to ensuring the protection and privacy of their data.

Chapter Review

Protecting assets, particularly information, is critical to any organization and must be incorporated into the comprehensive risk management process described in Chapter 2. This protection will probably require different controls at different phases in the data life cycle, so it is important to consider phase-specific risks when selecting controls. Rather than trying to protect all information equally, our organizations need classification standards that help us identify, handle, and protect data according to its sensitivity and criticality. We must also consider the roles played by various people in the organization. From the senior executives to the newest and most junior member of the team, everyone who interacts with our information has (and should understand) specific responsibilities with regard to protecting our assets.

A key responsibility is the protection of privacy of personal information. For various legal, regulatory, and operational reasons, we want to limit how long we hold on to personal information. There is no one-size-fits-all approach to data retention, so it is incumbent on the organization's leadership to consider a multitude of factors when developing privacy and data retention policies. These policies, in turn, should drive risk-based controls, baselines, and standards applied to the protection of our data. A key element in applying controls needs to be the proper use of strong cryptography.

Quick Review

- Data goes through a life cycle that starts with its acquisition and ends with its disposal.
- Each phase of the data life cycle requires different considerations when assessing risks and selecting controls.
- New information is prepared for use by adding metadata, including classification labels.

- Ensuring the consistency of data must be a deliberate process in organizations that use data replication.
- Cryptography can be an effective control at all phases of the data life cycle.
- The data retention policy drives the timeframe at which data transitions from the archival phase to the disposal phase of its life cycle.
- Information classification corresponds to the information's value to the organization.
- Each classification should have separate handling requirements and procedures pertaining to how that data is accessed, used, and destroyed.
- Senior executives are ultimately responsible to the shareholders for the successes and failures of their corporations, including security issues.
- The data owner is the manager in charge of a specific business unit and is ultimately responsible for the protection and use of a specific subset of information.
- Data owners specify the classification of data, and data custodians implement and maintain controls to enforce the set classification levels.
- The data retention policy must consider legal, regulatory, and operational requirements.
- The data retention policy should address what data is to be retained, where, how, and for how long.
- Electronic discovery (e-discovery) is the process of producing for a court or external attorney all electronically stored information (ESI) pertinent to a legal proceeding.
- Normal deletion of a file does not permanently remove it from media.
- NIST SP 800-88, Revision 1, *Guidelines for Media Sanitization*, describes the best practices for combating data remanence.
- Overwriting data entails replacing the 1's and 0's that represent it on storage media with random or fixed patterns of 1's and 0's to render the original data unrecoverable.
- Degaussing is the process of removing or reducing the magnetic field patterns on conventional disk drives or tapes.
- Privacy pertains to personal information, both from your employees and your customers.
- Generally speaking, organizations should collect the least amount of private personal data required for the performance of their business functions.
- Mobile devices are easily lost or stolen and should proactively be configured to mitigate the risks of data loss or leakage.
- Paper products oftentimes contain information that deserves controls commensurate to the sensitivity and criticality of that information.

Questions

Please remember that these questions are formatted and asked in a certain way for a reason. Keep in mind that the CISSP exam is asking questions at a conceptual level. Questions may not always have the perfect answer, and the candidate is advised against always looking for the perfect answer. Instead, the candidate should look for the best answer in the list.

1. Which of the following statements is true about the data life cycle?
   A. The data life cycle begins with its archival and ends with its classification.
   B. Most data must be retained indefinitely.
   C. The data life cycle begins with its acquisition/creation and ends with its disposal/destruction.
   D. Preparing data for use does not typically involve adding metadata to it.
2. Ensuring data consistency is important for all the following reasons, *except*
   A. Replicated data sets can become desynchronized.
   B. Multiple data items are commonly needed to perform a transaction.
   C. Data may exist in multiple locations within our information systems.
   D. Multiple users could attempt to modify data simultaneously.
3. Which of the following makes the most sense for a single organization's classification levels for data?
   A. Unclassified, Secret, Top Secret
   B. Public, Releasable, Unclassified
   C. Sensitive, Controlled unclassified information (CUI), Proprietary
   D. Proprietary, Trade Secret, Private
4. Which of the following is the most important criterion in determining the classification of data?
   A. The level of damage that could be caused if the data were disclosed
   B. The likelihood that the data will be accidentally or maliciously disclosed
   C. Regulatory requirements in jurisdictions within which the organization is not operating
   D. The cost of implementing controls for the data
5. Who bears ultimate responsibility for the protection of assets within the organization?
   A. Data owners
   B. Cyber insurance providers
   C. Senior management
   D. Security professionals

6. During which phase or phases of the data life cycle can cryptography be an effective control?
   - **A.** Use
   - **B.** Archival
   - **C.** Disposal
   - **D.** All the above
7. A transition into the disposal phase of the data life cycle is most commonly triggered by
   - **A.** Senior management
   - **B.** Insufficient storage
   - **C.** Acceptable use policies
   - **D.** Data retention policies
8. Information classification is most closely related to which of the following?
   - **A.** The source of the information
   - **B.** The information's destination
   - **C.** The information's value
   - **D.** The information's age
9. The data owner is most often described by all of the following *except*
   - **A.** Manager in charge of a business unit
   - **B.** Ultimately responsible for the protection of the data
   - **C.** Financially liable for the loss of the data
   - **D.** Ultimately responsible for the use of the data
10. Who has the primary responsibility of determining the classification level for information?
    - **A.** The functional manager
    - **B.** Senior management
    - **C.** The owner
    - **D.** The user
11. If different user groups with different security access levels need to access the same information, which of the following actions should management take?
    - **A.** Decrease the security level on the information to ensure accessibility and usability of the information.
    - **B.** Require specific written approval each time an individual needs to access the information.
    - **C.** Increase the security controls on the information.
    - **D.** Decrease the classification label on the information.

12. What should management consider the most when classifying data?
    A. The type of employees, contractors, and customers who will be accessing the data
    B. Availability, integrity, and confidentiality
    C. Assessing the risk level and disabling countermeasures
    D. The access controls that will be protecting the data
13. Which of the following requirements should the data retention policy address?
    A. Legal
    B. Regulatory
    C. Operational
    D. All the above
14. Which of the following is *not* addressed by the data retention policy?
    A. What data to keep
    B. For whom data is kept
    C. How long data is kept
    D. Where data is kept
15. Which of the following best describes the mitigation of data remanence by a physical destruction process?
    A. Replacing the 1's and 0's that represent data on storage media with random or fixed patterns of 1's and 0's
    B. Converting the 1's and 0's that represent data with the output of a cryptographic function
    C. Removing or reducing the magnetic field patterns on conventional disk drives or tapes
    D. Exposing storage media to caustic or corrosive chemicals that render it unusable
16. Which of the following best describes the mitigation of data remanence by a degaussing destruction process?
    A. Replacing the 1's and 0's that represent data on storage media with random or fixed patterns of 1's and 0's
    B. Converting the 1's and 0's that represent data with the output of a cryptographic function
    C. Removing or reducing the magnetic field patterns on conventional disk drives or tapes
    D. Exposing storage media to caustic or corrosive chemicals that render it unusable

17. Which of the following best describes the mitigation of data remanence by an overwriting process?
    A. Replacing the 1's and 0's that represent data on storage media with random or fixed patterns of 1's and 0's
    B. Converting the 1's and 0's that represent data with the output of a cryptographic function
    C. Removing or reducing the magnetic field patterns on conventional disk drives or tapes
    D. Exposing storage media to caustic or corrosive chemicals that render it unusable

Answers

1. **C.** Although various data life-cycle models exist, they all begin with the creation or acquisition of the data and end with its ultimate disposal (typically destruction).
2. **B.** Although it is typically true that multiple data items are needed for a transaction, this has much less to do with the need for data consistency than do the other three options. Consistency is important because we oftentimes keep multiple copies of a given data item.
3. **A.** This is a typical set of classification levels for government and military organizations. Each of the other options has at least two terms that are synonymous or nearly synonymous.
4. **A.** There are many criteria for classifying data, but it is most important to focus on the value of the data or the potential loss from its disclosure. The likelihood of disclosure, irrelevant jurisdictions, and cost considerations should not be central to the classification process.
5. **C.** Senior management always carries the ultimate responsibility for the organization.
6. **D.** Cryptography can be an effective control at every phase in the data life cycle. During data acquisition, a cryptographic hash can certify its integrity. When sensitive data is in use or in archives, encryption can protect it from unauthorized access. Finally, encryption can be an effective means of destroying the data.
7. **D.** Data retention policies should be the primary reason for the disposal of most of our information. Senior management or lack of resources should seldom, if ever, be the reason we dispose of data, while acceptable use policies have little, if anything, to do with it.
8. **C.** Information classification is very strongly related to the information's value and/or risk. For instance, trade secrets that are the key to a business's success are highly valuable, which will lead to a higher classification level. Similarly, information that could severely damage a company's reputation presents a high level of risk and is similarly classified at a higher level.

9. **C.** The data owner is the manager in charge of a specific business unit, and is ultimately responsible for the protection and use of a specific subset of information. In most situations, this person is not financially liable for the loss of his or her data.
10. **C.** A company can have one specific data owner or different data owners who have been delegated the responsibility of protecting specific sets of data. One of the responsibilities that goes into protecting this information is properly classifying it.
11. **C.** If data is going to be available to a wide range of people, more granular security should be implemented to ensure that only the necessary people access the data and that the operations they carry out are controlled. The security implemented can come in the form of authentication and authorization technologies, encryption, and specific access control mechanisms.
12. **B.** The best answer to this question is B, because to properly classify data, the data owner must evaluate the availability, integrity, and confidentiality requirements of the data. Once this evaluation is done, it will dictate which employees, contractors, and users can access the data, which is expressed in answer A. This assessment will also help determine the controls that should be put into place.
13. **D.** The data retention policy should follow the laws of any jurisdiction within which the organization's data resides. It must similarly comply with any regulatory requirements. Finally, the policy must address the organization's operational requirements.
14. **B.** The data retention policy should address what data to keep, where to keep it, how to store it, and for how long to keep it. The policy is not concerned with "for whom" the data is kept.
15. **D.** Two of the most common approaches to destroying data physically involve shredding the storage media or exposing it to corrosive or caustic chemicals. In certain highly sensitive government organizations, these approaches are used in tandem to make the risk of data remanence negligible.
16. **C.** Degaussing is typically accomplished by exposing magnetic media (such as hard disk drives or magnetic tapes) to powerful magnetic fields in order to change the orientation of the particles that physically represent 1's and 0's.
17. **A.** Data remanence can be mitigated by overwriting every bit on the storage medium. This is normally accomplished by writing all 0's, or all 1's, or a fixed pattern of them, or a random sequence of them. Better results can be obtained by repeating the process with different patterns multiple times.

CHAPTER 6

Data Security

This chapter presents the following:

- Data states
- Data security controls
- Data protection methods

Data is a precious thing and will last longer than the systems themselves.

—Tim Berners-Lee

Having addressed assets in general in the previous chapter, we now turn our attention to specific ways in which we go about protecting one of our most precious assets: data. One of the facts that makes securing data so difficult is that it can seemingly flow and rest anywhere in the world, literally. Even that virtual sticky note on your home computer's desktop reminding you to pick up some milk can be backed up automatically and its contents stored almost anywhere in the world unless you take steps to control it. The same issue arises, though with more significant consequences, when we consider data in our organizations' IT systems.

Clearly, the manner in which we protect our data depends on where it is and what it is doing (or having done to it). That sticky note on your desktop has different security implications than a confidential message being transmitted between two government organizations. Part of the decision deals with the data classification we discussed in Chapter 5, but another part deals with whether the data is just sitting somewhere, moving between places, or actively being worked on. These are the data states, and they determine what security controls make sense over time.

Data Security Controls

As described in Chapter 5, which types of controls should be implemented per classification depends upon the level of protection that management and the security team have determined is needed. The numerous types of controls available are discussed throughout this book. But some considerations pertaining to sensitive data and applications are common across most organizations:

- Strict and granular access control for all levels of sensitive data and programs
- Encryption of data while stored and while in transit

- Auditing and monitoring (determine what level of auditing is required and how long logs are to be retained)
- Separation of duties (determine whether two or more people must be involved in accessing sensitive information to protect against fraudulent activities; if so, define and document procedures)
- Periodic reviews (review classification levels, and the data and programs that adhere to them, to ensure they are still in alignment with business needs; data or applications may also need to be reclassified or declassified, depending upon the situation)
- Backup and recovery procedures (define and document)
- Change control procedures (define and document)
- Physical security protection (define and document)
- Information flow channels (where does the sensitive data reside and how does it traverse the network)
- Proper disposal actions, such as shredding, degaussing, and so on (define and document)
- Marking, labeling, and handling procedures

Clearly, this is not an exhaustive list. Still, it should be a good start as you delve into whatever specific compliance requirements apply to your organization. Keep in mind that the controls that constitute adequate data protections vary greatly between jurisdictions. When it comes to compliance, always be sure to consult your legal counsel.

Data States

Which controls we choose to use to mitigate risks to our information depend not only on the value we assign to that information but also on the dynamic state of that information. Generally speaking, data exists in one of three states: at rest, in motion, or in use. These states and their interrelations are shown in Figure 6-1. The risks to each state are different in significant ways, as described next.

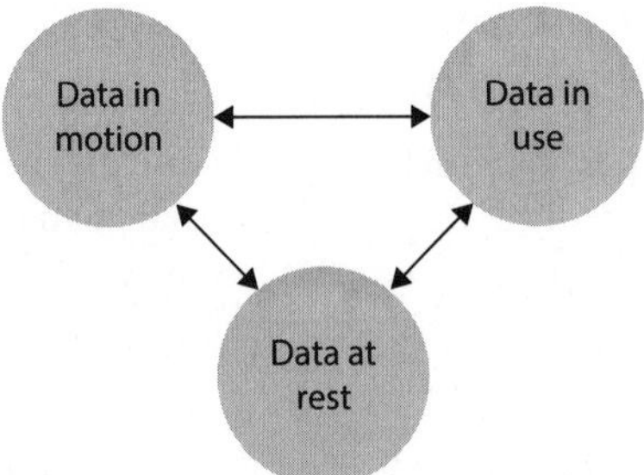

Figure 6-1
The states of data

Data at Rest

Information in an information system spends most of its time waiting to be used. The term *data at rest* refers to data that resides in external or auxiliary storage devices, such as hard disk drives (HDDs), solid-state drives (SSDs), optical discs (CD/DVD), or even on magnetic tape. A challenge with protecting data in this state is that it is vulnerable, not only to threat actors attempting to reach it over our systems and networks but also to anyone who can gain physical access to the device. It is not uncommon to hear of data breaches caused by laptops or mobile devices being stolen. In fact, one of the largest personal health information (PHI) breaches occurred in San Antonio, Texas, in September 2009 when an employee left unattended in his car backup tapes containing PHI on some 4.9 million patients. A thief broke into the vehicle and made off with the data. The solution to protecting data in such scenarios is as simple as it is ubiquitous: encryption.

Every major operating system now provides means to encrypt individual files or entire volumes in a way that is almost completely transparent to the user. Third-party software is also available to encrypt compressed files or perform whole-disk encryption. What's more, the current state of processor power means that there is no noticeable decrease in the performance of computers that use encryption to protect their data. Unfortunately, encryption is not yet the default configuration in any major operation system. The process of enabling it, however, is so simple that it borders on the trivial.

Many medium and large organizations now have policies that require certain information to be encrypted whenever it is stored in an information system. While typically this applies to PII, PHI, or other regulated information, some organizations are taking the proactive step of requiring whole-disk encryption to be used on all portable computing devices such as laptops and external hard drives. Beyond what are clearly easily pilfered devices, we should also consider computers we don't normally think of as mobile. Another major breach of PHI was reported by Sutter Health of California in 2011 when a thief broke a window and stole a desktop computer containing the unencrypted records on more than 4 million patients. We should resolve to encrypt all data being stored anywhere, and modern technology makes this easier than ever. This approach to "encrypt everywhere" reduces the risk of users accidentally storing sensitive information in unencrypted volumes.

NOTE NIST Special Publication 800-111, *Guide to Storage Encryption Technologies for End User Devices*, provides a good, if somewhat dated (2007), approach to this topic.

Data in Motion

Data in motion is data that is moving between computing nodes over a data network such as the Internet. This is perhaps the riskiest time for our data: when it leaves the confines of our protected enclaves and ventures into that Wild West that is the Internet. Fortunately, encryption once again rises to the challenge. The single best protection for our data while it is in motion (whether within or without our protected networks) is strong encryption such as that offered by Transport Layer Security (TLS version 1.2 and later) or IPSec. We will discuss strong (and weak) encryption in Chapter 8, but for now you should be aware that TLS and IPSec support multiple cipher suites and that some of these are not as strong as others. Weaknesses typically are caused by attempts to ensure backward compatibility, but result in unnecessary (or perhaps unknown) risks.

NOTE The terms data in motion, data in transit, and data in flight are all used interchangeably.

By and large, TLS relies on digital certificates (more on those in Chapter 8) to certify the identity of one or both endpoints. Typically, the server uses a certificate but the client doesn't. This one-way authentication can be problematic because it relies on the user to detect a potential impostor. A common exploit for this vulnerability is known as a man-in-the-middle (MitM) attack. The attacker intercepts the request from the client to the server and impersonates the server, pretending to be, say, Facebook. The attacker presents to the client a fake web page that looks exactly like Facebook and requests the user's credentials. Once the user provides that information, the attacker can forward the log-in request to Facebook and then continue to relay information back and forth between the client and the server over secure connections, intercepting all traffic in the process. A savvy client would detect this by noticing that the web browser reports a problem with the server's certificate. (It is extremely difficult for all but certain nation-states to spoof a legitimate certificate.) Most users, however, simply click through any such warnings without thinking of the consequences. This tendency to ignore the warnings underscores the importance of security awareness in our overall efforts to protect our information and systems.

Another approach to protecting our data in motion is to use trusted channels between critical nodes. Virtual private networks (VPNs) are frequently used to provide secure connections between remote users and corporate resources. VPNs are also used to securely connect campuses or other nodes that are physically distant from each other. The trusted channels we thus create allow secure communications over shared or untrusted network infrastructure.

Data in Use

Data in use is the term for data residing in primary storage devices, such as volatile memory (e.g., RAM), memory caches, or CPU registers. Typically, data remains in primary storage for short periods of time while a process is using it. Note, however, that anything stored in volatile memory could persist there for extended periods (until power is shut down) in some cases. The point is that data in use is being touched by the CPU or ALU in the computer system and will eventually go back to being data at rest, or end up being deleted.

As discussed earlier, data at rest should be encrypted. The challenge is that, in most operating systems today, the data must be decrypted before it is used. In other words, data in use generally cannot be protected by encrypting it. Many people think this is safe, the thought process being, "If I'm encrypting my data at rest and in transit already, why would I worry about protecting it during the brief period in which it is being used by the CPU? After all, if someone can get to my volatile memory, I probably have bigger problems than protecting this little bit of data, right?" Not really.

Various independent researchers have demonstrated effective side-channel attacks against memory shared by multiple processes. A *side-channel attack* exploits information that is being leaked by a cryptosystem. As we will see in our discussion of cryptology in Chapter 8, a cryptosystem can be thought of as connecting two channels: a plaintext channel and an encrypted one. A *side channel* is any information flow that is the electronic by-product of this process. As an illustration of this, imagine yourself being transported in the windowless back of a van. You have no way of knowing where you are going, but you can infer some aspects of the route by feeling the centrifugal force when the van makes a turn or follows a curve. You could also pay attention to the engine noise or the pressure in your ears as you climb or descend hills. These are all side channels. Similarly, if you are trying to recover the secret keys used to encrypt data, you could pay attention to how much power is being consumed by the CPU or how long it takes for other processes to read and write from memory. Researchers have been able to recover 2,048-bit keys from shared systems in this manner.

But the threats are not limited to cryptosystems alone. The infamous Heartbleed security bug of 2014 demonstrated how failing to check the boundaries of requests to read from memory could expose information from one process to others running on the same system. In that bug, the main issue was that anyone communicating with the server could request an arbitrarily long "heartbeat" message from it. Heartbeat messages are typically short strings that let the other end know that an endpoint is still there and wanting to communicate. The developers of the library being used for this never imagined that someone would ask for a string that was hundreds of characters in length. The attackers, however, did think of this and in fact were able to access crypto keys and other sensitive data belonging to other users.

More recently, the Meltdown, Spectre, and BranchScope attacks that came to light in 2018 show how a clever attacker can exploit hardware features in most modern CPUs. Meltdown, which affects Intel and ARM microprocessors, works by exploiting the manner in which memory mapping occurs. Since cache memory is a lot faster than main memory, most modern CPUs include ways to keep frequently used data in the faster cache. Spectre and BranchScope, on the other hand, take advantage of a feature called speculative execution, which is meant to improve the performance of a process by guessing what future instructions will be based on data available in the present. All three implement side-channel attacks to go after data in use.

So, how do we protect our data in use? The short answer is, we can't, at least for now. We can get close, however, by ensuring that our systems decrypt data at the very last possible moment, ideally as it gets loaded into the CPU registers, and encrypt it as it leaves those registers. This approach means that the data is encrypted even in memory, but it is an expensive approach that requires a cryptographic co-processor. You may encounter it if you work with systems that require extremely high security but are in places where adversaries can put their hands on them, such as automated teller machines (ATMs) and military weapon systems.

A promising approach, which is not quite ready for prime time, is called *homomorphic encryption*. This is a family of encryption algorithms that allows certain operations on the encrypted data. Imagine that you have a set of numbers that you protect with homomorphic encryption and give that set to me for processing. I could then perform certain operations on the numbers, such as common arithmetic ones like addition and multiplication, without decrypting them. I add the encrypted numbers together and send the sum back to you. When you decrypt them, you get a number that is the sum of the original set before encryption. If this is making your head hurt a little bit, don't worry. We're still a long ways from making this technology practical.

Standards

As we discussed in Chapter 1, *standards* are mandatory activities, actions, or rules that are formally documented and enforced within an organization. Asset security standards can be expensive in terms of both financial and opportunity costs, so we must select them carefully. This is where classification and controls come together. Since we already know the relative value of our data and other information assets and we understand many of the security controls we can apply to them, we can make cost-effective decisions about how to protect them. These decisions get codified as information asset protection standards.

The most important concept to remember when selecting information asset protection standards is to balance the value of the information with the cost of protecting it. Asset inventories and classification standards will help you determine the right security controls.

Scoping and Tailoring

One way to go about selecting standards that make sense for your organization is to adapt an existing standard (perhaps belonging to another organization) to your specific situation. *Scoping* is the process of taking a broader standard and trimming out the irrelevant or otherwise unwanted parts. For example, suppose your company is acquired by another company and you are asked to rewrite some of your company's standards based on the ones the parent company uses. That company allows employees to bring their own devices to work, but that is not permitted in your company. You remove those sections from their standard and scope it down to your size. *Tailoring*, on the other hand, is when you make changes to specific provisions so they better address your requirements. Suppose your new parent company uses a particular solution for centralized backup management that is different from the solution your company has been using. As you modify that part of the standard to account for your platform, you are tailoring it to your needs.

Data Protection Methods

As we have seen, data can exist in many forms and places. Even data in motion and data in use can be temporarily stored or cached on devices throughout our systems. Given the abundance of data in the typical enterprise, we have to narrow the scope of our data protection to the data that truly matters. A *digital asset* is anything that exists in digital form, has intrinsic value to the organization, and to which access should be restricted in some way. Since these assets are digital, we must also concern ourselves with the storage media on which they reside. These assets and storage media require a variety of controls to ensure data is properly preserved and that its integrity, confidentiality, and availability are not compromised. For the purposes of this discussion, "storage media" may include both electronic (disk, optical discs, tape, flash devices such as USB "thumb drives," and so on) and nonelectronic (paper) forms of information.

The operational controls that pertain to digital assets come in many flavors. The first are controls that prevent unauthorized access (protect confidentiality), which, as usual, can be physical, administrative, and technical. If the company's backup tapes are to be properly protected from unauthorized access, they must be stored in a place where only authorized people have access to them, which could be in a locked server room or an offsite facility. If storage media needs to be protected from environmental issues such as humidity, heat, cold, fire, and natural disasters (to maintain availability), the media should be kept in a fireproof safe in a regulated environment or in an offsite facility that controls the environment, so it is hospitable to data processing components.

Companies may have a digital asset library with a librarian in charge of protecting its resources. If so, most or all of the responsibilities described in this chapter for the protection of the confidentiality, integrity, and availability of media fall to the librarian. Users may be required to check out specific resources from the library, instead of having the resources readily available for anyone to access them. This is common when the library includes licensed software. It provides an accounting (audit log) of uses of assets, which can help in demonstrating due diligence in complying with license agreements and in protecting confidential information (such as PII, financial/credit card information, and PHI) in libraries containing those types of data.

Storage media should be clearly marked and logged, its integrity should be verified, and it should be properly erased of data when no longer needed. After a large investment is made to secure a network and its components, a common mistake is to replace old computers, along with their hard drives and other magnetic storage media, and ship the obsolete equipment out the back door along with all the data the company just spent so much time and money securing. This puts the information on the obsolete equipment and media at risk of disclosure and violates legal, regulatory, and ethical obligations of the company. Thus, overwriting (see Figure 6-2) and secure overwriting algorithms are required. Whenever storage media containing highly sensitive information cannot be cleared or purged, physical destruction must take place.

When storage media is erased (*cleared* of its contents), it is said to be *sanitized*. In military/government classified systems terms, this means erasing information so it is not readily retrievable using routine operating system commands or commercially available forensic/data recovery software. Clearing is acceptable when storage media will be reused in the same physical environment for the same purposes (in the same compartment of compartmentalized information security) by people with the same access levels for that compartment.

Not all clearing/purging methods are applicable to all storage media—for example, optical media is not susceptible to degaussing, and overwriting may not be effective when

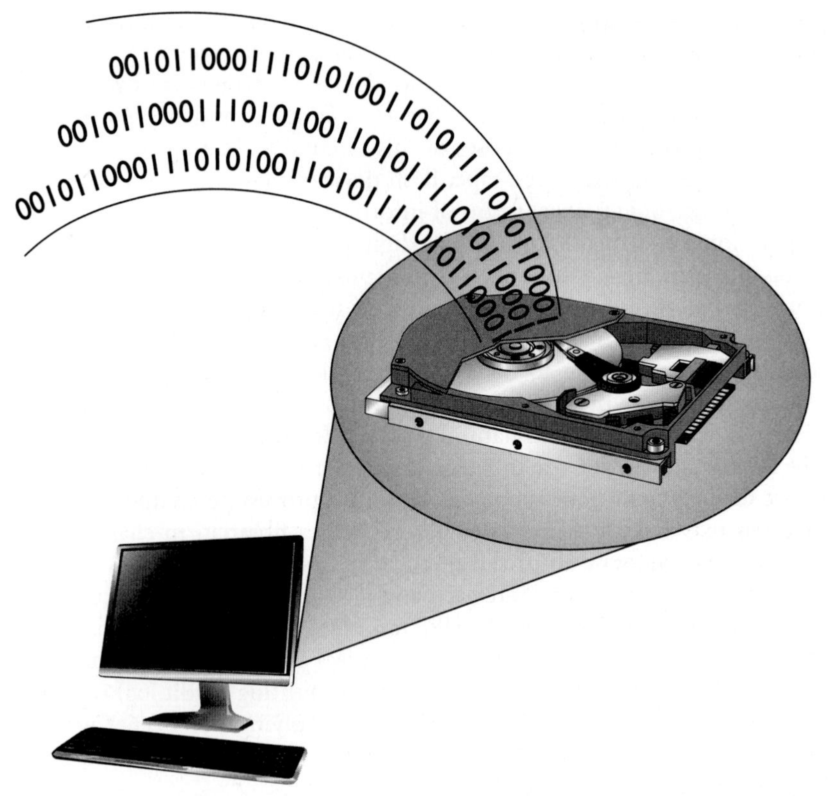

Figure 6-2 Overwriting storage media to protect sensitive data

dealing with solid-state devices. The degree to which information may be recoverable by a sufficiently motivated and capable adversary must not be underestimated or guessed at in ignorance. For the highest-value digital assets, and for all data regulated by government or military classification rules, read and follow the rules and standards.

The guiding principle for deciding what is the necessary method (and cost) of data erasure is to ensure that the enemies' cost of recovering the data exceeds the value of the data. "Sink the company" (or "sink the country") information has value that is so high that the destruction of the storage devices, which involves both the cost of the destruction and the total loss of any potential reusable value of the storage media, is justified. For most other categories of information, multiple or simple overwriting is sufficient. Each organization must evaluate the value of its digital assets and then choose the appropriate erasure/disposal method.

Chapter 5 discussed methods for secure clearing, purging, and destruction of electronic media. Other forms of information, such as paper, microfilm, and microfiche, also require secure disposal. "Dumpster diving" is the practice of searching through trash at homes and businesses to find valuable information that was simply thrown away without being first securely destroyed through shredding or burning.

Atoms and Data
A device that performs degaussing generates a coercive magnetic force that reduces the magnetic flux density of the storage media to zero. This magnetic force is what properly erases data from media. Data is stored on magnetic media by the representation of the polarization of the atoms. Degaussing changes this polarization (magnetic alignment) by using a type of large magnet to bring it back to its original flux (magnetic alignment).

Digital Asset Management

Digital asset management is the process by which organizations ensure their digital assets are properly stored, well protected, and easily available to authorized users. While specific implementations vary, they typically involve the following tasks:

- **Tracking** (audit logging) who has custody of each digital asset at any given moment. This creates the same kind of audit trail as any audit logging activity—to allow an investigation to determine where information was at any given time, who had it, and, for particularly sensitive information, why they accessed it. This enables an investigator to focus efforts on particular people, places, and times if a breach is suspected or known to have happened.
- **Effectively implementing access controls** to restrict who can access each asset to only those people defined by its owner and to enforce the appropriate security measures based on the classification of the digital asset. Certain types of media, due to their sensitivity and storage media, may require special handling. As an example, classified government information may require that the asset may only be removed from the library or its usual storage place under physical guard, and even then may not be removed from the building. Access controls will include *physical* (locked doors, drawers, cabinets, or safes), *technical* (access and authorization control of any automated system for retrieving contents of information in the library), and *administrative* (the actual rules for who is supposed to do what to each piece of information). Finally, the digital media may need to change format, as in printing electronic data to paper, and still needs to be protected at the necessary level, no matter what format it is in. Procedures must include how to continue to provide the appropriate protection. For example, sensitive material that is to be mailed should be sent in a sealable inner envelope and only via a courier service.
- **Tracking the number and location of backup versions** (both onsite and offsite). This is necessary to ensure proper disposal of information when the information reaches the end of its lifespan, to account for the location

and accessibility of information during audits, and to find a backup copy of information if the primary source of the information is lost or damaged.

- **Documenting the history of changes.** For example, when a particular version of a software application kept in the library has been deemed obsolete, this fact must be recorded so the obsolete version of the application is not used unless that particular obsolete version is required. Even once no possible need for the actual asset remains, retaining a log of the former existence and the time and method of its deletion may be useful to demonstrate due diligence.
- **Ensuring environmental conditions do not endanger storage media.** If you store digital assets on local storage media, each media type may be susceptible to damage from one or more environmental influences. For example, all types are susceptible to fire, and most are susceptible to liquids, smoke, and dust. Magnetic storage media are susceptible to strong magnetic fields. Magnetic and optical media are susceptible to variations in temperature and humidity. A media library and any other space where reference copies of information are stored must be physically built so all types of media will be kept within their environmental parameters, and the environment must be monitored to ensure conditions do not range outside of those parameters. Media libraries are particularly useful when large amounts of information must be stored and physically/environmentally protected so that the high cost of environmental control and media management may be centralized in a small number of physical locations and so that cost is spread out over the large number of items stored in the library.
- **Inventorying digital assets** to detect if any asset has been lost or improperly changed. This can reduce the amount of damage a violation of the other protection responsibilities could cause by detecting such violations sooner rather than later, and is a necessary part of the digital asset management life cycle by which the controls in place are verified as being sufficient.
- **Carrying out secure disposal activities.** Disposal activities usually begin at the point at which the information is no longer valuable and becomes a potential liability. Secure disposal of media/information can add significant cost to media management. Knowing that only a certain percentage of the information must be securely erased at the end of its life may significantly reduce the long-term operating costs of the company. Similarly, knowing that certain information must be disposed of securely can reduce the possibility of a storage device being simply thrown in a dumpster and then found by someone who publicly embarrasses or blackmails the company over the data security breach represented by that inappropriate disposal of the information. The business must take into account the useful lifetime of the information to the business, legal, and regulatory restrictions and, conversely, the requirements for retention and archiving when making these decisions. If a law or regulation requires the information to be kept beyond its normally useful lifetime for the business, then disposition may involve *archiving*—moving the information from the ready (and possibly more expensive) accessibility of a library to a long-term stable and (with some effort) retrievable format that has lower storage costs.

- **Internal and external labeling** of each piece of asset in the library should include
  - Date created
  - Retention period
  - Classification level
  - Who created it
  - Date to be destroyed
  - Name and version

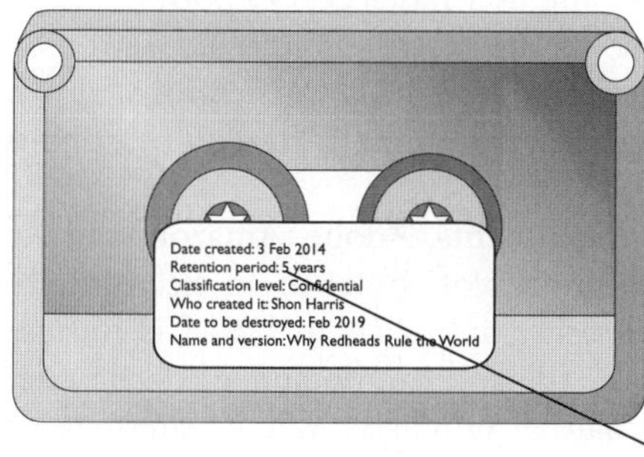

Date created: 3 Feb 2014
Retention period: 5 years
Classification level: Confidential
Who created it: Shon Harris
Date to be destroyed: Feb 2019
Name and version: Why Redheads Rule the World

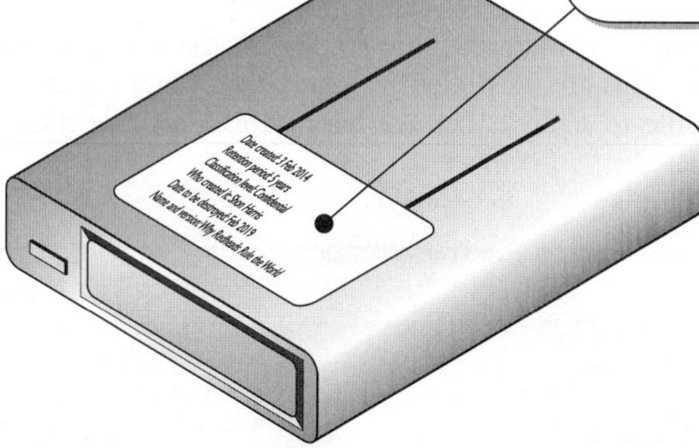

Digital Rights Management

So, how can we protect our digital assets when they leave our organizations? For example, if you share a sensitive file or software system with a customer, how can you ensure that only authorized users gain access to it? *Digital Rights Management (DRM)* refers to a set of technologies that is applied to controlling access to copyrighted data. The technologies themselves don't need to be developed exclusively for this purpose. It is the use of a technology that makes it DRM, not its design. In fact, many of the DRM technologies in use today are standard cryptographic ones. For example, when you buy a Software as a Service

(SaaS) license for, say, Office 365, Microsoft uses standard user authentication and authorization technologies to ensure that you only install and run the allowed number of copies of the software. Without these checks during the installation (and periodically thereafter), most of the features will stop working after a period of time. A potential problem with this approach is that the end-user device may not have Internet connectivity.

An approach to DRM that does not require Internet connectivity is the use of product keys. When you install your application, the key you enter is checked against a proprietary algorithm and, if it matches, the installation is activated. It might be tempting to equate this approach to symmetric key encryption, but in reality, the algorithms employed are not always up to cryptographic standards. Since the user has access to both the key and the executable code of the algorithm, the latter can be reverse-engineered with a bit of effort. This could allow a malicious user to develop a product-key generator with which to effectively bypass DRM. A common way around this threat is to require a one-time online activation of the key.

DRM technologies are also used to protect documents. Adobe, Amazon, and Apple all have their own approaches to limiting the number of copies of an electronic book (e-book) that you can download and read. Another approach to DRM is the use of digital watermarks, which are embedded into the file and can document details such as the owner of the file, the licensee (user), and date of purchase. While watermarks will not stop someone from illegally copying and distributing files, they could help the owner track, identify, and prosecute the perpetrator. An example technique for implementing watermarks is called steganography.

Steganography

Steganography is a method of hiding data in another media type so the very existence of the data is concealed. Common steps are illustrated in Figure 6-3. Only the sender and receiver are supposed to be able to see the message because it is secretly hidden

Figure 6-3 Main components of steganography

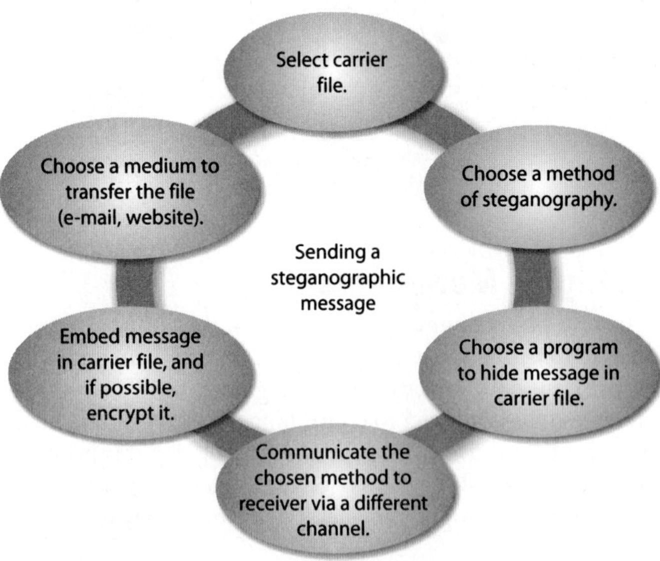
Select carrier file.
Choose a method of steganography.
Choose a program to hide message in carrier file.
Communicate the chosen method to receiver via a different channel.
Embed message in carrier file, and if possible, encrypt it.
Choose a medium to transfer the file (e-mail, website).
Sending a steganographic message

in a graphic, audio file, document, or other type of media. The message is often just hidden, and not necessarily encrypted. Encrypted messages can draw attention because the encryption tells the bad guy, "This is something sensitive." A message hidden in a picture of your grandmother would not attract this type of attention, even though the same secret message can be embedded into this image. Steganography is a type of security through obscurity.

Steganography includes the concealment of information within computer files. In digital steganography, electronic communications may include steganographic coding inside of a document file, image file, program, or protocol. Media files are ideal for steganographic transmission because of their large size. As a simple example, a sender might start with an innocuous image file and adjust the color of every 100th pixel to correspond to a letter in the alphabet, a change so subtle that someone not specifically looking for it is unlikely to notice it.

Let's look at the components that are involved with steganography:

- **Carrier** A signal, data stream, or file that has hidden information (payload) inside of it
- **Stegomedium** The medium in which the information is hidden
- **Payload** The information that is to be concealed and transmitted

A method of embedding the message into some types of media is to use the *least significant bit (LSB)*. Many types of files have some bits that can be modified and not affect the file they are in, which is where secret data can be hidden without altering the file in a visible manner. In the LSB approach, graphics with a high resolution or an audio file that has many different types of sounds (high bit rate) are the most successful for hiding information within. There is commonly no noticeable distortion, and the file is usually not increased to a size that can be detected. A 24-bit bitmap file will have 8 bits representing each of the three color values, which are red, green, and blue. These 8 bits are within each pixel. If we consider just the blue, there will be 2^8 different values of blue. The difference between 11111111 and 11111110 in the value for blue intensity is likely to be undetectable by the human eye. Therefore, the least significant bit can be used for something other than color information.

A digital graphic is just a file that shows different colors and intensities of light. The larger the file, the more bits that can be modified without much notice or distortion.

Data Loss Prevention

Unless we diligently apply the right controls to our data wherever it may be, we should expect that some of it will eventually end up in the wrong hands. In fact, even if we do everything right, the risk of this happening will never be eliminated. *Data loss* is the flow of sensitive information, such as PII, to unauthorized external parties. Leaks of personal information by an organization can cause large financial losses. The costs commonly include

- Investigating the incident and remediating the problem
- Contacting affected individuals to inform them about the incident

- Penalties and fines to regulatory agencies
- Contractual liabilities
- Mitigating expenses (such as free credit monitoring services for affected individuals)
- Direct damages to affected individuals

In addition to financial losses, a company's reputation may be damaged and individuals' identities may be stolen.

The most common cause of data breach for a business is a lack of awareness and discipline among employees—an overwhelming majority of all leaks are the result of negligence. The most common forms of negligent data breaches occur due to the inappropriate removal of information—for instance, from a secure company system to an insecure home computer so that the employee can work from home—or due to simple theft of an insecure laptop or tape from a taxi cab, airport security checkpoint, or shipping box. However, breaches also occur due to negligent uses of technologies that are inappropriate for a particular use—for example, reassigning some type of medium (say, a page frame, disk sector, or magnetic tape) that contained one or more objects to an unrelated purpose without securely ensuring that the media contained no residual data.

It would be too easy to simply blame employees for any inappropriate use of information that results in the information being put at risk, followed by breaches. Employees have a job to do, and their understanding of that job is almost entirely based on what their employer tells them. What an employer tells an employee about the job is not limited to, and may not even primarily be in, the "job description." Instead, it will be in the feedback the employee receives on a day-to-day and year-to-year basis regarding their work. If the company in its routine communications to employees and its recurring training, performance reviews, and salary/bonus processes does not include security awareness, then employees will not understand security to be a part of their job.

The more complex the environment and types of media used, the more communication and training that are required to ensure that the environment is well protected. Further, except in government and military environments, company policies and even awareness training will not stop the most dedicated employees from making the best use of up-to-date consumer technologies, including those technologies not yet integrated into the corporate environment, and even those technologies not yet reasonably secured for the corporate environment or corporate information. Companies must stay aware of new consumer technologies and how employees (wish to) use them in the corporate environment. Just saying "no" will not stop an employee from using, say, a personal smartphone, a USB thumb drive, or webmail to forward corporate data to their home e-mail address in order to work on the data when out of the office. Companies must include in their technical security controls the ability to detect and/or prevent such actions through, for example, computer lockdowns, which prevent writing sensitive data to non-company-owned storage devices, such as USB thumb drives, and e-mailing sensitive information to nonapproved e-mail destinations.

Data loss prevention (DLP) comprises the actions that organizations take to prevent unauthorized external parties from gaining access to sensitive data. That definition has some key terms. First, the data has to be considered *sensitive*, the meaning of which we spent a good chunk of the beginning of this chapter discussing. We can't keep every single datum safely locked away inside our systems, so we focus our attention, efforts, and funds on the truly important data. Second, DLP is concerned with *external parties.* If somebody in the accounting department gains access to internal R&D data, that is a problem, but technically it is not considered a data leak. Finally, the external party gaining access to our sensitive data must be *unauthorized* to do so. If former business partners have some of our sensitive data that they were authorized to get at the time they were employed, then that is not considered a leak either. While this emphasis on semantics may seem excessive, it is necessary to properly approach this tremendous threat to our organizations.

EXAM TIP The terms data loss and data leak are used interchangeably by most security professionals. Technically, however, data loss means we do not know where the data is (e.g., after the theft of a laptop), while data leak means that the confidentiality of the data has been compromised (e.g., when the laptop thief posts the files on the Internet).

The real challenge to DLP is in taking a holistic view of our organization. This perspective must incorporate our people, our processes, and then our information. A common mistake when it comes to DLP is to treat the problem as a technological one. If all we do is buy or develop the latest technology aimed at stopping leaks, we are very likely to leak data. If, on the other hand, we consider DLP a program and not a project, and we pay due attention to our business processes, policies, culture, and people, then we have a good fighting chance at mitigating many or even most of the potential leaks. Ultimately, like everything else concerning information system security, we have to acknowledge that despite our best efforts, we will have bad days. The best we can do is stick to the program and make our bad days less frequent and less bad.

General Approaches to DLP

There is no one-size-fits-all approach to DLP, but there are tried-and-true principles that can be helpful. One important principle is the integration of DLP with our risk management processes. This allows us to balance out the totality of risks we face and favor controls that mitigate those risks in multiple areas simultaneously. Not only is this helpful in making the most of our resources, but it also keeps us from making decisions in one silo with little or no regard to their impacts on other silos. In the sections that follow, we will look at key elements of any approach to DLP.

Data Inventories It is difficult to defend an unknown target. Similarly, it is difficult to prevent the leaking of data of which we are unaware or whose sensitivity is unknown. Some organizations try to protect all their data from leakage, but this is not a good approach. For starters, acquiring the resources required to protect everything is likely cost prohibitive to most organizations. Even if an organization is able to afford this level of protection, it runs a very high risk of violating the privacy of its employees and/or customers by examining every single piece of data in its systems.

A good approach is to find and characterize all the data in your organization before you even look at DLP solutions. The task can seem overwhelming at first, but it helps to prioritize things a bit. You can start off by determining what is the most important kind of data for your organization. A compromise of these assets could lead to direct financial losses or give your competitors an advantage in your sector. Are these healthcare records? Financial records? Product designs? Military plans? Once you figure this out, you can start looking for that data across your servers, workstations, mobile devices, cloud computing platforms, and anywhere else it may live. Keep in mind that this data can live in a variety of formats (e.g., database management system records or files) and media (e.g., hard drives or backup tapes). If your experience doing this for the first time is typical, you will probably be amazed at the places in which you find sensitive data.

Once you get a handle on what is your high-value data and where it resides, you can gradually expand the scope of your search to include less valuable, but still sensitive, data. For instance, if your critical data involves designs for next-generation radios, you would want to look for information that could allow someone to get insights into those designs even if they can't directly obtain them. So, for example, if you have patent filings, FCC license applications, and contracts with suppliers of electronic components, then an adversary may be able to use all this data to figure out what you're designing even without direct access to your new radio's plans. This is why it is so difficult for Apple to keep secret all the features of a new iPhone ahead of its launch. Often there is very little you can do to mitigate this risk, but some organizations have gone as far as to file patents and applications they don't intend to use in an effort to deceive adversaries as to their true plans. Obviously, and just as in any other security decision, the costs of these countermeasures must be weighed against the value of the information you're trying to protect. As you keep expanding the scope of your search, you will reach a point of diminishing returns in which the data you are inventorying is not worth the time you spend looking for it.

NOTE We cover the threats posed by adversaries compiling public information (aggregation) and using it to derive otherwise private information (inference) in Chapter 7.

Once you are satisfied that you have inventoried your sensitive data, the next step is to characterize it. We already covered the classification of information earlier in this chapter, so you should know all about data labels. Another element of this characterization is ownership. Who owns a particular set of data? Beyond that, who should be authorized to read or modify it? Depending on your organization, your data may have other characteristics of importance to the DLP effort, such as which data is regulated and how long it must be retained.

Data Flows Data that stays put is usually of little use to anyone. Most data will move according to specific business processes through specific network pathways. Understanding data flows at this intersection between business and IT is critical to implementing DLP. Many organizations put their DLP sensors at the perimeter of their networks, thinking that is where the leakages would occur. But if that's the only location these sensors are placed, a large number of leaks may not be detected or stopped. Additionally, as we will discuss in detail when we cover network-based DLP, perimeter sensors can often be bypassed by sophisticated attackers.

A better approach is to use a variety of sensors tuned to specific data flows. Suppose you have a software development team that routinely passes finished code to a quality assurance (QA) team for testing. The code is sensitive, but the QA team is authorized to read (and perhaps modify) it. However, the QA team is not authorized to access code under development or code from projects past. If an adversary compromises the computer used by a member of the QA team and attempts to access the source code for different projects, a DLP solution that is not tuned to that business process will not detect the compromise. The adversary could then repackage the data to avoid your perimeter monitors and successfully extract the data.

Data Protection Strategy The example just described highlights the need for a comprehensive, risk-based data protection strategy. The extent to which we attempt to mitigate these exfiltration routes depends on our assessment of the risk of their use. Obviously, as we increase our scrutiny of a growing set of data items, our costs will grow disproportionately. We usually can't watch everything all the time, so what do we do?

Once we have our data inventories and understand our data flows, we have enough information to do a risk assessment. Recall that we described this process in detail in Chapter 2. The trick is to incorporate data loss into that process. Since we can't guarantee that we will successfully defend against all attacks, we have to assume that sometimes our adversaries will gain access to our networks. Not only does our data protection strategy have to cover our approach to keeping attackers out, but it also must describe how we protect our data against a threat agent that is already inside. The following are some key areas to consider when developing data protection strategies:

- **Backup and recovery** Though we have been focusing our attention on data leaks, it is also important to consider the steps to prevent the loss of this data due to electromechanical or human failures. As we take care of this, we need to also consider the risk that, while we focus our attention on preventing leaks of our primary data stores, our adversaries may be focusing their attention on stealing the backups.
- **Data life cycle** Most of us can intuitively grasp the security issues at each of the stages of the data life cycle. However, we tend to disregard securing the data as it transitions from one stage to another. For instance, if we are archiving data at an offsite location, are we ensuring that it is protected as it travels there?
- **Physical security** While IT provides a wealth of tools and resources to help us protect our data, we must also consider what happens when an adversary just steals a hard drive left in an unsecured area, as happened to Sentara Heart Hospital in Norfolk, Virginia, in August 2015.
- **Security culture** Our information systems users can be a tremendous control if properly educated and incentivized. By developing a culture of security within our organizations, we not only reduce the incidence of users clicking on malicious links and opening attachments, but we also turn each of them into a security sensor, able to detect attacks that we may not otherwise be able to.

- **Privacy** Every data protection policy should carefully balance the need to monitor data with the need to protect our users' privacy. If we allow our users to check personal e-mail or visit social media sites during their breaks, would our systems be quietly monitoring their private communications?
- **Organizational change** Many large organizations grow because of mergers and acquisitions. When these changes happen, we must ensure that the data protection approaches of all entities involved are consistent and sufficient. To do otherwise is to ensure that the overall security posture of the new organization is the lesser of its constituents' security postures.

Implementation, Testing, and Tuning All the elements of a DLP process that we have discussed so far (i.e., data inventories, data flows, and data protection strategies) are administrative in nature. We finally get to discuss the part of DLP with which most of us are familiar: deploying and running a toolset. The sequence of our discussion so far has been deliberate in that the technological part needs to be informed by the other elements we've covered. Many organizations have wasted large sums of money on so-called solutions that, though well-known and highly regarded, are just not suitable for their particular environment.

Assuming we've done our administrative homework and have a good understanding of our true DLP requirements, we can evaluate products according to our own criteria, not someone else's. The following are some aspects of a possible solution that most organizations will want to consider when comparing competing products:

- **Sensitive data awareness** Different tools will use different approaches to analyzing the sensitivity of documents' contents and the context in which they are being used. In general terms, the more depth of analysis and breadth of techniques that a product offers, the better. Typical approaches to finding and tracking sensitive data include keywords, regular expressions, tags, and statistical methods.
- **Policy engine** Policies are at the heart of any DLP solution. Unfortunately, not all policy engines are created equal. Some allow extremely granular control but require obscure methods for defining these policies. Other solutions are less expressive but are simple to understand. There is no right answer here, so each organization will weigh this aspect of a set of solutions differently.
- **Interoperability** DLP tools must play nicely with existing infrastructure, which is why most vendors will assure you that their product is interoperable. The trick becomes to determine precisely how this integration takes place. Some products are technically interoperable but, in practice, require so much effort to integrate that they become infeasible.
- **Accuracy** At the end of the day, DLP solutions keep your data out of the hands of unauthorized entities. Therefore, the right solution is one that is accurate in its identification and prevention of incidents that result in the leakage of sensitive data. The best way to assess this criterion is by testing a candidate solution in an environment that mimics the actual conditions in the organization.

Once we select a DLP solution, the next interrelated tasks are integration, testing, and tuning. Obviously, we want to ensure that bringing the new toolset online won't disrupt any of our existing systems or processes, but testing needs to cover a lot more than that. The most critical elements when testing any DLP solution are to verify that it allows authorized data processing and to ensure that it prevents unauthorized data processing.

Verifying that authorized processes are not hampered by the DLP solution is fairly straightforward if we have already inventoried our data and the authorized flows. The data flows, in particular, will tell us exactly what our tests should look like. For instance, if we have a data flow for source code from the software development team to the QA team, then we should test that it is in fact allowed to occur by the new DLP tool. We probably won't have the resources to exhaustively test all flows, which means we should prioritize them based on their criticality to the organization. As time permits, we can always come back and test the remaining, and arguably less common or critical, processes (before our users do).

Testing the second critical element, that the DLP solution prevents unauthorized flows, requires a bit more work and creativity. Essentially, we are trying to imagine the ways in which threat agents might cause our data to leak. A useful tool in documenting these types of activities is called the misuse case. *Misuse cases* describe threat actors and the tasks they want to perform on the system. They are related to *use cases*, which are used by system analysts to document the tasks that authorized actors want to perform on a system. By compiling a list of misuse cases, we can keep a record of which data leak scenarios are most likely, most dangerous, or both. Just like we did when testing authorized flows, we can then prioritize which misuse cases we test first if we are resource constrained. As we test these potential misuses, it is important to ensure that the DLP system behaves in the manner we expect—that is to say, that it *prevents* a leak and doesn't just alert to it. Some organizations have been shocked to learn that their DLP solution has been alerting them about data leaks but doing nothing to stop them, letting their data leak right into the hands of their adversaries.

NOTE We cover misuse cases in detail in Chapter 18.

Finally, we must remember that everything changes. The solution that is exquisitely implemented, finely tuned, and effective immediately is probably going to be ineffective in the near future if we don't continuously monitor, maintain, and improve it. Apart from the efficacy of the tool itself, our organizations change as people, products, and services come and go. The ensuing cultural and environmental changes will also change the effectiveness of our DLP solutions. And, obviously, if we fail to realize that users are installing rogue access points, using thumb drives without restriction, or clicking malicious links, then it is just a matter of time before our expensive DLP solution will be circumvented.

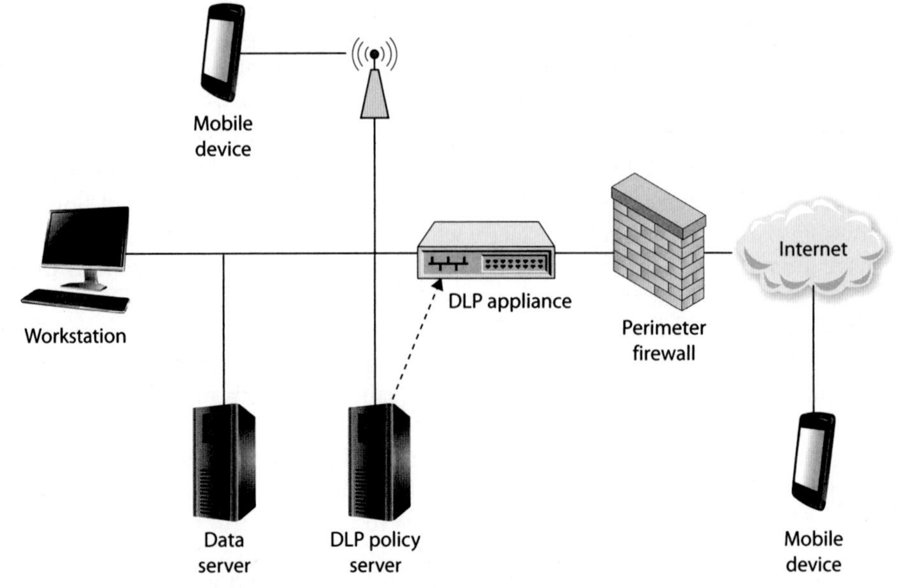

Figure 6-4 Network DLP

Network DLP

Network DLP (NDLP) applies data protection policies to data in motion. NDLP products are normally implemented as appliances that are deployed at the perimeter of an organization's networks. They can also be deployed at the boundaries of internal subnetworks and could be deployed as modules within a modular security appliance. Figure 6-4 shows how an NDLP solution might be deployed with a single appliance at the edge of the network and communicating with a DLP policy server.

DLP Resiliency

Resiliency is the ability to deal with challenges, damage, and crises and bounce back to normal or near-normal condition in short order. It is an important element of security in general and of DLP in particular.

Assume your organization's information systems have been compromised (and it wasn't detected): What does the adversary do next, and how can you detect and deal with *that*? It is a sad reality that virtually all organizations have been attacked and that most have been breached. A key differentiator between those who withstand attacks relatively unscathed and those who suffer tremendous damage is their attitude toward operating in contested environments. If an organization's entire security strategy hinges on keeping adversaries off its networks, then it will likely fail catastrophically when an adversary manages to break in. If, on the other hand, the strategy builds on the concept of resiliency and accounts for the continuation of critical processes even with adversaries operating inside the perimeter, then the failures will likely be less destructive and restoration may be much quicker.

From a practical perspective, the high cost of NDLP devices leads most organizations to deploy them at traffic choke points rather than throughout the network. Consequently, NDLP devices likely will not detect leaks that don't traverse the network segment on which the devices are installed. For example, suppose that an attacker is able to connect to a wireless access point and gain unauthorized access to a subnet that is not protected by an NDLP tool. This can be visualized in Figure 6-4 by supposing that the attacker is using the device connected to the WAP. Though this might seem like an obvious mistake, many organizations fail to consider their wireless subnets when planning for DLP. Alternatively, malicious insiders could connect their workstations directly to a mobile or external storage device, copy sensitive data, and remove it from the premises completely undetected.

The principal drawback of an NDLP solution is that it will not protect data on devices that are not on the organizational network. Mobile device users will be most at risk, since they will be vulnerable whenever they leave the premises. Since we expect the ranks of our mobile users to continue to increase into the future, this will be an enduring challenge for NDLP.

Endpoint DLP

Endpoint DLP (EDLP) applies protection policies to data at rest and data in use. EDLP is implemented in software running on each protected endpoint. This software, usually called a *DLP agent*, communicates with the DLP policy server to update policies and report events. Figure 6-5 illustrates an EDLP implementation.

EDLP allows a degree of protection that is normally not possible with NDLP. The reason is that the data is observable at the point of creation. When a user enters PII on

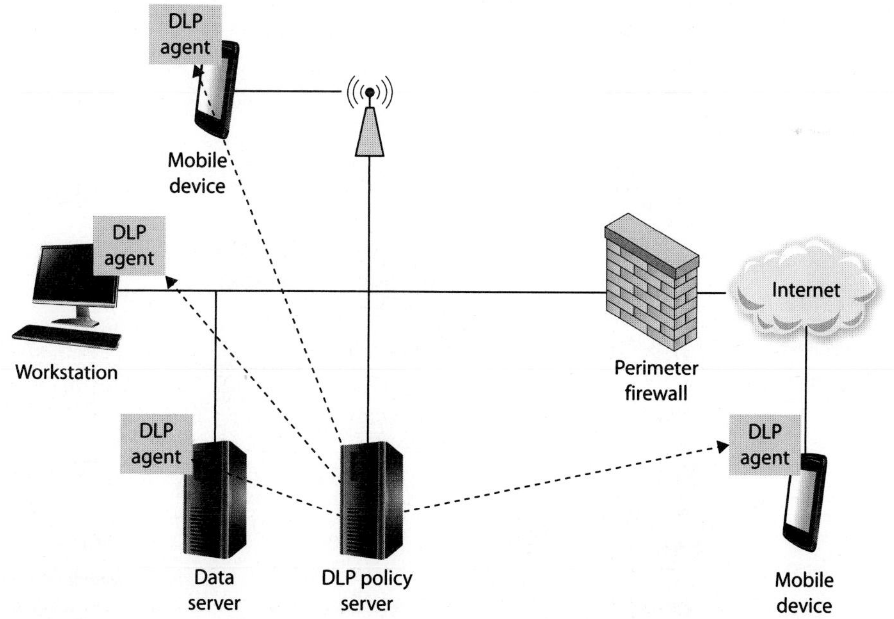

Figure 6-5 Endpoint DLP

the device during an interview with a client, the EDLP agent detects the new sensitive data and immediately applies the pertinent protection policies to it. Even if the data is encrypted on the device when it is at rest, it will have to be decrypted whenever it is in use, which allows for EDLP inspection and monitoring. Finally, if the user attempts to copy the data to a non-networked device such as a thumb drive, or if it is improperly deleted, EDLP will pick up on these possible policy violations. None of these examples would be possible using NDLP.

The main drawback of EDLP is complexity. Compared to NDLP, these solutions require a lot more presence points in the organization, and each of these points may have unique configuration, execution, or authentication challenges. Additionally, since the agents must be deployed to every device that could possibly handle sensitive data, the cost could be much higher than that of an NDLP solution. Another challenge is ensuring that all the agents are updated regularly, both for software patches and policy changes. Finally, since a pure EDLP solution is unaware of data-in-motion protection violations, it would be possible for attackers to circumvent the protections (e.g., by disabling the agent through malware) and leave the organization blind to the ongoing leakages. It is typically harder to disable NDLP, because it is normally implemented in an appliance that is difficult for attackers to exploit.

Hybrid DLP

Another approach to DLP is to deploy both NDLP and EDLP across the enterprise. Obviously, this approach is the costliest and most complex. For organizations that can afford it, however, it offers the best coverage. Figure 6-6 shows how a hybrid NDLP/EDLP deployment might look.

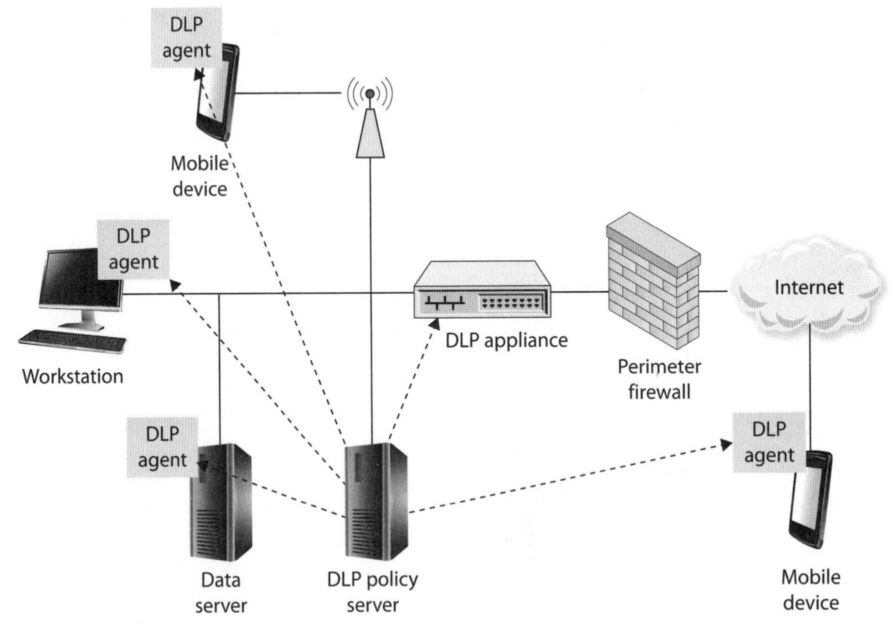

Figure 6-6 Hybrid NDLP/EDLP

Cloud Access Security Broker

The DLP approaches described so far work best (or perhaps only) in traditional network environments that have a clearly defined perimeter. But what about organizations that use cloud services, especially services that employees can access from their own devices? Whatever happens in the cloud is usually not visible (or controllable) by the organization. A *cloud access security broker (CASB)* is a system that provides visibility and security controls for cloud services. A CASB monitors what users do in the cloud and applies whatever policies and controls are applicable to that activity.

For example, suppose a nurse at a healthcare organization uses Microsoft 365 to take notes when interviewing a new patient. That document is created and exists only in the cloud and clearly contains sensitive healthcare information that must be protected under HIPAA. Without a CASB solution, the organization would depend solely on the nurse doing the right things, including ensuring the data is encrypted and not shared with any unauthorized parties. A CASB could automatically update the inventory of sensitive data, apply any labels in the document's metadata for tracking it, encrypt it, and ensure it is only shared with specific authorized entities.

Most CASBs do their work by leveraging one of two techniques: proxies or application programming interfaces (APIs). The proxy technique places the CASB in the data path between the endpoint and the cloud service provider, as shown on the left in Figure 6-7. For example, you could have an appliance in your network that automatically detects user connection requests to a cloud service, intercepts that user connection, and creates a tunnel to the service provider. In this way, all traffic to the cloud is routed through the CASB so that it can inspect it and apply the appropriate controls.

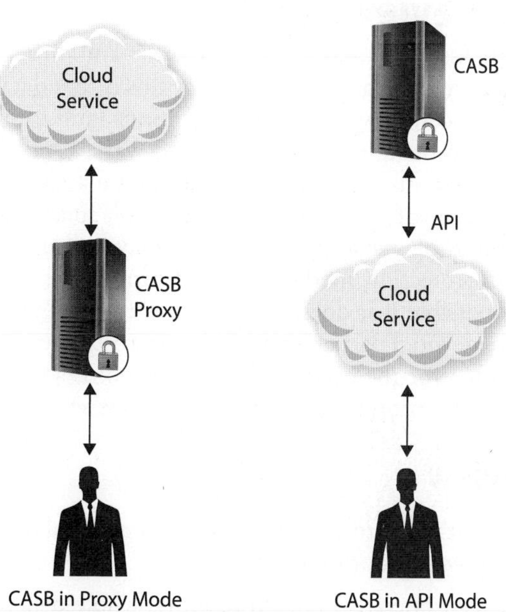

Figure 6-7 Two common approaches to implementing CASBs: proxy and API

PART II

But what if you have remote users who are not connected to your organization through a VPN? What about staff members trying to access the cloud services through a personal device (assuming that is allowed)? In those situations, you can set up a reverse proxy. The way this works is that the users log into the cloud service, which is configured to immediately route them back to the CASB, which then completes the connection back to the cloud.

There are a number of challenges with using proxies for CASBs. For starters, they need to intercept the users' encrypted traffic, which will generate browser alerts unless the browsers are configured to trust the proxy. While this works on organizational computers, it is a bit trickier to do on personally owned devices. Another challenge is that, depending on how much traffic goes to cloud service providers, the CASB can become a choke point that slows down the user experience. It also represents a single point of failure unless you deploy redundant systems. Perhaps the biggest challenge, however, has to do with the fast pace of innovation and updates to cloud services. As new features are added and others changed or removed, the CASB needs to be updated accordingly. The problem is not only that the CASB will miss something important but that it may actually break a feature by not knowing how to deal with it properly. For this reason, some vendors such as Google and Microsoft advise against using CASBs in proxy mode.

The other way to implement CASBs is by leveraging the APIs exposed by the service providers themselves, as you can see on the right side of Figure 6-7. An API is a way to have one software system directly access functionality in another one. For example, a properly authenticated CASB could ask Exchange Online (a cloud e-mail solution) for all the activities in the last 24 hours. Most cloud services include APIs to support CASB and, better yet, these APIs are updated by the vendors themselves. This ensures the CASB won't break anything as new features come up.

Chapter Review

Protecting data assets is a much more dynamic and difficult prospect than is protecting most other asset types. The main reason for this is that data is so fluid. It can be stored in unanticipated places, flow in multiple directions (and to multiple recipients) simultaneously, and end up being used in unexpected ways. Our data protection strategies must account for the various states in which our data may be found. For each state, there are multiple unique threats that our security controls must mitigate.

Still, regardless of our best efforts, data may end up in the wrong hands. We want to implement protection methods that minimize the risk of this happening, alert us as quickly as possible if it does, and allow us to track and, if possible, recover the data effectively. We devoted particular attention to three methods of protecting data that you should remember for the exam and for your job: Digital Rights Management (DRM), data loss/leak prevention (DLP), and cloud access security brokers (CASBs).

Quick Review

- Data at rest refers to data that resides in external or auxiliary storage devices, such as hard drives or optical discs.
- Every major operating system supports whole-disk encryption, which is a good way to protect data at rest.

- Data in motion is data that is moving between computing nodes over a data network such as the Internet.
- TLS, IPSec, and VPNs are typical ways to use cryptography to protect data in motion.
- Data in use is the term for data residing in primary storage devices, such as volatile memory (e.g., RAM), memory caches, or CPU registers.
- Scoping is taking a broader standard and trimming out the irrelevant or otherwise unwanted parts.
- Tailoring is making changes to specific provisions in a standard so they better address your requirements.
- A digital asset is anything that exists in digital form, has intrinsic value to the organization, and to which access should be restricted in some way.
- Digital asset management is the process by which organizations ensure their digital assets are properly stored, protected, and easily available to authorized users.
- Steganography is a method of hiding data in another media type so the very existence of the data is concealed.
- Digital Rights Management (DRM) refers to a set of technologies that is applied to controlling access to copyrighted data.
- Data leakage is the flow of sensitive information to unauthorized external parties.
- Data loss prevention (DLP) comprises the actions that organizations take to prevent unauthorized external parties from gaining access to sensitive data.
- Network DLP (NDLP) applies data protection policies to data in motion.
- Endpoint DLP (EDLP) applies data protection policies to data at rest and data in use.
- Cloud access security brokers (CASBs) provide visibility and control over user activities on cloud services.

Questions

Please remember that these questions are formatted and asked in a certain way for a reason. Keep in mind that the CISSP exam is asking questions at a conceptual level. Questions may not always have the perfect answer, and the candidate is advised against always looking for the perfect answer. Instead, the candidate should look for the best answer in the list.

1. Data at rest is commonly
   - **A.** Using a RESTful protocol for transmission
   - **B.** Stored in registers
   - **C.** Being transmitted across the network
   - **D.** Stored in external storage devices

2. Data in motion is commonly
   A. Using a RESTful protocol for transmission
   B. Stored in registers
   C. Being transmitted across the network
   D. Stored in external storage devices
3. Data in use is commonly
   A. Using a RESTful protocol for transmission
   B. Stored in registers
   C. Being transmitted across the network
   D. Stored in external storage devices
4. Which of the following best describes an application of cryptography to protect data at rest?
   A. VPN
   B. Degaussing
   C. Whole-disk encryption
   D. Up-to-date antivirus software
5. Which of the following best describes an application of cryptography to protect data in motion?
   A. Testing software against side-channel attacks
   B. TLS
   C. Whole-disk encryption
   D. EDLP
6. Which of the following is not a digital asset management task?
   A. Tracking the number and location of backup versions
   B. Deciding the classification of data assets
   C. Documenting the history of changes
   D. Carrying out secure disposal activities
7. Which data protection method would best allow you to detect a malicious insider trying to access a data asset within your corporate infrastructure?
   A. Digital Rights Management (DRM)
   B. Steganography
   C. Cloud access security broker (CASB)
   D. Data loss prevention (DLP)

8. What term best describes the flow of data assets to an unauthorized external party?
   A. Data leakage
   B. Data in motion
   C. Data flow
   D. Steganography

Answers

1. **D.** Data at rest is characterized by residing in secondary storage devices such as disk drives, DVDs, or magnetic tapes. Registers are temporary storage within the CPU and are used for data storage only when the data is being used.
2. **C.** Data in motion is characterized by network or off-host transmission. The RESTful protocol, while pertaining to a subset of data on a network, is not as good an answer as option C.
3. **B.** Registers are used only while data is being used by the CPU, so when data is resident in registers, it is, by definition, in use.
4. **C.** Data at rest is best protected using whole-disk encryption on the user workstations or mobile computers. None of the other options apply to data at rest.
5. **B.** Data in motion is best protected by network encryption solutions such as TLS, VPN, or IPSec. None of the other options apply to data in motion.
6. **B.** The classification of a data asset is determined by the asset owner before it starts being managed. Otherwise, how would the manager know how to handle it? All other answers are typically part of digital asset management.
7. **C.** Cloud access security brokers (CASBs) provide visibility and control over user activities on cloud services. Provided the asset in question is in the cloud, this would be your best option. Data loss prevention (DLP) systems are primarily concerned with preventing unauthorized external parties from gaining access to sensitive data.
8. **A.** Data leakage is the flow of sensitive information to unauthorized external parties.

PART III

Security Architecture and Engineering

CHAPTER 7

System Architectures

This chapter presents the following:

- General system architectures
- Industrial control systems
- Virtualized systems
- Cloud-based systems
- Pervasive systems
- Distributed systems

Computer system analysis is like child-rearing; you can do grievous damage, but you cannot ensure success.

—Tom DeMarco

As we have seen in previous chapters, most systems leverage other systems in some way, whether by sharing data with each other or by sharing services with each other. While each system has its own set of vulnerabilities, the interdependencies between them create a new class of vulnerabilities that we must address. In this chapter, we look at ways to assess and mitigate the vulnerabilities of security architectures, designs, and solution elements. We'll do this by looking at some of the most common system architectures. For each, we classify components based on their roles and the manner in which they interact with others. Along the way, we'll look at potential vulnerabilities in each architecture and also at the manner in which these vulnerabilities might affect other connected components.

General System Architectures

A *system* is a set of things working together in order to do something. An *architecture* describes the designed structure of something. A *system architecture*, then, is a description of how specific components are deliberately put together to perform some actions. Recall from the Chapter 4 discussion of TOGAF and the Zachman Framework that there are different perspectives or levels of abstraction at which a system architecture can be presented depending on the audience. In this chapter, we present what TOGAF would call application architectures. In other words, we describe how applications running in one or more computing devices interact with each other and with users.

Client-Based Systems

Let's start with the simplest computing system architecture, the one that ruled the early days of personal computing. *Client-based systems* are embodied in applications that execute entirely on one user device (such as a workstation or smartphone). The software is installed on a specific computer, and we can use it with no network connectivity. To be clear, the application may still reach out for software patches and updates or to save and retrieve files, but none of its core features require any processing on a remote device. Examples of these are the text and graphic applications that ship with almost every operating system. You could save documents on remote servers, but even with no networking the app is fully functional.

One of the main vulnerabilities of client-based systems is that they tend to have weak authentication mechanisms (if they have them at all). This means an adversary who gains access to the application would be able to also access its data on local or even remote data stores. Furthermore, this data is usually stored in plaintext (unless the underlying operating system encrypts it), which means that even without using the application, the adversary could read its data with ease.

Server-Based Systems

Unlike client-based systems, *server-based systems* (also called *client/server systems*) require that two (or more) separate applications interact with each other across a network connection in order for users to benefit from them. One application (the client) requests services over a network connection that the other application (the server) fulfills. Perhaps the most common example of a server-based application is your web browser, which is designed to connect to a web server. Sure, you could just use your browser to read local documents, but that's not really the way it's meant to be used. Most of us use our browsers to connect two tiers, a client and a server, which is why we call it a two-tier architecture.

Generally, server-based systems are known as *n*-tier architectures, where *n* is a numerical variable that can assume any value. The reason for this is that most of the time only the development team would know the number of tiers in the architecture (which could change over time) even if to the user it looks like just two. Consider the example of browsing the Web, which is probably a two-tier architecture if you are reading a static web page on a small web server. If, on the other hand, you are browsing a typical commercial site, you will probably be going through many more tiers. For example, your client (tier 1) could be connecting to a web server (tier 2) that provides the static HTML, CSS, and some images. The dynamic content, however, is pulled by the web server from an application server (tier 3) that in turn gets the necessary data from a back-end database (tier 4). Figure 7-1 shows what this four-tier architecture would look like.

As you can imagine by looking at Figure 7-1, there are multiple potential security issues to address in a server-based architecture. For starters, access to each tier needs to be deliberately and strictly controlled. Having users authenticate from their clients makes perfect sense, but we must not forget that each of the tiers needs to establish and maintain trust with the others. A common way to ensure this is by developing access control lists (ACLs) that determine which connections are allowed. For example, the database management system in Figure 7-1 might be listening on port 5432 (the default

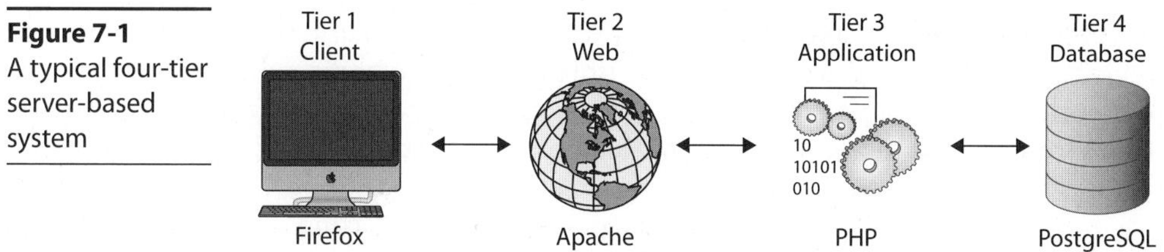

Figure 7-1 A typical four-tier server-based system

port for PostgreSQL, a popular open-source database server), so it makes perfect sense for the application server on tier 3 to connect to that port on the database server. However, it probably shouldn't be allowed to connect on port 3389 and establish a Remote Desktop Protocol (RDP) session because servers don't normally communicate this way.

The following are some other guidelines in securing server-based systems. Keep in mind, however, that this list is by no means comprehensive; it's just meant to give you food for thought.

- Block traffic by default between any components and allow only the specific set of connections that are absolutely necessary.
- Ensure all software is patched and updated as soon as possible.
- Maintain backups (ideally offline) of all servers.
- Use strong authentication for both clients and servers.
- Encrypt all network communications, even between the various servers.
- Encrypt all sensitive data stored anywhere in the system
- Enable logging of all relevant system events, ideally to a remote server.

Database Systems

Most interactive (as opposed to static) web content, such as that in the example four-tier architecture we just looked at, requires a web application to interact with some sort of data source. You may be looking at a catalog of products on an e-commerce site, updating customer data on a customer relationship management (CRM) system, or just reading a blog online. In any case, you need a system to manage your product, or customer, or blog data. This is where database systems come in.

A database management system (DBMS) is a software system that allows you to efficiently create, read, update, and delete (CRUD) any given set of data. Of course, you can always keep all the data in a text file, but that makes it *really* hard to organize, search, maintain, and share among multiple users. A DBMS makes this all easy. It is optimized for efficient storage of data, which means that, unlike flat files, it gives you ways to optimize the storage of all your information. A DBMS also provides the capability to speed up searches, for example, through the use of indexes. Another key feature of a DBMS is that it can provide mechanisms to prevent the accidental corruption of data while it is being manipulated. We typically call changes to a database *transactions*, which is a term to describe the sequence of actions required to change the state of the database.

A foundational principle in database transactions is referred to as their ACID properties, which stands for atomicity, consistency, isolation, and durability. *Atomicity* means that either the entire transactions succeeds or the DBMS rolls it back to its previous state (in other words, clicks the "undo" button). Suppose you are transferring funds between two bank accounts. This transaction consists of two distinct operations: first, you withdraw the funds from the first account, and then you deposit the same amount of funds into the second account. What would happen if there's a massive power outage right after the withdrawal is complete but before the deposit happens? In that case, the money could just disappear. If this was an atomic transaction, the system would detect the failure and put the funds back into the source account.

Consistency means that the transaction strictly follows all applicable rules (e.g., you can't withdraw funds that don't exist) on any and all data affected. *Isolation* means that if transactions are allowed to happen in parallel (which most of them are), then they will be isolated from each other so that the effects of one don't corrupt another. In other words, isolated transactions have the same effect whether they happen in parallel or one after the other. Finally, *durability* is the property that ensures that a completed transaction is permanently stored (for instance, in nonvolatile memory) so that it cannot be wiped by a power outage or other such failure.

Securing database systems mainly requires the same steps we listed for securing server-based systems. However, databases introduce two unique security issues you need to consider: aggregation and inference. *Aggregation* happens when a user does not have the clearance or permission to access specific information but she does have the permission to access components of this information. She can then figure out the rest and obtain restricted information. She can learn of information from different sources and combine it to learn something she does not have the clearance to know.

The following is a silly conceptual example. Let's say a database administrator does not want anyone in the Users group to be able to figure out a specific sentence, so he segregates the sentence into components and restricts the Users group from accessing it, as represented in Figure 7-2. However, Emily can access components A, C, and F. Because she is particularly bright, she figures out the sentence and now knows the restricted secret.

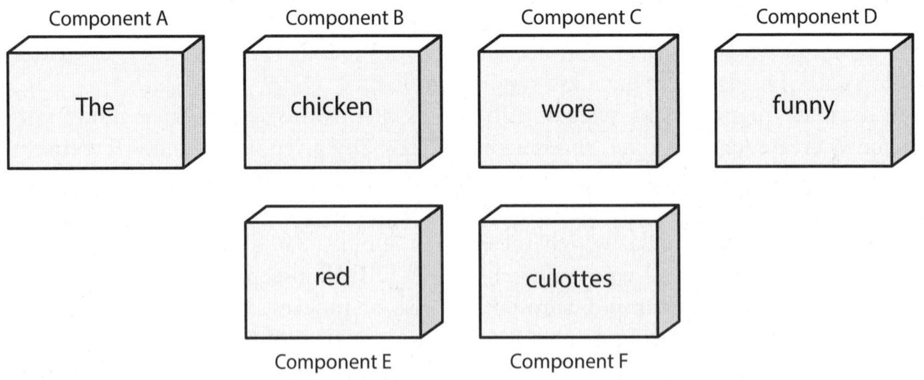

Figure 7-2 Because Emily has access to components A, C, and F, she can figure out the secret sentence through aggregation.

To prevent aggregation, the subject, and any application or process acting on the subject's behalf, needs to be prevented from gaining access to the whole collection, including the independent components. The objects can be placed into containers, which are classified at a higher level to prevent access from subjects with lower-level permissions or clearances. A subject's queries can also be tracked, and context-dependent access control can be enforced. This would keep a history of the objects that a subject has accessed and restrict an access attempt if there is an indication that an aggregation attack is underway.

EXAM TIP *Aggregation* is the act of combining information from separate sources. The combination of the data forms new information, which the subject does not have the necessary rights to access. The combined information has a sensitivity that is greater than that of the individual parts.

The other security issue is *inference*, which is the intended result of aggregation. The inference problem happens when a subject deduces the full story from the pieces he learned of through aggregation. This is seen when data at a lower security level indirectly portrays data at a higher level.

EXAM TIP *Inference* is the ability to derive information not explicitly available.

For example, if a clerk were restricted from knowing the planned movements of troops based in a specific country but did have access to food shipment requirement forms and tent allocation documents, he could figure out that the troops were moving to a specific place because that is where the food and tents are being shipped. The food shipment and tent allocation documents were classified as confidential, and the troop movement was classified as top secret. Because of the varying classifications, the clerk could access and ascertain top-secret information he was not supposed to know.

The trick is to prevent the subject, or any application or process acting on behalf of that subject, from indirectly gaining access to the inferable information. This problem is usually dealt with in the development of the database by implementing content- and context-dependent access control rules. *Content-dependent access control* is based on the sensitivity of the data. The more sensitive the data, the smaller the subset of individuals who can gain access to the data.

Context-dependent access control means that the software "understands" what actions should be allowed based upon the state and sequence of the request. So what does that mean? It means the software must keep track of previous access attempts by the user and understand what sequences of access steps are allowed. Content-dependent access control can go like this: "Does Julio have access to File A?" The system reviews the ACL on File A and returns with a response of "Yes, Julio can access the file, but can only read it." In a context-dependent access control situation, it would be more like this: "Does Julio have access to File A?" The system then reviews several pieces of data: What other access attempts has Julio made? Is this request out of sequence of how a safe series of requests takes place? Does this request fall within the allowed time period of system access (8 A.M. to 5 P.M.)? If the answers to all of these questions are within a set of preconfigured parameters, Julio can access the file. If not, he can't.

If context-dependent access control is being used to protect against inference attacks, the database software would need to keep track of what the user is requesting. So Julio makes a request to see field 1, then field 5, then field 20, which the system allows, but once he asks to see field 15, the database does not allow this access attempt. The software must be preprogrammed (usually through a rule-based engine) as to what sequence and how much data Julio is allowed to view. If he is allowed to view more information, he may have enough data to infer something we don't want him to know.

Obviously, content-dependent access control is not as complex as context-dependent access control because of the number of items that need to be processed by the system.

Some other common attempts to prevent inference attacks are cell suppression, partitioning the database, and noise and perturbation. *Cell suppression* is a technique used to hide specific cells that contain information that could be used in inference attacks. *Partitioning* the database involves dividing the database into different parts, which makes it much harder for an unauthorized individual to find connecting pieces of data that can be brought together and other information that can be deduced or uncovered. *Noise and perturbation* is a technique of inserting bogus information in the hopes of misdirecting an attacker or confusing the matter enough that the actual attack will not be fruitful.

Often, security is not integrated into the planning and development of a database. Security is an afterthought, and a trusted front end is developed to be used with the database instead. This approach is limited in the granularity of security and in the types of security functions that can take place.

A common theme in security is a balance between effective security and functionality. In many cases, the more you secure something, the less functionality you have. Although this could be the desired result, it is important not to excessively impede user productivity when security is being introduced.

High-Performance Computing Systems

All the architectures we've discussed so far in this chapter support significant amounts of computing. From high-end workstations used for high-resolution video processing to massive worldwide e-commerce sites supporting hundreds of millions of transactions per day, the power available to these systems today is very impressive indeed. As we will see shortly, the use of highly scalable cloud services can help turbo-charge these architectures, too. But what happens when even that is not enough? That's when we have to abandon these architectures and go for something altogether different.

High-performance computing (HPC) is the aggregation of computing power in ways that exceed the capabilities of general-purpose computers for the specific purpose of solving large problems. You may have already encountered this architecture if you've read about supercomputers. These are devices whose performance is so optimized that, even with electrons traveling at close to the speed of light down their wires, engineers spend significant design effort to make those wires even a few inches shorter. This is partially achieved by dividing the thousands (or tens of thousands) of processors in a typical system into tightly packed clusters, each with its own high-speed storage devices. Large problems can be broken down into individual jobs and assigned to the different clusters by a central scheduler. Once these smaller jobs are completed, they are progressively put together with other jobs (which, in turn, would be a job) until the final answer is computed.

While it may seem that most of us will seldom (if ever) work with HPC, the move toward big data analytics will probably drive us there sooner rather than later. For this reason, we need to be at least aware of some of the biggest security challenges with HPC. The first one is, quite simply, the very purpose of HPC's existence: efficiency. Large organizations spend millions of dollars building these custom systems for the purpose of crunching numbers really fast. Security tends to slow down (at least a little) just about everything, so we're already fighting an uphill battle. Fortunately, the very fact that HPC systems are so expensive and esoteric can help us justify the first rule for securing them, which is to put them in their own isolated enclave. Complete isolation is probably infeasible in many cases because raw data must flow in and solutions must flow out at some point. The goal would be to identify exactly how those flows should happen and then force them through a few gateways that can restrict who can communicate with the HPC system and under what conditions.

Another way in which HPC systems actually help us secure them is by following some very specific patterns of behavior during normal operations: jobs come in to the schedulers, which then assign them to specific clusters, which then return results in a specific format. Apart from some housekeeping functions, that's pretty much all that happens in an HPC system. It just happens *a lot*! These predictable patterns mean that anomaly detection is much easier than in a typical IT environment with thousands of users each doing their own thing.

Finally, since performance is so critical to HPC, most attacks are likely to affect it in noticeable ways. For this reason, simply monitoring the performance of the system will probably reveal nefarious activities. This noticeable impact on performance, as we will see shortly, affects other, less-esoteric systems, like those that control our factories, refineries, and electric grids.

Industrial Control Systems

Industrial control systems (ICS) consist of information technology that is specifically designed to control physical devices in industrial processes. ICS exist on factory floors to control conveyor belts and industrial robots. They exist in the power and water infrastructures to control the flows of these utilities. Because, unlike the majority of other IT systems, ICS control things that can directly cause physical harm to humans, safety must be paramount in operating and securing them. Another important consideration is that, due to the roles these systems typically fulfill in manufacturing and infrastructure, maintaining their "uptime" or availability is critical. For these two reasons (safety and availability), securing ICS requires a slightly different approach than that used to secure traditional IT systems.

EXAM TIP Safety is the paramount concern in operating and securing industrial control systems.

The term industrial control system actually is an umbrella term covering a number of somewhat different technologies that were developed independently to solve different problems. The term encompasses programmable logic controllers (PLCs) that open or close valves, remote terminal units (RTUs) that relay readings and execute commands, and specialized databases called data historians that capture all process data for analysis. ICS, with all its technologies, protocols, and devices, can generally be divided into two solution spaces:

- Controlling physical processes that take place in a (more or less) local area. This involves what are called distributed control systems (DCS).
- Controlling processes that take place at multiple sites separated by significant distances. This is addressed through supervisory control and data acquisition (SCADA).

We'll delve into both of these solution spaces shortly.

NOTE A good resource for ensuring ICS safety, security, and availability is NIST Special Publication 800-82, Revision 2, *Guide to Industrial Control Systems (ICS) Security*, discussed further later in this section.

Another umbrella term you may see is *operational technology (OT)*, which includes both ICS and some traditional IT systems that are needed to make sure all the ICS devices can talk to each other. Figure 7-3 shows the relationship between these terms. Note that there is overlap between DCS and SCADA, in this case shown by the PLC, which supports both types of systems. Before we discuss each of the two major categories of ICS, let's take a quick look at some of the devices, like PLCs, that are needed to make these systems work.

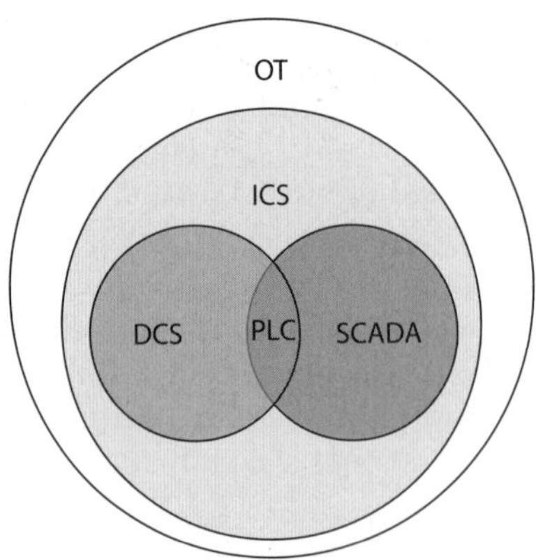

Figure 7-3 Relationship between OT terms

Devices

There are a lot of different types of devices in use in OT systems. Increasingly, the lines between these types are blurred as different features converge in newer devices. However, most OT environments will have PLCs, a human-machine interface (HMI), and a data historian, which we describe in the following sections. Please note that you don't need to memorize what any of the following devices do in order to pass the CISSP exam. However, being familiar with them will help you understand the security implications of ICS and how OT and IT systems intertwine in the real world.

Programmable Logic Controller

When automation (the physical kind, not the computing kind to which we're accustomed) first showed up on factory floors, it was bulky, brittle, and difficult to maintain. If, for instance, you wanted an automatic hammer to drive nails into boxes moving through a conveyor belt, you would arrange a series of electrical relays such that they would sequentially actuate the hammer, retrieve it, and then wait for the next box. Whenever you wanted to change your process or repurpose the hammer, you would have to suffer through a complex and error-prone reconfiguration process.

Programmable logic controllers (PLCs) are computers designed to control electromechanical processes such as assembly lines, elevators, roller coasters, and nuclear centrifuges. The idea is that a PLC can be used in one application today and then easily reprogrammed to control something else tomorrow. PLCs normally connect to the devices they control over a standard serial interface such as RS-232, and to the devices that control them over Ethernet cables. The communications protocols themselves, however, are not always standard. The dominant protocols are Modbus and EtherNet/IP, but this is not universal. While this lack of universality in communications protocols creates additional challenges to securing PLCs, we are seeing a trend toward standardization of these serial connection protocols. This is particularly important because, while early PLCs had limited or no network connectivity, it is now rare to see a PLC that is not network-enabled.

PLCs can present some tough security challenges. Unlike the IT devices with which many of us are more familiar, these OT devices tend to have very long lifetimes. It's not unusual for production systems to include PLCs that are ten years old or older. Depending on how the ICS was architected, it may be difficult to update or patch the PLCs. When you couple this difficulty with the risk of causing downtime to a critical industrial process, you may understand why some PLCs can go years without getting patched. To make things worse, we've seen plenty of PLCs using factory default passwords that are well documented. While modern PLCs come with better security features, odds are that an OT environment will have some legacy controllers hiding somewhere. The best thing to do is to ensure that all PLC network segments are strictly isolated from all nonessential devices and are monitored closely for anomalous traffic.

Human-Machine Interface

A *human-machine interface (HMI)* is usually a regular workstation running a proprietary supervisory system that allows operators to monitor and control an ICS. An HMI normally has a dashboard that shows a diagram or schematic of the system being controlled,

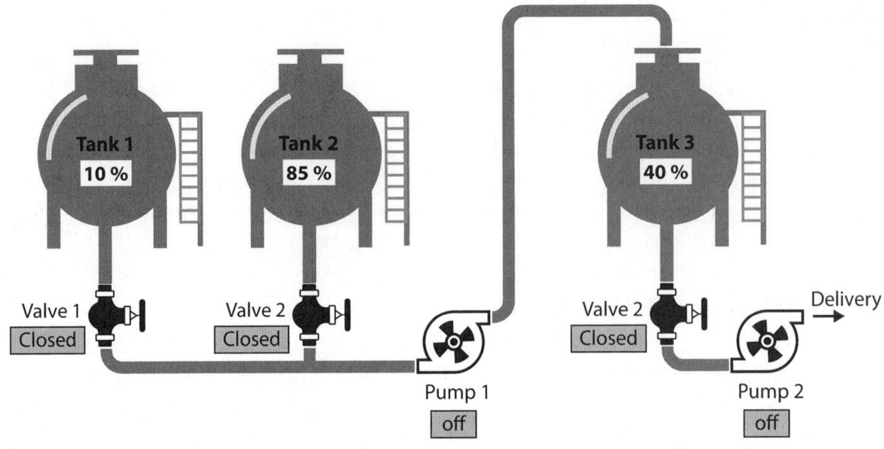

Figure 7-4 A simplified HMI screen

the readings from whatever sensors the system has in place, and buttons with which to control your actuators. Figure 7-4 shows a simplified HMI screen for a small fuel distribution system. Each of the three tanks shows how much fuel it contains. Three valves control the flow of fuel between the tanks, and all three are closed. If the operator wanted to move fuel around, she would simply click the CLOSED button, it would change to OPEN, and the fuel would be free to move. Similarly, clicking the OFF button on the pumps would turn them on to actually move the fuel around.

Another feature of HMIs is alarm monitoring. Each sensor (like those monitoring tank levels in our example) can be configured to alarm if certain values are reached. This is particularly important when it comes to the pressure in a pipeline, the temperature in a tank, or the load on a power line. HMIs usually include automation features that can automatically instruct PLCs to take certain actions when alarm conditions are met, such as tripping breakers when loads are too high.

HMIs simplify the myriad of details that make the ICS work so that the operators are not overwhelmed. In the simple example in Figure 7-4, Pump 1 would typically have a safety feature that would prevent it from being open unless Valve 1 and/or Valve 2 were open and the capacity in Tank 3 was not 100 percent. These features are manually programmed by the plant staff when the system is installed and are periodically audited for safety. Keep in mind that safety is of even more importance than security in OT environments.

Technically, securing an HMI is mostly the same as securing any IT system. Keep in mind that this is normally just a regular workstation that just happens to be running this proprietary piece of software. The challenge is that, because HMIs are part of mission-critical industrial systems where safety and efficiency are paramount, there can be significant resistance from OT staff to making any changes or taking any actions that can compromise either of these imperatives. These actions, of course, could include the typical security measures such as installing endpoint detection and response (EDR) systems, scanning them for vulnerabilities, conducting penetration tests, or even mandating unique credentials for each user with strong authentication. (Imagine what could happen if the HMI is locked, there is an emergency, and the logged-in user is on a break.)

Data Historian

As the name suggests, a *data historian* is a data repository that keeps a history of everything seen in the ICS. This includes all sensor values, alarms, and commands issued, all of which are timestamped. A data historian can communicate directly with other ICS devices, such as PLCs and HMIs. Sometimes, a data historian is embedded with (or at least running on the same workstation as) the HMI. Most OT environments, however, have a dedicated data historian (apart from the HMI) in a different network segment. The main reason for this is that this device usually communicates with enterprise IT systems for planning and accounting purposes. For example, the data historian in our fuel system example would provide data on how much fuel was delivered out of Tank 3.

One of the key challenges in securing the data historian stems from the fact that it frequently has to talk to both PLCs (and similar devices) and enterprise IT systems (e.g., for accounting purposes). A best practice when this is required is to put the data historian in a specially hardened network segment like a demilitarized zone (DMZ) and implement restrictive ACLs to ensure unidirectional traffic from the PLCs to the historian and from the historian to the enterprise IT systems. This can be done using a traditional firewall (or even a router), but some organizations instead use specialized devices called *data diodes*, which are security hardened and permit traffic to flow only in one direction.

Distributed Control System

A *distributed control system (DCS)* is a network of control devices within fairly close proximity that are part of one or more industrial processes. DCS usage is very common in manufacturing plants, oil refineries, and power plants, and is characterized by decisions being made in a concerted manner, but by different nodes within the system.

You can think of a DCS as a hierarchy of devices. At the bottom level, you will find the physical devices that are being controlled or that provide inputs to the system. One level up, you will find the microcontrollers and PLCs that directly interact with the physical devices but also communicate with higher-level controllers. Above the PLCs are the supervisory computers that control, for example, a given production line. You can also have a higher level that deals with plant-wide controls, which would require some coordination among different production lines.

As you can see, the concept of a DCS was born from the need to control fairly localized physical processes. Because of this, the communications protocols in use are not optimized for wide-area communications or for security. Another byproduct of this localized approach is that DCS users felt for many years that all they needed to do to secure their systems was to provide physical security. If the bad guys can't get into the plant, it was thought, then they can't break our systems. This is because, typically, a DCS consists of devices within the same plant. However, technological advances and converging technologies are blurring the line between a DCS and a SCADA system.

Supervisory Control and Data Acquisition

While DCS technology is well suited for local processes such as those in a manufacturing plant, it was never intended to operate across great distances. The *supervisory control and data acquisition (SCADA)* systems were developed to control large-scale physical processes involving nodes separated by significant distances. The main conceptual differences between DCS and SCADA are size and distances. So, while the control of a power plant is perfectly suited for a traditional DCS, the distribution of the generated power across a power grid would require a SCADA system.

SCADA systems typically involve three kinds of devices: endpoints, backends, and user stations. A *remote terminal unit (RTU)* is an endpoint that connects directly to sensors and/or actuators. Though there are still plenty of RTUs in use, many RTUs have been replaced with PLCs. The *data acquisition servers (DAS)* are backends that receive all data from the endpoints through a telemetry system and perform whatever correlation or analysis may be necessary. Finally, the users in charge of controlling the system interact with it through the use of the previously introduced *human-machine interface (HMI)*, the user station that displays the data from the endpoints and allows the users to issue commands to the actuators (e.g., to close a valve or open a switch).

One of the main challenges with operating at great distances is effective communications, particularly when parts of the process occur in areas with limited, spotty, or nonexistent telecommunications infrastructures. SCADA systems commonly use dedicated cables and radio links to cover these large expanses. Many legacy SCADA implementations rely on older proprietary communications protocols and devices. For many years, this led this community to feel secure because only someone with detailed knowledge of an obscure protocol and access to specialized communications gear could compromise the system. In part, this assumption is one of the causes of the lack of effective security controls on legacy SCADA communications. While this thinking may have been arguable in the past, today's convergence on IP-based protocols makes it clear that this is not a secure way of doing business.

ICS Security

The single greatest vulnerability in ICS is their increasing connectivity to traditional IT networks. This has two notable side effects: it accelerates convergence toward standard protocols, and it exposes once-private systems to anyone with an Internet connection. NIST SP 800-82 Rev. 2 has a variety of recommendations for ICS security, but we highlight some of the most important ones here:

- Apply a risk management process to ICS.
- Segment the network to place IDS/IPS at the subnet boundaries.
- Disable unneeded ports and services on all ICS devices.
- Implement least privilege through the ICS.
- Use encryption wherever feasible.
- Ensure there is a process for patch management.
- Monitor audit trails regularly.

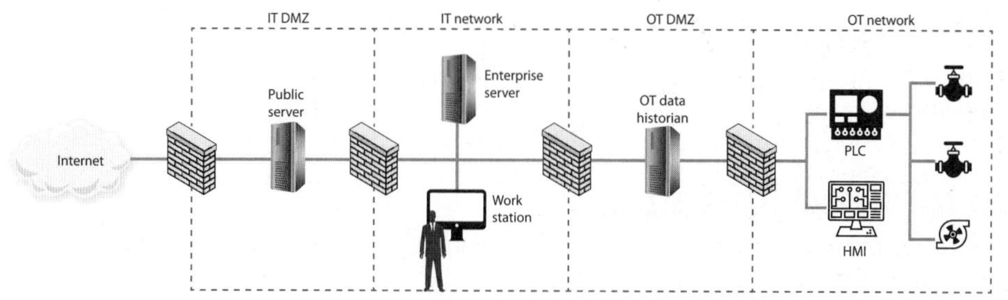

Figure 7-5 A simplified IT/OT environment

Let's look at a concrete (if seriously simplified) example in Figure 7-5. We're only showing a handful of IT and OT devices, but the zones are representative of a real environment. Starting from the right, you see the valves and pumps that are controlled by the PLC in the OT network. The PLC is directly connected to the HMI so that the PLC can be monitored and controlled by the operator. Both the PLC and the HMI are also connected (through a firewall) to the OT data historian in the OT DMZ. This is so that everything that happens in the OT network can be logged and analyzed. The OT data historian can also communicate with the enterprise server in the IT network to pass whatever data is required for planning, accounting, auditing, and reporting. If a user, say, in the accounting department, wants any of this data, he would get it from the enterprise server and would not be able to connect directly to the OT data historian. If a customer wanted to check via the Internet how much fuel they've been dispensed, they would log into their portal on the public server and that device would query the enterprise server for the relevant data.

Note that each segment is protected by a firewall (or data diode) that allows only specific devices in the next zone to connect in very restrictive ways to get only specific data. No device should ever be able to connect any further than one segment to the left or right.

Network segmentation also helps mitigate one of the common risks in many OT environments: unpatched devices. It is not rare to find devices that have been operating unpatched for several years. There are many reasons for this. First, ICS devices have very long shelf lives. They can remain in use for a decade or longer and may no longer receive updates from the manufacturer. They can also be very expensive, which means organizations may be unwilling or unable to set up a separate laboratory in which to test patches to ensure they don't cause unanticipated effects on the production systems. While this is a pretty standard practice in IT environments, it is pretty rare in the OT world. Without prior testing, patches could cause outages or safety issues and, as we know, maintaining availability and ensuring safety are the two imperatives of the OT world.

So, it is not all that strange for us to have to live with unpatched devices. The solution is to isolate them as best as we can. At a very minimum, it should be impossible for ICS devices to be reachable from the Internet. Better yet, we control access strictly from one zone to the next, as discussed previously. But for unpatched control devices, we have to be extremely paranoid and surround them with protective barriers that are monitored continuously.

EXAM TIP The most important principle in defending OT systems is to isolate them from the public Internet, either logically or physically.

Virtualized Systems

If you have been into computers for a while, you might remember computer games that did not have the complex, lifelike graphics of today's games. *Pong* and *Asteroids* were what we had to play with when we were younger. In those simpler times, the games were 16-bit and were written to work in a 16-bit MS-DOS environment. When our Windows operating systems moved from 16-bit to 32-bit, the 32-bit operating systems were written to be backward compatible, so someone could still load and play a 16-bit game in an environment that the game did not understand. The continuation of this little life pleasure was available to users because the OSs created virtual environments for the games to run in. Backward compatibility was also introduced with 64-bit OSs.

When a 32-bit application needs to interact with a 64-bit OS, it has been developed to make system calls and interact with the computer's memory in a way that would only work within a 32-bit OS—not a 64-bit system. So, the virtual environment simulates a 32-bit OS, and when the application makes a request, the OS converts the 32-bit request into a 64-bit request (this is called *thunking*) and reacts to the request appropriately. When the system sends a reply to this request, it changes the 64-bit reply into a 32-bit reply so the application understands it.

Today, virtual environments are much more advanced. *Virtualized systems* are those that exist in software-simulated environments. In our previous example of *Pong*, the 16-bit game "thinks" it is running on a 16-bit computer when in fact this is an illusion created by a layer of virtualizing software. In this case, the virtualized system was developed to provide backward compatibility. In many other cases, virtualization allows us to run multiple services or even full computers simultaneously on the same hardware, greatly enhancing resource (e.g., memory, processor) utilization, reducing operating costs, and even providing improved security, among other benefits.

Virtual Machines

Virtual machines (VMs) are entire computer systems that reside inside a virtualized environment. This means that you could have a legitimate Windows workstation running within a Linux server, complete with automatic updates from Microsoft, licensed apps from any vendor, and performance that is virtually indistinguishable (pun intended) from a similar Windows system running on "bare metal." This VM is commonly referred to as a *guest* that is executed in the *host* environment, which, in our example, would be the Linux server.

Virtualization allows a single host environment to execute multiple guests at once, with multiple VMs dynamically pooling resources from a common physical system. Computer resources such as RAM, processors, and storage are emulated through the host environment. The VMs do not directly access these resources; instead, they communicate with a *hypervisor* within the host environment, which is responsible for managing system resources. The hypervisor is the central program that controls the execution of the various guest operating

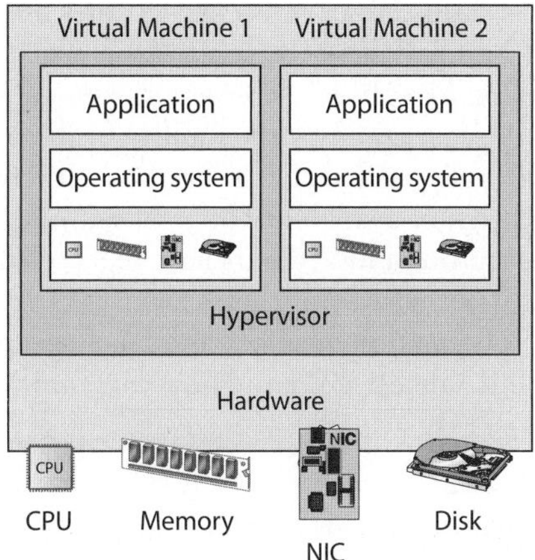

Figure 7-6 The hypervisor controls virtual machine instances.

systems and provides the abstraction level between the guest and host environments, as shown in Figure 7-6.

There are two types of hypervisors. A *type 1 hypervisor* runs directly on hardware or "bare metal" and manages access to it by its VMs. This is the sort of setup we use in server rooms and cloud environments. Examples of type 1 hypervisors are Citrix/Xen Server and VMware ESXi. A *type 2 hypervisor*, on the other hand, runs as an application on an OS. This allows users, for example, to host a Windows VM in their macOS computer. Type 2 hypervisors are commonly used by developers and security researchers to test their work in a controlled environment or use applications that are not available for the host OS. Examples of type 2 hypervisors are Oracle VM VirtualBox and VMware Workstation.

Hypervisors allow you to have one computer running several different operating systems at one time. For example, you can run a system with Windows 10, Linux, and Windows 2016 on one computer. Think of a house that has different rooms. Each OS gets its own room, but each shares the same resources that the house provides—a foundation, electricity, water, roof, and so on. An OS that is "living" in a specific room does not need to know about or interact with another OS in another room to take advantage of the resources provided by the house. The same concept happens in a computer: Each OS shares the resources provided by the physical system (memory, processor, buses, and so on). The OSs "live" and work in their own "rooms," which are the guest VMs. The physical computer itself is the host.

Why would we want to virtualize our machines? One reason is that it is cheaper than having a full physical system for each and every operating system. If they can all live on one system and share the same physical resources, your costs are reduced immensely. This is the same reason people get roommates. The rent can be split among different people, and all can share the same house and resources. Another reason to use virtualization is security. Providing to each OS its own "clean" environment to work within reduces the possibility of the various OSs negatively interacting with each other.

Furthermore, since every aspect of the virtual machine, including the contents of its disk drives and even its memory, is stored as files within the host, restoring a backup is a snap.

All you have to do is drop the set of backed-up files onto a new hypervisor and you will instantly restore a VM to whatever state it was in when the backup was made. Contrast this with having to rebuild a physical computer from backups, which can take a lot longer.

On the flip side of security, any vulnerability in the hypervisor would give an attacker unparalleled and virtually undetectable (pun not intended) power to compromise the confidentiality, integrity, or availability of VMs running on it. This is not a hypothetical scenario, as both VirtualBox and VMware have reported (and patched) such vulnerabilities in recent years. The takeaway from these discoveries is that we should assume that any component of an information system could be compromised and ask ourselves the questions "how would I detect it?" and "how can I mitigate it?"

Containerization

As virtualization matured, a new branch called *containerization* emerged. A container is an application that runs in its own isolated user space. Whereas virtual machines have their own complete operating systems running on top of hypervisors and share the resources provided by the bare metal, containers sit on top of OSs and share the resources provided by the host OS. Instead of abstracting the hardware for guest OSs, container software abstracts the kernel of the OS for the applications running above it. This allows for low overhead in running many applications and improved speed in deploying instances, because a whole VM doesn't have to be started for every application. Rather, the application, services, processes, libraries, and any other dependencies can be wrapped up into one unit.

Additionally, each container operates in a sandbox, with the only means to interact being through the user interface or application programming interface (API) calls. The big names to know in this space are Docker on the commercial side and Kubernetes as the open-source alternative. Containers have enabled rapid development operations because developers can test their code more quickly, changing only the components necessary in the container and then redeploying.

Securing containers requires a different approach than we'd take with full-sized VMs. Obviously, we want to harden the host OS. But we also need to pay attention to each container and the manner in which it interacts with clients and other containers. Keep in mind that containers are frequently used in rapid development. This means that, unless you build secure development right into the development team, you will likely end up with insecure code. We'll address the integration of development, security, and operations staff when we discuss DevSecOps in Chapters 24 and 25, but for now remember that it's really difficult to secure containers that have been developed insecurely.

NIST offers some excellent specific guidance on securing containers in NIST SP 800-190, *Application Container Security Guide*. Among the most important recommendations in that publication are the following:

- Use container-specific host OSs instead of general-purpose ones to reduce attack surfaces.
- Only group containers with the same purpose, sensitivity, and threat posture on a single host OS kernel to allow for additional defense in depth.

- Adopt container-specific vulnerability management tools and processes for images to prevent compromises.
- Use container-aware runtime defense tools such as intrusion prevention systems.

Microservices

A common use of containers is to host *microservices*, which is a way of developing software where, rather than building one large enterprise application, the functionality is divided into multiple smaller components that, working together in a distributed manner, implement all the needed features. Think of it as a software development version of the old "divide and conquer" approach. Microservices are considered an architectural style rather than a standard, but there is broad consensus that they consist of small, decentralized, individually deployable services built around business capabilities. They also tend to be *loosely coupled*, which means there aren't a lot of dependencies between the individual services. As a result, microservices are quick to develop, test, and deploy and can be exchanged without breaking the larger system. For many business applications, microservices are also more efficient and scalable than monolithic server-based architectures.

NOTE Containers and microservices don't have to be used together. It's just very common to do so.

The decentralization of microservices can present a security challenge. How can you track adversarial behaviors through a system of microservices, where each service does one discrete task? The answer is *log aggregation*. Whereas microservices are decentralized, we want to log them in a centralized fashion so we can look for patterns that span multiple services and can point to malicious intent. Admittedly, you will need automation and perhaps data analytics or artificial intelligence to detect these malicious events, but you won't have a chance at spotting them unless you aggregate the logs.

Serverless

If we gain efficiency and scalability by breaking up a big service into a bunch of microservices, can we gain even more by breaking up the microservices further? The answer, in many cases, is yes, because hosting a service (even a micro one) means that you have to provision, manage, update, and run the thing. So, if we're going to go further down this road of dividing and conquering, the next level of granularity is individual functions.

Hosting a service usually means setting up hardware, provisioning and managing servers, defining load management mechanisms, setting up requirements, and running the service. In a *serverless* architecture, the services offered to end users, such as compute, storage, or messaging, along with their required configuration and management, can be performed without a requirement from the user to set up any server infrastructure. The focus is strictly at the individual function level. These serverless models are designed primarily for massive scaling and high availability. Additionally, from a cost perspective, they are attractive, because billing occurs based on what cycles are actually used versus what is provisioned in advance.

Integrating security mechanisms into serverless models is not as simple as ensuring that the underlying technologies are hardened. Because visibility into host infrastructure operations is limited, implementing countermeasures for remote code execution or modifying access control lists isn't as straightforward as it would be with traditional server design. In the serverless model, security analysts are usually restricted to applying controls at the application or function level and then keeping a close eye on network traffic.

As you probably know by now, serverless architectures rely on the capability to automatically and securely provision, run, and then deprovision computing resources on demand. This capability undergirds their economic promise: you only pay for exactly the computing you need to perform just the functions that are required, and not a penny more. It is also essential to meet the arbitrary scalability of serverless systems. This capability is characteristic of cloud computing.

Comparing Server-Based, Microservice, and Serverless Architectures

A typical service houses a bunch of functions within it. Think of a very simple e-commerce web application server. It allows customers to log in, view the items that are for sale, and place orders. When placing an order, the server invokes a multitude of functions. For instance, it may have to charge the payment card, decrease inventory, schedule a shipment, and send a confirmation message. Here's how each of these three architectures handle this.

Server-based implementations provide all services (and their component functions) in the same physical or virtual server that houses the monolithic web application. The server must always be available (meaning powered on and connected to the Internet). If there's a sudden spike in orders, you better hope you have enough bandwidth, memory, and processing power to handle it. If you don't, you get to build a new server from scratch and either replace the original server with a beefier one or load-balance between the two. Either way, you now have more infrastructure to keep up and running.

Microservices can be created for each of the major features in the web application: view items and place orders. Each microservice lives in its own container and gets called as needed. If you see that spike in orders, you deploy a new container (in seconds), perhaps in a different host, and can destroy it when you no longer need it. Sure, you'll need some supervisory process to figure out when and how to spin up new containers, but at least you can dynamically respond to increased demands.

Serverless approaches would decompose each service into its fundamental functions and then dynamically provision those functions as needed. In other words, there is never a big web application server (like in the server-based approach) or even a microservice for order processing that is up and running. Instead, the charge_payment_card function is invoked in whatever infrastructure is available whenever a card needs to be processed. If that function is successful, it invokes the decrease_inventory function, again, in whatever infrastructure is available, and so on. After each function terminates, it simply evaporates so that no more resources are consumed than are absolutely needed. If there's a sudden spike in demand, the orchestrator spins up whatever additional resources are needed to run as many functions as are required.

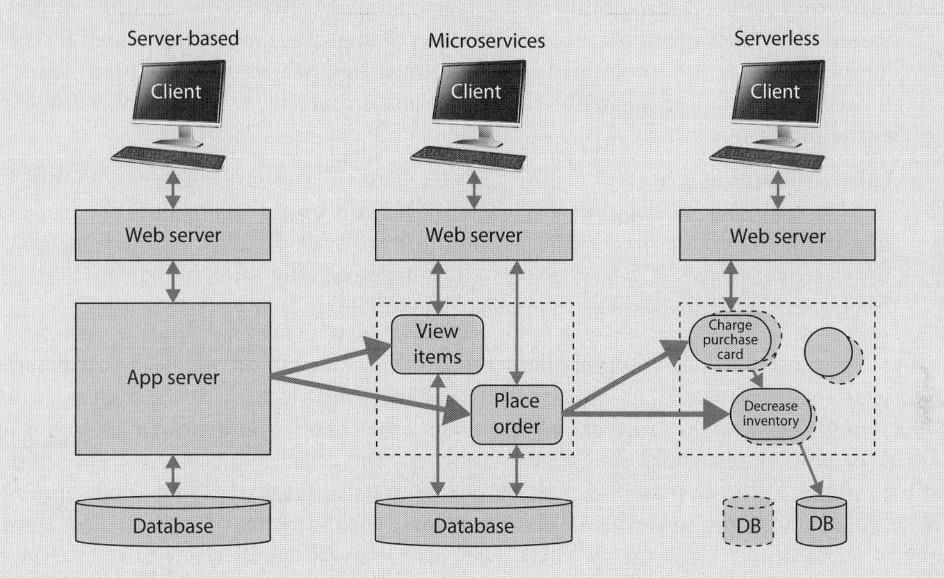

Cloud-Based Systems

If you were asked to install a brand-new server room for your organization, you would probably have to clear your calendar for weeks (or longer) to address the many tasks that would be involved. From power and environmental controls to hardware acquisition, installation, and configuration to software builds, the list is long and full of headaches. Now, imagine that you can provision all the needed servers in minutes using a simple graphical interface or a short script and that you can get rid of them just as quickly when you no longer need them. This is one of the benefits of cloud computing.

Cloud computing is the use of shared, remote computing devices for the purpose of providing improved efficiencies, performance, reliability, scalability, and security. These devices are usually based on virtual machines running on shared infrastructure and can be outsourced to a third-party cloud service provider (CSP) on a *public cloud* or provided in-house on a *private cloud*. If you don't feel comfortable sharing infrastructure with random strangers (though this is done securely), there is also a *virtual private cloud (VPC)* model in which you get your own walled garden inside an otherwise public cloud.

Generally speaking, there are three models for cloud computing services:

- **Software as a Service (SaaS)** The user of SaaS is allowed to use a specific application that executes on the CSP's environment. Examples of SaaS are Microsoft 365 and Google Apps, which you use via a web interface but someone else provisions and maintains everything for you.
- **Platform as a Service (PaaS)** In this model, the user gets access to a computing platform that is typically built on a server operating system. An example of this would be spawning an instance of Windows Server 2019 to provide a web server. The CSP is normally responsible for configuring and securing the platform, however, so the user normally doesn't get administrative privileges over the entire platform.
- **Infrastructure as a Service (IaaS)** If you want full, unfettered access to (and responsibility for securing) a cloud-based VM, you would want to use the IaaS model. Following up on the previous example, this would allow you to manage the patching of the Windows Server 2019 instance. The catch is that the CSP has no responsibility for security; it's all on you.

If you are a user of IaaS, you probably won't do things too differently than you already do to secure your systems. The only exception is that you wouldn't have physical access to the computers if a CSP hosts them. If, on the other hand, you use SaaS or PaaS, the security of your systems will almost always rely on the policies and contracts that you put into place. The policies will dictate how your users interact with the cloud services. This would include the information classification levels that would be allowed on those services, terms of use, and other policies. The contracts will specify the quality of service and what the CSP will do with or for you in responding to security events.

CAUTION It is imperative that you carefully review the terms of service when evaluating a potential contract for cloud services and consider them in the context of your organization's security. Though the industry is getting better all the time, security provisions are oftentimes lacking in these contracts at this time.

Software as a Service

SaaS is pervasively used by most enterprises. According to some estimates, the average company uses nearly 2,000 unique cloud services for everything from writing memos to managing their sales pipeline. The whole idea is that, apart from a fairly small amount of allowed customization, you just pay for the licenses and the vendor takes care of making sure all your users have access to the software, regardless of where they are.

Given the popularity of SaaS solutions, cloud service providers such as Microsoft, Amazon, Cisco, and Google often dedicate large teams to securing all aspects of their service infrastructure. Increasingly, however, most security incidents involving SaaS occur at the data-handling level, where these infrastructure companies do not have the responsibility or visibility required to take action. For example, how could the CSP be held liable when one of your employees shares a confidential file with an unauthorized third party?

So, visibility is one of our main concerns as security professionals when it comes to SaaS. Do you know what assets you have and how they are being used? The "McAfee 2019 Cloud Adoption and Risk Report" describes the disconnect between the number of cloud services that organizations believe are being accessed by their users and the number of cloud services that are actually being accessed. The discrepancy, according to the report, can be several orders of magnitude. As we have mentioned before, you can't protect what you don't know you have. This is where solutions like cloud access security brokers (CASBs) and data loss prevention (DLP) systems can come in very handy.

NOTE We already covered CASBs and DLP systems in Chapter 6.

Platform as a Service

What if, instead of licensing someone else's application, you have developed your own and need a place to host it for your users? You'd want to have a fair amount of flexibility in terms of configuring the hosting environment, but you probably could use some help in terms of provisioning and securing it. You can secure the app, for sure, but would like someone else to take care of things like hardening the host, patching the underlying OS, and maybe even monitoring access to the VM. This is where PaaS comes in.

PaaS has a similar set of functionalities as SaaS and provides many of the same benefits in that the CSP manages the foundational technologies of the stack in a manner transparent to the end user. You simply tell your provider, "I'd like a Windows Server 2019 with 64 gigabytes of RAM and eight cores," and, voilà, there it is. You get direct access to a development or deployment environment that enables you to build and host your own solutions on a cloud-based infrastructure without having to build your own infrastructure. PaaS solutions, therefore, are optimized to provide value focused on software development. PaaS, by its very nature, is designed to provide an organization with tools that interact directly with what may be its most important asset: its source code.

At the physical infrastructure, in PaaS, service providers assume the responsibility of maintenance and protection and employ a number of methods to deter successful exploits at this level. This often means PaaS providers require trusted sources for hardware, use strong physical security for its data centers, and monitor access to the physical servers and connections to and from them. Additionally, PaaS providers often enhance their protection against distributed denial-of-service (DDoS) attacks using network-based technologies that require no additional configuration from the user.

While the PaaS model makes a lot of provisioning, maintenance, and security problems go away for you, it is worth noting that it does nothing to protect the software systems you host there. If you build and deploy insecure code, there is very little your CSP will be able to do to keep it protected. PaaS providers focus on the infrastructure on which the service runs, but you still have to ensure that the software is secure and the appropriate controls are in place. We'll dive into how to build secure code in Chapters 24 and 25.

Infrastructure as a Service

Sometimes, you just have to roll up your sleeves, get your hands dirty, and build your own servers from the ground up. Maybe the applications and services you have developed require your IT and security teams to install and configure components at the OS level that would not be accessible to you in the PaaS model. You don't need someone to make platforms that they manage available to you; you need to build platforms from the ground up yourself. IaaS gives you just that. You upload an image to the CSP's environment and build your own hosts however you need them.

As a method of efficiently assigning hardware through a process of constant assignment and reclamation, IaaS offers an effective and affordable way for organizations to get all of the benefits of managing their own hardware without incurring the massive overhead costs associated with acquisition, physical storage, and disposal of the hardware. In this service model, the vendor provides the hardware, network, and storage resources necessary for the user to install and maintain any operating system, dependencies, and applications they want. The vendor deals with all hardware issues for you, leaving you to focus on the virtual hosts.

In the IaaS model, the majority of the security controls (apart from physical ones) are your responsibility. Obviously, you want to have a robust security team to manage these. Still, there are some risks that are beyond your control and for which you rely on your vendor, such as any vulnerabilities that could allow an attacker to exploit flaws in hard disks, RAM, CPU caches, and GPUs. One attack scenario affecting IaaS cloud providers could enable a malicious actor to implant persistent back doors for data theft into bare-metal cloud servers. A vulnerability either in the hypervisor supporting the visualization of various tenant systems or in the firmware of the hardware in use could introduce a vector for this attack. This attack would be difficult for the customer to detect because it would be possible for all services to appear unaffected at a higher level of the technology stack.

Though the likelihood of a successful exploit of this kind of vulnerability is quite low, defects and errors at this level may still incur significant costs unrelated to an actual exploit. Take, for example, the 2014 hypervisor update performed by Amazon Web Services (AWS), which essentially forced a complete restart of a major cloud offering, the Elastic Compute Cloud (EC2). In response to the discovery of a critical security flaw in the open-source hypervisor Xen, Amazon forced EC2 instances globally to restart to ensure the patch would take correctly and that customers remained unaffected. In most cases, though, as with many other cloud services, attacks against IaaS environments are possible because of misconfiguration on the customer side.

Everything as a Service

It's worth reviewing the basic premise of cloud service offerings: you save money by only paying for exactly the resources you actually use, while having the capacity to scale those up as much as you need to at a moment's notice. If you think about it, this model can apply to things other than applications and computers. *Everything as a Service (XaaS)* captures the trend to apply the cloud model to a large range of offerings, from entertainment (e.g., television shows and feature-length movies), to cybersecurity (e.g., Security as a Service), to serverless computing environments (e.g., Function as a Service). Get ready for the inevitable barrage of <fill-in-the-blank> as a Service offerings coming your way.

Cloud Deployment Models

By now you may be a big believer in the promise of cloud computing but may be wondering, "Where, exactly, *is* the cloud?" The answer, as in so many questions in our field, is "It depends." There are four common models for deploying cloud computing resources, each with its own features and limitations:

- A *public cloud* is the most prevalent model, in which a vendor like AWS owns all the resources and provides them as a service to all its customers. Importantly, the resources are shared among all customers, albeit in a transparent and secure manner. Public cloud vendors typically also offer a virtual private cloud (VPC) as an option, in which increased isolation between users provides added security.
- A *private cloud* is owned and operated by the organization that uses its services. Here, you own, operate, and maintain the servers, storage, and networking needed to provide the services, which means you don't share resources with anyone. This approach can provide the best security, but the tradeoff might be higher costs and a cap on scalability.
- A *community cloud* is a private cloud that is co-owned (or at least shared) by a specific set of partner organizations. This approach is commonly implemented in large conglomerates where multiple firms report to the same higher-tier headquarters.
- A *hybrid cloud* combines on-premises infrastructure with a public cloud, with a significant effort placed in the management of how data and applications leverage each solution to achieve organizational goals. Organizations that use a hybrid model often derive benefits offered by both public and private models.

Pervasive Systems

Cloud computing is all about the concentration of computing power so that it may be dynamically reallocated among customers. Going in the opposite conceptual direction, *pervasive computing* (also called *ubiquitous computing* or *ubicomp*) is the concept that small (even tiny) amounts of computing power are spread out everywhere and computing is embedded into everyday objects that communicate with each other, often with little or no user interaction, to do very specific things for particular customers. In this model, computers are everywhere and communicate on their own with each other, bringing really cool new features but also really thorny new security challenges.

Embedded Systems

An *embedded system* is a self-contained computer system (that is, it has its own processor, memory, and input/output devices) designed for a very specific purpose. An embedded device is part of (or embedded into) some other mechanical or electrical device or system. Embedded systems typically are cheap, rugged, and small, and they use very little power. They are usually built around *microcontrollers*, which are specialized devices that consist of a CPU, memory, and peripheral control interfaces. Microcontrollers have a very basic operating system, if they have one at all. A digital thermometer is an example of a very simple embedded system; other examples of embedded systems include traffic lights and factory assembly line controllers. As you can see from these examples, embedded systems are frequently used to sense and/or act on a physical environment. For this reason, they are sometimes called *cyber-physical systems*.

The main challenge in securing embedded systems is that of ensuring the security of the software that drives them. Many vendors build their embedded systems around commercially available microprocessors, but they use their own proprietary code that is difficult, if not impossible, for a customer to audit. Depending on the risk tolerance of your organization, this may be acceptable as long as the embedded systems are standalone. The problem, however, is that these systems are increasingly shipping with some sort of network connectivity. For example, some organizations have discovered that some of their embedded devices have "phone home" features that are not documented. In some cases, this has resulted in potentially sensitive information being transmitted to the manufacturer. If a full audit of the embedded device security is not possible, at a very minimum, you should ensure that you see what data flows in and out of it across any network.

Another security issue presented by many embedded systems concerns the ability to update and patch them securely. Many embedded devices are deployed in environments where they have no Internet connectivity. Even if this is not the case and the devices can check for updates, establishing secure communications or verifying digitally signed code, both of which require processor-intensive cryptography, may not be possible on a cheap device.

Internet of Things

The *Internet of Things (IoT)* is the global network of connected embedded systems. What distinguishes the IoT is that each node is connected to the Internet and is uniquely addressable. By some accounts, this network is expected to reach 31 billion devices by 2025, which makes this a booming sector of the global economy. Perhaps the most visible aspect of this explosion is in the area of smart homes in which lights, furnaces, and even refrigerators collaborate to create the best environment for the residents.

With this level of connectivity and access to physical devices, the IoT poses many security challenges. Among the issues to address by anyone considering adoption of IoT devices are the following:

- **Authentication** Embedded devices are not known for incorporating strong authentication support, which is the reason why most IoT devices have very poor (if any) authentication.

- **Encryption** Cryptography is typically expensive in terms of processing power and memory requirements, both of which are very limited in IoT devices. The fallout of this is that data at rest and data in transit can be vulnerable in many parts of the IoT.
- **Updates** Though IoT devices are networked, many vendors in this fast-moving sector do not provide functionality to automatically update their software and firmware when patches are available.

Perhaps the most dramatic illustration to date of what can happen when millions of insecure IoT devices are exploited by an attacker is the Mirai botnet. Mirai is a malware strain that infects IoT devices and was behind one of the largest and most effective botnets in recent history. The Mirai botnet took down major websites via massive DDoS attacks against several sites and service providers using hundreds of thousands of compromised IoT devices. In October 2016, a Mirai attack targeted the popular DNS provider Dyn, which provided name resolution to many popular websites such as Airbnb, Amazon, GitHub, HBO, Netflix, PayPal, Reddit, and Twitter. After taking down Dyn, Mirai left millions of users unable to access these sites for hours.

Distributed Systems

A distributed system is one in which multiple computers work together to do something. The earlier section "Server-Based Systems" already covered a specific example of a four-tier distributed system. It is this collaboration that more generally defines a distributed system. A server-based system is a specific kind of distributed system in which devices in one group (or tier) act as clients for devices in an adjacent group. A tier-1 client cannot work directly with the tier-4 database, as shown earlier in Figure 7-1. We could then say that a *distributed system* is any system in which multiple computing nodes, interconnected by a network, exchange information for the accomplishment of collective tasks.

Not all distributed systems are hierarchical like the example in Figure 7-1. Another approach to distributed computing is found in *peer-to-peer systems*, which are systems in which each node is considered an equal (as opposed to a client or a server) to all others. There is no overarching structure, and nodes are free to request services from any other node. The result is an extremely resilient structure that fares well even when large numbers of nodes become disconnected or otherwise unavailable. If you had a typical client/server model and you lost your server, you'd be down for the count. In a peer-to-peer system, you could lose multiple nodes and still be able to accomplish whatever task you needed to. Clearly, not every application lends itself to this model, because some tasks are inherently hierarchical or centralized. Popular examples of peer-to-peer systems are file sharing systems like BitTorrent, anonymizing networks like The Onion Router (TOR), and cryptocurrencies like bitcoin.

One of the most important issues in securing distributed systems is network communications, which are essential to these systems. While the obvious approach would be to encrypt all traffic, it can be challenging to ensure all nodes are using cryptography that is robust enough to mitigate attacks. This is particularly true when the system includes IoT or OT components that may not have the same crypto capabilities as traditional computers.

Even if you encrypt all traffic (and you really should) in a distributed system, there's still the issue of trust. How do we ensure that every user and every node is trustworthy? How could you tell if part of the system was compromised? Identity and access management is another key area to address, as is the ability to isolate users or nodes from the system should they become compromised.

NOTE We will discuss identity and access management (IAM) in Chapter 16.

Edge Computing Systems

An interesting challenge brought about by the proliferation of IoT devices is how to service them in a responsive, scalable, and cost-effective manner. To understand the problem, let's first consider a server-based example. Suppose you enjoy playing a massively multiplayer online game (MMOG) on your web browser. The game company would probably host the backend servers in the cloud to allow massive scalability, so the processing power is not an issue. Now suppose all these servers were provisioned in the eastern United States. Gamers in New York would have no problem enjoying the game, but those in Japan would probably have noticeable network latency issues because every one of their commands would have to be sent literally around the world to be processed by the U.S. servers, and then the resulting graphics sent back around the world to the player in Japan. That player would probably lose interest in the game really quickly. Now, suppose that the company kept its main servers in the United States but provisioned regional servers, with one of them in, say, Singapore. Most of the commands are processed in the regional server, which means that the user experience of players in Japan is a lot better, while the global leaderboard is maintained centrally in the United States. This is an example of edge computing.

Edge computing is an evolution of content distribution networks (CDNs), which were designed to bring web content closer to its clients. CDNs helped with internationalization of websites but were also very good for mitigating the effects of DDoS attacks. *Edge computing* is a distributed system in which some computational and data storage assets are deployed close to where they are needed in order to reduce latency and network traffic. As shown in Figure 7-7, an edge computing architecture typically has three layers: end devices, edge devices, and cloud infrastructure. The end devices can be anything from smart thermometers to self-driving cars. They have a requirement for processing data in real time, which means there are fairly precise time constraints. Think of a thermal sensor in one of your data centers and how you would need to have an alarm within minutes (at most) of it detecting rising or excessive heat.

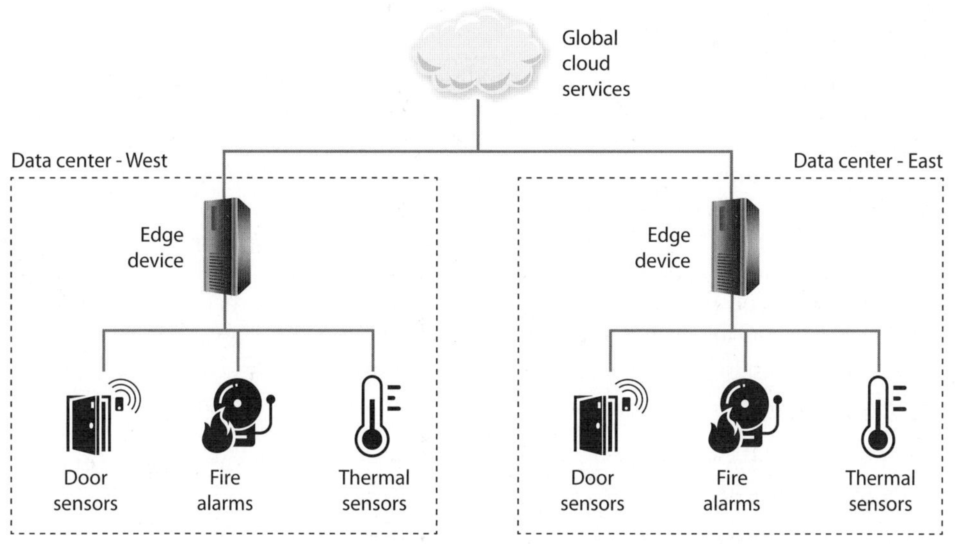

Figure 7-7 A sample edge computing architecture for facility management

PART III

To reduce the turnaround time for these computing requirements, we deploy edge devices that are closer to, and in some cases embedded within, the end devices. Returning to the thermometer example, suppose you have several of these devices in each of your two data centers. You also have a multitude of other sensors such as fire alarms and door sensors. Rather than configuring an alarm to sound whenever the data center gets too hot, you integrate all these sensors to develop an understanding of what is going in the facility. For example, maybe the temperature is rising because someone left the back door open on a hot summer day. If it keeps going up, you want to sound a door alarm, not necessarily a temperature alarm, and do it while there is still time for the cooling system to keep the ambient temperature within tolerance. The sensors (including the thermometer) would send their data to the edge device, which is located near or in the same facility. This reduces the time needed to compute solutions and also provides a degree of protection against network outages. The determination to sound the door alarm (and when) is made there, locally, at the edge device. All (or maybe some of) the data from all the sensors at both data centers is also sent to the global cloud services infrastructure. There, we can take our time and run data analytics to discover useful patterns that could tell us how to be more efficient in how we use our resources around the world.

NOTE As increased computing power finds its way into IoT devices, these too are becoming edge devices in some cases.

Chapter Review

Central to securing our systems is understanding their components and how they interact with each other—in other words, their architectures. While it may seem that architectural terminology overlaps quite a bit, in reality each approach brings some unique challenges and some not-so-unique challenges. As security professionals, we need to understand where architectures are similar and where they differ. We can mix and match, of course, but must also do so with a clear understanding of the underlying issues. In this chapter, we've classified the more common system architectures and discussed what makes them unique and what specific security challenges they pose. Odds are that you will encounter devices and systems in most, if not all, of the architectures we've covered here.

Quick Review

- Client-based systems execute all their core functions on the user's device and don't require network connectivity.
- Server-based systems require that a client make requests from a server across a network connection.
- Transactions are sequences of actions required to properly change the state of a database.
- Database transactions must be atomic, consistent, isolated, and durable (ACID).
- Aggregation is the act of combining information from separate sources and is a security problem when it allows unauthorized individuals to piece together sensitive information.
- Inference is deducing a whole set of information from a subset of its aggregated components. This is a security problem when it allows unauthorized individuals to infer sensitive information.
- High-performance computing (HPC) is the aggregation of computing power in ways that exceed the capabilities of general-purpose computers for the specific purpose of solving large problems.
- Industrial control systems (ICS) consist of information technology that is specifically designed to control physical devices in industrial processes.
- Any system in which computers and physical devices collaborate via the exchange of inputs and outputs to accomplish a task or objective is an embedded or cyber-physical system.
- The two main types of ICS are distributed control systems (DCS) and supervisory control and data acquisition (SCADA) systems. The main difference between them is that a DCS controls local processes while SCADA is used to control things remotely.
- ICS should always be logically or physically isolated from public networks.
- Virtualized systems are those that exist in software-simulated environments.
- Virtual machines (VMs) are systems in which the computing hardware has been virtualized for the operating systems running in them.

- Containers are systems in which the operating systems have been virtualized for the applications running in them.
- Microservices are software architectures in which features are divided into multiple separate components that work together in a distributed manner across a network.
- Containers and microservices don't have to be used together but it's very common to do so.
- In a serverless architecture, the services offered to end users can be performed without a requirement to set up any dedicated server infrastructure.
- Cloud computing is the use of shared, remote computing devices for the purpose of providing improved efficiencies, performance, reliability, scalability, and security.
- Software as a Service (SaaS) is a cloud computing model that provides users access to a specific application that executes in the service provider's environment.
- Platform as a Service (PaaS) is a cloud computing model that provides users access to a computing platform but not to the operating system or to the virtual machine on which it runs.
- Infrastructure as a Service (IaaS) is a cloud computing model that provides users unfettered access to a cloud device, such as an instance of a server, which includes both the operating system and the virtual machine on which it runs.
- An embedded system is a self-contained, typically ruggedized, computer system with its own processor, memory, and input/output devices that is designed for a very specific purpose.
- The Internet of Things (IoT) is the global network of connected embedded systems.
- A distributed system is a system in which multiple computing nodes, interconnected by a network, exchange information for the accomplishment of collective tasks.
- Edge computing is a distributed system in which some computational and data storage assets are deployed close to where they are needed in order to reduce latency and network traffic.

Questions

Please remember that these questions are formatted and asked in a certain way for a reason. Keep in mind that the CISSP exam is asking questions at a conceptual level. Questions may not always have the perfect answer, and the candidate is advised against always looking for the perfect answer. Instead, the candidate should look for the best answer in the list.

1. Which of the following lists two foundational properties of database transactions?
   - **A.** Aggregation and inference
   - **B.** Scalability and durability
   - **C.** Consistency and performance
   - **D.** Atomicity and isolation

2. Which of the following is *not* true about containers?
   A. They are embedded systems.
   B. They are virtualized systems.
   C. They commonly house microservices.
   D. They operate in a sandbox.
3. What is the term that describes a database attack in which an unauthorized user is able to combine information from separate sources to learn sensitive information to which the user should not have access?
   A. Aggregation
   B. Containerization
   C. Serialization
   D. Collection
4. What is the main difference between a distributed control system (DCS) and supervisory control and data acquisition (SCADA)?
   A. SCADA is a type of industrial control system (ICS), while a DCS is a type of bus.
   B. SCADA controls systems in close proximity, while a DCS controls physically distant ones.
   C. A DCS controls systems in close proximity, while SCADA controls physically distant ones.
   D. A DCS uses programmable logic controllers (PLCs), while SCADA uses remote terminal units (RTUs).
5. What is the main purpose of a hypervisor?
   A. Virtualize hardware resources and manage virtual machines
   B. Virtualize the operating system and manage containers
   C. Provide visibility into virtual machines for access control and logging
   D. Provide visibility into containers for access control and logging
6. Which cloud service model provides customers direct access to hardware, the network, and storage?
   A. SaaS
   B. PaaS
   C. IaaS
   D. FaaS
7. Which cloud service model do you recommend to enable access to developers to write custom code while also providing all employees access from remote offices?
   A. PaaS
   B. SaaS

C. FaaS

D. IaaS

8. Which of the following is not a major issue when securing embedded systems?

A. Use of proprietary code

B. Devices that "phone home"

C. Lack of microcontrollers

D. Ability to update and patch them securely

9. Which of the following is true about edge computing?

A. Uses no centralized computing resources, pushing all computation to the edge

B. Pushes computation to the edge while retaining centralized data management

C. Typically consists of two layers: end devices and cloud infrastructure

D. Is an evolution of content distribution networks

Use the following scenario to answer Questions 10–12. You were just hired as director of cybersecurity for an electric power company with facilities around your country. Carmen is the director of operations and offers to give you a tour so you can see the security measures that are in place on the operational technology (OT).

10. What system would be used to control power generation, distribution, and delivery to all your customers?

A. Supervisory control and data acquisition (SCADA)

B. Distributed control system (DCS)

C. Programmable logic controller

D. Edge computing system

11. You see a new engineer being coached remotely by a more senior member of the staff in the use of the human-machine interface (HMI). Carmen tells you that senior engineers are allowed to access the HMI from their personal computers at home to facilitate this sort of impromptu training. She asks what you think of this policy. How should you respond?

A. Change the policy. They should not access the HMI with their personal computers, but they could do so using a company laptop, assuming they also use a virtual private network (VPN).

B. Change the policy. ICS devices should always be isolated from the Internet.

C. It is acceptable because the HMI is only used for administrative purposes and not operational functions.

D. It is acceptable because safety is the fundamental concern in ICS, so it is best to let the senior engineers be available to train other staff from home.

12. You notice that several ICS devices have never been patched. When you ask why, Carmen tells you that those are mission-critical devices, and her team has no way of testing the patches before patching these production systems. Fearing that patching them could cause unexpected outages or, worse, injure someone, she has authorized them to remain as they are. Carmen asks whether you agree. How could you respond?
    - **A.** Yes. As long as we document the risk and ensure the devices are as isolated and as closely monitored as possible.
    - **B.** Yes. Safety and availability trump all other concerns when it comes to ICS security.
    - **C.** No. You should stand up a testing environment so you can safely test the patches and then deploy them to all devices.
    - **D.** No. These are critical devices and should be patched as soon as possible.

Answers

1. **D.** The foundational properties of database transactions are atomicity, consistency, isolation, and durability (ACID).
2. **A.** Containers are virtualized systems that commonly (though not always) house microservices and run in sandboxes. It would be highly unusual to implement a container as an embedded system.
3. **A.** Aggregation happens when a user does not have the clearance or permission to access specific information, but she does have the permission to access components of this information. She can then figure out the rest and obtain restricted information.
4. **C.** The main difference is that a DCS controls devices within fairly close proximity, while SCADA controls large-scale physical processes involving nodes separated by significant distances. They both can (and frequently use) PLCs, but RTUs are almost always seen in SCADA systems.
5. **A.** Hypervisors are almost always used to virtualize the hardware on which virtual machines run. They can also provide visibility and logging, but these are secondary functions. Containers are the equivalents of hypervisors, but they work at a higher level by virtualizing the operating system.
6. **C.** Infrastructure as a Service (IaaS) offers an effective and affordable way for organizations to get all the benefits of managing their own hardware without the massive overhead costs associated with acquisition, physical storage, and disposal of the hardware.
7. **A.** Platform as a Service (PaaS) solutions are optimized to provide value focused on software development, offering direct access to a development environment to enable an organization to build its own solutions on the cloud infrastructure, rather than providing its own infrastructure.

8. **C.** Embedded systems are usually built around microcontrollers, which are specialized devices that consist of a CPU, memory, and peripheral control interfaces. All the other answers are major issues in securing embedded systems.
9. **D.** Edge computing is an evolution of content distribution networks, which were designed to bring web content closer to its clients. It is a distributed system in which some computational and data storage assets are deployed close to where they are needed in order to reduce latency and network traffic. Accordingly, some computing and data management is handled in each of three different layers: end devices, edge devices, and cloud infrastructure.
10. **A.** SCADA was designed to control large-scale physical processes involving nodes separated by significant distances, as is the case with electric power providers.
11. **B.** It is a best practice to completely isolate ICS devices from Internet access. Sometimes this is not possible for operational reasons, so remote access through a VPN could be allowed even though it is not ideal.
12. **A.** It is all too often the case that organizations can afford neither the risk of pushing untested patches to ICS devices nor the costs of standing up a testing environment. In these conditions, the best strategy is to isolate and monitor the devices as much as possible.

CHAPTER 8

Cryptology

This chapter presents the following:

- Principles of cryptology
- Symmetric cryptography
- Asymmetric cryptography
- Public key infrastructure
- Cryptanalytic attacks

Three can keep a secret, if two of them are dead.

—Benjamin Franklin

Now that you have a pretty good understanding of system architectures from Chapter 7, we turn to a topic that is central to protecting these architectures. *Cryptography* is the practice of storing and transmitting information in a form that only authorized parties can understand. Properly designed and implemented, cryptography is an effective way to protect sensitive data throughout its life cycle. However, with enough time, resources, and motivation, hackers can successfully attack most cryptosystems and reveal the information. So, a more realistic goal of cryptography is to make obtaining the information too work intensive or time consuming to be worthwhile to the attacker.

Cryptanalysis is the name collectively given to techniques that aim to weaken or defeat cryptography. This is what the adversary attempts to do to thwart the defender's use of cryptography. Together, cryptography and cryptanalysis comprise *cryptology*. In this chapter, we'll take a good look at both sides of this topic. This is an important chapter in the book, because we can't defend our information systems effectively without understanding applied cryptology.

The History of Cryptography

Cryptography has roots in antiquity. Around 600 B.C., Hebrews invented a cryptographic method called *atbash* that required the alphabet to be flipped so each letter in the original message was mapped to a different letter in the flipped, or shifted, message. An example of an encryption key used in the atbash encryption scheme is shown here:

```
ABCDEFGHIJKLMNOPQRSTUVWXYZ
ZYXWVUTSRQPONMLKJIHGFEDCBA
```

If you want to encrypt the word "security" you would instead use "hvxfirgb." Atbash is an example of a *substitution cipher* because each character is replaced with another character. This type of substitution cipher is referred to as a *monoalphabetic substitution cipher* because it uses only one alphabet, whereas a *polyalphabetic substitution cipher* uses multiple alphabets.

TIP Cipher is another term for algorithm.

Around 400 B.C., the Spartans used a system of encrypting information in which they would write a message on a sheet of papyrus (a type of paper) that was wrapped around a staff (a stick or wooden rod), which was then delivered and wrapped around a different staff by the recipient. The message was only readable if it was wrapped around the correct size staff, which made the letters properly match up, as shown in Figure 8-1. When the papyrus was not wrapped around the staff, the writing appeared as just a bunch of random characters. This approach, known as the *scytale cipher*, is an example of a *transposition cipher* because it relies on changing the sequence of the characters to obscure their meaning. Only someone who knows how to rearrange them would be able to recover the original message.

Later, in Rome, Julius Caesar (100–44 B.C.) developed a simple method of shifting letters of the alphabet, similar to the atbash scheme. He simply shifted the alphabet by three positions. The following example shows a standard alphabet and a shifted alphabet. The alphabet serves as the algorithm, and the key is the number of locations it has been shifted during the encryption and decryption process.

- **Standard alphabet:**
  `ABCDEFGHIJKLMNOPQRSTUVWXYZ`
- **Cryptographic alphabet:**
  `DEFGHIJKLMNOPQRSTUVWXYZABC`

As an example, suppose we need to encrypt the message "MISSION ACCOMPLISHED." We take the first letter of this message, *M*, and shift up three locations within the alphabet. The encrypted version of this first letter is *P*, so we write

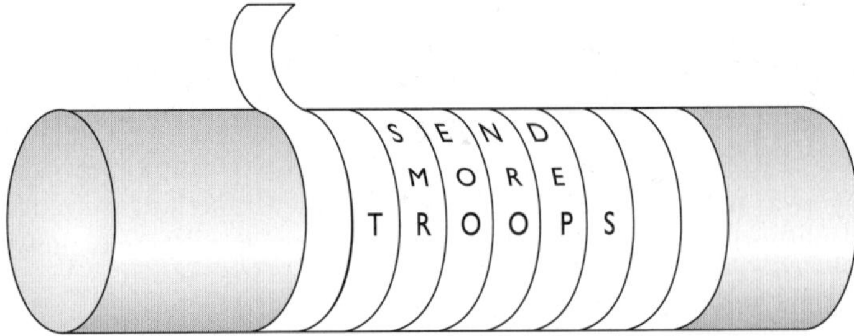

Figure 8-1 The scytale was used by the Spartans to decipher encrypted messages.

that down. The next letter to be encrypted is *I*, which matches *L* when we shift three spaces. We continue this process for the whole message. Once the message is encrypted, a carrier takes the encrypted version to the destination, where the process is reversed.

- **Original message:**
  `MISSION ACCOMPLISHED`
- **Encrypted message:**
  `PLVVLRQ DFFRPSOLVKHG`

Today, this technique seems too simplistic to be effective, but in the time of Julius Caesar, not very many people could read in the first place, so it provided a high level of protection. The Caesar cipher, like the atbash cipher, is an example of a monoalphabetic cipher. Once more people could read and reverse-engineer this type of encryption process, the cryptographers of that day increased the complexity by creating polyalphabetic ciphers.

In the 16th century in France, Blaise de Vigenère developed a polyalphabetic substitution cipher for Henry III. This was based on the Caesar cipher, but it increased the difficulty of the encryption and decryption process. As shown in Figure 8-2, we have a message that needs to be encrypted, which is SYSTEM SECURITY AND CONTROL. We have a key with the value of SECURITY. We also have a Vigenère table, or algorithm, which is really the Caesar cipher on steroids. Whereas the Caesar cipher used a single shift alphabet (letters were shifted up three places), the Vigenère cipher has 27 shift alphabets and the letters are shifted up only one place.

So, looking at the example in Figure 8-2, we take the first value of the key, *S*, and starting with the first alphabet in our algorithm, trace over to the *S* column. Then we look at the first character of the original message that needs to be encrypted, which is *S*, and go down to the *S* row. We follow the column and row and see that they intersect on the value *K*. That is the first encrypted value of our message, so we write down *K*. Then we go to the next value in our key, which is *E*, and the next character in the original message, which is *Y*. We see that the *E* column and the *Y* row intersect at the cell with the value of *C*. This is our second encrypted value, so we write that down. We continue this process for the whole message (notice that the key repeats itself, since the message is longer than the key). The result is an encrypted message that is sent to the destination. The destination must have the same algorithm (Vigenère table) and the same key (SECURITY) to properly reverse the process to obtain a meaningful message.

The evolution of cryptography continued as countries refined it using new methods, tools, and practices with varying degrees of success. Mary, Queen of Scots, lost her life in the 16th century when an encrypted message she sent was intercepted. During the American Revolutionary War, Benedict Arnold used a codebook cipher to exchange information on troop movement and strategic military advancements. By the late 1800s, cryptography was commonly used in the methods of communication between military factions.

During World War II, encryption devices were used for tactical communication, which drastically improved with the mechanical and electromechanical technology that provided the world with telegraphic and radio communication. The rotor cipher machine, which is a device that substitutes letters using different rotors within the

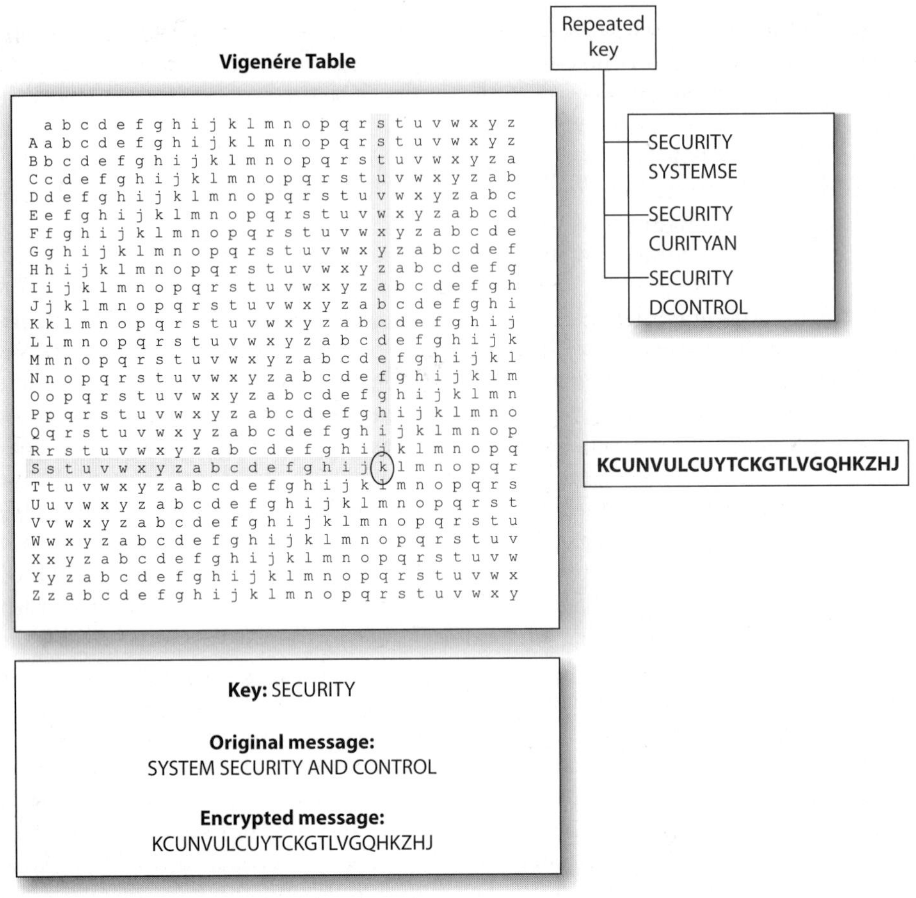

Figure 8-2 Polyalphabetic algorithms were developed to increase encryption complexity.

machine, was a huge breakthrough in military cryptography that provided complexity that proved difficult to break. This work gave way to the most famous cipher machine in history to date: Germany's *Enigma* machine. The Enigma machine had separate rotors, a plug board, and a reflecting rotor.

The originator of the message would configure the Enigma machine to its initial settings before starting the encryption process. The operator would type in the first letter of the message, and the machine would substitute the letter with a different letter and present it to the operator. This encryption was done by moving the rotors a predefined number of times. So, if the operator typed in a *T* as the first character, the Enigma machine might present an *M* as the substitution value. The operator would write down the letter *M* on his sheet. The operator would then advance the rotors and enter the next letter. Each time a new letter was to be encrypted, the operator would advance the rotors to a new setting. This process was followed until the whole message was encrypted. Then the encrypted text was transmitted over the airwaves, most likely to a German U-boat. The chosen substitution for each letter was dependent upon the rotor setting, so the crucial and secret part of this process (the key) was the initial setting and how the operators advanced the rotors when encrypting and decrypting a message. The operators at each end needed to know this sequence of increments to advance each rotor in order to enable the German military units to properly communicate.

When computers were invented, the possibilities for encryption methods and devices expanded exponentially and cryptography efforts increased dramatically. This era brought unprecedented opportunity for cryptographic designers to develop new encryption techniques. A well-known and successful project was *Lucifer*, which was developed at IBM. Lucifer introduced complex mathematical equations and functions that were later adopted and modified by the U.S. National Security Agency (NSA) to establish the U.S. Data Encryption Standard (DES) in 1976, a federal government standard. DES was used worldwide for financial and other transactions, and was embedded into numerous commercial applications. Though it was cracked in the late 1990s and is no longer considered secure, DES represented a significant advancement for cryptography. It was replaced a few years later by the Advanced Encryption Standard (AES), which continues to protect sensitive data to this day.

Cryptography Definitions and Concepts

Encryption is a method of transforming readable data, called *plaintext*, into a form that appears to be random and unreadable, which is called *ciphertext*. Plaintext is in a form that can be understood either by a person (a document) or by a computer (executable code). Once plaintext is transformed into ciphertext, neither human nor machine can properly process it until it is decrypted. This enables the transmission of confidential information over insecure channels without unauthorized disclosure. When sensitive data is stored on a computer, it is usually protected by logical and physical access controls. When this same sensitive information is sent over a network, it no longer has the advantage of these controls and is in a much more vulnerable state.

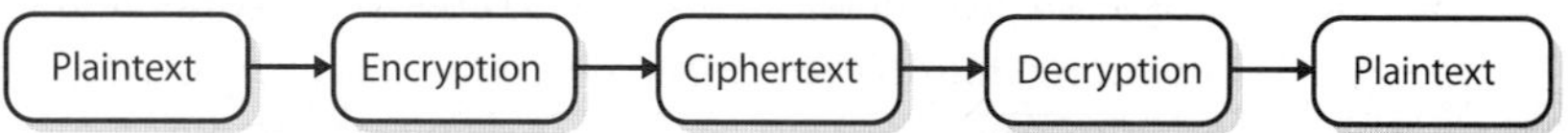

A system or product that provides encryption and decryption is referred to as a *cryptosystem* and can be created through hardware components or program code in an application. The cryptosystem uses an encryption algorithm (which determines how simple or complex the encryption process will be), keys, and the necessary software components and protocols. Most algorithms are complex mathematical formulas that are applied in a specific sequence to the plaintext. Most encryption methods use a secret value called a key (usually a long string of bits), which works with the algorithm to encrypt and decrypt the text.

The *algorithm*, the set of rules also known as the *cipher*, dictates how enciphering and deciphering take place. Many of the mathematical algorithms used in computer systems today are publicly known and are not the secret part of the encryption process. If the internal mechanisms of the algorithm are not a secret, then something must be: the key.

A common analogy used to illustrate this point is the use of locks you would purchase from your local hardware store. Let's say 20 people bought the same brand of lock. Just because these people share the same type and brand of lock does not mean they can now unlock each other's doors and gain access to their private possessions. Instead, each lock comes with its own key, and that one key can open only that one specific lock.

In encryption, the *key* (also known as *cryptovariable*) is a value that comprises a large sequence of random bits. Is it just any random number of bits crammed together? Not really. An algorithm contains a *keyspace*, which is a range of values that can be used to construct a key. When the algorithm needs to generate a new key, it uses random values from this keyspace. The larger the keyspace, the more available values that can be used to represent different keys—and the more random the keys are, the harder it is for intruders to figure them out. For example, if an algorithm allows a key length of 2 bits, the keyspace for that algorithm would be 4, which indicates the total number of different keys that would be possible. (Remember that we are working in binary and that 2^2 equals 4.) That would not be a very large keyspace, and certainly it would not take an attacker very long to find the correct key that was used.

A large keyspace allows for more possible keys. (Today, we are commonly using key sizes of 128, 256, 512, or even 1,024 bits and larger.) So a key size of 512 bits would provide 2^{512} possible combinations (the keyspace). The encryption algorithm should use the entire keyspace and choose the values to make up the keys as randomly as possible. If a smaller keyspace were used, there would be fewer values to choose from when generating a key, as shown in Figure 8-3. This would increase an attacker's chances of figuring out the key value and deciphering the protected information.

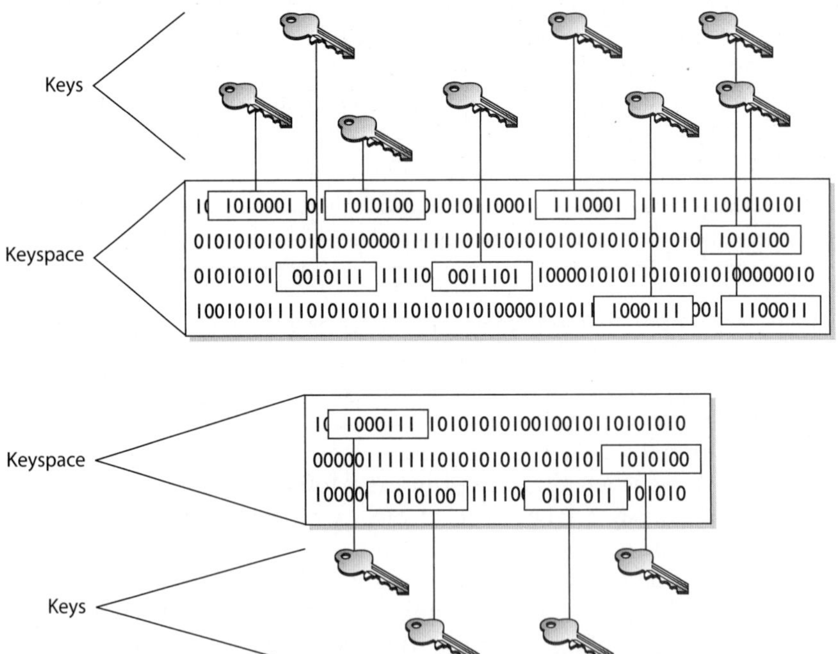

Figure 8-3 Larger keyspaces permit a greater number of possible key values.

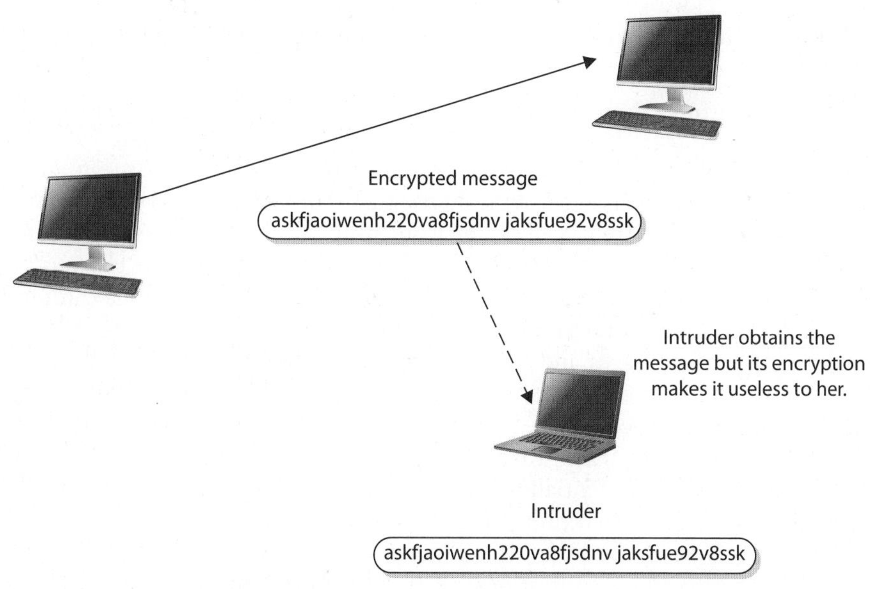

Figure 8-4 Without the right key, the captured message is useless to an attacker.

If an eavesdropper captures a message as it passes between two people, she can view the message, but it appears in its encrypted form and is therefore unusable. Even if this attacker knows the algorithm that the two people are using to encrypt and decrypt their information, without the key, this information remains useless to the eavesdropper, as shown in Figure 8-4.

Cryptosystems

A *cryptosystem* encompasses all of the necessary components for encryption and decryption to take place. Pretty Good Privacy (PGP) is just one example of a cryptosystem. A cryptosystem is made up of at least the following:

- Software
- Protocols
- Algorithms
- Keys

Cryptosystems can provide the following services:

- **Confidentiality** Renders the information unintelligible except by authorized entities.
- **Integrity** Ensures that data has not been altered in an unauthorized manner since it was created, transmitted, or stored.
- **Authentication** Verifies the identity of the user or system that created the information.

- **Authorization** Provides access to some resource to the authenticated user or system.
- **Nonrepudiation** Ensures that the sender cannot deny sending the message.

As an example of how these services work, suppose your boss sends you an e-mail message stating that you will be receiving a raise that doubles your salary. The message is encrypted, so you can be sure it really came from your boss (authenticity), that someone did not alter it before it arrived at your computer (integrity), that no one else was able to read it as it traveled over the network (confidentiality), and that your boss cannot deny sending it later when he comes to his senses (nonrepudiation).

Different types of messages and transactions require higher or lower degrees of one or all of the services that cryptography methods can supply. Military and intelligence agencies are very concerned about keeping information confidential, so they would choose encryption mechanisms that provide a high degree of secrecy. Financial institutions care about confidentiality, but they also care about the integrity of the data being transmitted, so the encryption mechanism they would choose may differ from the military's encryption methods. If messages were accepted that had a misplaced decimal point or zero, the ramifications could be far reaching in the financial world. Legal agencies may care most about the authenticity of the messages they receive. If information received ever needed to be presented in a court of law, its authenticity would certainly be questioned; therefore, the encryption method used must ensure authenticity, which confirms who sent the information.

NOTE If David sends a message and then later claims he did not send it, this is an act of repudiation. When a cryptography mechanism provides nonrepudiation, the sender cannot later deny he sent the message (well, he can try to deny it, but the cryptosystem proves otherwise).

The types and uses of cryptography have increased over the years. At one time, cryptography was mainly used to keep secrets secret (confidentiality), but today we use cryptography to ensure the integrity of data, to authenticate messages, to confirm that a message was received, to provide access control, and much more.

Kerckhoffs' Principle

Auguste Kerckhoffs published a paper in 1883 stating that the only secrecy involved with a cryptography system should be the key. He claimed that the algorithm should be publicly known. He asserted that if security were based on too many secrets, there would be more vulnerabilities to possibly exploit.

So, why do we care what some guy said almost 140 years ago? Because this debate is still going on. Cryptographers in certain sectors agree with *Kerckhoffs' principle*, because making an algorithm publicly available means that many more people can view the source code, test it, and uncover any type of flaws or weaknesses. It is the attitude of "many heads are better than one." Once someone uncovers some type of flaw, the developer can fix the issue and provide society with a much stronger algorithm.

But not everyone agrees with this philosophy. Governments around the world create their own algorithms that are not released to the public. Their stance is that if a smaller number of people know how the algorithm actually works, then a smaller number of people will know how to possibly break it. Cryptographers in the private sector do not agree with this practice and do not commonly trust algorithms they cannot examine. It is basically the same as the open-source versus compiled software debate that is in full force today.

The Strength of the Cryptosystem

The *strength* of an encryption method comes from the algorithm, the secrecy of the key, the length of the key, and how they all work together within the cryptosystem. When strength is discussed in encryption, it refers to how hard it is to figure out the algorithm or key, whichever is not made public. Attempts to break a cryptosystem usually involve processing an amazing number of possible values in the hopes of finding the one value (key) that can be used to decrypt a specific message. The strength of an encryption method correlates to the amount of necessary processing power, resources, and time required to break the cryptosystem or to figure out the value of the key.

Breaking a cryptosystem can be accomplished by a *brute-force attack*, which means trying every possible key value until the resulting plaintext is meaningful. Depending on the algorithm and length of the key, this can be an easy task or one that is close to impossible. If a key can be broken with an Intel Core i5 processor in three hours, the cipher is not strong at all. If the key can only be broken with the use of a thousand multiprocessing systems over 1.2 million years, then it is pretty darned strong. The introduction of commodity cloud computing has really increased the threat of brute-force attacks.

The goal when designing an encryption method is to make compromising it too expensive or too time consuming. Another name for cryptography strength is *work factor*, which is an estimate of the effort and resources it would take an attacker to penetrate a cryptosystem.

Even if the algorithm is very complex and thorough, other issues within encryption can weaken encryption methods. Because the key is usually the secret value needed to actually encrypt and decrypt messages, improper protection of the key can weaken the encryption. Even if a user employs an algorithm that has all the requirements for strong encryption, including a large keyspace and a large and random key value, if she shares her key with others, the strength of the algorithm becomes almost irrelevant.

Important elements of encryption are to use an algorithm without flaws, use a large key size, use all possible values within the keyspace selected as randomly as possible, and protect the actual key. If one element is weak, it could be the link that dooms the whole process.

One-Time Pad

A *one-time pad* is a perfect encryption scheme because it is considered unbreakable if implemented properly. It was invented by Gilbert Vernam in 1917, so sometimes it is referred to as the Vernam cipher.

This cipher does not use shift alphabets, as do the Caesar and Vigenère ciphers discussed earlier, but instead uses a pad made up of random values, as shown in Figure 8-5. Our plaintext message that needs to be encrypted has been converted into bits, and our one-time

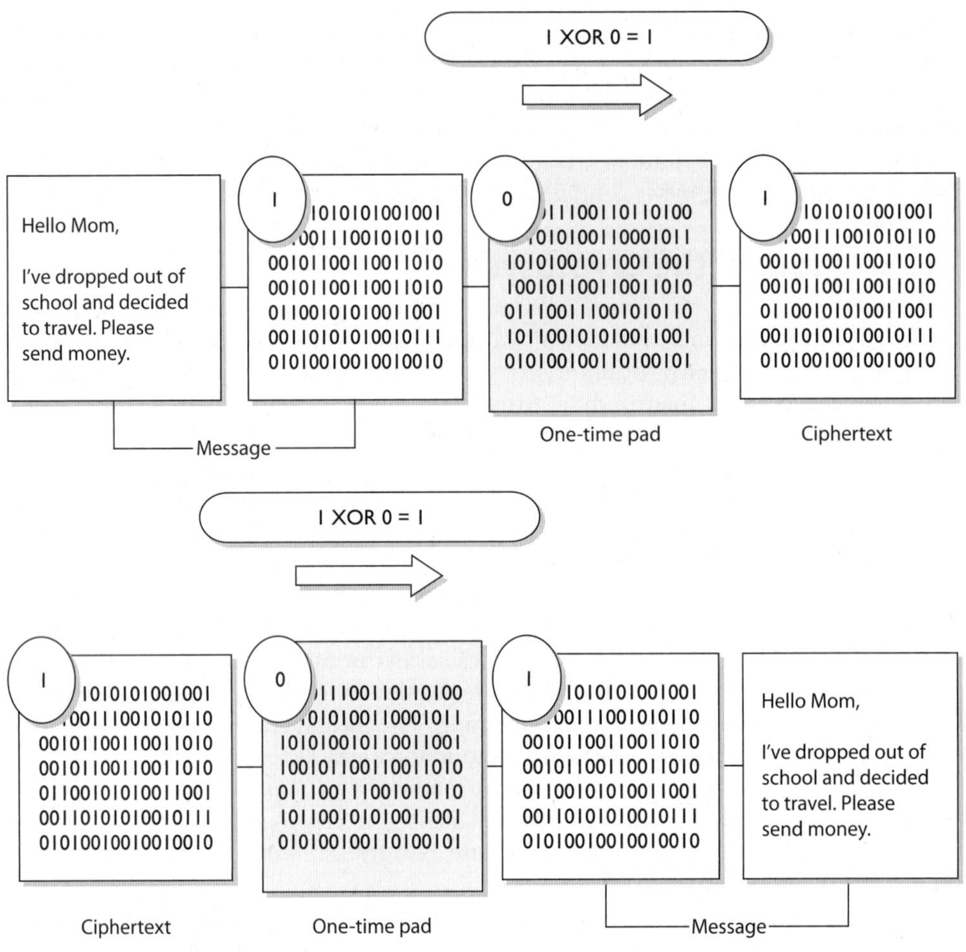

Figure 8-5 A one-time pad

pad is made up of random bits. This encryption process uses a binary mathematic function called exclusive-OR, usually abbreviated as XOR.

XOR is an operation that is applied to 2 bits and is a function commonly used in binary mathematics and encryption methods. When combining the bits, if both values are the same, the result is 0 (1 XOR 1 = 0). If the bits are different from each other, the result is 1 (1 XOR 0 = 1). For example:

Message stream:	1	0	0	1	0	1	0	1	1	1
Keystream:	0	0	1	1	1	0	1	0	1	0
Ciphertext stream:	1	0	1	0	1	1	1	1	0	1

So in our example, the first bit of the message is XORed to the first bit of the one-time pad, which results in the ciphertext value 1. The second bit of the message is XORed with the second bit of the pad, which results in the value 0. This process continues until the whole message is encrypted. The result is the encrypted message that is sent to the receiver.

In Figure 8-5, we also see that the receiver must have the same one-time pad to decrypt the message by reversing the process. The receiver takes the first bit of the encrypted message and XORs it with the first bit of the pad. This results in the plaintext value. The receiver continues this process for the whole encrypted message until the entire message is decrypted.

The one-time pad encryption scheme is deemed unbreakable only if the following things are true about the implementation process:

- *The pad must be used only one time.* If the pad is used more than one time, this might introduce patterns in the encryption process that will aid the eavesdropper in his goal of breaking the encryption.
- *The pad must be at least as long as the message.* If it is not as long as the message, the pad will need to be reused to cover the whole message. This would be the same thing as using a pad more than one time, which could introduce patterns.
- *The pad must be securely distributed and protected at its destination.* This is a very cumbersome process to accomplish, because the pads are usually just individual pieces of paper that need to be delivered by a secure courier and properly guarded at each destination.
- *The pad must be made up of truly random values.* This may not seem like a difficult task, but even our computer systems today do not have truly random number generators; rather, they have pseudorandom number generators.

NOTE Generating truly random numbers is very difficult. Most systems use an algorithmic *pseudorandom number generator (PRNG)* that takes as its input a seed value and creates a stream of pseudorandom values from it. Given the same seed, a PRNG generates the same sequence of values. Truly random numbers must be based on natural phenomena such as thermal noise and quantum mechanics.

Although the one-time pad approach to encryption can provide a very high degree of security, it is impractical in most situations because of all of its different requirements. Each possible pair of entities that might want to communicate in this fashion must receive, in a secure fashion, a pad that is as long as, or longer than, the actual message. This type of key management can be overwhelming and may require more overhead than it is worth. The distribution of the pad can be challenging, and the sender and receiver must be perfectly synchronized so each is using the same pad.

EXAM TIP The one-time pad, though impractical for most modern applications, is the only perfect cryptosystem.

> **One-Time Pad Requirements**
> For a one-time pad encryption scheme to be considered unbreakable, each pad in the scheme must be
>
> - Made up of truly random values
> - Used only one time
> - Securely distributed to its destination
> - Secured at sender's and receiver's sites
> - At least as long as the message

Cryptographic Life Cycle

Since most of us will probably not be using one-time pads (the only "perfect" system) to defend our networks, we have to consider that cryptography, like a fine steak, has a limited shelf life. Given enough time and resources, any cryptosystem can be broken, either through analysis or brute force. The *cryptographic life cycle* is the ongoing process of identifying your cryptography needs, selecting the right algorithms, provisioning the needed capabilities and services, and managing keys. Eventually, you determine that your cryptosystem is approaching the end of its shelf life and you start the cycle all over again.

How can you tell when your algorithms (or choice of keyspaces) are about to go stale? You need to stay up to date with the cryptologic research community. They are the best source for early warning that things are going sour. Typically, research papers postulating weaknesses in an algorithm are followed by academic exercises in breaking the algorithm under controlled conditions, which are then followed by articles on how it is broken in general cases. When the first papers come out, it is time to start looking for replacements.

Cryptographic Methods

By far, the most commonly used cryptographic methods today are *symmetric key cryptography*, which uses symmetric keys (also called secret keys), and *asymmetric key cryptography*, which uses two different, or asymmetric, keys (also called public and private keys). Asymmetric key cryptography is also called *public key cryptography* because one of its keys can be made public. As we will see shortly, public key cryptography typically uses powers of prime numbers for encryption and decryption. A variant of this approach uses elliptic curves, which allows much smaller keys to be just as secure and is (unsurprisingly) called *elliptic curve cryptography (ECC)*. Though you may not know it, it is likely that you've used ECC at some point to communicate securely on the Web. (More on that later.) Though these three cryptographic methods are considered secure today (given that you use good keys), the application of quantum computing to cryptology could dramatically change this situation. The following sections explain the key points of these four methods of encryption.

Symmetric Key Cryptography

In a cryptosystem that uses symmetric key cryptography, the sender and receiver use two instances of the same key for encryption and decryption, as shown in Figure 8-6. So the key has dual functionality in that it can carry out both encryption and decryption processes. Symmetric keys are also called *secret* keys, because this type of encryption relies on each user to keep the key a secret and properly protected. If an intruder were to get this key, he could decrypt any intercepted message encrypted with it.

Each pair of users who want to exchange data using symmetric key encryption must have two instances of the same key. This means that if Dan and Iqqi want to communicate, both need to obtain a copy of the same key. If Dan also wants to communicate using symmetric encryption with Norm and Dave, he needs to have three separate keys, one for each friend. This might not sound like a big deal until Dan realizes that he may communicate with hundreds of people over a period of several months, and keeping track and using the correct key that corresponds to each specific receiver can become a daunting task. If 10 people needed to communicate securely with each other using symmetric keys, then 45 keys would need to be kept track of. If 100 people were going to communicate, then 4,950 keys would be involved. The equation used to calculate the number of symmetric keys needed is

$$N(N - 1)/2 = \text{number of keys}$$

The security of the symmetric encryption method is completely dependent on how well users protect their shared keys. This should raise red flags for you if you have ever had to depend on a whole staff of people to keep a secret. If a key is compromised, then all messages encrypted with that key can be decrypted and read by an intruder. This is complicated further by how symmetric keys are actually shared and updated when necessary. If Dan wants to communicate with Norm for the first time, Dan has to figure out how to get the right key to Norm securely. It is not safe to just send it in an e-mail

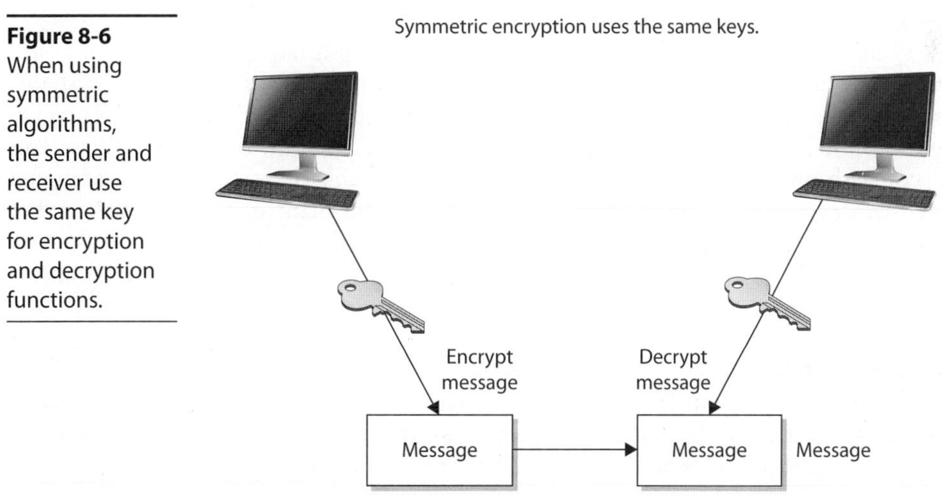

Figure 8-6 When using symmetric algorithms, the sender and receiver use the same key for encryption and decryption functions.

PART III

Symmetric Key Cryptosystems Summary

The following outlines the strengths and weaknesses of symmetric key algorithms.

Strengths:

- Much faster (less computationally intensive) than asymmetric systems.
- Hard to break if using a large key size.

Weaknesses:

- Requires a secure mechanism to deliver keys properly.
- Each pair of users needs a unique key, so as the number of individuals increases, so does the number of keys, possibly making key management overwhelming.
- Provides confidentiality but not authenticity or nonrepudiation.

Examples:

- Advanced Encryption Standard (AES)
- ChaCha20

message, because the key is not protected and can be easily intercepted and used by attackers. Thus, Dan must get the key to Norm through an *out-of-band method*. Dan can save the key on a thumb drive and walk over to Norm's desk, or have a secure courier deliver it to Norm. This is a huge hassle, and each method is very clumsy and insecure.

Because both users employ the same key to encrypt and decrypt messages, symmetric cryptosystems can provide confidentiality, but they cannot provide authentication or nonrepudiation. There is no way to prove through cryptography who actually sent a message if two people are using the same key.

If symmetric cryptosystems have so many problems and flaws, why use them at all? Because they are very fast and can be hard to break. Compared with asymmetric systems, symmetric algorithms scream in speed. They can encrypt and decrypt relatively quickly large amounts of data that would take an unacceptable amount of time to encrypt and decrypt with an asymmetric algorithm. It is also difficult to uncover data encrypted with a symmetric algorithm if a large key size is used. For many of our applications that require encryption, symmetric key cryptography is the only option.

The two main types of symmetric algorithms are block ciphers, which work on blocks of bits, and stream ciphers, which work on one bit at a time.

Block Ciphers

When a *block cipher* is used for encryption and decryption purposes, the message is divided into blocks of bits. These blocks are then put through mathematical functions, one block at a time. Suppose you need to encrypt a message you are sending to your mother and you are using a block cipher that uses 64 bits. Your message of 640 bits is chopped up into 10 individual blocks of 64 bits. Each block is put through a succession of mathematical formulas, and what you end up with is 10 blocks of encrypted text.

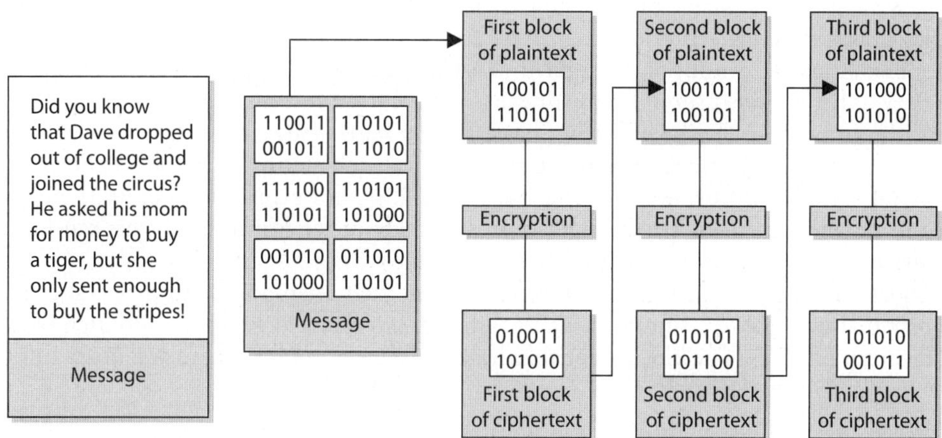

You send this encrypted message to your mother. She has to have the same block cipher and key, and those 10 ciphertext blocks go back through the algorithm in the reverse sequence and end up in your plaintext message.

A strong cipher contains the right level of two main attributes: confusion and diffusion. *Confusion* is commonly carried out through substitution, while *diffusion* is carried out by using transposition. For a cipher to be considered strong, it must contain both of these attributes to ensure that reverse-engineering is basically impossible. The randomness of the key values and the complexity of the mathematical functions dictate the level of confusion and diffusion involved.

In algorithms, diffusion takes place as individual bits of a block are scrambled, or *diffused*, throughout that block. Confusion is provided by carrying out complex substitution functions so the eavesdropper cannot figure out how to substitute the right values and come up with the original plaintext. Suppose you have 500 wooden blocks with individual letters written on them. You line them all up to spell out a paragraph (plaintext). Then you substitute 300 of them with another set of 300 blocks (confusion through substitution). Then you scramble all of these blocks (diffusion through transposition) and leave them in a pile. For someone else to figure out your original message, they would have to substitute the correct blocks and then put them back in the right order. Good luck.

Confusion pertains to making the relationship between the key and resulting ciphertext as complex as possible so the key cannot be uncovered from the ciphertext. Each ciphertext value should depend upon several parts of the key, but this mapping between the key values and the ciphertext values should seem completely random to the observer.

Diffusion, on the other hand, means that a single plaintext bit has influence over several of the ciphertext bits. Changing a plaintext value should change many ciphertext values, not just one. In fact, in a strong block cipher, if one plaintext bit is changed, it will change every ciphertext bit with the probability of 50 percent. This means that if one plaintext bit changes, then about half of the ciphertext bits will change.

A very similar concept of diffusion is the *avalanche effect*. If an algorithm follows strict avalanche effect criteria, this means that if the input to an algorithm is slightly modified, then the output of the algorithm is changed significantly. So a small change to the key or the plaintext should cause drastic changes to the resulting ciphertext. The ideas of diffusion and avalanche effect are basically the same—they were just derived from different people. Horst Feistel came up with the avalanche term, while Claude Shannon came up with the diffusion term. If an algorithm does not exhibit the necessary degree of the avalanche effect, then the algorithm is using poor randomization. This can make it easier for an attacker to break the algorithm.

Block ciphers use diffusion and confusion in their methods. Figure 8-7 shows a conceptual example of a simplistic block cipher. It has four block inputs, and each block is made up of 4 bits. The block algorithm has two layers of 4-bit substitution boxes called

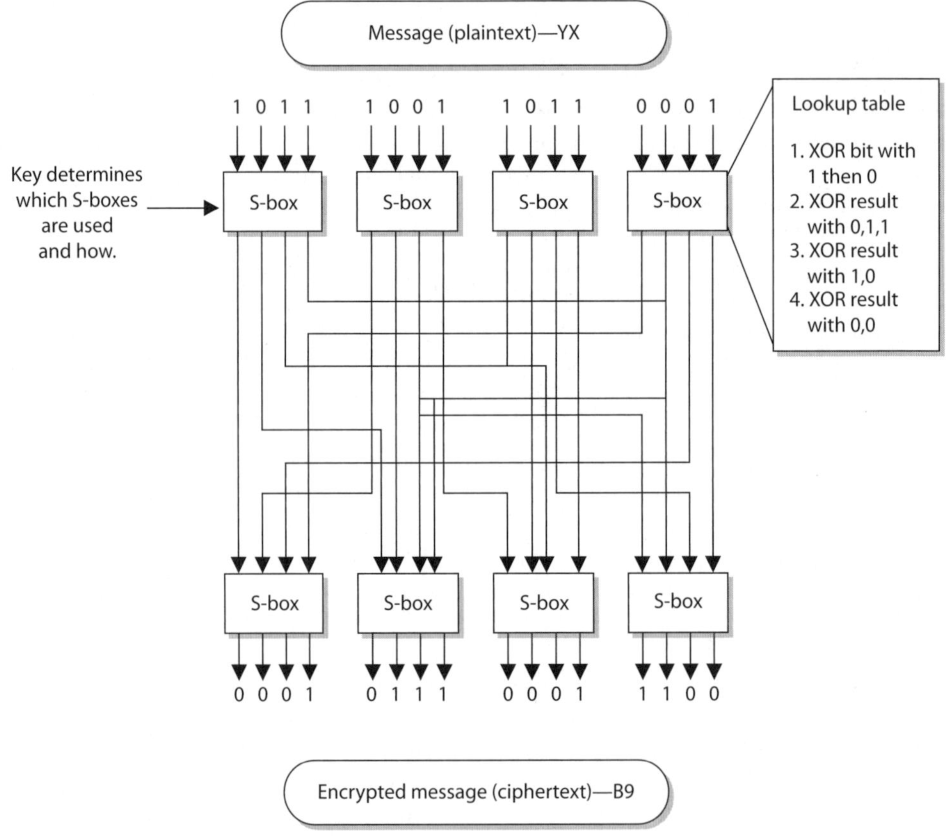

Figure 8-7 A message is divided into blocks of bits, and substitution and transposition functions are performed on those blocks.

S-boxes. Each S-box contains a lookup table used by the algorithm as instructions on how the bits should be encrypted.

Figure 8-7 shows that the key dictates what S-boxes are to be used when scrambling the original message from readable plaintext to encrypted nonreadable ciphertext. Each S-box contains the different substitution methods that can be performed on each block. This example is simplistic—most block ciphers work with blocks of 32, 64, or 128 bits in size, and many more S-boxes are usually involved.

Stream Ciphers

As stated earlier, a block cipher performs mathematical functions on blocks of bits. A stream cipher, on the other hand, does not divide a message into blocks. Instead, a *stream cipher* treats the message as a stream of bits and performs mathematical functions on each bit individually.

When using a stream cipher, a plaintext bit will be transformed into a different ciphertext bit each time it is encrypted. Stream ciphers use *keystream generators*, which produce a stream of bits that is XORed with the plaintext bits to produce ciphertext, as shown in Figure 8-8.

NOTE This process is very similar to the one-time pad explained earlier. The individual bits in the one-time pad are used to encrypt the individual bits of the message through the XOR function, and in a stream algorithm the individual bits created by the keystream generator are used to encrypt the bits of the message through XOR also.

In block ciphers, it is the key that determines what functions are applied to the plaintext and in what order. The key provides the randomness of the encryption process. As stated earlier, most encryption algorithms are public, so people know how they work. The secret to the secret sauce is the key. In stream ciphers, the key also provides randomness, so that the stream of bits that is XORed to the plaintext is as random as possible. This concept

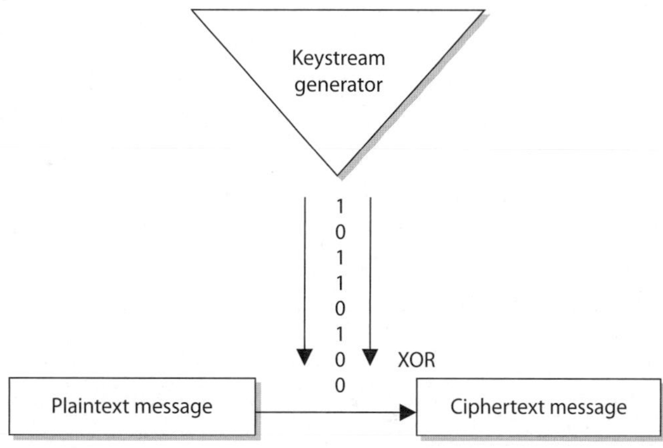

Figure 8-8 With stream ciphers, the bits generated by the keystream generator are XORed with the bits of the plaintext message.

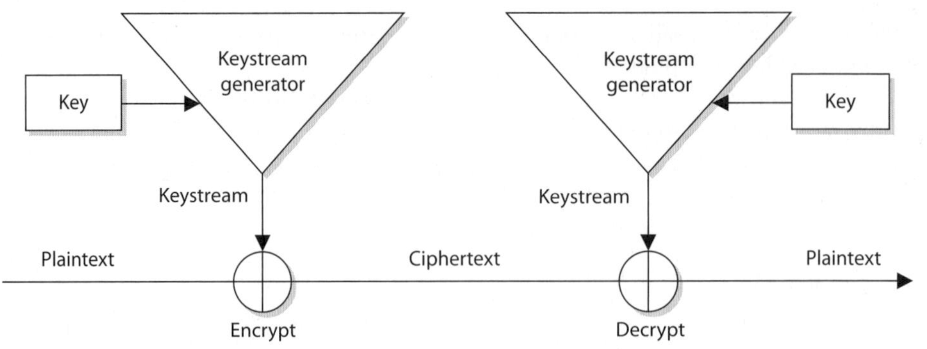

Figure 8-9 The sender and receiver must have the same key to generate the same keystream.

is shown in Figure 8-9. As you can see in this graphic, both the sending and receiving ends must have the same key to generate the same keystream for proper encryption and decryption purposes.

Initialization Vectors

Initialization vectors (IVs) are random values that are used with algorithms to ensure patterns are not created during the encryption process. They are used with keys and do not need to be encrypted when being sent to the destination. If IVs are not used, then two identical plaintext values that are encrypted with the same key will create the same ciphertext. Providing attackers with these types of patterns can make their job easier in breaking the encryption method and uncovering the key. For example, if we have the plaintext value of "See Spot run" two times within our message, we need to make sure that even though there is a pattern in the plaintext message, a pattern in the resulting ciphertext will not be created. So the IV and key are both used by the algorithm to provide more randomness to the encryption process.

A strong and effective stream cipher contains the following characteristics:

- **Easy to implement in hardware** Complexity in the hardware design makes it more difficult to verify the correctness of the implementation and can slow it down.
- **Long periods of no repeating patterns within keystream values** Bits generated by the keystream are not truly random in most cases, which will eventually lead to the emergence of patterns; we want these patterns to be rare.
- **A keystream not linearly related to the key** If someone figures out the keystream values, that does not mean she now knows the key value.
- **Statistically unbiased keystream (as many zeroes as ones)** There should be no dominance in the number of zeroes or ones in the keystream.

Stream ciphers require a lot of randomness and encrypt individual bits at a time. This requires more processing power than block ciphers require, which is why stream ciphers are better suited to be implemented at the hardware level. Because block ciphers do not require as much processing power, they can be easily implemented at the software level.

Asymmetric Key Cryptography

In symmetric key cryptography, a single secret key is used between entities, whereas in public key systems, each entity has different, *asymmetric keys*. The two different asymmetric keys are mathematically related. If a message is encrypted by one key, the other key is required in order to decrypt the message. One key is called public and the other one private. The *public key* can be known to everyone, and the *private key* must be known and used only by the owner. Many times, public keys are listed in directories and databases of e-mail addresses so they are available to anyone who wants to use these keys to encrypt or decrypt data when communicating with a particular person. Figure 8-10 illustrates the use of the different keys.

The public and private keys of an asymmetric cryptosystem are mathematically related, but if someone gets another person's public key, she should not be able to figure out the corresponding private key. This means that if an eavesdropper gets a copy of Bob's public key, she can't employ some mathematical magic and find out Bob's private key. But if someone gets Bob's private key, then there is big trouble—no one other than the owner should have access to a private key.

If Bob encrypts data with his private key, the receiver must have a copy of Bob's public key to decrypt it. The receiver can decrypt Bob's message and decide to reply to Bob in an encrypted form. All the receiver needs to do is encrypt her reply with Bob's public key, and then Bob can decrypt the message with his private key. It is not possible to encrypt and decrypt using the same key when using an asymmetric key encryption technology because, although mathematically related, the two keys are not the same key, as they are in symmetric cryptography. Bob can encrypt data with his private key, and the receiver can then decrypt it with Bob's public key. By decrypting the message with Bob's

Figure 8-10 An asymmetric cryptosystem

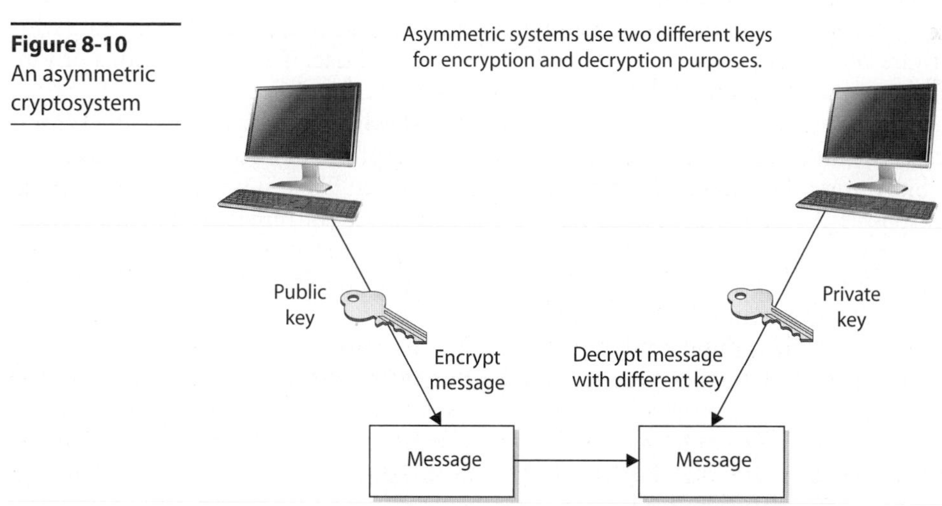

public key, the receiver can be sure the message really came from Bob. A message can be decrypted with a public key only if the message was encrypted with the corresponding private key. This provides authentication, because Bob is the only one who is supposed to have his private key. However, it does not truly provide confidentiality because anyone with the public key (which is, after all, public) can decrypt it. If the receiver wants to make sure Bob is the only one who can read her reply, she will encrypt the response with his public key. Only Bob will be able to decrypt the message because he is the only one who has the necessary private key.

The receiver can also choose to encrypt data with her private key instead of using Bob's public key. Why would she do that? Authentication—she wants Bob to know that the message came from her and no one else. If she encrypted the data with Bob's public key, it does not provide authenticity because anyone can get Bob's public key. If she uses her private key to encrypt the data, then Bob can be sure the message came from her and no one else. Symmetric keys do not provide authenticity, because the same key is used on both ends. Using one of the secret keys does not ensure the message originated from a specific individual.

If confidentiality is the most important security service to a sender, she would encrypt the file with the receiver's public key. This is called a *secure message format* because it can only be decrypted by the person who has the corresponding private key.

If authentication is the most important security service to the sender, then she would encrypt the data with her private key. This provides assurance to the receiver that the only person who could have encrypted the data is the individual who has possession of that private key. If the sender encrypted the data with the receiver's public key, authentication is not provided because this public key is available to anyone.

Encrypting data with the sender's private key is called an *open message format* because anyone with a copy of the corresponding public key can decrypt the message. Confidentiality is not ensured.

Each key type can be used to encrypt and decrypt, so do not get confused and think the public key is only for encryption and the private key is only for decryption. They both have the capability to encrypt and decrypt data. However, if data is encrypted with a private key, it cannot be decrypted with a private key. If data is encrypted with a private key, it must be decrypted with the corresponding public key.

An asymmetric algorithm works much more slowly than a symmetric algorithm, because symmetric algorithms carry out relatively simplistic mathematical functions on the bits during the encryption and decryption processes. They substitute and scramble (transposition) bits, which is not overly difficult or processor intensive. The reason it is hard to break this type of encryption is that the symmetric algorithms carry out this type of functionality over and over again. So a set of bits will go through a long series of being substituted and scrambled.

Asymmetric algorithms are slower than symmetric algorithms because they use much more complex mathematics to carry out their functions, which requires more processing time. Although they are slower, asymmetric algorithms can provide authentication and nonrepudiation, depending on the type of algorithm being used. Asymmetric systems also provide for easier and more manageable key distribution than symmetric systems and do not have the scalability issues of symmetric systems. The reason for these differences

Asymmetric Key Cryptosystems Summary

The following outlines the strengths and weaknesses of asymmetric key algorithms.

Strengths:

- Better key distribution than symmetric systems.
- Better scalability than symmetric systems.
- Can provide authentication and nonrepudiation.

Weaknesses:

- Works much more slowly than symmetric systems.
- Mathematically intensive tasks.

Examples:

- Rivest-Shamir-Adleman (RSA)
- Elliptic curve cryptography (ECC)
- Digital Signature Algorithm (DSA)

is that, with asymmetric systems, you can send out your public key to all of the people you need to communicate with, instead of keeping track of a unique key for each one of them. The "Hybrid Encryption Methods" section later in this chapter shows how these two systems can be used together to get the best of both worlds.

TIP Public key cryptography is asymmetric cryptography. The terms can be used interchangeably.

Table 8-1 summarizes the differences between symmetric and asymmetric algorithms.

Diffie-Hellman Algorithm

The first group to address the shortfalls of symmetric key cryptography decided to attack the issue of secure distribution of the symmetric key. Whitfield Diffie and Martin Hellman worked on this problem and ended up developing the first asymmetric key agreement algorithm, called, naturally, Diffie-Hellman.

To understand how *Diffie-Hellman* works, consider an example. Let's say that Tanya and Erika would like to communicate over an encrypted channel by using Diffie-Hellman. They would both generate a private and public key pair and exchange public keys. Tanya's software would take her private key (which is just a numeric value) and Erika's public key (another numeric value) and put them through the Diffie-Hellman algorithm. Erika's software would take her private key and Tanya's public key and insert them into the Diffie-Hellman algorithm on her computer. Through this process, Tanya and Erika derive the same shared value, which is used to create instances of symmetric keys.

Attribute	Symmetric	Asymmetric
Keys	One key is shared between two or more entities.	One entity has a public key, and the other entity has the corresponding private key.
Key exchange	Out-of-band through secure mechanisms.	A public key is made available to everyone, and a private key is kept secret by the owner.
Speed	The algorithm is less complex and faster.	The algorithm is more complex and slower.
Use	Bulk encryption, which means encrypting files and communication paths.	Key distribution and digital signatures.
Security service provided	Confidentiality.	Confidentiality, authentication, and nonrepudiation.

Table 8-1 Differences Between Symmetric and Asymmetric Systems

So, Tanya and Erika exchanged information that did not need to be protected (their public keys) over an untrusted network, and in turn generated the exact same symmetric key on each system. They both can now use these symmetric keys to encrypt, transmit, and decrypt information as they communicate with each other.

NOTE The preceding example describes key *agreement*, which is different from key *exchange*, the functionality used by the other asymmetric algorithms that will be discussed in this chapter. With key exchange functionality, the sender encrypts the symmetric key with the receiver's public key before transmission.

The Diffie-Hellman algorithm enables two systems to generate a symmetric key securely without requiring a previous relationship or prior arrangements. The algorithm allows for key distribution, but does not provide encryption or digital signature functionality. The algorithm is based on the difficulty of calculating discrete logarithms in a finite field.

The original Diffie-Hellman algorithm is vulnerable to a man-in-the-middle attack, because no authentication occurs before public keys are exchanged. In our example, when Tanya sends her public key to Erika, how does Erika really know it is Tanya's public key? What if Lance spoofed his identity, told Erika he was Tanya, and sent over his key? Erika would accept this key, thinking it came from Tanya. Let's walk through the steps of how this type of attack would take place, as illustrated in Figure 8-11:

1. Tanya sends her public key to Erika, but Lance grabs the key during transmission so it never makes it to Erika.
2. Lance spoofs Tanya's identity and sends over his public key to Erika. Erika now thinks she has Tanya's public key.

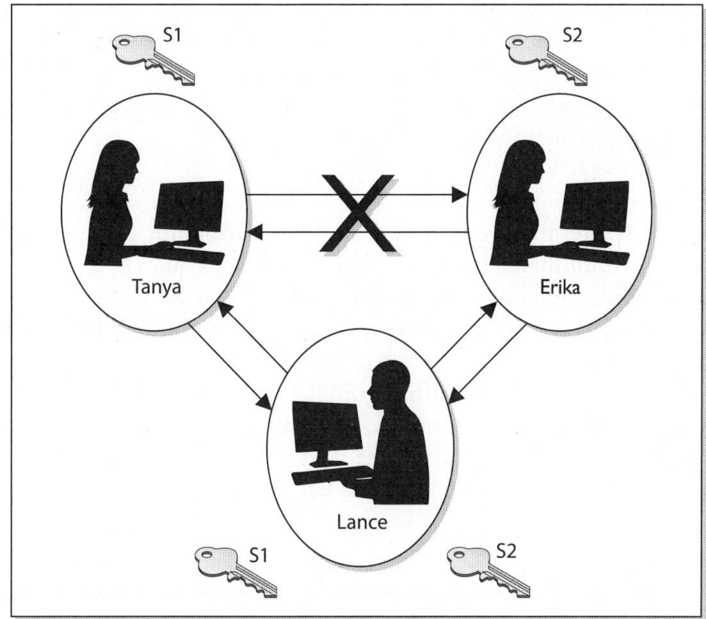

Figure 8-11 A man-in-the-middle attack against a Diffie-Hellman key agreement

3. Erika sends her public key to Tanya, but Lance grabs the key during transmission so it never makes it to Tanya.
4. Lance spoofs Erika's identity and sends over his public key to Tanya. Tanya now thinks she has Erika's public key.
5. Tanya combines her private key and Lance's public key and creates symmetric key S1.
6. Lance combines his private key and Tanya's public key and creates symmetric key S1.
7. Erika combines her private key and Lance's public key and creates symmetric key S2.
8. Lance combines his private key and Erika's public key and creates symmetric key S2.
9. Now Tanya and Lance share a symmetric key (S1) and Erika and Lance share a different symmetric key (S2). Tanya and Erika think they are sharing a key between themselves and do not realize Lance is involved.
10. Tanya writes a message to Erika, uses her symmetric key (S1) to encrypt the message, and sends it.
11. Lance grabs the message and decrypts it with symmetric key S1, reads or modifies the message and re-encrypts it with symmetric key S2, and then sends it to Erika.
12. Erika takes symmetric key S2 and uses it to decrypt and read the message.

The countermeasure to this type of attack is to have authentication take place before accepting someone's public key. The basic idea is that we use some sort of certificate to attest the identity of the party on the other side before trusting the data we receive from it. One of the most common ways to do this authentication is through the use of the RSA cryptosystem, which we describe next.

RSA

RSA, named after its inventors Ron Rivest, Adi Shamir, and Leonard Adleman, is a public key algorithm that is the most popular when it comes to asymmetric algorithms. RSA is a worldwide de facto standard and can be used for digital signatures, key exchange, and encryption. It was developed in 1978 at MIT and provides authentication as well as key encryption.

The security of this algorithm comes from the difficulty of factoring large numbers into their original prime numbers. The public and private keys are functions of a pair of large prime numbers, and the necessary activity required to decrypt a message from ciphertext to plaintext using a private key is comparable to factoring a product into two prime numbers.

NOTE A prime number is a positive whole number whose only factors (i.e., integer divisors) are 1 and the number itself.

One advantage of using RSA is that it can be used for encryption and digital signatures. Using its one-way function, RSA provides encryption and signature verification, and the inverse direction performs decryption and signature generation.

RSA has been implemented in applications; in operating systems; and at the hardware level in network interface cards, secure telephones, and smart cards. RSA can be used as a *key exchange protocol*, meaning it is used to encrypt the symmetric key to get it securely to its destination. RSA has been most commonly used with the symmetric algorithm AES. So, when RSA is used as a key exchange protocol, a cryptosystem generates a symmetric key to be used with the AES algorithm. Then the system encrypts the symmetric key with the receiver's public key and sends it to the receiver. The symmetric key is protected because only the individual with the corresponding private key can decrypt and extract the symmetric key.

Diving into Numbers Cryptography is really all about using mathematics to scramble bits into an undecipherable form and then using the same mathematics in reverse to put the bits back into a form that can be understood by computers and people. RSA's mathematics are based on the difficulty of factoring a large integer into its two prime factors. Put on your nerdy hat with the propeller and let's look at how this algorithm works.

The algorithm creates a public key and a private key from a function of large prime numbers. When data is encrypted with a public key, only the corresponding private key can decrypt the data. This act of decryption is basically the same as factoring the product of two prime numbers. So, let's say Ken has a secret (encrypted message), and for you to be able to uncover the secret, you have to take a specific large number and factor it and come up with the two numbers Ken has written down on a piece of paper. This may sound simplistic, but the number you must properly factor can be 2^{2048} in size. Not as easy as you may think.

The following sequence describes how the RSA algorithm comes up with the keys in the first place:

1. Choose two random large prime numbers, p and q.
2. Generate the product of these numbers: $n = pq$. n is used as the modulus.
3. Choose a random integer e (the public key) that is greater than 1 but less than $(p - 1)(q - 1)$. Make sure that e and $(p - 1)(q - 1)$ are relatively prime.
4. Compute the corresponding private key, d, such that $de - 1$ is a multiple of $(p - 1)(q - 1)$.
5. The public key = (n, e).
6. The private key = (n, d).
7. The original prime numbers p and q are discarded securely.

We now have our public and private keys, but how do they work together?

If someone needs to encrypt message m with your public key (e, n), the following formula results in ciphertext c:

$$c = m^e \bmod n$$

Then you need to decrypt the message with your private key (d), so the following formula is carried out:

$$m = c^d \bmod n$$

In essence, you encrypt a plaintext message by multiplying it by itself e times (taking the modulus, of course), and you decrypt it by multiplying the ciphertext by itself d times (again, taking the modulus). As long as e and d are large enough values, an attacker will have to spend an awfully long time trying to figure out through trial and error the value of d. (Recall that we publish the value of e for the whole world to know.)

You may be thinking, "Well, I don't understand these formulas, but they look simple enough. Why couldn't someone break these small formulas and uncover the encryption key?" Maybe someone will one day. As the human race advances in its understanding of mathematics and as processing power increases and cryptanalysis evolves, the RSA algorithm may be broken one day. If we were to figure out how to quickly and more easily factor large numbers into their original prime values, all of these cards would fall down, and this algorithm would no longer provide the security it does today. But we have not hit that bump in the road yet, so we are all happily using RSA in our computing activities.

One-Way Functions A *one-way function* is a mathematical function that is easier to compute in one direction than in the opposite direction. An analogy of this is when you drop a glass on the floor. Although dropping a glass on the floor is easy, putting all the pieces back together again to reconstruct the original glass is next to impossible. This concept is similar to how a one-way function is used in cryptography, which is what the RSA algorithm, and all other asymmetric algorithms, are based upon.

The easy direction of computation in the one-way function that is used in the RSA algorithm is the process of multiplying two large prime numbers. If I asked you to multiply two prime numbers, say 79 and 73, it would take you just a few seconds to punch that into a calculator and come up with the product (5,767). Easy. Now, suppose I asked you to find out which two numbers, when multiplied together, produce the value 5,767. This is called factoring and, when the factors involved are large prime numbers, it turns out to be a *really* hard problem. This difficulty in factoring the product of large prime numbers is what provides security for RSA key pairs.

As explained earlier in this chapter, *work factor* is the amount of time and resources it would take for someone to break an encryption method. In asymmetric algorithms, the work factor relates to the difference in time and effort that carrying out a one-way function in the easy direction takes compared to carrying out a one-way function in the hard direction. In most cases, the larger the key size, the longer it would take for the adversary to carry out the one-way function in the hard direction (decrypt a message).

The crux of this section is that all asymmetric algorithms provide security by using mathematical equations that are easy to perform in one direction and next to impossible to perform in the other direction. The "hard" direction is based on a "hard" mathematical problem. RSA's hard mathematical problem requires factoring large numbers into their original prime numbers.

Elliptic Curve Cryptography

The one-way function in RSA has survived cryptanalysis for over four decades but eventually will be cracked simply because we keep building computers that are faster. Sooner or later, computers will be able to factor the products of ever-larger prime numbers in reasonable times, at which point we would need to either ditch RSA or figure out how to use larger keys. Anticipating this eventuality, cryptographers found an even better trapdoor in elliptic curves. An *elliptic curve*, such as the one shown in Figure 8-12, is the set of points that satisfies a specific mathematical equation such as this one:

$$y^2 = x^3 + ax + b$$

Elliptic curves have two properties that are useful for cryptography. The first is that they are symmetrical about the X axis. This means that the top and bottom parts of the curve are mirror images of each other. The second useful property is that a straight line will intersect them in no more than three points. With these properties in mind, you can define a "dot" function that, given two points on the curve, gives you a third point on the flip side of it. Figure 8-12 shows how P dot Q = R. You simply follow the line through P and Q to find its third point of intersection on the curve (which could be between the two), and then drop down to that point R on the mirror image (in this case) below the X axis. You can keep going from there, so R dot P gives you another point that is

Figure 8-12
Elliptic curve

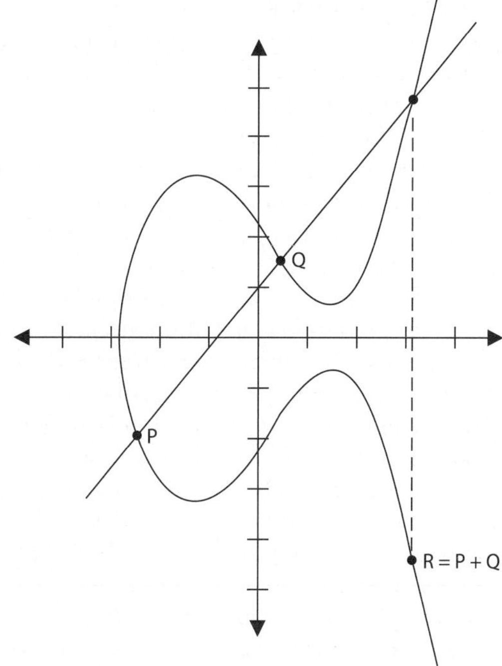

somewhere to the left and up from Q on the curve. If you keep "dotting" the original point P with the result of the previous "dot" operation *n* times (for some reasonably large value of *n*), you end up with a point that is really hard for anyone to guess or brute-force if they don't know the value of *n*. If you do know that value, then computing the final point is pretty easy. That is what makes this a great one-way function.

An *elliptic curve cryptosystem (ECC)* is a public key cryptosystem that can be described by a prime number (the equivalent of the modulus value in RSA), a curve equation, and a public point on the curve. The private key is some number *d*, and the corresponding public key *e* is the public point on the elliptic curve "dotted" with itself *d* times. Computing the private key from the public key in this kind of cryptosystem (i.e., reversing the one-way function) requires calculating the elliptic curve discrete logarithm function, which turns out to be really, really hard.

ECC provides much of the same functionality RSA provides: digital signatures, secure key distribution, and encryption. One differing factor is ECC's efficiency. ECC is more efficient than RSA and any other asymmetric algorithm. To illustrate this, an ECC key of 256 bits offers the equivalent protection of an RSA key of 3,072 bits. This is particularly useful because some devices have limited processing capacity, storage, power supply, and bandwidth, such as wireless devices and mobile telephones. With these types of devices, efficiency of resource use is very important. ECC provides encryption functionality, requiring a smaller percentage of the resources compared to RSA and other algorithms, so it is used in these types of devices.

Quantum Cryptography

Both RSA and ECC rely on the difficulty of reversing one-way functions. But what if we were able to come up with a cryptosystem in which it was impossible (not just difficult) to do this? This is the promise of quantum cryptography, which, despite all the hype, is still very much in its infancy. *Quantum cryptography* is the field of scientific study that applies quantum mechanics to perform cryptographic functions. The most promising application of this field, and the one we may be able to use soonest, provides a solution to the key distribution problem associated with symmetric key cryptosystems.

Quantum key distribution (QKD) is a system that generates and securely distributes encryption keys of any length between two parties. Though we could, in principle, use anything that obeys the principles of quantum mechanics, photons (the tiny particles that make up light) are the most convenient particles to use for QKD. It turns out photons are polarized or spin in ways that can be described as vertical, horizontal, diagonal left (–45°), and diagonal right (45°). If we put a polarized filter in front of a detector, any photon that makes it to that detector will have the polarization of its filter. Two types of filters are commonly used in QKD. The first is rectilinear and allows vertically and horizontally polarized photons through. The other is a (you guessed it) diagonal filter, which allows both diagonally left and diagonally right polarized photons through. It is important to note that the only way to measure the polarization on a photon is to essentially destroy it: either it is blocked by the filter if the polarizations are different or it is absorbed by the sensor if it makes it through.

Let's suppose that Alice wants to securely send an encryption key to Bob using QKD. They would use the following process.

1. They agree beforehand that photons that have either vertical or diagonal-right polarization represent the number zero and those with horizontal or diagonal-left polarization represent the number one.
2. The polarization of each photon is then generated randomly but is known to Alice.
3. Since Bob doesn't know what the correct spins are, he'll pass them through filters, randomly detect the polarization for each photon, and record his results. Because he's just guessing the polarizations, on average, he'll get half of them wrong, as we can see in Figure 8-13. He will, however, know which filter he applied to each photon, whether he got it right or wrong.
4. Once Alice is done sending bits, Bob will send her a message over an insecure channel (they don't need encryption for this), telling her the sequence of polarizations he recorded.
5. Alice will compare Bob's sequence to the correct sequence and tell him which polarizations he got right and which ones he got wrong.
6. They both discard Bob's wrong guesses and keep the remaining sequence of bits. They now have a shared secret key through this process, which is known as *key distillation*.

But what if there's a third, malicious, party eavesdropping on the exchange? Suppose this is Eve and she wants to sniff the secret key so she can intercept whatever messages

Figure 8-13 Key distillation between Alice and Bob

Alice's bit	0	1	1	0	1	0	0	1
Alice's basis	+	+	×	+	×	×	×	+
Alice's polarization	↑	→	↖	↑	↖	↗	↗	→
Bob's filter	+	×	×	×	+	×	+	+
Bob's measurement	↑	↗	↖	↗	→	↗	→	→
Shared secret key	0		1			0		1

Alice and Bob encrypt with it. Since the quantum state of photons is destroyed when they are filtered or measured, she would have to follow the same process as Bob intends to and then generate a new photon stream to forward to Bob. The catch is that Eve (just like Bob) will get 50 percent of the measurements wrong, but (unlike Bob) now has to guess what random basis was used and send these guesses to Bob. When Alice and Bob compare polarizations, they'll note a much higher error rate than normal and be able to infer that someone was eavesdropping.

If you're still awake and paying attention, you may be wondering, "Why use the polarization filters in the first place? Why not just capture the photon and see how it's spinning?" The answer gets complicated in a hurry, but the short version is that polarization is a random quantum state until you pass the photon through the filter and force the photon to "decide" between the two polarizations. Eve cannot just re-create the photon's quantum state like she would do with conventional data. Keep in mind that quantum mechanics are pretty weird but lead to unconditional security of the shared key.

Now that we have a basic idea of how QKD works, let's think back to our discussion of the only perfect and unbreakable cryptosystem: the one-time pad. You may recall that it has five major requirements that largely make it impractical. We list these here and show how QKD addresses each of them rather nicely:

- **Made up of truly random values** Quantum mechanics deals with attributes of matter and energy that are truly random, unlike the pseudo-random numbers we can generate algorithmically on a traditional computer.
- **Used only one time** Since QKD solves the key distribution problem, it allows us to transmit as many unique keys as we want, reducing the temptation (or need) to reuse keys.
- **Securely distributed to its destination** If someone attempts to eavesdrop on the key exchange, they will have to do so actively in a way that, as we've seen, is pretty much guaranteed to produce evidence of their tampering.
- **Secured at sender's and receiver's sites** OK, this one is not really addressed by QKD directly, but anyone going through all this effort would presumably not mess this one up, right?
- **At least as long as the message** Since QKD can be used for arbitrarily long key streams, we can easily generate keys that are at least as long as the longest message we'd like to send.

Now, before you get all excited and try to buy a QKD system for your organization, keep in mind that this technology is not quite ready for prime time. To be clear, commercial QKD devices are available as a "plug and play" option. Some banks in Geneva, Switzerland, use QKD to secure bank-to-bank traffic, and the Canton of Geneva uses it to secure online voting. The biggest challenge to widespread adoption of QKD at this point is the limitation on the distance at which photons can be reliably transmitted. As we write these lines, the maximum range for QKD is just over 500 km over fiber-optic wires. While space-to-ground QKD has been demonstrated using satellites and ground stations, drastically increasing the reach of such systems, it remains extremely difficult due to atmospheric interference. Once this problem is solved, we should be able to leverage a global, satellite-based QKD network.

Hybrid Encryption Methods

Up to this point, we have figured out that symmetric algorithms are fast but have some drawbacks (lack of scalability, difficult key management, and provide only confidentiality). Asymmetric algorithms do not have these drawbacks but are very slow. We just can't seem to win. So we turn to a hybrid system that uses symmetric and asymmetric encryption methods together.

Asymmetric and Symmetric Algorithms Used Together

Asymmetric and symmetric cryptosystems are used together very frequently. In this hybrid approach, the two technologies are used in a complementary manner, with each performing a different function. A symmetric algorithm creates keys used for encrypting bulk data, and an asymmetric algorithm creates keys used for automated key distribution. Each algorithm has its pros and cons, so using them together can be the best of both worlds.

When a symmetric key is used for bulk data encryption, this key is used to encrypt the message you want to send. When your friend gets the message you encrypted, you want him to be able to decrypt it, so you need to send him the necessary symmetric key to use to decrypt the message. You do not want this key to travel unprotected, because if the message were intercepted and the key were not protected, an eavesdropper could intercept the message that contains the necessary key to decrypt your message and read your information. If the symmetric key needed to decrypt your message is not protected, there is no use in encrypting the message in the first place. So you should use an asymmetric algorithm to encrypt the symmetric key, as depicted in Figure 8-14. Why use the symmetric key on the message and the asymmetric key on the symmetric key? As stated earlier, the asymmetric algorithm takes longer because the math is more complex. Because your message is most likely going to be longer than the length of the key, you use the faster algorithm (symmetric) on the message and the slower algorithm (asymmetric) on the key.

How does this actually work? Let's say Bill is sending Paul a message that Bill wants only Paul to be able to read. Bill encrypts his message with a secret key, so now Bill has ciphertext and a symmetric key. The key needs to be protected, so Bill encrypts the symmetric key with an asymmetric key. Remember that asymmetric algorithms use private and public keys, so Bill will encrypt the symmetric key with Paul's public key. Now Bill has ciphertext from the message and ciphertext from the symmetric key. Why did Bill encrypt the symmetric key with Paul's public key instead of his own private key? Because if Bill

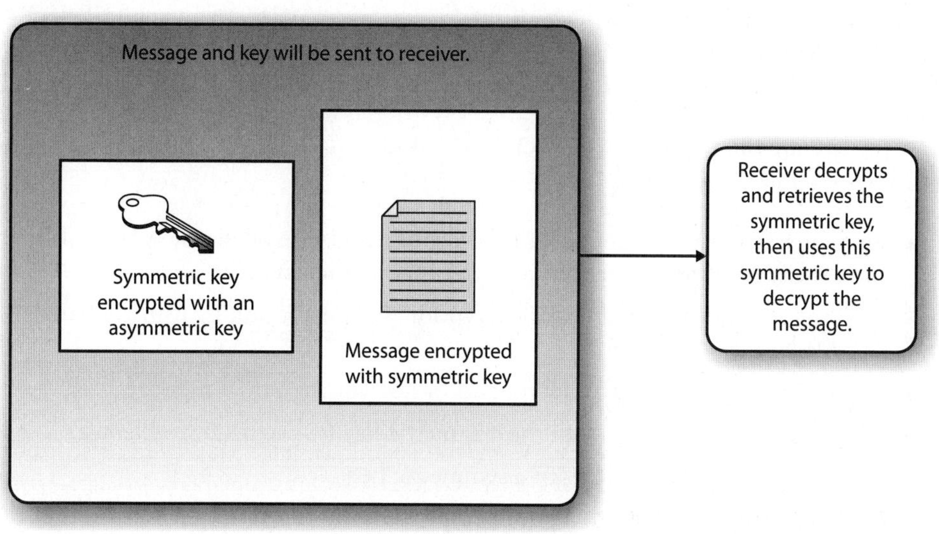

Figure 8-14 In a hybrid system, the asymmetric key is used to encrypt the symmetric key, and the symmetric key is used to encrypt the message

encrypted it with his own private key, then anyone with Bill's public key could decrypt it and retrieve the symmetric key. However, Bill does not want anyone who has his public key to read his message to Paul. Bill only wants Paul to be able to read it. So Bill encrypts the symmetric key with Paul's public key. If Paul has done a good job protecting his private key, he will be the only one who can read Bill's message.

Paul receives Bill's message, and Paul uses his private key to decrypt the symmetric key. Paul then uses the symmetric key to decrypt the message. Paul then reads Bill's very important and confidential message that asks Paul how his day is.

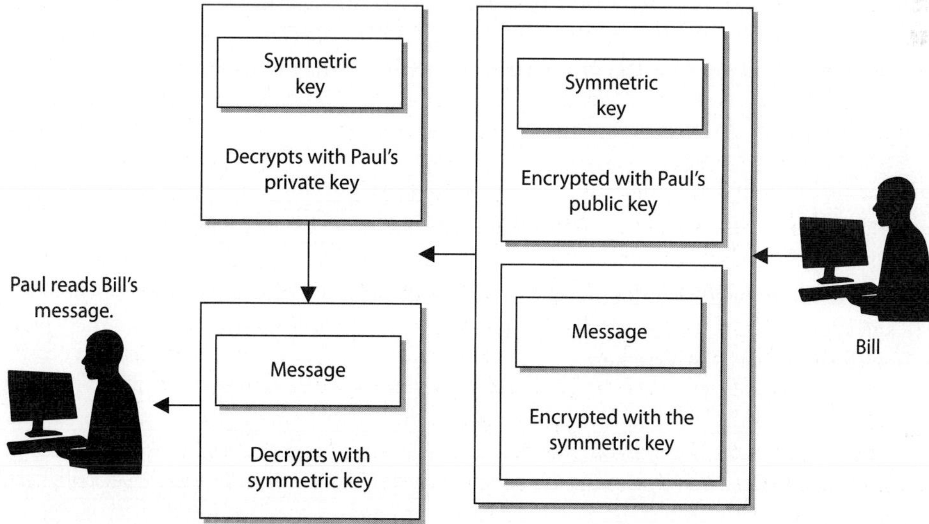

Now, when we say that Bill is using this key to encrypt and that Paul is using that key to decrypt, those two individuals do not necessarily need to find the key on their hard drive and know how to properly apply it. We have software to do this for us—thank goodness.

If this is your first time with these issues and you are struggling, don't worry. Just remember the following points:

- An asymmetric algorithm performs encryption and decryption by using public and private keys that are related to each other mathematically.
- A symmetric algorithm performs encryption and decryption by using a shared secret key.
- A symmetric key is used to encrypt and/or decrypt the actual message.
- Public keys are used to encrypt the symmetric key for secure key exchange.
- A secret key is synonymous with a symmetric key.
- An asymmetric key refers to a public or private key.

So, that is how a hybrid system works. The symmetric algorithm uses a secret key that will be used to encrypt the bulk, or the message, and the asymmetric key encrypts the secret key for transmission.

To ensure that some of these concepts are driven home, ask these questions of yourself without reading the answers provided:

1. If a symmetric key is encrypted with a receiver's public key, what security service(s) is (are) provided?
2. If data is encrypted with the sender's private key, what security service(s) is (are) provided?
3. If the sender encrypts data with the receiver's private key, what security services(s) is (are) provided?
4. Why do we encrypt the message with the symmetric key?
5. Why don't we encrypt the symmetric key with another symmetric key?

Now check your answers:

1. Confidentiality, because only the receiver's private key can be used to decrypt the symmetric key, and only the receiver should have access to this private key.
2. Authenticity of the sender and nonrepudiation. If the receiver can decrypt the encrypted data with the sender's public key, then she knows the data was encrypted with the sender's private key.

3. None, because no one but the owner of the private key should have access to it. Trick question.
4. Because the asymmetric key algorithm is too slow.
5. We need to get the necessary symmetric key to the destination securely, which can only be carried out through asymmetric cryptography via the use of public and private keys to provide a mechanism for secure transport of the symmetric key.

Session Keys

A *session key* is a single-use symmetric key that is used to encrypt messages between two users during a communication session. A session key is no different from the symmetric key described in the previous section, but it is only good for one communication session between users.

If Tanya has a symmetric key she uses to always encrypt messages between Lance and herself, then this symmetric key would not be regenerated or changed. They would use the same key every time they communicated using encryption. However, using the same key repeatedly increases the chances of the key being captured and the secure communication being compromised. If, on the other hand, a new symmetric key were generated each time Lance and Tanya wanted to communicate, as shown in Figure 8-15, it would be used only during their one dialogue and then destroyed. If they wanted to communicate an hour later, a new session key would be created and shared.

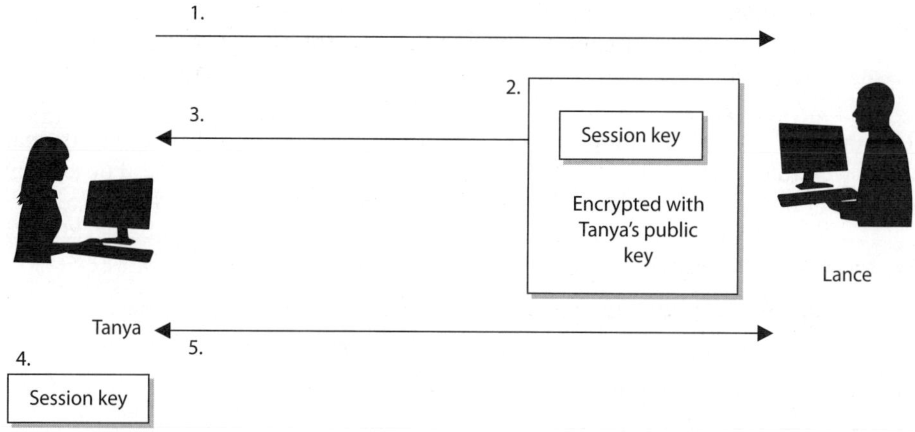

1) Tanya sends Lance her public key.
2) Lance generates a random session key and encrypts it using Tanya's public key.
3) Lance sends the session key, encrypted with Tanya's public key, to Tanya.
4) Tanya decrypts Lance's message with her private key and now has a copy of the session key.
5) Tanya and Lance use this session key to encrypt and decrypt messages to each other.

Figure 8-15 A session key is generated so all messages can be encrypted during one particular session between users.

A session key provides more protection than static symmetric keys because it is valid for only one session between two computers. If an attacker were able to capture the session key, she would have a very small window of time to use it to try to decrypt messages being passed back and forth.

In cryptography, almost all data encryption takes place through the use of session keys. When you write an e-mail and encrypt it before sending it over the wire, it is actually being encrypted with a session key. If you write another message to the same person one minute later, a brand-new session key is created to encrypt that new message. So if an eavesdropper happens to figure out one session key, that does not mean she has access to all other messages you write and send off.

When two computers want to communicate using encryption, they must first go through a handshaking process. The two computers agree on the encryption algorithms that will be used and exchange the session key that will be used for data encryption. In a sense, the two computers set up a virtual connection between each other and are said to be in session. When this session is done, each computer tears down any data structures it built to enable this communication to take place, releases the resources, and destroys the session key. These things are taken care of by operating systems and applications in the background, so a user would not necessarily need to be worried about using the wrong type of key for the wrong reason. The software will handle this, but it is important for security professionals to understand the difference between the key types and the issues that surround them.

CAUTION Private and symmetric keys should not be available in cleartext. This may seem obvious to you, but there have been several implementations over time that have allowed for this type of compromise to take place.

Unfortunately, we don't always seem to be able to call an apple an apple. In many types of technology, the exact same thing can have more than one name. For example, symmetric cryptography can be referred to as any of the following:

- Secret key cryptography
- Session key cryptography
- Shared key cryptography
- Private key cryptography

We know the difference between secret keys (static) and session keys (dynamic), but what is this "shared key" and "private key" mess? Well, using the term "shared key" makes sense, because the sender and receiver are sharing one single key. It's unfortunate that the term "private key" can be used to describe symmetric cryptography, because it only adds more confusion to the difference between symmetric cryptography (where one symmetric key is used) and asymmetric cryptography (where both a private and public key are used). You just need to remember this little quirk and still understand the difference between symmetric and asymmetric cryptography.

Integrity

Cryptography is mainly concerned with protecting the confidentiality of information. It can also, however, allow us to ensure its integrity. In other words, how can we be certain that a message we receive or a file we download has not been modified? For this type of protection, hash algorithms are required to successfully detect intentional and unintentional unauthorized modifications to data. However, as we will see shortly, it is possible for attackers to modify data, recompute the hash, and deceive the recipient. In some cases, we need a more robust approach to message integrity verification. Let's start off with hash algorithms and their characteristics.

Hashing Functions

A *one-way hash* is a function that takes a variable-length string (a message) and produces a fixed-length value called a *hash value*. For example, if Kevin wants to send a message to Maureen and he wants to ensure the message does not get altered in an unauthorized fashion while it is being transmitted, he would calculate a hash value for the message and append it to the message itself. When Maureen receives the message, she performs the same hashing function Kevin used and then compares her result with the hash value sent with the message. If the two values are the same, Maureen can be sure the message was not altered during transmission. If the two values are different, Maureen knows the message was altered, either intentionally or unintentionally, and she discards the message.

The hashing algorithm is not a secret—it is publicly known. The secrecy of the one-way hashing function is its "one-wayness." The function is run in only one direction, not the other direction. This is different from the one-way function used in public key cryptography, in which security is provided based on the fact that, without knowing a trapdoor, it is very hard to perform the one-way function backward on a message and come up with readable plaintext. However, one-way hash functions are never used in reverse; they create a hash value and call it a day. The receiver does not attempt to reverse the process at the other end, but instead runs the same hashing function one way and compares the two results.

EXAM TIP Keep in mind that hashing is not the same thing as encryption; you can't "decrypt" a hash. You can only run the same hashing algorithm against the same piece of text in an attempt to derive the same hash or fingerprint of the text.

Various Hashing Algorithms

As stated earlier, the goal of using a one-way hash function is to provide a fingerprint of the message. If two different messages produce the same hash value, it would be easier for an attacker to break that security mechanism because patterns would be revealed.

A strong one-hash function should not provide the same hash value for two or more different messages. If a hashing algorithm takes steps to ensure it does not create the same hash value for two or more messages, it is said to be *collision free*.

Algorithm	Description
Message Digest 5 (MD5) algorithm	Produces a 128-bit hash value. More complex than MD4.
Secure Hash Algorithm (SHA)	Produces a 160-bit hash value. Used with Digital Signature Algorithm (DSA).
SHA-1, SHA-256, SHA-384, SHA-512	Updated versions of SHA. SHA-1 produces a 160-bit hash value, SHA-256 creates a 256-bit value, and so on.

Table 8-2 Various Hashing Algorithms Available

Strong cryptographic hash functions have the following characteristics:

- The hash should be computed over the entire message.
- The hash should be a one-way function so messages are not disclosed by their values.
- Given a message and its hash value, computing another message with the same hash value should be impossible.
- The function should be resistant to birthday attacks (explained in the upcoming section "Attacks Against One-Way Hash Functions").

Table 8-2 and the following sections quickly describe some of the available hashing algorithms used in cryptography today.

MD5 *MD5* was created by Ron Rivest in 1991 as a better version of his previous message digest algorithm (MD4). It produces a 128-bit hash, but the algorithm is subject to collision attacks, and is therefore no longer suitable for applications like digital certificates and signatures that require collision attack resistance. It is still commonly used for file integrity checksums, such as those required by some intrusion detection systems, as well as for forensic evidence integrity.

SHA *SHA* was designed by the NSA and published by the National Institute of Standards and Technology (NIST) to be used with the Digital Signature Standard (DSS), which is discussed a bit later in more depth. SHA was designed to be used in digital signatures and was developed when a more secure hashing algorithm was required for U.S. government applications. It produces a 160-bit hash value, or message digest. This is then inputted into an asymmetric algorithm, which computes the signature for a message.

SHA is similar to MD5. It has some extra mathematical functions and produces a 160-bit hash instead of a 128-bit hash, which initially made it more resistant to collision attacks. Newer versions of this algorithm (collectively known as the SHA-2 and SHA-3 families) have been developed and released: SHA-256, SHA-384, and SHA-512. The SHA-2 and SHA-3 families are considered secure for all uses.

Attacks Against One-Way Hash Functions

A strong hashing algorithm does not produce the same hash value for two different messages. If the algorithm does produce the same value for two distinctly different messages, this is called a *collision*. An attacker can attempt to force a collision, which is referred to as a *birthday attack*. This attack is based on the mathematical birthday paradox that exists in standard statistics. Now hold on to your hat while we go through this—it is a bit tricky:

> How many people must be in the same room for the chance to be greater than even that another person has the same birthday as you?
> **Answer:** 253
>
> How many people must be in the same room for the chance to be greater than even that at least two people share the same birthday?
> **Answer:** 23

This seems a bit backward, but the difference is that in the first instance, you are looking for someone with a specific birthday date that matches yours. In the second instance, you are looking for any two people who share the same birthday. There is a higher probability of finding two people who share a birthday than of finding another person who shares your birthday. Or, stated another way, it is easier to find two matching values in a sea of values than to find a match for just one specific value.

Why do we care? The birthday paradox can apply to cryptography as well. Since any random set of 23 people most likely (at least a 50 percent chance) includes two people who share a birthday, by extension, if a hashing algorithm generates a message digest of 60 bits, there is a high likelihood that an adversary can find a collision using only 2^{30} inputs.

The main way an attacker can find the corresponding hashing value that matches a specific message is through a brute-force attack. If he finds a message with a specific hash value, it is equivalent to finding someone with a specific birthday. If he finds two messages with the same hash values, it is equivalent to finding two people with the same birthday.

The output of a hashing algorithm is n, and to find a message through a brute-force attack that results in a specific hash value would require hashing $2n$ random messages. To take this one step further, finding two messages that hash to the same value would require review of only $2n/2$ messages.

How Would a Birthday Attack Take Place?

Sue and Joe are going to get married, but before they do, they have a prenuptial contract drawn up that states if they get divorced, then Sue takes her original belongings and Joe takes his original belongings. To ensure this contract is not modified, it is hashed and a message digest value is created.

One month after Sue and Joe get married, Sue carries out some devious activity behind Joe's back. She makes a copy of the message digest value without anyone knowing. Then she makes a new contract that states that if Joe and Sue get a divorce, Sue owns both her own original belongings and Joe's original belongings. Sue hashes this new contract and compares the new message digest value with the message digest value that correlates with the contract. They don't match. So Sue tweaks her contract ever so slightly and creates another message digest value and compares them. She continues to tweak her contract until she forces a collision, meaning her contract creates the same message digest value as the original contract. Sue then changes out the original contract with her new contract and quickly divorces Joe. When Sue goes to collect Joe's belongings and he objects, she shows him that no modification could have taken place on the original document because it still hashes out to the same message digest. Sue then moves to an island.

Hash algorithms usually use message digest sizes (the value of *n*) that are large enough to make collisions difficult to accomplish, but they are still possible. An algorithm that has 256-bit output, like SHA-256, may require approximately 2^{128} computations to break. This means there is a less than 1 in 2^{128} chance that someone could carry out a successful birthday attack.

The main point of discussing this paradox is to show how important longer hashing values truly are. A hashing algorithm that has a larger bit output is less vulnerable to brute-force attacks such as a birthday attack. This is the primary reason why the new versions of SHA have such large message digest values.

Message Integrity Verification

Whether messages are encrypted or not, we frequently want to ensure that they arrive at their destination with no alterations, accidental or deliberate. We can use the principles we've discussed in this chapter to ensure the integrity of our traffic to various degrees of security. Let's look at three increasingly more powerful ways to do this, starting with a simple message digest.

Message Digest

A one-way hashing function takes place without the use of any keys. This means, for example, that if Cheryl writes a message, calculates a message digest, appends the digest to the message, and sends it on to Scott, Bruce can intercept this message, alter Cheryl's message, recalculate another message digest, append it to the message, and send it on to Scott. When Scott receives it, he verifies the message digest, but never knows the message was actually altered by Bruce. Scott thinks the message came straight from Cheryl and was never modified because the two message digest values are the same. This process is depicted in Figure 8-16 and consists of the following steps:

1. The sender writes a message.
2. The sender puts the message through a hashing function, generating a message digest.
3. The sender appends the message digest to the message and sends it to the receiver.
4. The receiver puts the message through a hashing function and generates his own message digest.
5. The receiver compares the two message digest values. If they are the same, the message has not been altered.

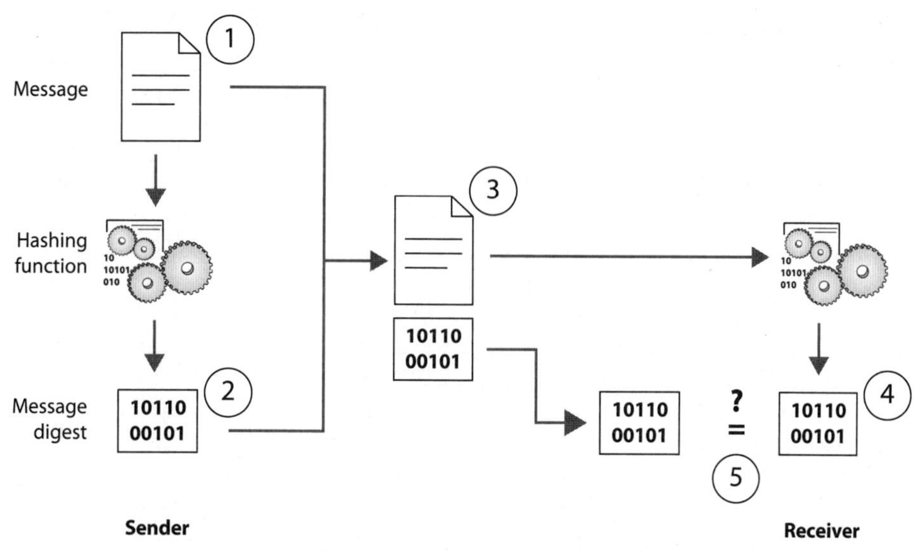

Figure 8-16 Verifying message integrity with a message digest

Message Authentication Code

If Cheryl wanted more protection than just described, she would need to use a *message authentication code (MAC)*, an authentication scheme derived by applying a secret key to a message in some form. This does not mean the symmetric key is used to encrypt the message, though. A good example of a MAC leverages hashing functions and is called a *hash MAC (HMAC)*.

In the previous example, if Cheryl were to use an HMAC function instead of just a plain hashing algorithm, a symmetric key would be concatenated with her message. The result of this process would be put through a hashing algorithm, and the result would be a MAC value. This MAC value would then be appended to her message and sent to Scott. If Bruce were to intercept this message and modify it, he would not have the necessary symmetric key to create the MAC value that Scott will attempt to generate. Figure 8-17 shows the following steps to use an HMAC:

1. The sender writes a message.
2. The sender concatenates a shared secret key with the message and puts them through a hashing function, generating a MAC.
3. The sender appends the MAC value to the message and sends it to the receiver. (Just the message with the attached MAC value. The sender does not send the symmetric key with the message.)
4. The receiver concatenates his copy of the shared secret key with the message and puts the results through a hashing algorithm to generate his own MAC.
5. The receiver compares the two MAC values. If they are the same, the message has not been modified.

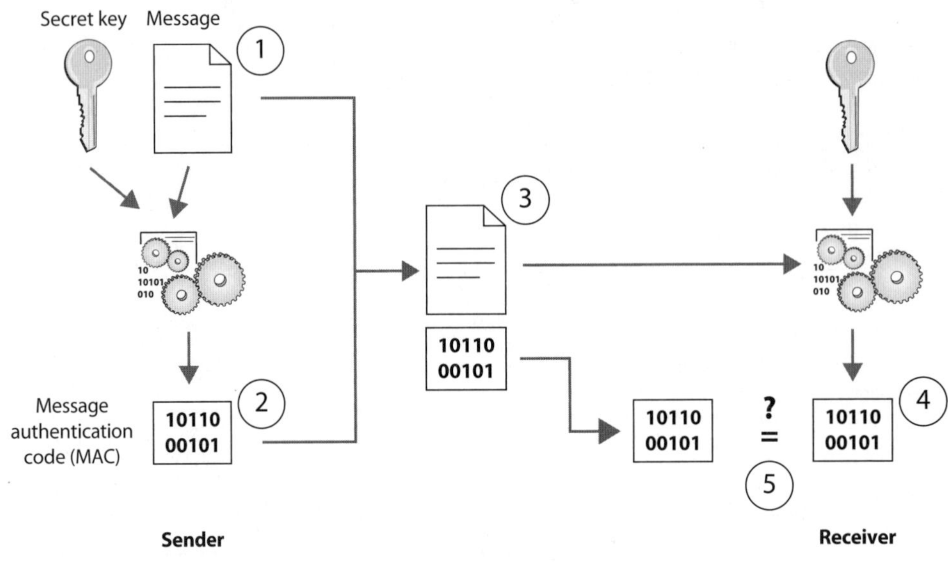

Figure 8-17 Verifying message integrity with a message digest

Now, when we say that the message is concatenated with a symmetric key, we don't mean a symmetric key is used to encrypt the message. The message is not encrypted in an HMAC function, so there is no confidentiality being provided. Think about throwing a message in a bowl and then throwing a symmetric key in the same bowl. If you dump the contents of the bowl into a hashing algorithm, the result will be a MAC value.

Digital Signatures

A MAC can ensure that a message has not been altered, but it cannot ensure that it comes from the entity that claims to be its source. This is because MACs use symmetric keys, which are shared. If there was an insider threat who had access to this shared key, that person could modify messages in a way that could not be easily detected. If we wanted to protect against this threat, we would want to ensure the integrity verification mechanism is tied to a specific individual, which is where public key encryption comes in handy.

A *digital signature* is a hash value that has been encrypted with the sender's private key. Since this hash can be decrypted by anyone who has the corresponding public key, it verifies that the message comes from the claimed sender and that it hasn't been altered. The act of signing means encrypting the message's hash value with a private key, as shown in Figure 8-18.

Continuing our example from the previous section, if Cheryl wants to ensure that the message she sends to Scott is not modified *and* she wants him to be sure it came only from her, she can digitally sign the message. This means that a one-way hashing function would be run on the message, and then Cheryl would encrypt that hash value with her private key.

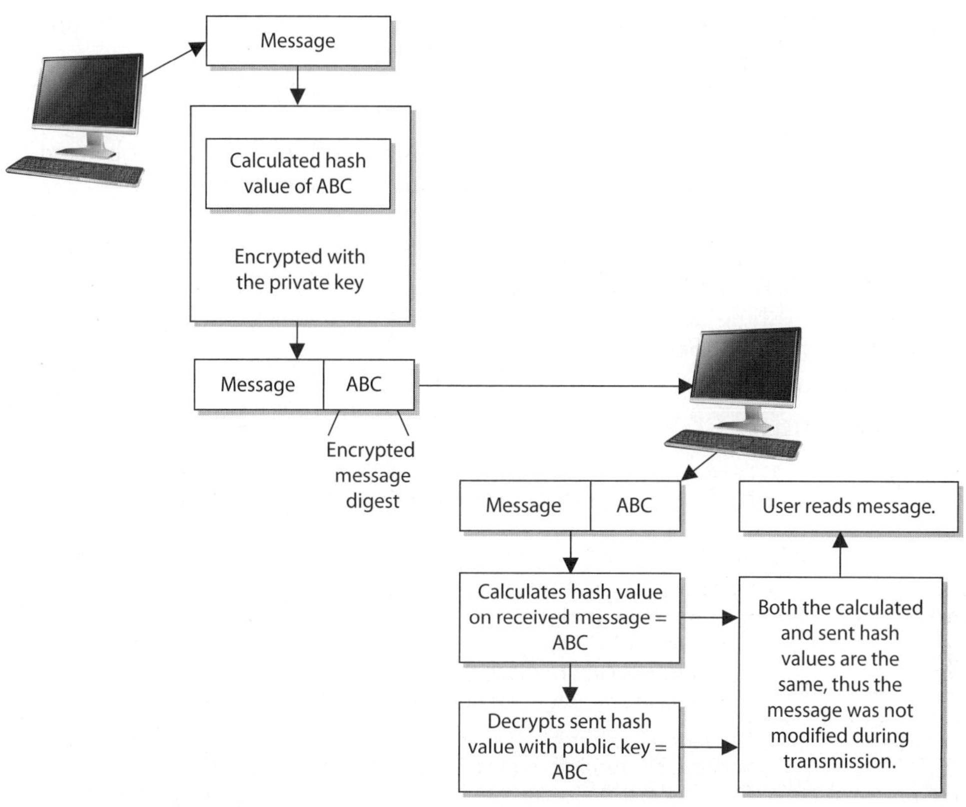

Figure 8-18 Creating a digital signature for a message

When Scott receives the message, he performs the hashing function on the message and comes up with his own hash value. Then he decrypts the sent hash value (digital signature) with Cheryl's public key. He then compares the two values, and if they are the same, he can be sure the message was not altered during transmission. He is also sure the message came from Cheryl because the value was encrypted with her private key.

The hashing function ensures the integrity of the message, and the signing of the hash value provides authentication and nonrepudiation. The act of signing just means the value was encrypted with a private key.

Because digital signatures are so important in proving who sent which messages, the U.S. federal government decided to establish standards pertaining to their functions and acceptable use. In 1991, NIST proposed a federal standard called the *Digital Signature Standard (DSS)*. It was developed for federal departments and agencies, but most vendors also designed their products to meet these specifications. The federal government requires its departments to use DSA, RSA, or the elliptic curve digital signature algorithm (ECDSA) and SHA-256. SHA creates a 256-bit message digest output, which is then inputted into one of the three mentioned digital signature algorithms. SHA is used to ensure the integrity of the message, and the other algorithms are used to digitally sign the message. This is an example of how two different algorithms are combined to provide the right combination of security services.

RSA and DSA are the best-known and most widely used digital signature algorithms. DSA was developed by the NSA. Unlike RSA, DSA can be used only for digital signatures, and DSA is slower than RSA in signature verification. RSA can be used for digital signatures, encryption, and secure distribution of symmetric keys.

Digests, HMACs, and Digital Signatures—Oh My!

MACs and hashing processes can be confusing. The following table simplifies the differences between them.

Function	Steps	Security Service Provided
Hash	1. Sender puts a message through a hashing algorithm and generates a message digest (MD) value. 2. Sender sends message and MD value to receiver. 3. Receiver runs just the message through the same hashing algorithm and creates an independent MD value. 4. Receiver compares both MD values. If they are the same, the message was not modified.	Integrity; not confidentiality or authentication. Can detect only unintentional modifications.
HMAC	1. Sender concatenates a message and secret key and puts the result through a hashing algorithm. This creates a MAC value. 2. Sender appends the MAC value to the message and sends it to the receiver. 3. The receiver takes just the message and concatenates it with her own symmetric key. This results in an independent MAC value. 4. The receiver compares the two MAC values. If they are identical, the receiver knows the message was not modified.	Integrity and data origin authentication; confidentiality is not provided.
Digital signature	1. The sender computes the hash of the message and encrypts it with her private key. 2. The sender appends the encrypted message digest to the message and sends it to the receiver. 3. The receiver computes the hash of the received message. 4. The receiver decrypts the received message digest using the sender's public key. 5. The receiver compares the two digests. If they are identical, the receiver knows the message was not modified and knows from which system it came.	Integrity, sender authentication, and nonrepudiation; confidentiality is not provided.

Public Key Infrastructure

Now that you understand the main approaches to modern cryptography, let's see how they come together to provide an infrastructure that can help us protect our organizations in practical ways. A *public key infrastructure (PKI)* consists of programs, data formats, procedures, communication protocols, security policies, and cryptosystems working in a comprehensive manner to enable a wide range of dispersed people to communicate in a secure and predictable fashion. In other words, a PKI establishes and maintains a high level of trust within an environment. It can provide confidentiality, integrity, nonrepudiation, authentication, and even authorization. As we will see shortly, it is a *hybrid* system of symmetric and asymmetric cryptosystems, which were discussed in earlier sections.

There is a difference between public key cryptography and PKI. Public key cryptography is another name for asymmetric algorithms, while PKI (as the name states) is an infrastructure that is partly built on public key cryptography. The central concept in PKI is the digital certificate, but it also requires certificate authorities, registration authorities, and effective key management.

Digital Certificates

Recall that, in asymmetric key cryptography, we keep a private key secret and widely share its corresponding public key. This allows anyone to send us an encrypted message that only we (or whoever is holding the private key) can decrypt. Now, suppose you receive a message from your boss asking you to send some sensitive information encrypted with her public key, which she attaches to the message. How can you be sure it really is her? After all, anybody could generate a key pair and send you a public key claiming to be hers.

A *digital certificate* is the mechanism used to associate a public key with a collection of components in a manner that is sufficient to uniquely identify the claimed owner. The most commonly used standard for digital certificates is the International Telecommunications Union's *X.509*, which dictates the different fields used in the certificate and the valid values that can populate those fields. The certificate includes the serial number, version number, identity information, algorithm information, lifetime dates, and the signature of the issuing authority, as shown in Figure 8-19.

Note that the certificate specifies the subject, which is the owner of the certificate and holder of the corresponding private key, as well as an issuer, which is the entity that is certifying that the subject is who they claim to be. The issuer attaches a digital signature to the certificate to prove that it was issued by that entity and hasn't been altered by others. There is nothing keeping anyone from issuing a self-signed certificate, in which the subject and issuer can be one and the same. While this might be allowed, it should be very suspicious when dealing with external entities. For example, if your bank presents to you a self-signed certificate, you should not trust it at all. Instead, we need a reputable third party to verify subjects' identities and issue their certificates.

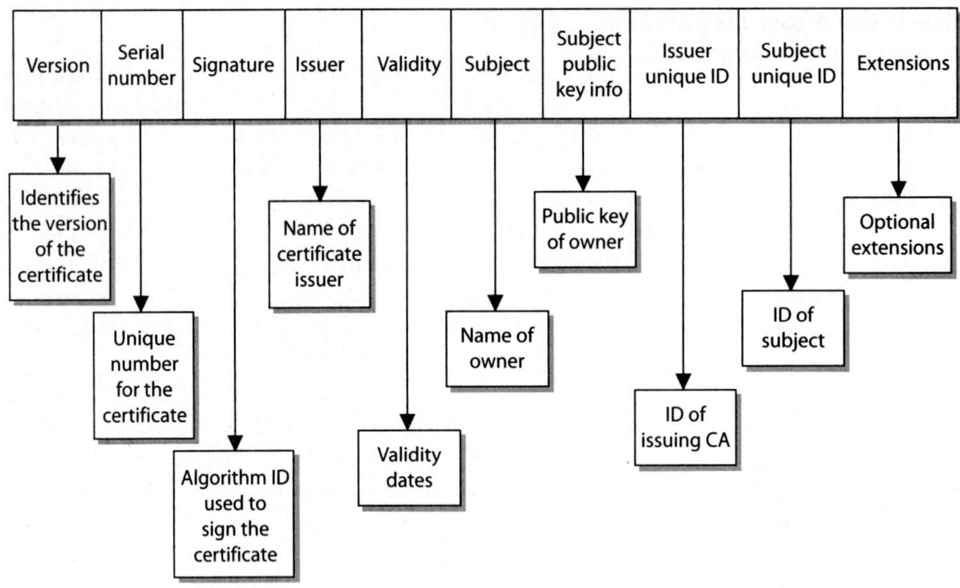

Figure 8-19 Each certificate has a structure with all the necessary identifying information in it.

Certificate Authorities

A *certificate authority (CA)* is a trusted third party that vouches for the identity of a subject, issues a certificate to that subject, and then digitally signs the certificate to assure its integrity. When the CA signs the certificate, it binds the subject's identity to the public key, and the CA takes liability for the authenticity of that subject. It is this trusted third party (the CA) that allows people who have never met to authenticate to each other and to communicate in a secure method. If Kevin has never met Dave but would like to communicate securely with him, and they both trust the same CA, then Kevin could retrieve Dave's digital certificate and start the process.

A CA is a trusted organization (or server) that maintains and issues digital certificates. When a person requests a certificate, a *registration authority (RA)* verifies that individual's identity and passes the certificate request off to the CA. The CA constructs the certificate, signs it, sends it to the requester, and maintains the certificate over its lifetime. When another person wants to communicate with this person, the CA basically vouches for that person's identity. When Dave receives a digital certificate from Kevin, Dave goes through steps to validate it. Basically, by providing Dave with his digital certificate, Kevin is stating, "I know you don't know or trust me, but here is this document that was created by someone you do know and trust. The document says I am legitimate and you should trust I am who I claim to be."

Once Dave validates the digital certificate, he extracts Kevin's public key, which is embedded within it. Now Dave knows this public key is bound to Kevin. He also knows that if Kevin uses his private key to create a digital signature and Dave can properly decrypt it using this public key, it did indeed come from Kevin.

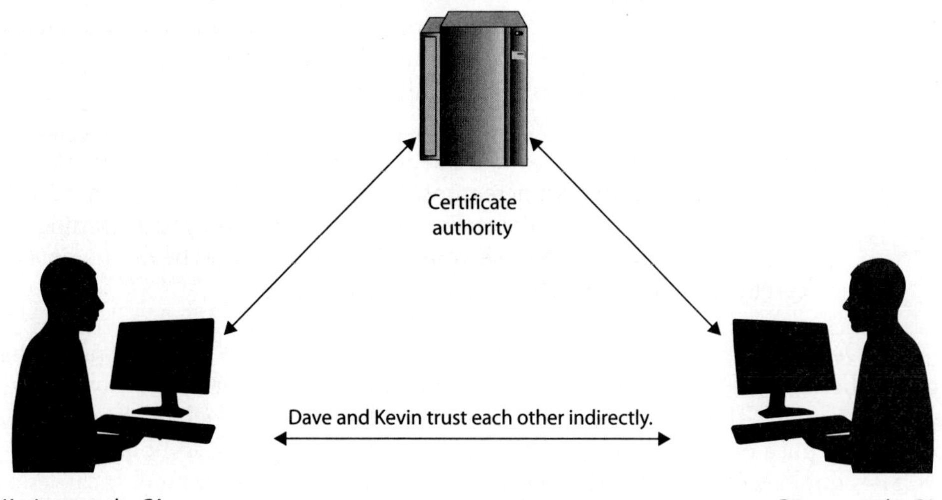
Certificate
authority
Dave and Kevin trust each other indirectly.
Kevin trusts the CA.
Dave trusts the CA.

The CA can be internal to an organization. Such a setup would enable the organization to control the CA server, configure how authentication takes place, maintain the certificates, and recall certificates when necessary. Other CAs are organizations dedicated to this type of service, and other individuals and companies pay them to supply it. Some well-known CAs are Symantec and GeoTrust. All browsers have several well-known CAs configured by default. Most are configured to trust dozens or hundreds of CAs.

NOTE More and more organizations are setting up their own internal PKIs. When these independent PKIs need to interconnect to allow for secure communication to take place (either between departments or between different companies), there must be a way for the two root CAs to trust each other. The two CAs do not have a CA above them they can both trust, so they must carry out cross-certification. *Cross-certification* is the process undertaken by CAs to establish a trust relationship in which they rely upon each other's digital certificates and public keys as if they had issued them themselves. When this is set up, a CA for one company can validate digital certificates from the other company and vice versa.

The CA is responsible for creating and handing out certificates, maintaining them, and revoking them if necessary. Revocation is handled by the CA, and the revoked certificate information is stored on a *certificate revocation list (CRL)*. This is a list of every certificate that has been revoked. This list is maintained and periodically updated by the issuing CA. A certificate may be revoked because the key holder's private key was compromised or because the CA discovered the certificate was issued to the wrong person. An analogy for the use of a CRL is how a driver's license is used by a police officer. If an officer pulls over Sean for speeding, the officer will ask to see Sean's license. The officer will then run a check on the license to find out if Sean is wanted for any other infractions of the law and to verify the license has not expired. The same thing happens when a person compares a certificate to a CRL. If the certificate became invalid for some reason, the CRL is the mechanism for the CA to let others know this information.

NOTE CRLs are the thorn in the side of many PKI implementations. They are challenging for a long list of reasons. By default, web browsers do not check a CRL to ensure that a certificate is not revoked. So when you are setting up a secure connection to an e-commerce site, you could be relying on a certificate that has actually been revoked. Not good.

The *Online Certificate Status Protocol (OCSP)* is being used more and more rather than the cumbersome CRL approach. When using just a CRL, either the user's browser must check a central CRL to find out if the certification has been revoked, or the CA has to continually push out CRL values to the clients to ensure they have an updated CRL. If OCSP is implemented, it does this work automatically in the background. It carries out real-time validation of a certificate and reports back to the user whether the certificate is valid, invalid, or unknown. OCSP checks the CRL that is maintained by the CA. So the CRL is still being used, but now we have a protocol developed specifically to check the CRL during a certificate validation process.

Registration Authorities

The previously introduced *registration authority (RA)* performs the certification registration duties. The RA establishes and confirms the identity of an individual, initiates the certification process with a CA on behalf of an end user, and performs certificate life-cycle management functions. The RA cannot issue certificates, but can act as a broker between the user and the CA. When users need new certificates, they make requests to the RA, and the RA verifies all necessary identification information before allowing a request to go to the CA. In many cases, the role of CA and RA are fulfilled by different teams in the same organization.

PKI Steps

Now that you know some of the main pieces of a PKI and how they actually work together, let's walk through an example. First, suppose that John needs to obtain a digital certificate for himself so he can participate in a PKI. The following are the steps to do so:

1. John makes a request to the RA.
2. The RA requests certain identification information from John, such as a copy of his driver's license, his phone number, his address, and other identifying information.
3. Once the RA receives the required information from John and verifies it, the RA sends his certificate request to the CA.

4. The CA creates a certificate with John's public key and identity information embedded. (The private/public key pair is generated either by the CA or on John's machine, which depends on the systems' configurations. If it is created at the CA, his private key needs to be sent to him by secure means. In most cases, the user generates this pair and sends in his public key during the registration process.)

Now John is registered and can participate in a PKI. John and Diane decide they want to communicate, so they take the following steps, shown in Figure 8-20:

1. John requests Diane's public key from a public directory.
2. The directory, sometimes called a repository, sends Diane's digital certificate.
3. John verifies the digital certificate and extracts her public key. John uses this public key to encrypt a session key that will be used to encrypt their messages. John sends the encrypted session key to Diane. John also sends his certificate, containing his public key, to Diane.
4. When Diane receives John's certificate, she verifies that she trusts the CA that digitally signed it. Diane trusts this CA and, after she verifies the certificate, decrypts the session key John sent her using her private key. Now, both John and Diane can communicate securely using symmetric key encryption and the shared session key.

A PKI may be made up of the following entities and functions:

- Certification authority
- Registration authority
- Certificate repository
- Certificate revocation system

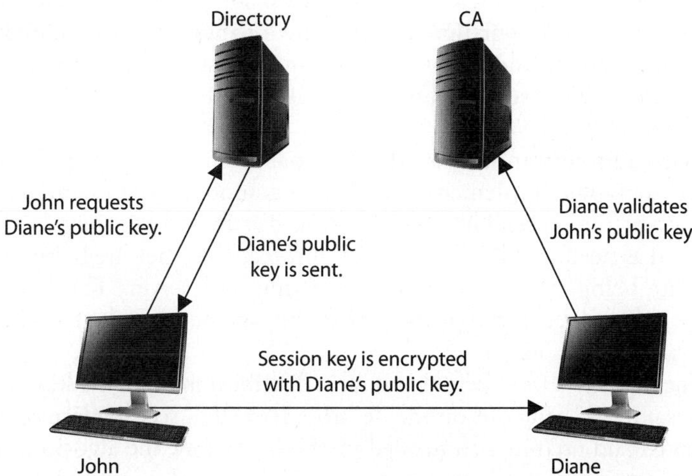
Directory
CA
John requests
Diane's public key.
Diane's public
key is sent.
Diane validates
John's public key.
Session key is encrypted
with Diane's public key.
John
Diane

Figure 8-20 CA and user relationships

- Key backup and recovery system
- Automatic key update
- Management of key histories
- Timestamping
- Client-side software

PKI supplies the following security services:

- Confidentiality
- Access control
- Integrity
- Authentication
- Nonrepudiation

A PKI must retain a key history, which keeps track of all the old and current public keys that have been used by individual users. For example, if Kevin encrypted a symmetric key with Dave's old public key, there should be a way for Dave to still access this data. This can only happen if the CA keeps a proper history of Dave's old certificates and keys.

NOTE Another important component that must be integrated into a PKI is a reliable time source that provides a way for secure timestamping. This comes into play when true nonrepudiation is required.

Key Management

Cryptography can be used as a security mechanism to provide confidentiality, integrity, and authentication, but not if the keys are compromised in any way. The keys can be captured, modified, corrupted, or disclosed to unauthorized individuals. Cryptography is based on a trust model. Individuals must trust each other to protect their own keys; trust the CA who issues the keys; and trust a server that holds, maintains, and distributes the keys.

Many administrators know that key management causes one of the biggest headaches in cryptographic implementation. There is more to key maintenance than using them to encrypt messages. The keys must be distributed securely to the right entities and updated as needed. They must also be protected as they are being transmitted and while they are being stored on each workstation and server. The keys must be generated, destroyed, and recovered properly. Key management can be handled through manual or automatic processes.

The keys are stored before and after distribution. When a key is distributed to a user, it does not just hang out on the desktop. It needs a secure place within the file system to be stored and used in a controlled method. The key, the algorithm that will use the key, configurations, and parameters are stored in a module that also needs to be protected.

If an attacker is able to obtain these components, she could masquerade as another user and decrypt, read, and re-encrypt messages not intended for her.

The Kerberos authentication protocol (which we will describe in Chapter 17) uses a Key Distribution Center (KDC) to store, distribute, and maintain cryptographic session and secret keys. This provides an automated method of key distribution. The computer that wants to access a service on another computer requests access via the KDC. The KDC then generates a session key to be used between the requesting computer and the computer providing the requested resource or service. The automation of this process reduces the possible errors that can happen through a manual process, but if the KDC gets compromised in any way, then all the computers and their services are affected and possibly compromised.

In some instances, keys are still managed through manual means. Unfortunately, although many organizations use cryptographic keys, they rarely, if ever, change them, either because of the hassle of key management or because the network administrator is already overtaxed with other tasks or does not realize the task actually needs to take place. The frequency of use of a cryptographic key has a direct correlation to how often the key should be changed. The more a key is used, the more likely it is to be captured and compromised. If a key is used infrequently, then this risk drops dramatically. The necessary level of security and the frequency of use can dictate the frequency of key updates. A mom-and-pop diner might only change its cryptography keys every month, whereas an information warfare military unit might change them daily. The important thing is to change the keys using a secure method.

Key management is the most challenging part of cryptography and also the most crucial. It is one thing to develop a very complicated and complex algorithm and key method, but if the keys are not securely stored and transmitted, it does not really matter how strong the algorithm is.

Key Management Principles

Keys should not be in cleartext outside the cryptography device. As stated previously, many cryptography algorithms are known publicly, which puts more stress on protecting the secrecy of the key. If attackers know how the actual algorithm works, in many cases, all they need to figure out is the key to compromise a system. This is why keys should not be available in cleartext—the key is what brings secrecy to encryption.

These steps, and all of key distribution and maintenance, should be automated and hidden from the user. These processes should be integrated into software or the operating system. It only adds complexity and opens the doors for more errors when processes are done manually and depend upon end users to perform certain functions.

Keys are at risk of being lost, destroyed, or corrupted. Backup copies should be available and easily accessible when required. If data is encrypted and then the user accidentally loses the necessary key to decrypt it, this information would be lost forever if there were not a backup key to save the day. The application being used for cryptography may have key recovery options, or it may require copies of the keys to be kept in a secure place.

Different scenarios highlight the need for key recovery or backup copies of keys. For example, if Bob has possession of all the critical bid calculations, stock value information, and corporate trend analysis needed for tomorrow's senior executive presentation, and Bob has an unfortunate confrontation with a bus, someone is going to need to access this data after the funeral. As another example, if an employee leaves the company and has encrypted important documents on her computer before departing, the company would probably still want to access that data later. Similarly, if the vice president did not know that running a large magnet over the USB drive that holds his private key was not a good idea, he would want his key replaced immediately instead of listening to a lecture about electromagnetic fields and how they rewrite sectors on media.

Of course, having more than one key increases the chance of disclosure, so an organization needs to decide whether it wants to have key backups and, if so, what precautions to put into place to protect them properly. An organization can choose to have multiparty control for emergency key recovery. This means that if a key must be recovered, more than one person is needed for this process. The key recovery process could require two or more other individuals to present their private keys or authentication information. These individuals should not all be members of the IT department. There should be a member from management, an individual from security, and one individual from the IT department, for example. All of these requirements reduce the potential for abuse and would require collusion for fraudulent activities to take place.

Rules for Keys and Key Management

Key management is critical for proper protection. The following are responsibilities that fall under the key management umbrella:

- The key length should be long enough to provide the necessary level of protection.
- Keys should be stored and transmitted by secure means.
- Keys should be random, and the algorithm should use the full spectrum of the keyspace.
- The key's lifetime should correspond with the sensitivity of the data it is protecting. (Less secure data may allow for a longer key lifetime, whereas more sensitive data might require a shorter key lifetime.)
- The more the key is used, the shorter its lifetime should be.
- Keys should be backed up or escrowed in case of emergencies.
- Keys should be properly destroyed when their lifetime comes to an end.

Key escrow is a process or entity that can recover lost or corrupted cryptographic keys; thus, it is a common component of key recovery operations. When two or more entities are required to reconstruct a key for key recovery processes, this is known as *multiparty key recovery*. Multiparty key recovery implements dual control, meaning that two or more people have to be involved with a critical task.

Of course, this creates a bit of a problem if two (or three, or whatever) people are required for key recovery but one of them is missing. What do you do at a point of crisis if Carlos is one of the people required to recover the key but he's on a cruise in the middle of the Pacific Ocean? To solve this, you can use an approach called *m-of-n control* (or *quorum authentication*), in which you designate a group of (*n*) people as recovery agents

> **The Web of Trust**
> An alternative approach to using certificate authorities is called the *web of trust*, which was introduced by Phil Zimmermann for use in Pretty Good Privacy (PGP) cryptosystems. In a web of trust, people sign each other's certificates if they have verified their identity and trust them. This can happen, for example, at key-signing parties where people meet and sign each other's certificates. Thereafter, anyone who has signed a certificate can either share it with others as trusted or subsequently vouch for that certificate if asked to. This decentralized approach is popular among many security practitioners but is not practical for most commercial applications.

and only need a subset (*m*) of them for key recovery. So, you could choose three people in your organization (n = 3) as key recovery agents, but only two of them (m = 2) would need to participate in the actual recovery process for it to work. In this case, your m-of-n control would be 2-of-3.

NOTE More detailed information on key management best practices can be found in NIST Special Publication 800-57, Part 1 Revision 5, *Recommendation for Key Management: Part 1 – General.*

Attacks Against Cryptography

We've referred multiple times in this chapter to adversaries attacking our cryptosystems, but how exactly do they carry out those attacks? Sometimes, it's as simple as listening to network traffic and picking up whatever messages they can. Eavesdropping and sniffing data as it passes over a network are considered *passive attacks* because the attacker is not affecting the protocol, algorithm, key, message, or any parts of the encryption system. Passive attacks are hard to detect, so in most cases methods are put in place to try to prevent them rather than to detect and stop them.

Altering messages, modifying system files, and masquerading as another individual are acts that are considered *active attacks* because the attacker is actually doing something instead of sitting back and gathering data. Passive attacks are usually used to gain information prior to carrying out an active attack.

The common attack vectors in cryptography are key and algorithm, implementation, data, and people. We should assume that the attacker knows what algorithm we are using and that the attacker has access to all encrypted text. The following sections address some active attacks that relate to cryptography.

Key and Algorithm Attacks

The first class of attack against cryptosystems targets the algorithms themselves or the keyspace they use. Except for brute forcing, these approaches require a significant level of knowledge of the mathematical principles underpinning cryptography. They are relatively rare among attackers, with the possible exception of state actors with significant intelligence capabilities. They are, however, much more common when a new algorithm is presented to the cryptographic community for analysis prior to their adoption.

Brute Force

Sometimes, all it takes to break a cryptosystem is to systematically try all possible keys until you find the right one. This approach is called a *brute-force* attack. Of course, cryptographers know this and develop systems that are resistant to brute forcing. They do the math and ensure that brute forcing takes so long to work that it is computationally infeasible for adversaries to try this approach and succeed. But there's a catch: computational power and, importantly, improved techniques to more efficiently use it are growing each year. We can make assumptions about where these capabilities will be in five or ten years, but we really can't be sure how long it'll be until that key that seemed strong enough all of a sudden is crackable through brute force.

Ciphertext-Only Attacks

In a *ciphertext-only attack*, the attacker has the ciphertext of one or more messages, each of which has been encrypted using the same encryption algorithm and key. The attacker's goal is to discover the key used in the encryption process. Once the attacker figures out the key, she can decrypt all other messages encrypted with the same key.

A ciphertext-only attack is the most common type of active attack because it is very easy to get ciphertext by sniffing someone's traffic, but it is the hardest attack to carry out successfully because the attacker has so little information about the encryption process. Unless the attackers have nation-state resources at their disposal, it is very unlikely that this approach will work.

Known-Plaintext Attacks

In a *known-plaintext attack*, the attacker has the plaintext and corresponding ciphertext of one or more messages and wants to discover the key used to encrypt the message(s) so that he can decipher and read other messages. This attack can leverage known patterns in message composition. For example, many corporate e-mail messages end with a standard confidentiality disclaimer, which the attacker can easily acquire by getting an unencrypted e-mail from anyone in that organization. In this instance, the attacker has some of the plaintext (the data that is the same on each message) and can capture encrypted messages, knowing that some of the ciphertext corresponds to this known plaintext. Rather than having to cryptanalyze the entire message, the attacker can focus on that part of it that is known. Some of the first encryption algorithms used in computer networks would generate the same ciphertext when encrypting the same plaintext with the same key. Known-plaintext attacks were used by the United States against the Germans and the Japanese during World War II.

Chosen-Plaintext Attacks

In a *chosen-plaintext attack*, the attacker has the plaintext and ciphertext, but can choose the plaintext that gets encrypted to see the corresponding ciphertext. This gives the attacker more power and possibly a deeper understanding of the way the encryption process works so that she can gather more information about the key being used. Once the attacker discovers the key, she can decrypt other messages encrypted with that key.

How would this be carried out? Doris can e-mail a message to you that she thinks you not only will believe, but will also panic about, encrypt, and send to someone else. Suppose Doris sends you an e-mail that states, "The meaning of life is 42." You may think you have received an important piece of information that should be concealed from others, everyone except your friend Bob, of course. So you encrypt Doris's message and send it to Bob. Meanwhile Doris is sniffing your traffic and now has a copy of the plaintext of the message, because she wrote it, and a copy of the ciphertext.

Chosen-Ciphertext Attacks

In a *chosen-ciphertext attack*, the attacker can choose the ciphertext to be decrypted and has access to the resulting decrypted plaintext. Again, the goal is to figure out the key. This is a harder attack to carry out compared to the previously mentioned attacks, and the attacker may need to have control of the system that contains the cryptosystem.

NOTE All of these attacks have a derivative form, the names of which are the same except for putting the word "adaptive" in front of them, such as adaptive chosen-plaintext and adaptive chosen-ciphertext. What this means is that the attacker can carry out one of these attacks and, depending upon what she gleaned from that first attack, modify her next attack. This is the process of reverse-engineering or cryptanalysis attacks: using what you learned to improve your next attack.

Differential Cryptanalysis

This type of attack also has the goal of uncovering the key that was used for encryption purposes. A *differential cryptanalysis attack* looks at ciphertext pairs generated by encryption of plaintext pairs with specific differences and analyzes the effect and result

Public vs. Secret Algorithms

The public mainly uses algorithms that are known and understood versus the secret algorithms where the internal processes and functions are not released to the public. In general, cryptographers in the public sector feel as though the strongest and best-engineered algorithms are the ones released for peer review and public scrutiny, because a thousand brains are better than five, and many times some smarty-pants within the public population can find problems within an algorithm that the developers did not think of. This is why vendors and companies have competitions to see if anyone can break their code and encryption processes. If someone does break it, that means the developers must go back to the drawing board and strengthen this or that piece.

Not all algorithms are released to the public, such as the ones developed by the NSA. Because the sensitivity level of what the NSA encrypts is so important, it wants as much of the process to be as secret as possible. The fact that the NSA does not release its algorithms for public examination and analysis does not mean its algorithms are weak. Its algorithms are developed, reviewed, and tested by many of the top cryptographic pros around, and are of very high quality.

of those differences. One such attack was effectively used in 1990 against the Data Encryption Standard, but turned out to also work against other block algorithms.

The attacker takes two messages of plaintext and follows the changes that take place to the blocks as they go through the different S-boxes. (Each message is being encrypted with the same key.) The differences identified in the resulting ciphertext values are used to map probability values to different possible key values. The attacker continues this process with several more sets of messages and reviews the common key probability values. One key value will continue to show itself as the most probable key used in the encryption processes. Since the attacker chooses the different plaintext messages for this attack, it is considered a type of chosen-plaintext attack.

Frequency Analysis

A *frequency analysis*, also known as a *statistical attack*, identifies statistically significant patterns in the ciphertext generated by a cryptosystem. For example, the number of zeroes may be significantly higher than the number of ones. This could show that the pseudorandom number generator (PRNG) in use may be biased. If keys are taken directly from the output of the PRNG, then the distribution of keys would also be biased. The statistical knowledge about the bias could be used to reduce the search time for the keys.

Implementation Attacks

All of the attacks we have covered thus far have been based mainly on the mathematics of cryptography. We all know that there is a huge difference between the theory of how something should work and how the widget that comes off the assembly line actually works. *Implementation flaws* are system development defects that could compromise a real system, and *implementation attacks* are the techniques used to exploit these flaws. With all the emphasis on developing and testing strong algorithms for encryption, it should come as no surprise that cryptosystems are far likelier to have implementation flaws than to have algorithmic flaws.

One of the best-known implementation flaws is the Heartbleed bug discovered in 2014 in the OpenSSL cryptographic software library estimated to have been in use by two-thirds of the world's servers. Essentially, a programmer used an insecure function call that allowed an attacker to copy arbitrary amounts of data from the victim computer's memory, including encryption keys, usernames, and passwords.

There are multiple approaches to finding implementation flaws, whether you are an attacker trying to exploit them or a defender trying to keep them from being exploited. In the sections that follow, we look at some of the most important techniques to keep in mind.

Source Code Analysis

The first, and probably most common, approach to finding implementation flaws in cryptosystems is to perform *source code analysis*, ideally as part of a large team of researchers, and look for bugs. Through a variety of software auditing techniques (which we will cover in Chapter 25), source code analysis examines each line of code and branch of execution to determine whether it is vulnerable to exploitation. This is most practical when the code is open source or you otherwise have access to its source. Sadly, as with Heartbleed, this approach can fail to reveal major flaws for many years.

Reverse Engineering

Another approach to discovering implementation flaws in cryptosystems involves taking a product and tearing it apart to see how it works. This is called *reverse engineering* and can be applied to both software and hardware products. When you buy software, you normally get binary executable programs, so you can't do the source code analysis discussed in the previous section. However, there are a number of ways in which you can disassemble those binaries and get code that is pretty close to the source code. Software reverse engineering requires a lot more effort and skill than regular source code analysis, but it is more common that most would think.

A related practice, which applies to hardware and firmware implementations, involves something called *hardware reverse engineering*. This means the researcher is directly probing integrated circuit (IC) chips and other electronic components. In some cases, chips are actually peeled apart layer by layer to show internal interconnections and even individual bits that are set in memory structures. This approach oftentimes requires destroying the device as it is dissected, probed, and analyzed. The effort, skill, and expense required can sometimes yield implementation flaws that would be difficult or impossible to find otherwise.

Side-Channel Attacks

Using plaintext and ciphertext involves high-powered mathematical tools that are needed to uncover the key used in the encryption process. But what if we took a different approach? What if we paid attention to what happens around the cryptosystem as it does its business? As an analogy, burglars can unlock a safe and determine its combination by feeling the change in resistance as they spin the dial and listening to the mechanical clicks inside the lock.

Similarly, in cryptography, we can review facts and infer the value of an encryption key. For example, we could detect how much power consumption is used for encryption and decryption (the fluctuation of electronic voltage). We could also intercept the radiation emissions released and then calculate how long the processes took. Looking around the cryptosystem, or its attributes and characteristics, is different from looking into the cryptosystem and trying to defeat it through mathematical computations.

If Omar wants to figure out what you do for a living, but he doesn't want you to know he is doing this type of reconnaissance work, he won't ask you directly. Instead, he will find out when you go to work and when you come home, the types of clothing you wear, the items you carry, and whom you talk to—or he can just follow you to work. These are examples of *side channels*.

So, in cryptography, gathering "outside" information with the goal of uncovering the encryption key is just another way of attacking a cryptosystem. An attacker could measure power consumption, radiation emissions, and the time it takes for certain types of data processing. With this information, he can work backward by reverse-engineering the process to uncover an encryption key or sensitive data. A power attack reviews the amount of heat released. This type of attack has been successful in uncovering confidential information from smart cards.

In 1995, RSA private keys were uncovered by measuring the relative time cryptographic operations took. This type of side-channel attack is also called a *timing attack* because it uses time measurements to determine the inner workings, states, and even data flows within a cryptosystem. Timing attacks can also result in theft of sensitive information, including keys. Although the Meltdown and Spectre attacks of 2017 were not technically examples of cryptanalysis, they could be used to steal keys and are probably the best-known examples of timing attacks.

The idea is that instead of attacking a device head on, just watch how it performs to figure out how it works. In biology, scientists can choose to carry out a noninvasive experiment, which involves watching an organism eat, sleep, mate, and so on. This type of approach learns about the organism through understanding its behaviors instead of killing it and looking at it from the inside out.

Fault Injection

Cryptanalysts can deliberately introduce conditions that are designed to cause the system to fail in some way. This can be done in connection with one of the previous implementation techniques, or on its own. *Fault injection attacks* attempt to cause errors in a cryptosystem in an attempt to recover or infer the encryption key. Though this attack is fairly rare, it received a lot of attention in 2001 after it was shown to be effective after only one injection against the RSA using Chinese Remainder Theorem (RSA-CRT). According to some experts, a fault injection attack is a special case of a side-channel attack.

Other Attacks

Unless you or your adversary are skilled cryptanalysts or are employed by a national intelligence organization, you are fairly unlikely to be on the receiving end of one of the previous attacks. You may, as happened with Heartbleed, be caught up in a broader attack, however. We now turn our attention to a set of attacks that are much more likely to be targeted against you or your organization.

Replay Attacks

A big concern in distributed environments is the *replay attack*, in which an attacker captures some type of data and resubmits it with the hopes of fooling the receiving device into thinking it is legitimate information. Many times, the data captured and resubmitted is authentication information, and the attacker is trying to authenticate herself as someone else to gain unauthorized access.

Pass the hash is a well-known replay attack that targets Microsoft Windows Active Directory (AD) single sign-on environments. As we will explore more deeply in Chapters 16 and 17, *single sign-on (SSO)* is any authentication approach that requires the user to authenticate only once and then automatically provides access to network resources as requested without manual user reauthentication. Microsoft implements SSO by storing a hash of the user password locally and then automatically using that for future service requests without any user interaction. The Local Security Authority Subsystem Service (LSASS) is a process in Microsoft Windows that is responsible for verifying user logins, handling password changes, and managing access tokens such as password hashes. Any user with local admin rights can dump LSASS memory from a Windows computer and recover password hashes for any user who has recently logged into that system.

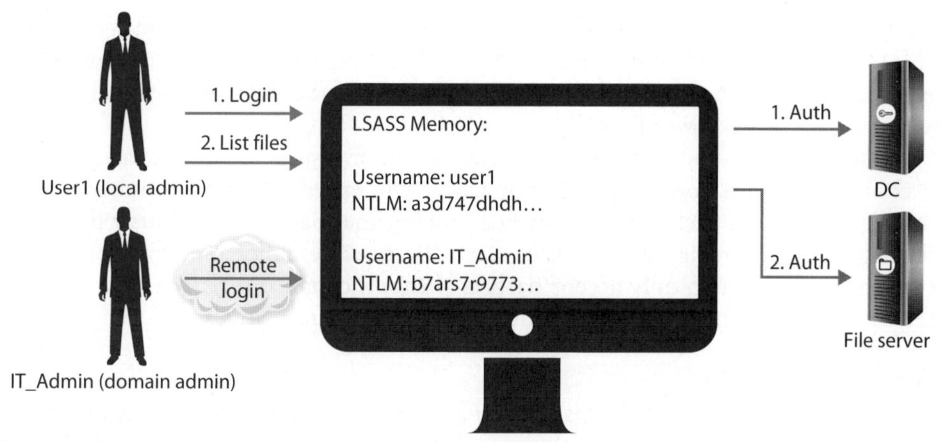

Figure 8-21 Single sign-on in Microsoft Windows Active Directory

In the example shown in Figure 8-21, User1 logs into the system locally. LSASS authenticates the user with the domain controller (DC) and then stores the username and New Technology LAN Manager (NTLM) password hash in memory for future use. User1 later browses files on the file server and, rather than having to reenter credentials, LSASS authenticates User1 automatically with the file server using the cached username and hash. A domain admin has also logged in remotely to update the host, so her username and hash are cached in memory, too.

Now, suppose an attacker sends a malicious attachment to User1, who then opens it and compromises the host, as shown in Figure 8-22. The attacker can now interact

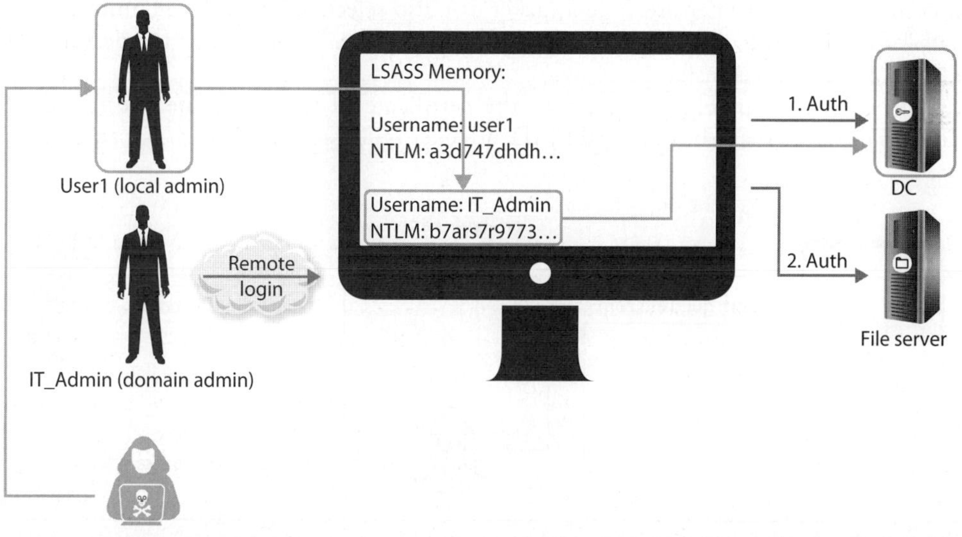

Figure 8-22 Pass-the-hash attack

with the compromised system using User1's permissions and, because that user is a local admin, is able to dump hashes from LSASS memory. Now the attacker has the hash of the domain admin's password, which grants him access to the domain controller without having to crack any passwords at all.

Timestamps and sequence numbers are two countermeasures to replay attacks. Packets can contain sequence numbers, so each machine will expect a specific number on each receiving packet. If a packet has a sequence number that has been previously used, that is an indication of a replay attack. Packets can also be timestamped. A threshold can be set on each computer to only accept packets within a certain timeframe. If a packet is received that is past this threshold, it can help identify a replay attack.

Man-in-the-Middle

Hashes are not the only useful things you can intercept if you can monitor network traffic. If you can't compromise the algorithms or implementations of cryptosystems, the next best thing is to insert yourself into the process by which secure connections are established. In *man-in-the-middle (MitM)* attacks, threat actors intercept an outbound secure connection request from clients and relay their own requests to the intended servers, terminating both and acting as a proxy. This allows attackers to defeat encrypted channels without having to find vulnerabilities in the algorithms or their implementations.

Figure 8-23 shows a MitM attack used in a phishing campaign. First, the attacker sends an e-mail message enticing the victim to click a link that looks like a legitimate one but leads to a server controlled by the attacker instead. The attacker then sends her own request to the server and establishes a secure connection to it. Next, the attacker completes the connection requested by the client but using her own certificate instead of the intended server's. The attacker is now invisibly sitting in the middle of two separate, secure connections. From this vantage point, the attacker can either relay information from one end to the other, perhaps copying some of it (e.g., credentials, sensitive documents, etc.) for later use. The attacker can also selectively modify the information sent from one end to the other. For example, the attacker could change the destination account for a funds transfer.

You will notice in Figure 8-23 that the certificate of the legitimate site (goodsite .com) is different than the one used by the attacker (g00dsite.com, which has two zeroes

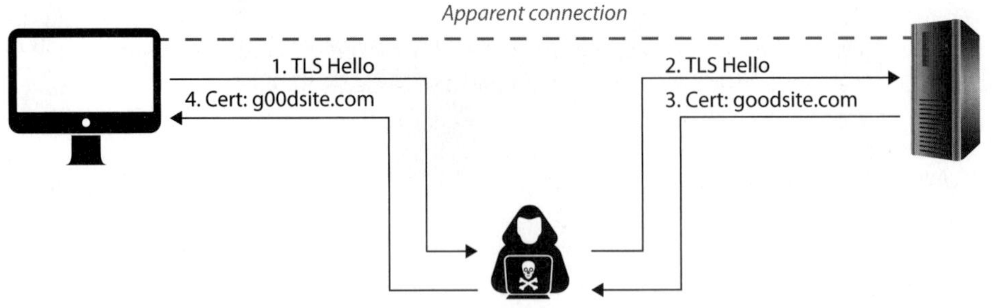

Figure 8-23 A web-based man-in-the-middle attack

instead of letters "o"). The attacker needs to present her own certificate because she needs the corresponding private key to complete the connection with the client and be able to share the secret session key. There are a few ways in which the attacker can make this less noticeable to the user. The first is to send the link to the server in an e-mail to the user. The HTML representation of the link is the legitimate site, while the actual (hidden) link points to the almost identical but malicious domain. A more sophisticated attacker can use a variety of techniques to compromise DNS resolution and have the client go to the malicious site instead of the legitimate one. Either way, the browser is likely to generate a warning letting the user know that something is not right. Fortunately for the attackers (and unfortunately for us), most users either do not pay attention to or actively disregard such warnings.

Social Engineering Attacks

It should come as no surprise that people can be fooled by clever attackers who can trick them into providing their cryptographic key material through various social engineering attack types. As discussed in earlier chapters, social engineering attacks are carried out on people with the goal of tricking them into divulging some type of sensitive information that can be used by the attacker. For example, an attacker may convince a victim that the attacker is a security administrator who requires the cryptographic data for some type of operational effort. The attacker could then use the data to decrypt and gain access to sensitive data. Social engineering attacks can be carried out through deception, persuasion, coercion (rubber-hose cryptanalysis), or bribery (purchase-key attack).

Ransomware

Ransomware is a type of malware that typically encrypts victims' files and holds them ransom until a payment is made to an account controlled by the attacker. When the victim pays, the attacker usually (but not always) provides the secret key needed to decrypt the files. It is not so much an attack against cryptography as it is an attack *employing* cryptography. Ransomware attacks are typically delivered through a phishing e-mail that contains a malicious attachment. After the initial compromise, however, the ransomware may be able to move laterally across the victim's network, infecting other hosts.

Chapter Review

Cryptographic algorithms provide the underlying tools to most security protocols used in today's infrastructures. They are, therefore, an integral tool for cybersecurity professionals. The cryptographic algorithms work off of mathematical functions and provide various types of functionality and levels of security. Every algorithm has strengths and weaknesses, so we tend to use them in hybrid systems such as public key infrastructures. Symmetric and asymmetric key cryptography, working with hashing functions, provide a solid foundation on which to build the security architectures we'll discuss in the next chapter.

Of course, there are many ways to attack these cryptosystems. Advanced adversaries may find vulnerabilities in the underlying algorithms. Others may target the manner in which these algorithms are implemented in software and hardware. Most attackers, however, simply attempt to bypass cryptography by replaying authentication data, inserting themselves in the middle of a trusted communications channel, or simply targeting the people involved through social engineering.

Quick Review

- Cryptography is the practice of storing and transmitting information in a form that only authorized parties can understand.
- A readable message is in a form called plaintext, and once it is encrypted, it is in a form called ciphertext.
- Cryptographic algorithms are the mathematical rules that dictate the functions of enciphering and deciphering.
- Cryptanalysis is the name collectively given to techniques that aim to weaken or defeat cryptography.
- Nonrepudiation is a service that ensures the sender cannot later falsely deny sending a message.
- The range of possible keys is referred to as the keyspace. A larger keyspace and the full use of the keyspace allow for more-random keys to be created. This provides more protection.
- The two basic types of encryption mechanisms used in symmetric ciphers are substitution and transposition. Substitution ciphers change a character (or bit) out for another, while transposition ciphers scramble the characters (or bits).
- A polyalphabetic cipher uses more than one alphabet to defeat frequency analysis.
- A key is a random string of bits inserted into an encryption algorithm. The result determines what encryption functions will be carried out on a message and in what order.
- In symmetric key algorithms, the sender and receiver use the same key for encryption and decryption purposes.
- In asymmetric key algorithms, the sender and receiver use different keys for encryption and decryption purposes.
- The biggest challenges in employing symmetric key encryption are secure key distribution and scalability. However, symmetric key algorithms perform much faster than asymmetric key algorithms.
- Symmetric key algorithms can provide confidentiality, but not authentication or nonrepudiation.
- Examples of symmetric key algorithms include AES and ChaCha20.
- Asymmetric algorithms are typically used to encrypt keys, and symmetric algorithms are typically used to encrypt bulk data.
- Asymmetric key algorithms are much slower than symmetric key algorithms but can provide authentication and nonrepudiation services.
- Examples of asymmetric key algorithms include RSA, ECC, and DSA.

- Two main types of symmetric algorithms are stream ciphers and block ciphers. Stream ciphers use a keystream generator and encrypt a message one bit at a time. A block cipher divides the message into groups of bits and encrypts them.
- Many algorithms are publicly known, so the secret part of the process is the key. The key provides the necessary randomization to encryption.
- RSA is an asymmetric algorithm developed by Rivest, Shamir, and Adleman and is the de facto standard for digital signatures.
- Elliptic curve cryptosystems (ECCs) are used as asymmetric algorithms and can provide digital signatures, secure key distribution, and encryption functionality. ECCs use fewer resources, which makes them better for wireless device and cell phone encryption use.
- Quantum cryptography is the field of scientific study that applies quantum mechanics to perform cryptographic functions. The most immediate application of this field is quantum key distribution (QKD), which generates and securely distributes encryption keys of any length between two parties.
- When symmetric and asymmetric key algorithms are used together, this is called a hybrid system. The asymmetric algorithm encrypts the symmetric key, and the symmetric key encrypts the data.
- A session key is a symmetric key used by the sender and receiver of messages for encryption and decryption purposes. The session key is only good while that communication session is active and then it is destroyed.
- A public key infrastructure (PKI) is a framework of programs, procedures, communication protocols, and public key cryptography that enables a diverse group of individuals to communicate securely.
- A certificate authority (CA) is a trusted third party that generates and maintains user certificates, which hold their public keys.
- The CA uses a certification revocation list (CRL) to keep track of revoked certificates.
- A certificate is the mechanism the CA uses to associate a public key to a person's identity.
- A registration authority (RA) validates the user's identity and then sends the request for a certificate to the CA. The RA cannot generate certificates.
- A one-way function is a mathematical function that is easier to compute in one direction than in the opposite direction.
- RSA is based on a one-way function that factors large numbers into prime numbers. Only the private key knows how to use the trapdoor and how to decrypt messages that were encrypted with the corresponding public key.
- Hashing algorithms provide data integrity only.
- When a hash algorithm is applied to a message, it produces a message digest, and this value is signed with a private key to produce a digital signature.
- Some examples of hashing algorithms include SHA-1, SHA-2, SHA-3, and MD5.
- SHA produces a 160-bit hash value and is used in DSS.

- A birthday attack is an attack on hashing functions through brute force. The attacker tries to create two messages with the same hashing value.
- A one-time pad uses a pad with random values that are XORed against the message to produce ciphertext. The pad is at least as long as the message itself and is used once and then discarded.
- A digital signature is the result of a user signing a hash value with a private key. It provides authentication, data integrity, and nonrepudiation. The act of signing is the actual encryption of the value with the private key.
- Key management is one of the most challenging pieces of cryptography. It pertains to creating, maintaining, distributing, and destroying cryptographic keys.
- Brute-force attacks against cryptosystems systematically try all possible keys against given ciphertext in hopes of guessing the key that was used.
- Ciphertext-only attacks against cryptosystems involve analyzing the ciphertext of one or more messages encrypted with the same algorithm and key in order to discover the key that was used.
- In a known-plaintext attack, the attacker has the plaintext and corresponding ciphertext of one or more messages and wants to discover the key that was used.
- A chosen-plaintext attack is like a known-plaintext attack but the attacker chooses the plaintext that gets encrypted to see the corresponding ciphertext.
- A chosen-ciphertext attack is like a chosen-plaintext attack except that the attacker chooses the ciphertext and then gets to see the corresponding decrypted plaintext.
- A frequency analysis, also known as a statistical attack, identifies statistically significant patterns in the ciphertext generated by a cryptosystem.
- Implementation attacks are the techniques used to exploit defects in the implementation of a cryptosystem.
- Side-channel attacks analyze changes in the environment around a cryptosystem in an attempt to infer an encryption key whose processing causes those changes.
- Timing attacks are side-channel attacks that use time measurements to determine the inner workings, states, and even data flows within a cryptosystem.
- Fault injection attacks attempt to cause errors in a cryptosystem in an attempt to recover or infer the encryption key.
- In man-in-the-middle (MitM) attacks, threat actors intercept an outbound secure connection request from clients and relay their own requests to the intended servers, terminating both and acting as a proxy.
- Pass the hash is a type of attack against Microsoft Windows Active Directory in which the attacker resubmits cached authentication tokens to gain illicit access to resources.
- Ransomware is a type of malware that encrypts victims' files and holds them ransom until a payment is made to an account controlled by the attacker.

Questions

Please remember that these questions are formatted and asked in a certain way for a reason. Keep in mind that the CISSP exam is asking questions at a conceptual level. Questions may not always have the perfect answer, and the candidate is advised against always looking for the perfect answer. Instead, the candidate should look for the best answer in the list.

1. What is the goal of cryptanalysis?
   - **A.** To determine the strength of an algorithm
   - **B.** To increase the substitution functions in a cryptographic algorithm
   - **C.** To decrease the transposition functions in a cryptographic algorithm
   - **D.** To determine the permutations used
2. Why has the frequency of successful brute-force attacks increased?
   - **A.** The use of permutations and transpositions in algorithms has increased.
   - **B.** As algorithms get stronger, they get less complex, and thus more susceptible to attacks.
   - **C.** Processor speed and power have increased.
   - **D.** Key length reduces over time.
3. Which of the following is not a property or characteristic of a one-way hash function?
   - **A.** It converts a message of arbitrary length into a value of fixed length.
   - **B.** Given the digest value, finding the corresponding message should be computationally infeasible.
   - **C.** Deriving the same digest from two different messages should be impossible or rare.
   - **D.** It converts a message of fixed length to an arbitrary length value.
4. What would indicate that a message had been modified?
   - **A.** The public key has been altered.
   - **B.** The private key has been altered.
   - **C.** The message digest has been altered.
   - **D.** The message has been encrypted properly.
5. Which of the following is a U.S. federal government algorithm developed for creating secure message digests?
   - **A.** Data Encryption Algorithm
   - **B.** Digital Signature Standard
   - **C.** Secure Hash Algorithm
   - **D.** Data Signature Algorithm

6. What is an advantage of RSA over DSA?
   A. It can provide digital signature and encryption functionality.
   B. It uses fewer resources and encrypts faster because it uses symmetric keys.
   C. It is a block cipher rather than a stream cipher.
   D. It employs a one-time encryption pad.
7. What is used to create a digital signature?
   A. The receiver's private key
   B. The sender's public key
   C. The sender's private key
   D. The receiver's public key
8. Which of the following best describes a digital signature?
   A. A method of transferring a handwritten signature to an electronic document
   B. A method to encrypt confidential information
   C. A method to provide an electronic signature and encryption
   D. A method to let the receiver of the message prove the source and integrity of a message
9. Why would a certificate authority revoke a certificate?
   A. If the user's public key has become compromised
   B. If the user changed over to using the PEM model that uses a web of trust
   C. If the user's private key has become compromised
   D. If the user moved to a new location
10. Which of the following best describes a certificate authority?
    A. An organization that issues private keys and the corresponding algorithms
    B. An organization that validates encryption processes
    C. An organization that verifies encryption keys
    D. An organization that issues certificates
11. Which of the following is a true statement pertaining to data encryption when it is used to protect data?
    A. It verifies the integrity and accuracy of the data.
    B. It requires careful key management.
    C. It does not require much system overhead in resources.
    D. It requires keys to be escrowed.

12. What is the definition of an algorithm's work factor?
    A. The time it takes to encrypt and decrypt the same plaintext
    B. The time it takes to break the encryption
    C. The time it takes to implement 16 rounds of computation
    D. The time it takes to apply substitution functions
13. What is the primary purpose of using one-way hashing on user passwords?
    A. It minimizes the amount of primary and secondary storage needed to store passwords.
    B. It prevents anyone from reading passwords in plaintext.
    C. It avoids excessive processing required by an asymmetric algorithm.
    D. It prevents replay attacks.
14. Which of the following is based on the fact that it is hard to factor large numbers into two original prime numbers?
    A. ECC
    B. RSA
    C. SHA
    D. MD5
15. What is the name given to attacks that involve analyzing changes in the environment around a cryptosystem to infer the encryption key whose processing causes those changes?
    A. Side-channel attack
    B. Timing attack
    C. Implementation attack
    D. Fault injection attack

Answers

1. **A.** Cryptanalysis is the process of trying to reverse-engineer a cryptosystem, with the possible goal of uncovering the key used. Once this key is uncovered, all other messages encrypted with this key can be accessed. Cryptanalysis is carried out by the white hats to test the strength of the algorithm.
2. **C.** A brute-force attack is resource intensive. It tries all values until the correct one is obtained. As computers have more powerful processors added to them, attackers can carry out more powerful brute-force attacks.

3. **D.** A hashing algorithm will take a string of variable length (the message can be any size) and compute a fixed-length value. The fixed-length value is the message digest. The MD family creates the fixed-length value of 128 bits, and SHA creates one of 160 bits.
4. **C.** Hashing algorithms generate message digests to detect whether modification has taken place. The sender and receiver independently generate their own digests, and the receiver compares these values. If they differ, the receiver knows the message has been altered.
5. **C.** SHA was created to generate secure message digests. Digital Signature Standard (DSS) is the standard to create digital signatures, which dictates that SHA must be used. DSS also outlines the digital signature algorithms that can be used with SHA: RSA, DSA, and ECDSA.
6. **A.** RSA can be used for data encryption, key exchange, and digital signatures. DSA can be used only for digital signatures.
7. **C.** A digital signature is a message digest that has been encrypted with the sender's private key. A sender, or anyone else, should never have access to the receiver's private key.
8. **D.** A digital signature provides authentication (knowing who really sent the message), integrity (because a hashing algorithm is involved), and nonrepudiation (the sender cannot deny sending the message).
9. **C.** The reason a certificate is revoked is to warn others who use that person's public key that they should no longer trust the public key because, for some reason, that public key is no longer bound to that particular individual's identity. This could be because an employee left the company or changed his name and needed a new certificate, but most likely it is because the person's private key was compromised.
10. **D.** A registration authority (RA) accepts a person's request for a certificate and verifies that person's identity. Then the RA sends this request to a certificate authority (CA), which generates and maintains the certificate.
11. **B.** Data encryption always requires careful key management. Most algorithms are so strong today that it is much easier to go after key management than to launch a brute-force attack. Hashing algorithms are used for data integrity, encryption does require a good amount of resources, and keys do not have to be escrowed for encryption.
12. **B.** The work factor of a cryptosystem is the amount of time and resources necessary to break the cryptosystem or its encryption process. The goal is to make the work factor so high that an attacker could not be successful in breaking the algorithm or cryptosystem.
13. **B.** Passwords are usually run through a one-way hashing algorithm so that the actual password is not transmitted across the network or stored on a system in plaintext. This greatly reduces the risk of an attacker being able to obtain the actual password.

14. **B.** The RSA algorithm's security is based on the difficulty of factoring large numbers into their original prime numbers. This is a one-way function. Calculating the product is easier than identifying the prime numbers used to generate that product.
15. **A.** Side-channel attack is the best answer. The question could also describe a timing attack, which is a kind of side-channel attack, but because there is no specific mention of timing, this option is not the best answer. An argument could also be made for this being a fault injection attack but, again, there is no specific mention of the attacker deliberately trying to cause errors. This question is representative of the harder questions in the CISSP exam, which provide one or more answers that could be correct but are not the best ones.

CHAPTER 9

Security Architectures

This chapter presents the following:

- Threat modeling
- Security architecture design principles
- Security models
- Addressing security requirements
- Security capabilities of information systems

Security is a process, not a product.

—Bruce Schneier

Having discussed the various information system architectures (in Chapter 7) and cryptology (in Chapter 8), our next step is to put these together as we develop an enterprise security architecture. We already discussed the various frameworks for this in Chapter 4, so what we need to do now is to apply tried and true principles, models, and system capabilities. Before we do this, however, we will explore threat modeling in a fair amount of detail, since it informs everything else we do.

Threat Modeling

Before we can develop effective defenses, it is imperative to understand the assets that we value, as well as the threats against which we are protecting them. Though multiple definitions exist for the term, for the purposes of our discussion we define *threat modeling* as the process of describing probable adverse effects on our assets caused by specific threat sources. That's quite a mouthful, so let's break it down.

When we build a model of the threats we face, we want to ground them in reality, so it is important to only consider dangers that are reasonably likely to occur. To do otherwise would dilute our limited resources to the point of making us unable to properly defend ourselves. Next, we want to focus our work on the potential impact of those threats to organizational assets or, in other words, to things and people that are of value to the organization. Lastly, the model needs to specify the threat sources if we are to develop effective means to thwart them. We must understand their capabilities and motivations if we are to make sense of their actions.

Attack Trees

An *attack tree* is a graph showing how individual actions by attackers can be chained together to achieve their goals. This methodology is based on the observation that, typically, there are multiple ways to accomplish a given objective. For example, if a disgruntled employee wanted to steal the contents of the president's mailbox, she could accomplish this by either accessing the e-mail server, obtaining the password, or stealing the president's smartphone. Accessing the e-mail server could be accomplished by using administrative credentials or by hacking in. To get the credentials, she could use brute force or social engineering. The options available to the attacker create the branches in the tree, an example of which is shown in Figure 9-1. Each of the leaf nodes represents a specific condition that must be met in order for the parent node to be effective. For instance, to effectively obtain the mailbox credentials, the disgruntled employee could have stolen a network access token. Given that the employee has met the condition of having the credentials, she would then be able to steal the contents of the president's mailbox. A successful attack, then, is one in which the attacker traverses from a leaf node all the way to the root node at the top of the tree, which represents the ultimate objective.

NOTE The terms "attack chain" and "kill chain" are commonly used. They refer to a specific type of attack tree that has no branches and simply proceeds from one stage or action to the next. The attack tree is much more expressive in that it shows many ways in which an attacker can accomplish each objective.

Reduction Analysis

The generation of attack trees for an organization usually requires a large investment of resources. Each vulnerability-threat-attack triad can be described in detail using an attack tree, so you end up with as many trees as you do triads. To defeat each of the attacks

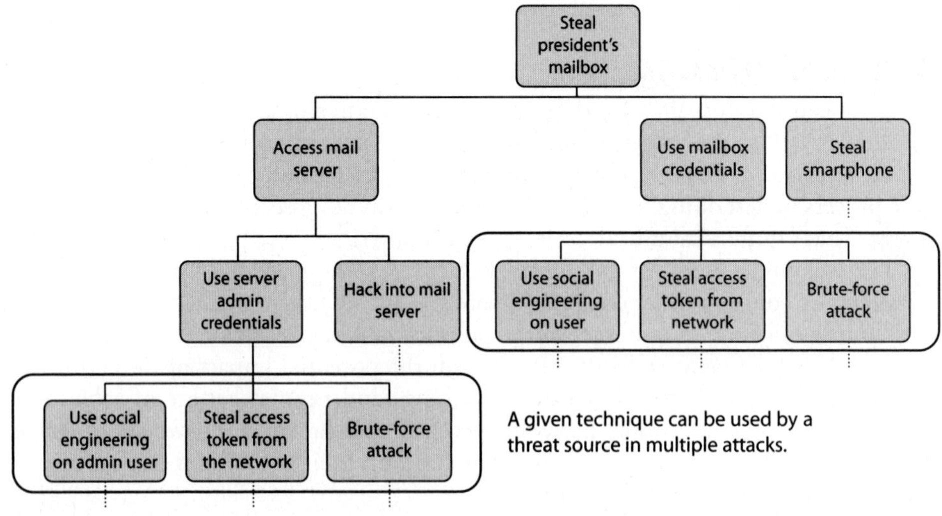

Figure 9-1 A simplified attack tree

you identify, you would typically need a control or countermeasure at each leaf node. Since one attack generates many leaf nodes, this has a multiplicative effect that could make it very difficult to justify the whole exercise. However, attack trees lend themselves to a methodology known as *reduction analysis*.

There are two aspects of reduction analysis in the context of threat modeling: one aspect is to reduce the number of attacks we have to consider, and the other is to reduce the threat posed by the attacks. The first aspect is evidenced by the commonalities in the example shown in Figure 9-1. To satisfy the conditions for logging into the mail server or the user's mailbox, an attacker can use the exact same three techniques. This means we can reduce the number of conditions we need to mitigate by finding these commonalities. When you consider that these three sample conditions apply to a variety of other attacks, you realize that we can very quickly cull the number of conditions to a manageable number.

The second aspect of reduction analysis is the identification of ways to mitigate or negate the attacks we've identified. This is where the use of attack trees can really benefit us. Recall that each tree has only one root but many leaves and internal nodes. The closer you are to the root when you implement a mitigation technique, the more leaf conditions you will defeat with that one control. This allows you to easily identify the most effective techniques to protect your entire organization. These techniques are typically called *controls* or *countermeasures*.

STRIDE

STRIDE is a threat modeling framework that evaluates a system's design using flow diagrams, system entities, and events related to a system. STRIDE is not an acronym, but a mnemonic for the six categories of security threats outlined in Table 9-1. STRIDE was developed in 1999 by Microsoft as a tool to help secure systems as they were being developed. STRIDE is among the most widely used threat-modeling frameworks and is suitable for application to logical and physical systems alike.

The Lockheed Martin Cyber Kill Chain

Threat modeling is really nothing new. It probably has its oldest roots in military operations, where it is used to anticipate the intent and actions of an enemy and then develop a plan to get inside their decision loop and defeat them. The term *kill chain* evolved to describe the process of identifying a target, determining the best way to engage it, amassing the required forces against it, engaging it, and destroying it. In 2011, Lockheed Martin released a paper defining a *Cyber Kill Chain* based on this methodology. It identifies the steps that threat actors generally must complete to achieve their objectives. This model specifies seven distinct stages of a cyberattack:

1. **Reconnaissance** The attacker selects a target, researches it, and attempts to identify vulnerabilities in the target network.
2. **Weaponization** The attacker either adapts an existing remote access malware weapon or creates a new one, tailored to one or more vulnerabilities identified in the previous step.

Threat	Property Affected	Definition	Example
Spoofing	Authentication	Impersonating someone or something else	An outside sender pretending to be an HR employee in an e-mail
Tampering	Integrity	Modifying data on disk, in memory, or elsewhere	A program modifying the contents of a critical system file
Repudiation	Nonrepudiation	Claiming to have not performed an action or to have no knowledge of who performed it	A user claiming that she did not receive a request
Information disclosure	Confidentiality	Exposing information to parties not authorized to see it	An analyst accidentally revealing the inner details of the network to outside parties
Denial of service	Availability	Denying or degrading service to legitimate users by exhausting resources needed for a service	A botnet flooding a website with thousands of requests a second, causing it to crash
Elevation of privilege	Authorization	Gaining capabilities without the proper authorization to do so	A user bypassing local restrictions to gain administrative access to a workstation

Table 9-1 STRIDE Threat Categories

3. **Delivery** The attacker transmits the weapon to the target (e.g., via e-mail attachments, links to malicious websites, or USB drives).
4. **Exploitation** The malware weapon triggers, which takes action on the target to exploit one or more vulnerabilities and compromise the host.
5. **Installation** The malware weapon installs an access point (e.g., backdoor) usable by the attacker.
6. **Command and Control** The malware enables the attacker to have "hands on the keyboard" persistent access to the target network.
7. **Actions on Objective** The attacker takes actions to achieve their goals, such as data exfiltration, data destruction, or encryption for ransom.

One of Lockheed Martin's key goals of developing this model was to allow defenders to map defensive measures to each stage and ensure that they have sufficient coverage to detect, deny, disrupt, degrade, deceive, or contain the attack. The earlier in the kill chain this is done, the better, because the adversary will not have attained their objective yet. Another key idea in the model is that of identifying indicators of adversarial activity at each stage of a cyberattack, which would allow defenders to detect the activities but also determine whether the defensive measures at a particular stage were effective. Though the Cyber Kill Chain is a high-level framework, it is one of the most commonly used ones for modeling threat activities.

The MITRE ATT&CK Framework

The MITRE Corporation developed a framework of adversarial tactics, techniques, and common knowledge called ATT&CK as a comprehensive matrix of tactics and techniques used by threat actors. It is a widely used tool to construct models of complex campaigns and operations using reusable common components. Like the Cyber Kill Chain, ATT&CK breaks down actions into (generally) sequential groupings called *tactics*, which can be mapped to those in the Lockheed Martin model. Each of the 14 tactics contains a number of *techniques* by which the adversary may achieve a particular purpose. The techniques, in turn, contain specific *sub-techniques* used by named threat actors.

For example, the eleventh tactic (T0011), Command and Control, describes techniques used by adversaries when trying to communicate with compromised systems to control them. One of these techniques (T1071) deals with the use of application layer protocols to establish communications in a discrete manner. One of the sub-techniques (T1071.004) involves the use of the Domain Name System (DNS) to send and receive messages covertly. This sub-technique, in turn, contains examples of procedures used by various known threat actors, such as OceanLotus (also known as APT32) using a DNS tunneling for command and control on its Denis Trojan.

Why Bother with Threat Modeling

A scientific model is a simplified representation of something that is difficult to understand. The model is built in a way that makes certain parts of the subject easier to observe and analyze. We use these models to study complex phenomena like the spread of disease, global financial markets, and, of course, cybersecurity threats. Threat modeling allows us to simplify some of the activities of our adversaries so we can drill into the parts that really matter to us as defenders. There are just too many threat actors doing too many discrete things in too many places for us to study each in detail. Instead, we look for likely attackers and patterns that allow us to mitigate a bunch of different attacks by defeating the techniques that they all have in common.

Let's continue our previous example of the Denis Trojan using DNS tunneling. Should we care about it? That depends on what organization we belong to. We would probably care if we happen to be part of a media and human rights organizations in or around Vietnam, where OceanLotus/APT32 appears to be focused. This is the power of threat modeling: it allows us to focus keenly on specific actors and specific techniques based on who and where our organization is.

A typical threat modeling effort would start by identifying threat actors that are likelier to target our organization. This can be general classes of actors, such as opportunistic ransomware gangs, or more specific ones, like OceanLotus. Where do we get this information? Maybe we read the news and look for attackers that are targeting organizations such as ours. Or maybe we are subscribed to threat intelligence services that specifically look for those who are coming after us. Either way, we start by answering a series of questions:

- Why might someone want to target our organization? (Motive)
- How could they go about accomplishing their objectives? (Means)
- When and where would they attack us? (Opportunity)

The answer to the first question comes from our asset inventory. What do we have that is of value to others? Intellectual property would be valuable to competitors. Cybercriminals would like to get any financial data. Foreign governments would be after national security information. Once we know what kind of threat actors would be interested in us, we can study how they go about attacking organizations like ours. Going back to our example, suppose we are in an organization that might be of interest to OceanLotus. We can research any available open or private sources to learn about their tactics, techniques, and procedures (TTPs). The MITRE ATT&CK framework, for instance, lists over 40 techniques and at least 13 tools used by OceanLotus. Knowing their motivation and means, we can examine our systems and determine where they could use those techniques. This is the power of threat modeling: it allows us to focus our attention on understanding the threats that are likeliest to be of concern to our organizations. Out of the countless TTPs used by adversaries around the world, we can focus our attention on those that matter most to us.

Secure Design Principles

Understanding our threats is foundational to building secure architectures, but so is applying the collective wisdom developed by the security community. This wisdom exists in certain secure design principles that are widely recognized as best practices. The sections that follow address the secure design principles that you should know for the CISSP exam. Think of them as a solid starting point, not as an all-inclusive list.

EXAM TIP You should be able to describe each of the 11 secure design principles (which include the previously covered threat modeling) in some detail and recognize when they are (and are not) being followed in a given scenario.

Defense in Depth

One of the bedrock principles in designing security architectures is the assumption that our jobs are not to determine *whether* our systems can be compromised, but rather to prepare for the inevitable reality that this *will* happen. Consequently, we want to provide *defense in depth*, which is the coordinated use of multiple security controls in a layered approach, as shown in Figure 9-2. A multilayered defense system reduces the probability of successful penetration and compromise because an attacker would have to get through several different types of protection mechanisms before she gained access to the

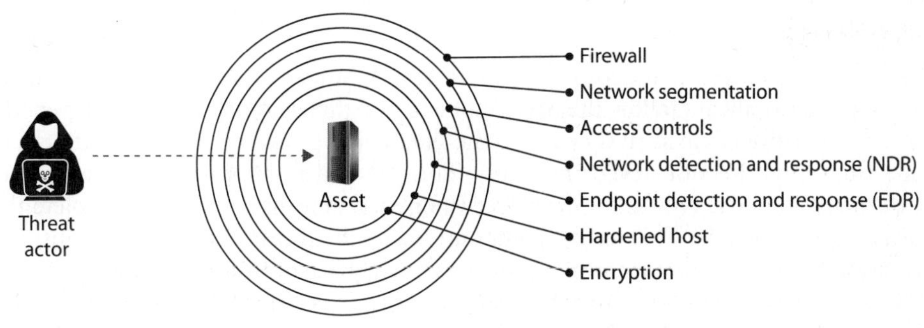

Figure 9-2 Defense in depth

critical assets. She may succeed at penetrating the perimeter and may get a foothold in the environment, but security controls are arranged in a way that will slow her down, improve the odds of detecting her, and provide means for defeating the attack or quickly recovering from it.

A well-designed security architecture considers the interplay of physical, technical, and administrative controls. For example, Company A can protect its facilities by using physical security controls such as the following:

- Perimeter fencing
- External lights
- Locked external and internal doors
- Security guard
- Security cameras

These measures would force the attacker, in many cases, to conduct the attack through the network. Technical controls would then have to provide adequate protection to the various assets in the company. Like their physical counterparts, you can think of these technical controls as creating concentric circles of protection around your assets. For example, as shown in Figure 9-2, you could have a perimeter firewall on the outer ring. If the attacker circumvents this, she'd have to navigate through a segmented network with strictly enforced access controls everywhere. Beyond this she'd have to defeat network detection and response (NDR) systems that can detect and stop the attack as it moves across your network. Deeper still, there are endpoint detection and response (EDR) systems that are deployed on hardened hosts. Finally, all data is encrypted, which makes exfiltrating anything useful out of the company's environment more difficult.

Physical and technical controls are integrated and augmented by administrative controls such as policies, procedures, and standards. The types of controls that are actually implemented must map to the threats the company faces, and the number of layers that are put into place must map to the sensitivity of the asset. The rule of thumb is the more sensitive the asset, the more layers of protection that must be put into place.

Zero Trust

The principle of defense in depth is certainly useful, but some people may think it suggests that attacks always follow the pattern of external threat actors sequentially penetrating each defensive circle until they get to the asset being protected. In reality, attacks can come from any direction (even internally) and proceed nonlinearly. Some adversaries lay dormant in our networks for days, weeks, or even months waiting to complete their attacks from the inside. This reality, compounded by the threat of malicious or just careless insiders, has led many security professionals to a place of healthy paranoia.

A *zero trust* model is one in which every entity is considered hostile until proven otherwise. It considers trust as a vulnerability and tries to reduce or eliminate it in order to make it harder for threat actors (external or internal) to accomplish their objectives. If defense in depth looks at security from the outside in, zero trust architectures are built from the inside out. These are not mutually exclusive approaches, however. It is best to incorporate both principles as we design our systems.

The catch is that it is very hard to implement a zero trust model throughout an enterprise environment because it would hinder productivity and efficiency. For this reason, this approach is most often focused only on a relatively small group of critical assets, access to which defines a "protect surface," which is where the tightest controls are placed.

Trust But Verify

Another principle of designing secure architectures is *trust but verify*, which basically means that, even when an entity and its behaviors are trusted, we should double-check both. It could seem that this is an alternative to (or even incompatible with) the zero trust model, but that is not necessarily true. You could, for instance, take a zero trust approach to defending your most critical assets, while allowing certain trust (that you verify) elsewhere. Of course, the zero trust assets would also be verified, and frequently. In this manner, the two approaches can coexist happily. On the other hand, you could take a hardline approach to one or the other and build your entire security architecture around it. It really depends on your organization and its environment.

At the heart of the trust but verify principle is the implementation of mechanisms that allow you to audit everything that happens on your systems. How else could you verify them, right? But what is equally important is the development of processes by which you pay the right amount of attention to auditing different elements of your environment. You won't have the ability to examine everything all the time so you have to figure out how you'll be able to analyze some things most of the time, and most things some of the time. The risk is that we leave some parts of our environment unexamined and therefore create a safe haven for attackers. Procedures matter just as much as technology.

Shared Responsibility

While the previous three principles (defense in depth, zero trust, and trust but verify) can apply equally well to traditional, cloud, and hybrid environments, cloud computing adds a bit of complexity in terms of defensive roles. *Shared responsibility* refers to the

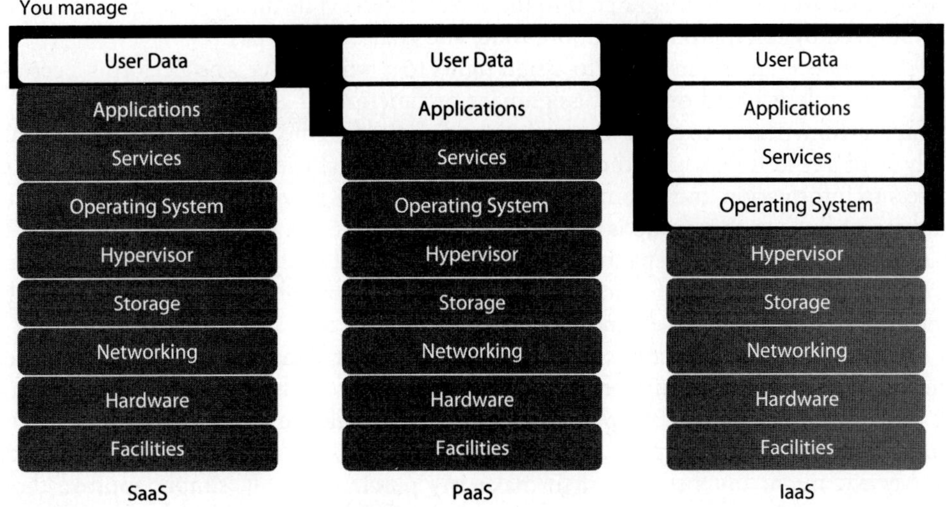

Figure 9-3 Shared responsibility in different cloud computing services

situation in which a service provider is responsible for certain security controls, while the customer is responsible for others. Typically, the service provider is responsible for security of the "thing" that they are providing. Think back to the three predominant cloud computing models we discussed in Chapter 7: Software as a Service (SaaS), Infrastructure as a Service (IaaS), and Platform as a Service (PaaS). Figure 9-3 shows the breakdown of responsibilities in each model.

The figure is, of course, a generalization. You should carefully read the fine print in the service agreements and discuss with your provider exactly what they will be doing for you and what they assume you'll do for yourself. Then, you need to periodically ensure that these parameters have not changed due to changes in the environment, a revised agreement, or new features offered by your provider. Many cloud compromises can be traced to organizations not understanding they were responsible for providing a certain aspect of security.

Separation of Duties

Regardless of your physical or logical architecture, people will be responsible for performing various business, infrastructure, and security functions based on their roles within the organization. It is important to consider the human element in designing our security architectures. Granting access rights to our teammates should be based on the level of trust the organization has in them and in their need to know and do certain things. Just because a company completely trusts Joyce with its files and resources does not mean she fulfills the need-to-know criteria to access the company's tax returns and profit margins. If Maynard fulfills the need-to-know criteria to access employees' work histories, it does not mean the company trusts him to access all of the company's other files. These issues must be identified and integrated into the access criteria. The different access criteria can be enforced by roles, groups, location, time, and transaction types.

Using *roles* is an efficient way to assign rights to a type of user who performs a certain task. This role is based on a job assignment or function. If there is a position within a company for a person to audit transactions and audit logs, the role this person fills would only need a read function to those types of files. If several users require the same type of access to information and resources, putting them into a *group* and then assigning rights and permissions to that group is easier to manage than assigning rights and permissions to each and every individual separately. If a specific printer is available only to the accounting group, when a user attempts to print to it, the group membership of the user will be checked to see if she is indeed in the accounting group.

Transaction-type restrictions can be used to further control what data is accessed during certain types of functions and what commands can be carried out on the data. A purchasing agent in a company may be able to make purchases of up to $2,000, but would need a supervisor's approval to buy more expensive items. The supervisor, conversely, might not be allowed to make any purchases at all, simply approve those submitted by a subordinate. This is an example of the principle of *separation of duties (SoD)*, in which important functions are divided among multiple individuals to ensure that no one person has the ability to intentionally or accidentally cause serious losses to the organization.

Least Privilege

A related principle, *least privilege*, states that people are granted exactly the access and authority that they require to do their jobs, and nothing more. The purchasing agent's supervisor from the example in the previous section is not really expected to swipe his corporate credit card as part of his daily duties, so why should he even have a card? His purchasing agent is expected to make small purchases on a regular basis, but anything over $2,000 would be fairly rare, so why have a purchase limit any higher than that?

The *need-to-know* principle is similar to the least-privilege principle. It is based on the concept that individuals should be given access only to the information they absolutely require in order to perform their job duties. Giving any more rights to a user just asks for headaches and the possibility of that user abusing the permissions assigned to him. An administrator wants to give a user the least amount of privileges she can, but just enough for that user to be productive when carrying out tasks. Management decides what a user needs to know, or what access rights are necessary, and the administrator configures the access control mechanisms to allow this user to have that level of access and no more, and thus the least privilege.

For example, if management has decided that Dan, the intern, needs to know where the files he needs to copy are located and needs to be able to print them, this fulfills Dan's need-to-know criteria. Now, an administrator could give Dan full control of all the files he needs to copy, but that would not be practicing the least-privilege principle. The administrator should restrict Dan's rights and permissions to only allow him to read and print the necessary files, and no more. Besides, if Dan accidentally deletes all the files on

Authorization Creep

As employees work at an organization over time and move from one department to another, they often are assigned more and more access rights and permissions. This is commonly referred to as *authorization creep*. It can be a large risk for an organization, because too many users have too much privileged access to organizational assets. In the past, it has usually been easier for network administrators to give more access than less, because then the user would not come back and require more work to be done on her profile. It is also difficult to know the exact access levels different individuals require. This is why user management and user provisioning are becoming more prevalent in identity management products today and why organizations are moving more toward role-based access control implementation. Enforcing least privilege on user accounts should be an ongoing job, which means each user's rights are permissions that should be reviewed to ensure the organization is not putting itself at risk.

the whole file server, who do you think management will hold ultimately responsible? Yep, the administrator.

It is important to understand that it is management's job to determine the security requirements of individuals and how access is authorized. The security administrator configures the security mechanisms to fulfill these requirements, but it is not her job to determine security requirements of users. Those should be left to the owners. If there is a security breach, management will ultimately be held responsible, so it should make these decisions in the first place.

Keep It Simple

The secure design principles we've discussed thus far can introduce complexity into our information systems. As many of us have learned the hard way, the more complex a system is, the more difficult it is to understand and protect it. This is where the principle of *simplicity* comes in: make everything as simple as possible and periodically check things to ensure we are not adding unnecessary complexity.

This principle has long been known in the software development community, where one of the metrics routinely tracked is errors per 1,000 lines of code, also known as defects per KLOC (kilo-lines of code). The idea is that the more code you write, the greater the odds you'll make an error without noticing it. Similarly, the more unique hosts, facilities, or policies you have, the greater the odds that a vulnerability will be introduced inadvertently.

Obviously, we can't force a global enterprise to use a small network, but we can simplify things by standardizing configurations. We can have 10,000 endpoints around the world, all configured in just a handful of ways with no exceptions allowed. We can similarly ensure that all our facilities use the same security protocols and that our policies are few in number, simple to understand, and uniformly enforced. The fewer variables we have to track, the simpler our systems become and, by extension, the easier they are to secure.

Secure Defaults

As many people in the technology field know, out-of-the-box implementations are oftentimes far from secure. Many systems come out of the box in an insecure state because settings have to be configured to properly integrate a system into different environments, and this is a friendlier way of installing the product for users. For example, if Mike is installing a new software package that continually throws messages of "Access Denied" when he is attempting to configure it to interoperate with other applications and systems, his patience might wear thin, and he might decide to hate that vendor for years to come because of the stress and confusion inflicted upon him.

Yet again, we are at a hard place for developers and architects. When a security application or device is installed, it should default to "No Access." This means that when Laurel installs a firewall, it should not allow any traffic to pass into the network that was not specifically granted access. A fine balance exists between security, functionality, and user friendliness. If an application is extremely user friendly or has lots of features, it is probably not as secure. It is up to us as security professionals to help our organizations balance these three competing needs.

NOTE Most operating systems nowadays ship with reasonably secure default settings, but users are still able to override the majority of these settings. This brings us closer to "default with no access," but we still have a ways to go.

The principle of *secure defaults* means that every system starts off in a state where security trumps user friendliness and functionality. It is later that, as deliberate decisions, security personnel can relax some restrictions, enable additional features, and generally make the system more user friendly. These decisions are integrated into the risk management program (see Chapter 2), typically through the configuration management processes (which we'll discuss in Chapter 20). The goal of secure defaults is to start everything in a place of extreme security and then intentionally loosen things until users can get their jobs done, but no further.

Fail Securely

A design principle that is related to secure defaults deals with the manner in which failures are handled. In the event of an error, information systems ought to be designed to behave in a predictable and noncompromising manner. This is also generally referred to as *failing securely*. We already saw how violating this principle can give adversaries an advantage when we discussed some of the cryptanalysis approaches in the previous chapter. If adversaries can induce a fault in a cryptosystem, they could recover a partial key or otherwise compromise it. The same holds for any information system.

A fail-secure system defaults to the highest level of security when it encounters a fault. For example, a firewall that is powered off unexpectedly may block all traffic when it reboots until an administrator can verify that it is still configured and operating securely. An EDR system may lock out a system if it encounters certain critical errors. Finally, a web browser could prevent a user from visiting a website if the connection is not secure or the digital certificate doesn't match, is not trusted, or is expired or revoked. Many a successful phishing campaign could've been defeated by implementing this last example alone!

Privacy by Design

The best way to ensure privacy of user data is to incorporate data protection as an integral part of the design of an information system, not as an afterthought or later-stage feature. This is the principle of *privacy by design* in a nutshell. Apart from making sense (we hope), this principle is part of the European Union's General Data Protection Regulation (GDPR), which means your organization may be required to abide by it already.

Privacy by design is not a new concept. It was originally introduced in the 1990s and formally described in a joint report by the Dutch Data Protection Authority and the Ontario Information Commissioner, titled *Privacy by Design: Delivering the Promises*, in 2010. This document describes the seven foundational principles of privacy by design, which are listed here:

1. Proactive, not reactive; preventative, not remedial
2. Privacy as the default setting
3. Privacy embedded into design
4. Full functionality—positive-sum, not zero-sum
5. End-to-end security—full life-cycle protection
6. Visibility and transparency—keep it open
7. Respect for user privacy—keep it user-centric

Security Models

A security model is a more formal way to capture security principles. Whereas a principle is a rule of thumb that can be adapted to different situations, the security models we describe here are very specific and verifiable. A security model is usually represented in mathematics and analytical ideas, which are mapped to system specifications and then implemented in software and/or hardware by product developers. So we have a policy that encompasses security goals, such as "each subject must be authenticated and authorized before accessing an object." The security model takes this requirement and provides the necessary mathematical formulas, relationships, and logic structure to be followed to accomplish this goal. From there, specifications are developed per operating system type

(Unix, Windows, macOS, and so on), and individual vendors can decide how they are going to implement mechanisms that meet these necessary specifications.

Several security models have been developed to enforce security policies. The following sections provide overviews of the models with which you must be familiar as a CISSP.

Bell-LaPadula Model

The *Bell-LaPadula model* enforces the *confidentiality* aspects of access control. It was developed in the 1970s to prevent secret information from being accessed in an unauthorized manner. It was the first mathematical model of a multilevel security policy used to define the concept of secure modes of access and outlined rules of access. Its development was funded by the U.S. government to provide a framework for computer systems that would be used to store and process sensitive information. A system that employs the Bell-LaPadula model is called a *multilevel security system* because users with different clearances use the system, and the system processes data at different classification levels.

EXAM TIP The Bell-LaPadula model was developed to make sure secrets stay secret; thus, *it provides and addresses confidentiality only*. This model does not address the integrity of the data the system maintains—only who can and cannot access the data and what operations can be carried out.

Three main rules are used and enforced in the Bell-LaPadula model:

- Simple security rule
- *-property (star property) rule
- Strong star property rule

The *simple security rule* states that a subject at a given security level cannot read data that resides at a higher security level. For example, if Bob is given the security clearance of secret, this rule states he cannot *read* data classified as top secret. If the organization wanted Bob to be able to read top-secret data, it would have given him that clearance in the first place.

The **-property rule* (star property rule) states that a subject in a given security level cannot *write* information to a lower security level. The simple security rule is referred to as the "no read up" rule, and the *-property rule is referred to as the "no write down" rule.

The *strong star property rule* states that a subject who has read and write capabilities can only perform both of those functions at the same security level; nothing higher and nothing lower. So, for a subject to be able to read and write to an object, the subject's clearance and the object classification must be equal.

Biba Model

The *Biba model* is a security model that addresses the *integrity* of data within a system. It is not concerned with security levels and confidentiality. The Biba model uses integrity levels to prevent data at any integrity level from flowing to a higher integrity level. Biba has three main rules to provide this type of protection:

- ***-integrity axiom** A subject cannot write data to an object at a higher integrity level (referred to as "no write up").
- **Simple integrity axiom** A subject cannot read data from a lower integrity level (referred to as "no read down").
- **Invocation property** A subject cannot request service (invoke) at a higher integrity.

A simple example might help illustrate how the Biba model could be used in a real context. Suppose that Indira and Erik are on a project team and are writing two documents: Indira is drafting meeting notes for internal use and Erik is writing a report for the CEO. The information Erik uses in writing his report must be very accurate and reliable, which is to say it must have a high level of integrity. Indira, on the other hand, is just documenting the internal work being done by the team, including ideas, opinions, and hunches. She could use unconfirmed and maybe even unreliable sources when writing her document. The **-integrity axiom* dictates that Indira would not be able to contribute (write) material to Erik's report, though there's nothing to say she couldn't use Erik's (higher integrity) information in her own document. The *simple integrity axiom*, on the other hand, would prevent Erik from even reading Indira's document because it could potentially introduce lower integrity information into his own (high integrity) report.

The *invocation property* in the Biba model states that a subject cannot invoke (call upon) a subject at a higher integrity level. How is this different from the other two Biba rules? The *-integrity axiom (no write up) dictates how subjects can *modify* objects. The simple integrity axiom (no read down) dictates how subjects can *read* objects. The invocation property dictates how one subject can communicate with and initialize other

Bell-LaPadula vs. Biba

The Bell-LaPadula and Biba models are informational flow models because they are most concerned about data flowing from one level to another. Bell-LaPadula uses security levels to provide data *confidentiality*, and Biba uses integrity levels to provide data *integrity*.

It is important for CISSP test takers to know the rules of Bell-LaPadula and Biba, and their rules sound similar. Both have "simple" and "* (star)" rules—one writing one way and one reading another way. A tip for how to remember them is if the word "simple" is used, the rule is about *reading*. If the rule uses * or "star," it is about *writing*. So now you just need to remember the reading and writing directions per model.

subjects at run time. An example of a subject invoking another subject is when a process sends a request to a procedure to carry out some type of task. Subjects are only allowed to invoke tools at a lower integrity level. With the invocation property, the system is making sure a dirty subject cannot invoke a clean tool to contaminate a clean object.

Clark-Wilson Model

The *Clark-Wilson model* was developed after Biba and takes some different approaches to protecting the integrity of information. This model uses the following elements:

- **Users** Active agents
- **Transformation procedures (TPs)** Programmed abstract operations, such as read, write, and modify
- **Constrained data items (CDIs)** Can be manipulated only by TPs
- **Unconstrained data items (UDIs)** Can be manipulated by users via primitive read and write operations
- **Integrity verification procedures (IVPs)** Check the consistency of CDIs with external reality

A distinctive feature of the Clark-Wilson model is that it focuses on well-formed transactions and separation of duties. A *well-formed transaction* is a series of operations that transforms a data item from one consistent state to another. Think of a consistent state as one wherein we know the data is reliable. This consistency ensures the integrity of the data and is the job of the TPs. Separation of duties is implemented in the model by adding a type of procedure (the IVPs) that audits the work done by the TPs and validates the integrity of the data.

When a system uses the Clark-Wilson model, it separates data into one subset that needs to be highly protected, which is referred to as a constrained data item (CDI), and another subset that does not require a high level of protection, which is called an unconstrained data item (UDI). Users cannot modify critical data (CDI) directly. Instead, software procedures (TPs) carry out the operations on behalf of the users. This is referred to as *access triple*: subject (user), program (TP), and object (CDI). A user cannot modify a CDI without using a TP. The UDI does not require such a high level of protection and can be manipulated directly by the user.

Remember that this is an integrity model, so it must have something that ensures that specific integrity rules are being carried out. This is the job of the IVP. The IVP ensures that all critical data (CDI) manipulation follows the application's defined integrity rules.

Noninterference Model

Multilevel security properties can be expressed in many ways, one being *noninterference*. This concept is implemented to ensure any actions that take place at a higher security level do not affect, or interfere with, actions that take place at a lower level. This type of model does not concern itself with the flow of data, but rather with what a subject knows about the state of the system. So, if an entity at a higher security level performs an action, it cannot change the state for the entity at the lower level. If a lower-level entity was aware of a certain activity that took place by an entity at a higher level and the state of the system changed for this lower-level entity, the entity might be able to deduce too much information about the activities of the higher state, which, in turn, is a way of leaking information.

Let's say that Tom and Kathy are both working on a multilevel mainframe at the same time. Tom has the security clearance of secret, and Kathy has the security clearance of top secret. Since this is a central mainframe, the terminal Tom is working at has the context of secret, and Kathy is working at her own terminal, which has a context of top secret. This model states that nothing Kathy does at her terminal should directly or indirectly affect Tom's domain (available resources and working environment). The commands she executes or the resources she interacts with should not affect Tom's experience of working with the mainframe in any way.

The real intent of the noninterference model is to address covert channels. The model looks at the shared resources that the different users of a system will access and tries to identify how information can be passed from a process working at a higher security clearance to a process working at a lower security clearance. Since Tom and Kathy are working on the same system at the same time, they will most likely have to share some types of resources. So the model is made up of rules to ensure that Kathy cannot pass data to Tom through covert channels.

Covert Channels

A *covert channel* is a way for an entity to receive information in an unauthorized manner. These communications can be very difficult to detect. Covert channels are of two types: storage and timing. In a *covert storage channel*, processes are able to communicate through some type of storage space on the system. For example, suppose Adam wants to leak classified information to Bob. Adam could create a user account on a web system. Bob pretends he will create an account on the same system and checks to see if the username is available. If it is available, that is the equivalent of a zero (no account existed). Otherwise, he records a one, and aborts the creation of the account. Either way, Bob waits a given amount of time. Adam either removes the account, effectively writing a zero, or ensures one exists (which would be a one). Bob tries again, recording the next bit of covertly communicated information.

In a *covert timing channel*, one process relays information to another by modulating its use of system resources. Adam could tie up a shared resource (such as a communications bus). Bob tries to access the resource and, if successful, records it as a zero bit (no wait). Otherwise, he records a one and waits a predetermined amount of time. Adam, meanwhile, is encoding his covert message by selectively tying up or freeing the shared resource. Think of this as a type of Morse code, but using some type of system resource.

Brewer and Nash Model

The *Brewer and Nash model*, also called the *Chinese Wall model*, states that a subject can write to an object if, and only if, the subject cannot read another object that is in a different dataset. It was created to provide access controls that can change dynamically depending upon a user's previous actions. The main goal of the model is to protect against conflicts of interest by users' access attempts. Suppose Maria is a broker at an investment firm that also provides other services to Acme Corporation. If Maria were able to access Acme information from the other service areas, she could learn of a phenomenal earnings report that is about to be released. Armed with that information, she could encourage her clients to buy shares of Acme, confident that the price will go up shortly. The Brewer and Nash Model is designed to mitigate the risk of this situation happening.

Graham-Denning Model

Remember that these are all models, so they are not very specific in nature. Each individual vendor must decide how it is going to actually meet the rules outlined in the chosen model. Bell-LaPadula and Biba do not define how the security and integrity levels are defined and modified, nor do they provide a way to delegate or transfer access rights. The *Graham-Denning model* addresses some of these issues and defines a set of basic rights in terms of commands that a specific subject can execute on an object. This model has eight primitive protection rights, or rules of how these types of functionalities should take place securely:

- How to securely create an object
- How to securely create a subject
- How to securely delete an object
- How to securely delete a subject
- How to securely provide the read access right
- How to securely provide the grant access right
- How to securely provide the delete access right
- How to securely provide transfer access rights

These functionalities may sound insignificant, but when you're building a secure system, they are critical. If a software developer does not integrate these functionalities in a secure manner, they can be compromised by an attacker and the whole system can be at risk.

Harrison-Ruzzo-Ullman Model

The *Harrison-Ruzzo-Ullman (HRU)* model deals with access rights of subjects and the integrity of those rights. A subject can carry out only a finite set of operations on an object. Since security loves simplicity, it is easier for a system to allow or disallow authorization of operations if one command is restricted to a single operation. For example, if a subject sent command X that only requires the operation of Y, this is pretty straightforward and the system can allow or disallow this operation to take place. But if a subject

Security Models Recap

All of these models can seem confusing. Most people are not familiar with all of them, which can make the information even harder to absorb. The following are the core concepts of the different models.

Bell-LaPadula Model This is the first mathematical model of a multilevel security policy that defines the concept of a secure state and necessary modes of access. It ensures that information only flows in a manner that does not violate the system policy and is confidentiality focused.

- **The simple security rule** A subject cannot read data within an object that resides at a higher security level (no read up).
- **The *-property rule** A subject cannot write to an object at a lower security level (no write down).
- **The strong star property rule** For a subject to be able to read and write to an object, the subject's clearance and the object's classification must be equal.

Biba Model A model that describes a set of access control rules designed to ensure data integrity.

- **The simple integrity axiom** A subject cannot read data at a lower integrity level (no read down).
- **The *-integrity axiom** A subject cannot modify an object at a higher integrity level (no write up).

Clark-Wilson Model This integrity model is implemented to protect the integrity of data and to ensure that properly formatted transactions take place. It addresses all three goals of integrity:

- Subjects can access objects only through authorized programs (access triple).
- Separation of duties is enforced.
- Auditing is required.

Noninterference Model This formal multilevel security model states that commands and activities performed at one security level should not be seen by, or affect, subjects or objects at a different security level.

Brewer and Nash Model This model allows for dynamically changing access controls that protect against conflicts of interest. Also known as the Chinese Wall model.

Graham-Denning Model This model shows how subjects and objects should be created and deleted. It also addresses how to assign specific access rights.

Harrison-Ruzzo-Ullman Model This model shows how a finite set of procedures can be available to edit the access rights of a subject.

sent a command M and to fulfill that command, operations N, B, W, and P have to be carried out, then there is much more complexity for the system to decide if this command should be authorized.

Also the integrity of the access rights needs to be ensured; thus, in this example, if one operation cannot be processed properly, the whole command fails. So although it is easy to dictate that subject A can only read object B, it is not always so easy to ensure each and every function supports this high-level statement. The HRU model is used by software designers to ensure that no unforeseen vulnerability is introduced and the stated access control goals are achieved.

Security Requirements

Whether we are building enterprise security architectures or software systems or anything in between, we always want to start from a set of requirements. These are what ultimately tell us whether or not the thing we built meets our needs. Security requirements should flow out of the organizational risk management processes, be informed by threat models, and be grounded in the principles and models we discussed earlier in this chapter. These requirements are then addressed within the frameworks we discussed in Chapter 4, and the whole thing is then assessed over time using a maturity model like the Capability Maturity Model Integration (CMMI), also discussed in Chapter 4.

One of the key tasks in addressing security requirements in our enterprise architectures is selecting the right controls for each requirement and then implementing, documenting, and verifying them. The exact process will vary depending on the framework you choose, but you may want to review the CRM example we discussed in Chapter 4 that applies NIST SP 800-53 (see Table 4-2 in particular).

Security Capabilities of Information Systems

Satisfying security requirements has become easier over the years as most vendors now incorporate advanced security capabilities into their products, particularly physical ones. After all, we can go to great lengths to ensure that the software we develop is secure, to run it on operating systems that have been hardened by a myriad of security controls, and to monitor everything using advanced security tools, but if the physical devices on which these systems run are untrustworthy, then all our efforts are for naught. In the sections that follow, we discuss a variety of hardware-based capabilities of many information systems that you should know.

Trusted Platform Module

A *Trusted Platform Module (TPM)* is a hardware component installed on the motherboard of modern computers that is dedicated to carrying out security functions involving the storage of cryptographic keys and digital certificates, symmetric and asymmetric encryption, and hashing. The TPM was devised by the Trusted Computing Group (TCG), an organization that promotes open standards to help strengthen computing platforms against security weaknesses and attacks.

The essence of a TPM lies in a protected and encapsulated microcontroller security chip that provides a safe haven for storing and processing critical security data such as keys, passwords, and digital certificates. The use of a dedicated and encoded hardware-based platform drastically improves the root of trust of the computing system, while allowing for a vastly superior implementation and integration of security features. The introduction of TPM has made it much harder to access information on computing devices without proper authorization and allows for effective detection of malicious configuration changes to a computing platform.

TPM Uses

The most common usage scenario of a TPM is to bind a hard disk drive, where the content of a given hard disk drive is affixed with a particular computing system. The content of the hard disk drive is encrypted, and the decryption key is stored away in a TPM chip. To ensure safe storage of the decryption key, it is further "wrapped" with another encryption key. Binding a hard disk drive makes its content basically inaccessible to other systems, and any attempt to retrieve the drive's content by attaching it to another system will be very difficult. However, in the event of a TPM chip's failure, the hard drive's content will be rendered useless, unless a backup of the key has been escrowed.

Another application of a TPM is *sealing* a system's state to a particular hardware and software configuration. Sealing a computing system through TPM is used to deter any attempts to tamper with a system's configurations. In practice, this is similar to how hashes are used to verify the integrity of files shared over the Internet (or any other untrusted medium). Sealing a system is fairly straightforward. The TPM generates hash values based on the system's configuration files and stores them in its memory. A sealed system will be activated only after the TPM verifies the integrity of the system's configuration by comparing it with the original "sealing" value.

A TPM is essentially a securely designed microcontroller with added modules to perform cryptographic functions. These modules allow for accelerated storage and processing of cryptographic keys, hash values, and pseudonumber sequences. A TPM's internal storage is based on random access memory (RAM), which retains its information when power is turned off and is therefore termed *nonvolatile RAM (NVRAM)*. A TPM's internal memory is divided into two different segments: persistent (static) and versatile (dynamic) memory modules, as shown in Figure 9-4.

Persistent Memory Two kinds of keys are present in the static memory:

- **Endorsement Key (EK)** A public/private key pair that is installed in the TPM at the time of manufacture and cannot be modified. The private key is always present inside the TPM, while the public key is used to verify the authenticity of the TPM itself. The EK, installed in the TPM, is unique to that TPM and its platform.
- **Storage Root Key (SRK)** The master wrapping key used to secure the keys stored in the TPM.

PART III

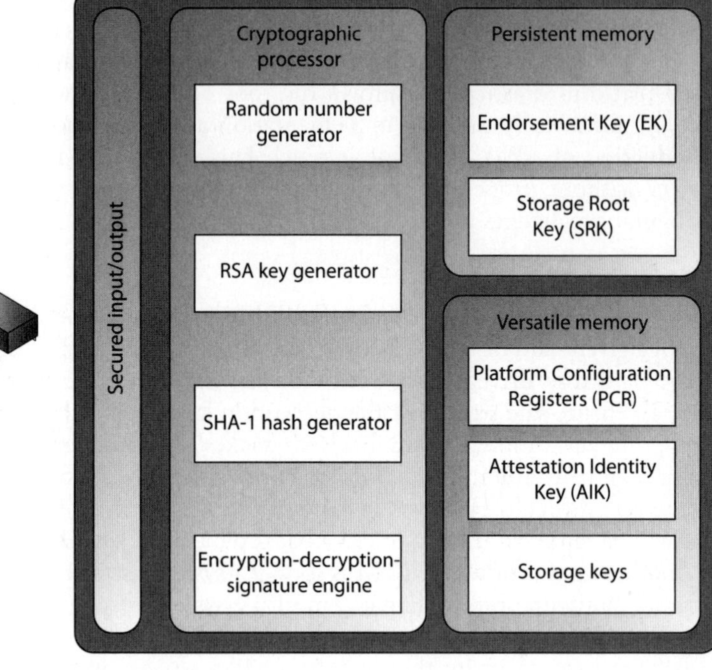

Figure 9-4 Functional components of a Trusted Platform Module

Versatile Memory Three kinds of keys (or values) are present in the versatile memory:

- **Platform Configuration Registers (PCRs)** Used to store cryptographic hashes of data used for TPM's sealing functionality.
- **Attestation Identity Keys (AIKs)** Used for the attestation of the TPM chip itself to service providers. The AIK is linked to the TPM's identity at the time of development, which in turn is linked to the TPM's EK. Therefore, the AIK ensures the integrity of the EK.
- **Storage keys** Used to encrypt the storage media of the computer system.

Hardware Security Module

Whereas a TPM is a microchip installed on a motherboard, a *hardware security module (HSM)* is a removable expansion card or external device that can generate, store, and manage cryptographic keys. HSMs are commonly used to improve encryption/decryption performance by offloading these functions to a specialized module, thus freeing up the general-purpose microprocessor to take care of, well, general-purpose tasks. HSMs have become critical components for data confidentiality and integrity in digital business transactions. The U.S. Federal Information Processing Standard (FIPS) 140-2 is perhaps the most widely recognized standard for evaluating the security of an HSM. This evaluation is important, because so much digital commerce nowadays relies on protections provided by HSM.

As with so many other cybersecurity technologies, the line between TPMs and HSMs gets blurred. TPMs are typically soldered onto a motherboard, but they can be added through a header. HSMs are almost always external devices, but you will occasionally see them as Peripheral Component Interconnect (PCI) cards. In general, however, TPMs are permanently mounted and used for hardware-based assurance and key storage, while HSMs are removable (or altogether external) and are used for both hardware-accelerated cryptography and key storage.

Self-Encrypting Drive

Full-disk encryption (FDE) refers to approaches used to encrypt the entirety of data at rest on a disk drive. This can be accomplished in either software or hardware. A *self-encrypting drive (SED)* is a hardware-based approach to FDE in which a cryptographic module is integrated with the storage media into one package. Typically, this module is built right into the disk controller chip. Most SEDs are built in accordance with the TCG Opal 2.0 standard specification.

NOTE Although SEDs can use onboard TPMs, that is not the norm.

The data stored in an SED is encrypted using symmetric key encryption, and it's decrypted dynamically whenever the device is read. A write operation works the other way—that is, the plaintext data arrives at the drive and is encrypted automatically before being stored on disk. Because the SED has its own hardware-based encryption engine, it tends to be faster than software-based approaches.

Encryption typically uses the Advanced Encryption Standard (AES) and a 128- or 256-bit key. This secret key is stored in nonvolatile memory within the cryptographic module and is itself encrypted with a password chosen by the user. If the user changes the password, the same secret key is encrypted with the new password, which means the whole disk doesn't have to be decrypted and then re-encrypted. If ever there is a need to securely wipe the contents of the SED, the cryptographic module is simply told to generate a new secret key. Since the drive contents were encrypted with the previous (now overwritten) key, that data is effectively wiped. As you can imagine, wiping an SED is almost instantaneous.

Bus Encryption

While the self-encrypting drive protects the data as it rests on the drive, it decrypts the data prior to transferring it to memory for use. This means that an attacker has three opportunities to access the plaintext data: on the external bus connecting the drive to the motherboard (which is sometimes an external cable), in memory, or on the bus between memory and the CPU. What if we moved the cryptographic module from the disk controller to the CPU? This would make it impossible for attackers to access the plaintext data outside the CPU itself, making their job that much harder.

Bus encryption means data and instructions are encrypted prior to being put on the internal bus, which means they are also encrypted everywhere else except when data is being processed. This approach requires a specialized chip, a *cryptoprocessor*, that combines traditional CPU features with a cryptographic module and specially protected memory for keys. If that sounds a lot like a TPM, it's because it usually is.

You won't see bus encryption in general-purpose computers, mostly because the cryptoprocessors are both more expensive and less capable (performance-wise) than regular CPUs. However, bus encryption is a common approach to protecting highly sensitive systems such as automated teller machines (ATMs), satellite television boxes, and military weapon systems. Bus encryption is also widely used for smart cards. All these examples are specialized systems that don't require a lot of processing power but do require a lot of protection from any attacker who gets his or her hands on them.

Secure Processing

By way of review, data can exist in one of three states: at rest, in transit, or in use. While we've seen how encryption can help us protect data in the first two states, it becomes a bit trickier when it is in use. The reason is that processors almost always need unencrypted code and data to work on.

There are three common ways to protect data while it's in use. The first is to create a specially protected part of the computer in which only trusted applications can run with little or no interaction with each other or those outside the trusted environment. Another approach is to build extensions into the processors that enable them to create miniature protected environments for each application (instead of putting them all together in one trusted environment). Finally, we can just write applications that temporarily lock the processor and/or other resources to ensure nobody interferes with them until they're done with a specific task. Let's take a look at these approaches in order.

Trusted Execution Environment

A *trusted execution environment (TEE)* is a software environment in which special applications and resources (such as files) have undergone rigorous checks to ensure that they are trustworthy and remain protected. Some TEEs, particularly those used in Apple products, are called *secure enclaves*, but the two terms are otherwise interchangeable. TEEs exist in parallel with untrusted *rich execution environments (REEs)* on the same platform, as shown in Figure 9-5. TEEs are widely used in mobile devices and increasingly included in embedded and IoT devices as well, to ensure that certain critical applications and their data have guaranteed confidentiality, integrity, and availability. TEEs are also starting to show up in other places, such as microservices and cloud services, where hardware resources are widely shared.

A TEE works by creating a trust boundary around itself and strictly controlling the way in which the untrusted REE interacts with the trusted applications. The TEE typically has its own hardware resources (such as a processor core, memory, and persistent storage) that are unavailable to the REE. It also runs its own trusted OS that is separate from and independent of the one in the REE. The two environments interact through a

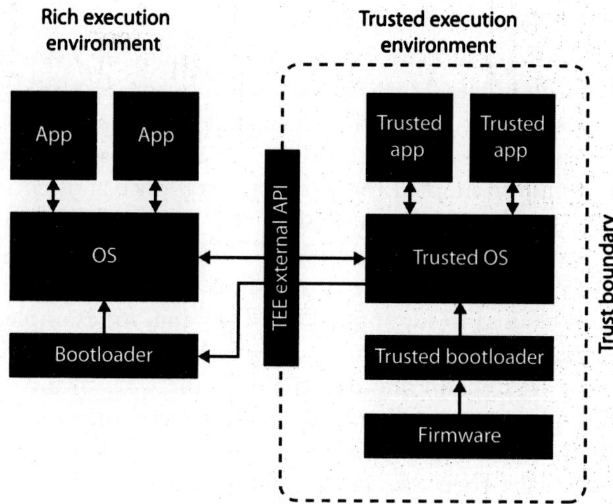

Figure 9-5 A typical TEE and its related REE

restricted external application programming interface (API) that enables the rich OS to call a limited set of services provided by the REE.

NOTE The term "secure enclave" is most commonly associated with Apple products such as the iPhone, but it is otherwise equivalent to the term "trusted execution environment."

So, how do TPMs, HSMs, and TEEs differ from each other? A TPM is usually a system on a chip (SoC) soldered onto the motherboard to provide limited cryptographic functions. An HSM is a big TPM that plugs into a computer system to provide these functions at a much larger scale. A TEE can perform the functions of a TPM, but, unlike both the TPM and HSM, it is specifically designed to run trusted applications that may have nothing to do with cryptography.

Trusted execution starts with a secure boot, in which the firmware verifies the integrity of the trusted OS bootloader before executing it. In fact, every executable and driver in the TEE is verified to the hardware root of trust and restricted to its own assigned resources. Only specific applications that have undergone rigorous security assessments at the hands of trusted parties are deployed in the TEE by the device manufacturer. This enables trusted applications such as cryptography, identity, and payment systems to enjoy high levels of protection that would otherwise be impossible to attain.

EXAM TIP TEEs (and, by extension, secure enclaves) do not implement hardware roots of trust because they are implemented in software. However, TEEs typically rely on an underlying root of trust provided by a TPM on the device.

Processor Security Extensions

TEEs need hardware support, which all the major chip manufacturers provide in their chipsets. Security is baked into the chips of most modern microprocessors. These CPU packages become a security perimeter outside of which all data and code can exist in encrypted form. Before encrypted data or code can cross into the secure perimeter, it can be decrypted and/or checked for integrity. Even once allowed inside, data and code are restricted by special controls that ensure what may be done with or to them. For all this to work, however, we need to enable the features through special instructions.

Processor security extensions are instructions that provide these security features in the CPU and can be used to support a TEE. They can, for example, enable programmers to designate special regions in memory as being encrypted and private for a given process. These regions are dynamically decrypted by the CPU while in use, which means any unauthorized process, including the OS or a hypervisor, is unable to access the plaintext stored in them. This feature is one of the building blocks of TEEs, which enables trusted applications to have their own protected memory.

Atomic Execution

Atomic execution is an approach to controlling the manner in which certain sections of a program run so that they cannot be interrupted between the start and end of a section. This prevents other processes from interfering with resources being used by the protected process. To enable this, the programmer designates a section of code as atomic by placing a lock around it. The compiler then leverages OS libraries that, in turn, invoke hardware protections during execution of that locked code segment. The catch is that if you do this too often, you will see some dramatic performance degradation in a modern multithreaded OS. You want to use atomic execution as little as possible to protect critical resources and tasks.

Atomic execution protects against a class of attacks called *time-of-check to time-of-use (TOC/TOU)*. This type of attack exploits the dependency on the timing of events that take place in a multitasking OS. When running a program, an OS must carry out instruction 1, then instruction 2, then instruction 3, and so on. This is how programs are normally written. If an attacker can get in between instructions 2 and 3 and manipulate something, she can control the result of these activities. Suppose instruction 1 verifies that a user is authorized to read an unimportant file that is passed as a link, say, a help file. Instruction 2 then opens the file pointed to by the link, and instruction 3 closes it after it's been read by the user. If an attacker can interrupt this flow of execution after instruction 1, change the link to point to a sensitive document, and then allow instruction 2 to execute, the attacker will be able to read the sensitive file even though she isn't authorized to do so. By enforcing atomic execution of instructions 1 and 2 together, we would protect against TOC/TOU attacks.

NOTE This type of attack is also referred to as an asynchronous attack. *Asynchronous* describes a process in which the timing of each step may vary. The attacker gets in between these steps and modifies something.

Putting It All Together: Where Can Data Be Encrypted?

Data in a computer system can exist in three different places: in the processor, in memory, and in secondary storage such as a disk drive. Standard systems do not encrypt data in any of these three places by default. You can opt to use FED, such as a self-encrypting drive, to encrypt the data in secondary storage, but that leaves it exposed everywhere else in the system, including the external bus. The third option is to use bus encryption, which requires a cryptoprocessor that is (relatively) expensive and underpowered. You are unlikely to want this unless you *really* have to protect the data in situations where you assume the adversary will be able to hack your hardware. Finally, the most flexible (and common) balance of protection, performance, and cost is the use of TEEs that can coexist with untrusted applications. Only the data within the TEE receives the full encryption treatment outside the CPU, leaving everything else to run on regular processor cores.

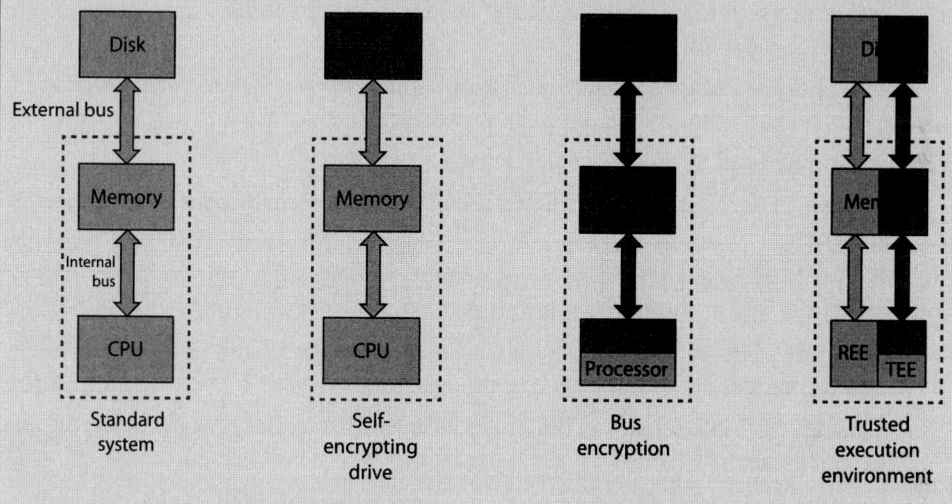

Chapter Review

One of the keys to providing the best security possible is to have a baseline understanding of adversaries that may target the organization, what their capabilities are, and what motivates them. We saw multiple ways to do that in this chapter, of which the MITRE ATT&CK framework is probably the one you want to dig into on your own. It seems like many professionals and organizations alike are converging on it as the *lingua franca* by which to describe adversarial behaviors.

A sound approach to defeating these threat actors is to apply the fundamental principles of secure design, of which we covered the 11 that ISC² stresses in the CISSP Certification

Exam Outline. There are other principles that you may be tracking, but these are the 11 you'll need to know for the exam. Likewise, the security models we discussed, which bring extra rigor to the study of security, are sure to make an appearance in the exam. Pay particular attention to Biba and Bell-LaPadula. Together, these principles and models provide a solid foundation on which to select controls based upon systems security requirements and build a solid security architecture.

Quick Review

- Threat modeling is the process of describing probable adverse effects on our assets caused by specific threat sources.
- An attack tree is a graph showing how individual actions by attackers can be chained together to achieve their goals.
- STRIDE is a threat modeling framework developed by Microsoft that evaluates a system's design using flow diagrams, system entities, and events related to a system.
- The Lockheed Martin Cyber Kill Chain identifies seven stages of cyberattacks.
- The MITRE ATT&CK framework is a comprehensive matrix of tactics and techniques used to model cyberattacks.
- Defense in depth is the coordinated use of multiple security controls in a layered approach.
- Zero trust is a model in which every entity is considered hostile until proven otherwise, and even that trust is limited.
- Trust but verify is the principle that, even when an entity and its behaviors are trusted, we should double-check both.
- Shared responsibility refers to the situation in which a service provider is responsible for certain security controls, while the customer is responsible for others.
- Separation of duties divides important functions among multiple individuals to ensure that no one person has the ability to intentionally or accidentally cause serious losses to the organization.
- Least privilege states that people are granted exactly the access and authority that they require to do their jobs, and nothing more.
- The need-to-know principle, which is similar to the least-privilege principle, is based on the concept that individuals should be given access only to the information they absolutely require in order to perform their job duties.
- The "keep it simple" principle drives us to make everything as simple as possible and periodically check things to ensure we are not adding unnecessary complexity.
- The principle of secure defaults means that every system starts off in a state where security trumps user friendliness and functionality.

- The principle of failing securely states that, in the event of an error, information systems ought to be designed to behave in a predictable and noncompromising manner.
- The principle of privacy by design states that the best way to ensure privacy of user data is to incorporate data protection as an integral part of the design of an information system, not as an afterthought or later-stage feature.
- The Bell-LaPadula model enforces the confidentiality aspects of access control.
- The Biba model is a security model that addresses the integrity of data within a system but is not concerned with security levels and confidentiality.
- The Brewer and Nash model, also called the Chinese Wall model, states that a subject can write to an object if, and only if, the subject cannot read another object that is in a different dataset.
- A Trusted Platform Module (TPM) is dedicated to carrying out security functions involving the storage of cryptographic keys and digital certificates, symmetric and asymmetric encryption, and hashing.
- A hardware security module (HSM) is a removable expansion card or external device that can generate, store, and manage cryptographic keys to improve encryption/decryption performance of the system into which it is installed.
- A self-encrypting drive (SED) provides full disk encryption (FDE) through a cryptographic module that is integrated with the storage media into one package.
- Data in SEDs is encrypted using symmetric key cryptography.
- Bus encryption systems use TPMs to encrypt data and instructions prior to being put on the internal bus, which means they are also encrypted everywhere else except when data is being processed.
- A trusted execution environment (TEE), or a secure enclave, is a software environment in which special applications and resources (such as files) have undergone rigorous checks to ensure that they are trustworthy and remain protected.
- Processor security extensions are instructions that provide additional security features in the CPU and can be used to support a TEE.
- Atomic execution is an approach to controlling the manner in which certain sections of a program run so that they cannot be interrupted between the start and end of the section.

Questions

Please remember that these questions are formatted and asked in a certain way for a reason. Keep in mind that the CISSP exam is asking questions at a conceptual level. Questions may not always have the perfect answer, and the candidate is advised against always looking for the perfect answer. Instead, the candidate should look for the best answer in the list.

PART III

1. Developed by Microsoft, which threat-modeling technique is suitable for application to logical and physical systems alike?
   A. Attack trees
   B. STRIDE
   C. The MITRE ATT&CK framework
   D. The Cyber Kill Chain
2. Which threat modeling framework provides detailed procedures followed by specific cyberthreat actors?
   A. Attack trees
   B. STRIDE
   C. The MITRE ATT&CK framework
   D. The Cyber Kill Chain
3. Which of the following security models is concerned with the confidentiality and not the integrity of information?
   A. Biba
   B. Bell-LaPadula
   C. Brewer and Nash
   D. Clark-Wilson
4. Which of the following security models is concerned with the integrity and not the confidentiality of information?
   A. Biba
   B. Bell-LaPadula
   C. Graham-Denning
   D. Brewer and Nash
5. Where is the data encrypted in a self-encrypting drive system?
   A. On the disk drive
   B. In memory
   C. On the bus
   D. All of the above
6. Where is the data encrypted in a bus encryption system?
   A. On the disk drive
   B. In memory
   C. On the bus
   D. All of the above

7. What is the difference between a Trusted Platform Module (TPM) and a hardware security module (HSM)?
   A. An HSM is typically on the motherboard and a TPM is an external device.
   B. Only an HSM can store multiple digital certificates.
   C. There is no difference, as both terms refer to the same type of device.
   D. A TPM is typically on the motherboard and an HSM is an external device.
8. Which of the following is *not* a required feature in a TPM?
   A. Hashing
   B. Certificate revocation
   C. Certificate storage
   D. Encryption
9. Which of the following is true about changing the password on a self-encrypting drive?
   A. It requires re-encryption of stored data.
   B. The new password is encrypted with the existing secret key.
   C. It has no effect on the encrypted data.
   D. It causes a new secret key to be generated.
10. Which of these is true about processor security extensions?
   A. They are after-market additions by third parties.
   B. They must be disabled to establish trusted execution environments.
   C. They enable developers to encrypt memory associated with a process.
   D. Encryption is not normally one of their features.

Answers

1. **B.** STRIDE is a threat-modeling framework that evaluates a system's design using flow diagrams, system entities, and events related to a system.
2. **C.** The MITRE ATT&CK framework maps cyberthreat actor tactics to the techniques used for them and the detailed procedures used by specific threat actors during cyberattacks.
3. **B.** The Bell-LaPadula model enforces the confidentiality aspects of access control.
4. **A.** The Biba model is a security model that addresses the integrity of data within a system but is not concerned with security levels and confidentiality.
5. **A.** Self-encrypting drives include a hardware module that decrypts the data prior to putting it on the external bus, so the data is protected only on the drive itself.

6. **D.** In systems that incorporate bus encryption, the data is decrypted only on the cryptoprocessor. This means that the data is encrypted everywhere else on the system.
7. **D.** In general, TPMs are permanently mounted on the motherboard and used for hardware-based assurance and key storage, while HSMs are removable or altogether external and are used for both hardware accelerated cryptography and key storage.
8. **B.** Certificate revocation is not a required feature in a TPM. TPMs must provide storage of cryptographic keys and digital certificates, symmetric and asymmetric encryption, and hashing.
9. **C.** When you change the password on a self-encrypting drive, the existing secret key is retained but is encrypted with the new password. This means the encrypted data on the disk remains unaltered.
10. **C.** Processor security extensions are instructions that provide security features in the CPU and can be used to support a trusted execution environment. They can, for example, enable programmers to designate special regions in memory as being encrypted and private for a given process.

CHAPTER 10

Site and Facility Security

This chapter presents the following:

- Security principles of facility design
- Designing facility security controls

A building has at least two lives—the one imagined by its maker and the life it lives afterward—and they are never the same.

—Rem Koolhaas

We close out the third domain of the CISSP Common Body of Knowledge (CBK) by turning our attention to a topic to which many of us cybersecurity professionals don't pay enough attention: the security of our facilities and buildings. Most of us are focused on people and technology, but without a secure physical environment, all these efforts could be for naught. If adversaries can put their hands on our computers at will, it becomes much more difficult to keep them from also getting their hands on our information.

In this chapter, we take a good look at all that goes into securing the facilities that house our people, equipment, and information. Whether you get to build a site from scratch, have to choose an existing one, or are already occupying one, you should know and be able to apply the security principles we'll discuss here. We'll start off with the planning and design processes. Next, we'll examine how to apply the secure design principles (discussed in the previous chapter) to the overall design of a site or facility. We'll then explore how to refine that design by selecting specific controls that mitigate risks to tolerable levels. Although we don't explicitly cover it in this chapter (and just as with any other aspect of security), we must periodically review and test our plans and controls so that they remain effective and are continuously improved.

Site and Facility Design

The terms site and facility are oftentimes used interchangeably, and although the CISSP exam does not make a strong distinction between them, we should clarify what they each mean for purposes of this discussion. A *site* is a geographic area with fixed boundaries that typically contains at least one building and its supporting structures (e.g., a parking lot or electric substation). A *facility* is a building or a part of a building dedicated to a specific purpose, such as corporate headquarters or a data center. So, a site would include one or more facilities within it. Sometimes, an organization will have a facility inside someone else's site or even building, such as when an organization rents a group of connected offices (the facility) in a corporate plaza (the site).

EXAM TIP Don't worry about differentiating the terms site and facility for purposes of the exam.

Site planning, like almost anything else, starts with a good set of requirements. These depend upon the level of protection required for the various assets and the organization as a whole. This required level of protection, in turn, is determined by the risk management processes we discussed in Chapter 2, particularly the risk assessment. Physical security is a combination of structures, people, processes, procedures, technology, and equipment to protect resources. The design of a solid physical security program should be methodical and should weigh the objectives of the program and the available resources. Although every organization is different, the approach to constructing and maintaining a physical security program is the same. The organization must first define the vulnerabilities, threats, threat agents, and targets, which may be different than the ones we normally track in cybersecurity.

NOTE Remember that a vulnerability is a weakness and a threat is the event or mechanism that could actually exploit this identified vulnerability. The threat agent is the person or thing that initiates the threat against this identified vulnerability.

Security Principles

Let's take a moment to review the security principles covered in Chapter 9, which are equally applicable to designing secure networks and designing secure facilities. In the sections that follow, we briefly point out some examples of how these principles are applied in real organizations. We could provide many more examples, but the point is to show how the principles apply, not to be all-inclusive.

EXAM TIP You should be prepared to identify the application of the principles of secure design in a given scenario on the exam.

Threat Modeling

Securing anything, physical facilities included, should start with the question: securing it from what? Depending on the nature of our organizations and their environments, our concerns may range from petty thieves to terrorists. If we were to hold a brainstorming session, we could probably think of a very large set of potential threat actors carrying out an even larger set of harmful actions. It is helpful to narrow things down a bit by considering the most likely threat and then the most dangerous one too. For example, suppose your organization develops and sells productivity software. After a bit of threat modeling, you determine that your likeliest physical security threat is a fire accidentally started by employees overloading circuits (say, with portable space heaters) and your most dangerous physical threat is a competitor sneaking into your facility and copying your source code. So, you focus your attention on mitigating the risk that stems from those two threats, which allows you to apply your limited resources to the threats that matter most to you.

Things change, however, so threat modeling (just as the broader risk management) activities are ongoing. You should periodically reassess your threat models to ensure they remain accurate and up to date. Threat modeling includes not only the source of the risk (i.e., the threat actor) but also the manner in which that risk becomes manifest (i.e., the threat actor's specific actions). Continuing our earlier example, suppose you realize that your competitors are likelier to bribe an insider to exfiltrate the source code on a removable drive than to sneak into your facility and steal it themselves, so you update your threat models and ensure the right controls are in place. Or maybe your company's CEO makes a controversial statement and now your most dangerous adversary's course of action is that angry demonstrators will vandalize your facility. Either way, threat models need to be updated and security controls adjusted periodically.

Defense in Depth

Just like we think in terms of concentric layers of protection around our logical assets, we do the same with our physical ones. Whether your organization has an existing facility or is planning a new one, what is the outermost layer? It could be a fence or simply a row of concrete planters. Maybe your organization is located in a single building and the lobby is this first layer. Whatever the case, you want to balance the (oftentimes) competing needs of making the facility attractive and welcoming to legitimate visitors, while conveying the message that security is treated seriously.

Beyond the outer perimeter, you want to maintain the message that security is part of the design. Visitors should have to sign in and be escorted. All staff should wear badges that are different from badges issued to visitors. Cameras should be conspicuous throughout. "Restricted area" signs should be visible. To gain access to these restricted areas, staff should be required to badge in so that an audit record of who enters and leaves exists. We'll get into specific controls later in this chapter, but the point is that as one travels from the outside of the facility toward the most sensitive areas, security controls should be visible and increasingly tight.

Zero Trust

A threat that is frequently overlooked, even in some fairly secure environments, is that of the malicious insider. Whether that person is a member of the organization, a contractor, a partner, or even an impostor, it is not hard to come across news stories describing the damage malicious insiders have caused from within. Applying the principle of zero trust to securing our facilities means we need to be able to tell whether someone should be in a given part of our facility doing whatever it is they're doing. To this end, we could use badges with different colors or icons. For example, you could divide a site into black, gray, and gold sections and then label the rooms, hallways, and badges with the appropriate colors. If you come across someone with a badge that doesn't match the section in which they are located, you can approach or report them. Similarly, you could have icons on the badges that denote other authorizations. The following list gives you some ideas of the types of staff badge icons that are used in real organizations to display a staff member's restrictions, permissions, or status:

- Escort required
- Allowed to escort visitors
- Custodial staff
- Data center (or operations center, or C-suite) access
- Top secret security clearance
- Allowed to carry weapons

Another aspect of zero trust applied to physical security is the notion of "see something, say something." Staff members should be required by policy and trained to pay attention to suspicious situations and respond appropriately. Examples are challenging unbadged personnel in the hallways, shutting doors that may have been propped open, and reporting a co-worker who is acting in an odd manner. Some organizations deliberately stage suspicious situations to see which employees respond correctly to them. Those who do get some token reward; those who don't get additional training.

Trust But Verify

As with logical security, the principles of zero trust and trust but verify can (and oftentimes) coexist within the same organization when it comes to physical security. Perhaps the most common implementation of the principle of trust but verify is the logging of physical events, which are then periodically checked by someone else. For example, if there is a safe or area that needs to be locked after work hours, it could be the responsibility of one individual to lock it (maybe the last one out) and another to verify that it was locked (maybe a security guard or rotating staff member assigned to after-hours checks).

The critical aspect of this principle is to actually verify that individuals are carrying out their responsibilities. For example, is anyone checking the physical access logs periodically and comparing them to what should be happening? Are employees who are on vacation badging in? This could indicate a stolen badge. Is a staff member coming in at odd hours for no apparent reason? In multiple, documented cases this has happened because employees were doing something they didn't want others noticing. Think of your own organization. Are there any things you or your team should be verifying regularly with regard to physical security? If not, should there be?

Shared Responsibility

Of course, not every aspect of site and facility security will rest on your shoulders as a security professional. In many cases, organizations share this responsibility with partners, landlords, and service providers. If you share office space in a building, whoever owns the building has certain responsibilities for its security. They may provide lobby guards and ensure that all the perimeter doors are locked except those leading to authorized access points. Or perhaps guards are provided to your organization by a security firm. They will have clearly defined responsibilities documented in the contract or service agreement.

All too often, however, the delineation of shared responsibilities is not clearly understood by all who should. A good way to discover points of confusion is to regularly conduct physical security drills, such as physical penetration tests and tabletop exercises involving all responsible entities, perhaps extending to local law enforcement as appropriate.

Separation of Duties

Duties can be deliberately separated with regard to physical security to mitigate theft and unauthorized physical access, among other risks. As an example, it is common for organizations to require one person (typically a receptionist or guard) to sign in guests and another person to escort them. This reduces the risk that a malicious insider sneaks in an external conspirator unnoticed. It also means that there are two pairs of eyes on each visitor to minimize the chances of accidentally letting an impostor in. Another example of separation of duties concerns receiving shipments. If only one person is involved in the process, how would we know whether a shipment that person reports as incomplete was truly incomplete or that person is stealing? To prevent this from easily happening, some organizations require only one person to sign for the delivery but require at least one other person to be present when the packages are opened and the property is added to the inventory.

Least Privilege

We previously mentioned the need to balance security with functionality, and this is especially true when it comes to staff authorizations. Staff should have the least amount of privileges that are absolutely necessary for their jobs, while enabling them to do those jobs efficiently and effectively. When it comes to site and facility security, this commonly takes the form of access to restricted areas. If employees have to badge in and out of different facilities, it is important to ensure that each staff member can effortlessly flow through the ones in which they do their jobs, and no others. For example, if some employees work at site A, their badges should not allow them entry to site B unless it is required.

Another example that comes to mind is access to server rooms or data centers. Oftentimes the racks that house the computing and storage devices in these facilities can and should be locked. Depending on the devices involved and their purpose, it is typical for different groups to need access to different racks. For example, the IT team may need access to the racks containing the domain controller and mail servers. The product team may need to get to the development servers that are on a different rack and subnet. The security team may need access to the security appliances, such as the network detection and response systems. Obviously, these groups probably shouldn't be able to access all the devices in the facility, but only the ones they need to do their jobs. Rather than leave all racks unlocked or use the same key for expediency, these staff members should be given only the minimum access possible to just the resources they need.

Simplicity

We discussed in Chapter 9 how complexity leads to the introduction of defects that, in turn, could create vulnerabilities. When it comes to our sites and facilities, the need for simplicity comes in at least two flavors: layout and procedural. The simpler the layout of our workplaces, the fewer hiding spots we create, the fewer cameras we need, and the more eyes that will naturally fall on everything that happens there. Whenever you have the choice, choose the simpler, more open layout to improve your organization's physical security.

Regardless of whether or not you can control the layout of your sites and facilities, you can almost always influence the security procedures that are implemented. Of course, you want to make these procedures so simple that they become second nature to all your organization's staff. From signing in and escorting visitors to safely evacuating the building in case of emergency, your organization needs procedures that are as simple as possible. These are normally validated and practiced during drills, which also provide a good opportunity to verify that no unnecessary complexity has crept into them.

Secure Defaults

As discussed in Chapter 9, secure defaults mean everything starts off in a place of extreme security that is then intentionally loosened until people can get their jobs done, but no further. Picture, then, your site schematics. Fence in every outdoor area, block off all vehicular travel around it, lock every door, and keep everyone out of every space. In other words, lock the place down as tightly as you know how. Now, take one of your teams, say IT, and walk through a day in their life. As you step through it, make note of how they'd drive in, what doors they'd have to use, which locks they need to open, and where they need to sit. Repeat this process for each organizational team, and then for your partners, vendors, and general visitors. You'll end up with the minimal relaxation to your extreme security plan that would be required for your staff members to do their jobs. This is what secure defaults look like for site security planning.

Fail Securely

This is a good point to discuss the difference between two principles that sound a lot alike but have very different implications. Recall that a *fail-secure* configuration is one in which things like doors default to being locked if there are any problems with the power, because that is the highest level of security for that system (the lock). If people do not need to use specific doors for escape during an emergency, then those doors can most likely default to fail-secure settings. On the other hand, a *fail-safe* setting means that if a power disruption occurs that affects the automated locking system, the doors default to being unlocked. Fail-safe deals directly with protecting people. If people work in an area in which a fire starts or the power is lost, it is a terrible idea to lock them in. Doorways with automatic locks can be configured in either mode, but we need to make careful decisions about which is appropriate and how we mitigate residual risks when we execute a fail-safe setting.

EXAM TIP The protection of human life trumps everything else. Be on the lookout for exam questions involving fail-safe versus fail-secure configurations.

Privacy by Design

Finally, we must keep in mind the need for privacy as we plan our site and facility security. This comes up in a number of areas and, frankly, varies widely between organizations. On one end of the spectrum, we have military and intelligence agencies wherein privacy in physical spaces is very limited due to the nature of the work being done. On the other end, consider healthcare organizations, in which privacy is absolutely essential. Regardless of where your organization falls in that spectrum, privacy definitely plays some role (e.g., restrooms) in shaping the manner in which you develop your site security. At a minimum, you should consider what private conversations (e.g., employee counseling, patient intakes, etc.) will take place in your site and where those would take place.

The Site Planning Process

Site and facility planning involves much more than physical security. Organizations should also be addressing issues like functionality, efficiency, cost, compliance, and aesthetics, just to name a few. However, as these (and other) issues are being addressed by the planning team, it is best to consider how each relates to physical security. For example, functionality and efficiency can frequently hinder security (and vice versa). So, we should balance the various requirements to ensure we are enabling the organization's functions while also protecting it from the various threats we've modeled for it. These threats include the following:

- **Natural environmental threats** Floods, earthquakes, storms, volcanic eruptions, pandemics, and so forth
- **Supply system threats** Power distribution outages, communications interruptions, and interruption of other resources such as water, gas, and air filtration
- **Manmade threats** Deliberate or accidental actions of humans, including fire, burglary, equipment loss/destruction, active shooters, and even terrorism

In all situations, the primary consideration, above all else, is that nothing should impede *life safety* goals. Protecting human life is the first priority. Good planning helps balance life safety concerns and other security measures. For example, barring a door to prevent unauthorized physical intrusion might prevent individuals from being able to escape in the event of a fire. Life safety goals should always take precedence over all other types of goals; thus, this door might allow insiders to exit through it after pushing an emergency bar, but not allow external entities in.

As with any type of security, most attention and awareness surround the exciting and headline-grabbing tidbits about large crimes being carried out and criminals being captured. In information security, most people are aware of viruses and hackers, but not of the components that make up a corporate security program. The same is true for physical security. Many "water cooler" conversations include talk about current robberies, murders, and other criminal activity, but not much attention is paid to the necessary framework that should be erected and maintained to reduce these types of activities.

An organization's physical security program should address the following goals:

- **Crime and disruption prevention through deterrence** Fences, security guards, warning signs, and so forth
- **Reduction of damage through the use of delaying mechanisms** Layers of defenses that slow down the adversary, such as locks, security personnel, and barriers
- **Crime or disruption detection** Smoke detectors, motion detectors, security cameras, and so forth
- **Incident assessment** Response of security guards to detected incidents and determination of damage level
- **Response procedures** Fire suppression mechanisms, emergency response processes, law enforcement notification, and consultation with outside security professionals

So, an organization should try to prevent crimes and disruptions from taking place, but must also plan to deal with them when they do happen. Criminals should be delayed in their activities by having to penetrate several layers of controls before gaining access to a resource. All types of crimes and disruptions should be able to be detected through components that make up the physical security program. Once an intrusion is discovered, a security guard should be called upon to assess the situation. The security guard must then know how to properly respond to a large range of potentially dangerous activities. The emergency response activities could be carried out by the organization's internal security team or by outside experts.

This all sounds straightforward enough, until the team responsible for developing the physical security program looks at all the possible threats, the finite budget that the team has to work with, and the complexity of choosing the right combination of countermeasures and ensuring that they all work together in a manner that ensures no gaps of protection. All of these components must be understood in depth before the design of a physical security program can begin.

As with all security programs, it is possible to determine how beneficial and effective your organization's physical security program is only if it is monitored through a *performance-based approach*. This means you should devise measurements and metrics to gauge the effectiveness of your countermeasures. This enables management to make informed business decisions when investing in the protection of the organization's physical security. The goal is to increase the performance of the physical security program and decrease the risk to the organization in a cost-effective manner. You should establish a baseline of performance and thereafter continually evaluate performance to make sure that the organization's protection objectives are being met. The following list provides some examples of possible performance metrics:

- Number of crimes committed
- Number of disruptions experienced
- Number of crimes attempted
- Number of disruptions prevented
- Time between detection, assessment, and recovery steps

- Business impact of disruptions
- Number of false-positive detection alerts
- Time it took for a criminal to defeat a control
- Time it took to restore the operational environment
- Financial loss of a successful crime
- Financial loss of a successful disruption

Capturing and monitoring these types of metrics enables the organization to identify deficiencies, evaluate improvement measures, and perform cost/benefit analyses.

NOTE Metrics are important in all domains of security because organizations need to allocate the necessary controls and countermeasures to mitigate risks in a cost-beneficial manner. You can't manage what you can't measure.

The physical security team needs to carry out a risk analysis, which will identify the organization's vulnerabilities, threats, and business impacts. The team should present these findings to management and work with management to define an acceptable risk level for the physical security program. From there, the team must develop baselines (minimum levels of security) and metrics in order to evaluate and determine if the baselines are being met by the implemented countermeasures. Once the team identifies and implements the countermeasures, the performance of these countermeasures should be continually evaluated and expressed in the previously created metrics. These performance values are compared to the set baselines. If the baselines are continually maintained, then the security program is successful because the organization's acceptable risk level is not being exceeded. This is illustrated in Figure 10-1.

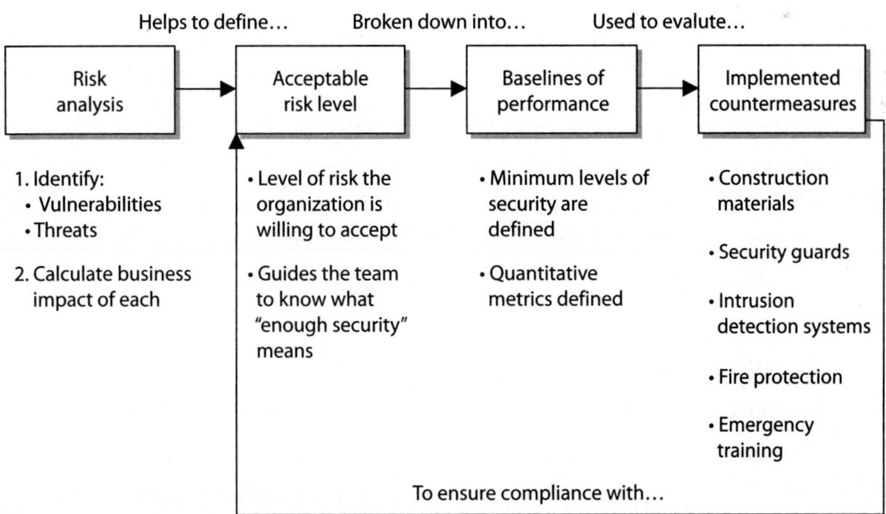

Figure 10-1 Relationships of risk, baselines, and countermeasures

Similarities in Approaches

The risk analysis steps that need to take place for the development of a physical security program are similar to the steps outlined for the development of an organizational security program and for business impact analysis, because each of these processes (development of an information security program, a physical security program, or a business continuity plan) accomplishes goals that are similar to the goals of the other two processes, but with different focuses. Each process requires a team to carry out a risk analysis to determine the organization's threats and risks. An information security program looks at the internal and external threats to resources and data through business processes and technological means. Business continuity planning looks at how natural disasters and disruptions could damage the organization, while a physical security program looks at internal and external physical threats to the organization's resources.

Each requires a solid risk analysis process. Review Chapter 2 to understand the core components of every risk analysis.

So, before an effective physical security program can be rolled out, the following steps must be taken:

1. Identify a team of internal employees and/or external consultants who will build the physical security program through the following steps.
2. Define the scope of the effort: site or facility.
3. Carry out a risk analysis to identify the vulnerabilities and threats and to calculate the business impact of each threat.
4. Identify regulatory and legal requirements that the organization must meet and maintain.
5. Work with management to define an acceptable risk level for the physical security program.
6. Derive the required performance baselines from the acceptable risk level.
7. Create countermeasure performance metrics.
8. Develop criteria from the results of the analysis, outlining the level of protection and performance required for the following categories of the security program:
    - Deterrence
    - Delaying
    - Detection
    - Assessment
    - Response
9. Identify and implement countermeasures for each program category.
10. Continuously evaluate countermeasures against the set baselines to ensure the acceptable risk level is not exceeded.

Legal Requirements

In physical security there are some regulatory and high-level legal requirements that must be met, but many of them just have high-level statements, as in "protect personnel" or "implement lifesaving controls." It is up to the organization to figure out how to actually meet these requirements in a practical manner. In the United States there is a lot of case law that pertains to physical security requirements, which is built upon precedence. This means that there have been lawsuits pertaining to specific physical security instances and a judgment was made on liability. For example, there is no law that dictates that you must put up a yellow sign indicating that a floor is wet. Many years ago someone somewhere slipped on a wet floor and sued the company, and the judge ruled that the company was negligent and liable for the person's injuries because it didn't warn the person about the wet floor. Now it is built into many company procedures that after a floor is mopped or there is a spill, this yellow sign is put in place so no one will fall and sue the company. It is hard to think about and cover all of these issues since there is no specific checklist to follow. This is why it is a good idea to consult with a physical security expert when developing a physical security program.

Once these steps have taken place, the team is ready to move forward in its actual design phase. The design will incorporate the controls required for each category of the program: deterrence, delaying, detection, assessment, and response. We will dig deeper into these categories and their corresponding controls later in the chapter in the section "Designing a Physical Security Program."

One of the most commonly used approaches in physical security program development is described in the following section.

Crime Prevention Through Environmental Design

Crime Prevention Through Environmental Design (CPTED) is a discipline that outlines how the proper design of a physical environment can reduce crime by directly affecting human behavior. It provides guidance in loss and crime prevention through proper facility construction and environmental components and procedures.

CPTED concepts were developed in the 1960s. They have been expanded upon and have matured as our environments and crime types have evolved. CPTED has been used not just to develop corporate physical security programs but also for large-scale activities such as development of neighborhoods, towns, and cities. It addresses landscaping, entrances, facility and neighborhood layouts, lighting, road placement, and traffic circulation patterns. It looks at microenvironments, such as offices and restrooms, and macroenvironments, like campuses and cities. The crux of CPTED is that the physical environment can be manipulated to create behavioral effects that will reduce crime and the fear of crime. It looks at the components that make up the relationship between humans and their environment. This encompasses the physical, social, and psychological needs of the users of different types of environments and predictable behaviors of these users and of potential offenders.

CPTED provides guidelines on items some of us might not consider. For example, planters should be placed away from buildings so they cannot be used to gain access to a window. A data center should be located at the center of a facility so the facility's walls will absorb any damages from external forces, instead of the data center itself. Street furnishings (benches and tables) encourage people to sit and watch what is going on around them, which discourages criminal activity. A corporation's landscape should not include wooded areas or other places where intruders can hide. Security cameras should be mounted in full view so that criminals know their activities will be captured and other people know that the environment is well monitored and thus safer.

CPTED and target hardening are two different approaches. *Target hardening* focuses on denying access through physical and artificial barriers (alarms, locks, fences, and so on). Traditional target hardening can lead to restrictions on the use, enjoyment, and aesthetics of an environment. Sure, we can implement hierarchies of fences, locks, and intimidating signs and barriers—but how pretty would that be? If your environment is a prison, this look might be just what you need. But if your environment is an office building, you're not looking for Fort Knox décor. Nevertheless, you still must provide the necessary levels of protection, but your protection mechanisms should be more subtle and unobtrusive.

Let's say your organization's team needs to protect a side door at your facility. The traditional target-hardening approach would be to put locks, alarms, and cameras on the door; install an access control mechanism, such as a proximity reader; and instruct security guards to monitor this door. The CPTED approach would be to ensure there is no sidewalk leading to this door from the front of the building if you don't want customers using it. The CPTED approach would also ensure no tall trees or bushes block the ability to view someone using this door. Barriers such as trees and bushes may make intruders feel more comfortable in attempting to break in through a secluded door.

The best approach is usually to build an environment from a CPTED approach and then apply the target-hardening components on top of the design where needed.

If a parking garage were developed using the CPTED approach, the stair towers and elevators within the garage might have glass windows instead of metal walls, so people would feel safer, and potential criminals would not carry out crimes in this more visible environment. Pedestrian walkways would be created such that people could look out across the rows of cars and see any suspicious activities. The different rows for cars to park in would be separated by low walls and structural pillars, instead of solid walls, to allow pedestrians to view activities within the garage. The goal is to not provide any hidden areas where criminals can carry out their crimes and to provide an open-viewed area so if a criminal does attempt something malicious, there is a higher likelihood of someone seeing it.

CPTED provides four main strategies to bring together the physical environment and social behavior to increase overall protection: natural access control, natural surveillance, territorial reinforcement, and maintenance.

Natural Access Control

Natural access control is the guidance of people entering and leaving a space by the placement of doors, fences, lighting, and even landscaping. For example, an office building may have external bollards with lights in them, as shown in Figure 10-2. These bollards actually carry out different safety and security services. The bollards themselves protect

Figure 10-2 Sidewalks, lights, and landscaping can be used for protection.

the facility from physical destruction by preventing people from driving their cars into the building. The light emitted helps ensure that criminals do not have a dark place to hide. And the lights and bollard placement guide people along the sidewalk to the entrance, instead of using signs or railings. As shown in Figure 10-2, the landscape, sidewalks, lighted bollards, and clear sight lines are used as natural access controls. They work together to give individuals a feeling of being in a safe environment and help dissuade criminals by working as deterrents.

NOTE Bollards are short posts commonly used to prevent vehicular access and to protect a building or people walking on a sidewalk from vehicles. They can also be used to direct foot traffic.

Clear lines of sight and transparency can be used to discourage potential offenders, because of the absence of places to hide or carry out criminal activities.

The CPTED model shows how *security zones* can be created. An environment's space should be divided into zones with different security levels, depending upon who needs to be in that zone and the associated risk. The zones can be labeled as controlled, restricted, public, or sensitive. This is conceptually similar to asset classification, as described in Chapter 5, in which different classifications are created, along with data handling procedures and the level of protection that each classification requires. The same is true of physical zones. Each zone should have a specific protection level required of it, which will help dictate the types of controls that should be put into place.

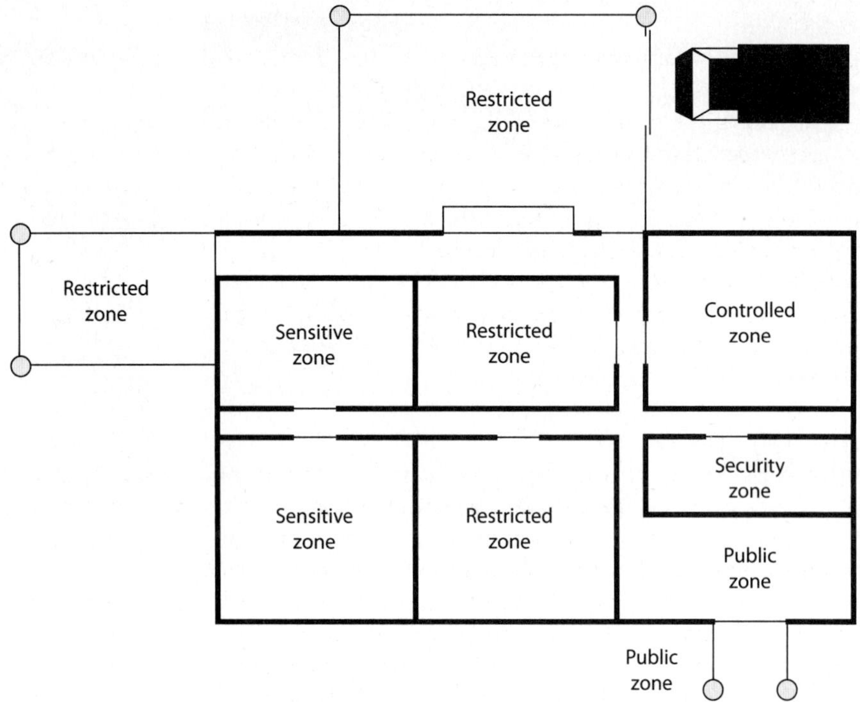

Access control should be in place to control and restrict individuals from going from one security zone to the next. Access control should also be in place for all facility entrances and exits. The security program development team needs to consider other ways in which intruders can gain access to buildings, such as by climbing adjacent trees to access skylights, upper-story windows, and balconies. The following controls are commonly used for access controls within different organizations:

- Limit the number of entry points.
- Force all guests to go to a front desk and sign in before entering the environment.
- Reduce the number of entry points even further after hours or during the weekend, when not as many employees are around.
- Implement sidewalks and landscaping to guide the public to a main entrance.
- Implement a back driveway for suppliers and deliveries that is not easily accessible to the public.
- Provide lighting for the pathways the public should follow to enter a building to help encourage use of only one entry for access.

- Implement sidewalks and grassy areas to guide vehicle traffic to only enter and exit through specific locations.
- Provide parking in the front of the building (not the back or sides) so people will be directed to enter the intended entrance.

These types of access controls are used all of the time, and we usually do not think about them. They are built into the natural environment to manipulate us into doing what the owner of the facility wants us to do. When you are walking on a sidewalk that leads to an office front door and there are pretty flowers on both sides of the sidewalk, know that they are put there because people tend not to step off a sidewalk and crush pretty flowers. Flowers are commonly placed on both sides of a sidewalk to help ensure that people stay on the sidewalk. Subtle and sneaky, but these control mechanisms work.

More obvious access barriers can be naturally created (cliffs, rivers, hills), existing manmade elements (railroad tracks, highways), or artificial forms designed specifically to impede movement (fences, closing streets). These can be used in tandem or separately to provide the necessary level of access control.

Natural Surveillance

Surveillance can also take place through organized means (security guards), mechanical means (security cameras), and natural strategies (straight lines of sight, low landscaping, raised entrances). The goal of *natural surveillance* is to make criminals feel uncomfortable by providing many ways observers could potentially see them and to make all other people feel safe and comfortable by providing an open and well-designed environment.

Natural surveillance is the use and placement of physical environmental features, personnel walkways, and activity areas in ways that maximize visibility. Figure 10-3 illustrates a stairway in a parking garage designed to be open and allow easy observation.

Next time you are walking down a street and see a bench next to a building or you see a bench in a park, know that the city has not allocated funds for these benches just in case your legs get tired. These benches are strategically placed so that people will sit and watch other people. This is a very good surveillance system. The people who are watching others do not realize that they are actually protecting the area, but many criminals will identify them and not feel as confident in carrying out some type of malicious deed.

Walkways and bicycle paths are commonly installed so that there will be a steady flow of pedestrians who could identify malicious activity. Buildings might have large windows that overlook sidewalks and parking lots for the same reason. Shorter fences might be installed so people can see what is taking place on both sides of the fence. Certain high-risk areas have more lighting than what is necessary so that people from a distance can see what is going on. These high-risk areas could be stairs, parking areas, bus stops, laundry rooms, children's play areas, dumpsters, and recycling stations. These constructs help people protect people without even knowing it.

Territorial Reinforcement

The third CPTED strategy is *territorial reinforcement*, which creates physical designs that emphasize or extend the organization's physical sphere of influence so legitimate users feel a sense of ownership of that space. Territorial reinforcement can be

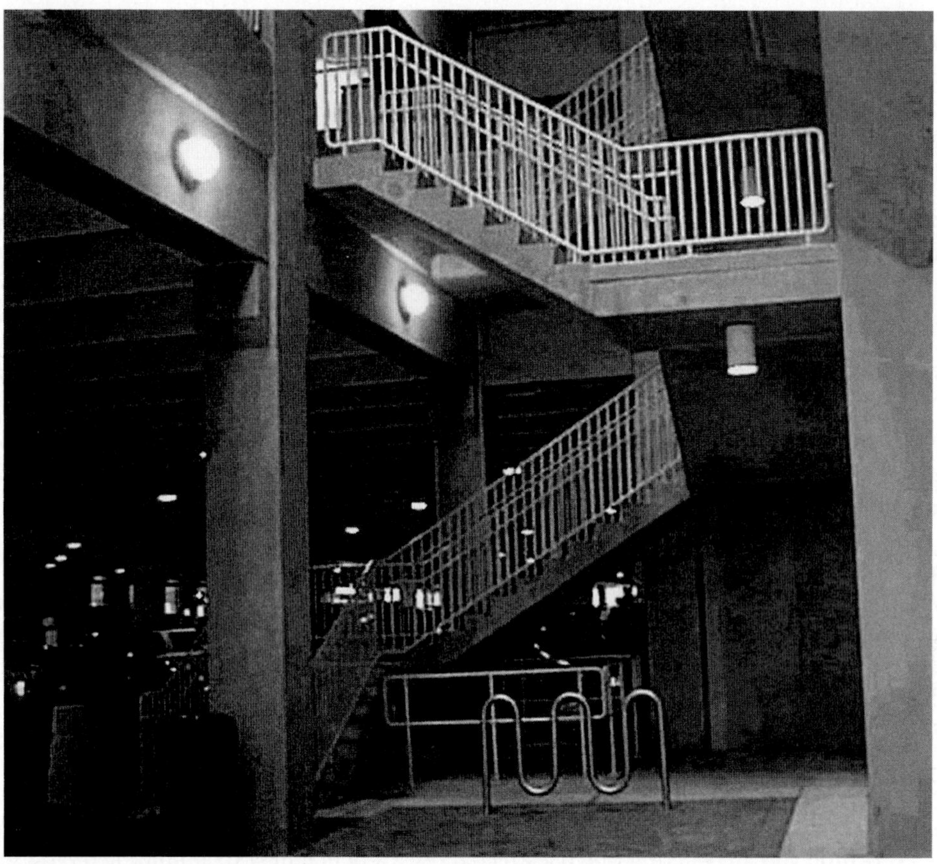

Figure 10-3 Open areas reduce the likelihood of criminal activity.

implemented through the use of walls, fences, landscaping, light fixtures, flags, clearly marked addresses, and decorative sidewalks. The goal of territorial reinforcement is to create a sense of a dedicated community. Organizations implement these elements so employees feel proud of their environment and have a sense of belonging, which they will defend if required to do so. These elements are also implemented to give potential offenders the impression that they do not belong there, that their activities are at risk of being observed, and that their illegal activities will not be tolerated or ignored.

Most corporate environments use a mix of the CPTED and target-hardening approaches. CPTED deals mainly with the construction of the facility, its internal and external designs, and exterior components such as landscaping and lighting. If the environment is built based on CPTED, then the target hardening is like icing on the cake. The target-hardening approach applies more granular protection mechanisms, such as locks and motion detectors.

Maintenance

In the mid-1980s, crime was rampant in New York City subways. Looking for creative solutions, the Metropolitan Transit Authority (MTA) hired George L. Kelling as a consultant. Kelling had written an influential book titled *Broken Windows* in which he presented his theory that visible signs of crime create an environment that encourages more crime. Make the signs go away, the theory goes, and so does the crime. In a large-scale experiment involving the "broken windows" theory that extended into 2001, NYC saw a dramatic decrease in crime, which strongly suggested the theory is valid.

The fourth and final CPTED strategy, *maintenance*, is an extension of the broken windows theory. It basically states that criminals will be more attracted to facilities that look unkept because they'll assume that the occupants don't care as much about them and probably lack the resources to properly maintain and secure them. Faced with a well-kept facility with no burned-out lamps, no broken windows, and with manicured lawns, criminals will think those inside the facility are more attentive, well resourced, and possibly alert.

Designing a Physical Security Program

If a team is organized to assess the protection level of an existing facility, it needs to investigate the following:

- Construction materials of walls and ceilings
- Power distribution systems
- Communication paths and types (copper, telephone, fiber)
- Surrounding hazardous materials
- Exterior components:
  - Topography
  - Proximity to airports, highways, railroads
  - Potential electromagnetic interference from surrounding devices
  - Climate
  - Soil
  - Existing fences, detection sensors, cameras, barriers
  - Operational activities that depend upon physical resources
  - Vehicle activity
  - Neighbors

To properly obtain this information, the team should do physical surveys and interview various employees. All of this collected data will help the team to evaluate the current controls, identify weaknesses, and ensure operational productivity is not negatively affected by implementing new controls.

Although there are usually written policies and procedures on what *should* be taking place pertaining to physical security, policies and reality do not always match up. It is important for the team to observe how the facility is used, note daily activities that could introduce vulnerabilities, and determine how the facility is protected. This information should be documented and compared to the information within the written policy and procedures. In most cases, existing gaps must be addressed and fixed. Just writing out a policy helps no one if it is not actually followed.

Every organization must comply with various regulations, whether they be safety and health regulations; fire codes; state and local building codes; military, energy, or labor requirements; or some other agency's regulations. The organization may also have to comply with requirements of the Occupational Safety and Health Administration (OSHA) and the Environmental Protection Agency (EPA), if it is operating in the United States, or with the requirements of equivalent organizations within another country. The physical security program development team must understand all the regulations the organization must comply with and how to reach compliance through physical security and safety procedures.

Legal issues must be understood and properly addressed as well. These issues may include access availability for the disabled, liability issues, the failure to protect assets, and so on. This long laundry list of items can get an organization into legal trouble if it is not doing what it is supposed to. Occasionally, the legal trouble may take the form of a criminal case—for example, if doors default to being locked when power is lost (fail-secure) and, as a result, several employees are trapped and killed during a fire, criminal negligence may be alleged. Legal trouble can also come in the form of civil cases—for instance, if a company does not remove the ice on its sidewalks and a pedestrian falls and breaks his ankle, the pedestrian may sue the company. The company may be found negligent and held liable for damages.

Every organization should have a *facility safety officer*, whose main job is to understand all the components that make up the facility and what the organization needs to do to protect its assets and stay within compliance. This person should oversee facility management duties day in and day out, but should also be heavily involved with the team that has been organized to evaluate the organization's physical security program.

A physical security program is a collection of controls that are implemented and maintained to provide the protection levels necessary to be in compliance with the physical security policy. The policy should embody all the regulations and laws that must be adhered to and should set the risk level the organization is willing to accept.

By this point, the team has carried out a risk analysis, which consisted of identifying the organization's vulnerabilities, threats, and business impact pertaining to the identified threats. The program design phase should begin with a structured outline, which will evolve into a framework. This framework will then be fleshed out with the necessary controls and countermeasures. The outline should contain the program categories and the necessary countermeasures. The following is a simplistic example:

I. Deterrence of criminal activity

- **A.** Fences
- **B.** Warning signs
- **C.** Security guards
- **D.** Dogs

II. Delay of intruders to help ensure they can be caught
   A. Locks
   B. Defense-in-depth measures
   C. Access controls
III. Detection of intruders
   A. External intruder sensors
   B. Internal intruder sensors
IV. Assessment of situations
   A. Security guard procedures
   B. Damage assessment criteria
V. Response to intrusions and disruptions
   A. Communication structure (calling tree)
   B. Response force
   C. Emergency response procedures
   D. Police, fire, medical personnel

The team can then start addressing each phase of the security program, usually starting with the facility.

Facility

When an organization decides to erect a building, it should consider several factors before pouring the first batch of concrete. Of course, it should review land prices, customer population, and marketing strategies, but as security professionals, we are more interested in the confidence and protection that a specific location can provide. Some organizations that deal with top-secret or confidential information and processes make their facilities unnoticeable so they do not attract the attention of would-be attackers. The building may be hard to see from the surrounding roads, the organization's signs and logos may be small and not easily noticed, and the markings on the building may not give away any information that pertains to what is going on inside that building. It is a type of urban camouflage that makes it harder for the enemy to seek out that organization as a target. This is very common for telecommunication facilities that contain critical infrastructure switches and other supporting technologies. When driving down the road you might pass three of these buildings, but because they have no features that actually stand out, you likely would not even give them a second thought—which is the goal.

An organization should evaluate how close the facility would be to a police station, fire station, and medical facilities. Many times, the proximity of these entities raises the real estate value of properties, but for good reason. If a chemical company that manufactures highly explosive materials needs to build a new facility, it may make good business sense to put it near a fire station. (Although the fire station might not be so happy.) If another company that builds and sells expensive electronic devices is expanding and needs to move operations into another facility, police reaction time may be looked at when choosing one facility location over another. Each of these issues—police station, fire station, and medical facility proximity—can also reduce insurance rates and must be looked at carefully. Remember that a key goal of physical security is to ensure the safety of personnel. Always keep that in mind when implementing any sort of physical security control. Protect your fellow humans, be your brother's keeper, and *then* run.

Some buildings are placed in areas surrounded by hills or mountains to help prevent eavesdropping of electrical signals emitted by the facility's equipment. In some cases, the organization itself will build hills or use other landscaping techniques to guard against eavesdropping. Other facilities are built underground or right into the side of a mountain for concealment and disguise in the natural environment and for protection from radar tools, spying activities, and aerial bomb attacks.

In the United States there is an Air Force base built into a mountain close to Colorado Springs, Colorado. The underground Cheyenne Mountain complex is made up of buildings, rooms, and tunnels. It has its own air intake supply, as well as water, fuel, and sewer lines. This is where the North American Aerospace Defense Command (NORAD) carries out its mission and apparently, according to many popular movies, is where you should be headed if the world is about to be blown up.

Construction

Physical construction materials and structure composition need to be evaluated for their appropriateness to the site environment, their protective characteristics, their utility, and their costs and benefits. Different building materials provide various levels of fire protection and have different rates of combustibility, which correlate with their fire ratings. When making structural decisions, the decision of what type of construction material to use (wood, concrete, or steel) needs to be considered in light of what the building is going to be used for. If an area will be used to store documents and old equipment, it has far different needs and legal requirements than if it is going to be used for employees to work in every day.

The *load* (how much weight can be held) of a building's walls, floors, and ceilings needs to be estimated and projected to ensure the building will not collapse in different situations. In most cases, this is dictated by local building codes. The walls, ceilings, and floors must contain the necessary materials to meet the required fire rating and to protect against water damage. The windows (interior and exterior) may need to provide ultraviolet (UV) protection, may need to be shatterproof, or may need to be translucent or opaque, depending on the placement of the window and the contents of the building. The doors (exterior and interior) may need to have directional openings, have the same fire rating as the surrounding walls, prohibit forcible entries, display emergency egress markings, and—depending on placement—have monitoring and attached alarms. In most buildings, raised floors are used to hide and protect wires and pipes, and it is important to ensure any raised outlets are properly grounded.

Building codes may regulate all of these issues, but there are still many options within each category that the physical security program development team should review for extra security protection. The right options should accomplish the organization's security and functionality needs and still be cost-effective.

When designing and building a facility, the following major items need to be addressed from a physical security point of view.

Walls:

- Combustibility of material (wood, steel, concrete)
- Fire rating
- Reinforcements for secured areas

Doors:

- Combustibility of material (wood, pressed board, aluminum)
- Fire rating
- Resistance to forcible entry
- Emergency marking
- Placement
- Locked or controlled entrances
- Alarms
- Secure hinges
- Directional opening
- Electric door locks that revert to an unlocked state for safe evacuation in power outages
- Type of glass—shatterproof or bulletproof glass requirements

Ceilings:

- Combustibility of material (wood, steel, concrete)
- Fire rating
- Weight-bearing rating
- Drop-ceiling considerations

Windows:

- Translucent or opaque requirements
- Shatterproof
- Alarms
- Placement
- Accessibility to intruders

Flooring:

- Weight-bearing rating
- Combustibility of material (wood, steel, concrete)
- Fire rating
- Raised flooring
- Nonconducting surface and material

Heating, ventilation, and air conditioning:

- Positive air pressure
- Protected intake vents
- Dedicated power lines
- Emergency shutoff valves and switches
- Placement

Electric power supplies:

- Backup and alternative power supplies
- Clean and steady power source
- Dedicated feeders to required areas
- Placement and access to distribution panels and circuit breakers

Water and gas lines:

- Shutoff valves—labeled and brightly painted for visibility
- Positive flow (material flows out of building, not in)
- Placement—properly located and labeled

Fire detection and suppression:

- Placement of sensors and detectors
- Placement of suppression systems
- Type of detectors and suppression agents

The risk analysis results will help the team determine the type of construction material that should be used when constructing a new facility. Several grades of building construction are available. For example, *light frame construction material* provides the least amount of protection against fire and forcible entry attempts. It is composed of untreated lumber that would be combustible during a fire. Light frame construction material is usually used to build homes, primarily because it is cheap, but also because homes typically are not under the same types of fire and intrusion threats that office buildings are.

Heavy timber construction material is sometimes used for office buildings. Combustible lumber is still used in this type of construction, but there are requirements on the thickness and composition of the materials to provide more protection from fire. The construction materials must be at least 4 inches in thickness. Denser woods are used and are fastened with metal bolts and plates. Whereas light frame construction material has a fire survival rate of 30 minutes, the heavy timber construction material has a fire survival rate of one hour.

A building could be made up of *incombustible material*, such as steel, which provides a higher level of fire protection than the previously mentioned materials, but loses its strength under extreme temperatures, something that may cause the building to collapse. So, although the steel will not burn, it may melt and weaken. If a building consists of *fire-resistant material*, the construction material is fire retardant and may have steel rods encased inside of concrete walls and support beams. This provides the most protection against fire and forced-entry attempts.

The team should choose its construction material based on the identified threats of the organization and the fire codes to be complied with. If a company is just going to have some office workers in a building and has no real adversaries interested in destroying the facility, then the light frame or heavy timber construction material would be used. Facilities for government organizations, which are under threat by domestic and foreign terrorists, would be built with fire-resistant materials. A financial institution would also use fire-resistant and reinforcement material within its building. This is especially true for its exterior walls, through which thieves may attempt to drive vehicles to gain access to the vaults.

Calculations of approximate penetration times for different types of explosives and attacks are based on the thickness of the concrete walls and the gauge of rebar used. (*Rebar*, short for *reinforcing bar*, refers to the steel rods encased within the concrete.) So even if the concrete were damaged, it would take longer to actually cut or break through the rebar. Using thicker rebar and properly placing it within the concrete provides even more protection.

Reinforced walls, rebar, and the use of double walls can be used as delaying mechanisms. The idea is that it will take the bad guy longer to get through two reinforced walls, which gives the response force sufficient time (hopefully) to arrive at the scene and stop the attacker.

Entry Points

Understanding the organization's needs and types of entry points for a specific building is critical. The various types of entry points may include doors, windows, roof access, fire escapes, chimneys, and service delivery access points. Second and third entry points must also be considered, such as internal doors that lead into other portions of the building and to exterior doors, elevators, and stairwells. Windows at the ground level should be fortified because they could be easily broken. Fire escapes, stairwells to the roof, and chimneys often are overlooked as potential entry points.

NOTE Ventilation ducts and utility tunnels can also be used by intruders and thus must be properly protected with sensors and access control mechanisms.

The weakest portion of the structure, usually its doors and windows, will likely be attacked first. With regard to doors, the weaknesses usually lie within the frames, hinges, and door material. The bolts, frames, hinges, and material that make up the door should all provide the same level of strength and protection. For example, if a company implements a heavy, nonhollow steel door but uses weak hinges that could be easily extracted, the company is just wasting money. The attacker can just remove the hinges and remove this strong and heavy door.

The door and surrounding walls and ceilings should also provide the same level of strength. If another company has an extremely fortified and secure door, but the surrounding wall materials are made out of regular light frame wood, then it is also wasting money on doors. There is no reason to spend a lot of money on one countermeasure that can be easily circumvented by breaking a weaker countermeasure in proximity.

Doors Different door types for various functionalities include the following:

- Vault doors
- Personnel doors
- Industrial doors
- Vehicle access doors
- Bullet-resistant doors

Doors can be hollow-core or solid-core. The team needs to understand the various entry types and the potential forced-entry threats, which will help the team determine what type of door should be implemented. Hollow-core doors can be easily penetrated by kicking or cutting them; thus, they are usually used internally. The team also has a choice of solid-core doors, which are made up of various materials to provide different fire ratings and protection from forced entry. As stated previously, the fire rating and protection level of the door need to match the fire rating and protection level of the surrounding walls.

Bulletproof doors are also an option if there is a threat that damage could be done to resources by shooting through the door. These types of doors are constructed in a manner that involves sandwiching bullet-resistant and bulletproof material between wood or steel veneers to still give the door some aesthetic qualities while providing the necessary levels of protection.

Hinges and strike plates should be secure, especially on exterior doors or doors used to protect sensitive areas. The hinges should have pins that cannot be removed, and the door frames must provide the same level of protection as the door itself.

Fire codes dictate the number and placement of doors with panic bars on them. These are the crossbars that release an internal lock to allow a locked door to open. Panic bars can be on regular entry doors and also on emergency exit doors. Those are the ones that usually have the sign that indicates the door is not an exit point and that an alarm will go off if the door is opened. It might seem like fun and a bit tempting to see if the alarm will *really* go off or not—but don't try it. Security people are not known for their sense of humor.

Mantraps and turnstiles can be used so unauthorized individuals entering a facility cannot get in or out if it is activated. A *mantrap* is a small room with two doors. The first door is locked; a person is identified and authenticated by a security guard, biometric system, smart card reader, or swipe card reader. Once the person is authenticated and access is authorized, the first door opens and allows the person into the mantrap. The first door locks and the person is trapped. The person must be authenticated again before the second door unlocks and allows him into the facility. Some mantraps use biometric systems that weigh the person who enters to ensure that only one person at a time is entering the mantrap area. This is a control to counter piggybacking.

Window Types Though most of us would probably think of doors as the obvious entry points, windows deserve every bit as much attention in the design of secure facilities. Like doors, different types of windows afford various degrees of protection against intrusions. The following sums up the types of windows that can be used:

- **Standard** No extra protection. The cheapest and lowest level of protection.
- **Tempered** Glass is heated and then cooled suddenly to increase its integrity and strength.
- **Acrylic** A type of plastic instead of glass. Polycarbonate acrylics are stronger than regular acrylics.
- **Wired** A mesh of wire is embedded between two sheets of glass. This wire helps prevent the glass from shattering.
- **Laminated** The plastic layer between two outer glass layers. The plastic layer helps increase its strength against breakage.
- **Solar window film** Provides extra security by being tinted and offers extra strength due to the film's material.
- **Security film** Transparent film is applied to the glass to increase its strength.

Site and Facility Controls

Having covered the general processes and principles we should use in planning security for our sites and facilities, we now turn our attention to examples of specific controls we should consider. The following section discuss the most common or important controls you should know both for the exam and in the conduct of your job.

Work Area Security

The largest total area in an organization's facilities is usually devoted to workspaces for its staff. In terms of facility security, these spaces comprise the largest attack surface for the organization. This is where malicious insiders, thieves, and active shooters will find the most target-rich environment. For this reason, we need to consider the threats to our workforce occupying those spaces and implement controls to keep them and their assets protected. Just like we segment our networks to limit where digital intruders can operate, we should separate our workspaces to make it harder for physical intruders to accomplish their objectives. *Internal partitions* are used to create barriers between one area and another. These partitions can be used to segment separate work areas, but should not be used in protected areas that house sensitive systems and devices because they would limit the ability to detect malicious activity on those systems.

Movement from one area to another should ideally be restricted using *keycard entry systems*, which are electronic locks that are unlocked by keycards. Keycards are plastic cards with magnetic or radio frequency identification (RFID) components that act as physical keys on special electronic locks. Alternatively, doors between areas could be remotely locked and unlocked by security guards to restrict the movement of an assailant, protect occupants, or facilitate evacuations. To facilitate this remote operation, all work areas should be covered by security cameras that automatically record all activity and save the video files, at least for several days.

Beware of the dropped ceilings that many office buildings have. These can cause the interior partitions or even walls to not extend to the true ceiling—only to the dropped ceiling. An intruder can lift a ceiling panel and climb over the partition. This example of intrusion is shown in Figure 10-4. In many situations, this would not require forced entry, specialized tools, or much effort. (In some office buildings, this may even be possible from a common public-access hallway.) These types of internal partitions should not be relied upon to provide protection for sensitive areas.

Another common control for work areas is a clean desk policy. This means that, before staff members leave their desks for extended periods (e.g., lunch, end of day), they remove all documents and pilferable items and store them in locked drawers. This ensures that sensitive documents are not lying around for wandering eyes (or cameras) to see. At the

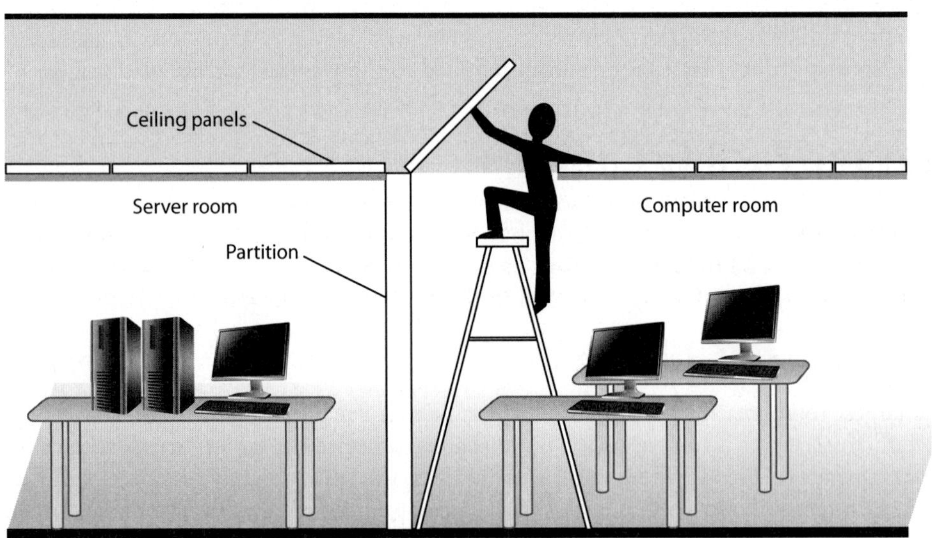

Figure 10-4 An intruder can lift ceiling panels and enter a secured area with little effort.

> **Restricted Areas**
> In some cases, a work area can be so sensitive that we must take extreme measures to ensure only authorized personnel are allowed in. Examples of these types of work areas are sensitive compartmented information facilities (SCIFs) used by governments to protect top secret information; police crime labs, where the integrity of evidence is absolutely paramount; research and development laboratories conducting particularly sensitive work; and many data centers. The controls we would use in these sensitive areas are similar to the ones previously discussed but are much stricter and more rigorously enforced.

end of the shift or work day, somebody is assigned the task of checking all desks to ensure compliance with the policy.

Data Processing Facilities

With the growing trend toward cloud computing, data processing facilities such as server rooms and data centers are less common than once was the case. Still, many organizations, not to mention providers of cloud services, can't get away from having these facilities. Since most servers, routers, switches, mainframes, and data centers can be controlled remotely and seldom require physical interaction, our data processing facilities have few people milling around and potentially spilling coffee. This lack of personnel sitting and working in them for long periods means these data centers can be constructed in a manner that is efficient for equipment instead of people.

On the other hand, there are situations in which people may have to be physically in the data center, perhaps for very extended periods of time (equipment installations/upgrades, data center infrastructure upgrades and reconfigurations, incident response, forensic data acquisition, etc.). Consequently, the inhospitable conditions (cold, dry environment; lack of comfortable workspaces; extremely high decibel levels) should be taken into account when deploying such personnel.

Data centers and server rooms should be located in the core areas of a facility, with strict access control mechanisms and procedures. The access control mechanisms may be smart card readers, biometric readers, or combination locks. These restricted areas should have only one *access* door, but fire code requirements typically dictate there must be at least two doors to most data centers and server rooms. Only one door should be used for daily entry and exit, and the other door should be used only in emergency situations. This second door should not be an access door, which means people should not be able to come in through this door. It should be locked, but should have a panic bar that will release the lock if pressed, possibly sounding an alarm.

These restricted areas ideally should not be directly accessible from public areas like stairways, corridors, loading docks, elevators, and restrooms. This helps ensure that the people who are by the doors to secured areas have a specific purpose for being there, versus being on their way to the restroom or standing around in a common area gossiping about the CEO.

Because data centers usually hold expensive equipment and the organization's critical data, their protection should be thoroughly thought out before implementation. A data center should not be located on an upper floor of a building, because that would make accessing it in a timely fashion in case of a fire more difficult for an emergency crew. By the same token, data centers should not be located in basements where flooding can affect the systems. And if a facility is in a hilly area, the data center should be located well above ground level. Data centers should be located at the core of a building so that if there is some type of attack on the building, the exterior walls and structures will absorb the hit and hopefully the data center will not be damaged.

Which access controls and security measures should be implemented for the data center depends upon the sensitivity of the data being processed and the protection level required. Alarms on the doors to the data processing center should be activated during off-hours, and there should be procedures dictating how to carry out access control during normal business hours, after hours, and during emergencies. If a combination lock is used to enter the data processing center, the combination should be changed at least every six months and also after an employee who knows the code leaves the organization.

The various controls discussed next are shown in Figure 10-5. The team responsible for designing a new data center (or evaluating a current data center) should understand all the controls shown in Figure 10-5 and be able to choose what is needed.

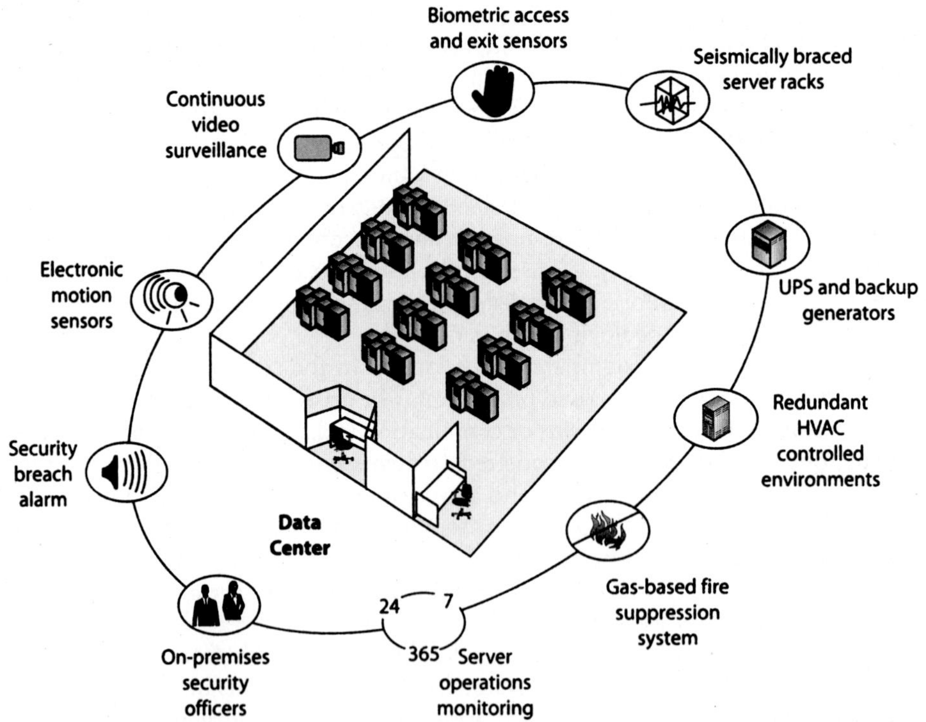

Figure 10-5 A data center should have many physical security controls.

The data processing center should be constructed as one room rather than different individual rooms. The room should be away from any of the building's water pipes in case a break in a line causes a flood. The vents and ducts from the heating, ventilation, and air conditioning (HVAC) system should be protected with some type of barrier bars and should be too small for anyone to crawl through and gain access to the center. The data center must have positive air pressure, so no contaminants can be sucked into the room and into the computers' fans.

Smoke detectors or fire sensors should be implemented, and portable fire extinguishers should be located close to the equipment and should be easy to see and access (see "Fire Safety" later in the chapter for details). Water sensors should be placed under the raised floors. Since most of the wiring and cables run under the raised floors, it is important that water does not get to these places and, if it does, that an alarm sound if water is detected.

TIP If there is any type of water damage in a data center or facility, mold and mildew could easily become a problem. Instead of allowing things to "dry out on their own," many times it is better to use industry-strength dehumidifiers, water movers, and sanitizers to ensure secondary damage does not occur.

Water can cause extensive damage to equipment, flooring, walls, computers, and facility foundations. It is important that an organization be able to detect leaks and unwanted water. The detectors should be under raised floors and on dropped ceilings (to detect leaks from the floor above it). The location of the detectors should be documented, and their position marked for easy access. As smoke and fire detectors should be tied to an alarm system, so should water detectors. The alarms usually just alert the necessary staff members and not everyone in the building. The staff members who are responsible for following up when an alarm sounds should be trained properly on how to reduce any potential water damage. Before anyone pokes around to see where water is or is not pooling in places it does not belong, the electricity for that particular zone of the building should be temporarily turned off.

Water detectors can help prevent damage to

- Equipment
- Flooring
- Walls
- Computers
- Facility foundations

Location of water detectors should be

- Under raised floors
- On dropped ceilings

It is important to maintain the proper temperature and humidity levels within data centers, which is why an HVAC system should be implemented specifically for this room. Too high a temperature can cause components to overheat and turn off; too low a temperature can cause the components to work more slowly. If the humidity is high, then corrosion of the computer parts can take place; if humidity is low, then static electricity can be introduced. Because of this, the data center must have its own temperature and humidity controls that are separate from those for the rest of the building.

It is best if the data center is on a different electrical system than the rest of the building, if possible. Thus, if anything negatively affects the main building's power, it will not carry over and affect the center. The data center may require redundant power supplies, which means two or more feeders coming in from two or more electrical substations. The idea is that if one of the power company's substations were to go down, the organization would still be able to receive electricity from the other feeder. But just because an organization has two or more electrical feeders coming into its facility does not mean true redundancy is automatically in place. Many organizations have paid for two feeders to come into their building, only to find out both feeders were coming from the same substation! This defeats the whole purpose of having two feeders in the first place.

Data centers need to have their own backup power supplies, either an uninterrupted power supply (UPS) or generators. The different types of backup power supplies are discussed later in the chapter, but it is important to know at this point that the power backup must be able to support the load of the data center.

Many organizations choose to use large glass panes for the walls of the data center so personnel within the center can be viewed at all times. This glass should be shatter-resistant since the window is acting as an exterior wall. The center's doors should not be hollow, but rather secure solid-core doors. Doors should open out rather than in, so they don't damage equipment when opened. Best practices indicate that the door frame should be fixed to adjoining wall studs and that there should be at least three hinges per door. These characteristics would make the doors much more difficult to break down.

Distribution Facilities

Distribution facilities are systems that distribute communications lines, typically dividing higher-bandwidth lines into multiple lower-bandwidth lines. A building typically has one main distribution facility (MDF) where one or more external data lines are fed into the server room, data center, and/or other smaller intermediate distribution facilities (IDFs). An IDF usually provides individual lines or drops to multiple endpoints, though it is possible to daisy-chain IDFs as needed.

Larger IDFs are usually installed in small rooms normally called *wiring closets*. All of the design considerations for unstaffed server rooms and data centers discussed in the previous section also apply to these facilities. It is critical to think of these as the sensitive IT facilities that they are and not as just closets. We've seen too many organizations that allow their IDF rooms to do double duty as janitors' closets.

Smaller IDFs are oftentimes installed in rooms that have a large number of network endpoints. They can be as small as a single switch and small patch panel on a shelf or as big as a cabinet. Unlike an MDF, an IDF is usually not enclosed in its own room, which makes it more susceptible to tampering and accidental damage. Whenever possible, an IDF should be protected by a locked enclosure. Ideally, it is elevated to reduce the risk of flood or collision damage and to make it more visible should someone tamper with it. Another consideration that is oftentimes overlooked is placing the IDF away from overhead sprinklers, pipes, or HVAC ducts.

Storage Facilities

Storage facilities are often overlooked when it comes to security considerations other than, perhaps, locking them. While a simple lock may be all we need to think of when we're storing office supplies and basic tools, we should really think about what it is that we are protecting. In many cases, the physical locks we use are either low grade (in other words, easily picked) or have keys that are shared by multiple people. Unlike their modern electronic counterparts, these locks lack built-in auditing tools to see who opened them and when. If you are storing anything that you'd hate to have go missing, you probably want to think long and hard about who gets a key, how it's signed out, and how to periodically inventory the storage area.

This is particularly true of storage facilities in which you store computing equipment. Depending on your organizational procedures, you may be storing computers with storage devices that have not yet been securely wiped or baselined. This means there are security risks if someone gets their hands on them apart from that of theft. You also need to worry about the environmental conditions of the storage facility, since computers don't do so well in hot, humid areas over long periods.

These are just examples to get you thinking. Whatever is stored in the facility should impact the security controls you put on it. There are two types of storage facilities that deserve special attention, which are those we use to store media and those we use to store evidence. Let's take a closer look at each.

Media Storage

We discussed in Chapter 5 that the information life cycle includes an archival phase during which information is not regularly used but we still need to retain it. This happens, for example, when we close accounts but still need to keep the records for a set number of years, or when we do backups. In any event, we have to keep a large number of disks, magnetic tapes, or even paper files for prolonged periods until we either need them or are able to dispose of them. This has to happen in a secure location that meets the requirements discussed for server rooms and data centers. Unfortunately, media storage is sometimes not given the importance it deserves, which can result in the loss or compromise of important information.

Evidence Storage

Evidence storage facilities are even more sensitive because any compromise, real or perceived, could render evidence inadmissible in court. We will cover forensic investigations in Chapter 22, but every organization with a dedicated IT staff should probably have a secure facility in which to store evidence. The two key requirements for evidence storage facilities are that they are properly secured and that all access and transfers are logged.

Ideally, only select incident handlers and forensic investigators have access to the facility. Unless forensic investigations are part of your business, you will likely only need a rugged cabinet with a good lock and a register in which to record who opened/closed it and what was done in it. This is yet another example of a situation in which a technical control alone (like the cabinet or safe) won't do the job. You also have to have a good policy (like logging all access to the contents) that is rigorously enforced.

Utilities

Utilities, as with storage, is another area on which many of us don't spend a lot of time thinking about security. Still, utilities can pose significant risks to our sites and facilities. Local construction codes may address safety issues, but they do very little to otherwise help us protect our organizations.

Water and Wastewater

As the saying goes, water is life. Without clean water and wastewater services, our staffed facilities would not be able to operate safely for any length of time. Interruptions to these services, therefore, could require the evacuation of most or all personnel from a facility, which could degrade its security posture and create a window of opportunity for nefarious activity.

An abundance of water in the wrong place can also cause serious problems. As we discussed previously with regard to data centers and distribution facilities, it is critical to route water pipes (or, more realistically, position assets) so that a ruptured or leaking pipe will not cause equipment damage.

During facility construction, the physical security team must make certain that water, steam, and gas lines have proper shutoff valves, as shown in Figure 10-6, and *positive drains*, which means their contents flow out instead of in. If there is ever a break in a main water pipe, the valve to shut off water flow must be readily accessible. Similarly, in case of fire in a building, the valve to shut off the gas lines must be readily accessible. In case of a flood, an organization wants to ensure that material cannot travel up through the water pipes and into its water supply or facility. Facility, operations, and security personnel should know where these shutoff valves are, and there should be strict procedures to follow in these types of emergencies. This will help reduce the potential damage.

Electric Power

Power failure, particularly over a long stretch of time, can be devastating to an unprepared organization. Having good plans to fall back on is crucial to ensure that a business will not be drastically affected by storms, high winds, hardware failure, lightning, or other events that can stop or disrupt power supplies. A continuous supply of electricity assures the availability of organizational resources; thus, a security professional must be familiar with the threats to electric power and the corresponding countermeasures.

Power Backup Several types of power backup capabilities exist. Before you choose one, you should calculate the total cost of anticipated downtime and its effects. This information can be gathered from past records and other businesses in the same area on the same power grid and plugged into the annualized loss expectancy (ALE) formula we

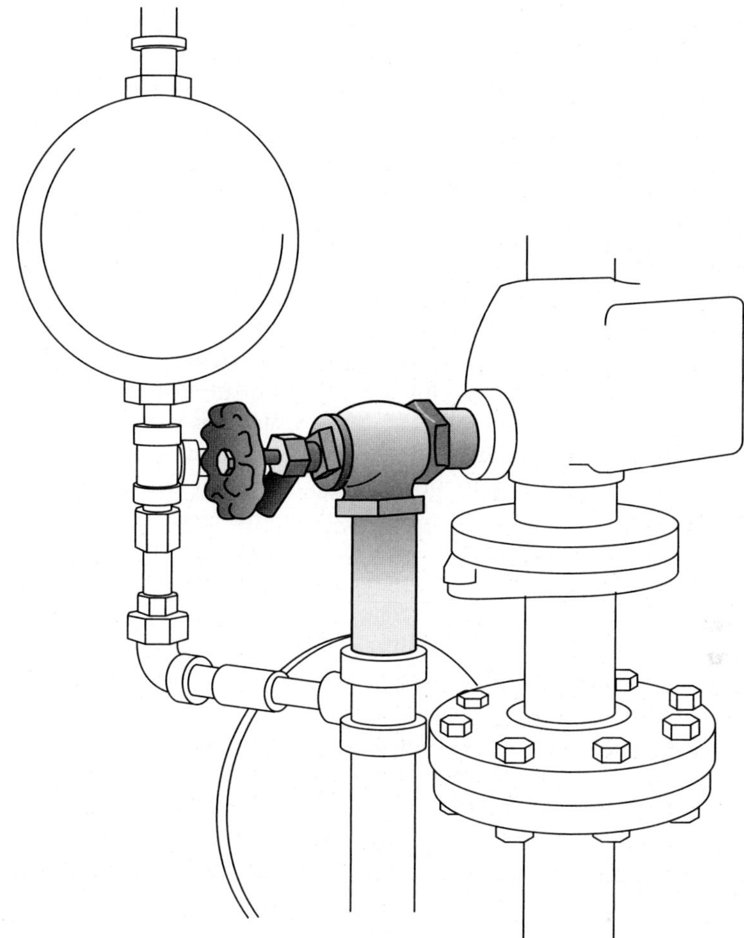

Figure 10-6 Water, steam, and gas lines should have emergency shutoff valves.

discussed in Chapter 2. Essentially, you want to calculate the annual expected cost of power outages in terms of lost revenue, recovery costs, and the like. This amount will tell you whether it makes sense to run a secondary line that is fed by a different grid or to buy a backup generator, both of which are significant investments.

If you plan to buy a generator, you also have to determine how long it will be expected to run each year, which tells you how big of a fuel storage tank you need and what the expected fuel costs are. Keep in mind that you will have to periodically run the generator to ensure that it remains ready, and also be aware that some fuels go bad after sitting around for several months. As always, we have to ensure the cure is not worse than the illness.

Just having a generator in the backyard should not give you that warm fuzzy feeling of protection. An alternative power source should be tested periodically to make sure it works and to the extent expected. Power interruption drills should be performed periodically to avoid nasty surprises. It is never good to find yourself in an emergency only to discover that the organization added a bunch of power-hungry assets since you bought the generator and it is now too small to power them all.

Electric Power Issues Electric power enables us to be productive and functional in many different ways, but if it is not installed, monitored, and respected properly, it can do us great harm. When *clean* power is being provided, the power supply contains no interference or voltage fluctuation. The possible types of interference (*line noise*) are *electromagnetic interference (EMI)* and *radio frequency interference (RFI)*, which can cause disturbance to the flow of electric power while it travels across a power line, as shown in Figure 10-7.

EMI is the effect of unwanted energy on an electrical system caused by radiations from another, nearby, electrical system. EMI can be created by the difference between three wires—hot, neutral, and ground—and the magnetic field they create. Lightning and electrical motors can induce EMI, which could then interrupt the proper flow of electrical current as it travels over wires to, from, and within buildings. RFI, which is the subset of EMI that occurs in the radio frequency (RF) portion of the electromagnetic (EM) spectrum, can be caused by anything that creates radio waves. Fluorescent lighting is one of the main causes of RFI within buildings today. So, does that mean we need to rip out all the fluorescent lighting? That's one choice, but we could also just use shielded cabling where fluorescent lighting could cause a problem. If you take a break from your reading, climb up into your office's dropped ceiling, and look around, you would probably see wires bundled and tied up to the *true* ceiling. If your office is using fluorescent lighting, the power and data lines should not be running over, or on top of, the fluorescent lights. This is because the radio frequencies being given off can interfere with the data or power current as it travels through these wires. Now, get back down from the ceiling. We have work to do.

Interference interrupts the flow of an electrical current, and fluctuations can actually deliver a different level of voltage than what was expected. Each fluctuation can be

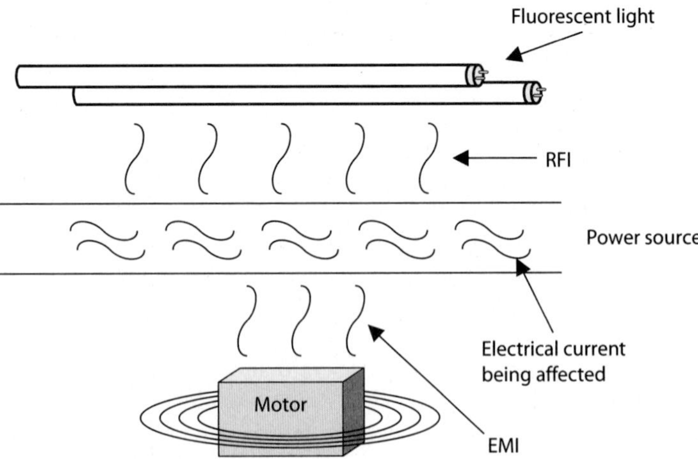

Figure 10-7 RFI and EMI can cause line noise on power lines.

damaging to devices and people. The following explains the different types of voltage fluctuations possible with electric power:

Power excess:

- **Spike** Momentary high voltage
- **Surge** Prolonged high voltage

Power loss:

- **Fault** Momentary power outage
- **Blackout** Prolonged, complete loss of electric power

Power degradation:

- **Sag/dip** Momentary low-voltage condition, from one cycle to a few seconds
- **Brownout** Prolonged power supply that is below normal voltage
- **In-rush current** Initial surge of current required to start a load

When an electrical device is turned on, it can draw a large amount of current, which is referred to as *in-rush current*. If the device sucks up enough current, it can cause a *sag* in the available power for surrounding devices. This could negatively affect their performance. As stated earlier, it is a good idea to have the data processing center and devices on a different electrical wiring segment from that of the rest of the facility, if possible, so the devices will not be affected by these issues. For example, if you are in a building or house without efficient wiring and you turn on a vacuum cleaner or microwave, you may see the lights quickly dim because of this in-rush current. The drain on the power supply caused by in-rush currents still happens in other environments when these types of electrical devices are used—you just might not be able to see the effects. Any type of device that would cause such a dramatic in-rush current should not be used on the same electrical segment as data processing systems.

Because these and other occurrences are common, mechanisms should be in place to detect unwanted power fluctuations and protect the integrity of your data processing environment. *Voltage regulators* and *line conditioners* can be used to ensure a clean and smooth distribution of power. The primary power runs through a regulator or conditioner. They have the capability to absorb extra current if there is a spike and to store energy to add current to the line if there is a sag. The goal is to keep the current flowing at a nice, steady level so neither motherboard components nor employees get fried.

Many data centers are constructed to take power-sensitive equipment into consideration. Because surges, sags, brownouts, blackouts, and voltage spikes frequently cause data corruption, the centers are built to provide a high level of protection against these events. Other types of environments usually are not built with these things in mind and do not provide this level of protection. Offices usually have different types of devices connected and plugged into the same outlets. Outlet strips are plugged into outlet strips, which are connected to extension cords. This causes more line noise and a reduction of voltage to each device. Figure 10-8 depicts an environment that can cause line noise, voltage problems, and possibly a fire hazard.

Figure 10-8 This configuration can cause a lot of line noise and poses a fire hazard.

Power Protection Protecting power can be done in three ways: through online UPSs, through standby UPSs, and through the power line conditioners discussed in the previous section. UPSs use battery packs that range in size and capacity. *Online UPS systems* use AC line voltage to charge a bank of batteries. When in use, the UPS has an inverter that changes the DC output from the batteries into the required AC form and regulates the voltage as it powers computer devices. This conversion process is shown in Figure 10-9.

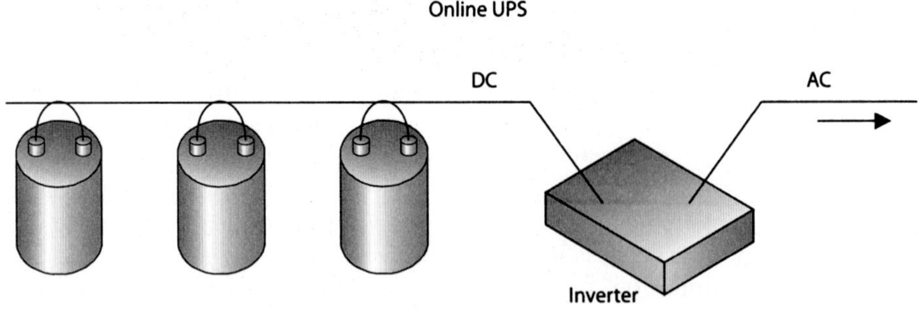

Figure 10-9 A UPS device converts DC current from its internal or external batteries to usable AC by using an inverter.

Online UPS systems have the normal primary power passing through them day in and day out. They constantly provide power from their own inverters, even when the electric power is in proper use. Since the environment's electricity passes through this type of UPS all the time, the UPS device is able to quickly detect when a power failure takes place. An online UPS can provide the necessary electricity and picks up the load after a power failure much more quickly than a standby UPS.

Standby UPS devices stay inactive until a power line fails. The system has sensors that detect a power failure, and the load is switched to the battery pack. The switch to the battery pack is what causes the small delay in electricity being provided. So an online UPS picks up the load much more quickly than a standby UPS, but costs more, of course.

An organization should identify critical systems that need protection from interrupted power supplies and then estimate how long secondary power would be needed and how much power is required per device. Some UPS devices provide just enough power to allow systems to shut down gracefully, whereas others allow the systems to run for a longer period. An organization needs to determine whether systems should only have a big enough power supply to allow the organization to shut down properly or should have sufficient power to keep the organization up and running so that critical operations remain available.

Heating, Ventilation, and Air Conditioning

Improper environmental controls can cause damage to services, hardware, and lives. Interruption of some services can cause unpredicted and unfortunate results. HVAC systems and air-quality controls can be complex and contain many variables. They all need to be operating properly and to be monitored regularly.

Most electronic equipment must operate in a climate-controlled atmosphere. Although it is important to keep the atmosphere at a proper working temperature, you must also be aware that the components within the equipment can suffer from overheating even in a climate-controlled atmosphere if the internal computer fans are not cleaned or are blocked. When devices are overheated, the components can expand and contract, which causes components to change their electronic characteristics, reducing their effectiveness or damaging the system overall.

NOTE The climate issues involved with a data processing environment are why it needs its own separate HVAC system. Maintenance procedures should be documented and properly followed. HVAC activities should be recorded and reviewed annually.

Maintaining appropriate temperature and humidity is important in any facility, especially facilities with computer systems. Improper levels of either can cause damage to computers and electrical devices. High humidity can cause corrosion, and low humidity can cause excessive static electricity. This static electricity can short out devices and cause the loss of information.

Lower temperatures can cause mechanisms to slow or stop, and higher temperatures can cause devices to use too much fan power and eventually shut down. Table 10-1 lists different components and their corresponding damaging temperature levels.

Table 10-1 Components Affected by Specific Temperatures

Material or Component	Damaging Temperature
Computer systems and peripheral devices	175°F
Magnetic storage devices	100°F
Paper products	350°F

Fire Safety

The subject of physical security would not be complete without a discussion on fire safety. Every site and facility must meet national and local standards pertaining to fire prevention, detection, and suppression methods. *Fire prevention* includes training employees on how to prevent fires, how to react properly when faced with a fire, supplying the right equipment and ensuring it is in working order, making sure there is an easily reachable fire suppression supply, and storing combustible elements in the proper manner. Fire prevention may also include using proper noncombustible construction materials and designing the facility with containment measures that provide barriers to minimize the spread of fire and smoke. These thermal or fire barriers can be made up of different types of construction material that is noncombustible and has a fire-resistant coating applied.

Fire detection response systems come in many different forms. Manual detection response systems are the red pull boxes you see on many building walls. Automatic detection response systems have sensors that react when they detect the presence of fire or smoke. We will review different types of detection systems in the next section.

Fire suppression is the use of a suppression agent to put out a fire. Fire suppression can take place manually through handheld portable extinguishers or through automated systems such as water sprinkler systems or CO_2 discharge systems. The upcoming "Fire Suppression" section reviews the different types of suppression agents and where they are best used. Automatic sprinkler systems are widely used and highly effective in protecting buildings and their contents. When deciding upon the type of fire suppression systems to install, an organization needs to evaluate many factors, including an estimate of the occurrence rate of a possible fire, the amount of damage that could result, the types of fires that would most likely take place, and the types of suppression systems to choose from.

Fire protection processes should consist of implementing early smoke or fire detection devices and shutting down systems until the source of the fire is eliminated. A warning signal may be sounded by a smoke or fire detector before the suppression agent is released so that if it is a false alarm or a small fire that can be handled without the automated suppression system, someone has time to shut down the suppression system.

Types of Fire Detection

Fires present a dangerous security threat because they can damage hardware and data and risk human life. Smoke, high temperatures, and corrosive gases from a fire can cause devastating results. It is important to evaluate the fire safety measurements of a building and the different sections within it.

A fire begins because something ignited a combustible substance (the fuel). Ignition sources can be failure of an electrical device, improper storage of combustible materials, carelessly discarded cigarettes, malfunctioning heating devices, and arson. A fire needs fuel (paper, wood, liquid, and so on) and oxygen to continue to burn and grow. The more fuel per square foot, the more intense the fire will become. A facility should be built, maintained, and operated to minimize the accumulation of fuels that can feed fires.

There are six classes (A, B, C, D, E, and F) of fire, which are explained in the "Fire Suppression" section. You need to know the differences between the types of fire so you know how to properly extinguish each type. Portable fire extinguishers have markings that indicate what type of fire they should be used on, as illustrated in Figure 10-10. The markings denote what types of chemicals are within the canisters and what types of fires they have been approved to be used on. Portable fire extinguishers should be located within 50 feet of any electrical equipment and also near exits. The extinguishers should be marked clearly, with an unobstructed view. They should be easily reachable and operational by employees and inspected quarterly.

A lot of computer systems are made of components that are not combustible but that will melt or char if overheated. Most computer circuits use only 2 to 5 volts of direct current, which usually cannot start a fire. If a fire does happen in a server room, it will most likely be an electrical fire caused by overheating of wire insulation or by overheating components that ignite surrounding plastics. Prolonged smoke usually occurs before combustion.

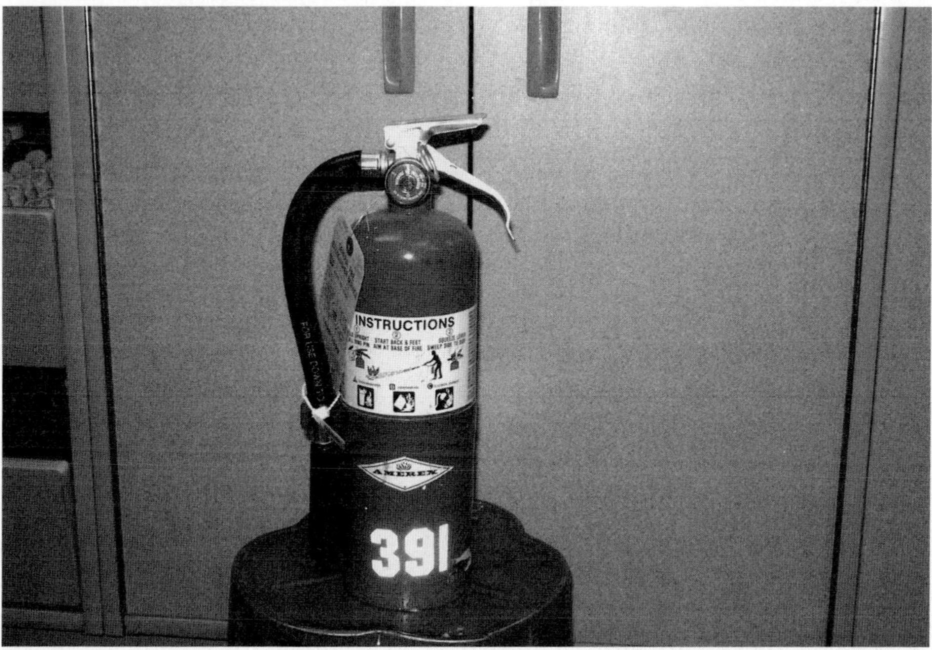

Figure 10-10 Portable extinguishers are marked to indicate what type of fire they should be used on.

Fire Resistance Ratings

Fire resistance ratings are the result of tests carried out in laboratories using specific configurations of environmental settings. ASTM International is the organization that creates the standards that dictate how these tests should be performed and how to properly interpret the test results. ASTM International accredited testing centers carry out the evaluations in accordance with these standards and assign fire resistance ratings that are then used in federal and state fire codes. The tests evaluate the fire resistance of different types of materials in various environmental configurations. Fire resistance represents the ability of a laboratory-constructed assembly to contain a fire for a specific period. For example, a 5/8-inch-thick drywall sheet installed on each side of a wood stud provides a one-hour rating. If the thickness of this drywall is doubled, then this would be given a two-hour rating. The rating system is used to classify different building components.

Several types of detectors are available, each of which works in a different way. The detector can be activated by smoke or heat.

Smoke Activated Smoke-activated detectors are good for early warning devices. They can be used to sound a warning alarm before the suppression system activates. A photoelectric device, also referred to as an optical detector, detects the variation in light intensity. The detector produces a beam of light across a protected area, and if the beam is obstructed, the alarm sounds. Figure 10-11 illustrates how a photoelectric device works.

Another type of photoelectric device samples the surrounding air by drawing air into a pipe. If the light source is obscured, the alarm will sound.

Heat Activated Heat-activated detectors can be configured to sound an alarm either when a predefined temperature (fixed temperature) is reached or when the temperature increases over time (rate of rise). Rate-of-rise temperature sensors usually provide a quicker warning than fixed-temperature sensors because they are more sensitive, but they

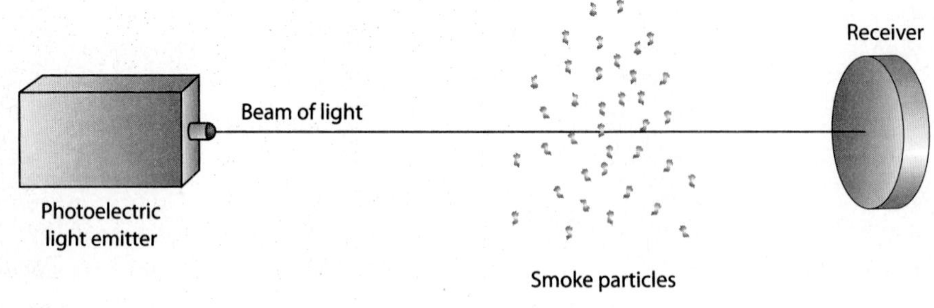

Figure 10-11 A photoelectric device uses a light emitter and a receiver.

Figure 10-12 Smoke detectors should be located above suspended ceilings, below raised floors, and in air vents.

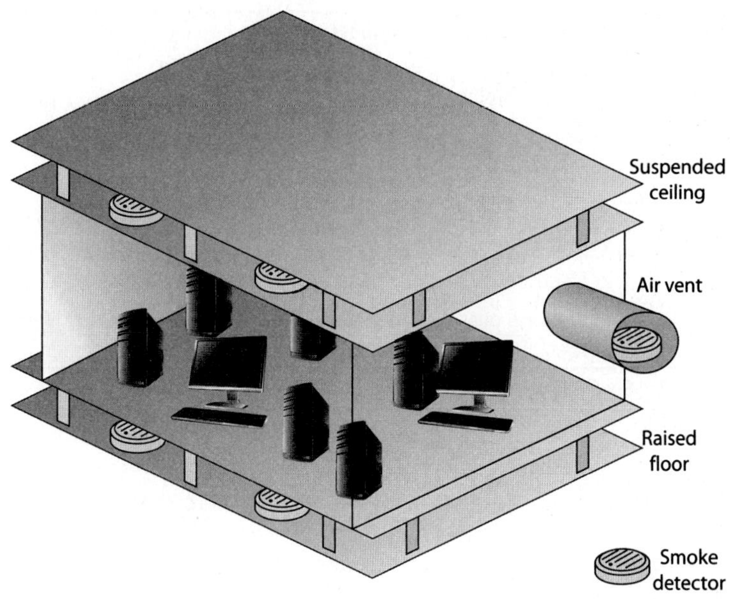

can also cause more false alarms. The sensors can either be spaced uniformly throughout a facility or implemented in a line type of installation, which is operated by a heat-sensitive cable.

It is not enough to have these fire and smoke detectors installed in a facility; they must be installed in the right places. Detectors should be installed both on and above suspended ceilings and raised floors because organizations run many types of wires in both places that could start an electrical fire. No one would know about the fire until it broke through the floor or dropped ceiling if detectors were not placed in these areas. Detectors should also be located in enclosures and air ducts because smoke can gather in these areas before entering other spaces. It is important that people are alerted about a fire as quickly as possible so damage may be reduced, fire suppression activities may start quickly, and lives may be saved. Figure 10-12 illustrates the proper placement of smoke detectors.

Fire Suppression

It is important to know the different types of fire and what should be done to properly suppress each type. Each fire type has a class that indicates what materials are burning and how to suppress the fire. Unfortunately, three slightly different classifications are in use around the world today (United States, European Union, and Australia). Table 10-2 shows the EU classification fires and their suppression agents. We show this classification because it provides the most granularity. More important than memorizing the letter assigned to each class is to know which suppression methods work best for the different types of fire.

EU Fire Class	Type of Fire	Elements of Fire	Suppression Agent
A	Common combustibles	Wood products, paper, and laminates	Water, foam, dry powders, wet chemicals
B	Liquid	Petroleum products and coolants	CO_2, foam, dry powders
C	Gases	Butane, propane, or methane	Dry powders
D	Combustible metals	Aluminum, lithium, or magnesium	Dry powders
E	Electrical	Electrical equipment and wires	CO_2, dry powders
F	Cooking oils and fats	Typically found in food preparation and storage areas	Wet chemicals

Table 10-2 Six EU Types of Fires and Their Suppression Methods

At the risk of confusing things, we also list here the U.S. classification of fires for reference.

U.S. Class	Type of Fire
A	Common combustibles (same as EU)
B	Liquids and gases (EU Classes B and C combined)
C	Electrical (EU Class E)
D	Metals (same as EU)
K	Cooking oils and fats (EU Class F)

You can suppress a fire in several ways, all of which require taking certain precautions. A fire suppression agent is the substance used to extinguish it. The agent can be delivered in a variety of ways such as a portable fire extinguisher or an overhead distribution system (e.g., water sprinklers). When designing and implementing fire controls, it is critical to match the right suppression agent with the specific facility we're trying to protect. Overhead water sprinklers may be fine for regular work areas but would be catastrophic in a data center. Gases, such as CO_2 will reduce damage to our data assets but could suffocate humans in confined spaces. If you use CO_2, the suppression-releasing device should have a delay mechanism within it that makes sure the agent does not start applying CO_2 to the area until after an audible alarm has sounded and people have been given time to evacuate. CO_2 is a colorless, odorless substance that is potentially lethal because it removes oxygen from the air. Gas masks do not provide protection against CO_2. This type of fire suppression mechanism is best used in unattended facilities and areas.

For all types of fires except those involving cooking oils and fats, specific types of dry powders can be used, which include sodium or potassium bicarbonate, calcium carbonate, or monoammonium phosphate. The first three powders interrupt the chemical combustion of a fire. Monoammonium phosphate melts at low temperatures and excludes oxygen from the fuel.

Combustion Element	Suppression Agent	How Suppression Works
Fuel	Soda acid	Removes fuel
Oxygen	Carbon dioxide	Displaces oxygen
Temperature	Water	Reduces temperature
Chemical reaction	FM-200 (Halon substitute)	Interferes with the chemical reactions between elements

Table 10-3 How Different Substances Interfere with Elements of Fire

Foams are mainly water-based and contain a foaming agent that allows them to float on top of a burning substance to exclude the oxygen.

Wet chemical fire extinguishers contain a potassium solution that cools the fire. However, they have an added benefit of chemically reacting with hot oil or fat, creating a soapy film on the surface of these fuels, which starves the fire. For this reason, wet chemical extinguishers are the preferred way of putting out fires involving cooking oils and fats. These extinguishers are also useful for putting put out Class A fires.

A fire needs fuel, oxygen, and high temperatures to sustain its chemical reactions. Fire suppression approaches target one of these three required elements, or the chemical reaction itself. Table 10-3 shows how different suppression substances interfere with these elements of fire.

The HVAC system should be connected to the fire alarm and suppression system so that it properly shuts down if a fire is identified. A fire needs oxygen, and this type of system can feed oxygen to the fire. Plus, the HVAC system can spread deadly smoke into all areas of the building. Many fire systems can configure the HVAC system to shut down if a fire alarm is triggered.

Water Sprinklers

Water sprinklers are typically the simpler and less expensive fire suppression systems but can cause water damage. In an electrical fire, the water can increase the intensity of the fire because it can work as a conductor for electricity—only making the situation worse. If water is going to be used in any type of environment with electrical equipment, the electricity must be turned off before the water is released. Sensors should be used to shut down the electric power before water sprinklers activate. Each sprinkler head should activate individually to avoid wide-area damage, and there should be shutoff valves so the water supply can be stopped if necessary.

Plenum Area

Wiring and cables are strung through *plenum areas*, such as the space above dropped ceilings, the space in wall cavities, and the space under raised floors. Plenum areas should have fire detectors. Also, only plenum-rated cabling should be used in plenum areas, which is cabling that is made out of material that does not release hazardous gases if it burns.

An organization should take great care in deciding which suppression agent and system is best for it. Four main types of water sprinkler systems are available:

- **Wet pipe** Wet pipe systems always contain water in the pipes and are usually discharged by temperature control–level sensors. One disadvantage of wet pipe systems is that the water in the pipes may freeze in colder climates. Also, if there is a nozzle or pipe break, it can cause extensive water damage. These types of systems are also called closed-head systems.
- **Dry pipe** In dry pipe systems, the water is not actually held in the pipes. The water is contained in a "holding tank" until it is released. The pipes hold pressurized air, which is reduced when a fire or smoke alarm is activated, allowing the water valve to be opened by the water pressure. Water is not allowed into the pipes that feed the sprinklers until an actual fire is detected. First, a heat or smoke sensor is activated; then, the water fills the pipes leading to the sprinkler heads, the fire alarm sounds, the electric power supply is disconnected, and finally water is allowed to flow from the sprinklers. These pipes are best used in colder climates because the pipes will not freeze. Figure 10-13 depicts a dry pipe system.
- **Preaction** Preaction systems are similar to dry pipe systems in that the water is not held in the pipes, but is released when the pressurized air within the pipes is reduced. Once this happens, the pipes are filled with water, but it is not released right away. A thermal-fusible link on the sprinkler head has to melt before the water is released. The purpose of combining these two techniques is to give people more time to respond to false alarms or to small fires that can be handled by other means. Putting out a small fire with a handheld extinguisher is better than losing a lot of electrical equipment to water damage. These systems are usually used only in data processing environments rather than the whole building because of the higher cost of these types of systems.
- **Deluge** A deluge system has its sprinkler heads wide open to allow a larger volume of water to be released in a shorter period. Because the water being released is in such large volumes, these systems are usually not used in data processing environments.

Figure 10-13 Dry pipe systems do not hold water in the pipes.

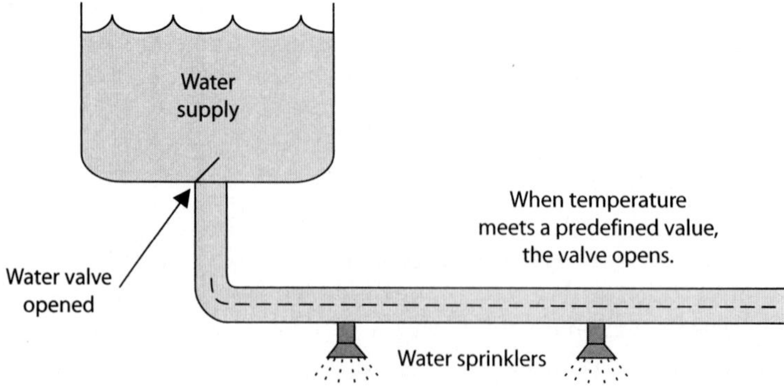

Environmental Issues

In drier climates, or during the winter, the air contains less moisture, which can cause static electricity when two dissimilar objects touch each other. This electricity usually travels through the body and produces a spark from a person's finger that can release several thousand volts. This can be more damaging than you would think. Usually, the charge is released on a system casing and is of no concern, but sometimes it is released directly to an internal computer component and causes damage. People who work on the internal parts of a computer usually wear antistatic armbands to reduce the chance of this happening.

In more humid climates, or during the summer, more humidity is in the air, which can also affect components. Particles of silver can begin to move away from connectors onto copper circuits, which cement the connectors into their sockets. This can adversely affect the electrical efficiency of the connection. A *hygrometer* is usually used to monitor humidity. It can be manually read, or an automatic alarm can be set up to go off if the humidity passes a set threshold.

Chapter Review

Physical security of our sites and facilities requires a deliberate planning, execution, and review process. In this chapter, we have discussed the most important topics you'll need to know about to ensure that your organization's physical spaces are secure, but it's up to you to apply them in your particular situations. One of the most important aspects of securing a facility is controlling access in and out of it. In our experience, it is rare for an auditor (such as a physical penetration tester) to not be able to breach this perimeter through social engineering, lockpicking, or simply waiting for someone to leave a door propped open when they shouldn't. This underscores the importance of applying defense in depth and the other principles we discussed in the first half of the chapter.

The practical application of these secure design principles happens through security controls. Though our focus is on physical security, these controls can be administrative (e.g., policies and procedures), technical (e.g., keycard entry systems and security cameras), or physical (e.g., fences and guards). By carefully balancing threats, resources, and controls in a deliberate manner, we can provide effective site and facility security.

Quick Review

- A site is a geographic area with fixed boundaries that typically contains at least one building and its supporting structures (e.g., a parking lot or electric substation).
- A facility is a building or a part of a building dedicated to a specific purpose, such as corporate headquarters or a data center.
- The secure design principles covered in Chapter 9 for information systems are just as applicable to the design of physical security.
- The value of property within the facility and the value of the facility itself need to be ascertained to determine the proper budget for physical security so that security controls are cost-effective.

- Some physical security controls may conflict with the safety of people. These issues need to be addressed; human life is always more important than protecting a facility or the assets it contains.
- When looking at locations for a facility, consider local crime; natural disaster possibilities; and distance to hospitals, police and fire stations, airports, and railroads.
- Crime Prevention Through Environmental Design (CPTED) combines the physical environment and sociology issues that surround it to reduce crime rates and the fear of crime.
- CPTED provides four main strategies, which are natural access control, natural surveillance, territorial reinforcement, and maintenance.
- Natural access control is the guidance of people entering and leaving a space by the placement of doors, fences, lighting, and even landscaping.
- The goal of natural surveillance is not only to make criminals feel uncomfortable by providing many ways observers could potentially see them but also to make authorized personnel feel safe and comfortable by providing an open and well-designed environment.
- Territorial reinforcement creates physical designs (e.g., using walls, fences, landscaping) that emphasize or extend the organization's physical sphere of influence so legitimate users feel a sense of ownership of that space.
- CPTED's maintenance principle focuses on deterring criminal activity by making sites look well cared for, thus implying that site personnel are more attentive, well resourced, and alert.
- Target hardening focuses on denying access through physical and artificial barriers (alarms, locks, fences, and so on).
- If interior partitions do not go all the way up to the true ceiling, an intruder can remove a ceiling tile and climb over the partition into a critical portion of the facility.
- The primary power source is what is used in day-to-day operations, and the alternative power source is a backup in case the primary source fails.
- Smoke detectors should be located on and above suspended ceilings, below raised floors, and in air ducts to provide maximum fire detection.
- A fire needs high temperatures, oxygen, and fuel. To suppress it, one or more of those items needs to be reduced or eliminated.
- Portable fire extinguishers should be located within 50 feet of electrical equipment and should be inspected quarterly.
- CO_2 is a colorless, odorless, and potentially lethal substance because it removes the oxygen from the air in order to suppress fires.
- Window types that should be understood are standard, tempered, acrylic, wired, and laminated.

Questions

Please remember that these questions are formatted and asked in a certain way for a reason. Keep in mind that the CISSP exam is asking questions at a conceptual level. Questions may not always have the perfect answer, and the candidate is advised against always looking for the perfect answer. Instead, the candidate should look for the best answer in the list.

1. When should a CO_2 fire extinguisher be used?
   A. When electrical equipment is on fire
   B. When gases are on fire
   C. When a combustible metal is on fire
   D. In workspaces with paper products
2. When should a water sprinkler system be used?
   A. When electrical equipment is on fire
   B. When gases are on fire
   C. When a combustible metal is on fire
   D. In workspaces with paper products
3. Which of the following is not a main component of CPTED?
   A. Natural access control
   B. Natural surveillance
   C. Territorial reinforcement
   D. Target hardening
4. Which problems may be caused by humidity in an area with electrical devices?
   A. High humidity causes excess electricity, and low humidity causes corrosion.
   B. High humidity causes corrosion, and low humidity causes static electricity.
   C. High humidity causes power fluctuations, and low humidity causes static electricity.
   D. High humidity causes corrosion, and low humidity causes power fluctuations.
5. The fourth principle of Crime Prevention Through Environmental Design (CPTED) is maintenance. What does this principle entail?
   A. Ensuring that target hardening controls remain in working order
   B. Periodically assessing designs to ensure they remain effective
   C. Maintaining visibility over all elements of the environmental design
   D. Deterring criminal activity by making sites look well cared for

6. Which of the following answers contains a category of controls that does not belong in a physical security program?
   A. Deterrence and delaying
   B. Response and detection
   C. Assessment and detection
   D. Delaying and lighting

Use the following scenario to answer Questions 7–9. You are the CISO for a data analytics company and, after reading this chapter, have decided to review the physical security of your facility. You currently lease the top three floors of a high-rise building in a major metropolitan area. The top floor contains the executive suites and conference facilities. The next floor down houses your data center and research and development (R&D) and software development teams. The lower floor is where your administrative and sales staff workspaces are located.

7. As part of your lease agreement, the building owners provide a reception area in the lobby with receptionists, security guards, keycard-based access controls, and security cameras. What secure design principle is this arrangement an example of?
   A. Zero trust
   B. Trust but verify
   C. Shared responsibility
   D. Separation of duties
8. As you ride the elevator up, you notice that your company employees can use their keycards to access any of the top three floors. What secure design principle could this violate?
   A. Shared responsibility
   B. Simplicity
   C. Defense in depth
   D. Secure defaults
9. Based on your preliminary findings, you are concerned about the security of your facility and decide to redo the entire plan. What would you do first?
   A. Determine the resources available to you
   B. Conduct an audit of the current posture
   C. Apply the secure design principles
   D. Conduct a risk assessment

Answers

1. **A.** CO_2 fire extinguishers work by displacing oxygen and thus choking the fire. This approach can put human lives in danger of also choking, so it should not be used in workspaces. It is also not ideal for gas or metal fires. It is, however, very well suited for electrical fires since it minimizes the risk of electric shock and damage to the equipment.
2. **D.** Water sprinklers are very effective against wood and paper fires and are safe for humans, so they are a good choice for use in regular workspaces. They are, however, particularly bad choices to use against the other types of fires listed (electric, gas, metal).
3. **D.** Target hardening has to do with implementing locks, security guards, and proximity devices. Natural access control is the use of the environment to control access to entry points, such as using landscaping and bollards. An example of natural surveillance is the construction of pedestrian walkways so there is a clear line of sight of all the activities in the surroundings. Territorial reinforcement gives people a sense of ownership of a property, giving them a greater tendency to protect it. These concepts are all parts of CPTED.
4. **B.** High humidity can cause corrosion, and low humidity can cause excessive static electricity. Static electricity can short out devices or cause loss of information.
5. **D.** CPTED's maintenance principle focuses on deterring criminal activity by making sites look well cared for, thus implying that site personnel are more attentive, well resourced, and possibly alert.
6. **D.** The categories of controls that should make up any physical security program are deterrence, delaying, detection, assessment, and response. Lighting is a control itself, not a category of controls.
7. **C.** Shared responsibility usually involves different organizations that have a services agreement, such as leasing office spaces and having the landlord provide security in the entry points. Separation of duties is similar but applies to staff responsibilities divided between individuals to deter and prevent any one party from damaging the company. While elements of zero trust and trust but verify are present in the scenario, they are not the salient ones.
8. **C.** Defense in depth means you should create concentric rings around your most critical resources. In this case, only certain individuals should have access to the executive spaces and, possibly, the data center floor, unless you have additional security controls in place as soon as someone enters those two floors.
9. **D.** Site and facility security, like any other type of security, must start with an understanding of the risks faced by the organization. These risks determine the required resources for the effort and the manner in which the secure design principles are applied to your particular situation.

PART IV

Communication and Network Security

CHAPTER 11

Networking Fundamentals

This chapter presents the following:

- Data communications foundations
- Networking protocols
- Local, metropolitan, and wide area networks

The Internet…it's a series of tubes.

—Ted Stevens

Before we dive into communications and network security, it makes sense to review (and maybe pick up a bit of new information on) the fundamentals of data communications networks. Data communications and networking are complex topics, mainly because so many technologies are involved. Our current technologies are constantly evolving, and every month there seems to be new "emerging" ones that we have to learn, understand, implement, and secure. As security professionals, we need a solid grasp of networking software, protocols, services, and devices. We have to be able to identify and deal with interoperability issues (ideally before developing or acquiring a new system). Armed with all this knowledge and skill, we need to anticipate or discover vulnerabilities, both in individual components and in their interactions with each other, and devise effective controls for them. This can be a challenging task. However, if you are knowledgeable, have a solid practical skill set, and are willing to continue to learn, you can have more career opportunities than you know what to do with.

In this chapter we will start with the basics of data communications and networking, and then build upon them and identify many of the security issues that are involved. We'll follow up in the next chapter with a discussion of wireless technologies that take the place of the cables described in this chapter. Then, in Chapter 13 we'll dive into the protocols that drive the Internet. This will set the stage for understanding how we secure this hodgepodge of technologies, the focus of Chapters 14 and 15.

Data Communications Foundations

Data communications have made amazing advances in a relatively short period of time. In the beginning of the Computer Age, mainframes were the name of the game. They were isolated powerhouses, and many had "dumb" terminals hanging off them, but this was not true networking. In the late 1960s and early 1970s, some technical researchers came up with ways of connecting all the mainframes and Unix systems to enable them to communicate. This marked the Internet's first baby steps.

While access to shared resources was a major drive in the evolution of networking, today the infrastructure that supports these shared resources and the services these components provide is really the secret to the secret sauce. As we will see, networks are made up of routers, switches, servers, proxies, firewalls, intrusion detection/prevention systems (IDS/IPSs), storage systems, virtual private network (VPN) concentrators, public key infrastructure, private branch exchanges (PBXs), and more. While functionality is critical, there are other important requirements that need to be understood when architecting a network, such as scalability, redundancy, performance, security, manageability, and maintainability.

Infrastructure provides foundational capabilities that support almost every aspect of our lives. When most people think of technology, they focus on the end systems that they interact with—laptops, mobile phones, tablet PCs, workstations, and so on—or the applications they use, such as e-mail, Facebook, websites, instant messaging, Twitter, and online banking. Most people do not even give a thought to how this stuff works under the covers, and many people do not fully realize all the other stuff that is dependent upon technology: medical devices, critical infrastructure, weapon systems, transportation, satellites, telephony, and so forth. People say it is love that makes the world go around, but let them experience one day without the Internet. We are all more dependent upon the Matrix than we fully realize, and as security professionals we need to not only understand the Matrix but also secure it.

Before we get into the weeds of actual devices, systems, and services, it will be helpful to have a reference model so that we can put like pieces in the same bin. This will allow us to compare things that perform similar functions so that we can better see how they differ and what those differences may mean for security. Let's start off by introducing the two most common models for understanding networked systems: the OSI model and the TCP/IP model.

Network Reference Models

In the early 1980s, the International Organization for Standardization (as it is referred to internationally, but commonly abbreviated as ISO) worked to develop a protocol set that would be used by all vendors throughout the world to allow the interconnection of network devices. This movement was fueled with the hopes of ensuring that all vendor products and technologies could communicate and interact across international and technical boundaries. The actual protocol set did not catch on as a standard, but the *Open Systems Interconnection (OSI) reference model* was adopted and is used as an abstract framework to which most operating systems and protocols adhere.

Many people think that the OSI reference model arrived at the beginning of the computing age as we know it and helped shape and provide direction for many, if not all, networking technologies. However, this is not true. In fact, it was introduced in 1984, at which time the basics of the Internet had already been developed and implemented, and the basic Internet protocols had been in use for many years.

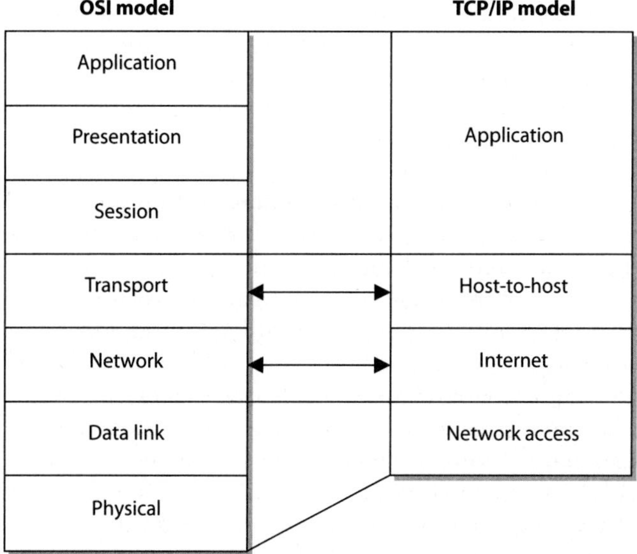

Figure 11-1 The OSI and TCP/IP networking models

The Transmission Control Protocol/Internet Protocol (TCP/IP) suite actually has its own model that predates the OSI model by several years. As a bit of background, the Internet as we know it grew from the Advanced Research Project Agency Network (ARPANET) program that started in the late 1960s. By 1978, ARPANET researchers realized that a monolithic approach to networking was not going to scale well. That's when they split what had until then been known as the Transmission Control Program (which encompassed all aspects of getting data from point A to point B) into two distinct layers: TCP and IP. Everything that happened below IP was the domain of network access engineers, and everything above TCP was the domain of application developers. The idea caught on and the TCP/IP reference model was born. It is often used today when examining and understanding networking issues. Figure 11-1 shows the differences between the OSI and TCP/IP networking models. In this chapter, we will focus on the OSI model.

NOTE The host-to-host layer is sometimes called the transport layer in the TCP/IP model. The application layer in the TCP/IP architecture model is equivalent to a combination of the application, presentation, and session layers in the OSI model.

Protocols

Before we delve into the details of each layer of the OSI model, we need to examine the concept of network protocols. A *network protocol* is a standard set of rules that determines how systems will communicate across networks. Two different systems that use the same protocol can communicate and understand each other despite their differences, similar to how two people can communicate and understand each other by using the same language.

The OSI reference model, as described by ISO Standard 7498-1, provides important guidelines used by vendors, engineers, developers, and others. The model segments the networking tasks, protocols, and services into different layers. Each layer has its own responsibilities regarding how two computers communicate over a network. Each layer has certain functionalities, and the services and protocols that work within that layer fulfill them.

The OSI model's goal is to help vendors develop products that will work within an open network architecture. An *open network* architecture is one that no vendor owns, that is not proprietary, and that can easily integrate various technologies and vendor implementations of those technologies. Vendors have used the OSI model as a jumping-off point for developing their own networking frameworks. These vendors use the OSI model as a blueprint and develop their own protocols and services to produce functionality that is different from, or overlaps, that of other vendors. However, because these vendors use the OSI model as their starting place, integration of other vendor products is an easier task, and the interoperability issues are less burdensome than if the vendors had developed their own networking framework from scratch.

Although computers communicate in a physical sense (electronic signals are passed from one computer over a wire to the other computer), they also communicate through logical channels. Each protocol at a specific OSI layer on one computer communicates with a corresponding protocol operating at the same OSI layer on another computer. This happens through *encapsulation*.

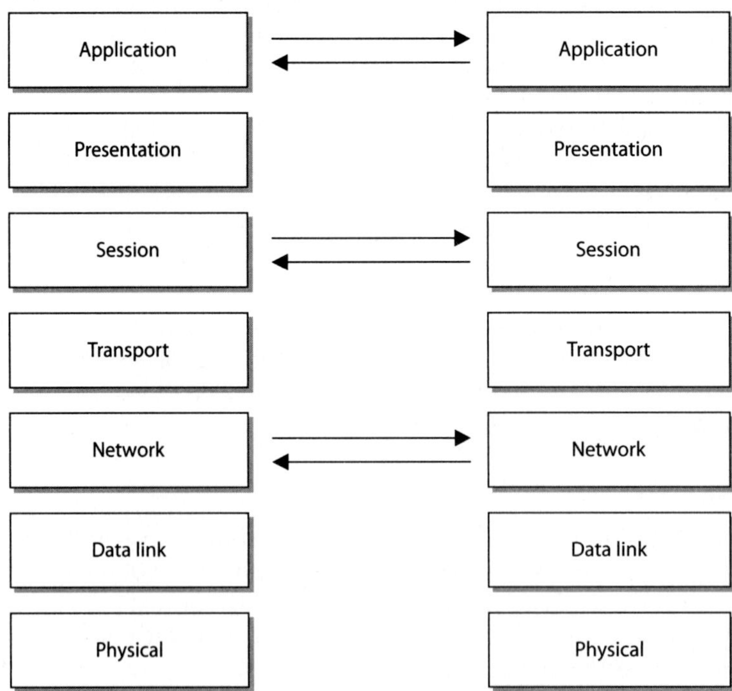

Here's how encapsulation works: A message is constructed within a program on one computer and is then passed down through the network protocol's stack. A protocol at each layer adds its own information to the message, creating a *protocol data unit (PDU)*. Thus, the message grows in size as it goes down the protocol stack. The message is then sent to the destination computer, and the encapsulation is reversed by taking the packet apart through the same steps used by the source computer that encapsulated it. At the data link layer, the PDU pertaining to the data link layer is deconstructed, and the packet is sent up to the next layer. Then at the network layer, the network layer PDU is stripped and processed, and the message is again passed up to the next layer, and so on. This is how computers communicate logically. The information stripped off at the destination computer informs it how to interpret and process the packet properly. Data encapsulation is shown in Figure 11-2.

A protocol at each layer has specific responsibilities and control functions it performs, as well as data format syntaxes it expects. Each layer has a special interface (connection point) that allows it to interact with three other layers: (1) communications from the interface of the layer above it, (2) communications to the interface of the layer below it, and (3) communications with the same layer in the interface of the target packet address. The control functions, added by the protocols at each layer, are in the form of headers and trailers of the packet.

The benefit of modularizing these layers, and the functionality within each layer, is that various technologies, protocols, and services can interact with each other and provide the proper interfaces to enable communications. This means a computer can use an application protocol developed by Microsoft, a transport protocol developed by Apple,

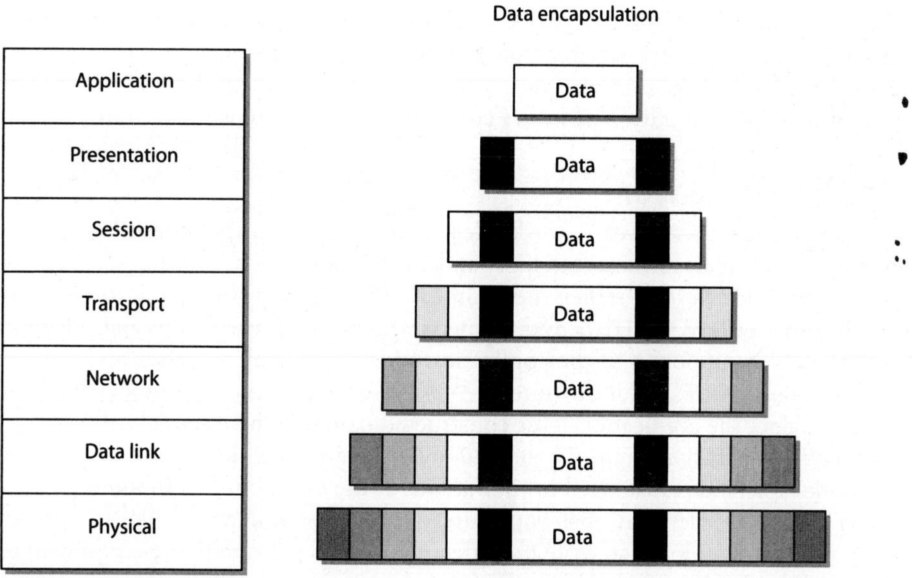

Figure 11-2 Each OSI layer protocol adds its own information to the data packet.

Attacks at Different Layers

As we examine the different layers of a common network stack, we will also look at the specific attack types that can take place at each layer. One concept to understand at this point is that a network can be used as a *channel for an attack*, or the network can be the *target of an attack*. If the network is a channel for an attack, this means the attacker is using the network as a resource. For example, when an attacker sends a virus from one system to another system, the virus travels through the network channel. If an attacker carries out a denial-of-service (DoS) attack, which sends a large amount of bogus traffic over a network link to bog it down, then the network itself is the target. As you will see throughout this book, it is important to understand how attacks take place and where they take place so that the correct countermeasures can be put into place.

and a data link protocol developed by Cisco to construct and send a message over a network. The protocols, technologies, and computers that operate within the OSI model are considered *open systems*. Open systems are capable of communicating with other open systems because they implement international standard protocols and interfaces. The specification for each layer's interface is very structured, while the actual code that makes up the internal part of the software layer is not defined. This makes it easy for vendors to write plug-ins in a modularized manner. Systems are able to integrate the plug-ins into the network stack seamlessly, gaining the vendor-specific extensions and functions.

Understanding the functionalities that take place at each OSI layer and the corresponding protocols that work at those layers helps you understand the overall communication process between computers. Once you understand this process, a more detailed look at each protocol will show you the full range of options each protocol provides and the security weaknesses embedded into each of those options.

Application Layer

The *application layer*, layer 7, works closest to the user and provides file transmissions, message exchanges, terminal sessions, and much more. This layer does not include the actual applications, but rather the protocols that support the applications. When an application needs to send data over the network, it passes instructions and the data to the protocols that support it at the application layer. This layer processes and properly formats the data and passes it down to the next layer within the OSI model. This happens until the data the application layer constructed contains the essential information from each layer necessary to transmit the data over the network. The data is then put on the network cable and transmitted until it arrives at the destination computer.

As an analogy, let's say that you write a letter that you would like to send to your congressman. Your job is to write the letter, your clerk's job is to figure out how to get it to him, and the congressman's job is to read your letter and respond to it. You (the application) create the content (message) and hand it to your assistant (application layer protocol).

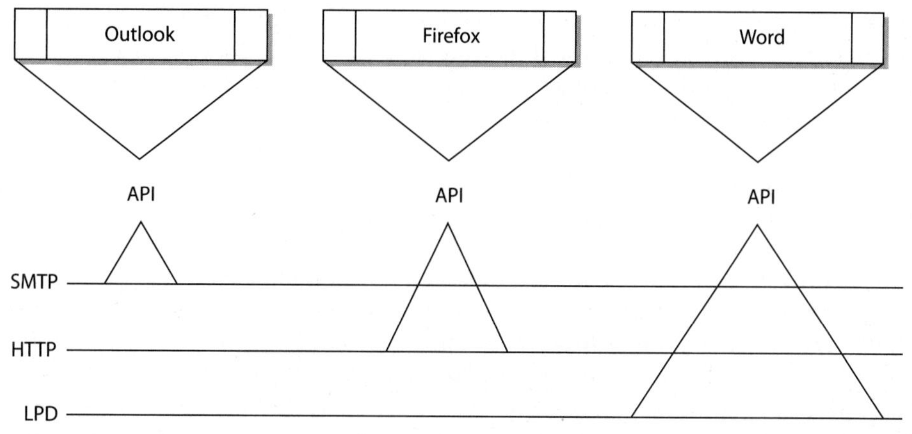

Figure 11-3 Applications send requests to an API, which is the interface to the supporting protocol.

Your assistant puts the content into an envelope, writes the congressman's address on the envelope (inserts headers and trailers), and puts it into the mailbox (passes it on to the next protocol in the network stack). When your assistant checks the mailbox a week later, there is a letter from the congressman (the remote application) addressed to you. Your assistant opens the envelope (strips off headers and trailers) and gives you the message (passes the message up to the application).

Some examples of the protocols working at the application layer are the Simple Mail Transfer Protocol (SMTP), the Hypertext Transfer Protocol (HTTP), and the Line Printer Daemon (LPD) protocol. Figure 11-3 shows how applications communicate with the underlying protocols through application programming interfaces (APIs). If a user makes a request to send an e-mail message through her e-mail client Outlook, the e-mail client sends this information to SMTP. SMTP adds its information to the user's message and passes it down to the presentation layer.

Presentation Layer

The *presentation layer*, layer 6, receives information from the application layer protocol and puts it in a format that any process operating at the same layer on a destination computer following the OSI model can understand. This layer provides a common means of representing data in a structure that can be properly processed by the end system. This means that when a user creates a Word document and sends it out to several people, it does not matter whether the receiving computers have different word processing programs; each of these computers will be able to receive this file and understand and present it to its user as a document. It is the data representation processing that is done at the presentation layer that enables this to take place. For example, when a Windows 10 computer receives a file from another computer system, information within the file's header indicates what type of file it is. The Windows 10 operating system has a list of file types it understands and a table describing what program should be used to open and manipulate each of these file types. For example, suppose the sender e-mails a Portable Document Format (PDF) file created in Word and the receiver uses a Linux system. The receiver can open this file because the presentation layer on the sender's system encoded the file and added a descriptive header in accordance with the Multipurpose Internet Mail Extensions (MIME) standards, and the receiver's computer interprets the header's MIME type (Content-Type: application/pdf), decodes the file, and knows to open it with its PDF viewer application.

The presentation layer is concerned not with the meaning of data but with the syntax and format of that data. It works as a translator, translating the format an application is using to a standard format used for passing messages over a network. If a user uses a graphics application to save a file, for example, the graphic could be a Tagged Image File Format (TIFF), Graphic Interchange Format (GIF), or Joint Photographic Experts Group (JPEG) format. The presentation layer adds information to tell the destination computer the file type and how to process and present it. This way, if the user sends this graphic to another user who does not have the same graphics application, the receiving user's operating system can still present the graphic because it has been saved in a standard format. Figure 11-4 illustrates the conversion of a file into different standard file types.

This layer also handles data compression and encryption issues. If a program requests a certain file to be compressed and encrypted before being transferred over the network, the presentation layer provides the necessary information for the destination computer. It provides information on how the file was encrypted and/or compressed so that the receiving system knows what software and processes are necessary to decrypt and decompress the file. Let's say Sara compresses a file using WinZip and sends it to you. When your system receives this file, it looks at data within the header (Content-Type: application/zip) and knows what application can decompress the file. If your system has WinZip installed, then the file can be decompressed and presented to you in its original form. If your system does not have an application that understands the compression/decompression instructions, the file will be presented to you with an unassociated icon.

Figure 11-4 The presentation layer receives data from the application layer and puts it into a standard format.

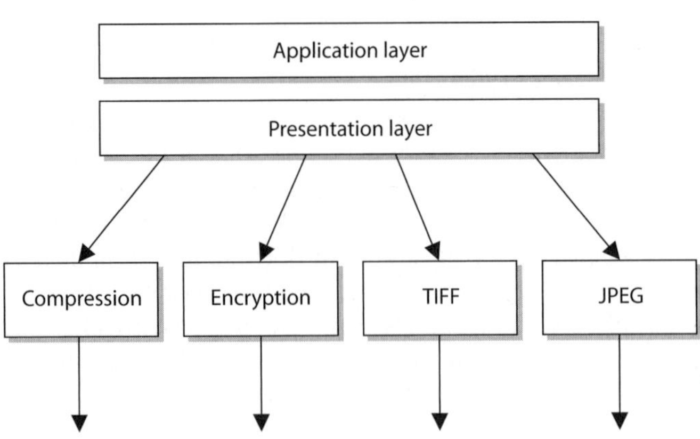

Session Layer

When two applications need to communicate or transfer data between themselves, a connection may need to be set up between them. The *session layer*, layer 5, is responsible for establishing a connection between the two applications, maintaining it during the transfer of data, and controlling the release of this connection. A good analogy for the functionality within this layer is a telephone conversation. When Kandy wants to call a friend, she uses the telephone. The telephone network circuitry and protocols set up the connection over the telephone lines and maintain that communication path, and when Kandy hangs up, they release all the resources they were using to keep that connection open.

Similar to how telephone circuitry works, the session layer works in three phases: connection establishment, data transfer, and connection release. It provides session restart and recovery if necessary and provides the overall maintenance of the session. When the conversation is over, this path is broken down and all parameters are set back to their original settings. This process is known as *dialog management*. Figure 11-5 depicts the three phases of a session. Some protocols that work at this layer are the Layer 2 Tunneling Protocol (L2TP), Point-to-Point Tunneling Protocol (PPTP), and Remote Procedure Call (RPC).

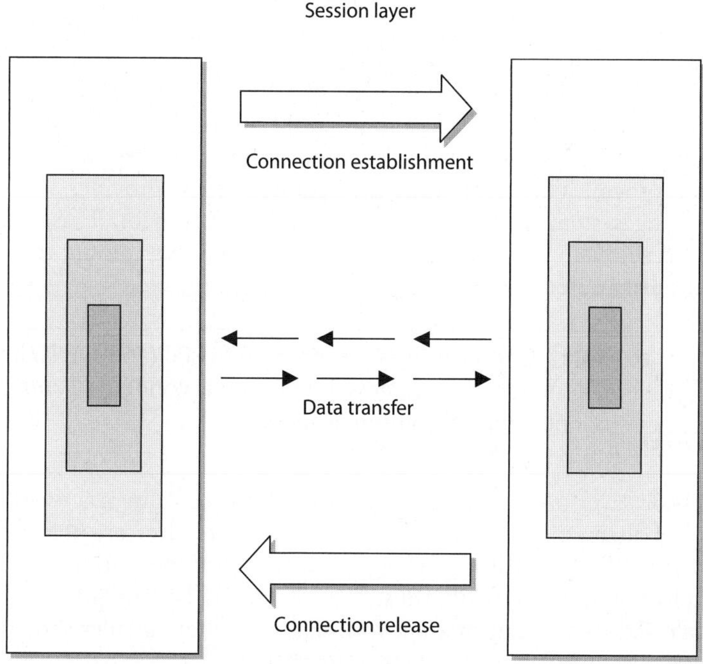

Figure 11-5 The session layer sets up the connection, maintains it, and tears it down once communication is completed.

The session layer protocol can enable communication between two applications to happen in three different modes:

- **Simplex** Communication takes place in one direction, though in practice this is very seldom the case.
- **Half-duplex** Communication takes place in both directions, but only one application can send information at a time.
- **Full-duplex** Communication takes place in both directions, and both applications can send information at the same time.

Many people have a hard time understanding the difference between what takes place at the session layer versus the transport layer because their definitions sound similar. Session layer protocols control application-to-application communication, whereas the transport layer protocols handle computer-to-computer communication. For example, if you are using a product that is working in a client/server model, in reality you have a small piece of the product on your computer (client portion) and the larger piece of the software product is running on a different computer (server portion). The communication between these two pieces of the same software product needs to be controlled, which is why session layer protocols even exist. Session layer protocols take on the functionality of middleware, which allows software on two different computers to communicate.

Session layer protocols provide interprocess communication channels, which allow a piece of software on one system to call upon a piece of software on another system without the programmer having to know the specifics of the software on the receiving system. The programmer of a piece of software can write a function call that calls upon a subroutine. The subroutine could be local to the system or be on a remote system. If the subroutine is on a remote system, the request is carried over a session layer protocol. The result that the remote system provides is then returned to the requesting system over the same session layer protocol. This is how RPC works. A piece of software can execute components that reside on another system. This is the core of distributed computing.

NOTE One security issue common to RPC (and similar interprocess communication systems) is improperly configured authentication or the use of unencrypted communications.

Session layer protocols are the least used protocols in a network environment; thus, many of them should be disabled on systems to decrease the chance of them being exploited. RPC, NetBIOS, and similar distributed computing calls usually only need to take place within a network; thus, firewalls should be configured so this type of traffic is not allowed into or out of a network. Firewall filtering rules should be in place to stop this type of unnecessary and dangerous traffic.

Transport Layer

When two computers are going to communicate through a connection-oriented protocol, they first agree on how much information each computer will send at a time, how to verify the integrity of the data once received, and how to determine whether a packet was lost along the way. The two computers agree on these parameters through a handshaking process at the *transport layer*, layer 4. The agreement on these issues before transferring data helps provide more reliable data transfer, error detection, correction, recovery, and flow control, and it optimizes the network services needed to perform these tasks. The transport layer provides end-to-end data transport services and establishes the logical connection between two communicating computers.

NOTE Connection-oriented protocols, such as Transmission Control Protocol (TCP), provide reliable data transmission when compared to connectionless protocols, such as User Datagram Protocol (UDP). This distinction is covered in more detail in the "Internet Protocol Networking" section, later in the chapter.

The functionality of the session and transport layers is similar insofar as they both set up some type of session or virtual connection for communication to take place. The difference is that protocols that work at the session layer set up connections between *applications*, whereas protocols that work at the transport layer set up connections between *computer systems*. For example, we can have three different applications on computer A communicating with three applications on computer B. The session layer protocols keep track of these different sessions. You can think of the transport layer protocol as the bus. It does not know or care what applications are communicating with each other. It just provides the mechanism to get the data from one system to another.

The transport layer receives data from many different applications and assembles the data into a stream to be properly transmitted over the network. The main protocols that work at this layer are the Transmission Control Protocol (TCP) and the User Datagram Protocol (UDP). Information is passed down from different entities at higher layers to the transport layer, which must assemble the information into a stream, as shown in Figure 11-6. The stream is made up of the various data segments passed to it. Just like a bus can carry a variety of people, the transport layer protocol can carry a variety of application data types.

NOTE Different references can place specific protocols at different layers. For example, many references place the Transport Layer Security (TLS) protocol in the session layer, while other references place it in the transport layer. Neither placement is right or wrong. The OSI model tries to draw boxes around reality, but some protocols straddle the different layers.

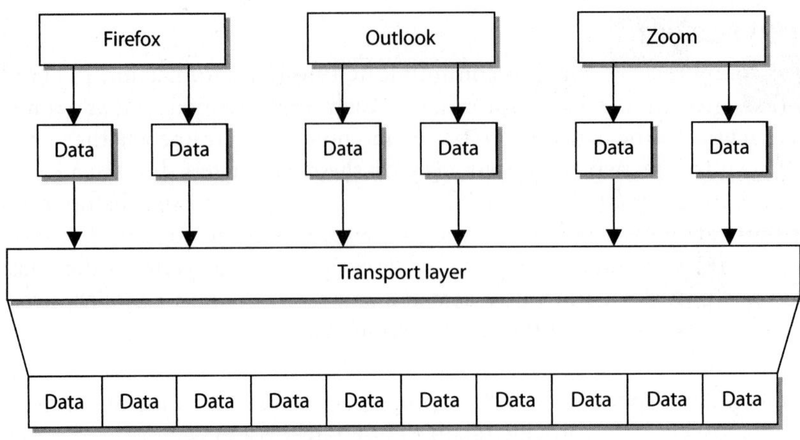

Figure 11-6 TCP formats data from applications into a stream to be prepared for transmission.

Network Layer

The main responsibilities of the *network layer*, layer 3, are to insert information into the packet's header so it can be properly addressed and routed, and then to actually route the packet to its proper destination. In a network, many routes can lead to one destination. The protocols at the network layer must determine the best path for the packet to take. Routing protocols build and maintain their routing tables. These tables are maps of the network, and when a packet must be sent from computer A to computer M, the protocols check the routing table, add the necessary information to the packet's header, and send it on its way.

The protocols that work at this layer do not ensure the delivery of the packets. They depend on the protocols at the transport layer to catch any problems and resend packets if necessary. The Internet Protocol (IP) is the predominant protocol working at the network layer, although other routing and routed protocols work there as well. Some of the other protocols are the Internet Control Message Protocol (ICMP), Routing Information Protocol (RIP), Open Shortest Path First (OSPF), Border Gateway Protocol (BGP), and Internet Group Management Protocol (IGMP). Figure 11-7 shows that a packet can take many routes and that the network layer enters routing information into the header to help the packet arrive at its destination.

Data Link Layer

As we continue down the protocol stack, we are getting closer to the actual transmission channel (e.g., network wire) over which all the data will travel. The network layer has already figured out how to route the packet through the various network devices to its final destination, but we still need to get the data over to the next, directly connected device. This happens at the *data link layer*, layer 2.

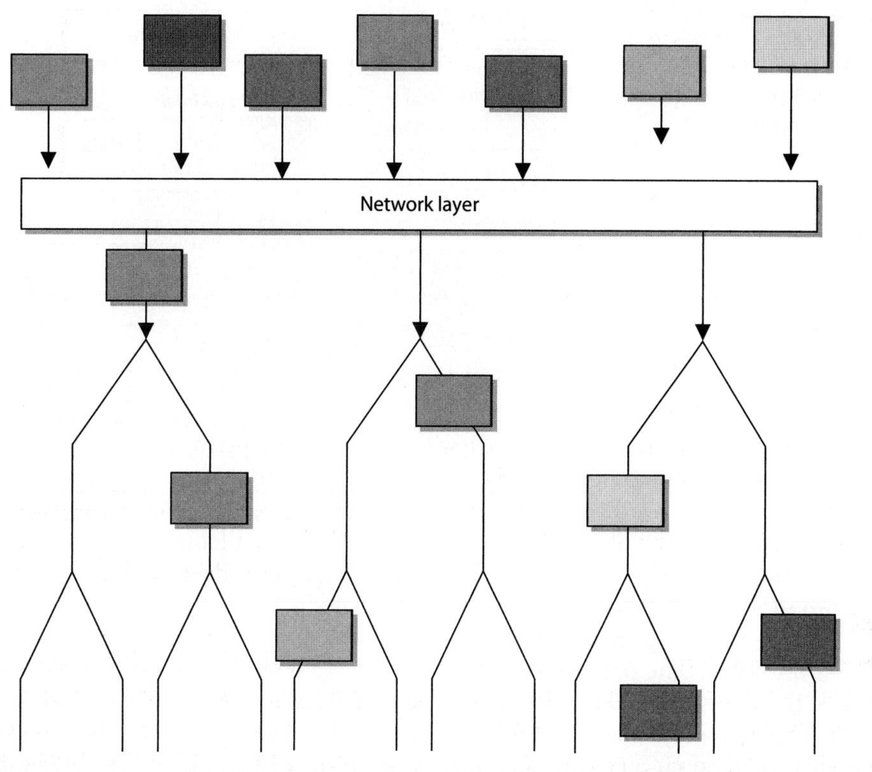

Figure 11-7 The network layer determines the most efficient path for each packet to take.

Different networking technologies, as we will shortly discuss in detail, can use different protocols, network interface cards (NICs), cables, and transmission methods. Each of these components has a different header data format structure, and they interpret electromagnetic signals in different ways. The data link layer is where the network stack knows in what format the data frame must be in order to transmit it properly over Ethernet, wireless, or frame relay links. If the network is an Ethernet network, for example, all the computers will expect packet headers to be a certain length, the flags to be positioned in certain field locations within the header, and the trailer information to be in a certain place with specific fields. Compared to Ethernet, frame relay network technology has different frame header lengths, flag values, and header formats.

The data link layer can be further divided into two functional sublayers: *Logical Link Control (LLC)*, whose job is to interface with the network layer above, and *Media Access Control (MAC)*, which is designed to interface with the physical layer below. Let's drill into this a bit. The LLC sublayer, which is defined in the ISO/IEC 8802-2 standard for Ethernet networks, receives a message (say, an IP packet) from layer 3 and negotiates the manner in which it should be sent out over the network link. This could include keeping track of which layer 3 protocol was used, determining what kind of service (e.g.,

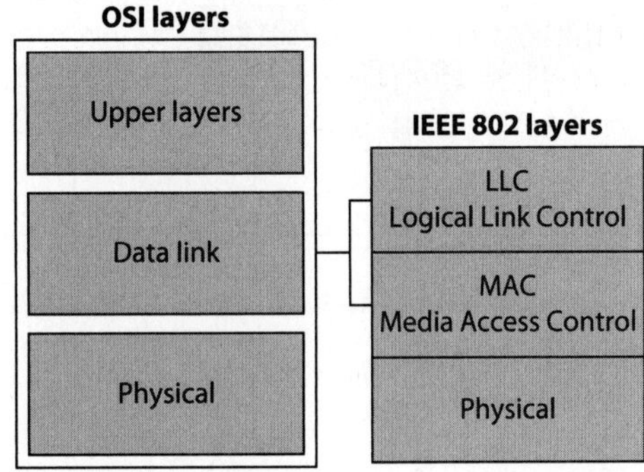

Figure 11-8 The data link layer is made up of two sublayers.

connectionless or connection-oriented) will be used, and performing flow control so the link doesn't get saturated. The LLC sublayer then hands over the data to the MAC sublayer, which encapsulates it into a frame of the right type depending on the networking technology in use by the physical layer. Generally, LLC is implemented in software (as a device driver), while MAC is built in firmware on a physical device. Figure 11-8 shows these two sublayers that make up the data link layer.

As data is passed down the network stack, it has to go from the network layer to the data link layer. The protocol at the network layer does not know if the underlying network is Ethernet, wireless, or frame relay—it does not need to have this type of insight. The protocol at the network layer just adds its header and trailer information to the packet and passes it on to the next layer, which is the LLC sublayer. The LLC sublayer takes care of flow control and error checking. Data coming from the network layer passes down through the LLC sublayer and goes to the MAC sublayer. The technology at the MAC sublayer knows if the network is Ethernet, wireless, or frame relay, so it knows how to put the last header and trailer on the packet before it "hits the wire" for transmission.

Some of the protocols that work at the data link layer are the Point-to-Point Protocol (PPP), Asynchronous Transfer Mode (ATM), Layer 2 Tunneling Protocol (L2TP), Fiber Distributed Data Interface (FDDI), Ethernet, and Token Ring.

Each network technology (Ethernet, wireless, frame relay, and so on) defines the compatible physical transmission type (coaxial, twisted pair, fiber, wireless) that is required to enable network communication. Each network technology also has defined electronic signaling and encoding patterns. For example, if we were transmitting a bit with the value of 1 over an Ethernet network, the MAC sublayer would tell the physical layer to create a +0.5-volt electric signal. In the "language of Ethernet" this means that 0.5 volts is the encoding value for a bit with the value of 1. If the next bit the MAC sublayer receives is 0, the MAC layer would tell the physical layer to transmit 0 volts. The different network types will have different encoding schemes.

NICs bridge the data link and physical layers. Data is passed down through the first six layers and reaches the NIC at the data link layer. Depending on the network technology being used, the NIC encodes the bits at the data link layer, which are then turned into electricity states at the physical layer and placed onto the wire for transmission.

EXAM TIP When the data link layer applies the last header and trailer to the data message, this is referred to as *framing*. The unit of data is now called a *frame*.

Physical Layer

The *physical layer*, layer 1, converts bits into electromagnetic signals for transmission. Signals and voltage schemes have different meanings for different LAN and WAN technologies, as covered earlier. If a user sends data through the radio transceiver on a smartphone, the data format, electrical signals, and control functionality are much different than if that user sends data through an Ethernet NIC and onto an unshielded twisted pair (UTP) wire for LAN communication. The mechanisms that control this data going onto the radio waves, or the UTP wire, work at the physical layer. This layer controls synchronization, data rates, line noise, and transmission techniques. Specifications for the physical layer include the timing of voltage changes, voltage levels, and the physical connectors for electrical, optical, and mechanical transmission.

EXAM TIP To remember all the layers within the OSI model in the correct order, memorize "All People Seem To Need Data Processing." Remember that you are starting at layer 7, the application layer, at the top.

Functions and Protocols in the OSI Model

For the CISSP exam, you will need to know the functionality that takes place at the different layers of the OSI model, along with specific protocols that work at each layer. The following is a quick overview of each layer and its components.

Application

The protocols at the application layer handle file transfer, virtual terminals, network management, and fulfilling networking requests of applications. A few of the protocols that work at this layer include

- File Transfer Protocol (FTP)
- Network Time Protocol (NTP)
- Simple Mail Transfer Protocol (SMTP)
- Internet Message Access Protocol (IMAP)
- Hypertext Transfer Protocol (HTTP)

Presentation

The services of the presentation layer handle translation into standard formats, data compression and decompression, and data encryption and decryption. No protocols work at this layer, just services. The following lists some of the presentation layer standards:

- American Standard Code for Information Interchange (ASCII)
- Tagged Image File Format (TIFF)

- Joint Photographic Experts Group (JPEG)
- Motion Picture Experts Group (MPEG)
- Musical Instrument Digital Interface (MIDI)

Session

The session layer protocols set up connections between applications; maintain dialog control; and negotiate, establish, maintain, and tear down the communication channel. Some of the protocols that work at this layer include

- Layer 2 Tunneling Protocol (L2TP)
- Network Basic Input Output System (NetBIOS)
- Password Authentication Protocol (PAP)
- Point-to-Point Tunneling Protocol (PPTP)
- Remote Procedure Call (RPC)

Transport

The protocols at the transport layer handle end-to-end transmission and segmentation of a data stream. The following protocols work at this layer:

- Transmission Control Protocol (TCP)
- User Datagram Protocol (UDP)
- Stream Control Transmission Protocol (SCTP)
- Resource Reservation Protocol (RSVP)
- QUIC (not an acronym)

Network

The responsibilities of the network layer protocols include internetworking service, addressing, and routing. The following lists some of the protocols that work at this layer:

- Internet Protocol (IP)
- Internet Control Message Protocol (ICMP)
- Internet Group Management Protocol (IGMP)
- Routing Information Protocol (RIP)
- Open Shortest Path First (OSPF)

Data Link

The protocols at the data link layer convert data into LAN or WAN frames for transmission and define how a computer accesses a network. This layer is divided into the Logical Link Control (LLC) and the Media Access Control (MAC) sublayers. Some protocols that work at this layer include the following:

- Address Resolution Protocol (ARP)
- Reverse Address Resolution Protocol (RARP)
- Serial Line Internet Protocol (SLIP)
- Ethernet (IEEE 802.3)
- Wireless Ethernet (IEEE 802.11)

Physical

Network interface cards and drivers convert bits into electrical signals and control the physical aspects of data transmission, including optical, electrical, and mechanical requirements. The following are some of the standard interfaces at this layer:

- RS/EIA/TIA-422, RS/EIA/TIA-423, RS/EIA/TIA-449, RS/EIA/TIA-485
- 10Base-T, 10Base2, 10Base5, 100Base-TX, 100Base-FX, 100Base-T, 1000Base-T, 1000Base-SX
- Integrated Services Digital Network (ISDN)
- Digital subscriber line (DSL)
- Synchronous Optical Networking (SONET)

Tying the Layers Together

The OSI model is used as a framework for many network-based products and is used by many types of vendors. Various types of devices and protocols work at different parts of this seven-layer model. The main reason that a Cisco switch, a Microsoft web server, a Barracuda firewall, and a Belkin wireless access point can all communicate properly on one network is because they all work within the OSI model. They do not have their own individual ways of sending data; they follow a standardized manner of communication, which allows for interoperability and allows a network to be a network. If a product does not follow the OSI model, it will not be able to communicate with other devices on the network because the other devices will not understand its proprietary way of communicating.

The different device types work at specific OSI layers. For example, computers can interpret and process data at each of the seven layers, but routers can understand information only up to the network layer because a router's main function is to route packets, which does not require knowledge about any further information within the packet. A router peels back the header information until it reaches the network layer data, where the routing and IP address information is located. The router looks at this information to make its decisions on where the packet should be routed. Bridges and switches understand only up to the data link layer, and repeaters understand traffic only at the physical layer. So if you hear someone mention a "layer 3 device," the person is referring to a device that works at the network layer. A "layer 2 device" works at the data link layer. Figure 11-9 shows what layer of the OSI model each type of device works within.

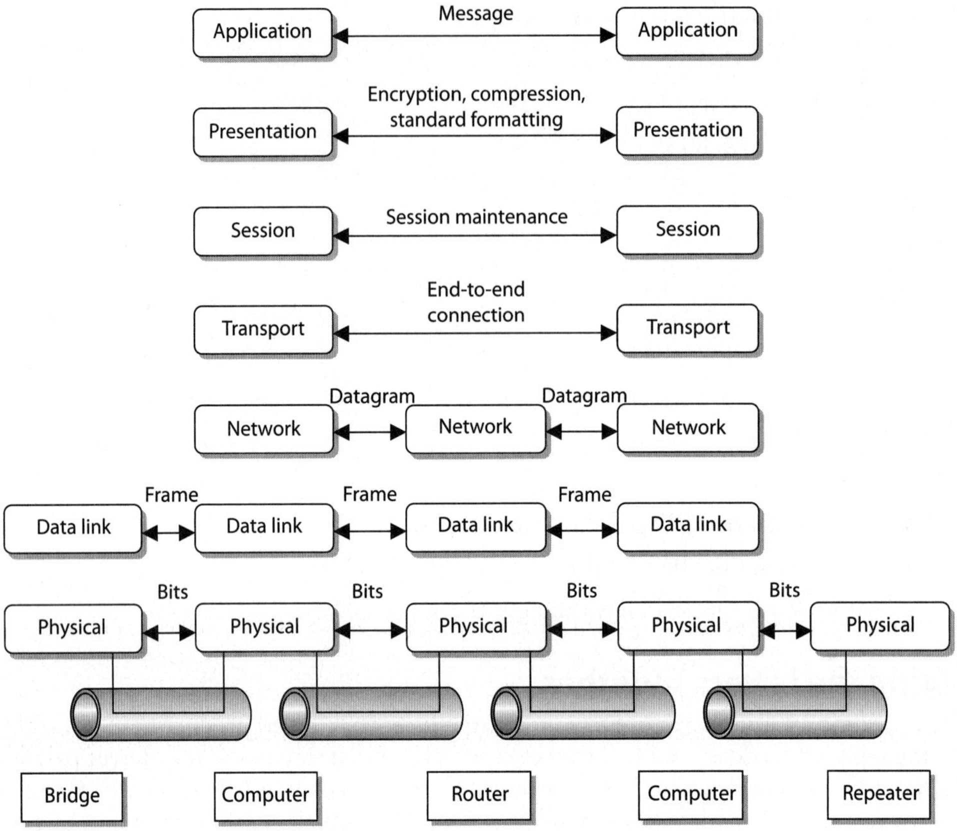

Figure 11-9 Each device works at a particular layer within the OSI model.

NOTE Some techies like to joke that all computer problems reside at layer 8. The OSI model does not have an eighth layer, and what these people are referring to is the user of a computer. So if someone states that there is a problem at layer 8, this is code for "the user is the problem."

Let's walk through an example. You just logged into a website and the landing page includes an image that your web browser automatically requests from the server. The web server now has to move this file over the network to your computer, so it generates an HTTP response, which includes a handle to the file, and hands it over to the presentation layer for encoding. HTTP doesn't directly handle binary files like JPEG images, so the file must first be "serialized" or converted to a sequence of printable characters, which is what the presentation layer does.

Once the response is "presentable" (pardon the pun), the presentation layer hands it to the session layer to figure out which of the clients currently communicating with the server should receive this image; the session layer figures out that it is for you and that you have been authenticated. The session layer then forwards the response to the transport layer, telling it the connection (or network socket) on which it should go out. Based on this connection identifier, the transport layer encapsulates the payload it just got from the session layer in a TCP datagram (which is what HTTP runs on), writes the protocol and port numbers in its header, and passes it on to layer 3.

The image you're requesting is quite large, so the network layer breaks it up into a numbered sequence of chunks, encapsulates each in its own IP packet, figures out how to route the packets, and then hands each to the data link layer. Layer 2 takes each packet and, based on its destination IP address, determines the next hop on its journey back to you, which is probably the DMZ firewall. It encapsulates the packet into an Ethernet frame, writes the MAC address of the firewall in it, and sends it down to the physical layer, which turns the 1's and 0's into electric currents on the network cable. And, just like that, your image starts its journey toward your screen.

Local Area Networks

Now that we've taken a quick look down all seven layers of the OSI model, let's circle back and take a more detailed look from the ground up. If you connect two general-purpose computers that are right next to each other, you create a local area network. A *local area network (LAN)* is a group of interconnected computers in close physical proximity to each other. A LAN is the basic building block for most organizational networks. As we'll shortly see, there are multiple ways to build LANs both physically and logically. In the following sections, we'll discuss the various technologies that allow us to physically interconnect devices.

PART IV

Network Topology

The arrangement of computers and devices is called a *network topology*. Topology refers to the manner in which a network is physically connected and shows the layout of resources and systems. A difference exists between the physical network topology and the logical topology. A network can be configured as a physical star but work logically as a ring, as in the Token Ring technology.

The best topology for a particular network depends on such things as how nodes are supposed to interact; which protocols are used; the types of applications that are available; the reliability, expandability, and physical layout of a facility; existing wiring; and the technologies implemented. The wrong topology or combination of topologies can negatively affect the network's performance, productivity, and growth possibilities.

This section describes the basic types of network topologies. Most networks are much more complex and are usually implemented using a combination of topologies.

Bus Topology

In a simple *bus topology*, a single cable runs the entire length of the network. Nodes are attached to the network through drop points on this cable. Data communications transmit the length of the medium, and each packet transmitted has the capability of being "looked at" by all nodes. Each node decides to accept or ignore the packet, depending upon the packet's destination address.

Bus topologies are of two main types: linear and tree. The *linear bus topology* has a single cable with nodes attached. A *tree topology* has branches from the single cable, and each branch can contain many nodes. In simple implementations of a bus topology, if one workstation fails, other systems can be negatively affected because of the degree of interdependence. In addition, because all nodes are connected to one main cable, the cable itself becomes a potential single point of failure.

Bus topologies were common years ago on the first Ethernet networks. Today, you are very unlikely to encounter them in local area networks. However, this topology is prevalent in vehicular networks, of which the Controller Area Network (CAN) bus is by far the most popular standard.

Star Topology

In a *star topology*, all nodes connect to a central device such as a switch. Each node has a dedicated link to the central device. The central device needs to provide enough throughput that it does not become a detrimental bottleneck for the network as a whole. Because a central device is required, it is a potential single point of failure, so redundancy may need to be implemented. Switches can be configured in flat or hierarchical implementations so larger organizations can use them.

When one workstation fails on a star topology, it does not affect other systems, as in the bus topologies. In a star topology, each system is not as dependent on others as it is dependent on the central connection device. This topology generally requires less cabling than other types of topologies. As a result, cut cables are less likely, and detecting cable problems is an easier task.

Mesh Topology

In a *mesh topology*, all systems and resources are connected to each other in a way that does not follow the uniformity of the previous topologies, as shown in Figure 11-10. This arrangement is usually a network of interconnected routers and switches that provides

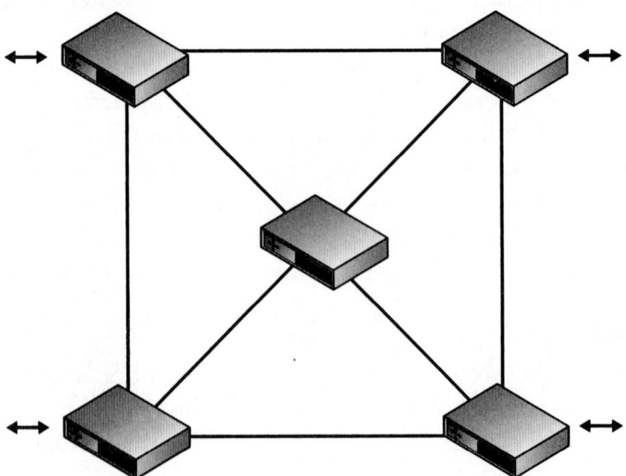

Figure 11-10 In a mesh topology, each node is connected to all other nodes, which provides for redundant paths.

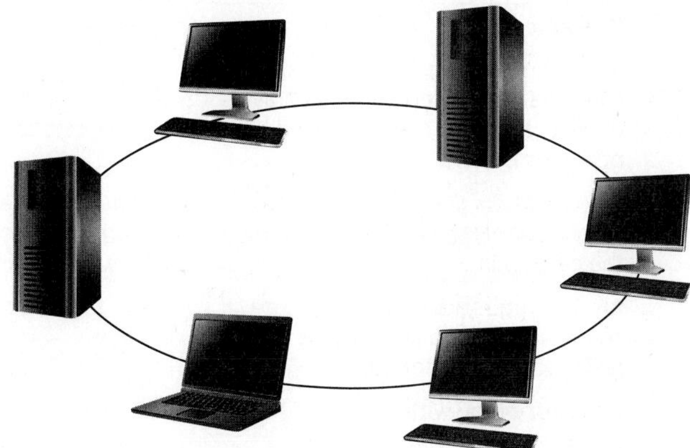

Figure 11-11 A ring topology forms a closed-loop connection.

multiple paths to all the nodes on the network. In a full mesh topology, every node is directly connected to every other node, which provides a great degree of redundancy. A typical Internet of Things (IoT) home automation network using ZigBee is an example of a full mesh topology. In a partial mesh topology, every node is not directly connected. The Internet is an example of a partial mesh topology.

Ring Topology

A *ring topology* has a series of devices connected by unidirectional transmission links, as shown in Figure 11-11. These links form a closed loop and do not connect to a central system, as in a star topology. In a physical ring formation, each node is dependent upon the preceding nodes. In simple networks, if one system fails, all other systems could be negatively affected because of this interdependence. Compensating for such failures, coupled with the difficulty of installing a ring network in the first place, makes ring topologies more expensive than other topologies. Although you have to know about ring topologies for the CISSP exam, you are extremely unlikely to find them in the real world. Still, who knows? Maybe one day they'll make a comeback.

Network Topologies Summary

A summary of the different network topologies and their important characteristics is provided in Table 11-1.

Medium Access Control Mechanisms

The physical topology of a network is the lower layer, or foundation, of a network. It determines what type of physical media will be used to connect network devices and what these connections look like. *Medium access control (MAC)* mechanisms deal with how computer systems communicate over these media and are built into the network interfaces. MAC mechanisms set up the rules of how computers will communicate on a LAN, how errors are handled, the maximum transmission unit (MTU) size of frames, and much more. These rules enable all computers and devices to communicate and

Topology	Characteristics	Problems
Bus	Uses a linear, single cable for all computers attached. All traffic travels the full cable and can be viewed by all other computers.	If one station experiences a problem, it can negatively affect surrounding computers on the same cable.
Ring	All computers are connected by a unidirectional transmission link, and the cable is in a closed loop.	If one station experiences a problem, it can negatively affect surrounding computers on the same ring.
Star	All computers are connected to a central device, which provides more resilience for the network.	The central device is a single point of failure.
Tree	A bus topology with branches off of the main cable.	Multiple single points of failure.
Mesh	Computers are connected to each other, which provides redundancy.	Requires more expense in cabling and extra effort to track down cable faults.

Table 11-1 Summary of Network Topologies

recover from problems, and enable users to be productive in accomplishing their networking tasks. Each participating entity needs to know how to communicate properly so all other systems will understand the transmissions, instructions, and requests.

LAN MAC mechanisms reside at the data link layer of the OSI model. Remember that as a message is passed down through a network stack, it is encapsulated by the protocols and services at each layer. When the data message reaches the data link layer, the protocol at this layer adds the necessary headers and trailers that will allow the message to traverse a specific type of network (Ethernet, Token Ring, FDDI, etc.)

No matter what type of medium access technology is being used, the main resource that has to be shared by all systems and devices on the network is the network transmission channel. This transmission channel could be coaxial cabling, UTP cabling, optical fibers, or free space (e.g., using radio waves). There must be methods in place to make sure that each system gets its fair share of access to the channel, that the system's data is not corrupted during transmission, and that there is a way to control traffic in peak times. Let's take a closer look at the three most common approaches to MAC: carrier sense multiple access, Token Ring, and polling.

Carrier Sense Multiple Access

By far, the most common approach to MAC is called *carrier sense multiple access (CSMA)*, which provides a standard way to access the shared medium, communicate, and recover from any errors that may occur. A transmission is called a *carrier*, so if a computer is transmitting frames, it is performing a carrier activity. Despite their best efforts, networked computers sometimes talk over each other, which creates what is called a *collision*. Think about it: it takes time for electromagnetic signals to move from point A (where one transmitter sits) to point B (where another computer also wants to transmit). Both computers listen to the medium and, detecting no other traffic on it, simultaneously transmit their messages.

Sometime later, these messages meet each other on the medium and *collide*, or corrupt each other. There are two variants of CSMA with which you should be familiar: collision detection (CSMA/CD) and collision avoidance (CSMA/CA).

When computers use the *carrier sense multiple access with collision detection (CSMA/CD)* protocol, they monitor the transmission activity, or carrier activity, on the wire so they can determine when would be the best time to transmit data. Each node monitors the wire continuously and waits until the wire is free before it transmits its data. As an analogy, consider several people gathered in a group talking here and there about this and that. If a person wants to talk, she usually listens to the current conversation and waits for a break before she proceeds to talk. If she does not wait for the first person to stop talking, she will be speaking at the same time as the other person, and the people around them may not be able to understand fully what each is trying to say. If a computer puts frames on the wire and its frames collide with another computer's frames, it will abort its transmission and alert all other stations that a collision just took place. All stations will start a random collision timer to force a delay before they attempt to transmit data. This random collision timer is called the *back-off algorithm*. CSMA/CD was important in the early days of Ethernet LANs when hubs and bridges were common, but is now largely deprecated.

The other variant of CSMA is *carrier sense multiple access with collision avoidance (CSMA/CA)*, in which all stations with data to transmit first check the medium to see if it's quiet. If it is, they send their data. If it isn't, they start a random timer before they check again. In some implementations, the station wishing to send data first sends a request to send (RTS) frame to a controller or the destination and then waits for a clear to send (CTS) frame before transmitting its data. CSMA/CA is most commonly used in wireless networks.

Token Passing

Some of North America's indigenous people devised a clever way to ensure only one of them spoke (and was not interrupted) at meetings. It was called the talking stick, and only the one holding it was allowed to speak. Once that person was done, they would put it down, allowing the next individual to pick it up and speak. This token ensured that all participants had a chance to speak uninterrupted. Some MAC technologies also use tokens, which are 24-bit control frames used to control which computers communicate at what intervals. The token is passed from computer to computer, and only the computer that has the token can actually put frames onto the wire. The token grants a computer the right to communicate. The token contains the data to be transmitted and source and destination address information. When a system has data it needs to transmit, it has to wait to receive the token. The computer then connects its message to the token and puts it on the wire. Each computer checks this message to determine whether it is addressed to it, which continues until the destination computer receives the message. The destination computer makes a copy of the message and flips a bit to tell the source computer it did indeed get its message. Once this gets back to the source computer, it removes the frames from the network. The destination computer makes a copy of the message, but only the originator of the message can remove the message from the token and the network.

Carrier-Sensing and Token-Passing Access Methods
Overall, carrier-sensing access methods are faster than token-passing access methods, but the former do have the problem of collisions. A network segment with many devices can cause too many collisions and slow down the network's performance. Token-passing technologies do not have problems with collisions, but they do not perform at the speed of carrier-sensing technologies. Network routers can help significantly in isolating the network resources for both the CSMA/CD and the token-passing methods.

If a computer that receives the token does not have a message to transmit, it sends the token to the next computer on the network. An empty token has a header, data field, and trailer, but a token that has an actual message has a new header, destination address, source address, and a new trailer. This type of media-sharing method is used by Token Ring and FDDI technologies.

NOTE Some applications and network protocols work better if they can communicate at determined intervals, instead of "whenever the data arrives." In token-passing technologies, traffic arrives in this type of deterministic nature because not all systems can communicate at one time; only the system that has control of the token can communicate.

NOTE When there is just one transmission medium (i.e., UTP cable) that has to be shared by all nodes and devices in a network, this is referred to as a *contention-based* environment. Each system has to "compete" to use the transmission line, which can cause contention.

Collision and Broadcast Domains

As previously indicated, a collision occurs on Ethernet networks when two computers transmit data at the same time. Other computers on the network detect this collision because the overlapping signals of the collision increase the voltage of the signal above a specific threshold. The more devices on a contention-based network, the more likely collisions will occur, which increases network latency (data transmission delays). A *collision domain* is a group of devices that are contending, or competing, for the same shared communication medium. For example, all devices that are connected to a particular wireless access point (WAP) belong to the same collision domain.

NOTE Collision domains used to be a problem in wired networks back when hubs were more prevalent than switches. You may still come across these examples, but they are exceptionally rare in real networks nowadays.

Sometimes, a network device will want to send a message to all its neighbors. For example, it may need to send a message to Priya, so it shouts out "which of you have Priya?" In Ethernet networks, the broadcast address is the one consisting of all 1's, which in hexadecimal looks like this: FF:FF:FF:FF:FF:FF. A *broadcast domain* consists of all devices that can receive layer 2 (data link) broadcast messages from each other. If a group of devices are in the same collision domain, then they must also be in the same broadcast domain. However, there are cases in which these two domains are different. For example, as shown in Figure 11-12, you can have wireless and wired clients on a hybrid network in which all devices are in the same broadcast domain, but there will be different collision domains. Note that network switches create a separate collision domain for each port. If there is a single device on each port, collisions are avoided altogether.

EXAM TIP *Broadcast domains* are sets of computing nodes that all receive a layer 2 broadcast frame. These are normally all nodes that are interconnected, with no routers in between them. *Collision domains* are sets of computing nodes that may produce collisions when they transmit data. These are normally nodes connected by hubs, repeaters, or wireless access points.

Another benefit of restricting and controlling broadcast and collision domains is that it makes sniffing the network and obtaining useful information more difficult for an intruder as he traverses the network. A useful tactic for attackers is to install a Trojan horse that sets up a network sniffer on the compromised computer. The sniffer is usually configured to look for a specific type of information, such as usernames and passwords. If broadcast and collision domains are in effect, the compromised system will have access only to the broadcast and collision traffic within its specific subnet or broadcast domain.

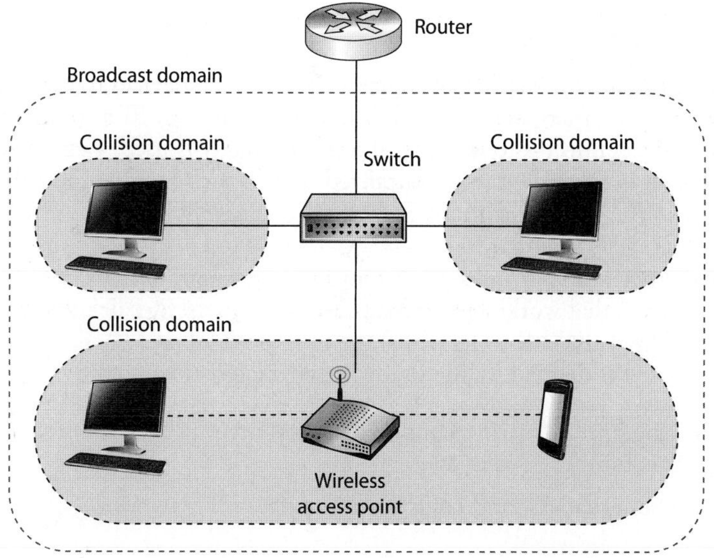

Figure 11-12 Collision domains within one broadcast domain

PART IV

The compromised system will not be able to listen to traffic on other broadcast and collision domains, and this can greatly reduce the amount of traffic and information available to an attacker.

Polling

The third type of media-sharing method, besides CSMA and token passing, is polling. *Polling* is a medium access control mechanism that relies on a primary station that periodically polls all others in its collision domain. Each polled device responds by stating whether or not it has anything to send. In some implementations, the secondary stations (devices) can also let the primary station know how much data they want to send, where it's going to, and how urgent it is. After polling all secondary stations, the primary station allocates the channel according to whatever policy it follows. It could, for example, prioritize traffic from one station, or type, or evenly divide the channel among all stations that asked to access it.

The main thing to remember about polling MAC is that each device needs to wait until the primary station completes a poll and then tells that device how much of the channel it can use. Only then can a secondary station transmit data. This approach is very uncommon in LANs, though it is used in some wireless networks. Polling is much more common in wide area networks.

Layer 2 Protocols

Now that we've discussed LAN topologies and MAC mechanisms, let's look at how these are implemented in reality. For the CISSP exam, you should know three layer 2 protocols: Ethernet, Token Ring, and FDDI. In reality, you are almost certainly to only use Ethernet and its wireless cousin Wi-Fi. Token Ring and FDDI are exceptionally rare in LANs, though FDDI is still used as the backbone of metropolitan area networks (MANs).

Ethernet

Ethernet is a set of technologies that enables several devices to communicate on the same network. Ethernet usually uses a bus or star topology. If a linear bus topology is used, all devices connect to one cable. If a star topology is used, each device is connected to a cable that is connected to a centralized device, such as a switch. Ethernet was developed in the 1970s, became commercially available in 1980, and was officially defined through the IEEE 802.3 standard.

Ethernet has seen quite an evolution in its short history, from purely coaxial cable installations that worked at 10 Mbps to mostly twisted-pair cable that works at speeds of 100 Mbps, 1,000 Mbps (1 Gbps), and up to 40 Gbps.

Ethernet is defined by the following characteristics:

- Contention-based technology (all resources use the same shared communication medium)
- Uses broadcast and collision domains

Table 11-2 Ethernet Implementation Types

Ethernet Type	IEEE Standard	Cable Type (minimum)	Speed
10Base-T	802.3i-1990	Cat3 UTP	10 Mbps
100Base-TX, Fast Ethernet	802.3u-1995	Cat5 UTP	100 Mbps
1000Base-T, Gigabit Ethernet	802.3ab-1999	Cat5 UTP	1,000 Mbps
10GBase-T	802.3an-2006	Cat6a UTP	10,000 Mbps

- Uses the CSMA access method
- Supports full-duplex communication
- Can use coaxial, twisted-pair, or fiber-optic cabling types, but most commonly uses UTP cables
- Is defined by the IEEE 802.3 family of standards

Ethernet addresses how computers share a common network and how they deal with collisions, data integrity, communication mechanisms, and transmission controls. These are the common characteristics of Ethernet, but Ethernet does vary in the type of cabling schemes and transfer rates it can supply. Several types of Ethernet implementations are available, as outlined in Table 11-2.

10Base-T was considered heaven-sent when it first arrived on the networking scene, but soon many users were demanding more speed and power. It is now considered a legacy standard and is very rarely seen in organizational networks. There are ongoing efforts, however, to develop variants of this obsolete standard for use in automotive and IoT applications. Today, the most widely deployed type of Ethernet in organizational networks is 1000Base-T.

PART IV

Token Ring

The *Token Ring* technology was originally developed by IBM and then defined by the IEEE 802.5 standard. At first, Token Ring technology had the ability to transmit data at 4 Mbps. Later, it was improved to transmit at 16 Mbps. It uses a token-passing technology with a star-configured topology. The *ring* part of the name pertains to how the signals travel, which is in a logical ring. Each computer is connected to a central hub, called a *Multistation Access Unit (MAU)*. Physically, the topology can be a star, but the signals and transmissions are passed in a logical ring.

As previously described, *token-passing technology* is one in which a device cannot put data on the network wire without having possession of a *token*, a control frame that travels in a logical circle and is "picked up" when a system needs to communicate. This is different from Ethernet, in which all the devices attempt to communicate at the same time. This is why Ethernet is referred to as a "chatty protocol" and has collisions. Token Ring does not endure collisions, since only one system can communicate at a time, but this also means communication takes place more slowly compared to Ethernet.

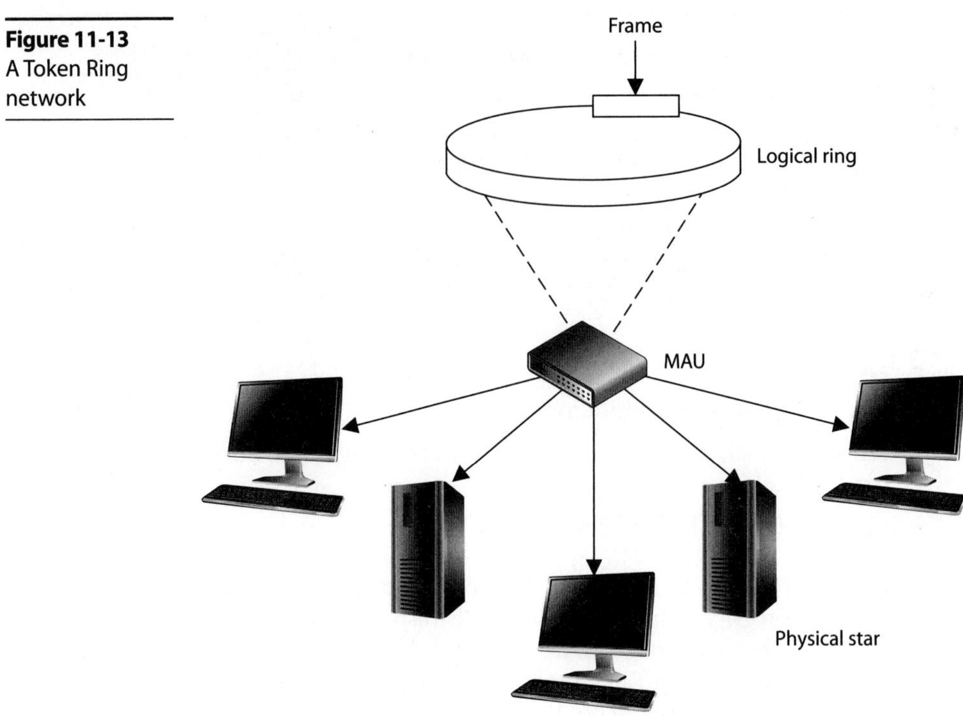

Figure 11-13 A Token Ring network

Token Ring employs a couple of mechanisms to deal with problems that can occur on this type of network. The *active monitor* mechanism removes frames that are continuously circulating on the network. This can occur if a computer locks up or is taken offline for one reason or another and cannot properly receive a token destined for it. With the *beaconing* mechanism, if a computer detects a problem with the network, it sends a beacon frame. This frame generates a failure domain, which is between the computer that issued the beacon and its neighbor downstream. The computers and devices within this failure domain will attempt to reconfigure certain settings to try to work around the detected fault. Figure 11-13 depicts a Token Ring network in a physical star configuration. Token Ring networks were popular in the 1980s and 1990s, and although some are still around, Ethernet is much more popular.

FDDI

Fiber Distributed Data Interface (FDDI) technology, developed by the American National Standards Institute (ANSI), is a high-speed, token-passing, medium access technology. FDDI has a data transmission speed of up to 100 Mbps and is usually used as a backbone network using fiber-optic cabling. FDDI also provides fault tolerance by offering a second counter-rotating fiber ring. The primary ring has data traveling clockwise and is used for regular data transmission. The second ring transmits data in a counterclockwise fashion and is invoked only if the primary ring goes down. Sensors watch the primary ring and, if it goes down, invoke a ring *wrap* so the data will be diverted to the second

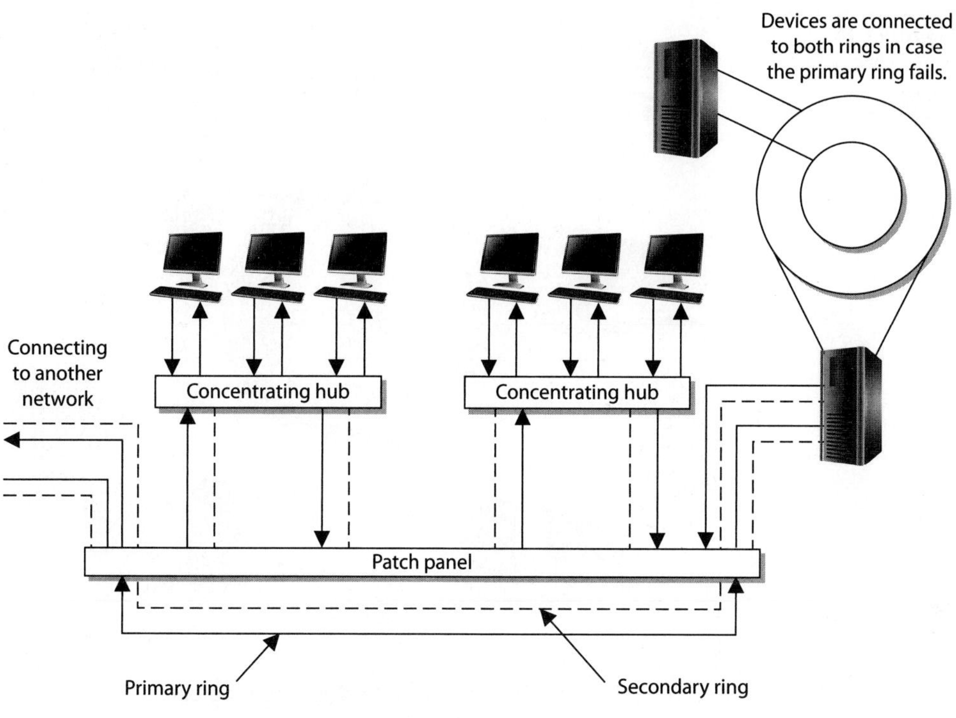

Figure 11-14 FDDI rings can be used as backbones to connect different LANs.

ring. Each node on the FDDI network has relays that are connected to both rings, so if a break in the ring occurs, the two rings can be joined.

When FDDI is used as a backbone network, it usually connects several different networks, as shown in Figure 11-14.

Before Fast Ethernet and Gigabit Ethernet hit the market, FDDI was used mainly as campus and service provider backbones. Because FDDI can be employed for distances up to 100 kilometers, it was often used in MANs. The benefit of FDDI is that it can work over long distances and at high speeds with minimal interference. It enables several tokens to be present on the ring at the same time, causing more communication to take place simultaneously, and it provides predictable delays that help connected networks and devices know what to expect and when.

NOTE A version of FDDI, Copper Distributed Data Interface (CDDI), can work over UTP cabling.

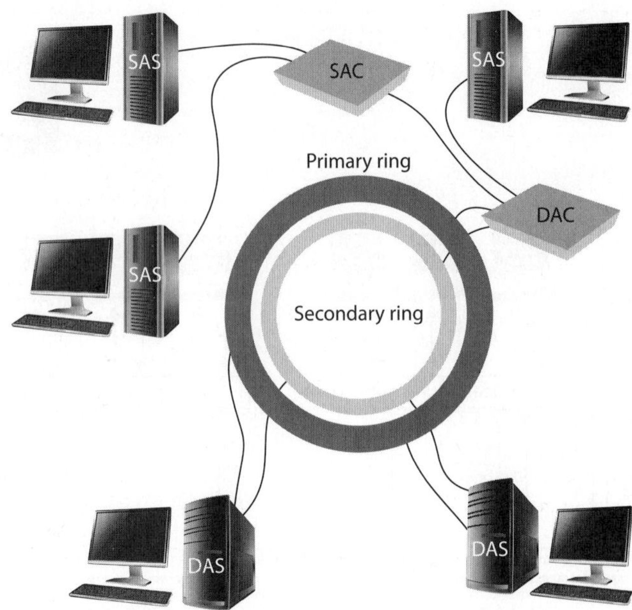

Figure 11-15 FDDI device types

Devices that connect to FDDI rings fall into one of the following categories:

- **Single-attachment station (SAS)** Attaches to only one ring (the primary) through a concentrator
- **Dual-attachment station (DAS)** Has two ports and each port provides a connection for both the primary and the secondary rings
- **Single-attached concentrator (SAC)** Concentrator that connects an SAS device to the primary ring
- **Dual-attached concentrator (DAC)** Concentrator that connects DAS, SAS, and SAC devices to both rings

The different FDDI device types are illustrated in Figure 11-15.

NOTE Ring topologies are considered deterministic, meaning that the rate of the traffic flow can be predicted. Since traffic can only flow if a token is in place, the maximum time that a node will have to wait to receive traffic can be determined. This can be beneficial for time-sensitive applications.

Layer 2 Network Protocol Summary

Table 11-3 sums up the important characteristics of the technologies described in the preceding sections.

LAN Implementation	Standard	Characteristics
Ethernet	IEEE 802.3	Uses broadcast and collision domains. Uses CSMA medium access control method. Can use coaxial, twisted-pair, or fiber-optic media. Transmission speeds of 10 Mbps to 10 Gbps.
Token Ring	IEEE 802.5	Token-passing media access method. Transmission speeds of 4 to 16 Mbps. Uses an active monitor and beaconing. Effectively defunct.
FDDI	ANSI standard Based on IEEE 802.4	Dual counter-rotating rings for fault tolerance. Transmission speeds of 100 Mbps. Operates over long distances at high speeds and is therefore used as a backbone. CDDI works over UTP. Very rarely seen in the enterprise.

Table 11-3 LAN Media Access Methods

Transmission Methods

A packet may need to be sent to only one workstation, to a set of workstations, or to all workstations on a particular subnet. If a packet needs to go from the source computer to one particular system, a *unicast* transmission method is used. If the packet needs to go to a specific group of systems, the sending system uses the *multicast* method. If a system wants all computers on its subnet to receive a message, it uses the *broadcast* method.

Unicast is pretty simple because it has a source address and a destination address. The data goes from point A to point B, it is a one-to-one transmission, and everyone is happy. Multicast is a bit different in that it is a one-to-many transmission. Multicasting enables one computer to send data to a selective group of computers. A good example of multicasting is tuning into a radio station on a computer. Some computers have software that enables the user to determine whether she wants to listen to rock, Latin, or a talk radio station, for example. Once the user selects one of these genres, the software must tell the NIC driver to pick up not only packets addressed to its specific MAC address but also packets that contain a specific multicast address.

The difference between broadcast and multicast is that in a broadcast one-to-all transmission, everyone gets the data, whereas in a multicast, only certain nodes receive the data. So how does a server three states away multicast to one particular computer on a specific network and no other networks in between? Suppose a user tunes in to her favorite Internet radio station. An application running on her computer (say, a web browser) has to tell her local router she wants to get frames with this particular multicast address passed her way. The local router must tell the router upstream, and this process continues so each router between the source and destination knows where to pass this multicast data. This ensures that the user can get her rock music without other networks being bothered with this extra data.

IPv4 multicast protocols use a Class D address (224.0.0.0 to 239.255.255.255), which is a special address space reserved for multicasting. IPv6 multicast addresses start with eight 1's (that is, 1111 1111). Multicasting can be used to send out information; multimedia data; and even real-time video, music, and voice clips.

Internet Group Management Protocol (IGMP) is used to report multicast group memberships to routers. When a user chooses to accept multicast traffic, she becomes a member of a particular multicast group. IGMP is the mechanism that allows her computer to inform the local routers that she is part of this group and to send traffic with a specific multicast address to her system. IGMP can be used for online streaming video and gaming activities. The protocol allows for efficient use of the necessary resources when supporting these types of applications.

Like most protocols, IGMP has gone through a few different versions, each improving upon the earlier one. In version 1, multicast agents periodically send queries to systems on the network they are responsible for and update their databases, indicating which system belongs to which group membership. Version 2 provides more granular query types and allows a system to signal to the agent when it wants to leave a group. Version 3 allows the systems to specify the sources it wants to receive multicast traffic from. Each version is backward-compatible because versions 1 and 2 are still in use in legacy equipment.

NOTE The previous statements are true pertaining to IPv4. IPv6 is more than just an upgrade to the original IP protocol; it functions differently in many respects, including how it handles multicasting, which has caused many interoperability issues and delay in its full deployment.

Layer 2 Security Standards

As frames pass from one network device to another device, attackers could sniff the data; modify the headers; redirect the traffic; spoof traffic; carry out man-in-the-middle attacks, DoS attacks, and replay attacks; and indulge in other malicious activities. It has become necessary to secure network traffic at the frame level, which is layer 2 of the OSI model.

802.1AE is the IEEE MAC Security (MACSec) standard, which defines a security infrastructure to provide data confidentiality, data integrity, and data origin authentication. Where a VPN connection provides protection at the higher networking layers, MACSec provides hop-by-hop protection at layer 2, as shown in Figure 11-16.

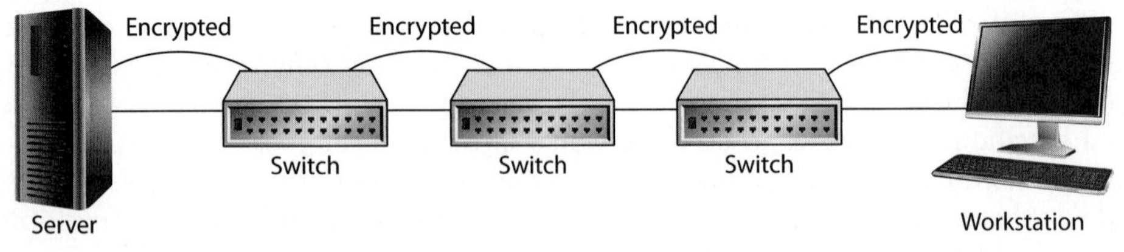

Figure 11-16 MACSec provides layer 2 frame protection.

MACSec integrates security protection into wired Ethernet networks to secure LAN-based traffic. Only authenticated and trusted devices on the network can communicate with each other. Unauthorized devices are prevented from communicating via the network, which helps prevent attackers from installing rogue devices and redirecting traffic between nodes in an unauthorized manner. When a frame arrives at a device that is configured with MACSec, the MACSec Security Entity (SecY) decrypts the frame if necessary and computes an integrity check value (ICV) on the frame and compares it with the ICV that was sent with the frame. If the ICVs match, the device processes the frame. If they do not match, the device handles the frame according to a preconfigured policy, such as discarding it.

The *IEEE 802.1AR* standard specifies unique per-device identifiers (DevID) and the management and cryptographic binding of a device (router, switch, access point) to its identifiers. A verifiable unique device identity allows establishment of the trustworthiness of devices, and thus facilitates secure device provisioning.

As a security administrator you really only want devices that are allowed on your network to be plugged into your network. But how do you properly and uniquely identify devices? The manufacturer's serial number is not available for a protocol to review. MAC addresses, hostnames, and IP addresses are easily spoofed. 802.1AR defines a globally unique per-device secure identifier cryptographically bound to the device through the use of public cryptography and digital certificates. These unique hardware-based credentials can be used with the Extensible Authentication Protocol-Transport Layer Security (EAP-TLS) authentication framework. Each device that is compliant with IEEE 802.1AR comes with a single built-in initial secure device identity (iDevID). The iDevID is an instance of the general concept of a DevID, which is intended to be used with authentication protocols such as EAP, which is supported by IEEE 802.1X.

So 802.1AR provides a unique ID for a device. 802.1AE provides data encryption, integrity, and origin authentication functionality. 802.1AF carries out key agreement functions for the session keys used for data encryption. Each of these standards provides specific parameters to work within an 802.1X EAP-TLS framework, as shown in Figure 11-17.

As Figure 11-17 shows, when a new device is installed on the network, it cannot just start communicating with other devices, receive an IP address from a Dynamic Host Configuration Protocol (DHCP) server, resolve names with the Domain Name System (DNS) server, and so on. The device cannot carry out any network activity until it is authorized to do so. So 802.1X port authentication kicks in, which means that only authentication data is allowed to travel from the new device to the authenticating server. The authentication data is the digital certificate and hardware identity associated with that device (802.1AR), which is processed by EAP-TLS. Once the device is authenticated, usually by a Remote Authentication Dial-In User Server (RADIUS) server, encryption keying material is negotiated and agreed upon between surrounding network devices. Once the keying material is installed, then data encryption and frame integrity checking can take place (802.1AE) as traffic goes from one network device to the next.

These IEEE standards are new and evolving and at different levels of implementation by various vendors. One way the unique hardware identity and cryptographic material

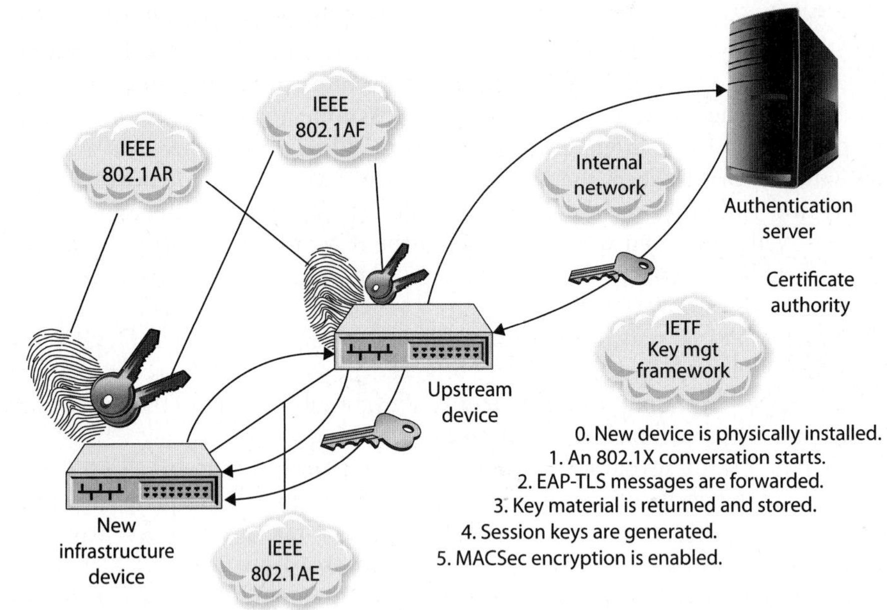
IEEE
802.1AF
IEEE
802.1AR
Internal
network
Authentication
server
Certificate
authority
IETF
Key mgt
framework
Upstream
device
0. New device is physically installed.
1. An 802.1X conversation starts.
2. EAP-TLS messages are forwarded.
3. Key material is returned and stored.
4. Session keys are generated.
5. MACSec encryption is enabled.
New
infrastructure
device
IEEE
802.1AE

Figure 11-17 Layer 2 security protocols

are embedded in new network devices is through the use of a Trusted Platform Module (TPM; described in Chapter 9).

Internet Protocol Networking

Unless your network consists of only a few devices, isolated from the Internet (and what good is that?), you will need to move from layer 2 into layer 3 and above to do anything meaningful. Recall that the data link layer is concerned with exchanging data between devices that are directly connected to each other (in other words, in the same collision domain). Beyond that, we need layer 3 (network) and 4 (transport) protocols, such as TCP/IP.

The *Transmission Control Protocol/Internet Protocol (TCP/IP)* is a suite of protocols that governs the way data travels from one device to another. IP is a network layer protocol and provides datagram routing services. IP's main task is to support internetwork addressing and packet routing. It is a connectionless protocol that envelops data passed to it from the transport layer. The IP protocol addresses the datagram with the source and destination IP addresses. The protocols within the TCP/IP suite work together to break down the data passed from the application layer into pieces that can be moved along a network. They work with other protocols to transmit the data to the destination

IP

IP is a connectionless protocol that provides the addressing and routing capabilities for each package of data. The data, IP, and network relationship can be compared to the relationship between a letter and the postal system:

- Data = Letter
- IP = Addressed envelope
- Network = Postal system

The message is the letter, which is enveloped and addressed by IP, and the network and its services enable the message to be sent from its origin to its destination, like the postal system.

computer and then reassemble the data back into a form that the application layer can understand and process.

Two main protocols work at the transport layer: TCP and UDP. *TCP* is a reliable and *connection-oriented protocol*, which means it ensures packets are delivered to the destination computer. If a packet is lost during transmission, TCP has the ability to identify this issue and resend the lost or corrupted packet. TCP also supports packet sequencing (to ensure each and every packet was received), flow and congestion control, and error detection and correction. *UDP*, on the other hand, is a *best-effort* and *connectionless protocol*. It has neither packet sequencing nor flow and congestion control, and the destination does not acknowledge every packet it receives.

TCP

TCP is referred to as a connection-oriented protocol because before any user data is actually sent, handshaking takes place between the two systems that want to communicate. Once the handshaking completes successfully, a virtual connection is set up between the two systems. UDP is considered a connectionless protocol because it does not go through these steps. Instead, UDP sends out messages without first contacting the destination computer and does not know if the packets were received properly or dropped. Figure 11-18 shows the difference between a connection-oriented protocol and a connectionless protocol.

UDP and TCP sit together on the transport layer, and developers can choose which to use when developing applications. Many times, TCP is the transport protocol of choice because it provides reliability and ensures the packets are delivered. TCP provides a full-duplex, reliable communication mechanism, and if any packets are lost or damaged, they are re-sent; however, TCP requires a lot of system overhead compared to UDP.

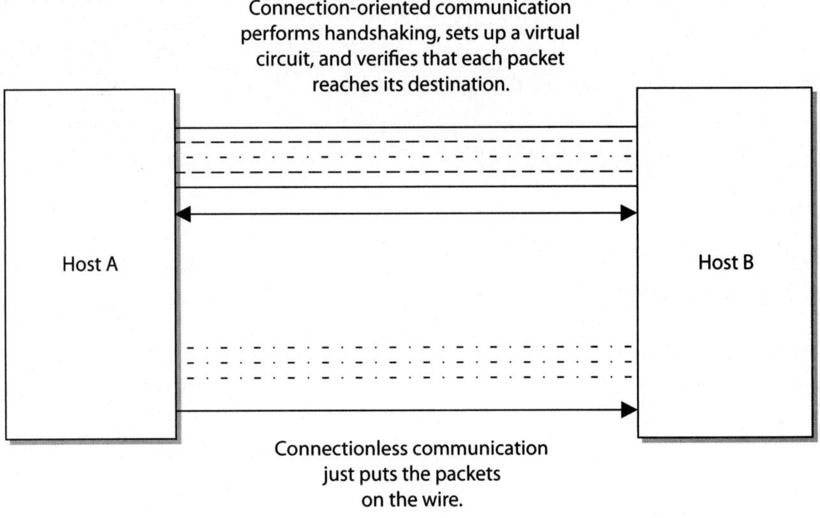
Connection-oriented communication performs handshaking, sets up a virtual circuit, and verifies that each packet reaches its destination.
Host A
Host B
Connectionless communication just puts the packets on the wire.

Figure 11-18 Connection-oriented protocol vs. connectionless protocol functionality

If developers know that data being dropped during transmission is not detrimental to the application, they may choose to use UDP because it is faster and requires fewer resources. For example, UDP is a better choice than TCP when a server sends status information to all listening nodes on the network. A node will not be negatively affected if, by some chance, it did not receive this status information, because the information will be re-sent every 60 seconds.

UDP and TCP are transport protocols that applications use to get their data across a network. They both use *ports* to communicate with upper OSI layers and to keep track of various conversations that take place simultaneously. The ports are also the mechanism used to identify how other computers access services. When a TCP or UDP message is formed, source and destination ports are contained within the header information along with the source and destination IP addresses. The combination of protocol (TCP or UDP), port, and IP address makes up a *socket*, and is how packets know where to go (by the address) and how to communicate with the right service or protocol on the other computer (by the port number). The IP address acts as the doorway to a computer, and the port acts as the doorway to the actual protocol or service. To communicate properly, the packet needs to know these doors. Figure 11-19 shows how packets communicate with applications and services through ports.

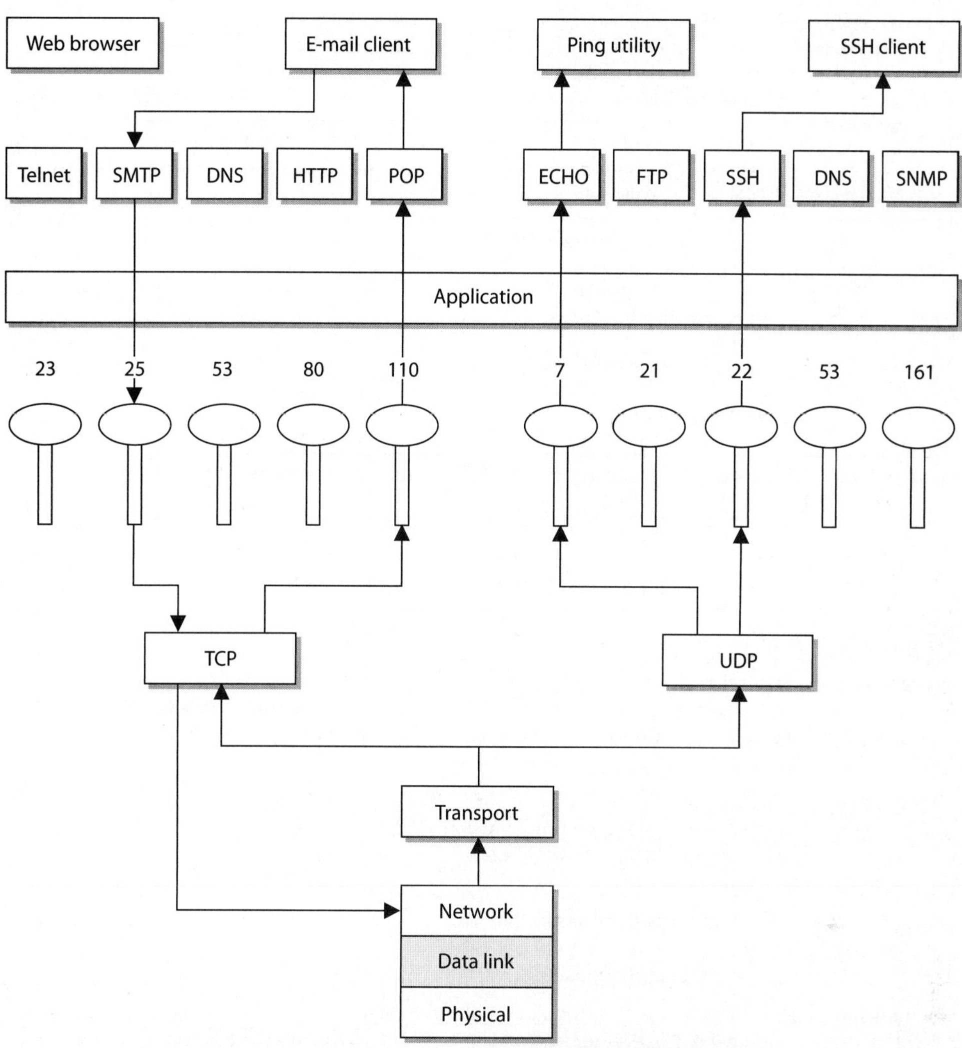

Figure 11-19 The packet can communicate with upper-layer protocols and services through a port.

The difference between TCP and UDP can also be seen in the message formats. Because TCP offers more services than UDP, it must contain much more information within its packet header format, as shown in Figure 11-20. Table 11-4 lists the major differences between TCP and UDP.

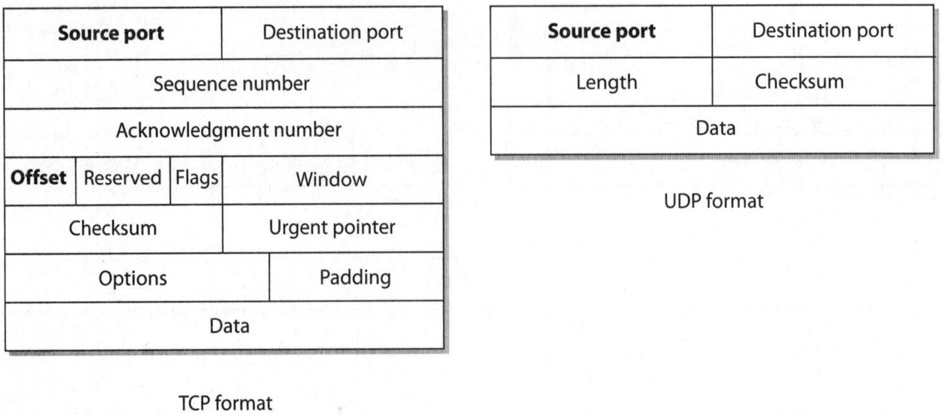

Source port | Destination port
Sequence number
Acknowledgment number
Offset | Reserved | Flags | Window
Checksum | Urgent pointer
Options | Padding
Data

TCP format

Source port | Destination port
Length | Checksum
Data

UDP format

Figure 11-20 TCP carries a lot more information within its segment because it offers more services than UDP.

Property	TCP	UDP
Reliability	Ensures that packets reach their destinations, returns ACKs when packets are received, and is a reliable protocol.	Does not return ACKs and does not guarantee that a packet will reach its destination. Is an unreliable protocol.
Connection	Connection-oriented. It performs handshaking and develops a virtual connection with the destination computer.	Connectionless. It does no handshaking and does not set up a virtual connection.
Packet sequencing	Uses sequence numbers within headers to make sure each packet within a transmission is received.	Does not use sequence numbers.
Congestion controls	The destination computer can tell the source if it is overwhelmed and thus slow the transmission rate.	The destination computer does not communicate back to the source computer about flow control.
Usage	Used when reliable delivery is required. Intended for relatively small amounts of data transmission.	Used when reliable delivery is not required and high volumes of data need to be transmitted, such as in streaming video and status broadcasts.
Speed and overhead	Uses a considerable amount of resources and is slower than UDP.	Uses fewer resources and is faster than TCP.

Table 11-4 Major Differences Between TCP and UDP

Port Types

Port numbers up to 1023 (0 to 1023) are called *well-known ports*, and almost every computer in the world has the exact same protocol mapped to the exact same port number. That is why they are called well known—everyone follows this same standardized approach. This means that on almost every computer, port 25 is mapped to SMTP, port 80 is mapped to HTTP, and so on. This mapping between lower-numbered ports and specific protocols is a de facto standard, which just means that we all do this and that we do not have a standards body dictating that it absolutely has to be done this way. The fact that almost everyone follows this approach translates to more interoperability among systems all over the world.

Because this is a de facto standard and not a standard that absolutely must be followed, administrators can map different protocols to different port numbers if that fits their purpose. However, one thing to note is that ports 0 to 1023 can be used only by privileged system or root processes.

The following shows some of the most commonly used protocols and the ports to which they are usually mapped:

- Secure Shell (SSH) port 22
- SMTP port 25
- DNS port 53
- HTTP port 80
- NTP port 123
- IMAP port 143
- HTTP Secure (HTTPS) port 443

Registered ports are 1024 to 49151, which can be registered with the Internet Assigned Numbers Authority (IANA) for a particular use. Vendors register specific ports to map to their proprietary software. *Dynamic ports* (also known as *ephemeral ports*) are 49152 to 65535 and are available to be used by any application on an "as needed" basis. Typically, these ports are used on the client side of a connection. For instance, if you look at a specific connection between your web browser and a website you visit, you may notice that the destination port is 80 and the source port (on your client) is 53042. In some cases, however, the server may be listening on a well-known port (e.g., 135 for RPC) and hand off the server port to an ephemeral one. This means that in some cases, you will see both the client and the server port for a connection in the range of 49152 to 65535.

TCP Handshake

TCP must set up a virtual connection between two hosts before any data is sent. This means the two hosts must agree on certain parameters, data flow, windowing, error detection, and options. These issues are negotiated during the handshaking phase, as shown in Figure 11-21.

The host that initiates communication sends a synchronization (SYN) packet to the receiver. The receiver acknowledges this request by sending a SYN/ACK packet. This packet translates into, "I have received your request and am ready to communicate with you." The sending host acknowledges this with an acknowledgment (ACK) packet, which translates into, "I received your acknowledgment. Let's start transmitting our data." This completes the handshaking phase, after which a virtual connection is set up, and actual data can now be passed. The connection that has been set up at this point is considered *full duplex*, which means transmission in both directions is possible using the same transmission line.

If an attacker sends a target system SYN packets with a spoofed address, then the victim system replies to the spoofed address with SYN/ACK packets. Each time the victim system receives one of these SYN packets, it sets aside resources to manage the new connection. If the attacker floods the victim system with SYN packets, eventually the victim system allocates all of its available TCP connection resources and can no longer process new requests. This is a type of DoS attack that is referred to as a *SYN flood*. To thwart this type of attack you can use a number of mitigations, the most common of which are described in the Internet Engineering Task Force's (IETF) Request for Comments (RFC) 4987. One of the most effective techniques described in RFC 4987 is the use of SYN caches, which delays the allocation of a socket until the handshake is completed.

Another attack vector we need to understand is TCP sequence numbers. One of the values that is agreed upon during a TCP handshake between two systems is the sequence numbers that will be inserted into the packet headers. Once the sequence number is agreed upon, if a receiving system receives a packet from the sending system that does not have this predetermined value, it disregards the packet. This means that an attacker cannot just spoof the address of a sending system to fool a receiving system; the attacker has to spoof the sender's address and use the correct sequence number values. If an attacker can correctly predict the TCP sequence numbers that two systems will use, then she can create packets containing those numbers and fool the receiving system into thinking that the packets are coming from the authorized sending system. She can then take over the TCP connection between the two systems, which is referred to as *TCP session hijacking*.

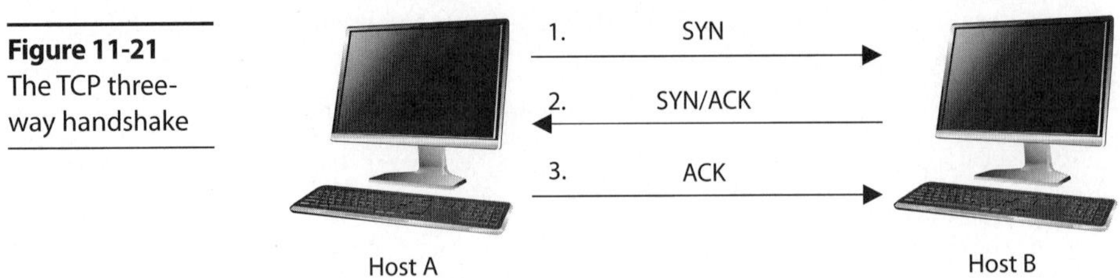

Figure 11-21 The TCP three-way handshake

Data Structures

As stated earlier, the message is formed and passed to the application layer from a program and sent down through the protocol stack. Each protocol at each layer adds its own information to the message to create a PDU and passes it down to the next layer. This activity is referred to as *encapsulation*. As the message is passed down the stack, it goes through a sort of evolution, and each stage has a specific name that indicates what is taking place. When an application formats data to be transmitted over the network, the PDU is called a *message* or *data*. The message is sent to the transport layer, where TCP does its magic on it. The PDU is now a *segment*. The segment is sent to the network layer. The network layer adds routing and addressing, and now the PDU is called a *packet*. The network layer passes off the packet to the data link layer, which frames the packet with a header and a trailer, and now it is called a *frame*. Figure 11-22 illustrates these stages.

EXAM TIP If the message is being transmitted over TCP, it is referred to as a "segment." If it is being transmitted over UDP, it is referred to as a "datagram."

Sometimes when an author refers to a segment, she is specifying the stage in which the data is located within the protocol stack. If the literature is describing routers, which work at the network layer, the author might use the word "packet" because the data at this layer has routing and addressing information attached. If an author is describing network traffic and flow control, she might use the word "frame" because all data actually ends up in the frame format before it is put on the network wire. The important thing here is that you understand the various steps a data package goes through when it moves up and down the protocol stack.

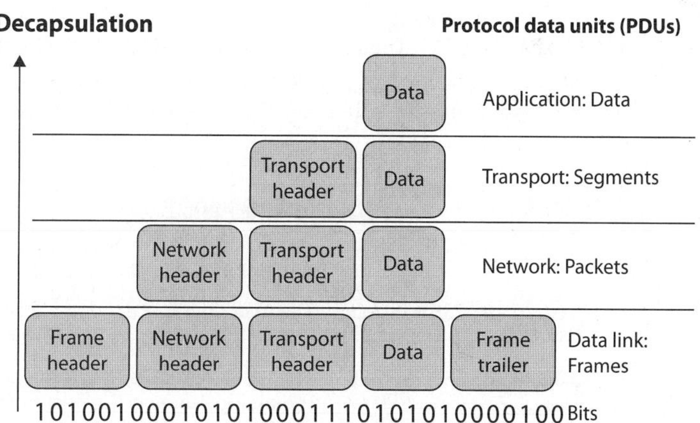

Figure 11-22 Data goes through its own evolutionary stages as it passes through the layers within the network stack.

PART IV

IP Addressing

Each node on a network must have a unique IP address. Today, the most commonly used version of IP is *IP version 4 (IPv4)*, which is used by roughly 70 percent of Internet hosts as we write these words. *IP version 6 (IPv6)*, which was created in part to address the shortage of IPv4 addresses (IPv6 also has many security features built into it that are not part of IPv4), is steadily gaining ground, however. IPv6 is covered later in this chapter.

IPv4 uses 32 bits for its addresses, whereas IPv6 uses 128 bits; thus, IPv6 provides more possible addresses with which to work. Each address has a host portion and a network portion, and the addresses are grouped into *classes* and then into *subnets*. The subnet mask of the address differentiates the groups of addresses that define the subnets of a network. IPv4 address classes are listed in Table 11-5.

For any given IP network within an organization, all nodes connected to the network can have different host addresses but a common network address. The host address identifies every individual node, whereas the network address is the identity of the network all the nodes are connected to; therefore, it is the same for each one of them. Any traffic meant for nodes on this network will be sent to the prescribed network address.

A *subnet* is created from the host portion of an IP address to designate a "sub" network. This allows us to further break the host portion of the address into two or more logical groupings, as shown in Figure 11-23. A network can be logically partitioned to reduce administration headaches, increase traffic performance, and potentially strengthen security. As an analogy, let's say you work at Toddlers R Us and you are responsible for babysitting 100 toddlers. If you kept all 100 toddlers in one room, you would probably end up crazy. To better manage these kids, you could break them up into groups. The three-year-olds go in the yellow room, the four-year-olds go in the green room, and the five-year-olds go in the blue room. This is what a network administrator would do—break up and separate computer nodes to be able to better control them. Instead of putting them into physical rooms, the administrator puts them into logical rooms (subnets).

To continue with our analogy, when you put your toddlers in different rooms, you would have physical barriers that separate them—walls. Network subnetting is not physical; it is logical. This means you would not have physical walls separating your individual subnets, so how do you keep them separate? This is where subnet masks

Class	Address Range	Description
A	0.0.0.0 to 127.255.255.255	The first byte is the network portion, and the remaining 3 bytes are the host portion.
B	128.0.0.0 to 191.255.255.255	The first 2 bytes are the network portion, and the remaining 2 bytes are the host portion.
C	192.0.0.0 to 223.255.255.255	The first 3 bytes are the network portion, and the remaining 1 byte is the host portion.
D	224.0.0.0 to 239.255.255.255	Used for multicast addresses.
E	240.0.0.0 to 255.255.255.255	Reserved for research.

Table 11-5 IPv4 Addressing

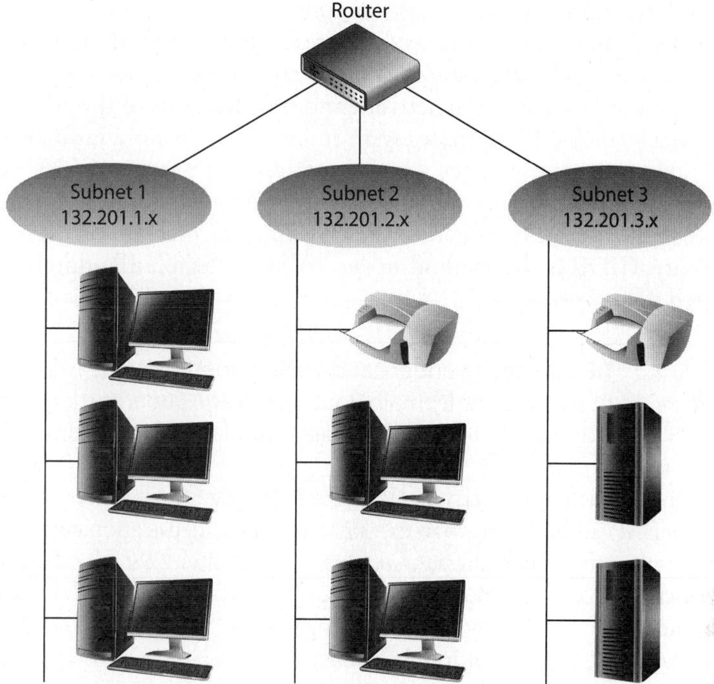

Figure 11-23 Subnets create logical partitions.

come into play. A *subnet mask* defines smaller networks inside a larger network, just like individual rooms are defined within a building.

Subnetting allows larger IP address ranges to be divided into smaller, logical, and more tangible network segments. Consider an organization with several divisions, such as IT, Accounting, HR, and so on. Creating subnets for each division breaks the networks into logical partitions that route traffic directly to recipients without dispersing data all over the network. This drastically reduces the traffic load across the network, reducing the possibility of network congestion and excessive broadcast packets in the network. Implementing network security policies is also much more effective across logically categorized subnets with a demarcated perimeter, as compared to a large, cluttered, and complex network.

Subnetting is particularly beneficial in keeping down routing table sizes because external routers can directly send data to the actual network segment without having to worry about the internal architecture of that network and getting the data to individual hosts. This job can be handled by the internal routers, which can determine the individual hosts in a subnetted environment and save the external routers the hassle of analyzing all 32 bits of an IP address and just look at the "masked" bits.

TIP You should not have to calculate any subnets for the CISSP exam, but for a better understanding of how this stuff works under the hood, check out the article "IP Tutorial: Subnet Mask and Subnetting" at https://www.lifewire.com/internet-protocol-tutorial-subnets-818378 (keep in mind that URLs are subject to change from time to time).

If the traditional subnet masks are used, they are referred to as *classful* or *classical* IP addresses. If an organization needs to create subnets that do not follow these traditional sizes, then it would use *classless* IP addresses. This just means a different subnet mask would be used to define the network and host portions of the addresses. After it became clear that available IP addresses were running out as more individuals and corporations participated on the Internet, *classless interdomain routing (CIDR)* was created. A Class B address range is usually too large for most organizations, and a Class C address range is too small, so CIDR provides the flexibility to increase or decrease the class sizes as necessary. CIDR is the method to specify more flexible IP address classes. CIDR is also referred to as *supernetting*.

TIP To better understand CIDR, a good resource is "IP Classless Addressing: Classless Inter-Domain Routing (CIDR)/"Supernetting": www.tcpipguide.com/free/t_IPClasslessAddressingClasslessInterDomainRoutingCI.htm.

Although each node has an IP address, people usually refer to their hostname rather than their IP address. Hostnames, such as www.mheducation.com, are easier for humans to remember than IP addresses, such as 198.105.254.228. However, the use of these two nomenclatures requires mapping between the hostnames and IP addresses because the computer understands only the numbering scheme. This process is addressed in the "Domain Name Service" section later in this chapter.

NOTE IP provides addressing, packet fragmentation, and packet timeouts. To ensure that packets do not continually traverse a network forever, IP provides a *Time to Live (TTL)* value that is decremented every time the packet passes through a router.

IPv6

IPv6, also called *IP next generation (IPng)*, not only has a larger address space than IPv4 to support more IP addresses; it has some capabilities that IPv4 does not and it accomplishes some of the same tasks differently. All of the specifics of the new functions within IPv6 are beyond the scope of this book, but we will look at a few of them, because IPv6 is the way of the future. IPv6 allows for scoped addresses, which enables an administrator to restrict specific addresses for specific servers or file and print sharing, for example. IPv6 has Internet Protocol Security (IPSec) integrated into the protocol stack, which provides end-to-end secure transmission and authentication. IPv6 has more flexibility and routing capabilities and allows for Quality of Service (QoS) priority values to be assigned to time-sensitive transmissions. The protocol offers autoconfiguration, which makes administration much easier, and it does not require network address translation (NAT) to extend its address space.

NAT was developed because IPv4 addresses were running out. Although the NAT technology is extremely useful, it has caused a lot of overhead and transmission problems because it breaks the client/server model that many applications use today. One reason the industry did not jump on the IPv6 bandwagon when it came out years ago is that NAT was developed, which reduced the speed at which IP addresses were being depleted.

Although the conversion rate from IPv4 to IPv6 is slow in some parts of the world and the implementation process is quite complicated, the industry is making the shift because of all the benefits that IPv6 brings to the table.

NOTE NAT is covered in the "Network Address Translation" section later in this chapter.

The IPv6 specification, as outlined in RFC 8200, lays out the differences and benefits of IPv6 over IPv4. A few of the differences are as follows:

- IPv6 increases the IP address size from 32 bits to 128 bits to support more levels of addressing hierarchy, a much greater number of addressable nodes, and simpler autoconfiguration of addresses.
- The scalability of multicast routing is improved by adding a "scope" field to multicast addresses. Also, a new type of address called an *anycast address* is defined, which is used to send a packet to any one of a group of nodes.
- Some IPv4 header fields have been dropped or made optional to reduce the common-case processing cost of packet handling and to limit the bandwidth cost of the IPv6 header. This is illustrated in Figure 11-24.

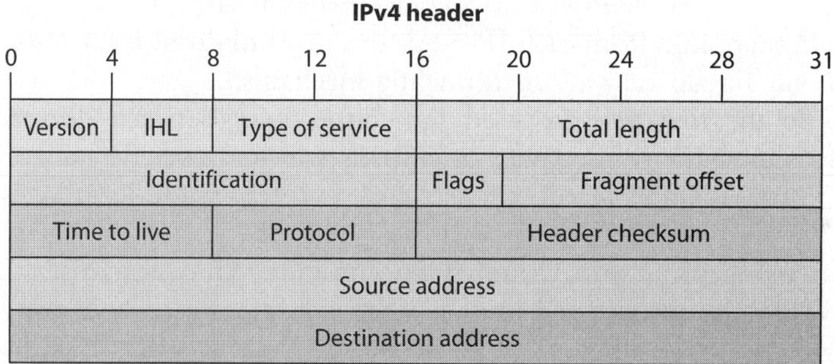

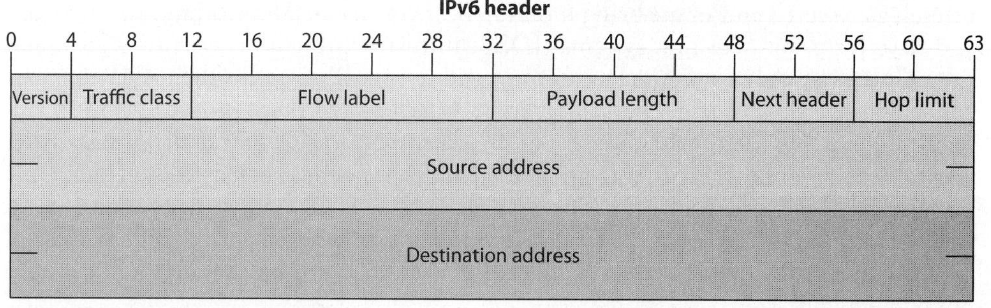

Figure 11-24 IPv4 vs. IPv6 headers

- Changes in the way IP header options are encoded allow for more efficient forwarding, less stringent limits on the length of options, and greater flexibility for introducing new options in the future.
- A new capability is added to enable the labeling of packets belonging to particular traffic "flows" for which the sender requests special handling, such as nondefault QoS or "real-time" service.
- Extensions to support authentication, data integrity, and (optional) data confidentiality are also specified for IPv6.

IPv4 limits packets to 65,535 bytes of payload, and IPv6 extends this size to 4,294,967,295 bytes. These larger packets are referred to as *jumbograms* and improve performance over high-MTU links. Currently most of the world still uses IPv4, but IPv6 is being deployed more rapidly. This means that there are "pockets" of networks using IPv4 and "pockets" of networks using IPv6 that still need to communicate. This communication takes place through different tunneling techniques, which either encapsulate IPv6 packets within IPv4 packets or carry out automated address translations. *Automatic tunneling* is a technique where the routing infrastructure automatically determines the tunnel endpoints so that protocol tunneling can take place without preconfiguration. In the *6to4* tunneling method, the tunnel endpoints are determined by using a well-known IPv4 anycast address on the remote side and embedding IPv4 address data within IPv6 addresses on the local side. *Teredo* is another automatic tunneling technique that uses UDP encapsulation so that NAT address translations are not affected. *Intra-Site Automatic Tunnel Addressing Protocol (ISATAP)* treats the IPv4 network as a virtual IPv6 local link, with mappings from each IPv4 address to a link-local IPv6 address.

The 6to4 and Teredo are *intersite* tunneling mechanisms, and ISATAP is an *intrasite* mechanism. So the first two are used for connectivity between different networks, and ISATAP is used for connectivity of systems within a specific network. Notice in Figure 11-25 that 6to4 and Teredo are used on the Internet and ISATAP is used within an intranet.

While many of these automatic tunneling techniques reduce administration overhead, because network administrators do not have to configure each and every system and network device with two different IP addresses, there are security risks that need to be understood. Many times users and network administrators do not know that automatic tunneling capabilities are enabled, and thus they do not ensure that these different tunnels are secured and/or are being monitored. If you are an administrator of a network and have intrusion detection systems (IDSs), intrusion prevention systems (IPSs), and firewalls that are only configured to monitor and restrict IPv4 traffic, then all IPv6 traffic could be traversing your network insecurely. Attackers use these protocol tunnels and misconfigurations to get past these types of security devices so that malicious activities can take place unnoticed. If you are a user and have a host-based firewall that only understands IPv4 and your operating system has a dual IPv4/IPv6 networking stack, traffic could be bypassing your firewall without being monitored and logged. The use of Teredo can actually open ports in NAT devices that allow for unintended traffic in and out of a network.

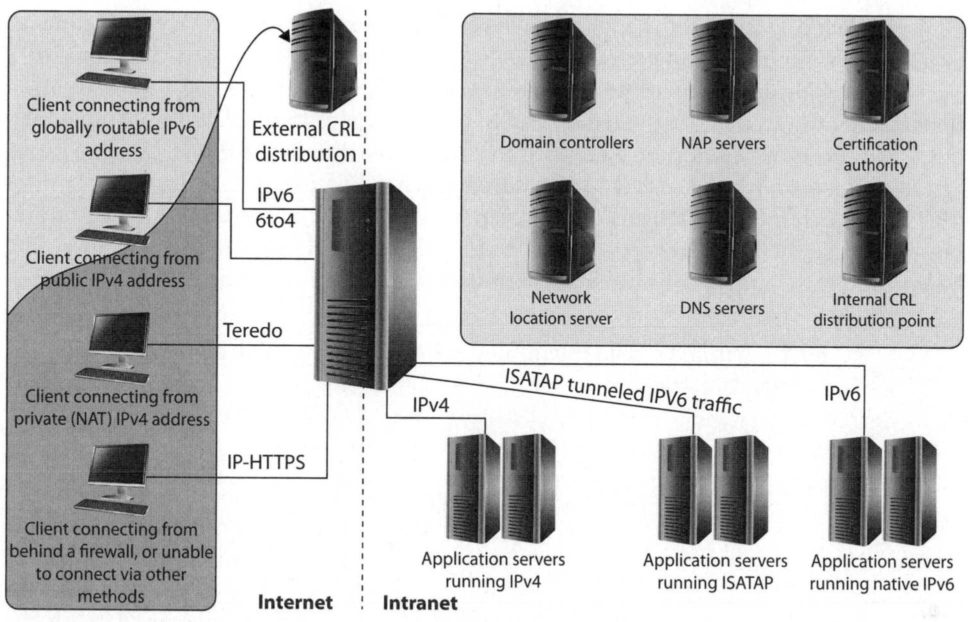

Figure 11-25 Various IPv4 to IPv6 tunneling techniques

It is critical that people who are responsible for configuring and maintaining systems and networks understand the differences between IPv4 and IPv6 and how the various tunneling mechanisms work so that all vulnerabilities are identified and properly addressed. Products and software may need to be updated to address both traffic types, proxies may need to be deployed to manage traffic communication securely, IPv6 should be disabled if not needed, and security appliances need to be configured to monitor all traffic types.

Address Resolution Protocol

On a TCP/IP network, each computer and network device requires a unique IP address and a unique physical hardware address. Each NIC has a unique 48-bit physical address that is programmed by the manufacturer into the ROM chips on the card. The physical address is also referred to as the *Media Access Control (MAC)* address. The network layer works with and understands IP addresses, and the data link layer works with and understands physical MAC addresses. So, how do these two types of addresses work together while operating at different layers?

NOTE A MAC address is unique because the first 24 bits represent the manufacturer code and the last 24 bits represent the unique serial number assigned by the manufacturer.

When data comes from the application layer, it goes to the transport layer for sequence numbers, session establishment, and streaming. The data is then passed to the network layer, where routing information is added to each packet and the source and destination IP addresses are attached to the data bundle. Then this goes to the data link layer, which must find the MAC address and add it to the header portion of the frame. When a frame hits the wire, it only knows what MAC address it is heading toward. At this lower layer of the OSI model, the mechanisms do not even understand IP addresses. So if a computer cannot resolve the IP address passed down from the network layer to the corresponding MAC address, it cannot communicate with that destination computer.

NOTE A *frame* is data that is fully encapsulated, with all of the necessary headers and trailers.

MAC and IP addresses must be properly mapped so they can be correctly resolved. This happens through the *Address Resolution Protocol (ARP)*. When the data link layer receives a frame, the network layer has already attached the destination IP address to it, but the data link layer cannot understand the IP address and thus invokes ARP for help. ARP broadcasts a frame requesting the MAC address that corresponds with the destination IP address. Each computer on the broadcast domain receives this frame, and all but the computer that has the requested IP address ignore it. The computer that has the destination IP address responds with its MAC address. Now ARP knows what hardware address corresponds with that specific IP address. The data link layer takes the frame, adds the hardware address to it, and passes it on to the physical layer, which enables the frame to hit the wire and go to the destination computer. ARP maps the hardware address and associated IP address and stores this mapping in its table for a predefined amount of time. This caching is done so that when another frame destined for the same IP address needs to hit the wire, ARP does not need to broadcast its request again. It just looks in its table for this information.

Sometimes attackers alter a system's ARP table so it contains incorrect information. This is called *ARP table cache poisoning*. The attacker's goal is to receive packets intended for another computer. This is a type of masquerading attack. For example, let's say that Bob's computer has an IP address of 10.0.0.1 and a MAC address of bb:bb:bb:bb:bb:bb, Alice's computer has an IP address of 10.0.0.7 and a MAC address of aa:aa:aa:aa:aa:aa, and an attacker has an IP address of 10.0.0.3 and a MAC address of cc:cc:cc:cc:cc:cc, as shown in Figure 11-26. Suppose Bob wants to send a message to Alice. The message is encapsulated at the IP layer with information including Alice's IP address and then handed off to the data link layer. If this is the first message for Alice's computer, the data link process on Bob's computer has no way of knowing her MAC address, so it crafts an ARP query that (literally) says "Who has 10.0.0.7?" This ARP frame is broadcast to the network, where it is received by both Alice's computer and the attacker's computer. Both respond claiming to be the rightful owners of that IP address. What does Bob's computer do when faced with multiple different responses? The answer in most cases is that it uses the most recent response. If the attacker wants to ensure that Bob's ARP table remains poisoned, then he will have to keep pumping out bogus ARP replies.

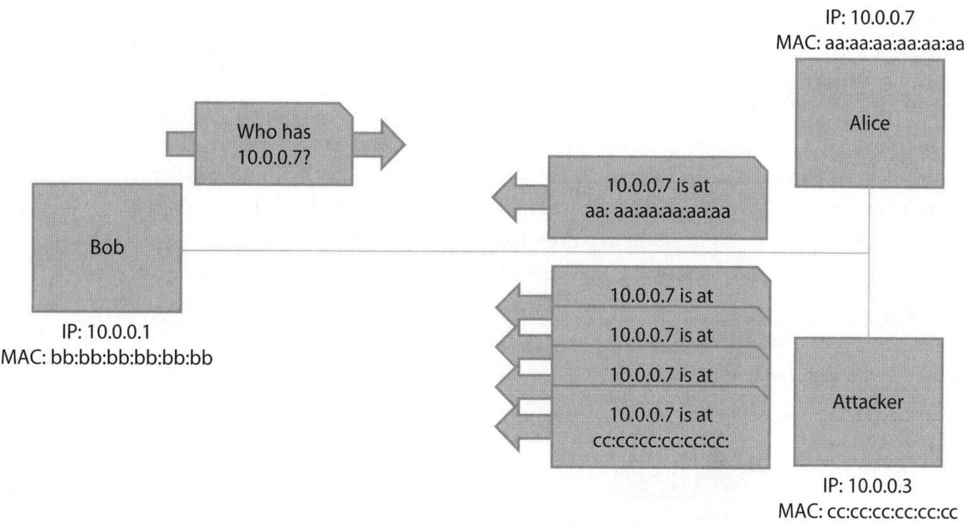

Figure 11-26 ARP poisoning attack

So ARP is critical for a system to communicate, but it can be manipulated to allow traffic to be sent to unintended systems. ARP is a rudimentary protocol and does not have any security measures built in to protect itself from these types of attacks. Networks should have IDS sensors monitoring for this type of malicious activity so that administrators can be alerted if it is underway. This is not difficult to detect, since, as already noted, the attacker will have to constantly (or at least frequently) transmit bogus ARP replies.

Dynamic Host Configuration Protocol

A computer can receive its IP addresses in a few different ways when it first boots up. If it has a statically assigned address, nothing needs to happen. It already has the configuration settings it needs to communicate and work on the intended network. If a computer depends upon a DHCP server to assign it the correct IP address, it boots up and makes a request to the DHCP server. The DHCP server assigns the IP address, and everyone is happy.

DHCP is a UDP-based protocol that allows servers to assign IP addresses to network clients in real time. Unlike static IP addresses, where IP addresses are manually configured, the DHCP server automatically checks for available IP addresses and correspondingly assigns an IP address to the client. This eliminates the possibility of IP address conflicts that occur if two systems are assigned identical IP addresses, which could cause loss of service. On the whole, DHCP considerably reduces the effort involved in managing large-scale IP networks.

The DHCP server assigns IP addresses in real time from a specified range when a client connects to the network; this is different from static addresses, where each system is individually assigned a specific IP address when coming online. In a standard DHCP-based network, the client computer broadcasts a DHCPDISCOVER message on the network in search of the DHCP server. Once the respective DHCP server receives the DHCPDISCOVER request, the server responds with a DHCPOFFER packet, offering the client an IP address. The server assigns the IP address based on the subject of the availability of that IP address and in compliance with its network administration policies. The DHCPOFFER packet that the server responds with contains the assigned IP address information and configuration settings for client-side services.

Once the client receives the settings sent by the server through the DHCPOFFER packet, it responds to the server with a DHCPREQUEST packet confirming its acceptance of the allotted settings. The server now acknowledges with a DHCPACK packet, which includes the validity period (lease) for the allocated parameters.

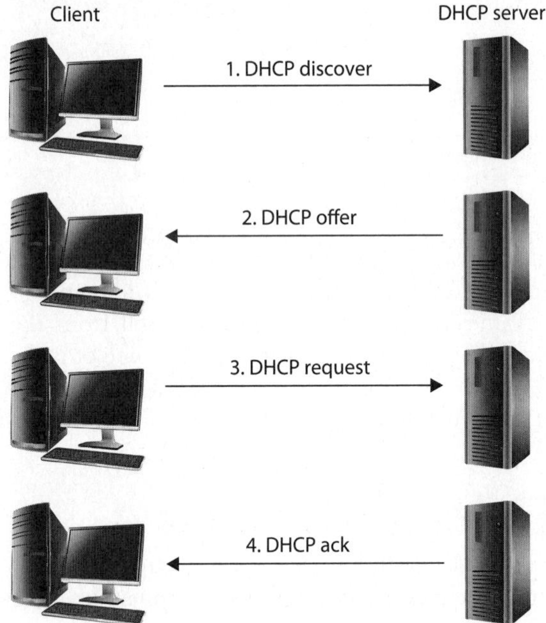

So as shown in Figure 11-27, the DHCP client yells out to the network, "Who can help me get an address?" The DHCP server responds with an offer: "Here is an address and the parameters that go with it." The client accepts this gracious offer with the DHCPREQUEST message, and the server acknowledges this message. Now the client can start interacting with other devices on the network and the user can surf the Web and check her e-mail.

Unfortunately, both the client and server segments of DHCP are vulnerable to falsified identity. On the client end, attackers can masquerade their systems to appear as valid network clients. This enables rogue systems to become a part of an organization's network and potentially infiltrate other systems on the network. An attacker may create an unauthorized DHCP server on the network and start responding to clients searching

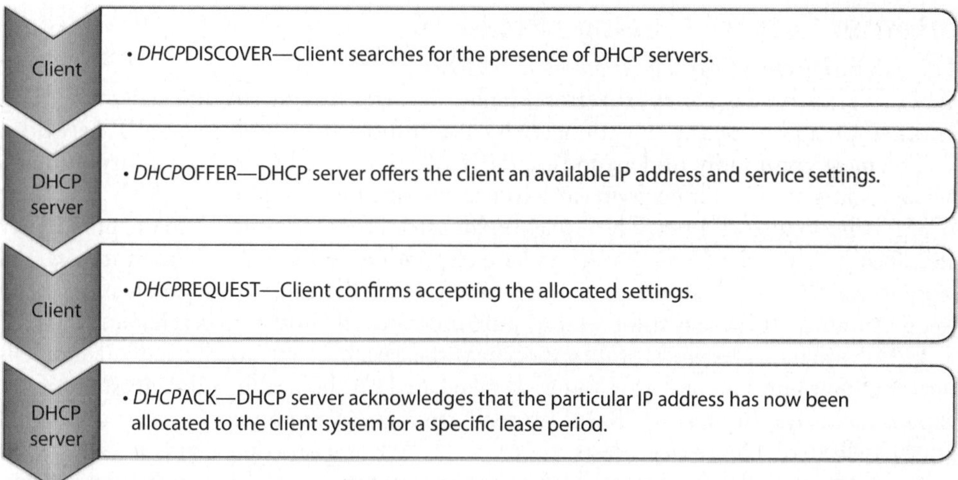

Figure 11-27 The four stages of the Discover, Offer, Request, and Acknowledgment (D-O-R-A) process

for a DHCP server. A DHCP server controlled by an attacker can compromise client system configurations, carry out man-in-the-middle attacks, route traffic to unauthorized networks, and a lot more, with the end result of jeopardizing the entire network.

An effective method to shield networks from unauthenticated DHCP clients is through the use of *DHCP snooping* on network switches. DHCP snooping ensures that DHCP servers can assign IP addresses to only selected systems, identified by their MAC addresses. Also, advanced network switches have the capability to direct clients toward legitimate DHCP servers to get IP addresses and restrict rogue systems from becoming DHCP servers on the network.

Diskless workstations do not have a full operating system but have just enough code to know how to boot up and broadcast for an IP address, and they may have a pointer to the server that holds the operating system. The diskless workstation knows its hardware address, so it broadcasts this information so that a listening server can assign it the correct IP address. As with ARP, *Reverse Address Resolution Protocol (RARP)* frames go to all systems on the subnet, but only the RARP server responds. Once the RARP server receives this request, it looks in its table to see which IP address matches the broadcast hardware address. The server then sends a message that contains its IP address back to the requesting computer. The system now has an IP address and can function on the network.

The *Bootstrap Protocol (BOOTP)* was created after RARP to enhance the functionality that RARP provides for diskless workstations. The diskless workstation can receive its IP address, the name server address for future name resolutions, and the default gateway address from the BOOTP server. BOOTP usually provides more functionality to diskless workstations than does RARP.

Internet Control Message Protocol

The *Internet Control Message Protocol (ICMP)* is basically IP's "messenger boy." ICMP delivers status messages, reports errors, replies to certain requests, and reports routing information and is used to test connectivity and troubleshoot problems on IP networks.

The most commonly understood use of ICMP is its use by the *ping* utility. When a person wants to test connectivity to another system, he may ping it, which sends out ICMP Echo Request frames. The replies on his screen that are returned to the ping utility are called ICMP Echo Reply frames and are responding to the Echo Request frames. If a reply is not returned within a predefined time period, the ping utility sends more Echo Request frames. If there is still no reply, ping indicates the host is unreachable.

ICMP also indicates when problems occur with a specific route on the network and tells surrounding routers about better routes to take based on the health and congestion of the various pathways. Routers use ICMP to send messages in response to packets that could not be delivered. The router selects the proper ICMP response and sends it back to the requesting host, indicating that problems were encountered with the transmission request.

ICMP is used by other connectionless protocols, not just IP, because connectionless protocols do not have any way of detecting and reacting to transmission errors, as do connection-oriented protocols. In these instances, the connectionless protocol may use ICMP to send error messages back to the sending system to indicate networking problems.

As you can see in Table 11-6, ICMP is used for many different networking purposes. This table lists the various messages that can be sent to systems and devices through ICMP.

Attacks Using ICMP

ICMP was developed to send status messages, not to hold or transmit user data. But someone figured out how to insert some data inside of an ICMP packet, which can be used to communicate to an already compromised system. This technique is called *ICMP tunneling*, and is an older, but still effective, client/server approach that can be used by hackers to set up and maintain covert communication channels to compromised systems. The attacker would target a computer and install the server portion of the tunneling software. This server portion would "listen" on a port, which is the back door an attacker can use to access the system. To gain access and open a remote shell to this computer, an attacker would send commands inside of ICMP packets. This is usually successful because many routers and firewalls are configured to allow ICMP traffic to come and go out of the network, based on the assumption that this is safe because ICMP was developed to not hold any data or a payload.

Just as any tool that can be used for good can also be used for evil, attackers commonly use ICMP to redirect traffic. The redirected traffic can go to the attacker's dedicated system, or it can go into a "black hole." Routers use ICMP messages to update each other on network link status. An attacker could send a bogus ICMP message with incorrect information, which could cause the routers to divert network traffic to where the attacker indicates it should go.

ICMP is also used as the core protocol for a network tool called Traceroute. Traceroute is used to diagnose network connections, but since it gathers a lot of important network statistics, attackers use the tool to map out a victim's network. This is similar to a burglar

Table 11-6 ICMP Message Types

Type	Name
0	Echo Reply
1	Unassigned
2	Unassigned
3	Destination Unreachable
4	Source Quench
5	Redirect
6	Alternate Host Address
7	Unassigned
8	Echo Request
9	Router Advertisement
10	Router Solicitation
11	Time Exceeded
12	Parameter Problem
13	Timestamp
14	Timestamp Reply
15	Information Request
16	Information Reply
17	Address Mask Request
18	Address Mask Reply
19	Reserved (for Security)
20–29	Reserved (for Robustness Experiment)
30	Traceroute
31	Datagram Conversion Error
32	Mobile Host Redirect
33	IPv6 Where-Are-You
34	IPv6 I-Am-Here
35	Mobile Registration Request
36	Mobile Registration Reply
37	Domain Name Request
38	Domain Name Reply
39	SKIP
40	Photuris (Disambiguation)
41	ICMP messages utilized by experimental mobility protocols such as Seamoby

"casing the joint," meaning that the more the attacker learns about the environment, the easier it can be for her to exploit some critical targets. So while the Traceroute tool is a valid networking program, a security administrator might configure the IDS sensors to monitor for extensive use of this tool because it could indicate that an attacker is attempting to map out the network's architecture.

The countermeasures to these types of attacks are to use firewall rules that only allow the necessary ICMP packets into the network and the use of an IDS or IPS to watch for suspicious activities. Host-based protection (host firewalls and host IDS) can also be installed and configured to identify this type of suspicious behavior.

Simple Network Management Protocol

The *Simple Network Management Protocol (SNMP)* was released to the networking world in 1988 to help with the growing demand of managing network IP devices. Organizations use many types of products that use SNMP to view the status of their network, traffic flows, and the hosts within the network. Since these tasks are commonly carried out using graphical user interface (GUI)–based applications, many people do not have a full understanding of how the protocol actually works. The protocol is important to understand because it can provide a wealth of information to attackers, and you should understand the amount of information that is available to the ones who wish to do you harm, how they actually access this data, and what can be done with it.

The two main components within SNMP are managers and agents. The *manager* is the server portion, which polls different devices to check status information. The server component also receives trap messages from agents and provides a centralized place to hold all network-wide information. The *agent* is a piece of software that runs on a network device, which is commonly integrated into the operating system. The agent has a list of objects that it is to keep track of, which is held in a database-like structure called the *Management Information Base (MIB)*. A MIB is a logical grouping of managed objects that contain data used for specific management tasks and status checks.

When the SNMP manager component polls the individual agent installed on a specific device, the agent pulls the data it has collected from the MIB and sends it to the manager. Figure 11-28 illustrates how data pulled from different devices is located in one centralized location (SNMP manager). This allows the network administrator to have a holistic view of the network and the devices that make up that network.

NOTE The trap operation allows the agent to inform the manager of an event, instead of having to wait to be polled. For example, if an interface on a router goes down, an agent can send a trap message to the manager. This is the only way an agent can communicate with the manager without first being polled.

It might be necessary to restrict which managers can request information of an agent, so *communities* were developed to establish a trust between specific agents and managers. A *community string* is basically a password a manager uses to request data from the agent, and there are two main community strings with different levels of access: read-only and

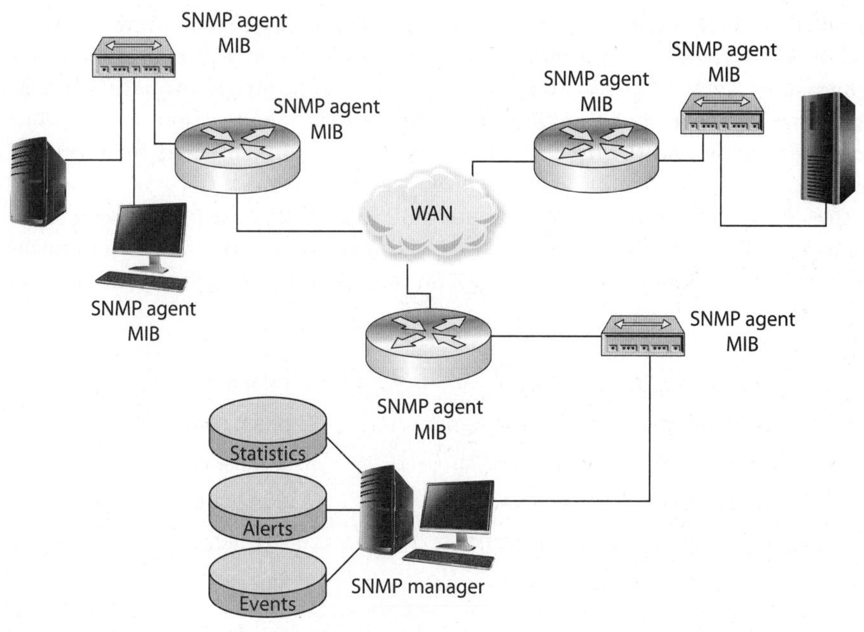

Figure 11-28 Agents provide the manager with SNMP data.

read-write. As the names imply, the read-only community string allows a manager to read data held within a device's MIB, and the read-write string allows a manager to read the data and modify it. If an attacker can uncover the read-write string, she could change values held within the MIB, which could reconfigure the device.

Since the community string is a password, it should be hard to guess and be protected. It should contain mixed-case alphanumeric strings that are not dictionary words. This practice is not always the case in many networks. The usual default read-only community string is "public" and the read-write string is "private." Many organizations do not change these, so anyone who can connect to port 161 can read the status information of a device and potentially reconfigure it. Different vendors may put in their own default community string values, but organizations may still not take the necessary steps to change them. Attackers usually have lists of default vendor community string values, so they can be easily discovered and used against networks.

To make matters worse, the community strings are sent in cleartext in SNMP v1 and v2, so even if a company does the right thing by changing the default values, the strings are still easily accessible to any attacker with a sniffer. If you absolutely have to use v1 or v2 (and you really shouldn't because they are obsolete), make sure that different network segments use different community strings, so that if one string is compromised an attacker cannot gain access to all the devices in the network. The SNMP ports (161 and 162) should not be open to untrusted networks, like the Internet, and if needed they should be filtered to ensure only authorized individuals can connect to them. If these ports need to be available to an untrusted network, configure the router or firewall to only allow UDP traffic to come and go from preapproved network-management stations. While versions 1 and 2 of this protocol send the community string values in cleartext, version 3 has cryptographic functionality, which provides encryption, message integrity, and authentication security. So, SNMP v3 should be implemented for more granular protection.

If the proper countermeasures are not put into place, then an attacker can gain access to a wealth of device-oriented data that can be used in her follow-up attacks. The following are just some data sets held within MIB SNMP objects that attackers would be interested in:

.server.svSvcTable.svSvcEntry.svSvcName	Running services
.server.svShareTable.svShareEntry.svShareName	Share names
.server.sv.ShareTable.svShareEntry.svSharePath	Share paths
.server.sv.ShareTable.svShareEntry.svShareComment	Comments on shares
.server.svUserTable.svUserEntry.svUserName	Usernames
.domain.domPrimaryDomain8	Domain names

Gathering this type of data allows an attacker to map out the target network and enumerate the nodes that make up the network.

As with all tools, SNMP is used for good purposes (network management) and for bad purposes (target mapping, device reconfiguration). We need to understand both sides of all tools available to us.

Domain Name Service

Imagine how hard it would be to use the Internet if we had to remember actual specific IP addresses to get to various websites. The *Domain Name Service (DNS)* is a method of resolving hostnames to IP addresses so names can be used instead of IP addresses within networked environments.

The first iteration of the Internet was made up of about 100 computers (versus over 22 billion now), and a list was kept that mapped every system's hostname to its IP address. This list was kept on an FTP server so everyone could access it. It did not take long for the task of maintaining this list to become overwhelming, and the computing community looked to automate it.

When a user types a uniform resource locator (URL) into his web browser, the URL is made up of words or letters that are in a sequence that makes sense to that user, such as www.google.com. However, these words are only for humans—computers work with IP addresses. So after the user enters this URL and presses ENTER, behind the scenes his computer is actually being directed to a DNS server that will resolve this URL, or hostname, into an IP address that the computer understands. Once the hostname has been resolved into an IP address, the computer knows how to get to the web server holding the requested web page.

Many organizations have their own DNS servers to resolve their internal hostnames. These organizations usually also use the DNS servers at their Internet service providers (ISPs) to resolve hostnames on the Internet. An internal DNS server can be used to resolve hostnames on the entire LAN, but usually more than one DNS server is used so the load can be split up and so redundancy and fault tolerance are in place.

Within DNS servers, DNS namespaces are split up administratively into *zones*. One zone may contain all hostnames for the marketing and accounting departments, and another zone may contain hostnames for the administration, research, and legal departments. The DNS server that holds the files for one of these zones is said to be the *authoritative* name server for that particular zone. A zone may contain one or more domains, and the DNS server holding those host records is the authoritative name server for those domains.

The DNS server contains records that map hostnames to IP addresses, which are referred to as *resource records*. When a user's computer needs to resolve a hostname to an IP address, it looks to its networking settings to find its DNS server. The computer then sends a request, containing the hostname, to the DNS server for resolution. The DNS server looks at its resource records and finds the record with this particular hostname, retrieves the address, and replies to the computer with the corresponding IP address.

It is recommended that a primary and a secondary DNS server cover each zone. The primary DNS server contains the actual resource records for a zone, and the secondary DNS server contains copies of those records. Users can use the secondary DNS server to resolve names, which takes a load off of the primary server. If the primary server goes down for any reason or is taken offline, users can still use the secondary server for name resolution. Having both a primary DNS server and a secondary DNS server provides fault tolerance and redundancy to ensure users can continue to work if something happens to one of these servers.

The primary and secondary DNS servers synchronize their information through a *zone transfer*. After changes take place to the primary DNS server, those changes must be replicated to the secondary DNS server. It is important to configure the DNS server to allow zone transfers to take place only between the specific servers. For years now, attackers have been carrying out unauthorized zone transfers to gather very useful network information from victims' DNS servers.

An unauthorized zone transfer provides the attacker with information on almost every system within the network, including the hostname and IP address of each system, system alias names, public key infrastructure (PKI) server, DHCP server, DNS servers, and so on. This allows an attacker to carry out very targeted attacks on specific systems. If you were the attacker and you had a new exploit for DHCP software, now you would know the IP address of the company's DHCP server and could send your attack parameters directly to that system. Also, since the zone transfer can provide data on all of the systems in the network, the attacker can map out the network. He knows what subnets are being used, which systems are in each subnet, and where the critical network systems reside. This is analogous to you allowing a burglar into your house with the freedom of identifying where you keep your jewels, expensive stereo equipment, piggy bank, and keys to your car, which will allow him to more easily steal these items when you are on vacation. Unauthorized zone transfers can take place if the DNS servers are not properly configured to restrict this type of activity.

Internet DNS and Domains

Networks on the Internet are connected in a hierarchical structure, as are the different DNS servers, as shown in Figure 11-29. While performing routing tasks, if a router does not know the necessary path to the requested destination, that router passes the packet up to a router above it. The router above it knows about all the routers below it. This router has a broader view of the routing that takes place on the Internet and has a better chance of getting the packet to the correct destination. This holds true with DNS servers also. If one DNS server does not know which DNS server holds the necessary resource record to resolve a hostname, it can pass the request up to a DNS server above it.

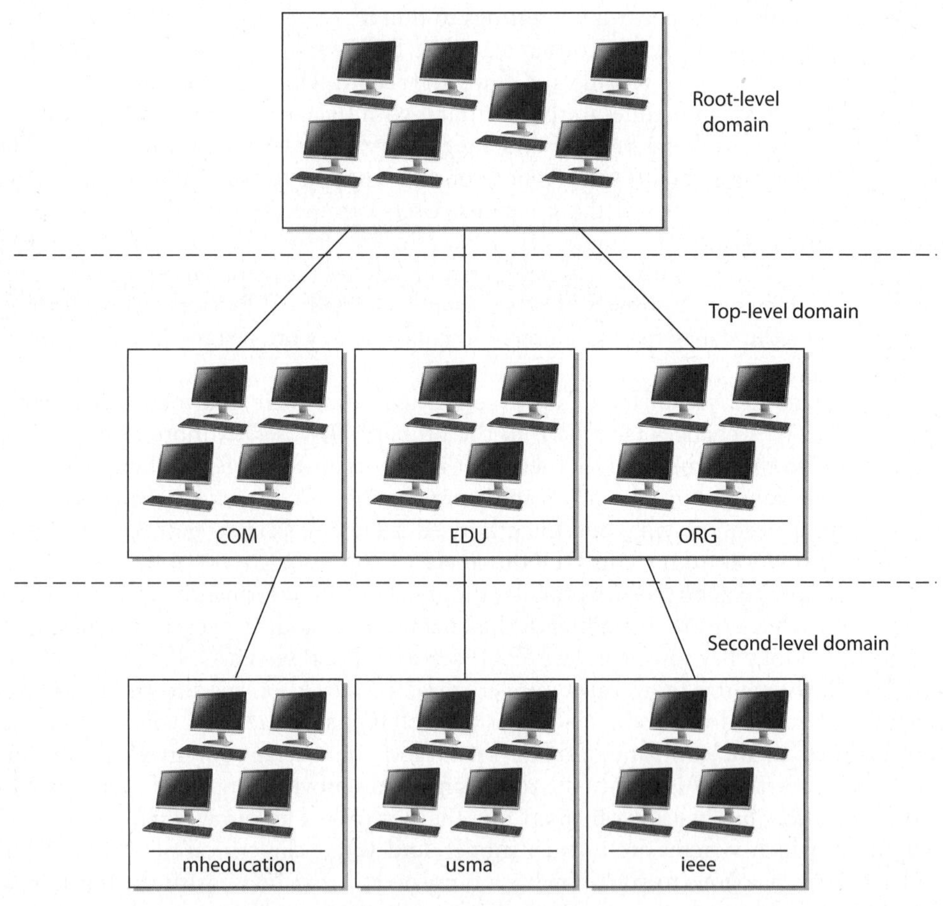

Figure 11-29 The DNS naming hierarchy is similar to the routing hierarchy on the Internet.

The naming scheme of the Internet resembles an inverted tree with the root servers at the top. Lower branches of this tree are divided into top-level domains, with second-level domains under each. The most common top-level domains are as follows:

- **COM** Commercial
- **EDU** Education
- **MIL** U.S. military organization
- **INT** International treaty organization
- **GOV** Government
- **ORG** Organizational
- **NET** Networks

So how do all of these DNS servers play together in the Internet playground? When a user types in a URL to access a website that sells computer books, for example, his computer asks its local DNS server if it can resolve this hostname to an IP address. If the primary DNS server cannot resolve the hostname, it must query a higher-level DNS server, ultimately ending at an authoritative DNS server for the specified domain. Because this website is most likely not on the corporate network, the local LAN DNS server will not usually know the necessary IP address of that website. The DNS server does not reject the user's request, but rather passes it on to another DNS server on the Internet. The request for this hostname resolution continues through different DNS servers until it reaches one that knows the IP address. The requested host's IP information is reported back to the user's computer. The user's computer then attempts to access the website using the IP address, and soon the user is buying computer books, happy as a clam.

DNS server and hostname resolution is extremely important in corporate networking and Internet use. Without it, users would have to remember and type in the IP address for each website and individual system instead of the name. That would be a mess.

DNS Resolution Components

Your computer has a *DNS resolver*, which is responsible for sending out requests to DNS servers for host IP address information. If your system did not have this resolver, when you type in www.google.com in your browser, you would not get to this website because your system does not actually know what www.google.com means. When you type in this URL, your system's resolver has the IP address of a DNS server it is supposed to send its hostname-to-IP address request to. Your resolver can send out a nonrecursive query or a recursive query to the DNS server. A *nonrecursive query* means that the request just goes to that specified DNS server and either the answer is returned to the resolver or an error is returned. A *recursive query* means that the request can be passed on from one DNS server to another one until the DNS server with the correct information is identified.

(*Continued*)

In the following illustration, you can follow the succession of requests that commonly takes place. Your system's resolver first checks to see if it already has the necessary hostname-to-IP address mapping cached or if it is in a local HOSTS file. If the necessary information is not found, the resolver sends the request to the local DNS server. If the local DNS server does not have the information, it sends the request to a different DNS server.

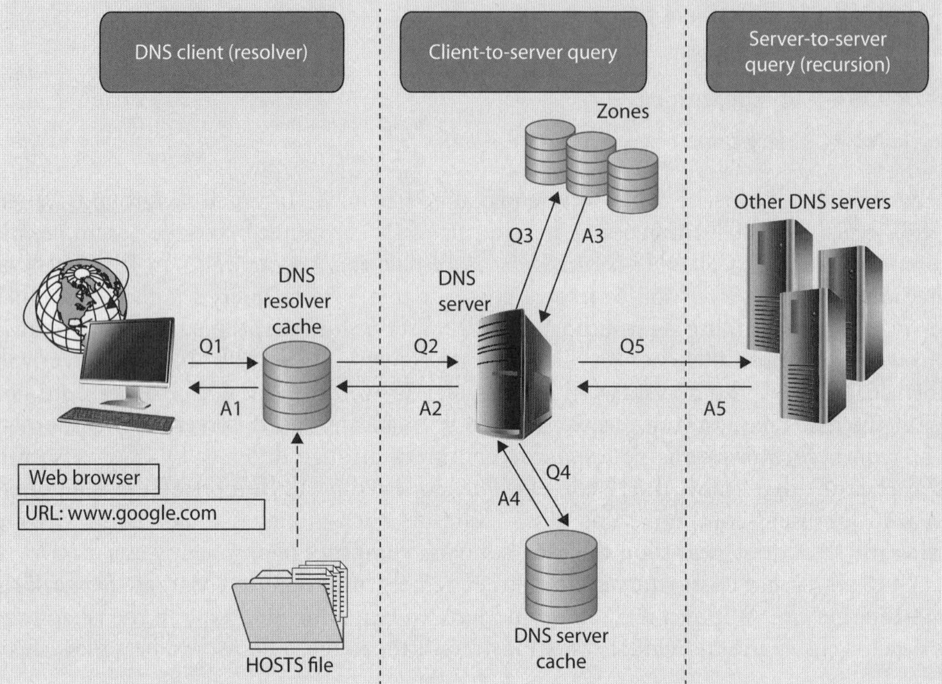

The HOSTS file resides on the local computer and can contain static hostname-to-IP address mapping information. If you do not want your system to query a DNS server, you can add the necessary data in the HOSTS file, and your system will check its contents before reaching out to a DNS server. HOSTS files are like two-edged swords: on the one hand they offer a degree of security by ensuring that certain hosts resolve to specific IP addresses, but on the other hand they are attractive targets for attackers who want to redirect your traffic to specific hosts. The key, as always, is to carefully analyze and mitigate the risks.

DNS Threats

As stated earlier, not every DNS server knows the IP address of every hostname it is asked to resolve. When a request for a hostname-to-IP address mapping arrives at a DNS server (server A), the server reviews its resource records to see if it has the necessary information to fulfill this request. If the server does not have a resource record for this hostname, it forwards the request to another DNS server (server B), which in turn reviews its resource records and, if it has the mapping information, sends the information back to server A. Server A caches this hostname-to-IP address mapping in its memory (in case another client requests it) and sends the information on to the requesting client.

With the preceding information in mind, consider a sample scenario. Andy the attacker wants to make sure that any time one of his competitor's customers tries to visit the competitor's website, the customer is instead pointed to Andy's website. Therefore, Andy installs a tool that listens for requests that leave DNS server A asking other DNS servers if they know how to map the competitor's hostname to its IP address. Once Andy sees that server A sends out a request to server B to resolve the competitor's hostname, Andy quickly sends a message to server A indicating that the competitor's hostname resolves to Andy's website's IP address. Server A's software accepts the first response it gets, so server A caches this incorrect mapping information and sends it on to the requesting client. Now when the client tries to reach Andy's competitor's website, she is instead pointed to Andy's website. This will happen subsequently to any user who uses server A to resolve the competitor's hostname to an IP address because this information is cached on server A.

Previous vulnerabilities that have allowed this type of activity to take place have been addressed, but this type of attack is still taking place because when server A receives a response to its request, it does not authenticate the sender.

Mitigating DNS threats consists of numerous measures, the most important of which is the use of stronger authentication mechanisms such as the *DNSSEC* (DNS security, which is part of many current implementations of DNS server software). DNSSEC implements PKI and digital signatures, which allows DNS servers to validate the origin of a message to ensure that it is not spoofed and potentially malicious. If DNSSEC were enabled on server A, then server A would, upon receiving a response, validate the digital signature on the message before accepting the information to make sure that the response is from an authorized DNS server. So even if an attacker sends a message to a DNS server, the DNS server would discard it because the message would not contain a valid digital signature. DNSSEC allows DNS servers to send and receive authorized messages between themselves and thwarts the attacker's goal of poisoning a DNS cache table.

This sounds simple enough, but for DNSSEC to be rolled out properly, all of the DNS servers on the Internet would have to participate in a PKI to be able to validate digital signatures. The implementation of Internet-wide PKIs simultaneously and seamlessly has proved to be difficult.

Despite the fact that DNSSEC requires more resources than the traditional DNS, more and more organizations globally are opting to use DNSSEC. As of this writing, 91 percent of the top-level domains implement DNSSEC. However, across the entire Internet, barely 3 percent of domains have implemented it. So we are getting there, slowly but surely.

DNS Splitting

Organizations should implement *split DNS*, which means a DNS server in the DMZ handles external hostname-to-IP address resolution requests, while an internal DNS server handles only internal requests. This helps ensure that the internal DNS server has layers of protection and is not exposed by being "Internet facing." The internal DNS server should only contain resource records for the internal computer systems, and the external DNS server should only contain resource records for the systems the organization wants the outside world to be able to connect to. If the external DNS server is compromised and it has the resource records for all of the internal systems, now the attacker has a lot of "inside knowledge" and can carry out targeted attacks. External DNS servers should only contain information on the systems within the DMZ that the organization wants others on the Internet to be able to communicate with (web servers, external mail server, etc.).

Now let's discuss another (indirectly related) predicament in securing DNS traffic—manipulation of the HOSTS file, a technique frequently used by malware. The HOSTS file is used by the operating system to map hostnames to IP addresses as described before. The HOSTS file is a plaintext file located in the *%systemroot%\system32\drivers\etc* folder in Windows, in */etc/hosts* in Unix/Linux systems, and in */private/etc/hosts* in macOS. The HOSTS file simply consists of a list of IP addresses with their corresponding hostnames.

Depending on its configuration, the computer refers to the HOSTS file before issuing a DNS request to a DNS server. Most operating systems give preference to details of IP addresses returned by the HOSTS file rather than querying the DNS server because the HOSTS file is generally under the direct control of the local system administrator.

As covered previously, in the early days of the Internet and prior to the adoption of DNS, HOSTS files were the primary source of determining a host's network addresses from its hostname. With the increase in the number of hosts connected to the Internet, maintaining HOSTS files became next to impossible and ultimately led to the creation of DNS.

Due to the important role of HOSTS files, they are frequently targeted by malware to propagate across systems connected on a local network. Once a malicious program takes over the HOSTS file, it can divert traffic from its intended destination to websites hosting malicious content, for example. A common example of HOSTS file manipulation carried out by malware involves blocking users from visiting antivirus update websites. This is usually done by mapping target hostnames to the loopback interface IP address 127.0.0.1. The most effective technique for preventing HOSTS file intrusions is to set it as a read-only file and implement a host-based IDS that watches for critical file modification attempts.

Attackers don't always have to go through all this trouble to divert traffic to rogue destinations. They can also use some very simple techniques that are surprisingly effective in routing naive users to unintended destinations. The most common approach is known as *URL hiding*. Hypertext Markup Language (HTML) documents and e-mail messages allow users to attach or embed hyperlinks in any given text, such as the "Click Here" links you commonly see in e-mail messages or web pages. Attackers misuse hyperlinks to deceive unsuspecting users into clicking rogue links.

Let's say a malicious attacker creates an unsuspicious text, www.good.site, but embeds the link to an abusive website, www.bad.site. People are likely to click the www.good.site link without knowing that they are actually being taken to the bad site. In addition, attackers also use character encoding to obscure web addresses that may arouse user suspicion.

Network Address Translation

When computers need to communicate with each other, they must use the same type of addressing scheme so everyone understands how to find and talk to one another. The Internet uses the IP address scheme as discussed earlier in the chapter, and any computer or network that wants to communicate with other users on the network must conform to this scheme; otherwise, that computer will sit in a virtual room with only itself to talk to. However, IP addresses have become scarce (until the full adoption of IPv6) and expensive. So some smart people came up with *network address translation (NAT)*, which enables a network that does not follow the Internet's addressing scheme to communicate over the Internet.

Private IP addresses have been reserved for internal LAN address use, as outlined in RFC 1918. These addresses can be used within the boundaries of an organization, but they cannot be used on the Internet because they will not be properly routed. NAT enables an organization to use these private addresses and still be able to communicate transparently with computers on the Internet.

The following lists current private IP address ranges:

- 10.0.0.0–10.255.255.255 Class A networks
- 172.16.0.0–172.31.255.255 Class B networks
- 192.168.0.0–192.168.255.255 Class C networks

NAT is a gateway that lies between a network and the Internet (or another network) that performs transparent routing and address translation. Because IP addresses were depleting fast, IPv6 was developed in 1999, and was intended to be the long-term fix to the address shortage problem. NAT was developed as the short-term fix to enable more organizations to participate on the Internet. However, to date, IPv6 is slow in acceptance and implementation, while NAT has caught on like wildfire. Many firewall vendors have implemented NAT into their products, and it has been found that NAT actually provides a great security benefit. When attackers want to hack a network, they first do what they can to learn all about the network and its topology, services, and addresses. Attackers cannot easily find out an organization's address scheme and its topology when NAT is in place, because NAT acts like a large nightclub bouncer by standing in front of the network and hiding the true IP scheme.

NAT hides internal addresses by centralizing them on one device, and any frames that leave that network have only the source address of that device, not of the actual internal computer that sends the message. So when a message comes from an internal computer with the address of 10.10.10.2, for example, the message is stopped at the device running NAT software, which happens to have the IP address of 1.2.3.4. NAT changes the header of the packet from the internal address, 10.10.10.2, to the IP address of the NAT device, 1.2.3.4. When a computer on the Internet replies to this message, it replies to the address 1.2.3.4. The NAT device changes the header on this reply message to 10.10.10.2 and puts it on the wire for the internal user to receive.

Three basic types of NAT implementations can be used:

- **Static mapping** The NAT software has a pool of public IP addresses configured. Each private address is statically mapped to a specific public address. So computer A always receives the public address x, computer B always receives the public address y, and so on. This is generally used for servers that need to keep the same public address at all times.
- **Dynamic mapping** The NAT software has a pool of IP addresses, but instead of statically mapping a public address to a specific private address, it works on a first-come, first-served basis. So if Bob needs to communicate over the Internet, his system makes a request to the NAT server. The NAT server takes the first IP address on the list and maps it to Bob's private address. The balancing act is to estimate how many computers will most likely need to communicate outside the internal network at one time. This estimate is the number of public addresses the organization purchases, instead of purchasing one public address for each computer.
- **Port address translation (PAT)** The organization owns and uses only one public IP address for all systems that need to communicate outside the internal network. How in the world could all computers use the exact same IP address? Good question. Here's an example: The NAT device has an IP address of 127.50.41.3. When computer A needs to communicate with a system on the Internet, the NAT device documents this computer's private address and source port number (10.10.44.3; port 43,887). The NAT device changes the IP address in the computer's packet header to 127.50.41.3, with the source port 40,000. When computer B also needs to communicate with a system on the Internet, the NAT device documents the private address and source port number (10.10.44.15; port 23,398) and changes the header information to 127.50.41.3 with source port 40,001. So when a system responds to computer A, the packet first goes to the NAT device, which looks up the port number 40,000 and sees that it maps to computer A's real information. So the NAT device changes the header information to address 10.10.44.3 and port 43,887 and sends it to computer A for processing. An organization can save a lot more money by using PAT because it needs to buy only a few public IP addresses, which are used by all systems in the network.

Most NAT implementations are *stateful*, meaning they keep track of a communication between the internal host and an external host until that session is ended. The NAT device needs to remember the internal IP address and port to send the reply messages back. This stateful characteristic is similar to stateful-inspection firewalls, but NAT does not perform scans on the incoming packets to look for malicious characteristics. Instead, NAT is a service usually performed on routers or gateway devices within an organization's screened subnet.

Although NAT was developed to provide a quick fix for the depleting IP address problem, it has actually put the problem off for quite some time. The more organizations that implement private address schemes, the less likely IP addresses will become scarce. This has been helpful to NAT and the vendors that implement this technology, but it has put the acceptance and implementation of IPv6 much farther down the road.

Routing Protocols

Individual networks on the Internet are referred to as *autonomous systems (ASs)*. These ASs are independently controlled by different service providers and organizations. An AS is made up of routers, which are administered by a single entity and use a common Interior Gateway Protocol (IGP) within the boundaries of the AS. The boundaries of these ASs are delineated by border routers. These routers connect to the border routers of other ASs and run interior and exterior routing protocols. Internal routers connect to other routers within the same AS and run interior routing protocols. So, in reality, the Internet is just a network made up of ASs and routing protocols.

NOTE As an analogy, just as the world is made up of different countries, the Internet is made up of different ASs. Each AS has delineated boundaries just as countries do. Countries can have their own languages (e.g., Spanish, Arabic, Russian). Similarly, ASs have their own internal routing protocols. Countries that speak different languages need to have a way of communicating with each other, which could happen through interpreters. ASs need to have a standardized method of communicating and working together, which is where external routing protocols come into play.

The architecture of the Internet that supports these various ASs is created so that no entity that needs to connect to a specific AS has to know or understand the interior routing protocols that are being used. Instead, for ASs to communicate, they just have to be using the same exterior routing protocols (see Figure 11-30). As an analogy, suppose you want to deliver a package to a friend who lives in another state. You give the package to your brother, who is going to take a train to the edge of the state and hand it to the postal system at that junction. Thus, you know how your brother will arrive at the edge of the state—by train. You do not know how the postal system will then deliver your package to your friend's house (truck, car, bus), but that is not your concern. It will get to its destination without your participation. Similarly, when one network communicates with another network, the first network puts the data packet (package) on an exterior protocol (train), and when the data packet gets to the border router (edge of the state), the data is transferred to whatever interior protocol is being used on the receiving network.

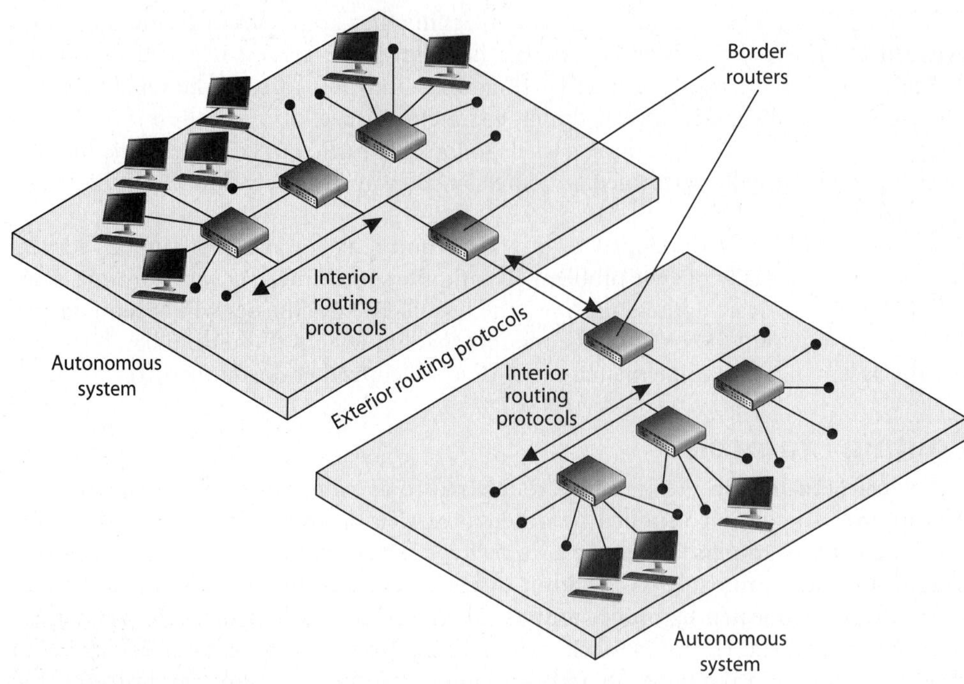

Figure 11-30 Autonomous systems

NOTE Routing protocols are used by routers to identify a path between the source and destination systems.

Dynamic vs. Static

Routing protocols can be dynamic or static. A *dynamic routing protocol* can discover routes and build a routing table. Routers use these tables to make decisions on the best route for the packets they receive. A dynamic routing protocol can change the entries in the routing table based on changes that take place to the different routes. When a router that is using a dynamic routing protocol finds out that a route has gone down or is congested, it sends an update message to the other routers around it. The other routers use this information to update their routing table, with the goal of providing efficient routing functionality. A *static routing protocol* requires the administrator to manually configure the router's routing table. If a link goes down or there is network congestion, the routers cannot tune themselves to use better routes.

NOTE *Route flapping* refers to the constant changes in the availability of routes. Also, if a router does not receive an update that a link has gone down, the router will continue to forward packets to that route, which is referred to as a *black hole*.

Distance-Vector vs. Link-State

Two main types of routing protocols are used: distance-vector and link-state routing. *Distance-vector routing protocols* make their routing decisions based on the distance (or number of hops) and a vector (a direction). The protocol takes these variables and uses them with an algorithm to determine the best route for a packet. *Link-state routing protocols* build a more accurate routing table because they build a topology database of the network. These protocols look at more variables than just the number of hops between two destinations. They use packet size, link speed, delay, network load, and reliability as the variables in their algorithms to determine the best routes for packets to take.

So, a distance-vector routing protocol only looks at the number of hops between two destinations and considers each hop to be equal. A link-state routing protocol sees more pieces to the puzzle than just the number of hops, but understands the status of each of those hops and makes decisions based on these factors also. As you will see in the next section, RIP is an example of a distance-vector routing protocol, and OSPF is an example of a link-state routing protocol. OSPF is preferred and is used in large networks. RIP is still around but should only be used in smaller networks.

Interior Routing Protocols

Interior routing protocols (also known as Interior Gateway Protocols) route traffic within the same AS. Just like the process for flying from one airport to another is different if you travel domestically or internationally, routing protocols are designed differently depending on which side of the AS boundary they operate. De facto and proprietary interior protocols are being used today. The following are just a few of them:

- **Routing Information Protocol** RIP is a standard that outlines how routers exchange routing table data and is considered a distance-vector protocol, which means it calculates the shortest distance between the source and destination. It is considered a legacy protocol because of its slow performance and lack of functionality. It should only be used in small networks. RIP version 1 has no authentication, and RIP version 2 sends passwords in cleartext or hashed with MD5. RIPng is the third generation of this venerable protocol. It is very similar to version 2 but is designed for IPv6 routing.
- **Open Shortest Path First** OSPF uses link-state algorithms to send out routing table information. The use of these algorithms allows for smaller, more frequent routing table updates to take place. This provides a more stable network than RIP, but requires more memory and CPU resources to support this extra processing. OSPF allows for a hierarchical routing network that has a backbone link connecting all subnets together. OSPF has replaced RIP in many networks today. Authentication can take place with cleartext passwords or hashed passwords, or

you can choose to configure no authentication on the routers using this protocol. The latest OSPF is version 3. Though it was designed to support IPv6, it also supports IPv4. Among the most important improvements is that OSPFv3 uses IPSec for authentication.

- **Interior Gateway Routing Protocol** IGRP is a distance-vector routing protocol that was developed by, and is proprietary to, Cisco Systems. Whereas RIP uses one criterion to find the best path between the source and destination, IGRP uses five criteria to make a "best route" decision. A network administrator can set weights on these different metrics so that the protocol works best in that specific environment.
- **Enhanced Interior Gateway Routing Protocol** EIGRP is a Cisco-proprietary and advanced distance-vector routing protocol. It allows for faster router table updates than its predecessor IGRP and minimizes routing instability, which can occur after topology changes. Routers exchange messages that contain information about bandwidth, delay, load, reliability, and MTU of the path to each destination as known by the advertising router. The latest version is 4.
- **Virtual Router Redundancy Protocol** VRRP is used in networks that require high availability where routers as points of failure cannot be tolerated. It is designed to increase the availability of the default gateway by advertising a "virtual router" as a default gateway. Two physical routers (primary and secondary) are mapped to one virtual router. If one of the physical routers fails, the other router takes over the workload.
- **Intermediate System to Intermediate System** IS-IS is a link-state protocol that allows each router to independently build a database of a network's topology. Similar to the OSPF protocol, it computes the best path for traffic to travel. It is a classless and hierarchical routing protocol that is vendor neutral. Unlike other protocols (e.g., RIP and OSPF), IS-IS does not use IP addresses. Instead, it uses ISO addresses, which means that the protocol didn't have to be redesigned to support IPv6.

NOTE Although most routing protocols have authentication functionality, many routers do not have this functionality enabled.

Exterior Routing Protocols

The exterior routing protocols used by routers connecting different ASs are generically referred to as *exterior gateway protocols (EGPs)*. The *Border Gateway Protocol (BGP)* enables routers on different ASs to share routing information to ensure effective and efficient routing between the different AS networks. BGP is commonly used by Internet service providers to route data from one location to the next on the Internet.

NOTE There is an exterior routing protocol called Exterior Gateway Protocol, but it has been widely replaced by BGP, and now the term "exterior gateway protocol" and the acronym EGP are used to refer generically to a type of protocol rather than to specify the outdated protocol.

BGP uses a combination of link-state and distance-vector routing algorithms. It creates a network topology by using its link-state functionality and transmits updates on a periodic basis instead of continuously, which is how distance-vector protocols work. Network administrators can apply weights to the different variables used by link-state routing protocols when determining the best routes. These configurations are collectively called the *routing policy*.

Routing Protocol Attacks

Several types of attacks can take place on routers through their routing protocols. A majority of the attacks have the goal of misdirecting traffic through the use of spoofed ICMP messages. An attacker can masquerade as another router and submit routing table information to the victim router. After the victim router integrates this new information, it may be sending traffic to the wrong subnets or computers, or even to a nonexistent address (black hole). These attacks are successful mainly when routing protocol authentication is not enabled. When authentication is not required, a router can accept routing updates without knowing whether or not the sender is a legitimate router. An attacker could divert a company's traffic to reveal confidential information or to just disrupt traffic, which would be considered a DoS attack.

Intranets and Extranets

Web technologies and their uses have exploded with functionality, capability, and popularity. Organizations set up internal websites for centralized business information such as employee phone numbers, policies, events, news, and operations instructions. Many organizations have also implemented web-based terminals that enable employees to perform their daily tasks, access centralized databases, make transactions, collaborate on projects, access global calendars, use videoconferencing tools and whiteboard applications, and obtain often-used technical or marketing data.

Web-based clients are different from workstations that log into a network and have their own desktop. Web-based clients limit a user's ability to access the computer's system files, resources, and hard drive space; access backend systems; and perform other tasks. The web-based client can be configured to provide a GUI with only the buttons, fields, and pages necessary for the users to perform tasks. This gives all users a standard universal interface with similar capabilities.

When an organization uses web-based technologies that are only available inside its networks, it is using an *intranet*, a "private" network. The organization has web servers and client machines using web browsers, and it uses the TCP/IP protocol suite. The web pages are written in HTML or XML (eXtensible Markup Language) and are accessed via HTTP.

Using web-based technologies has many pluses. They have been around for quite some time, they are easy to implement, no major interoperability issues occur, and with just the click of a link, a user can be taken to the location of the requested resource. Web-based technologies are not platform dependent, meaning all websites and pages may be maintained on various platforms and different flavors of client workstations can access them—they only need a web browser.

An *extranet* extends outside the bounds of the organization's network to enable two or more organizations to share common information and resources. Business partners commonly set up extranets to accommodate business-to-business communication. An extranet enables business partners to work on projects together; share marketing information; communicate and work collaboratively on issues; post orders; and share catalogs, pricing structures, and information on upcoming events. Trading partners often use *electronic data interchange (EDI)*, which provides structure and organization to electronic documents, orders, invoices, purchase orders, and a data flow. EDI has evolved into web-based technologies to provide easy access and easier methods of communication.

For many organizations, an extranet can create a weakness or hole in their security if the extranet is not implemented and maintained properly. Properly configured firewalls need to be in place to control who can use the extranet communication channels. Extranets used to be based mainly on dedicated transmission lines, which are more difficult for attackers to infiltrate, but today many extranets are set up over the Internet, which requires properly configured VPNs and security policies.

Metropolitan Area Networks

A *metropolitan area network (MAN)* is usually a backbone that connects LANs to each other and LANs to WANs, the Internet, and telecommunications and cable networks. A majority of today's MANs are *Synchronous Optical Networks (SONETs)* or FDDI rings and Metro Ethernet provided by the telecommunications service providers. (FDDI technology was discussed earlier in the chapter.) The SONET and FDDI rings cover a large area, and businesses can connect to the rings via T1, fractional T1, and T3 lines. Figure 11-31 illustrates two companies connected via a SONET ring and the devices usually necessary to make this type of communication possible. This is a simplified example of a MAN. In reality, several businesses are usually connected to one ring.

SONET is a standard for telecommunications transmissions over fiber-optic cables. Carriers and telephone companies have deployed SONET networks for North America, and if they follow the SONET standards properly, these various networks can intercommunicate

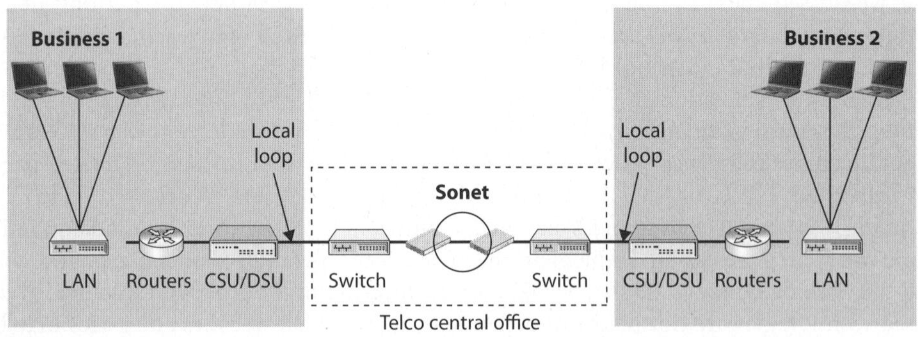

Figure 11-31 A MAN covers a large area and enables businesses to connect to each other, to the Internet, or to other WAN connections.

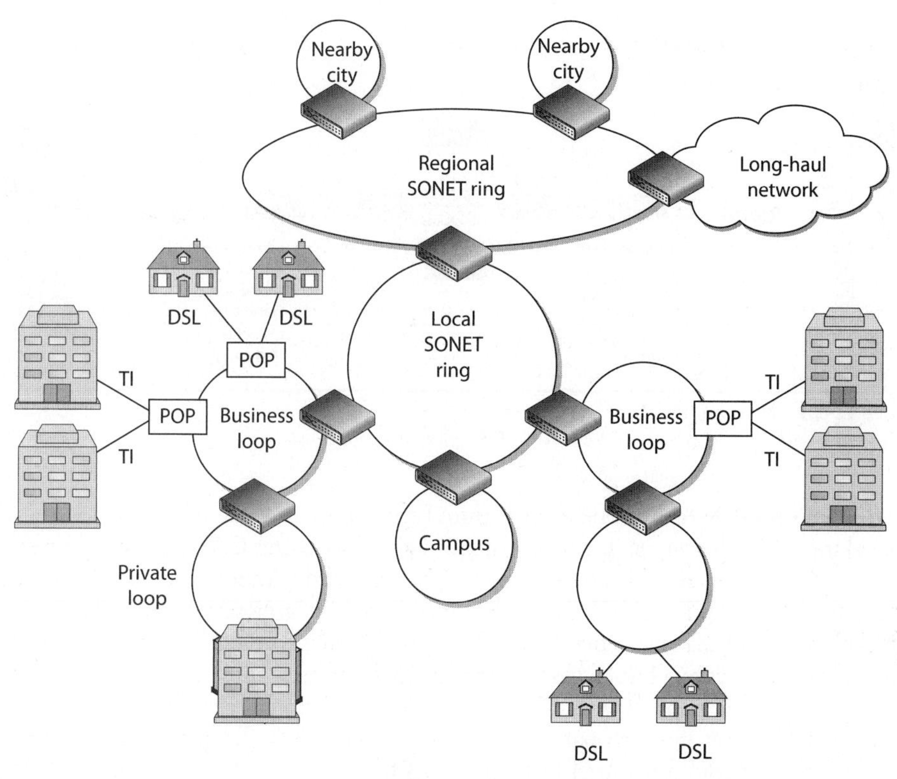

Figure 11-32 Smaller SONET rings connect to larger SONET rings to construct individual MANs.

with little difficulty. SONET is *self-healing*, meaning that if a break in the line occurs, it can use a backup redundant ring to ensure transmission continues. All SONET lines and rings are fully redundant. The redundant line waits in the wings in case anything happens to the primary ring.

SONET networks can transmit voice, video, and data over optical networks. Slower-speed SONET networks often feed into larger, faster SONET networks, as shown in Figure 11-32. This enables businesses in different cities and regions to communicate.

MANs can be made up of wireless infrastructures, optical fiber, or Ethernet connections. Ethernet has evolved from just being a LAN technology to being used in MAN environments. Due to its prevalent use within organizations' networks, Ethernet is easily extended and interfaced into MAN networks. A service provider commonly uses layer 2 and 3 switches to connect optical fibers, which can be constructed in a ring, star, or partial mesh topology.

Metro Ethernet

Ethernet has been around for many years and is embedded in almost every LAN. Ethernet LANs can connect to the previously mentioned MAN technologies, or they can be extended to cover a metropolitan area, which is called *Metro Ethernet*.

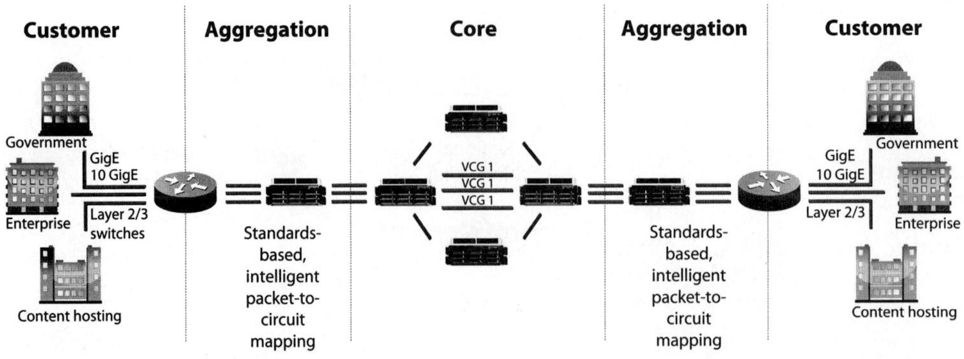

Figure 11-33 MAN architecture

Ethernet on the MAN can be used as pure Ethernet or Ethernet integrated with other networking technologies, as in Multiprotocol Label Switching (MPLS). Pure Ethernet is less expensive but less reliable and scalable. MPLS-based deployments are more expensive but highly reliable and scalable, and are typically used by large service providers.

MAN architectures are commonly built upon three layers: access, aggregation/distribution, and core. The access layer provides services directly to the customers, typically at data rates of 10 Gbps or less. The aggregation layer provides routing for customer data, most of which passes on to the core layer, which operates at data rates of 100 Gbps or higher as illustrated in Figure 11-33.

Access devices exist at a customer's premises and connect the customer's equipment to the service provider's network. The service provider's distribution network aggregates the traffic and sends it to the provider's core network. From there, the traffic is moved to the next aggregation network that is closest to the destination. This is similar to how smaller highways are connected to larger interstates with on and off ramps that allow people to quickly travel from one location to a different one.

Wide Area Networks

LAN technologies provide communication capabilities over a small geographic area, whereas *wide area network (WAN)* technologies are used when communication needs to travel over a larger geographical area. LAN technologies encompass how a computer puts its data onto a network cable, the rules and protocols of how that data is formatted and transmitted, how errors are handled, and how the destination computer picks up this data from the cable. When a computer on one network needs to communicate with a network on the other side of the country or in a different country altogether, WAN technologies kick in.

The network must have some avenue to other networks, which is most likely a router that communicates with the organization's service provider's switches or telephone company facilities. Just as several types of technologies lie within the LAN arena, several technologies lie within the WAN arena. The following sections discuss the dedicated links that oftentimes connect LANs to WANs and the various technologies used in WANs.

Dedicated Links

A *dedicated link* is also called a *leased line* or *point-to-point link*. It is one single link that is pre-established for the purposes of WAN communications between two destinations. It is dedicated, meaning only the destination points can communicate with each other. This link is not shared by any other entities at any time. This was the main way organizations communicated in the past, because there were not as many choices available as there are today. Establishing a dedicated link is a good idea for two locations that will communicate often and require fast transmission and a specific bandwidth, but it is expensive compared to other possible technologies that enable several organizations to share the same bandwidth and also share the cost. This does not mean that dedicated lines are not in use; they definitely are used, but many other options are now available, including X.25, frame relay, and ATM technologies.

T-Carriers

T-carriers are dedicated lines that can carry voice and data information over trunk lines. They were developed by AT&T and were initially implemented in the early 1960s to support pulse-code modulation (PCM) voice transmission. This was first used to digitize the voice over a dedicated, point-to-point, high-capacity connection line. The most commonly used T-carriers are T1 lines and T3 lines. Both are digital circuits that multiplex several individual channels into a higher-speed channel.

These lines can have multiplex functionality through *time-division multiplexing (TDM)*. What does this multiplexing stuff really mean? It means that each channel gets to use the path only during a specific time slot. It's like having a time-share property on the beach; each co-owner gets to use it, but only one can do so at a time and can only remain for a fixed number of days. Consider a T1 line, which can multiplex up to 24 channels. If a company has a PBX connected to a T1 line, which in turn connects to the telephone company switching office, 24 calls can be chopped up and placed on the T1 line and transferred to the switching office. If this company did not use a T1 line, it would need 24 individual twisted pairs of wire to handle this many calls.

As shown in Figure 11-34, data is input into these 24 channels and transmitted. Each channel gets to insert up to 8 bits into its established time slot. Twenty-four of these 8-bit time slots make up a T1 frame. That does not sound like much information, but 8,000 frames are built per second. Because this happens so quickly, the receiving end

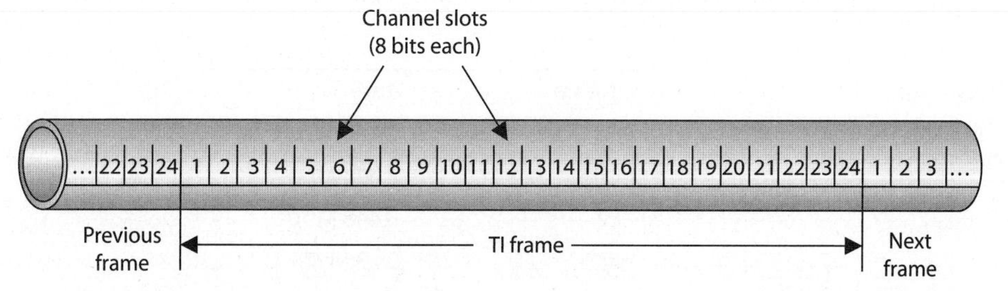

Figure 11-34 Multiplexing puts several phone calls, or data transmissions, on the same wire.

PART IV

Table 11-7 A T-Carrier Hierarchy Summary Chart

Carrier	# of T1s	# of Channels	Speed (Mbps)
Fractional	1/24	1	0.064
T1	1	24	1.544
T2	4	96	6.312
T3	28	672	44.736
T4	168	4,032	274.760

does not notice a delay and does not know it is sharing its connection and bandwidth with up to 23 other devices.

Originally, T1 and T3 lines were used by the carrier companies, but they have been replaced mainly with optical lines. Now T1 and T3 lines feed data into these powerful and super-fast optical lines. The T1 and T3 lines are leased to organizations and ISPs that need high-capacity transmission capability. Sometimes, T1 channels are split up between organizations that do not need the full bandwidth of 1.544 Mbps. These are called *fractional* T lines. The different carrier lines and their corresponding characteristics are listed in Table 11-7.

As mentioned earlier, dedicated lines have their drawbacks. They are expensive and inflexible. If a company moves to another location, a T1 line cannot easily follow it. A dedicated line is expensive because organizations have to pay for a dedicated connection with a lot of bandwidth even when they do not use the bandwidth. Not many organizations require this level of bandwidth 24 hours a day. Instead, they may have data to send out here and there, but not continuously.

The cost of a dedicated line is determined by the distance to the destination. A T1 line run from one building to another building 2 miles away is much cheaper than a T1 line that covers 50 miles or a full state.

E-Carriers

E-carriers are similar to T-carrier telecommunication connections, where a single physical wire pair can be used to carry many simultaneous voice conversations by time-division multiplexing. Within this technology 30 channels interleave 8 bits of data in a frame. While the T-carrier and E-carrier technologies are similar, they are not interoperable. E-carriers are used by European countries. The E-carrier channels and associated rates are shown in Table 11-8.

The most commonly used channels are E1 and E3 and fractional E-carrier lines.

Table 11-8 E-Carrier Characteristics

Signal	Rate
E0	64 Kbps
E1	2.048 Mbps
E2	8.448 Mbps
E3	34.368 Mbps
E4	139.264 Mbps
E5	565.148 Mbps

Table 11-9 OC Transmission Rates

Optical Carrier	Speed
OC-1	51.84 Mbps
OC-3	155.52 Mbps
OC-9	466.56 Mbps
OC-12	622.08 Mbps
OC-19	933.12 Mbps
OC-24	1.244 Gbps
OC-36	1.866 Gbps
OC-48	2.488 Gbps
OC-96	4.977 Gbps
OC-192	9.953 Gbps
OC-768	40 Gbps
OC-3072	160 Gbps

Optical Carrier

High-speed fiber-optic connections are measured in *optical carrier (OC)* transmission rates. The transmission rates are defined by rate of the bit stream of the digital signal and are designated by an integer value of the multiple of the basic unit of rate. They are generically referred to as OC*x*, where *x* represents a multiplier of the basic OC-1 transmission rate, which is 51.84 Mbps. The carrier levels and speeds are shown in Table 11-9.

Small and medium-sized organizations that require high-speed Internet connectivity may use OC-3 or OC-12 connections. Service providers that require much larger amounts of bandwidth may use one or more OC-48 connections. OC-192 and greater connections are commonly used for the Internet backbone, which connects the largest networks in the world together.

WAN Technologies

Several varieties of WAN technologies are available to organizations today. The information that an organization evaluates to decide which is the most appropriate WAN technology for it usually includes functionality, bandwidth demands, service level agreements, required equipment, cost, and what is available from service providers. The following sections go over some of the WAN technologies available today.

CSU/DSU

A *channel service unit/data service unit (CSU/DSU)* is required when digital equipment will be used to connect a LAN to a WAN. This connection can take place with T1 and T3 lines, as shown in Figure 11-35. A CSU/DSU is necessary because the signals and frames can vary between the LAN equipment and the WAN equipment used by service providers.

More Multiplexing

Here are some other types of multiplexing functionalities you should be aware of:

Statistical time-division multiplexing (STDM):

- Transmits several types of data simultaneously across a single transmission cable or line (such as a T1 or T3 line).
- Analyzes statistics related to the typical workload of each input device (printer, fax, computer) and determines in real time how much time each device should be allocated for data transmission.

Frequency-division multiplexing (FDM):

- An available wireless spectrum is used to move data.
- Available frequency band is divided into narrow frequency bands and used to have multiple parallel channels for data transfer.

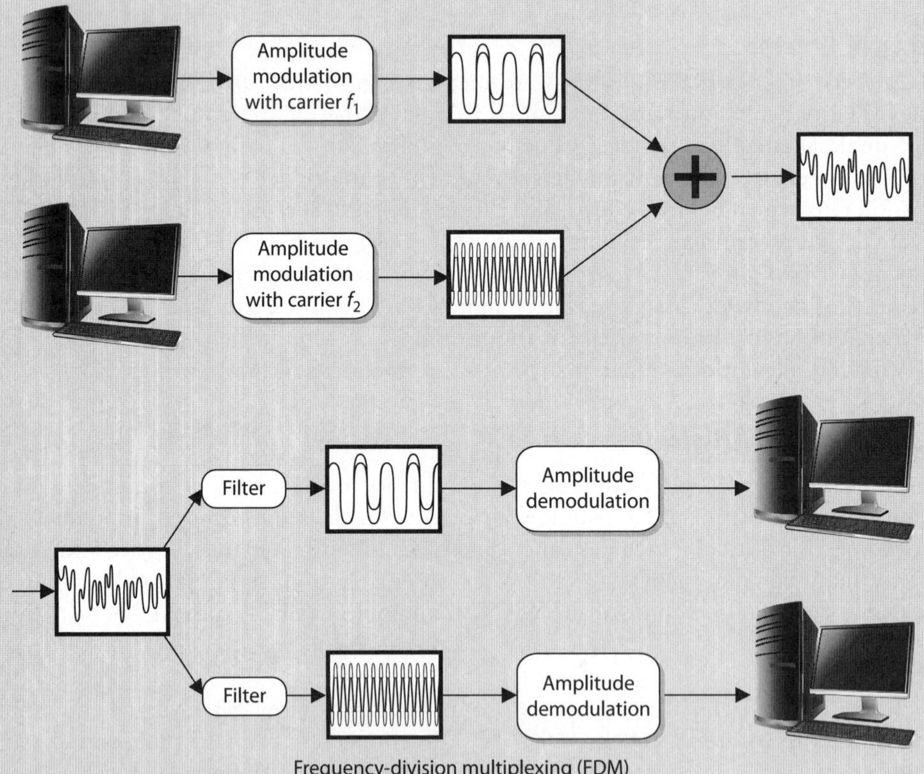

Frequency-division multiplexing (FDM)

Wave-division multiplexing (WDM):

- Used in fiber-optic communication.
- Multiplexes a number of optical carrier signals onto a single optical fiber.

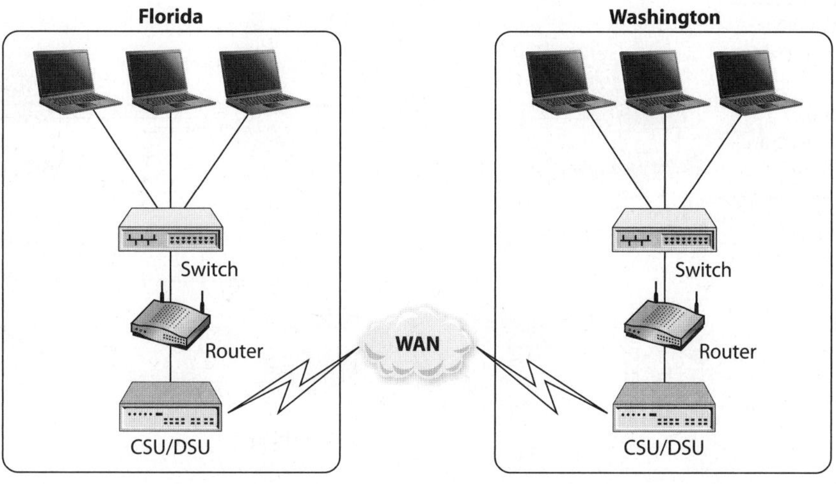

Figure 11-35 A CSU/DSU is required for digital equipment to communicate with telecommunications lines.

The DSU device converts digital signals from routers, switches, and multiplexers into signals that can be transmitted over the service provider's digital lines. The DSU device ensures that the voltage levels are correct and that information is not lost during the conversion. The CSU connects the network directly to the service provider's line. The CSU/DSU is not always a separate device and can be part of a networking device.

The CSU/DSU provides a digital interface for data terminal equipment (DTE), such as terminals, multiplexers, or routers, and an interface to the data circuit–terminating equipment (DCE) device, such as a carrier's switch. The CSU/DSU basically works as a translator and, at times, as a line conditioner.

Switching

Dedicated links have one single path to traverse; thus, there is no complexity when it comes to determining how to get packets to different destinations. Only two points of reference are needed when a packet leaves one network and heads toward the other. It gets much more complicated when thousands of networks are connected to each other, which is often when switching comes into play.

Two main types of switching can be used: circuit switching and packet switching. *Circuit switching* sets up a virtual connection that acts like a dedicated link between two systems. ISDN and telephone calls are examples of circuit switching, which is shown in the lower half of Figure 11-36.

When the source system makes a connection with the destination system, they set up a communication channel. If the two systems are local to each other, fewer devices need to be involved with setting up this channel. The farther the two systems are from each other, the more the devices are required to be involved with setting up the channel and connecting the two systems.

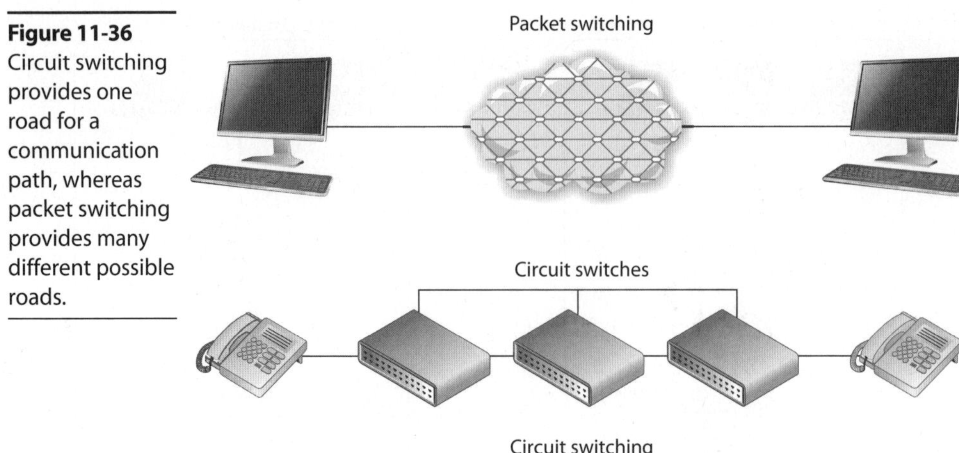

Figure 11-36 Circuit switching provides one road for a communication path, whereas packet switching provides many different possible roads.

An example of how a circuit-switching system works is daily telephone use. When one person calls another, the same type of dedicated virtual communication link is set up. Once the connection is made, the devices supporting that communication channel do not dynamically move the call through different devices, which is what takes place in a packet-switching environment. The channel remains configured at the original devices until the call (connection) is done and torn down.

Packet switching, on the other hand, does not set up a dedicated virtual link, and packets from one connection can pass through a number of different individual devices (see the top of Figure 11-36), instead of all of them following one another through the same devices. Some examples of packet-switching technologies are the Internet, X.25, and frame relay. The infrastructure that supports these methods is made up of routers and switches of different types. They provide multiple paths to the same destinations, which offers a high degree of redundancy.

In a packet-switching network, the data is broken up into packets containing frame check sequence (FCS) numbers. These packets go through different devices, and their paths can be dynamically altered by a router or switch that determines a better route for a specific packet to take. Once the packets are received at the destination computer, all the packets are reassembled according to their FCS numbers and processed.

Because the path a packet will take in a packet-switching environment is not set in stone, there could be variable delays when compared to a circuit-switching technology. This is okay, because packet-switching networks usually carry data rather than voice. Because voice connections clearly detect these types of delays, in many situations a circuit-switching network is more appropriate for voice connections. Voice calls usually provide a steady stream of information, whereas a data connection is "burstier" in nature. When you talk on the phone, the conversation keeps a certain rhythm. You and your friend do not talk extremely fast and then take a few minutes in between conversations to stop talking and create a void with complete silence. However, this is usually how a data connection works. A lot of data is sent from one end to the other at one time, and then dead time occurs until it is time to send more data.

Circuit Switching vs. Packet Switching

The following points provide a concise summary of the differences between circuit- and packet-switching technologies:

Circuit switching:

- Connection-oriented virtual links.
- Traffic travels in a predictable and constant manner.
- Fixed delays.
- Usually carries voice-oriented data.

Packet switching:

- Packets can use many different dynamic paths to get to the same destination.
- Traffic is usually bursty in nature.
- Variable delays.
- Usually carries data-oriented data.

Frame Relay

For a long time, many organizations used dedicated links to communicate with other organizations. Company A had a pipeline to company B that provided a certain bandwidth 24 hours a day and was not used by any other entities. This was great because only the two companies could use the line, so a certain level of bandwidth was always available, but it was expensive, and most organizations did not use the full bandwidth each and every hour the link was available. Thus, organizations spent a lot of money for a service they did not use all the time. Later, to avoid this unnecessary cost, organizations turned to using frame relay instead of dedicated lines.

EXAM TIP Frame relay is an obsolescent technology. It is still in limited use, however, and you should be familiar with it for the CISSP exam.

Frame relay is a WAN technology that operates at the data link layer. It is a WAN solution that uses packet-switching technology to let multiple organizations and networks share the same WAN medium, devices, and bandwidth. Whereas direct point-to-point links have a cost based on the distance between the endpoints, the frame relay cost is based on the amount of bandwidth used. Because several organizations and networks use the same medium and devices (routers and switches), the cost can be greatly reduced per organization compared to dedicated links.

If a company knows it will usually require a certain amount of bandwidth each day, it can pay a certain fee to make sure this amount of bandwidth is always available to it. If another company knows it will not have a high bandwidth requirement, it can pay a lower fee that does not guarantee the higher bandwidth allocation. This second company will have the higher bandwidth available to it anyway—at least until that link gets busy, and then the bandwidth level will decrease. (Organizations that pay more to ensure that a higher level of bandwidth will always be available pay a *committed information rate*, or *CIR*.)

Two main types of equipment are used in frame relay connections: DTE and DCE, both of which were previously introduced in the discussion of CSU/DSU. The DTE is usually a customer-owned device, such as a router or switch, that provides connectivity between the organization's own network and the frame relay network. DCE is the service provider's device, or telecommunications company's device, that does the actual data transmission and switching in the frame relay cloud. So the DTE is an organization's ramp onto the frame relay network, and the DCE devices actually do the work within the frame relay cloud.

The frame relay cloud is the collection of DCE devices that provides switching and data communications functionality. Several service providers offer this type of service, and some providers use other providers' equipment—it can all get confusing because a packet can take so many different routes. This collection is called a *cloud* to differentiate it from other types of networks and because when a packet hits this cloud, users do not usually know the route their frames will take. The frames will be sent either through permanent or switched virtual circuits that are defined within the DCE or through carrier switches.

NOTE The term cloud is used in several technologies: Internet cloud, ATM cloud, frame relay cloud, cloud computing, and so on. The cloud is like a black box—we know our data goes in and we know it comes out, but we do not normally care about all the complex things that are taking place internally.

Frame relay is an any-to-any service that is shared by many users. As stated earlier, this is beneficial because the costs are much lower than those of dedicated leased lines. Because frame relay is shared, if one subscriber is not using its bandwidth, it is available for others to use. On the other hand, when traffic levels increase, the available bandwidth decreases. This is why subscribers who want to ensure a certain bandwidth is always available to them pay a higher CIR.

Figure 11-37 shows five sites being connected via dedicated lines versus five sites connected through the frame relay cloud. The first solution requires many dedicated lines that are expensive and not flexible. The second solution is cheaper and provides organizations much more flexibility.

Virtual Circuits

Frame relay (and X.25) forwards frames across virtual circuits. These circuits can be either *permanent*, meaning they are programmed in advance, or *switched*, meaning the circuit is quickly built when it is needed and torn down when it is no longer needed.

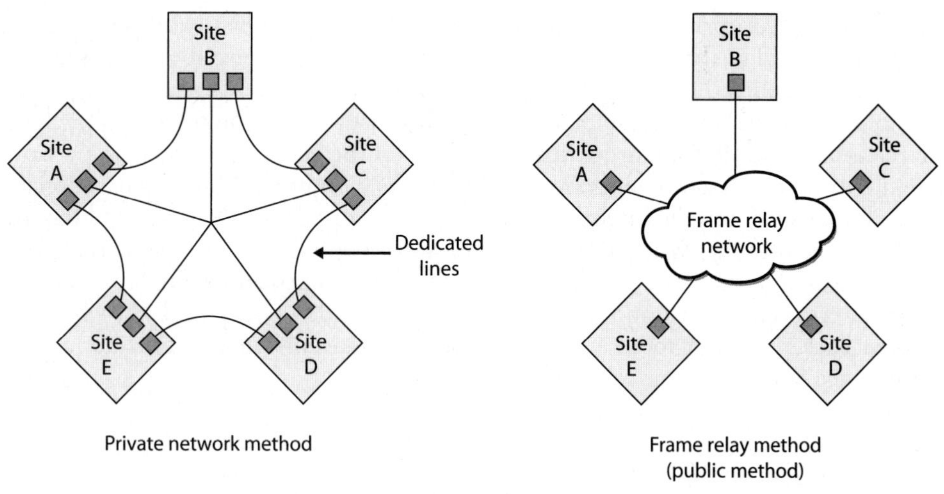

Figure 11-37 A private network connection requires several expensive dedicated links. Frame relay enables users to share a public network.

The *permanent virtual circuit (PVC)* works like a private line for a customer with an agreed-upon bandwidth availability. When a customer decides to pay for the CIR, a PVC is programmed for that customer to ensure it will always receive a certain amount of bandwidth.

Unlike PVCs, *switched virtual circuits (SVCs)* require steps similar to a dial-up and connection procedure. The difference is that a permanent path is set up for PVC frames, whereas when SVCs are used, a circuit must be built. It is similar to setting up a phone call over the public network. During the setup procedure, the required bandwidth is requested, the destination computer is contacted and must accept the call, a path is determined, and forwarding information is programmed into each switch along the SVC's path. SVCs are used for teleconferencing, establishing temporary connections to remote sites, data replication, and voice calls. Once the connection is no longer needed, the circuit is torn down and the switches forget it ever existed.

Although a PVC provides a guaranteed level of bandwidth, it does not have the flexibility of an SVC. If a customer wants to use her PVC for a temporary connection, as mentioned earlier, she must call the carrier and have it set up, which can take hours.

X.25

X.25 is an older WAN protocol that defines how devices and networks establish and maintain connections. Like frame relay, X.25 is a switching technology that uses carrier switches to provide connectivity for many different networks. It also provides an any-to-any connection, meaning many users use the same service simultaneously. Subscribers are charged based on the amount of bandwidth they use, unlike dedicated links, for which a flat fee is charged.

Data is divided into 128 bytes and encapsulated in High-level Data Link Control (HDLC) frames. The frames are then addressed and forwarded across the carrier switches. Much of this sounds the same as frame relay—and it is—but frame relay is much more advanced and efficient when compared to X.25, because the X.25 protocol was developed and released in the 1970s. During this time, many of the devices connected to networks were dumb terminals and mainframes, the networks did not have built-in functionality and fault tolerance, and the Internet overall was not as foundationally stable and resistant to errors as it is today. When these characteristics were not part of the Internet, X.25 was required to compensate for these deficiencies and to provide many layers of error checking, error correcting, and fault tolerance. This made the protocol fat, which was required back then, but today it slows down data transmission and provides a lower performance rate than frame relay or ATM.

ATM

Asynchronous Transfer Mode (ATM) is another switching technology, but instead of being a packet-switching method, it uses a cell-switching method. ATM is a high-speed networking technology used for LAN, MAN, WAN, and service provider connections. Like frame relay, it is a connection-oriented switching technology, and creates and uses a fixed channel. IP is an example of a connectionless technology. Within the TCP/IP protocol suite, IP is connectionless and TCP is connection oriented. This means IP segments can be quickly and easily routed and switched without each router or switch in between having to worry about whether the data actually made it to its destination—that is TCP's job. TCP works at the source and destination ends to ensure data was properly transmitted, and it resends data that ran into some type of problem and did not get delivered properly. When using ATM or frame relay, the devices in between the source and destination have to ensure that data gets to where it needs to go, unlike when a purely connectionless protocol is being used.

Since ATM is a cell-switching technology rather than a packet-switching technology, data is segmented into fixed-size cells of 53 bytes instead of variable-size packets. This provides for more efficient and faster use of the communication paths. ATM sets up virtual circuits, which act like dedicated paths between the source and destination. These virtual circuits can guarantee bandwidth and QoS. For these reasons, ATM is a good carrier for voice and video transmission.

ATM technology is used by carriers and service providers, and is the core technology of the Internet, but ATM technology can also be used for an organization's private use in backbones and connections to the service provider's networks.

Traditionally, organizations used dedicated lines, usually T-carrier lines, to connect to the public networks. However, organizations have also moved to implementing an ATM switch on their network, which connects them to the carrier infrastructure. Because the fee is based on bandwidth used instead of a continual connection, it can be much cheaper. Some organizations have replaced their Fast Ethernet and FDDI backbones with ATM. When an organization uses ATM as a private backbone, the organization has ATM switches that take the Ethernet frames, or whatever data link technology is being used, and frame them into the 53-byte ATM cells.

Quality of Service *Quality of Service (QoS)* is a capability that allows a protocol to distinguish between different classes of messages and assign priority levels. Some applications, such as video conferencing, are time sensitive, meaning delays would cause unacceptable performance of the application. A technology that provides QoS allows an administrator to assign a priority level to time-sensitive traffic. The protocol then ensures this type of traffic has a specific or minimum rate of delivery.

QoS allows a service provider to guarantee a level of service to its customers. QoS began with ATM and then was integrated into other technologies and protocols responsible for moving data from one place to another. Four different types of ATM QoS services (listed next) are available to customers. Each service maps to a specific type of data that will be transmitted.

- **Constant bit rate (CBR)** A connection-oriented channel that provides a consistent data throughput for time-sensitive applications, such as voice and video applications. Customers specify the necessary bandwidth requirement at connection setup.
- **Variable bit rate (VBR)** A connection-oriented channel best used for delay-insensitive applications because the data throughput flow is uneven. Customers specify their required peak and sustained rate of data throughput.
- **Unspecified bit rate (UBR)** A connectionless channel that does not promise a specific data throughput rate. Customers cannot, and do not need to, control their traffic rate.
- **Available bit rate (ABR)** A connection-oriented channel that allows the bit rate to be adjusted. Customers are given the bandwidth that remains after a guaranteed service rate has been met.

ATM was the first protocol to provide true QoS, but as the computing society has increased its desire to send time-sensitive data throughout many types of networks, developers have integrated QoS into other technologies.

QoS has three basic levels:

- **Best-effort service** No guarantee of throughput, delay, or delivery. Traffic that has priority classifications goes before traffic that has been assigned this classification. Most of the traffic that travels on the Internet has this classification.
- **Differentiated service** Compared to best-effort service, traffic that is assigned this classification has more bandwidth, shorter delays, and fewer dropped frames.
- **Guaranteed service** Ensures specific data throughput at a guaranteed speed. Time-sensitive traffic (voice and video) is assigned this classification.

Administrators can set the classification priorities (or use a policy manager product) for the different traffic types, which the protocols and devices then carry out.

Controlling network traffic to allow for the optimization or the guarantee of certain performance levels is referred to as *traffic shaping*. Using technologies that have QoS

WAN Technology	Characteristics
Dedicated line	Dedicated, leased line that connects two locations Expensive compared to other WAN options Secure because only two locations are using the same medium
Frame relay	High-performance WAN protocol that uses packet-switching technology, which works over public networks Shared media among organizations Uses SVCs and PVCs Fee based on bandwidth used
X.25	First packet-switching technology developed to work over public networks Lower speed than frame relay because of its extra overhead Uses SVCs and PVCs Basically obsolete and replaced with other WAN protocols
ATM	High-speed bandwidth switching and multiplexing technology that has a low delay Uses 53-byte fixed-size cells Very fast because of the low overhead
HSSI	DTE/DCE interface to enable high-speed communication over WAN links

Table 11-10 Characteristics of WAN Technologies

capabilities allows for traffic shaping, which can improve latency and increase bandwidth for specific traffic types, bandwidth throttling, and rate limiting.

HSSI

High-Speed Serial Interface (HSSI) is an interface used to connect multiplexers and routers to high-speed communications services such as ATM and frame relay. It supports speeds up to 52 Mbps, as in T3 WAN connections, which are usually integrated with router and multiplex devices to provide serial interfaces to the WAN. These interfaces define the electrical and physical interfaces to be used by DTE/DCE devices; thus, HSSI works at the physical layer.

WAN Technology Summary

We have covered several WAN technologies in the previous sections. Table 11-10 provides a snapshot of the important characteristics of each.

Chapter Review

Before we can delve into communication and network security, we must first understand how networks are put together from the ground up. In this chapter, we started with a high-level overview of the OSI reference model because it will be the framework within which we will build the rest of our discussion of network security. You really need to become comfortable mapping technologies and protocols to the OSI reference model both for the CISSP exam and for your daily work.

We next took a look at the various technologies that allow us to build networks from the ground up. There are three types of LANs that you need to remember for the exam: Ethernet, Token Ring, and FDDI. Recall that LANs are limited in geographical scope but can be linked together using technologies like dedicated links, frame relay, SONET, and ATM to form MANs and WANs. Once you extend past the local area (and oftentimes even within it), you'll need routers to break up broadcast domains and link together the pieces of your MAN or WAN.

Quick Review

- A protocol is a set of rules that dictates how computers communicate over networks.
- The application layer, layer 7, has services and protocols required by the user's applications for networking functionality.
- The presentation layer, layer 6, formats data into a standardized format and deals with the syntax of the data, not the meaning.
- The session layer, layer 5, sets up, maintains, and breaks down the dialog (session) between two applications. It controls the dialog organization and synchronization.
- The transport layer, layer 4, provides end-to-end transmissions.
- The network layer, layer 3, provides routing, addressing, and fragmentation of packets. This layer can determine alternative routes to avoid network congestion. Routers work at the network layer, layer 3.
- The data link layer, layer 2, prepares data for the network medium by framing it. This is where the different LAN and WAN technologies work.
- The physical layer, layer 1, provides physical connections for transmission and performs the electrical encoding of data. This layer transforms bits to electrical signals.
- A network topology describes the arrangement of computers and devices.
- In a bus topology, a single cable runs the entire length of the network and nodes attach to it through drop points.
- In a star topology, all nodes connect to a central device such as a switch using a dedicated link.
- In a mesh topology, all nodes are connected to each other in a non-uniform manner that provides multiple paths to most or all the nodes on the network.
- A ring topology has a series of devices connected by unidirectional transmission links that form a closed loop and do not connect to a central system.
- Ethernet uses CSMA/CD, which means all computers compete for the shared network cable, listen to learn when they can transmit data, and are susceptible to data collisions.

- Token Ring, IEEE 802.5, is an older LAN implementation that uses a token-passing technology.
- FDDI is a LAN and MAN technology, usually used for backbones, that uses token-passing technology and has redundant rings in case the primary ring goes down.
- TCP/IP is a suite of protocols that is the de facto standard for transmitting data across the Internet. TCP is a reliable, connection-oriented protocol, while IP is an unreliable, connectionless protocol.
- Data is encapsulated as it travels down the network stack on the source computer, and the process is reversed on the destination computer. During encapsulation, each layer adds its own information so the corresponding layer on the destination computer knows how to process the data.
- Two main protocols at the transport layer are TCP and UDP.
- UDP is a connectionless protocol that does not send or receive acknowledgments when a datagram is received. It does not ensure data arrives at its destination. It provides "best-effort" delivery.
- TCP is a connection-oriented protocol that sends and receives acknowledgments. It ensures data arrives at the destination.
- ARP translates the IP address into a MAC address (physical Ethernet address), while RARP translates a MAC address into an IP address.
- ICMP works at the network layer and informs hosts, routers, and devices of network or computer problems. It is the major component of the ping utility.
- DNS resolves hostnames into IP addresses and has distributed databases all over the Internet to provide name resolution.
- Altering an ARP table so an IP address is mapped to a different MAC address is called ARP poisoning and can redirect traffic to an attacker's computer or an unattended system.
- Routers link two or more network segments, where each segment can function as an independent network. A router works at the network layer, works with IP addresses, and has more network knowledge than bridges, switches, or repeaters.
- IPv4 uses 32 bits for its addresses, whereas IPv6 uses 128 bits; thus, IPv6 provides more possible addresses with which to work.
- NAT is used when organizations do not want systems to know internal hosts' addresses, and it enables organizations to use private, nonroutable IP addresses.
- Subnetting allows large IP address ranges to be divided into smaller, logical, and easier-to-maintain network segments.
- Dedicated links are usually the most expensive type of WAN connectivity method because the fee is based on the distance between the two destinations rather than on the amount of bandwidth used. T1 and T3 are examples of dedicated links.
- Frame relay and X.25 are packet-switched WAN technologies that use virtual circuits instead of dedicated ones.

- ATM transfers data in fixed cells, is a WAN technology, and transmits data at very high rates. It supports voice, data, and video applications.
- Circuit-switching technologies set up a circuit that will be used during a data transmission session. Packet-switching technologies do not set up circuits—instead, packets can travel along many different routes to arrive at the same destination.
- Three main types of multiplexing are statistical time division, frequency division, and wave division.

Questions

Please remember that these questions are formatted and asked in a certain way for a reason. Keep in mind that the CISSP exam is asking questions at a conceptual level. Questions may not always have the perfect answer, and the candidate is advised against always looking for the perfect answer. Instead, the candidate should look for the best answer in the list.

1. Which of the following protocols is considered connection-oriented?
   A. IP
   B. ICMP
   C. UDP
   D. TCP
2. Which of the following shows the layer sequence as layers 2, 5, 7, 4, and 3?
   A. Data link, session, application, transport, and network
   B. Data link, transport, application, session, and network
   C. Network, session, application, network, and transport
   D. Network, transport, application, session, and presentation
3. Metro Ethernet is a MAN protocol that can work in network infrastructures made up of access, aggregation, metro, and core layers. Which of the following best describes these network infrastructure layers?
   A. The access layer connects the customer's equipment to a service provider's aggregation network. Aggregation occurs on a core network. The metro layer is the metropolitan area network. The core connects different metro networks.
   B. The access layer connects the customer's equipment to a service provider's core network. Aggregation occurs on a distribution network at the core. The metro layer is the metropolitan area network.
   C. The access layer connects the customer's equipment to a service provider's aggregation network. Aggregation occurs on a distribution network. The metro layer is the metropolitan area network. The core connects different access layers.
   D. The access layer connects the customer's equipment to a service provider's aggregation network. Aggregation occurs on a distribution network. The metro layer is the metropolitan area network. The core connects different metro networks.

4. Systems that are built on the OSI model are considered open systems. What does this mean?
   A. They do not have authentication mechanisms configured by default.
   B. They have interoperability issues.
   C. They are built with internationally accepted protocols and standards so they can easily communicate with other systems.
   D. They are built with international protocols and standards so they can choose what types of systems they will communicate with.
5. Which of the following protocols work in the following layers: application, data link, network, and transport?
   A. FTP, ARP, TCP, and UDP
   B. FTP, ICMP, IP, and UDP
   C. TFTP, ARP, IP, and UDP
   D. TFTP, RARP, IP, and ICMP
6. What takes place at the data link layer?
   A. End-to-end connection
   B. Dialog control
   C. Framing
   D. Data syntax
7. What takes place at the session layer?
   A. Dialog control
   B. Routing
   C. Packet sequencing
   D. Addressing
8. Which best describes the IP protocol?
   A. A connectionless protocol that deals with dialog establishment, maintenance, and destruction
   B. A connectionless protocol that deals with the addressing and routing of packets
   C. A connection-oriented protocol that deals with the addressing and routing of packets
   D. A connection-oriented protocol that deals with sequencing, error detection, and flow control

9. Which of the following is not one of the messages exchanged during the DHCP lease process?
   i. Discover
   ii. Offer
   iii. Request
   iv. Acknowledgment
   A. All of them are exchanged
   B. None of them are exchanged
   C. i, ii
   D. ii, iii
10. An effective method to shield networks from unauthenticated DHCP clients is through the use of __________ on network switches.
   A. DHCP snooping
   B. DHCP protection
   C. DHCP shielding
   D. DHCP caching

Answers

1. **D.** TCP is the only connection-oriented protocol listed. A connection-oriented protocol provides reliable connectivity and data transmission, while a connectionless protocol provides unreliable connections and does not promise or ensure data transmission.
2. **A.** The OSI model is made up of seven layers: application (layer 7), presentation (layer 6), session (layer 5), transport (layer 4), network (layer 3), data link (layer 2), and physical (layer 1).
3. **D.** The access layer connects the customer's equipment to a service provider's aggregation network. Aggregation occurs on a distribution network. The metro layer is the metropolitan area network. The core connects different metro networks.
4. **C.** An open system is a system that has been developed based on standardized protocols and interfaces. Following these standards allows the systems to interoperate more effectively with other systems that follow the same standards.
5. **C.** Different protocols have different functionalities. The OSI model is an attempt to describe conceptually where these different functionalities take place in a networking stack. The model attempts to draw boxes around reality to help people better understand the stack. Each layer has a specific functionality and has several different protocols that can live at that layer and carry out that specific functionality. These listed protocols work at these associated layers: TFTP (application), ARP (data link), IP (network), and UDP (transport).

6. **C.** The data link layer, in most cases, is the only layer that understands the environment in which the system is working, whether it be Ethernet, Token Ring, wireless, or a connection to a WAN link. This layer adds the necessary headers and trailers to the frame. Other systems on the same type of network using the same technology understand only the specific header and trailer format used in their data link technology.
7. **A.** The session layer is responsible for controlling how applications communicate, not how computers communicate. Not all applications use protocols that work at the session layer, so this layer is not always used in networking functions. A session layer protocol sets up the connection to the other application logically and controls the dialog going back and forth. Session layer protocols allow applications to keep track of the dialog.
8. **B.** The IP protocol is connectionless and works at the network layer. It adds source and destination addresses to a packet as it goes through its data encapsulation process. IP can also make routing decisions based on the destination address.
9. **B.** The four-step DHCP lease process is
    1. **DHCPDISCOVER message:** This message is used to request an IP address lease from a DHCP server.
    2. **DHCPOFFER message:** This message is a response to a DHCPDISCOVER message, and is sent by one or numerous DHCP servers.
    3. **DHCPREQUEST message:** The client sends this message to the initial DHCP server that responded to its request.
    4. **DHCPACK message:** This message is sent by the DHCP server to the DHCP client and is the process whereby the DHCP server assigns the IP address lease to the DHCP client.
10. **A.** DHCP snooping ensures that DHCP servers can assign IP addresses to only selected systems, identified by their MAC addresses. Also, advance network switches now have the capability to direct clients toward legitimate DHCP servers to get IP addresses and to restrict rogue systems from becoming DHCP servers on the network.

CHAPTER 12

Wireless Networking

This chapter presents the following:

- Wireless networking
- Wireless LAN security
- Cellular networks
- Satellite communications

When wireless is perfectly applied the whole earth will be converted into a huge brain...

—Nikola Tesla

Wireless communications take place much more often than most people realize, and they involve a vast number of technologies working over a multitude of radio frequency ranges. These radio signals occupy frequency bands that may be shared with microwave, satellite, radar, and ham radio use, for example. We use these technologies for satellite communications, cellular phones, metropolitan and local area networking, and even for locking doors and controlling lights in our smart homes, as illustrated in Figure 12-1. All these interconnected networks rely on different communications techniques, using different radio frequencies and implementing different protocols. This extremely complex ecosystem makes many of our modern conveniences possible, but also introduces significant security challenges.

In this chapter, we'll cover the fundamentals of radio communications techniques and the most important protocols you should be aware of. We then put this theoretical information into real-world contexts as we discuss the opportunities and challenges they represent. Along the way, we'll talk about security threats and how to mitigate them.

Wireless Communications Techniques

Wireless communication involves transmitting information via radio waves that move through free space. These radio signals are typically described in terms of frequency and amplitude. The *frequency* of a signal indicates how many radio waves travel through a fixed place each second (i.e., how close each radio wave is to the one before it). Frequency is measured in hertz (Hz) and dictates the amount of data that can be carried and how far. The higher the frequency, the more data the signal can carry, but the shorter its range.

Figure 12-1 Various wireless networks

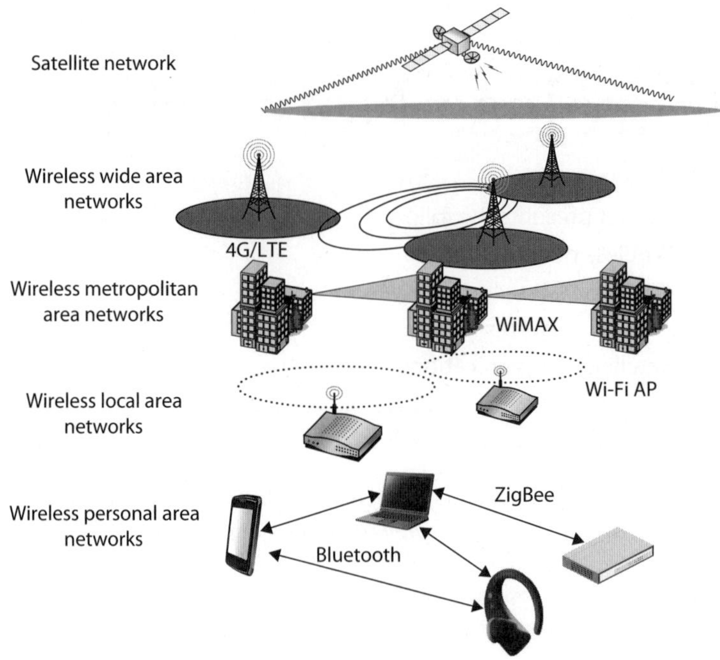

The *amplitude* of a radio signal indicates its power, which in turn dictates how far it can go. Amplitude usually is measured in watts or milliwatts (one-thousandth of a watt), but you may also see it expressed in decibels per milliwatt (dBm or dBmW), which is a measure of comparison to one milliwatt. For example, a wireless access point may allow you to configure the transmit power in increments from 0 dBm (1 mW) up to 23 dBm (200 mW).

In a wired network, each computer and device has its own cable connecting it to the network in some fashion. In wireless technologies, each device must instead share the allotted radio frequency spectrum with all other wireless devices that need to communicate. This spectrum of frequencies is finite in nature, which means it cannot grow if more and more devices need to use it. The same thing happens with Ethernet—all the computers on a segment share the same medium, and only one computer can send data at any given time. Otherwise, a collision can take place. Wired networks using Ethernet employ the CSMA technology (described in Chapter 11). Wireless LAN (WLAN) technology is actually very similar to Ethernet, but it uses CSMA/CA (collision avoidance). The wireless device sends out a broadcast indicating it is going to transmit data. This is received by other devices on the shared medium, which causes them to hold off on transmitting information. It is all about trying to eliminate or reduce collisions.

A number of techniques have been developed to allow wireless devices to access and share this limited amount of medium for communication purposes. The goal of each of these wireless technologies is to split the available frequency into usable portions, since it is a limited resource, and to allow the devices to share those portions efficiently. The most popular approach is called spread spectrum, though orthogonal frequency division multiplexing (OFDM) is widely used also. Because spread-spectrum technology is so prevalent, we'll get into it in a fair amount of detail in the next section.

Spread Spectrum

Radio frequencies cover a wide range, or *spectrum*, of frequencies. Some parts of this spectrum are allocated by national governments or international agreements for specific purposes. A radio *frequency band* is a subset of the radio spectrum designated for a specific use. For example, the range of radio frequencies between 1.8 and 29.7 megahertz (MHz) is almost universally considered the amateur radio band. A well-known frequency band is frequently labeled using just a single frequency, such as when we refer to the 2.4-GHz band used in many Wi-Fi systems. This band actually corresponds to the range of frequencies between 2.4 and 2.5 GHz. The challenge is how to dynamically allocate individual frequencies to specific sets of transmitters and receivers without them stepping all over each other. This is where spread-spectrum techniques come in handy.

Spread spectrum means that something is distributing individual signals across the allocated frequencies in some fashion. So, when a spread-spectrum technique is used, the sender spreads its data across the frequencies over which it has permission to communicate. This allows for more effective use of the available spectrum, because the sending system can use more than one frequency at a time.

Think of spread spectrum in terms of investments. In conventional radio transmissions, all the data is transmitted on a specific frequency (as in amplitude modulated [AM] radio systems) or on a narrow band of frequencies (as in frequency modulated [FM] radio). This is like investing only in one stock; it is simple and efficient, but may not be ideal in risky environments. The alternative is to diversify your portfolio, which is normally done by investing a bit of your money in each of many stocks across a wide set of industries. This is more complex and inefficient, but can save your bottom line when the stock in one of your selected companies takes a nose-dive. This example is akin to direct sequence spread spectrum (DSSS), which we discuss in an upcoming section.

There is in theory another way to minimize your exposure to volatile markets. Suppose the cost of buying and selling was negligible. You could then invest all your money in a single stock, but only for a brief period of time, sell it as soon as you turn a profit, and then reinvest all your proceeds in another stock. By jumping around the market, your exposure to the problems of any one company are minimized. This approach would be comparable to frequency hopping spread spectrum (FHSS), discussed next. The point is that spread-spectrum communications are used primarily to reduce the effects of adverse conditions such as crowded radio bands, interference, and eavesdropping.

Frequency Hopping Spread Spectrum

Frequency hopping spread spectrum (FHSS) takes the total amount of spectrum and splits it into smaller subchannels. The sender and receiver work at one of these subchannels for a specific amount of time and then move to another subchannel. The sender puts the first piece of data on one frequency, the second on a different frequency, and so on. The FHSS algorithm determines the individual frequencies that will be used and in what order, and this is referred to as the sender and receiver's *hop sequence*.

Interference is a large issue in wireless transmissions because it can corrupt signals as they travel. Interference can be caused by other devices working in the same frequency space. The devices' signals step on each other's toes and distort the data being sent. The FHSS approach to this is to hop between different frequencies so that if another device is operating at the same frequency, it will not be drastically affected. Consider another analogy: Suppose George and Marge work in the same room. They could get into each other's way and affect each other's work. But if they periodically change rooms, the probability of them interfering with each other is reduced.

A hopping approach also makes it much more difficult for eavesdroppers to listen in on and reconstruct the data being transmitted when used in technologies other than WLAN. FHSS has been used extensively in military wireless communications devices because the only way the enemy could intercept and capture the transmission is by knowing the hopping sequence. The receiver has to know the sequence to be able to obtain the data. But in today's WLAN devices, the hopping sequence is known and does not provide any security.

So how does this FHSS stuff work? The sender and receiver hop from one frequency to another based on a predefined hop sequence. Several pairs of senders and receivers can move their data over the same set of frequencies because they are all using different hop sequences. Let's say you and Marge share a hop sequence of 1, 5, 3, 2, 4, and Nicole and Ed have a sequence of 4, 2, 5, 1, 3. Marge sends her first message on frequency 1, and Nicole sends her first message on frequency 4 at the same time. Marge's next piece of data is sent on frequency 5, the next on 3, and so on until each reaches its destination, which is your wireless device. So your device listens on frequency 1 for a half-second, and then listens on frequency 5, and so on, until it receives all of the pieces of data that are on the line on those frequencies at that time. Ed's device is listening to the same frequencies but at different times and in a different order, so his device never receives Marge's message because it is out of sync with his predefined sequence. Without knowing the right code, Ed treats Marge's messages as background noise and does not process them.

Direct Sequence Spread Spectrum

Direct sequence spread spectrum (DSSS) takes a different approach by applying sub-bits to a message. The sub-bits are used by the sending system to generate a different format of the data before the data is transmitted. The receiving end uses these sub-bits to reassemble the signal into the original data format. The sub-bits are called *chips*, and the sequence of how the sub-bits are applied is referred to as the *chipping code*.

When the sender's data is combined with the chip, the signal appears as random noise to anyone who does not know the chipping sequence. This is why the sequence is sometimes called a pseudo-noise sequence. Once the sender combines the data with the chipping sequence, the new form of the information is modulated with a radio carrier signal, and it is shifted to the necessary frequency and transmitted. What the heck does that mean? When using wireless transmissions, the data is actually moving over radio signals that work in specific frequencies. Any data to be moved in this fashion must have a carrier signal, and this carrier signal works in its own specific range, which is a frequency. So you can think of it this way: once the data is combined with the chipping code, it is put into a car (carrier signal), and the car travels down its specific road (frequency) to get to its destination.

> **Spread Spectrum Types**
> This technology transmits data by "spreading" it over a broad range of frequencies:
>
> - FHSS moves data by changing frequencies.
> - DSSS takes a different approach by applying sub-bits to a message and uses all of the available frequencies at the same time.

The receiver basically reverses the process, first by demodulating the data from the carrier signal (removing it from the car). The receiver must know the correct chipping sequence to change the received data into its original format. This means the sender and receiver must be properly synchronized.

The sub-bits provide error-recovery instructions, just as parity does in RAID technologies. If a signal is corrupted using FHSS, it must be re-sent; but by using DSSS, even if the message is somewhat distorted, the signal can still be regenerated because it can be rebuilt from the chipping code bits. The use of this code allows for prevention of interference, allows for tracking of multiple transmissions, and provides a level of error correction.

FHSS vs. DSSS

FHSS uses only a portion of the total spectrum available at any one time, while the DSSS technology uses all of the available spectrum continuously. DSSS spreads the signals over a wider frequency band, whereas FHSS uses a narrowband carrier that changes frequently across a wide band.

Since DSSS sends data across all frequencies at once, it has higher data rates than FHSS. The first wireless WAN standard, 802.11, used FHSS, but as data requirements increased, DSSS was implemented. By using FHSS, the 802.11 standard can provide a data throughput of only 1 to 2 Mbps. By using DSSS instead, 802.11b provides a data throughput of up to 11 Mbps.

Orthogonal Frequency Division Multiplexing

Besides spread-spectrum techniques, another common approach to trying to move even more data over wireless frequency signals is called *orthogonal frequency division multiplexing (OFDM)*. OFDM is a digital multicarrier modulation scheme that compacts multiple modulated carriers tightly together, reducing the required spectrum. The modulated signals are orthogonal (perpendicular) and do not interfere with each other. OFDM uses a composite of narrow channel bands to enhance its performance in high-frequency bands. OFDM is officially a multiplexing technology and not a spread-spectrum technology, but is used in a similar manner.

A large number of closely spaced orthogonal subcarrier signals are used, and the data is divided into several parallel data streams or channels, one for each subcarrier. Channel equalization is simplified because OFDM uses many slowly modulated narrowband signals rather than one rapidly modulated wideband signal.

OFDM is used for several wideband digital communication types such as digital television, audio broadcasting, DSL broadband Internet access, wireless networks, and 4G/5G mobile communications.

Wireless Networking Fundamentals

The techniques we've covered so far deal with how we create radio links between devices, but how do we build on those links to create networks? Fundamentally, there are three topologies used to build wireless networks: star, mesh, and point to point. The star topology is by far the most prevalent because it is used in both WLANs and cellular networks, both of which have endpoints connecting to a specialized network device that handles layer 2 forwarding and, in some cases, layer 3 routing. The mesh topology is common for low-power devices in close proximity to each other, such as those used in smart homes, as well as in devices that span a large area, such as environmental sensors in wildlife refuges. Finally, point-to-point wireless topologies are common when connecting buildings as part of a metropolitan area network (MAN).

Before we get into the myriad of wireless protocols that enable the various types of wireless networks, let's take a closer look at what makes a typical WLAN work.

WLAN Components

A WLAN uses a transceiver, called an *access point (AP)*, also known as a wireless access point (WAP), which connects to an Ethernet cable that is the link wireless devices use to access resources on the wired network, as shown in Figure 12-2. When the AP is connected to the LAN Ethernet by a wired cable, it is the component that connects the wired

Figure 12-2 Access points allow wireless devices to participate in wired LANs.

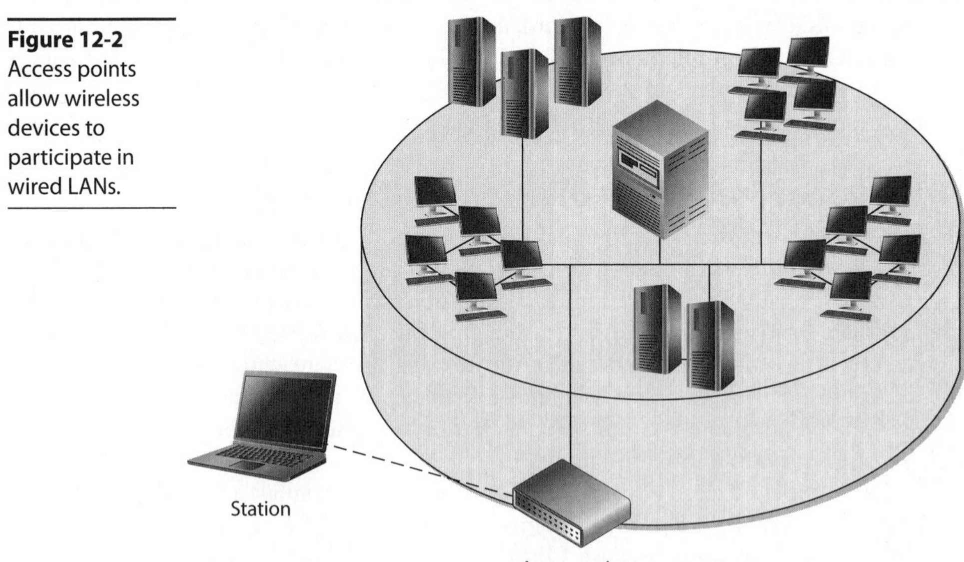

and the wireless worlds. The APs are in fixed locations throughout a network and work as communication beacons. Let's say a wireless user has a device with a wireless network interface card (NIC), which modulates the user's data onto radio frequency signals that are accepted and processed by the AP. The signals transmitted from the AP are received by the wireless NIC and converted into a digital format, which the device can understand.

When APs are used to connect wireless and wired networks, this is referred to as an *infrastructure WLAN*, which is used to extend an existing wired network. When there is just one AP and it is not connected to a wired network, it is considered to be in *stand-alone* mode and just acts as a wireless hub. An *ad hoc WLAN* has no APs; the wireless devices communicate with each other through their wireless NICs instead of going through a centralized device.

EXAM TIP Ad hoc WLANs are inherently less secure than infrastructure WLANs.

For a wireless device and AP to communicate, they must be configured to communicate over the same channel. A *channel* is a certain frequency within a given frequency band. The AP is configured to transmit over a specific channel, and the wireless device "tunes" itself to be able to communicate over this same frequency.

Any hosts that wish to participate within a particular WLAN must be configured with the proper *Service Set ID (SSID)*. Various hosts can be segmented into different WLANs by using different SSIDs. The reasons to segment a WLAN into portions are the same reasons wired systems are segmented on a network: the users require access to different resources, have different business functions, or have different levels of trust.

NOTE When wireless devices work in infrastructure mode, the AP and wireless clients form a group referred to as a Basic Service Set (BSS). This group is assigned a name, which is the SSID value.

When WLAN technologies first came out, authentication was simple and largely ineffective against many attackers. As wireless communication increased in use and many deficiencies were identified in these networks, a steady stream of improved approaches were developed and standardized. These covered both performance and security issues.

WLAN Standards

Standards are developed so that many different vendors can create various products that will work together seamlessly. Standards are usually developed on a consensus basis among the different vendors in a specific industry. The IEEE develops standards for a wide range of technologies—wireless being one of them.

The first WLAN standard, 802.11, was developed in 1997 and provided a 1- to 2-Mbps transfer rate. It worked in the 2.4-GHz frequency band, which is one of the free industrial, scientific, and medical (ISM) bands established by the International

Table 12-1 Generational Wi-Fi

Technology Supported	Wi-Fi Generation
802.11b	Wi-Fi 1
802.11a	Wi-Fi 2
802.11g	Wi-Fi 3
802.11n	Wi-Fi 4
802.11ac	Wi-Fi 5
802.11ax	Wi-Fi 6

Telecommunication Union (ITU). This means that organizations and users in most countries do not need a license to use this range. The 802.11 standard outlines how wireless clients and APs communicate; lays out the specifications of their interfaces; dictates how signal transmission should take place; and describes how authentication, association, and security should be implemented.

Now just because life is unfair, a long list of standards actually fall under the 802.11 main standard. You have probably seen the alphabet soup of 802.11a, 802.11b, 802.11g, 802.11n, 802.11ac, and 802.11ax (and a bunch of others). While the original 802.11 standard created the world of WLANs, the unrelenting pace of progress required changes and improvements over time. To try and make sense of things, the Wi-Fi Alliance created a scheme for numbering the generations of 802.11 protocols in 2018. This was done to help consumers differentiate products based on the most advanced 802.11-based technology supported by a given device. Table 12-1 lists the six generations of Wi-Fi, which we describe in the following sections.

NOTE Wi-Fi generations 1–3 are not formally defined by the Wi-Fi Alliance but are commonly understood to map to the technologies shown in Table 12-1.

802.11b

This standard was the first extension to the 802.11 WLAN standard. (Although 802.11a was conceived and approved first, it was not released first because of the technical complexity involved with this proposal.) 802.11b provides a transfer rate of up to 11 Mbps and works in the 2.4-GHz frequency range. It uses DSSS and is backward-compatible with 802.11 implementations.

802.11a

This standard uses a different method of modulating data onto the necessary radio carrier signals. Whereas 802.11b uses DSSS, 802.11a uses OFDM and works in the 5-GHz frequency band. Because of these differences, 802.11a is not backward-compatible with 802.11b or 802.11. Several vendors have developed products that can work with both 802.11a and 802.11b implementations; the devices must be properly configured or be able to sense the technology already being used and configure themselves appropriately.

As previously discussed, OFDM is a modulation scheme that splits a signal over several narrowband channels. The channels are then modulated and sent over specific frequencies. Because the data is divided across these different channels, any interference from the environment will degrade only a small portion of the signal. This allows for greater throughput. Like FHSS and DSSS, OFDM is a physical layer specification. It can be used to transmit high-definition digital audio and video broadcasting as well as WLAN traffic.

This technology offers advantages in two areas: speed and frequency. 802.11a provides up to 54 Mbps, and it does not work in the already very crowded 2.4-GHz spectrum. The 2.4-GHz frequency band is referred to as a "dirty" frequency because several devices already work there—microwaves, cordless phones, baby monitors, and so on. In many situations, this means that contention for access and use of this frequency can cause loss of data or inadequate service. But because 802.11a works at a higher frequency, it does not provide the same range as the 802.11b and 802.11g standards. The maximum speed for 802.11a is attained at short distances from the AP, up to 25 feet.

802.11g

The 802.11g standard provides for higher data transfer rates—up to 54 Mbps. This is basically a speed extension for 802.11b products. If a product meets the specifications of 802.11b, its data transfer rates are up to 11 Mbps, and if a product is based on 802.11g, that new product can be backward-compatible with older equipment but work at a much higher transfer rate.

802.11n (Wi-Fi 4)

This standard is designed to be much faster than 802.11g, with throughput at 100 Mbps, and it works at the same frequency range as 802.11a (5 GHz). The intent is to maintain some backward-compatibility with current Wi-Fi standards, while combining a mix of the current technologies. This standard uses a concept called multiple input, multiple output (MIMO) to increase the throughput. This requires the use of two receive and two transmit antennas to broadcast in parallel using a 20-MHz channel.

802.11ac (Wi-Fi 5)

The IEEE 802.11ac WLAN standard is an extension of 802.11n. It also operates on the 5-GHz band, but increases throughput to 1.3 Gbps. 802.11ac is backward compatible with 802.11a, 802.11b, 802.11g, and 802.11n, but if in compatibility mode it slows down to the speed of the slower standard. A major improvement is the use of multiuser MIMO (MU-MIMO) technology, which supports up to four data streams, allowing that many endpoints to simultaneously use a channel. Another benefit of this newer standard is its support for *beamforming*, which is the shaping of radio signals to improve their performance in specific directions. In simple terms, this means that 802.11ac is better able to maintain high data rates at longer ranges than its predecessors.

802.11ax (Wi-Fi 6)

Higher data rates are not always the best way to solve problems, and in the race for faster standards, we took a bunch of shortcuts that made them inefficient. The 802.11ax standard aims to address efficiency rather than faster speeds. A significant improvement it has is a new multiuser OFDM technology that replaces the single-user focused technology used in the 802.11a/g/n/ac standards. This means that multiple stations get to use available channels much more efficiently. In addition, the new standard doubles the number of streams supported by MU-MIMO, which means more stations can use it at the same time. These and many other improvements make 802.11ax much faster and better able to handle very crowded environments.

Other Wireless Network Standards

So far, we've focused pretty heavily on radio-based WLANs. There are other wireless network standards that you should know, at least at a superficial level. These include light-based WLANs and radio-based MANs and PANs. We describe the most important of these standards in the following sections.

Li-Fi

Li-Fi is a wireless networking technology that uses light rather than radio waves to transmit and receive data. It is essentially Wi-Fi using lights instead of radios. You can also think of it as fiber-optic communications without the fiber (i.e., over free space). It turns out that light, like radio, is an electromagnetic wave. The difference is that light is on a much higher frequency range and, thus, can carry significantly more information, at least in theory. Imagine if every light fixture in your home or workplace was able to modulate data onto the light it generates, while your computing device (laptop, smartphone, or whatever) could sense it and use its own light source (maybe the flash on your smartphone) to send data back to the light bulb. Because of the frequencies involved, our eyes are not able to perceive the tiny fluctuations in frequency. Besides, Li-Fi can work over infrared light too, which we can't see anyway.

One of the key benefits of Li-Fi (besides speed and ubiquity) is that it is very constrained to a particular space. Each light bulb has a cone of illumination within which it communicates with specific devices. You don't have to worry about an attacker with a sophisticated antenna picking up your signals a mile away. You can also be pretty confident of who you are communicating with because they have to be right there under the light source. These relatively small areas of service (by a given light source) are called *attocells*. The prefix atto- means quintillionth (which is a pretty small number), but, importantly, it's the next prefix down after femto-, as in *femtocells*, which are tiny cells used in some cellular networks.

At the time of this writing, Li-Fi technology is in its infancy but holds great promise. There are still many challenges to overcome, including co-channel interference (where multiple light sources overlap each other), roaming (seamlessly transferring a communications channel to an adjacent attocell or to an RF-based system if the user wanders out of the supported area), and endpoint interface devices (the sensors and light sources that would have to be built into each laptop, smartphone, etc.). Still, the benefits are many. Apart from the ones mentioned in the previous paragraph, Li-Fi promises to support much higher densities of endpoints, with much lower latencies, and in places where RF can be problematic (e.g., healthcare facilities, aircraft cabins, and power plants).

802.16

IEEE standard 802.16 is a MAN wireless standard that allows for wireless traffic to cover a much wider geographical area, where stations can be as far as 70 km apart. It uses some of the same bands as WLAN standards, specifically 2.4 GHz and 5 GHz, but uses up to 256 subcarriers with variable data rates to efficiently handle lots of traffic across large distances. This technology is also referred to as *broadband* wireless access.

A commercial technology that is based on 802.16 is WiMAX, which was widely touted as a replacement for second-generation (2G) digital cellular networks, particularly in rural areas. While this did not happen across the board (it largely lost out to Long Term Evolution or LTE), 802.16, and WiMAX in particular, remains in widespread use, especially outside the United States. A common implementation of 802.16 technology is shown in Figure 12-3.

NOTE IEEE 802.16 is a standard for vendors to follow to allow for interoperable broadband wireless connections. IEEE does not test for compliance to this standard. The WiMAX Forum runs a certification program that is intended to guarantee compliance with the standard and interoperability with equipment between vendors.

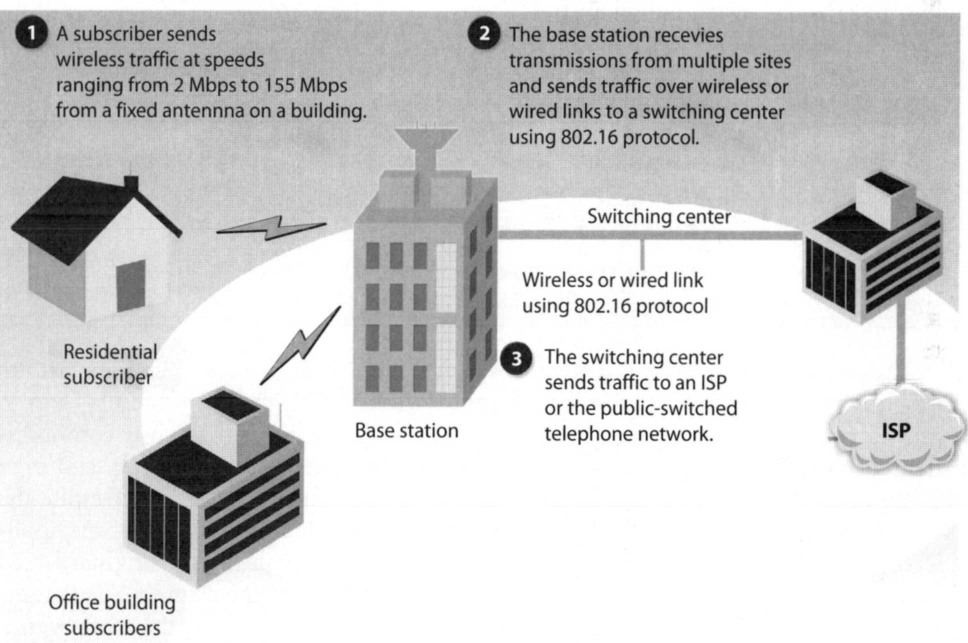

Figure 12-3 Broadband wireless in MAN

802.15.4

The IEEE 802.15.4 standard deals with a much smaller geographical network, which is referred to as a *wireless personal area network (WPAN)*. This technology allows for connectivity to take place among "disadvantaged" devices, which are the ubiquitous low-cost, low-data-rate, low-power, extended-life ones such as the embedded devices introduced in Chapter 7. For example, if you are using active radio frequency identification (RFID) or Industrial Internet of Things (IIoT) devices, odds are that you are using 802.15.4. This standard is optimized for situations in which machines communicate directly with other machines over relatively short distances (typically no more than 100 meters). For this reason, this standard is a key enabler of the Internet of Things (IoT), in which everything from your thermostat to your door lock is (relatively) smart and connected.

The 802.15.4 standard defines the physical (PHY) layer and Media Access Control (MAC) sublayer of the data link layer in the OSI model. At the physical layer, it uses DSSS. For MAC, it uses CSMA-CA. In terms of topology, this standard supports star, tree, and mesh networks. The catch is that, regardless of the topology, 802.15.4 requires a full-function device (FFD) that acts as a central node for the network (even if it is not logically or physically placed at its center). This central device is called the *coordinator* for one or more connected reduced-function devices (RFDs). This makes a lot of sense in a star or tree topology, where you have a regular computer as the hub or root node. It might be a bit less intuitive when you think of mesh networks such as you would find in a smart home network, but we'll get into that when we discuss ZigBee in the next section.

There are multiple extensions to the base 802.15.4 standard that optimize it for specific geographic regions or applications. You may come across the following:

802.15.4c	For use in China
802.15.4d	For use in Japan
802.15.4e	For industrial applications
802.15.4f	For active (i.e., battery powered) radio frequency identification (RFID)
802.15.4g	For smart utility networks (SUNs)

Because this standard was intended to support embedded devices in close proximity to each other, the typical range is only about 10 meters (though it could reach 1 km in optimal conditions) and the data rates are quite low. While nodes frequently communicate at the maximum rate of 250 Kbps, there are also lower rates of 100, 20, and even 10 Kbps for smaller devices that have to last a long time on small batteries. Despite the low data rates, devices that implement this standard are able to support real-time applications (i.e., those that require extremely low latencies) through the use of Guaranteed Time Slot (GTS) reservations. Note that when a GTS is used, the channel access technique used has to be time division multiple access (TDMA) instead of the more typical CSMA/CA. TDMA is a technique that divides each communications channel into multiple time slots to increase the data rates by taking advantage of the fact that not every station will be transmitting all the time.

Security-wise, 802.15.4 implements access control lists (ACLs) by default, so nodes can decide whether to communicate with other nodes based on their claimed physical address. Keep in mind, however, that spoofing a physical address is trivial. The standard also offers (but does not require) two other security mechanisms that you should know. The first is support for symmetric key encryption using the Advanced Encryption Standard (AES) with 128-bit keys, used to protect message confidentiality and integrity. The second is a frame counter feature that protects against replay attacks by tracking the last message received from another node and ensuring a new message is more recent than it.

ZigBee

ZigBee is one of the most popular standards based on IEEE 802.15.4. It sits right on top of the layer 1 and layer 2 services provided by 802.15.4 and adds networking and application layer support.

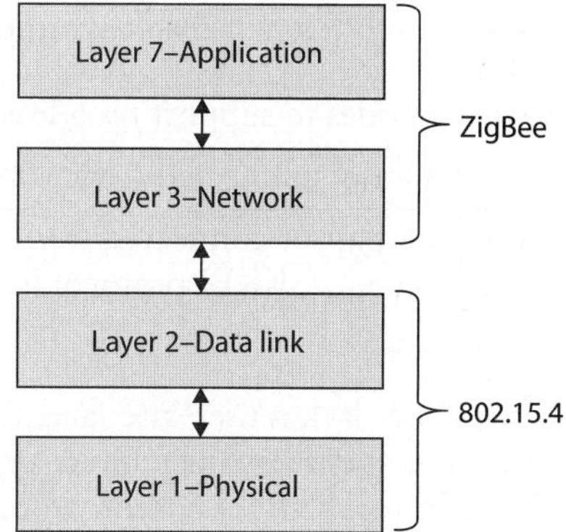

ZigBee is intended to be simpler and cheaper than most WPAN protocols and is very popular in the embedded device market. You can find ZigBee in a variety of home automation, industrial control, medical, and sensor network applications. Figure 12-4

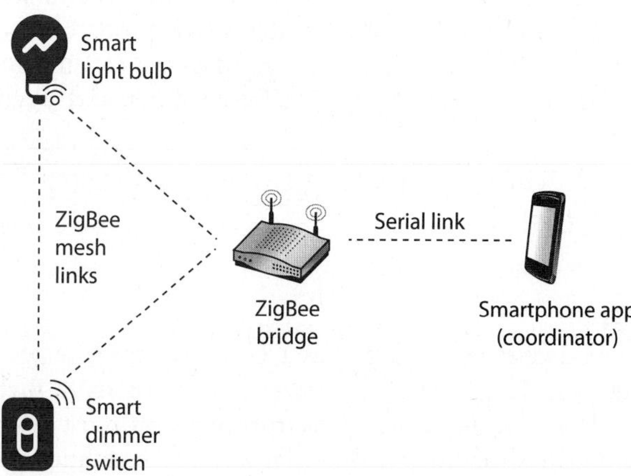

Figure 12-4 ZigBee in a smart home

shows a typical implementation of this standard for controlling lights in a smart home. All light bulbs and switches are able to talk to each other either directly, through the bridge, or by relaying traffic for destination nodes that are too far from the source node. Note that the connection between the bridge and the controller is over a serial link, but this could be implemented as a connection over Wi-Fi, Bluetooth, or any other means.

Because ZigBee is meant to be used in embedded devices that don't have (and can't afford) a bunch of operating system overhead, it assumes what is called an *open trust model.* This means that all applications within a device trust each other, which indirectly extends to all devices in a network as well. It also means that perimeter protection is absolutely critical. This protection should be implemented both physically and logically. At the physical level, ZigBee devices should be tamper-resistant to prevent attackers from simply reading encryption keys or otherwise gaining physical control of a node and using it as a beachhead for future attacks. At the logical level, it means controlling access to the network, which is done primarily through key management.

The ZigBee standard defines three different 128-bit symmetric keys:

- **Network key** Shared by all nodes to support broadcasts
- **Link key** Unique for each pair of connected devices and used for unicasts
- **Master key** Unique for each pair of connected devices and used for the Symmetric-Key Key Establishment (SKKE) protocol from which the other keys are derived

Since embedded devices oftentimes lack a user interface, the ZigBee standard allows multiple ways to distribute and subsequently manage these keys. The most secure way is based on a centralized security model in which the coordinator node acts as a Trust Center. This node is responsible for authenticating new devices that attempt to join the network and then securely sending them the keys they need. To facilitate this, manufacturers of ZigBee devices can install unique certificates at the factory, which are then used by the Trust Center to authenticate them and distribute keys using the Certificate-Based Key Establishment (CBKE) protocol. This is not all that common of an approach apart from high-security commercial systems. More commonly, manufacturers install a unique key in each device, which is then used by the SKKE protocol to derive keys, much like we would do using the Diffie-Hellman algorithm we covered in Chapter 8. This second approach is less secure, doesn't require a Trust Center, and is typical in consumer systems.

EXAM TIP ZigBee is most secure when a coordinator node acts as a Trust Center.

Bluetooth

The *Bluetooth wireless* technology has a 1- to 3-Mbps transfer rate and works in a range of approximately 1, 10, or 100 meters. It was originally invented as an alternative to connecting devices using cables. Unsurprisingly, its most common application today is in cordless headsets for smartphones. However, the technology has plenty of other uses.

If you have a cell phone and a tablet that are both Bluetooth-enabled and both have calendar functionality, you could have them update each other without any need to connect them physically. If you added some information to your cell phone contacts list and task list, for example, you could just place the phone close to your tablet. The tablet would sense that the other device is nearby, and it would then attempt to set up a network connection with it. Once the connection was made, synchronization between the two devices would take place, and the tablet would add the new contacts list and task list data. Bluetooth works in a portion of the frequency band used by 802.11 devices (2.4 GHz).

In early versions of Bluetooth, real security risks existed due to protocol vulnerabilities, but they have been largely mitigated. Still, as with any other technology, it is possible for attackers to compromise the confidentiality, integrity, or availability of Bluetooth devices. One attack type to which these devices are vulnerable is called *Bluesnarfing*, which is the unauthorized access from a wireless device through a Bluetooth connection. This allows attackers to read, modify, or delete calendar events, contacts, e-mails, text messages, and so on. While recent versions of the Bluetooth standard make this much harder, it is still possible to trick unwary users into accepting an attacker's connection attempts.

Another attack type that Bluetooth is vulnerable to is referred to as *Bluejacking*. In this attack, someone sends an unsolicited message to a device that is Bluetooth-enabled. Bluejackers look for a receiving device (phone, tablet, laptop) and then send a message to it. The countermeasure is to put the Bluetooth-enabled device into nondiscoverable mode so others cannot identify this device in the first place. If you receive some type of message this way, just look around you. Bluetooth only works within a 10-meter distance, so it is coming from someone close by.

Other Important Standards

The wireless standards we've covered so far cover the ways in which devices connect to each other and send data over the radio links they create. Over the years, we've discovered that there are a bunch of other features we want in our wireless networks, regardless of the communications standards being used by the radios themselves. These include Quality of Service (QoS), roaming, and spectrum management issues. Let's take a look at another set of standards you should know.

802.11e

This standard provides QoS and support of multimedia traffic in wireless transmissions. Voice, streaming video, and other types of time-sensitive applications have a lower tolerance for delays in data transmission. The problem is that the original 802.11 protocol treated all traffic equally. In other words, an e-mail message that could safely take minutes to get through had exactly the same priority as a video packet whose tolerable latency is measured in fractions of a second. To address this, the 802.11e standard defines four access categories (ACs) in increasing priority: background, best effort, video, and voice. This QoS provides the capability to prioritize traffic and affords guaranteed delivery. This standard and its capabilities have opened the door to allow many different types of data to be transmitted over wireless connections.

802.11f

When a user moves around in a WLAN, her wireless device often needs to communicate with different APs. An AP can cover only a certain distance, and as the user moves out of the range of the first AP, another AP needs to pick up and maintain her signal to ensure she does not lose network connectivity. This is referred to as *roaming*, and for this to happen seamlessly, the APs need to communicate with each other. If the second AP must take over this user's communication, it needs to be assured that this user has been properly authenticated and must know the necessary settings for this user's connection. This means the first AP needs to be able to convey this information to the second AP. The conveying of this information between the different APs during roaming is what 802.11f deals with. The process of transferring between one AP and another is sometimes called *handoff*. It outlines how this information can be properly shared.

802.11h

Because the ISM bands are unlicensed, devices that operate in them are expected to deal well with interference from other devices. This was all good and well before the explosion of WLANs and Bluetooth devices, but quickly became an issue as crowding increased. To make things worse, the 5-GHz band is used not only for Wi-Fi but also for certain radar and satellite communications systems. In this increasingly busy portion of the spectrum, something had to be done to deal with interference.

The 802.11h standard was originally developed to address these issues in Europe, where interference in the 5-GHz band was particularly problematic. However, the techniques it implements are applicable in many countries around the world. Two specific technologies included in the standard are *Dynamic Frequency Selection (DFS)* and *Transmit Power Control (TPC)*. DFS is typically implemented in the WLAN AP and causes it to automatically select channels that have less interference, particularly from radars. TPC causes any device to automatically reduce its power output when it detects interference from other networks.

802.11j

Japan regulates its radio spectrum differently than many other countries, particularly in the 4.9- and 5-GHz bands. Specifically, Japan uses different frequencies, radio channel widths, and wireless operating settings. In order to allow international devices to be interoperable in Japan, the IEEE developed the 802.11j standard. The need for this standard underscores the fact that each country has the sovereign right to regulate its radio spectrum as it sees fit.

Evolution of WLAN Security

To say that security was an afterthought in the first WLANs would be a remarkable understatement. As with many new technologies, wireless networks were often rushed to market with a focus on functionality, even if that sometimes came at the expense of security. Over time, vendors and standards bodies caught on and tried to correct these omissions. While we have made significant headway in securing our wireless networks, as security professionals we must acknowledge that whenever we transmit anything over the electromagnetic spectrum, we are essentially putting our data in the hands (or at least within the grasp) of our adversaries.

802.11

When WLANs were being introduced, there was industry-wide consensus that some measures would have to be taken to assure users that their data (now in the air) would be protected from eavesdropping to the same degree that data on a wired LAN was already protected. This was the genesis of *Wired Equivalent Privacy (WEP)*. This first WLAN standard, codified as part of the original IEEE 802.11, had a tremendous number of security flaws. These were found within the core standard itself, as well as in different implementations of this standard. Before we delve into these deficiencies, it will be useful to spend a bit of time with some of the basics of 802.11.

EXAM TIP If you ever come across WEP in the context of wireless security, you know it's the wrong answer (unless the question is asking for the least secure standard).

The wireless devices using this protocol can authenticate to the AP in two main ways: *open system authentication (OSA)* and *shared key authentication (SKA)*. OSA does not require the wireless device to prove to the AP it has a specific cryptographic key to allow for authentication purposes. In many cases, the wireless device needs to provide only the correct SSID value. In OSA implementations, all transactions are in cleartext because no encryption is involved. So an intruder can sniff the traffic, capture the necessary steps of authentication, and walk through the same steps to be authenticated and associated to an AP.

When an AP is configured to use SKA, the AP sends a random value to the wireless device. The device encrypts this value with a preshared key (PSK) and returns it. The AP decrypts and extracts the response, and if it is the same as the original value, the device is authenticated. In this approach, the wireless device is authenticated to the network by proving it has the necessary encryption key. The PSK, commonly known as the Wi-Fi password, is a 64- or 128-bit key.

The three core deficiencies with WEP are the use of static encryption keys, the ineffective use of initialization vectors, and the lack of packet integrity assurance. The WEP protocol uses the RC4 algorithm, which is a stream-symmetric cipher. *Symmetric* means the sender and receiver must use the exact same key for encryption and decryption purposes. The 802.11 standard does not stipulate how to update these keys through an automated process, so in most environments, the RC4 symmetric keys are never changed out. And usually all of the wireless devices and the AP share the exact same key. This is like having everyone in your company use the exact same password. Not a good idea. So that is the first issue—static WEP encryption keys on all devices.

The next flaw is how initialization vectors (IVs) are used. An IV is a numeric seeding value that is used with the symmetric key and RC4 algorithm to provide more randomness to the encryption process. Randomness is extremely important in encryption because any patterns can give the bad guys insight into how the process works, which may allow them to uncover the encryption key that was used. The key and 24-bit IV value are inserted into the RC4 algorithm to generate a key stream. The values (1's and 0's) of the key stream are XORed with the binary values of the individual packets. The result is ciphertext, or encrypted packets.

In most WEP implementations, the same IV values are used over and over again in this process, and since the same symmetric key (or shared secret) is generally used, there is no way to provide effective randomness in the key stream that is generated by the algorithm. The appearance of patterns allows attackers to reverse-engineer the process to uncover the original encryption key, which can then be used to decrypt future encrypted traffic.

So now we are onto the third mentioned weakness, which is the integrity assurance issue. WLAN products that use only the 802.11 standard introduce a vulnerability that is not always clearly understood. An attacker can actually change data within the wireless packets by flipping specific bits and altering the Integrity Check Value (ICV) so the receiving end is oblivious to these changes. The ICV works like a cyclic redundancy check (CRC) function; the sender calculates an ICV and inserts it into a frame's header. The receiver calculates his own ICV and compares it with the ICV sent with the frame. If the ICVs are the same, the receiver can be assured that the frame was not modified during transmission. If the ICVs are different, it indicates a modification did indeed take place and thus the receiver discards the frame. In WEP, there are certain circumstances in which the receiver cannot detect whether an alteration to the frame has taken place; thus, there is no true integrity assurance.

So the problems identified with the 802.11 standard include poor authentication, static WEP keys that can be easily obtained by attackers, IV values that are repetitive and do not provide the necessary degree of randomness, and a lack of data integrity. The next section describes the measures taken to remedy these problems.

NOTE 802.11 and WEP were deprecated years ago, are inherently insecure, and should not be used.

802.11i

IEEE came out with a standard in 2004 that deals with the security issues of the original 802.11 standard, which is called IEEE 802.11i or *Wi-Fi Protected Access 2 (WPA2)*. Why the number 2? Because while the formal standard was being ratified by the IEEE, the Wi-Fi Alliance pushed out WPA (the first one) based on the draft of the standard. For this reason, WPA is sometimes referred to as the *draft* IEEE 802.11i. This rush to push out WPA required the reuse of elements of WEP, which ultimately made WPA vulnerable to some of the same attacks that doomed its predecessor. Let's start off by looking at WPA in depth, since this protocol is still in use despite its weaknesses.

WPA employs different approaches that provide much more security and protection than the methods used in the original 802.11 standard. For starters, the PSK size was increased to 256 bits and is salted with the SSID of the WLAN to make it harder to crack. This is good, but the greatest enhancement of security is accomplished through specific protocols, technologies, and algorithms. The first protocol is *Temporal Key Integrity Protocol (TKIP)*, which is backward-compatible with the WLAN devices based upon the original 802.11 standard. TKIP actually works with WEP by feeding it keying material, which is data to be used for generating new dynamic keys. TKIP generates a new key for every frame that is transmitted. These changes constitute the variety of this standard known as WPA Personal, which is geared at consumers.

NOTE TKIP was developed by the IEEE 802.11i task group and the Wi-Fi Alliance. The goal of this protocol was to increase the strength of WEP or replace it fully without the need for hardware replacement. TKIP provides a key mixing function, which allows the RC4 algorithm to provide a higher degree of protection. It also provides a sequence counter to protect against replay attacks and implements a message integrity check mechanism.

There is also a more robust version called WPA Enterprise. The main difference is that it also integrates 802.1X port authentication and Extensible Authentication Protocol (EAP) authentication methods. The use of the 802.1X technology (which we'll discuss in its own section shortly) provides access control by restricting network access until full authentication and authorization have been completed, and provides a robust authentication framework that allows for different EAP modules to be plugged in. These two technologies (802.1X and EAP) work together to enforce mutual authentication between the wireless device and authentication server. So what about the static keys, IV value, and integrity issues?

TKIP addresses the deficiencies of WEP pertaining to static WEP keys and inadequate use of IV values. Two hacking tools, AirSnort and WEPCrack, can be used to easily crack WEP's encryption by taking advantage of these weaknesses and the ineffective use of the key scheduling algorithm within the WEP protocol. If a company is using products that implement only WEP encryption and is not using a third-party encryption solution (such as a VPN), these programs can break its encrypted traffic within minutes. There is no "maybe" pertaining to breaking WEP's encryption. Using these tools means it will be broken whether a 40-bit or 128-bit key is being used—it doesn't matter. This is one of the most serious and dangerous vulnerabilities pertaining to the original 802.11 standard.

The use of TKIP provides the ability to rotate encryption keys to help fight against these types of attacks. The protocol increases the length of the IV value and ensures that every frame has a different IV value. This IV value is combined with the transmitter's MAC address and the original WEP key, so even if the WEP key is static, the resulting encryption key will be different for every frame. (WEP key + IV value + MAC address = new encryption key.) So what does that do for us? This brings more randomness to the encryption process, and it is randomness that is necessary to properly thwart cryptanalysis and attacks on cryptosystems. The changing IV values and resulting keys make the resulting key stream less predictable, which makes it much harder for the attacker to reverse-engineer the process and uncover the original key.

TKIP also deals with the integrity issues by using a message integrity check (MIC) instead of an ICV function. If you are familiar with a message authentication code

(MAC) function, this is the same thing. A symmetric key is used with a hashing function, which is similar to a CRC function but stronger. The use of a MIC instead of an ICV function ensures the receiver will be properly alerted if changes to the frame take place during transmission. The sender and receiver calculate their own separate MIC values. If the receiver generates a MIC value different from the one sent with the frame, the frame is seen as compromised and it is discarded.

The types of attacks that have been carried out on WEP devices and networks that just depend upon WEP are numerous and unnerving. Wireless traffic can be easily sniffed, data can be modified during transmission without the receiver being notified, rogue APs can be erected (which users can authenticate to and communicate with, not knowing it is a malicious entity), and encrypted wireless traffic can be decrypted quickly and easily. Unfortunately, these vulnerabilities usually provide doorways to the actual wired network where the more destructive attacks can begin.

The full 802.11i (WPA2) has a major advantage over WPA by providing encryption protection with the use of the AES algorithm in counter mode with CBC-MAC (CCM), which is referred to as the Counter Mode Cipher Block Chaining Message Authentication Code Protocol (CCM Protocol or CCMP). AES is a more appropriate algorithm for wireless than RC4 and provides a higher level of protection. WPA2 defaults to CCMP, but can switch down to TKIP and RC4 to provide backward compatibility with WPA devices and networks.

802.11w

WPA2 was a huge step forward for WLAN security because it provided effective encryption for most wireless traffic. However, there are certain frames that cannot be encrypted because every station (even those that have not yet joined the network) must be able to receive. These are called *management frames*, and they take care of things like beaconing, association, and authentication. While we can't encrypt them, we can take measures to ensure their integrity. The IEEE 802.11w standard provides Management Frame Protection (MFP) that prevents certain types of attacks, such as replay and denial-of-service (DoS) attacks.

A particularly problematic type of DoS attack on WLANs is called a deauthentication (or deauth) attack and it exploits a feature of Wi-Fi that allows WAPs to disconnect rogue devices by sending a deauthentication management frame. You can see how, in an environment without MFP, it would be trivial for an attacker to spoof such messages, claiming to be the real WAP. 802.11w solves this problem for WLANs that are not yet on WPA3.

WPA3

Like any other security mechanism, WPA2 began to crack under intensifying attacks. By 2018, the Wi-Fi Alliance decided that a new approach was needed. The result is WPA3, which is not directly equivalent to any IEEE standard, though it does require 802.11w to protect management frames. Like its predecessor WPA2, WPA3 comes in two flavors: Personal and Enterprise.

WPA3 Personal is aimed at the consumer market and tries to make security transparent to the average user. One of the most important innovations of this standard is that it allows users to choose passwords that, though they might be easily guessable, still provide adequate security. This is done through Simultaneous Authentication of Equals (SAE), which is defined in IEEE 802.11s, instead of relying on WPA2's preshared keys. SAE uses the Diffie-Hellman key exchange method but adds an authentication element based on the (potentially weak) password. The result is a secret session key that is remarkably resistant to password-cracking attempts.

WPA3 Enterprise is similar to its predecessor (WPA2 Enterprise) but makes use of stronger cryptography. It does this by restricting the allowed algorithms to a handful of strong ones that use 192-bit keys. It also requires certificates on both the AP and the wireless device for mutual authentication. The challenge with deploying WPA3 is that many older wireless interfaces, particularly those on most embedded devices, cannot support it, which means you may have to upgrade many (or all) of your endpoints.

802.1X

The 802.11i standard can be understood as three main components in two specific layers. The lower layer contains the improved encryption algorithms and techniques (TKIP and CCMP), while the layer that resides on top of it contains 802.1X. They work together to provide more layers of protection than the original 802.11 standard.

The 802.1X standard is a port-based network access control protocol that ensures a user cannot make a full network connection until he is properly authenticated. This means a user cannot access network resources and no traffic is allowed to pass, other than authentication traffic, from the wireless device to the network until the user is properly authenticated. An analogy is having a chain on your front door that enables you to open the door slightly to identify a person who knocks before you allow him to enter your house.

NOTE 802.1X is not a wireless protocol. It is an access control protocol that can be implemented on both wired and wireless networks.

By incorporating 802.1X, the new standard allows for the user to be authenticated, whereas using only WPA provides *system* authentication. User authentication provides a higher degree of confidence and protection than system authentication. The 802.1X technology actually provides an authentication framework and a method of dynamically distributing encryption keys. The three main entities in this framework are the supplicant (wireless device), the authenticator (AP), and the authentication server (usually a RADIUS server).

The AP controls all communication and allows the wireless device to communicate with the authentication server and wired network only when all authentication steps are completed successfully. This means the wireless device cannot send or receive HTTP, DHCP, SMTP, or any other type of traffic until the user is properly authorized. WEP does not provide this type of strict access control.

PART IV

Another disadvantage of the original 802.11 standard is that mutual authentication is not possible. When using WEP alone, the wireless device can authenticate to the AP, but the authentication server is not required to authenticate to the wireless device. This means a rogue AP can be set up to capture users' credentials and traffic without the users being aware of this type of attack. 802.11i deals with this issue by using EAP. EAP allows for mutual authentication to take place between the authentication server and wireless device and provides flexibility in that users can be authenticated by using passwords, tokens, one-time passwords, certificates, smart cards, or Kerberos. This allows wireless users to be authenticated using the current infrastructure's existing authentication technology. The wireless device and authentication server that are 802.11i-compliant have different authentication modules that plug into 802.1X to allow for these different options. So, 802.1X provides the framework that allows for the different EAP modules to be added by a network administrator. The two entities (supplicant and authenticator) agree upon one of these authentication methods (EAP modules) during their initial handshaking process.

The 802.11i standard does not deal with the full protocol stack, but addresses only what is taking place at the data link layer of the OSI model. Authentication protocols reside at a higher layer than this, so 802.11i does not specify particular authentication protocols. The use of EAP, however, allows different protocols to be used by different vendors. For example, Cisco uses a purely password-based authentication framework called Lightweight Extensible Authentication Protocol (LEAP). Other vendors, including Microsoft, use EAP and Transport Layer Security (EAP-TLS), which carries out authentication through digital certificates. And yet another choice is Protected EAP (PEAP), where only the server uses a digital certificate.

EAP-Tunneled Transport Layer Security (EAP-TTLS) is an EAP protocol that extends TLS. EAP-TTLS is designed to provide authentication that is as strong as EAP-TLS, but it does not require that each user be issued a certificate. Instead, only the authentication servers are issued certificates. User authentication is performed by password, but the password credentials are transported in a securely encrypted tunnel established based upon the server certificates.

If EAP-TLS is being used, the authentication server and wireless device exchange digital certificates for authentication purposes. If PEAP is being used instead, the user of the wireless device sends the server a password and the server authenticates to the wireless device with its digital certificate. In both cases, some type of public key infrastructure (PKI) needs to be in place. If a company does not have a PKI currently implemented, it can be an overwhelming and costly task to deploy a PKI just to secure wireless transmissions.

When EAP-TLS is being used, the steps the server takes to authenticate to the wireless device are basically the same as when a TLS connection is being set up between a web server and web browser. Once the wireless device receives and validates the server's digital certificate, it creates a master key, encrypts it with the server's public key, and sends it over to the authentication server. Now the wireless device and authentication server have a master key, which they use to generate individual symmetric session keys. Both entities use these session keys for encryption and decryption purposes, and it is the use of these keys that sets up a secure channel between the two devices.

Organizations may choose to use PEAP instead of EAP-TLS because they don't want the hassle of installing and maintaining digital certificates on every wireless device.

Before you purchase a WLAN product, you should understand the requirements and complications of each method to ensure you know what you are getting yourself into and if it is the right fit for your environment.

A large concern with any WLANs using just WEP is that if individual wireless devices are stolen, they can easily be authenticated to the wired network. 802.11i has added steps to require the user to authenticate to the network instead of just requiring the wireless device to authenticate. By using EAP, the user must send some type of credential set that is tied to his identity. When using only WEP, the wireless device authenticates itself by proving it has a symmetric key that was manually programmed into it. Since the user does not need to authenticate using WEP, a stolen wireless device can allow an attacker easy access to your precious network resources.

The Answer to All Our Prayers?

So, does the use of EAP, 802.1X, AES, and TKIP result in secure and highly trusted WLAN implementations? Maybe, but we need to understand what we are dealing with here. TKIP was created as a quick fix to WEP's overwhelming problems. It does not provide an overhaul for the wireless standard itself because WEP and TKIP are still based on the RC4 algorithm, which is not the best fit for this type of technology. The use of AES is closer to an actual overhaul, but it is not backward-compatible with the original 802.11 implementations. In addition, we should understand that using all of these new components and mixing them with the current 802.11 components will add more complexity and steps to the process. Security and complexity do not usually get along. The highest security is usually accomplished with simplistic and elegant solutions to ensure all of the entry points are clearly understood and protected. These newer technologies add more flexibility to how vendors can choose to authenticate users and authentication servers, but can also bring us interoperability issues because the vendors will not all choose the same methods. This means that if an organization buys an AP from company A, then the wireless cards the organization buys from companies B and C may not work seamlessly.

So, does that mean all of this work has been done for naught? No. 802.11i provides much more protection and security than WEP ever did. The working group has had very knowledgeable people involved and some very large and powerful companies aiding in the development of these new solutions. But the customers who purchase these new products need to understand what will be required of them *after* their purchase. For example, with the use of EAP-TLS, each wireless device needs its own digital certificate. Are your current wireless devices programmed to handle certificates? How will the certificates be properly deployed to all the wireless devices? How will the certificates be maintained? Will the devices and authentication server verify that certificates have not been revoked by periodically checking a certificate revocation list (CRL)? What if a rogue authentication server or AP was erected with a valid digital certificate? The wireless device would just verify this certificate and trust that this server is the entity it is supposed to be communicating with.

Today, WLAN products are being developed following the stipulations of this 802.11i wireless standard. Many products will straddle the fence by providing TKIP for backward-compatibility with current WLAN implementations and AES for organizations that are just now thinking about extending their current wired environments with a wireless component. Before buying wireless products, customers should review the Wi-Fi Alliance's certification findings, which assess systems against the 802.11i proposed standard.

Best Practices for Securing WLANs

There is no silver bullet to protect any of our devices or networks. That being said, there are a number of things we can do that will increase the cost of the attack for the adversary. Some of the best practices pertaining to WLAN implementations are as follows:

- Change the default SSID. Each AP comes with a preconfigured default SSID value that may reveal the manufacturer and even model number, which may advertise systems with known vulnerabilities.
- Implement WPA3 Enterprise to provide centralized user authentication (e.g., RADIUS, Kerberos). Before users can access the network, require them to authenticate.
- Use separate VLANs for each class of users, just as you would on a wired LAN.
- If you must support unauthenticated users (e.g., visitors), ensure they are connected to an untrusted VLAN that remains outside your network's perimeter.
- Deploy a wireless intrusion detection system (WIDS).
- Physically put the AP at the center of the building to limit how far outside the facility the signal will reach (and be reachable). The AP has a specific zone of coverage it can provide.
- Logically put the AP in a DMZ with a firewall between the DMZ and internal network. Allow the firewall to investigate the traffic before it gets to the wired network.
- Implement VPN for wireless devices to use. This adds another layer of protection for data being transmitted.
- Configure the AP to allow only known MAC addresses into the network. Allow only known devices to authenticate. But remember that these MAC addresses are sent in cleartext, so an attacker could capture them and masquerade himself as an authenticated device.
- Carry out penetration tests on the WLAN. Use the tools described in this section to identify APs and attempt to break the current encryption scheme being used.

Mobile Wireless Communication

Mobile wireless has now exploded into a trillion-dollar industry, with over 14 billion devices worldwide, fueled by a succession of new technologies and by industry and international standard agreements. So what is a mobile phone anyway? It is a device that can send voice and data over wireless radio links. It connects to a cellular network, which is connected to the public switched telephone network (PSTN). So instead of needing a physical cord and connection that connects your phone and the PSTN, you have a device that allows you to indirectly connect to the PSTN as you move around a wide geographic area.

A cellular network distributes radio signals over delineated areas, called *cells*. Each cell has at least one fixed-location transceiver (base station) and is joined to other cells to provide connections over large geographic areas. So as you are talking on your mobile phone and you move out of one cell, the base station in the original cell sends your connection information to the base station in the next cell so that your call is not dropped and you can continue your conversation.

We do not have an infinite number of frequencies to work with when it comes to mobile communication. Millions of people around the world are using their cell phones as you read this. How can all of these calls take place if we only have one set of frequencies to use for such activity? Individual cells can use the same frequency range, as long as they are not right next to each other. So the same frequency range can be used in every other cell, which drastically decreases the amount of ranges required to support simultaneous connections. A rudimentary depiction of a cellular network, in which nonadjacent cells reuse the frequency sets F0, F1, F2, F3, and F4, is shown in Figure 12-5.

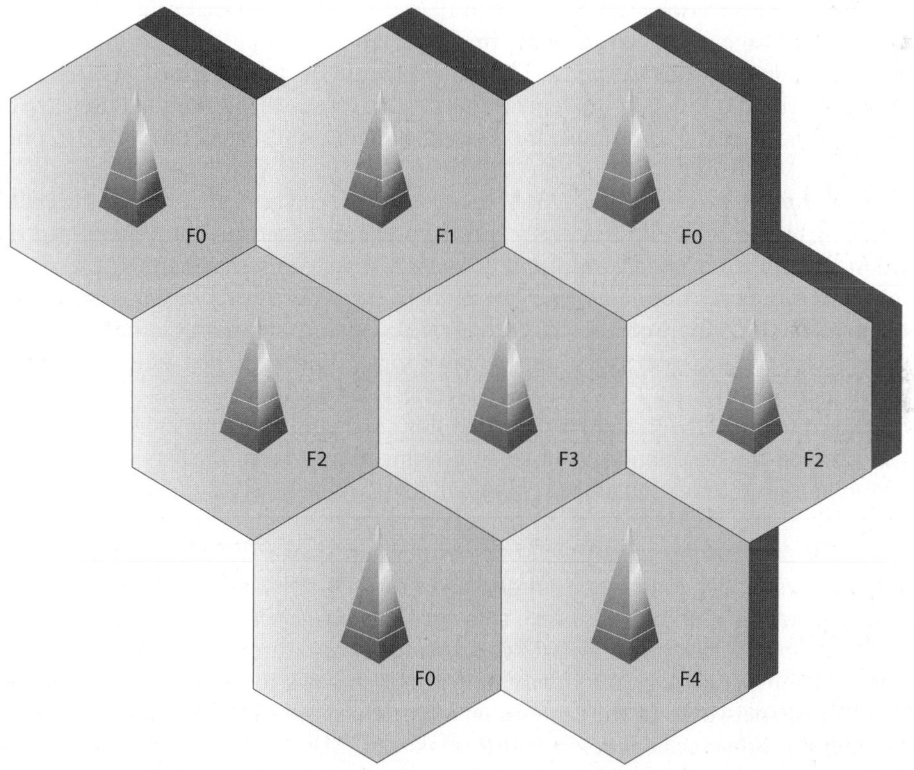

Figure 12-5 Nonadjacent cells can use the same frequency ranges.

Multiple Access Technologies

The industry has had to come up with other ways to allow millions of users to be able to use this finite resource (frequency range) in a flexible manner. Over time, mobile wireless has been made up of progressively more complex and more powerful "multiple access" technologies, listed here:

- Frequency division multiple access (FDMA)
- Time division multiple access (TDMA)
- Code division multiple access (CDMA)
- Orthogonal frequency division multiple access (OFDMA)

We'll quickly go over the characteristics of each of these technologies because they are the foundational constructs of the various cellular network generations.

Frequency division multiple access (FDMA) was the earliest multiple access technology put into practice. The available frequency range is divided into sub-bands (channels), and one channel is assigned to each subscriber (cell phone). The subscriber has exclusive use of that channel while the call is made, or until the call is terminated or handed off; no other calls or conversations can be made on that channel during that call. Using FDMA in this way, multiple users can share the frequency range without the risk of interference between the simultaneous calls. FDMA was used in the first generation (1G) of cellular networks. Various 1G mobile implementations, such as Advanced Mobile Phone System (AMPS), Total Access Communication System (TACS), and Nordic Mobile Telephone (NMT), used FDMA.

Time division multiple access (TDMA) increases the speed and efficiency of the cellular network by taking the radio frequency spectrum channels and dividing them into time slots. At various time periods, multiple users can share the same channel; the systems within the cell swap from one user to another user, in effect, reusing the available frequencies. TDMA increased speeds and service quality. A common example of TDMA in action is a conversation. One person talks for a time and then quits, and then a different person talks. In TDMA systems, time is divided into frames. Each frame is divided into slots. TDMA requires that each slot's start and end time are known to both the source and the destination. Mobile communication systems such as Global System for Mobile Communication (GSM), Digital AMPS (D-AMPS), and Personal Digital Cellular (PDC) use TDMA.

Code division multiple access (CDMA) was developed after FDMA, and as the term "code" implies, CDMA assigns a unique code to each voice call or data transmission to uniquely identify it from all other transmissions sent over the cellular network. In a CDMA "spread spectrum" network, calls are spread throughout the entire radio frequency band. CDMA permits every user of the network to simultaneously use every channel in the network. At the same time, a particular cell can simultaneously interact with multiple other cells. These features make CDMA a very powerful technology.

It is the main technology for the mobile cellular networks that presently dominate the wireless space.

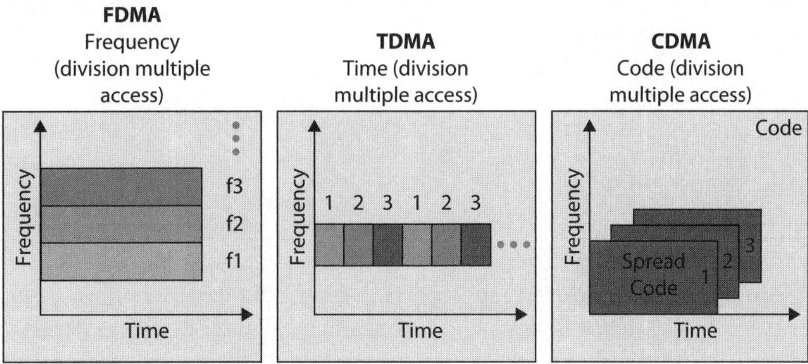

Orthogonal frequency division multiple access (OFDMA) is derived from a combination of FDMA and TDMA. In earlier implementations of FDMA, the different frequencies for each channel were widely spaced to allow analog hardware to separate the different channels. In OFDMA, each of the channels is subdivided into a set of closely spaced orthogonal frequencies with narrow subchannels. Each of the different subchannels can be transmitted and received simultaneously in a multiple input, multiple output (MIMO) manner. The use of orthogonal frequencies and MIMO allows signal processing techniques to reduce the impacts of any interference between different subchannels and to correct for channel impairments, such as noise and selective frequency fading. 4G and 5G require that OFDMA be used.

Generations of Mobile Wireless

Multiple access technology development was driven by the dramatic growth in mobile subscribers worldwide. Mobile wireless technologies have gone through a whirlwind of confusing generations. The first generation (1G) dealt with analog transmissions of voice-only data over circuit-switched networks. This generation provided a throughput of around 19.2 Kbps. The second generation (2G) allows for digitally encoded voice and data to be transmitted between wireless devices, such as cell phones, and content providers. TDMA, CDMA, GSM, and PCS all fall under the umbrella of 2G mobile telephony. This technology can transmit data over circuit-switched networks and supports data encryption, fax transmissions, and short message services (SMSs).

The third-generation (3G) networks became available around the turn of the century. Incorporating FDMA, TDMA, and CDMA, 3G has the flexibility to support a great variety of applications and services. Further, 3G replaced circuit switching with packet switching. Modular in design to allow ready expandability, backward compatibility with 2G networks, and stressing interoperability among mobile systems, 3G services greatly expanded the applications available to users, such as global roaming (without changing one's cell phone or cell phone number), as well as Internet services and multimedia.

In addition, reflecting the ever-growing demand from users for greater speed, latency in 3G networks was much reduced as transmission speeds were enhanced. More enhancements

Mobile Technology Generations

Like many technologies, the mobile communication technology has gone through several different generations.

First generation (1G):

- Analog services
- Voice service only

Second generation (2G):

- Primarily voice, some low-speed data (circuit switched)
- Phones were smaller in size
- Added functionality of e-mail, paging, and caller ID

Generation 2½ (2.5G):

- Higher data rates than 2G
- "Always on" technology for e-mail and pages

Third generation (3G):

- Integration of voice and data
- Packet-switched technology, instead of circuit-switched

Generation 3.5 G (3GPP)

- Higher data rates
- Use of OFDMA technology

Fourth generation (4G)

- Based on an all-IP packet-switched network
- Data exchange at 100 Mbps to 1 Gbps

Fifth generation (5G)

- Higher frequency ranges, which cut down range and make interference a bigger deal
- Data rates of 20 Gbps possible
- Supports dense deployment of high-speed, low-latency services

to 3G networks, often referred to as 3.5G or as mobile broadband, took place under the rubric of the Third Generation Partnership Project (3GPP). 3GPP resulted in a number of new or enhanced technologies. These include Enhanced Data Rates for GSM Evolution (EDGE), High-Speed Downlink Packet Access (HSDPA), CDMA2000, and Worldwide Interoperability for Microwave Access (WiMAX).

At the time of writing, 4th generation (4G) mobile networks are dominant (though, as we're about to see, that's going to change soon). Initially, there were two competing technologies that fell under the umbrella of 4G: Mobile WiMAX and Long-Term Evolution (LTE). Eventually, however, LTE won out and WiMAX is no longer used in mobile wireless networks. (Though, as we've already discussed, WiMAX is still used as an alternative to traditional ISP services in WANs.) A 4G system does not support traditional circuit-switched telephony service as 3G does, but works over a purely packet-based network. 4G devices are IP-based and are based upon OFDMA instead of the previously used multiple carrier access technologies. In theory, 4G devices should be able to reach 2-Gbps data rates, though that is seldom the case in practice.

Fifth generation (5G) is the technology that is all the rage right now. Its biggest advantage, at least from users' perspectives, over 4G is speed. 5G is capable of reaching a whopping 20 Gbps, which puts it in the neighborhood of the latest Wi-Fi 6 standard. What are the drawbacks of 5G? In order to achieve those jaw-dropping speeds, 5G uses higher frequencies that, as we already discussed, have shorter ranges and are more susceptible to interference. This means that carriers will have to put up more cellular towers.

Each of the different mobile communication generations has taken advantage of the improvement of hardware technology and processing power. The increase in hardware has allowed for more complicated data transmission between users and hence the desire for more users to use mobile communications.

Table 12-2 illustrates some of the main features of the 2G through 5G networks. It is important to note that this table does not and cannot easily cover all the aspects of each generation. Earlier generations of mobile communication have considerable variability between countries. The variability was due to country-sponsored efforts before agreed-upon international standards were established. Various efforts between the ITU and countries have attempted to minimize the differences.

NOTE While it would be great if the mobile wireless technology generations broke down into clear-cut definitions, they do not. This is because various parts of the world use different foundational technologies, and there are several competing vendors in the space with their own proprietary approaches.

	2G	3G	4G	5G
Spectrum	1,800 MHz	2 GHz	Various	Various 3–86 GHz
Bandwidth	25 MHz	25 MHz	100 MHz	30–300 MHz
Multiplexing Type	TDMA	CDMA	OFDMA	OFDMA
New Features Introduced	Digital voice, SMS, MMS	Mobile Internet access, video	Mobile broadband, HD video	Ultra-HD and 3D video
Data Rate	115–128 Kbps	384 kbps	100 Mbps (moving) 1 Gbps (stationary)	Up to 10 Gbps
Introduction	1993	2001	2009	2018

Table 12-2 The Different Characteristics of Mobile Technology

PART IV

Hacking Mobile Phones

2G networks (which are still around, believe it or not) lack the ability to authenticate towers to phones. In other words, an attacker can easily set up a rogue tower with more power than the nearby legitimate ones and cause the target's mobile phone to connect to it. This type of attack allows attackers to intercept all mobile phone traffic. Though 3G and 4G networks corrected this serious vulnerability, it is sometimes still possible to force most phones to switch down to 2G mode by jamming 3G, 4G, and 5G towers. In an effort to maintain some form of connectivity, handsets may then switch down to the vulnerable 2G mode, making the attack possible again.

Devices designed to perform this type of attack are called International Mobile Subscriber Identity (IMSI) catchers. Initially intended for law enforcement and intelligence agency use, IMSI catchers are increasingly available to criminals in the black markets. Moreover, it is possible for anyone to build one of these attack platforms for less than $1,500, as Chris Paget demonstrated at DefCon in 2010. This is yet another example of how backward compatibility can perpetuate vulnerabilities in older protocols.

Satellites

Today, satellites are used to provide wireless connectivity between distant stations. For two different locations to communicate via satellite links, they must be within the satellite's line of sight and *footprint* (area covered by the satellite), which tends to be large even for low Earth orbit satellites. The sender of information (ground station) modulates the data onto a radio signal that is transmitted to the satellite. A transponder on the satellite receives this signal, amplifies it, and relays it to the receiver. The receiver must have a type of antenna—one of those circular, dish-like things we see on top of buildings. The antenna contains one or more microwave receivers, depending upon how many satellites it is accepting data from.

Satellites provide broadband transmission that is commonly used for television channels and Internet access. If a user is receiving TV data, then the transmission is set up as a one-way (broadcast) network. If a user is using this connection for Internet connectivity, then the transmission is set up as a two-way network. The available bandwidth depends upon the antenna and terminal type and the service provided by the service provider. Time-sensitive applications, such as voice and video conferencing, can suffer from the delays experienced as the data goes to and from the satellite.

There are two types of orbits that are commonly used in satellite communications networks: geosynchronous and low Earth. Traditional networks, like the ones that broadcast TV and carry transoceanic data links for the major carriers, orbit at an altitude of 22,236 miles, which means they rotate at the same rate as the Earth does. This is called a *geosynchronous orbit*, and it makes the satellites appear to be stationary over the same spot on the ground. The key benefit is that the ground station antenna doesn't have to move. The main drawbacks are that, with that kind of range, you need a pretty big antenna and have to wait about a second for a radio wave to go up to the satellite and come back to Earth. This latency can create challenges for real-time communications like video conferencing.

Other satellites use a low Earth orbit (LEO), which is typically between 99 and 1,243 miles above the surface of the Earth. This means there is not as much distance between the ground stations and the satellites as in other types of satellites. In turn, this means smaller receivers can be used, which makes LEO satellites ideal for international cellular communication and Internet use. The catch is that the data rates tend to be much smaller than geosynchronous satellites and the service plans are pretty expensive.

In most cases, organizations use a system known as a very small aperture terminal (VSAT), which links a station (such as a remote office) to the Internet through a satellite gateway facility run by a service provider, as shown in Figure 12-6. Alternatively, VSATs can be deployed in stand-alone networks in which the organization also places a VSAT at a central location and has all the remote ones reach into it with no need for a gateway facility. The data rates available can range from a few Kbps to several Mbps. Dropping prices have rendered this technology affordable to many midsized organizations, though it is still far from being inexpensive.

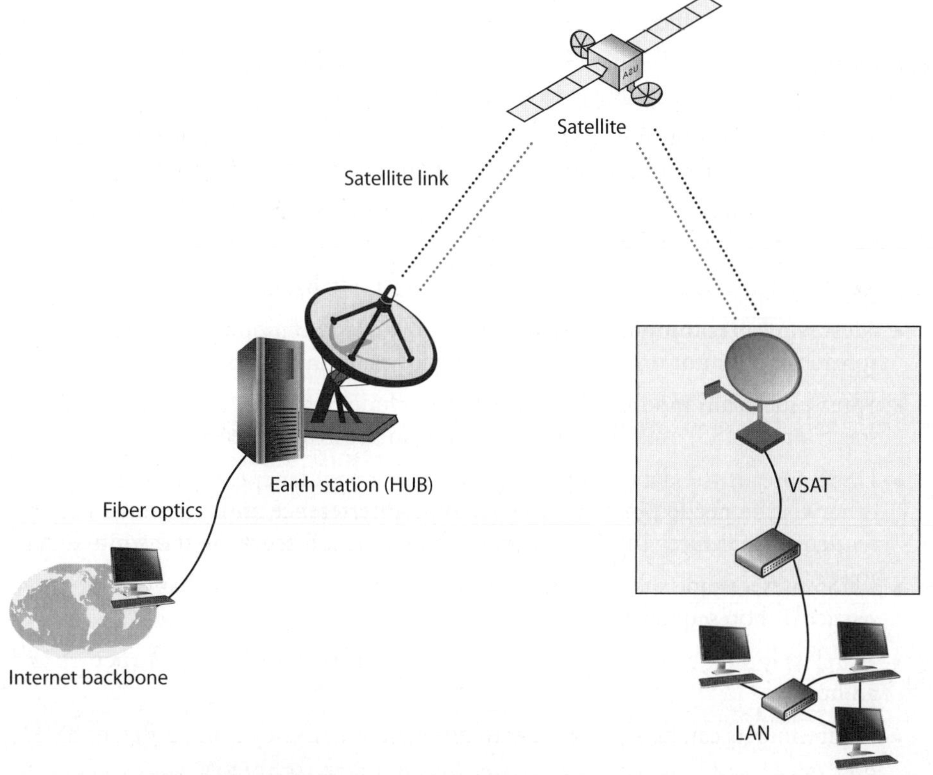

Figure 12-6 Satellite broadband

Chapter Review

Wireless networking is ubiquitous and, over the years, the security community has made great strides to ensure the confidentiality, integrity, and availability of our systems using these technologies. Still, risk can never be driven to zero, and this is particularly true when you transmit into free space, whether you do so using radio or light waves. Best practices for securing wireless networks include using strong cryptography, controlling access, and periodically testing the effectiveness of our controls.

As security professionals, we must always be aware of the myriad of new wireless technologies being developed and sold. For each, we have to compare the benefits (which are always touted by the vendors) to the risks (which may be less obvious and more difficult to identify). The market will constantly push products that promise new features and functionality, even if they come at the cost of security. To be clear, most new technologies incorporate at least some basic security features (and in many cases, advanced security features too), but these are not always implemented in a systematic manner by their adopters. That's where security professionals need to weigh in.

Quick Review

- Wireless communication systems modulate data onto electromagnetic signals like radio and light waves.
- Normally, a higher frequency can carry more data, but over a shorter distance and with more susceptibility to interference.
- Wireless communication systems typically use carrier sense multiple access with collision avoidance (CSMA/CA) as a medium access control (MAC) protocol.
- A radio frequency band is a subset of the radio spectrum designated for a specific use.
- Wi-Fi systems operate in the 2.4-GHz and 5-GHz bands.
- Most wireless communication systems use one of two modulation techniques: spread spectrum or orthogonal frequency division multiplexing (OFDM).
- Spread spectrum modulation techniques include frequency hopping spread spectrum (FHSS) and direct sequence spread spectrum (DSSS).
- DSSS spreads the data being transmitted over a wider spectrum than would otherwise be needed in order to overcome interference and relies on a chip sequence to let receiving stations know how to reconstruct the transmitted data.
- FHSS uses a single subchannel at a time, but rapidly changes channels in a particular hop sequence.
- Wireless local area networks (WLANs) come in two forms: infrastructure and ad hoc.
- Environments can be segmented into different WLANs by using different SSIDs.
- 802.11a provides up to 54 Mbps and operates in the 5-GHz band.

- 802.11b provides a transfer rate of up to 11 Mbps and works in the 2.4-GHz frequency range.
- 802.11g operates in the 2.4-GHz band and supports data rates of up to 54 Mbps.
- 802.11n, also known as Wi-Fi 4, supports throughputs of up to 100 Mbps and works in the 5-GHz band.
- IEEE 802.11ac (Wi-Fi 5) is an extension of 802.11n that increases throughput to 1.3 Gbps and is backward compatible with 802.11a, 802.11b, 802.11g, and 802.11n.
- The 802.11ax standard aims to address efficiency rather than faster speeds.
- Li-Fi is a wireless networking technology that uses light rather than radio waves to transmit and receive data.
- 802.16 is a metropolitan area network (MAN) wireless standard that allows wireless traffic to cover large geographical areas where stations can be as far as 70 km apart, using the 2.4-GHz and 5-GHz bands.
- The 802.15.4 standard defines the physical layer and Media Access Control sublayer of wireless personal area networks (WPANs).
- ZigBee is a standard for layers 3 (network) and 7 (application) that is built on top of 802.15.4 and is most commonly used in Internet of Things (IoT) and Industrial IoT systems.
- Bluetooth is another standard for WPANs, which is most commonly used to replace the cables connecting peripherals to computers and mobile devices.
- The 802.11e standard provides Quality of Service (QoS) and support of multimedia traffic in wireless transmissions.
- 802.11f standardizes the processes by which access points transfer active connections among themselves, enabling users to roam across APs.
- The 802.11h standard was developed to address interference issues in the 5-GHz band, particularly with regard to radar and satellite systems, through Dynamic Frequency Selection (DFS) and Transmit Power Control (TPC) techniques.
- 802.11j is an example of standards that allow common technologies such as WLANs to be employed in countries (in this case Japan) where local regulations conflict with portions of a broader standard (in this case 802.11).
- 802.11 was the original WLAN standard, which included Wired Equivalent Privacy (WEP); it is now obsolete.
- 802.11i defines Wi-Fi Protected Access 2 (WPA2) and is the most common standard in use in WLANs today.
- The IEEE 802.11w standard provides Management Frame Protection (MFP) that prevents certain types of attacks, such as replay and DoS attacks.
- WPA3 was developed by the Wi-Fi alliance (not IEEE) and is quickly replacing WPA2 for both personal and enterprise use.

- 802.1X is an access control protocol that can be implemented on both wired and wireless networks for user authentication and key distribution.
- Mobile telephony has gone through different generations and multiple access technologies: 1G (FDMA), 2G (TDMA), 3G (CDMA), 4G (OFDM), and 5G (OFDM).
- Satellite communications links provide connectivity across very long distances and in places that would otherwise not be reachable, but may introduce latency challenges.

Questions

Please remember that these questions are formatted and asked in a certain way for a reason. Keep in mind that the CISSP exam is asking questions at a conceptual level. Questions may not always have the perfect answer, and the candidate is advised against always looking for the perfect answer. Instead, the candidate should look for the best answer in the list.

1. Which of the following is not a characteristic of the IEEE 802.11a standard?
   A. It works in the 5-GHz range.
   B. It uses the OFDM spread-spectrum technology.
   C. It provides 52 Mbps in bandwidth.
   D. It covers a smaller distance than 802.11b.
2. Wireless LAN technologies have gone through different versions over the years to address some of the inherent security issues within the original IEEE 802.11 standard. Which of the following provides the correct characteristics of WPA2 in Enterprise mode?
   A. IEEE 802.1X, WEP, MAC
   B. IEEE 802.1X, EAP, TKIP
   C. IEEE 802.1X, EAP, WEP
   D. IEEE 802.1X, EAP, CCMP
3. Which of the following is *not* a characteristic of Li-Fi networks?
   A. Support for high client densities
   B. High latency
   C. Constrained coverage area
   D. Can work on the infrared spectrum
4. How would you best ensure the security of a ZigBee system?
   A. Ensure a coordinator acts as a Trust Center
   B. Use 256-bit encryption keys
   C. Deploy in a ring topology with preassigned slots for each device
   D. Use the Symmetric-Key Key Establishment (SKKE) protocol to derive keys

5. Which of the following is a Bluetooth-specific attack that allows unauthorized read/write access from a wireless device?
   A. Bluejacking
   B. Replay attack
   C. Smurf attack
   D. Bluesnarfing
6. What does the IEEE 802.1X standard cover?
   A. A Management Frame Protection (MFP) that prevents replay and denial-of-service (DoS) attacks
   B. Wi-Fi Protected Access 2 (WPA2)
   C. Security extensions to the physical layer (PHY) and Media Access Control (MAC) sublayer of the data link layer in the OSI model
   D. An access control protocol for user authentication and key distribution
7. Which of the following is not a disadvantage of satellite networks compared to terrestrial ones?
   A. Latency
   B. Cost
   C. Bandwidth
   D. Video conferencing

Use the following scenario to answer Questions 8–10. You are planning an upgrade for the wireless network at one of your manufacturing sites and want to use this as an opportunity to improve network security. The current system is based on 10-year-old wireless access points (WAPs) that implement 802.11g. You're using WPA2 in Personal mode because you have multiple Industrial Internet of Things (IIoT) devices. You can update the firmware on the WAPs, but you really think it's time for an upgrade.

8. What could make it harder for you to switch from WPA2 Personal mode to Enterprise mode?
   A. Enterprise mode requires licenses that can be costly.
   B. The WAPs may not support Enterprise mode.
   C. IIoT devices may not support Enterprise mode.
   D. The return on investment is insufficient.
9. What is the best technology to which you should consider upgrading?
   A. IEEE 802.16
   B. IEEE 802.11w
   C. IEEE 802.11f
   D. IEEE 802.11ax

10. The existing wireless network has recently become unusable, and you suspect you may be the target of a persistent Wi-Fi deauthentication attack. How can you best mitigate this threat?
    A. Deploy WPA3 access points across the facility
    B. Perform MAC address filtering to keep the rogue stations off the network
    C. Immediately update the firmware on the access points to support 802.11w
    D. Change the channel used by the WAPs

Answers

1. **C.** The IEEE standard 802.11a uses the OFDM spread-spectrum technology, works in the 5-GHz frequency band, and provides bandwidth of up to 54 Mbps. The operating range is smaller because it works at a higher frequency.
2. **D.** Wi-Fi Protected Access 2 requires IEEE 802.1X or preshared keys for access control, Extensible Authentication Protocol (EAP) or preshared keys for authentication, and the Advanced Encryption Standard (AES) algorithm in counter mode with CBC-MAC Protocol (CCMP) for encryption.
3. **B.** Latency is the delay in data transfers, which is extremely low in Li-Fi networks.
4. **A.** Using a Trust Center provides a way to centrally authenticate devices and securely manage encryption keys, which are 128 bits (not 256). Without a Trust Center, the SKKE protocol can be used to derive keys, but this approach is not as secure. ZigBee does not support ring topologies.
5. **D.** Bluesnarfing could allow an attacker to read, modify, or delete calendar events, contacts, e-mails, text messages, and so on. Bluejacking is the only other Bluetooth attack option, but this refers to someone sending an unsolicited message to a device.
6. **D.** 802.1X is an access control protocol that can be implemented on both wired and wireless networks for user authentication and key distribution. MFP is covered in 802.11w, WPA2 is covered in 802.11i, and the other option (security extensions) was a distracter.
7. **C.** If you have the budget for it, data rates on satellite networks are comparable with other modes of communication. These systems, however, are typically more expensive and have high latencies, which means they are not well suited for time-sensitive applications, such as voice and video conferencing.
8. **D.** If a WAP supports WPA2, it would do so in either Personal or Enterprise mode as long as it can be connected to the needed backend services (e.g., a RADIUS server), with no need for additional licensing. Thus, the change would not typically be expected to have ROI issues. However, many embedded devices, including IIoT, do not support this mode and would have to be replaced.

9. **D.** 802.11ax is the only standard describing a WLAN among the list of options. 802.16 is used in metropolitan area networks (MANs). 802.11w covers Management Frame Protection (MFP) in wireless networks. 802.11f deals with users roaming among access points.
10. **C.** 802.11w provides Management Frame Protection (MFP) capabilities that would mitigate this type of attack. This is included in WPA3, so either answer would generally work. However, it is probably faster, cheaper, and safer to roll out 802.11w upgrades first, which would likely have no negative effects on the networks, while research and planning continue on how to best implement a WPA3 solution across the enterprise. This is a good example of the types of ambiguous questions you'll see on the CISSP exam.

CHAPTER 13

Securing the Network

This chapter presents the following:

- Secure networking
- Secure protocols
- Multilayer protocols
- Converged protocols
- Micro-segmentation

More connections to more devices means more vulnerabilities.

—Marc Goodman

Having developed a foundational understanding of networking technologies, we now turn our attention to building secure networks upon this foundation. In this chapter, we circle back to the core networking and service protocols introduced in Chapter 11 and discuss the threats against them and how to mitigate those threats. This discussion is grounded in the secure design principles covered in Chapter 9. We'll take the same approach as we expand our scope of interest from those core protocols and services to include other services, such as e-mail, that are critical to modern networks.

These networks are not as neatly divided as the OSI model could lead us to believe. Increasingly, we are relying on multilayer and converged protocols where concepts from different layers and even network components overlap in ways that have important security implications. The goal of this chapter is to show how, through a thoughtful application of secure protocols and best practices, we can secure our networks and the services they provide.

Applying Secure Design Principles to Network Architectures

A network architecture is just a model of a network. Like any model, it is not 100 percent representative of reality and uses abstractions to simplify some details so that we can focus on the others. By ignoring the little details (for now), we make it easier on ourselves to focus on the more important elements. For example, before we decide how many web servers we need and which operating systems and software we need to run on them, we should first identify the classes of servers and where we would put them. We might have a set of externally accessible servers for our web presence, but we may also need some servers that are for internal use only by all employees, and yet another set that is only for web developers. Where do we put each set and how might we need different controls for them? Maybe we need a demilitarized zone (DMZ), an internal sharing cluster, and a development virtual local area network (VLAN), each with specific sets of controls meant to mitigate their differing risk profiles. A network architecture allows us to answer these high-level questions before we start configuring any boxes.

Now, once we go through all the trouble of coming up with an architecture that works, we shouldn't have to reinvent the wheel. Network architectures also serve as templates for future systems. What's more, they can be codified and shared among similar organizations to reduce work and ensure we all follow best practices. Even if a lot of the details are different, a sound architecture can be reused time and again.

Many of these best practices relate to security. Since we intend our architectures to be reusable, it is imperative that we apply secure design principles when we implement them. In the sections that follow, we will discuss a (wide) variety of networking concepts and technologies that you will need to understand to implement secure design principles in network architectures. Periodically, we circle back and discuss some of these important secure design principles. It is important to note that there is no one-size-fits-all solution in this effort, so you will have to be selective about which of these principles you apply in any specific situation. Still, as a CISSP, you are expected to be conversant with all of them.

Let's start by reviewing the 11 secure design principles we covered in Chapter 9 and look at how they apply to network architectures.

- **Threat modeling** Everything we do in cybersecurity should be grounded in a good understanding of the threats we face. In this chapter, we focus our attention on network security, so we'll illustrate the threats we face as we discuss the various technologies and protocols involved in operating and securing our networks.
- **Least privilege** Traffic should be allowed to flow between any two points that are required to communicate in order to satisfy a valid organizational requirement, and nowhere else. We cover this in depth when we address network segmentation later in this chapter.
- **Defense in depth** While some IT and security professionals equate this principle with having a DMZ for public-facing servers, the principle applies throughout the network and requires that we build concentric defenses around our most valuable assets.
- **Secure defaults** Perhaps the simplest illustration of this principle as it applies to our networks is ensuring firewalls' default configurations are to deny all traffic from any source to any destination (deny all all). However, the principle should apply throughout our network and be consistent with least privilege.
- **Fail securely** The key to applying this principle is asking two questions: What happens when this network system fails? What happens when a packet doesn't match an "allow" rule on the firewall? (Hint: it should not be allowed through.)

- **Separation of duties** Speaking of firewall (and other security appliance) rules, who is in charge of those in your organization? Any sensitive duties should be split up among vetted staff members. At a minimum, if you don't have enough staff, everybody's sensitive work should be regularly checked by someone else.
- **Keep it simple** Unless you are architecting a global network for a multinational corporation, you should try to develop an architecture that can be depicted in a single PowerPoint slide and still describe all the important components.
- **Zero trust** Services and traffic on your network should all be authenticated and encrypted. When two servers are part of a system (e.g., the web server and its backend database), they should authenticate each other and have rules around what requests each is allowed to make of the other.
- **Privacy by design** Encrypting your network traffic is a good start toward protecting privacy, but where is the data being collected and for what purpose? For example, as we prepare for auditability (see the next principle), we need to ensure that we are not casting too wide of a net in terms of the data we log.
- **Trust but verify** Everything that happens on the network should be auditable, meaning that there should be a record of who is talking with whom, when, and why. This is normally done by ensuring logs are properly configured and protected against tampering or accidental loss.
- **Shared responsibility** Odds are that your network architecture will include at least a handful of service providers. Whether these are Internet service providers, cloud service providers, or managed services providers, it is critical to agree on who has responsibility over which aspects of your network.

EXAM TIP You should be prepared to map the various secure design principles to specific scenarios.

With these principles in mind, let's look at specific ways in which we can assess and implement network architectures securely.

Secure Networking

The most prevalent networking standards and protocols we use today (Ethernet, TCP/IP, and so on) were born decades ago (before many of us). Back then, the world was kinder and gentler (at least in the digital realm) and security just wasn't the sort of thing folks thought about when it came to computers and networks. With the explosion of the Internet came immense opportunities for both the law abiding and the criminals. The need for secure networking became apparent, but it was too late. We've been trying to catch up ever since by bolting security onto insecure technologies. One of the most common ways of securing our networks is through the use of encryption, particularly in trusted tunnels through untrusted networks.

Link Encryption vs. End-to-End Encryption

In each of the networking technologies discussed in this chapter, encryption can be performed at different levels, each with different types of protection and implications. Two general modes of encryption implementation are link encryption and end-to-end encryption. *Link encryption* encrypts all the data along a specific communication path, as in a satellite link, a terrestrial T3 leased line, or even between hosts on the same LAN. Because link encryption happens at layers 1 and 2, not only is the user information encrypted, but the (layer 3 and higher) headers, trailers, addresses, and routing data that are part of the packets are also encrypted. The only traffic not encrypted in this technology is the data link control messaging information, which includes instructions and parameters that the different link devices use to synchronize communication methods. Reading this information won't give an attacker any insights into what is being transmitted or where it is ultimately going.

End-to-end encryption (E2EE) occurs at the session layer (or higher), which means the headers, addresses, routing information, and trailer information are not encrypted, enabling attackers to learn more about a captured packet and where it is headed. Transport Layer Security (TLS), which we will discuss shortly, is the most common example of E2EE. Because the routing information is sent in plaintext, attackers can perform traffic analysis to learn details about the network, such as which hosts play which roles in it.

Link encryption, which is sometimes called *online encryption*, is usually provided by service providers and is incorporated into network protocols. All of the information is encrypted, and the packets must be decrypted at each hop so the router, or other intermediate device, knows where to send the packet next. The router must decrypt the header portion of the packet, read the routing and address information within the header, and then re-encrypt it and send it on its way.

With end-to-end encryption, the packets do not need to be decrypted and then encrypted again at each hop because the headers and trailers are not encrypted. The devices in between the origin and destination just read the necessary routing information and pass the packets on their way.

End-to-end encryption is usually initiated by the user of the originating computer. It provides more flexibility for the user to be able to determine whether or not certain

Encryption at Different Layers

Encryption can (and typically does) happen at different layers of an operating system and network stack. The following are just a few examples:

- End-to-end encryption happens within the applications.
- TLS encryption takes place at the session layer.
- Point-to-Point Tunneling Protocol (PPTP) encryption takes place at the data link layer.
- Link encryption takes place at the data link and physical layers.

messages will get encrypted. It is called "end-to-end encryption" because the message stays encrypted from one end of its journey to the other. Link encryption has to decrypt the packets at every device between the two ends.

Link encryption occurs at the data link and physical layers, as depicted in Figure 13-1. Hardware encryption devices interface with the physical layer and encrypt all data that passes through them. Because no part of the data is available to an attacker, the attacker cannot learn basic information about how data flows through the environment. This is referred to as *traffic-flow security*.

NOTE A *hop* is a device that helps a packet reach its destination. It is usually a router that looks at the packet address to determine where the packet needs to go next. Packets usually go through many hops between the sending and receiving computers.

Advantages of end-to-end encryption include the following:

- It provides more flexibility to the user in choosing what gets encrypted and how.
- Higher granularity of functionality is available because each application or user can choose specific configurations.
- Each hop device on the network does not need to have a key to decrypt each packet.

The disadvantage of end-to-end encryption is the following:

- Headers, addresses, and routing information are not encrypted, and therefore not protected.

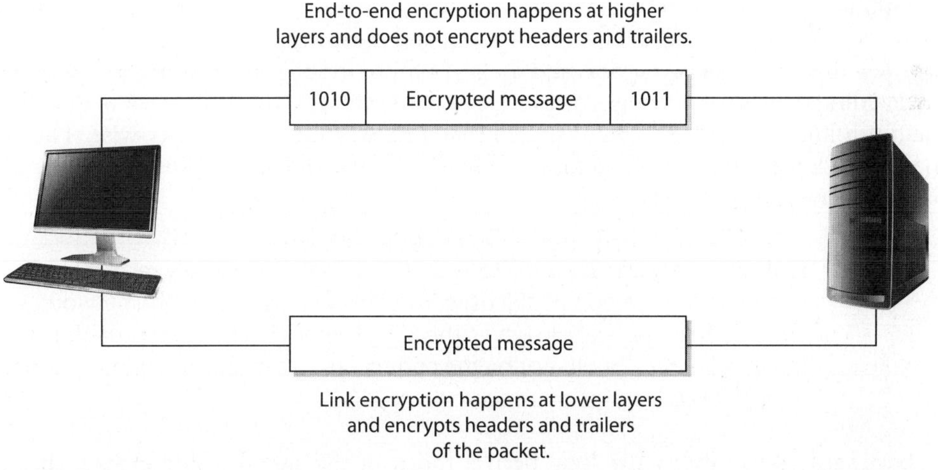
End-to-end encryption happens at higher layers and does not encrypt headers and trailers.
1010
Encrypted message
1011
Encrypted message
Link encryption happens at lower layers and encrypts headers and trailers of the packet.

Figure 13-1 Link and end-to-end encryption happen at different OSI layers.

> **Hardware vs. Software Cryptography Systems**
> Encryption can be done through software or hardware, and there are trade-offs with each. Generally, software is less expensive and provides a slower throughput than hardware mechanisms. Software cryptography methods can be more easily modified and disabled compared to hardware systems, but it depends on the application and the hardware product.
>
> If an organization needs to perform high-end encryption functions at a higher speed, it will most likely implement a hardware solution.

Advantages of link encryption include the following:

- All data is encrypted, including headers, addresses, and routing information.
- Users do not need to do anything to initiate it. It works at a lower layer in the OSI model.

Disadvantages of link encryption include the following:

- Key distribution and management are more complex because each hop device must receive a key, and when the keys change, each must be updated.
- Packets are decrypted at each hop; thus, more points of vulnerability exist.

TLS

The most prevalent form of end-to-end encryption is *Transport Layer Security (TLS)*. TLS is a security protocol that provides confidentiality and data integrity for network communications. It replaced the (now insecure) Secure Sockets Layer (SSL) standard. These two protocols coexisted for many years, and most people thought that there were very few differences between SSL and TLS (TLS is currently in version 1.3). However, the Padding Oracle On Downgraded Legacy Encryption (POODLE) attack in 2014 was the death knell of SSL and demonstrated that TLS was superior security-wise. The key to the attack was to force SSL to downgrade its security, which was allowed for the sake of interoperability.

EXAM TIP Because SSL and TLS were (for a time) very closely related, the terms are sometimes still used interchangeably to describe network encryption in general. However, the SSL protocol has been insecure for many years and should not be the correct answer to an encryption question (unless it is asking for an insecure protocol).

Backward compatibility has long been a thorn in the side of those of us trying to improve cybersecurity. TLS 1.3 represents a switch to a focus on security, which shows in the limited number of cipher suites that it supports (just five). This means attackers can no longer trick a server into using an insecure cryptosystem during the connection establishment negotiation. One of the key features of TLS 1.3 is that the handshake used to establish a new connection requires only one client message to the server and one response from the server. There's a lot that happens in there, though, so let's take a look at a summarized version of this handshake.

1. Client "Hello" message, which includes
   - A list of cipher suites and protocols supported by the client
   - Client inputs for the key exchange
2. Server "Hello" message, which includes
   - The server's selection of cipher suite and protocol version
   - Server inputs for the key exchange
3. Server authentication, which includes
   - The server's digital certificate
   - Proof that the server owns the certificate's private key
4. (Optionally) Client authentication, which includes
   - The client's digital certificate
   - Proof that the client owns the certificate's private key

NOTE While TLS 1.3 minimizes the plaintext information transferred between hosts, TLS 1.2 (and earlier) passes a lot more information in the clear, potentially including the server name (e.g., www.goodsite.com).

As mentioned, TLS 1.3 has dramatically reduced the number of recommended cipher suites from 37 (in previous versions) to just five. This is an important improvement because some of those 37 suites were known (or suspected) to be vulnerable to cryptanalysis. By reducing the suites to five and ensuring these provide strong protection, TLS 1.3 makes it harder for attackers to downgrade the security of a system by forcing a server to use a weaker suite. The allowed suites in the latest version of TLS are as follows:

- **TLS_AES_256_GCM_SHA384** The encryption algorithm here is AES with a 256-bit key in Galois/Counter Mode (GCM). GCM is a mode of operation that provides message authentication. The hashing algorithm is SHA-384. This suite provides the best protection but requires the most computing resources.
- **TLS_AES_128_GCM_SHA256** This suite is almost identical to the preceding one, but saves on resources by using a smaller 128-bit key for encryption and a slightly faster SHA-256 for hashing. It is ideally suited for systems with hardware support for encryption.
- **TLS_AES_128_CCM_SHA256** In this suite, AES (again, with a 128-bit key) runs in Counter mode with CBC-MAC (CCM), which uses 16-byte tags to provide message authentication (much like GCM does).

- **TLS_AES_128_CCM_8_SHA256** This suite is almost identical to the preceding one, but Counter mode with CBC-MAC uses 8-byte tags (instead of 16-byte ones), which makes it better suited for embedded devices.
- **TLS_CHACHA20_POLY1305_SHA256** The ChaCha stream cipher (doing 20 rounds), combined with the Poly1305 message authentication code (MAC), is a cipher suite that is a good choice for software-based encryption systems. Many modern systems rely on hardware-based encryption, so the authors of TLS 1.3 wanted to ensure the recommended suites supported multiple devices. Besides, it just makes sense to have at least one encryption algorithm that is not AES.

We already discussed AES (and briefly mentioned ChaCha20) in Chapter 8, and CCM in Chapter 12, but this is the first time we bring up GCM and Poly1305. These are approaches to provide authenticated symmetric key encryption. *Authenticated encryption (AE)* provides assurances that a message was not modified in transit and could only come from a sender who knows the secret key. This is similar to the MAC approach discussed in Chapter 8 but is applied to stream ciphers. TLS 1.3 takes the AE concept to the next level in what is known as *authenticated encryption with additional data (AEAD).* AEAD essentially computes the MAC over both ciphertext and plaintext when these are sent together. For example, when sending network traffic, there are certain fields (e.g., source and destination addresses) that cannot be encrypted. An attacker could replay an encrypted message later using a different packet, but if we're using AEAD (as TLS 1.3 requires), this bogus packet would automatically be discarded.

Another key feature of TLS 1.3 (which was optional in TLS 1.2 and prior) is its use of *ephemeral keys*, which are only used for one communication session and then discarded, using the Diffie-Hellman Ephemeral (DHE) algorithm. This provides *forward secrecy* (sometimes called *perfect forward secrecy*), which means that if attackers were somehow able to crack or otherwise obtain the secret key, it would only give them the ability to decrypt a small portion of the ciphertext. They wouldn't be able to decrypt everything going forward.

Attackers Use TLS Too!

While TLS is often our first line of defense in protecting our network traffic from prying eyes, attackers use it too, precisely for the same reason. There are many known examples of malware using TLS. Banking Trojans, such as TrickBot, Emotet, and Dyre, make use of TLS to communicate data back to their master server. Ransomware families, such as Jigsaw, Locky, and Petya, have also used TLS to infect machines and transfer information. They way in which attackers use TLS, however, is usually quite different from how it is used in legitimate connections. Analyzing network traffic can often point out some of these differences, such as:

- Offering weak or obsolete cipher suites
- Rarely offering more than one extension (enterprise clients use up to nine)
- Using self-signed certificates

While we focused on TLS 1.3 in this section, it is worth noting that, as of this writing, the Internet Society reports that only 58 percent of the world's top 1,000 websites support this latest version. What does this mean to you? You should balance the enhanced security of this protocol with the needs of your stakeholders. If you are not on TLS 1.3 yet, you may want to ask what percentage of your user base would not be able to communicate securely if you switched. All major browsers support it, so odds are that you'd be in good shape. But even if you're still on TLS 1.2, keep in mind that most of the features described in this section that make 1.3 so much better are optional in the previous version. This should give you a path to gradually improve your security while taking care of your stakeholders. Whatever your situation, TLS is probably the most important encryption technology for securing our networks, particularly our virtual private ones.

NOTE TLS 1.0 and TLS 1.1 were never formally deprecated but are widely considered insecure.

VPN

A *virtual private network (VPN)* is a secure, private connection through an untrusted network, as shown in Figure 13-2. It is a private connection because the encryption and tunneling protocols are used to ensure the confidentiality and integrity of the data in transit. It is important to remember that VPN technology requires a tunnel to work and it assumes encryption.

We need VPNs because we send so much confidential information from system to system and network to network. The information can be credentials, bank account data, Social Security numbers, medical information, or any other type of data we do not want to share with the world. The demand for securing data transfers has increased over the years, and as our networks have increased in complexity, so have our VPN solutions.

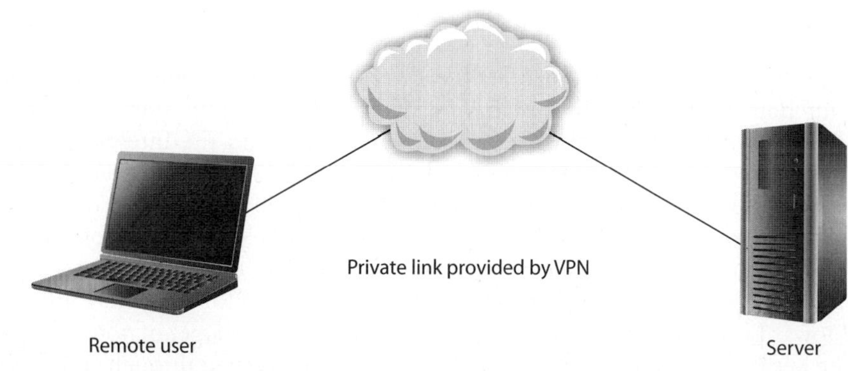

Figure 13-2 A VPN provides a virtual dedicated link between two entities across a public network.

PART IV

Point-to-Point Tunneling Protocol

One of the early approaches to building VPNs was Microsoft's *Point-to-Point Tunneling Protocol (PPTP)*, which uses Generic Routing Encapsulation (GRE) and TCP to encapsulate Point-to-Point Protocol (PPP) connections and extend them through an IP network (running on TCP port 1723, by default). Since most Internet-based communication first started over telecommunication links, the industry needed a way to secure PPP connections, which were prevalent back then. The original goal of PPTP was to provide a way to tunnel PPP connections through an IP network, but most implementations included security features also since protection was becoming an important requirement for network transmissions at that time. PPTP, like many security protocols, did not age well and is now considered insecure and obsolete.

Layer 2 Tunneling Protocol

The *Layer 2 Tunneling Protocol (L2TP)*, currently in version 3, is a combination of Cisco's *Layer 2 Forwarding (L2F)* protocol and Microsoft's PPTP. L2TP tunnels PPP traffic over various network types (IP, ATM, X.25, etc.); thus, it is not just restricted to IP networks as PPTP was. PPTP and L2TP have very similar focuses, which is to get PPP traffic to an end point that is connected to some type of network that does not understand PPP. Unlike PPTP, L2TP runs on UDP (default port 1701), which makes it a bit more efficient. However, just like PPTP, L2TP does not actually provide much protection for the PPP traffic it is moving around, but it integrates with protocols that *do* provide security features. L2TP inherits PPP authentication and integrates with IPSec to provide confidentiality, integrity, and potentially another layer of authentication.

It can get confusing when several protocols are involved with various levels of encapsulation, but if you do not understand how they work together, you cannot identify if certain traffic links lack security. To figure out if you understand how these protocols work together and why, ask yourself these questions:

1. If the Internet is an IP-based network, why do we even need PPP?
2. If L2TP does not actually secure data, then why does it even exist?
3. If a connection is using IP, PPP, and L2TP, where does IPSec come into play?

Let's go through the answers together. Let's say that you are a remote user and work from your home office. You do not have a dedicated link from your house to your company's network; instead, your traffic needs to go through the Internet to be able to communicate with the corporate network. The line between your house and your ISP is a point-to-point telecommunications link, one point being your home router and the other point being the ISP's switch, as shown in Figure 13-3. Point-to-point telecommunication devices do not understand IP, so your router has to encapsulate your traffic in a protocol the ISP's device will understand—PPP. Now your traffic is not headed toward some website on the Internet; instead, it has a target of your company's corporate network. This means that your traffic has to be "carried through" the Internet to its ultimate destination through a tunnel. The Internet does not understand PPP, so your PPP traffic has to be encapsulated with a protocol that can work on the Internet and create the needed tunnel.

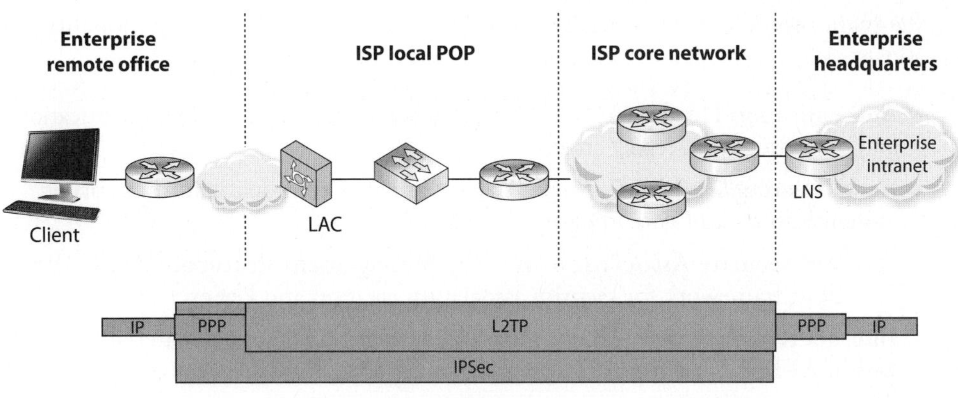

Figure 13-3 IP, PPP, L2TP, and IPSec can work together.

So your IP packets are wrapped up in PPP, and are then wrapped up in L2TP. But you still have no encryption involved, so your data is actually not protected. This is where IPSec comes in. IPSec is used to encrypt the data that will pass through the L2TP tunnel. Once your traffic gets to the corporate network's perimeter device, it will decrypt the packets, take off the L2TP and PPP headers, add the necessary Ethernet headers, and send these packets to their ultimate destination.

Here are the answers to our questions:

1. If the Internet is an IP-based network, why do we even need PPP?
   Answer: The point-to-point line devices that connect individual systems to the Internet do not understand IP, so the traffic that travels over these links has to be encapsulated in PPP.
2. If L2TP does not actually secure data, then why does it even exist?
   Answer: It extends PPP connections by providing a tunnel through networks that do not understand PPP.
3. If a connection is using IP, PPP, and L2TP, where does IPSec come into play?
   Answer: IPSec provides the encryption, data integrity, and system-based authentication.

Here is another question: Does all of this PPP, L2TP, and IPSec encapsulation have to happen for every single VPN used on the Internet? No, only when connections over point-to-point connections are involved. When two gateway routers are connected over the Internet and provide VPN functionality, they only have to use IPSec.

Internet Protocol Security

Internet Protocol Security (IPSec) is a suite of protocols that was developed to specifically protect IP traffic. IPv4 does not have any integrated security, so IPSec was developed to "bolt onto" IP and secure the data the protocol transmits. Where L2TP works at the data link layer, IPSec works at the network layer of the OSI model.

The main protocols that make up the IPSec suite and their basic functionality are as follows:

- **Authentication Header (AH)** Provides data integrity, data-origin authentication, and protection from replay attacks
- **Encapsulating Security Payload (ESP)** Provides confidentiality, data-origin authentication, and data integrity
- **Internet Security Association and Key Management Protocol (ISAKMP)** Provides a framework for security association creation and key exchange
- **Internet Key Exchange (IKE)** Provides authenticated keying material for use with ISAKMP

AH and ESP can be used separately or together in an IPSec VPN configuration. The AH protocols can provide data-origin authentication (system authentication) and protection from unauthorized modification, but do not provide encryption capabilities. If the VPN needs to provide confidentiality, then ESP has to be enabled and configured properly.

When two routers need to set up an IPSec VPN connection, they have a list of security attributes that need to be agreed upon through handshaking processes. The two routers have to agree upon algorithms, keying material, protocol types, and modes of use, which will all be used to protect the data that is transmitted between them.

Let's say that you and Juan are routers that need to protect the data you will pass back and forth to each other. Juan sends you a list of items that you will use to process the packets he sends to you. His list contains AES-128, SHA-1, and ESP tunnel mode. You take these parameters and store them in a security association (SA). When Juan sends you packets one hour later, you will go to this SA and follow these parameters so that you know how to process this traffic. You know what algorithm to use to verify the integrity of the packets, the algorithm to use to decrypt the packets, and which protocol to activate and in what mode. Figure 13-4 illustrates how SAs are used for inbound and outbound traffic.

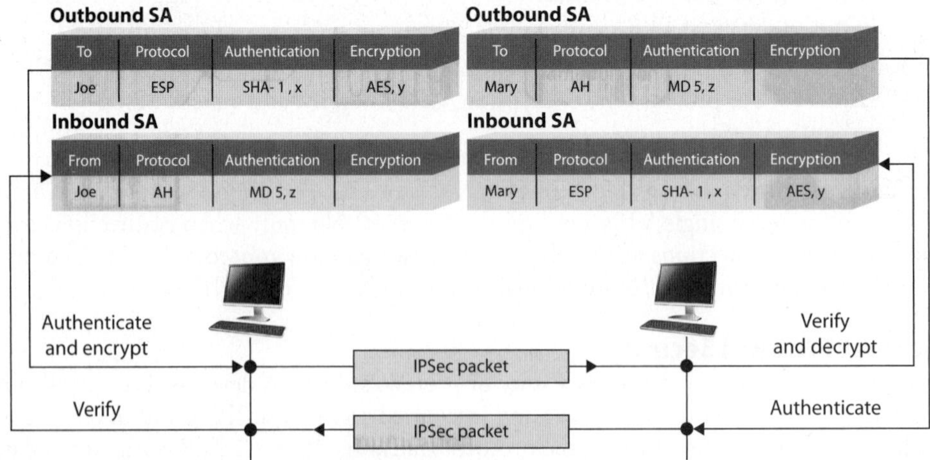

Figure 13-4 IPSec uses security associations to store VPN parameters.

NOTE The U.S. National Security Agency (NSA) uses a protocol encryptor that is based upon IPSec. A *HAIPE (High Assurance Internet Protocol Encryptor)* is a Type 1 encryption device that is based on IPSec with additional restrictions, enhancements, and capabilities. A HAIPE is typically a secure gateway that allows two enclaves to exchange data over an untrusted or lower-classification network. Since this technology works at the network layer, secure end-to-end connectivity can take place in heterogeneous environments. This technology has largely replaced link layer encryption technology implementations.

IPSec

IPSec can be configured to provide *transport adjacency*, which just means that more than one security protocol (ESP and AH) is used in a VPN tunnel. IPSec can also be configured to provide *iterated tunneling*, in which an IPSec tunnel is tunneled through another IPSec tunnel, as shown in the following diagram. Iterated tunneling would be used if the traffic needed different levels of protection at different junctions of its path. For example, if the IPSec tunnel started from an internal host and terminated at an internal border router, this may not require encryption, so only the AH protocol would be used. But when that data travels from that border router throughout the Internet to another network, then the data requires more protection. So the first packets travel through a semisecure tunnel until they get ready to hit the Internet and then they go through a very secure second tunnel.

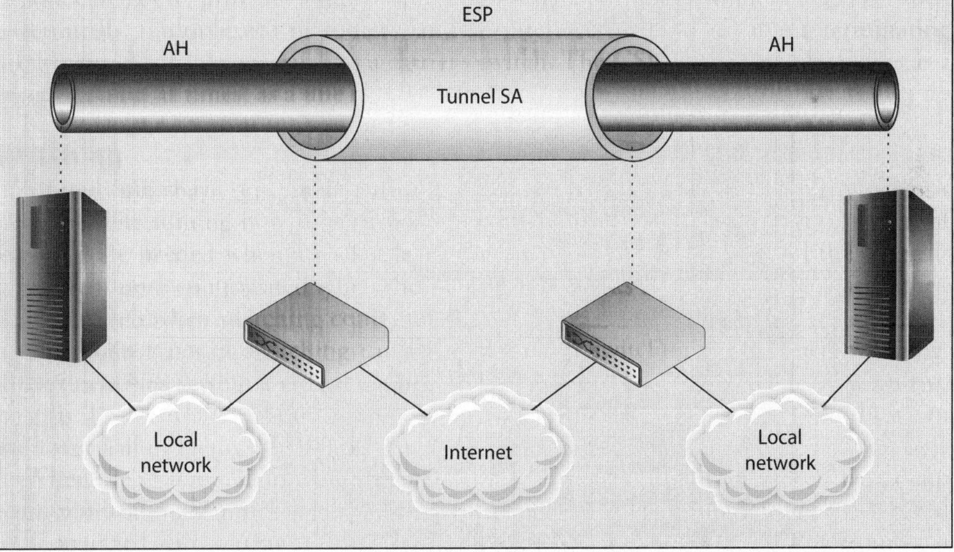

The most common implementation types of TLS VPN are as follows:

- **TLS portal VPN** An individual uses a single standard TLS connection to a website to securely access multiple network services. The website accessed is typically called a *portal* because it is a single location that provides access to other resources. The remote user accesses the TLS VPN gateway using a web browser, is authenticated, and is then presented with a web page that acts as the portal to the other services.
- **TLS tunnel VPN** An individual uses a web browser to securely access multiple network services, including applications and protocols that are not web-based, through a TLS tunnel. This commonly requires custom programming to allow the services to be accessible through a web-based connection.

Summary of Tunneling Protocols

Layer 2 Tunneling Protocol (L2TP):

- Hybrid of L2F and PPTP
- Extends and protects PPP connections
- Works at the data link layer
- Transmits over multiple types of networks, not just IP
- Combined with IPSec for security

IPSec:

- Handles multiple VPN connections at the same time
- Provides secure authentication and encryption
- Supports only IP networks
- Focuses on LAN-to-LAN communication rather than user-to-user communication
- Works at the network layer and provides security on top of IP

Transport Layer Security (TLS):

- Works at the session layer and protects mainly web and e-mail traffic
- Offers granular access control and configuration
- Easy to deploy since TLS is already embedded into web browsers
- Can only protect a small number of protocol types, thus is not an infrastructure-level VPN solution

Since TLS VPNs are closer to the application layer, they can provide more granular access control and security features compared to the other VPN solutions. But since they are dependent on the application layer protocol, there are a smaller number of traffic types that can be protected through this VPN type.

One VPN solution is not necessarily better than the other; they just have their own focused purposes:

- L2TP is used when a PPP connection needs to be extended through a network.
- IPSec is used to protect IP-based traffic and is commonly used in gateway-to-gateway connections.
- TLS VPN is used when a specific application layer traffic type needs protection.

Secure Protocols

TLS may be one of the most talked-about technologies when it comes to network security. Still, there are other protocols, and other applications of TLS, that you should know. This section addresses each of the main network services, web, DNS, and e-mail. Let's start with how we secure web services.

Web Services

Many people hear the term "web services" and think of websites and the web servers that do the work behind the scenes. In reality, however, this is but a portion of what the term actually covers. A *web service* is a client/server system in which clients and servers communicate using HTTP over a network such as the Internet. Sure, this definition covers static web pages written in HTML being served out of an old Apache server somewhere, but it can also cover much more.

For example, suppose you are a retailer and don't want to pay for a huge storage space for merchandise that may or may not sell anytime soon. You could implement a just-in-time logistics system that keeps track of your inventory and past selling patterns, and then automatically order merchandise so that it arrives just before you start running low. This kind of system is typically implemented using a business-to-business (B2B) web service and is depicted in Figure 13-5. Each icon in the figure represents a distinct web service component.

When we look at web services this way, it becomes clear that we have much more to worry about than simply the interaction between customers and our website. Let's look at ways in which we could implement some of the secure design principles in this example. The following list is meant to be illustrative, not all-inclusive:

- **Least privilege** The forecasting service should have read-only access to some of the data in the inventory system. It doesn't need any additional access.
- **Secure defaults** The inventory service should refuse all connection requests from any endpoint other than those explicitly authorized (point of sale and forecasting). If any other connections are required, those should be added as exceptions after a careful review.

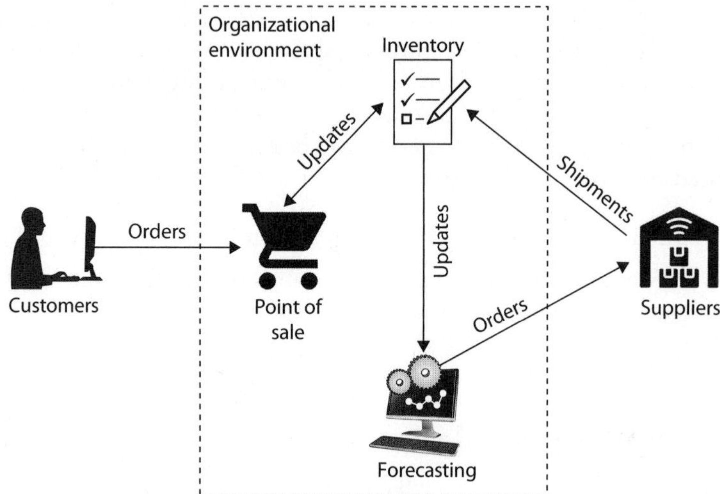

Figure 13-5 Example just-in-time logistics B2B web service

- **Fail securely** The forecasting service has the ability to spend money by placing orders from suppliers. It should not process any order that is malformed or otherwise fails any checks.
- **Separation of duties** The forecasting service can place orders but cannot receive shipments and update inventory. Ordering and receiving should be two separate duties performed by different people/systems to mitigate the risk of fraud.
- **Zero trust** Before any two components collaborate, they should both be required to authenticate with each other and encrypt all communications. This is particularly true (and the authentication protocol should be more rigorous) when dealing with external parties like customers and suppliers.
- **Privacy by design** Customer information should not be shared outside the point-of-sale (PoS) system, particularly since the other two internal systems (inventory and forecasting) communicate with an external third party. This example is overly simplistic, but the point is that customer data should be limited to the components that absolutely need it.
- **Trust but verify** All components (with the possible exception of the user) should generate logs that are sufficient to detect attacks or errors. Ideally, these logs are centrally collected to make them easier to correlate and harder to tamper with.
- **Shared responsibility** The security obligations of the organization and of the supplier should be codified in a legally binding contract and audited periodically.

Again, the list is not exhaustive, but it should give you an idea of how the secure design principles can be applied to a web services scenario. You should be prepared to do likewise with a variety of other scenarios for the CISSP exam.

How are these web services actually delivered? The key is to focus on *what* service is being delivered, and not on *how* it is implemented or *where* it is hosted (as long as it is available). A *service-oriented architecture (SOA)* describes a system as a set of interconnected but self-contained components that communicate with each other and with their clients through standardized protocols. These protocols, called *application programming interfaces (APIs)*, establish a "language" that enables a component to make a request from another component and then interpret that second component's response. The requests that are defined by these APIs correspond to discrete business functions (such as estimated shipping costs to a postal code) that can be useful by themselves or can be assembled into more complex business processes. An SOA has three key characteristics: self-contained components, a standardized protocol (API) for requests/responses, and components that implement business functions.

SOAs are commonly built using web services standards that rely on HTTP as a standard communication protocol. Examples of these are SOAP (which used to stand for the Simple Object Access Protocol) and the Representational State Transfer (REST) architectures. Let's look at these three (HTTP, SOAP and REST) in turn.

Hypertext Transfer Protocol

HTTP is a TCP/IP-based communications protocol used for transferring resources (e.g., HTML files and images) between a server and a client. It also allows clients to send queries to the server. The two basic features of HTTP are that it is connectionless and stateless. Connectionless protocols do not set up a connection (obviously) and instead send their messages in a best-effort manner. They rely on some other protocol (in this case TCP) to ensure the message gets across. *Stateless* means that the server is amnesiac; it doesn't remember any previous conversations with any clients. Thus, whatever is needed for the server to "remember" has to be provided with each request. This is a role commonly played by session identifiers and cookies.

NOTE A cookie is just a small text file containing information that only one website can write or read.

Uniform Resource Identifiers A foundational component of HTTP is the use of the uniform resource identifier (URI), which uniquely identifies a resource on the Internet. A typical URI looks like this: http://www.goodsite.com:8080/us/en/resources/search.php?term=cissp. Let's look at its components in sequence:

1. **Scheme** This is another name for the protocol being used (e.g., HTTP or HTTPS) and ends in a colon (:).
2. **Authority** There are three possible subcomponents here, but the second is the most prevalent:
   - Username (optional) (and optional password, separated by a colon) followed by an at (@) symbol.
   - Host in either hostname (e.g., www.goodsite.com) or IP address format.
   - Port number (optional), preceded by a colon (e.g., :8080). Note that port 80 is assumed for HTTP schemes and port 443 for HTTPS schemes.

3. **Path** The path to the requested resource on the server. If the path is not specified by the client, it is assumed to be a single slash (/), which is the default document at the root of the website (e.g., the homepage). Subdirectories are indicated as they are in Linux/Unix by successive slashes (e.g., /us/en/resources/search.php).
4. **Query (optional)** An attribute-value pair preceded by a question mark (?) (e.g., ?term=cissp). Each additional pair is separated from the previous one by an ampersand (&).

Request Methods HTTP uses a request-response model in which the client requests one or more resources from the server, and the latter provides the requested resources (assuming, of course, they are available to the client). The protocol defines two request methods: GET and POST. The main difference for our discussion is that a GET request must include all parameters in the URI, while POST allows us to include additional information (e.g., parameters) in the body of the request, where it will not be revealed in the URI. So, in the previous example we can safely guess that the method used was GET because we see the search term (cissp) in the URI.

Hypertext Transfer Protocol Secure *HTTP Secure (HTTPS)* is HTTP running over Transport Layer Security (TLS). Ensuring that all your web services require HTTPS is probably the most important security control you can apply to them. Recall that unencrypted requests can provide an awful lot of sensitive data, including credentials, session IDs, and URIs. Ideally, you require TLS 1.3 on all your web servers and ensure they do not allow unencrypted communications (by enforcing secure defaults).

An important consideration before you jump to HTTPS everywhere is whether you want to perform deep packet analysis on all your internal traffic. If you force use of HTTPS, you will need to deploy TLS decryption proxies, which can be pricey and require careful configuration on all your endpoints. The way these proxies work is by performing what is essentially a (benign) man-in-the-middle attack in which they terminate the clients' secure sessions and establish the follow-on session to their intended server. This allows the proxy to monitor all HTTPS traffic, which provides a measure of defense in depth but may pose some challenges to the privacy by design principle. Many organizations deal with this challenge by whitelisting connections to certain types of servers (e.g., healthcare and financial services organizations), while intercepting all others.

SOAP

SOAP is a messaging protocol that uses XML over HTTP to enable clients to invoke processes on a remote host in a platform-agnostic way. SOAP was one of the first SOAs to become widely adopted. SOAP consists of three main components:

- A message envelope that defines the messages that are allowed and how they are to be processed by the recipient
- A set of encoding rules used to define data types
- Conventions regarding what remote procedures can be called and how to interpret their responses

Extensible Markup Language

The term XML keeps coming up for good reasons. Extensible Markup Language is a popular language to use if you want to mark up parts of a text document. If you've ever looked at raw HTML documents, you probably noticed the use of tags such as <title>CISSP</title> to mark up the beginning and end of a page's title. These tags enable both humans and machines to interpret text and process it (such as rendering it in a web browser) as the author intended. Similarly, XML enables the author of a text document to "explain" to a receiving computer what each part of the file means so that a receiving process knows what to do with it. Before XML, there was no standard way to do this, but nowadays there are a number of options, including JavaScript Object Notation (JSON) and YAML Ain't Markup Language (YAML).

SOAP security is enabled by a set of protocol extensions called the Web Services Security (WS-Security or WSS) specification, which provides message confidentiality, integrity, and authentication. Note that, in keeping with HTTP's stateless nature, the focus here is on message-level security. Confidentiality is provided through XML encryption, integrity through XML digital signatures, and single-message authentication through security tokens. These tokens can take on various forms (the specification is intentionally broad here), which include username tokens, X.509 digital certificates, SAML assertions, and Kerberos tickets (we'll cover the last two in Chapter 17).

One of the key features of SOAP is that the message envelope allows the requester to describe the actions that it expects from the various nodes that respond. This feature supports options such as routing tables that specify the sequence and manner in which a series of SOAP nodes will take action on a given message. This can make it possible to finely control access as well as efficiently recover from failures along the way. This richness of features, however, comes at a cost: SOAP is not as simple as its name implies. In fact, SOAP systems tend to be fairly complex and cumbersome, which is why many web service developers prefer more lightweight options like REST.

Representational State Transfer

Unlike SOAP, which is a messaging protocol, Representational State Transfer (REST) is an architectural pattern used to develop web services using a variety of languages. In REST, HTTP is used to provide an API that allows clients to make programmatic requests from servers. For example, a client of a RESTful service could insert a new user record using the HTTP POST method (which lets you send additional information in the body of the request) by sending the following URI: https://www.goodsite.com/UserService/Add/1. The server would know to read the body of the POST to get the new user's details, create it, and then send a HTTP confirmation (or error). As you can see, REST essentially creates a programming language in which every statement is an HTTP URI.

Because every interaction with the system is spelled out in the URI, it is essential to use HTTPS as a secure default communications protocol. Of course, in keeping with the principle of zero trust, we want to authenticate clients and servers to each other, as well as put limits on what resources are available to each client. Another good security practice for RESTful services, which applies to any software system, is to validate all inputs before processing them. This mitigates a large number of possible injection attacks in which the adversary deliberately provides malformed inputs in order to trigger a system flaw.

Domain Name System

We covered the Domain Name System (DNS) in a fair amount of detail back in Chapter 11. Let's return to it now in the context of its role in helping us to secure our networks. Early on in its history, DNS was most commonly targeted by attackers to hijack requests, redirecting the unwitting requesters to malicious hosts instead of the legitimate ones they were seeking. While this is still a concern that we'll address in a bit, we also have to consider the much more common use of DNS to assist threat actors in conducting attacks, rather than being the target of attacks.

Since some of the most problematic adversarial uses of DNS depend on how this system works, let's review the process by which DNS performs recursive queries. Recall from Chapter 11 that a *recursive query* means that the request can be passed on from one DNS server to another one until the DNS server with the correct information is identified. This is illustrated in Figure 13-6. First, the client queries its local DNS server, which may either be an authoritative source for it or have cached it after some other client's request. Failing that, the server will typically start by consulting the root DNS server. The root server (there are actually a few of them for redundancy) will probably say something like "No, but here is the address of the name server for all .com domains." The local server will then query that server, which will probably result in it responding "No, but here is the address of the name server responsible for ironnet.com." Finally, the local server will query that other server, which will respond with an A record containing the IP address of the www host.

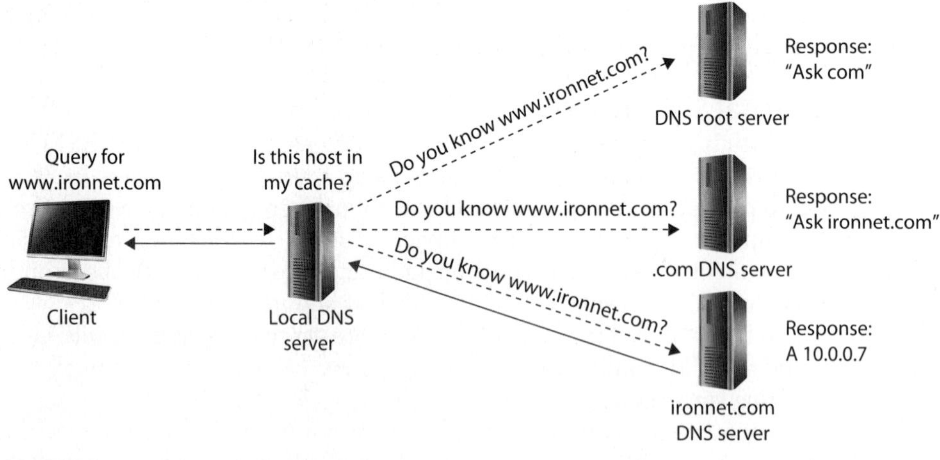

Figure 13-6 A recursive DNS query

Preventing Common DNS Attacks

DNS is the Internet's ubiquitous messenger; its queries and responses go everywhere, and without them the Internet as we know it would not work. Because of its importance to most other network systems, DNS traffic is seldom blocked by firewalls or routers. Attackers quickly figured out that this ubiquity makes DNS a preferred tool to manipulate and use for their own nefarious purposes. Perhaps the cleverest application of DNS for unintended purposes is its use to reach out and touch hosts in ways that are difficult to block using pseudo-randomly generated domain names.

EXAM TIP You will not be tested on the material that covers the following DNS attacks, but note that these attacks are both important to know and illustrative of the challenges we face in securing networks. If you are preparing for the exam only, feel free to move to the "Domain Name System Security Extensions" section.

Domain Generation Algorithms Once malware is implanted on target systems, the adversaries still need to communicate with those hosts. Since inbound connection attempts would easily be blocked at the firewall, most malware initiates outbound connections to the attacker's command and control (C2) infrastructure instead. The problem for the attackers is that if they provide a hostname or IP address in the malware, defenders will eventually find it, share it as an indicator of compromise (IOC), and reduce or negate the effectiveness of the C2 system.

To bypass signature detection by intrusion detection systems (IDSs) and intrusion prevention systems (IPSs) that use these IOCs, malware authors developed algorithms that can generate different domain names in a manner that appears random but produces a predictable sequence of domain names for those who know the algorithm. Suppose I am an attacker and want to hide my real C2 domains to keep them from being blocked or removed. I develop a domain generation algorithm (DGA) that produces a new (seemingly) random domain name each time it is run. Sprinkled somewhere in that (very long) list of domains are the ones I actually want to use. The infected host then attempts to resolve each domain to its corresponding IP address using DNS. Most of the domains do not exist and others may be benign, so either way there is no malicious C2 communications that follow. However, since I know the sequence of domains generated by the DGA and I know how quickly the malware will generate them, I can determine approximately when a particular infected host will query a specific domain. I can then register it the day before and rendezvous with the malware on that domain so I can receive its report and/or issue commands. The defenders won't know which domains are my malicious ones and which are just noise meant to distract them.

Figure 13-7 shows three domains being generated by an infected host. The first two that are queried do not exist, and thus result in an NXDOMAIN response from the server, which means the domain was not found. The third domain resolves to a malicious domain. When the authoritative (malicious) server for that domain receives the request, it knows it comes from a compromised system and sends a response that, when decoded, means "sleep for 7 hours."

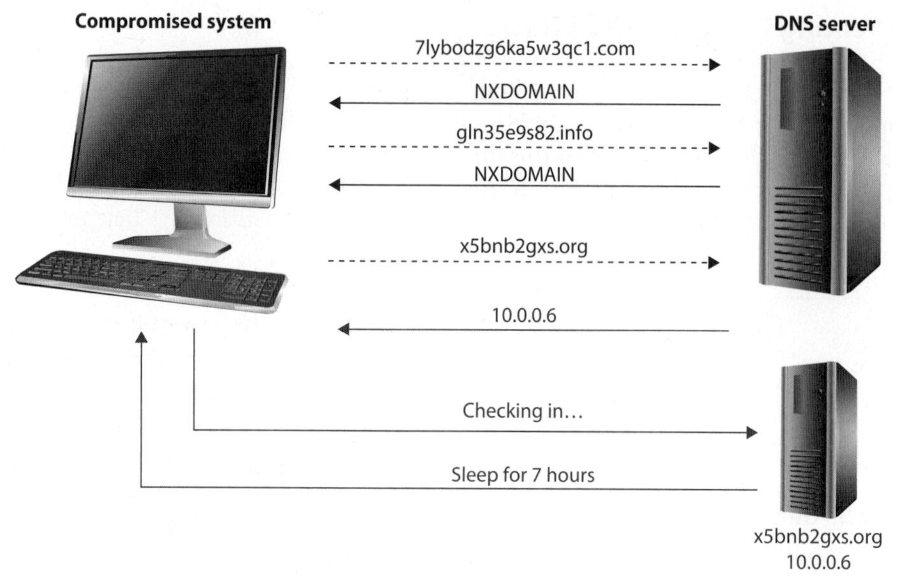

Figure 13-7 DGA in use by a compromised system

How can we detect and stop this kind of adversarial behavior? There are two general approaches. The first is to capture the malware and reverse engineer its DGA. We then play it forward (just like the attacker does) to determine which domains will be generated and when. Knowing this timeline, you can blacklist the domains and use the fact that a host attempted to reach them to infer that the querying system is compromised. Keep in mind that different compromised systems will be generating domain names at different times, so the task is onerous even for organizations that are mature enough to reverse engineer malware in the first place.

The second approach to detecting and stopping the use of DGAs is to analyze the domain names in each query to determine the probability of the query being legitimate. You can see from Figure 13-7 that most domains generated by these algorithms look, well, random. They are not the sort of domain names that you would expect someone to pay money to register. If you find a domain that is highly suspicious, you can investigate the host to see if it is infected, or you could block or monitor the DNS query and response to see if there is anything suspicious in either. For example, in some cases, the response will come as an encoded or encrypted message in a TXT record. This approach is only practical if you have a fairly sophisticated artificial intelligence analysis system that can examine every DNS request and learn over time which ones are likely to be bad.

NOTE There are legitimate uses of DGAs. For example, some systems use them to test whether or not a system can reach the Internet and perhaps track who that system is. This is done by some developers for licensing, updating, or diagnostic purposes.

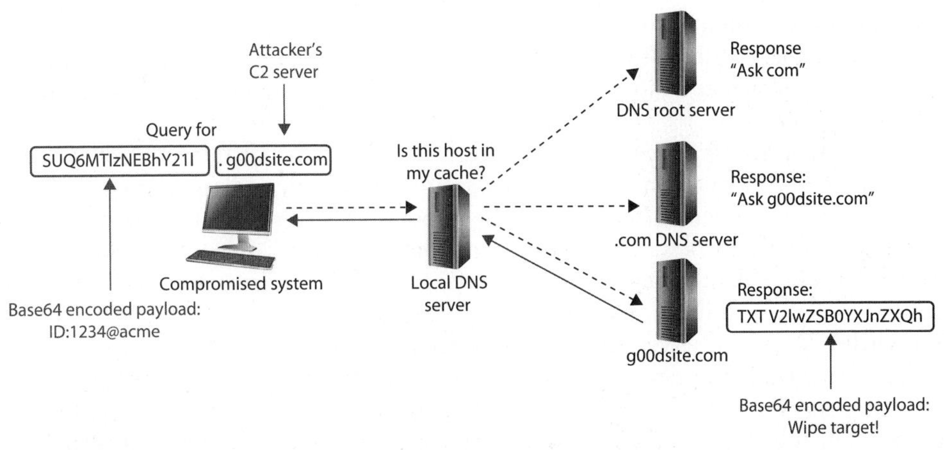

Figure 13-8 Covert communication over a DNS tunnel

DNS Tunneling Malicious use of a DGA can be very hard to stop unless you have advanced capabilities at your disposal. Fortunately, however, this use is limited to simple messaging between a compromised host and an external threat actor. But what if we could use DNS to transfer more information? A lot more? It turns out that data can be hidden in DNS queries using encoded host and other resource labels. *DNS tunneling* is the practice of encoding messages in one or a series of DNS queries or responses for exfiltrating or infiltrating data into an environment.

Figure 13-8 shows a very simple example of DNS tunneling that builds on our discussion of recursive queries in Figure 13-6. In this case, the compromised system wants to check in with its C2 server, so it uses Base64 encoding to obfuscate its message, which contains its identifier. Let's say that this is an infected host in the Acme Corporation, so its ID is 1234@acme. The recursive DNS query eventually is sent to the server that owns the malicious domain g00dsite.com. It decodes the hostname field, sees which of its bots this is from, and decides it is time to wipe the file system on the infected system. This command comes in the form of a TXT response that is also Base64 encoded.

A similar, but much less noticeable, use of DNS tunneling is to slowly exfiltrate data from the compromised system. Since DNS allows names of up to 63 characters between each dot, attackers can break down a longer file (e.g., a secret document) and exfiltrate it in a sequence of DNS queries to the same server or different servers.

Defending against DNS tunneling is similarly difficult to countering DGAs. Again, we could use network detection and response (NDR) solutions that use artificial intelligence to look for this type of behavior. However, because this type of attack (unlike DGAs) tends to rely on just a few domains, we could use domain reputation tools to determine whether any of our systems are making queries for suspicious or malicious domains.

Distributed Denial of Service The third type of DNS attack targets someone else's infrastructure using your DNS servers. An attacker who owns (or can rent) a large army of compromised systems (bots) can use them to overwhelm a target with name resolution responses to queries it didn't send out in the first place. To see how this attack works, we must first consider that DNS is based on UDP, which means spoofing the source address of a query is trivial.

In a *DNS reflection attack*, the threat actor instructs each bot they control to send a query to one of many open DNS servers around the world, while spoofing the source addresses on those queries. Collectively, the responding servers then bombard the target with traffic. If you have a sufficient number of bots and servers doing this quickly enough, the results could take the target system offline. Even if the target is not a DNS server, it still has to process millions (or more) of UDP packets arriving each second, which can overwhelm the typical server. But what if we could amplify the effects?

A *DNS amplification attack* is characterized by small queries that result in very much larger responses. A typical query is about 30 bytes and its response is around 45 bytes on average. The following are three techniques that are used to turn this relatively equal ratio of query to response size by a factor of up to 50 times:

- **DNS ANY** DNS has a (deprecated in 2019, but still used) diagnostic feature that allows a client to request all the information a server has on a given domain name. By sending a query of type ANY, an attacker can cause the server to send all the records in that domain up to the maximum size of a DNS message, which is 512 bytes. Having a 30-byte query produce a 512-byte response is a 17× amplification.
- **EDNS(0)** There are several situations in which the 512-byte limit on DNS messages over UDP becomes problematic. In particular, it is not possible to implement DNS Security Extensions (DNSSEC) with this constraint. Therefore, the Internet Engineering Task Force (IETF) developed EDNS(0), the Extension Mechanisms for DNS, which allows for up to 4096-byte responses. Properly used by an attacker, this new maximum size represents a 136× amplification given a 30-byte query.
- **DNSSEC** One of the most practical ways to exploit the maximum size defined in EDNS(0) is, ironically, using DNSSEC. Going back to Figure 13-6, when the local DNS server requests the A record from the authoritative server for that domain (the bottom left one), it also requests the DNSSEC associated with the zone. This is done to ensure the identity of the authoritative server (and hence the response) but results in a significantly larger response (because it includes a digital signature). So, all an attacker needs to do is find open DNS servers that have DNSSEC enabled and direct the bots at them.

Domain Name System Security Extensions

DNSSEC is a set of standards IETF developed to protect DNS from a variety of attacks. Specifically, DNSSEC is focused on ensuring the integrity of DNS records, not their confidentiality or availability. In plain-old DNS, a client makes a recursive query that, eventually, is responded to by some server that claims to be authoritative and provides an IP address. As we discussed in Chapter 11, however, this led to impersonation attacks where unwitting clients were pointed to malicious hosts. In response to this threat, the IETF came up with DNSSEC.

DNSSEC works by grouping records in a DNS zone according to their name and type (e.g., A, NS, MAIL) into Resource Record Sets (RRSets) that are then digitally signed, with the resulting signature going into a resource record signature (RRSig) record. The corresponding public key is published in a DNSKey record. So, when we want to resolve a fully qualified domain name (FQDN) using DNSSEC, we first retrieve the RRSet containing the name, then we request the RRSig for that set, and finally we verify that the record has not been tampered with. While this approach prevents impersonation and cache poisoning attacks, it has, as we just saw, also opened the door to crippling amplification attacks.

DNS over HTTPS

While DNSSEC ensures the integrity of DNS data, it does nothing to protect the confidentiality or privacy of queries. Sure, you can be confident that the IP address you got back was the right one, but what if anyone on the network can now see that you went to a domain called embarrassingmedicalcondition.com? We know from our discussion of TLS 1.3 earlier in this chapter that this URL will not go out in plaintext over HTTPS (which, by the way, it will in TLS 1.2 and earlier), but it will still be visible before the TLS handshake when the DNS query goes out. This is particularly problematic when we are connected to public networks such as the Wi-Fi network at the local coffee shop.

DNS over HTTPS (DoH) is a (yet to be ratified) approach to protecting the privacy and confidentiality of DNS queries by sending them over HTTPS/TCP/IP instead of unsecured UDP/IP. As of this writing, DoH is available on most platforms, though it is an optional feature that has to be configured. Keep in mind, however, that DoH provides confidentiality but (unlike DNSSEC) not integrity protections. Also, DoH was conceived as a privacy mechanism when using public networks. If you think back to the DNS-enabled attacks we discussed earlier in this chapter (especially DGA and DNS tunneling), DoH would actually make these much harder to detect unless you have a TLS decryption proxy in place. This is one of the reasons why the U.S. NSA recommended in 2021 that DoH not use external resolvers in enterprise networks.

DNS Filtering

Our final topic on securing DNS is perhaps the most obvious. Instead of allowing any DNS request to go out of our organizational networks, what if we first filtered them to block known malicious (or otherwise disallowed) domains from being resolved in the first place? A DNS filter performs a similar role as a web proxy that blocks content that is inappropriate, except that it works on DNS instead of HTTP traffic. There are many commercial solutions that provide this functionality, but keep in mind they should be deployed as part of a broader, defense-in-depth approach to securing DNS.

Electronic Mail

Let's now shift our attention to the third major service (along with web and DNS services) that is required for virtually all major organizations: e-mail. Though it has lost some ground to other business communication platforms such as Slack, Microsoft Teams,

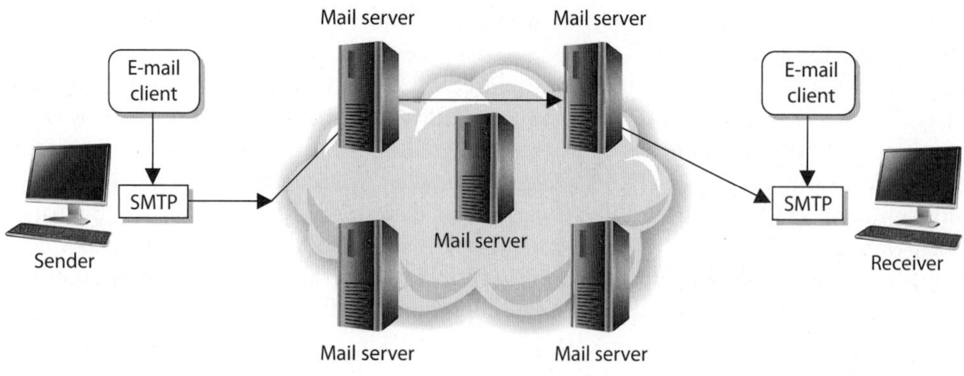

Figure 13-9 SMTP works as a transfer agent for e-mail messages.

and Google Hangouts, e-mail remains a critical service in virtually all organizations. An e-mail message, however, is of no use unless it can actually be sent somewhere. This is where *Simple Mail Transfer Protocol (SMTP)* comes in. In e-mail clients, SMTP works as a message transfer agent, as shown in Figure 13-9, and moves the message from the user's computer to the mail server when the user clicks the Send button. SMTP also functions as a message transfer protocol between e-mail servers. Lastly, SMTP is a message-exchange addressing standard, and most people are used to seeing its familiar addressing scheme: something@somewhere.com.

Many times, a message needs to travel throughout the Internet and through different mail servers before it arrives at its destination mail server. SMTP is the protocol that carries this message, and it works on top of TCP because it is a reliable protocol and provides sequencing and acknowledgments to ensure the e-mail message arrived successfully at its destination.

The user's e-mail client must be SMTP-compliant to be properly configured to use this protocol. The e-mail client provides an interface to the user so the user can create and modify messages as needed, and then the client passes the message off to the SMTP application layer protocol. So, to use the analogy of sending a letter via the post office, the e-mail client is the typewriter that a person uses to write the message, SMTP is the mail courier who picks up the mail and delivers it to the post office, and the post office is the mail server. The mail server has the responsibility of understanding where the message is heading and properly routing the message to that destination.

It is worth noting that basic SMTP doesn't include any security controls. This is why the IETF published Extended SMTP (ESMTP), which, among other features, allows servers to negotiate a TLS session in which to exchange the messages. This implementation, referred to as SMTP Secure (SMTPS), can provide authentication, confidentiality, and integrity protections for mail transfers.

The mail server is often referred to as an SMTP server. The most common SMTP server software in the world is Exim, which is an open-source mail transfer agent (MTA). SMTP works closely with two mail server protocols, POP and IMAP, which are explained in the following sections.

E-mail Threats

E-mail spoofing is a technique used by malicious users to forge an e-mail to make it appear to be from a legitimate source. Usually, such e-mails appear to be from known and trusted e-mail addresses when they are actually generated from a malicious source. This technique is widely used by attackers these days for spamming and phishing purposes. An attacker tries to acquire the target's sensitive information, such as username and password or bank account credentials. Sometimes, the e-mail messages contain a link of a known website when it is actually a fake website used to trick the user into revealing his information.

E-mail spoofing is done by modifying the fields of e-mail headers, such as the From, Return-Path, and Reply-To fields, so the e-mail appears to be from a trusted source. This results in an e-mail looking as though it is from a known e-mail address. Mostly the From field is spoofed, but some scams have modified the Reply-To field to the attacker's e-mail address. E-mail spoofing is caused by the lack of security features in SMTP. When SMTP technologies were developed, the concept of e-mail spoofing didn't exist, so countermeasures for this type of threat were not embedded into the protocol. A user could use an SMTP server to send e-mail to anyone from any e-mail address. We'll circle back to these threats when we describe e-mail security later in this section.

POP

Post Office Protocol (POP) is an Internet mail server protocol that supports incoming and outgoing messages. The current version is 3, so you'll also see it referred to as POP3. A mail server that uses POP, apart from storing and forwarding e-mail messages, works with SMTP to move messages between mail servers. By default, POP servers listen on TCP port 110.

A smaller organization may have only one POP server that holds all employee mailboxes, whereas larger organizations could have several POP servers, one for each department within the organization. There are also Internet POP servers that enable people all over the world to exchange messages. This system is useful because the messages are held on the mail server until users are ready to download their messages, instead of trying to push messages right to a person's computer, which may be down or offline.

The e-mail server can implement different authentication schemes to ensure an individual is authorized to access a particular mailbox, but this is usually handled through usernames and passwords. Connections to these clients can be encrypted using TLS by using the secure version of POP, known as POP3S, which typically listens on port 995.

IMAP

Internet Message Access Protocol (IMAP) is also an Internet protocol that enables users to access mail on a mail server (the default TCP port is 143). IMAP provides all the functionalities of POP, but has more capabilities. If a user is using POP, when he accesses his mail server to see if he has received any new messages, all messages are automatically downloaded to his computer. Once the messages are downloaded from the POP server, they are usually deleted from that server, depending upon the configuration. POP can cause frustration for mobile users because the messages are automatically pushed down to their computer or device and they may not have the necessary space to hold all the messages. This is especially true for mobile devices that can be used to access e-mail servers. This is also inconvenient for people checking their mail on other people's computers. If Christina checks her e-mail on Jessica's computer, all of Christina's new mail could be downloaded to Jessica's computer.

If a user uses IMAP instead of POP, she can download all the messages or leave them on the mail server within her remote message folder, referred to as a mailbox. The user can also manipulate the messages within this mailbox on the mail server as if the messages resided on her local computer. She can create or delete messages, search for specific messages, and set and clear flags. This gives the user much more freedom and keeps the messages in a central repository until the user specifically chooses to download all messages from the mail server.

IMAP is a store-and-forward mail server protocol that is considered POP's successor. IMAP also gives administrators more capabilities when it comes to administering and maintaining the users' messages. Just like SMTP and POP, IMAP can run over TLS, in which case the server listens for connections on TCP port 993.

E-mail Authorization

POP has the capability to integrate *Simple Authentication and Security Layer (SASL)*, a protocol-independent framework for performing authentication. This means that any protocol that knows how to interact with SASL can use its various authentication mechanisms without having to actually embed the authentication mechanisms within its code.

To use SASL, a protocol includes a command for identifying and authenticating a user to an authentication server and for optionally negotiating protection of subsequent protocol interactions. If its use is negotiated, a security layer is inserted between the protocol and the connection. The data security layer can provide data integrity, data confidentiality, and other services. SASL's design is intended to allow new protocols to reuse existing mechanisms without requiring redesign of the mechanisms and allows existing protocols to make use of new mechanisms without redesign of protocols.

The use of SASL is not unique just to POP; other protocols, such as IMAP, Internet Relay Chat (IRC), Lightweight Directory Access Protocol (LDAP), and SMTP, can also use SASL and its functionality.

Sender Policy Framework

A common way to deal with the problem of forged e-mail messages is by using *Sender Policy Framework (SPF)*, which is an e-mail validation system designed to prevent e-mail spam by detecting e-mail spoofing by verifying the sender's IP address. SPF allows administrators to specify which hosts are allowed to send e-mail from a given domain by creating a specific SPF record in DNS. Mail exchanges use DNS to check that mail from a given domain is being sent by a host sanctioned by that domain's administrators.

DomainKeys Identified Mail

We can also leverage public key infrastructure (PKI) to validate the origin and integrity of each message. The *DomainKeys Identified Mail (DKIM)* standard, codified in RFC 6376, allows e-mail servers to digitally sign messages to provide a measure of confidence for the receiving server that the message is from the domain it claims to be from. These digital signatures are normally invisible to the user and are just used by the servers sending and receiving the messages. When a DKIM-signed message is received, the server requests the sending domain's certificate through DNS and verifies the signature. As long as the private key is not compromised, the receiving server is assured that the message came from the domain it claims and that it has not been altered in transit.

Domain-Based Message Authentication

SPF and DKIM were brought together to define the Domain-based Message Authentication, Reporting and Conformance (DMARC) system. DMARC, which today is estimated to protect 80 percent of mailboxes worldwide, defines how domains communicate to the rest of the world whether they are using SPF or DKIM (or both). It also codifies the mechanisms by which receiving servers provide feedback to the senders on the results of their validation of individual messages. Despite significant advances in securing e-mail, phishing e-mail remains one of the most common and effective attack vectors.

Secure/Multipurpose Internet Mail Extensions

Multipurpose Internet Mail Extensions (MIME) is a technical specification indicating how multimedia data and e-mail binary attachments are to be transferred. The Internet has mail standards that dictate how mail is to be formatted, encapsulated, transmitted, and opened. If a message or document contains a binary attachment, MIME dictates how that portion of the message should be handled.

When an attachment contains an audio clip, graphic, or some other type of multimedia component, the e-mail client sends the file with a header that describes the file type. For example, the header might indicate that the MIME type is Image and that the subtype is jpeg. Although this information is in the header, many times, systems also use the file's extension to identify the MIME type. So, in the preceding example, the file's name might be stuff.jpeg. The user's system sees the extension .jpeg, or sees the data in the header field, and looks in its association list to see what program it needs to initialize to open this particular file. If the system has JPEG files associated with the Explorer application, then Explorer opens and presents the image to the user.

Sometimes systems either do not have an association for a specific file type or do not have the helper program necessary to review and use the contents of the file. When a file has an unassociated icon assigned to it, it might require the user to choose the Open With command and choose an application in the list to associate this file with that program. So when the user double-clicks that file, the associated program initializes and presents the file. If the system does not have the necessary program, the website might offer the necessary helper program, like Acrobat or an audio program that plays WAV files.

MIME is a specification that dictates how certain file types should be transmitted and handled. This specification has several types and subtypes, enables different computers to exchange data in varying formats, and provides a standardized way of presenting the data. So if Sean views a funny picture that is in GIF format, he can be sure that when he sends it to Debbie, it will look exactly the same.

Secure MIME (S/MIME) is a standard for encrypting and digitally signing e-mail and for providing secure data transmissions. S/MIME extends the MIME standard by providing support for the encryption of e-mail and attachments. The encryption and hashing algorithms can be specified by the user of the mail application, instead of having it dictated to them. S/MIME follows the Public Key Cryptography Standards (PKCS). It provides confidentiality through encryption algorithms, integrity through hashing algorithms, authentication through the use of X.509 public key certificates, and nonrepudiation through cryptographically signed message digests.

Multilayer Protocols

Not all protocols fit neatly within the layers of the OSI model. This is particularly evident among devices and networks that were never intended to interoperate with the Internet. For this same reason, they tend to lack robust security features aimed at protecting the availability, integrity, and confidentiality of the data they communicate. The problem is that as the Internet of old becomes the Internet of Things (IoT), these previously isolated devices and networks find themselves increasingly connected to a host of threats they were never meant to face.

As security professionals, we need to be aware of these nontraditional protocols and their implications for the security of the networks to which they are connected. In particular, we should be vigilant when it comes to identifying nonobvious cyber-physical systems. In December 2015, attackers were able to cut power to over 80,000 homes in Ukraine apparently by compromising the utilities' supervisory control and data acquisition (SCADA) systems in what is considered the first known blackout caused by a cyberattack. A few years later, in 2017, attackers were able to exploit a previously unknown vulnerability and reprogram a Schneider Electric safety instrumented system (SIS) at an undisclosed target, causing the facility to shut down. At the heart of most SCADA systems used by power and water utilities is a multilayer protocol known as DNP3.

Distributed Network Protocol 3

The *Distributed Network Protocol 3 (DNP3)* is a communications protocol designed for use in SCADA systems, particularly those within the power sector. It is not a general-purpose protocol like IP, nor does it incorporate routing functionality. SCADA systems typically have a very flat hierarchical architecture in which sensors and actuators are connected to remote terminal units (RTUs). The RTUs aggregate data from one or more of these devices and relay it to the SCADA master, which includes a human–machine interface (HMI) component. Control instructions and configuration changes are sent from the SCADA master to the RTUs and then on to the sensors and actuators.

At the time DNP3 was designed, there wasn't a need to route traffic among the components (most of which were connected with point-to-point circuits), so networking was not needed or supported in DNP3. Instead of using the OSI seven-layer model, its developers opted for a simpler three-layer model called the Enhanced Performance Architecture (EPA) that roughly corresponds to layers 2, 4, and 7 of the OSI model. There was no encryption or authentication, since the developers did not think network attacks were feasible on a system consisting of devices connected to each other and to nothing else.

Over time, SCADA systems were connected to other networks and then to the Internet for a variety of very valid business reasons. Unfortunately, security wasn't considered until much later. Encryption and authentication features were added as an afterthought, though not all implementations have been thus updated. Network segmentation is not always present either, even in some critical installations. Perhaps most concerning is the shortage of effective IPSs and IDSs that understand the interconnections between DNP3 and IP networks and can identify DNP3-based attacks.

Controller Area Network Bus

Another multilayer protocol that had almost no security features until very recently is the one that runs most automobiles worldwide. The *Controller Area Network (CAN) bus* is a protocol designed to allow microcontrollers and other embedded devices to communicate with each other on a shared bus. Over time, these devices have diversified so that today they can control almost every aspect of a vehicle's functions, including steering, braking, and throttling. CAN bus was never meant to communicate with anything outside the vehicle except for a mechanic's maintenance computer, so there never appeared to be a need for security features.

As automobiles started getting connected via Wi-Fi and cellular data networks, their designers didn't fully consider the new attack vectors this would introduce to an otherwise undefended system. That is, until Charlie Miller and Chris Valasek famously hacked a Jeep in 2015 by connecting to it over a cellular data network and bridging the head unit (which controls the sound system and GPS) to the CAN bus (which controls all the vehicle sensors and actuators) and causing it to run off a road. As automobiles become more autonomous, security of the CAN bus becomes increasingly important.

Modbus

Like CAN bus, the Modbus system was developed to prioritize functionality over security. A communications system created in the late 1970s by Modicon, now Schneider Electric, Modbus enables communications among SCADA devices quickly and easily. Since its inception, Modbus has quickly become the de facto standard for communications between programmable logic controllers (PLCs). But as security was not built in, Modbus offers little protection against attacks. An attacker residing on the network can simply collect traffic using a tool like Wireshark, find a target device, and issue commands directly to the device.

Converged Protocols

Converged protocols are those that started off independent and distinct from one another but over time converged to become one. How is this possible? Think about the phone and data networks. Once upon a time, these were two different entities and each had its own protocols and transmission media. For a while, in the 1990s, data networks sometimes rode over voice networks using data modems. This was less than ideal, which is why we flipped it around and started using data networks as the carrier for voice communications. Over time, the voice protocols converged onto the data protocols, which paved the way for Voice over IP (VoIP).

IP convergence, which addresses a specific type of converged protocols, is the transition of services from disparate transport media and protocols to IP. It is not hard to see that IP has emerged as the dominant standard for networking, so it makes sense that any new protocols would leverage this existing infrastructure rather than create a separate one.

Technically, the term *converged* implies that the two protocols became one. Oftentimes, however, the term is used to describe cases in which one protocol was originally independent of another but over time started being encapsulated (or tunneled) within that other one.

Encapsulation

We already saw (in Chapter 9) how encapsulation enables the transmission of data down the seven layers of the OSI reference model. We came across encapsulation again earlier in this chapter when we discussed techniques to tunnel (or encapsulate) one protocol's traffic inside some other protocol. The next two sections describe two more examples. It should be obvious that encapsulation can be helpful in architecting our networks, but it can also have significant security implications.

When we covered DNS tunneling, we saw another, less helpful application of encapsulation. Threat actors develop their own protocols for controlling compromised hosts and they can encapsulate those protocols within legitimate systems. It is important, therefore, to not assume that just because we have a network link that should be transporting data of a certain protocol, it won't have something else embedded in it. Whether encapsulation is malicious or benign, the point is that we need to be aware of what traffic should be where and have the means to inspect it to ensure we are not surprised.

Fiber Channel over Ethernet

Fibre Channel (FC) (also called Fiber Channel in the United States) was developed by the American National Standards Institute (ANSI) in 1988 as a way to connect supercomputers using optical fibers. FC is now used to connect servers to data storage devices in data centers and other high-performance environments. One of its best features is that it can support speeds of up to 128 Gbps over distances of up to 500 meters. (Distances of up to 50 km are possible at lower data rates.) While the speed and other features of FC are pretty awesome for data centers and storage area network (SAN) applications, the need to maintain both Ethernet and fiber-optic cabling adds costs and complexity to its use in enterprise environments.

Fibre Channel over Ethernet (FCoE) is a protocol encapsulation that allows FC frames to ride over Ethernet networks. Its use allows data centers to be almost exclusively wired using Ethernet cabling. It is important to note, however, that FCoE rides on top of Ethernet and is, therefore, a non-routable protocol. It is only intended for LAN environments where devices are in close proximity to each other and efficiency is essential.

Internet Small Computer Systems Interface

A much different approach to encapsulation is exemplified by the Internet Small Computer Systems Interface (iSCSI), which encapsulates SCSI data in TCP segments. SCSI is a set of technologies that allows peripherals to be connected to computers. The problem with the original SCSI is that it has limited range, which means that connecting a remote peripheral (e.g., camera or storage device) is not normally possible. The solution was to let SCSI ride on TCP segments so that a peripheral device could be literally anywhere in the world and still appear as local to a computer.

Network Segmentation

Once upon a time, networks were flat (i.e., almost everyone within an organization was in the same layer 2 broadcast domain) so that everyone could easily communicate with everyone else inside the "trusted" perimeter. Network defenses were mostly (sometimes solely) outward-facing. This led to the networks that were "crunchy on the outside but soft and chewy on the inside." Believe it or not, this was the design mantra for many organizations for many years. Eventually, they realized that this design was a really bad idea. For starters, they recognized that at least some attackers will get through their perimeter defenses. Also, they learned that insider threats could be just as dangerous as external ones, and these insiders would have no problem moving through the soft and chewy interior network. Furthermore, they realized that most networks no longer have a neat concept of "inside" and "outside." Instead, organizations increasingly rely on external systems such as those provided by cloud service providers.

Network segmentation is the practice of dividing networks into smaller subnetworks. An example is to divide the network by department, so that the finance department and marketing department are each in their own LAN. If they need to communicate directly, they have to go through a gateway (e.g., a router or firewall) that allows network administrators to block or detect suspicious traffic. This is a classic implementation of the zero trust security design principle.

The decision to segment a network begs a couple of questions. How many subnetworks should we have? Are more subnets better? There really is no one-size-fits-all answer, but generally, the smaller the subnetworks (and the more you have), the better. In fact, many organizations are implementing *micro-segmentation*, which is the practice of isolating individual assets (e.g., data servers) in their own protected network environment. Think of it as a subnet where the only devices are the protected asset and a security gateway.

So, how do we go about segmenting networks? We can do it either physically (using devices like switches and routers) or logically (using virtualization software). We'll cover devices in detail in the next chapter, so let's turn our attention to the most important technologies that enable segmentation and micro-segmentation.

VLANs

One of the most commonly used technologies used to segment LANs is the *virtual local area network (VLAN)*. A LAN can be defined as a set of devices on the same layer 2 (data link layer) broadcast domain. This typically means hosts that are *physically* connected to the same layer 2 switches. A VLAN is a set of devices that *behave* as though they were all directly connected to the same switch, when in fact they aren't. This allows you to, for instance, ensure that all members of the finance team are on the same (virtual) LAN, even though they are scattered across multiple countries. The ability to segment networks of users in this manner is critical for both functional and security reasons.

Virtually all modern enterprise-grade switches have the capability to use VLANs. VLANs enable administrators to separate and group computers logically based on resource requirements, security, or business needs instead of the standard physical location of the systems. When repeaters, bridges, and routers are used, systems and resources are grouped in a manner dictated by their physical location. Figure 13-10 shows how computers that are physically located next to each other can be grouped logically into different VLANs. Administrators can form these groups based on the users' and organization's needs instead of the physical location of systems and resources.

Figure 13-10 VLANs enable administrators to manage logical networks.

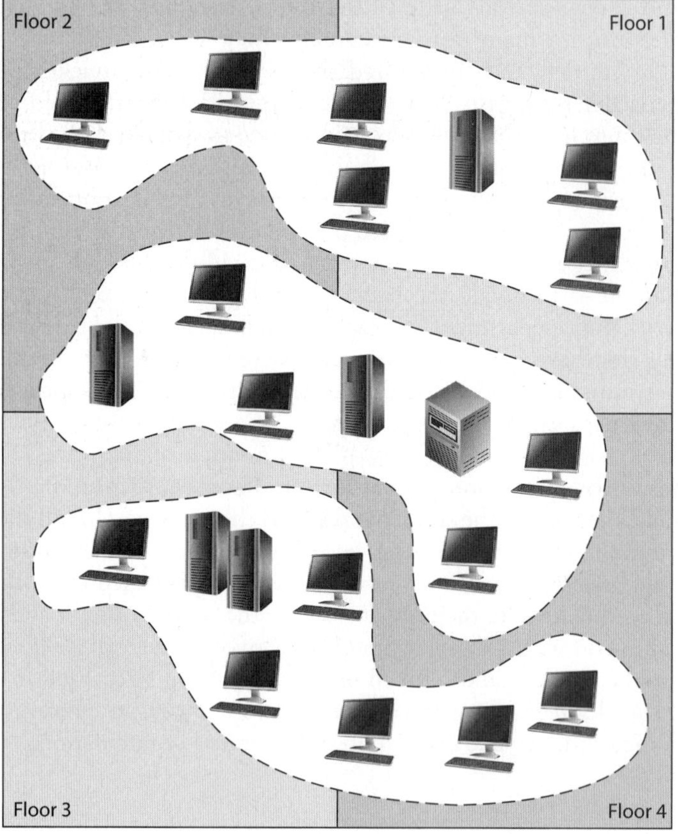

An administrator may want to segment the computers of all users in the marketing department in the same VLAN network, for example, so all users receive the same broadcast messages and can access the same types of resources. This arrangement could get tricky if a few of the users are located in another building or on another floor, but VLANs provide the administrator with this type of flexibility. VLANs also enable an administrator to apply particular security policies to respective zones or segments. This way, if tighter security is required for the payroll department, for example, the administrator can develop a policy, add all payroll systems to a specific VLAN, and apply the security policy only to the payroll VLAN.

A VLAN exists on top of the physical network, as shown in Figure 13-11. Each Ethernet frame is prepended with a VLAN identifier (VID), which is a 12-bit field. This means that we can define up to 4,095 VLANs in the same network. (The first and last VID values are reserved.) If workstation P1 wants to communicate with workstation D1, the message has to be routed—even though the workstations are physically next to each other—because they are on different logical networks.

NOTE The IEEE standard that defines how VLANs are to be constructed and how tagging should take place to allow for interoperability is IEEE 802.1Q.

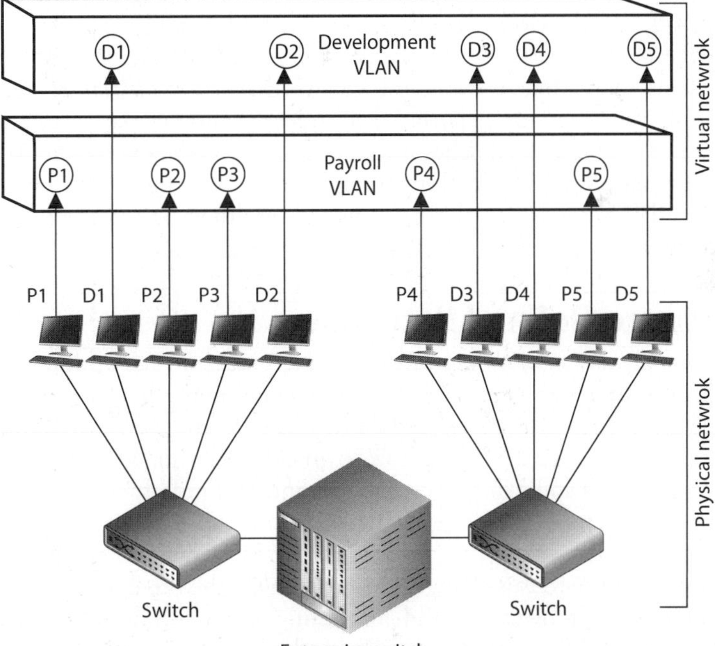

Figure 13-11 VLANs exist on a higher level than the physical network and are not bound to it.

While VLANs are used to segment traffic, attackers can still gain access to traffic that is supposed to be "walled off" in another VLAN segment. *VLAN hopping attacks* allow attackers to gain access to traffic in various VLAN segments. An attacker can have a system act as though it is a switch. The system understands the tagging values being used in the network and the trunking protocols and can insert itself between other VLAN devices and gain access to the traffic going back and forth. This is called a *switch spoofing attack*. An attacker can also insert VLAN tags to manipulate the control of traffic at the data link layer in what is known as a *double tagging attack*. Proper configuration of all switches mitigates VLAN hopping attacks.

Virtual eXtensible Local Area Network

VLANs, however, have some significant limitations. For starters, remember that you're limited to around 4,000 VLANs because the VID is 12 bits. While this sounds like a lot, it really isn't if you happen to be a cloud-based service provider supporting hundreds of customers. Another challenge is that VLANs are layer 2 constructs separated by layer 3 routers. This means that all the hosts on a given VLAN must be on the same port of the same router. In other words, if the hosts are in different countries, it becomes really hard to join them to the same VLAN.

The *Virtual eXtensible Local Area Network (VxLAN)* is a network virtualization technology that encapsulates layer 2 frames onto UDP (layer 4) datagrams for distribution anywhere in the world. Whereas VLANs have VIDs, VxLANs have a virtual network identifier (VNI) that is 24 bits long, which gives us over 16 million segments. VxLANs are mostly used in cloud environments where hosts and networks are virtualized.

VxLANs are overlay networks on top of UDP/IP underlay networks. Each network switch or router that is part of a VxLAN has a *virtual tunnel end point (VTEP)* that provides the interface between the underlay and overlay networks. When a VTEP receives a frame, it establishes a virtual tunnel on the overlay network connecting it to the destination VTEP just long enough to deliver the frame. The VTEP encapsulates this overlay frame in UDP datagrams that are then passed to the underlay network for delivery.

Software-Defined Networks

Software-defined networking (SDN) is an approach to networking that relies on distributed software to provide unprecedented agility and efficiency. Using SDN, it becomes much easier to dynamically route traffic to and from newly provisioned services and platforms. This means a new server can be quickly provisioned using a cloud service provider in response to a spike in service requests and the underlying network can just as quickly adapt to the new traffic patterns. It also means that a service or platform can be quickly moved from one location to another and the SDN will just as quickly update traffic-flow rules in response to this change. Unsurprisingly, the three biggest drivers to the adoption of SDN are the growth in cloud computing, big data, and mobile computing.

How does SDN differ from traditional networking? Whereas traditional networking relies on network devices that coordinate with one another in a mostly decentralized manner, SDN centralizes the configuration and control of devices. In a decentralized environment, it takes time for routers to converge onto (or agree on) good routes. These devices must normally be manually configured whenever any changes take place, which is also a time-consuming task. In SDN, on the other hand, all changes are pushed out to the devices either reactively (i.e., in response to requests from the devices) or proactively (i.e., because the admins know a change is being made, such as the addition of 100 servers). Because it is centrally controlled, the SDN approach allows traffic to be routed much more efficiently and securely. Perhaps the most important element of SDN is the abstraction of control and forwarding planes.

Control and Forwarding Planes

The *control plane* is where the internetwork routing decisions are being made. Think of this as the part of your router that runs the routing protocol, such as Open Shortest Path First (OSPF). (The analogy is not perfect, but it is useful for now.) The control plane is responsible for discovering the topology of neighboring networks and maintaining a table of routes for outbound packets. Since most networks are pretty dynamic places in which congestion along different routes is always changing, the control plane is a pretty dynamic place as well. New routes are routinely being discovered, just as old routes are dropped or at least flagged as slow or expensive. As you can see, the control plane is mostly interested in effects that are more than one hop away.

The *forwarding plane*, by contrast, is where traffic forwarding decisions are made. Think of this as that part of your router that decides (very quickly) that a packet received on network interface eth0 needs to be forwarded to network interface eth3. How does the forwarding plane decide this? By using the products developed by the control plane. The control plane is the strategic, methodical planner of traffic routing, while the forwarding plane is the tactical, fast executioner of those plans. Unsurprisingly, the forwarding plane is typically implemented in hardware such as an application-specific integrated chip (ASIC).

NOTE Because traditional routing decisions are made by the controller in an SDN architecture, the network devices behave (and are referred to) as switches.

In a traditional network architecture, each networking device has its own control plane and its own forwarding plane, both of which run on some sort of proprietary operating system (e.g., Cisco IOS). The normal way of reconfiguring these traditional devices is via a terminal connection of some sort. This means that an administrator must remotely log into each device in order to change its configuration. Let's suppose that we want to support a distinct QoS for a new user. In order to do this, we'd modify the configuration in each networking device that would be involved in providing services to this user. Even assuming that we are able to do this without making any mistakes, we still face the onerous task of manually changing these parameters whenever the terms of the contract change, or when equipment is replaced or upgraded, or when the network architecture changes. There are exceptions to these challenges, of course, but the point is that making frequent, granular configuration changes is tough.

PART IV

What About Automation?

One of the challenges of network administration is that most network devices (apart from those that support SDN) do not have comprehensive mechanisms for programmatically and remotely changing the configuration of the device. This is why administrators have to manually log into each device and update the configuration. Reading information is easier because these devices typically support SNMP, but writing meaningful changes to the devices almost always requires manual interaction or some third-party tool that comes with its own set of constraints.

Further complicating the issue of making dynamic changes, vendors typically use their own proprietary operating system, which makes it harder to write a script that makes the same changes to all devices in heterogeneous environments that implement products from multiple vendors. This is the reason why many organizations implement homogeneous network architectures in which all the devices are manufactured by the same vendor. A big downside of this homogeneity is that it leads to vendor lockdown because it is hard (and expensive) to change vendors when that means you must change every single device on your network. Furthermore, homogeneity is bad for security, because an exploit that leverages a vulnerability in a network operating system will likely affect every device in a homogeneous network.

In SDN, by contrast, the control plane is implemented in a central node that is responsible for managing all the devices in the network. For redundancy and efficiency, this node can actually be a federation of nodes that coordinate their activities with one another. The network devices are then left to do what they do best: forward packets very efficiently. So the forwarding plane lives in the network devices and the control plane lives in a centralized SDN controller. This allows us to abstract the network devices (heterogeneous or otherwise) from the applications that rely on them to communicate in much the same way Windows abstracts the hardware details from the applications running on a workstation.

Approaches to SDN

The concept of network abstraction is central to all implementations of SDN. The manner in which this abstraction is implemented, however, varies significantly among flavors of SDN. There are at least three common approaches to SDN, each championed by a different community and delivered primarily through a specific technology:

- **Open** The SDN approach championed by the Open Networking Foundation (ONF) (https://opennetworking.org) is, by most accounts, the most common. It relies on open-source code and standards to develop the building blocks of an SDN solution. The controller communicates with the switches using OpenFlow, a standardized, open-source communications interface between controllers and network devices in an SDN architecture. OpenFlow allows the devices implementing the forwarding plane to provide information (such as utilization data) to the controller, while allowing the controller to update the flow tables (akin to traditional routing tables) on the devices. Applications communicate with the controller using the RESTful or Java APIs.

- **API** Another approach to SDN, and one that is championed by Cisco, is built on the premise that OpenFlow is not sufficient to fully leverage the promise of SDN in the enterprise. In addition to OpenFlow, this approach leverages a rich API on proprietary switches that allows greater control over traffic in an SDN. Among the perceived shortcomings that are corrected are the inability of OpenFlow to do deep packet inspection and manipulation and its reliance on a centralized control plane. This proprietary API approach to SDN is seen as enriching rather than replacing ONF's SDN approach.
- **Overlays** Finally, one can imagine a virtualized network architecture as an overlay on a traditional one. In this approach, we virtualize all network nodes, including switches, routers, and servers, and treat them independently of the physical networks upon which this virtualized infrastructure exists. The SDN exists simply as a virtual overlay on top of a physical (underlay) network.

Software-Defined Wide Area Network

Software-defined wide area networking (SD-WAN) is the use of software (instead of hardware) to control the connectivity, management, and services between distant sites. Think of it as SDN applied to WANs instead of LANs. Similarly to SDN, SD-WAN separates the control plane from the forwarding plane. This means that network links, whether they are leased lines or 5G wireless, are better utilized. Also, since the control plane is centralized, security policies can be consistently applied throughout.

Another advantage of SD-WANs is that they are application-aware, meaning they know the difference between supporting video conferencing (low latency, loss tolerance), supporting file transfers (latency tolerance, loss intolerant), or supporting any other sort of traffic. This means SD-WANs use the right path for the traffic and are able to switch things around as links become congested or degraded.

Chapter Review

Securing our networks is a lot more effective if we first understand the underlying technologies and then apply secure design principles to their selection and integration. This chapter built on the foundations of the previous two chapters to show common approaches to building and operating secure networking architectures. We focused our attention on network encryption and service security techniques but also covered how to deal with dispersed networks and those with cloud service components. A key aspect of our discussion was the application of the secure design principles at multiple points. We'll continue this theme in the next chapter as we talk about securing the components of our networks.

Quick Review

- Link encryption encrypts all the data along a specific communication path.
- End-to-end encryption (E2EE) occurs at the session layer (or higher) and does not encrypt routing information, enabling attackers to learn more about a captured packet and where it is headed.
- Transport Layer Security (TLS) is an E2EE protocol that provides confidentiality and data integrity for network communications.
- Secure Sockets Layer (SSL) is the predecessor of TLS and is deprecated and considered insecure.
- A virtual private network (VPN) is a secure, private connection through an untrusted network.
- The Point-to-Point Tunneling Protocol (PPTP) is an obsolete and insecure means of providing VPNs.
- The Layer 2 Tunneling Protocol (L2TP) tunnels PPP traffic over various network types (IP, ATM, X.25, etc.) but does not encrypt the user traffic.
- Internet Protocol Security (IPSec) is a suite of protocols that provides authentication, integrity, and confidentiality protections to data at the network layer.
- TLS can be used to provide VPN connectivity at layer 5 in the OSI model.
- A web service is client/server system in which clients and servers communicate using HTTP over a network such as the Internet.
- A service-oriented architecture (SOA) describes a system as a set of interconnected but self-contained components that communicate with each other and with their clients through standardized protocols.
- Application programming interfaces (APIs) establish a "language" that enables a system component to make a request from another component and then interpret that second component's response.
- The Hypertext Transfer Protocol (HTTP) is a TCP/IP-based communications protocol used for transferring data between a server and a client in a connectionless and stateless manner.
- A uniform resource identifier (URI) uniquely identifies a resource on the Internet.
- HTTP Secure (HTTPS) is HTTP running over TLS.
- The Simple Object Access Protocol (SOAP) is a messaging protocol that uses XML over HTTP to enable clients to invoke processes on a remote host in a platform-agnostic way.
- SOAP security is enabled by a set of protocol extensions called the Web Services Security (WS-Security or WSS) specification, which provides message confidentiality, integrity, and authentication.

- Representational State Transfer (REST) is an architectural pattern used to develop web services without using SOAP.
- A domain generation algorithm (DGA) produces seemingly random domain names in a way that is predictable by anyone who knows the algorithm.
- DNS tunneling is the practice of encoding messages in one or a series of DNS queries or responses for exfiltrating or infiltrating data into an environment.
- DNS reflection attacks involve sending a query to a server while spoofing the source address to be that of the intended target.
- A DNS amplification attack is characterized by small queries that result in very much larger responses.
- Domain Name System Security Extensions (DNSSEC) is a set of IETF standards that ensures the integrity of DNS records but not their confidentiality or availability.
- DNS over HTTPS (DoH) is a (yet to be ratified) approach to protecting the privacy and confidentiality of DNS queries by sending them over HTTPS/TCP /IP instead of unsecured UDP/IP.
- E-mail spoofing is a technique used by malicious users to forge an e-mail to make it appear to be from a legitimate source.
- Simple Authentication and Security Layer (SASL) is a protocol-independent framework for performing authentication that is typically used in POP3 e-mail systems.
- The Sender Policy Framework (SPF) is an e-mail validation system designed to prevent e-mail spam by detecting e-mail spoofing by verifying the sender's IP address.
- The DomainKeys Identified Mail (DKIM) standard allows e-mail servers to digitally sign messages to provide a measure of confidence for the receiving server that the message is from the domain it claims to be from.
- Domain-based Message Authentication, Reporting and Conformance (DMARC) systems incorporate both SPF and DKIM to protect e-mail.
- Secure MIME (S/MIME) is a standard for encrypting and digitally signing e-mail and for providing secure data transmissions.
- The Distributed Network Protocol 3 (DNP3) is a multilayer communications protocol designed for use in SCADA systems, particularly those within the power sector.
- The Controller Area Network (CAN) bus is a multilayer protocol designed to allow microcontrollers and other embedded devices to communicate with each other on a shared bus.
- Converged protocols are those that started off independent and distinct from one another but over time converged to become one.

- Fibre Channel over Ethernet (FCoE) is a protocol encapsulation that allows Fibre Channel (FC) frames to ride over Ethernet networks.
- The Internet Small Computer Systems Interface (iSCSI) protocol encapsulates SCSI data in TCP segments so that computer peripherals could be located at any physical distance from the computer they support.
- Network segmentation is the practice of dividing networks into smaller subnetworks.
- A virtual LAN (VLAN) is a set of devices that behave as though they were all directly connected to the same switch, when in fact they aren't.
- Virtual eXtensible LAN (VxLAN) is a network virtualization technology that encapsulates layer 2 frames onto UDP (layer 4) datagrams for distribution anywhere in the world.
- Software-defined networking (SDN) is an approach to networking that relies on distributed software to separate the control and forwarding planes of a network.
- Software-defined wide area networking (SD-WAN) is the use of software (instead of hardware) to control the connectivity, management, and services between distant sites in a manner that is similar to SDN but applied to WANs.

Questions

Please remember that these questions are formatted and asked in a certain way for a reason. Keep in mind that the CISSP exam is asking questions at a conceptual level. Questions may not always have the perfect answer, and the candidate is advised against always looking for the perfect answer. Instead, the candidate should look for the best answer in the list.

1. Which of the following provides secure end-to-end encryption?
   - **A.** Transport Layer Security (TLS)
   - **B.** Secure Sockets Layer (SSL)
   - **C.** Layer 2 Tunneling Protocol (L2TP)
   - **D.** Domain Name System Security Extensions (DNSSEC)
2. Which of the following can take place if an attacker is able to insert tagging values into network- and switch-based protocols with the goal of manipulating traffic at the data link layer?
   - **A.** Open relay manipulation
   - **B.** VLAN hopping attack
   - **C.** Hypervisor denial-of-service attack
   - **D.** DNS tunneling

3. Which of the following provides an incorrect definition of the specific component or protocol that makes up IPSec?
   A. Authentication Header protocol provides data integrity, data origin authentication, and protection from replay attacks.
   B. Encapsulating Security Payload protocol provides confidentiality, data origin authentication, and data integrity.
   C. Internet Security Association and Key Management Protocol provides a framework for security association creation and key exchange.
   D. Internet Key Exchange provides authenticated keying material for use with encryption algorithms.
4. Alice wants to send a message to Bob, who is several network hops away from her. What is the best approach to protecting the confidentiality of the message?
   A. PPTP
   B. S/MIME
   C. Link encryption
   D. SSH
5. Which technology would best provide confidentiality to a RESTful web service?
   A. Web Services Security (WS-Security)
   B. Transport Layer Security (TLS)
   C. HTTP Secure (HTTPS)
   D. Simple Object Access Protocol (SOAP)
6. Which of the following protections are provided by Domain Name System Security Extensions (DNSSEC)?
   A. Confidentiality and integrity
   B. Integrity and availability
   C. Integrity and authentication
   D. Confidentiality and authentication
7. Which approach provides the best protection against e-mail spoofing?
   A. Internet Message Access Protocol (IMAP)
   B. Domain-based Message Authentication, Reporting and Conformance (DMARC)
   C. Sender Policy Framework (SPF)
   D. DomainKeys Identified Mail (DKIM)

8. Which of the following is a multilayer protocol developed for use in supervisory control and data acquisition (SCADA) systems?
   A. Controller Area Network (CAN) bus
   B. Simple Authentication and Security Layer (SASL)
   C. Control Plane Protocol (CPP)
   D. Distributed Network Protocol 3 (DNP3)
9. All of the following statements are true of converged protocols *except* which one?
   A. Distributed Network Protocol 3 (DNP3) is a converged protocol.
   B. Fibre Channel over Ethernet (FCoE) is a converged protocol.
   C. IP convergence addresses a specific type of converged protocols.
   D. The term includes certain protocols that are encapsulated within each other.
10. Suppose you work at a large cloud service provider that has thousands of customers around the world. What technology would best support segmentation of your customers' environments?
   A. Virtual local area network (VLAN)
   B. Virtual eXtensible Local Area Network (VxLAN)
   C. Software-defined wide area networking (SD-WAN)
   D. Layer 2 Tunneling Protocol (L2TP)

Answers

1. **A.** TLS and SSL are the only two answers that provide end-to-end encryption, but SSL is insecure, so it's not a good answer.
2. **B.** VLAN hopping attacks allow attackers to gain access to traffic in various VLAN segments. An attacker can have a system act as though it is a switch. The system understands the tagging values being used in the network and the trunking protocols and can insert itself between other VLAN devices and gain access to the traffic going back and forth. Attackers can also insert tagging values to manipulate the control of traffic at this data link layer.
3. **D.** Authentication Header protocol provides data integrity, data origin authentication, and protection from replay attacks. Encapsulating Security Payload protocol provides confidentiality, data origin authentication, and data integrity. Internet Security Association and Key Management Protocol provides a framework for security association creation and key exchange. Internet Key Exchange provides authenticated keying material for use with ISAKMP.
4. **B.** Secure Multipurpose Internet Mail Extensions (S/MIME) is a standard for encrypting and digitally signing e-mail and for providing secure data transmissions using public key infrastructure (PKI).

5. **C.** Either TLS or HTTPS would be a correct answer, but since web services in general and RESTful ones in particular require HTTP, HTTPS is the best choice. Keep in mind that you are likely to come across similar questions where multiple answers are correct but only one is best. SOAP is an alternative way to deliver web services and uses WS-Security for confidentiality.
6. **C.** Domain Name System Security Extensions (DNSSEC) is a set of IETF standards that ensures the integrity and authenticity of DNS records but not their confidentiality or availability.
7. **B.** Domain-based Message Authentication, Reporting and Conformance (DMARC) systems incorporate both SPF and DKIM to protect e-mail. IMAP does not have any built-in protections against e-mail spoofing.
8. **D.** DNP3 is a multilayer communications protocol designed for use in SCADA systems, particularly those within the power sector.
9. **A.** DNP3 is a multilayer communications protocol that was designed for use in SCADA systems and has not converged with other protocols. All other statements are descriptive of converged protocols.
10. **B.** Since there are thousands of customers to support, VxLAN is the best choice because it can support over 16 million subnetworks. Traditional VLANs are capped at just over 4,000 subnetworks, which would not be able to provide more than a few segments to each customer.

CHAPTER 14

Network Components

This chapter presents the following:

- Transmission media
- Network devices
- Endpoint security
- Content distribution networks

The hacker didn't succeed through sophistication. Rather he poked at obvious places, trying to enter through unlocked doors. Persistence, not wizardry, let him through.

—Clifford Stoll, *The Cuckoo's Egg*

In the previous chapter, we covered how to defend our networks. Let's now talk about securing the components of those networks. We need to pay attention to everything from the cables, to the network devices, to the endpoints, because our adversaries will poke at all of it, looking for ways to get in. We (defenders) have to get it right all the time; they (attackers) only need to find that one chink in our armor to compromise our systems. In this chapter, we focus on physical devices. In the next chapter, we'll drill into the software systems that run on them.

Transmission Media

We've already talked a fair bit about the protocols that allow us to move data from point A to point B, but we haven't really covered what actually carries this information. A transmission medium is a physical thing through which data is moved. If we are speaking with each other, our vocal chords create vibrations in the air that we expel from our lungs, in which case the air is the transmission medium. Broadly speaking, we use three different types of transmission media:

- **Electrical wires** Encode information as changes in the voltage level of an electric current. Typically, we use cables, which are two or more wires encased within a sheath.
- **Optical fibers** Transmit data that is encoded in the wavelength (color), phase, or polarization of the light. The light is generated by either an LED or a laser diode. As with electrical wires, we usually bundle multiple fibers into cables for longer distances.

- **Free space** The medium we use for wireless communications, covered in Chapter 12. Any electromagnetic signal can travel through free space even outside our atmosphere. We tend to use mostly radio signals in free space, but every now and then you may encounter a system that uses light, such as infrared laser beams.

Types of Transmission

Physical data transmission can happen in different ways (analog or digital); can use different synchronization schemes (synchronous or asynchronous); can use either one sole channel over a transmission medium (baseband) or several different channels over a transmission medium (broadband); and can take place as electrical voltage, radio waves, or optical signals. These transmission types and their characteristics are described in the following sections.

Analog vs. Digital

A *signal* is just some way of moving information in a physical format from one point to another point. You can signal a message to another person through nodding your head, waving your hand, or giving a wink. Somehow you are transmitting data to that person through your signaling method. In the world of technology, we have specific carrier signals that are in place to move data from one system to another system. The carrier signal is like a horse, which takes a rider (data) from one place to another place. Data can be transmitted through analog or digital signaling formats. If you are moving data through an analog transmission technology (e.g., radio), then the data is represented by the characteristics of the waves that are carrying it. For example, a radio station uses a transmitter to put its data (music) onto a radio wave that travels all the way to your antenna. The information is stripped off by the receiver in your radio and presented to you in its original format—a song. The data is encoded onto the carrier signal and is represented by various amplitude and frequency values, as shown in Figure 14-1.

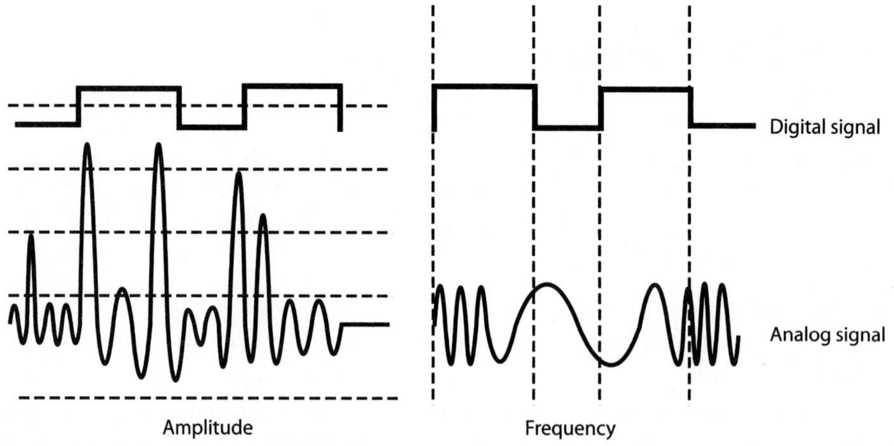

Figure 14-1 Analog signals are measured in amplitude and frequency, whereas digital signals represent binary digits as electrical pulses.

Data being represented in wave values (analog) is different from data being represented in discrete voltage values (digital). As an analogy, compare an analog clock and a digital clock. An analog clock has hands that continuously rotate on the face of the clock. To figure out what time it is, you have to interpret the position of the hands and map their positions to specific values. So you have to know that if the small hand is on the number 1 and the large hand is on the number 6, this actually means 1:30. The individual and specific location of the hands corresponds to a value. A digital clock does not take this much work. You just look at it and it gives you a time value in the format of hour:minutes. There is no mapping work involved with a digital clock because it provides you with data in clear-cut formats.

An analog clock can represent different values as the hands move forward—1:35 and 1 second, 1:35 and 2 seconds, 1:35 and 3 seconds. Each movement of the hands represents a specific value just like the individual data points on a wave in an analog transmission. A digital clock provides discrete values without having to map anything. The same is true with digital transmissions: the values are almost always binary, meaning they are either a 1 or a 0—no need for mapping to find the actual value.

Computers have always worked in a binary manner (1 or 0). When our telecommunication infrastructure was purely analog, each system that needed to communicate over a telecommunication line had to have a modem (modulator/demodulator), which would modulate the digital data into an analog signal. The sending system's modem would modulate the data on to the signal, and the receiving system's modem would demodulate the data off the signal.

Digital signals are more reliable than analog signals over a long distance and provide a clear-cut and efficient signaling method because the voltage is either on (1) or not on (0), compared to interpreting the waves of an analog signal. Extracting digital signals from a noisy carrier is relatively easy. It is difficult to extract analog signals from background noise because the amplitudes and frequencies of the waves slowly lose form. This is because an analog signal could have an infinite number of values or states, whereas a digital signal exists in discrete states. A digital signal is a square wave, which does not have all of the possible values of the different amplitudes and frequencies of an analog signal. Digital systems can implement compression mechanisms to increase data throughput, provide signal integrity through repeaters that "clean up" the transmissions, and multiplex different types of data (voice, data, video) onto the same transmission channel.

Asynchronous vs. Synchronous

Analog and digital transmission technologies deal with the characteristics of the physical carrier on which data is moved from one system to another. Asynchronous and synchronous transmission types are similar to the cadence rules we use for conversation *synchronization*. Asynchronous and synchronous network technologies provide synchronization rules to govern how systems communicate to each other. If you have ever spoken over a satellite phone, you have probably experienced problems with communication synchronization. Commonly, when two people are new to using satellite phones, they do not allow for the necessary delay that satellite communication requires, so they "speak over" one another. Once they figure out the delay in the connection, they resynchronize their timing so that only one person's data (voice) is transmitting at one time, enabling each person to properly understand the full conversation. Proper pauses frame your words in a way to make them understandable.

Synchronization through communication also happens when we write messages to each other. Properly placed commas, periods, and semicolons provide breaks in text so that the person reading the message can better understand the information. If you see "stickwithmekidandyouwillweardiamonds" without the proper punctuation, it is more difficult for you to understand. This is why we have grammar rules. If someone writes a letter to you that starts from the bottom and right side of a piece of paper, and that person does not inform you of this unconventional format, you will not be able to read the message properly, at least initially.

Technological communication protocols also have their own grammar and synchronization rules when it comes to the transmission of data. If two systems are communicating over a network protocol that employs asynchronous timing, they use start and stop bits. The sending system sends a "start" bit, then sends its character, and then sends a "stop" bit. This happens for the whole message. The receiving system knows when a character is starting and stopping; thus, it knows how to interpret each character of the message. This is akin to our previous example of using punctuation marks in written communications to convey pauses. If the systems are communicating over a network protocol that uses synchronous timing, then they don't add start and stop bits. The whole message is sent without artificial breaks, but with a common timing signal that allows the receiver to know how to interpret the information without these bits. This is similar to our satellite phone example in which we use a timing signal (i.e., we count off seconds in our head) to ensure we don't talk over the other person's speech.

If two systems are going to communicate using a synchronous transmission technology, they do not use start and stop bits, but the synchronization of the transfer of data takes place through a timing sequence, which is initiated by a clock pulse.

It is the data link protocol that has the synchronization rules embedded into it. So when a message goes down a system's network stack, if a data link protocol, such as High-level Data Link Control (HDLC), is being used, then a clocking sequence is in place. (The receiving system must also be using this protocol so that it can interpret the data.) If the message is going down a network stack and a protocol such as Asynchronous Transfer Mode (ATM) is at the data link layer, then the message is framed with start and stop indicators.

Data link protocols that employ synchronous timing mechanisms are commonly used in environments that have systems that transfer large amounts of data in a predictable manner (i.e., data center environment). Environments that contain systems that send data in a nonpredictable manner (i.e., Internet connections) commonly have systems with protocols that use asynchronous timing mechanisms.

So, synchronous communication protocols transfer data as a stream of bits instead of framing it in start and stop bits. The synchronization can happen between two systems using a clocking mechanism, or a signal can be encoded into the data stream to let the receiver synchronize with the sender of the message. This synchronization needs to take place before the first message is sent. The sending system can transmit a digital clock pulse to the receiving system, which translates into, "We will start here and work in this type of synchronization scheme." Many modern bulk communication systems,

Asynchronous	Synchronous
Simpler, less costly implementation	More complex, costly implementation
No timing component	Timing component for data transmission synchronization
Parity bits used for error control	Robust error checking, commonly through cyclic redundancy checking (CRC)
Used for irregular transmission patterns	Used for high-speed, high-volume transmissions
Each byte requires three bits of instruction (start, stop, parity)	Minimal protocol overhead compared to asynchronous communication

Table 14-1 Main Differences Between Asynchronous and Synchronous Transmissions

such as high-bandwidth satellite links, use Global Positioning System (GPS) clock signals to synchronize their communications without the need to include a separate channel for timing.

Table 14-1 provides an overview of the differences between asynchronous and synchronous transmissions.

Broadband vs. Baseband

As you read, analog transmission means that data is being moved as waves, and digital transmission means that data is being moved as discrete electric pulses. Synchronous transmission means that two devices control their conversations with a clocking mechanism, and asynchronous means that systems use start and stop bits for communication synchronization. Now let's look at how many individual communication sessions can take place at one time.

A *baseband* technology uses the entire communication channel for its transmission, whereas a *broadband* technology divides the communication channel into individual and independent subchannels so that different types of data can be transmitted simultaneously. Baseband permits only one signal to be transmitted at a time, whereas broadband carries several signals over different subchannels. For example, a coaxial cable TV (CATV) system is a broadband technology that delivers multiple television channels over the same cable. This system can also provide home users with Internet access, but this data is transmitted at a different frequency range than the TV channels.

As an analogy, baseband technology only provides a one-lane highway for data to get from one point to another point. A broadband technology provides a data highway made up of many different lanes, so that not only can more data be moved from one point to another point, but different types of data can travel over the individual lanes.

Any transmission technology that "chops up" one communication channel into multiple channels is considered broadband. The communication channel is usually a specific range of frequencies, and the broadband technology provides delineation between these frequencies and provides techniques on how to modulate the data onto the individual subchannels. To continue with our analogy, we could have one large highway that *could* fit eight individual lanes—but unless we have something that defines

How Do These Technologies Work Together?

If you are new to networking, it can be hard to understand how the OSI model, analog and digital, synchronous and asynchronous, and baseband and broadband technologies interrelate and differentiate. You can think of the OSI model as a structure to build different languages. If you and Luigi are going to speak to each other in English, you have to follow the rules of this language to be able to understand each other. If you are going to speak French, you still have to follow the rules of that language (OSI model), but the individual letters that make up the words are in a different order. The OSI model is a generic structure that can be used to define many different "languages" for devices to be able to talk to each other. Once you and Luigi agree that you are going to communicate using English, you can *speak* your message to Luigi, and thus your words move over continuous airwaves (analog). Or you can choose to send your message to Luigi through Morse code, which uses individual discrete values (digital). You can send Luigi all of your words with no pauses or punctuation (synchronous) or insert pauses and punctuation (asynchronous). If you are the only one speaking to Luigi at a time, this would be analogous to baseband. If ten people are speaking to Luigi at one time, this would be broadband.

these lanes and have rules for how these lanes are used, this is a baseband connection. If we take the same highway and lay down painted white lines, post traffic signs, add on and off ramps, and establish rules that drivers have to follow, now we are talking about broadband.

A digital subscriber line (DSL) uses one single phone line and constructs a set of high-frequency channels for Internet data transmissions. A cable modem uses the available frequency spectrum that is provided by a cable TV carrier to move Internet traffic to and from a household. Mobile broadband devices implement individual channels over a cellular connection, and Wi-Fi broadband technology moves data to and from an access point over a specified frequency set. The point is that there are different ways of cutting up one channel into subchannels for higher data transfer and that they provide the capability to move different types of traffic at the same time.

Cabling

The different types of transmission techniques we just covered eventually end up being used to send signals over either a cable or free space. We already covered wireless communications in Chapter 12, so let's talk about cabling now.

Electrical signals travel as currents through cables and can be negatively affected by many factors within the environment, such as motors, fluorescent lighting, magnetic forces, and other electrical devices. These items can corrupt the data as it travels through the cable, which is why cable standards are used to indicate cable type, shielding, transmission rates, and maximum distance a particular type of cable can be used.

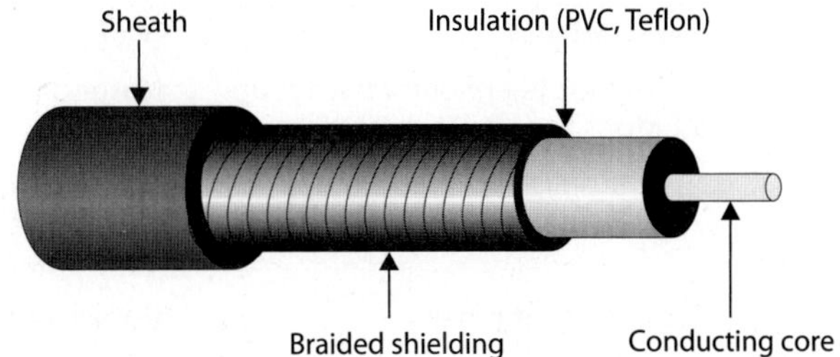

Figure 14-2 Coaxial cable

Coaxial Cable

Coaxial cable has a copper core that is surrounded by a shielding layer and grounding wire, as shown in Figure 14-2. This is all encased within a protective outer jacket. Compared to twisted-pair cable, coaxial cable is more resistant to electromagnetic interference (EMI), provides a higher bandwidth, and supports the use of longer cable lengths. So, why is twisted-pair cable more popular? Twisted-pair cable is cheaper and easier to work with, and the move to switched environments that provide hierarchical wiring schemes has overcome the cable-length issue of twisted-pair cable.

Coaxial cabling is used as a transmission line for radio frequency signals. If you have cable TV, you have coaxial cabling entering your house and the back of your TV. The various TV channels are carried over different radio frequencies. Modems allow us to use some of the "empty" TV frequencies for Internet connectivity.

Twisted-Pair Cable

Twisted-pair cabling has insulated copper wires surrounded by an outer protective jacket. If the cable has an outer foil shielding, it is referred to as *shielded twisted pair (STP)*, which adds protection from radio frequency interference (RFI) and EMI. Twisted-pair cabling, which does not have this extra outer shielding, is called *unshielded twisted pair (UTP)*.

The twisted-pair cable contains copper wires that twist around each other, as shown in Figure 14-3. This twisting of the wires protects the integrity and strength of the signals they carry. Each wire forms a balanced circuit, because the voltage in each pair uses the same amplitude, just with opposite phases. The tighter the twisting of the wires, the more

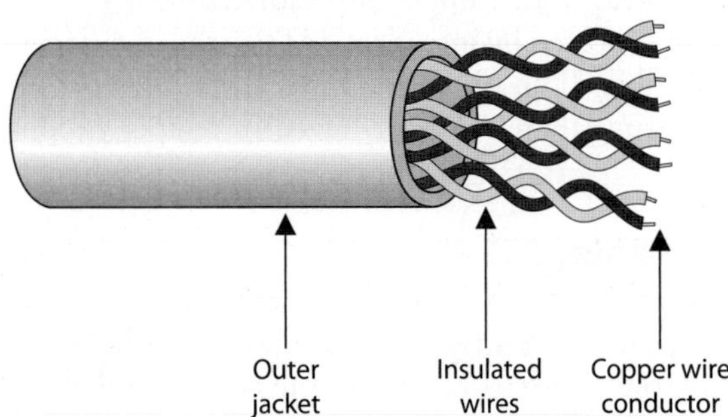

Figure 14-3 Twisted-pair cabling uses copper wires.

UTP Category	Characteristics	Usage
Category 1	Voice-grade telephone cable for up to 1 Mbps transmission rate	No longer in use for data or phones.
Category 2	Data transmission up to 4 Mbps	Historically used in mainframe and minicomputer terminal connections, but no longer in common use.
Category 3	10 Mbps for Ethernet	Used in older 10Base-T network installations and legacy phone lines.
Category 4	16 Mbps	Normally used in Token Ring networks.
Category 5	100 Mbps; two twisted pairs	Sometimes used in legacy 100Base-TX; deprecated in 2001 for data but still used for telephone and video.
Category 5e	1 Gbps; four twisted pairs, providing reduced crosstalk	Widely used in modern networks.
Category 6	1 Gbps, but can support 10 Gbps up to 55 meters	Used in newer network installations requiring high-speed transmission. Standard for Gigabit Ethernet.

Table 14-2 UTP Cable Ratings

resistant the cable is to interference and attenuation. UTP has several categories of cabling, each of which has its own unique characteristics.

The twisting of the wires, the type of insulation used, the quality of the conductive material, and the shielding of the wire determine the rate at which data can be transmitted. The UTP ratings indicate which of these components were used when the cables were manufactured. Some types are more suitable and effective for specific uses and environments. Table 14-2 lists the cable ratings.

Copper cable has been around for many years. It is inexpensive and easy to use. A majority of the telephone systems today use copper cabling with the rating of voice grade. Twisted-pair wiring is the preferred network cabling, but it also has its drawbacks. Copper actually resists the flow of electrons, which causes a signal to degrade after it has traveled a certain distance. This is why cable lengths are recommended for copper cables; if these recommendations are not followed, a network could experience signal loss and data corruption. Copper also radiates energy, which means information can be monitored and captured by intruders. UTP is the least secure networking cable compared to coaxial and fiber. If an organization requires higher speed, higher security, and cables to have longer runs than what is allowed in copper cabling, fiber-optic cable may be a better choice.

Fiber-Optic Cable

Twisted-pair cable and coaxial cable use copper wires as their data transmission media, but fiber-optic cable uses a type of glass that carries light waves, onto which we modulate the data being transmitted. The glass core is surrounded by a protective cladding, which in turn is encased within an outer jacket.

Fiber Components

Fiber-optic cables are made up of a light source, an optical fiber cable, and a light detector.

Light Sources Convert electrical signal into light signal.

- Light-emitting diodes (LEDs)
- Diode lasers

Optical Fiber Cable Data travels as light.

- **Single mode** Small glass core, used for high-speed data transmission over long distances. They are less susceptible to attenuation than multimode fibers.
- **Multimode** Large glass core, able to carry more data than single mode fibers, though they are best for shorter distances because of their higher attenuation levels.

Light Detector Converts light signal back into electrical signal.

Because it uses glass, *fiber-optic* cabling has higher transmission speeds that allow signals to travel over longer distances. Fiber-optic cabling is not as affected by attenuation and EMI when compared to cabling that uses copper. It does not radiate signals, as does UTP cabling, and is difficult to eavesdrop on; therefore, fiber-optic cabling is much more secure than UTP, STP, or coaxial.

Using fiber-optic cable sounds like the way to go, so you might wonder why you would even bother with UTP, STP, or coaxial. Unfortunately, fiber-optic cable is expensive and difficult to work with. It is usually used in backbone networks and environments that require high data transfer rates. Most networks use UTP and connect to a backbone that uses fiber.

NOTE The price of fiber and the cost of installation have been steadily decreasing, while the demand for more bandwidth only increases. More organizations and service providers are installing fiber directly to the end user.

Cabling Problems

Cables are extremely important within networks, and when they experience problems, the whole network could experience problems. This section addresses some of the more common cabling issues many networks experience.

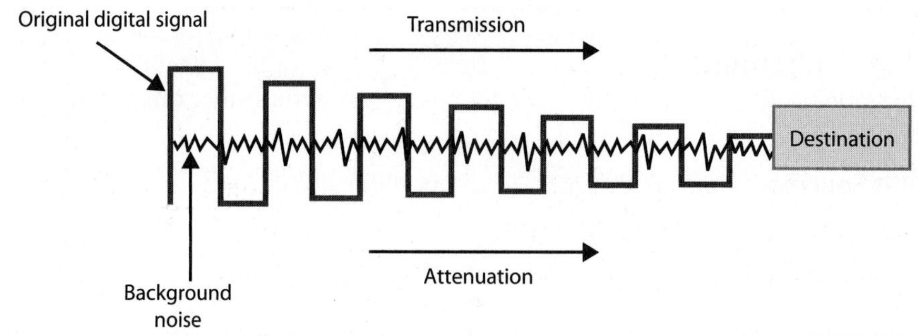

Figure 14-4 Background noise can merge with an electronic signal and alter the signal's integrity.

Noise The term *line noise* refers to random fluctuations in electrical-magnetic impulses that are carried along a physical medium. Noise on a line is usually caused by surrounding devices or by characteristics of the wiring's environment. Noise can be caused by motors, computers, copy machines, fluorescent lighting, and microwave ovens, to name a few. This background noise can combine with the data being transmitted over the cable and distort the signal, as shown in Figure 14-4. The more noise there is interacting with the cable, the more likely the receiving end will not receive the data in the form originally transmitted.

Attenuation *Attenuation* is the loss of signal strength as it travels. This is akin to rolling a ball down the floor; as it travels, air causes resistance that slows it down and eventually stops it. In the case of electricity, the metal in the wire also offers resistance to the flow of electricity. Though some materials such as copper and gold offer very little resistance, it is still there. The longer a wire, the more attenuation occurs, which causes the signal carrying the data to deteriorate. This is why standards include suggested cable-run lengths.

The effects of attenuation increase with higher frequencies; thus, 100Base-TX at 80 MHz has a higher attenuation rate than 10Base-T at 10 MHz. This means that cables used to transmit data at higher frequencies should have shorter cable runs to ensure attenuation does not become an issue.

If a networking cable is too long, attenuation will become a problem. Basically, the data is in the form of electrons, and these electrons have to "swim" through a copper wire. However, this is more like swimming upstream, because there is a lot of resistance on the electrons working in this media. After a certain distance, the electrons start to slow down and their encoding format loses form. If the form gets too degraded, the receiving system cannot interpret the electrons any longer. If a network administrator needs to run a cable longer than its recommended segment length, she needs to insert a repeater or some type of device that amplifies the signal and ensures that it gets to its destination in the right encoding format.

Attenuation can also be caused by cable breaks and malfunctions. This is why cables should be tested. If a cable is suspected of attenuation problems, cable testers can inject signals into the cable and read the results at the end of the cable.

EXAM TIP Most implementations of Ethernet over UTP have a maximum cable length of 100 meters, partly to deal with attenuation.

Crosstalk *Crosstalk* is a phenomenon that occurs when electrical signals of one wire spill over to the signals of another wire. When electricity flows through a wire, it generates a magnetic field around it. If another wire is close enough, the second wire acts as an antenna that turns this magnetic field into an electric current. When the different electrical signals mix, their integrity degrades and data corruption can occur. UTP mitigates crosstalk by twisting the wires around each other. Because crosstalk is greatest wherever wires are parallel to each other, this twisting makes it harder for this condition to exist. Still, UTP is much more vulnerable to crosstalk than STP or coaxial because it does not have extra layers of shielding to help protect against it.

Fire Rating of Cables Just as buildings must meet certain fire codes, so must wiring schemes. A lot of organizations string their network wires in drop ceilings—the space between the ceiling and the next floor—or under raised floors. This hides the cables and prevents people from tripping over them. However, when wires are strung in places like this, they are more likely to catch on fire without anyone knowing about it. Some cables produce hazardous gases when on fire that would spread throughout the building quickly. Network cabling that is placed in these types of areas, called *plenum space*, must meet a specific fire rating to ensure the cable will not produce and release harmful chemicals in case of a fire. A ventilation system's components are usually located in this plenum space, so if toxic chemicals were to get into that area, they could easily spread throughout the building in minutes.

Nonplenum cables usually have a polyvinyl chloride (PVC) jacket covering, whereas plenum-rated cables have jacket covers made of fluoropolymers. When setting up a network or extending an existing network, it is important that you know which wire types are required in which situation.

Cables should be installed in unexposed areas so they are not easily tripped over, damaged, or eavesdropped upon. The cables should be strung behind walls and in the protected spaces, such as in dropped ceilings. In environments that require extensive security, wires can be encapsulated within *pressurized conduits* so if someone attempts to access a wire, the pressure of the conduit changes, causing an alarm to sound and a message to be sent to the security staff. A better approach to high-security requirements is probably to use fiber-optic cable, which is much more difficult to covertly tap.

NOTE While a lot of the world's infrastructure is wired and thus uses one of these types of cables, remember that a growing percentage of our infrastructure is not wired, but rather uses some form of wireless technology (Bluetooth, Wi-Fi, satellite, etc.), particularly to reach end devices.

Bandwidth and Throughput

Whatever type of transmission you use over any given cable, there is a limit to how much information you can encode within it. In computer networks, we use two different but related terms to measure this limit. *Bandwidth* is the amount of information that theoretically can be transmitted over a link within a second. In a perfect world, this is the data transfer capability of a connection and is commonly associated with the number of available frequencies and speed of a link. Data *throughput* is the actual amount of data that can be carried over a real link. Throughput is always less than or equal to a link's bandwidth. In fact, it is most often the case that throughput is notably less than bandwidth. Why?

As mentioned, bandwidth is a theoretical limit determined by analyzing a medium (e.g., category 5 UTP cable) and a physical layer protocol (e.g., 100BaseT Ethernet) and then doing the math to calculate the maximum possible amount of data we could push through it. Now, of course, when you put that medium and protocol into a real environment, a multitude of issues come into play and make it hard to achieve that optimal data rate.

The throughput of our networks is affected by many factors. There could be EMI (or line noise) in the medium, as previously discussed. However, in a well-engineered facility and network, this should not be a big problem. Typically, you'll be more concerned about packet delays and losses. *Latency* is the amount of time it takes a packet to get from its source to its destination. This could be measured as either time to first byte (TTFB) or round-trip time (RTT). Latency can be caused by multiple factors, including

- **Transmission medium** Even though electricity and light move at the speed of light, it still takes time to get from one place to another. If your links are very long, or if the cables have too many imperfections, the medium itself will cause latency.
- **Network devices** Routers and firewalls take some time to examine packets, even if they're just deciding which outbound interface to use. If you have too many rules in your routing or security devices, this is invariably going to introduce delays.

To reduce latency, you should keep your physical links as short as possible. You should also look at how many hops your packets must take to get to their destinations. Virtual LANs (VLANs) can help keep devices that communicate frequently "closer" to each other. For international organizations, using a content distribution network (CDN), which we address later in this chapter, keeps most data close to where it is needed. Finally, the use of proxies can reduce latency by bringing frequently requested data closer to your users.

Another issue that negatively impacts your data throughputs (compared to a link's rated bandwidth) is congestion. Since some links in your network are shared, if you have too many packets moving around, it will inevitably bog things down. You may have a 1-GBps (bandwidth) connection to your home, but if every house in your neighborhood has one too and you all share a 1-GBps link from the local switch to the first router, your throughput will be way lower than advertised unless you log on when everyone else is sleeping. The best way to prevent congestion is through careful design and implementation of your network. Keep your broadcast domains as small as possible, ensure that your shared links are able to support peak traffic rates, and consider prioritizing certain types of traffic so that if your staff decides to livestream news, that doesn't slow down your ability to get real work done.

Network Devices

Several types of devices are used in LANs, MANs, and WANs to provide intercommunication among computers and networks. We need to have physical devices throughout the network to actually use all the protocols and services we have covered up to this point. The different network devices vary according to their functionality, capabilities, intelligence, and network placement. We will look at the following devices:

- Repeaters
- Bridges
- Switches
- Routers
- Gateways
- Proxy servers
- PBXs
- Network access control devices

The typical network has a bunch of these devices, and their purposes and operation can get confusing really quickly. Therefore, we will also look at network diagram techniques that can help us create different (simpler) views into complex environments. We'll also consider operational issues like power requirements, warranties, and support agreements.

Repeaters

A *repeater* provides the simplest type of connectivity because it only repeats electrical signals between cable segments, which enables it to extend a network. Repeaters work at the physical layer and are add-on devices for extending a network connection over a greater distance. The device amplifies signals because signals attenuate the farther they have to travel.

Repeaters can also work as line conditioners by actually cleaning up the signals. This works much better when amplifying digital signals than when amplifying analog signals because digital signals are discrete units, which makes extraction of background noise from them much easier for the amplifier. If the device is amplifying analog signals, any accompanying noise often is amplified as well, which may further distort the signal.

A *hub* is a multiport repeater. A hub is often referred to as a *concentrator* because it is the physical communication device that allows several computers and devices to communicate with each other. A hub does not understand or work with IP or MAC addresses. When one system sends a signal to go to another system connected to it, the signal is broadcast to all the ports, and thus to all the systems connected to the concentrator.

NOTE Hubs are exceptionally rare nowadays but you may still come across them.

Bridges

A *bridge* is a LAN device used to connect LAN segments (or VLAN segments) and thus extends the range of a LAN. It works at the data link layer and therefore works with MAC addresses. A repeater does not work with addresses; it just forwards all signals it receives. When a frame arrives at a bridge, the bridge determines whether or not the MAC address is on the local network segment. If it is not, the bridge forwards the frame to the necessary network segment. A bridge amplifies the electrical signal, as does a repeater, but it has more intelligence than a repeater and is used to extend a LAN and enable the administrator to filter frames to control which frames go where.

When using bridges, you have to watch carefully for *broadcast storms*. While bridges break up a collision domain by port (i.e., computers on the same bridge port are in the same collision domain), all ports are on the same broadcast domain. Because bridges can forward all traffic, they forward all broadcast packets as well. This can overwhelm the network and result in a broadcast storm, which degrades the network bandwidth and performance.

The international standard for bridges on Ethernet networks is IEEE 802.1Q. It describes the principal elements of bridge operation as follows:

- Relaying and filtering frames (based on MAC addresses and port numbers)
- Maintenance of the information required to make frame filtering and relaying decisions (i.e., the forwarding tables)
- Management of the elements listed (e.g., aging off forwarding table entries)

EXAM TIP Do not confuse routers with bridges. Routers work at the network layer and filter packets based on IP addresses, whereas bridges work at the data link layer and filter frames based on MAC addresses. Routers usually do not pass broadcast information, but bridges do pass broadcast information.

Forwarding Tables

A bridge must know how to get a frame to its destination—that is, it must know to which port the frame must be sent and where the destination host is located. Years ago, network administrators had to type route paths into bridges so the bridges had static paths indicating where to pass frames that were headed for different destinations. This was a tedious task and prone to errors. Today, most bridges use *transparent bridging*.

In transparent bridging, a bridge starts to learn about the network's environment as soon as it is powered on and continues to learn as the network changes. It does this by examining frames and making entries in its forwarding tables. When a bridge receives a frame from a new source computer, the bridge associates this new source address and the

Connecting Two LANS: Bridge vs. Router

What is the difference between two LANs connected via a bridge versus two LANs connected via a router? If two LANs are connected with a bridge, the LANs have been extended because they are both in the same broadcast domain. A router separates broadcast domains, so if two LANs are connected with a router, an internetwork results. An *internetwork* is a group of networks connected in a way that enables any node on any network to communicate with any other node. The Internet is an example of an internetwork.

port on which it arrived. It does this for all computers that send frames on the network. Eventually, the bridge knows the address of each computer on the various network segments and to which port each is connected. If the bridge receives a request to send a frame to a destination that is not in its forwarding table, it sends out a query frame on each network segment except for the source segment. The destination host is the only one that replies to this query. The bridge updates its table with this computer address and the port to which it is connected and forwards the frame.

Many bridges use the *Spanning Tree Protocol (STP)*, which adds more intelligence to the bridges. STP ensures that frames do not circle networks forever, provides redundant paths in case a bridge goes down, assigns unique identifiers to each bridge, assigns priority values to these bridges, and calculates path costs. This creates much more efficient frame-forwarding processes by each bridge. STP also enables an administrator to indicate whether he wants traffic to travel certain paths instead of others. Newer bridges implement the Shortest Path Bridging (SPB) protocol, which is defined in IEEE 802.1aq and is more efficient and scalable than STP.

PART IV

Switches

Switches are, essentially, multiport bridges that typically have additional management features. Because bridges are intended to connect and extend LANs (and not necessarily individual hosts), they tend to have few ports. However, if you take the exact same functionality and add a bunch of ports to it, you could use the ports to connect to each individual host or to other switches. Figure 14-5 illustrates a typical, hierarchical network configuration in which computers are directly connected to access switches within close proximity (100 m or less). Access switches are, in turn, connected to distribution switches, which usually connect different departments or floors in a building. This distribution layer is a great place to implement access control lists (ACLs) and filtering to provide security. Finally, the upper tier of core switches provides a high-speed switching and routing backbone for the organization and is designed to pass network traffic as fast as possible. In this layer, only switches are connected to each other (i.e., there are no computers directly connected to them).

On Ethernet networks, computers have to compete for the same shared network medium. Each computer must listen for activity on the network and transmit its data when it thinks the coast is clear. This contention and the resulting collisions cause

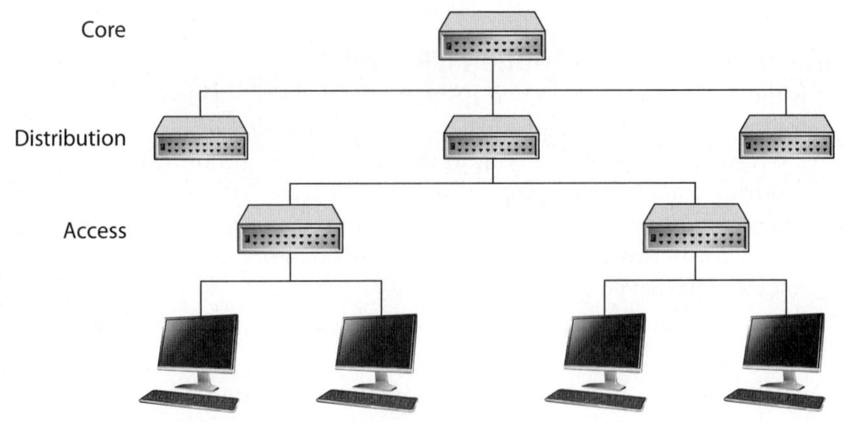

Figure 14-5 Hierarchical model of a switched network

traffic delays and use up precious bandwidth. When switches are used, contention and collisions are not issues, which results in more efficient use of the network's bandwidth and decreased latency. Switches reduce or remove the sharing of the network medium and the problems that come with it.

Since a switch is a multiport bridging device where each port is connected to exactly one other device, each port provides dedicated bandwidth to the device attached to it. A port is bridged to another port so the two devices have an end-to-end private link. The switch employs full-duplex communication, so one wire pair is used for sending and another pair is used for receiving. This ensures the two connected devices do not compete for the same bandwidth.

Basic switches work at the data link layer and forward traffic based on MAC addresses. However, today's layer 3, layer 4, and other layer switches have more enhanced functionality than layer 2 switches. These higher-level switches offer routing functionality, packet inspection, traffic prioritization, and QoS functionality. These switches are referred to as *multilayered switches* because they combine data link layer, network layer, and other layer functionalities.

Multilayered switches use hardware-based processing power, which enables them to look deeper within the frame, to make more decisions based on the information encapsulated within the frame, and then to provide forwarding and traffic management tasks. Usually this amount of work creates a lot of overhead and traffic delay, but multilayered switches perform these activities within an application-specific integrated circuit (ASIC). This means that most of the functions of the switch are performed at the hardware and chip level rather than at the software level, making it much faster than routers.

CAUTION While it is harder for attackers to sniff traffic on switched networks, they should not be considered safe just because switches are involved. Attackers commonly poison cache memory used on switches to divert traffic to their desired location.

Layer 3 and 4 Switches

Layer 2 switches only have the intelligence to forward a frame based on its MAC address and do not have a higher understanding of the network as a whole. A layer 3 switch has the intelligence of a router. It not only can route packets based on their IP addresses but also can choose routes based on availability and performance. A layer 3 switch is basically a router on steroids, because it moves the route lookup functionality to the more efficient switching hardware level.

The basic distinction between layer 2, 3, and 4 switches is the header information the device looks at to make forwarding or routing decisions (data link, network, or transport OSI layers). But layer 3 and 4 switches can use tags, which are assigned to each destination network or subnet. When a packet reaches the switch, the switch compares the destination address with its tag information base, which is a list of all the subnets and their corresponding tag numbers. The switch appends the tag to the packet and sends it to the next switch. All the switches in between this first switch and the destination host just review this tag information to determine which route it needs to take, instead of analyzing the full header. Once the packet reaches the last switch, this tag is removed and the packet is sent to the destination. This process increases the speed of routing of packets from one location to another.

The use of these types of tags, referred to as *Multiprotocol Label Switching (MPLS)*, not only allows for faster routing but also addresses service requirements for the different packet types. Some time-sensitive traffic (such as video conferencing) requires a certain level of service (QoS) that guarantees a minimum rate of data delivery to meet the requirements of a user or application. When MPLS is used, different priority information is placed into the tags to help ensure that time-sensitive traffic has a higher priority than less sensitive traffic, as shown in Figure 14-6.

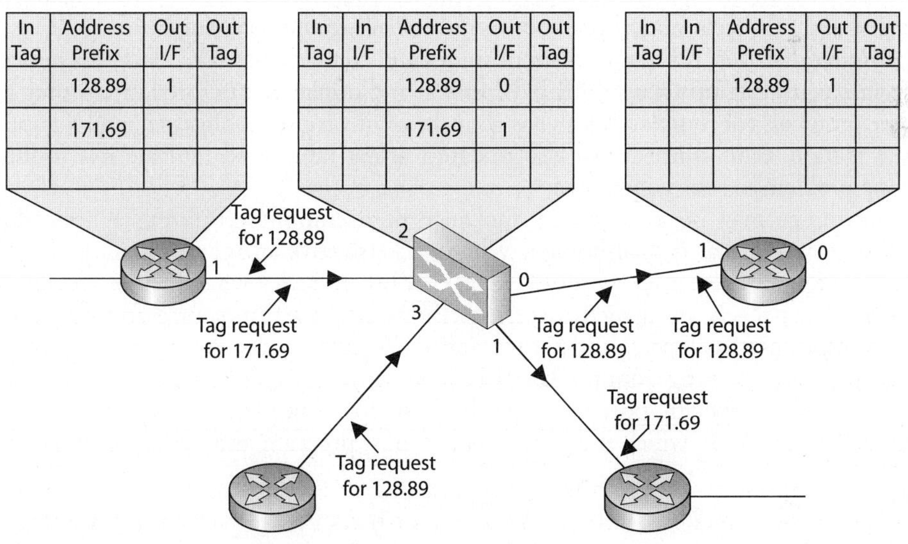

Figure 14-6 MPLS uses tags and tables for routing functions.

Because security requires control over who can access specific resources, more intelligent devices can provide a higher level of protection because they can make more detail-oriented decisions regarding who can access resources. When devices can look deeper into the packets, they have access to more information to make access decisions, which provides more granular access control.

As previously stated, switching makes it more difficult for intruders to sniff and monitor network traffic because no broadcast and collision information is continually traveling throughout the network. Switches provide a security service that other devices cannot provide. VLANs (described in depth in Chapter 13) are an important part of switching networks, because they enable administrators to have more control over their environment and they can isolate users and groups into logical and manageable entities.

Routers

We are going up the chain of the OSI layers while discussing various network devices. Repeaters work at the physical layer, bridges and switches work at the data link layer, and routers work at the network layer. As we go up each layer, each corresponding device has more intelligence and functionality because it can look deeper into the frame. A repeater looks at the electrical signal. The switch can look at the MAC address within the header. The router can peel back the first header information and look farther into the frame and find out the IP address and other routing information. The farther a device can look into a frame, the more decisions it can make based on the information within the frame.

Routers are layer 3, or network layer, devices that are used to connect similar or different networks. (For example, they can connect two Ethernet LANs or an Ethernet LAN to a Frame Relay link.) A router is a device that has two or more interfaces and a routing table, so it knows how to get packets to their destinations. It can filter traffic based on an access control list (ACL), and it fragments packets when necessary. Because routers have more network-level knowledge, they can perform higher-level functions, such as calculating the shortest and most economical path between the sending and receiving hosts.

A router discovers information about routes and changes that take place in a network through its routing protocols (RIP, BGP, OSPF, and others, as discussed in Chapter 11). These protocols tell routers if a link has gone down, if a route is congested, and if another route is more economical. They also update routing tables and indicate if a router is having problems or has gone down.

The router may be a dedicated appliance or a computer running a networking operating system that is dual-homed. When packets arrive at one of the interfaces, the router compares those packets to its ACL. This list indicates what packets are allowed in and what packets are denied. Access decisions are based on source and destination IP addresses, protocol type, and source and destination ports. An administrator may block all packets coming from the 10.10.12.0 network, any FTP requests, or any packets headed toward a specific port on a specific host, for example. This type of control is provided by the ACL, which the administrator must program and update as necessary.

What actually happens inside the router when it receives a packet? Let's follow the steps:

1. A packet is received on one of the interfaces of a router. The router views the routing data.
2. The router retrieves the destination IP network address from the packet.
3. The router looks at its routing table to see which port matches the requested destination IP network address.
4. If the router does not have information in its table about the destination address, it sends out an ICMP error message to the sending computer indicating that the message could not reach its destination.
5. If the router does have a route in its routing table for this destination, it decrements the TTL value and sees whether the maximum transmission unit (MTU) is different for the destination network. If the destination network requires a smaller MTU, the router fragments the packet.
6. The router changes header information in the packet so that the packet can go to the next correct router, or if the destination computer is on a connecting network, the changes made enable the packet to go directly to the destination computer.
7. The router sends the packet to its output queue for the necessary interface.

Table 14-3 provides a quick review of how routers differ from bridges and switches.

When is it best to use a repeater, bridge, or router? A repeater is used if an administrator needs to expand a network and amplify signals so they do not weaken on longer cables. However, a repeater also extends collision and broadcast domains.

Bridges and switches work at the data link layer and have a bit more intelligence than a repeater. Bridges can do simple filtering and separate collision domains, but not broadcast domains. A switch should be used when an administrator wants to connect multiple computers in a way that reduces traffic congestion and excessive collisions.

A router splits up a network into collision domains and broadcast domains. A router gives more of a clear-cut division between network segments than repeaters or bridges.

Bridge/Switch	Router
Reads header information but does not alter it	Creates a new header for each packet
Builds forwarding tables based on MAC addresses	Builds routing tables based on IP addresses
Has no concept of network addresses	Assigns a different network address per port
Filters traffic based on MAC addresses	Filters traffic based on IP addresses
Forwards broadcast traffic	Does not forward broadcast traffic
Forwards traffic if a destination address is unknown to the bridge	Does not forward traffic that contains a destination address unknown to the router

Table 14-3 Main Differences Between Bridges/Switches and Routers

A router should be used if an administrator wants to have more defined control of where the traffic goes, because more sophisticated filtering is available with routers, and when a router is used to segment a network, the result is more controllable sections.

Gateways

Gateway is a general term for software running on a device that connects two different environments and that many times acts as a translator for them or somehow restricts their interactions. Usually a gateway is needed when one environment speaks a different language, meaning it uses a certain protocol that the other environment does not understand. The gateway can translate mail from one type of mail server and format it so that another type of mail server can accept and understand it, or it can connect and translate different data link technologies such as Fiber Distributed Data Interface (FDDI) to Ethernet (both of which are discussed in Chapter 11).

Gateways perform much more complex tasks than connection devices such as routers and bridges. However, some people refer to routers as gateways when they connect two unlike networks (Token Ring and Ethernet) because the router has to translate between the data link technologies. Figure 14-7 shows how a network access server (NAS) functions as a gateway between telecommunications and network connections.

When networks connect to a backbone, a gateway can translate the different technologies and frame formats used on the backbone network versus the connecting LAN protocol frame formats. If a bridge were set up between an FDDI backbone and an Ethernet LAN, the computers on the LAN would not understand the FDDI protocols and frame formats. In this case, a LAN gateway would be needed to translate the protocols used between the different networks.

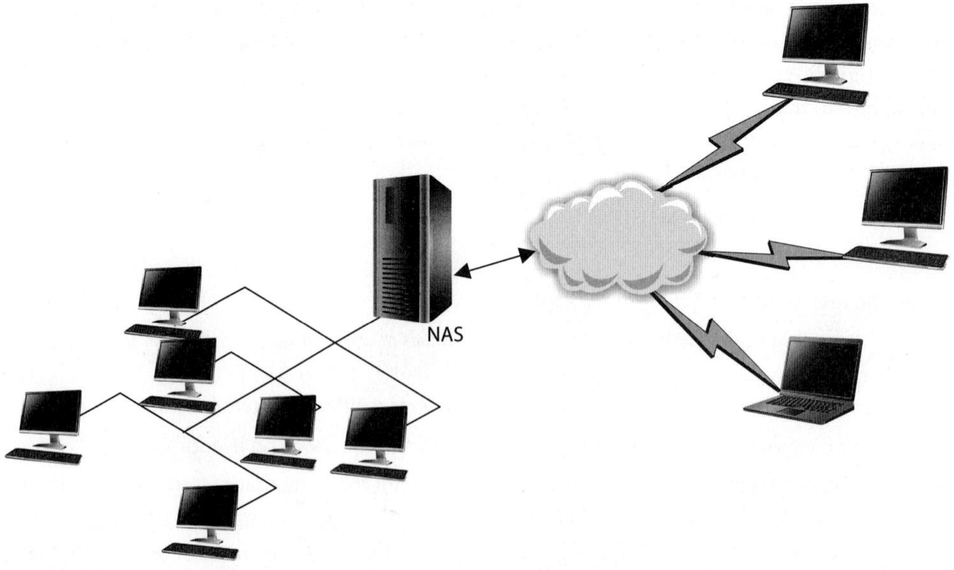

Figure 14-7 Several types of gateways can be used in a network. A NAS is one example.

A popular type of gateway is an *e-mail* gateway. Because several e-mail vendors have their own syntax, message format, and way of dealing with message transmission, e-mail gateways are needed to convert messages between e-mail server software. For example, suppose that David, whose corporate network uses Sendmail, writes an e-mail message to Dan, whose corporate network uses Microsoft Exchange. The e-mail gateway converts the message into a standard that all mail servers understand—usually X.400—and passes it on to Dan's mail server.

Proxy Servers

Proxy servers act as an intermediary between the clients that want access to certain services and the servers that provide those services. As a security professional, you do not want internal systems to directly connect to external servers without some type of control taking place. For example, if users on your network could connect directly to websites without some type of filtering and rules in place, the users could allow malicious traffic into the network or could surf websites your organization deems inappropriate. To prevent this situation, all internal web browsers should be configured to send their web requests to a web proxy server. The proxy server validates that the request is safe and then sends an independent request to the website on behalf of the user. A very basic proxy server architecture is shown in Figure 14-8.

The proxy server may cache the response it receives from the server so that when other clients make the same request, the proxy server doesn't have to make a connection out to the actual web server again but rather can serve up the necessary data directly. This drastically reduces latency and allows the clients to get the data they need much more quickly.

There are different types of proxies that provide specific services. A *forwarding proxy* is one that allows the client to specify the server it wants to communicate with, as in our scenario earlier. An *open proxy* is a forwarding proxy that is open for anyone to use. An anonymous open proxy allows users to conceal their IP address while browsing websites

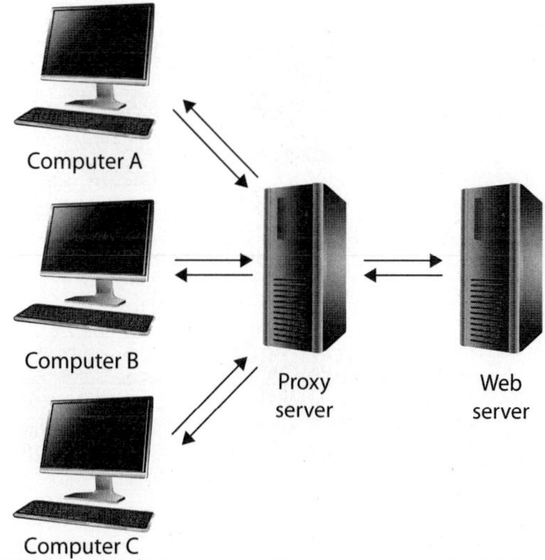

Figure 14-8 Proxy servers control traffic between clients and servers.

or using other Internet services. A *reverse proxy* appears to the clients as the original server. The client sends a request to what it thinks is the original server, but in reality this reverse proxy makes a request to the actual server and provides the client with the response. The forwarding and reverse proxy functionality seems similar, but as Figure 14-9 illustrates, a forwarding proxy server is commonly on an internal network controlling traffic that is exiting the network. A reverse proxy server is commonly on the network that fulfills clients' requests; thus, it is handling traffic that is entering its network. The reverse proxy can carry out load balancing, encryption acceleration, security, and caching.

Web proxy servers are commonly used to carry out content filtering to ensure that Internet use conforms to the organization's acceptable use policy (AUP). These types of proxies can block unacceptable web traffic, provide logs with detailed information pertaining to the websites specific users visited, monitor bandwidth usage statistics, block restricted website usage, and screen traffic for specific keywords (e.g., porn, confidential, Social Security numbers). The proxy servers can be configured to act mainly as caching servers, which keep local copies of frequently requested resources, allowing organizations to significantly reduce their upstream bandwidth usage and costs while significantly increasing performance.

While the most common use of proxy servers is for web-based traffic, they can be used for other network functionality and capabilities, as in DNS proxy servers. Proxy servers are a critical component of almost every network today. They need to be properly placed, configured, and monitored.

NOTE The use of proxy servers to allow for online anonymity has increased over the years. Some people use a proxy server to protect their browsing behaviors from others, with the goal of providing personal freedom and privacy. Attackers use the same functionality to help ensure their activities cannot be tracked back to their local systems.

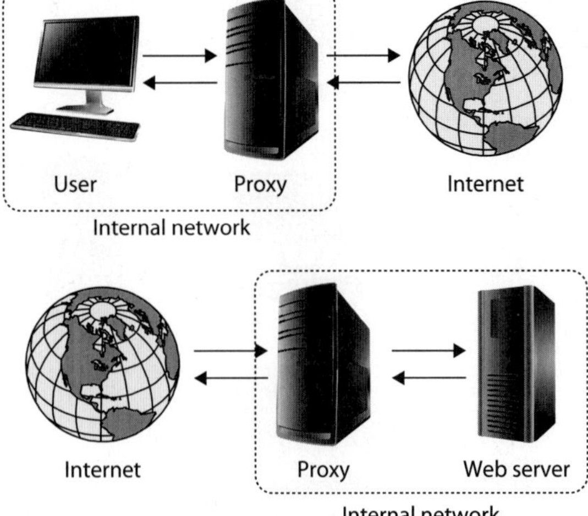

Figure 14-9 Forward vs. reverse proxy services

The Tor Network

Tor (originally known as The Onion Router) is a volunteer-operated network of computers around the world that work together to route encrypted web traffic. The goal of Tor is to keep your identity private online, or at least as close to private as is possible. (Misconfigurations or exploitable software on your local machine can still reveal your identity.) Every computer (or node) in Tor receives data from another node and passes it on to the next. Each node only knows where the encrypted data came from and where it's going next. After several hops, someone at the destination has no way of knowing who initiated the connection when you pop back up in the open Internet.

Tor can also provide access to so-called "hidden services" in the deep web that run only inside Tor. The infamous drug marketplace The Silk Road was an example of this. Tor is very popular among privacy advocates and people who live in countries that have strong censorship laws. However, Tor also is commonly used by criminal and even nation-state actors who want to protect their source location. Therefore, you should be extremely suspicious if you see Tor traffic in any enterprise network.

PBXs

Telephone companies use switching technologies to transmit phone calls to their destinations. A telephone company's central office houses the switches that connect towns, cities, and metropolitan areas through the use of optical fiber rings. So, for example, when

Putting It All Together: Network Devices

The network devices we've covered so far are the building blocks of almost any network architecture. Table 14-4 lists them and points out their important characteristics.

Device	OSI Layer	Functionality
Repeater	Physical	Amplifies the signal and extends networks
Bridge	Data link	Forwards packets and filters based on MAC addresses; forwards broadcast traffic, but not collision traffic
Switch	Data link	Provides a private virtual link between communicating devices; allows for VLANs; reduces collisions; impedes network sniffing
Router	Network	Separates and connects LANs creating internetworks; filters based on IP addresses
Gateway	Application	Connects different types of networks; performs protocol and format translations
Web proxy	Application	Acts as an intermediary between clients and servers, typically to improve security and/or performance

Table 14-4 Main Differences Between Network Devices

Dusty makes a landline phone call from his house, the call first hits the local central office of the telephone company that provides service to Dusty, and then the switch within that office decides whether it is a local or long-distance call and where it needs to go from there. A *Private Branch Exchange (PBX)* is a private telephone switch that is located on an organization's property. This switch performs some of the same switching tasks that take place at the telephone company's central office. The PBX has a dedicated connection to its local telephone company's central office, where more intelligent switching takes place.

A PBX can interface with several types of devices and provides a number of telephone services. The voice data is multiplexed onto a dedicated line connected to the telephone company's central office. Figure 14-10 shows how data from different data sources can be placed on one line at the PBX and sent to the telephone company's switching facility.

PBXs use digital switching devices that can control analog and digital signals. While these modern exchanges are more secure than their analog predecessors, that in no way means PBX systems are free from vulnerabilities. Many PBX systems have system administrator passwords that are hardly ever changed. These passwords are set by default; therefore, if 100 companies purchase and implement 100 PBX systems from the PBX vendor ABC and they do not reset the password, a *phreaker* (a phone hacker) who knows this default password now has access to 100 PBX systems. Once a phreaker breaks into a PBX system, she can cause mayhem by rerouting calls, reconfiguring switches, or configuring the system to provide her and her friends with free long-distance calls. This type of fraud happens more often than most organizations realize because many of them do not closely audit their phone bills. Though the term is not used as much nowadays, phreakers are very much an issue to our telecommunications systems. Toll fraud (as most of their activities are called) associated with PBX systems are estimated to cost over $3 billion in annual losses worldwide, according to the Communications Fraud Control Association's (CFCA) 2019 Fraud Loss Survey.

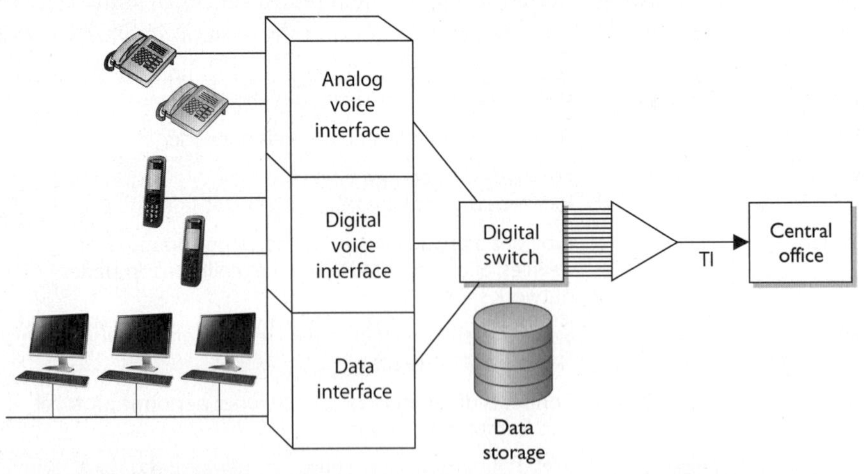

Figure 14-10 A PBX combines different types of data on the same lines.

PBX systems are also vulnerable to brute force and other types of attacks, in which phreakers use scripts and dictionaries to guess the necessary credentials to gain access to the system. In some cases, phreakers have listened to and changed people's voice messages. So, for example, when people call Bob and reach his voicemail, they might hear not his usual boring message but a new message that is screaming obscenities and insults.

Unfortunately, many security people do not even think about a PBX when they are assessing a network's vulnerabilities and security level. This is because telecommunication devices have historically been managed by service providers and/or by someone on the staff who understands telephony. The network administrator is usually not the person who manages the PBX, so the PBX system commonly does not even get assessed. The PBX is just a type of switch and it is directly connected to the organization's infrastructure; thus, it is a doorway for the bad guys to exploit and enter. These systems need to be assessed and monitored just like any other network device.

So, what should we do to secure PBX systems? Since many of these systems nowadays ride on IP networks, some of the basic security measures will sound familiar. Start by ensuring you know all accounts on the system and that their passwords are strong. Then, ensure that your PBX is updated regularly and that it sits behind your firewall with the appropriate ACLs in place. Other security measures are more specific to a PBX. For example, consider separating your voice and data traffic through these systems by placing them on different VLANs. If one of the VLANs is penetrated, the other could remain secure. Also, limiting the rate of traffic to IP telephony VLANs can slow down an outside attack.

Network Access Control Devices

Network access control (NAC) is any set of policies and controls that we use to, well, control access to our networks. The term implies that we will verify that a device satisfies certain requirements before we let it in. At its simplest level, this could just be user authentication, which was the theme of our discussion of the IEEE 802.1X standard when we were covering wireless network security in Chapter 12. The 802.1X protocol allows devices to connect in a very limited manner (i.e., only to the network authenticator) until we can verify the user credentials it presents.

To fully leverage the power of NAC, however, we should do much more. For starters, we can (and should) authenticate a device. Endpoint/device authentication should be familiar to you because you already use it whenever you establish an HTTPS connection to a web server. When a client requests a secure connection, the server responds with its certificate, which contains its public key issued by a trusted certificate authority (CA). The client then encrypts a secret session key using the server's public key, so only the server can decrypt it and then establish a symmetrically encrypted secure link. It is possible to configure a NAC device to authenticate itself in a similar manner, but also require the client device to do the same. Obviously, we'd need a certificate (and matching private key) installed on the client device for this to work. An alternative approach to using certificates is to use a hardware Trusted Platform Module (TPM) if the endpoint has one. We discussed TPMs in Chapter 9.

A common use of NAC is to ensure the endpoint is properly configured prior to it being allowed to connect to the network. For example, it is pretty common to check the version of the OS as well as the signatures for the antimalware software. If either of these is not current, the device may be placed in an untrusted LAN segment from which it can download and install the required updates. Once the device meets the access policy requirements, it is allowed to connect to the protected network.

Network Diagramming

In many cases, you cannot capture a full network in a diagram because of the complexity of most organizations' networks. Sometimes we have a false sense of security when we have a pretty network diagram that we can all look at and be proud of, but let's dig deeper into why this can be deceiving. From what perspective should you look at a network? Many possibilities exist:

- A cabling diagram that shows how everything is physically connected (coaxial, UTP, fiber) and a wireless portion that describes the WLAN structure
- A network diagram that illustrates the network in infrastructure layers of access, aggregation, edge, and core
- A diagram that illustrates how the various networking routing takes place (VLANs, MPLS connections, OSPF, IGRP, and BGP links)
- A diagram that shows how different data flows take place (FTP, IPSec, HTTP, TLS, L2TP, PPP, Ethernet, FDDI, ATM, etc.)
- A diagram that separates workstations and the core server types that almost every network uses (DNS, DHCP, web farm, storage, print, SQL, PKI, mail, domain controllers, RADIUS, etc.)
- A view of a network based upon trust zones, which are enforced by filtering routers, firewalls, and DMZ structures
- A view of a network based upon its IP subnet structure

But what if you look at a network diagram from a Microsoft perspective, which illustrates many of these things but in forest, tree, domain, and OU containers? Then you need to show remote access connections, VPN concentrators, extranets, and the various MAN and WAN connections. How do we illustrate our IP telephony structure? How do we integrate our mobile device administration servers into the diagram? How do we document our new cloud computing infrastructure? How do we show the layers of virtualization within our database? How are redundant lines and fault-tolerance solutions marked? How does this network correlate and interact with our offsite location that carries out parallel processing? And we have not even gotten to our security components (firewalls, IDS, IPS, DLP, antimalware, content filters, etc.). And in the real world, whatever network diagrams an organization does have are usually out of date because they take a lot of effort to create and maintain.

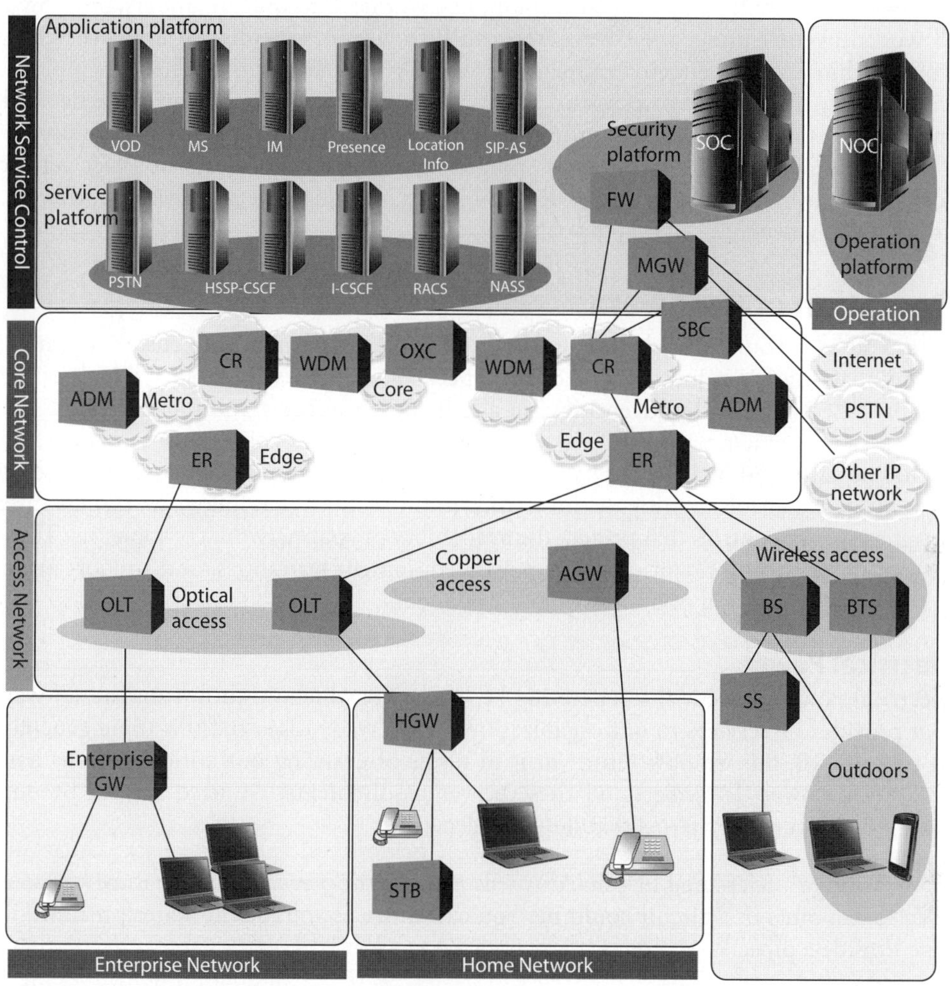

The point is that a network is a complex beast that cannot really be captured on one piece of paper. Compare it to a human body. When you go into the doctor's office, you see posters on the wall. One poster shows the circulatory system, one shows the muscles, one shows bones, another shows organs, and another shows tendons and ligaments; a dentist's office has a bunch of posters on teeth; if you are at an acupuncture clinic, there will be a poster on acupuncture and reflexology points. And then there is a ton of stuff no one makes posters for—hair follicles, skin, toenails, eyebrows—but these are all part of one system.

So what does this mean to the security professional? You have to understand a network from many different aspects if you are actually going to secure it. You start by learning all this network stuff in a modular fashion, but you need to quickly understand how it all works together under the covers. You can be a complete genius on how everything works within your current environment but not fully understand that when an employee connects her iPhone to her company laptop that is connected to the corporate network and uses it as a modem, this is an unmonitored WAN connection that can be used as a doorway by an attacker. Security is complex and demanding, so do not ever get too cocky, and always remember that a diagram is just showing a perspective of a network, not the whole network.

Operation of Hardware

Once you have your network designed and implemented, you need to ensure it remains operational. Keep in mind that one of the aspects of security is availability, which can be compromised not only by adversaries but also by power outages, equipment defects, and human error. Remember that all risks, not just the ones that come from human actors, should be addressed by your risk management program. This ensures that you can select cost-effective controls to mitigate those risks. In the sections that follow, we discuss three specific types of controls that protect the availability of your network components. These control types are redundant electrical power, equipment warranties, and support agreements on the operation of our network components.

Electrical Power

Electrical power is essential to operating IT hardware, which, in turn, runs the software that provides IT services to our organizations. We already discussed this topic generally in Chapter 10, but we now return to it in terms of ensuring our critical systems have redundant power. To understand these power requirements, we need to first become familiar with three key terms that describe electricity:

- **Voltage** Measured in volts, this tells us what the *potential* electric force between two points in a circuit could be. You can think of volts as the water pressure inside a pipe.
- **Current** Measured in amps, this is the *actual* electric flow through the circuit. If you think of volts as the pressure inside a water pipe, you can think of current as the diameter of a valve attached to it; the bigger the valve, the faster the water can come out.
- **Power** There are two ways to measure power. We measure electrical power in watts, which we calculate by multiplying voltage by amperage. In other words, if your server rack is running on 240 volts and drawing 9 amps of current, it is consuming 2,160 watts or 2.16 kilowatts (kW). Another related term is kilowatt-hours (kWh), which is simply the amount of power consumed during a 1-hour period. So, that same server rack would draw 2.16 kWh in one hour, or 51.84 kWh in a day (assuming the current draw is constant).

What we actually care about is whether or not we have enough electric power to run our equipment. There are two ways to measure power: apparent and real. You can think of *apparent power* as the maximum amount of electricity that could get through a circuit in a perfect case. This value is simply the product of the voltage and current of a system, and is measured in volt-amps (VA). So, if you have a 120-volt computer that can draw up to 3 amps, its apparent power would be 360 VA.

Typically, however, the real power drawn by a system is less than its apparent power. This is because of certain complexities of alternating current (AC) circuits that we won't dive into. Suffice it to say that AC, which is the type of current produced from virtually every power outlet, is constantly changing. This variance means that the *real power* drawn by a server will be some value, measured in watts, equal to or (much more frequently) lower than the apparent power. Thankfully, we don't have to calculate this value; most computing equipment is labeled with the real power value in watts (or kilowatts).

Why should you care? Because real power (watts) determines the actual power you purchase from the utility company, the size of any backup generators you might need, and the heat generated by the equipment. Apparent power (VA) is used for sizing wiring and circuit breakers, so the former don't melt (or worse, catch fire) and the latter don't trip. The ratio of real power to apparent power is called the *work factor*, which can never be greater than one (since the denominator is the ideal apparent power).

With all this discussion under our belts, we can now (finally) talk about redundant power, which typically comes in the two forms presented in Chapter 10: uninterruptable power supplies (UPSs) and backup power sources. Suppose one of your organization's facilities has (what will eventually turn out to be) an extended power outage lasting multiple days. Your business continuity plan (BCP; covered in Chapter 2) should identify your mission-critical systems and determine how long they can remain unavailable before your organizational losses are intolerable. You would have addressed this in your facility planning (Chapter 10) by implementing a backup power source. Typically, there is a period between the start of a power outage and when the backup power source comes online and is usable. This is the amount of time during which your UPS systems will have to keep your critical assets running.

To determine how much power you need from your backup power source, you simply add up the power consumption of your critical assets (in kW), keeping in mind the need for cooling and any other supporting systems. Let's say this comes out to be 6 kW and your backup source is a generator. Since generators run optimally at 75 percent to 80 percent of their rated loads, you'd need an 8-kW generator or greater. You also want to factor in room for growth, which should be no less than 25 percent, so you end up getting a 10-kW generator. Now, suppose you also get an automatic transfer switch that will start the generator and transfer the load from critical circuits 60 seconds after the outage is detected. How much UPS capacity do you need?

Whereas the real power consumption that you used to estimate your generator needs probably came from actual readings of how many kilowatts your critical servers drew, your apparent power needs are probably higher because they capture peaks in consumption that are averaged out by real power readings. Remember that apparent power is at least as much as (and usually higher than) your real power. If you look at your equipment's technical descriptions (or labels) you may see a value measured in volt-ampere (VA or kVA), and all you have to do is add up these values and get a UPS that is rated for that value. Alternatively, a good rule of thumb is to multiply your real power by 1.4 kWA (kilowatt-ampere) per kVA. The resulting number of kVAs should give you sufficient UPS capacity until the generator kicks in.

Equipment Warranty

Of course, many other things can go wrong with our assets with or without power outages. Equipment failures due to manufacturing defects are, unfortunately, unavoidable in the long run. The good news is that most original equipment manufacturers (OEMs) provide a three-year warranty against such defects. However, you have to read the fine print and may want to upgrade the protections. Suppose that you have a critical server fail and you can only afford to have it down for 24 hours. The standard warranty includes next-day replacement delivery, so you're covered, right? Well, not if you factor in the time it'll take you to reconfigure the server, load up all the data it needs, and put it back into production. Since it is difficult and expensive to get better than next-day support, you may want to build in the cost of having a spare server (or two) in addition to the warranty to ensure you meet your maximum tolerable downtime (MTD).

Most OEMs also offer extended warranties at an additional cost. Depending on your hardware refresh cycle (i.e., how long you will operate equipment before replacing it with new systems), you may want to add one, two, or three more years to the base three-year warranty. This is usually cheaper to purchase when you buy the hardware, as opposed to purchasing it a year or two later. Seven to eight years after the initial purchase, however, warranty offers tend to expire, as the hardware will be too old for the OEM to continue supporting it.

Support Agreements

Even if your hardware doesn't fail, it could become unavailable (or insufficiently available) with regard to supporting your organizational processes. For example, suppose that a server slows down to the point where your users sit around for several seconds (or even minutes) waiting for a response. This would not only be frustrating but also lead to a loss of productivity that could add up to significant financial losses. If you have a large and well-staffed organization, you probably have a resident expert who can troubleshoot the server and get it back to peak performance. If you don't have such an expert, what do you do?

Many organizations use support agreements with third parties to deal with issues that are outside the expertise of their IT or security staff. Sometimes this support can be provided by the OEM as part of the purchase of a system. Other times, organizations hire a managed services provider (MSP), who not only responds when things go badly but continuously monitors the systems' performance to detect and fix problems as early as possible. Most MSPs charge flat monthly fees per device and include 24/7 remote monitoring, maintenance, and, when needed, onsite support. Think of this as an insurance policy against loss of availability.

Endpoint Security

An *endpoint* is any computing device that communicates through a network and whose principal function is not to mediate communications for other devices on that network. In other words, if a device is connected to a network but is not part of the routing, relaying, or managing of traffic on that network, then it is an endpoint. That definition leaves out all of the network devices we've discussed in the preceding sections. Endpoints include devices that you would expect, such as desktops, laptops, servers, smartphones, and tablets. However, they also include other devices that many of us don't normally think of, such as point of sale (POS) terminals at retail stores, building automation devices like smart thermostats and other Internet of Things (IoT) devices, and sensors and actuators in industrial control systems (ICS).

One of the greatest challenges in dealing with (and securing) endpoints is knowing they are present in the first place. While it would be extremely unusual (not to say frightening) for your routers and switches to unexpectedly drop in and out of the network, this is what mobile devices do by their very nature. The intermittent connectivity of mobile devices is also a problem when it comes to ensuring that they are properly configured and running the correct firmware, OS, and software versions. An approach to dealing with some of these issues is to use network access control (NAC), as discussed earlier in this chapter.

But mobile devices are not the only problem. Our increasing reliance on embedded systems like IoT and ICS devices poses additional challenges. For starters, embedded devices normally have lesser computing capabilities than other endpoints. You usually can't install security software on them, which means that many organizations simply

Securing Endpoints

Endpoint security really boils down to a handful of best practices. Sure, you should thoroughly analyze risks to your endpoints and implement cost-effective controls as part of a broader risk management program, but if you don't take care of the basic "tackling and blocking," then whatever else you do won't really make much of a difference. Here's a short list to get you started:

- Know what every single endpoint is, where it is, who uses it, and what it should (and should not) be doing.
- Strictly enforce least privilege (i.e., no regular users with local admin rights).
- Keep everything updated (ideally, do this automatically).
- Use endpoint protection and response (EDR) solutions.
- Back up everything (ideally in a way that is difficult for an attacker to compromise).
- Export endpoint logs to a security information and event management (SIEM) solution.

create security perimeters or bubbles around them and hope for the best. Just to make things even more interesting, IoT and ICS devices oftentimes control physical processes like heating, ventilation, and air conditioning (HVAC) that can have effects on the health and safety of the people in our organizations.

Content Distribution Networks

So far, our discussion of networking has sort of implied that there is *a* (singular) web server, a (singular) database server, and so on. While this simplifies our discussion of network foundations, protocols, and services, we all know that this is a very rare scenario in all but the smallest networks. Instead, we tend to implement multiples of each service, whether to segment systems, provide redundancy, or both. We may have a couple of web servers connected by a load balancer and interfacing with multiple backend database servers. This sort of redundant deployment can improve performance, but all clients still have to reach the same physical location regardless of where in the world they may be. Wouldn't it be nice if users in Europe did not have to ride transatlantic cables or satellite links to reach a server in the United States and instead could use one closer to them?

A *content distribution network (CDN)* consists of multiple servers distributed across a large region, each of which provides content that is optimized for users closest to it. This optimization can come in many flavors. For example, if you were a large streaming video distribution entity like Netflix, you would want to keep your movie files from having to traverse multiple links between routers, since each hop would incur a delay and potential loss of packets (which could cause jitter in the video). Reducing the number of network hops for your video packets would also usually mean having a server geographically closer to the other node, offering you the opportunity to tailor the content for users in that part of the world. Building on our video example, you could keep movies dubbed in Chinese on servers that are in or closer to Asia and those dubbed in French closer to Europe. So when we talk about optimizing content, we can mean many things.

Another benefit of using CDNs is that they make your Internet presence more resistant to distributed denial-of-service (DDoS) attacks. These attacks rely on having a large number of computers flood a server until it becomes unresponsive to legitimate requests. If an attacker can muster a DDoS attack that can send a million packets per second (admittedly fairly small by today's standards) and aim it at a single server, then it could very well be effective. However, if the attacker tries that against a server that is part of a CDN, the clients will simply start sending their requests to other servers in the network. If the attacker then directs a portion of his attack stream to each server on the CDN in hopes of bringing the whole thing down, the attack will obviously be diffused and would likely require many times more packets. Unsurprisingly, using CDNs is how many organizations protect themselves against DDoS attacks.

Chapter Review

The physical components that make up our networks are foundational to our information systems. Without these cables and switches and routers, nothing else would work. This may seem obvious, but when was the last time you inspected any of them to ensure that they are secure, in good condition, properly configured, and well supported by appropriate third parties? The two classes of threat actors with which we should concern ourselves in this context are attackers and nature. We take care of the first by applying the principles of secure design we've discussed throughout the book and, particularly, by physically securing these cables and devices as discussed in Chapter 10. As far as natural threats, we need to be on the lookout for the wear and tear that is natural over time and that can exacerbate small product defects that may not have been apparent during our initial inspections of new products. This boils down to having qualified staff that is augmented, as necessary, by third parties that provide warranty and support services.

Quick Review

- Analog signals represent data as continuously changing wave values, while digital signals encode data in discrete voltage values.
- Digital signals are more reliable than analog signals over a long distance and provide a clear-cut and efficient signaling method because the voltage is either on (1) or not on (0), compared to interpreting the waves of an analog signal.
- Synchronous communications require a timing component but ensure reliability and higher speeds; asynchronous communications require no timing component and are simpler to implement.
- A baseband technology uses the entire communication channel for its transmission, whereas a broadband technology divides the communication channel into individual and independent subchannels so that different types of data can be transmitted simultaneously.
- Coaxial cable has a copper core that is surrounded by a shielding layer and grounding wire, which makes it more resistant to electromagnetic interference (EMI), provides a higher bandwidth, and supports the use of longer cable lengths.
- With twisted-pair cable, the twisting of the wires, the type of insulation used, the quality of the conductive material, and the shielding of the wire determine the rate at which data can be transmitted.
- Fiber-optic cabling carries data as light waves, is expensive, can transmit data at high speeds, is difficult to tap into, and is resistant to EMI and RFI. If security is extremely important, fiber-optic cabling should be used.
- Because it uses glass, fiber-optic cabling has higher transmission speeds that allow signals to travel over longer distances.
- Depending on the material used, network cables may be susceptible to noise, attenuation, and crosstalk.
- Line noise refers to random fluctuations in electrical-magnetic impulses that are carried along a physical medium.
- Attenuation is the loss of signal strength as it travels.
- Crosstalk is a phenomenon that occurs when electrical signals of one wire spill over to the signals of another wire.

- Bandwidth is the amount of information that can theoretically be transmitted over a link within a second.
- Data throughput is the actual amount of data that can actually be carried over a real link.
- A repeater provides the simplest type of connectivity because it only repeats electrical signals between cable segments, which enables it to extend a network.
- A bridge is a LAN device used to connect LAN segments (or VLAN segments) and thus extends the range of a LAN.
- A transparent bridge starts to learn about the network's environment as soon as it is powered on and continues to learn as the network changes by examining frames and making entries in its forwarding tables.
- Spanning Tree Protocol (STP) ensures that forwarded frames do not circle networks forever, provides redundant paths in case a bridge goes down, assigns unique identifiers to each bridge, assigns priority values to these bridges, and calculates path costs.
- The Shortest Path Bridging (SPB) protocol is defined in IEEE 802.1aq and is more efficient and scalable than STP; it is used in newer bridges.
- Switches are multiport bridges that typically have additional management features.
- Routers are layer 3, or network layer, devices that are used to connect similar or different networks.
- Routers link two or more network segments, where each segment can function as an independent network. A router works at the network layer, works with IP addresses, and has more network knowledge than bridges, switches, or repeaters.
- Gateway is a general term for software running on a device that connects two different environments and that many times acts as a translator for them or somehow restricts their interactions.
- A Private Branch Exchange (PBX) is a private telephone switch that is located on an organization's property and performs some of the same switching tasks that take place at the telephone company's central office.
- Proxy servers act as an intermediary between the clients that want access to certain services and the servers that provide those services.
- Network access control (NAC) is any set of policies and controls that restrict access to our networks.
- An endpoint is any computing device that communicates through a network and whose principal function is not to mediate communications for other devices on that network.
- A content distribution network (CDN) consists of multiple servers distributed across a large region, each of which provides content that is optimized for users closest to it.

Questions

Please remember that these questions are formatted and asked in a certain way for a reason. Keep in mind that the CISSP exam is asking questions at a conceptual level. Questions may not always have the perfect answer, and the candidate is advised against always looking for the perfect answer. Instead, the candidate should look for the best answer in the list.

1. Which of the following is true of asynchronous transmission signals?
   - **A.** Used for high-speed, high-volume transmissions
   - **B.** Robust error checking
   - **C.** Used for irregular transmission patterns
   - **D.** More complex, costly implementation
2. Which of the following technologies divides a communication channel into individual and independent subchannels?
   - **A.** Baseband
   - **B.** Broadband
   - **C.** Circuit-switched
   - **D.** Crosstalk
3. What type of cabling would you use if you needed inexpensive networking in an environment prone to electromagnetic interference?
   - **A.** Fiber-optic
   - **B.** Unshielded twisted pair (UTP)
   - **C.** Plenum
   - **D.** Coaxial
4. Which of the following issues would be likeliest to cause problems in a cable tray where large numbers of cables run in parallel and close proximity?
   - **A.** Thermal noise
   - **B.** Line noise
   - **C.** Crosstalk
   - **D.** Attenuation
5. What problem is inevitable as the length of a cable run increases?
   - **A.** Thermal noise
   - **B.** Line noise
   - **C.** Crosstalk
   - **D.** Attenuation

6. What is the term for the maximum amount of data that actually traverses a given network link?
   - A. Latency
   - B. Bandwidth
   - C. Throughput
   - D. Maximum transmission unit (MTU)
7. Which protocol ensures that frames being forwarded by switches do not circle networks forever?
   - A. Open Shortest Path First (OSPF)
   - B. Border Gateway Protocol (BGP)
   - C. Intermediate System-to-Intermediate System (IS-IS)
   - D. Spanning Tree Protocol (STP)
8. Which standard specifically addresses issues in network access control?
   - A. IEEE 802.1Q
   - B. IEEE 802.1aq
   - C. IEEE 802.AE
   - D. IEEE 802.1X
9. Which of the following would not be considered an endpoint?
   - A. Point of sale (POS) terminal
   - B. Industrial control system (ICS)
   - C. Internet of Things (IoT) device
   - D. Multiprotocol Label Switching (MPLS) system
10. All of the following are good reasons to implement a content distribution network except for which one?
   - A. Reduced latency
   - B. Reduced total cost of ownership (TCO)
   - C. Protection against distributed denial-of-service (DDoS) attacks
   - D. Tailoring content to users around the world

Answers

1. **C.** Asynchronous communications are typically used when data transfers happen at lower volumes and with unpredictable intervals. All other answers describe synchronous signaling, which is best suited for regular, high-volume traffic.

2. **B.** A broadband technology divides the communication channel into individual and independent subchannels so that different types of data can be transmitted simultaneously. A baseband technology, on the other hand, uses the entire communication channel for its transmission.
3. **D.** Coaxial cable has a copper core that is surrounded by a shielding layer and grounding wire, which makes it more resistant to electromagnetic interference (EMI). It is significantly cheaper than fiber-optic cable, which is the other EMI-resistant answer listed, while still allowing higher bandwidths.
4. **C.** Crosstalk is a phenomenon that occurs when electrical signals of one wire spill over to the signals of another wire. The more cables you have in close proximity, the worse this issue can be unless you use shielded cables.
5. **D.** Attenuation is the loss of signal strength as it travels. Regardless of which type of cabling is used, attenuation is inevitable given a long enough distance, which is why repeaters were invented.
6. **C.** Data throughput is the actual amount of data that can be carried over a real link. Bandwidth, on the other hand, is the amount of information that can theoretically be transmitted over a link within a second.
7. **D.** Spanning Tree Protocol (STP) ensures that forwarded frames do not circle networks forever, provides redundant paths in case a bridge goes down, assigns unique identifiers to each bridge, assigns priority values to these bridges, and calculates path costs. The other answers are all routing (layer 3) protocols.
8. **D.** The 802.1X protocol allows devices to connect in a very limited manner (i.e., only to the network authenticator) until the device and/or user can be authenticated. The other standards listed all pertain to layer 2 bridging and security.
9. **D.** An endpoint is any computing device that communicates through a network and whose principal function is not to mediate communications for other devices on that network. MPLS functionality is built into networking devices to help them move packets between endpoints more efficiently.
10. **B.** A content distribution network (CDN) consists of multiple servers distributed across a large region, each of which provides content that is optimized for users closest to it. This improves latency and localization. The very distributed nature of the CDN also provides DDoS protections. It all comes at significant costs and increases the complexity of deploying systems and content, which may require additional organizational resources apart from the service itself.

CHAPTER 15

Secure Communications Channels

This chapter presents the following:

- Voice communications
- Multimedia collaboration
- Remote access
- Data communications
- Virtualized networks
- Third-party connectivity

Mr. Watson—come here—I want to see you.

—Alexander Graham Bell

Up to this point, we've treated all the data as if it were equal. While it is true that a packet is a packet regardless of its contents, there are a number of common cases in which the purpose of a communication matters a lot. If we're downloading a file from a server, we normally don't care (or even know about) the variation in delay times between consecutive packets. This variation, known as *packet jitter*, could mean that some packets follow each other closely (no variance) while others take a lot longer (or shorter) time to arrive. While packet jitter is largely inconsequential to our file download, it could be very problematic for voice, video, or interactive collaboration communications channels.

Implementing secure communications channels has always been important to most organizations. However, the sudden shift to remote working brought on by COVID-19 has made the security of these channels critical due to the convergence of increased demand by legitimate users and increased targeting by threat actors. In this chapter, we look at some of the most prevalent communications channels that ride on our networks. These include voice, multimedia collaboration, remote access, and third-party channels. Let's start with the one we're most accustomed to: voice communications.

Voice Communications

Voice communications have come a long way since Alexander Graham Bell made that first call in 1876. It is estimated that 95 percent of the global population has access to telephone service, with most of those being cellular systems. What ties global voice networks together is a collection of technologies, some of which we've discussed before (e.g., ATM in Chapter 11 and LTE in Chapter 12), and some to which we now turn our attention.

Public Switched Telephone Network

The traditional telephone system is based on a circuit-switched, voice-centric network called the *public switched telephone network (PSTN)*. The PSTN uses circuit switching instead of packet switching. When a phone call is made, the call is placed at the PSTN interface, which is the user's telephone. This telephone is connected to the telephone company's local loop via electric wires, optical fibers, or a radio channel. Once the signals for this phone call reach the telephone company's central office (the end of the local loop), they are part of the telephone company's circuit-switching world. A connection is made between the source and the destination, and as long as the call is in session, the data flows through the same switches.

When a phone call is made, the phone numbers have to be translated, the connection has to be set up, signaling has to be controlled, and the session has to be torn down. This takes place through the Signaling System 7 (SS7) protocol. Figure 15-1 illustrates how calls are made in the PSTN using SS7. Suppose Meeta calls Carlos. Meeta's phone is directly connected to a signal switching point (SSP) belonging to the telephone company (telco) that provides her service. Her telco's SSP finds the SSP of the telco providing Carlos's phone service and they negotiate the call setup. The call itself is routed over

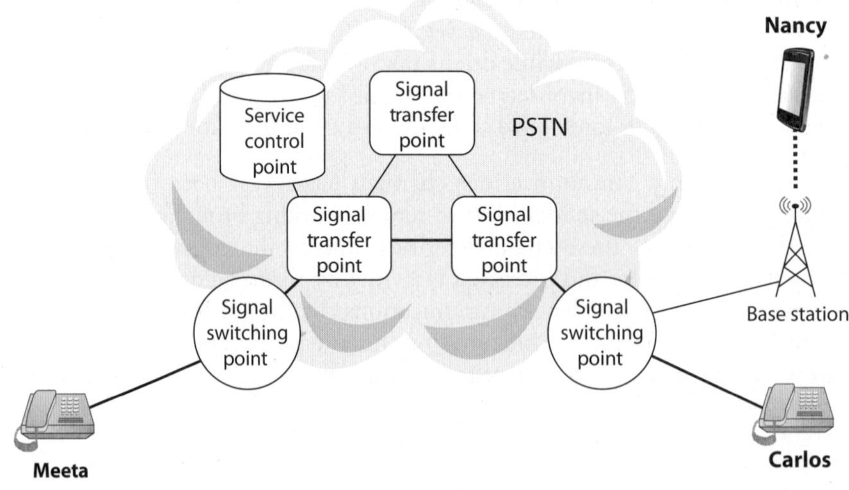

Figure 15-1 Major components of a public switched telephone network

the two signal transfer points (STPs) that interconnect the two SSPs. STPs perform a similar function in a circuit-switched network as routers do in an IP network. If Meeta wanted to call (or conference in) Nancy on her mobile phone, her SSP could query a service control point (SCP), which controls advanced features such as finding mobile subscribers' SSPs and enabling conference calls involving multiple networks.

NOTE PSTNs are being replaced with IP telephony. In the UK, for example, the service provider BT announced that it will switch off its PSTN in 2025.

DSL

It turns out that PSTN local loops (i.e., the telephone wires that go into our homes and offices) are able to support much more bandwidth than the small amount required for voice communications. In the 1980s, telcos figured out that they could transmit digital data at frequencies above those used for voice calls without interference. This was the birth of *digital subscriber line (DSL)*, which is a high-speed communications technology that simultaneously transmits analog voice and digital data between a home or business and the service provider's central office.

Figure 15-2 shows a typical DSL network. In the subscriber's home, a DSL modem creates a LAN to which computers and wireless access points can be connected. This modem, in turn, is connected to a DSL splitter if the home also has analog phone service. A bunch of DSL subscribers in the same neighborhood are then connected to a DSL access multiplexer (DSLAM) in the central office, where analog signals are sent to a voice switch (and on to the PSTN) and digital signals are routed out to the Internet. The tricky part is that the maximum distance between the DSLAM and the DSL splitter

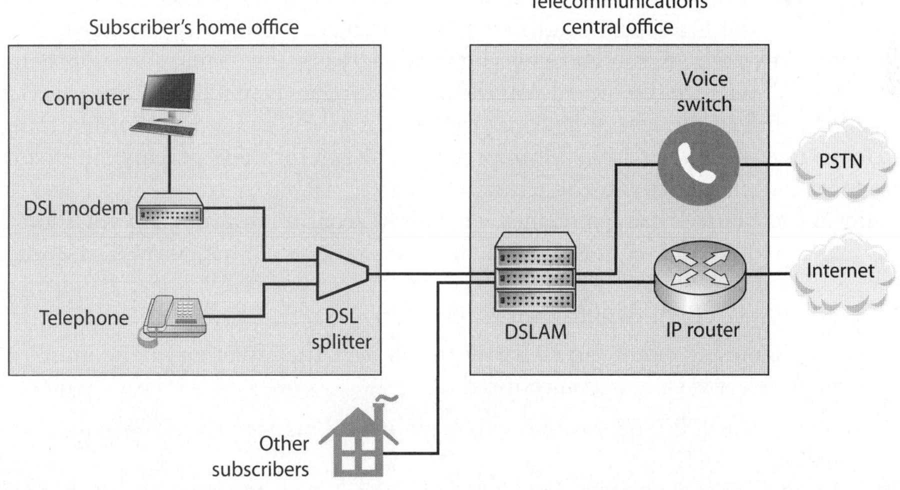

Figure 15-2 DSL network

in the subscriber's home cannot be greater than about 2.5 miles unless you put extenders in place to boost the signal strength.

DSL offers two broad types of services. With *symmetric services*, traffic flows at the same speed upstream and downstream (to and from the Internet or destination). With *asymmetric services*, the downstream speed is much higher than the upstream speed. The vast majority of DSL lines in use today are asymmetric, because most users usually download much more data from the Internet than they upload. The following are some of the most common types of DSL service:

- **Asymmetric DSL (ADSL)** These lines allocate more bandwidth for downstream data than for upstream. The technology has gone through multiple upgrades, with ADSL2+ (ITU standard G.992.5) being the latest and fastest. It has data rates of up to 24 Mbps downstream and 1.4 Mbps upstream, but can only support distances of about a mile from the central office. ADSL is generally used by residential users.
- **Very high-data-rate DSL (VDSL)** VDSL is basically ADSL at much higher data rates (up to 300 Mbps downstream and 100 Mbps upstream). It is capable of supporting high-bandwidth applications such as HDTV, telephone services (Voice over IP), and general Internet access over a single connection.
- **G.fast** Since the biggest challenge with DSL is the length of the subscriber loop, why not run fiber-optic cable from the central office to a distribution point near the home and then finish the last few hundred feet using the copper wires that are already in place? This is what G.fast (ITU standards G.9700 and G.9701) does. It can deliver data rates of up to 1 Gbps.

Dial-up Connections

Dial-up modems using PSTN were the dominant form of remote access in the early days of the Internet. Antiquated as they may seem, some organizations still have modems enabled, sometimes without the network staff being aware of them. For example, we once discovered that the facilities manager at a large school district installed a dial-up modem so he could control the HVAC systems remotely during inclement weather. Therefore, it is important to search for these systems and ensure no unauthorized modems are attached and operational.

If you find yourself using modems, some of the security measures that you should put in place for dial-up connections include

- Disable and remove nonessential modems.
- Configure the remote access server to call back the initiating phone number to ensure it is valid and authorized.
- Consolidate all modems into one location and manage them centrally, if possible.
- Whenever possible, implement use of two-factor authentication, VPNs, and NAC for remote access connections.

NOTE Despite being in wide use, DSL is an obsolescent technology. Major telecommunications companies around the world have announced plans to phase out DSL by 2025.

ISDN

Integrated Services Digital Network (ISDN) is another technology that leverages legacy telephone lines to enable data, voice, and signaling traffic to travel over a medium in a digital manner previously used only for analog voice transmission. ISDN uses the same wires and transmission medium used by analog dial-up technologies, but it works in a digital fashion. If a computer uses a modem to communicate with an ISP, the modem converts the data from digital to analog to be transmitted over the phone line. If that same computer was configured to use ISDN and had the necessary equipment, it would not need to convert the data from digital to analog, but would keep it in a digital form. This, of course, means the receiving end would also require the necessary equipment to receive and interpret this type of communication properly. Communicating in a purely digital form provides higher bit rates that can be sent more economically.

ISDN is a set of telecommunications services that can be used over public and private telecommunications networks. It provides a digital, point-to-point, circuit-switched medium and establishes a circuit between the two communicating devices. An ISDN connection can be used for anything a modem can be used for, but it provides more functionality and higher bandwidth. This digital service can provide bandwidth on an

ISDN Examined

ISDN breaks the telephone line into different channels and transmits data in a digital form rather than the old analog form. Three ISDN implementations are in use:

- **Basic Rate Interface (BRI) ISDN** This implementation operates over existing copper lines at the local loop and provides digital voice and data channels. It uses two B channels (at 64 Kbps each) to support user data or voice and one D channel (at 16 Kbps) for signaling, with a combined bandwidth of 144 Kbps. BRI ISDN is generally used for home and small office subscribers.
- **Primary Rate Interface (PRI) ISDN** This implementation has up to 23 B channels and 1 D channel, at 64 Kbps per channel. The total bandwidth is equivalent to a T1, which is 1.544 Mbps. This would be more suitable for an organization that requires a higher amount of bandwidth compared to BRI ISDN.
- **Broadband ISDN (BISDN)** This implementation can handle many different types of services simultaneously and is mainly used within telecommunications carrier backbones. When BISDN is used within a backbone, ATM is commonly employed to encapsulate data at the data link layer into cells, which travel over a SONET network.

as-needed basis and can be used for LAN-to-LAN on-demand connectivity, instead of using an expensive dedicated link.

Analog telecommunication signals use a full channel for communication, but ISDN can break up this channel into multiple channels to move various types of data and provide full-duplex communication and a higher level of control and error handling. ISDN provides two basic services: *Basic Rate Interface (BRI)* and *Primary Rate Interface (PRI)*.

BRI has two B channels that enable data to be transferred and one D channel that provides for call setup, connection management, error control, caller ID, and more. The bandwidth available with BRI is 144 Kbps, and BRI service is aimed at the small office and home office (SOHO) market. The D channel provides for a quicker call setup and process in making a connection compared to dial-up connections. An ISDN connection may require a setup connection time of only 2 to 5 seconds, whereas a modem may require a timeframe of 45 to 90 seconds. This D channel is an out-of-band communication link between the local loop equipment and the user's system. It is considered "out-of-band" because the control data is not mixed in with the user communication data. This makes it more difficult for a would-be defrauder to send bogus instructions back to the service provider's equipment in hopes of causing a denial of service (DoS), obtaining services not paid for, or conducting some other type of destructive behavior.

PRI has 23 B channels and one D channel, and is more commonly used in corporations. The total bandwidth is equivalent to a T1, which is 1.544 Mbps.

ISDN is not usually the primary telecommunications connection for organizations, but it can be used as a backup in case the primary connection goes down. An organization can also choose to implement *dial-on-demand routing (DDR)*, which can work over ISDN. DDR allows an organization to send WAN data over its existing telephone lines and use the PSTN as a temporary type of WAN link. It is usually implemented by organizations that send out only a small amount of WAN traffic and is a much cheaper solution than a real WAN implementation. The connection activates when it is needed and then idles out.

NOTE ISDN has lost popularity over the years and is now a legacy technology that is seldom used. Some organizations still rely on it as a backup for communications.

Cable Modems

The cable television companies have been delivering television services to homes for years, and then they started delivering data transmission services for users who have cable modems and want to connect to the Internet at high speeds. *Cable modems* provide high-speed access to the Internet through existing cable coaxial and fiber lines. The cable modem provides upstream and downstream conversions.

Coaxial and fiber cables are used to deliver hundreds of television stations to users, and one or more of the channels on these lines are dedicated to carrying data. The bandwidth is shared between users in a local area; therefore, it will not always stay at a static rate. So, for example, if Mike attempts to download a program from the Internet at 5:30 P.M., he most likely will have a much slower connection than if he had attempted it at 10:00 A.M., because many people come home from work and hit the Internet at the same time. As more people access the Internet within his local area, Mike's Internet access performance drops.

Most cable providers comply with *Data-Over-Cable Service Interface Specifications (DOCSIS)*, which is an international telecommunications standard that allows for the addition of high-speed data transfer to an existing cable TV (CATV) system. DOCSIS includes MAC layer security services in its Baseline Privacy Interface/Security (BPI/SEC) specifications. This protects individual user traffic by encrypting the data as it travels over the provider's infrastructure.

IP Telephony

Internet Protocol (IP) telephony is an umbrella term that describes carrying telephone traffic over IP networks. So, if we have all these high-speed digital telecommunications services and the ability to transmit Voice over IP (VoIP) networks, do we even need analog telephones anymore? The answer is a resounding no. PSTN is being replaced by data-centric, packet-oriented networks that can support voice, data, and video. The new IP telephony networks use more efficient and secure switches, protocols, and communication links compared to PSTN but must still coexist (for now) with this older network. This means that VoIP is still going through a tricky transition stage that enables the old systems and infrastructures to communicate with the new systems until the old systems are dead and gone.

This technology gets around some of the barriers present in the PSTN today. The PSTN interface devices (telephones) have limited embedded functions and logic, and the PSTN environment as a whole is inflexible in that new services cannot be easily added. In VoIP, the interface to the network can be a computer, server, PBX, or anything else that runs a telephone application. This provides more flexibility when it comes to adding new services and provides a lot more control and intelligence to the interfacing devices. The traditional PSTN has basically dumb interfaces (telephones without much functionality), and the telecommunication infrastructure has to provide all the functionality. In VoIP, the interfaces are the "smart ones" and the network just moves data from one point to the next.

Because VoIP is a packet-oriented switching technology, the arrival times of different packets may not be regular. You may get a bunch of packets close to each other and then have random delays until the next ones arrive. This irregularity in arrival rates is referred to as *jitter*, which can cause loss of synchronicity in the conversation. It typically means the packets holding the other person's voice message got queued somewhere within the network or took a different route. VoIP includes protocols to help smooth out these issues and provide a more continuous telephone call experience.

EXAM TIP Applications that are time sensitive, such as voice and video signals, need to work over an isochronous network. An isochronous network contains the necessary protocols and devices that guarantee regular packet interarrival times.

Four main components are normally used for VoIP: an IP telephony device, a call-processing manager, a voicemail system, and a voice gateway. The *IP telephony device* is just a phone that has the necessary software that allows it to work as a network device. Traditional phone systems require a "smart network" and a "dumb phone." In VoIP, the phone must be "smart" by having the necessary software to take analog signals, digitize them, break them into packets, and create the necessary headers and trailers for the packets to find their destination. The *voicemail system* is a storage place for messages and provides user directory lookups and call-forwarding functionality. A *voice gateway* carries out packet routing and provides access to legacy voice systems and backup calling processes.

When a user makes a call, his VoIP phone sends a message to the *call-processing manager* to indicate a call needs to be set up. When the person at the call destination takes her phone off the hook, this notifies the call-processing manager that the call has been accepted. The call-processing manager notifies both the sending and receiving phones that the channel is active, and voice data is sent back and forth over a traditional data network line.

Moving voice data through packets is more involved than moving regular data through packets. This is because voice (and video) data must be sent as a steady stream, whereas other types of traffic are more tolerant to burstiness and jitter. A delay in data transmission is not noticed as much as is a delay in voice transmission. VoIP systems have advanced features to provide voice data transmission with increased bandwidth, while reducing variability in delay, round-trip delay, and packet loss issues. These features are covered by two relevant standards: H.323 and the Session Initiation Protocol (SIP).

NOTE A media gateway is the translation unit between disparate telecommunications networks. VoIP media gateways perform the conversion between TDM voice and VoIP, for example.

VoIP vs. IP Telephony

The terms "IP telephony" and "Voice over IP" are used interchangeably, but there is a distinction:

- The term "VoIP" is widely used to refer to the actual services offered: caller ID, QoS, voicemail, and so on.
- IP telephony is an umbrella term for all real-time applications over IP, including voice over instant messaging (IM) and video conferencing.

So, "IP telephony" means that telephone and telecommunications activities are taking place over an IP network instead of the traditional PSTN. "Voice over IP" means voice data is being moved over an IP network instead of the traditional PSTN. They are basically the same thing, but VoIP focuses more on the telephone call services.

H.323

The ITU-T *H.323* recommendation is a standard that deals with audio and video calls over packet-based networks. H.323 defines four types of components: terminals, gateways, multipoint control units, and gatekeepers. The *terminals* can be dedicated VoIP telephone sets, videoconferencing appliances, or software systems running on a traditional computer. *Gateways* interface between H.323 and non-H.323 networks, providing any necessary protocol translation. These gateways are needed, for instance, when using the PSTN to connect H.323 systems. *Multipoint control units (MCUs)* allow three or more terminals to be conferenced together and are sometimes referred to as *conference call bridges*. Finally, the H.323 *gatekeeper* is the central component of the system in that it provides call control services for all registered terminals.

Session Initiation Protocol

An alternative standard for voice and video calls is the *Session Initiation Protocol (SIP)*, which can be used to set up and break down the call sessions, just as SS7 does for PSTN calls. SIP is an application layer protocol that can work over TCP or UDP. It provides the foundation to allow the phone-line features that SS7 provides, such as causing a phone to ring, dialing a phone number, generating busy signals, and so on. SIP is used in applications such as video conferencing, multimedia, instant messaging, and online gaming.

SIP consists of two major components: the *User Agent Client (UAC)* and *User Agent Server (UAS)*. The UAC is the application that creates the SIP requests for initiating a communication session. UACs are generally messaging tools and soft-phone applications that are used to place VoIP calls. The UAS is the SIP server, which is responsible for handling all routing and signaling involved in VoIP calls.

SIP relies on a three-way-handshake process to initiate a session. To illustrate how a SIP-based call kicks off, let's look at an example of two people, Bill and John, trying to communicate using their VoIP phones. Bill's system starts by sending an INVITE message to John's system. Since Bill's system is unaware of John's location, the INVITE message is sent to the SIP server, which looks up John's address in the SIP *registrar* server. Once the location of John's system has been determined, the INVITE message is forwarded to his system. During this entire process, the server keeps the caller (Bill) updated by sending his system a Trying response, indicating the process is underway. Once the INVITE message reaches John's system, it starts ringing. While John's system rings and waits for John to respond, it sends a Ringing response to Bill's system, notifying Bill that the INVITE has been received and John's system is waiting for John to accept the call. As soon as John answers the call, an OK packet is sent to Bill's system (through the server). Bill's system now issues an ACK packet to begin call setup. It is important to note here that SIP itself is not used to stream the conversation because it's just a signaling protocol. The actual voice stream is carried on media protocols such as the *Real-time Transport Protocol (RTP)*. RTP provides a standardized packet format for delivering audio and video over IP networks. Once Bill and John are done communicating, a BYE message is sent from the system terminating the call. The other system responds with an OK, acknowledging the session has ended. This handshake is illustrated in Figure 15-3.

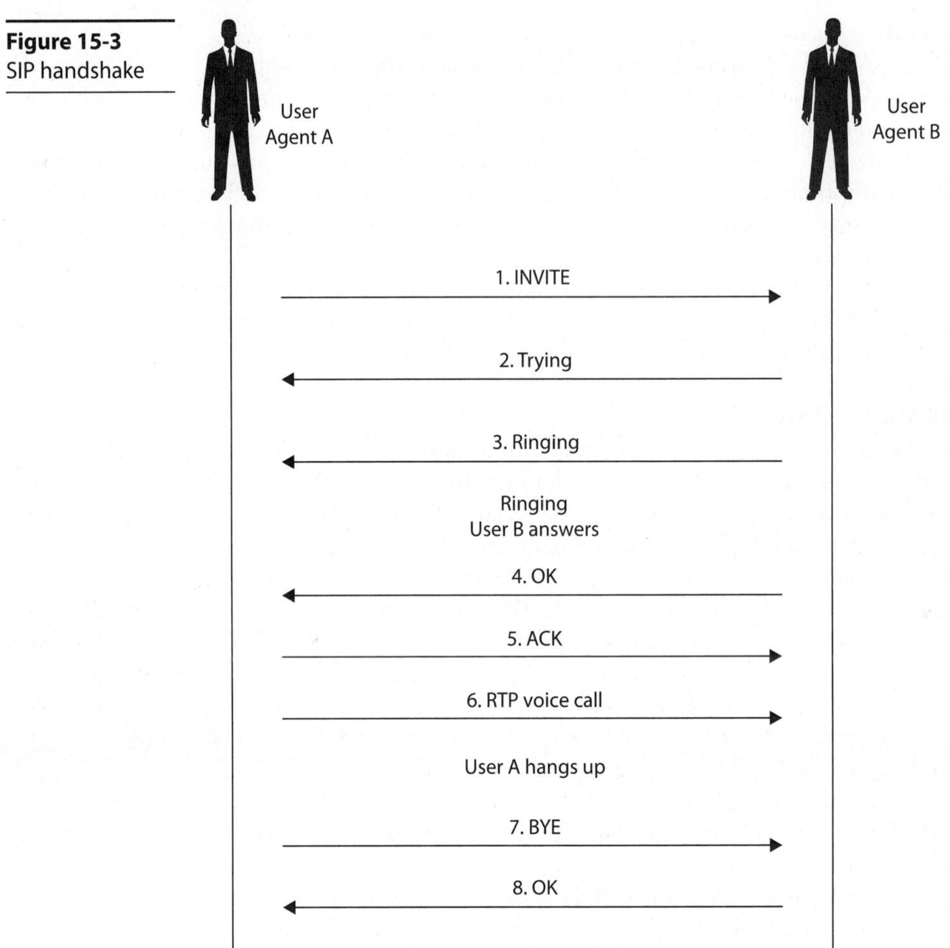

Figure 15-3 SIP handshake

The SIP architecture consists of three different types of servers, which play an integral role in the entire communication process of the VoIP system:

- **Proxy server** Is used to relay packets within a network between the UACs and the UAS. It also forwards requests generated by callers to their respective recipients. Proxy servers are also generally used for name mapping, which allows the proxy server to interlink an external SIP system to an internal SIP client.
- **Registrar server** Keeps a centralized record of the updated locations of all the users on the network. These addresses are stored on a location server.

- **Redirect server** Allows SIP devices to retain their SIP identities despite changes in their geographic location. This allows a device to remain accessible when its location is physically changed and hence while it moves through different networks. The use of redirect servers allows clients to remain within reach while they move through numerous network coverage zones. This configuration is generally known as an *intraorganizational* configuration. Intraorganizational routing enables SIP traffic to be routed within a VoIP network without being transmitted over the PSTN or external network.

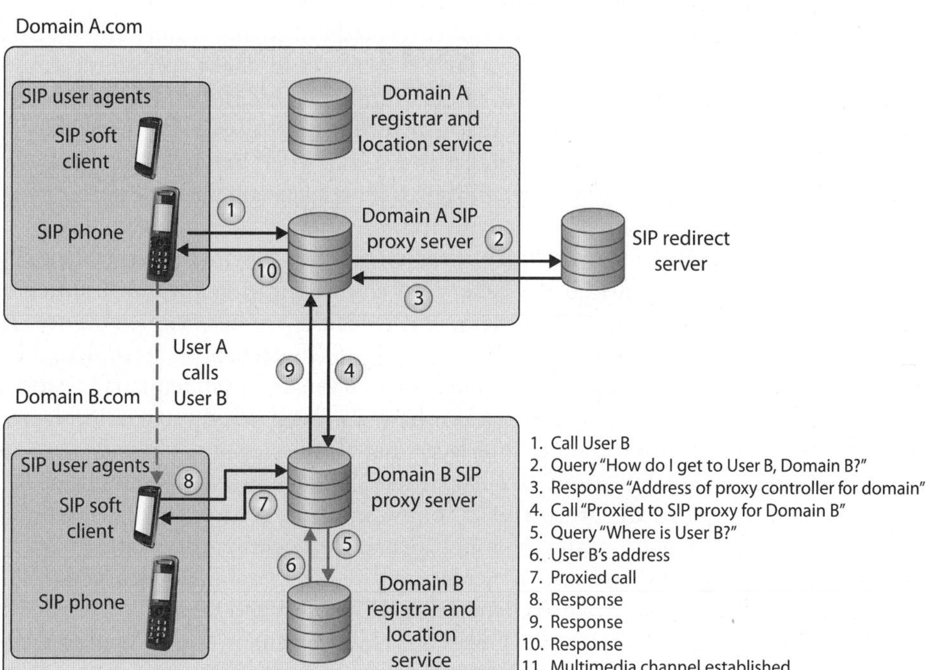

Streaming Protocols

The Real Time Protocol (RTP) is a session layer protocol that carries data in media stream format, as in audio and video, and is used extensively in VoIP, telephony, video conferencing, and other multimedia streaming technologies. It provides end-to-end delivery services and is commonly run over the transport layer protocol UDP. *RTP Control Protocol (RTCP)* is used in conjunction with RTP and is also considered a session layer protocol. It provides out-of-band statistics and control information to provide feedback on QoS levels of individual streaming multimedia sessions.

IP Telephony Issues

VoIP's integration with the TCP/IP protocol has brought about some security challenges because it allows threat actors to leverage their TCP/IP experience to probe for flaws in both the architecture and the implementation of VoIP systems. Also involved are the traditional security issues associated with networks, such as unauthorized access, exploitation of communication protocols, and the spreading of malware. The promise of financial benefit derived from stolen call time is a strong incentive for most attackers. In short, the VoIP telephony network faces all the flaws that traditional computer networks have faced, plus the ones from legacy telephone systems too.

SIP-based signaling suffers from the lack of encrypted call channels and authentication of control signals. Attackers can tap into the SIP server and client communication to sniff out login IDs, passwords/PINs, and phone numbers. Once an attacker gets a hold of such information, she can use it to place unauthorized calls on the network. Toll fraud is considered to be the most significant threat that VoIP networks face, but illicit surveillance is also a threat for some organizations. If attackers are able to intercept voice packets, they may eavesdrop on ongoing conversations.

Attackers can also masquerade identities by redirecting SIP control packets from a caller to a forged destination to mislead the caller into communicating with an unintended end system. Like in any networked system, VoIP devices are also vulnerable to DoS attacks. Just as attackers would flood TCP servers with SYN packets on an IP network to exhaust a device's resources, attackers can flood RTP servers with call requests in order to overwhelm its processing capabilities. Attackers have also been known to connect laptops simulating IP phones to the Ethernet interfaces that IP phones use. These systems can then be used to carry out intrusions and DoS attacks. Attackers can also intercept RTP packets containing the media stream of a communication session to inject arbitrary audio/video data that may be a cause of annoyance to the actual participants.

Attackers can also impersonate a server and issue commands such as BYE, CHECKSYNC, and RESET to VoIP clients. The BYE command causes VoIP devices to close down while in a conversation, the CHECKSYNC command can be used to reboot VoIP terminals, and the RESET command causes the server to reset and reestablish the connection, which takes considerable time.

Combating VoIP security threats requires a well-thought-out infrastructure implementation plan. With the convergence of traditional and VoIP networks, balancing security while maintaining unconstrained traffic flow is crucial. VoIP calls can (and probably should) be encrypted over TLS. The use of authorization on the network is also an important step in limiting the possibilities of rogue and unauthorized entities on the network. Authorization of individual IP terminals ensures that only prelisted devices are allowed to access the network. Although not absolutely foolproof, this method can prevent rogue devices from connecting and flooding the network with illicit packets.

The use of secure cryptographic protocols such as TLS ensures that all SIP packets are conveyed within an encrypted and secure tunnel. The use of TLS can provide a secure channel for VoIP client/server communication and prevents the possibility of eavesdropping and packet manipulation.

VoIP Security Measures Broken Down

Hackers can intercept incoming and outgoing calls, carry out DoS attacks, spoof phone calls, and eavesdrop on sensitive conversations. Many of the countermeasures to these types of attacks are the same ones used with traditional data-oriented networks:

- Keep patches updated on each network device involved with VoIP transmissions:
  - The call-processing manager server
  - The voicemail server
  - The gateway server
- Encrypt VoIP traffic whenever possible.
- Identify unidentified or rogue telephony devices:
  - Implement authentication so only authorized telephony devices are working on the network.
- Install and maintain
  - Stateful firewalls
  - VPN for sensitive voice data
  - Intrusion detection
- Disable unnecessary ports and services on routers, switches, PCs, and IP telephones.
- Employ real-time monitoring that looks for attacks, tunneling, and abusive call patterns through IDS/IPS:
  - Employ content monitoring.
  - Use encryption when data (voice, fax, video) crosses an untrusted network.
  - Use a two-factor authentication technology.
  - Limit the number of calls via media gateways.
  - Close the media sessions after completion.

PART IV

Multimedia Collaboration

The term *multimedia collaboration* is very broad and includes remotely sharing any combination of voice, video, messages, telemetry, and files during an interactive session. The term encompasses conferencing applications like Zoom, WebEx, and Google Meetings but also many other applications in disciplines such as project management, e-learning, science, telemedicine, and military. What distinguishes multimedia collaboration applications is their need to simultaneously share a variety of data formats, each of which has different loss, latency, jitter, and bandwidth requirements. Of course, as we work to meet these performance requirements and allow maximum participation from authorized users (potentially around the world), we also have to ensure the security of this communication channel.

Meeting Applications

Imagine this scenario: You are hosting an online leadership meeting with your international partners to discuss the year ahead. Suddenly, a participant with a name you don't recognize starts sharing pornographic images and hate speech for all to see. You've just been "Zoom-bombed." (A term that doesn't necessarily mean you were using that particular platform.) This is what happens when access controls to your online meeting are inadequate. Many naïve users of meeting applications simply share a link with their guests, usually via e-mail or some other messaging application. Anyone with that link could then join the call if other precautions aren't taken.

The rise in popularity of meeting applications and their increased importance to the business of our organizations have put them in the crosshairs of a wide range of attackers beyond the Zoom-bombing troll we described. To prevent these attacks, consider the following best practices for securing online meeting applications:

- *Don't use consumer-grade products.* There is much wisdom in the old adage "you get what you pay for." Consumer-grade products are much cheaper than enterprise-grade ones (or even free), but they lack most security controls that we need to secure our organizational meetings.
- *Use AES 256-bit encryption.* It is rare to be able to support true end-to-end encryption for online meetings because most service providers need access to the traffic for things like recording, closed captioning, and echo cancelation. Still, you should ensure all call traffic is encrypted between each participant and the service provider.
- *Control access to every meeting.* Enterprise-grade conferencing services can integrate with your identity and access management service to ensure strong authentication. Failing that, ensure that, at a minimum, each meeting is password-protected.
- *Enable the waiting room feature, particularly for external participants.* Many services place participants in a virtual waiting room when they sign in to the meeting until the host lets them in. This gives you an opportunity to screen each participant prior to allowing them to join. At a minimum, ensure participants cannot connect to the call before the host does.
- *Restrict participants' sharing of their screens or cameras as appropriate.* This is particularly important when the meeting involves external parties such as partners or clients. While cameras may be desirable for a variety of reasons, it is rare for all participants to need unfettered screen sharing. Either way, ensure this is a deliberate decision by the host or organizer and enforceable by the platform.

Telepresence

Sometimes, you and other meeting participants need to do more than just see and hear each other and share slides remotely. *Telepresence* is the application of various technologies to allow people to be virtually present somewhere other than where they physically are. Consider a bomb disposal specialist trying to disarm an explosive device remotely using a robot, or a surgeon performing a delicate operation on a patient who would otherwise be inaccessible. The possibilities are endless and include the far more mundane applications that most of our organizations would consider, such as trade shows, pipeline inspections, and virtual reality (VR) training.

Because telepresence systems are not yet prevalent, there is no consensus yet on how to best secure them as a whole. Still, the secure design principles we've covered in this book (to which we'll return later in this chapter) apply to these systems.

- *Keep your software updated.* Online meeting software is no different than any other in the need for patch and update management. Even if you don't use dedicated clients and use web browsers to connect, you should ensure whatever you use is up to date.
- *Don't record meetings unless necessary.* It is helpful to record meetings, particularly when some participants cannot join in real time and must watch it later. However, the recordings can contain sensitive data that could be stolen or lead to other types of liability. If you do record the meeting, ensure it is for good reasons and that the recorded data is encrypted.
- *Know how to eject unwanted participants.* If you do get Zoom-bombed, that is not the time to figure out how to eject (and lock out) an offending participant. Ensure all hosts know how to do this beforehand and, while they're at it, learn also how to mute their microphones (and cameras) if needed.

Unified Communications

While meeting applications like videoconferencing systems have received a lot of attention recently, there is a broader application of multimedia collaboration services known as *unified communications (UC)*. UC is the integration of real-time and non-real-time communications technologies in one platform. Real-time communications are those that are instantaneous and interactive, such as telephone and video conferencing. Non-real-time communications, on the other hand, don't require our immediate attention and are exemplified by technologies such as e-mail and text messaging. The whole point of UC is that it integrates multiple modes of communication, as shown in Figure 15-4.

One of the key features of UC is the concept of *presence information*, which is an indicator of a subject's availability and willingness to communicate. If you have ever used a platform like Slack or Microsoft Teams, you will have noticed the presence icon next to your teammates. It may show that they are available, sleeping, on a call, or on a meeting. Presence information allows you to choose how to interact with your colleagues. If you

Figure 15-4 Unified communications components

need to get a message to Mohammed, who happens to be in a meeting, you can send him a text message. If, on the other hand, you see that Carmen is available, you may want to reach out to her on a voice or video call. Presence information can also show where in the world your colleagues are. For example, if you want to meet Bob and notice that he happens to be in the same city as you are, you may opt for a face-to-face meeting request.

Securing UC involves similar security controls that we would apply to any other communications platform, but with a couple of important caveats. For starters, UC relies on centralized data and access controls. This means that, whether your organization hosts its services on premises or in the cloud, there is a hub that supports and enables them. You want to ensure that this hub is adequately protected against physical and logical threats. Obviously, you want to protect your data, whether at rest or in motion, with strong encryption, but this will only get you so far if you allow anyone to access it. Consequently, you want to apply strict access controls that still allow the business processes to run efficiently. Finally, you want to ensure that demand spikes don't cause self-inflicted denial-of-service conditions. Instead, ensure that you have enough spare capacity to handle these inevitable (if rare) spikes.

Remote Access

Remote access covers several technologies that enable remote and home users to connect to resources that they need to perform their tasks. Most of the time, these users must first gain access to the Internet through an ISP, which sets up a connection to the destination network. For many organizations, remote access is a necessity because it enables users to access centralized network resources; it reduces networking costs by using the Internet as the access medium instead of expensive dedicated lines; and it extends the workplace for employees to their home computers, laptops, and mobile devices. Remote access can streamline access to resources and information through Internet connections and provides a competitive advantage by letting partners, suppliers, and customers have closely controlled links.

VPN

We discussed VPNs in Chapter 13 as a general concept, but let's circle back and see how to best employ them to provide secure remote connectivity for our staff members. VPNs are typically implemented using a client application that connects to a VPN server (commonly called a concentrator) in our organization. In a perfect world, you would have enough bandwidth and concentrator capacity to ensure all your remote staff members can simultaneously connect over the VPN. Then, you could enforce *always-on VPN*, which is a system configuration that automatically connects the device to the VPN with no user interaction. Obviously, this would only be possible with devices owned by the organization, but it can provide strong access controls if properly implemented. For even better results, you can implement a *VPN kill switch*, which automatically cuts off Internet access unless a VPN session is established.

Alas, things are usually a bit more complicated. Perhaps you don't have enough VPN capacity for your entire workforce, or you allow use of personal devices. If you cannot implement always-on VPN, the next best thing is to ensure you use multifactor authentication (MFA) and network access control (NAC). NAC is particularly important because you want to be able to check that the user device is safe before allowing it to access your corporate network. Since not everyone will be connecting to the VPN, you want to ensure that remote users have access to the resources they need and no others, possibly by putting them on the right VLANs and ensuring you have the right access control lists (ACLs) in your internal routers.

Regardless, you want to ensure your VPN systems (clients and concentrators) are updated and properly configured. Many clients allow you to select the cryptosystem to use, in which case you want to select the strongest option you can. Finally, carefully consider whether you will allow split tunnels.

A *VPN split tunnel* is a configuration that routes certain traffic (e.g., to the corporate data center) through the VPN while allowing other traffic (such as web searches) to access the Internet directly (without going through the VPN tunnel). The advantage of this approach is that users will be less likely to experience latency induced by an overworked concentrator. It also allows them to print to their local printer at home while on VPN. The disadvantage is that, should they pick up malware or otherwise become compromised on the Internet, the adversary will automatically get a free ride into your corporate network through the VPN. To prevent this from happening, you can enforce a *VPN full tunnel*, which routes all traffic through the concentrators.

VPN Authentication Protocols

While we're talking about VPN configuration, let's go over some of the authentication protocols you may come across, so you know what each brings to the table.

PAP The *Password Authentication Protocol (PAP)* is used by remote users to authenticate over Point-to-Point Protocol (PPP) connections such as those used in some VPNs. PAP requires a user to enter a password before being authenticated. The password and the username credentials are sent over the network to the authentication server after a connection has been established via PPP. The authentication server has a database of user credentials that are compared to the supplied credentials to authenticate users. PAP is one of the least secure authentication methods because the credentials are sent in cleartext, which renders them easy to capture by network sniffers. PAP is also vulnerable to man-in-the-middle attacks. Although this protocol is not recommended for use anywhere, some (improperly configured) systems can revert to PAP if they cannot agree on any other authentication protocol.

EXAM TIP PAP has been considered insecure for decades. If you see it on the exam, consider it a bad choice.

CHAP The *Challenge Handshake Authentication Protocol (CHAP)* addresses some of the vulnerabilities found in PAP. It uses a challenge/response mechanism to authenticate the user instead of having the user send a password over the wire. When a user wants to establish a PPP connection and both ends have agreed that CHAP will be used for authentication purposes, the user's computer sends the authentication server a logon request. The server sends the user a challenge (called a nonce), which is a random value. This challenge is encrypted with the use of a predefined password as an encryption key, and the encrypted challenge value is returned to the server. The authentication server also uses the predefined password as an encryption key and decrypts the challenge value, comparing it to the original value sent. If the two results are the same, the authentication server deduces that the user must have entered the correct password and grants authentication. The steps that take place in CHAP are depicted in Figure 15-5. Unlike PAP, CHAP is not vulnerable to man-in-the-middle attacks because it continues this challenge/response activity throughout the connection to ensure the authentication server is still communicating with a user who holds the necessary credentials.

EXAM TIP MS-CHAP is Microsoft's version of CHAP and provides mutual authentication functionality. It has two versions, which are incompatible with each other.

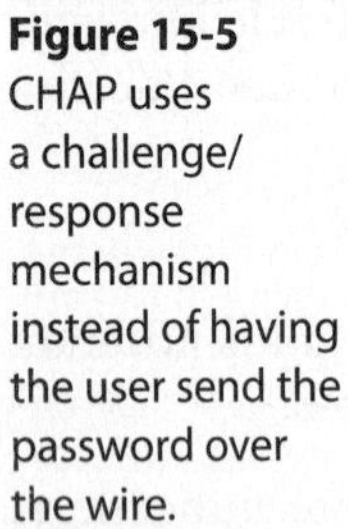

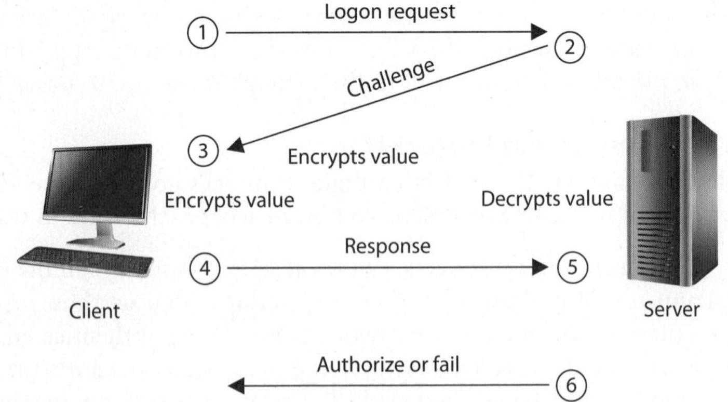

Figure 15-5 CHAP uses a challenge/response mechanism instead of having the user send the password over the wire.

EAP The *Extensible Authentication Protocol (EAP)* is also supported by PPP. Actually, EAP is not a specific authentication protocol as are PAP and CHAP. Instead, it provides a framework to enable many types of authentication techniques to be used when establishing network connections. As the name states, it *extends* the authentication possibilities from the norm (PAP and CHAP) to other methods, such as one-time passwords, token cards, biometrics, Kerberos, digital certificates, and future mechanisms. So when a user connects to an authentication server and both have EAP capabilities, they can negotiate between a longer list of possible authentication methods.

NOTE EAP has been defined for use with a variety of technologies and protocols, including PPP, Point-to-Point Tunneling Protocol (PPTP), Layer 2 Tunneling Protocol (L2TP), IEEE 802 wired networks, and wireless technologies such as 802.11 and 802.16.

There are many different variants of EAP, as shown in Table 15-1, because EAP is an extensible framework that can be morphed for different environments and needs.

Desktop Virtualization

Desktop virtualization technologies allow users to remotely interact with computers as if they were physically using them. In essence, these technologies present a virtual copy of a desktop that is running on some computer (physical or virtual) somewhere else

Protocol	Description
EAP-TLS	Digital certificate–based authentication, considered one of the most secure EAP standards
EAP-PSK	Provides mutual authentication and session key derivation using a preshared key
EAP-TTLS	Tunneled TLS, which requires the server to have a CA-issued certificate, but makes this optional for the client
EAP-IKE2	Internet Key Exchange version 2 (IKE2), which provides mutual authentication and session key establishment using asymmetric or symmetric keys or passwords
PEAPv0/EAP-MSCHAPv2	Similar in design to EAP-TTLS but only requires a server-side digital certificate
PEAPv1/EAP-GTC	Cisco variant based on Generic Token Card (GTC) authentication
EAP-FAST	Cisco-proprietary replacement for Lightweight EAP (LEAP) based on Flexible Authentication via Secure Tunneling (FAST)
EAP-SIM	For Global System for Mobile Communications (GSM), based on Subscriber Identity Module (SIM), a variant of PEAP for GSM
EAP-AKA	For Universal Mobile Telecommunication System (UMTS) Subscriber Identity Module (USIM) and provides Authentication and Key Agreement (AKA)
EAP-GSS	Based on Generic Security Service (GSS), uses Kerberos

Table 15-1 EAP Variants

in the network. IT staff frequently use desktop virtualization to manage rack-mounted servers (without having to attach a monitor, keyboard, and mouse to each), to log into jump boxes, and to manage and troubleshoot user workstations. In some organizations, remote desktop solutions allow staff to work from home and, through their personal devices, securely use an organizational computer. The upside of desktop virtualization is that the asset is protected by the organization's security architecture but still is accessible from almost anywhere. There are two main approaches to desktop virtualization: remote desktops and virtual desktop infrastructure.

NOTE A *jump box* (also called a *jump host* or *jump server*) is a hardened host that acts as a secure entry point or gateway into a sensitive part of a network.

Remote Desktops

Two of the most common approaches to providing remote desktops are Microsoft's *Remote Desktop Protocol (RDP)* and the open-source *Virtual Network Computing (VNC)* system. At a high level, both are very similar. They both require that a special server is running on the computer that will be controlled remotely and that the remote device has a software client installed and connected to the server, by default over port 3389 for RDP and 5900 for VNC. Although there are clients and servers for every major operating system, RDP is more common in Windows environments and VNC is more common in Linux environments.

The most important security consideration when deploying either RDP or VNC is to ensure that the connections are encrypted. Neither of these systems has robust security controls, so you have to tunnel them over a secure channel. If you are providing this service to remote users outside your organizational network, then you should ensure they are connected to the VPN. Having external RDP or VNC servers is a recipe for a security disaster, so their corresponding ports should be blocked at your firewall.

One of the advantages or disadvantages (depending on how you look at it) of RDP and VNC is that they allow a client to remotely control a specific computer. That computer must be provisioned somewhere on the network, specifically configured to allow remote access, and then must remain available. If it is powered off or is otherwise unavailable, there is nothing to remotely control.

Virtual Desktop Infrastructure

By combining virtualization and remote desktop technologies, we can create an environment in which users access the desktops of virtual machines (VMs) that look and behave exactly as the users have configured them, but that can be spun up or down, migrated, wiped, and re-created centrally as needed. *Virtual desktop infrastructure (VDI)* is a technology that hosts multiple virtual desktops in a centralized manner and makes them available to authorized users. Each virtual desktop can be directly tied to a VM (very similarly to the remote desktops described in the previous section) or can be a composite of multiple virtual components, such as a desktop template combined with virtual applications running on multiple different VMs. This flexibility allows organizations to tailor desktops to specific departments, roles, or even individuals in a scalable and resource-effective manner.

VDI deployments can be either persistent or nonpersistent. In a *persistent VDI*, a given user connects to the same virtual desktop every time and is able to customize it as allowed by whatever organizational policies are in place. In a persistent model, users' desktops look the same at the beginning of one session as they did at the end of the last one, creating continuity that is helpful for long-term use and for complex workflows. By contrast, users of a *nonpersistent VDI* are presented with a standard desktop that is wiped at the end of each session. Nonpersistent infrastructures are useful when providing occasional access for very specific purposes or in extremely secure environments.

VDI is particularly helpful in regulated environments because of the ease with which it supports data retention, configuration management, and incident response. If a user's system is compromised, it can quickly be isolated for remediation or investigation, while a clean desktop is almost instantly spawned and presented to the user, reducing the downtime to seconds. VDI is also attractive when the workforce is highly mobile and may log in from a multitude of physical devices in different locations. Obviously, this approach is highly dependent on network connectivity. For this reason, organizations need to consider carefully their own network speed and latency when deciding how (or whether) to implement it.

Secure Shell

We don't always need a graphical user interface (GUI) to interact with our devices. In fact, there are many advanced use cases in which users, especially experienced and administrative ones, are more productive using a command-line interface (CLI). The tool of choice in many of these cases (particularly in Linux environments) is *Secure Shell (SSH)*, which functions as a type of tunneling mechanism that provides terminal-like access to remote computers. SSH is the equivalent of remote desktops but without the GUI. For example, the program can let Paul, who is on computer A, access computer B's files, run applications on computer B, and retrieve files from computer B without ever physically touching that computer. SSH provides authentication and secure transmission over vulnerable channels like the Internet.

NOTE SSH can also be used for secure channels for file transfer and port redirection.

SSH should be used instead of Telnet, FTP, rlogin, rexec, or rsh, which provide the same type of functionality SSH offers but in a much less secure manner. SSH is a program and a set of protocols that work together to provide a secure tunnel between two computers. The two computers go through a handshaking process and exchange (via Diffie-Hellman) a session key that will be used during the session to encrypt and protect the data sent. The steps of an SSH connection are outlined in Figure 15-6.

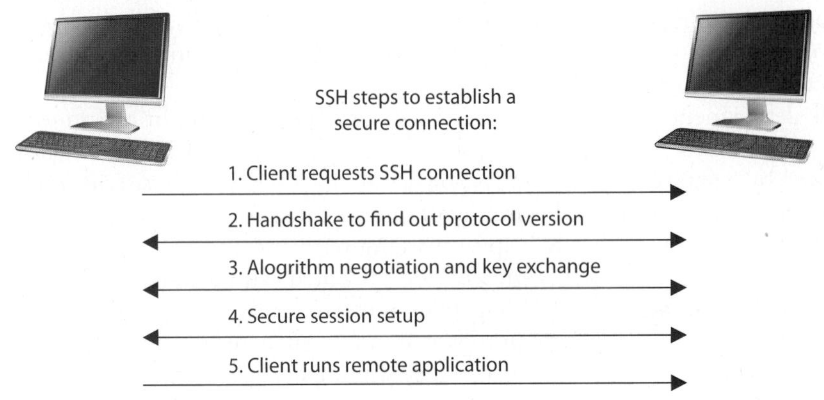
SSH steps to establish a
secure connection:
1. Client requests SSH connection
2. Handshake to find out protocol version
3. Alogrithm negotiation and key exchange
4. Secure session setup
5. Client runs remote application

Figure 15-6 SSH is used for remote terminal-like functionality.

EXAM TIP Telnet is similar in overall purpose to SSH but provides none of the latter's security features. It is insecure and probably not the right answer to any question.

Once the handshake takes place and a secure channel is established, the two computers have a pathway to exchange data with the assurance that the information will be encrypted and its integrity will be protected.

Secure channel

Data Communications

Up to this point in this chapter, we've been focused on communications channels used by users. It is probably a good idea to also consider machine to machine data communications. Recall from Chapter 7 that there are multiple system architectures that require quite a bit of backend chatter between system components. For example, in an n-tier architecture, you may have an application server communicating quite regularly with a database. We must also map out and secure all these not-so-obvious data communications channels.

Network Sockets

A *network socket* is an endpoint for a data communications channel. A socket is a layer 4 (transport) construct that is defined by five parameters: source address, source port, destination address, destination port, and protocol (TCP or UDP). At any given time, a typical workstation has dozens of open sockets, each representing an existing data communications channel. (Servers can have thousands or even tens of thousands of them.) Each of these channels represents an opportunity for an attacker to compromise our systems. Do you know what all your data channels are?

This is one of the reasons why understanding our systems architectures is so critical. Many systems use default installation configurations that are inherently insecure. In addition to the proverbial (weak) default password, a brand-new server probably includes a number of services that are not needed and could provide an open door to attackers. Here are some best practices for securing sockets-based communications channels:

- Map out every authorized data communications channel to and from each server.
- Apply ACLs to block every connection except authorized ones.
- Use segmentation to ensure servers that communicate with each other regularly are in the same network segment.
- Whenever possible, encrypt all data communications channels.
- Authenticate all connection requests.

One of the challenges of securing data communications channels is that they rely on service accounts that usually run with elevated privileges. Oftentimes, these service accounts are excluded from the password policies that are enforced for user accounts. As a result, service account passwords are seldom changed and sometimes are documented in an unsecure manner. For example, we know of organizations that keep a list of their service accounts and passwords on a SharePoint or Confluence page for their IT team. These passwords should be protected just like any other privileged account and securely stored in a password vault.

Remote Procedure Calls

Moving up one level to the session layer (layer 5), a *remote procedure call (RPC)* allows a program somewhere in your network to execute a function or procedure on some other host. RPC is commonly used in distributed systems because it allows systems to divide larger tasks into subtasks and then hand those subtasks to other systems. Although the IETF defined an RPC protocol for Open Network Computing (ONC), the RPC concept can take many different forms in practice. In most networks (especially Windows ones), RPC services listen on TCP port 135. RPC use is ubiquitous in many enterprise environments because it is so powerful. However, by default, it doesn't provide any security beyond basic authentication.

If your organization uses RPC, then you should really consider upgrading its security. Secure RPC (S-RPC) provides authentication of both users and hosts as well as traffic encryption. As of February 9, 2021, Windows Active Directory (AD) systems require S-RPC. The IETF also released a standard for RPC security (RPCSEC) years ago, but because it is difficult to implement, it was never widely adopted. Instead, many organizations require TLS for authenticating hosts and encrypting RPC traffic. Other, vendor-specific implementations of RPC security exist, so you should research whatever versions are being used in your environment and ensure they are secure.

Virtualized Networks

A lot of the network functionality we have covered in this chapter can take place in virtual environments. You should remember from our coverage of virtual machines (VMs) in Chapter 7 that a host system can have virtual guest systems running on it, enabling multiple operating systems to run on the same hardware platform simultaneously. But the industry has advanced much further than this when it comes to virtualized technology. Routers and switches can be virtualized, which means you do not actually purchase a piece of hardware and plug it into your network, but instead you deploy software products that carry out routing and switching functionality. Obviously, you still need a robust hardware infrastructure on which to run the VMs, but virtualization can save you a lot of money, power, heat, and physical space.

These VMs, whether they implement endpoints or networking equipment, communicate with each other over virtual networks that behave much like their real counterparts, with a few exceptions. In order to understand some of these, let us first consider the simple virtual infrastructure shown in Figure 15-7. Let's suppose that VM-1 is an endpoint (perhaps a server), VM-2 is a firewall, and VM-3 is an IDS on the external side of the firewall. Two of these devices (VM-1 and VM-3) have a single virtual NIC (vNIC), while the other one (VM-2) has two vNICs. Every vNIC is connected to a virtual port on a virtual switch. Unlike the real world, any data that flows from one vNIC

Figure 15-7 Virtualized networks

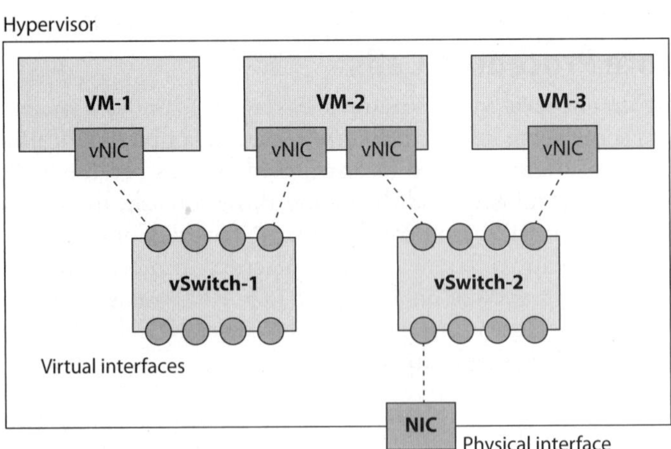

to another vNIC is usually just copied from one memory location (on the physical host) to another; it only pretends to travel the virtual network.

The single physical NIC in our example is connected to vSwitch-2, but it could just as easily have been directly connected to a vNIC on a VM. In this virtual network, VM-2 and VM-3 have connectivity to the physical network but VM-1 does not. The hypervisor stores in memory any data arriving at the physical NIC, asks the virtual switch where to send it, and then copies it into the memory location for the intended vNIC. This means that the hypervisor has complete visibility over all the data traversing its virtualized networks, whether or not it touches the physical NIC.

It should come as no surprise that one of the greatest strengths of virtualization, the hypervisor, is potentially also its greatest weakness. Any attacker who compromises the hypervisor could gain access to all virtualized devices and networks within it. So, both the good and the bad guys are intensely focused on finding any vulnerabilities in these environments. What should you do to ensure the security of your virtualized networks and devices? First, just as you should do for any other software, ensure you stay on top of any security patches that come out. Second, beware of third-party add-ons that extend the functionality of your hypervisor or virtual infrastructure. Ensure these are well tested and acquired from reputable vendors. Last, ensure that whoever provisions and maintains your virtualized infrastructure is competent and diligent, but also check their work. Many vulnerabilities are the result of misconfigured systems, and hypervisors are no different.

Third-Party Connectivity

We can't wrap up our discussion of securing the multitude of communications channels in our systems without talking about third parties. In Chapter 2, we covered the risks that third parties bring to our organizations and how to mitigate them. These third parties cover a broad spectrum that includes suppliers, service providers, and partners. Each of them may have legitimate needs to communicate digitally with our organizations, potentially in an automated manner. How can we provide this required connectivity to third parties without sacrificing our security? The answer can be found by applying the secure design principles we've been revisiting throughout the book:

- **Threat modeling** Always start by identifying the threats. What might malicious (or just careless) third parties be able to do with the communications channels we provide that would cause us harm? What are their likeliest and most dangerous actions? This deliberate exercise in understanding the threats is foundational.
- **Least privilege** Third parties will have legitimate connectivity requirements that we should minimally provide. If a contractor needs to monitor and control our HVAC systems remotely, we should segment those systems on the same VLAN and ensure that only specific calls from specific hosts to specific devices are allowed, and nothing more.

- **Defense in depth** Based on the threat model, we put in place controls to mitigate risks. But what happens if the first layer of controls fails to contain the threat? If that HVAC contractor is compromised in an island-hopping attack and the adversary is able to escape the VLAN, how do we detect the breach and then contain the attack?
- **Secure defaults** While ensuring that default configurations are secure is generally a best practice, it is particularly important on systems that will be used by third parties. One of the keys here is to enforce strict configuration management. For any system that will be accessible by a third party, we must ensure that all defaults are secure by testing them.
- **Fail securely** Speaking of testing, we should test the system under a range of conditions to see what happens when it breaks. For example, stress testing (under heavy usage loads), fuzzing, and power and network failure testing can show us what happens when a system fails. This is not specific to third-party systems, by the way.
- **Separation of duties** Giving third parties the least privileges needed actually makes separating duties easier. For example, it may be that the HVAC contractor does not normally start or stop the furnace, but this may be occasionally required. Because this can have an impact on our facility, the action must be approved by our site manager.
- **Keep it simple** This principle is centered on the statement of work (SoW) that describes the agreement with the third party and in the processes we build to support that work. A policy of "deny by default, allow by exception" can keep things simple, supports the least-privilege principle, and should be paired with a simple process for handling exceptions.
- **Zero trust** It goes without saying that we should not trust third parties when it comes to access to our systems. For every interaction of third parties with our systems, we must ensure that authentication, nonrepudiation, and audit controls are sufficient to detect and mitigate any threat (deliberate or otherwise) that they introduce into our environments.
- **Privacy by design** If we use this principle to guide the development of our entire security architecture (and we really ought to), then we really shouldn't have to do anything else to account for third parties using our systems, particularly if we couple privacy with least privilege in the first place.
- **Trust but verify** We already talked about auditability in the context of zero trust, but there is a difference between logging activities and analyzing those logs periodically (or even continually). What is the process by which our security staff verifies that the actions of third parties are appropriate? How are suspicious or malicious activities handled?
- **Shared responsibility** Finally, who is contractually responsible for what? As the saying goes, "good fences make good neighbors." It is important to define responsibilities in the service or partnership agreement so that there are no misunderstandings and, should someone fail, we can take financial or legal actions to recover our losses.

Chapter Review

With this chapter, we have finished our coverage of the fourth domain of the CISSP Common Body of Knowledge, Communication and Network Security, by discussing the myriad of technologies that allow us to create secure communications channels in our organizations. Though most people (particularly in the technology fields) would not consider voice to be their primary means of communication, it remains important for many reasons, not the least of which is the fact that traditional voice channels are more commonly used nowadays for digital data traffic. It is important to understand how these technologies blend in different ways so that we can better secure them.

The COVID-19 pandemic forced most organizations around the world to quickly move toward (or improve their ability at) supporting a remote workforce largely based in home offices. While the news media regularly featured stories on the vulnerabilities and attacks on our multimedia collaboration and remote access systems, it is remarkable how well these held up to the sudden increase in use (and attacks). We hope that this chapter has given you a better understanding of how security professionals can continue to improve the security of these systems while supporting a remote workforce and third-party connectivity.

Quick Review

- The public switched telephone network (PSTN) uses circuit switching instead of packet routing to connect calls.
- The Signaling System 7 (SS7) protocol is used for establishing and terminating calls in the PSTN.
- The main components of a PSTN network are signal switching points (SSPs) that terminate subscriber loops, signal transfer points (STPs) that interconnect SSPs and other STPs to route calls through the network, and service control points (SCPs) that control advanced features.
- A digital subscriber line (DSL) is a high-speed communications technology that simultaneously transmits analog voice and digital data between a home or business and a PSTN service provider's central office.
- Asymmetric DSL (ADSL) has data rates of up to 24 Mbps downstream and 1.4 Mbps upstream but can only support distances of about a mile from the central office without signal boosters.
- Very high-data-rate DSL (VDSL) is a higher-speed version of ADSL (up to 300 Mbps downstream and 100 Mbps upstream).
- G.fast is DSL that runs over fiber-optic cable from the central office to a distribution point near the home and then uses legacy copper wires for the last few hundred feet to the home or office. It can deliver data rates of up to 1 Gbps.
- Integrated Services Digital Network (ISDN) is an obsolescent pure digital technology that uses legacy phone lines for both voice and data.

- Basic Rate Interface (BRI) ISDN is intended to support a single user with two channels each with data throughput of 64 Kbps.
- Primary Rate Interface (PRI) ISDN has up to 23 usable channels, at 64 Kbps each, which is equivalent to a T1 leased line.
- Cable modems provide high-speed access to the Internet through existing cable coaxial and fiber lines, but the shared nature of these media result in inconsistent throughputs.
- Internet Protocol (IP) telephony is an umbrella term that describes carrying telephone traffic over IP networks.
- The terms "IP telephony" and "Voice over IP" are used interchangeably.
- Jitter is the irregularity in the arrival times of consecutive packets, which is problematic for interactive voice and video communications.
- The H.323 recommendation is a standard that deals with audio and video calls over packet-based networks.
- The Session Initiation Protocol (SIP) is an application layer protocol used for call setup and teardown in IP telephony, video and multimedia conferencing, instant messaging, and online gaming.
- The Real-time Transport Protocol (RTP) is a session layer protocol that carries data in media stream format, as in audio and video, and is used extensively in VoIP, telephony, video conferencing, and other multimedia streaming technologies.
- RTP Control Protocol (RTCP) is used in conjunction with RTP and is also considered a session layer protocol. It provides out-of-band statistics and control information to provide feedback on QoS levels of individual streaming multimedia sessions.
- Multimedia collaboration is a broad term that includes remotely and simultaneously sharing any combination of voice, video, messages, telemetry, and files in an interactive session.
- Telepresence is the application of various technologies to allow people to be virtually present somewhere other than where they physically are.
- Unified communications (UC) is the integration of real-time and non-real-time communications technologies in one platform.
- An always-on VPN is a system configuration that automatically connects the device to the VPN with no user interaction.
- A VPN kill switch is a system configuration that automatically cuts off Internet access unless a VPN session is established.
- A VPN split tunnel is a configuration that routes certain traffic through the VPN while allowing other traffic to access the Internet directly.

- The Password Authentication Protocol (PAP) is an obsolete and insecure authentication protocol that sends user credentials in plaintext and should not be allowed.
- The Challenge Handshake Authentication Protocol (CHAP) uses a challenge/response mechanism using the password as an encryption key to authenticate the user instead of having the user send a password over the wire.
- The Extensible Authentication Protocol (EAP) is a framework that enables many types of authentication techniques to be used when establishing network connections.
- Desktop virtualization technologies, such as remote desktops and virtual desktops, allow users to remotely interact with computers as if they were physically using them.
- Two of the most common approaches to providing remote desktops are Microsoft's Remote Desktop Protocol (RDP) and the open-source Virtual Network Computing (VNC) system.
- Virtual desktop infrastructure (VDI) is a technology that hosts multiple virtual desktops in a centralized manner and makes them available to authorized users.
- Secure Shell (SSH) is a secure tunneling mechanism that provides terminal-like access to remote computers.
- A network socket is an endpoint for a data communications channel, defined by five parameters: source address, source port, destination address, destination port, and protocol (TCP or UDP).
- Remote procedure calls allow a program somewhere in your network to execute a function or procedure on some other host.

Questions

Please remember that these questions are formatted and asked in a certain way for a reason. Keep in mind that the CISSP exam is asking questions at a conceptual level. Questions may not always have the perfect answer, and the candidate is advised against always looking for the perfect answer. Instead, the candidate should look for the best answer in the list.

1. In which type of networks is the Signaling System 7 (SS7) protocol used?
   A. Integrated Services Digital Network (ISDN)
   B. IP telephony network
   C. Real-time Transport Protocol (RTP) network
   D. Public switched telephone network (PSTN)

2. Which of the following is true about the Session Initiation Protocol (SIP)?
   A. Used to establish virtual private network (VPN) sessions
   B. Framework for authenticating network connections
   C. Session layer protocol for out-of-band statistics
   D. Application layer protocol used in online gaming communications
3. Which of the following is not considered a best practice for securing multimedia collaboration platforms?
   A. Don't record meetings unless necessary
   B. Use consumer-grade products
   C. Use AES 256-bit encryption
   D. Restrict participants' sharing of their screens or cameras as appropriate
4. How could you best protect a unified communications (UC) platform?
   A. Protect it as you would any other systems
   B. Enable Password Authentication Protocol (PAP)
   C. Use the Session Initiation Protocol (SIP) for every new session
   D. Ensure the hub is protected against physical and logical threats

Use the following scenario to answer Questions 5–7. You are the CISO of a research and development company that is transitioning to a 100 percent remote workforce, so your entire staff will be working from home. You don't have enough laptops for all your staff, so those without one will be using their personal computers and printers for work. Your VPN concentrators are sufficient to support the entire workforce, and you will be requiring all staff members to connect to the VPN.

5. Which authentication protocol would be best for your VPN connections?
   A. Password Authentication Protocol (PAP)
   B. Challenge Handshake Authentication Protocol (CHAP)
   C. Extensible Authentication Protocol (EAP)
   D. Session Initiation Protocol (SIP)
6. Which of the following additional VPN configurations should you also enable?
   A. Split tunneling
   B. Full tunneling
   C. VPN kill switch
   D. Hybrid tunneling

7. Which of the following will best protect the confidentiality of your sensitive research data?
   A. Secure Shell (SSH)
   B. Virtualized networks
   C. Virtual desktop infrastructure (VDI)
   D. Remote Procedure Calls (RPC)
8. During a recent review of your enterprise architecture, you realize that many of your mission-critical systems rely on Remote Procedure Call (RPC). What measures should you take to ensure remote procedure calls are secured?
   A. Implement ITU standard H.323
   B. Tunnel RPC through Transport Layer Security (TLS)
   C. Use the Password Authentication Protocol (PAP) for authentication
   D. Enforce client-side authentication
9. Which of the following is not an advantage of virtual desktops?
   A. Reduced user downtime during incident response
   B. Support for both persistent and nonpersistent sessions
   C. Support for both physical and remote logins
   D. Better implementation of data retention standards

Answers

1. **D.** The SS7 protocol is used in a PSTN to set up, control, and disconnect calls.
2. **D.** SIP is an application layer protocol used for call setup and teardown in IP telephony, video and multimedia conferencing, instant messaging, and online gaming.
3. **B.** Consumer-grade products almost always lack the security controls and management features that we need to properly secure multimedia collaboration platforms.
4. **D.** Securing UC involves similar security controls that we would apply to any other communications platform, but with a couple of important caveats. Unified communications rely on a central hub that integrates, coordinates, and synchronizes the various technologies. You want to ensure that this hub is adequately protected against physical and logical threats.
5. **C.** EAP is considered much more secure than both PAP (which is not secure at all) and CHAP. SIP does not provide authentication mechanisms at all.
6. **A.** Because your staff will be using printers on their home networks, you will have to enable split tunneling, which allows some traffic to be sent over the VPN and other traffic to go to the local network or to the Internet directly.

7. **C.** VDI allows your sensitive data to remain in your protected network even as users are able to work with it over a virtual desktop. Properly configured, this infrastructure prevents any sensitive research data from being stored on the remote user's computer.
8. **B.** Since many implementations of RPC lack security controls, many organizations require TLS for authenticating hosts and encrypting RPC traffic.
9. **C.** VDI is particularly helpful in regulated environments because of the ease with which it supports data retention, configuration management, and incident response through persistent and nonpersistent sessions. However, since VDI relies on VMs in a data center, there is not a computer at which a user could physically log in.

PART V

Identity and Access Management

CHAPTER 16

Identity and Access Fundamentals

This chapter presents the following:

- Identification, authentication, authorization, and accountability
- Credential management
- Identity management
- Federated identity management with a third-party service

The value of identity of course is that so often with it comes purpose.

—Richard Grant

The concept of identity is foundational to controlling access to our assets because everyone (and everything) that touches them must have a legitimate purpose in doing so. What makes access control tricky is that most of us have multiple identities that depend on the context in which we find ourselves. A person could simultaneously be an asset owner, custodian, and processor (roles we discussed in Chapter 5), depending on which asset we consider and at what time. On top of the challenge of handling multiple identities, we also have to ensure that each identity belongs to the person claiming it.

In this chapter, we discuss the fundamentals of user identification, authentication, and authorization. We do this while considering a variety of real-world contexts, such as complex enterprise environments and the interaction with third parties. Of course, we must be able to verify that things are being done correctly, so we also talk about accountability in these efforts. This all sets the stage for the next chapter, in which we delve into how to actually manage identities and access.

Identification, Authentication, Authorization, and Accountability

For users to be permitted to access any resource, they first must prove they are who they claim to be, have the necessary credentials, and have been given the necessary rights or privileges to perform the actions they are requesting. Once these steps are completed successfully, it is necessary to track users' activities and enforce accountability for their actions. *Identification* describes a method by which a subject (user, program, or process) claims to have a specific identity (username, account number, or e-mail address). *Authentication* is the process by which a system verifies the identity of the subject, usually by requiring a piece of information that only the claimed identity should have. This piece could be a password, passphrase, cryptographic key, personal identification number (PIN), physiological characteristic, or token. Together, the identification and authentication information (for example, username and password) make up the subject's *credentials*. These credentials are compared to information that has been previously stored for this subject. If these credentials match the stored information, the subject is authenticated. But we are not done yet.

Once the subject provides its credentials and is properly authenticated, the system it is trying to access needs to determine if this subject has been given the necessary rights and privileges to carry out the requested actions. The system may look at an access control matrix or compare security labels to verify that this subject may indeed access the requested resource and perform the actions it is attempting. If the system determines that the subject may access the resource, it *authorizes* the subject.

Although identification, authentication, authorization, and accountability have close and complementary definitions, each has distinct functions that fulfill a specific requirement in the process of access control. A user may be properly identified and authenticated to the network, but may not have the authorization to access certain files on the file server. On the other hand, a user may be authorized to access the files on the file server, but until she is properly identified and authenticated, those resources are out of reach. Figure 16-1 illustrates the four steps that must happen for a subject to access an object.

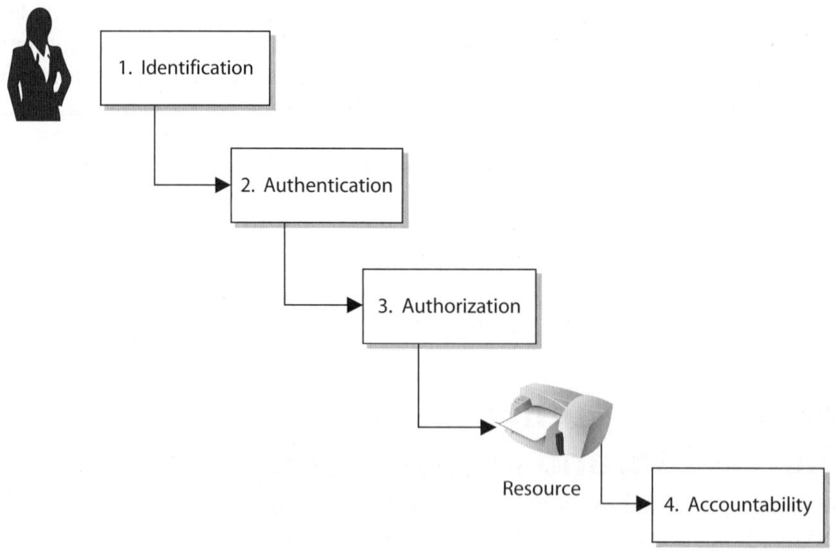

Figure 16-1 Four steps must happen for a subject to access an object: identification, authentication, authorization, and accountability.

Race Condition

A *race condition* occurs when processes carry out their tasks on a shared resource in an incorrect order. A race condition is possible when two or more processes use a shared resource, such as data within a variable. It is important that the processes carry out their functionality in the correct sequence. If process 2 carried out its task on the data before process 1, the result would be much different than if process 1 carried out its tasks on the data before process 2.

In software, when the authentication and authorization steps are split into two functions, there is a possibility an attacker could use a race condition to force the authorization step to be completed *before* the authentication step. This would be a flaw in the software that the attacker has figured out how to exploit. A race condition occurs when two or more processes use the same resource and the sequence of steps within the software can be carried out in an improper order, something that can drastically affect the output. So, an attacker can force the authorization step to take place before the authentication step and gain unauthorized access to a resource.

The subject needs to be held accountable for the actions taken within a system or domain. The only way to ensure accountability is if the subject is uniquely identified and the subject's actions are recorded.

Logical access controls are technical tools used for identification, authentication, authorization, and accountability. They are software components that enforce access control measures for systems, programs, processes, and information. The logical access controls can be embedded within operating systems, applications, add-on security packages, or database and telecommunication management systems. It can be challenging to synchronize all access controls and ensure all vulnerabilities are covered without producing overlaps of functionality. However, if it were easy, security professionals would not be getting paid the big bucks!

EXAM TIP The words "logical" and "technical" can be used interchangeably in this context. It is conceivable that the CISSP exam would refer to logical and technical controls interchangeably.

An individual's identity must be verified during the authentication process. Authentication usually involves a two-step process: entering public information (a username, employee number, account number, or department ID), and then entering private information (a static password, smart token, cognitive password, one-time password, or PIN). Entering public information is the identification step, while entering private information is the authentication step of the two-step process. Each technique used for identification and authentication has its pros and cons. Each should be properly evaluated to determine the right mechanism for the correct environment.

Identification and Authentication

Once a person has been identified through the user ID or a similar value, she must be authenticated, which means she must prove she is who she says she is. Three main types of factors can be used for authentication: *something a person knows*, *something a person has*, and *something a person is*. Sometimes, these factors are combined with two additional factors: *somewhere a person is* (logical or physical location) and *something a person does* (behavioral factor). These location and behavioral factors may not be all that strong by themselves, but when combined with other factors they can significantly improve the effectiveness of the authentication process.

Something a person knows (knowledge-based authentication [KBA]) can be, for example, a password, PIN, mother's maiden name, or the combination to a lock. Authenticating a person by something that she knows is usually the least expensive method to implement. The downside to this method is that another person may acquire this knowledge and gain unauthorized access to a resource.

Something a person has (ownership-based authentication) can be a key, swipe card, access card, or badge. This method is common for accessing facilities but could also be used to access sensitive areas or to authenticate systems. A downside to this method is that the item can be lost or stolen, which could result in unauthorized access.

Something specific to a person (biometric authentication) becomes a bit more interesting. This is not based on whether the person is an American, a geek, or an athlete—it is based on a physical attribute. Authenticating a person's identity based on a unique physical attribute is referred to as biometrics.

Strong authentication contains two or all of these three methods: something a person knows, has, or is. Using a biometric system by itself does not provide strong authentication because it provides only one out of the three methods. Biometrics supplies what a person is, not what a person knows or has. For a strong authentication process to be in place, a biometric system needs to be coupled with a mechanism that checks for one of the other two methods. For example, many times the person has to type a PIN into a keypad before the biometric scan is performed. This satisfies the "something the person knows" category. Conversely, the person could be required to swipe a magnetic card through a

One-to-One and One-to-Many

Verification 1:1 is the measurement of an identity against a single claimed identity. The conceptual question is, "Is this person who he claims to be?" So if Bob provides his identity and credential set, this information is compared to the data kept in an authentication database. If they match, we know that it is really Bob. If the identification is *1:N (many)*, the measurement of a single identity is compared against multiple identities. The conceptual question is, "Who is this person?" An example is if fingerprints were found at a crime scene, the cops would run them through their database to identify the suspect.

reader prior to the biometric scan. This would satisfy the "something the person has" category. Whatever identification system is used, for strong authentication to be in the process, it must include multiple factors.

TIP Strong authentication is also sometimes referred to as *multifactor authentication (MFA)*, which just means that more than one authentication method is used. While two-factor authentication (2FA) is common, *three-factor authentication* (for example, smart card, PIN, and retinal scan) is sometimes used.

Identity is a complicated concept with many varied nuances, ranging from the philosophical to the practical. A person may have multiple digital identities. For example, a user could be JPublic in a Windows domain environment, JohnP on a Unix server, JohnPublic on the mainframe, JJP in instant messaging, JohnCPublic in the certification authority, and JohnnyPub on Facebook. If the organization that employs that user wants to centralize all of its access control, these various identity names for the same person may cause the security administrator undue stress.

NOTE *Mutual authentication* is when the two communicating entities must authenticate to each other before passing data. For example, an authentication server may be required to authenticate to a user's system before allowing data to flow back and forth.

While most of this chapter deals with user authentication, it is important to realize system-based authentication is possible also. Computers and devices can be identified, authenticated, monitored, and controlled based upon their hardware addresses (media access control) and/or Internet Protocol (IP) addresses. Networks may have network access control (NAC) technology that authenticates systems before they are allowed access to the network. Every network device has a hardware address that is integrated into its network interface card (NIC) and a software-based address (IP) that either is assigned by a Dynamic Host Configuration Protocol (DHCP) server or locally configured.

Identification Component Requirements

When issuing identification values to users, the following should be in place:

- Each identifier should be unique, for user accountability.
- A standard naming scheme should be followed.
- The value should be nondescriptive of the user's position or tasks.
- The value should not be shared between users.

Knowledge-Based Authentication

We start off our discussion of authentication methods by looking at the most commonly used approach: using something that a person knows. This knowledge-based approach typically uses a password, passphrase, or cognitive password. Let's take a closer look at each.

Passwords

User identification coupled with a reusable password is the most common form of system identification and authorization mechanisms. A *password* is a protected string of characters that is used to authenticate an individual. As stated previously, authentication factors are based on what a person knows, has, or is. A password is something the user knows, and in order to ensure its effectiveness for authentication, it must be kept secret.

Password Policies Although passwords are prevalent, they are also considered one of the weakest security mechanisms available. Why? Users usually choose passwords that are easily guessed (a spouse's name, a user's birth date, or a dog's name), or tell others their passwords, and many times write the passwords down on a sticky note and hide it under the keyboard. To most users, security is usually not the most important or interesting part of using their computers—except when someone hacks into their computer and steals confidential information, that is. Then security is all the rage.

This is where password policies step in. If passwords are properly generated, updated, and kept secret, they can provide effective security. Password generators can be used to create passwords for users. This ensures that a user will not be using "Bob" or "Spot" for a password, but if the generator spits out "kdjasijew284802h," the user will surely scribble it down on a piece of paper and stick it to the monitor, which defeats the whole purpose. If a password generator is going to be used, the tools should create uncomplicated, pronounceable, nondictionary words to help users remember them so they aren't tempted to write them down.

If users can choose their own passwords, the operating system should enforce certain password requirements. The operating system can require that a password contain a certain number of characters, unrelated to the user ID, and not be easily guessable. The operating system can keep track of the passwords a specific user generates so as to ensure no passwords are reused. In March of 2020 the National Institute of Standards and Technology (NIST) updated its guidelines concerning passwords in SP 800-63B. These include the following recommendations:

- **Increased password length** The longer the password, the harder it is to guess. The recommended minimum password length is 8 characters for user-selected ones and 6 characters for computer-generated passwords. The maximum recommended length is 64 characters.
- **Allow special characters** Users should be allowed to use any special character, and even emojis, in their passwords. Special characters, however, should not be required.
- **Disallow password hints** On the surface, password hints may seem to make sense because they allow users to remember complex passwords and reduce reliance on password resetting features. However, they mostly help attackers.

If an attacker is after a password, she can try a few different techniques:

- **Electronic monitoring** Listening to network traffic to capture information, especially when a user is sending her password to an authentication server. The password can be copied and reused by the attacker at another time, which is called a *replay attack*.
- **Access the password file** Usually done on the authentication server. The password file contains many users' passwords and, if compromised, can be the source of a lot of damage. This file should be protected with access control mechanisms and encryption.
- **Brute-force attacks** Performed with tools that cycle through many possible character, number, and symbol combinations to uncover a password.
- **Dictionary attacks** Comparing files of thousands of words to the user's password until a match is found.
- **Social engineering** Falsely convincing an individual that she has the necessary authorization to access specific resources.
- **Rainbow table** Using a table that contains all possible passwords already in a hash format.

Certain techniques can be implemented to provide another layer of security for passwords and their use. After each successful logon, a message can be presented to a user indicating the date and time of the last successful logon, the location of this logon, and whether there were any unsuccessful logon attempts. This alerts the user to any suspicious activity and whether anyone has attempted to log on using his credentials. An administrator can set system parameters that allow a certain number of failed logon attempts to be accepted before a user is locked out; this is a type of *clipping level*. The user can be locked out for five minutes or a full day, for example, after the threshold (or clipping level) has been exceeded. It depends on how the administrator configures this mechanism. An audit trail can also be used to track password usage and both successful and unsuccessful logon attempts. This audit information should include the date, time, user ID, and workstation the user logged in from.

NOTE *Clipping level* is an older term that just means threshold. If the number of acceptable failed login attempts is set to three, three is the threshold (clipping level) value.

Policies can also specify other conditions that make passwords more difficult to exploit. Many organizations maintain a password history so users cannot reuse passwords within a certain timeframe. A variation on this is having the system remember the last *n* (where *n* is some number greater than or equal to one) passwords to prevent their reuse. Policies can also specify maximum age (that is, expiration) and minimum age (so the password can't be changed immediately to bypass the other policies) requirements.

As with many things in life, education is the key. Password requirements, protection, and generation should be addressed in security awareness programs so users understand what is expected of them, why they should protect their passwords, and how passwords can be stolen. Users should be an extension to a security team, not the opposition.

NOTE Rainbow tables contain passwords already in their hashed format. The attacker just compares a captured hashed password with one that is listed in the table to uncover the plaintext password. This takes much less time than carrying out a dictionary or brute-force attack.

Password Checkers Several organizations test user-chosen passwords using tools that perform dictionary and/or brute-force attacks to detect the weak passwords. This helps make the environment as a whole less susceptible to dictionary and exhaustive attacks used to discover users' passwords. Many times the same tools employed by an attacker to crack a password are used by a network administrator to make sure the password is strong enough. Most security tools have this dual nature. They are used by security professionals and IT staff to test for vulnerabilities within their environment in the hope of uncovering and fixing them before an attacker finds the vulnerabilities. An attacker uses the same tools to uncover vulnerabilities to exploit before the security professional can fix them. It is the never-ending cat-and-mouse game.

If a tool is called a *password checker*, it is used by a security professional to test the strength of a password. If a tool is called a *password cracker*, it is usually used by a hacker; however, most of the time, these tools are one and the same.

You need to obtain management's approval before attempting to test (break) employees' passwords with the intent of identifying weak passwords. Explaining you are trying to help the situation, not hurt it, *after* you have uncovered the CEO's password is not a good situation to be in.

Password Hashing and Encryption In most situations, if an attacker sniffs your password from the network wire, she still has some work to do before she actually knows your password value because most systems hash the password with a hashing algorithm, commonly Message Digest 5 (MD5) or Secure Hash Algorithm (SHA), to ensure passwords are not sent in cleartext.

Although some people think the world is run by Microsoft, other types of operating systems are out there, such as Unix and Linux. These systems do not use registries and SAM databases but contain their user passwords in a file cleverly called "shadow." This shadow file does not contain passwords in cleartext; instead, your password is run through a hashing algorithm, and the resulting value is stored in this file. Unix-type systems zest things up by using salts in this process. *Salts* are random values added to passwords prior to hashing to add more complexity and randomness. The more randomness entered into the hashing process, the harder it is for the bad guy to decrypt and uncover your password. The use of a salt means that the same password can be encrypted into several thousand different hashes. This makes it much more difficult for an adversary to attack the passwords in your system using approaches like rainbow tables.

Limit Logon Attempts A threshold can be set to allow only a certain number of unsuccessful logon attempts. After the threshold is met, the user's account can be locked for a period of time or indefinitely, which requires an administrator to manually unlock the account. This protects against dictionary and other exhaustive attacks that continually submit credentials until the right combination of username and password is discovered.

Passphrase

A *passphrase* is a sequence of characters that is longer than a password (thus a "phrase") and, in some cases, takes the place of a password during an authentication process. The user enters this phrase into an application, and the application transforms the value into a *virtual password*, making the passphrase the length and format that are required by the application. (For example, an application may require your virtual password to be 128 bits to be used as a key with the AES algorithm.) If a user wants to authenticate to an application, such as Pretty Good Privacy (PGP), he types in a passphrase, let's say StickWithMeKidAndYouWillWearDiamonds. The application converts this phrase into a virtual password that is used for the actual authentication. The user usually generates the passphrase in the same way a user creates a password the first time he logs on to a computer. A passphrase is more secure than a password because it is longer, and thus harder to obtain by an attacker. In many cases, the user is more likely to remember a passphrase than a password.

Cognitive Password

Cognitive passwords are fact- or opinion-based information used to verify an individual's identity. A user is enrolled by answering several questions based on her life experiences. Passwords can be hard for people to remember, but that same person will not likely forget the first person they kissed, the name of their best friend in 8th grade, or their favorite cartoon character. After the enrollment process, the user can answer the questions asked of her to be authenticated instead of having to remember a password. This authentication process is best for a service the user does not use on a daily basis, because it takes longer than other authentication mechanisms. This can work well for help-desk services. The user can be authenticated via cognitive means. This way, the person at the help desk can be sure he is talking to the right person, and the user in need of help does not need to remember a password that may be used once every three months.

EXAM TIP Knowledge-based authentication means that a subject is authenticated based upon something she knows. This could be a PIN, password, passphrase, cognitive password, personal history information, or through the use of a CAPTCHA, which is the graphical representation of data. A CAPTCHA is a skewed representation of characteristics a person must enter to prove that the subject is a human and not an automated tool as in a software robot.

Biometric Authentication

Biometrics verifies an individual's identity by analyzing a unique personal characteristic, which is one of the most effective and accurate methods of verifying identification. Biometrics is a very sophisticated technology; thus, it is much more expensive and complex than the other types of identity verification processes. Biometric systems typically base authentication decisions on physical attributes (such as iris, retina, or fingerprint), which provides more accuracy because physical attributes typically don't change, absent some disfiguring injury, and are harder to impersonate.

Biometrics is typically broken up into two different categories:

- **Physiological** This category of biometrics uses physical attributes unique to a specific individual to verify that person's identity. Fingerprints are a common example of a physiological trait used in biometric systems. Physiological is "what you are."
- **Behavioral** This approach is based on something an individual does uniquely to confirm her identity. An example is signature dynamics. Behavioral is "what you do."

A biometric system scans a person's physiological attribute or behavioral trait and compares it to a record created in an earlier enrollment process. Because this system inspects the grooves of a person's fingerprint, the pattern of someone's retina, or the pitches of someone's voice, it must be extremely sensitive. The system must perform accurate and repeatable measurements of anatomical or behavioral characteristics. This type of sensitivity can easily cause false positives or false negatives. The system must be calibrated so these false positives and false negatives occur infrequently and the results are as accurate as possible.

When a biometric system rejects an authorized individual, it is called a *Type I error* (false rejection rate [FRR]). When the system accepts impostors who should be rejected, it is called a *Type II error* (false acceptance rate [FAR]). The goal is to obtain low numbers for each type of error, but Type II errors are the most dangerous and thus the most important to avoid.

When comparing different biometric systems, many different variables are used, but one of the most important metrics is the *crossover error rate (CER)*. This rating is stated as a percentage and represents the point at which the FRR equals the FAR. This rating is the most important measurement when determining the system's accuracy. A biometric system that delivers a CER of 3 will be more accurate than a system that delivers a CER of 4.

NOTE Crossover error rate (CER) is also called equal error rate (EER).

What is the purpose of this CER value anyway? Using the CER as an impartial judgment of a biometric system helps create standards by which products from different vendors can be fairly judged and evaluated. If you are going to buy a biometric system, you need a way to compare the accuracy between different systems. You can just go by the different vendors' marketing material (they all say they are the best), or you can compare the different CER values of the products to see which one really is more accurate than the others. It is also a way to keep the vendors honest. One vendor may tell you, "We have absolutely no Type II errors." This would mean that their product would not allow any imposters to be improperly authenticated. But what if you asked the vendor how many Type I errors their product had and the rep sheepishly replied, "We average around 90 percent of Type I errors." That would mean that 90 percent of the authentication attempts would be rejected, which would negatively affect your employees' productivity. So you can ask a vendor about their product's CER value, which represents when the Type I and Type II errors are equal, to give you a better understanding of the product's overall accuracy.

Individual environments have specific security level requirements, which will dictate how many Type I and Type II errors are acceptable. For example, a military institution that is very concerned about confidentiality would be prepared to accept a certain rate of Type I errors, but would absolutely not accept any false accepts (Type II errors). Because all biometric systems can be calibrated, if you lower the Type II error rate by adjusting the system's sensitivity, it will typically result in an increase in Type I errors. The military institution would obviously calibrate the biometric system to lower the Type II errors to zero, but that would mean it would have to accept a higher rate of Type I errors.

Biometric authentication is the most expensive method of verifying a person's identity, and it faces other barriers to becoming widely accepted. These include user acceptance, enrollment timeframe, and throughput. Many people are reluctant to let a machine read the pattern of their retina or scan the geometry of their hand. The enrollment phase requires an action to be performed several times to capture a clear and distinctive reference record. People are not particularly fond of expending this time and energy when they are used to just picking a password and quickly typing it into their console. When a person attempts to be authenticated by a biometric system, sometimes the system will request an action to be completed several times. If the system is unable to get a clear reading of an iris scan or cannot capture a full voice verification print, the individual may have to repeat the action. This causes low throughput, stretches the individual's patience, and reduces acceptability.

During enrollment, the user provides the biometric data (e.g., fingerprint, voice print, or retina scan), and the biometric reader converts this data into binary values. Depending on the system, the reader may create a hash value of the biometric data, or it may encrypt the data, or do both. The biometric data then goes from the reader to a backend authentication database where the user's account has been created. When the user needs to later authenticate to a system, she provides the necessary biometric data, and the binary format of this information is compared to what is in the authentication database. If they match, then the user is authenticated.

In Figure 16-2, we see that biometric data can be stored on a smart card and used for authentication. Also, you might notice that the match is 95 percent instead of 100 percent. Obtaining a 100 percent match every time is very difficult because of the level of sensitivity of the biometric systems. A smudge on the reader, oil on the person's finger, and other small environmental issues can stand in the way of matching 100 percent. If your biometric system was calibrated so it required 100 percent matches, this would mean you would not allow any Type II errors and that users would commonly not be authenticated in a timely manner.

Figure 16-2 Biometric data is turned into binary data and compared for identity validation.

> **Processing Speed**
> When reviewing biometric devices for purchase, one component to take into consideration is the length of time it takes to actually authenticate users. From the time a user inserts data until she receives an accept or reject response should take five to ten seconds.

The following is an overview of the different types of biometric systems and the physiological or behavioral characteristics they examine.

Fingerprint

Fingerprints are made up of ridge endings and bifurcations exhibited by friction ridges and other detailed characteristics called minutiae. It is the distinctiveness of these minutiae that gives each individual a unique fingerprint. An individual places his finger on a device that reads the details of the fingerprint and compares this to a reference file. If the two match, the individual's identity has been verified.

NOTE Fingerprint systems store the full fingerprint, which is actually a lot of information that takes up hard drive space and resources. The finger-scan technology extracts specific features from the fingerprint and stores just that information, which takes up less hard drive space and allows for quicker database lookups and comparisons.

Palm Scan

The palm holds a wealth of information and has many aspects that are used to identify an individual. The palm has creases, ridges, and grooves throughout that are unique to a specific person. The palm scan also includes the fingerprints of each finger. An individual places his hand on the biometric device, which scans and captures this information. This information is compared to a reference file, and the identity is either verified or rejected.

Hand Geometry

The shape of a person's hand (the shape, length, and width of the hand and fingers) defines hand geometry. This trait differs significantly between people and is used in some biometric systems to verify identity. A person places her hand on a device that has grooves for each finger. The system compares the geometry of each finger, and the hand as a whole, to the information in a reference file to verify that person's identity.

Retina Scan

A system that reads a person's retina scans the blood-vessel pattern of the retina on the backside of the eyeball. This pattern is unique for each person. A camera is used to project a beam inside the eye and capture the pattern and compare it to a reference file recorded previously.

NOTE Retina scans are extremely invasive and involve a number of privacy issues. Since the information obtained through this scan can be used in the diagnosis of medical conditions, it could very well be considered protected health information (PHI) subject to healthcare information privacy regulations such as HIPAA.

Iris Scan

The iris is the colored portion of the eye that surrounds the pupil. The iris has unique patterns, rifts, colors, rings, coronas, and furrows. The uniqueness of each of these characteristics within the iris is captured by a camera and compared with the information gathered during the enrollment phase. Of the biometric systems, iris scans are the most accurate. The iris remains constant through adulthood, which reduces the type of errors that can happen during the authentication process. Sampling the iris offers more reference coordinates than any other type of biometric. Mathematically, this means it has a higher accuracy potential than any other type of biometric.

NOTE When using an iris pattern biometric system, the optical unit must be positioned so the sun does not shine into the aperture; thus, when the system is implemented, it must be properly placed within the facility.

Signature Dynamics

When a person writes a signature, usually they do so in the same manner and at the same speed each time. Writing a signature produces electrical signals that can be captured by a biometric system. The physical motions performed when someone is signing a document create these electrical signals. The signals provide unique characteristics that can be used to distinguish one individual from another. Signature dynamics provides more information than a static signature, so there are more variables to verify when confirming an individual's identity and more assurance that this person is who he claims to be.

Signature dynamics is different from a digitized signature. A digitized signature is just an electronic copy of someone's signature and is not a biometric system that captures the speed of signing, the way the person holds the pen, and the pressure the signer exerts to generate the signature.

Keystroke Dynamics

Whereas signature dynamics is a method that captures the electrical signals when a person signs a name, keystroke dynamics captures electrical signals when a person types a certain phrase. As a person types a specified phrase, the biometric system captures the speed and motions of this action. Each individual has a certain style and speed of typing, which translate into unique signals. This type of authentication is more effective than typing in a password, because a password is easily obtainable. It is much harder to repeat a person's typing style than it is to acquire a password.

Voice Print

People's speech sounds and patterns have many subtle distinguishing differences. A biometric system that is programmed to capture a voice print and compare it to the information held in a reference file can differentiate one individual from another. During the enrollment process, an individual is asked to say several different words. Later, when this individual needs to be authenticated, the biometric system jumbles these words and presents them to the individual. The individual then repeats the sequence of words given. This technique is used so others cannot attempt to record the session and play it back in hopes of obtaining unauthorized access.

Facial Scan

A system that scans a person's face takes many attributes and characteristics into account. People have different bone structures, nose ridges, eye widths, forehead sizes, and chin shapes. These are all captured during a facial scan and compared to an earlier captured scan held within a reference record. If the information is a match, the person is positively identified.

A naïve implementation of this technology could be fooled by a photograph of the legitimate user. To thwart this approach, the scanner can perform a three-dimensional measurement of the user's face by projecting thousands of infrared dots on it. This is how Apple's Face ID works.

Hand Topography

Whereas hand geometry looks at the size and width of an individual's hand and fingers, hand topology looks at the different peaks and valleys of the hand, along with its overall shape and curvature. When an individual wants to be authenticated, she places her hand on the system. Off to one side of the system, a camera snaps a side-view picture of the

Biometric Issues and Concerns

Biometric systems are not without their own sets of issues and concerns. Because they depend upon the specific and unique traits of living things, problems can arise. Living things are notorious for not remaining the same, which means they won't present static biometric information for every login attempt. Voice recognition can be hampered by a user with a cold. Retinas can detach. Someone could lose a finger. Or all three could happen. You just never know in this crazy world.

Some biometric systems actually check for the pulsation and/or heat of a body part to make sure it is alive. So if you are planning to cut someone's finger off or pluck out someone's eyeball so you can authenticate yourself as a legitimate user, it may not work. Although not specifically stated, this type of activity definitely falls outside the bounds of the CISSP ethics you will be responsible for upholding once you receive your certification.

hand from a different view and angle than that of systems that target hand geometry, and thus captures different data. This attribute is not unique enough to authenticate individuals by itself and is commonly used in conjunction with hand geometry.

Ownership-Based Authentication

Authentication can also be based on something that the subject has. This is almost always some sort of physical or logical token. It can be a device such as a phone, identification card, or even an implanted device. It can also be a cryptographic key, such as a private key in public key infrastructure (PKI). Sometimes, access to the token is protected by some other authentication process, such as when you have to unlock your phone to get to a software-based token generator.

PART V

One-Time Password

A *one-time password (OTP)*, also called a *dynamic password*, is used for authentication purposes and is valid only once. After the password is used, it is no longer valid; thus, it can't be reused if a hacker obtains it. The password is generated by a token device, which is something the person owns (or at least carries around). This device is the most common implementation mechanism for OTP and generates the one-time password for the user to submit to an authentication server. It is commonly implemented in three formats: as a dedicated physical device with a small screen that displays the OTP, as a smartphone application, and as a service that sends an SMS message to your phone. The following sections explain the concepts behind this technology.

NOTE SMS was deprecated as a means of providing 2FA by the NIST in 2017. It is widely considered an insecure channel but is unfortunately still in common use.

The Token Device The token device, or password generator, is usually a handheld device that has a display and possibly a keypad. This hardware is separate from the computer the user is attempting to access. The token device and authentication service must be synchronized in some manner to be able to authenticate a user. The token device presents the user with a list of characters to be entered as a password when logging on to a computer. Only the token device and authentication service know the meaning of these characters. Because the two are synchronized, the token device presents the exact password the authentication service is expecting. This is a one-time password, also called a token, and is no longer valid after initial use.

Synchronous A *synchronous token device* requires the device and the authentication service to advance to the next OTP in sync with each other. This change can be triggered by time (e.g., every 30 seconds a new OTP is in play) or by simply going down a pre-agreed sequence of passwords, each of which is used only once before both the device and the server advance to the next one. The device displays the OTP to the user, who then enters this value and a user ID. The authentication service decrypts credentials and compares the OTP to the value it expects. If the two match, the user is authenticated and allowed to access the system.

RSA SecurID

RSA SecurID, from RSA Security LLC, is a well-known time-based token. One version of the product generates the OTP by using a mathematical function on the time, date, and ID of the token card. Another version of the product requires a PIN to be entered into the token device.

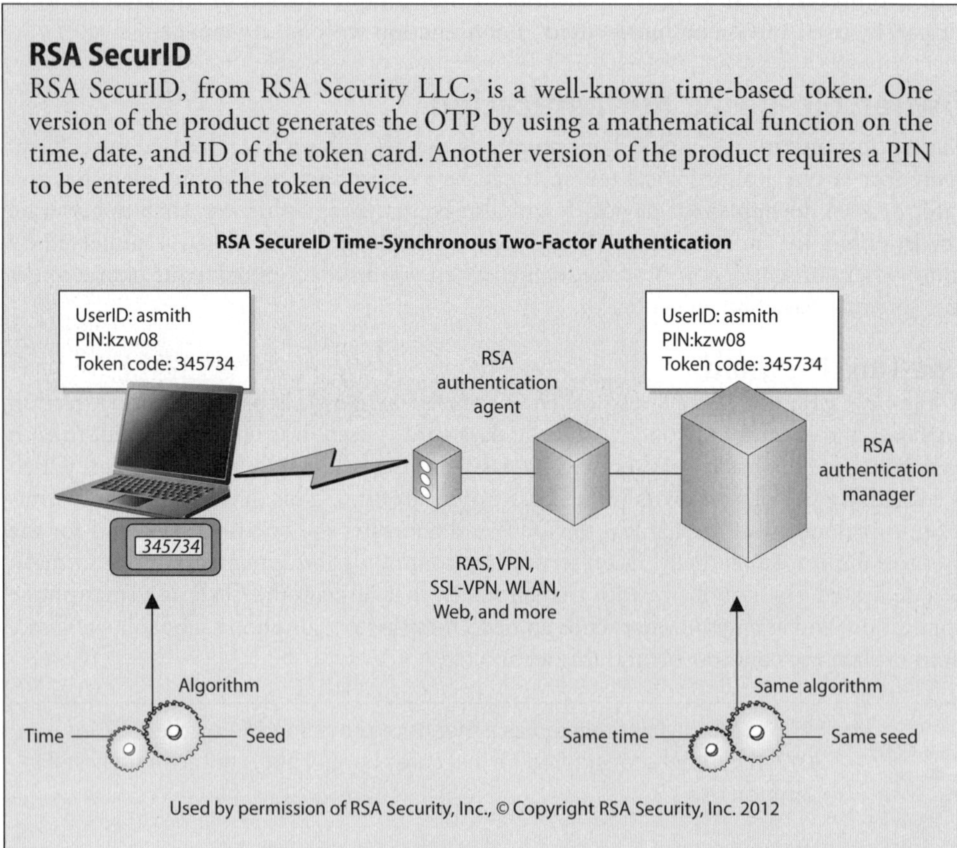

EXAM TIP Synchronous token-based OTP generation can be time-based or counter-based. Another term for counter-based is event-based. Counter-based and event-based are interchangeable terms, and you could see either or both on the CISSP exam.

Asynchronous A token device using an *asynchronous token*–generating method employs a challenge/response scheme to authenticate the user. In this situation, the authentication server sends the user a challenge, a random value, also called a *nonce*. The user enters this random value into the token device, which encrypts it and returns a value the user uses as an OTP. The user sends this value, along with a username, to the authentication server. If the authentication server can decrypt the value and it is the same challenge value sent earlier, the user is authenticated, as shown in Figure 16-3.

EXAM TIP The actual implementation and process that these devices follow can differ between different vendors. What is important to know is that asynchronous is based on challenge/response mechanisms, while synchronous is based on time- or counter-driven mechanisms.

Both token systems can fall prey to masquerading if a user shares his identification information (ID or username) and the token device is shared or stolen. The token device can also have battery failure or other malfunctions that would stand in the way of a successful authentication. However, this type of system is not vulnerable to electronic eavesdropping, sniffing, or password guessing.

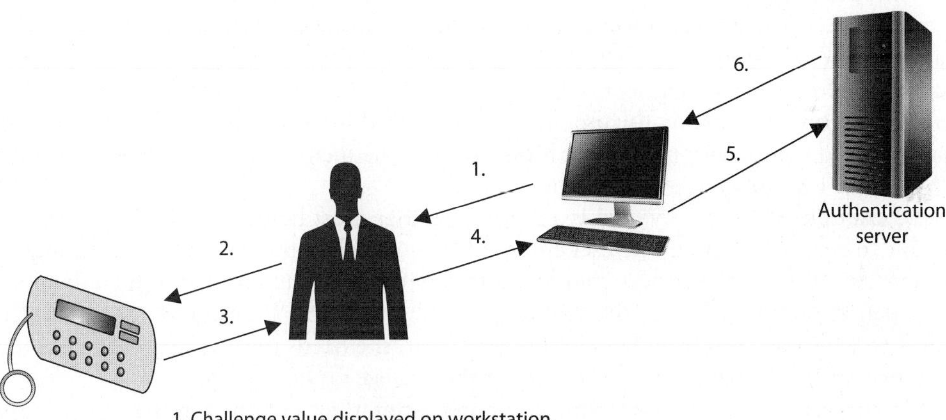
6.
5.
1.
4.
2.
3.
Authentication server
1. Challenge value displayed on workstation.
2. User enters challenge value and PIN into token device.
3. Token device presents a different value to the user.
4. User enters new value into the workstation.
5. Value sent to authentication service on server.
6. AS sends an "allow access" response.

Figure 16-3 Authentication using an asynchronous token device includes a workstation, token device, and authentication service.

PART V

If the user has to enter a password or PIN into the token device before it provides an OTP, then strong authentication is in effect because it is using two factors—something the user knows (PIN) and something the user has (the token device).

NOTE One-time passwords can also be generated in software, in which case a piece of hardware such as a token device is not required. These are referred to as *soft tokens* and require that the authentication service and application contain the same base secrets, which are used to generate the OTPs.

Cryptographic Keys

Another way to prove one's identity is to use asymmetric cryptography and let the users' private keys show they are who they claim to be. Recall that the private key is kept secret by an individual and should never be shared. So, if the authentication server has (or gets a hold of) the user's public key, it can use that key to encrypt a challenge and send it to the user. Only the person owning the corresponding private key would be able to decrypt it and respond to it. Ideally, the user then encrypts the response using the server's public key to provide mutual authentication. This approach is commonly used in Secure Shell (SSH) instead of passwords, which are the weakest form of authentication and can be easily sniffed as they travel over a network.

Memory Cards

The main difference between memory cards and smart cards is their capacity to process information. A *memory card* holds information but cannot process information. A *smart card* holds information and has the necessary hardware and software to actually process that information. A memory card can hold a user's authentication information so the user only needs to type in a user ID or PIN and present the memory card, and if the data that the user enters matches the data on the memory card, the user is successfully authenticated. If the user presents a PIN value, then this is an example of two-factor authentication—something the user knows and something the user has. A memory card can also hold identification data that is pulled from the memory card by a reader. It travels with the PIN to a backend authentication server.

An example of a memory card is a swipe card that must be used for an individual to be able to enter a building. The user enters a PIN and swipes the memory card through a card reader. If this is the correct combination, the reader flashes green and the individual can open the door and enter the building. Another example is an ATM card. If Buffy wants to withdraw $40 from her checking account, she needs to slide the ATM card (or memory card) through the reader and enter the correct PIN.

Memory cards can be used with computers, but they require a reader to process the information. The reader adds cost to the process, especially when one is needed per computer, and card generation adds cost and effort to the whole authentication process. Using a memory card provides a more secure authentication method than using a password because the attacker would need to obtain the card and know the correct PIN. Administrators and management must weigh the costs and benefits of a memory token–based card implementation to determine if it is the right authentication mechanism for their environment.

Smart Card

A *smart card* has the capability of processing information because it has a microprocessor and integrated circuits incorporated into the card itself. Memory cards do not have this type of hardware and lack this type of functionality. The only function they can perform is simple storage. A smart card, which adds the capability to process information stored on it, can also provide a two-factor authentication method because the user may have to enter a PIN to unlock the smart card. This means the user must provide something she knows (PIN) and something she has (smart card).

Two general categories of smart cards are the contact and the contactless types. The *contact* smart card has a gold seal on the face of the card. When this card is fully inserted into a card reader, electrical fingers wipe against the card in the exact position that the chip contacts are located. This supplies power and data I/O to the chip for authentication purposes. The *contactless* smart card has an antenna wire that surrounds the perimeter of the card. When this card comes within an electromagnetic field of the reader, the antenna within the card generates enough energy to power the internal chip. Now, the results of the smart card processing can be broadcast through the same antenna, and the conversation of authentication can take place. The authentication can be completed by using a one-time password, by employing a challenge/response value, or by providing the user's private key if it is used within a PKI environment.

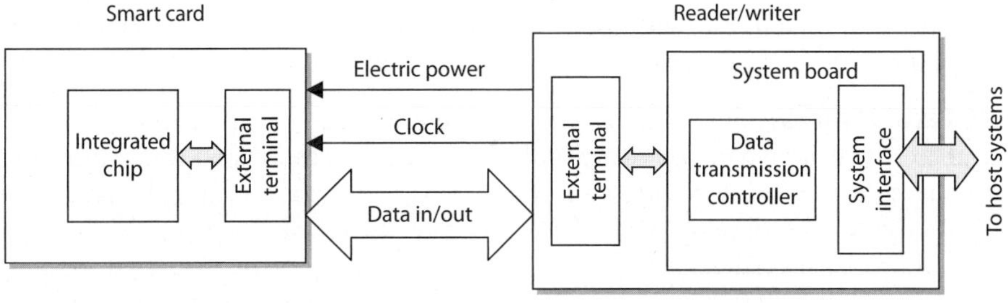

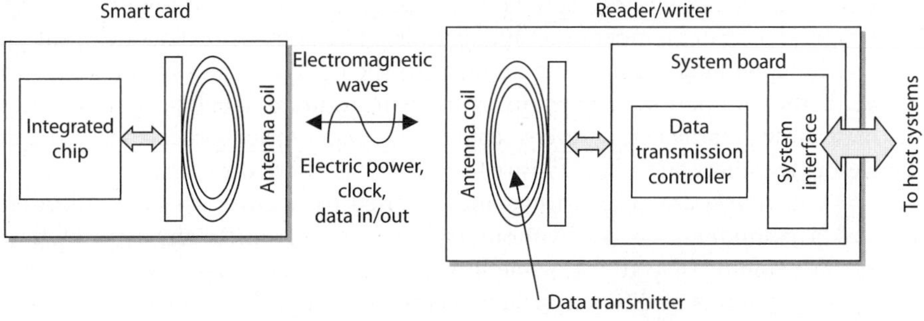

PART V

TIP Two types of contactless smart cards are available: hybrid and combi. The hybrid card has two chips, with the capability of utilizing both the contact and contactless formats. A combi card has one microprocessor chip that can communicate to contact or contactless readers.

The information held within the memory of a smart card is not readable until the correct PIN is entered. This fact and the complexity of the smart token make these cards resistant to reverse-engineering and tampering methods. If George loses the smart card he uses to authenticate to the domain at work, the person who finds the card would need to know his PIN to do any real damage. The smart card can also be programmed to store information in an encrypted fashion, as well as detect any tampering with the card itself. In the event that tampering is detected, the information stored on the smart card can be automatically wiped.

The drawbacks to using a smart card are the extra cost of the readers and the overhead of card generation, as with memory cards, although this cost is decreasing. The smart cards themselves are more expensive than memory cards because of the extra integrated circuits and microprocessor. Essentially, a smart card is a kind of computer, and because of that it has many of the operational challenges and risks that can affect a computer.

Smart cards have several different capabilities, and as the technology develops and memory capacities increase for storage, they will gain even more. They can store personal information in a storage manner that is tamper resistant. This also gives them the capability to isolate security-critical computations within themselves. They can be used in encryption systems to store keys and have a high level of portability as well as security. The memory and integrated circuit also provide the capacity to use encryption algorithms on the actual card and use them for secure authorization that can be utilized throughout an entire organization.

Smart Card Attacks Smart cards are more tamperproof than memory cards, but where there is sensitive data, there are individuals who are motivated to circumvent any countermeasure the industry throws at them. Over the years, criminals have become very inventive in the development of various ways to attack smart cards. Smart card attacks tend to be special cases of the cryptanalysis techniques we discussed in Chapter 8. For example, attackers have introduced computational errors into smart cards with the goal of uncovering the encryption keys used and stored on the cards. These "errors" are introduced by manipulating some environmental component of the card (changing input voltage, clock rate, temperature fluctuations). The attacker reviews the result of an encryption function after introducing an error to the card, and also reviews the correct result, which the card performs when no errors are introduced. Analysis of these different results may allow an attacker to reverse-engineer the encryption process, with the hope of uncovering the encryption key. This type of attack is referred to as *fault generation*.

Side-channel attacks are nonintrusive and are used to uncover sensitive information about how a component works, without trying to compromise any type of flaw or weakness. So a noninvasive attack is one in which the attacker watches how something works and how it reacts in different situations instead of trying to "invade" it with more

Interoperability

In the industry today, lack of interoperability is a big problem. An ISO/IEC standard, 14443, outlines the following items for smart card standardization:

- **ISO/IEC 14443-1** Physical characteristics
- **ISO/IEC 14443-2** Radio frequency power and signal interface
- **ISO/IEC 14443-3** Initialization and anticollision
- **ISO/IEC 14443-4** Transmission protocol

intrusive measures. Some examples of side-channel attacks that have been carried out on smart cards are *differential power analysis* (examining the power emissions released during processing), *electromagnetic analysis* (examining the frequencies emitted), and *timing* (how long a specific process takes to complete). These types of attacks are used to uncover sensitive information about how a component works without trying to compromise any type of flaw or weakness. They are commonly used for data collection. Attackers monitor and capture the analog characteristics of all supply and interface connections and any other electromagnetic radiation produced by the processor during normal operation. They can also collect the time it takes for the smart card to carry out its function. From the collected data, the attacker can deduce specific information she is after, which could be a private key, sensitive financial data, or an encryption key stored on the card.

Software attacks are also considered noninvasive attacks. A smart card has software just like any other device that does data processing, and anywhere there is software, there is the possibility of software flaws that can be exploited. The main goal of this type of attack is to input into the card instructions that will allow the attacker to extract account information, which he can use to make fraudulent purchases. Many of these types of attacks can be disguised by using equipment that looks just like the legitimate reader.

A more intrusive smart card attack is called *microprobing*, which uses needleless and ultrasonic vibration to remove the outer protective material on the card's circuits. Once this is completed, data can be accessed and manipulated by directly tapping into the card's ROM chips.

Near Field Communications

Near Field Communication (NFC) is a short-range (i.e., a few centimeters) radio frequency (RF) communications technology that provides data communication on a base frequency of 13.56 MHz. Manufacturers of NFC devices abide by ISO/IEC 18092 for international interoperability. While this technology is perhaps best known for contactless payments using mobile phones, it is also used for contactless smart cards.

Credential Management

Credential management deals with creating user accounts on all systems, assigning and modifying the account details and privileges when necessary, and decommissioning the accounts when they are no longer needed. In many environments, the IT department creates accounts manually on the different systems, users are given excessive rights and permissions, and when an employee leaves the organization, many or all of the accounts stay active. This typically occurs because a centralized credential management technology has not been put into place.

Credential management products attempt to attack these issues by allowing an administrator to manage user accounts across multiple systems. When there are multiple directories containing user profiles or access information, the account management software allows for replication between the directories to ensure each contains the same up-to-date information. This automated workflow capability not only reduces the potential errors that can take place in account management, it also logs and tracks each step (including account approval). This allows for accountability and provides documentation for use in backtracking if something goes wrong. Automated workflow also helps ensure that only the necessary amount of access is provided to the account and that there are no "orphaned" accounts still active when employees leave the organization. In addition, these types of processes are the kind your auditors will be looking for—and we always want to make the auditors happy!

NOTE These types of credential management products are commonly used to set up and maintain internal accounts. Web access control management is used mainly for external users.

Enterprise credential management products are usually expensive and can take time to properly roll out across the enterprise. Regulatory requirements, however, are making more and more organizations spend the money for these types of solutions—which the vendors love! In the following sections, we'll explore the many facets of a good credential management solution.

Password Managers

Two of the best practices when it comes to password-based authentication are to use complex passwords/passphrases and to have a different one for each account; accomplishing both from memory is a tall order for most of us. A popular solution to address this challenge is to use software products that remember our credentials for us. These products, known as *password managers* or *password vaults*, come in two flavors: as a stand-alone application or as a feature within another application (such as a web browser). In either case, the application stores user identifiers and passwords in a password-encrypted data store. The user need only remember this master password and the application maintains all others. These products typically provide random password generation and allow the user to store other information such as URLs and notes. Most modern web browsers also provide features that remember the user identifiers and passwords for specific websites.

An obvious problem with using password vaults is that they provide one-stop-shopping for malicious actors. If they can exploit this application, they gain access to all of the user's credentials. Developers of these applications go to great lengths to ensure they are secure, but as we all know there is no such thing as a 100 percent secure system. In fact, there have been multiple documented vulnerabilities that allowed adversaries to steal these (supposedly secure) credentials.

Password Synchronization

Another approach to credential management is to use password synchronization technologies that can allow a user to maintain just one password across multiple systems. The product synchronizes the password to other systems and applications, which happens transparently to the user. The goal is to require the user to memorize only one password, which enables the organization to enforce more robust and secure password requirements. If a user needs to remember only one password, he is more likely to not have a problem with longer, more complex strings of values. This reduces help-desk call volume and allows the administrator to keep her sanity for just a little bit longer.

One criticism of this approach is that since only one password is used to access different resources, the hacker only has to figure out one credential set to gain unauthorized access to all resources. But if the password requirements are more demanding (12 characters, no dictionary words, three symbols, upper- and lowercase letters, and so on) and the password is changed out regularly, the balance between security and usability can be acceptable.

Self-Service Password Reset

Some products are implemented to allow users to reset their own passwords. This does not mean that the users have any type of privileged permissions on the systems to allow them to change their own credentials. Instead, during the registration of a user account, the user can be asked to provide several personal questions (first car, favorite teacher, favorite color, and so on) in a question-and-answer form. When the user forgets his password, he may be required to provide another authentication mechanism (smart card, token, etc.) and to answer these previously answered questions to prove his identity.

Products are available that allow users to change their passwords through other means. For example, if you forgot your password, you may be asked to answer some of the questions answered during the registration process of your account (i.e., a cognitive password). If you do this correctly, an e-mail is sent to you with a link you must click. The password management product has your identity tied to the answers you gave to the questions during your account registration process and to your e-mail address. If you do everything correctly, you are given a screen that allows you to reset your password.

CAUTION The product should not ask for information that is publicly available, as in your mother's maiden name, because anyone can find that out and attempt to identify himself as you.

PART V

Assisted Password Reset

Some products are created for help-desk employees who need to work with individuals when they forget their password. The help-desk employee should not know or ask the individual for her password. This would be a security risk since only the owner of the password should know the value. The help-desk employee also should not just change a password for someone calling in without authenticating that person first. This can allow social engineering attacks where an attacker calls the help desk and indicates she is someone who she is not. If this were to take place, an attacker would have a valid employee password and could gain unauthorized access to the organization's jewels.

The products that provide assisted password reset functionality allow the help-desk individual to authenticate the caller before resetting the password. This authentication process is commonly performed through the use of cognitive passwords described in the previous section. The help-desk individual and the caller must be identified and authenticated through the password management tool before the password can be changed. Once the password is updated, the system that the user is authenticating to should require the user to change her password again. This would ensure that only she (and not she and the help-desk person) knows her password. The goal of an assisted password reset product is to reduce the cost of support calls and ensure all calls are processed in a uniform, consistent, and secure fashion.

Just-in-Time Access

You probably don't want your general users having administrative privileges on their computers. However, if you apply the security principle of least privilege (described in Chapter 9), your users will probably lack the authorization to perform many functions that you would like them to be able to perform in certain circumstances. From having their laptops "forget" wireless networks to which they may have connected, to updating software, there are many scenarios in which a regular user may need administrative (or otherwise elevated) credentials. The traditional approach is to have the user put in a ticket and wait for an IT administrator to perform the action for the user. This is a costly way of doing business, particularly if you have a large organization.

Just-in-time (JIT) access is a provisioning methodology that elevates users to the necessary privileged access to perform a specific task. This is a way to allow users to take care of routine tasks that would otherwise require IT staff intervention (and possibly decrease user productivity). This approach mitigates the risk of privileged account abuse by reducing the time a threat actor has to gain access to a privileged account. JIT access is usually granted in a granular manner, so that it applies to a specific resource or action in a given timeframe. For example, if users need administrative rights to allow a conferencing application access to their desktop, they can be granted one-time access to change that particular setting in their systems and then it's gone.

Registration and Proofing of Identity

Now let's think about how accounts are set up. In many environments, when a new user needs an account, a network administrator sets up the account(s) and provides some type of privileges and permissions. But how would the network administrator know what resources this new user should have access to and what permissions should be assigned to the new account? In most situations, she doesn't—she just wings it. This is how users end up with too much access to too many resources. What should take place instead is implementation of a workflow process that allows for a request for a new user account. Since hardly anyone in the organization likely knows the new employee, we need someone to vouch for this person's identity. This process, sometimes called *proofing of identity*, is almost always carried out by human resources (HR) personnel who would've had to verify the new employee's identity for tax and benefit purposes. The new account request is then sent to the employee's manager, who verifies the permissions that this person needs, and a ticket is generated for the technical staff to set up the account(s).

If there is a request for a change to the permissions on the account or if an account needs to be decommissioned, it goes through the same process. The request goes to a manager (or whoever is delegated with this approval task), the manager approves it, and the changes to the various accounts take place.

Over time, this new user will commonly have different identity attributes, which will be used for authentication purposes, stored in different systems in the network. When a user requests access to a resource, all of his identity data has already been copied from other identity stores and the HR database and held in this centralized directory (sometimes called the *identity repository*). When this employee parts with the organization for any reason, this new information goes from the HR database to the directory. An e-mail is automatically generated and sent to the manager to allow this account to be decommissioned. Once this is approved, the account management software disables all of the accounts that had been set up for this user.

User provisioning refers to the creation, maintenance, and deactivation of user objects and attributes as they exist in one or more systems, directories, or applications, in response to business processes. User provisioning software may include one or more of the following components: change propagation, self-service workflow, consolidated user administration, delegated user administration, and federated change control.

Authoritative System of Record

The authoritative source is the "system of record," or the location where identity information originates and is maintained. It should have the most up-to-date and reliable identity information. An *authoritative system of record (ASOR)* is a hierarchical tree-like structure system that tracks subjects and their authorization chains. Organizations need an automated and reliable way of detecting and managing unusual or suspicious changes to user accounts and a method of collecting this type of data through extensive auditing capabilities. The ASOR should contain the subject's name, associated accounts, authorization history per account, and provision details. This type of workflow and accounting is becoming more in demand for regulatory compliance because it allows auditors to understand how access is being centrally controlled within an environment.

User objects may represent employees, contractors, vendors, partners, customers, or other recipients of a service. Services may include e-mail, access to a database, access to a file server or database, and so on.

Great. So we create, maintain, and deactivate accounts as required based on business needs. What else does this mean? The creation of the account also is the creation of the access rights to organizational assets. It is through provisioning that users either are given access or have access taken away. Throughout the life cycle of a user identity, access rights, permissions, and privileges should change as needed in a clearly understood, automated, and audited process.

Profile Update

Most companies do not just contain the information "Bob Smith" for a user and make all access decisions based on this data. There can be a plethora of information on a user that is captured (e-mail address, home address, phone number, and so on). When this collection of data is associated with the identity of a user, it is called a *profile*.

Profiles should be centrally located to enable administrators to efficiently create, edit, or delete these profiles in an automated fashion when necessary. Many user profiles contain nonsensitive data that users can update themselves (called *self-service*). So, if George moved to a new house, there should be a profile update tool that allows him to go into his profile and change his address information. Now, his profile may also contain sensitive data that should not be available to George—for example, his access rights to resources or information that he is going to be laid off on Friday.

You have interacted with a profile update technology if you have requested to update your personal information on any e-commerce website. These companies provide you with the capability to sign in and update the information they allow you to access. This could be your contact information, home address, purchasing preferences, or credit card data. They then use this information to update their customer relationship management (CRM) systems so they know where to send you their junk mail advertisements and spam messages!

Session Management

A *session* is an agreement between two parties to communicate interactively. Think of it as a phone call: you dial your friend's number, she decides whether to answer, and if she does then you talk with each other until something happens to end the call. That "something" could be that you (or her) are out of time and have to go, or maybe one of you runs out of things to say and there's an awkward silence on the line, or maybe one of you starts acting weird and the other is bothered and hangs up. Technically, the call could go on forever, though in practice that doesn't happen.

Information systems use sessions all the time. When you show up for work and log onto your computer, you establish an authenticated session with the operating system that allows you to launch your e-mail client. When that application connects to the mail server, it establishes a different authenticated session (perhaps using the same credentials you used to log onto your computer). So, a session, in the context of information systems security, can exist between a user and an information system or between two information systems (e.g., two running programs). If the session is an authenticated one, as in the previous two examples, then authentication happens at the beginning and then everything else is trusted until the session ends.

That trust is the reason we need to be very careful about how we deal with our sessions. Threat actors often try to inject themselves into an authenticated session and hijack it for their own purposes. Session management is the process of establishing, controlling, and terminating sessions, usually for security reasons. The session establishment usually entails authentication and authorization of one or both endpoints. Controlling the session can involve logging the start and end and anything in between. It could also keep track of time, activity, and even indicia of malicious activity. These are three of the most common triggers for session termination:

- **Timeout** When sessions are established, the endpoints typically agree on how long they will last. You should be careful to make this time window as short as possible without unduly impacting the organization. For example, a VPN concentrator could enforce sessions of no more than eight hours for your teleworkers.
- **Inactivity** Some sessions could go on for very long periods of time, provided that the user is active. Sessions that are terminated for inactivity tend to have a shorter window than those that are triggered only by total duration (i.e., timeout). For example, many workstations lock the screen if the user doesn't use the mouse or keyboard for 15 minutes.
- **Anomaly** Usually, anomaly detection is an additional control added to a session that is triggered by timeouts or inactivity (or both). This control looks for suspicious behaviors in the session, such as requests for data that are much larger than usual or communication with unusual or forbidden destinations. These can be indicators of session hijacking.

Accountability

Auditing capabilities ensure users are accountable for their actions, verify that the security policies are enforced, and can be used as investigation tools. There are several reasons why network administrators and security professionals want to make sure accountability mechanisms are in place and configured properly: to deter wrongdoing, be able to track bad deeds back to individuals, detect intrusions, reconstruct events and system conditions, provide legal recourse material, and produce problem reports. Audit documentation and log files hold a mountain of information—the trick is usually deciphering it and presenting it in a useful and understandable format.

Accountability is enabled by recording user, system, and application activities. This recording is done through auditing functions and mechanisms within an operating system or application. Audit trails contain information about operating system activities, application events, and user actions. Audit trails can be used to verify the health of a system by checking performance information or certain types of errors and conditions. After a system crashes, a network administrator often will review audit logs to try and piece together the status of the system and attempt to understand what events could be attributed to the disruption.

Audit trails can also be used to provide alerts about any suspicious activities that can be investigated at a later time. In addition, they can be valuable in determining exactly how far an attack has gone and the extent of the damage that may have been caused. It is important to make sure a proper chain of custody is maintained to ensure any data collected can later be properly and accurately represented in case it needs to be used for later events such as criminal proceedings or investigations.

Keep the following in mind when dealing with auditing:

- Store the audits securely.
- Use audit tools that keep the size of the logs under control.
- Protect the logs from any unauthorized changes in order to safeguard data.
- Train staff to review the data in the right manner while protecting privacy.
- Make sure the ability to delete logs is only available to administrators.
- Configure logs to contain activities of all high-privileged accounts (root, administrator).

An administrator configures what actions and events are to be audited and logged. In a high-security environment, the administrator would configure more activities to be captured and set the threshold of those activities to be more sensitive. The events can be reviewed to identify where breaches of security occurred and if the security policy has been violated. If the environment does not require such levels of security, the events analyzed would be fewer, with less-demanding thresholds.

Without proper oversight, items and actions to be audited can become an endless list. A security professional should be able to assess an environment and its security goals, know what actions should be audited, and know what is to be done with that information after it is captured—without wasting too much disk space, CPU power, and staff time. The following is a broad overview of the items and actions that can be audited and logged.

System-level events:

- System performance
- Logon attempts (successful and unsuccessful)
- Logon ID
- Date and time of each logon attempt
- Lockouts of users and terminals
- Use of administration utilities
- Devices used
- Functions performed
- Requests to alter configuration files

Application-level events:

- Error messages
- Files opened and closed
- Modifications of files
- Security violations within applications

User-level events:

- Identification and authentication attempts
- Files, services, and resources used
- Commands initiated
- Security violations

The threshold (clipping level) and parameters for each of these items must be deliberately configured. For example, an administrator can audit each logon attempt or just each failed logon attempt. System performance can look at the amount of memory used within an eight-hour period or the memory, CPU, and hard drive space used within an hour.

Intrusion detection systems (IDSs) continually scan audit logs for suspicious activity. If an intrusion or harmful event takes place, audit logs are usually kept to be used later to prove guilt and prosecute if necessary. If severe security events take place, the IDS alerts the administrator or staff member so they can take proper actions to end the destructive activity. If a dangerous virus is identified, administrators may take the mail server offline. If an attacker is accessing confidential information within the database, this computer may be temporarily disconnected from the network or Internet. If an attack is in progress, the administrator may want to watch the actions taking place so she can track down the intruder. IDSs can watch for this type of activity during real time and/or scan audit logs and watch for specific patterns or behaviors.

Review of Audit Information

Audit trails can be reviewed manually or through automated means—either way, they must be reviewed and interpreted. If an organization reviews audit trails manually, it needs to establish a system of how, when, and why they are viewed. Usually audit logs are very popular items right after a security breach, unexplained system action, or system disruption. An administrator or staff member rapidly tries to piece together the activities that led up to the event. This type of audit review is event-oriented. Audit trails can also be viewed periodically to watch for unusual behavior of users or systems and to help understand the baseline and health of a system. Then there is a real-time, or near real-time, audit analysis that can use an automated tool to review audit information as it is created. Administrators should have a scheduled task of reviewing audit data. The audit material usually needs to be parsed and saved to another location for a certain time period. This retention information should be stated in the organization's security policy and procedures.

Reviewing audit information manually can be overwhelming. Fortunately, there are applications and audit trail analysis tools that reduce the volume of audit logs to review and improve the efficiency of manual review procedures. A majority of the time, audit logs contain information that is unnecessary, so these tools parse out specific events and present them in a useful format.

An *audit-reduction tool* does just what its name suggests—reduces the amount of information within an audit log. This tool discards mundane task information and records system performance, security, and user functionality information that can be useful to a security professional or administrator.

Today, more organizations are implementing *security information and event management (SIEM)* systems. These products gather logs from various devices (servers, firewalls, routers, etc.) and attempt to correlate the log data and provide analysis capabilities. Reviewing logs manually looking for suspicious activity in a continuous manner is not only mind-numbing; it is close to impossible to be successful. So many packets and network communication data sets are passing along a network, humans cannot collect all the data in real or near real time, analyze it, identify current attacks, and react—it is just too overwhelming.

Organizations also have different *types* of systems on a network (routers, firewalls, IDS, IPS, servers, gateways, proxies) collecting logs in various proprietary formats, which requires centralization, standardization, and normalization. Log formats are different per product type and vendor. The format of logs created by Juniper network device systems is different from the format of logs created by Cisco systems, which in turn is different from the format created by Palo Alto and Barracuda firewalls. It is important to gather logs from various different systems within an environment so that some type of situational awareness can take place. Once the logs are gathered, intelligence routines need to be processed on them so that data mining can take place to identify patterns. The goal is to piece together seemingly unrelated event data so that the security team can fully understand what is taking place within the network and react properly.

NOTE Situational awareness means that you understand the current environment even though it is complex, dynamic, and made up of seemingly unrelated data points. You need to be able to understand each data point in its own context within the surrounding environment so that you can make the best possible decisions.

Protecting Audit Data and Log Information

If an intruder breaks into your house, he will do his best to cover his tracks by not leaving fingerprints or any other clues that can be used to tie him to the criminal activity. The same is true in computer fraud and illegal activity. The intruder will work to cover his tracks. Attackers often delete audit logs that hold this incriminating information. (Deleting specific incriminating data within audit logs is called *scrubbing*.) Deleting this information can cause the administrator to not be alerted or aware of the security breach and can destroy valuable data. Therefore, audit logs should be protected by strict access control and stored on a remote host.

Only certain individuals (the administrator and security personnel) should be able to view, modify, and delete audit trail information. No other individuals should be able to view this data, much less modify or delete it. The integrity of the data can be ensured with the use of digital signatures, hashing tools, and strong access controls. Its confidentiality can be protected with encryption and access controls, if necessary, and it can be stored on *write-once media* (optical discs) to prevent loss or modification of the data. Unauthorized access attempts to audit logs should be captured and reported.

Audit logs may be used in a trial to prove an individual's guilt, demonstrate how an attack was carried out, or corroborate a story. The integrity and confidentiality of these logs will be under scrutiny. Proper steps need to be taken to ensure that the confidentiality and integrity of the audit information are not compromised in any way.

NOTE We cover investigative techniques and evidence handling in Chapter 22.

Identity Management

Identity management (IdM) is a broad term that encompasses the use of different products to identify, authenticate, and authorize users through automated means. It usually includes user account management, access control, credential management, single sign-on (SSO) functionality, managing rights and permissions for user accounts, and auditing and monitoring all of these items. It is important for security professionals to understand all the technologies that make up a full enterprise IdM solution. IdM requires managing uniquely identified entities, their attributes, credentials, and entitlements. IdM allows organizations to create and manage digital identities' life cycles (create, maintain, terminate) in a timely and automated fashion. An enterprise IdM solution must meet business needs and scale from internally facing systems to externally facing systems. In this section, we cover many of these technologies and how they work together.

NOTE Identity and access management (IAM) is another term that is used interchangeably with IdM, though ISC^2 considers IdM to be a subset of IAM.

Selling identity management products is a flourishing market that focuses on reducing administrative costs, increasing security, meeting regulatory compliance, and improving upon service levels throughout enterprises. The continual increase in complexity and diversity of networked environments also increases the complexity of keeping track of who can access what and when. Organizations have different types of applications, network operating systems, databases, enterprise resource management (ERM) systems, customer relationship management (CRM) systems, directories, and mainframes—all used for different business purposes. Organizations also have partners, contractors, consultants, employees, and temporary employees. (Figure 16-4 provides a simplistic

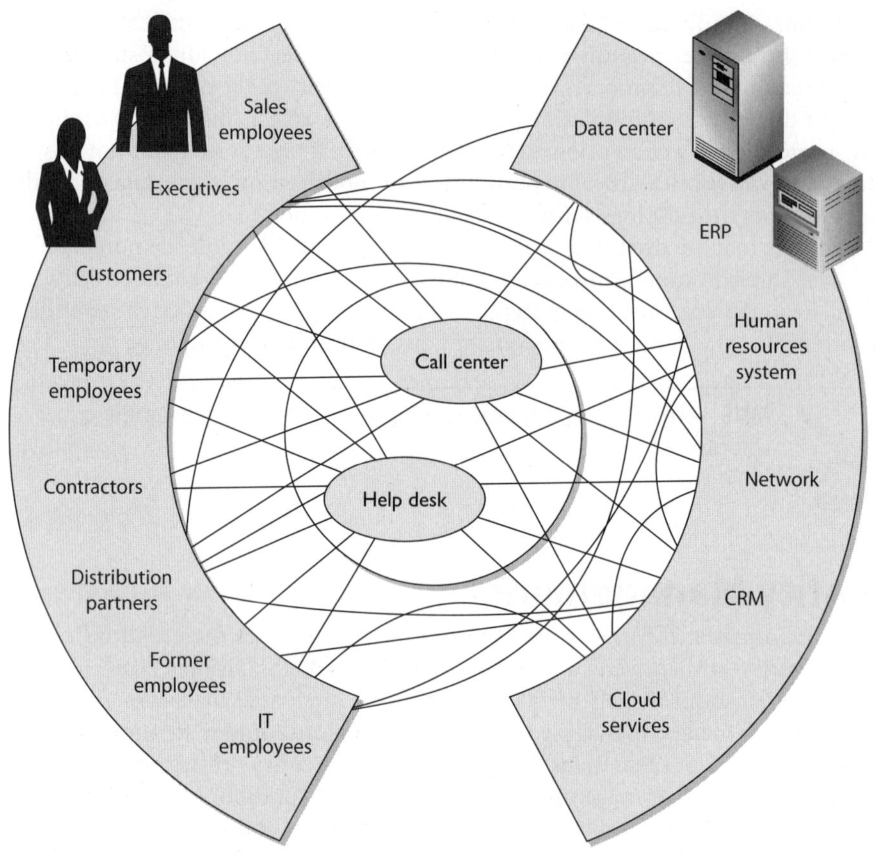

Figure 16-4 Most environments are complex in terms of access.

view of most environments.) Users usually access several different types of systems throughout their daily tasks, which makes controlling access and providing the necessary level of protection on different data types difficult and full of obstacles. This complexity usually results in unforeseen and unidentified holes in asset protection, overlapping and contradictory controls, and policy and regulation noncompliance. It is the goal of IdM technologies to simplify the administration of these tasks and bring order to chaos.

The following are some of the common questions enterprises deal with regarding IdM implementation:

- What should each user have access to?
- Who approves and allows access?
- How do the access decisions map to policies?
- Do former employees still have access?
- How do we keep up with our dynamic and ever-changing environment?

- What is the process of revoking access?
- How is access controlled and monitored centrally?
- Why do employees have eight passwords to remember?
- We have five different operating platforms. How do we centralize access when each platform (and application) requires its own type of credential set?
- How do we control access for our employees, customers, and partners?
- How do we make sure we are compliant with the necessary regulations?

The traditional identity management process has been manual, using directory services with permissions, access control lists (ACLs), and profiles. This labor-intensive approach has proven incapable of keeping up with complex demands and thus has been replaced with automated applications rich in functionality that work together to create an IdM infrastructure. The main goal of IdM technologies is to streamline the management of identity, authentication, authorization, and auditing of subjects on multiple systems throughout the enterprise. The sheer diversity of a heterogeneous enterprise makes proper implementation of IdM a huge undertaking.

Directory Services

Directory services, much like DNS, map resource names to their corresponding network addresses, allowing discovery of and communication with devices, files, users, or any other asset. Network directory services provide users access to network resources transparently, meaning that users don't need to know the exact location of the resources or the steps required to access them. The network directory services handle these issues for the user in the background.

Most organizations have some type of directory service that contains information pertaining to the organization's network resources and users. Most directories follow a hierarchical database format, originally established by the ITU X.500 standard but now most commonly implemented with the Lightweight Directory Access Protocol (LDAP), that allows subjects and applications to interact with the directory. Applications can request information about a particular user by making an LDAP request to the directory, and users can request information about a specific resource by using a similar request.

The objects within the directory are managed by a directory service. The directory service allows an administrator to configure and manage how identification, authentication, authorization, and access control take place within the network and on individual systems. The objects within the directory are labeled and identified with namespaces.

In a Windows Active Directory (AD) environment, when you log in, you are logging into a domain controller (DC), which has a hierarchical LDAP directory in its database. The database organizes the network resources and carries out user access control functionality. So once you successfully authenticate to the DC, certain network resources are available to you (print service, file server, e-mail server, and so on) as dictated by the configuration of AD.

How does the directory service keep all of these entities organized? By using *namespaces*. Each directory service has a way of identifying and naming the objects they manage. In LDAP, the directory service assigns distinguished names (DNs) to each object. Each DN represents a collection of attributes about a specific object and is stored in the directory as an entry. In the following example, the DN is made up of a common name (cn) and domain components (dc). Since this is a hierarchical directory, .com is the top, LogicalSecurity is one step down from .com, and Shon is at the bottom.

```
dn: cn=Shon Harris,dc=LogicalSecurity,dc=com
cn: Shon Harris
```

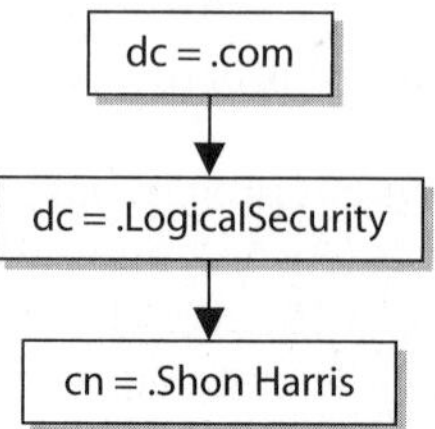

This is a very simplistic example. Companies usually have large trees (directories) containing many levels and objects to represent different departments, roles, users, and resources.

A directory service manages the entries and data in the directory and also enforces the configured security policy by carrying out access control and identity management functions. For example, when you log into the DC, the directory service determines which resources you can and cannot access on the network.

Directories' Role in Identity Management

A directory service is a general-purpose resource that can be used for IdM. When used in this manner it is optimized for reading and searching operations and becomes the central component of an IdM solution. This is because all resource information, users' attributes, authorization profiles, roles, access control policies, and more are stored in this one location. When other IdM features need to carry out their functions (authorization, access control, assigning permissions), they now have a centralized location for all of the information they need.

A lot of the information that is catalogued in an IdM directory is scattered throughout the enterprise. User attribute information (employee status, job description, department, and so on) is usually stored in the HR database, authentication information could be in a Kerberos server, role and group identification information might be in a SQL database, and resource-oriented authentication information may be stored in Active Directory on a domain controller. These are commonly referred to as *identity stores* and are located in different places on the network.

Something nifty that many IdM products do is create meta-directories or virtual directories. A *meta-directory* gathers the necessary information from multiple sources and stores it in one central directory. This provides a unified view of all users' digital identity information throughout the enterprise. The meta-directory synchronizes itself with all of the identity stores periodically to ensure the most up-to-date information is being used by all applications and IdM components within the enterprise.

Organizing All of This Stuff

In an LDAP system, the following rules are used for object organization:

- The directory has a tree structure to organize the entries using a parent-child configuration.
- Each entry has a unique name made up of attributes of a specific object.
- The attributes used in the directory are dictated by the defined schema.
- The unique identifiers are called distinguished names.

The schema describes the directory structure and what names can be used within the directory, among other things. The following diagram shows how an object (Kathy Conlon) can have the attributes of ou=General, ou=NCTSW, ou=WNY, ou=locations, ou=Navy, ou=DoD, ou=U.S. Government, and C=US. Kathy's distinguished name is made up by listing all of the nodes starting at the root of the tree (C=US) all the way to her leaf node (cn=Kathy Conlon), separated by commas.

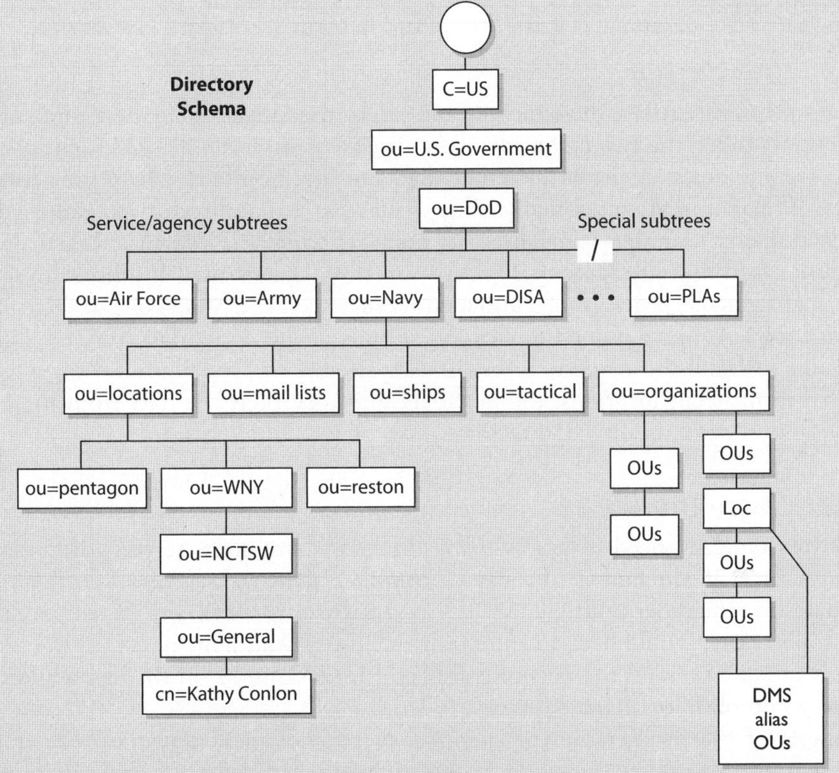

Note that OU stands for organizational unit. OUs are used as containers of other similar OUs, users, and resources. CN stands for common name.

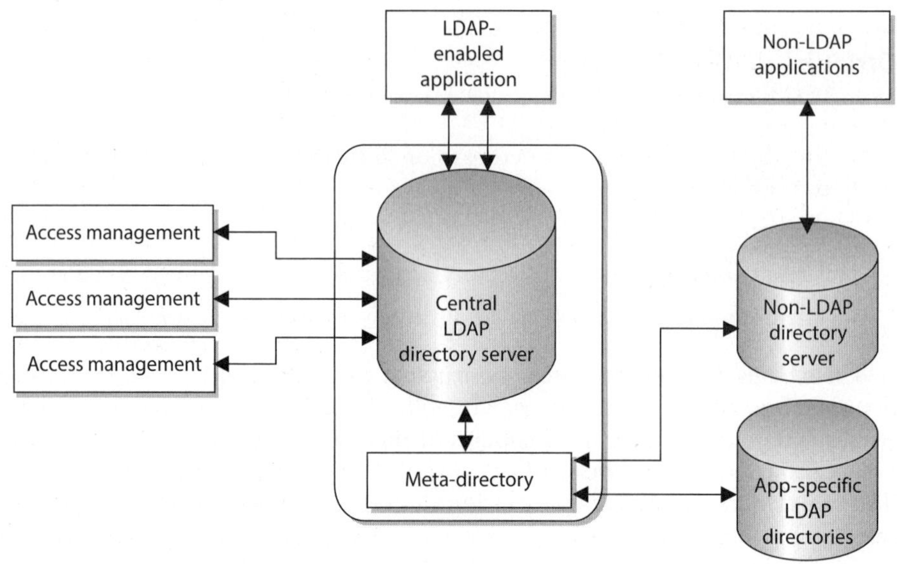

Figure 16-5 Meta-directories pull data from other sources to populate the IdM directory.

A *virtual directory* plays the same role and can be used instead of a meta-directory. The difference between the two is that the meta-directory physically has the identity data in its directory, whereas a virtual directory does not and points to where the actual data resides. When an IdM component makes a call to a virtual directory to gather identity information on a user, the virtual directory points to where the information actually lives.

Figure 16-5 illustrates a central LDAP directory that is used by the IdM services: access management, provisioning, and identity management. When one of these services accepts a request from a user or application, it pulls the necessary data from the directory to be able to fulfill the request. Since the data needed to properly fulfill these requests is stored in different locations, the metadata directory pulls the data from these other sources and updates the LDAP directory.

Single Sign-On

Employees typically need to access many different computers, servers, databases, and other resources in the course of a day to complete their tasks. This often requires the employees to remember multiple user IDs and passwords for these different computers. In a utopia, a user would need to enter only one user ID and one password to be able to access all resources in all the networks this user is working in. In the real world, this is hard to accomplish for all system types.

Because of the proliferation of client/server technologies, networks have migrated from centrally controlled networks to heterogeneous, distributed environments. The propagation of open systems and the increased diversity of applications, platforms, and operating systems have caused the end user to have to remember several user IDs and passwords just to be able to access and use the different resources within his own network. Although the different IDs and passwords are supposed to provide a greater level of security, they often end up compromising security (because users write them down) and causing more effort and overhead for the staff that manages and maintains the network.

As any network staff member or administrator can attest to, too much time is devoted to resetting passwords for users who have forgotten them. More than one employee's productivity is affected when forgotten passwords have to be reassigned. The network staff member who has to reset the password could be working on other tasks, and the user who forgot the password cannot complete his task until the network staff member is finished resetting the password. Depending on the enterprise, between 20 percent and 50 percent of all IT help-desk calls are for password resets, according to the Gartner Group. Forrester Research estimates that each of these calls costs $70 in the United States. System administrators have to manage multiple user accounts on different platforms, which all need to be coordinated in a manner that maintains the integrity of the security policy. At times the complexity can be overwhelming, which results in poor access control management and the generation of many security vulnerabilities. A lot of time is spent on multiple passwords, and in the end they do not provide us with more security.

The increased cost of managing a diverse environment, security concerns, and user habits, coupled with the users' overwhelming desire to remember one set of credentials, has brought about the idea of *single sign-on (SSO)* capabilities. These capabilities would allow a user to enter credentials one time and be able to access all resources in primary and secondary network domains. This reduces the amount of time users spend authenticating to resources and enables the administrator to streamline user accounts and better control access rights. It improves security by reducing the probability that users will write down passwords and also reduces the administrator's time spent on adding and removing user accounts and modifying access permissions. If an administrator needs to disable or suspend a specific account, she can do it uniformly instead of having to alter configurations on each and every platform.

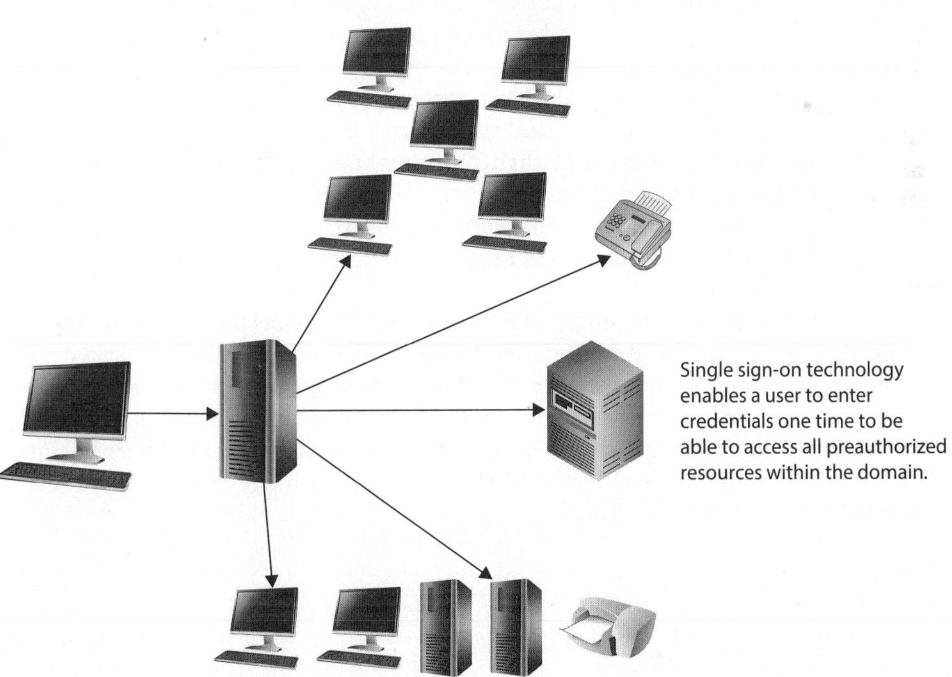

Single sign-on technology enables a user to enter credentials one time to be able to access all preauthorized resources within the domain.

So that is our utopia: log on once and you are good to go. What bursts this bubble? Mainly interoperability issues. For SSO to actually work, every platform, application, and resource needs to accept the same type of credentials, in the same format, and interpret their meanings the same. When Steve logs on to his Windows workstation and gets authenticated by a mixed-mode Windows domain controller, it must authenticate him to the resources he needs to access on the Apple MacBook, the Linux server running NIS, the PrinterLogic print server, and the Windows computer in a trusted domain that has the plotter connected to it. A nice idea, until reality hits.

There is also a security issue to consider in an SSO environment. Once an individual is in, he is in. If an attacker is able to uncover one credential set, he has access to every resource within the environment that the compromised account has access to. This is certainly true, but one of the goals is that if a user only has to remember one password, and not ten, then a more robust password policy can be enforced. If the user has just one password to remember, then it can be more complicated and secure because he does not have nine other ones to remember also.

Federated Identity Management

The world continually gets smaller as technology brings people and companies closer together. Many times, when we are interacting with just one website, we are actually interacting with several different companies—we just don't know it. The reason we don't know it is because these companies are sharing our identity and authentication information behind the scenes. This is not done for nefarious purposes necessarily, but to make our lives easier and to allow merchants to sell their goods without much effort on our part.

For example, a person wants to book an airline flight and a hotel room. If the airline company and hotel company use a federated identity management (FIM) system, this means they have set up a trust relationship between the two companies and share customer identification and, potentially, authentication information. So when you book a flight on United Airlines, the website asks if you want to also book a hotel room. If you click Yes, you could then be brought to the Marriott website, which provides information on the closest hotel to the airport you're flying into. Now, to book a room you don't have to log in again. You logged in on the United website, and that website sent your information over to the Marriott website, all of which happened transparently to you.

A *federated identity* is a portable identity, and its associated entitlements, that can be used across business boundaries. It allows a user to be authenticated across multiple IT systems and enterprises. Identity federation is based upon linking a user's otherwise distinct identities at two or more locations without the need to synchronize or consolidate directory information. Federated identity offers businesses and consumers a more convenient way of accessing distributed resources and is a key component of e-commerce.

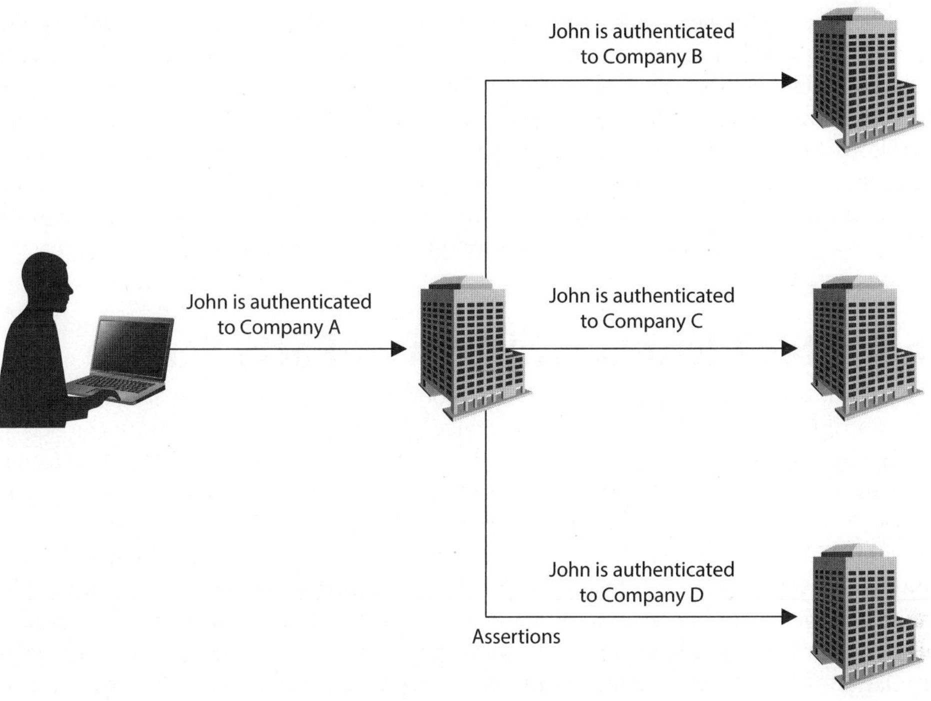

Web portal functions are parts of a website that act as a point of access to information. A portal presents information from diverse sources in a unified manner. It can offer various services, as in e-mail, news updates, stock prices, data access, price lookups, access to databases, and entertainment. Web portals provide a way for organizations to present one consistent interface with one "look and feel" and various functionality types. For example, you log into your company web portal and it provides access to many different systems and their functionalities, but it seems as though you are only interacting with one system because the interface is "clean" and organized. Portals combine web services (web-based functions) from several different entities and present them in one central website.

A web portal is made up of *portlets*, which are pluggable user-interface software components that present information from other systems. A portlet is an interactive application that provides a specific type of web service functionality (e-mail, news feed, weather updates, forums, etc.). A portal is made up of individual portlets to provide a plethora of services through one interface. It is a way of centrally providing a set of web services. Users can configure their view to the portal by enabling or disabling these various portlet functions.

Since each of these portlets can be provided by different entities, how user authentication information is handled must be tightly controlled, and there must be a high level of trust between these different entities. A college, for example, might have one web portal available to students, parents, faculty members, and the public. The public should only be able to view and access a small subset of available portlets and not have access to more powerful web services (such as e-mail and database access). Students could be able to log in and gain access to their grades, assignments, and a student forum. Faculty members can gain access to all of these web services, including the school's e-mail service and access to the central database, which contains all of the students' information. If there is a software flaw or misconfiguration, it is possible that someone can gain access to something they are not supposed to.

Federated Identity with a Third-Party Service

It should not be surprising to consider that cloud service providers are also able to provide identification services. Identity as a Service (IDaaS) is a type of Software as a Service (SaaS) offering that is normally configured to provide SSO, FIM, and password management services. Though most IDaaS vendors are focused on cloud- and web-centric systems, it is also possible to leverage their products for FIM on legacy platforms within the enterprise network. Many organizations are transitioning to IDaaS providers for compliance reasons because this approach allows them to centralize access control and monitoring across the enterprise. This, in turn reduces risk and improves auditability, meaning there's a much lower chance of getting hit with a huge General Data Protection Regulation (GDPR) fine because some obscure part of the system didn't have proper access controls.

There are three basic approaches to architecting identity management services: on-premise, cloud-based, and a hybrid of both. The first approach, on-premise, is simple because all the systems and data are located within the enterprise. In the cloud-based model, on the other hand, most or all of the systems or data are hosted by an external party in the cloud. A hybrid FIM system includes both on-premise and cloud-based IdM components, each responsible for its environment but able to coordinate with each other. Regardless of the approach, it is important to ensure that all components play nice with each other. In the following sections we will explore some of the considerations that are common to the successful integration of these services.

Integration Issues

Integration of any set of different technologies or products is typically one of the most complex and risky phases of any deployment. In order to mitigate both the complexities and risks, it is necessary to carefully characterize each product or technology as well as the systems and networks into which they will be incorporated. Regardless of whether you ultimately use an on-premise or cloud-based (or hybrid) approach, you should carefully plan how you will address connectivity, trust, testing, and federation issues. As the old carpentry adage goes, "Measure twice and cut once."

Establishing Connectivity

A critical requirement is to ensure that the components are able to communicate with one another in a secure manner. The big difference between the in-house and outsourced models here is that in the former, the chokepoints are all internal to the organization's network, while in the latter, they also exist in the public Internet. Clearing a path for this traffic typically means creating new rules for firewalls and IDS/IPS. These rules must be restrictive enough to allow the FIM traffic, but nothing else, to flow between the various nodes. Depending on the systems being used, ports, protocols, and user accounts may also need to be configured to enable bidirectional communication.

Establishing Trust

All traffic between nodes engaged in identity services must be encrypted. (To do otherwise would defeat the whole point of this effort.) From a practical perspective, this almost certainly means that PKI in general and certificate authorities (CAs) in particular will be needed. A potential issue here is that the CAs may not be trusted by default by all the nodes. This is especially true if the enterprise has implemented its own CA internally and is deploying an outsourced service. This is easy to plan ahead of time, but could lead to some big challenges if discovered during the actual rollout. Trust may also be needed between domains.

Incremental Testing

When dealing with complex systems, it is wise to assume that some important issue will not be covered in the plan. This is why it is important to incrementally test the integration of identity services instead of rolling out the entire system at once. Many organizations choose to roll out new services first to test accounts (i.e., not real users), then to one department or division that is used as the test case, and finally to the entire organization. For critical deployments (and one would assume that identity services would fall in this category), it is best to test as thoroughly as possible in a testbed or sandbox environment. Only then should the integration progress to real systems.

Legacy Systems

Unless your entire infrastructure is in the cloud, odds are that you have at least a handful of legacy systems that don't play nice with the FIM service or provider. To mitigate this risk, you should first ensure that you have an accurate asset inventory that clearly identifies any systems (or system dependencies) that will not integrate well. Then, you should get together with all stakeholders (e.g., business, IT, security, partners) to figure out which of these systems can be retired, replaced, or upgraded. The change management process we'll discuss in Chapter 20 is a great way to handle this. Finally, for any legacy systems that must remain as they are (and hence, not integrated into FIM), you want to minimize their authorized users and put additional controls in place to ensure they are monitored in an equivalent manner as the systems that fall under IdM.

On-Premise

An *on-premise* (or *on-premises*) FIM system is one in which all needed resources remain under your physical control. This usually means that you purchase or lease the necessary hardware, software, and licenses and then use your own team to build, integrate, and maintain the system. This kind of deployment, though rare, makes sense in cases where different organizations' networks are interconnected but not directly connected to the Internet, such as those of some critical infrastructure and military organizations. Though most on-premise FIM solution providers offer installation, configuration, and support services, day-to-day operation and management of the system falls on your team. This requires them to have not only the needed expertise but also the time to devote to managing the system's life cycle.

Cloud

Arguably, the most cost-effective and secure way to implement FIM across an enterprise is to use a cloud-only solution. The economies of scale that IDaaS providers enjoy translate into cost savings for their customers. Even if you have the talent in your workforce to implement IdM on-premises, it would almost certainly be cheaper to outsource it to one of the many established vendors in this space. The visibility that an IDaaS provider has not only across your organization but also across the entire space of its customers allows it to detect and respond to threats faster and better than might otherwise be possible. This should be a dream come true, if only your entire infrastructure were cloud-based.

Hybrid

Most likely, your organization has a combination of cloud-based and on-premise systems. Some of the latter ones probably don't lend themselves to a cloud-based FIM solution, at least not without incurring exorbitant upgrade or integration costs. So, what should you do? You can implement a hybrid approach in which you have on-premise and cloud-based FIM platforms that are integrated with each other. One would be the primary and the other would be the secondary. As long as they are interoperable and properly configured, you get to have the best of both worlds. Most major IDaaS providers have solutions that support hybrid deployments.

Chapter Review

Identification, authentication, and authorization of users and systems are absolutely essential to cybersecurity. After all, how can we differentiate good and bad actors unless we know (at least) who the good ones are? This is why we spent so much time going over knowledge-based, biometric, and ownership-based authentication techniques and technologies. These, together with credential management products and practices, allow us to ensure we know who it is that our systems are interacting with.

The purpose of this chapter was to expose you to the multiple processes and technologies that make identity management possible, both at an individual level and at aggregate enterprise scales. This all sets the stage for the next chapter, in which we will delve into how to operationalize these concepts and build on them to ensure authorized parties (and no others) have access to the right assets (and no others).

Quick Review

- Identification describes a method by which a subject (user, program, or process) claims to have a specific identity (e.g., username, account number, or e-mail address).
- Authentication is the process by which a system verifies the identity of the subject, usually by requiring a piece of information that only the claimed identity should have.
- Credentials consist of an identification claim (e.g., username) and authentication information (e.g., password).
- Authorization is the determination of whether a subject has been given the necessary rights and privileges to carry out the requested actions.
- The three main types of factors used for authentication are something a person knows (e.g., password), something a person has (e.g., token), and something a person is (e.g., fingerprint), which can be combined with two additional factors: somewhere a person is (e.g., geolocation) and something a person does (e.g., keystroke behavior).
- Knowledge-based authentication uses information a person knows, such as a password, passphrase, or life experience.
- Salts are random values added to plaintext passwords prior to hashing to add more complexity and randomness.
- Cognitive passwords are fact- or opinion-based questions, typically based on life experiences, used to verify an individual's identity.
- A Type I biometric authentication error occurs when a legitimate individual is denied access; a Type II error occurs when an impostor is granted access.
- The crossover error rate (CER) of a biometric authentication system represents the point at which the false rejection rate (Type I errors) is equal to the false acceptance rate (Type II errors).
- Ownership-based authentication is based on something a person owns, such as a token device.
- A token device, or password generator, is usually a handheld device that has a display (and possibly a keypad), is synchronized in some manner with the authentication server, and displays to the user a one-time password (OTP).
- A synchronous token device requires the device and the authentication service to advance to the next OTP in sync with each other; an asynchronous token device employs a challenge/response scheme to authenticate the user.
- A memory card holds information but cannot process information; a smart card holds information and has the necessary hardware and software to actually process that information.

- Password managers or password vaults are a popular solution to remembering a myriad of complex passwords.
- Just-in-time (JIT) access is a provisioning methodology that elevates users to the necessary privileged access to perform a specific task.
- User provisioning refers to the creation, maintenance, and deactivation of user objects and attributes as they exist in one or more systems, directories, or applications, in response to business processes.
- An authoritative system of record (ASOR) is a hierarchical tree-like structure system that tracks subjects and their authorization chains.
- User provisioning refers to the creation, maintenance, and deactivation of user objects and attributes as they exist in one or more systems, directories, or applications, in response to business processes.
- A session is an agreement between two parties to communicate interactively.
- Auditing capabilities ensure users are accountable for their actions, verify that the security policies are enforced, and can be used as investigation tools.
- Deleting specific incriminating data within audit logs is called scrubbing.
- Identity management (IdM) is a broad term that encompasses the use of different products to identify, authenticate, and authorize users through automated means.
- Directory services map resource names to their corresponding network addresses, allowing discovery of and communication with devices, files, users, or any other asset.
- The most commonly implemented directory services, such as Microsoft Windows Active Directory (AD), implement the Lightweight Directory Access Protocol (LDAP).
- Single sign-on (SSO) systems allow users to authenticate once and be able to access all authorized resources, which reduces the amount of time users spend authenticating and enables administrators to streamline user accounts and better control access rights.
- A federated identity is a portable identity, and its associated entitlements, that allows a user to be authenticated across multiple IT systems and enterprises.
- Identity as a Service (IDaaS) is a type of Software as a Service (SaaS) offering that is normally configured to provide SSO, FIM, and password management services.
- There are three basic approaches to architecting identity management services: on-premise, cloud-based, and a hybrid of both.

Questions

Please remember that these questions are formatted and asked in a certain way for a reason. Keep in mind that the CISSP exam is asking questions at a conceptual level. Questions may not always have the perfect answer, and the candidate is advised against always looking for the perfect answer. Instead, the candidate should look for the best answer in the list.

1. Which of the following statements correctly describes biometric methods of authentication?
   A. They are the least expensive and provide the most protection.
   B. They are the most expensive and provide the least protection.
   C. They are the least expensive and provide the least protection.
   D. They are the most expensive and provide the most protection.
2. Which of the following statements correctly describes the use of passwords for authentication?
   A. They are the least expensive and most secure.
   B. They are the most expensive and least secure.
   C. They are the least expensive and least secure.
   D. They are the most expensive and most secure.
3. How is a challenge/response protocol utilized with token device implementations?
   A. This type of protocol is not used; cryptography is used.
   B. An authentication service generates a challenge, and the smart token generates a response based on the challenge.
   C. The token challenges the user for a username and password.
   D. The token challenges the user's password against a database of stored credentials.
4. The process of mutual authentication involves _______________.
   A. a user authenticating to a system and the system authenticating to the user
   B. a user authenticating to two systems at the same time
   C. a user authenticating to a server and then to a process
   D. a user authenticating, receiving a ticket, and then authenticating to a service
5. What role does biometrics play in access control?
   A. Authorization
   B. Authenticity
   C. Authentication
   D. Accountability

6. Which of the following is the best description of directories that are used in identity management technology?
   A. Most are hierarchical and follow the X.500 standard.
   B. Most have a flat architecture and follow the X.400 standard.
   C. Most have moved away from LDAP.
   D. Most use RADIUS.
7. Which of the following is not part of user provisioning?
   A. Creation and deactivation of user accounts
   B. Business process implementation
   C. Maintenance and deactivation of user objects and attributes
   D. Delegating user administration
8. What is a technology that allows a user to remember just one password?
   A. Password generation
   B. Password dictionaries
   C. Password rainbow tables
   D. Password synchronization
9. This graphic covers which of the following?

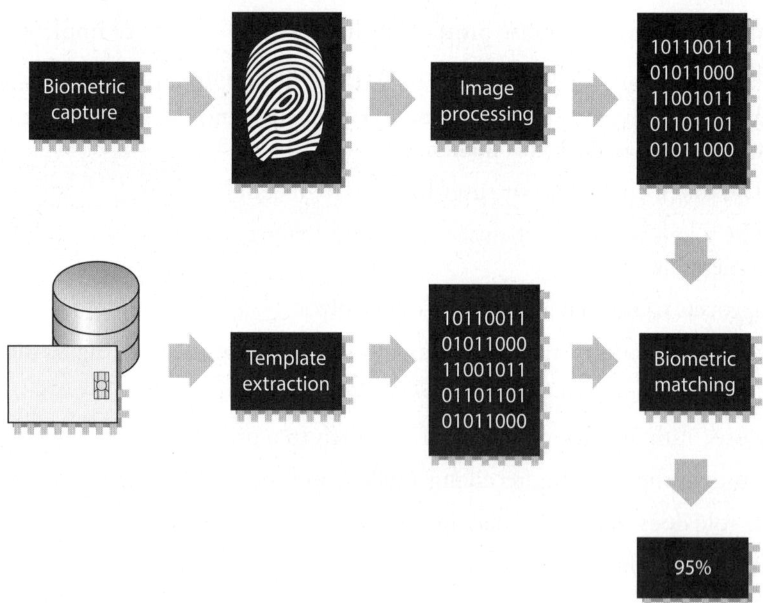

   A. Crossover error rate
   B. Identity verification
   C. Authorization rates
   D. Authentication error rates

10. The diagram shown here explains which of the following concepts?

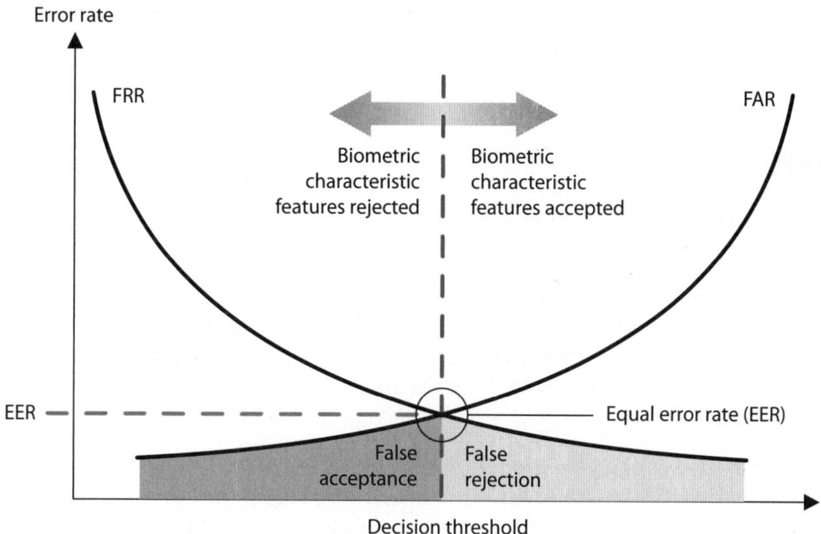

A. Crossover error rate.

B. Type III errors.

C. FAR equals FRR in systems that have a high crossover error rate.

D. Biometrics is a high acceptance technology.

11. The graphic shown here illustrates how which of the following works?

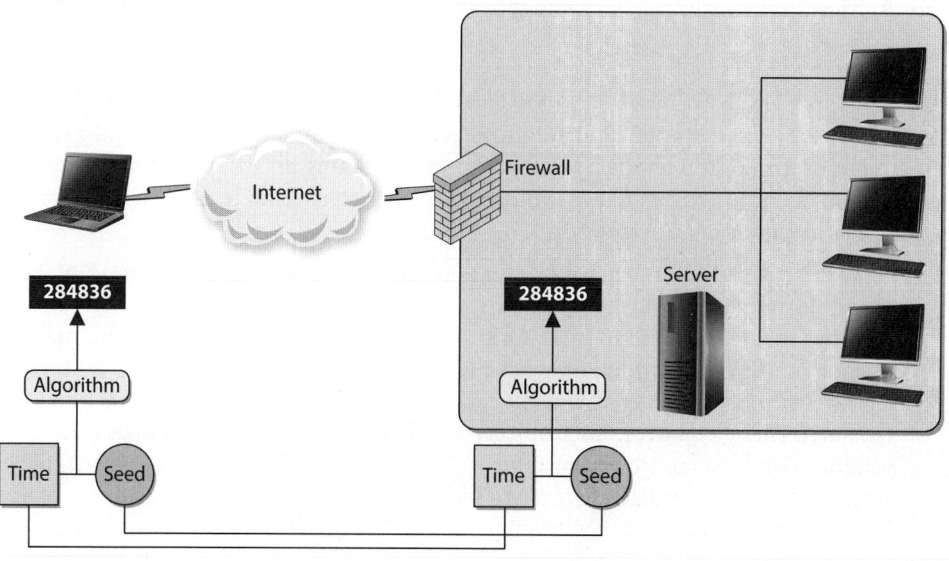

A. Rainbow tables
B. Dictionary attack
C. One-time password
D. Strong authentication

Answers

1. **D.** Compared with the other available authentication mechanisms, biometric methods provide the highest level of protection and are the most expensive.
2. **C.** Passwords provide the least amount of protection, but are the cheapest because they do not require extra readers (as with smart cards and memory cards), do not require devices (as do biometrics), and do not require a lot of overhead in processing (as in cryptography). Passwords are the most common type of authentication method used today.
3. **B.** An asynchronous token device is based on challenge/response mechanisms. The authentication service sends the user a challenge value, which the user enters into the token. The token encrypts or hashes this value, and the user uses this as her one-time password.
4. **A.** Mutual authentication means it is happening in both directions. Instead of just the user having to authenticate to the server, the server also must authenticate to the user.
5. **C.** Biometrics is a technology that validates an individual's identity by reading a physical attribute. In some cases, biometrics can be used for identification, but that was not listed as an answer choice.
6. **A.** Most organizations have some type of directory service that contains information pertaining to the organization's network resources and users. Most directories follow a hierarchical database format, based on the X.500 standard, and a type of protocol, as in Lightweight Directory Access Protocol (LDAP), that allows subjects and applications to interact with the directory. Applications can request information about a particular user by making an LDAP request to the directory, and users can request information about a specific resource by using a similar request.
7. **B.** User provisioning refers to the creation, maintenance, and deactivation of user objects and attributes as they exist in one or more systems, directories, or applications, in response to business processes. User provisioning software may include one or more of the following components: change propagation, self-service workflow, consolidated user administration, delegated user administration, and federated change control. User objects may represent employees, contractors, vendors, partners, customers, or other recipients of a service. Services may include e-mail, access to a database, access to a file server or mainframe, and so on.

8. **D.** Password synchronization technologies can allow a user to maintain just one password across multiple systems. The product synchronizes the password to other systems and applications, which happens transparently to the user.
9. **B.** These steps are taken to convert the biometric input for identity verification:
   i. A software application identifies specific points of data as match points.
   ii. An algorithm is used to process the match points and translate that information into a numeric value.
   iii. Authentication is approved or denied when the database value is compared with the end user input entered into the scanner.
10. **A.** This rating is stated as a percentage and represents the point at which the false rejection rate equals the false acceptance rate. This rating is the most important measurement when determining a biometric system's accuracy.
    - **Type I error, false rejection rate (FRR)** Rejects authorized individual
    - **Type II error, false acceptance rate (FAR)** Accepts impostor
11. **C.** Different types of one-time passwords are used for authentication. This graphic illustrates a synchronous token device, which synchronizes with the authentication service by using time or a counter as the core piece of the authentication process.

CHAPTER 17

Managing Identities and Access

This chapter presents the following:

- Authorization mechanisms
- Implementing authentication systems
- Managing the identity and access provisioning life cycle
- Controlling physical and logical access

Locks keep out only the honest.

—Proverb

Identification and authentication of users and systems, which was the focus of the previous chapter, is only half of the access control battle. You may be able to establish that you are truly dealing with Ahmed, but what assets should he be allowed to access? It really depends on the sensitivity of the asset, Ahmed's role, and any applicable rules on how these assets are supposed be used. Access control can also depend on any number of other attributes of the user, the asset, and the relationship between the two. Finally, access control can be based on risk.

Once you decide what access control model is best for your organization, you still have to implement the right authentication and authorization mechanism. There are many choices, but in this chapter we'll focus on the technologies that you are likeliest to encounter in the real world (and on the CISSP exam). We'll talk about how to manage the user access life cycle, which is where a lot of organizations get in trouble by not changing authorizations as situations change. After we cover all these essentials, we'll see how it all fits together in the context of controlling access to physical and logical assets. Let's start by looking at authorization mechanisms.

Authorization Mechanisms

Authorization is the process of ensuring authenticated users have access to the resources they are authorized to use and don't have access to any other resources. This is preceded by authentication, of course, but unlike that process, which tends to be a one-time activity, authorization controls every interaction of every user with every resource. It is an ongoing, all-seeing, access control mechanism.

An *access control mechanism* dictates how subjects access objects. It uses access control technologies and security mechanisms to enforce the rules and objectives of an *access control model.* As discussed in this section, there are six main types of access control models: discretionary, mandatory, role-based, rule-based, attribute-based, and risk-based. Each model type uses different methods to control how subjects access objects, and each has its own merits and limitations. The business and security goals of an organization, along with its culture and habits of conducting business, help prescribe what access control model it should use. Some organizations use one model exclusively, whereas others combine models to provide the necessary level of protection.

Regardless of which model or combination of models your organization uses, your security team needs a mechanism that consistently enforces the model and its rules. The *reference monitor* is an abstract machine that mediates all access subjects have to objects, both to ensure that the subjects have the necessary access rights and to protect the objects from unauthorized access and destructive modification. It is an access control concept, not an actual physical component, which is why it is normally referred to as the "reference monitor concept" or an "abstract machine." However the reference monitor is implemented, it must possess the following three properties to be effective:

- **Always invoked** To access an object, you have to go through the monitor first.
- **Tamper-resistant** It must ensure a threat actor cannot disable or modify it.
- **Verifiable** It must be capable of being thoroughly analyzed and tested to ensure that it works correctly all the time.

Let's explore the different approaches to implement and manage authorization mechanisms. The following sections explain the six different models and where they should be implemented.

Discretionary Access Control

If a user creates a file, he is the owner of that file. An identifier for this user is placed in the file header and/or in an access control matrix within the operating system. Ownership might also be granted to a specific individual. For example, a manager for a certain department might be made the owner of the files and resources within her department. A system that uses *discretionary access control (DAC)* enables the owner of the resource to specify which subjects can access specific resources. This model is called discretionary because the control of access is based on the discretion of the owner. Many times department managers or business unit managers are the owners of the data within their specific department. Being the owner, they can specify who should have access and who should not.

In a DAC model, access is restricted based on the authorization granted to the users. This means users are allowed to specify what type of access can occur to the objects they own. If an organization is using a DAC model, the network administrator can allow resource owners to control who has access to their files. The most common

> **Identity-Based Access Control**
> DAC systems grant or deny access based on the identity of the subject. The identity can be a user identity or a group membership. So, for example, a data owner can choose to allow Bob (user identity) and the Accounting group (group membership identity) to access his file. If Bob as a user is only granted Read access but he happens to be a member of the Accounting group, which has Change access, Bob would get the greater of the two: Change. The exception to this "greater access" rule is when No Access is set. In that case, it doesn't matter what other access levels a user may have gotten as an individual or through group membership, since that rule trumps all others.

implementation of DAC is through access control lists (ACLs), which are dictated and set by the owners and enforced by the operating system.

Most of the operating systems you may be used to dealing with (e.g., Windows, Linux, and macOS systems and most flavors of Unix) are based on DAC models. When you look at the properties of a file or directory and see the choices that allow you to control which users can have access to this resource and to what degree, you are witnessing an instance of ACLs enforcing a DAC model.

DAC can be applied to both the directory tree structure and the files it contains. The Microsoft Windows world has access permissions of No Access, Read (r), Write (w), Execute (x), Delete (d), Change (c), and Full Control. The Read attribute lets you read the file but not make changes. The Change attribute allows you to read, write, execute, and delete the file but does not let you change the ACLs or the owner of the files. Obviously, the attribute of Full Control lets you make any changes to the file and its permissions and ownership.

PART V

Access Control Lists

Access control lists (ACLs) are lists of subjects that are authorized to access a specific object, and they define what level of authorization is granted. Authorization can be specific to an individual, group, or role. ACLs are used in several operating systems, applications, and router configurations.

ACLs map values from the access control matrix to the object. Whereas a capability corresponds to a row in the access control matrix, the ACL corresponds to a column of the matrix. The ACL for a notional File1 object is shown in Table 17-1.

Table 17-1 The ACL for a Notional File1 Object

User	File1
Diane	Full control
Katie	Read and execute
Chrissy	Read, write, and execute
John	Read and execute

Challenges When Using DAC

While DAC systems provide a lot of flexibility to the user and less administration for IT, it is also the Achilles' heel of operating systems. Malware can install itself and work under the security context of the user. For example, if a user opens an attachment that is infected with a virus, the code can install itself in the background without the user's being aware of this activity. This code basically inherits all the rights and permissions that the user has and can carry out all the activities the user can on the system. It can send copies of itself out to all the contacts listed in the user's e-mail client, install a back door, attack other systems, delete files on the hard drive, and more. The user is actually giving rights to the virus to carry out its dirty deeds, because the user has discretionary rights and is considered the owner of many objects on the system. This is particularly problematic in environments where users are assigned local administrator or root accounts, because once malware is installed, it can do anything on a system.

While we may want to give users some freedom to indicate who can access the files that they create and other resources on their systems that they are configured to be "owners" of, we really don't want them dictating all access decisions in environments with assets that need to be protected. We just don't trust them that much, and we shouldn't if you think back to the zero-trust principle. In most environments, user profiles are created and loaded on user workstations that indicate the level of control the user does and does not have. As a security administrator you might configure user profiles so that users cannot change the system's time, alter system configuration files, access a command prompt, or install unapproved applications. This type of access control is referred to as *nondiscretionary*, meaning that access decisions are not made at the discretion of the user. Nondiscretionary access controls are put into place by an authoritative entity (usually a security administrator) with the goal of protecting the organization's most critical assets.

Mandatory Access Control

In a *mandatory access control (MAC)* model, users do not have the discretion of determining who can access objects as in a DAC model. For security purposes, an operating system that is based on a MAC model greatly reduces the amount of rights, permissions, and functionality that a user has. In most systems based on the MAC model, a user cannot install software, change file permissions, add new users, and so on. The system can be used by the user for very focused and specific purposes, and that is it. These systems are usually very specialized and are in place to protect highly classified data. Most people have never interacted directly with a MAC-based system because they are mainly used by government-oriented agencies that maintain top-secret information.

However, MAC is used behind the scenes in some environments you may have encountered at some point. For example, the optional Linux kernel security module called AppArmor allows system administrators to implement MAC for certain kernel resources. There is also a version of Linux called SELinux, developed by the NSA, that implements a flexible MAC model for enhanced security.

The MAC model is based on a security label system. Users are given a security clearance (secret, top secret, confidential, and so on), and data is classified in the same way. The clearance and classification data is stored in the security labels, which are bound to the specific subjects and objects. When the system makes a decision about fulfilling a request to access an object, it is based on the clearance of the subject, the classification of the object, and the security policy of the system. This means that even if a user has the right clearance to read a file, specific policies (e.g., requiring "need to know") could still prevent access to it. The rules for how subjects access objects are made by the organization's security policy, configured by the security administrator, enforced by the operating system, and supported by security technologies.

NOTE Traditional MAC systems are based upon multilevel security policies, which outline how data at different classification levels is to be protected. Multilevel security (MLS) systems allow data at different classification levels to be accessed and interacted with by users with different clearance levels simultaneously.

When the MAC model is being used, every subject and object must have a security label, also called a sensitivity label. This label contains the object's security classification and any categories that may apply to it. The classification indicates the sensitivity level, and the categories enforce need-to-know rules. Figure 17-1 illustrates the use of security labels.

The classifications follow a hierarchical structure, with one level being more trusted than another. However, the categories do not follow a hierarchical scheme, because they represent compartments of information within a system. The categories can correspond to departments (intelligence, operations, procurement), project codenames (Titan, Jack Voltaic, Threatcasting), or management levels, among others. In a military environment, the classifications could be top secret, secret, confidential, and unclassified. Each classification is more trusted than the one below it. A commercial organization might use confidential, proprietary, corporate, and sensitive. The definition of the classification is up to the organization and should make sense for the environment in which it is used.

The categories portion of the label enforces need-to-know rules. Just because someone has a top secret clearance does not mean she now has access to all top secret information.

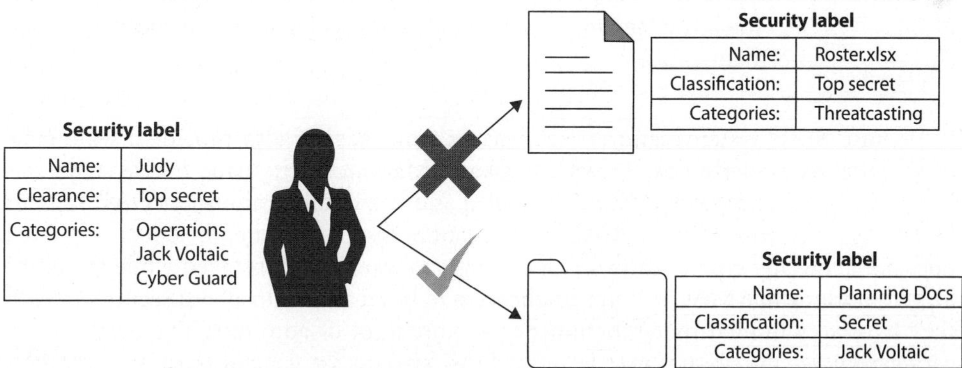

Figure 17-1 A security label is made up of a classification and categories.

She must also have a need to know. As shown in Figure 17-1, Judy is cleared top secret and has the codename Jack Voltaic as one of her categories. She can, therefore, access the folder with the planning documents for Jack Voltaic because her clearance is at least that of the object, and all the categories listed in the object match her own. Conversely, she cannot access the roster spreadsheet because, although her clearance is sufficient, she does not have a need to know that information. We know this last bit because whoever assigned the categories to Judy did not include Threatcasting among them.

EXAM TIP In MAC implementations, the system makes access decisions by comparing the subject's clearance and need-to-know level to the object's security label. In DAC implementations, the system compares the subject's identity to the ACL on the resource.

Software and hardware guards allow the exchange of data between trusted (high assurance) and less trusted (low assurance) systems and environments. For instance, if you were working on a MAC system (working in the dedicated security mode of secret) and you needed it to communicate to a MAC database (working in multilevel security mode, which goes up to top secret), the two systems would provide different levels of protection. If a system with lower assurance can directly communicate with a system of high assurance, then security vulnerabilities and compromises could be introduced.

A *software guard* is really just a front-end product that allows interconnectivity between systems working at different security levels. Different types of guards can be used to carry out filtering, processing requests, data blocking, and data sanitization. A *hardware guard* is a system with two network interface cards (NICs) connecting the two systems that need to communicate with one another. Guards can be used to connect different MAC systems working in different security modes, and they can be used to connect different networks working at different security levels. In many cases, the less trusted system can send messages to the more trusted system and can only receive acknowledgments back. This is common when e-mail messages need to go from less trusted systems to more trusted classified systems.

TIP The terms "security labels" and "sensitivity labels" can be used interchangeably.

Because MAC systems enforce strict access control, they also provide a wide range of security, particularly dealing with malware. Malware is the bane of DAC systems. Viruses, worms, and rootkits can be installed and run as applications on DAC systems. Since users that work within a MAC system cannot install software, the operating system does not allow any type of software, including malware, to be installed while the user is logged in. But while MAC systems might seem to be an answer to all our security prayers, they have very limited user functionality, require a lot of administrative overhead, are very expensive, and are not user friendly. DAC systems are general-purpose computers, while MAC systems serve a very specific purpose.

EXAM TIP Unlike DAC systems, MAC systems are considered nondiscretionary because users cannot make access decisions based on their own discretion (choice).

Role-Based Access Control

A *role-based access control (RBAC)* model uses a centrally administrated set of controls to determine how subjects and objects interact. The access control levels are based on the necessary operations and tasks a user needs to carry out to fulfill her responsibilities within an organization. This type of model lets access to resources be based on the role the user holds within the organization. The more traditional access control administration is based on just the DAC model, where access control is specified at the object level with ACLs. This approach is more complex because the administrator must translate an organizational authorization policy into permission when configuring ACLs. As the number of objects and users grows within an environment, users are bound to be granted unnecessary access to some objects, thus violating the least-privilege rule and increasing the risk to the organization. The RBAC approach simplifies access control administration by allowing permissions to be managed in terms of user job roles.

In an RBAC model, a role is defined in terms of the operations and tasks the role will carry out, whereas a DAC model outlines which subjects can access what objects based upon the individual user identity. Let's say we need a research and development analyst role. We develop this role not only to allow an individual to have access to all product and testing data but also, and more importantly, to outline the tasks and operations that the role can carry out on this data. When the analyst role makes a request to access the new testing results on the file server, in the background the operating system reviews the role's access levels before allowing this operation to take place.

NOTE Introducing roles also introduces the difference between rights being assigned explicitly and implicitly. If rights and permissions are assigned explicitly, they are assigned directly to a specific individual. If they are assigned implicitly, they are assigned to a role or group and the user inherits those attributes.

An RBAC model is the best system for an organization that has high employee turnover. If John, who is mapped to the Contractor role, leaves the organization, then Chrissy, his replacement, can be easily mapped to this role. That way, the administrator does not need to continually change the ACLs on the individual objects. He only needs to create a role (Contractor), assign permissions to this role, and map the new user to this role. Optionally, he can define roles that inherit access from other roles higher up in a hierarchy. These features are covered by two components of RBAC: core and hierarchical.

Core RBAC

There is a core component that is integrated into every RBAC implementation because it is the foundation of the model. Users, roles, permissions, operations, and sessions are defined and mapped according to the security policy. The core RBAC

- Has a many-to-many relationship among individual users and privileges
- Uses a session as a mapping between a user and a subset of assigned roles
- Accommodates traditional but robust group-based access control

Many users can belong to many groups with various privileges outlined for each group. When the user logs in (this is a session), the various roles and groups this user has been assigned are available to the user at one time. If you are a member of the Accounting role, RD group, and Administrative role, when you log on, all of the permissions assigned to these various groups are available to you.

This model provides robust options because it can include other components when making access decisions, instead of just basing the decision on a credential set. The RBAC system can be configured to also include time of day, location of role, day of the week, and so on. This means other information, not just the user ID and credential, is used for access decisions.

Hierarchical RBAC

This component allows the administrator to set up an organizational RBAC model that maps to the organizational structures and functional delineations required in a specific environment. This is very useful since organizations are already set up in a personnel hierarchical structure. In most cases, the higher you are in the chain of command, the more access you most likely have. Hierarchical RBAC has the following features:

- Uses role relations in defining user membership and privilege inheritance. For example, the Nurse role can access a certain set of files, and the Lab Technician role can access another set of files. The Doctor role inherits the permissions and access rights of these two roles and has more elevated rights already assigned to the Doctor role. So hierarchical RBAC is an accumulation of rights and permissions of other roles.
- Reflects organizational structures and functional delineations.
- Supports two types of hierarchies:
    - **Limited hierarchies** Only one level of hierarchy is allowed (Role 1 inherits from Role 2 and no other role)
    - **General hierarchies** Allows for many levels of hierarchies (Role 1 inherits Role 2's and Role 3's permissions)

Hierarchies are a natural means of structuring roles to reflect an organization's lines of authority and responsibility. Role hierarchies define an inheritance relation among roles. Different separations of duties are provided through RBAC:

- **Static separation of duty (SSD) relations** Deters fraud by constraining the combination of privileges (e.g., the user cannot be a member of both the Cashier and Accounts Receivable roles).
- **Dynamic separation of duty (DSD) relations** Deters fraud by constraining the combination of privileges that can be activated in any session (e.g., the user cannot be in both the Cashier and Cashier Supervisor roles at the same time, but the user can be a member of both). This one warrants a bit more explanation. Suppose José is a member of both the Cashier and Cashier Supervisor roles. If he logs in as a Cashier, the Supervisor role is unavailable to him during that session. If he logs in as Cashier Supervisor, the Cashier role is unavailable to him during that session.
- Role-based access control can be managed in the following ways:
  - **Non-RBAC** Users are mapped directly to applications and no roles are used.
  - **Limited RBAC** Users are mapped to multiple roles and mapped directly to other types of applications that do not have role-based access functionality.
  - **Hybrid RBAC** Users are mapped to multiapplication roles with only selected rights assigned to those roles.
  - **Full RBAC** Users are mapped to enterprise roles.

PART V

RBAC, MAC, and DAC

A lot of confusion exists regarding whether RBAC is a type of DAC model or a type of MAC model. Different sources claim different things, but in fact RBAC is a model in its own right. In the 1960s and 1970s, the U.S. military and NSA did a lot of research on the MAC model. DAC, which also sprang to life in the 1960s and 1970s, has its roots in the academic and commercial research laboratories. The RBAC model, which started gaining popularity in the 1990s, can be used in combination with MAC and DAC systems. For the most up-to-date information on the RBAC model, go to https://csrc.nist.gov/projects/role-based-access-control, which has documents that describe an RBAC standard and independent model, with the goal of clearing up this continual confusion.

In reality, operating systems can be created to use one, two, or all three of these models in some form, but just because they can be used together does not mean that they are not their own individual models with their own strict access control rules.

Rule-Based Access Control

Rule-based access control uses specific rules that indicate what can and cannot happen between a subject and an object. This access control model is built on top of traditional RBAC and is thus commonly called RB-RBAC to disambiguate the otherwise overloaded RBAC acronym. It is based on the simple concept of "if this, then that" (IFTTT) programming rules, which can be used to provide finer-grained access control to resources. Before a subject can access an object in a certain circumstance, the subject must meet a set of predefined rules. This can be simple and straightforward, as in, "If the subject's ID matches the unique ID value in the provided digital certificate, then the subject can gain access." Or there could be a set of complex rules that must be met before a subject can access an object. For example, "If the subject is accessing the object on a weekday between 8 A.M. and 5 P.M., and if the subject is accessing the object while physically in the office, and if the subject is in the procurement role, then the subject can access the object."

Rule-based access allows a developer to define specific and detailed situations in which a subject can or cannot access an object and what that subject can do once access is granted. Traditionally, rule-based access control has been used in MAC systems as an enforcement mechanism of the complex rules of access that MAC systems provide. Today, rule-based access is used in other types of systems and applications as well. Many routers and firewalls use rules to determine which types of packets are allowed into a network and which are rejected. Rule-based access control is a type of compulsory control, because the administrator sets the rules and the users cannot modify these controls.

Attribute-Based Access Control

Attribute-based access control (ABAC) uses attributes of any part of a system to define allowable access. These attributes can belong to subjects, objects, actions, or contexts. Here are some possible attributes we could use to describe our ABAC policies:

- **Subjects** Clearance, position title, department, years with the organization, training certification on a specific platform, member of a project team, location
- **Objects** Classification, files pertaining to a particular project, human resources (HR) records, location, security system component
- **Actions** Review, approve, comment, archive, configure, restart
- **Context** Time of day, project status (open/closed), fiscal year, ongoing audit

As you can see, ABAC provides the most granularity of any of the access control models. It would be possible, for example, to define and enforce a policy that allows only directors to comment on (but not edit) files pertaining to a project that is currently being audited. This specificity is a two-edged sword, since it can lead to an excessive number of policies that could interact with each other in ways that are difficult to predict.

Risk-Based Access Control

The access control models we've discussed so far all require that we decide exactly what is and is not allowed ahead of time. Whether these decisions involve users, security labels, roles, rules, or attributes, we codify them in our systems and, barring the occasional update, the policies are pretty static. But what if we were to make access control decisions dynamically based on the conditions surrounding the subjects' requests?

Risk-based access control (in case the term RBAC wasn't already ambiguous) estimates the risk associated with a particular request in real time and, if it doesn't exceed a given threshold, grants the subject access to the requested resource. It is an attempt to more closely align risk management and access control while striving to share objects as freely as possible. For example, suppose David works for a technology manufacturer that is about to release a super-secret new product that will revolutionize the world. If the details of this product are leaked before the announcement, it will negatively impact revenues and the return on investment of the marketing campaigns. Obviously, the product's specification sheet will be very sensitive until the announcement. Should David be granted access it?

Risk-based access control would look at it from the perspective of risk, which is the likelihood of an event multiplied by its impact. Suppose that the event about which we are concerned is a leak of the product details ahead of the official announcement. The impact is straightforward, so the real question is how likely it is that David's request will lead to a leak. That depends on several factors, such as his role (is he involved in the rollout?), trustworthiness (is he suspected of leaking anything before?), context (what is he doing that requires access to the specification sheet?), and possibly many others. The system would gather the necessary information, estimate the risk, compare it to the maximum tolerable threshold, and then make a decision.

Figure 17-2 illustrates the main components of risk-based access control. The risk factors are generally divided into categories like user context, resource sensitivity, action severity, and risk history. We've already touched on the first three of these in our example, but we also may want to learn from previous decisions. What is the risk history of similar requests? If the organization doesn't have a culture of secrecy and has experienced leaks

PART V

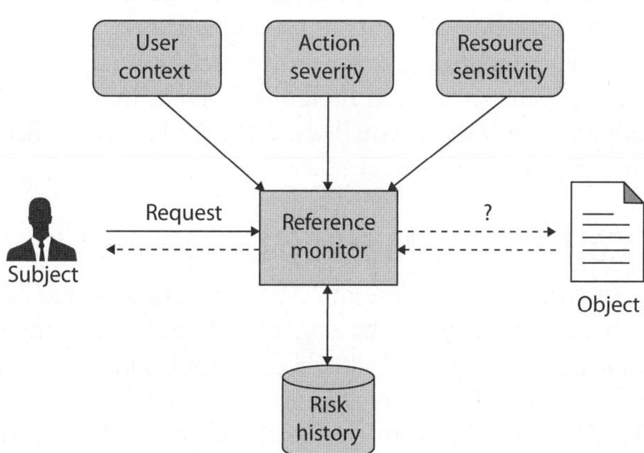

Figure 17-2 Components of a risk-based access control model

Access Control Models

The main characteristics of the six different access control models are important to understand.

- **DAC** Data owners decide who has access to resources, and ACLs are used to enforce these access decisions.
- **MAC** Operating systems enforce the system's security policy through the use of security labels.
- **RBAC** Access decisions are based on each subject's role and/or functional position.
- **RB-RBAC** Adds on to RBAC by imposing rules that further restrict access decisions.
- **ABAC** Access decisions are based on attributes of any component of or action on the system.
- **Risk BAC** Estimates the risk associated with a particular request in real time.

in the past, that drives risk way up. If a particular subject has a history of making bad decisions, that likewise points toward denying access. Regardless of how the decision is arrived at, there is an element of monitoring the user activities to add to this history so we can improve the accuracy of our risk estimates over time.

Implementing Authentication and Authorization Systems

Now that you know the theory and principles behind authorization mechanisms, let's turn our attention to how they are integrated with the authentication systems discussed in Chapter 16. Together, authentication and authorization are at the heart of cybersecurity. The following sections give you some technical details on the most common technologies with which you should be familiar. First, however, we have to talk a bit about markup languages, which, as you'll see shortly, play an important role in authentication and authorization.

Access Control and Markup Languages

If you can remember when *Hypertext Markup Language (HTML)* was *all* we had to make a static web page, you might be considered "old" in terms of the technology world; HTML came out in the early 1990s. HTML evolved from Standard Generalized Markup Language (SGML), which evolved from the Generalized Markup Language (GML). We still use HTML, so it is certainly not dead and gone; the industry has just improved upon the markup languages available for use to meet today's needs.

A *markup language* is a way to structure text and data sets, and it dictates how these will be viewed and used. When you adjust margins and other formatting capabilities in a word processor, you are marking up the text in the word processor's markup language. If you develop a web page, you are using some type of markup language. You can control how it looks and some of the actual functionality the page provides. The use of a standard markup language also allows for interoperability. If you develop a web page and follow basic markup language standards, the page will basically look and act the same no matter what web server is serving up the web page or what browser the viewer is using to interact with it.

As the Internet grew in size and the World Wide Web (WWW) expanded in functionality, and as more users and organizations came to depend upon websites and web-based communication, the basic and elementary functions provided by HTML were not enough. And instead of every website having its own proprietary markup language to meet its specific functionality requirements, the industry had to have a way for functionality needs to be met and still provide interoperability for all web server and web browser interaction. This is the reason that *Extensible Markup Language (XML)* was developed. XML is a universal and foundational standard that provides a structure for other independent markup languages to be built from and still allow for interoperability. Markup languages with various functionalities were built from XML, and while each language provides its own individual functionality, if they all follow the core rules of XML, then they are interoperable and can be used across different web-based applications and platforms.

As an analogy, let's look at the English language. Samir is a biology scientist, Trudy is an accountant, and Val is a network administrator. They all speak English, so they have a common set of communication rules, which allow them to talk with each other, but each has their own "spin-off" language that builds upon and uses the English language as its core. Samir uses words like "mitochondrial amino acid genetic strains" and "DNA polymerase." Trudy uses words such as "accrual accounting" and "acquisition indigestion." Val uses terms such as "multiprotocol label switching" and "subkey creation." Each profession has its own "language" to meet its own needs, but each is based off the same core language—English. In the world of the WWW, various websites need to provide different types of functionality through the use of their own language types but still need a way to communicate with each other and their users in a consistent manner, which is why they are based upon the same core language structure (XML). There are hundreds of markup languages based upon XML, but we are going to focus on the ones that are used for identity management and access control purposes.

The *Service Provisioning Markup Language (SPML)* allows for the exchange of provisioning data between applications, which could reside in one organization or many; allows for the automation of user management (account creation, amendments, revocation) and access entitlement configuration related to electronically published services across multiple provisioning systems; and allows for the integration and interoperation of service provisioning requests across various platforms.

When an organization hires a new employee, that employee usually needs access to a wide range of systems, servers, and applications. Setting up new accounts on every system, properly configuring access rights, and then maintaining those accounts throughout their lifetimes is time-consuming, laborious, and error-prone. What if the organization has 20,000 employees and thousands of network resources that each employee needs various access rights to? This opens the door for confusion, mistakes, vulnerabilities, and a lack of standardization.

SPML allows for all these accounts to be set up and managed simultaneously across the various systems and applications. SPML is made up of three main entities: the Requesting Authority (RA), which is the entity that is making the request to set up a new account or make changes to an existing account; the Provisioning Service Provider (PSP), which is the software that responds to the account requests; and the Provisioning Service Target (PST), which is the entity that carries out the provisioning activities on the requested system.

So when a new employee is hired, there is a request to set up the necessary user accounts and access privileges on several different systems and applications across the enterprise. This request originates in a piece of software carrying out the functionality of the RA. The RA creates SPML messages, which provide the requirements of the new account, and sends them to a piece of software that is carrying out the functionality of the PSP. This piece of software reviews the requests and compares them to the organization's approved account creation criteria. If these requests are allowed, the PSP sends new SPML messages to the end systems (PST) that the user actually needs to access. Software on the PST sets up the requested accounts and configures the necessary access rights. If this same employee is fired three months later, the same process is followed and all necessary user accounts are deleted. This allows for consistent account management in complex environments. These steps are illustrated in Figure 17-3.

Figure 17-3 SPML provisioning steps

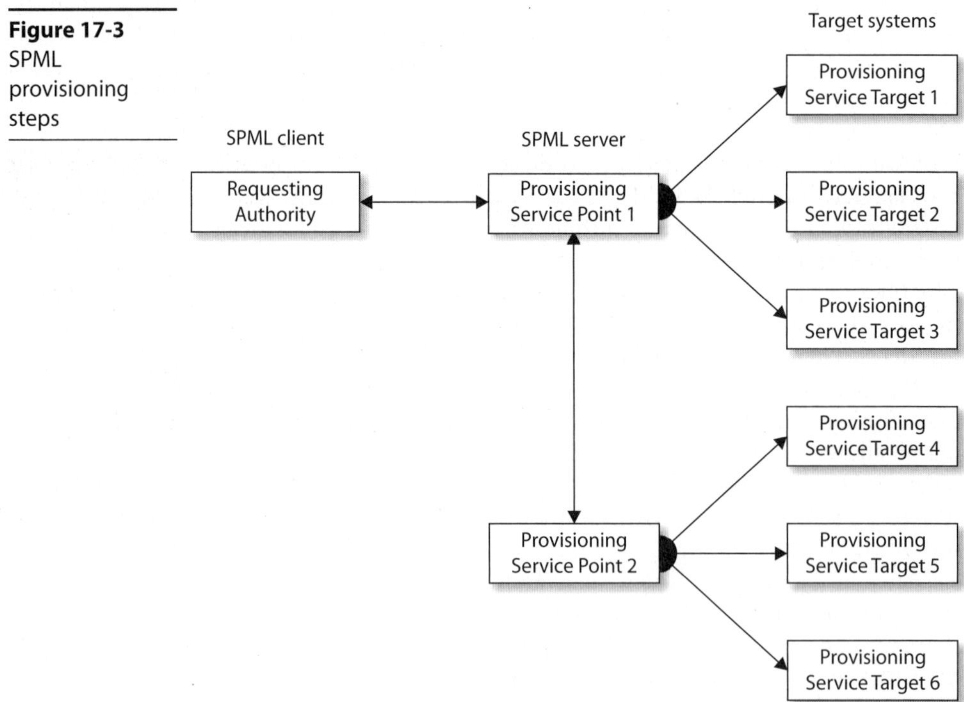

When there is a need to allow a user to log in one time and gain access to different and separate web-based applications, the actual authentication data has to be shared between the systems maintaining those web applications securely and in a standardized manner. This is the role that the *Security Assertion Markup Language (SAML)* plays. It is an XML standard that allows the exchange of authentication and authorization data to be shared between security domains. Suppose your organization, Acme Corp., uses Gmail as its corporate e-mail platform. You would want to ensure that you maintain control over user access credentials so that you could enforce password policies and, for example, prevent access to the e-mail account of an employee who just got fired. You could set up a relationship with Google that would allow you to do just this using SAML. Whenever one of your organization's users attempted to access their corporate Gmail account, Gmail would redirect their request to Acme's single sign-on (SSO) service, which would authenticate the user and relay (through the user) a SAML response. Figure 17-4 depicts this process, though its multiple steps are largely transparent to the user.

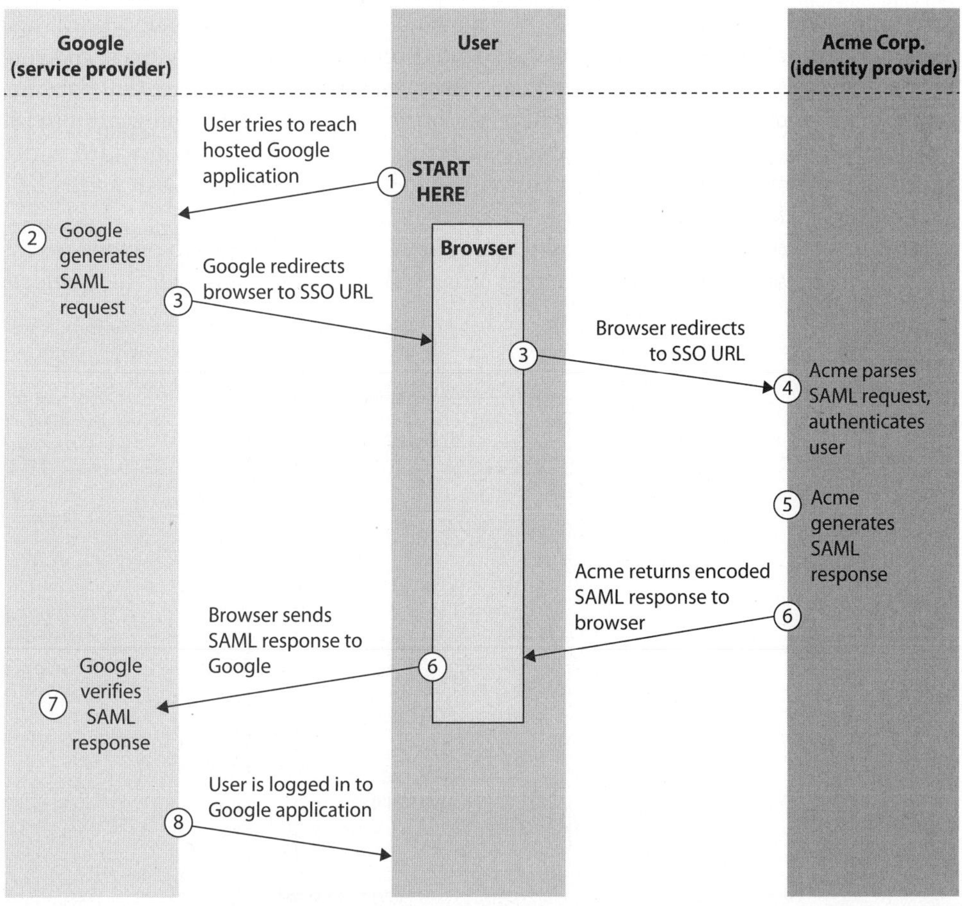

Figure 17-4 SAML authentication

SAML provides the authentication pieces to federated identity management systems to allow business-to-business (B2B) and business-to-consumer (B2C) transactions. In our previous example, the user is considered the *principal*, Acme Corporation is the *identity provider*, and Gmail is the *service provider*.

This is not the only way that the SAML language can be used. The digital world has evolved to being able to provide extensive services and functionality to users through web-based machine-to-machine communication standards. As we discussed in Chapter 13, *web services* is a collection of technologies and standards that allow services (weather updates, stock tickers, e-mail, customer resource management, etc.) to be provided on distributed systems and be "served up" in one place.

Transmission of SAML data can take place over different protocol types, but a common one is *Simple Object Access Protocol (SOAP)*. As you may recall from Chapter 13, SOAP is a specification that outlines how information pertaining to web services is exchanged in a structured manner. It provides the basic messaging framework, which allows users to request a service and, in exchange, the service is made available to that user. Let's say you need to interact with your company's CRM system, which is hosted and maintained by the vendor—for example, Salesforce.com. You would log into your company's portal and double-click a link for Salesforce. Your company's portal would take this request and your authentication data and package it up in an SAML format and encapsulate that data into a SOAP message. This message would be transmitted over an HTTP connection to the Salesforce vendor site, and once you were authenticated, you would be provided with a screen that shows you the company's customer database. The SAML, SOAP, and HTTP relationship is illustrated in Figure 17-5.

The use of web services in this manner also allows for organizations to provide *service-oriented architecture (SOA)* environments. An SOA is a way to provide independent

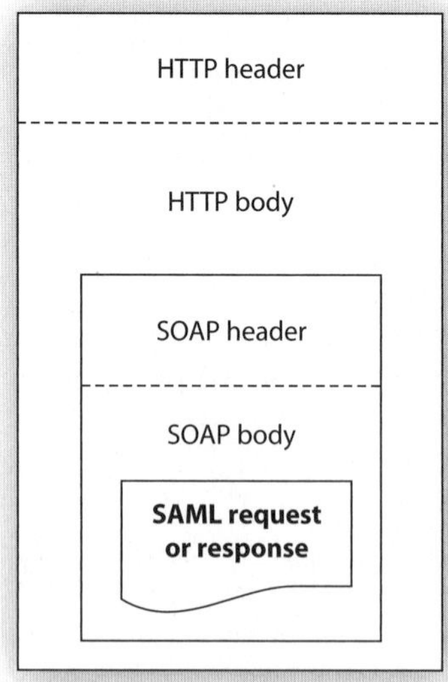

Figure 17-5 SAML material embedded within an HTTP message

services residing on different systems in different business domains in one consistent manner. For example, if your organization has a web portal that allows you to access the organization's CRM, an employee directory, and a help-desk ticketing application, this is most likely being provided through an SOA. The CRM system may be within the marketing department, the employee directory may be within the HR department, and the ticketing system may be within the IT department, but you can interact with all of them through one interface. SAML is a way to send your authentication information to each system, and SOAP allows this type of information to be presented and processed in a unified manner.

The last XML-based standard we will look at is *Extensible Access Control Markup Language (XACML).* XACML is used to express security policies and access rights to assets provided through web services and other enterprise applications. SAML is just a way to send around your authentication information, as in a password, key, or digital certificate, in a standard format. SAML does not tell the receiving system how to interpret and use this authentication data. Two systems have to be configured to use the same type of authentication data. If you log into System A and provide a password and try to access System B, which only uses digital certificates for authentication purposes, your password is not going to give you access to System B's service. So both systems have to be configured to use passwords. But just because your password is sent to System B does not mean you have complete access to all of System B's functionality. System B has access policies that dictate the operations that specific subjects can carry out on its resources. The access policies can be developed in the XACML format and enforced by System B's software.

XACML is both an access control policy language and a processing model that allows for policies to be interpreted and enforced in a standard manner. When your password is sent to System B, there is a rules engine on that system that interprets and enforces the XACML access control policies. If the access control policies are created in the XACML format, they can be installed on both System A and System B to allow for consistent security to be enforced and managed.

XACML uses a Subject element (requesting entity), a Resource element (requested entity), and an Action element (types of access). So if you request access to your company's CRM, you are the Subject, the CRM application is the Resource, and your access parameters are outlined in the Action element.

NOTE Who develops and keeps track of all of these standardized languages? The *Organization for the Advancement of Structured Information Standards (OASIS)*. This organization develops and maintains the standards for how various aspects of web-based communication are built and maintained.

Web services, SOA environments, and the implementation of these different XML-based markup languages vary in nature because they allow for extensive flexibility. Because so much of the world's communication takes place through web-based processes, it is increasingly important for security professionals to understand these issues and technologies.

OAuth

OAuth is an open standard for authorization (not authentication) to third parties. The general idea is that this lets you authorize a website to use something that you control at a different website. For instance, if you have a LinkedIn account, the system might ask you to let it have access to your Google contacts in order to find your friends who already have accounts in LinkedIn. If you agree, you next see a pop-up from Google asking whether you want to authorize LinkedIn to manage your contacts. If you agree to this, LinkedIn gains access to all your contacts until you rescind this authorization. With OAuth a user allows a website to access a third party. The latest version of OAuth, which is version 2.0, is defined in Request for Comments (RFC) 6749. It defines four roles as described here:

- **Client** A process that requests access to a protected resource. It is worth noting that this term describes the relationship of an entity with a resource provider in a client/server architecture. This means the "client" could actually be a web service (e.g., LinkedIn) that makes requests from another web service (e.g., Google).
- **Resource server** The server that controls the resource that the client is trying to access.
- **Authorization server** The system that keeps track of which clients are allowed to use which resources and issues access tokens to those clients.
- **Resource owner** Whoever owns a protected resource and is able to grant permissions for others to use it. These permissions are usually granted through a consent dialog box. The resource owner is typically an end user, but could be an application or service.

Figure 17-6 shows a resource owner granting an OAuth client access to protected resources in a resource server. This could be a user who wants to tweet directly from

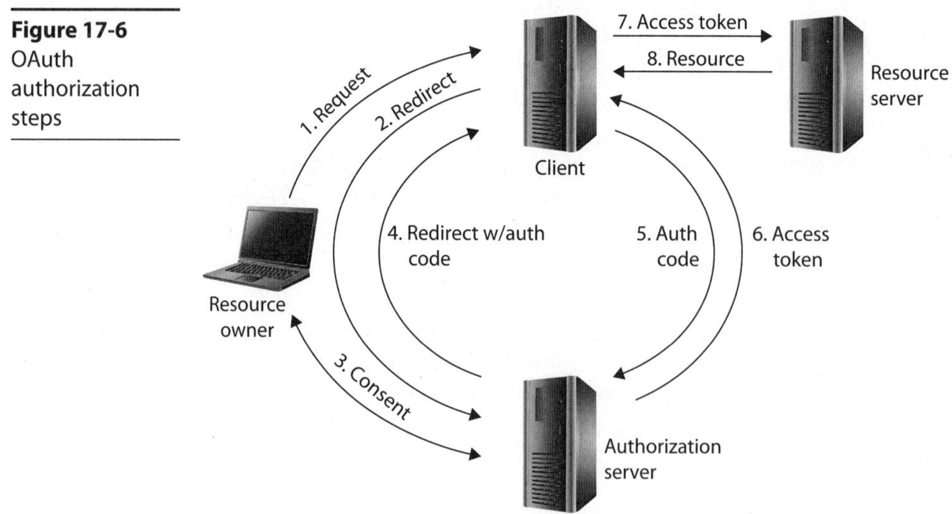

Figure 17-6 OAuth authorization steps

a LinkedIn page, for example. The resource owner sends a request to the client, which is redirected to an authorization server. This server negotiates consent with the resource owner and then redirects an HTTPS-secured message back to the client, including in the message an authorization code. The client next contacts the authorization server directly with the authorization code and receives in return an access token for the protected resource. Thereafter, as long as the token has not expired or the authorization is not rescinded by the resource owner, the client is able to present the token to the resource server and access the resource. Note that it is possible (and indeed fairly common) for the resource server and authorization server to reside on the same computing node.

Although OAuth is an authorization framework, it relies on some sort of authentication mechanism to verify the identity of the resource owner whenever permissions are changed on a protected resource. This authentication is outside the scope of the OAuth standard, but can be implicitly used, as described in the following section.

OpenID Connect

OpenID Connect (OIDC) is a simple authentication layer built on top of the OAuth 2.0 protocol. It allows transparent authentication and authorization of client resource requests, as shown in Figure 17-7. Most frequently, OIDC is used to allow a web application (relying party) to not only authenticate an end user using a third-party identity provider (IdP) but also get information about that user from that IdP. When end users attempt to log into the web service, they see a login prompt from the IdP (e.g., Google) and, after correctly authenticating, are asked for consent to share information (e.g., name, e-mail address) with the web service. The information shared can be arbitrary as long as it is configured at the IdP, the relying party explicitly requests it, and the end user consents to it being shared.

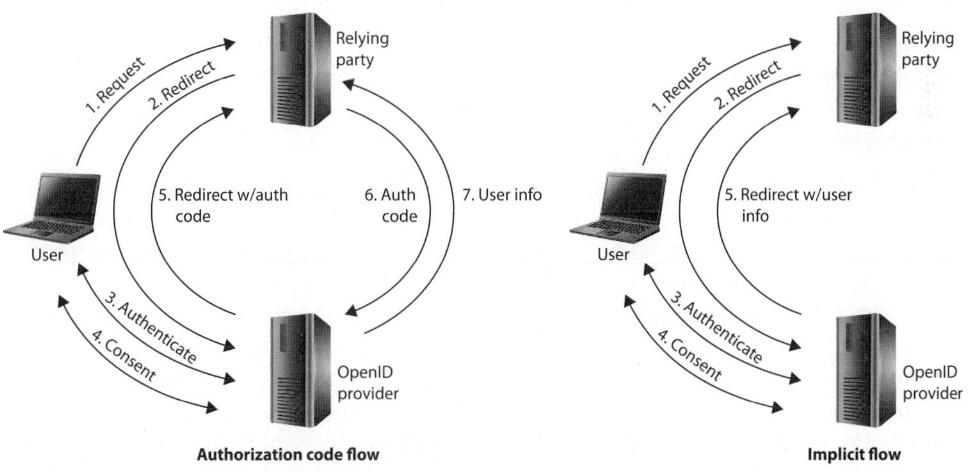

Figure 17-7 Two common OpenID Connect process flows

OIDC supports three flows:

- **Authorization code flow** The relying party is provided an authorization code (or token) and must use it to directly request the ID token containing user information from the IdP.
- **Implicit flow** The relying party receives the ID token containing user information with the redirect response from the IdP after user authentication and consent. The token is passed through the user's browser, potentially exposing it to tampering.
- **Hybrid flow** Essentially a combination of the previous two flows.

Figure 17-7 illustrates the first two flows, which are the most common ones in use. In the *authorization code flow*, the user requests a protected resource on the relying party's server, which triggers a redirect to the OpenID provider for authentication. The OpenID provider authenticates the user and then requests user consent to sharing specific kinds of information (e.g., e-mail, phone, profile, address), which are called *scope values*. The OpenID provider then redirects the user's browser back to the relying party and includes an authorization code. The relying party then presents this code to the OpenID provider and requests the user information, which is delivered to it in an ID token.

The *implicit flow* is similar to the authorization code flow, but the relying party includes the requested scope values in the authentication redirect to the OpenID provider. After the user is authenticated and consents to sharing the information, the OpenID provider includes the ID token with the user's information in the redirect back to the relying party.

The authorization code flow is preferred because it is more secure. The client app on the relying party obtains the ID token directly from the IdP, which means the user is unable to tamper with it. It also allows the OpenID provider to authenticate the client app that is requesting the user's information. This flow requires that the client app have a server backend. If the client app is browser-based (e.g., JavaScript) and doesn't have a server backend, then the implicit flow can be used. It is considered less secure because the ID token with the user information is given to the user's browser, where it could be compromised or manipulated.

Kerberos

The previous access control technologies were focused on service-oriented architectures and web services. Alas, not every system fits those architectures. We still need authentication and authorization when we log into our work computers and in many other scenarios. Enter Kerberos.

Kerberos is the name of a three-headed dog that guards the entrance to the underworld in Greek mythology. This is a great name for a security technology that provides authentication functionality, with the purpose of protecting an organization's assets. Kerberos is an authentication protocol and was designed in the mid-1980s as part of MIT's Project Athena. It works in a client/server model and is based on symmetric key cryptography. The protocol has been used for years in Unix systems and is the default authentication method for Windows operating systems. In addition, Apple macOS, Oracle Solaris, and Red Hat Enterprise Linux all use Kerberos authentication. Commercial products supporting Kerberos are fairly common, so this one might be a keeper.

Kerberos is an example of an SSO system for distributed environments, and it has become a de facto standard for heterogeneous networks. Kerberos incorporates a wide range of security capabilities, which gives organizations much more flexibility and scalability when they need to provide an encompassing security architecture. It has four elements necessary for enterprise access control: scalability, transparency, reliability, and security. However, this open architecture also invites interoperability issues. When vendors have a lot of freedom to customize a protocol, it usually means no two vendors will customize it in the same fashion. This creates interoperability and incompatibility issues.

Kerberos uses symmetric key cryptography and provides end-to-end security. Although it allows the use of passwords for authentication, it was designed specifically to eliminate the need to transmit passwords over the network. Most Kerberos implementations work with shared secret keys.

Main Components in Kerberos

The *Key Distribution Center (KDC)* is the most important component within a Kerberos environment. The KDC holds all users' and services' secret keys. It provides an authentication service, as well as key distribution functionality. The clients and services trust the integrity of the KDC, and this trust is the foundation of Kerberos security.

The KDC provides security services to *principals*, which can be users, applications, or network services. The KDC must have an account for, and share a secret key with, each principal. For users, a password is transformed into a secret key value. The secret key can be used to send sensitive data back and forth between the principal and the KDC, and is used for user authentication purposes.

A *ticket* is generated by the *ticket granting service (TGS)* on the KDC and given to a principal when that principal, let's say a user, needs to authenticate to another principal, let's say a print server. The ticket enables one principal to authenticate to another principal. If Emily needs to use the print server, she must prove to the print server she is who she claims to be and that she is authorized to use the printing service. So Emily requests a ticket from the TGS. The TGS gives Emily the ticket, and in turn, Emily passes this ticket on to the print server. If the print server approves this ticket, Emily is allowed to use the print service.

A KDC provides security services for a set of principals. This set is called a *realm* in Kerberos. The KDC is the trusted authentication server for all users, applications, and services within a realm. One KDC can be responsible for one realm or several realms. Realms enable an administrator to logically group resources and users.

So far, we know that principals (users, applications, and services) require the KDC's services to authenticate to each other; that the KDC has a database filled with information about every principal within its realm; that the KDC holds and delivers cryptographic keys and tickets; and that tickets are used for principals to authenticate to each other. So how does this process work?

The Kerberos Authentication Process

The user and the KDC share a secret key, while the service and the KDC share a different secret key. The user and the requested service do not share a symmetric key in the beginning. The user trusts the KDC because they share a secret key. They can encrypt and decrypt data they pass between each other, and thus have a protected communication path. Once the user authenticates to the service, they, too, will share a symmetric key (session key) that is used for authentication purposes.

Here are the exact steps:

1. Emily comes in to work and enters her username and password into her workstation at 8:00 A.M. The Kerberos software on Emily's computer sends the username to the authentication service (AS) on the KDC, which in turn sends Emily a ticket granting ticket (TGT) that is encrypted with the TGS's secret key.
2. If Emily has entered her correct password, the TGT is decrypted and Emily gains access to her local workstation desktop.
3. When Emily needs to send a print job to the print server, her system sends the TGT to the TGS, which runs on the KDC, and a request to access the print server. (The TGT allows Emily to prove she has been authenticated and allows her to request access to the print server.)
4. The TGS creates and sends a second ticket to Emily, which she will use to authenticate to the print server. This second ticket contains two instances of the same session key, one encrypted with Emily's secret key and the other encrypted with the print server's secret key. The second ticket also contains an *authenticator*, which contains identification information on Emily, her system's IP address, sequence number, and a timestamp.
5. Emily's system receives the second ticket, decrypts and extracts the embedded session key, adds a second authenticator set of identification information to the ticket, and sends the ticket on to the print server.
6. The print server receives the ticket, decrypts and extracts the session key, and decrypts and extracts the two authenticators in the ticket. If the print server can decrypt and extract the session key, it knows the KDC created the ticket, because only the KDC has the secret key used to encrypt the session key. If the authenticator information that the KDC and the user put into the ticket matches, then the print server knows it received the ticket from the correct principal.
7. Once this is completed, it means Emily has been properly authenticated to the print server and the server prints her document.

This is an extremely simplistic overview of what is going on in any Kerberos exchange, but it gives you an idea of the dance taking place behind the scenes whenever you interact with any network service in an environment that uses Kerberos. Figure 17-8 provides a simplistic view of this process.

The authentication service is the part of the KDC that authenticates a principal, and the TGS is the part of the KDC that makes the tickets and hands them out to the principals. TGTs are used so the user does not have to enter his password each time he needs to communicate with another principal. After the user enters his password, it is temporarily stored on his system, and any time the user needs to communicate with another principal, he just reuses the TGT.

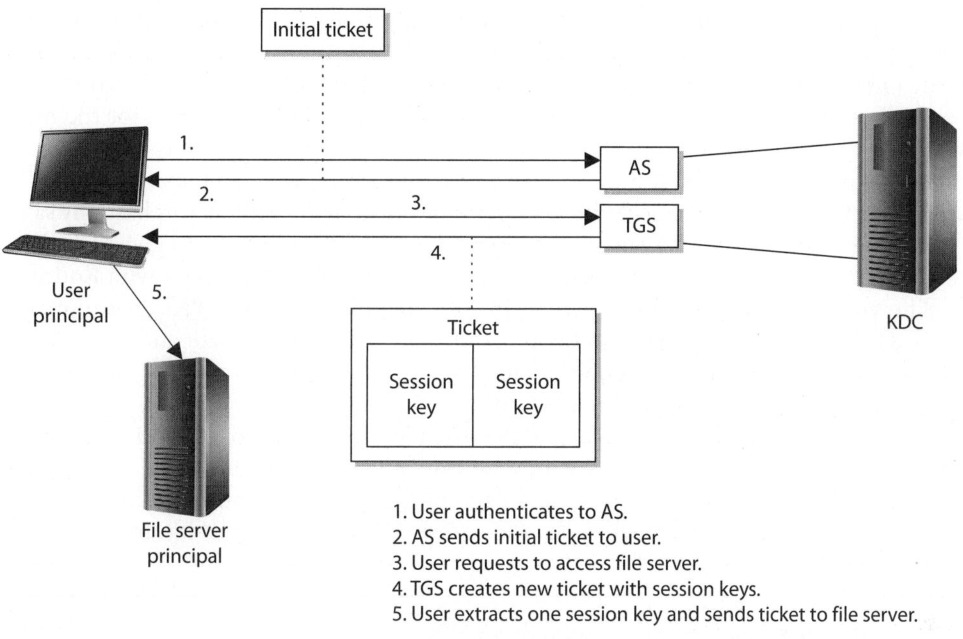

Figure 17-8 The user must receive a ticket from the KDC before being able to use the requested resource.

EXAM TIP Be sure you understand that a session key is different from a secret key. A secret key is shared between the KDC and a principal and is static in nature. A session key is shared between two principals and is generated when needed and is destroyed after the session is completed.

If a Kerberos implementation is configured to use an *authenticator*, the user sends to the print server her identification information and a timestamp and sequence number encrypted with the session key they share. The print server decrypts this information and compares it with the identification data the KDC sent to it about this requesting user. If the data is the same, the print server allows the user to send print jobs. The timestamp is used to help fight against replay attacks. The print server compares the sent timestamp with its own internal time, which helps determine if the ticket has been sniffed and copied by an attacker and then submitted at a later time in hopes of impersonating the legitimate user and gaining unauthorized access. The print server checks the sequence number to make sure that this ticket has not been submitted previously. This is another countermeasure to protect against replay attacks.

NOTE A replay attack is when an attacker captures and resubmits data (commonly a credential) with the goal of gaining unauthorized access to an asset.

The primary reason to use Kerberos is that the principals do not trust each other enough to communicate directly. In our example, the print server will not print anyone's print job without that entity authenticating itself. So none of the principals trust each other directly; they only trust the KDC. The KDC creates tickets to vouch for the individual principals when they need to communicate. Suppose Rodrigo needs to communicate directly with you, but you do not trust him enough to listen and accept what he is saying. If he first gives you a ticket from something you do trust (KDC), this basically says, "Look, the KDC says I am a trustworthy person. The KDC asked me to give this ticket to you to prove it." Once that happens, *then* you will communicate directly with Rodrigo.

The same type of trust model is used in PKI environments. In a PKI environment, users do not trust each other directly, but they all trust the certificate authority (CA). The CA vouches for the individuals' identities by using digital certificates, the same as the KDC vouches for the individuals' identities by using tickets.

So why are we talking about Kerberos? Because it is one example of an SSO technology. The user enters a user ID and password one time and one time only. The tickets have time limits on them that administrators can configure. Many times, the lifetime of a TGT is eight to ten hours, so when the user comes in the next day, he has to present his credentials again.

NOTE Kerberos is an open protocol, meaning that vendors can manipulate it to work properly within their products and environments. The industry has different "flavors" of Kerberos, since various vendors require different functionality.

Weaknesses of Kerberos

The following are some of the potential weaknesses of Kerberos:

- The KDC can be a single point of failure. If the KDC goes down, no one can access needed resources. Redundancy is necessary for the KDC.
- The KDC must be able to handle the number of requests it receives in a timely manner. It must be scalable.
- Secret keys are temporarily stored on the users' workstations, which means it is possible for an intruder to obtain these cryptographic keys.
- Session keys are decrypted and reside on the users' workstations, either in a cache or in a key table. Again, an intruder might capture these keys.
- Kerberos is vulnerable to password guessing. The KDC does not know if a dictionary attack is taking place.
- Network traffic is not protected by Kerberos if encryption is not enabled.
- If the keys are too short, they can be vulnerable to brute-force attacks.
- Kerberos needs all client and server clocks to be synchronized.

> **Kerberos and Password-Guessing Attacks**
> Just because an environment uses Kerberos does not mean the systems are vulnerable to password-guessing attacks. The operating system itself will (should) provide the protection of tracking failed login attempts. The Kerberos protocol does not have this type of functionality, so another component must be in place to counter these types of attacks. No need to start ripping Kerberos out of your network environment after reading this section; your operating system provides the protection mechanism for this type of attack.

Kerberos must be transparent (work in the background without the user needing to understand it), scalable (work in large, heterogeneous environments), reliable (use distributed server architecture to ensure there is no single point of failure), and secure (provide authentication and confidentiality).

Remote Access Control Technologies

The following sections present some examples of centralized remote access control technologies. Each of these authentication protocols is referred to as an AAA protocol, which stands for authentication, authorization, and auditing. (Some resources have the last A stand for accounting, but it is the same functionality—just a different name.)

Depending upon the protocol, there are different ways to authenticate a user in this client/server architecture. The traditional authentication protocol is the Challenge Handshake Authentication Protocol (CHAP), but many systems are now using Extensible Authentication Protocol (EAP). We discussed each of these authentication protocols at length in Chapter 15.

RADIUS

Remote Authentication Dial-In User Service (RADIUS) is a network protocol that provides client/server authentication and authorization and audits remote users. A network may have access servers, DSL, ISDN, or a T1 line dedicated for remote users to communicate through. The access server requests the remote user's logon credentials and passes them back to a RADIUS server, which houses the usernames and password values. The remote user is a client to the access server, and the access server is a client to the RADIUS server.

Most ISPs today use RADIUS to authenticate customers before they are allowed access to the Internet. The access server and customer's software negotiate through a handshake procedure and agree upon an authentication protocol (CHAP or EAP). The customer provides to the access server a username and password. This communication takes place over a Point-to-Point Protocol (PPP) connection. The access server and RADIUS server communicate over the RADIUS protocol. Once the authentication is completed properly, the customer's system is given an IP address and connection parameters and is allowed access to the Internet. The access server notifies the RADIUS server when the session starts and stops for billing purposes.

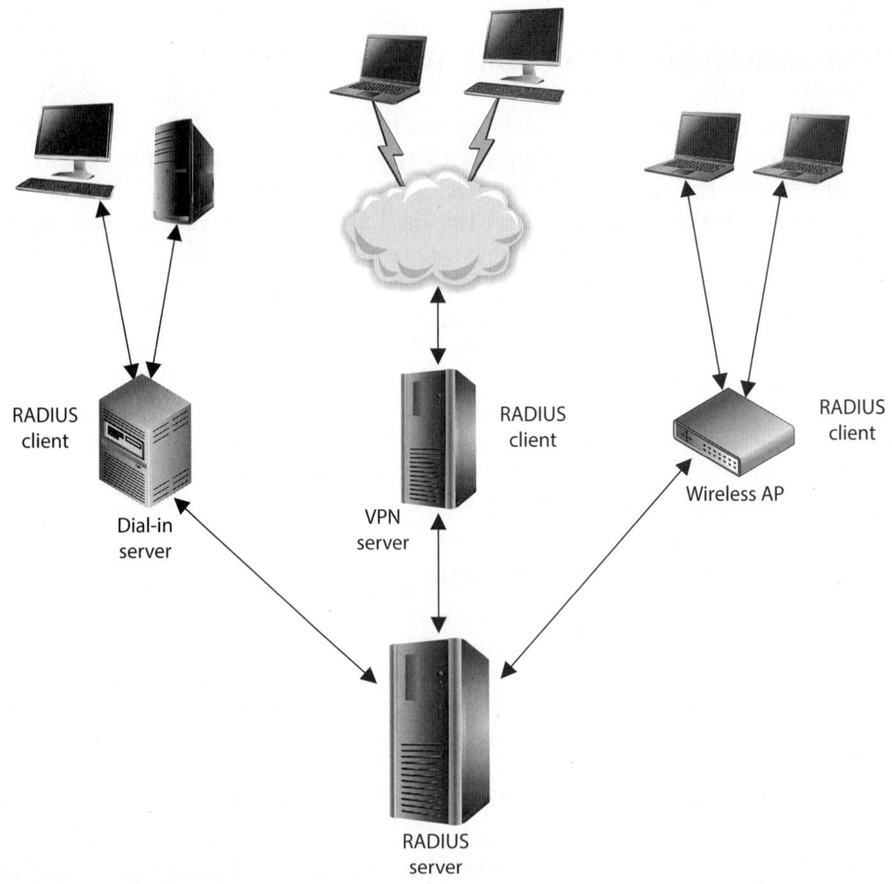

Figure 17-9 Environments can implement different RADIUS infrastructures.

RADIUS was developed by Livingston Enterprises for its network access server product series, but was then published as a set of standards (RFC 2865 and RFC 2866). This means it is an open protocol that any vendor can use and manipulate so that it works within its individual products. Because RADIUS is an open protocol, it can be used in different types of implementations. The format of configurations and user credentials can be held in LDAP servers, various databases, or text files. Figure 17-9 shows some examples of possible RADIUS implementations.

TACACS

Terminal Access Controller Access Control System (TACACS) has a very funny name. Not funny ha-ha, but funny "huh?" TACACS has been through three generations: TACACS, Extended TACACS (XTACACS), and TACACS+. TACACS combines its authentication and authorization processes; XTACACS separates authentication, authorization, and auditing processes; and TACACS+ is XTACACS with extended two-factor user authentication.

TACACS uses fixed passwords for authentication, while TACACS+ allows users to employ dynamic (one-time) passwords, which provides more protection. Although TACACS+ is now an open standard, both it and XTACACS started off as Cisco-proprietary protocols that were inspired by, but are not compatible with, TACACS.

NOTE TACACS+ is really not a new generation of TACACS and XTACACS; it is a distinct protocol that provides similar functionality and shares the same naming scheme. Because it is a totally different protocol, it is not backward-compatible with TACACS or XTACACS.

TACACS+ provides basically the same functionality as RADIUS with a few differences in some of its characteristics. First, TACACS+ uses TCP as its transport protocol, while RADIUS uses UDP. "So what?" you may be thinking. Well, any software that is developed to use UDP as its transport protocol has to be "fatter" with intelligent code that looks out for the items that UDP will not catch. Since UDP is a connectionless protocol, it will not detect or correct transmission errors. So RADIUS must have the necessary code to detect packet corruption, long timeouts, or dropped packets. Since the developers of TACACS+ chose to use TCP, the TACACS+ software does not need to have the extra code to look for and deal with these transmission problems. TCP is a connection-oriented protocol, and that is its job and responsibility.

RADIUS encrypts the user's password only as it is being transmitted from the RADIUS client to the RADIUS server. Other information, as in the username, accounting, and authorized services, is passed in cleartext. This is an open invitation for attackers to capture session information for replay attacks. Vendors who integrate RADIUS into their products need to understand these weaknesses and integrate other security mechanisms to protect against these types of attacks. TACACS+ encrypts all of this data between the client and server and thus does not have the vulnerabilities inherent in the RADIUS protocol.

The RADIUS protocol combines the authentication and authorization functionality. TACACS+ uses a true AAA architecture, which separates the authentication, authorization, and accounting functionalities. This gives a network administrator more flexibility in how remote users are authenticated. For example, if Tomika is a network administrator and has been assigned the task of setting up remote access for users, she must decide between RADIUS and TACACS+. If the current environment already authenticates all of the local users through a domain controller using Kerberos, then Tomika can configure the remote users to be authenticated in this same manner, as shown in Figure 17-10. Instead of having to maintain a remote access server database of remote user credentials and a database within Active Directory for local users, Tomika can just configure and maintain one database. The separation of authentication, authorization, and accounting functionality provides this capability. TACACS+ also enables the network administrator to define more granular user profiles, which can control the actual commands users can carry out.

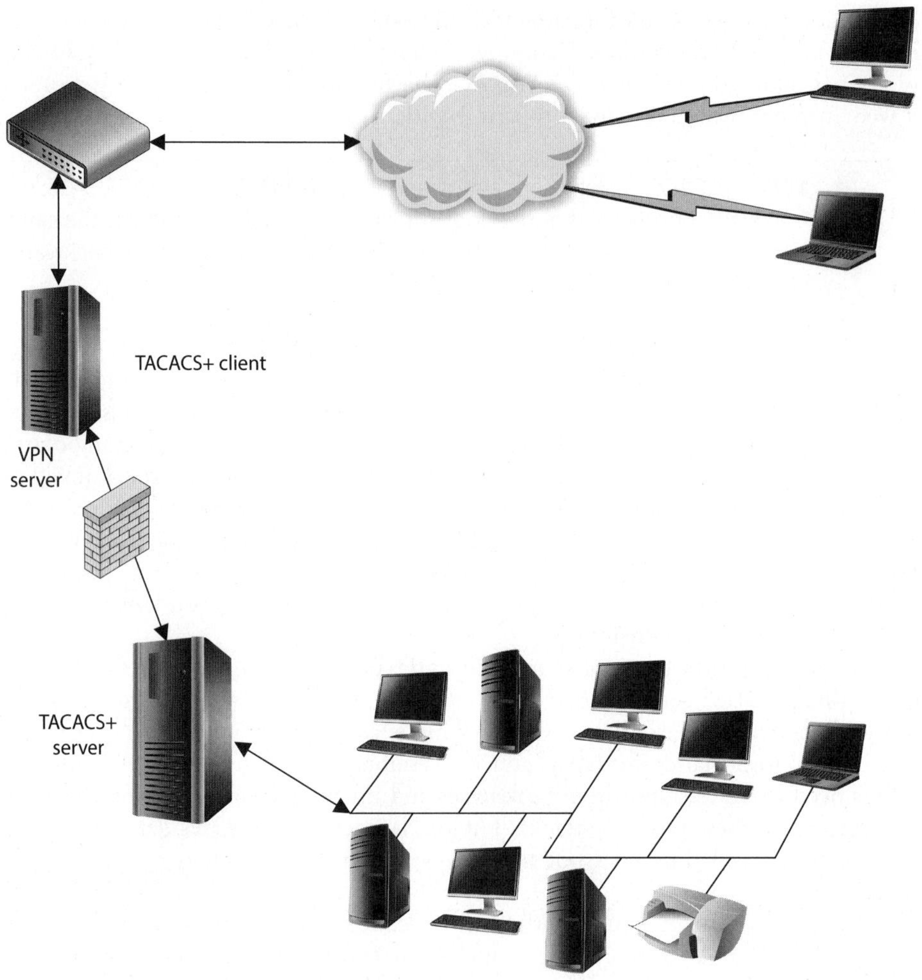

Figure 17-10 TACACS+ works in a client/server model.

Remember that RADIUS and TACACS+ are both protocols, and protocols are just agreed-upon ways of communication. When a RADIUS client communicates with a RADIUS server, it does so through the RADIUS protocol, which is really just a set of defined fields that will accept certain values. These fields are referred to as *attribute-value pairs (AVPs)*. As an analogy, suppose Ivan sends you a piece of paper that has several different boxes drawn on it. Each box has a headline associated with it: first name, last name, hair color, shoe size. You fill in these boxes with your values and send it back to Ivan. This is basically how protocols work; the sending system just fills in the boxes (fields) with the necessary information for the receiving system to extract and process.

	RADIUS	TACACS+
Packet delivery	UDP	TCP
Packet encryption	Encrypts only the password from the RADIUS client to the server.	Encrypts all traffic between the client and server.
AAA support	Combines authentication and authorization services.	Uses the AAA architecture, separating authentication, authorization, and auditing.
Multiprotocol support	Works over PPP connections.	Supports other protocols, such as AppleTalk, NetBIOS, and IPX.
Responses	Uses single-challenge response when authenticating a user, which is used for all AAA activities.	Uses multiple-challenge response for each of the AAA processes. Each AAA activity must be authenticated.

Table 17-2 Specific Differences Between These Two AAA Protocols

Since TACACS+ allows for more granular control on what users can and cannot do, TACACS+ has more AVPs, which allows the network administrator to define ACLs, filters, user privileges, and much more. Table 17-2 points out the differences between RADIUS and TACACS+.

So, RADIUS is the appropriate protocol when simplistic username/password authentication can take place and users only need an Accept or Deny for obtaining access, as in ISPs. TACACS+ is the better choice for environments that require more sophisticated authentication steps and tighter control over more complex authorization activities, as in corporate networks.

Diameter

Diameter is a protocol that has been developed to build upon the functionality of RADIUS and overcome many of its limitations. The creators of this protocol decided to call it Diameter as a play on the term RADIUS—as in *the diameter is twice the radius.*

Diameter is another AAA protocol that provides the same type of functionality as RADIUS and TACACS+ but also provides more flexibility and capabilities to meet the demands of today's complex and diverse networks. Today, we want our wireless devices and smartphones to be able to authenticate themselves to our networks, and we use roaming protocols, Mobile IP, Ethernet over PPP, Voice over IP (VoIP), and other crazy stuff that the traditional AAA protocols cannot keep up with. So the smart people came up with a new AAA protocol, Diameter, that can deal with these issues and many more.

Mobile IP

This technology allows a user to move from one network to another and still use the same IP address. It is an improvement upon the IP protocol because it allows a user to have a *home IP address*, associated with his home network, and a *care-of address*. The care-of address changes as the user moves from one network to the other. All traffic that is addressed to his home IP address is forwarded to his care-of address.

The Diameter protocol consists of two portions. The first is the base protocol, which provides the secure communication among Diameter entities, feature discovery, and version negotiation. The second is the extensions, which are built on top of the base protocol to allow various technologies to use Diameter for authentication.

Up until the conception of Diameter, the Internet Engineering Task Force (IETF) had individual working groups who defined how VoIP, Fax over IP (FoIP), Mobile IP, and remote authentication protocols work. Defining and implementing them individually in any network can easily result in too much confusion and interoperability. It requires customers to roll out and configure several different policy servers and increases the cost with each new added service. Diameter provides a base protocol, which defines header formats, security options, commands, and AVPs. This base protocol allows for extensions to tie in other services, such as VoIP, FoIP, Mobile IP, wireless, and cell phone authentication. So Diameter can be used as an AAA protocol for all of these different uses.

As an analogy, consider a scenario in which ten people all need to get to the same hospital, which is where they all work. They all have different jobs (doctor, lab technician, nurse, janitor, and so on), but they all need to end up at the same location. So, they can either all take their own cars and their own routes to the hospital, which takes up more hospital parking space and requires the gate guard to authenticate each car, or they can take a bus. The bus is the common element (base protocol) to get the individuals (different services) to the same location (networked environment). Diameter provides the common AAA and security framework that different services can work within.

RADIUS and TACACS+ are client/server protocols, which means the server portion cannot send unsolicited commands to the client portion. The server portion can only speak when spoken to. Diameter is a peer-based protocol that allows either end to initiate communication. This functionality allows the Diameter server to send a message to the access server to request the user to provide another authentication credential if she is attempting to access a secure resource.

Diameter is not directly backward-compatible with RADIUS but provides an upgrade path. Diameter uses TCP and AVPs and provides proxy server support. It has better error detection and correction functionality than RADIUS, as well as better failover properties, and thus provides better network resilience.

Diameter has the functionality and ability to provide the AAA functionality for other protocols and services because it has a large AVP set. RADIUS has 2^8 (256) AVPs, while Diameter has 2^{32} (a whole bunch). Recall from earlier in the chapter that AVPs are like boxes drawn on a piece of paper that outline how two entities can communicate back and forth. So, having more AVPs allows for more functionality and services to exist and communicate between systems.

Diameter provides the AAA functionality, as listed next.

Authentication:

- CHAP and EAP
- End-to-end protection of authentication information
- Replay attack protection

Authorization:

- Redirects, secure proxies, relays, and brokers
- State reconciliation
- Unsolicited disconnect
- Reauthorization on demand

Accounting:

- Reporting, roaming operations (ROAMOPS) accounting, event monitoring

Managing the Identity and Access Provisioning Life Cycle

Once an organization develops access control policies and determines the appropriate mechanisms, techniques, and technologies, it needs to implement procedures to ensure that identity and access are deliberately and systematically being issued to (and taken away from) users and systems. Many of us have either heard of or experienced the dismay of discovering that the credentials for someone who was fired months or years ago are still active in a domain controller. Some of us have even had to deal with that account having been used long after the individual left.

Identity and access have a life cycle, as illustrated in Figure 17-11. It begins with provisioning of an account, which we've already touched on in Chapter 16 in the context of registration and proofing of identities. Identities spend most of their lives being used for access control, which, as discussed in this chapter and the previous one, entails identification, authentication, and authorization of accounts. Changes invariably occur in organizations, and these changes impact identity and access control. For example, an employee gets promoted and her authorizations change. When changes occur, we want to ensure that our access control configurations remain up to date and effective. At some point, we need to

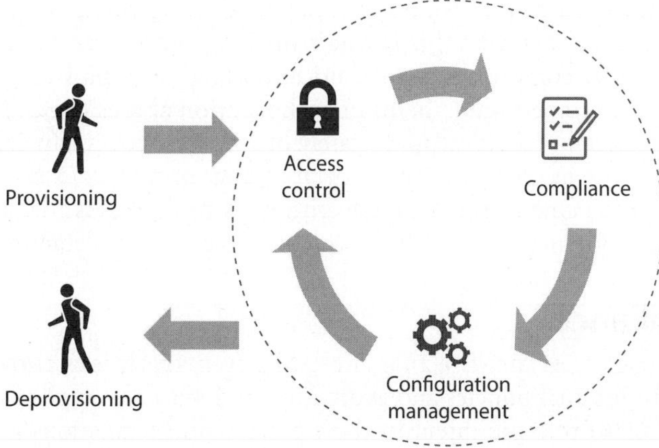

Figure 17-11 The identity and access management life cycle

ensure that we are in compliance with all applicable policies and regulations, so we also have to periodically review all the identities in the organization and their accesses. If all checks out, we let them continue to be used for access control. Inevitably, however, accounts need to be deprovisioned, which pops them out of the life-cycle model.

Provisioning

As introduced in Chapter 5, *provisioning* is the set of all activities required to provide one or more new information services to a user or group of users ("new" meaning previously not available to that user or group). In terms of identification and access management, this pertains to the creation of user objects or accounts and the assignment of permissions to those accounts. Sometimes, the term provisioning is used to describe the whole life cycle, but our focus in this section is on the first phase only, which is generating the account.

Normally, provisioning happens when a new user or system is added to an organization. For people, this is part of onboarding, which we discussed in Chapter 1. It is important to have an established process for ensuring that digital identities are issued only to the right folks. This usually involves reviews and approvals from HR staff, the individual's supervisor, and the IT department. The process is crucial for the rest of the life cycle because it answers the important question "Why did we provision this account?" The answer determines whether the account remains active or is deprovisioned at some point in the future. Keep in mind that some accounts are used for long periods of time, and rationales for provisioning accounts that were obvious in the beginning may be forgotten with the passage of time and with staffing changes.

Identity and access provisioning also pertains to system accounts, which are usually associated with services and automated agents and oftentimes require privileged access. A challenge here is that most organizations have a lot of system accounts that are largely invisible on a day-to-day basis. Just as for user identity and access, the trick here is to document what accounts were created, where they were created, and why they were created.

Access Control

We've already covered much of what happens in this phase of the life cycle, but it bears highlighting the fact that this is where most of the risk resides. Most security incidents are enabled by compromised authentication (e.g., user passwords are guessed, allowing adversaries to impersonate them) or authorization abuses (e.g., data to which users have legitimate access is used inappropriately or leaked). This is why it is essential to continuously monitor access controls, detect suspicious or malicious events, and generate alerts automatically. One of the most effective ways to do this is through the use of user and entity behavior analytics (UEBA), which we'll discuss in detail in Chapter 21.

Compliance

Monitoring access and detecting interesting events early is essential to ensure compliance both with internal policies and procedures and with any applicable external regulations. Keep in mind that the intent of these policies and regulations is to ensure information systems security, so being able to attest that we are doing things "by the book" is good all around. It gives us personal peace of mind, protects our systems, and ensures our organizations don't get hit with hefty fines. Note that rights and permission reviews have been incorporated into many regulatory-induced processes. For example, as part of the Sarbanes-Oxley Act (SOX) regulations (introduced in Chapter 1), managers have to review their employees' permissions to data on an annual basis.

Compliance can be summed up in three major components:

- Written standards must exist that assign responsibilities to individuals. This could range from acceptable use policies to national laws like SOX.
- There must be a program by which applicable aspects of the security program are compared against the standard. In terms of identity and access management, this program is centered on user and system access reviews.
- Any discrepancies between the standard and reality must be addressed and resolved in a systemic way that ensures the issues are not likely to resurface next month.

We've already covered the first part (policies, regulations, and such) in Chapter 3, so let's look at user and system access reviews (in turn) and resolving discrepancies.

User Access Review

One day, every user account will be deprovisioned because no one works (or lives) forever. It may also be necessary to change permissions (such as when a user changes roles) or temporarily disable accounts (such as when a user goes on an extended leave of absence or is under some sort of adverse administrative action). The list of conditions under which an account is disabled or deprovisioned will vary by organization, but we all need to have such a list. We need a process by which we periodically (or upon certain conditions) check every user account against that list. The purpose of these user access reviews is to ensure we don't have excessive authorizations or active accounts that are no longer needed.

Ideally, we conduct reviews periodically (say, every six months) for all accounts (or, at least, a sampling of them). A review should also be triggered by certain administrative actions. A best practice is to integrate these reviews into the HR procedures because HR typically is involved in administrative actions anyway. Though it is obvious that user accounts should be disabled or deprovisioned when an employee is terminated, other situations are not as clear-cut, such as the following, and require a deliberate review by the individual's supervisor and/or the IT department:

- Promotion
- Transfer
- Extended vacation or sabbatical
- Hospitalization
- Long-term disability (with an expected future return)
- Investigation for possible wrongdoing
- Unexpected disappearance

System Account Access Review

As with user access, we should conduct system account access reviews both periodically and when certain conditions are met. Though HR would not be involved in these reviews, the principle is the same: every system account eventually needs to be changed, disabled, or deprovisioned. What makes reviewing systems accounts a bit trickier is that it is easy to forget they exist in the first place. It is not unusual for a service to require multiple accounts with which nobody interacts directly and yet are absolutely critical for the system. What's worse, sometimes software updates can remove the need for legacy system accounts that are not deprovisioned as part of the updating process and remain in place as a potential vulnerability. A systematic approach to system account access review is your best way to avoid ending up with unneeded, potentially privileged accounts.

Although these two terms are synonymous to most IT and security professionals, the CISSP CBK distinguishes between a system account and a service account. Technically, a *system account* is created by the operating system for use by a particular process, not by a human. Most OSs have a "system" context in which they run privileged operations. A *service account* is a system account for a process that runs as a service (i.e., it listens for and responds to requests from other processes).

Resolving Discrepancies

So, you just completed an account access review (user, service, and/or system) and have found some discrepancies. What do you do? A possible approach would be to change, disable, or deprovision the accounts and go on your merry way. This solves the immediate problem but may result in your having to repeat this process after every review if the cause for the discrepancies is systemic. That is why you are much better off treating the discrepancies as symptoms of a problem, not the end problems themselves.

A good approach is to list all the deficiencies and, for each one, answer the four guiding questions listed here. For each, we offer an example answer for illustration purposes.

- *What happened?* You came across an account used by a service that was removed during a software upgrade months ago. The service is gone, but its account remains.
- *Why did it happen?* Because your team didn't fully understand the impact of the software update and didn't check the state of the system after it was applied.
- *What can we infer from it about discrepancies in other places and/or the future?* There may be other similarly orphaned service accounts in the environment, so we should audit them all.
- *How do we best correct this across the board?* We should create a process by which all services are characterized prior to being updated, the effects of the update are determined ahead of time, and any changes to access controls are implemented during the update process. This should all be included in our configuration management program going forward.

The example shouldn't be surprising, since many of us have come across this (or a very similar) situation. We find an account that is still enabled even though the staff member left the organization a year ago and we rush to fix it without thinking about how this happened in the first place. Fixing a broken process is way more effective than fixing a single discrepancy that was caused by it, and there is no more important process in the identity and access life cycle than configuration management.

Configuration Management

Configuration management is a broad subject that we'll discuss in detail in Chapter 20. However, with regard to the identity and access management life cycle, it really boils down to having a firm grasp (and control) of all the subjects and objects in our environment and of the manner in which they interrelate. If you think of the identity and access management (IAM) configuration of your systems in this way, you'll see that there are three drivers of change to your systems' configurations: users change, objects change, and authorizations change. The first of these (users change) is covered here in the provisioning and deprovisioning sections. We already gave an example of the second (objects change) in our previous example of a system account access review earlier in this chapter. Let's turn our attention in the sections that follow to what is, perhaps, the thorniest of the three: authorizations change.

Role Definitions

We tend to be very thorough in assigning the right authorizations to our staff members when we onboard them and provision their accounts. Usually, we follow lots of processes and ensure that various forms are signed by the correct people. We tend to not be as thorough, however, when somebody's role in the organization changes. This could be a promotion, a transfer to a new role, or a merger (or split) of roles. It is just as important to be thorough in these cases to ensure we maintain proper access controls.

A good way to do this is for the HR, IT, security, and business teams to jointly develop a role matrix that specifies who should have access to what and to periodically review and update the matrix as needed. Then, whenever there is a personnel action, the HR team notifies the IT staff of it. IT, in turn, updates the person's authorizations and everyone is happy.

More commonly, however, staff members are often assigned more and more access rights and permissions over time as their roles change and they move from one department to another. This is commonly referred to as *authorization creep*. It can be a large risk for an organization because it leads to too many users having too much privileged access to the organization's assets. In the past, it has usually been easier for network administrators to give more access than less, because then the user would not come back and require more work to be done on her profile. It is also difficult to know the exact access levels different individuals require unless something like a role matrix exists. Enforcing least privilege on user accounts should be an ongoing job, which means it should be part of a formal configuration management process.

Privilege Escalation

If we apply the principle of least privilege effectively, then everyone should be running with minimal access to get their day-to-day tasks done. Even system administrators should have to temporarily elevate their privileges to perform sensitive tasks. In Linux environments, this is normally done using the `sudo` command, which temporarily changes the authorizations of a user, typically to the root user. The Windows graphical user interface gives you the option to "run as administrator," which is similar to `sudo` but not as powerful or flexible. If you want that level of power, you need to drop to the Windows command line and use the `runas` command.

Privilege escalation, necessary as it might be, should be minimized in any environment. That means you want the least number of folks with admin privileges running around. It also means that you want to put in place policies regarding when and why account privileges should be escalated. Lastly, you want to log any such escalation so the use of newly escalated privileges use can be audited. We get into managing privileged accounts in Chapter 20, but these principles are worth keeping in mind (and repeating a few times).

Managed Service Accounts

Closely related to privilege escalation is the concept of service accounts that need to be accessible to certain administrators. Service accounts can be tricky because they are typically privileged but are not normally used by a human user. It is (sadly) all too common to see administrators install and configure a service, create an account for it to run under, and forget about the account. Passwords for these accounts are frequently exempt from password policy enforcement (e.g., complexity, expiration), so you can have some well-intentioned admins set an easy-to-remember password (because it could be disastrous if they ever forgot it) that never expired on a privileged account that few knew existed in the first place. Not good.

Microsoft Windows includes a feature that helps solve this challenge. *Managed service accounts (MSAs)* are Active Directory (AD) domain accounts that are used by services and provide automatic password management. MSAs can be used by multiple users and systems without any of them having to know the password. The way MSAs work is that AD creates policy-compliant passwords for these accounts and regularly changes them (every 30 days by default). Systems and users that are authorized to use these accounts need only be authenticated themselves on a domain controller and be included in that MSA's ACL. Think of it as an extension to SSO where you get to be authenticated as yourself or as any MSA that you are authorized to access.

Deprovisioning

As we already said, sooner or later every account should get deprovisioned. For users, this is usually part of the termination procedures we covered in Chapter 1. For system accounts, this could happen because we got rid of a system or because some configuration change rendered an account unnecessary. Whatever the type of account or the reason for getting rid of it, it is important to document the change so we no longer track that account for reviewing purposes.

A potential challenge with deprovisioning accounts is that it could leave orphaned resources. Suppose that Jonathan is the owner of project files on a shared folder to which no one else has access. If he leaves the company and has his account deprovisioned, that shared folder would be left on the server, but nobody (except administrators) could do anything with it. Apart from being wasteful, this situation could hinder the business if those files were important later on. When deprovisioning an account, therefore, it is important to transfer ownership of its resources to someone else.

Controlling Physical and Logical Access

We've focused our discussion so far on logical access control to our information, applications, and systems. The mechanisms we've covered can be implemented at various layers of a network and individual systems. Some controls are core components of operating systems or embedded into applications and devices, and some security controls require third-party add-on packages. Although different controls provide different functionality, they should all work together to keep the bad guys out and the good guys in and to provide the necessary quality of protection.

We also need to consider physical access controls to protect the devices on which these assets run as well as the facilities in which they reside. No organization wants people to be able to walk into their buildings arbitrarily, sit down at an employee's workstation, and be able to access any assets. While the mechanisms we've discussed in this chapter are mostly not applicable to physical security, most of the access control models (with the possible exception of risk-based access control) are.

Information Access Control

Controlling access to information assets is particularly tricky. Sure, we can implement the mechanisms described in the preceding sections to ensure only authorized subjects can read, write, or modify information in digital files. However, information can exist in a multitude of other places. Consider a fancy briefing room with a glass wall or doors leading into it. Inside, one of our staff members is giving a presentation on a product we'll soon be releasing that will turn our company's fortunes around. The slides are being projected, but the presenter provided hard copies for all attendees so they could take notes on them. Consider all the media on which our sensitive product information can exist:

- **Secondary storage** The slides exist in a file somewhere in the presenter's computer or in some network share (though this is probably the easiest medium to secure using the mechanisms discussed in this chapter).
- **Screen** Anyone walking by the room can see (or take a photo of) the slides being presented.
- **Handouts** If the attendees don't protect the hard copies of the slides or dispose of them improperly (say, by dumping them in a trash or recycling bin), the custodial staff (or anyone up for some dumpster diving) could get the information.
- **Voices** Not only can the presenter's remarks be overheard by unauthorized individuals but so can conversations that attendees have with each other in the break area.

The point is that our information access controls need to consider the variety of media and contexts in which sensitive information can exist. This is why it is important to consider both logical and physical controls for it. We've covered the logical side in depth here (though you may want to review Chapter 6 on data security); for a similar coverage of physical security, we refer you to Chapter 10's discussion of site and facility controls.

System and Application Access Control

Systems are a lot more closely aligned with the logical controls we described in this chapter, compared to the information assets we just covered. We kind of lumped all software together when we covered access controls. There is, however, a subtlety between systems and applications that bears pointing out, particularly with regard to the CISSP exam. Technically, a system is a type of software that provides services to other software. Web, e-mail, and authentication services are all examples of systems. An application is a type of software that interacts directly with a human user. A web browser, e-mail client, and even the authentication box that pops up to request your credentials are all examples of applications, as are stand-alone products like word processors and spreadsheets.

Access Control to Devices

All information that is stored in electronic media and all software exist within hardware devices. Whether it is the smartphone in your pocket, the laptop on your desk, or the server in the data center (or the cloud), you have to concern yourself with who can physically access them just as much as you worry about who can logically do so. After all, if an attacker can physically touch a device, then he can own it. We make the threat actors' jobs significantly more difficult by controlling physical access to our devices and assets. We can install and configure physical controls on each computer, such as install locks on the cover so the internal parts cannot be stolen, remove the USB and optical drives to prevent copying of confidential information, and implement a protection device that reduces the electrical emissions to thwart attempts to gather information through airwaves.

Speaking of electrical signals, different types of cabling can be used to carry information throughout a network. As a review of some of the cabling issues from Chapter 14, recall that some cable types have sheaths that protect the data from being affected by the electrical interference of other devices that emit electrical signals. Some types of cable have protection material around each individual wire to ensure there is no crosstalk between the different wires. Choosing the right kind of cable can help protect the devices they connect from accidental or environmental interferences. There is also, of course, the issue of deliberate tapping of these cables. If an adversary cannot get to a device but can tap its network cable, we could have issues unless all traffic is end-to-end encrypted (which it almost never is). Recall that distribution facilities (where one end of these cables terminates) need security controls and that some types of cables (UTP) are easier to tap than others (fiber optic).

Facilities Access Control

We discussed facility security in Chapter 10, but it is worthwhile to review and perhaps extend our conversation around access control. An example of facilities access controls is having a security guard verify individuals' identities prior to allowing them to enter a facility. How might the guard make that decision? In a classified facility, the guard may check that the clearance of the individual meets or exceeds that of the facility she is trying to enter and that she has a need to be there (perhaps from an access roster). This would be a simplified implementation of a MAC model. If the facility had different floors for different departments, another approach would be to check the person's department and grant her access to that floor only, which would be a form of RBAC. We could refine that access control by putting some rules around it, such as access is only granted during working hours, unless the person is an executive or a manager. We would then be using an RB-RBAC model.

These examples are simply meant to illustrate that physical access controls, just like their logical counterparts, should be deliberately designed and implemented. To this end, the models we discussed at the beginning of this chapter are very helpful. They can then inform the specific controls we implement. In the sections that follow, we take a closer look at some of the major considerations when thinking of facilities access control.

Perimeter Security

Perimeter security is concerned with controlling physical access to facilities. How it is implemented depends upon the organization and the security requirements of that environment. One environment may require employees to be authorized by a security guard by showing a security badge that contains a picture identification before being allowed to enter a section. Another environment may require no authentication process and let anyone and everyone into different sections. Perimeter security can also encompass closed-circuit TVs that scan the parking lots and waiting areas, fences surrounding a building, the lighting of walkways and parking areas, motion detectors, sensors, alarms, and the location and visual appearance of a building. These are examples of perimeter security mechanisms that provide physical access control by providing protection for individuals, facilities, and the components within facilities.

Work Area Separation

Some environments might dictate that only particular individuals can access certain areas of the facility. For example, research companies might not want office personnel to be able to enter laboratories, so that they can't disrupt or taint experiments or access test data. Most network administrators allow only network staff in the server rooms and wiring closets to reduce the possibilities of errors or sabotage attempts. In financial institutions, only certain employees can enter the vaults or other restricted areas. These examples of work area separation are physical controls used to support access control and the overall security policy of the company.

Control Zone

An organization's facility should be split up into zones that are based on the sensitivity of the activity that takes place per zone. The front lobby could be considered a public area, the product development area could be considered top secret, and the executive offices could be considered secret. It does not matter what classifications are used, but it should be understood that some areas are more sensitive than others, which will require different access controls based on the needed protection level. The same is true of the organization's network. It should be segmented, and access controls should be chosen for each zone based on the criticality of devices and the sensitivity of data being processed.

Chapter Review

This is one of the more important chapters in the book for a variety of reasons. First, access control is central to security. The models and mechanisms discussed in this chapter are security controls you should know really well and be able to implement in your own organization. Also, the CISSP exam has been known to include lots of questions covering the topics discussed in this chapter, particularly the access control models.

We chose to start this chapter with these models because they set the foundations for the discussion. You may think that they are too theoretical to be useful in your daily job, but you might be surprised how often we've seen them crop up in the real world. They also inform the mechanisms we discussed in more detail, like OAuth, OpenID Connect, and Kerberos. While these technologies are focused on logical access control, we wrapped up the chapter with a section on how physical and logical controls need to work together to protect our organizations.

Quick Review

- An access control mechanism dictates how subjects access objects.
- The reference monitor is an abstract machine that mediates all access subjects have to objects, both to ensure that the subjects have the necessary access rights and to protect the objects from unauthorized access and destructive modification.
- There are six main access control models: discretionary, mandatory, role-based, rule-based, attribute-based, and risk-based.
- Discretionary access control (DAC) enables data owners to dictate what subjects have access to the files and resources they own.
- Access control lists are bound to objects and indicate what subjects can use them.
- The mandatory access control (MAC) model uses a security label system. Users have clearances, and resources have security labels that contain data classifications. MAC systems compare these two attributes to determine access control capabilities.
- The terms "security labels" and "sensitivity labels" can be used interchangeably.
- Role-based access control (RBAC) is based on the user's role and responsibilities (tasks) within the company.
- Rule-based RBAC (RB-RBAC) builds on RBAC by adding "if this, then that" (IFTTT) rules that further restrict access.
- Attribute-based access control (ABAC) is based on attributes of any component of the system. It is the most granular of the access control models.
- Risk-based access control estimates the risk associated with a particular request in real time and, if it doesn't exceed a given threshold, grants the subject access to the requested resource.
- Extensible Markup Language (XML) is a set of rules for encoding documents in machine-readable form to allow for interoperability between various web-based technologies.

- The Service Provisioning Markup Language (SPML) allows for the automation of user management (account creation, amendments, revocation) and access entitlement configuration related to electronically published services across multiple provisioning systems.
- The Security Assertion Markup Language (SAML) allows for the exchange of authentication and authorization data to be shared between security domains.
- Extensible Access Control Markup Language (XACML), which is both a declarative access control policy language implemented in XML and a processing model, describes how to interpret security policies.
- OAuth is an open standard that allows a user to grant authority to some web resource, like a contacts database, to a third party.
- OpenID Connect is an authentication layer built on the OAuth 2.0 protocol that allows transparent authentication and authorization of client resource requests.
- Kerberos is a client/server authentication protocol based on symmetric key cryptography that can provide single sign-on (SSO) for distributed environments.
- The Key Distribution Center (KDC) is the most important component within a Kerberos environment because it holds all users' and services' secret keys, provides an authentication service, and securely distributes keys.
- Kerberos users receive a ticket granting ticket (TGT), which allows them to request access to resources through the ticket granting service (TGS), which in turn generates a new ticket with the session keys.
- The following are weaknesses of Kerberos: the KDC is a single point of failure; it is susceptible to password guessing; session and secret keys are locally stored; KDC needs to always be available; and management of secret keys is required.
- Some examples of remote access control technologies are RADIUS, TACACS+, and Diameter.
- The identity and access provisioning life cycle consists of provisioning, access control, compliance, configuration management, and deprovisioning.
- A system account is created by the operating system for use by a particular process, not by a human. A service account is a system account for a process that runs as a service (i.e., it listens for and responds to requests from other processes).
- Authorization creep takes place when a user gains too much access rights and permissions over time.
- Managed service accounts (MSAs) are Active Directory domain accounts that are used by services and provide automatic password management.

Questions

Please remember that these questions are formatted and asked in a certain way for a reason. Keep in mind that the CISSP exam is asking questions at a conceptual level. Questions may not always have the perfect answer, and the candidate is advised against always looking for the perfect answer. Instead, the candidate should look for the best answer in the list.

1. Which access control method is considered user directed?
   A. Nondiscretionary
   B. Mandatory
   C. Identity-based
   D. Discretionary
2. Which item is not part of a Kerberos authentication implementation?
   A. Message authentication code
   B. Ticket granting service
   C. Authentication service
   D. Users, applications, and services
3. If a company has a high turnover rate, which access control structure is best?
   A. Role-based
   B. Decentralized
   C. Rule-based
   D. Discretionary
4. In discretionary access control security, who has delegation authority to grant access to data?
   A. User
   B. Security officer
   C. Security policy
   D. Owner
5. Who or what determines if an organization is going to operate under a discretionary, mandatory, or nondiscretionary access control model?
   A. Administrator
   B. Security policy
   C. Culture
   D. Security levels
6. Which of the following best describes what role-based access control offers organizations in terms of reducing administrative burdens?
   A. It allows entities closer to the resources to make decisions about who can and cannot access resources.
   B. It provides a centralized approach for access control, which frees up department managers.

C. User membership in roles can be easily revoked and new ones established as job assignments dictate.

D. It enforces enterprise-wide security policies, standards, and guidelines.

Use the following scenario to answer Questions 7–9. Tanya is working with the company's internal software development team. Before a user of an application can access files located on the company's centralized server, the user must present a valid one-time password, which is generated through a challenge/response mechanism. The company needs to tighten access control for these files and reduce the number of users who can access each file. The company is looking to Tanya and her team for solutions to better protect the data that has been classified and deemed critical to the company's missions. Tanya has also been asked to implement a single sign-on technology for all internal users, but she does not have the budget to implement a public key infrastructure.

7. Which of the following best describes what is currently in place?
   A. Capability-based access system
   B. Synchronous tokens that generate one-time passwords
   C. RADIUS
   D. Kerberos
8. Which of the following is one of the easiest and best solutions Tanya can consider for proper data protection?
   A. Implementation of mandatory access control
   B. Implementation of access control lists
   C. Implementation of digital signatures
   D. Implementation of multilevel security
9. Which of the following is the best single sign-on technology for this situation?
   A. PKI
   B. Kerberos
   C. RADIUS
   D. TACACS+

Use the following scenario to answer Questions 10–12. Harry is overseeing a team that has to integrate various business services provided by different company departments into one web portal for both internal employees and external partners. His company has a diverse and heterogeneous environment with different types of systems providing customer relationship management, inventory control, e-mail, and help-desk ticketing capabilities. His team needs to allow different users access to these different services in a secure manner.

10. Which of the following best describes the type of environment Harry's team needs to set up?
    A. RADIUS
    B. Service-oriented architecture
    C. Public key infrastructure
    D. Web services
11. Which of the following best describes the types of languages and/or protocols that Harry needs to ensure are implemented?
    A. Security Assertion Markup Language, Extensible Access Control Markup Language, Service Provisioning Markup Language
    B. Service Provisioning Markup Language, Simple Object Access Protocol, Extensible Access Control Markup Language
    C. Extensible Access Control Markup Language, Security Assertion Markup Language, Simple Object Access Protocol
    D. Service Provisioning Markup Language, Security Association Markup Language
12. The company's partners need to integrate compatible authentication functionality into their web portals to allow for interoperability across the different company boundaries. Which of the following will deal with this issue?
    A. Service Provisioning Markup Language
    B. Simple Object Access Protocol
    C. Extensible Access Control Markup Language
    D. Security Assertion Markup Language

Answers

1. **D.** The discretionary access control (DAC) model allows users, or data owners, the discretion of letting other users access their resources. DAC is implemented by ACLs, which the data owner can configure.
2. **A.** Message authentication code (MAC) is a cryptographic function and is not a key component of Kerberos. Kerberos is made up of a Key Distribution Center (KDC), a realm of principals (users, applications, services), an authentication service, tickets, and a ticket granting service.
3. **A.** A role-based structure is easier on the administrator because she only has to create one role, assign all of the necessary rights and permissions to that role, and plug a user into that role when needed. Otherwise, she would need to assign and extract permissions and rights on all systems as each individual joined the company and left the company.

4. **D.** Although user might seem to be the correct choice, only the data owner can decide who can access the resources she owns. She may or may not be a user. A user is not necessarily the owner of the resource. Only the actual owner of the resource can dictate what subjects can actually access the resource.
5. **B.** The security policy sets the tone for the whole security program. It dictates the level of risk that management and the company are willing to accept. This in turn dictates the type of controls and mechanisms to put in place to ensure this level of risk is not exceeded.
6. **C.** With role-based access control, an administrator does not need to revoke and reassign permissions to individual users as they change jobs. Instead, the administrator assigns permissions and rights to a role, and users are plugged into those roles.
7. **A.** A capability-based access control system means that the subject (user) has to present something, which outlines what it can access. The item can be a ticket, token, or key. A capability is tied to the subject for access control purposes. A synchronous token is not being used, because the scenario specifically states that a challenge\response mechanism is being used, which indicates an asynchronous token.
8. **B.** Systems that provide mandatory access control (MAC) and multilevel security are very specialized, require extensive administration, are expensive, and reduce user functionality. Implementing these types of systems is not the easiest approach out of the list. Since there is no budget for a PKI, digital signatures cannot be used because they require a PKI. In most environments, access control lists (ACLs) are in place and can be modified to provide tighter access control. ACLs are bound to objects and outline what operations specific subjects can carry out on them.
9. **B.** The scenario specifies that PKI cannot be used, so the first option is not correct. Kerberos is based upon symmetric cryptography; thus, it does not need a PKI. RADIUS and TACACS+ are remote centralized access control protocols.
10. **B.** A service-oriented architecture (SOA) will allow Harry's team to create a centralized web portal and offer the various services needed by internal and external entities.
11. **C.** The most appropriate languages and protocols for the purpose laid out in the scenario are Extensible Access Control Markup Language, Security Assertion Markup Language, and Simple Object Access Protocol. Harry's group is not necessarily overseeing account provisioning, so the Service Provisioning Markup Language is not necessary, and there is no language called "Security Association Markup Language."
12. **D.** Security Assertion Markup Language allows the exchange of authentication and authorization data to be shared between security domains. It is one of the most commonly used approaches to allow for single sign-on capabilities within a web-based environment.

PART VI

Security Assessment and Testing

CHAPTER 18

Security Assessments

This chapter presents the following:

- Test, assessment, and audit strategies
- Testing technical security controls
- Conducting or facilitating security audits

Trust, but verify.

—Russian proverb

You can hire the best people, develop sound policies and procedures, and deploy world-class technology in an effort to secure your information systems, but if you do not regularly assess the effectiveness of these measures, your organization will not be secure for long. Unfortunately, thousands of well-intentioned organizations have learned the truth of this statement the hard way, realizing only after a security breach has occurred that the state-of-the-art controls they put into place initially have become less effective over time. So, unless your organization is continuously assessing and improving its security posture, that posture will become ineffective over time.

This chapter covers some of the most important elements of security assessments and testing. It is divided into three sections. We start by discussing assessment, test, and audit strategies, particularly how to design and assess them. From there, we get into the nitty-gritty of various common forms of testing with which you should be familiar. The third and final section discusses the various kinds of formal security audits and how you can conduct or facilitate them.

Test, Assessment, and Audit Strategies

Let's start by establishing some helpful definitions in the context of information systems security. A *test* is a procedure that records some set of properties or behaviors in a system being tested and compares them against predetermined standards. If you install a new device on your network, you might want to test its attack surface by running a network scanner against it, recording the open ports, and then comparing them against the appropriate security standards used in your organization. An *assessment* is a series of planned tests that are somehow related to each other. For example, we could conduct a vulnerability assessment against a new software system to determine how secure it is.

This assessment would include some specific (and hopefully relevant) vulnerability tests together with static and dynamic analysis of its software. An *audit* is a systematic assessment of significant importance to the organization that determines whether the system or process being audited satisfies some external standards. By "external" we mean that the organization being audited did not author the standards all by itself.

EXAM TIP You don't have to memorize these definitions. They are presented simply to give you an idea of the different scopes. Many security professionals use the terms almost interchangeably.

Each of these three types of system evaluations plays an important role in ensuring the security of our organizations. Our job as cybersecurity leaders is to integrate them into holistic strategies that, when properly executed, give us a complete and accurate picture of our security posture. It all starts with the risk management concepts we discussed in Chapter 2. Remember that risks determine which security controls we use, which are the focus of any tests, assessments, or audits we perform. So, a good security assessment strategy verifies that we are sufficiently protected against the risks we're tracking.

The security assessment strategy guides the development of standard testing and assessment procedures. This standardization is important because it ensures these activities are done in a consistent, repeatable, and cost-effective manner. We'll cover testing procedures later in this chapter, so let's take a look at how to design and validate a security assessment.

Designing an Assessment

The first step in designing anything is to figure out what it is that we are trying to accomplish. Are we getting ready for an external audit? Did we suffer a security incident because a control was not properly implemented? The answers to these sample questions point to significantly different types of assessment. In the first case, the assessment would be a very broad effort to verify an external standard with which we are supposed to be compliant. In the second case, the assessment would be focused on a specific control, so it would be much narrower in scope. Let's elaborate on the second case as we develop a notional assessment plan.

Suppose the security incident happened because someone clicked a link on a phishing e-mail and downloaded malware that the endpoint detection and response (EDR) solution was able to block. The EDR solution worked fine, but we are now concerned about our e-mail security controls. The objective of our assessment, therefore, is to determine the effectiveness of our e-mail defenses.

Once we have the objective identified, we can determine the necessary scope to accomplish it. When we talk about the scope of an assessment, we really mean which specific controls we will test. In our example, we would probably want to look at our e-mail security gateway, but we should also look at our staff members' security awareness. Next, we have to decide how many e-mail messages and how many users we need to assess to have confidence in our results.

The scope, in turn, informs the methods we use. We'll cover some of the testing techniques shortly, but it's important to note that it's not just *what* we do but *how* we do it that matters. We should develop standardized methodologies so that different tests are consistent and comparable. Otherwise, we won't necessarily know whether our posture is deteriorating from one assessment to the next.

Another reason to standardize the methodologies is to ensure we take into account business and operational impacts. For example, if we decide to test the e-mail security gateway using a penetration test, then there is a chance that we will interfere with e-mail service availability. This could present operational risks that we need to mitigate. Furthermore, on the off-chance that we break something during our assessment, we need to have a contingency plan that allows for the quick restoration of all services and capabilities.

A key decision is whether the assessment will be performed by an internal team or by a third party. If you don't have the in-house expertise, then this decision may very well already have been made for you. But even if your team has this expertise, you may still choose to bring in external auditors for any of a variety of reasons. For example, there may be a regulatory requirement that an external party test your systems; or you may want to benchmark your own internal assets against an external team; or perhaps your own team of testers is not large enough to cover all the auditing requirements and thus you want to bring in outside help.

Finally, once the assessment plan is complete, we need to get it approved for execution. This doesn't just involve our direct bosses but should also involve any stakeholders that might be affected (especially if something goes wrong and services are interrupted). The approval is not just for the plan itself, but also for any needed resources (e.g., funding for an external assessor) as well as for the scheduling. There is nothing worse than to schedule a security assessment that we later find out coincides with a big event like end-of-month accounting and reporting.

Validating an Assessment

Once the tests are over and the interpretation and prioritization are done, management will have in its hands a compilation of many of the ways the organization could be successfully attacked. This is the input to the next cycle in the remediation strategy. Every organization has only so much money, time, and personnel to commit to defending its network, and thus can mitigate only so much of the total risk. After balancing the risks and risk appetite of the organization and the costs of possible mitigations and the value gained from each, management must direct the system and security administrators as to where to spend those limited resources. An oversight program is required to ensure that the mitigations work as expected and that the estimated cost of each mitigation action is closely tracked by the actual cost of implementation. Any time the cost rises significantly or the value is found to be far below what was expected, the process should be briefly paused and reevaluated. It may be that a risk-versus-cost option initially considered less desirable now makes more sense than continuing with the chosen path.

Finally, when all is well and the mitigations are underway, everyone can breathe easier…except the security engineer who has the task of monitoring vulnerability announcements and discussion mailing lists, as well as the early warning services offered by some vendors. To put it another way, the risk environment keeps changing. Between tests, monitoring may make the organization aware of newly discovered vulnerabilities that would be found the next time the test is run but that are too high risk to allow to wait that long. And so another, smaller cycle of mitigation decisions and actions must be taken, and then it is time to run the tests again.

Table 18-1 provides an example of a testing schedule that each operations and security department should develop and carry out.

Test Type	Frequency	Benefits
Network scanning	Continuously to quarterly	• Enumerates the network structure and determines the set of active hosts and associated software • Identifies unauthorized hosts connected to a network • Identifies open ports • Identifies unauthorized services
Log reviews	Daily for critical systems	• Validates that the system is operating according to policy
Password cracking	Continuously to same frequency as expiration policy	• Verifies the policy is effective in producing passwords that are difficult to break • Verifies that users select passwords compliant with the organization's security policy
Vulnerability scanning	Quarterly or bimonthly (more often for high-risk systems), or whenever the vulnerability database is updated	• Enumerates the network structure and determines the set of active hosts and associated software • Identifies a target set of computers to focus vulnerability analysis • Identifies potential vulnerabilities on the target set • Validates operating systems and major applications are up to date with security patches and software versions
Penetration testing	Annually	• Determines how vulnerable an organization's network is to penetration and the level of damage that can be incurred • Tests the IT staff's response to perceived security incidents and their knowledge and implementation of the organization's security policy and the system's security requirements
Integrity checkers	Monthly and in case of a suspicious event	• Detects unauthorized file modifications

Table 18-1 Example Testing Schedules for Each Operations and Security Department

Testing Technical Controls

A *technical control* is a security control implemented through the use of an IT asset. This asset is usually, but not always, some sort of software or hardware that is configured in a particular way. When we test our technical controls, we are verifying their ability to mitigate the risks that we identified in our risk management process (see Chapter 2 for a detailed discussion). This linkage between controls and the risks they are meant to mitigate is important because we need to understand the context in which specific controls were implemented.

Once we understand what a technical control was intended to accomplish, we are able to select the proper means of testing whether it is being effective. We may be better off testing third-party software for vulnerabilities than attempting a code review. As security professionals, we must be familiar, and ideally experienced, with the most common approaches to testing technical controls so that we are able to select the right one for the job at hand.

Vulnerability Testing

Vulnerability testing, whether manual, automated, or—preferably—a combination of both, requires staff and/or consultants with a deep security background and the highest level of trustworthiness. Even the best automated vulnerability scanning tool will produce output that can be misinterpreted as crying wolf (false positive) when there is only a small puppy in the room, or alert you to something that is indeed a vulnerability but that either does not matter to your environment or is adequately compensated for elsewhere. There may also be two individual vulnerabilities that exist, which by themselves are not very important but when put together are critical. And, of course, false negatives will also crop up, such as an obscure element of a single vulnerability that matters greatly to your environment but is not called out by the tool.

NOTE Before carrying out vulnerability testing, a written agreement from management is required! This protects the tester against prosecution for doing his job and ensures there are no misunderstandings by providing in writing what the tester should—and should not—do.

The goals of the assessment are to

- Evaluate the true security posture of an environment (don't cry wolf, as discussed earlier).
- Identify as many vulnerabilities as possible, with honest evaluations and prioritizations of each.
- Test how systems react to certain circumstances and attacks, to learn not only what the known vulnerabilities are (such as this version of the database, that version of the operating system, or a user ID with no password set) but also how the unique elements of the environment might be abused (SQL injection attacks, buffer overflows, and process design flaws that facilitate social engineering).

- Before the scope of the test is decided and agreed upon, the tester must explain the testing ramifications. Vulnerable systems could be knocked offline by some of the tests, and production could be negatively affected by the loads the tests place on the systems.

Management must understand that results from the test are just a "snapshot in time." As the environment changes, new vulnerabilities can arise. Management should also understand that various types of assessments are possible, each one able to expose different kinds of vulnerabilities in the environment, and each one limited in the completeness of results it can offer:

- *Personnel testing* includes reviewing employee tasks and thus identifying vulnerabilities in the standard practices and procedures that employees are instructed to follow, demonstrating social engineering attacks and the value of training users to detect and resist such attacks, and reviewing employee policies and procedures to ensure those security risks that cannot be reduced through physical and logical controls are met with the final control category: administrative.
- *Physical testing* includes reviewing facility and perimeter protection mechanisms. For instance, do the doors actually close automatically, and does an alarm sound if a door is held open too long? Are the interior protection mechanisms of server rooms, wiring closets, sensitive systems, and assets appropriate? (For example, is the badge reader working, and does it really limit access to only authorized personnel?) Is dumpster diving a threat? (In other words, is sensitive information being discarded without proper destruction?) And what about protection mechanisms for manmade, natural, or technical threats? Is there a fire suppression system? Does it work, and is it safe for the people and the equipment in the building? Are sensitive electronics kept above raised floors so they survive a minor flood? And so on.
- *System and network testing* are perhaps what most people think of when discussing information security vulnerability testing. For efficiency, an automated scanning product identifies known system vulnerabilities, and some may (if management has signed off on the performance impact and the risk of disruption) attempt to exploit vulnerabilities.

Because a security assessment is a point-in-time snapshot of the state of an environment, assessments should be performed regularly. Lower-priority, better-protected, and less-at-risk parts of the environment may be scanned once or twice a year. High-priority, more vulnerable targets, such as e-commerce web server complexes and the middleware just behind them, should be scanned nearly continuously.

To the degree automated tools are used, more than one tool—or a different tool on consecutive tests—should be used. No single tool knows or finds every known vulnerability. The vendors of different scanning tools update their tools' vulnerability databases at different rates, and may add particular vulnerabilities in different orders. Always update the vulnerability database of each tool just before the tool is used. Similarly, from time to time different experts should run the test and/or interpret the results. No single expert always sees everything there is to be seen in the results.

Most networks consist of many heterogeneous devices, each of which will likely have its own set of potential vulnerabilities, as shown in Figure 18-1. The potential issues we would seek in, say, the perimeter router ("1." in Figure 18-1) are very different than those in a wireless access point (WAP) ("7." in Figure 18-1) or a back-end database management server (DBMS) ("11." in Figure 18-1). Vulnerabilities in each of these devices, in turn, will depend on the specific hardware, software, and configurations in use. Even if you were able to find an individual or tool who had expert knowledge on the myriad of devices and device-specific security issues, that person or tool would come with its own inherent biases. It is best to leverage team/tool heterogeneity in order to improve the odds of covering blind spots.

Other Vulnerability Types

As noted earlier, vulnerability scans find the potential vulnerabilities. Penetration testing is required to identify those vulnerabilities that can actually be exploited in the environment and cause damage.

Commonly exploited vulnerabilities include the following:

- **Kernel flaws** These are problems that occur below the level of the user interface, deep inside the operating system. Any flaw in the kernel that can be reached by an attacker, if exploitable, gives the attacker the most powerful level of control over the system.

  Countermeasure: Ensure that security patches to operating systems—after sufficient testing—are promptly deployed in the environment to keep the window of vulnerability as small as possible.

- **Buffer overflows** Poor programming practices, or sometimes bugs in libraries, allow more input than the program has allocated space to store it. This overwrites data or program memory after the end of the allocated buffer, and sometimes allows the attacker to inject program code and then cause the processor to execute it. This gives the attacker the same level of access as that held by the program that was attacked. If the program was run as an administrative user or by the system itself, this can mean complete access to the system.

  Countermeasure: Good programming practices and developer education, automated source code scanners, enhanced programming libraries, and strongly typed languages that disallow buffer overflows are all ways of reducing this extremely common vulnerability.

- **Symbolic links** Though the attacker may be properly blocked from seeing or changing the content of sensitive system files and data, if a program follows a symbolic link (a stub file that redirects the access to another place) and the attacker can compromise the symbolic link, then the attacker may be able to gain unauthorized access. (Symbolic links are used in Unix and Linux systems.) This may allow the attacker to damage important data and/or gain privileged access to the system. A historical example of this was to use a symbolic link to cause a

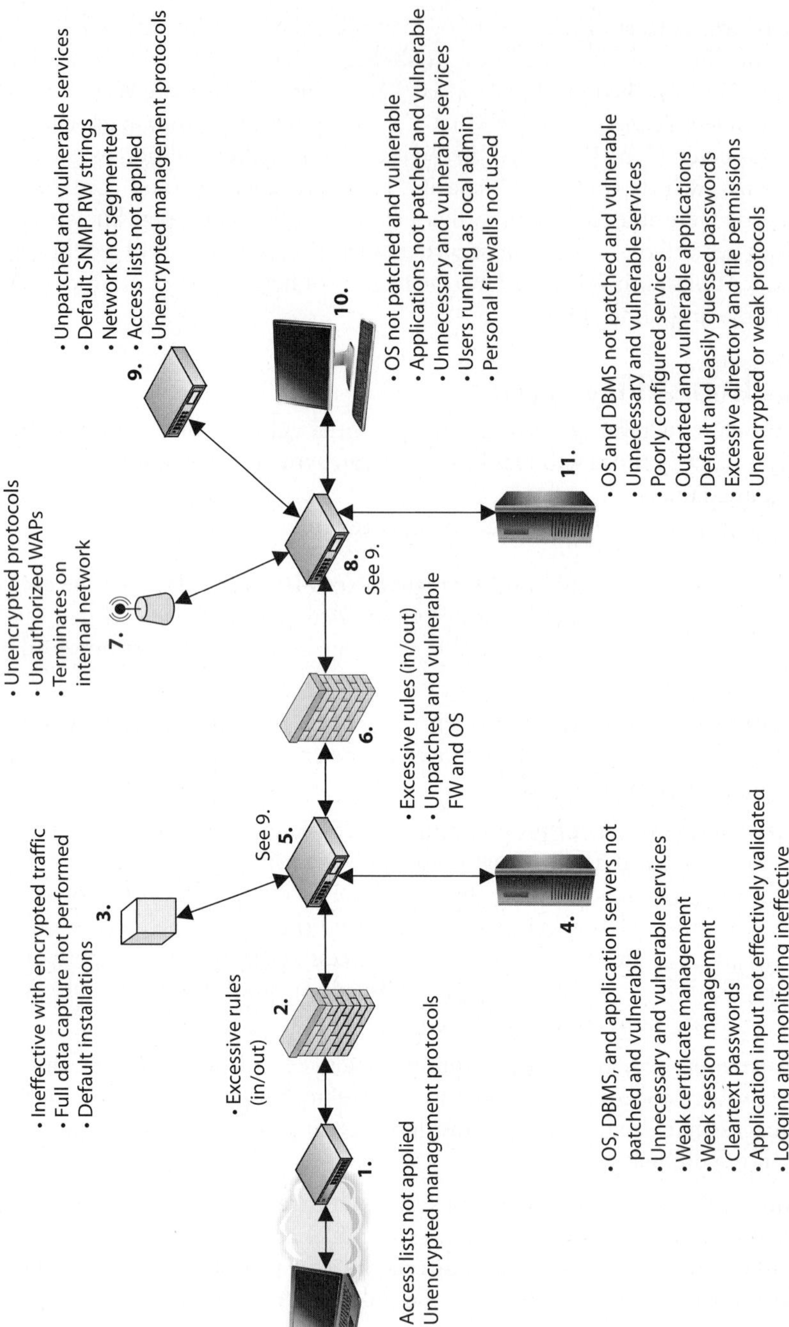

Figure 18-1 Vulnerabilities in heterogeneous networks

program to delete a password database, or replace a line in the password database with characters that, in essence, created a password-less root-equivalent account.

Countermeasure: Programs, and especially scripts, must be written to ensure that the full path to the file cannot be circumvented.

- **File descriptor attacks** File descriptors are numbers many operating systems use to represent open files in a process. Certain file descriptor numbers are universal, meaning the same thing to all programs. If a program makes unsafe use of a file descriptor, an attacker may be able to cause unexpected input to be provided to the program, or cause output to go to an unexpected place with the privileges of the executing program.

  Countermeasure: Good programming practices and developer education, automated source code scanners, and application security testing are all ways of reducing this type of vulnerability.

- **Race conditions** Race conditions exist when the design of a program puts it in a vulnerable condition before ensuring that those vulnerable conditions are mitigated. Examples include opening temporary files without first ensuring the files cannot be read or written to by unauthorized users or processes, and running in privileged mode or instantiating dynamic link library (DLL) functions without first verifying that the DLL path is secure. Either of these may allow an attacker to cause the program (with its elevated privileges) to read or write unexpected data or to perform unauthorized commands. An example of a race condition is a time-of-check to time-of-use (TOC/TOU) attack, discussed in Chapter 2.

  Countermeasure: Good programming practices and developer education, automated source code scanners, and application security testing are all ways of reducing this type of vulnerability.

- **File and directory permissions** Many of the previously described attacks rely on inappropriate file or directory permissions—that is, an error in the access control of some part of the system, on which a more secure part of the system depends. Also, if a system administrator makes a mistake that results in decreasing the security of the permissions on a critical file, such as making a password database accessible to regular users, an attacker can take advantage of this to add an unauthorized user to the password database or an untrusted directory to the DLL search path.

  Countermeasure: File integrity checkers, which should also check expected file and directory permissions, can detect such problems in a timely fashion, hopefully before an attacker notices and exploits them.

Many, many types of vulnerabilities exist, and we have covered some, but certainly not all, here in this book. The previous list includes only a few specific vulnerabilities you should be aware of for exam purposes.

Vulnerability Scanning Recap

Vulnerability scanners provide the following capabilities:

- The identification of active hosts on the network
- The identification of active and vulnerable services (ports) on hosts
- The identification of operating systems
- The identification of vulnerabilities associated with discovered operating systems and applications
- The identification of misconfigured settings
- Test for compliance with host applications' usage/security policies
- The establishment of a foundation for penetration testing

Penetration Testing

Penetration testing (also known as *pen testing*) is the process of simulating attacks on a network and its systems at the request of the owner, senior management. Penetration testing uses a set of procedures and tools designed to test and possibly bypass the security controls of a system. Its goal is to measure an organization's level of resistance to an attack and to uncover any exploitable weaknesses within the environment. Organizations need to determine the effectiveness of their security measures and not just trust the promises of the security vendors. Good computer security is based on reality, not on some lofty goals of how things are supposed to work.

A penetration test emulates the same methods attackers would use. Attackers can be clever, creative, and resourceful in their techniques, so penetration test attacks should align with the newest hacking techniques along with strong foundational testing methods. The test should look at each and every computer in the environment, as shown in Figure 18-2, because an attacker will not necessarily scan one or two computers only and call it a day.

The type of penetration test that should be used depends on the organization, its security objectives, and the management's goals. Some organizations perform periodic penetration tests on themselves using different types of tools. Other organizations ask a third party to perform the vulnerability and penetration tests to provide a more objective view.

Penetration tests can evaluate web servers, Domain Name System (DNS) servers, router configurations, workstation vulnerabilities, access to sensitive information, open ports, and available services' properties that a real attacker might use to compromise the organization's overall security. Some tests can be quite intrusive and disruptive. The timeframe for the tests should be agreed upon so productivity is not affected and personnel can bring systems back online if necessary.

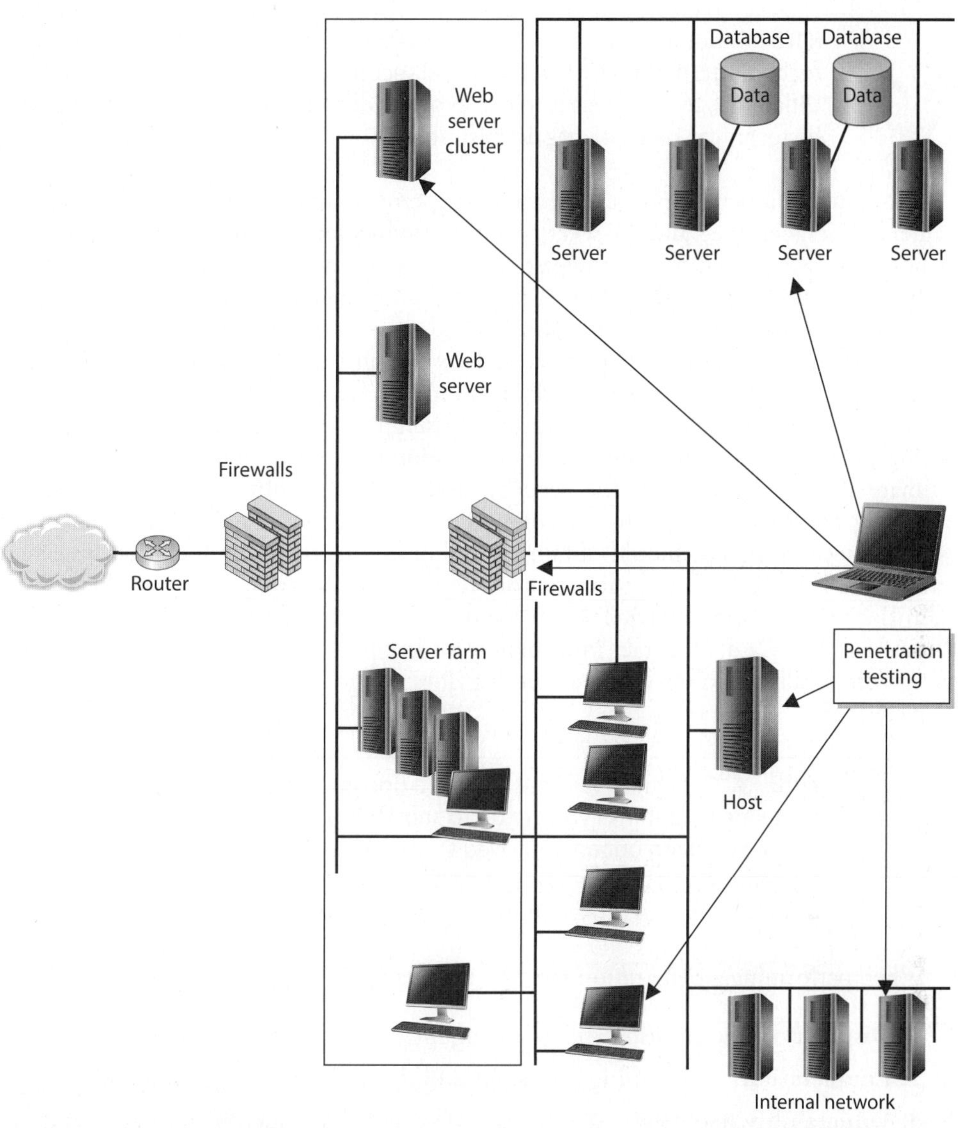

Figure 18-2 Penetration testing is used to prove an attacker can actually compromise systems.

NOTE Penetration tests are not necessarily restricted to information technology, but may include physical security as well as personnel security. Ultimately, the purpose is to compromise one or more controls, which could be technical, physical, or administrative.

The result of a penetration test is a report given to management that describes the vulnerabilities identified and the severity of those vulnerabilities, along with descriptions of how they were exploited by the testers. The report should also include suggestions on how to deal with the vulnerabilities properly. From there, it is up to management to determine how to address the vulnerabilities and what countermeasures to implement.

It is critical that senior management be aware of any risks involved in performing a penetration test before it gives the authorization for one. In rare instances, a system or application may be taken down inadvertently using the tools and techniques employed during the test. As expected, the goal of penetration testing is to identify vulnerabilities, estimate the true protection the security mechanisms within the environment are providing, and see how suspicious activity is reported—but accidents can and do happen.

Security professionals should obtain an authorization letter that includes the extent of the testing authorized, and this letter or memo should be available to members of the team during the testing activity. This type of letter is commonly referred to as a "Get Out of Jail Free Card." Contact information for key personnel should also be available, along with a call tree in the event something does not go as planned and a system must be recovered.

NOTE A "Get Out of Jail Free Card" is a document you can present to someone who thinks you are up to something malicious, when in fact you are carrying out an approved test. More than that, it's also the legal agreement you have between you and your customer that protects you from liability, and prosecution.

When performing a penetration test, the team goes through a five-step process:

1. **Discovery** Footprinting and gathering information about the target
2. **Enumeration** Performing port scans and resource identification methods
3. **Vulnerability mapping** Identifying vulnerabilities in identified systems and resources
4. **Exploitation** Attempting to gain unauthorized access by exploiting vulnerabilities

5. **Report to management** Delivering to management documentation of test findings along with suggested countermeasures

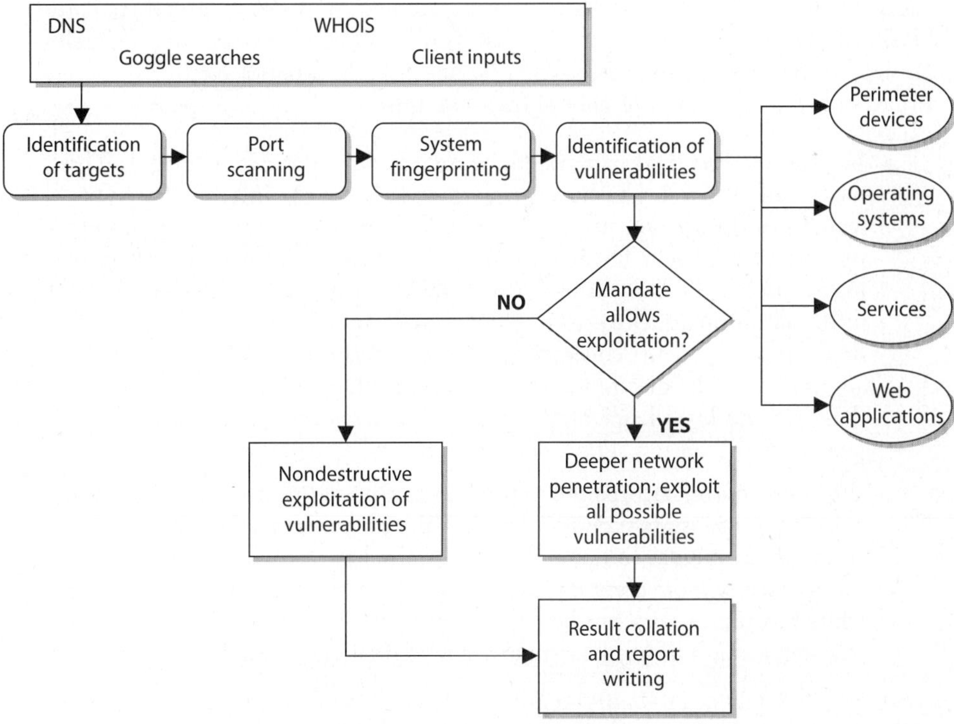

The penetration testing team can have varying degrees of knowledge about the penetration target before the tests are actually carried out:

- **Zero knowledge** The team does not have any knowledge of the target and must start from ground zero.
- **Partial knowledge** The team has some information about the target.
- **Full knowledge** The team has intimate knowledge of the target.

Security testing of an environment may take several forms, in the sense of the degree of knowledge the tester is permitted to have up front about the environment, and also the degree of knowledge the environment is permitted to have up front about the tester.

Tests can be conducted externally (from a remote location) or internally (meaning the tester is within the network). Combining both can help better understand the full scope of threats from either domain (internal and external).

Penetration tests may be blind, double-blind, or targeted. A *blind test* is one in which the testers only have publicly available data to work with (which is also known as zero knowledge or black box testing). The network security staff is aware that this type of test will take place, and will be on the lookout for pen tester activities. Part of the planning

Vulnerability and Penetration Testing: What Color Is Your Box?

Vulnerability testing and penetration testing come in boxes of at least three colors: black, white, and gray. The color, of course, is metaphorical, but security professionals need to be aware of the three types. None is clearly superior to the others in all situations, so it is up to us to choose the right approach for our purposes.

- *Black box testing* treats the system being tested as completely opaque. This means that the tester has no *a priori* knowledge of the internal design or features of the system. All knowledge will come to the tester only through the assessment itself. This approach simulates an external attacker best and may yield insights into information leaks that can give an adversary better information on attack vectors. The disadvantage of black box testing is that it probably won't cover all of the internal controls since some of them are unlikely to be discovered in the course of the audit. Another issue is that, with no knowledge of the innards of the system, the test team may inadvertently target a subsystem that is critical to daily operations.
- *White box testing* affords the pen tester complete knowledge of the inner workings of the system even before the first scan is performed. This approach allows the test team to target specific internal controls and features and should yield a more complete assessment of the system. The downside is that white box testing may not be representative of the behaviors of an external attacker, though it may be a more accurate depiction of an insider threat.
- *Gray box testing* meets somewhere between the other two approaches. Some, but not all, information on the internal workings is provided to the test team. This helps guide their tactics toward areas we want to have thoroughly tested, while also allowing for a degree of realism in terms of discovering other features of the system. This approach mitigates the issues with both white and black box testing.

for this type of test involves determining what actions, if any, the defenders are allowed to take. Stopping every detected attack will slow down the pen testing team and may not show the depths they could've reached without forewarning to the staff.

A *double-blind test* (stealth assessment) is also a blind test to the assessors, as mentioned previously, but in this case the network security staff is not notified. This enables the test to evaluate the network's security level and the staff's responses, log monitoring, and escalation processes, and is a more realistic demonstration of the likely success or failure of an attack.

Targeted tests can involve external consultants and internal staff carrying out focused tests on specific areas of interest. For example, before a new application is rolled out, the team might test it for vulnerabilities before installing it into production. Another example is to focus specifically on systems that carry out e-commerce transactions and not the other daily activities of the organization.

Vulnerability Test vs. Penetration Test

A vulnerability assessment identifies a wide range of vulnerabilities in the environment. This is commonly carried out through a scanning tool. The idea is to identify any vulnerabilities that *potentially* could be used to compromise the security of our systems. By contrast, in a penetration test, the security professional exploits one or more vulnerabilities to prove to the customer (or your boss) that a hacker can *actually* gain access to the organization's resources.

It is important that the team start off with only basic user-level access to properly simulate different attacks. The team needs to utilize a variety of different tools and attack methods and look at all possible vulnerabilities because actual attackers only need to find one vulnerability that the defenders missed.

Red Teaming

While penetration testing is intended to uncover as many exploitable vulnerabilities as possible in the allotted time, it doesn't really emulate threat actor behaviors all that well. Adversaries almost always have very specific objectives when they attack, so just because your organization passed its pen test doesn't mean there isn't a creative way for adversaries to get in. *Red teaming* is the practice of emulating a specific threat actor (or type of threat actor) with a particular set of objectives. Whereas pen testing answers the question "How many ways can I get in?" red teaming answers the question "How can I get in and accomplish this objective?"

Red teaming more closely mimics the operational planning and attack processes of advanced threat actors that have the time, means, and motive to defeat even advanced defenses and remain undetected for long periods of time. A red team operation begins by determining the adversary to be emulated and a set of objectives. The red team then conducts reconnaissance (typically with a bit of insider help) to understand how the systems work and locate the team's objectives. The next step is to draw up a plan on how to accomplish the objectives while remaining undetected. In the more elaborate cases, the red team may create a replica of the target environment inside a cyber range in which to perform mission rehearsals and ensure the team's actions will not trigger any alerts. Finally, the red team launches the attack on the actual system and tries to reach its objectives.

As you can imagine, red teaming as described here is very costly and beyond the reach of all but the most well-resourced organizations. Most often, what you'll see is a hybrid approach that is more focused than pen testing but less intense than red teaming. We all have to do what we can with the resources we have. This is why many organizations (even very small ones) establish an internal red team that periodically comes together to think like an adversary would about some aspect of the business. It could be a new or critical information system, or a business process, or even a marketing campaign. Their job is to ask the question "If we were adversaries, how would we exploit this aspect of the business?"

EXAM TIP Don't worry about differentiating penetration testing and red teaming during the exam. If the term "red team" shows up on your test, it will most likely describe the group of people who conduct both penetration tests and red teaming.

Breach Attack Simulations

One of the problems with both pen testing and red teaming is that they amount to a point-in-time snapshot of the organizational defenses. Just because your organization did very well against the penetration testers last week doesn't necessarily mean it would do well against a threat actor today. There are many reasons for this, but the two most important ones are that things change and the test (no matter how long it takes) is never 100 percent thorough. What would be helpful as a complement to human testing would be automated testing that could happen periodically or even continually.

Breach and attack simulations (BAS) are automated systems that launch simulated attacks against a target environment and then generate reports on their findings. They are meant to be realistic but not cause any adverse effect to the target systems. For example, a ransomware simulation might use "defanged" malware that looks and propagates just like the real thing but, when successful, will only encrypt a sample file on a target host as a proof of concept. Its signature should be picked up by your network detection and response (NDR) or your endpoint detection and response (EDR) solutions. Its communications with a command-and-control (C2) system via the Internet will follow the same processes that the real thing would. In other words, each simulation is very realistic and meant to test your ability to detect and respond to it.

BAS is typically offered as a Software as a Service (SaaS) solution. All the tools, automation, and reporting take place in the provider's cloud. BAS agents can also be deployed in the target environment for better coverage under an assumed breach scenario. This covers the cases in which the adversary breached your environment using a zero-day exploit or some other mechanism that successfully evaded your defenses. In that case, you're trying to determine how well your defense in depth is working.

Log Reviews

A *log review* is the examination of system log files to detect security events or to verify the effectiveness of security controls. Log reviews actually start way before the first event is examined by a security specialist. In order for event logs to provide meaningful information, they must capture a very specific but potentially large amount of information that is grounded on both industry best practices and the organization's risk management process. There is no one-size-fits-all set of event types that will help you assess your security posture. Instead, you need to constantly tune your systems in response to the ever-changing threat landscape.

Another critical element when setting up effective log reviews for an organization is to ensure that time is standardized across all networked devices. If an incident affects three devices and their internal clocks are off by even a few seconds, then it will be significantly more difficult to determine the sequence of events and understand the overall flow of the attack. Although it is possible to normalize differing timestamps, it is an extra step that adds complexity to an already challenging process of understanding an adversary's behavior on our networks. Standardizing and synchronizing time is not a difficult thing to do. The Network Time Protocol (NTP) version 4, described in RFC 5905, is the industry standard for synchronizing computer clocks between networked devices.

Now that you have carefully defined the events you want to track and ensured all timestamps are synchronized across your network, you still need to determine where the events will be stored. By default, most log files are stored locally on the corresponding device. The challenge with this approach is that it makes it more difficult to correlate events across devices to a given incident. Additionally, it makes it easier for attackers to alter the log files of whatever devices they compromise. By centralizing the location of all log files across the organization, you address both issues and also make it easier to archive the logs for long-term retention.

Efficient archiving is important because the size of these logs will likely be significant. In fact, unless your organization is extremely small, you will likely have to deal with thousands (or perhaps even millions) of events each day. Most of these are mundane and probably irrelevant, but we usually don't know which events are important and which

Network Time Protocol

The Network Time Protocol (NTP) is one of the oldest protocols used on the Internet and is still in widespread use today. It was originally developed in the 1980s in part to solve the problem of synchronizing trans-Atlantic network communications. Its current version, 4, still leverages statistical analysis of round-trip delays between a client and one or more time servers. The time itself is sent in a UDP datagram that carries a 64-bit timestamp on port 123.

Despite its client/server architecture, NTP employs a hierarchy of time sources organized into strata, with stratum 0 being the most authoritative. A network device on a lower stratum acts as a client to a server on a higher stratum, but could itself be a server to a node further downstream from it. Furthermore, nodes on the same stratum can and often do communicate with each other to improve the accuracy of their times.

(*Continued*)

Stratum 0 consists of highly accurate time sources such as atomic clocks, global positioning system (GPS) clocks, or radio clocks. Stratum 1 consists of primary time sources, typically network appliances with highly accurate internal clocks that are connected directly to a stratum 0 source. Stratum 2 is where you would normally see your network servers, such as your local NTP servers and your domain controllers. Stratum 3 can be thought of as other servers and the client computers on your network, although the NTP standard does not define this stratum as such. Instead, the standard allows for a hierarchy of up to 16 strata wherein the only requirement is that each strata gets its time from the higher one and serves time to the lower strata if it has any.

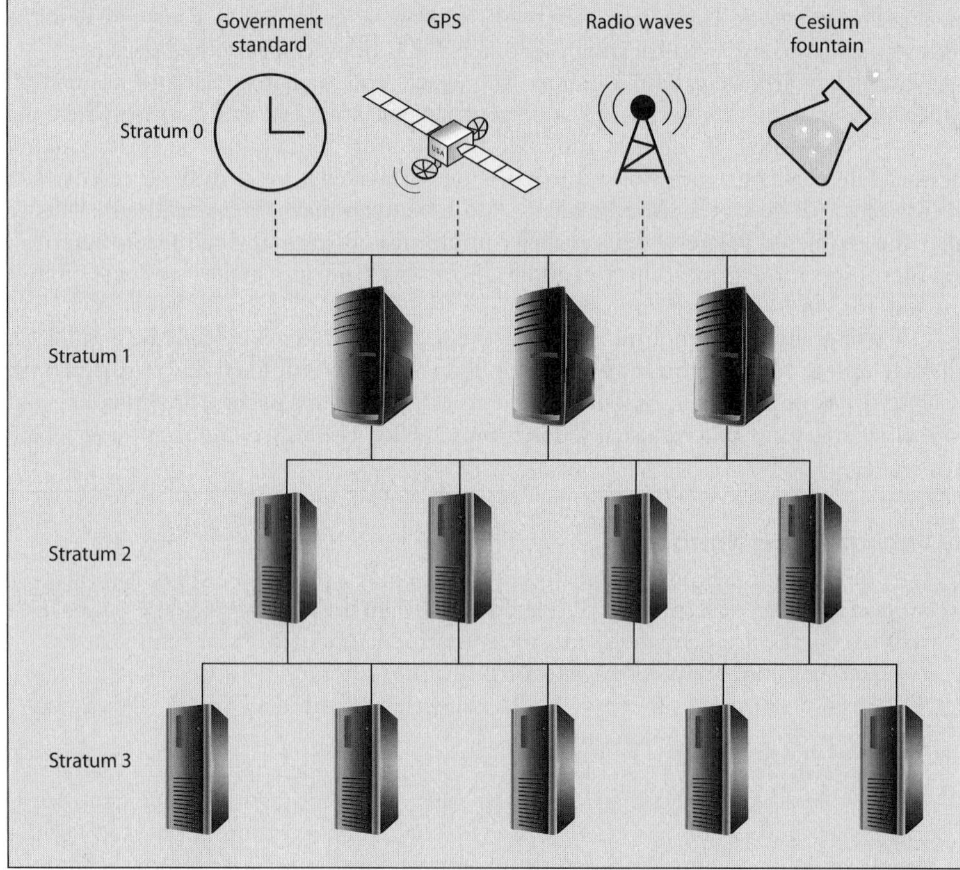

aren't until we've done some analysis. In many investigations, the seemingly unimportant events of days, weeks, or even months ago turn out to be the keys to understanding a security incident. So while retaining as much as possible is necessary, we need a way to quickly separate the wheat from the chaff.

Preventing Log Tampering

Log files are often among the first artifacts that attackers will use to attempt to hide their actions. Knowing this, it is up to us as security professionals to do what we can to make it infeasible, or at least very difficult, for attackers to successfully tamper with our log files. The following are the top five steps we can take to raise the bar for the bad folks:

- **Remote logging** When attackers compromise a device, they often gain sufficient privileges to modify or erase the log files on that device. Putting the log files on a separate box requires the attackers to target that box too, which at the very least buys you some time to notice the intrusion.
- **Simplex communication** Some high-security environments use one-way (or simplex) communications between the reporting devices and the central log repository. This is easily accomplished by severing the "receive" pairs on an Ethernet cable. The term *data diode* is sometimes used to refer to this approach to physically ensuring a one-way path.
- **Replication** It is never a good idea to keep a single copy of such an important resource as the consolidated log entries. By making multiple copies and keeping them in different locations, you make it harder for attackers to alter the log files, particularly if at least one of the locations is not accessible from the network (e.g., a removable device).
- **Write-once media** If one of the locations to which you back up your log files can be written to only once, you make it impossible for attackers to tamper with that copy of the data. Of course, they can still try to physically steal the media, but now you force them to move into the physical domain, which many attackers (particularly ones overseas) will not do.
- **Cryptographic hash chaining** A powerful technique for ensuring events that are modified or deleted are easily noticed is to use cryptographic hash chaining. In this technique, each event is appended the cryptographic hash (e.g., SHA-256) of the preceding event. This creates a chain that can attest to the completeness and the integrity of every event in it.

Fortunately, many solutions, both commercial and free, now exist for analyzing and managing log files and other important event artifacts. *Security information and event management (SIEM)* systems enable the centralization, correlation, analysis, and retention of event data in order to generate automated alerts. Typically, a SIEM provides a dashboard interface that highlights possible security incidents. It is then up to the security specialists to investigate each alert and determine if further action is required. The challenge, of course, is ensuring that the number of false positives is kept fairly low and that the number of false negatives is kept even lower.

Synthetic Transactions

Many of our information systems operate on the basis of transactions. A user (typically a person) initiates a transaction that could be anything from a request for a given web page to a wire transfer of half a million dollars to an account in Switzerland. This transaction is processed by any number of other servers and results in whatever action the requestor wanted. This is considered a real transaction. Now suppose that a transaction is not generated by a person but by a script. This is considered a *synthetic transaction.*

The usefulness of synthetic transactions is that they allow us to systematically test the behavior and performance of critical services. Perhaps the simplest example is a scenario in which you want to ensure that your home page is up and running. Rather than waiting for an angry customer to send you an e-mail saying that your home page is unreachable, or spending a good chunk of your day visiting the page on your browser, you could write a script that periodically visits your home page and ensures that a certain string is returned. This script could then alert you as soon as the page is down or unreachable, allowing you to investigate before you would've otherwise noticed it. This could be an early indicator that your web server was hacked or that you are under a distributed denial-of-service (DDoS) attack.

Synthetic transactions can do more than simply tell you whether a service is up or down. They can measure performance parameters such as response time, which could alert you to network congestion or server overutilization. They can also help you test new services by mimicking typical end-user behaviors to ensure the system works as it ought to. Finally, these transactions can be written to behave as malicious users by, for example, attempting a cross-site scripting (XSS) attack and ensuring your controls are effective. This is an effective way of testing software from the outside.

Real User Monitoring vs. Synthetic Transactions

Real user monitoring (RUM) is a passive way to monitor the interactions of real users with a web application or system. It uses agents to capture metrics such as delay, jitter, and errors from the user's perspective. RUM differs from synthetic transactions in that it uses real people instead of scripted commands. While RUM more accurately captures the actual user experience, it tends to produce noisy data (e.g., incomplete transactions due to users changing their minds or losing mobile connectivity) and thus may require more back-end analysis. It also lacks the elements of predictability and regularity, which could mean that a problem won't be detected during low utilization periods.

Synthetic transactions, on the other hand, are very predictable and can be very regular, because their behaviors are scripted. They can also detect rare occurrences more reliably than waiting for a user to actually trigger that behavior. Synthetic transactions also have the advantage of not having to wait for a user to become dissatisfied or encounter a problem, which makes them a more proactive approach.

It is important to note that RUM and synthetic transactions are different ways of achieving the same goal. Neither approach is the better one in all cases, so it is common to see both employed contemporaneously.

Code Reviews

So far, all the security testing we have discussed looks at the behaviors of our systems. This means that we are only assessing the externally visible features without visibility into the inner workings of the system. If you want to test your own software system from the inside, you could use a *code review*, a systematic examination of the instructions that comprise a piece of software, performed by someone other than the author of that code. This approach is a hallmark of mature software development processes. In fact, in many organizations, developers are not allowed to push out their software modules until someone else has signed off on them after doing a code review. Think of this as proofreading an important document before you send it to an important person. If you try to proofread it yourself, you will probably not catch all those embarrassing typos and grammatical errors as easily as someone else could who is checking it for you.

Code reviews go way beyond checking for typos, though that is certainly one element of it. It all starts with a set of coding standards developed by the organization that wrote the software. This could be an internal team, an outsourced developer, or a commercial vendor. Obviously, code reviews of commercial off-the-shelf (COTS) software are extremely rare unless the software is open source or you happen to be a major government agency. Still, each development shop will have a style guide or a set of documented coding standards that covers everything from how to indent the code to when and how to use existing code libraries. So a preliminary step to the code review is to ensure the author followed the team's style guide or standards. In addition to helping the maintainability of the software, this step gives the code reviewer a preview of the magnitude of the work ahead; a sloppy coder will probably have a lot of other, harder-to-find defects in his code.

After checking the structure and format of the code, the reviewer looks for uncalled or unneeded functions or procedures. These lead to "code bloat," which makes it harder to maintain and secure the application. For this same reason, the reviewer looks for modules that are excessively complex and should be restructured or split into multiple routines. Finally, in terms of reducing complexity, the reviewer looks for blocks of repeated code that could be refactored. Even better, these could be pulled out and turned into external reusable components such as library functions.

An extreme example of unnecessary (and dangerous) procedures are the code stubs and test routines that developers often include in their developmental software. There have been too many cases in which developers left test code (sometimes including hard-coded credentials) in final versions of software. Once adversaries discover this condition, exploiting the software and bypassing security controls is trivial. This problem is insidious, because developers sometimes comment out the code for final testing, just in case the tests fail and they have to come back and rework it. They may make a mental note to revisit the file and delete this dangerous code, but then forget to do so. While commented code is unavailable to an attacker after a program is compiled (unless they have access to the source code), the same is not true of the scripts that are often found in distributed applications.

Defensive programming is a best practice that all software development operations should adopt. In a nutshell, it means that as you develop or review the code, you are constantly looking for opportunities for things to go badly. Perhaps the best example of defensive programming is the practice of treating all inputs, whether they come from a keyboard, a file,

A Code Review Process

1. Identify the code to be reviewed (usually a specific function or file).
2. The team leader organizes the inspection and makes sure everyone has access to the correct version of the source code, along with all supporting artifacts.
3. Everyone on the team prepares for inspection by reading through the code and making notes.
4. A designated team member collates all the obvious errors offline (not in a meeting) so they don't have to be discussed during the inspection meeting (which would be a waste of time).
5. If everyone agrees the code is ready for inspection, then the meeting goes ahead.
6. The team leader displays the code (with line numbers) via an overhead projector so everyone can read through it. Everyone discusses bugs, design issues, and anything else that comes up about the code. A scribe (not the author of the code) writes everything down.
7. At the end of the meeting, everyone agrees on a "disposition" for the code:
   - Passed: Code is good to go
   - Passed with rework: Code is good so long as small changes are fixed
   - Reinspect: Fix problems and have another inspection
8. After the meeting, the author fixes any mistakes and checks in the new version.
9. If the disposition of the code in step 7 was passed with rework, the team leader checks off the bugs that the scribe wrote down and makes sure they're all fixed.
10. If the disposition of the code in step 7 was reinspect, the team leader goes back to step 2 and starts over again.

or the network, as untrusted until proven otherwise. This user input validation can be a bit trickier than it sounds, because you must understand the context surrounding the input. Are you expecting a numerical value? If so, what is the acceptable range for that value? Can this range change over time? These and many other questions need to be answered before we can decide whether the inputs are valid. Keep in mind that many of the oft-exploited vulnerabilities we see have a lack of input validation as their root cause.

Code Testing

We will discuss in Chapters 24 and 25 the multiple types of tests to which we must subject our code as part of the software development process. However, once the code comes out of development and before we put it into a production environment, we must ensure that it meets our security policies. Does it encrypt all data in transit? Is it possible to bypass authentication or authorization controls? Does it store sensitive data in unencrypted temporary files? Does it reach out to any undocumented external resources (e.g., for library updates)? The list goes on, but the point is that security personnel are incentivized differently than software developers. The programmer gets paid to implement features in software, while the security practitioner gets paid to keep systems secure.

Most mature organizations have an established process to certify that software systems are secure enough to be installed and operated on their networks. There is typically a follow-on to that process, which is when a senior manager (hopefully after reading the results of the certification) authorizes (or accredits) the system.

Misuse Case Testing

Use cases are structured scenarios that are commonly used to describe required functionality in an information system. Think of them as stories in which an external actor (e.g., a user) wants to accomplish a given goal on the system. The use case describes the sequence of interactions between the actor and the system that result in the desired outcome. Use cases are textual but are often summarized and graphically depicted using a Unified Modeling Language (UML) use case diagram such as the one shown in Figure 18-3. This figure illustrates a very simple view of a system in which a customer places online orders. According to the UML, actors such as our user are depicted using stick figures, and the actors' use cases are depicted as verb phrases inside ovals. Use cases can be related to one another in a variety of ways, which we call *associations*. The most common ways in which use cases are associated are by including another use case (that is, the included use case is always executed when the preceding one is) or by extending a use case (meaning that the second use case may or may not be executed depending on a decision point in the main use case). In Figure 18-3, our customer attempts to place an order and may be prompted to log in if she hasn't already done so, but she will always be asked to provide her credit card information.

Figure 18-3 UML use case diagram

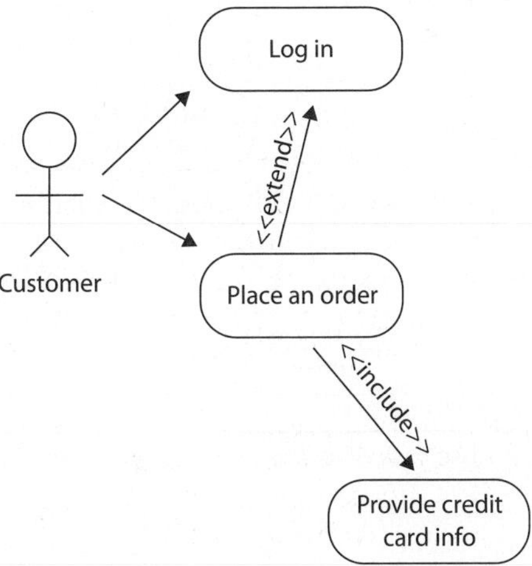

PART VI

While use cases are very helpful in analyzing requirements for the normal or expected behavior of a system, they are not particularly useful for assessing its security. That is what misuse cases do for us. A *misuse case* is a use case that includes threat actors and the tasks they want to perform on the system. Threat actors are normally depicted as stick figures with shaded heads and their actions (or misuse cases) are depicted as shaded ovals, as shown in Figure 18-4. As you can see, the attacker in this scenario is interested in guessing passwords and stealing credit card information.

Misuse cases introduce new associations to our UML diagram. The threat actor's misuse cases are meant to threaten a specific portion or legitimate use case of our system. You will typically see shaded ovals connected to unshaded ones with an arrow labeled <<threaten>> to denote this relationship. On the other hand, system developers and security personnel can implement controls that mitigate these misuses. These create new unshaded ovals connected to shaded ones with arrows labeled <<mitigate>>.

The idea behind misuse case testing is to ensure we have effectively addressed each of the risks we identified and decided to mitigate during our risk management process and that are applicable to the system under consideration. This doesn't mean that misuse case testing needs to include all the possible threats to our system, but it should include the ones we decided to address. This process forces system developers and integrators to incorporate the products of our risk management process into the early stages of any system development effort. It also makes it easier to quickly step through a complex system and ensure that effective security controls are in the right places without having to get deep into the source code, which is what we describe next.

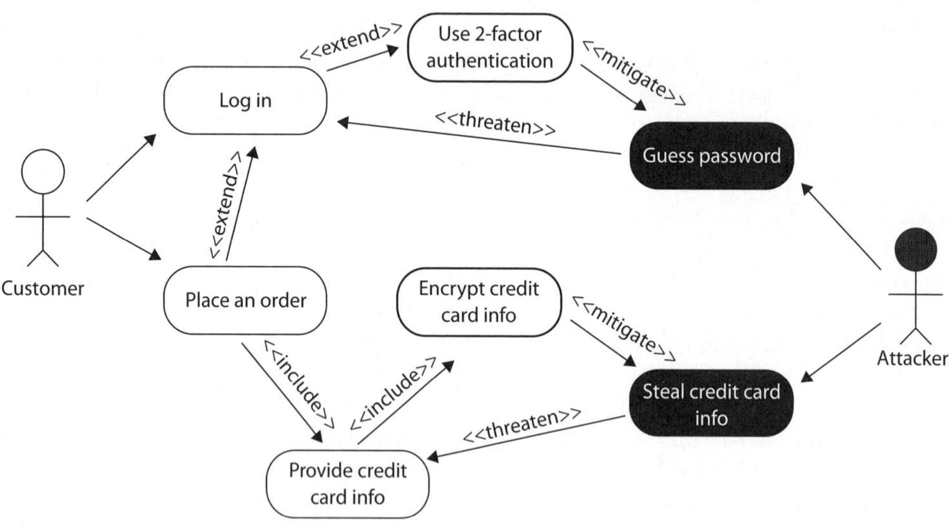

Figure 18-4 UML misuse case diagram

Test Coverage

Test coverage is a measure of how much of a system is examined by a specific test (or group of tests), which is typically expressed as a percentage. For example, if you are developing a software system with 1,000 lines of code and your suite of unit tests executes 800 of those, then you would have 80 percent test coverage. Why wouldn't we just go for 100 percent? Because it likely would be too expensive for the benefit we would get from it. We normally only see this full coverage being required in safety-critical systems like those used in aviation and medical devices.

Test coverage also applies to things other than software. Suppose you have 100 security controls in your organization. Testing all of them in one assessment or audit may be too disruptive or expensive (or both), so you schedule smaller evaluations throughout the year. Each quarter, for instance, you run an assessment with tests for one quarter of the controls. In this situation, your quarterly test coverage is 25 percent but your annual coverage is 100 percent.

Interface Testing

When we think of interfaces, we usually envision a graphical user interface (GUI) for an application. While GUIs are one kind of interface, there are others that are potentially more important. At its essence, an interface is an exchange point for data between systems and/or users. You can see this in your computer's network interface card (NIC), which is the exchange point for data between your computer (a system) and the local area network (another system). Another example of an interface is an application programming interface (API), a set of points at which a software system (e.g., the application) exchanges information with another software system (e.g., the libraries).

Interface testing is the systematic evaluation of a given set of these exchange points. This assessment should include both known good exchanges and known bad exchanges in order to ensure the system behaves correctly at both ends of the spectrum. The real rub is in finding test cases that are somewhere in between. In software testing, these are called *boundary conditions* because they lie at the boundary that separates the good from the bad. For example, if a given packet should contain a payload of no more than 1024 bytes, how would the system behave when presented with 1024 bytes plus one bit (or byte) of data? What about exactly 1024 bytes? What about 1024 bytes minus one bit (or byte) of data? As you can see, the idea is to flirt with the line that separates the good from the bad and see what happens when we get really close to it.

There are many other test cases we could consider, but the most important lesson here is that the primary task of interface testing is to dream up all the test cases ahead of time, document them, and then insert them into a repeatable and (hopefully) automated test engine. This way you can ensure that as the system evolves, a specific interface is always tested against the right set of test cases. We will talk more about software testing in Chapter 24, but for now you should remember that interface testing is a special case of something called *integration testing*, which is the assessment of how different parts of a system interact with each other.

Compliance Checks

We have framed our discussion of security tests in terms of evaluating the effectiveness of our technical controls. That really should be our first concern. However, many of us work in organizations that must comply with some set of regulations. If you are not in a (formally) regulated sector, you may still have regulations or standards with which you voluntarily comply. Finally, if you have an information security management system (ISMS) in place like we discussed in Chapter 1 (and you really should), you want to ensure the controls that are listed in there are actually working. In any of these three cases you can use the testing techniques we've discussed to demonstrate compliance.

Compliance checks are point-in-time verifications that specific security controls are implemented and performing as expected. For example, your organization may process payment card transactions for its customers and, as such, be required by PCI DSS to run annual penetration tests and quarterly vulnerability scans by an approved vendor. Your compliance checks would be the reports for each of these tests. Or, you may have an SPF record check as one of the e-mail security controls in your ISMS. (Recall from Chapter 13 that the Sender Policy Framework mitigates the risk of forged e-mail sources.) You could perform a log review to perform and document a compliance check on that control. If your e-mail server performed SPF checks on all e-mail messages in a selected portion of its logs, then you know the control is in place and performing as expected.

Conducting Security Audits

While compliance checks are point-in-time tests, audits tend to cover a longer period of time. The question is not "Is this control in place and working?" but rather "Has this control been in place for the last year?" Audits, of course, can leverage compliance checks. In the SPF record check example at the end of the previous section, the auditor would simply look through the compliance checks and, if they were performed and documented regularly, use those as evidence of compliance during an audit.

As simple as it sounds, establishing a clear set of goals is probably the most important step of planning a security audit. Since we usually can't test everything, we have to focus our efforts on whatever it is that we are most concerned about. An audit could be driven by regulatory or compliance requirements, by a significant change to the architecture of the information system, or by new developments in the threat facing the organization. There are many other possible scenarios, but these examples are illustrative of the vastly different objectives for our assessments.

Once our goals are established, we need to define the scope of the assessment:

- Which subnets and systems are we going to test?
- Are we going to look at user artifacts, such as passwords, files, and log entries, or at user behaviors, such as their response to social engineering attempts?
- Which information will we assess for confidentiality, integrity, and availability?
- What are the privacy implications of our audit?
- How will we evaluate our processes, and to what extent?

If our goals are clearly laid out, answering these questions should be a lot easier.

The scope of the audit should be determined in coordination with business unit managers. All too often security professionals focus on IT and forget about the business cases. In fact, business managers should be included early in the audit planning process and should remain engaged throughout the event. This not only helps bridge the gap between the two camps but also helps identify potential areas of risk to the organization brought on by the audit itself. Just imagine what would happen if your assessment interfered with a critical but nonobvious business process and ended up costing the organization a huge amount of money. (We call that an RGE, or résumé-generating event.)

Having decided who will actually conduct our audit, we are now in a position to plan the event. The plan is important for a variety of reasons:

- We must ensure that we are able to address whatever risks we may be introducing into the business processes. Without a plan, these risks are unknown and not easily mitigated.
- Documenting the plan ensures that we meet each of our audit goals. Audit teams sometimes attempt to follow their own scripted plan, which may or may not address all of the organization's goals for a specific audit.
- Documenting the plan will help us remember the items that were *not* in the scope of the assessment. Recall that we already acknowledged that we can't possibly test everything, so this specifies the things we did not test.
- The plan ensures that the audit process is repeatable. Like any good science experiment, we should be able to reproduce the results by repeating the process. This is particularly important because we may encounter unexpected results worth further investigation.

Information System Security Audit Process

1. **Determine the goals**, because everything else hinges on this.
2. **Involve the right business unit leaders** to ensure the needs of the business are identified and addressed.
3. **Determine the scope**, because not everything can be tested.
4. **Choose the audit team**, which may consist of internal or external personnel, depending on the goals, scope, budget, and available expertise.
5. **Plan the audit** to ensure all goals are met on time and on budget.
6. **Conduct the audit** while sticking to the plan and documenting any deviations therefrom.
7. **Document the results**, because the wealth of information generated is both valuable and volatile.
8. **Communicate the results** to the right leaders to achieve and sustain a strong security posture.

Having developed a detailed plan for the audit, we are finally in a position to get to the fun stuff. No matter how much time and effort we put into planning, inevitably we will find tasks we have to add, delete, change, or modify. Though we clearly want to minimize the number of these changes, they are really a part of the process that we just have to accept. The catch is that we must consciously decide to accept them, and then we absolutely must document them.

NOTE In certain cases, such as regulatory compliance, the parameters of the audit may be dictated and performed by an external team of auditors. This means that the role of the organization is mostly limited to preparing for the audit by ensuring all required resources are available to the audit team.

The documentation we start during the planning process must continue all the way through to the results. In all but the most trivial assessments, we are likely to generate reams of data and information. This information is invaluable in that it captures a snapshot in time of our security posture. If nothing else, it serves to benchmark the effectiveness of our controls so that we can compare audits and determine trends. Typically, however, this detailed documentation allows the security staff to drill into unexpected or unexplainable results and do some root cause analysis. If you capture all the information, it will be easier to produce reports for target audiences without concern that you may have deleted (or failed to document) any important data points.

Ultimately, the desired end state of any audit is to effectively communicate the results to the target audiences. The manner in which we communicate results to executives is very different from the manner in which we communicate results to the IT team members. This gets back to the point made earlier about capturing and documenting both the plan and the details and products of its execution. It is always easier to distill information from a large data set than to justify a conclusion when the facts live only in our brains. Many a security audit has been ultimately unsuccessful because the team has not been able to communicate effectively with the key stakeholders.

Internal Audits

In a perfect world, every organization would have an internal team capable of performing whatever audits were needed. Alas, we live in a far-from-perfect world in which even some of the best-resourced organizations lack this capability. But if your organization does have such a team on hand, its ability to implement continuous improvement of your organization's security posture offers some tremendous advantages.

One of the benefits of using your own personnel to do an audit is that they are familiar with the inner workings of your organization. This familiarity allows them to get right to work and not have to spend too much time getting oriented to the cyber terrain. Some may say that this insider knowledge gives them an unrealistic advantage because few adversaries could know as much about the systems as those who operate and defend them. It is probably more accurate to state that advanced adversaries can often approach the level of knowledge about an organization that an internal audit team would have. In any case, if the purpose of the audit is to leave no stone unturned and test the weakest, most obscure parts of an information system, then an internal team will likely get closer to that goal than any other.

Using internal assets also allows the organization to be more agile in its assessment efforts. Since the team is always available, all that the leadership would need to do is to reprioritize their tests to adapt to changing needs. For example, suppose a business unit is scheduled to be audited yearly, but the latest assessment's results from a month ago were abysmal and represent increased risk to the organization. The security management could easily reschedule other tests to conduct a follow-up audit three months later. This agility comes at no additional cost to the organization, which typically would not be true if engaging a third-party team.

The downsides of using an internal team include the fact that they likely have limited exposure to other approaches to both securing and exploiting information systems. Unless the team has some recent hires with prior experience, the team will probably have a lot of depth in the techniques they know, but not a lot of breadth, since they will have developed mostly the skills needed to test only their own organization.

A less obvious disadvantage of using internal auditors is the potential for conflicts of interest to exist. If the auditors believe that their bosses or coworkers may be adversely affected by a negative report or even by the documented presence of flaws, the auditors may be reluctant to accurately report their findings. The culture of the organization is probably the most influential factor in this potential conflict. If the climate is one of openness and trust, then the auditors are less likely to perceive any risk to their higher-ups or coworkers regardless of their findings. Conversely, in very rigid bureaucratic organizations with low tolerance for failures, the potential for conflicts of interest will likely be higher.

Another aspect of the conflict-of-interest issue is that the team members or their bosses may have an agenda to pursue with the audit. If they are intent on securing better

Conducting Internal Audits

Here are some best practices to get the most bang out of internal audits that you conduct:

- **Mark your calendars** Nothing takes the wind out of your audit's sails quicker than not having all key personnel and resources available. Book them early.
- **Prepare the auditors** Rehearse the process with the auditors so everyone is on the same sheet of music. Ensure everyone knows the relevant policies and procedures.
- **Document everything** Consider having note-takers follow the auditors around documenting everything they do and observe.
- **Make the report easy to read** Keep in mind that you will have at least two audiences: managers and technical personnel. Make the report easy to read for both.

funding, they may be tempted to overstate or even fabricate security flaws. Similarly, if they believe that another department needs to be taught a lesson (perhaps to get them to improve their willingness to "play nice" with the security team), the results could deliberately or subconsciously be less than objective. Politics and team dynamics clearly should be considered when deciding whether to use internal audit teams.

External Audits

When organizations come together to work in an integrated manner, special care must be taken to ensure that each party promises to provide the necessary level of protection, liability, and responsibility, which should be clearly defined in the contracts each party signs. Auditing and testing should be performed to ensure that each party is indeed holding up its side of the bargain. An *external audit* (sometimes called a second-party audit) is one conducted by (or on behalf of) a business partner.

External audits are tied to contracts. In today's business and threat environments, it is becoming commonplace for contracts to have security provisions. For example, a contract for disposing of computers may require the service provider to run background checks on all its employees, to store the computers in secure places until they are wiped, to overwrite all storage devices with alternating 1's and 0's at least three times, and to agree to being audited for any or all of these terms. Once the contract is in place, the client organization could demand access to people, places, and information to verify that the security provisions are being met by the contractor.

To understand why external audits are important, you don't have to go any further than the Target data breach of 2013. That incident was possible because Target was doing

Conducting and Facilitating External Audits

It would be pretty unusual for you to conduct an external audit on a contractor. Instead, you would normally ask the contractor to perform an internal audit (scoped in accordance with the contract) or bring in a third-party auditor (described in the next section). Regardless, here are some tips to consider whether you are on the giving or receiving end of the deal:

- **Learn the contract** An external audit, by definition, is scoped to include only the contractual obligations of an organization. Be sure the audit doesn't get out of control.
- **Schedule in- and out-briefs** Schedule an in-brief to occur right before the audit starts to bring all stakeholders together. Schedule an out-brief to occur immediately after the audit is complete to give the audited organization a chance to address any misconceptions or errors.
- **Travel in pairs** Ensure the organization being audited has someone accompanying each team of auditors. This will make things go smoother and help avoid misunderstandings.
- **Keep it friendly** The whole goal of this process is to engender trust.

business with Fazio Mechanical Services, who provided Target with heating, ventilation, and air conditioning (HVAC) services. The security postures of both organizations were vastly different, so the attackers targeted the weaker link: Fazio. Admittedly, Target made some costly mistakes that got it into that mess, but had its IT security personnel understood the information system security management practices of its partner, they may have been able to avoid the breach. How could they have learned of Fazio's weaknesses? By auditing them.

Third-Party Audits

Sometimes, you have no choice but to bring in a third party to audit your information systems' security. This is most often the case when you need to demonstrate compliance with some government regulation or industry standard. Even if you do have a choice, bringing in external auditors has advantages over using an internal team. For starters, the external auditors probably have seen and tested many information systems in different organizations. This means that they will almost certainly bring to your organization knowledge that it wouldn't otherwise be able to acquire. Even if you have some internal auditors with prior experience, they are unlikely to approach the breadth of experience that contractors who regularly test a variety of organizations will bring to the table.

Another advantage of third-party auditors is that they are unaware of the internal dynamics and politics of the target organization. This means that they have no favorites or agendas other than the challenge of finding flaws. This objectivity may give them an edge in testing, particularly if the alternative would've been to use internal personnel who played a role in implementing the controls in the first place and thus may overlook or subconsciously impede the search for defects in those controls.

The obvious disadvantage of hiring an external team is cost. Price tags in the tens of thousands of dollars are not uncommon, even on the low end of the scale. If nothing else, this probably means that you won't be able to use external auditors frequently (if at all). Even at the high end of the pay scale, it is not uncommon to find testers who rely almost exclusively on high-end scanners that do all the work (and thinking) for them. It is truly unfortunate when an organization spends a significant amount of money only to find out the tester simply plugs his laptop into the network, runs a scanner, and prints a report.

Even if you find an affordable and competent team to test your information systems, you still have to deal with the added resources required to orient them to the organization and supervise their work. Even with signed nondisclosure agreements (NDAs), most companies don't give free rein to their external auditors without some level of supervision. In addition, the lack of knowledge of the inner workings of the organization typically translates into the auditors taking a longer time to get oriented and be able to perform the test.

NOTE Signing a nondisclosure agreement is almost always a prerequisite before a third-party team is permitted to audit an organization's systems.

Facilitating Third-Party Audits

Your organization will typically pay for the third party to audit you, but if you're doing the audit for compliance or contractual reasons, the auditor won't be working for you. The job of a third-party auditor is to certify (using their own reputation) that you are meeting whatever standards are in scope. Regardless, the following are useful tips:

- **Know the requirements** Go through the audit requirements line by line to ensure you know exactly what the third-party auditor will be looking at. Call the auditor if you have any questions.
- **Pre-audit** Conduct your own internal audit using the same list of requirements to minimize the number of surprises.
- **Lock in schedules** Ensure the right staff will be available when the auditors show up, even if there's only a small chance they'll be needed.
- **Get organized** The audit team will likely need access to a large and diverse set of resources, so make sure you have them all assembled in one place and organized.
- **Keep the boss informed** A third-party audit, by definition, is an important event for the organization, and we all know that bad news doesn't get better with time. Be sure to keep the senior managers informed, especially of any potential deficient areas.

While there is no clear winner between using internal auditors and third-party auditors, sometimes the latter is the only choice where regulatory requirements such as the Sarbanes-Oxley Act force an organization to outsource the test. These are called *compliance audits* and must be performed by external parties.

EXAM TIP You will most likely see questions on external audits in the context of supply-chain risk management. Third-party audits will show up in questions dealing with compliance issues.

Chapter Review

As security professionals, evaluating the security posture of our organizations is an iterative and continuous process. This chapter discussed a variety of techniques that are helpful in determining how well you are mitigating risks with your technical and administrative controls. Whether you are doing your own audits or validating the audit plans provided by a third party, you should now know what to look for and how to evaluate proposals. Along the way, this chapter also covered some specific threats and opportunities that should play a role in your assessment plan. It is important to keep in mind that everything covered in this chapter is grounded in the risk management discussed in Chapter 2. If you do not keep in mind the specific threats and risks with which your organization is concerned, then it is very difficult to properly address them.

Quick Review

- An audit is a systematic assessment of the security controls of an information system.
- Setting a clear set of goals is probably the most important step of planning a security audit.
- A vulnerability test is an examination of a system for the purpose of identifying, defining, and ranking its vulnerabilities.
- Penetration testing is the process of simulating attacks on a network and its systems at the request of the owner.
- Red teaming is the practice of emulating a specific threat actor (or type of threat actor) with a particular set of objectives.
- Black box testing treats the system being tested as completely opaque.
- White box testing affords the auditor complete knowledge of the inner workings of the system even before the first scan is performed.
- Gray box testing gives the auditor some, but not all, information about the internal workings of the system.
- A blind test is one in which the assessors only have publicly available data to work with and the network security staff is aware that the testing will occur.
- A double-blind test (stealth assessment) is a blind test in which the network security staff is not notified that testing will occur.
- Breach and attack simulations (BAS) are automated systems that launch simulated attacks against a target environment and then generate reports on their findings.
- A log review is the examination of system log files to detect security events or to verify the effectiveness of security controls.
- Synthetic transactions are scripted events that mimic the behaviors of real users and allow security professionals to systematically test the performance of critical services.
- A code review is a systematic examination of the instructions that comprise a piece of software, performed by someone other than the author of that code.
- A misuse case is a use case that includes threat actors and the tasks they want to perform on the system.
- Test coverage is a measure of how much of a system is examined by a specific test (or group of tests).

- Interface testing is the systematic evaluation of a given set of exchange points for data between systems and/or users.
- Compliance checks are point-in-time verifications that specific security controls are implemented and performing as expected.
- Internal audits benefit from the auditors' familiarity with the systems, but may be hindered by a lack of exposure to how others attack and defend systems.
- External audits happen when organizations have a contract in place that includes security provisions. The contracting party can demand to audit the contractor to ensure those provisions are being met.
- Third-party audits typically bring a much broader background of experience that can provide fresh insights, but can be expensive.

Questions

Please remember that these questions are formatted and asked in a certain way for a reason. Keep in mind that the CISSP exam is asking questions at a conceptual level. Questions may not always have the perfect answer, and the candidate is advised against always looking for the perfect answer. Instead, the candidate should look for the best answer in the list.

1. Internal audits are the preferred approach when which of the following is true?
   - **A.** The organization lacks the organic expertise to conduct them.
   - **B.** Regulatory requirements dictate the use of a third-party auditor.
   - **C.** The budget for security testing is limited or nonexistent.
   - **D.** There is concern over the spillage of proprietary or confidential information.
2. All of the following are steps in the security audit process *except*
   - **A.** Document the results.
   - **B.** Convene a management review.
   - **C.** Involve the right business unit leaders.
   - **D.** Determine the scope.
3. Which of the following is an advantage of using third-party auditors?
   - **A.** They may have knowledge that an organization wouldn't otherwise be able to leverage.
   - **B.** Their cost.
   - **C.** The requirement for NDAs and supervision.
   - **D.** Their use of automated scanners and reports.

4. Choose the term that describes an audit performed to demonstrate that an organization is complying with its contractual obligations to another organization.
   A. Internal audit
   B. Third-party audit
   C. External audit
   D. Compliance audit
5. Which of the following is true of a vulnerability assessment?
   A. The aim is to identify as many vulnerabilities as possible.
   B. It is not concerned with the effects of the assessment on other systems.
   C. It is a predictive test aimed at assessing the future performance of a system.
   D. Ideally it is fully automated, with no human involvement.
6. An assessment whose goal is to assess the susceptibility of an organization to social engineering attacks is best classified as
   A. Physical testing
   B. Personnel testing
   C. Vulnerability testing
   D. Network testing
7. Which of the following is an assessment that affords the auditor detailed knowledge of the system's architecture before conducting the test?
   A. White box testing
   B. Gray box testing
   C. Black box testing
   D. Zero knowledge testing
8. Vulnerability scans normally involve all the following *except*
   A. The identification of active hosts on the network
   B. The identification of malware on all hosts
   C. The identification of misconfigured settings
   D. The identification of operating systems
9. Security event logs can best be protected from tampering by which of the following?
   A. Encrypting the contents using asymmetric key encryption
   B. Ensuring every user has administrative rights on their own workstations
   C. Using remote logging over simplex communications media
   D. Storing the event logs on DVD-RW

10. Synthetic transactions are best described as
    - **A.** Real user monitoring (RUM)
    - **B.** Transactions that fall outside the normal purpose of a system
    - **C.** Transactions that are synthesized from multiple users' interactions with the system
    - **D.** A way to test the behavior and performance of critical services
11. Suppose you want to study the actions an adversary may attempt against your system and test the effectiveness of the controls you have emplaced to mitigate the associated risks. Which of the following approaches would best allow you to accomplish this goal?
    - **A.** Misuse case testing
    - **B.** Use case testing
    - **C.** Real user monitoring (RUM)
    - **D.** Fuzzing
12. Code reviews include all of the following *except*
    - **A.** Ensuring the code conforms to applicable coding standards
    - **B.** Discussing bugs, design issues, and anything else that comes up about the code
    - **C.** Agreeing on a "disposition" for the code
    - **D.** Fuzzing the code
13. Interface testing could involve which of the following?
    - **A.** The application programming interface (API)
    - **B.** The graphical user interface (GUI)
    - **C.** Both of the above
    - **D.** None of the above

Answers

1. **C.** Third-party auditors are almost always fairly expensive, so if the organization's budget does not support their use, it may be necessary to use internal assets to conduct the audit.
2. **B.** The management review is not a part of any audit. Instead, this review typically uses the results of one or more audits in order to make strategic decisions.
3. **A.** Because they perform audits in multiple other organizations, and since their knowledge is constantly refreshed, third-party auditors almost always have knowledge and insights that would otherwise be unavailable to the organization.

4. **C.** External audits are used to ensure that contractors are meeting their contractual obligations, so that is the best answer. A compliance audit would apply to regulatory or industry standards and would almost certainly be a third-party audit, which makes answer D a poor fit in most cases.
5. **A.** One of the principal goals of a vulnerability assessment is to identify as many security flaws as possible within a given system, while being careful not to disrupt other systems.
6. **B.** Social engineering is focused on people, so personnel testing is the best answer.
7. **A.** White box testing gives the tester detailed information about the internal workings of the system under study. Gray box testing provides *some* information, so it is not the best answer to this question.
8. **B.** Vulnerability testing does not normally include scanning hosts for malware. Instead, it focuses on finding flaws that malware could potentially exploit.
9. **C.** Using a remote logging host raises the bar for attackers because if they are able to compromise one host, they would have to compromise the remote logger in order to tamper with the logs. The use of a simplex channel further hinders the attackers.
10. **D.** Synthetic transactions are those that simulate the behavior of real users, but are not the result of real user interactions with the system. They allow an organization to ensure that services are behaving properly without having to rely on user complaints to detect problems.
11. **A.** Misuse case testing allows us to document both an adversary's desired actions on a system and the controls that are meant to thwart that adversary. It is similar to developing use cases, but with a malicious user's actions in mind instead of those of legitimate users.
12. **D.** Fuzzing is a technique for detecting flaws in the code by bombarding it with massive amounts of random data. This is not part of a code review, which focuses on analyzing the source code, not its response to random data.
13. **C.** Interface testing covers the exchange points within different components of the system. The API is the exchange point between the system and the libraries it leverages, while the GUI is the exchange point between the system and the users. Testing either of these would constitute an interface test.

CHAPTER 19

Measuring Security

This chapter presents the following:

- Security metrics
- Security process data
- Reporting
- Management review and approval

One accurate measurement is worth a thousand expert opinions.

—Grace Hopper

The reason we conduct security assessments is that we want to answer specific questions. Is the firewall blocking dangerous traffic? How many systems are vulnerable? Can we detect (and block) phishing attacks? (The list goes on.) These questions all are important but also are very tactical. The typical board of directors or C-suite won't understand or care about them. What they do care about is how the organization is generating value for its stakeholders. Part of our job as cybersecurity leaders is to turn tactical observations into strategic insights. To do this, we need to be able to measure the right parts of our information security management system (ISMS) over time, analyze the results, and present them in an actionable manner to other leaders in our organizations. This is what this chapter is all about.

Quantifying Security

How can you tell whether you are moving toward or away from your destination? In the physical world, we use all sorts of environmental cues such as road signs and landmarks. Oftentimes, we can also use visual cues to assess the likely risk in our travels. For instance, if a sign on a hiking trail is loose and can pivot around its pole, then we know that there is a chance that the direction in which it points is not the right one. If a landmark is a river crossing and the waters are much higher than normal, we know we run the risk of being swept downstream. But when it comes to our security posture, how can we tell whether we're making progress and whether we're taking risks?

Attempting to run an ISMS without adequate metrics is perhaps more dangerous than not managing security at all. The reason is that, like following misplaced trail signs, using the wrong metrics can lead the organization down the wrong path and result in worse outcomes than would be seen if all is left to chance. Fortunately, the International Organization for Standardization (ISO) has published an industry standard for developing and using metrics that measure the effectiveness of a security program. ISO/IEC 27004, *Information security management — Monitoring, measurement, analysis and evaluation*, outlines a process by which to measure the performance of security controls and processes. Keep in mind that a key purpose of this standard is to support continuous improvement in an organization's security posture.

At this point, it is helpful to define a handful of terms:

- **Factor** An attribute of a system (such as an ISMS) that has a value that can change over time. Examples of factors are the number of alerts generated by an intrusion detection system (IDS) or the number of events investigated by the incident response (IR) team.
- **Measurement** A quantitative observation of a factor at a particular point in time. In other words, this is raw data. Two examples of measurements would be 356 IDS alerts in the last 24 hours and 42 verified events investigated by the IR team in the month of January.
- **Baseline** A value for a factor that provides a point of reference or denotes that some condition is met by achieving some threshold. For example, a baseline could be the historic trend in the number of IDS alerts over the past 12 months (a reference line) or a goal that the IR team will investigate 100 events or less in any given month (a threshold value).
- **Metric** A derived value that is generated by comparing multiple measurements against each other or against a baseline. Metrics are, by their very nature, comparative. Building upon the previous examples, an effective metric could be the ratio of verified incidents to IDS alerts during a 30-day period.
- **Indicator** A particularly important metric that describes a key element of the effectiveness of a system (such as an ISMS). In other words, indicators are meaningful to business leaders. If one of management's goals is to minimize the number of high-severity incidents, then an indicator could be the ratio of such incidents declared during a reporting period compared to an established baseline.

To put this all together visually, Figure 19-1 shows the relationship between these terms. Suppose you have a bunch of processes that make up your ISMS but there are two factors that are particularly important for you to track. Let's call them Factor A and Factor B, which could be anything, but for this hypothetical scenario, assume that they are network detection and response (NDR) system alerts and incidents declared. You intend to periodically take measurements for these factors, and the very first time you do so you get measurements A1 (say, 42 alerts) and B1 (7 incidents). You compare these measurements to each other and get your first metric A1:B1, which is the ratio of alerts generated to incidents declared (in this case, six). This metric might tell you how well tuned your NDR solution is; the higher the metric, the higher the number of false positives you're having to track down and, therefore, the less efficient your time is spent.

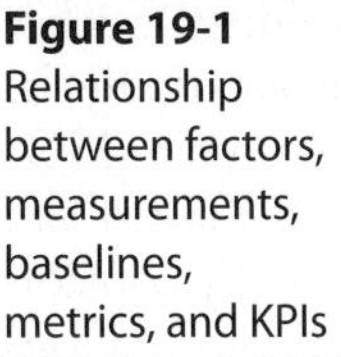

Figure 19-1 Relationship between factors, measurements, baselines, metrics, and KPIs

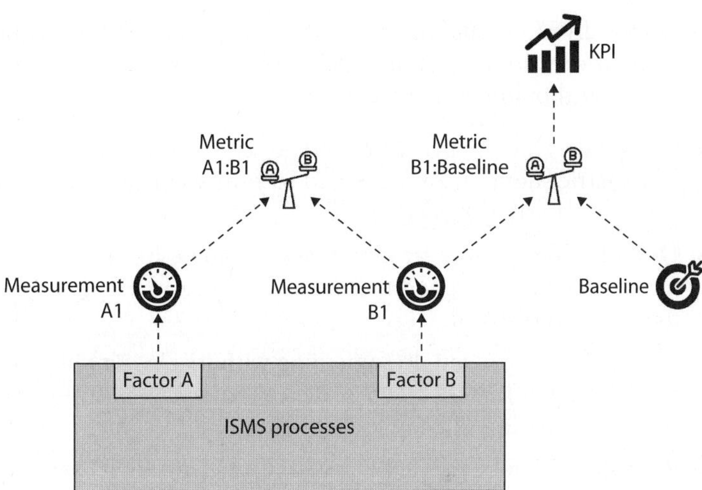

The second metric is a bit different. It is the comparison of B1 (the measurement of incidents) to some baseline you've established. Assume that management has determined that anything over five incidents per reporting period is a bad thing and might show that either your risk assessment is off (i.e., the threat is higher than you thought) or your ISMS is not doing well (i.e., your controls are not working as you need them to). This metric is particularly important to tracking your strategic business goals and thus becomes a key performance indicator (KPI). KPIs are discussed a bit later in this section.

Security Metrics

Security metrics sometimes get a bad reputation as tedious, burdensome, or even irrelevant. Many organizations pay lip service to them by latching on to the simple things that can easily be measured, such as the number of open tickets or how long it takes analysts to close each ticket. The problem with this approach is that it doesn't really generate valuable insights into how we are doing and how can we do better. In fact, if we measure the wrong things, we can end up doing more harm than good. For example, plenty of organizations rate their analysts based on how many tickets they close in a shift. This approach incentivizes throughput rather than careful analysis and oftentimes leads to missing evidence of ongoing attacks.

The best information security professionals use metrics to tell stories and, like any good storyteller, know their audience. What metrics we need and how we link them together depends on both the story we want to tell and the people to whom we'll be telling it. Board members typically like to hear about strategic threats and opportunities for the organization. Business managers may want to know how protected their business units are. Security operations leaders usually are most interested in how their teams are performing. In order to effectively engage each of these audiences, you need a different type of security metric.

Before we dive into the different types of metrics, it is important to identify what makes a good security metric in the first place. There are six characteristics of a good metric that you should consider:

- **Relevant** Does it align with your goals? Is it correlated with improved outcomes? The metric should be directly tied to your security goals and indirectly tied to your organization's business goals.
- **Quantifiable** Can it be objectively measured in a consistent manner? Could someone game it? A good metric should be relatively easy to measure with the tools at your disposal.
- **Actionable** Can you do something with it? Does it tell you what you must do to make things better? The best metrics inform your immediate actions, justify your requests, and directly lead to improved outcomes.
- **Robust** Will it be relevant in a year? Can you track it over many years? A good metric must allow you to track your situation over time to detect trends. It should capture information whose value endures.
- **Simple** Does it make intuitive sense? Will all stakeholders "get it?" Will they know what was measured and why it matters to them? If you can't explain the metric in a simple sentence, it probably is not a good one.
- **Comparative** Can it be evaluated against something else? Good metrics are the result of comparing measurements to each other or to some baseline or standard. This is why the best metrics are ratios, or percentages, or changes over time.

NOTE Another commonly used approach is to ensure metrics are SMART (specific, measurable, achievable, relevant, and time-bound).

Risk Metrics

Risk metrics capture the organizational risk and how it is changing over time. These are the metrics you're most likely to use if you are communicating with an executive audience, because these metrics are not technical. They are also forward-looking because they address things that may happen in the future. For these reasons, risk metrics are the best ones to support strategic analyses.

Depending on your organization's risk management program, you may already have risk metrics defined. Recall from Chapter 2 that quantitative risk management requires that you identify and capture risk metrics. Even if you use a qualitative approach, you probably have a good place from which to start. All you have to do is identify the variables that make your risks more or less likely to be realized and then start tracking those. Here are some examples of commonly used risk metrics:

- The percentage of change in your aggregated residual risks
- The percentage of change in your current worst-case risk
- The ratio of organizational security incidents to those reported by comparable organizations

Preparedness Metrics

There is another type of metric that indicates how prepared your organization is to deal with security incidents. These metrics are sometimes useful when dealing with executives, but they are more commonly used to monitor the security program as a whole. Preparedness metrics look at all your controls and how well they are being maintained. For example, are your policies and procedures being followed? Do your staff members know what they're supposed to (and not supposed to) do? What about your business partners?

Given the importance (and difficulty) of securing your organization's supply chain, your preparedness metrics should include the preparedness of organizations that are upstream from yours (in other words, your organization's suppliers of goods and services). Depending on your organization's relationship with them, you may have a lot of visibility into their security programs, which makes your assessment and measuring of them a lot easier. Even if they are fairly opaque and unwilling to give you enough information, you should develop a mechanism for rating their security, perhaps using an external or third-party audit, as discussed in Chapter 18.

Here are some examples of preparedness metrics used by many organizations:

- Monthly change in the mean time to patch a system
- Percentage of systems that are fully patched
- Percentage of staff that is up to date on security awareness training
- Ratio of privileged accounts to nonprivileged accounts
- Annual change in vendor security rating (i.e., how prepared is your organization's supply chain)

Performance Metrics

If risk metrics are fairly strategic and preparedness metrics are more operational, performance metrics are as tactical as they come. They measure how good your team and systems are at detecting, blocking, and responding to security incidents. In other words, performance metrics tell you how good you are at defeating your adversaries day in and day out.

If you've ever worked in or led a security operations center, performance metrics are the metrics you're probably most used to seeing. Some examples are listed here:

- Number of alerts analyzed this week/month compared to last week/month
- Number of security incidents declared this week/month compared to last week/month
- Percent change in mean time to detect (MTTD)
- Percent change in mean time to resolve (MTTR)

Key Performance and Risk Indicators

There is no shortage of security metrics in the industry, but not all are created equal. There are some that are important for tracking our processes and day-to-day operations. Other metrics, however, can tell us whether or not we are meeting strategic business goals.

These are the key performance indicators (KPIs) and key risk indicators (KRIs). KPIs measure how well things are going now, while KRIs measure how badly things could go in the future.

Key Performance Indicators

A *key performance indicator* is an indicator that is particularly significant in showing the performance of an ISMS compared to its stated goals. KPIs are carefully chosen from among a larger pool of indicators to show at a high level whether our ISMS is keeping pace with the threats to our organization or showing decreased effectiveness. KPIs should be easily understood by business and technical personnel alike and should be aligned with one or (better yet) multiple organizational goals.

Choosing KPIs really forces us to wrestle with the question "What is it that we're trying to accomplish here?" The process by which we choose KPIs is really driven by organizational goals. In an ideal case, the senior leadership sets (or perhaps approves) goals for the security of the organization. The ISMS team then gets to work on how to show whether we are moving toward or away from those goals. The process can be summarized as follows:

1. Choose the factors that can show the state of our security. In doing this, we want to strike a balance between the number of data sources and the resources required to capture all their data.
2. Define baselines for some or all of the factors under consideration. As we do this, it is helpful to consider which measurements will be compared to each other and which to some baseline. Keep in mind that a given baseline may apply to multiple factors' measurements.
3. Develop a plan for periodically capturing the values of these factors, and fix the sampling period. Ideally, we use automated means of gathering this data so as to ensure the periodicity and consistency of the process.
4. Analyze and interpret the data. While some analysis can (and probably should) be automated, there will be situations that require human involvement. In some cases, we'll be able to take the data at face value, while in others we will have to dig into it and get more information before reaching a conclusion about it.
5. Communicate the indicators to all stakeholders. In the end, we need to package the findings in a way that is understandable by a broad range of stakeholders. A common approach is to start with a nontechnical summary that is supported by increasingly detailed layers of supporting technical information. On the summary side of this continuum is where we select and put our KPIs.

This process is not universally accepted but represents some best security industry practices. At the end of the day, the KPIs are the product of distilling a large amount of information with the goal of answering one specific question: "Are we managing our information security well enough?" There is no such thing as perfect security, so what we are really trying to do is find the sweet spot where the performance of the ISMS is adequate and sustainable using an acceptable amount of resources. Clearly, this spot is a moving target given the ever-changing threat and risk landscape.

Key Risk Indicators

While KPIs tell us where we are today with regard to our goals, *key risk indicators* tell us where we are today in relation to our risk appetite. They measure how risky an activity is so that leadership can make informed decisions about that activity, all the while taking into account potential resource losses. Like KPIs, KRIs are selected for their impact on the decisions of the senior leaders in the organization. This means that KRIs often are not specific to one department or business function, but rather affect multiple aspects of the organization. KRIs have, by definition, a very high business impact.

When considering KRIs, it is useful to relate them to single loss expectancy (SLE) equations. Recall from Chapter 2 that SLE is the organization's potential monetary loss if a specific threat were to be realized. It is the product of the loss and the likelihood that the threat will occur. In other words, if we have a proprietary process for building widgets valued at $500,000 and we estimate a 5 percent chance of an attacker stealing and monetizing that process, then our SLE would be $25,000. Now, clearly, that 5 percent figure is affected by a variety of activities within the organization, such as IDS tuning, IR team proficiency, and end-user security awareness.

Over time, the likelihood of the threat being realized will change based on multiple activities going on within the organization. As this value changes, the risk changes too. A KRI would capture this and allow us to notice when we have crossed a threshold that makes our current activities too risky for our stated risk appetite. This trigger condition enables the organization to change its behavior to compensate for excessive risk. For instance, it could trigger an organizational stand-down for security awareness training.

In the end, the important thing to remember about KRIs is that they are designed to work much as coal mine canaries: they alert us when something bad is likely to happen so that we can change our behavior and defeat the threat.

EXAM TIP KPIs and KRIs are used to measure progress toward attainment of strategic business goals.

Security Process Data

Most of our metrics and indicators come from the security processes that make up our ISMS. There are other sources of measures, of course, but if we want to assess the effectiveness of our security controls, clearly we have to look at them first. To determine whether our controls are up to speed, we need to collect security process data from a variety of places. From how we manage our accounts to how we verify backups to the security awareness of our employees, administrative controls are probably more pervasive and less visible than our technical controls. It shouldn't be surprising that sophisticated threat actors often try to exploit administrative controls.

We covered a number of technical processes in the previous chapter. These included vulnerability assessments, various forms of attack simulations, and log reviews, to name a few. In the sections that follow, we look at some of the more administrative processes from which we can also collect data to help us determine our current posture and help us improve it over time. This is by no means an exhaustive list; it is simply a sampling that (ISC)² emphasizes in the CISSP exam objectives.

Account Management

A preferred technique of attackers is to become "normal" privileged users of the systems they compromise as soon as possible. They can accomplish this in at least three ways: compromise an existing privileged account, create a new privileged account, or elevate the privileges of a regular user account. The first approach can be mitigated through the use of strong authentication (e.g., strong passwords or, better yet, multifactor authentication) and by having administrators use privileged accounts only for specific tasks. The second and third approaches can be mitigated by paying close attention to the creation, modification, or misuse of user accounts. These controls all fall in the category of *account management.*

Adding Accounts

When new employees arrive, they should be led through a well-defined process that is aimed at ensuring not only that they understand their duties and responsibilities, but also that they are assigned the required organizational assets and that these are properly configured, protected, and accounted for. While the specifics of how this is accomplished vary from organization to organization, there are some specific administrative controls that should be universal.

First, all new users should be required to read through and acknowledge they understand (typically by signing) all policies that apply to them. At a minimum, every organization should have (and every user should sign) an acceptable use policy (AUP) that specifies what the organization considers acceptable use of the information systems that are made available to the employee. Using a workplace computer to view pornography, send hate e-mail, or hack other computers is almost always specifically forbidden in the AUP. On the other hand, many organizations allow their employees limited personal use, such as checking personal e-mail or surfing the Web during breaks. The AUP is a useful first line of defense, because it documents when each user was made aware of what is and is not acceptable use of computers (and other resources) at work. This makes it more difficult for a user to claim ignorance if they subsequently violate the AUP.

Testing that all employees are aware of the AUP and other applicable policies can be the first step in auditing user accounts. Since every user should have a signed AUP, for instance, all we need is to get a list of all users in the organization and then compare it to the files containing the signed documents. In many cases, all the documents a new employee signs are maintained by human resources (HR) and the computer accounts are maintained by IT. Cross-checking AUPs and user accounts can also verify that these two departments are communicating effectively.

The policies also should dictate the default expiration date of accounts, the password policy, and the information to which a user should have access. This last part becomes difficult because the information needs of individual users typically vary over time.

Modifying Accounts

Suppose a newly hired IT technician is initially assigned the task of managing backups for a set of servers. Over time, you realize this individual is best suited for internal user support, including adding new accounts, resetting passwords, and so forth. The privileges needed in each role are clearly different, so how should you handle this? Many organizations, unfortunately, resort to giving all privileges that a user may need. We have all been in, seen, or heard of organizations where every user is a local admin on his or her computer and every member of the IT department is a domain admin. This is an exceptionally dangerous practice, especially if they all use these elevated credentials by default. This is often referred to as *authorization creep*, which we discussed in Chapter 17.

Adding, removing, or modifying the permissions that a user has should be a carefully controlled and documented process. When are the new permissions effective? Why are they needed? Who authorized the change? Organizations that are mature in their security processes have a change control process in place to address user privileges. While many auditors focus on who has administrative privileges in the organization, there are many custom sets of permissions that approach the level of an admin account. It is important, then, to have and test processes by which elevated privileges are issued.

The Problem with Running as Root

It is undoubtedly easier to do all your work from one user account, especially if that account has all the privileges you could ever need. The catch, as you may well know, is that if your account is compromised, the malicious processes will run with whatever privileges the account has. If you run as root (or admin) all the time, you can be certain that if an attacker compromises your box, he instantly has the privileges to do whatever he needs or wants to do.

A better approach is to do as much of your daily work as you can using a restricted account and elevate to a privileged account only when you must. The way in which you do this varies by operating system:

- Windows operating systems allow you to right-click any program and select Run As to elevate your privileges. From the command prompt, you can use the command `runas /user:<AccountName>` to accomplish the same goal.
- In Linux operating systems, you can simply type `sudo<SomeCommand>` at the command line to run a program as the super (or root) user. Some Linux GUI desktop environments also offer the user the option of running with sudo (usually by checking a box) and prompting for a password.
- In macOS, you use `sudo` from the Terminal app just like you would do from a Linux terminal. However, if you want to run a GUI app with elevated privileges, you need to use `sudo open -a <AppName>` since there is no `gksudo` or `kdesudo` command.

PART VI

Suspending Accounts

Another important practice in account management is to suspend accounts that are no longer needed. Every large organization eventually stumbles across one or more accounts that belong to users who are no longer part of the organization. In extreme cases, an organization discovers that a user who left several months ago still has privileged accounts. The unfettered presence of these accounts on our networks gives adversaries a powerful means to become seemingly legitimate users, which makes our job of detecting and repulsing them that much more difficult.

Accounts may become unneeded, and thus require suspension, for a variety of reasons, but perhaps the most common one would be that the user of the account was terminated or otherwise left the organization. Other reasons for suspension include reaching the account's default expiration date, and temporary, but extended, absences of employees (e.g., maternity leave, military deployment). Whatever the reason, we must ensure that the account of someone who is not present to use it is suspended until that person returns or the term of our retention policy is met.

Testing the administrative controls on suspended accounts follows the same pattern already laid out in the preceding two sections: look at each account (or take a representative sample of all of them) and compare it with the status of its owner according to our HR records. Alternatively, we can get a list of employees who are temporarily or permanently away from the organization and check the status of those accounts. It is important that accounts are deleted only in strict accordance with the data retention policy. Many investigations into terminated employees have been thwarted because administrators have prematurely deleted user accounts and/or files.

Backup Verification

Modern organizations deal with vast amounts of data, which must be protected for a variety of reasons, including disaster recovery. We have all been in at least one situation in which we have lost data and needed to get it back. Some of us have had a rude awakening upon discovering that the data was lost permanently. The specific nature of the backup media is not as important as the fact that the data must be available when we need it most.

Magnetic tapes are now able to hold over 180 terabytes of data, which makes this seemingly antiquated technology the best in terms of total cost of ownership. That being said, many organizations prefer other technologies for daily operations, and relegate tapes to the role of backup to the backup. In other words, it is not uncommon for an organization to back up its user and enterprise data to a storage area network (SAN) on a daily basis, and back up these backups to tape on a weekly basis. Obviously, the frequency of each backup (hourly, daily, weekly) is driven by the risk management process discussed in Chapter 1.

Whatever the approach to backing up our organizational data, we need to periodically test it to ensure that the backups will work as promised when we need them. There are some organizations that have faced an event or disaster that required them to restore some or all data from backups, only to discover that the backups were missing, corrupted, or outdated. This section discusses some approaches to assess whether the data will be there when we need it.

CAUTION Never back up your data to the same device on which the original data exists.

Types of Data

Not all data is created equal, and different types may have unique requirements when it comes to backups. The following sections discuss some of the major categories of data that most of us deal with and some considerations when planning to preserve that data. Keep in mind, however, that there are many other types of data that we will not discuss here for the sake of brevity.

User Data Files This is the type of data with which most of us are familiar. These are the documents, presentations, and spreadsheets that we create or use on a daily basis. Though backing up these files may seem simple, challenges arise when users put "backup" copies in multiple locations for safekeeping. Users, if left to their own devices, may very well end up with inconsistently preserved files and may even violate retention requirements. The challenge with this type of data is ensuring that it is consistently backed up in accordance with all applicable policies, regulations, and laws.

Databases Databases are different from regular files in that they typically store the entire database in a special file that has its own file system within it. To make sense of this embedded file system, your database software uses metadata that lives in other files within your system. This architecture can create complex interdependencies among files on the database server. Fortunately, all major database management systems (DBMSs) include one or more means to back up their databases. The challenge is in ensuring that the backup will be sufficient to reconstitute the databases if necessary. To verify the backups, many organizations use a test database server that is periodically used to verify that the databases can be recovered from backup and that the queries will execute properly from the restored data.

Virtualization as a Backup and Security Strategy

Many organizations have virtualized their server infrastructure for performance and maintenance reasons. Some are also virtualizing their client systems and turning their workstations into thin clients on a virtualization infrastructure. The next step in this evolution is the use of virtual machine (VM) snapshots as a backup strategy. The main advantage to this approach is that restoration is almost instantaneous. All you typically have to do is click a button or issue a scripted command and the VM will revert to the designated state. Another key advantage is that this approach lends itself to automation and integration with other security systems so that if, for example, a workstation is compromised because the user clicked a link and an IDS detected this incident, then the VM can be instantly quarantined for later analysis while the user is dropped into the most recent snapshot automatically with very little impact to productivity.

Mailbox Data By some estimates, as much as 75 percent of an average organization's data lives in its mailboxes. Depending on the mail system your organization is running, the backup process may be very different. Still, some commonalities exist across all platforms, such as the critical need to document in excruciating detail every aspect of the configuration of the mail servers. Most medium-sized to large organizations have multiple mail servers (perhaps backing each other up), so it is a good idea not to back them up at the same time. Finally, whatever backup mechanism you have in place for your mail servers should facilitate compliance with e-discovery.

Verification

Having data backups is not particularly helpful unless we are able to use them to recover from mistakes, accidents, attacks, or disasters. Central to verifying this capability is understanding the sorts of things that can go wrong and which of them would require backups. Recall from our discussion on threat modeling in Chapter 9 that an important step in understanding risk is to consider what can happen or be done to our systems that would destroy, degrade, or disrupt our ability to operate. It is helpful to capture these possibilities in scenarios that can then inform how we go about ensuring that we are prepared for the likely threats to our information systems. It is also helpful to automate as much of the testing as possible, particularly in large organizations. This ensures that we cover the likely contingencies in a very methodical and predictable manner.

Some tests may cause disruptions to our business processes. It is difficult to imagine how a user's backups can be fully tested without involving that user in the process to some extent. If, for instance, our users store files locally and we want to test Mary's workstation backup, an approach could be to restore her backup to a new computer and have Mary log into and use the new computer as if it were the original. She would be in a better position than anyone else to determine whether everything works as expected. This kind of thorough testing is expensive and disruptive, but it ensures that we have in place what we need. Obviously, we have to be very selective about when and how we impact our business processes, so it becomes a trade-off.

However you decide to implement your backup verification, you must ensure that you are able to assert that all critical data is backed up and that you will be able to restore it in time of need. This means that you probably have to develop an inventory of data and a schedule for testing it as part of your plan. This inventory will be a living document, so you must have a means to track and document changes to it. Fortunately, major items such as mail and database servers don't change very frequently. The challenge is in verifying the backups of user data.

This brings us back to our policies. We already discussed the importance of the organization's data retention policy, but an equally important one is the policy that dictates how user data is backed up. Many organizations require their staff to maintain their files on file shares on network servers, but we all know that users don't necessarily always do this. It is not uncommon for users to keep a local folder with the data that is most important to them. If the local files are not being backed up, then we risk losing the most critical files, particularly if backups can be disabled by the user. The point of this is that policies need to be carefully thought out and aggressively enforced if we are to be ready for the day when things go badly for us.

Testing Data Backups

It is important to develop formal processes for testing your data backups to ensure they are available when needed. The following are some elements that should be included in these processes:

- *Develop scenarios* that capture specific sets of events that are representative of the threats facing the organization.
- *Develop a plan* that tests all the mission-critical data backups in each of the scenarios.
- *Leverage automation* to minimize the effort required by the auditors and ensure tests happen periodically.
- *Minimize impact on business* processes of the data backup test plan so that it can be executed regularly.
- *Ensure coverage* so that every system is tested, though not necessarily in the same test.
- *Document the results* so you know what is working and what needs to be worked on.
- *Fix or improve* any issues you documented.

Security Training and Security Awareness Training

As should be clear from the preceding discussions, having a staff that is well trained in security issues is crucial to the security of our organizations. The terms security training and security awareness training are often used interchangeably, but they have subtly different meanings. *Security training* is the process of teaching a skill or set of skills that enables people to perform specific security functions better. *Security awareness training*, on the other hand, is the process of exposing people to security issues so that they are able to recognize and respond to them better. Security training is typically provided to security personnel, while security awareness training should be provided to every member of the organization.

Assessing the effectiveness of our security training programs is fairly straightforward because the training is tied to specific security functions. Therefore, to test the effectiveness of a training program, all we have to do is test the performance of an individual on those functions before and after the training. If the performance improves, then the training was probably effective. Keep in mind that skills atrophy over time, so the effectiveness of the training should be measured immediately after it concludes. Otherwise, we are assessing the long-term retention of the functional skills.

We now turn our attention to the somewhat more difficult issue of assessing the effectiveness of a security awareness training program. As we broach this subject, keep in mind that the end state is to better equip our teammates to recognize and deal with security issues that arise while they are performing their everyday tasks. This implies that a key measure of the effectiveness of the security awareness program is the degree to which people change their behaviors when presented with certain situations. If this change is toward a better security posture, then we can infer that the program was effective. In the following sections, we take a look at specific components of a security awareness training program that are common to many organizations.

EXAM TIP Security awareness (and the training required to attain it) is one of the most critical controls in any ISMS. Expect exam questions on this topic.

Social Engineering

Social engineering, in the context of information security, is the process of manipulating individuals so that they perform actions that violate security protocols. Whether the action is divulging a password, letting someone into the building, or simply clicking a link, it has been carefully designed by the adversaries to help them exploit our information systems. A common misconception is that social engineering is an art of improvisation. While improvising may help the attacker better respond to challenges, the reality is that most effective social engineering is painstakingly designed against a particular target, sometimes a specific individual.

Perhaps the most popular form of social engineering is *phishing*, which is social engineering conducted through a digital communication. Figure 19-2 depicts the flow of a typical e-mail phishing attack. (While e-mail phishing receives a lot of attention, text messages can also be used to similar effect.) Like casting a baited fishing line into a

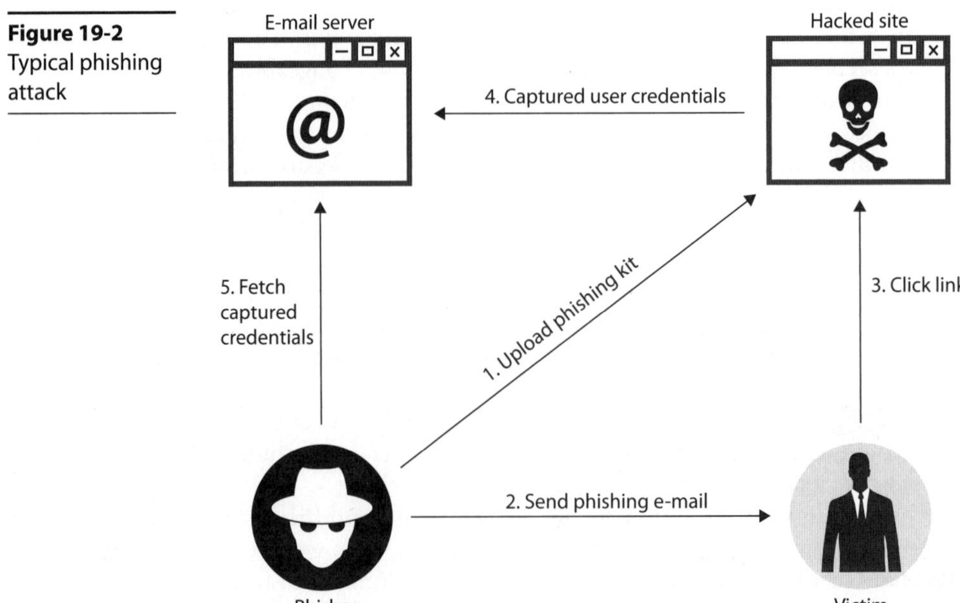

Figure 19-2 Typical phishing attack

pond full of fish, phishing relies on the odds that if enough people receive an enticing or believable message, at least one of them will click an embedded link within it.

Some adversaries target specific individuals or groups, which is referred to as *spear-phishing*. In some cases, the targets are senior executives, in which case it is called *whaling*. In whatever variety it comes, the desired result of phishing is usually to have the target click a link that will take them to a website under the control of the attacker. Sometimes the website looks like the legitimate logon page of a trusted site, such as that of the user's bank. Other times, the website is a legitimate one that has been compromised by the attacker to redirect users somewhere else. In the case of a *drive-by download*, the site invisibly redirects the user to a malware distribution server, as shown in Figure 19-3.

Pretexting is a form of social engineering, typically practiced in person or over the phone, in which the attacker invents a believable scenario in an effort to persuade the target to violate a security policy. A common example is a call received from (allegedly) customer service or fraud prevention at a bank in which the attacker tries to get the target to reveal account numbers, personal identification numbers (PINs), passwords, or similarly valuable information. Remarkably, pretexting was legal in the United States until 2007, as long as it was not used to obtain financial records. In 2006, Hewlett-Packard became embroiled in a scandal dealing with its use of pretexting in an effort to identify the sources of leaks on its board of directors. Congress responded by passing the Telephone Records and Privacy Protection Act of 2006, which imposes stiff criminal penalties on anyone who uses pretexting to obtain confidential information.

So how does one go about assessing security awareness programs aimed at countering social engineering in all its forms? One way is to keep track of the number of times users fall victim to these attacks before and after the awareness training effort. The challenge with this approach is that victims may not spontaneously confess to falling for

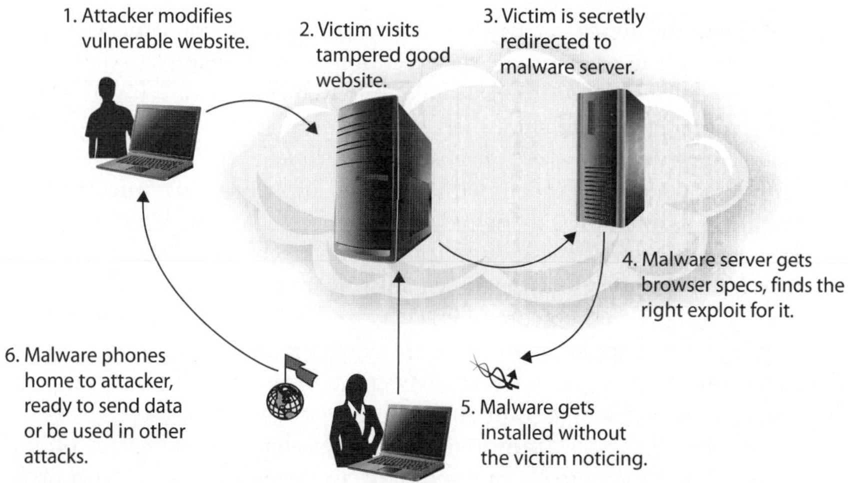
1. Attacker modifies vulnerable website.
2. Victim visits tampered good website.
3. Victim is secretly redirected to malware server.
4. Malware server gets browser specs, finds the right exploit for it.
5. Malware gets installed without the victim noticing.
6. Malware phones home to attacker, ready to send data or be used in other attacks.

Figure 19-3 Drive-by downloads

these tricks, and our security systems will certainly not detect all instances of successful attacks. Another approach is to have auditors (internal or external) conduct benign social engineering campaigns against our users. When users click a link inserted by the auditors, they are warned that they did something wrong and perhaps are redirected to a web page or short video explaining how to avoid such mistakes in the future. All the while, our automated systems are keeping tabs on which users are most susceptible and how often these attacks are successful. Anecdotal evidence suggests that there is a group of users who will not respond to remedial training, so the leadership should decide what to do with individuals who repeatedly make the wrong choices.

Online Safety

Oftentimes users don't have to be tricked into doing something wrong, but willingly go down that path. This is often the result of ignorance of the risks, and the remediation of this ignorance is the whole point of the security awareness campaign. An effective security awareness program should include issues associated with unsafe online behavior that could represent risk for the organization.

Perhaps one of the most important elements of safe online behavior is the proper use of social media. A good starting point is the proper use of privacy settings, particularly considering that all major social media sites have means to restrict what information is shared with whom. The default settings are not always privacy-focused, so it is important for users to be aware of their options. This becomes particularly important when users post information concerning their workplace. Part of the security awareness program should be to educate users about the risks they can pose to their employers if their posts reveal sensitive information. Once posted, the information cannot be recalled; it is forevermore out there.

Sometimes it is not what goes out to the Internet but what comes in from it that should concern users. Simply surfing to the wrong website, particularly from a workplace computer, may be all it takes to bring down the whole organization. In the case of a drive-by download, the attack is triggered simply by visiting a malicious website. While the mechanisms vary, the effect can be the execution of malware on the client computer, with or without additional user interaction. While web filters can mitigate some of the risk of surfing to inappropriate sites, malicious websites sometimes are legitimate ones that have been compromised, which means that the filters may not be effective.

While some downloads happen without user knowledge or interaction, others are intentional. It is not unusual for naïve users to attempt to download and install unauthorized and potentially risky applications on their computers. Unfortunately, many organizations do not use software whitelisting and even allow their users to have administrative privileges on their computers, which allows them to install any application they desire. Even benign applications can be problematic for the security of our systems, but when you consider that the software may come from an untrusted and potentially malicious source, the problem is compounded.

Assessing the effectiveness of an awareness campaign that promotes users' online safety is not easy and typically requires a multipronged approach. Social media posts may be detected using something as simple as Google Alerts, which trigger whenever Google's robots find a term of interest online. A simple script can then filter out the alerts by source in order to separate, say, a news outlet report on our organization from an ill-advised social media post. The software download problem (whether intentional or not) can be assessed by a well-tuned IDS. Over time, with an effective awareness campaign, we should see the number of incidents go down, which will allow us to focus our attention on repeat offenders.

Data Protection

We already covered data protection in Chapter 6, but for the purposes of assessing a security awareness program, it bears repeating that sensitive data must always be encrypted whether at rest or in transit. It is possible for users to circumvent controls and leave this data unprotected, so awareness is a key to preventing this type of behavior. Unencrypted data is vulnerable to leaks if it is stored in unauthorized online resources or intentionally (but perhaps not maliciously) shared with others. Another important topic is the proper destruction of sensitive data when it is no longer needed and falls out of the mandatory retention period (see Chapter 5).

Testing the degree to which our users are aware of data protection requirements and best practices can best be done by using tags in our files' metadata. The information classification labels we discussed in Chapter 5 become an effective means of tracking where our data is. Similarly, data loss prevention (DLP) solutions can help stop leaks and identify individuals who are maliciously or inadvertently exposing our sensitive information. This allows us to target those users either with additional awareness training or with disciplinary actions.

Culture

At the end of the day, the best way to test the security awareness of an organization may be by assessing its security culture. Do we have the kind of environment in which users feel safe self-reporting? Are they well incentivized to do so? Do they actively seek information and guidance when encountering a strange or suspicious situation? Self-reports and requests for information by users provide a good indicator of whether the organizational culture is helping or hindering us in securing our systems.

Disaster Recovery and Business Continuity

Most organizations cannot afford to be incapable of performing their business processes for very long. Depending on the specific organization, the acceptable downtime can be measured in minutes, hours, or, in some noncritical sectors, maybe days. Consequently, we all need to have procedures in place for ensuring we can go on working regardless of what happens around or to us. As introduced in Chapter 2, *business continuity* is the term used to describe the processes enacted by an organization to ensure that its vital business processes remain unaffected or can be quickly restored following a serious incident. Business continuity looks holistically at the entire organization. A subset of this effort, called *disaster recovery*, focuses on restoring the information systems after a disastrous event. Like any other business process, these processes must be periodically assessed to ensure they are still effective.

Often, the initial response to an emergency affects the ultimate outcome. Emergency response procedures are the prepared actions that are developed to help people in a crisis situation better cope with the disruption. These procedures are the first line of defense when dealing with a crisis situation. People who are up to date on their knowledge of these procedures will perform the best, which is why training and drills are very important. Emergencies are unpredictable, and no one knows when they will be called upon to perform their disaster recovery duties.

Protection of life is of the utmost importance and should be dealt with first before attempting to save material objects. Emergency procedures should show the people in charge how to evacuate personnel safely (see Table 19-1). All personnel should know their designated emergency exits and destinations. Emergency gathering spots should take into consideration the effects of seasonal weather. One person in each designated group is often responsible for making sure all people are accounted for. One person in particular should be responsible for notifying the appropriate authorities: the police department, security guards, fire department, emergency rescue, and management. With proper training, employees will be better equipped to handle emergencies and avoid the reflex to just run to the exit.

EXAM TIP Protection of human life is always the top priority in situations where it is threatened.

If the situation is not life threatening, designated staff should shut down systems in an orderly fashion, and remove critical data files or resources during evacuation for safekeeping. There is a reason for the order of activities. As with all processes, there are

Procedure: Personnel Evacuation Description	Location	Names of Staff Trained to Carry Out Procedure	Date Last Carried Out
Each floor within the building must have two individuals who will ensure that all personnel have been evacuated from the building after a disaster. These individuals are responsible for performing employee head count, communicating with the business continuity plan (BCP) coordinator, and assessing emergency response needs for their employees.	West wing parking lot	David Miller Michelle Lester	Drills were carried out on May 4, 2021.
Comments: These individuals are responsible for maintaining an up-to-date listing of employees on their specific floor. These individuals must have a company-issued walkie-talkie and proper training for this function.			

Table 19-1 Sample Emergency Response Procedure

dependencies with everything we do. Deciding to skip steps or add steps could in fact cause more harm than good.

Once things have approached a reasonable plateau of activity, one or more people will most likely be required to interface with external entities, such as the press, customers, shareholders, and civic officials. One or more people should be prepped in their reaction and response to the recent disaster so a uniform and reasonable response is given to explain the circumstances, how the organization is dealing with the disaster, and what customers and others should now expect from the organization. The organization should quickly present this information instead of allowing others to come to their own conclusions and start false rumors. At least one person should be available to the press to ensure proper messages are being reported and sent out.

Another unfortunate issue needs to be addressed prior to an emergency: potential looting, vandalism, and fraud opportunities from both a physical perspective and a logical perspective. After an organization is hit with a large disturbance or disaster, it is usually at its most vulnerable, and others may take advantage of this vulnerability. Careful thought and planning, such as provision of sufficient security personnel on site, enable the organization to deal with these issues properly and provide the necessary and expected level of protection at all times.

Ideally, we collect most of the data we need for assessing our disaster recovery and business continuity processes before any real emergencies arise. This allows us to ensure we are prepared and to improve the effectiveness of our organizational responses to these unforeseen events. Still, the best data is captured during an actual emergency situation. After any real or training events, it is imperative that we have a debriefing immediately after it. This event, sometimes called a *hot wash*, must happen while memories are still fresh. It is an ad hoc discussion of what happened, how we dealt with it, what went well, and how we can do better in the future. Ideally, it is followed by a more deliberate *after-action review (AAR)* that takes place later, once the stakeholders have had a chance to think through the events and responses and analyze them in more detail. Hot wash notes and AAR reports are excellent sources of security process data for disaster recovery and business continuity.

Reporting

For many security professionals, report writing is perhaps one of the least favorite activities, and yet it is often one of the most critical tasks for our organizations. While we all thrive on putting hands on keyboards and patch panels when it comes to securing our networks, we often cringe at the thought of putting in writing what it is that we've done and what it means to the organization. This is probably the task that best distinguishes the true security professional from the security practitioner: the professional understands the role of information systems security within the broader context of the business and is able to communicate this to both technical and nontechnical audiences alike.

It seems that many of us have no difficulty (though perhaps a bit of reluctance) describing the technical details of a plan we are proposing, a control we have implemented, or an audit we have conducted. It may be a bit tedious, but we've all done this at some point in our careers. The problem with these technical reports, important though they are, is that they are written by and for technical personnel. If your CEO is a technical person running a technical company, this may work fine. However, sooner or later most of us will work with decision-makers that are not inherently technical. These leaders will probably not be as excited about the details of an obscure vulnerability you just discovered as they will be about its impact on the business. If you want your report to have a business impact, it must be both technically sound and written in the language of the business.

Analyzing Results

Before you start typing that report, however, you probably want to take some time to review the outputs, ensure you understand them, and then infer what they mean to your organization. Only after analyzing the results can you provide insights and recommendations that will help maintain or improve your organization's security.

The goal of this analysis process is to move logically from facts to actionable information. A list of vulnerabilities and policy violations is of little value to business leaders unless it is placed in context. Once you have analyzed all the results in this manner, you'll be ready to start writing the official report.

You can think of analyzing results as a three-step process to determine the following: What?, So what?, and Now what? First you gather all your data, organize it, and study it carefully. You find out *what* is going on. This is where you establish the relevant and interesting facts. For example, you may have determined the fact that 12 of your servers are not running on the latest software release. Worse yet, you may have found that three of those servers have vulnerabilities that are being exploited in the wild. The instinctive reaction of many would be to say this is a big deal that needs to be corrected immediately. But wait.

The second step in your analysis is to determine the business impact of those facts. This is the *so what?* Though we tend to focus on the technology and security aspects of our environments, we have a responsibility to consider facts in a broader organizational context. Continuing with the previous example, you may find that those 12 servers provide a critical business function and cannot be updated in the near term for perfectly legitimate operations reasons. You may also discover that you already have compensatory administrative or technical controls that mitigate the risk they pose. So maybe it's not that big of a deal after all.

The third step is to figure out the *now what?* The whole point of measuring security is to ensure it is sufficient or to improve it so that it is sufficient. The analysis process leads to results, and these are only valuable if they are actionable. They must point to one or more sound recommendations that address the broader organizational needs. In our example, you clearly don't want to leave those servers as they are indefinitely. Maybe you have considered two courses of action: either leave things as they are but reassess every 30 days or update the servers immediately despite the resulting business impact. You evaluate the alternatives using risk and business impact as decision criteria and ultimately decide that keeping an extra-close eye on the unpatched servers for a few more weeks is the better course of action. You put down a date for the next decision point and go from there. The point is that your decision is based on a sound analysis of the facts.

Remediation

Most assessments uncover vulnerabilities. While many cybersecurity practitioners think of vulnerabilities in terms of software defects to be patched, the reality is that most vulnerabilities in the average organization tend to come from misconfigured systems, inadequate policies, unsound business processes, or unaware staff. Correcting most of these vulnerabilities requires engagement by more than just the IT or security teams. Even the more mundane system patches need to be carefully coordinated with all affected departments within the organization. Vulnerability remediation should include all stakeholders, especially those who don't have the word "security" anywhere in their job titles.

The fact that you're leveraging a multifunctional extended team to remediate vulnerabilities highlights the need for the sound analyses described in the previous section. You'll need the support of everyone from the very top of the organization on down, which is why you want to educate them on your findings, why they are impacted, and what you must all do about them. It is likely that remediation will impact the business, so it is also critical to have contingency plans and be able to handle exceptional cases.

Exception Handling

Sometimes, vulnerabilities simply can't be patched (at least, not in any reasonable amount of time). Some of us have dealt with very big and expensive medical devices that require Food and Drug Administration accreditations that preclude their patching without putting them through an expensive and time-consuming recertification process. The solution is to implement compensatory controls around the problem, document the exception, and revisit the vulnerability over time to see if can be remediated directly at some point in the future. For example, a medical device may be micro-segmented in its own VLAN behind a firewall that would only allow one other device to communicate with it, and then using only a specific port and protocol.

The Language of Your Audience

You cannot be an effective communicator if you don't know your audience. Learning to speak the language(s) of those you are trying to inform, advise, or lead is absolutely critical. It has been said that accounting is the language of business, which means you can generally do well communicating in terms of the financial impacts of your findings. The fact that risks are expressed as the probability of a certain amount of loss should make this fairly easy as long as you have some sort of risk management program in place.

Still, in order to up your game, you want to be able to communicate in the language of the various disciplines that make up a business. Human resource leaders will care most about issues like staff turnover and organizational culture. Your marketing (or public affairs) team will be focused on what external parties think about your organization. Product managers will be very reluctant to support proposals that can slow down their delivery tempo. We could go on, but the point is that, while the facts and analyses must be unassailable, you should always try to communicate them in the language of…whoever it is you're trying to persuade.

> **Ethical Disclosure**
>
> Occasionally, security assessments lead to discoveries of vulnerabilities that were not known and which affect other organizations. Perhaps you were performing a code review on one of the products your company sells and you discovered a vulnerability, or maybe your pentesting team was conducting a pen test on a system your organization bought from one of its vendors and they found a previously unknown way to exploit the system. However you discover the vulnerability, you have an ethical obligation to properly disclose it to the appropriate parties. If the vulnerability is in your own product, you need to notify your customers and partners as soon as possible. If it is in someone else's product, you need to notify the vendor or manufacturer immediately so they can fix it. The goal of ethical disclosure is to inform anyone who might be affected as soon as feasible, so a patch can be developed before any threat actors become aware of the vulnerability.

More commonly, exception handling is required because something crashed while we were attempting to patch a system. Though we should always test patches in a sandbox environment before pushing them out to production systems, we can never be 100 percent certain that something won't go wrong. In those cases, particularly if the system is mission-critical, we roll back the patch, get the system back online as quickly and securely as we can, document the exception, and move on with remediation of other systems. We circle back, of course, but exception handling is typically a time-intensive effort that should not delay the larger remediation effort.

Writing Technical Reports

After analyzing the assessment results, the next step is to document. A technical report should be much more than the output of an automated scanning tool or a generic checklist with yes and no boxes. There are way too many so-called auditors that simply push the start button on a scanning tool, wait for it to do its job, and then print a report with absolutely none of the analysis we just discussed.

A good technical report tells a story that is interesting and compelling *for its intended audience*. It is very difficult to write one without a fair amount of knowledge about its readers, at least the most influential ones. Your goal, after all, is to persuade them to take whatever actions are needed to balance risks and business functions for the betterment of the organization. Simultaneously, you want to anticipate likely objections that could undermine the conversation. Above all else, you must be absolutely truthful and draw all conclusions directly from empirical facts. To improve your credibility, you should always provide in an appendix the relevant raw data, technical details, and automated reports.

The following are key elements of a good technical audit report:

- **Executive Summary** We'll get into the weeds of this in the next section, but you should always consider that some readers may not be able to devote more than a few minutes to your report. Preface it with a hard-hitting summary of key take-aways.

- **Background** Explain why you conducted the experiment/test/assessment/audit in the first place. Describe the scope of the event, which should be tied to the reason for doing it in the first place. This is a good place to list any relevant references such as policies, industry standards, regulations, or statutes.
- **Methodology** As most of us learned in our science classes, experiments (and audits) must be repeatable. Describe the process by which you conducted the study. This is also a good section in which to list the personnel who participated, dates, times, locations, and any parts of the system that were excluded (and why).
- **Findings** You should group your findings to make them easier to search and read for your audience. If the readers are mostly senior managers, you may want to group your findings by business impact. Technologists may prefer groupings by class of system. Each finding should include the answer to "so what?" from your analysis.
- **Recommendations** This section should mirror the organization of your findings and provide the "now what?" from your analysis. This is the actionable part of the report, so you should make it compelling. When writing it, you should consider how each key reader will react to your recommendations. For instance, if you know the CFO is reluctant to make new capital investments, then you could frame expensive recommendations in terms of operational costs instead.
- **Appendices** You should include as much raw data as possible, but you certainly want to include enough to justify your recommendations. Pay attention to how you organize the appendices so that readers can easily find whatever data they may be looking for.

If you are on the receiving end of this process, always be wary of reports that look auto-generated, which usually points to an ineffective auditing team. Also be careful about reports that, having failed to find any significant vulnerabilities, overemphasize the importance of less important flaws. If the security posture of the organization is good, then the auditors should not shy away from saying so.

Executive Summaries

Getting into the technical weeds with an audit report is wonderful for techies, but it doesn't do the business folks any good. The next step in writing impactful reports is to translate the key findings and recommendations into language that is approachable and meaningful to the senior leadership of your organization. After all, it is their support that will allow you to implement the necessary changes. They will provide both the authority and resources that you will need.

Typically, technical reports (among others) include an executive summary of no more than a page or two, which highlights what senior leaders need to know from the report. The goal is to get their attention and effect the desired change. One way to get a business leader's attention is to explain the audit findings in terms of risk exposure. Security is almost always perceived as a cost center for the business. A good way to show return on investment (ROI) for a department that doesn't generate profits is by quantifying how much money a recommended change could potentially save the company.

One way to quantify risk is to express it in monetary terms. We could say that the risk (in dollars) is the value of an asset multiplied by the probability of the loss of that asset. In other words, if our customer's data is worth $1 million and there is a 10 percent chance that this data will be breached, then our risk for this data breach would be $100,000. How can we come up with these values? There are different ways in which accountants valuate other assets, but the most common are the following.

- The *cost approach* simply looks at the cost of acquiring or replacing the asset. This is the approach we oftentimes take to valuating our IT assets (minus information, of course). How might it be applied to information? Well, if an information asset is a file containing a threat intelligence report that cost the organization $10,000, then the cost approach would attach that value to this asset.
- The *income approach* considers the expected contribution of the asset to the firm's revenue stream. The general formula is value equals expected (or potential) income divided by capitalization rate. The capitalization rate is the actual net income divided by the value of the asset. So, for instance, if that $10,000 threat intelligence report brought in $1,000 in net income last year (so the capitalization rate is 0.10) and our projections are that it will bring in $2,000 this year, then its present value would be $2,000 ÷ 0.10, or $20,000. As you should be able to see, the advantage of this approach is that it takes into account the past and expected business conditions.
- The *market approach* is based on determining how much other firms are paying for a similar asset in the marketplace. It requires a fair amount of transparency in terms of what other organizations are doing. For instance, if we have no way of knowing how much others paid for that threat intelligence report, then we couldn't use a market approach to valuating it. If, on the other hand, we were able to find out that the going rate for the report is actually $12,000, then we can use that value for our report (asset) and celebrate that we got a really good deal.

So, as long as the life-cycle costs of implementing our proposed controls (say, $180,000) are less than the risks they mitigate (say, $1,000,000), it should be obvious that we should implement the control, right? Not quite. The controls, after all, are not perfect. They will not be able to eliminate the risk altogether, and will sometimes fail. This means that we need to know the likelihood that the control will be effective at thwarting an attack. Let's say that we are considering a solution that has been shown to be effective about 80 percent of the time and costs $180,000. We know that we have a 10 percent chance of being attacked and, if we are, that we have a 20 percent chance of our control failing to protect us. This means that the residual risk is 2 percent of $1,000,000, or $20,000. This is then added to the cost of our control ($180,000) to give us the total effective cost of $200,000.

This is the sort of content that is impactful when dealing with senior leaders. They want to know the answers to questions such as these: How likely is this control to work? How much will it save us? How much will it cost? The technical details are directly important to the ISMS team and only indirectly important to the business leaders. Keep that in mind the next time you package an audit report for executive-level consumption.

Management Review and Approval

A management review is a formal meeting of senior organizational leaders to determine whether the management systems are effectively accomplishing their goals. In the context of the CISSP, we are particularly interested in the performance of the ISMS. While we restrict our discussion here to the ISMS, you should be aware that the management review is typically much broader in scope.

While management reviews have been around for a very long time, the modern use of the term is perhaps best grounded in quality standards such as the ISO 9000 series. These standards define a Plan-Do-Check-Act loop, depicted in Figure 19-4. This cycle of continuous improvement elegantly captures the essence of most topics we cover in this book. The Plan phase is the foundation of everything else we do in an ISMS, because it determines our goals and drives our policies. The Do phase of the loop is the focal point of Part VII of this book ("Security Operations"). The Check phase is the main topic of this chapter and the previous one. Lastly, the Act phase is what we formally do in the management review. We take all the information derived from the preceding stages and decide whether we need to adjust our goals, standards, or policies in order to continuously improve our posture.

The management review, unsurprisingly, looks at the big picture in order to help set the strategy moving forward. For this reason, a well-run review will not be drawn into detailed discussions on very specific technical topics. Instead, it takes a holistic view of the organization and makes strategic decisions, which is the primary reason why the management review must include all the key decision makers in the organization. This top-level involvement is what gives our ISMS legitimacy and power.

When communicating with senior executives, it is important to speak the language of the business and to do so in a succinct manner. We already discussed this style of communication when we covered reports in the previous section, but it bears repeating here. If we are not able to clearly and quickly get the point across to senior leaders on the first try, we may not get another chance to do so.

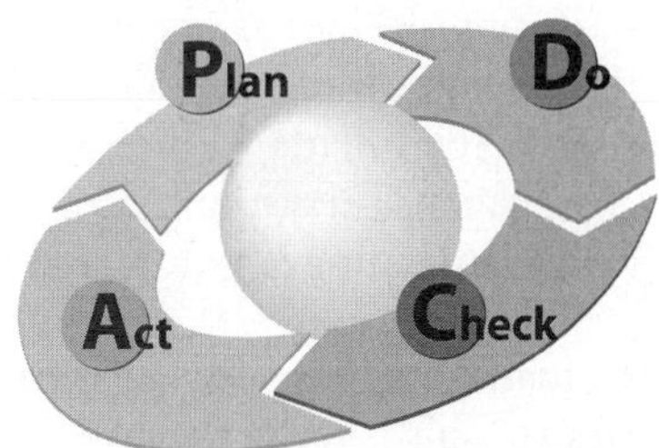

Figure 19-4 The Plan-Do-Check-Act loop

Before the Management Review

The management review should happen periodically. The more immature the management system and/or the organization, the more frequent these reviews should take place. Obviously, the availability of the key leaders will be a limiting factor during scheduling. This periodicity helps ensure that the entire organization is able to develop an operational rhythm that feeds the senior-level decision-making process. Absent this regularity, the reviews risk becoming reactive rather than proactive.

The frequency of the meetings should also be synchronized with the length of time required to implement the decisions of the preceding review. If, for instance, the leaders decided to implement sweeping changes that will take a year to develop, integrate, and measure, then having a review before the year is up may not be particularly effective. This is not to say that enough time must lapse to allow every single change to yield measurable results, but if these reviews are conducted too frequently, management won't be able to make decisions that are informed by the results of the previous set of actions.

Reviewing Inputs

The inputs to the management review come from a variety of sources. A key input is the results of relevant audits, both external and internal. These are, in part, the reports described earlier in the chapter. In addition to making the audit reports available for review, it is also necessary to produce executive summaries that describe the key findings, the impact to the organization, and the recommended changes (if any). Remember to write these summaries in business language.

Another important input to the review is the list of open issues and action items from the previous management review. Ideally, all these issues have been addressed and all actions have been completed and verified. If that is not the case, it is important to highlight whatever issues (e.g., resources, regulations, changes in the landscape) prevented them from being closed. Senior leaders normally don't like surprises (particularly unpleasant ones), so it might be wise to warn them of any unfinished business before the review is formally convened.

In addition to the feedback from auditors and action officers, customer feedback is an important input to the management review. Virtually every organization has customers, and they are normally the reason for the organization to exist in the first place. Their satisfaction, or lack thereof, is crucial to the organization's success. Chapter 18 mentioned real user monitoring (RUM) as one way of measuring their interactions with our information systems. Organizations are also increasingly relying on social media analysis to measure customer sentiments with regard to the organization in general and specific issues. Finally, we can use questionnaires or surveys, although these tend to have a number of challenges, including very low response rates and negative bias among respondents.

The final inputs to the management review are the recommendations for improvement based on all the other inputs. This is really the crux of the review. (While it is technically possible for a review to include no substantive change recommendations, it would be extremely unusual since it would mean that the ISMS team cannot think of any way to improve the organizational posture.) The ISMS team presents proposed high-level changes that require the approval and/or support of the senior leaders. This is not the place to discuss low-level tactical changes; we can take care of those ourselves. Instead, we would want to ask for changes to key policies or additional resources. These recommendations must logically follow from the other inputs that have been presented to the review panel.

In setting the stage for the senior leaders' decision-making process, it is often useful to present them with a range of options. Many security professionals typically offer three to five choices, depending on the complexity of the issues. For instance, one option could be "do nothing," which describes what happens if no changes are made. At the other end of the spectrum, we could state an option that amounts to the solid-gold approach in which we pull out all the stops and make bold and perhaps costly changes that are all but guaranteed to take care of the problems. In between, we would offer one to three other choices with various levels of risk, resource requirements, and business appeal.

When we present the options, we should also present objective evaluative criteria for management to consider. A criterion that is almost always required in the presentation is the monetary cost of the change. This factor should be the life-cycle cost of the option, not just the cost of implementation. It is a common mistake to overlook the maintenance costs over the life of the system/process, disregarding the fact that these costs are often much greater than the acquisition price tag. Other factors you may want to consider presenting are risk, impact on existing systems or processes, training requirements, and complexity. But whatever evaluative factors you choose, you should apply them to each of the options in order to assess which is the best one.

Management Approval

The senior leadership considers all the inputs; typically asks some pretty pointed questions; and then decides to approve, reject, or defer the recommendations. The amount of debate or discussion at this point is typically an indicator of how effective the ISMS team was at presenting sound arguments for changes that are well nested within (and supportive of) the business processes. Obviously, the leadership's decisions are the ultimate testament to how convincing the ISMS team's arguments were.

Typically, senior management will decide to either approve the recommendation in its entirety, approve it with specific changes, reject the recommendation, or send the ISMS team back to either get more supporting data or redesign the options. Regardless of the outcome, there will likely be a list of deliverables for the next management review that will have to be addressed. It is a good idea to conclude the management review with a review of open and action items, who will address them, and when each is due. These all become inputs to the next management review in a cycle that continues indefinitely.

Chapter Review

Whereas the focus of Chapter 18 was assessing and testing technical controls, this chapter discussed administrative controls, analyzing results, and communicating them effectively. We also introduced a couple of tools that will make this effort a whole lot easier (and more effective) for you: security metrics, KPIs, and KRIs. Together with the topics discussed in the previous chapter, we hope to have given you useful insights into how to measure and improve your ISMS, particularly when improvements depend on your ability to persuade other leaders in your organization to support your efforts. This all sets the stage for the next part of this book: "Security Operations."

Quick Review

- A factor is an attribute of an ISMS that has a value that can change over time.
- A measurement is a quantitative observation of a factor at a particular point in time.
- A baseline is a value for a factor that provides a point of reference or denotes that some condition is met by achieving some threshold value.
- A metric is a derived value that is generated by comparing multiple measurements against each other or against a baseline.
- Good metrics are relevant, quantifiable, actionable, robust, simple, and comparative.
- An indicator is a particularly important metric that describes a key element of the effectiveness of an ISMS.
- A key performance indicator (KPI) is an indicator that is particularly significant in showing the performance of an ISMS compared to its stated goals.
- Key risk indicators (KRIs) measure the risk inherent in performing a given action or set of actions.
- Privileged user accounts pose significant risk to the organization and should be carefully managed and controlled.
- User accounts should be promptly suspended whenever the user departs the organization permanently or for an extended period.
- Data backups should not be considered reliable unless they have been verified to be usable to restore data.
- Business continuity is the term used to describe the processes enacted by an organization to ensure that its vital business processes remain unaffected or can be quickly restored following a serious incident.
- Disaster recovery focuses on restoring the information systems after a disastrous event and is a subset of business continuity.
- Security training is the process of teaching a skill or set of skills that enables people to perform specific functions better.
- Security awareness training is the process of exposing people to security issues so that they are able to recognize and respond to them better.
- Social engineering, in the context of information security, is the process of manipulating individuals so that they perform actions that violate security protocols.
- Phishing is social engineering conducted through a digital communication.

- A drive-by download is an automatic attack that is triggered simply by visiting a malicious website.
- Disaster recovery and business continuity processes both need to be evaluated regularly to ensure they remain effective in the face of environmental changes in and around the organization.
- Reports must be written with a specific audience in mind if they are to be effective.
- A management review is a formal meeting in which senior organizational leaders determine whether the information security management systems are effectively accomplishing their goals.

Questions

Please remember that these questions are formatted and asked in a certain way for a reason. Keep in mind that the CISSP exam is asking questions at a conceptual level. Questions may not always have the perfect answer, and the candidate is advised against always looking for the perfect answer. Instead, the candidate should look for the best answer in the list.

1. What is a key performance indicator (KPI)?
   A. A value for a factor that denotes that some condition is met
   B. The result of comparing multiple measurements
   C. A significant indicator that shows the performance of an ISMS
   D. A quantitative observation of a factor of an ISMS at a point in time
2. Which of the following is true about key risk indicators (KRIs)?
   A. They tell managers where an organization stands with regard to its goals.
   B. They are inputs to the calculation of single loss expectancy (SLE).
   C. They tell managers where an organization stands with regard to its risk appetite.
   D. They represent an interpretation of one or more metrics that describes the effectiveness of the ISMS.
3. All of the following are normally legitimate reasons to suspend rather than delete user accounts *except*
   A. Regulatory compliance
   B. Protection of the user's privacy
   C. Investigation of a subsequently discovered event
   D. Data retention policy
4. Data backup verification efforts should
   A. Have the smallest scope possible
   B. Be based on the threats to the organization
   C. Maximize impact on business
   D. Focus on user data

5. What is the difference between security training and security awareness training?
   A. Security training is focused on skills, while security awareness training is focused on recognizing and responding to issues.
   B. Security training must be performed, while security awareness training is an aspirational goal.
   C. Security awareness training is focused on security personnel, while security training is geared toward all users.
   D. There is no difference. These terms refer to the same process.
6. Which of the following is *not* a form of social engineering?
   A. Pretexting
   B. Fishing
   C. Whaling
   D. Blackmailing
7. When assessing the performance of your organization during a disaster recovery drill, which is the highest priority?
   A. Safeguarding sensitive assets
   B. Notifying the appropriate authorities
   C. Preventing looting and vandalism
   D. Protection of life
8. Which of the following is true about vulnerability remediation after an organizational security assessment?
   A. All vulnerabilities uncovered must be remediated as soon as possible.
   B. It entails applying patches to all vulnerable software systems.
   C. Properly done, it should never impact the business.
   D. It requires the support of everyone from the very top of the organization.
9. Which of the following is true of management reviews?
   A. They happen periodically and include results of audits as a key input.
   B. They happen in an ad hoc manner as the needs of the organization dictate.
   C. They are normally conducted by mid-level managers, but their reports are presented to the key business leaders.
   D. They are focused on assessing the management of the information systems.

Answers

1. **C.** Key performance indicators (KPIs) are indicators that are particularly significant in showing the performance of an ISMS compared to its stated goals. Because every KPI is a metric, answer B (the partial definition of a metric) would also be correct but would not be the best answer since it leaves out the significance and purpose of the metric.
2. **C.** Key risk indicators (KRIs) allow managers to understand when specific activities of the organization are moving it toward a higher level of risk. They are useful to understanding changes and managing the overall risk.
3. **B.** If the organization was intentionally attempting to protect the privacy of its user, suspension of the account would be a poor privacy measure compared to outright deletion.
4. **B.** The verification of data backups should focus on assessing the organization's ability to respond to the threats identified during the threat modeling and risk management processes. If the organization can't respond to these threats, then its backups may be useless.
5. **A.** Security training is the process of teaching a skill or set of skills that will enable people to perform specific functions better. Security awareness training, on the other hand, is the process of exposing people to security issues so that they are able to recognize and respond to them better. Security training is typically provided to security personnel, while security awareness training should be provided to every member of the organization.
6. **B.** The correct term for social engineering conducted over digital communications means is phishing, not fishing.
7. **D.** In any situation where loss or harm to human lives is a possible outcome, protection of life is the top priority. The other options are all part of a disaster recovery process, but are never the top priority.
8. **D.** Because most remediations will have some impact on the business, they require the support of everyone. This is particularly true of organizational (as opposed to system-specific) assessments because not all vulnerabilities will involve just a software patch.
9. **A.** Management reviews work best when they are regularly scheduled events involving the key organizational leaders, because this allows the subordinate leaders to plan and conduct the assessments, such as audits that provide inputs to the review.

PART VII

Security Operations

CHAPTER 20

Managing Security Operations

This chapter presents the following:

- Foundational security operations concepts
- Change management processes
- Configuration management
- Resource protection
- Patch and vulnerability management
- Physical security management
- Personnel safety and security

Management is keeping the trains running on time.

—Andy Dunn

Security operations is a broad field, but the image that comes to many of our minds when we hear the term is a security operations center (SOC) where analysts, threat hunters, and incident responders fight off cyberthreats day in and day out. That is, in fact, an important aspect of security operations, but it isn't the complete scope. A lot of other work goes into ensuring our spaces are protected, our systems are optimized, and our people are doing the right things. This chapter covers many of the issues that we, as security leaders, must tackle to create a secure operational environment for our organizations. Security operations is the business of managing security. It may not be as exciting as hunting down a threat actor in real time, but it is just as important.

Foundational Security Operations Concepts

Security operations revolves around people much more than around computers and networks. A good chunk of our jobs as CISSPs is to lead security teams who prevent teams of attackers from causing us harm; our computers and networks are just the battlefields on which these groups fight each other. Sometimes, it is our own teammates who can become the enemy, either deliberately or through carelessness. So, we can't really manage security operations without first understanding the roles we need our teammates to fill and the ways in which we keep the people filling those roles honest.

Table 20-1 shows some of the common IT and security roles within organizations and their corresponding job definitions. Each role needs to have a completed and well-defined job description. Security personnel should use these job descriptions when assigning access rights and permissions in order to ensure that individuals have access only to those resources needed to carry out their tasks.

Table 20-1 contains just a few roles with a few tasks per role. Organizations should create a *complete* list of roles used within their environment, with each role's associated tasks and responsibilities. This should then be used by data owners and security personnel when determining who should have access to specific resources and the type of access. A clear and unambiguous understanding of roles and responsibilities across the organization is critical to managing security. Without it, ensuring that everyone has the right access they need for their jobs, and no more, becomes very difficult. In the sections that follow we look at other foundational concepts we all need to be able to apply to our security operations.

Organizational Role	Core Responsibilities
Cybersecurity Analyst	Monitors the organization's IT infrastructure and identifies and evaluates threats that could result in security incidents
Help Desk/Support	Resolves end-user and system technical or operations problems
Incident Responder	Investigates, analyzes, and responds to cyber incidents within the organization
IT Engineer	Performs the day-to-day operational duties on systems and applications
Network Administrator	Installs and maintains the local area network/wide area network (LAN/WAN) environment
Security Architect	Assesses security controls and recommends and implements enhancements
Security Director	Develops and enforces security policies and processes to maintain the security and safety of all organizational assets
Security Manager	Implements security policies and monitors security operations
Software Developer	Develops and maintains production software
System Administrator	Installs and maintains specific systems (e.g., database, e-mail)
Threat Hunter	Proactively finds cybersecurity threats and mitigates them before they compromise the organization

Table 20-1 Roles and Associated Tasks

SecOps

In many organizations the security and IT operations teams become misaligned because their responsibilities have different (and oftentimes conflicting) focuses. The operations staff is responsible for ensuring systems are operational, highly available, performing well, and providing users with the functionality they need. As new technology becomes available, they come under pressure by business leaders to deploy it as soon as possible to improve the organization's competitiveness. But many times this focus on operations and user functionality comes at the cost of security. Security mechanisms commonly decrease performance, delay provisioning, and reduce the functionality available to the users.

The conflicts between the priorities and incentives of the IT operations and security teams can become dysfunctional in many organizations. Many of us have witnessed the finger pointing and even outright hostility that can crop up when things go wrong. A solution that is catching on is *SecOps* (Security + Operations), which is the integration of security and IT operations people, technology, and processes to reduce risks while improving business agility. The goal is to create a culture in which security is baked into the entire life cycle of every system and process in the organization. This is accomplished by building multifunctional teams where, for instance, a cloud system administrator and a cloud security engineer work together under the leadership of a manager who is responsible for delivering agile *and* secure functionality to the organization.

Accountability

Users' access to resources must be limited and properly controlled to ensure that excessive privileges do not provide the opportunity to cause damage to an organization and its resources. Users' access attempts and activities while using a resource need to be properly monitored, audited, and logged. The individual user ID needs to be included in the audit logs to enforce individual responsibility. Each user should understand his responsibility when using organizational resources and be accountable for his actions.

Capturing and monitoring audit logs helps determine if a violation has actually occurred or if system and software reconfiguration is needed to better capture only the activities that fall outside of established boundaries. If user activities were not captured and reviewed, it would be very hard to determine if users have excessive privileges or if there has been unauthorized access.

Auditing needs to take place in a routine manner. Also, security analysts and managers need to review audit and log events. If no one routinely looks at the output, there really is no reason to create logs. Audit and function logs often contain too much cryptic or mundane information to be interpreted manually. This is why products and services are available that parse logs for organizations and report important findings. Logs should be monitored and reviewed, through either manual or automatic methods, to uncover suspicious activity and to identify an environment that is shifting away from its original baselines. This is how administrators can be warned of many problems before they become too big and out of control.

When reviewing events, administrators need to ask certain questions that pertain to the users, their actions, and the current level of security and access:

- *Are users accessing information and performing tasks that are not necessary for their job description?* The answer indicates whether users' rights and permissions need to be reevaluated and possibly modified.
- *Are repetitive mistakes being made?* The answer indicates whether users need to have further training.
- *Do too many users have rights and privileges to sensitive or restricted data or resources?* The answer indicates whether access rights to the data and resources need to be reevaluated, whether the number of individuals accessing them needs to be reduced, and/or whether the extent of their access rights should be modified.

Need-to-Know/Least Privilege

Least privilege (one of the secure design principles introduced in Chapter 9) means an individual should have just enough permissions and rights to fulfill her role in the organization and no more. If an individual has excessive permissions and rights, it could open the door to abuse of access and put the organization at more risk than is necessary. For example, if Dusty is a technical writer for a company, he does not necessarily need to have access to the company's source code. So, the mechanisms that control Dusty's access to resources should not let him access source code.

Another way to protect resources is enforcing *need to know*, which means we must first establish that an individual has a legitimate, job role–related need for a given resource. Least privilege and need to know have a symbiotic relationship. Each user should have a need to know about the resources that she is allowed to access. If Mikela does not have a need to know how much the company paid last year in taxes, then her system rights should not include access to these files, which would be an example of exercising least privilege. The use of identity management software that combines traditional directories; access control systems; and user provisioning within servers, applications, and systems is becoming the norm within organizations. This software provides the capabilities to ensure that only specific access privileges are granted to specific users, and it often includes advanced audit functions that can be used to verify compliance with legal and regulatory directives.

Separation of Duties and Responsibilities

The objective of separation of duties (another of the secure design principles introduced in Chapter 9) is to ensure that one person acting alone cannot compromise the organization's security in any way. High-risk activities should be broken up into different parts and distributed to different individuals or departments. That way, the organization does not need to put a dangerously high level of trust in certain individuals. For fraud to take place, collusion would need to be committed, meaning more than one person would have to be involved in the fraudulent activity. Separation of duties, therefore, is a preventive measure that requires collusion to occur for someone to commit an act that is against policy.

Separation of duties helps prevent mistakes and minimize conflicts of interest that can take place if one person is performing a task from beginning to end. For instance, a programmer should not be the only one to test her own code. Another person with a different job and agenda should perform functionality and integrity testing on the programmer's code, because the programmer may have a focused view of what the program is supposed to accomplish and thus may test only certain functions and input values, and only in certain environments.

Another example of separation of duties is the difference between the functions of a computer user and the functions of a security administrator. There must be clear-cut lines drawn between system administrator duties and computer user duties. These will vary from environment to environment and will depend on the level of security required within the environment. System and security administrators usually have the responsibility of installing and configuring software, performing backups and recovery procedures, setting permissions, adding and removing users, and developing user profiles. The computer user, on the other hand, may set or change passwords, create/edit/delete files, alter desktop configurations, and modify certain system parameters. The user should not be able to modify her own security profile, add and remove users globally, or make critical access decisions pertaining to network resources. This would breach the concept of separation of duties.

Privileged Account Management

Separation of duties also points to the need for *privileged account management* processes that formally enforce the principle of least privilege. A *privileged account* is one with elevated rights. When we hear this term, we usually think of system administrators, but it is important to consider that privileges often are gradually attached to user accounts for legitimate reasons but never reviewed again to see if they're still needed. In some cases, regular users end up racking up significant (and risky) permissions without anyone being aware of it (known as *authorization creep*).

More commonly, you will hear this concept under the label of *privileged account management (PAM)* because many organizations have very granular, role-based access controls. PAM consists of the policies and technologies used by an organization to control elevated (or privileged) access to any asset. It consists of processes for addressing the needs for individual elevated privileges, periodically reviewing those needs, reducing them to least privilege when appropriate, and documenting the whole thing.

Job Rotation

Job rotation means that, over time, more than one person fulfills the tasks of one position within the organization. This enables the organization to have more than one person who understands the tasks and responsibilities of a specific job title, which provides backup and redundancy if a person leaves the organization or is absent. Job rotation also helps identify fraudulent activities, and therefore can be considered a detective type of control. If Keith has performed David's position, Keith knows the regular tasks and routines that must be completed to fulfill the responsibilities of that job. Thus, Keith is better able to identify whether David does something out of the ordinary and suspicious.

A related practice is *mandatory vacations*. Chapter 1 touched on reasons to make sure employees take their vacations. Reasons include being able to identify fraudulent activities and enabling job rotation to take place. If an accounting employee has been performing a "salami attack" by shaving off pennies from multiple accounts and putting the money into his own account, the employee's company would have a better chance of figuring this out if that employee is required to take a vacation for a week or longer. When the employee is on vacation, another employee has to fill in. She might uncover questionable documents and clues of previous activities, or the company may see a change in certain patterns once the employee who is committing fraud is gone for a week or two.

It is best for auditing purposes if the employee takes two contiguous weeks off from work, which allows more time for fraudulent evidence to appear. Again, the idea behind mandatory vacations is that, traditionally, those employees who have committed fraud are usually the ones who have resisted going on vacation because of their fear of being found out while away.

Service Level Agreements

As we discussed briefly in Chapter 2, a service level agreement (SLA) is a contractual agreement that states that a service provider guarantees a certain level of service. For example, a web server will be down for no more than 52 minutes per year (which is approximately a 99.99 percent availability). SLAs help service providers, whether they are an internal IT operation or an outsourcer, decide what type of availability technology is appropriate. From this determination, the price of a service or the budget of the IT operation can be set. Most frequently, organizations use SLAs with external service providers to guarantee specific performance and, if it is not delivered, to penalize (usually monetarily) the vendor.

The process of developing an internal SLA (that is, one between the IT operations team and one or more internal departments) can also be beneficial to an organization. For starters, it drives a deeper conversation between IT and whoever is requesting the service. This alone can help both sides get a clearer understanding of the opportunities and threats the service brings with it. The requestor will then better understand the tradeoffs between service levels and costs and be able to negotiate the most cost-effective service with the IT team. The IT team can then use this dialogue to justify resources such as budget or staffing. Finally, internal SLAs allow all parties to know what "right" looks like.

Whether the SLA is internal or external, the organization must collect metrics to determine whether or not it is being met. After all, if nobody measures the service, what's the point of requiring a certain level of it? Identifying these metrics, in and of itself, allows the organization to determine whether a particular requirement is important or not. If both parties are having a hard time figuring out how much scheduled downtime is acceptable, that requirement probably doesn't need to be included in the SLA.

Change Management

The Greek philosopher Heraclitus said that "the only constant in life is change," and most of us would agree with him, especially when it comes to IT and security operations in our organizations. Change is needed to remain relevant and competitive, but it can bring risks that we must carefully manage. *Change management*, from an IT perspective, is the practice of minimizing the risks associated with the addition, modification, or removal of anything that could have an effect on IT services. This includes obvious IT actions like adding new software applications, segmenting LANs, and retiring network services. But it also includes changes to policies, procedures, staffing, and even facilities. Consequently, any change to security controls or practices probably falls under the umbrella of change management.

Change Management Practices

Well-structured change management practices are essential to minimizing the risks of changes to an environment. The process of devising these practices should include representatives for all stakeholders, so it shouldn't just be limited to IT and security staff. Most organizations that follow this process formally establish a group that is responsible for approving changes and overseeing the activities of changes that take place within the organization. This group can go by one of many names, but for this discussion we will refer to it as the change advisory board (CAB).

The CAB and change management practices should be laid out in the change management policy. Although the types of changes vary, a standard list of procedures can help keep the process under control and ensure it is carried out in a predictable manner. The following steps are examples of the types of procedures that should be part of any change management policy:

- **Request for a change to take place** The individual requesting the change must do so in writing, justify the reasons, clearly show the benefits and possible pitfalls of (that is, risk introduced by) the change. The Request for Change (RFC) is the standard document for doing this and contains all information required to approve a change.
- **Evaluate the change** The CAB reviews the RFC and analyzes its potential impacts across the entire organization. Sometimes the requester is asked to conduct more research and provide more information before the change is approved. The CAB then completes a change evaluation report and designates the individual or team responsible for planning and implementing the change.
- **Plan the change** Once the change is approved, the team responsible for implementing it gets to work planning the change. This includes figuring out all the details of how the change interfaces with other systems or processes, developing a timeline, and identifying specific actions to minimize the risks. The change must also be fully tested to uncover any unforeseen results. Regardless of how well we test, there is always a chance that the change will cause an unacceptable loss or outage, so every change request should also have a rollback plan that restores the system to the last known-good configuration.

- **Implementation** Once the change is planned and fully tested, it is implemented and integrated into any other affected processes and systems. This may include reconfiguring other systems, changing or developing policies and procedures, and providing training for affected staff. These steps should be fully documented and progress should be monitored.
- **Review the change** Once the change is implemented, it is brought back to the CAB for a final review. During this step, the CAB verifies that the change was implemented as planned, that any unanticipated consequences have been properly addressed, and that the risks remain within tolerable parameters.
- **Close or sustain** Once the change is implemented and reviewed, it should be entered into a change log. A full report summarizing the change may also be submitted to management, particularly for changes with large effects across the organization.

These steps, of course, usually apply to large changes that take place within an organization. These types of changes are typically expensive and can have lasting effects on an organization. However, smaller changes should also go through some type of change control process. If a server needs to have a patch applied, it is not good practice to have an engineer just apply it without properly testing it on a nonproduction server, without having the approval of the IT department manager or network administrator, and without having backup and backout plans in place in case the patch causes some negative effect on the production server. Of course, these changes still need to be documented. For this reason, ITIL 4 (introduced in Chapter 4) specifies three types of changes that follow the same basic process but tailored for specific situations:

- **Standard changes** Preauthorized, low-risk changes that follow a well-known procedure. Examples include patching a server or adding memory or storage to it.
- **Emergency changes** Changes that must be implemented immediately. Examples include implementing a security patch for a zero-day exploit or isolating the network from a DDoS attack.
- **Normal changes** All other changes that are not standard changes or emergency changes. Examples include adding a server that will provide new functionality or introducing a new application to (or removing a legacy one from) the golden image.

Regardless of the type of change, it is critical that the operations department create approved backout plans before implementing changes to systems or the network. It is very common for changes to cause problems that were not properly identified before the implementation process began. Many network engineers have experienced the headaches of applying poorly developed "fixes" or patches that end up breaking something else in the system. Developing a backout plan ensures productivity is not negatively affected by these issues. This plan describes how the team will restore the system to its original state before the change was implemented.

Change Management Documentation

Failing to document changes to systems and networks is only asking for trouble, because no one will remember, for example, what was done to that one server in the demilitarized zone (DMZ) six months ago or how the main router was fixed when it was acting up last year. Changes to software configurations and network devices take place pretty often in most environments, and keeping all of these details properly organized is impossible, unless someone maintains a log of this type of activity.

Numerous changes can take place in an organization, some of which are as follows:

- New computers installed
- New applications installed
- Different configurations implemented
- Patches and updates installed
- New technologies integrated
- Policies, procedures, and standards updated
- New regulations and requirements implemented
- Network or system problems identified and fixes implemented
- Different network configurations implemented
- New networking devices integrated into the network
- Company acquired by, or merged with, another company

The list could go on and on and could be general or detailed. Many organizations have experienced some major problem that affects the network and employee productivity. The IT department may run around trying to figure out the issue and go through hours or days of trial-and-error exercises to find and apply the necessary fix. If no one properly documents the incident and what was done to fix the issue, the organization may be doomed to repeat the same scramble six months to a year down the road.

Configuration Management

At every point in the O&M part of assets' life cycles (which we discussed in Chapter 5), we need to also ensure that we get (and keep) a handle on how these assets are configured. Sadly, most default configurations are woefully insecure. This means that if we do not configure security when we provision new hardware or software, we are virtually guaranteeing successful attacks on our systems. *Configuration management (CM)* is the process of establishing and maintaining consistent configurations on all our systems to meet organizational requirements.

Configuration management processes vary among organizations but have certain elements in common. Virtually everyone that practices it starts off by defining and establishing organization-wide agreement on the required configurations for all systems in the scope of the effort. At a minimum, this should include the users' workstations and all business-critical systems. These configurations are then applied to all systems. There will be exceptions, of course, and special requirements that lead to nonstandard configurations, which need to be approved by the appropriate individuals and documented. There will also be changes over time, which should be dealt with through the change management practices defined in the previous section. Finally, configurations need to be periodically audited to ensure continued compliance with them.

Baselining

A *baseline* is the configuration of a system at a point in time as agreed upon by the appropriate decision makers. For a typical user workstation, a baseline defines the software that is installed (both operating system and applications), policies that are applied (e.g., disabling USB thumb drives), and any other configuration setting such as the domain name, DNS server address, and many others. Baselining allows us to build a system once, put it through a battery of tests to ensure it works as expected, and then provision it out consistently across the organization.

In a perfect world, all systems that provide the same functionality are configured identically. This makes it easier to manage them throughout their life cycles. As we all know, however, there are plenty of exceptions in the real world. System configuration exceptions often have perfectly legitimate business reasons, so we can't just say "no" to exception requests and keep our lives simple. The system baseline allows us to narrow down what makes these exceptional systems different. Rather than document every single configuration parameter again (which could introduce errors and omissions), all we have to do is document what is different from a given baseline.

Baselines do more than simply tell us what systems (should) look like at a given point in time; they also document earlier configuration states for those systems. We want to keep old baselines around because they tell the story of how a system evolved. Properly annotated, baselines tell us not only the "what" but also the "why" of configurations over time.

A related concept to baselining is the golden image, which is a preconfigured, standard template from which all user workstations are provisioned. A golden image is known by many other names including gold master, clone image, master image, and base image. Whatever name you use, it saves time when provisioning systems because all you have to do is clone the image onto a device, enter a handful of parameters unique to the system (such as the hostname), and it's ready for use. Golden images also improve security by consistently applying security controls to every cloned system. Another advantage is a reduction in configuration errors, which also means a lower risk of inadvertently introduced vulnerabilities.

Provisioning

We already addressed secure provisioning in Chapter 5 but the topic bears revisiting in the context of configuration management. Recall that provisioning is the set of all activities required to provide one or more new information services to a user or group of users ("new" meaning previously not available to that user or group). Technically, provisioning and

Configuration Management vs. Change Management

Change management is a *business* process aimed at deliberately regulating the changing nature of business activities such as projects or IT services. It is concerned with issues such as changing the features in a system being developed or changing the manner in which remote workers connect to the internal network. While IT and security personnel are involved in change management, they are usually not in charge of it.

Configuration management is an *operational* process aimed at ensuring that controls are configured correctly and are responsive to the current threat and operational environments. As an information security professional, you would likely lead in configuration management but simply participate in change management processes.

configuration are two different but related activities. Provisioning generally entails acquiring, installing, and launching a new service. Depending on how this is done, that service may still need to be configured (and possibly even baselined).

Automation

As you can imagine, configuration management requires tracking and updating a lot of information on many different systems. This is why mature organizations leverage automation for many of the required tasks, including maintaining individual configuration items in a *configuration management database (CMDB)*. The CMDB can store information about all organizational assets, their baselines, and their relationships to one another. Importantly, a CMDB provides versioning so that, if a configuration error is made, reverting to a previous baseline is easy.

More elaborate automation tools are capable of not only tracking configurations but also provisioning systems that implement them. Perhaps the best-known tool in this regard, particularly for virtualized or cloud infrastructures, is Ansible, which is an open-source configuration management, deployment, and orchestration tool. Through the use of playbooks written in YAML (which, recursively, stands for "YAML Ain't Markup Language"), Ansible allows automated asset provisioning and configuration.

Resource Protection

In Chapter 5, we defined assets as anything of worth to the organization. A related concept is a *resource*, which is anything that is required to perform an activity or accomplish a goal. So, a resource can also be an asset if you own it and it has inherent value to you. In the context of security operations, a resource is anything the organization needs to accomplish any of its tasks. This includes hardware, software, data, and the media on which the last two are stored.

EXAM TIP Though assets and resources are, technically, slightly different things, you should treat them as synonymous in the exam.

We will discuss how to protect hardware resources later in this chapter when we cover physical security. Though we already covered software, data, and media protections in Chapter 6, the topic is worth revisiting as it applies to managing security operations. There are three types of digital resources that are of particular interest in this regard: system images, source files, and backups.

System Images

Because system images are essential to efficiently provisioning systems, they are a key resource both during normal operations and when we are responding to a security incident. Presumably, the images we use to clone new (or replacement) systems are secure because (as a best practice) we put a lot of work into hardening them and ensuring they contain no known vulnerabilities. However, if adversaries were able to modify the images so as to introduce vulnerabilities, they would have free access to any system provisioned using the tainted images. Similarly, if the images were destroyed (deliberately, accidentally, or through an act of nature), recovering from a large-scale incident would be much more difficult and time-consuming.

Source Files

If the images were unavailable or otherwise compromised, we would have to rebuild everything from scratch. There are also cases in which we just need to install specific software. Either way, we need reliable source files. Source files contain the code that executes on a computer to provide applications or services. This code can exist in either executable form or as a sequence of statements in a high-level language such as C/C++, Java, or Python. Either way, it is possible for adversaries to insert malicious code into source files so that any system provisioned using them will be vulnerable. Worse yet, if you work for a software company with clients around the world, your company may be a much more interesting target for advanced persistent threats (APTs) who may want to compromise your software to breach your customers. This kind of software supply-chain attack is best exemplified by the SolarWinds attack of 2020.

Even if your organization is not likely to be targeted by APTs, you are probably concerned about ransomware attacks. Having good backups is the key to quickly recovering from ransomware (without having to pay the ransom), but it hinges on the integrity and availability of the backup data. Many cybercriminals deliberately look for backups and encrypt them also to force their victims to pay the ransom.

Backups

Backing up software and having backup hardware devices are two large parts of network availability. You need to be able to restore data if a hard drive fails, a disaster takes place, or some type of software corruption occurs.

Every organization should develop a policy that indicates what gets backed up, how often it gets backed up, and how these processes should occur. If users have important information on their workstations, the operations department needs to develop a method that indicates that backups include certain directories on users' workstations or that users move their critical data to a server share at the end of each day to ensure it gets backed up. Backups may occur once or twice a week, every day, or every three hours. It is up to the organization to determine this interval. The more frequent the backups, the more resources will be dedicated to it, so there needs to be a balance between backup costs and the actual risk of potentially losing data.

An organization may find that conducting automatic backups through specialized software is more economical and effective than spending IT work-hours on the task. The integrity of these backups needs to be checked to ensure they are happening as expected—rather than finding out right after two major servers blow up that the automatic backups were saving only temporary files.

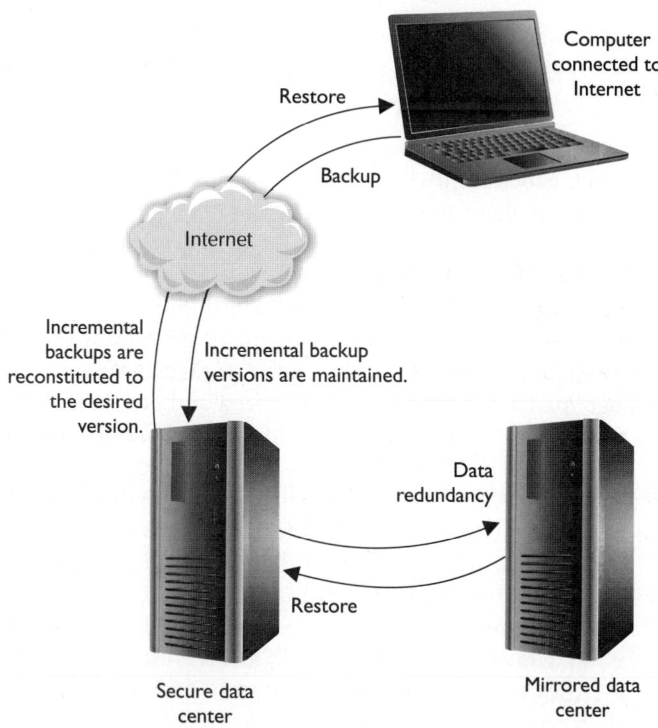

Protecting Backups from Ransomware

The best way to minimize your risks due to ransomware is to have effective backups that are beyond the reach of the cybercriminals and can quickly restore affected systems. This means putting the greatest distance (and security controls) possible between a system and its backups. Obviously, you should never store backups on the system itself or on a directly connected external drive. The following are some tips on how to keep your backups away from threat actors:

- *Use a different OS for your backup server.* Most ransomware today targets a single type of OS (mostly Windows). Even if the attack is not automated, threat actors are likelier to be proficient in whatever OS they are attacking, so having your backups managed by a system running a different OS automatically gives you a leg up.
- *Get your backups out of town.* Whatever you do, make sure your backups are not on a drive that is directly attached to the asset you are protecting, or even on the same LAN segment (like in the same data center). The more distance, the better, especially if you can layer controls like ACLs or even use data diodes. We know of data so sensitive that its backups are physically transported to other states or countries periodically.
- *Go old school.* Consider using older technologies like optical discs and magnetic tapes. You may get some weird looks from your early-adopter colleagues, but you may save the day when things go sideways on you.
- *Protect your backups like your career depends on it.* (It may!) Stay up to date on the latest techniques cybercriminals are using to attack backups and ensure you have adequate controls in place to prevent them from being effective.

Hierarchical Storage Management

Hierarchical storage management (HSM) provides continuous online backup functionality. It combines hard disk technology with the cheaper and slower optical or tape jukeboxes. The HSM system dynamically manages the storage and recovery of files, which are copied to storage media devices that vary in speed and cost. The faster media holds the files that are accessed more often, and the seldom-used files are stored on the slower devices, or *near-line* devices, as shown in Figure 20-1. The storage media could include optical discs, magnetic disks, and tapes. This functionality happens in the background without the knowledge of the user or any need for user intervention.

HSM works, according to tuning based on the trade-off between the cost of storage and the availability of information, by migrating the actual content of less used files to lower-speed, lower-cost storage, while leaving behind a "stub," which looks to the user like it contains the full data of the migrated file. When the user or an application accesses the stub, the HSM uses the information in the stub to find the real location of the information and then retrieve it transparently for the user.

This type of technology was created to save money and time. If all data was stored on hard drives, that would be expensive. If a lot of the data was stored on tapes, it would take too long to retrieve the data when needed. So HSM provides a terrific approach by providing you with the data you need, when you need it, without having to bother the administrator to track down some tape or optical disc.

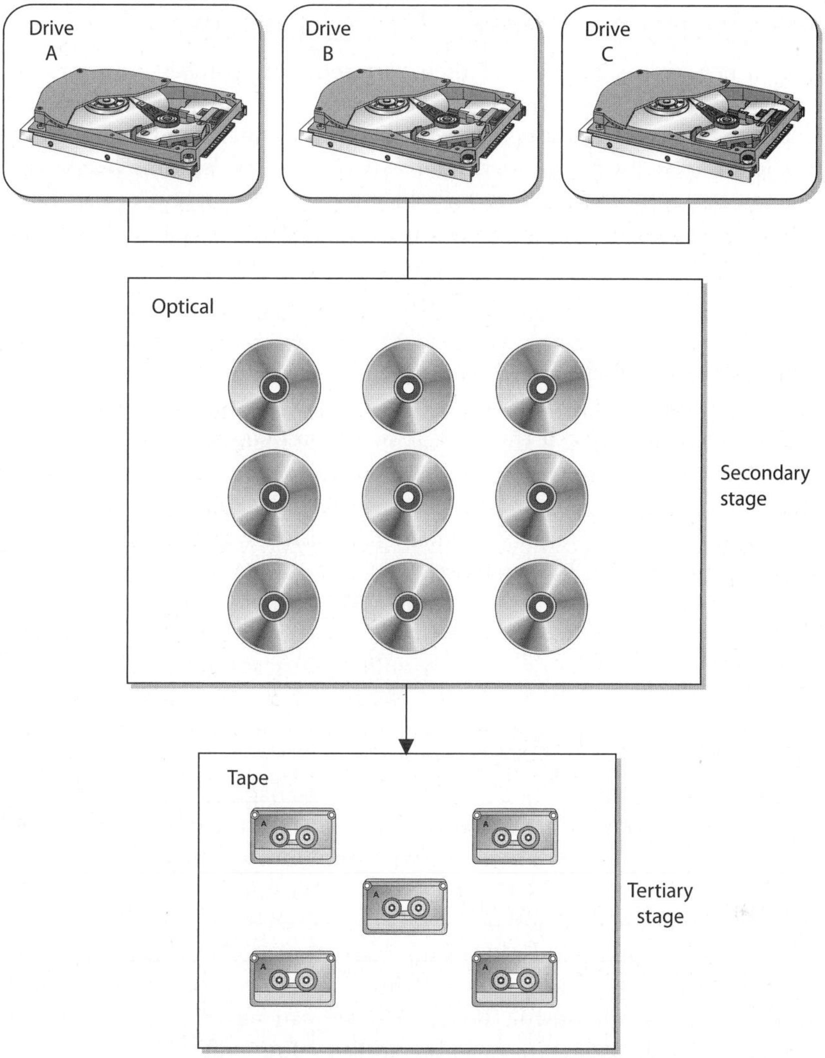

Figure 20-1 HSM provides an economical and efficient way of storing data.

Backups should include the underlying operating system and applications, as well as the configuration files for both. Systems are attached to networks, and network devices can experience failures and data losses as well. Data loss of a network device usually means the configuration of the network device is lost completely (and the device will not even boot up), or that the configuration of the network device reverts to defaults (which, though it will boot up, does your network little good). Therefore, the configurations of network and other nonsystem devices (for example, the phone system) in the environment are also necessary.

Vulnerability and Patch Management

Dealing with new vulnerabilities and their corresponding patches is an inevitability in cybersecurity. The trick is to deal with these in an informed and deliberate manner. While the following sections treat vulnerability management and patch management separately, it is important to consider them as two pieces of the same puzzle in real life. We may learn of a new vulnerability for which a patch does not yet exist. Equally bad would be applying a patch that brings down a critical business system. For these reasons (among many others), we should manage vulnerabilities and patches in a synchronized and coordinated manner across our organizations.

Vulnerability Management

No sufficiently complex information system can ever be completely free of vulnerabilities. *Vulnerability management* is the cyclical process of identifying vulnerabilities, determining the risks they pose to the organization, and applying security controls that bring those risks to acceptable levels. Many people equate vulnerability management with periodically running a vulnerability scanner against their systems, but the process must include more than just that. Vulnerabilities exist not only in software, which is what the scanners assess, but also in business processes and in people. Flawed business processes, such as sharing proprietary information with parties who have not signed a nondisclosure agreement (NDA), cannot be detected by vulnerability scanners. Nor can they detect users who click malicious links in e-mails. What matters most is not the tool or how often it is run, but having a formal process that looks at the organization holistically and is closely tied to the risk management process.

Vulnerability management is part of our risk management process. We identify the things that we have that are of value to us and the threat actors that might take those away from us or somehow interfere with our ability to benefit from them. Then we figure out how these actors might go about causing us losses (in other words, exploiting our vulnerabilities) and how likely these events might be. As we discussed in Chapter 2, this gives us a good idea of our risk exposure. The next step is to decide which of those risks we will address and how. The "how" is typically through the application of a security control. Recall that we can never bring our risk to zero, which means we will always have vulnerabilities for which we have no effective controls. These unmitigated risks exist because we think the chance of them being realized or their impact on the organization (or both) is low enough for the risk to be tolerable. In other words, the cost of mitigating the risk is not worth the return on our investment. For those risks, the best we can do is continually monitor for changes in their likelihood or potential impact.

As you can see, vulnerability management is all about finding vulnerabilities, understanding their impact on the organization, and determining what to do about them. Since information system vulnerabilities can exist in software, processes, or people, it is worthwhile to discuss how we implement and support vulnerability management in each of these areas.

Software Vulnerabilities

Vulnerabilities are usually discovered by security researchers who notify vendors and give them some time (at least two weeks) to work on a patch before the researchers make their findings public. This is known as responsible or ethical disclosure. The Computer Emergency Response Team Coordination Center (CERT/CC) is the main clearinghouse for vulnerability disclosures. Once a vulnerability is discovered, vulnerability scanner vendors release plug-ins for their tools. These plug-ins are essentially simple programs that look for the presence of one specific flaw.

NOTE Some organizations have their own in-house vulnerability research capability or can write their own plug-ins. In our discussion, we assume the more general case in which vulnerability scanning is done using third-party commercial tools whose licenses include subscriptions to vulnerability feeds and related plug-ins.

As previously mentioned, software vulnerability scanning is what most people think of when they hear the term vulnerability management. Scanning is simply a common type of vulnerability assessment that can be divided into four phases:

1. **Prepare** First, you have to determine the scope of the vulnerability assessment. What are you testing and how? Having defined the scope, you schedule the event and coordinate it with affected asset and process owners to ensure it won't interfere with critical business processes. You also want to ensure you have the latest vulnerability signatures or plug-ins for the systems you will be testing.
2. **Scan** For best results, the scan is automated, follows a script, and happens outside of the regular hours of operation for the organization. This reduces the chance that something goes unexpectedly wrong or that you overlook a system. During the scan, it is helpful to monitor resource utilization (like CPU and bandwidth) to ensure you are not unduly interfering with business operations.
3. **Remediate** In a perfect world, you don't find any of the vulnerabilities for which you were testing. Typically, however, you find a system that somehow slipped through the cracks, so you patch it and rescan just to be sure. Sometimes, however, there are legitimate business reasons why a system can't be patched (at least right away), so remediation may require deploying a compensating control or (in the worst case) accepting the risk as is.
4. **Document** This important phase is often overlooked because some organizations rely on the reports that are automatically generated by the scanning tools. These reports, however, don't normally include important details like why a vulnerability may intentionally be left unpatched, the presence of compensating controls elsewhere, or the need for more/less frequent scanning of specific systems. Proper documentation ensures that assumptions, facts, and decisions are preserved to inform future decisions.

Process Vulnerabilities

A process vulnerability exists whenever there is a flaw or weakness in a business process, independent of the use of automation. For example, suppose a user account provisioning process requires only an e-mail from a supervisor asking for an account for the new hire. Since e-mail messages can be spoofed, a threat actor could send a fake e-mail impersonating a real supervisor. If the system administrator creates the account and responds with the new credentials, the adversary would now have a legitimate account with whatever authorizations were requested.

Process vulnerabilities frequently are overlooked, particularly when they exist at the intersection of multiple departments within the organization. In the example, the account provisioning process vulnerability exists at the intersection of a business area (where the fictitious user will supposedly work), IT, and human resources.

A good way to find process vulnerabilities is to periodically review existing processes using a red team. As introduced in Chapter 18, a red team is a group of trusted individuals whose job is to look at something from an adversary's perspective. Red teaming is useful in many contexts, including identifying process vulnerabilities. The red team's task in this context would be to study the processes, understand the organization's environment, and then look for ways to violate its security policies. Ideally, red team exercises should be conducted whenever any new process is put in place. Realistically, however, these events take place much less frequently (if at all).

NOTE The term *red team exercise* is often used synonymously with *penetration test*. In reality, a red team exercise can apply to any aspect of an organization (people, processes, facilities, products, ideas, information systems) and aims to emulate the actions of threat actors seeking specific objectives. A penetration test, on the other hand, is focused on testing the effectiveness of security controls in facilities and/or information systems.

Human Vulnerabilities

By many accounts, over 90 percent of security incidents can be traced back to a member of an organization doing something they shouldn't have, maliciously or otherwise. This implies that if your vulnerability management is focused exclusively on hardware and software systems, you may not be reducing your attack surface by much. A common approach to managing human vulnerabilities is social engineering assessments. We briefly introduced social engineering in Chapter 18 as a type of attack but return to it now as a tool in your vulnerability management toolkit.

Chris Hadnagy, one of the world's leading experts on the subject, defines social engineering as "the act of manipulating a person to take an action that *may* or *may not* be in the 'target's' best interest." A social engineering assessment involves a team of trained personnel attempting to exploit vulnerabilities in an organization's staff. This could result in targets revealing sensitive information, allowing the social engineers into restricted areas, clicking malicious links, or plugging into their computer a thumb drive laden with malware.

A social engineering assessment, much like its nefarious counterpart, consists of three phases:

1. **Open-source intelligence (OSINT) collection** Before manipulating a target, the social engineer needs to learn as much as possible about that person. This phase is characterized by searches for personal information in social media sites; web searches; and observation, eavesdropping, and casual conversations. Some OSINT tools allow quick searches of a large number of sources for information on specific individuals or organizations.
2. **Assessment planning** The social engineer could go on gathering OSINT forever but at some point (typically very quickly) will have enough information to formulate a plot to exploit one or more targets. Some people respond emotionally to certain topics, while others may best be targeted by impersonating someone in a position of authority. The social engineer identifies the kinds of engagements, topics, and pretexts that are likeliest to work against one or more targets.
3. **Assessment execution** Regardless of how well planned an assessment may be, we know that no plan survives first contact. Social engineers have to think quickly on their feet and be very perceptive of their targets' states of mind and emotions. In this phase, they engage targets through some combination of personal face-to-face, telephonic, text, or e-mail exchange and persuade them to take some action that compromises the security of the organization.

Rarely is a social engineering assessment not effective. At the end of the event, the assessors report their findings and use them to educate the organization on how to avoid falling for these tricks. Perhaps the most common type of assessment is in the form of phishing, but a real human vulnerability assessment should be much more comprehensive.

Patch Management

According to NIST Special Publication 800-40, Revision 3, *Guide to Enterprise Patch Management Technologies*, patch management is "the process for identifying, acquiring, installing, and verifying patches for products and systems." *Patches* are software updates intended to remove a vulnerability or defect in the software, or to provide new features or functionality for it. Patch management is, at least in a basic way, an established part of organizations' IT or security operations already.

Unmanaged Patching

One approach to patch management is to use a decentralized or unmanaged model in which each software package on each device periodically checks for updates and, if any are available, automatically applies them. While this approach may seem like a simple solution to the problem, it does have significant issues that could render it unacceptably risky for an organization. Among these risks are the following:

- **Credentials** Installing patches typically requires users to have admin credentials, which violates the principle of least privilege.
- **Configuration management** It may be difficult (or impossible) to attest to the status of every application in the organization, which makes configuration management much more difficult.
- **Bandwidth utilization** Having each application or service independently download the patches will lead to network congestion, particularly if there is no way to control when this will happen.
- **Service availability** Servers are almost never configured to automatically update themselves because this could lead to unscheduled outages that have a negative effect on the organization.

There is almost no advantage to decentralized patch management, except that it is better than doing nothing. The effort saved by not having management overhead is more than balanced by the additional effort you'll have to put into responding to incidents and solving configuration and interoperability problems. Still, there may be situations in which it is not possible to actively manage some devices. For instance, if your users are allowed to work from home using personal devices, then it would be difficult to implement the centralized approach we discuss next. In such situations, the decentralized model may be the best to take, provided you also have a way to periodically (say, each time users connect back to the mother ship) check the status of their updates.

Centralized Patch Management

Centralized patch management is considered a best practice for security operations. There are multiple approaches to implementing it, however, so you must carefully consider the pluses and minuses of each. The most common approaches are

- **Agent based** An update agent is installed on each device. This agent communicates with one or more update servers and compares available patches with software and versions on the local host, updating as needed.
- **Agentless** One or more hosts remotely connect to each device on the network using admin credentials and check the remote device for needed updates. A spin on this is the use of Active Directory objects in a domain controller to manage patch levels.
- **Passive** Depending on the fidelity that an organization requires, it may be possible to passively monitor network traffic to infer the patch levels on each networked application or service. While minimally intrusive to the end devices, this approach is also the least effective since it may not always be possible to uniquely identify software versions through their network traffic artifacts.

Regardless of the approach you take, you want to apply the patches as quickly as possible. After all, every day you delay is an extra day that your adversaries have to exploit your vulnerabilities. The truth is that you can't (or at least shouldn't) always roll out the patch as soon as it comes out. There is no shortage of reports of major outages caused by rolling out patches without first testing their effects. Sometimes the fault lies with the vendor, who, perhaps in its haste to remove a vulnerability, failed to properly test that the patch wouldn't break any other functionality of the product. Other times the patch may be rock solid and yet have a detrimental second- or third-order effect on other systems on your hosts or networks. This is why testing the patch before rolling it out is a good idea.

Virtualization technologies make it easier to set up a patch test lab. At a minimum, you want to replicate your critical infrastructure (e.g., domain controller and production servers) in this virtual test environment. Most organizations also create at least one virtual machine (VM) that mimics each deployed operating system, with representative services and applications.

NOTE It is often possible to mitigate the risk created by a software vulnerability using other controls, such as rules for your firewalls, intrusion detection system (IDS), or intrusion protection system (IPS). This can buy time for you to test the patches. It also acts as a compensatory control.

Whether or not you are able to test the patches before pushing them out (and you really should), it is also a good idea to patch your subnets incrementally. It may take longer to get to all systems, but if something goes wrong, it will only affect a subset of

Reverse Engineering Patches

Zero-day exploits are able to successfully attack vulnerabilities that are not known to the software vendor or users of its software. For that reason, zero-day exploits are able to bypass the vast majority of controls such as firewalls, antimalware, and IDS/IPS. Though zero-day exploits are very powerful, they are also exceptionally hard to develop and very expensive to buy in the underground markets.

There is an easier and cheaper way for attackers to exploit recent vulnerabilities, and that is by reverse engineering the software patches that vendors push out. This approach takes advantage of the delay between a patch being available and it getting pushed to all the vulnerable computers in the organization. If the attacker can reverse engineer the patch faster than the defenders use it to update all computers, then the attacker wins. Some vendors are mitigating this threat by using *code obfuscation*, which, in an ironic turn of events, is a technique developed by attackers almost 30 years ago in an effort to thwart the then simple pattern-matching approach of antimalware solutions.

Even with code obfuscation, it is just a matter of time before the bad guys figure out what the vulnerability is. This puts pressure on the defenders to roll out the patches across the entire organization as quickly as possible. In this haste, organizations sometimes overlook problem indicators. Add to this a healthy application of Murphy's law and you see why it is imperative to have a way to deal with these unknowns. A *rollback plan* (previously discussed in the "Change Management" section of this chapter) describes the steps by which a change is reversed in order to restore functionality or integrity.

your users and services. This gradual approach to patching also serves to reduce network congestion that could result from all systems attempting to download patches at the same time. Obviously, the benefits of gradual patching need to be weighed against the additional exposure that the inherent delays will cause.

Physical Security

We already discussed physical security in Chapter 10, but our focus then was on the design of sites and facilities. The CISSP CBK breaks physical security into design, which falls under Domain 3 (Security Architecture and Engineering), and operations, which falls in the current Domain 7 (Security Operations). We follow the same approach here.

As with any other defensive technique, physical security should be implemented using the defense-in-depth secure design principle. For example, before an intruder can get to the written recipe for your company's secret barbeque sauce, she will need to climb or cut a fence, slip by a security guard, pick a door lock, circumvent a biometric access control reader that protects access to an internal room, and then break into the safe that holds the recipe. The idea is that if an attacker breaks through one control layer, there will be others in her way before she can obtain the company's crown jewels.

NOTE It is also important to have a diversity of controls. For example, if one key works on four different door locks, the intruder has to obtain only one key. Each entry should have its own individual key or authentication combination.

This defense model should work in two main modes: one mode during normal facility operations and another mode during the time the facility is closed. When the facility is closed, all doors should be locked with monitoring mechanisms in strategic positions to alert security personnel of suspicious activity. When the facility is in operation, security gets more complicated because authorized individuals need to be distinguished from unauthorized individuals. Perimeter security controls deal with facility and personnel access controls and with external boundary protection mechanisms. Internal security controls deal with work area separation and personnel badging. Both perimeter and internal security also address intrusion detection and corrective actions. The following sections describe the elements that make up these categories.

External Perimeter Security Controls

Your first layer of defense is your external perimeter. This could be broken down into distinct, concentric areas of increasing security. Let's consider an example taken from the *Site Security Design Guide*, published by the U.S. General Services Administration (GSA) Public Buildings Service, which is shown in Figure 20-2. In it, we see the entire site is fenced off, which actually creates two security zones: the (external) neighborhood (zone 1) and the standoff perimeter (zone 2). Depending on risk levels, the organization may want to restrict site access and parking by creating a third zone. Even if the risk is fairly low, it may be desirable to ensure that vehicles are unable to get too close to the building.

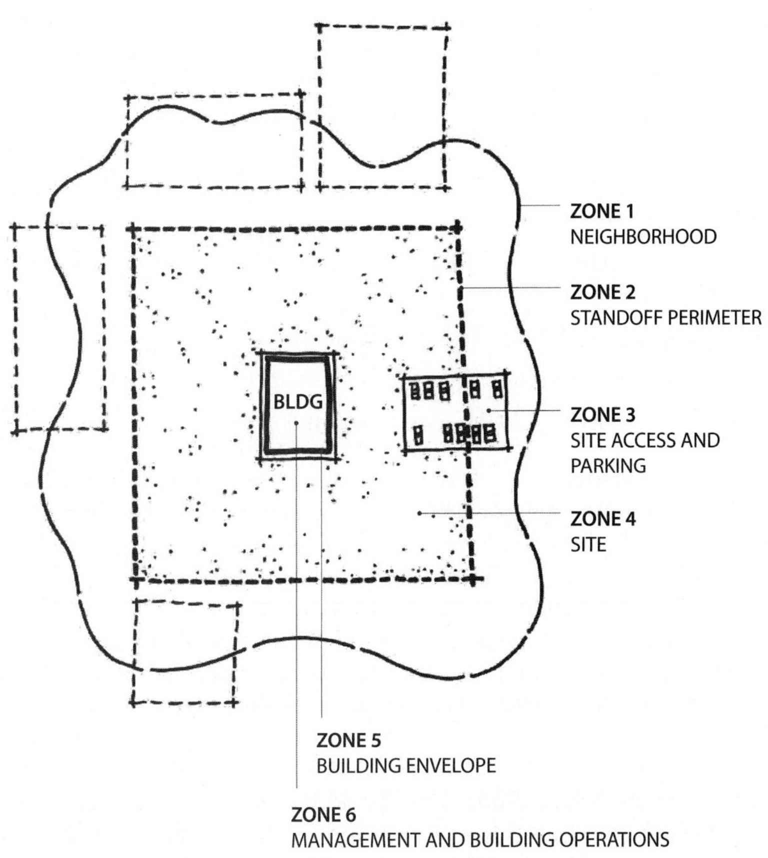

Figure 20-2 Security zones around a facility (Source: https://www.wbdg.org/FFC/GSA/site_security_dg.pdf)

This protects the facility against accidents, but also against explosions. (A good rule of thumb is to ensure there is a 200-foot standoff distance between any vehicles and buildings.) Then there is the rest of the enclosed site (zone 4), which could include break areas for employees, backup power plants, and anything else around the building exterior. Finally, there's the inside of the building, which we'll discuss later in this chapter. Each of these zones has its own set of requirements, which should be increasingly restrictive the closer someone gets to the building.

External perimeter security controls are usually put into place to provide one or more of the following services:

- Control pedestrian and vehicle traffic flows
- Provide various levels of protection for different security zones
- Establish buffers and delaying mechanisms to protect against forced entry attempts
- Limit and control entry points

These services can be provided by using the following control types (which are not all-inclusive):

- **Access control mechanisms** Locks and keys, an electronic card access system, personnel awareness
- **Physical barriers** Fences, gates, walls, doors, windows, protected vents, vehicular barriers
- **Intrusion detection** Perimeter sensors, interior sensors, annunciation mechanisms
- **Assessment** Guards, surveillance cameras
- **Response** Guards, local law enforcement agencies
- **Deterrents** Signs, lighting, environmental design

Several types of perimeter protection mechanisms and controls can be put into place to protect an organization's facility, assets, and personnel. They can deter would-be intruders, detect intruders and unusual activities, and provide ways of dealing with these issues when they arise. Perimeter security controls can be natural (hills, rivers) or manmade (fencing, lighting, gates). Landscaping is a mix of the two. In Chapter 10, we explored Crime Prevention Through Environmental Design (CPTED) and how this approach is used to reduce the likelihood of crime. Landscaping is a tool employed in the CPTED method. Sidewalks, bushes, and created paths can point people to the correct entry points, and trees and spiky bushes can be used as natural barriers. These bushes and trees should be placed such that they cannot be used as ladders or accessories to gain unauthorized access to unapproved entry points. Also, there should not be an overwhelming number of trees and bushes, which could provide intruders with places to hide. In the following sections, we look at the manmade components that can work within the landscaping design.

Fencing

Fencing can be quite an effective physical barrier. Although the presence of a fence may only delay dedicated intruders in their access attempts, it can work as a psychological deterrent by telling the world that your organization is serious about protecting itself.

Fencing can provide crowd control and helps control access to entrances and facilities. However, fencing can be costly and unsightly. Many organizations plant bushes or trees in front of the fencing that surrounds their buildings for aesthetics and to make the building less noticeable. But this type of vegetation can damage the fencing over time or negatively affect its integrity. The fencing needs to be properly maintained, because if a company has a sagging, rusted, pathetic fence, it is equivalent to telling the world that the company is not truly serious and disciplined about protection. But a nice, shiny, intimidating fence can send a different message—especially if the fencing is topped with three rungs of barbed wire.

When deciding upon the type of fencing, several factors should be considered. For example, when using metal fencing, the gauge of the metal should correlate to the types of physical threats the organization most likely faces. After carrying out the risk analysis (covered in Chapter 2), the physical security team should understand the probability of enemies attempting to cut the fencing, drive through it, or climb over or crawl under it. Understanding these threats will help the team determine the requirements for security fencing.

The risk analysis results will also help indicate what height of fencing the organization should implement. Fences come in varying heights, and each height provides a different level of security:

- Fences *three to four feet high* only deter casual trespassers.
- Fences *six to seven feet high* are considered too high to climb easily.
- Fences *eight feet high* (possibly with strands of barbed or razor wire at the top) deter the more determined intruder and clearly demonstrate your organization is serious about protecting its property.

The barbed wire on top of fences can be tilted in or out, which also provides extra protection. A prison would have the barbed wire on top of the fencing pointed in, which makes it harder for prisoners to climb and escape. Most organizations would want the barbed wire tilted out, making it harder for someone to climb over the fence and gain access to the premises.

Critical areas should have fences at least eight feet high to provide the proper level of protection. The fencing must be taut (not sagging in any areas) and securely connected to the posts. The fencing should not be easily circumvented by pulling up its posts.

Fencing: Gauges, Mesh Sizes, and Security

The gauge of fence wiring is the thickness of the wires used within the fence mesh. The lower the gauge number, the larger the wire diameter:

- **11 gauge** = 0.0907-inch diameter
- **9 gauge** = 0.1144-inch diameter
- **6 gauge** = 0.162-inch diameter

The mesh sizing is the minimum clear distance between the wires. Common mesh sizes are 2 inches, 1 inch, and 3/8 inch. It is more difficult to climb or cut fencing with smaller mesh sizes, and the heavier-gauged wiring is harder to cut. The following list indicates the strength levels of the most common gauge and mesh sizes used in chain-link fencing today:

- **Extremely high security** 3/8-inch mesh, 11 gauge
- **Very high security** 1-inch mesh, 9 gauge
- **High security** 1-inch mesh, 11 gauge
- **Greater security** 2-inch mesh, 6 gauge
- **Normal industrial security** 2-inch mesh, 9 gauge

PIDAS Fencing

Perimeter Intrusion Detection and Assessment System (PIDAS) is a type of fencing that has sensors located on the wire mesh and at the base of the fence. It is used to detect if someone attempts to cut or climb the fence. It has a passive cable vibration sensor that sets off an alarm if an intrusion is detected. PIDAS is very sensitive and can cause many false alarms.

The posts should be buried sufficiently deep in the ground and should be secured with concrete to ensure they cannot be dug up or tied to vehicles and extracted. If the ground is soft or uneven, this might provide ways for intruders to slip or dig under the fence. In these situations, the fencing should actually extend into the dirt to thwart these types of attacks.

Fences work as "first line of defense" mechanisms. A few other controls can be used also. Strong and secure gates need to be implemented. It does no good to install a highly fortified and expensive fence and then have an unlocked or flimsy gate that allows easy access.

Gates basically have four distinct classifications:

- **Class I** Residential usage
- **Class II** Commercial usage, where general public access is expected; examples include a public parking lot entrance, a gated community, or a self-storage facility
- **Class III** Industrial usage, where limited access is expected; an example is a warehouse property entrance not intended to serve the general public
- **Class IV** Restricted access; this includes a prison entrance that is monitored either in person or via closed circuitry

Each gate classification has its own long list of implementation and maintenance guidelines to ensure the necessary level of protection. These classifications and guidelines are developed by UL (formerly Underwriters Laboratory), a nonprofit organization that tests, inspects, and classifies electronic devices, fire protection equipment, and specific construction materials. This is the group that certifies these different items to ensure they are in compliance with national building codes. A specific UL code, UL 325, deals with garage doors, drapery, gates, and louver and window operators and systems.

So, whereas in the information security world we look to NIST for our best practices and industry standards, in the physical security world, we look to UL for the same type of direction.

Bollards

Bollards usually look like small concrete pillars outside a building. Sometimes companies try to dress them up by putting flowers or lights in them to soften the look of a protected environment. They are placed by the sides of buildings that have the most immediate threat of someone driving a vehicle through the exterior wall. They are usually placed between the facility and a parking lot and/or between the facility and a road that runs close to an exterior wall. An alternative, particularly in more rural environments, is to use very large boulders to surround and protect sensitive sites. They provide the same type of protection that bollards provide.

Lighting

Many of the items mentioned in this chapter are things people take for granted day in and day out during our usual busy lives. Lighting is certainly one of those items you probably wouldn't give much thought to, unless it wasn't there. Unlit (or improperly lit) parking lots and parking garages have invited many attackers to carry out criminal activity that they may not have engaged in otherwise with proper lighting. Breaking into cars, stealing cars, and attacking employees as they leave the office are the more common types of attacks that take place in such situations. A security professional should understand that the right illumination needs to be in place, that no dead spots (unlit areas) should exist between the lights, and that all areas where individuals may walk should be properly lit. A security professional should also understand the various types of lighting available and where they should be used.

Wherever an array of lights is used, each light covers its own zone or area. The size of the zone each light covers depends on the illumination of light produced, which usually has a direct relationship to the wattage capacity of the bulbs. In most cases, the higher the lamp's wattage, the more illumination it produces. It is important that the zones of illumination coverage overlap. For example, if a company has an open parking lot, then light poles must be positioned within the correct distance of each other to eliminate any dead spots. If the lamps that will be used provide a 30-foot radius of illumination, then the light poles should be erected less than 30 feet apart so there is an overlap between the areas of illumination.

NOTE Critical areas need to have illumination that reaches at least eight feet with the illumination of two foot-candles. Foot-candle is a unit of measure of the intensity of light.

If an organization does not implement the right types of lights and ensure they provide proper coverage, the probability of criminal activity, accidents, and lawsuits increases.

Exterior lights that provide protection usually require less illumination intensity than interior working lighting, except for areas that require security personnel to inspect identification credentials for authorization. It is also important to have the correct lighting when using various types of surveillance equipment. The correct contrast between a potential intruder and background items needs to be provided, which only happens with the correct illumination and placement of lights. If the light is going to bounce off of dark, dirty, or darkly painted surfaces, then more illumination is required for the necessary contrast between people and the environment. If the area has clean concrete and light-colored painted surfaces, then not as much illumination is required. This is because when the same amount of light falls on an object and the surrounding background, an observer must depend on the contrast to tell them apart.

When lighting is installed, it should be directed toward areas where potential intruders would most likely be coming from and directed away from the security force posts. For example, lighting should be pointed at gates or exterior access points, and the guard locations should be more in the shadows, or under a lower amount of illumination. This is referred to as *glare protection* for the security force. If you are familiar with military operations, you might know that when you are approaching a military entry point, there is a fortified guard building with lights pointing toward the oncoming cars. A large sign instructs you to turn off your headlights, so the guards are not temporarily blinded by your lights and have a clear view of anything coming their way.

Lights used within the organization's security perimeter should be directed outward, which keeps the security personnel in relative darkness and allows them to easily view intruders beyond the organization's perimeter.

An array of lights that provides an even amount of illumination across an area is usually referred to as *continuous lighting*. Examples are the evenly spaced light poles in a parking lot, light fixtures that run across the outside of a building, or a series of fluorescent lights used in parking garages. If an organization's building is relatively close to someone else's developed property, a railway, an airport, or a highway, the organization may need to ensure the lighting does not "bleed over" property lines in an obtrusive manner. Thus, the illumination needs to be *controlled*, which just means the organization should erect lights and use illumination in such a way that it does not blind its neighbors or any passing cars, trains, or planes.

You probably are familiar with the special home lighting gadgets that turn certain lights on and off at predetermined times, giving the illusion to potential burglars that a house is occupied even when the residents are away. Organizations can use a similar technology, which is referred to as *standby lighting*. The security personnel can configure the times that different lights turn on and off, so potential intruders think different areas of the facility are populated.

NOTE Redundant or backup lights should be available in case of power failures or emergencies. Special care must be given to understand what type of lighting is needed in different parts of the facility in these types of situations. This lighting may run on generators or battery packs.

Responsive area illumination takes place when an IDS detects suspicious activities and turns on the lights within a specific area. When this type of technology is plugged into automated IDS products, there is a high likelihood of false alarms. Instead of continually having to dispatch a security guard to check out these issues, an organization can install a CCTV camera (described in the upcoming section "Visual Recording Devices") to scan the area for intruders.

If intruders want to disrupt the security personnel or decrease the probability of being seen while attempting to enter an organization's premises or building, they could attempt to turn off the lights or cut power to them. This is why lighting controls and switches should be in protected, locked, and centralized areas.

Surveillance Devices

Usually, installing fences and lights does not provide the necessary level of protection an organization needs to protect its facility, equipment, and employees. Therefore, an organization needs to ensure that all areas are under surveillance so that security personnel notice improper actions and address them before damage occurs. Surveillance can happen through visual detection or through devices that use sophisticated means of detecting abnormal behavior or unwanted conditions. It is important that every organization have a proper mix of lighting, security personnel, IDSs, and surveillance technologies and techniques.

Visual Recording Devices

Because surveillance is based on sensory perception, surveillance devices usually work in conjunction with guards and other monitoring mechanisms to extend their capabilities and range of perception. A *closed-circuit TV (CCTV)* system is a commonly used monitoring device in most organizations, but before purchasing and implementing a CCTV system, you need to consider several items:

- **The purpose of CCTV** To detect, assess, and/or identify intruders
- **The type of environment the CCTV camera will work in** Internal or external areas
- **The field of view required** Large or small area to be monitored
- **Amount of illumination of the environment** Lit areas, unlit areas, areas affected by sunlight
- **Integration with other security controls** Guards, IDSs, alarm systems

The reason you need to consider these items before you purchase a CCTV product is that there are so many different types of cameras, lenses, and monitors that make up the different CCTV products. You must understand what is expected of this physical security control, so that you purchase and implement the right type.

CCTVs are made up of cameras, a controller and digital video recording (DVR) system, and a monitor. Remote storage and remote client access are usually added to prevent threat actors (criminals, fire) from destroying the recorded videos and to allow off-duty staff to report to alarms generated by the system without having to drive back to the office. The camera captures the data and transmits it to the controller, which allows the data to be displayed on a local monitor. The data is recorded so that it can be reviewed at a later time if needed. Figure 20-3 shows how multiple cameras can be connected to one controller, which allows several different areas to be monitored at one time. The controller accepts video feed from all the cameras and interleaves these transmissions over one line to the central monitor.

A CCTV sends the captured data from the cameras to the controller using a special network, which can be wired or wireless. The term "closed-circuit" comes from the fact that the very first systems used this special closed network instead of broadcasting the signals over a public network. This network should be encrypted so that an intruder

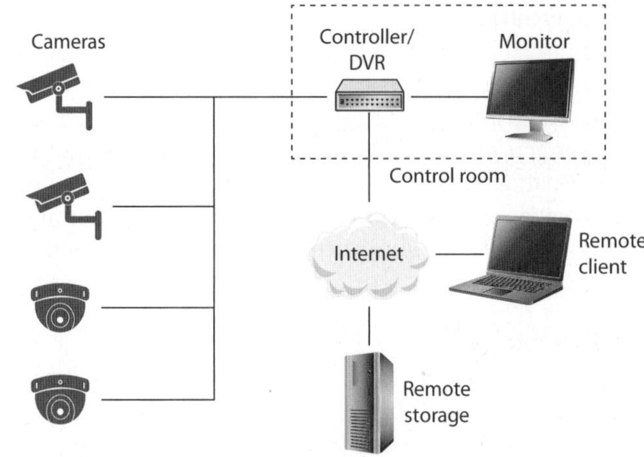

Figure 20-3 Several cameras can be connected to a DVR that can provide remote storage and access.

cannot manipulate the video feed that the security guard is monitoring. The most common type of attack is to replay previous recordings without the security personnel knowing it. For example, if an attacker is able to compromise a company's CCTV and play the recording from the day before, the security guard would not know an intruder is in the facility carrying out some type of crime. This is one reason why CCTVs should be used in conjunction with intruder detection controls, which we address in the next section.

Most of the CCTV cameras in use today employ light-sensitive chips called *charged-coupled devices (CCDs)*. The CCD is an electrical circuit that receives input light from the lens and converts it into an electronic signal, which is then displayed on the monitor. Images are focused through a lens onto the CCD chip surface, which forms the electrical representation of the optical image. It is this technology that allows for the capture of extraordinary detail of objects and precise representation, because it has sensors that work in the infrared range, which extends beyond human perception. The CCD sensor picks up this extra "data" and integrates it into the images shown on the monitor to allow for better granularity and quality in the video.

Two main types of lenses are used in CCTV: fixed focal length and zoom (varifocal). The *focal length* of a lens defines its effectiveness in viewing objects from a horizontal and vertical view. The focal length value relates to the angle of view that can be achieved. Short focal length lenses provide wider-angle views, while long focal length lenses provide a narrower view. The size of the images shown on a monitor, along with the area covered by one camera, is defined by the focal length. For example, if a company implements a CCTV camera in a warehouse, the focal length lens values should be between 2.8 and 4.3 millimeters (mm) so the whole area can be captured. If the company implements another CCTV camera that monitors an entrance, that lens value should be around 8 mm, which allows a smaller area to be monitored.

NOTE Fixed focal length lenses are available in various fields of views: wide, medium, and narrow. A lens that provides a "normal" focal length creates a picture that approximates the field of view of the human eye. A wide-angle lens has a short focal length, and a telephoto lens has a long focal length. When an organization selects a fixed focal length lens for a particular view of an environment, it should understand that if the field of view needs to be changed (wide to narrow), the lens must be changed.

So, if we need to monitor a large area, we use a lens with a smaller focal length value. Great, but what if a security guard hears a noise or thinks she sees something suspicious? A fixed focal length lens does not allow the user to optically change the area that fills the monitor. Though digital systems exist that allow this change to happen in logic, the resulting image quality is decreased as the area being studied becomes smaller. This is because the logic circuits are, in effect, cropping the broader image without increasing the number of pixels in it. This is called *digital zoom* (as opposed to optical zoom) and is a common feature in many cameras. The *optical zoom* lenses provide flexibility by allowing the viewer to change the field of view while maintaining the same number of pixels in the resulting image, which makes it much more detailed. The security personnel usually have a remote-control component integrated within the centralized CCTV monitoring area that allows them to move the cameras and zoom in and out on objects as needed. When both wide scenes and close-up captures are needed, an optical zoom lens is best.

To understand the next characteristic, depth of field, think about pictures you might take while on vacation with your family. For example, if you want to take a picture of your spouse with the Grand Canyon in the background, the main object of the picture is your spouse. Your camera is going to zoom in and use a *shallow depth of focus*. This provides a softer backdrop, which will lead the viewers of the photograph to the foreground, which is your spouse. Now, let's say you get tired of taking pictures of your spouse and want to get a scenic picture of just the Grand Canyon itself. The camera would use a *greater depth of focus*, so there is not such a distinction between objects in the foreground and background.

The depth of field is necessary to understand when choosing the correct lenses and configurations for your organization's CCTV. The *depth of field* refers to the portion of the environment that is in focus when shown on the monitor. The depth of field varies depending on the size of the lens opening, the distance of the object being focused on, and the focal length of the lens. The depth of field increases as the size of the lens opening decreases, the subject distance increases, or the focal length of the lens decreases. So, if you want to cover a large area and not focus on specific items, it is best to use a wide-angle lens and a small lens opening.

CCTV lenses have *irises*, which control the amount of light that enters the lens. *Manual iris lenses* have a ring around the CCTV lens that can be manually turned and controlled. A lens with a manual iris would be used in areas that have fixed lighting, since the iris cannot self-adjust to changes of light. An *auto iris lens* should be used in environments where the light changes, as in an outdoor setting. As the environment brightens, this is sensed by the iris, which automatically adjusts itself. Security personnel will configure the CCTV to have a specific fixed exposure value, which the iris is responsible for maintaining. On a sunny day, the iris lens closes to reduce the amount of light entering the camera, while at night, the iris opens to capture more light—just like our eyes.

When choosing the right CCTV for the right environment, you must determine the amount of light present in the environment. Different CCTV camera and lens products have specific illumination requirements to ensure the best quality images possible. The illumination requirements are usually represented in the *lux* value, which is a metric used to represent illumination strengths. The illumination can be measured by using a light meter. The intensity of light (illumination) is measured and represented in measurement units of lux or foot-candles. (The conversion between the two is one foot-candle = 10.76 lux.) The illumination measurement is not something that can be accurately provided by the vendor of a light bulb, because the environment can directly affect the illumination. This is why illumination strengths are most effectively measured where the light source is implemented.

Next, you need to consider the mounting requirements of the CCTV cameras. The cameras can be implemented in a *fixed mounting* or in a mounting that allows the cameras to move when necessary. A fixed camera cannot move in response to security personnel commands, whereas cameras that provide *PTZ capabilities* can pan, tilt, or zoom (PTZ) as necessary. Either way, there is deterrence value in ensuring the cameras (or at least some of them) are visible. You should also place signs stating that everyone in the area is being monitored through CCTV. Threat actors may be less likely to engage in illicit behavior if they know they're being recorded on video doing so.

NOTE You should be mindful of the privacy implications of camera placement. Areas like restrooms, locker rooms, and medical exam rooms are examples of places where you should not install cameras unless you are certain you comply with all applicable laws, regulations, and ethical standards.

Now, it would be nice if someone actually watched the monitors for suspicious activities. Realizing that monitor watching is a mentally deadening activity may lead your team to implement a type of *annunciator system*. Different types of annunciator products are available that can either "listen" for noise and activate electrical devices, such as lights, sirens, or CCTV cameras, or detect movement. Instead of expecting a security guard to stare at a CCTV monitor for eight hours straight, the guard can carry out other activities and be alerted by an annunciator if movement is detected on a screen.

Facility Access Control

Access control needs to be enforced through physical and technical components when it comes to physical security. Physical access controls use mechanisms to identify individuals who are attempting to enter a facility or area. They make sure the right individuals get in and the wrong individuals stay out and provide an audit trail of these actions. Having personnel within sensitive areas is one of the best security controls because they can personally detect suspicious behavior. However, they need to be trained on what activity is considered suspicious and how to report such activity.

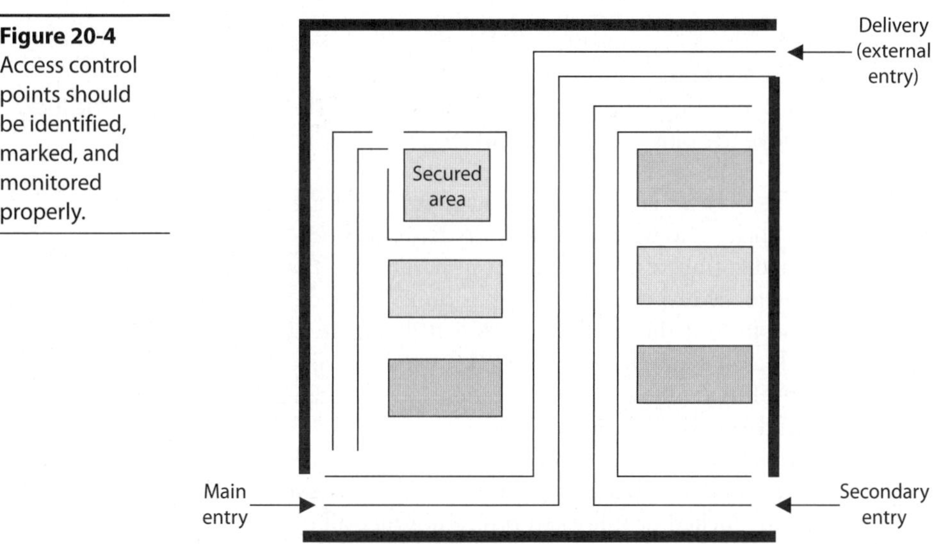

Figure 20-4 Access control points should be identified, marked, and monitored properly.

Before an organization can put into place the proper protection mechanisms, it needs to conduct a detailed review to identify which individuals should be allowed into what areas. Access control points can be identified and classified as external, main, and secondary entrances. Personnel should enter and exit through a specific entry, deliveries should be made to a different entry, and sensitive areas should be restricted. Figure 20-4 illustrates the different types of access control points into a facility. After an organization has identified and classified the access control points, the next step is to determine how to protect them.

Locks

Locks are inexpensive access control mechanisms that are widely accepted and used. They are considered *delaying* devices to intruders. The longer it takes to break or pick a lock, the longer a security guard or police officer has to arrive on the scene if the intruder has been detected. Almost any type of a door can be equipped with a lock, but keys can be easily lost and duplicated, and locks can be picked or broken. If an organization depends solely on a lock-and-key mechanism for protection, an individual who has the key can come and go as he likes without control and can remove items from the premises without detection. Locks should be used as part of the protection scheme, but should not be the sole protection scheme.

Locks vary in functionality. Padlocks can be used on chained fences, preset locks are usually used on doors, and programmable locks (requiring a combination to unlock) are used on doors or vaults. Locks come in all types and sizes. It is important to have the right type of lock so it provides the correct level of protection.

To the curious mind or a determined thief, a lock can be considered a little puzzle to solve, not a deterrent. In other words, locks may be merely a challenge, not necessarily something to stand in the way of malicious activities. Thus, you need to make the challenge difficult, through the complexity, strength, and quality of the locking mechanisms.

NOTE The delay time provided by the lock should match the penetration resistance of the surrounding components (door, door frame, hinges). A smart thief takes the path of least resistance, which may be to pick the lock, remove the pins from the hinges, or just kick down the door.

Mechanical Locks Two main types of mechanical locks are available: the warded lock and the tumbler lock. The warded lock is the basic padlock, as shown in Figure 20-5. It has a spring-loaded bolt with a notch cut in it. The key fits into this notch and slides the bolt from the locked to the unlocked position. The lock has wards in it, which are metal projections around the keyhole, as shown in Figure 20-6. The correct key for a specific warded lock has notches in it that fit in these projections and a notch to slide the bolt back and forth. These are the cheapest locks, because of their lack of any real sophistication, and are also the easiest to pick.

The *tumbler lock* has more pieces and parts than a ward lock. As shown in Figure 20-7, the key fits into a cylinder, which raises the lock metal pieces to the correct height so the bolt can slide to the locked or unlocked position. Once all of the metal pieces are at the correct level, the internal bolt can be turned. The proper key has the required size and sequences of notches to move these metal pieces into their correct position.

The three types of tumbler locks are the pin tumbler, wafer tumbler, and lever tumbler. The *pin tumbler lock*, shown in Figure 20-7, is the most commonly used tumbler lock. The key has to have just the right grooves to put all the spring-loaded pins in the right position so the lock can be locked or unlocked.

Figure 20-5
A warded lock

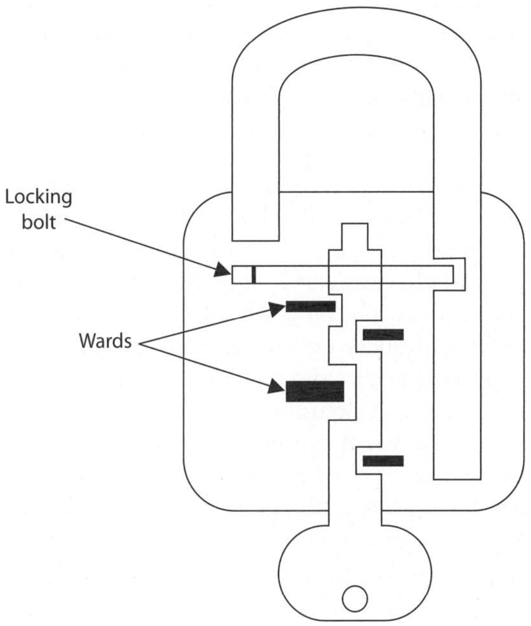

Figure 20-6 A key fits into a notch to turn the bolt to unlock the lock.

Wafer tumbler locks (also called *disc tumbler locks*) are the small, round locks you usually see on file cabinets. They use flat discs (wafers) instead of pins inside the locks. They often are used as car and desk locks. This type of lock does not provide much protection because it can be easily circumvented.

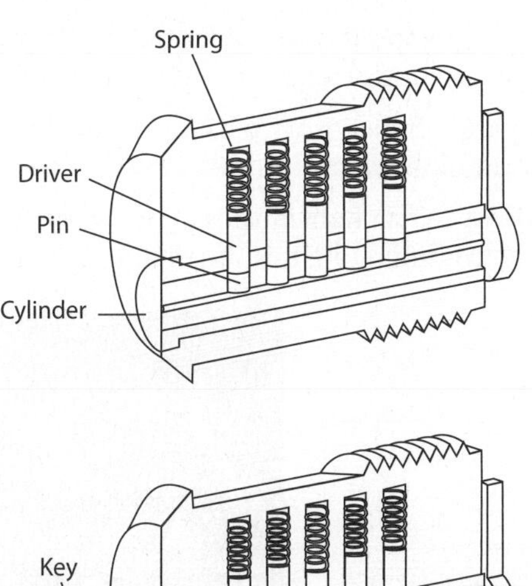

Figure 20-7 Tumbler lock

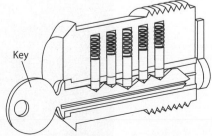

NOTE Some locks have interchangeable cores, which allow for the core of the lock to be taken out. You would use this type of lock if you wanted one key to open several locks. You would just replace all locks with the same core.

Combination locks, of course, require the correct combination of numbers to unlock them. These locks have internal wheels that have to line up properly before being unlocked. A user spins the lock interface left and right by so many clicks, which lines up the internal wheels. Once the correct turns have taken place, all the wheels are in the right position for the lock to release and open the door. The more wheels within the locks, the more protection provided. Electronic combination locks do not use internal wheels, but rather have a keypad that allows a person to type in the combination instead of turning a knob with a combination faceplate. An example of an electronic combination lock is shown in Figure 20-8.

Cipher locks, also known as *programmable locks*, are keyless and use keypads to control access into an area or facility. The lock requires a specific combination to be entered into the keypad and possibly a swipe card. Cipher locks cost more than traditional locks, but their combinations can be changed, specific combination sequence values can be locked out, and personnel who are in trouble or under duress can enter a specific code that will open the door and initiate a remote alarm at the same time. Thus, compared to traditional locks, cipher locks can provide a much higher level of security and control over who can access a facility.

The following are some functionalities commonly available on many cipher combination locks that improve the performance of access control and provide for increased security levels:

- **Door delay** If a door is held open for a given time, an alarm triggers to alert personnel of suspicious activity.
- **Key override** A specific combination can be programmed for use in emergency situations to override normal procedures or for supervisory overrides.
- **Master keying** Supervisory personnel can change access codes and other features of the cipher lock.
- **Hostage alarm** If an individual is under duress and/or held hostage, a combination he enters can communicate this situation to the guard station and/or police station.

Figure 20-8
An electronic combination lock

If a door is accompanied by a cipher lock, it should have a corresponding visibility shield so a bystander cannot see the combination as it is keyed in. Automated cipher locks must have a backup battery system and be set to unlock during a power failure so personnel are not trapped inside during an emergency. *Fail safe* systems are those that are designed and configured to ensure the safety of humans in the event of failure. Contrast this principle with *fail secure*, which we discussed in Chapter 9. These two imperatives (safety versus security) must be carefully balanced, while keeping in mind that human safety must always be the highest priority.

CAUTION It is important to change the combination of locks and to use random combination sequences. Often, people do not change their combinations or clean the keypads, which allows an intruder to know what key values are used in the combination, because they are the dirty and worn keys. The intruder then just needs to figure out the right combination of these values.

Some cipher locks require all users to know and use the same combination, which does not allow for any individual accountability. Some of the more sophisticated cipher locks permit specific codes to be assigned to unique individuals. This provides more accountability, because each individual is responsible for keeping his access code secret, and entry and exit activities can be logged and tracked. These are usually referred to as *smart locks*, because they are designed to allow only authorized individuals access at certain doors at certain times.

NOTE Hotel key cards are also known as smart cards. The access code on the card can allow access to a hotel room, workout area, business area, and better yet—the mini bar.

Device Locks Unfortunately, hardware has a tendency to "walk away" from facilities; thus, device locks are necessary to thwart these attempts. Cable locks consist of a vinyl-coated steel cable that can secure a computer or peripheral to a desk or other stationary components, as shown in Figure 20-9.

The following are some of the device locks available and their capabilities:

- **Switch controls** Cover on/off power switches
- **Slot locks** Secure the system to a stationary component by the use of steel cable that is connected to a bracket mounted in a spare expansion slot
- **Port controls** Block access to disk drives or unused serial or parallel ports
- **Peripheral switch controls** Secure a keyboard by inserting an on/off switch between the system unit and the keyboard input slot
- **Cable traps** Prevent the removal of input/output devices by passing their cables through a lockable unit

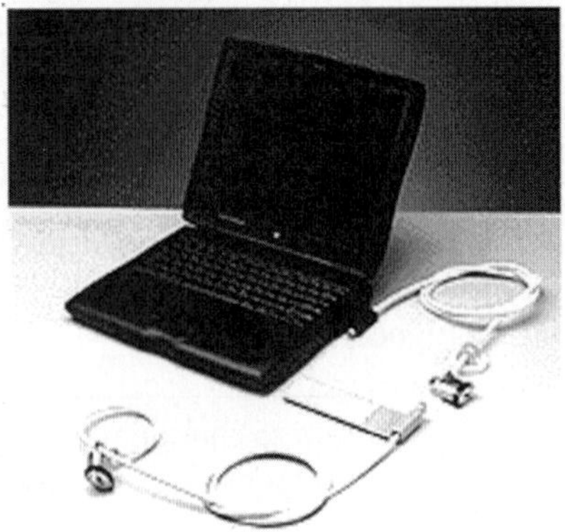

Figure 20-9 Laptop security cable kits secure a computer by enabling the user to attach the device to a stationary component within an area.

Administrative Responsibilities It is important for an organization not only to choose the right type of lock for the right purpose but also to follow proper maintenance and procedures. Keys should be assigned by facility management, and this assignment should be documented. Procedures should be written out detailing how keys are to be assigned, inventoried, and destroyed when necessary and what should happen if and when keys are lost. Someone on the organization's facility management team should be assigned the responsibility of overseeing key and combination maintenance.

Most organizations have master keys and submaster keys for the facility management staff. A master key opens all the locks within the facility, and the submaster keys open one or more locks. Each lock has its own individual unique keys as well. So if a facility has 100 offices, the occupant of each office can have his or her own key. A master key allows access to all offices for security personnel and for emergencies. If one security guard is responsible for monitoring half of the facility, the guard can be assigned one of the submaster keys for just those offices.

Since these master and submaster keys are powerful, they must be properly guarded and not widely shared. A security policy should outline what portions of the facility and which device types need to be locked. As a security professional, you should understand what type of lock is most appropriate for each situation, the level of protection provided by various types of locks, and how these locks can be circumvented.

Circumventing Locks Each lock type has corresponding tools that can be used to pick it (open it without the key). A tension wrench is a tool shaped like an L and is used to apply tension to the internal cylinder of a lock. The lock picker uses a lock pick to manipulate the individual pins to their proper placement. Once certain pins are "picked" (put in their correct place), the tension wrench holds these down while the lock picker figures out the correct settings for the other pins. After the intruder determines the proper pin placement, the wrench is used to then open the lock.

Intruders may carry out another technique, referred to as *raking*. To circumvent a pin tumbler lock, a lock pick is pushed to the back of the lock and quickly slid out while providing upward pressure. This movement makes many of the pins fall into place. A tension wrench is also put in to hold the pins that pop into the right place. If all the pins do not slide to the necessary height for the lock to open, the intruder holds the tension wrench and uses a thinner pick to move the rest of the pins into place.

Lock Strengths

Basically, three grades of locks are available:

- **Grade 1** Commercial and industrial use
- **Grade 2** Heavy-duty residential/light-duty commercial
- **Grade 3** Residential/consumer

The cylinders within the locks fall into three main categories:

- **Low security** No pick or drill resistance provided (can fall within any of the three grades of locks)
- **Medium security** A degree of pick-resistance protection provided (uses tighter and more complex keyways [notch combination]; can fall within any of the three grades of locks)
- **High security** Pick-resistance protection through many different mechanisms (only used in grade 1 and 2 locks)

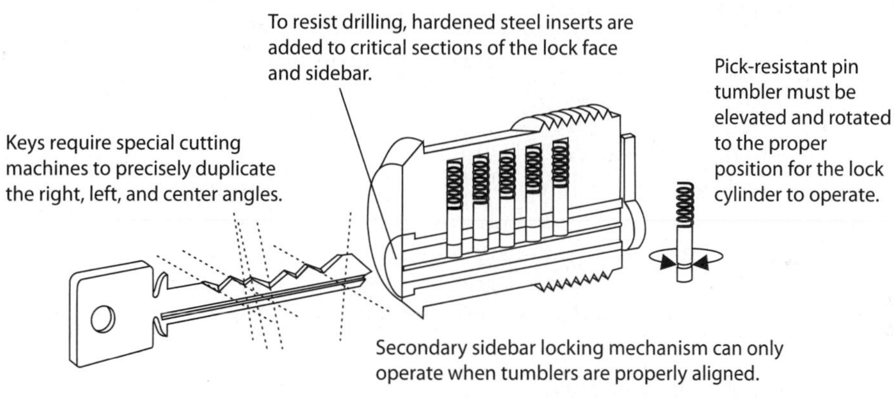

To resist drilling, hardened steel inserts are added to critical sections of the lock face and sidebar.
Pick-resistant pin tumbler must be elevated and rotated to the proper position for the lock cylinder to operate.
Keys require special cutting machines to precisely duplicate the right, left, and center angles.
Secondary sidebar locking mechanism can only operate when tumblers are properly aligned.

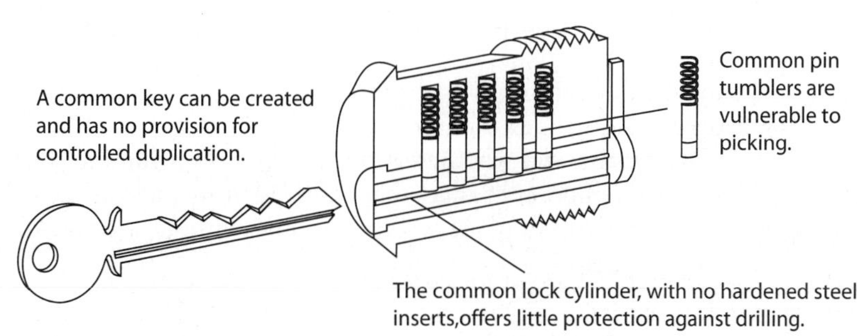

A common key can be created and has no provision for controlled duplication.
Common pin tumblers are vulnerable to picking.
The common lock cylinder, with no hardened steel inserts,offers little protection against drilling.

Lock bumping is a tactic that intruders can use to force the pins in a tumbler lock to their open position by using a special key called a *bump key*. The stronger the material that makes up the lock, the smaller the chance that this type of lock attack will be successful.

Now, if this is all too much trouble for the intruder, she can just drill the lock, use bolt cutters, attempt to break through the door or the doorframe, or remove the hinges. There are just so many choices for the bad guys.

Internal Security Controls

The physical security controls we've discussed so far have been focused on the perimeter. It is also important, however, to implement and manage internal security controls to mitigate risks when threat actors breach the perimeter or are insider threats. One type of control we already discussed in Chapter 10 is work area separation, in which we create internal perimeters around sensitive areas. For example, only designated IT and security personnel should be allowed in the server room. Access to these areas can then be restricted using locks and self-closing doors.

When implementing work area separation, we can start with a concentric zone model similar to the one we used for the external perimeter. Most staff will probably be able to move freely across the largest zone so that they can do their jobs. This general zone would have some controls, but not a bunch of them. Some staff members will also be allowed to go into more sensitive areas such as the operations center and the executive suite. These areas require some sort of access control like swiping a badge, but they're generally staffed so the people working there act as a sort of intrusion detection system when they see someone who doesn't belong. There can also be a highly sensitive zone that includes spaces where you really can't have any unauthorized persons, particularly if the spaces are not always staffed. Examples of these highly sensitive areas are server rooms, narcotic storage spaces (in healthcare facilities), and hazardous materials storerooms.

Physical security teams could include roving guards that move around the facility looking for potential security violations and unauthorized personnel. These teams could also monitor internal security cameras and be trained on how to respond to incidents such as medical emergencies and active shooters.

Personnel Access Controls

Proper identification verifies whether the person attempting to access a facility or area should actually be allowed in. Identification and authentication can be verified by matching an anatomical attribute (biometric system), using smart or memory cards (swipe cards), presenting a photo ID to a security guard, using a key, or providing a card and entering a password or PIN.

Personnel should be identified with badges that must be worn visibly while in the facility. The badges could include a photo of the individual and be color-coded to show clearance level, department, and whether or not that person is allowed to escort visitors. Visitors could be issued temporary badges that clearly identify them as such. All personnel would be trained to challenge anyone walking around without a badge or call security personnel to deal with them.

A common problem with controlling authorized access into a facility or area is called *piggybacking*. This occurs when an individual gains unauthorized access by using someone else's legitimate credentials or access rights. Usually, an individual just follows another person closely through a door without providing any credentials. The best preventive measures against piggybacking are to have security guards at access points and to educate employees about good security practices.

If an organization wants to use a card badge reader, it has several types of systems to choose from. Most systems are based on issuing to personnel cards that have embedded magnetic strips that contain access information. The reader can just look for simple access information within the magnetic strip, or it can be connected to a more sophisticated system that scans the information, makes more complex access decisions, and logs badge IDs and access times.

If the card is a memory card, then the reader just pulls information from it and makes an access decision. If the card is a smart card, the individual may be required to enter a PIN or password, which the reader compares against the information held within the card or in an authentication server.

These access cards can be used with *user-activated readers*, which just means the user actually has to do something—swipe the card or enter a PIN. *System sensing access control readers*, also called *transponders*, recognize the presence of an approaching object within a specific area. This type of system does not require the user to swipe the card through the reader. The reader sends out interrogating signals and obtains the access code from the card without the user having to do anything.

EXAM TIP *Electronic access control (EAC) tokens* is a generic term used to describe proximity authentication devices, such as proximity readers, programmable locks, or biometric systems, which identify and authenticate users before allowing them entrance into physically controlled areas.

Intrusion Detection Systems

Surveillance techniques are used to watch an area, whereas intrusion detection devices are used to sense changes that take place in an environment. Both are monitoring methods, but they use different devices and approaches. This section addresses the types of technologies that can be used to detect the presence of an intruder. One such technology, a perimeter scanning device, is shown in Figure 20-10.

IDSs are used to detect unauthorized entries and to alert a responsible entity to respond. These systems can monitor entries, doors, windows, devices, or removable coverings of equipment. Many work with magnetic contacts or vibration-detection devices that are sensitive to certain types of changes in the environment. When a change is detected, the IDS device sounds an alarm either in the local area or in both the local area and a remote police or guard station.

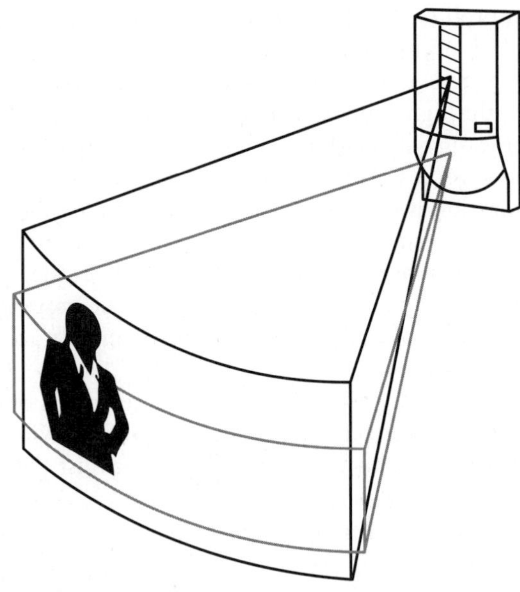

Figure 20-10 Different perimeter scanning devices work by covering a specific area.

IDSs can be used to detect changes in the following:

- Beams of light
- Sounds and vibrations
- Motion
- Different types of fields (microwave, ultrasonic, electrostatic)
- Electrical circuit

IDSs can be used to detect intruders by employing electromechanical systems (magnetic switches, metallic foil in windows, pressure mats) or volumetric systems. *Volumetric systems* are more sensitive because they detect changes in subtle environmental characteristics, such as vibration, microwaves, ultrasonic frequencies, infrared values, and photoelectric changes.

Electromechanical systems work by detecting a change or break in a circuit. The electrical circuits can be strips of foil embedded in or connected to windows. If the window breaks, the foil strip breaks, which sounds an alarm. Vibration detectors can detect movement on walls, screens, ceilings, and floors when the fine wires embedded within the structure are broken. Magnetic contact switches can be installed on windows and doors. If the contacts are separated because the window or door is opened, an alarm sounds. Another type of electromechanical detector is a pressure pad. This is placed underneath a rug or portion of the carpet and is activated after hours. If someone steps on the pad, an alarm is triggered.

A *photoelectric system*, or *photometric system*, detects the change in a light beam and thus can be used only in windowless rooms. These systems work like photoelectric smoke detectors, which emit a beam that hits the receiver. If this beam of light is interrupted, an alarm sounds. The beams emitted by the photoelectric cell can be cross-sectional and can be invisible or visible beams. *Cross-sectional* means that one area can have several different light beams extending across it, which is usually carried out by using hidden mirrors to bounce the beam from one place to another until it hits the light receiver. These are the systems commonly depicted in movies. You have probably seen James Bond and other noteworthy movie spies or criminals use night-vision goggles to see the invisible beams and then step over them.

A *passive infrared (PIR) system* identifies the changes of heat waves in an area it is configured to monitor. If the particles' temperature within the air rises, it could be an indication of the presence of an intruder, so an alarm is sounded.

An *acoustical detection system* uses microphones installed on floors, walls, or ceilings. The goal is to detect any sound made during a forced entry. Although these systems are easily installed, they are very sensitive and cannot be used in areas open to sounds of storms or traffic. *Vibration sensors* are similar and are also implemented to detect forced entry. Financial institutions may choose to implement these types of sensors on exterior walls, where bank robbers may attempt to drive a vehicle through. They are also commonly used around the ceiling and flooring of vaults to detect someone trying to make an unauthorized bank withdrawal.

Wave-pattern motion detectors differ in the frequency of the waves they monitor. The different frequencies are microwave, ultrasonic, and low frequency. All of these devices generate a wave pattern that is sent over a sensitive area and reflected back to a receiver. If the pattern is returned undisturbed, the device does nothing. If the pattern returns altered because something in the room is moving, an alarm sounds.

A *proximity detector*, or *capacitance detector*, emits a measurable magnetic field. The detector monitors this magnetic field, and an alarm sounds if the field is disrupted. These devices are usually used to protect specific objects (e.g., artwork, cabinets, or a safe) versus protecting a whole room or area. Capacitance change in an electrostatic field can be used to catch a bad guy, but first you need to understand what capacitance change means. An electrostatic IDS creates an electrostatic magnetic field, which is just an electric field associated with static electric charges. Most objects have a measurable static electric charge. They are all made up of many subatomic particles, and when everything is stable and static, these particles constitute one holistic electric charge. This means there is a balance between the electric capacitance and inductance. Now, if an intruder enters the area, his subatomic particles will mess up this lovely balance in the electrostatic field, causing a capacitance change, and an alarm will sound. So if you want to rob a company that uses these types of detectors, leave the subatomic particles that make up your body at home.

The type of motion detector that an organization chooses to implement, its power capacity, and its configurations dictate the number of detectors needed to cover a sensitive area. Also, the size and shape of the room and the items within the room may cause barriers, in which case more detectors would be needed to provide the necessary level of coverage.

Intrusion Detection Systems Characteristics

IDSs are very valuable controls to use in every physical security program, but several issues need to be understood before implementing them:

- They are expensive and require human intervention to respond to the alarms.
- They require a redundant power supply and emergency backup power.
- They can be linked to a centralized security system.
- They should have a fail-safe configuration, which defaults to "activated."
- They should detect, and be resistant to, tampering.

IDSs are support mechanisms intended to detect and announce an attempted intrusion. They will not prevent or apprehend intruders, so they should be seen as an aid to the organization's security forces.

Patrol Force and Guards

One of the best intrusion detection mechanisms is a security guard and/or a patrol force to monitor a facility's grounds. This type of security control is more flexible than other security mechanisms, provides good response to suspicious activities, and works as a great deterrent. However, it can be a costly endeavor because it requires a salary, benefits, and time off. People sometimes are unreliable. Screening and bonding is an important part of selecting a security guard, but this only provides a certain level of assurance. One issue is if the security guard decides to make exceptions for people who do not follow the organization's approved policies. Because basic human nature is to trust and help people, a seemingly innocent favor can put an organization at risk.

IDSs and physical protection measures ultimately require human intervention. Security guards can be at a fixed post or can patrol specific areas. Different organizations will have different needs from security guards. They may be required to check individual credentials and enforce filling out a sign-in log. They may be responsible for monitoring IDSs and expected to respond to alarms. They may need to issue and recover visitor badges, respond to fire alarms, enforce rules established by the company within the building, and control what materials can come into or go out of the environment. The guard may need to verify that doors, windows, safes, and vaults are secured; report identified safety hazards; enforce restrictions of sensitive areas; and escort individuals throughout facilities.

The security guard should have clear and decisive tasks that she is expected to fulfill. The guard should be fully trained on the activities she is expected to perform and on the responses expected from her in different situations. She should also have a central control point to check in to, two-way radios to ensure proper communication, and the necessary access into areas she is responsible for protecting.

The best security has a combination of security mechanisms and does not depend on just one component of security. Thus, a security guard should be accompanied by other surveillance and detection mechanisms.

Dogs

Dogs have proven to be highly useful in detecting intruders and other unwanted conditions. Their senses of smell and hearing outperform those of humans, and their intelligence and loyalty can be used for protection. The best security dogs go through intensive training to respond to a wide range of commands and to perform many tasks. Dogs can be trained to hold an intruder at bay until security personnel arrive or to chase an intruder and attack. Some dogs are trained to smell smoke so they can alert personnel to a fire.

Of course, dogs cannot always know the difference between an authorized person and an unauthorized person, so if an employee goes into work after hours, he can have more on his hands than expected. Dogs can provide a good supplementary security mechanism.

EXAM TIP Because the use of guard dogs introduces significant risks to personal safety, which is paramount for CISSPs, exam answers that include dogs are likelier to be incorrect. Be on the lookout for these.

Auditing Physical Access

Physical access control systems can use software and auditing features to produce audit trails or access logs pertaining to access attempts. The following information should be logged and reviewed:

- The date and time of the access attempt
- The entry point at which access was attempted
- The user ID employed when access was attempted
- Any unsuccessful access attempts, especially if during unauthorized hours

As with audit logs produced by computers, access logs are useless unless someone actually reviews them. A security guard may be required to review these logs, but a security professional or a facility manager should also review these logs periodically. Management needs to know where entry points into the facility exist and who attempts to use them.

Audit and access logs are detective controls, not preventive controls. They are used to piece together a situation after the fact instead of attempting to prevent an access attempt in the first place.

Personnel Safety and Security

The single most valuable asset for an organization, and the one that involves the highest moral and ethical standards, is its people. Our safety focus in security operations will be on our own employees, but we also need to take proper steps to ensure the safety of visitors, clients, and anyone who enters into our physical or virtual spaces. While the scope of safety is broader than information systems security, information security professionals make important contributions to this effort.

EXAM TIP Human safety almost always trumps all other concerns. If an exam question has a possible answer that focuses on safety, it is likelier to be the right one.

Travel

Personnel safety in the workplace is one thing, but how do we protect our staff while they are traveling? There are a host of considerations we should take. The most basic one is to determine the threat landscape at the destination. Some organizations go as far as having country-specific briefings that are regularly updated and required for all staff traveling overseas. This is obviously a resource-intensive proposition, but there are free alternatives you can leverage. Many governments have departments or ministries that publish this information for their citizens traveling abroad. For example, the U.S. Department of State publishes travel advisories on its website for virtually any destination.

Speaking of these government entities, it is also important for traveling staff to know the location and contact information for the nearest embassy or consulate. In case of emergency, these offices provide a variety of important services. Depending on the threat condition at the destination, it may be a good idea to notify these offices of staff members' contact information, dates of travel, and places of lodging.

Hotel security starts by doing a bit of research ahead of the trip. If you've never stayed in a specific hotel, a few minutes of web searching will give you a good indication of whether or not it's safe. Here are some other best practices that your organization's staff should consider when traveling:

- Ask for a room on the second floor. It reduces the risk of random criminal activity and is still close enough to the ground to escape in case of an emergency even if you can't use the front door.
- Ask for and keep a hotel business card on your person at all times in case you have to call the local police or embassy and provide your location in an emergency.
- Secure valuables in the in-room safe. It may not really be totally secure, but it raises the bar on would-be thieves.
- Always use the security latch on the door when in the room.
- Keep your passport with you at all times when in a foreign country. Before the trip leave a photocopy of the passport with a trusted individual at home.

Security Training and Awareness

All these personal safety measures are good only if your organization's staff actually knows what they are and how and when to use them. Many organizations have mandatory training events for all staff, and personal security should be part of it. Keep in mind that emergency procedures, panic codes/passwords, and travel security measures are quickly forgotten if they are not periodically reinforced.

Emergency Management

A common tool for ensuring the safety of personnel during emergencies is the occupant emergency plan (OEP). The OEP describes the actions that facility occupants should take to ensure their safety during an emergency situation. This plan should address the range of emergencies from individual to facility-wide, and it should be integrated into the security operations of the organization.

Perhaps the best example of the intersection of safety and security occurs in the area of physical access control. A well-designed system of physical access controls constrains the movement of specific individuals in and out of certain spaces. For instance, we only want authorized persons to enter the server room. But what if the server room offers the best escape route for people who would normally not be allowed in it? While we would not design a facility in which this would be the case, we sometimes end up occupying less-than-ideal facilities. If this were the case, what process would we implement to ensure we can get people out of the building quickly and not force them to take a circuitous route that could put them in danger, but keeps them out of the sensitive area?

Another example involves access for emergency responders. If a fire alarm is triggered in the building, how do we ensure we can evacuate all personnel while giving fire fighters access to all spaces (without requiring them to break down doors)? In this context, how do we simultaneously ensure the safety of our personnel while maintaining security of our information systems?

Lastly, many modern physical access controls require electricity. If an electronic lock does not have a battery backup, will it automatically unlock in the absence of power or will it remain in the locked state? A *fail-safe device* is one that automatically moves to the state that ensures safety in the event of a failure such as loss of power. Fail-safe controls, while critical to human safety, must be carefully considered because they introduce risks to the security of our information systems.

Duress

Duress is the use of threats or violence against someone in order to force them to do something they don't want to do or otherwise wouldn't do. Like any other threat, we need to factor in duress in our risk assessment and figure out what (if anything) to do about it. A popular example of a countermeasure for duress is the use of panic buttons by bank tellers. The button is hidden where an assailant can't see it but where the teller can easily and discretely activate it to warn the police. A twist on this is the use of duress codes in some alarm systems. The alarm has a keypad where an authorized person can enter a secret code to deactivate it. The system can have two different codes: a regular one that disarms the alarm, and a second one that also disarms the alarm but also alerts authorities to an emergency. If someone was forcing you to disarm an alarm, you'd enter the second code and they wouldn't be able to know that you just summoned the police.

Duress codes can also be verbal. For example, some alarm systems have an attendant call the facility to ensure everything is fine. If someone is under duress (and perhaps on speakerphone next to the assailant) you would want a discrete way for that person to convey that they are in danger. You could set up two possible responses, like "apple pie," which would mean you are in danger, and "sunshine," which would mean everything is truly fine. The key is to make the duress response sound completely benign.

Another situation to consider is when an assailant forces an employee to log into their account. You could set up a duress account with a username that is very similar to the real one. Upon login, the duress account looks just like the real one, except that it doesn't include sensitive content. The twist is that the duress password could do a range of things from activating full monitoring (like camera, keyboard, and packet logging) to quietly wiping the device in the background (useful for laptops being used away from the office). Obviously, it would also generate an alert to security personnel that the user is in danger.

Chapter Review

This chapter was a bit of a whirlwind tour of many of the issues we need to manage as part of security operations. We covered a lot of ground, but keep in mind that these are all important topics you need to address in your organization if you want to operationalize security. Collectively, this chapter lays the foundation for the tasks many of us prefer to be doing: blocking bad actors from gaining access, finding the ones that sneak in, and frustrating their efforts to cause us harm. We dive into those in the next three chapters as we delve into day-to-day security operations, incident response, and dealing with disasters.

Quick Review

- SecOps (Security + Operations) is the integration of security and IT operations people, technology, and processes to reduce risks while improving business agility.
- Access to resources should be limited to authorized personnel, applications, and services and should be audited for compliance to stated policies.
- Least privilege means an individual should have just enough permissions and rights to fulfill his role in the company and no more.
- Need to know means we must first establish that an individual has a legitimate, job role–related need for a given resource before granting access to it.
- Separation of duties and responsibilities should be in place so that fraud cannot take place without collusion of two or more people.
- Privileged account management formally enforces the principle of least privilege on accounts with elevated rights.
- Job rotation means that, over time, more than one person fulfills the tasks of one position within the organization, which provides backup and redundancy but also helps identify fraudulent activities.

- A service level agreement (SLA) is a contract that states that a service provider guarantees a certain level of service to a customer.
- Change management is the practice of minimizing the risks associated with the addition, modification, or removal of anything that could have an effect on IT services.
- Activities that involve change management include requesting, evaluating, planning, implementing, reviewing, and closing or sustaining a change.
- Configuration management is the process of establishing and maintaining consistent configurations on all our systems to meet organizational requirements.
- A baseline is the configuration of a system at a point in time as agreed upon by the appropriate decision makers.
- Vulnerability management is the cyclical process of identifying vulnerabilities, determining the risks they pose to the organization, and applying security controls that bring those risks to acceptable levels.
- Patch management is the process for identifying, acquiring, installing, and verifying patches for products and systems.
- Facilities that house systems that process sensitive information should have physical access controls to limit access to authorized personnel only.
- Exterior fencing can be costly and unsightly, but can provide crowd control and help control access to the facility, particularly if the fencing is eight feet or higher.
- Closed-circuit TV (CCTV) systems are made up of cameras, a controller and digital video recording (DVR) system, and a monitor, but frequently also include remote storage and remote client access.
- Locks are considered delaying devices to intruders.
- Some physical security controls may conflict with the safety of people. These issues need to be addressed; human life is always more important than protecting a facility or the assets it contains.
- Piggybacking occurs when an individual gains unauthorized access by using someone else's legitimate credentials or access rights, usually when the intruder closely follows an authorized person through a door or gate.
- Proximity identification devices can be user activated (action needs to be taken by a user) or system sensing (no action needs to be taken by the user).
- A transponder is a proximity-based access control reader that does not require action by the user. The reader transmits signals to the device, and the device responds with an access code.
- Intrusion detection devices include motion detectors, CCTVs, vibration sensors, and electromechanical devices.
- Intrusion detection devices can be penetrated, are expensive to install and monitor, require human response, and are subject to false alarms.

- Security guards are expensive but provide flexibility in response to security breaches and can deter intruders from attempting an attack.
- Dogs are very effective at detecting and deterring intruders, but introduce significant risks to personal safety.
- Duress is the use of threats or violence against someone in order to force them to do something they don't want to do or otherwise wouldn't do.

Questions

Please remember that these questions are formatted and asked in a certain way for a reason. Keep in mind that the CISSP exam is asking questions at a conceptual level. Questions may not always have the perfect answer, and the candidate is advised against always looking for the perfect answer. Instead, the candidate should look for the best answer in the list.

1. Why should employers make sure employees take their vacations?
   A. They have a legal obligation.
   B. It is part of due diligence.
   C. It is a way for fraud to be uncovered.
   D. To ensure employees do not get burned out.
2. Which of the following best describes separation of duties and job rotation?
   A. Separation of duties ensures that more than one employee knows how to perform the tasks of a position, and job rotation ensures that one person cannot perform a high-risk task alone.
   B. Separation of duties ensures that one person cannot perform a high-risk task alone, and job rotation can uncover fraud and ensure that more than one person knows the tasks of a position.
   C. They are the same thing, but with different titles.
   D. They are administrative controls that enforce access control and protect the organization's resources.
3. If a programmer is restricted from updating and modifying production code, what is this an example of?
   A. Rotation of duties
   B. Due diligence
   C. Separation of duties
   D. Controlling input values

4. What is the difference between least privilege and need to know?
   A. A user should have least privilege that restricts her need to know.
   B. A user should have a security clearance to access resources, a need to know about those resources, and least privilege to give her full control of all resources.
   C. A user should have a need to know to access particular resources, and least privilege should be implemented to ensure she only accesses the resources she has a need to know.
   D. They are two different terms for the same issue.
5. Which of the following would not require updated documentation?
   A. An antivirus signature update
   B. Reconfiguration of a server
   C. A change in security policy
   D. The installation of a patch to a production server
6. A company needs to implement a CCTV system that will monitor a large area outside the facility. Which of the following is the correct lens combination for this?
   A. A wide-angle lens and a small lens opening
   B. A wide-angle lens and a large lens opening
   C. A wide-angle lens and a large lens opening with a small focal length
   D. A wide-angle lens and a large lens opening with a large focal length
7. Which of the following is not a true statement about CCTV lenses?
   A. Lenses that have a manual iris should be used in outside monitoring.
   B. Zoom lenses carry out focus functionality automatically.
   C. Depth of field increases as the size of the lens opening decreases.
   D. Depth of field increases as the focal length of the lens decreases.
8. What is true about a transponder?
   A. It is a card that can be read without sliding it through a card reader.
   B. It is a biometric proximity device.
   C. It is a card that a user swipes through a card reader to gain access to a facility.
   D. It exchanges tokens with an authentication server.
9. When is a security guard the best choice for a physical access control mechanism?
   A. When discriminating judgment is required
   B. When intrusion detection is required
   C. When the security budget is low
   D. When access controls are in place

10. Which of the following is not a characteristic of an electrostatic intrusion detection system?
    A. It creates an electrostatic field and monitors for a capacitance change.
    B. It can be used as an intrusion detection system for large areas.
    C. It produces a balance between the electric capacitance and inductance of an object.
    D. It can detect if an intruder comes within a certain range of an object.
11. What is a common problem with vibration-detection devices used for perimeter security?
    A. They can be defeated by emitting the right electrical signals in the protected area.
    B. The power source is easily disabled.
    C. They cause false alarms.
    D. They interfere with computing devices.
12. Which of the following is not considered a delaying mechanism?
    A. Locks
    B. Defense-in-depth measures
    C. Warning signs
    D. Access controls
13. What are the two general types of proximity identification devices?
    A. Biometric devices and access control devices
    B. Swipe card devices and passive devices
    C. Preset code devices and wireless devices
    D. User-activated devices and system sensing devices
14. Which is not a drawback of an intrusion detection system?
    A. It's expensive to install.
    B. It cannot be penetrated.
    C. It requires human response.
    D. It's subject to false alarms.
15. What is a cipher lock?
    A. A lock that uses cryptographic keys
    B. A lock that uses a type of key that cannot be reproduced
    C. A lock that uses a token and perimeter reader
    D. A lock that uses a keypad

16. If a cipher lock has a door delay option, what does that mean?
    A. After a door is open for a specific period, the alarm goes off.
    B. It can only be opened during emergency situations.
    C. It has a hostage alarm capability.
    D. It has supervisory override capability.

Answers

1. **C.** Many times, employees who are carrying out fraudulent activities do not take the vacation they have earned because they do not want anyone to find out what they have been doing. Forcing an employee to take a vacation means that someone else has to do that person's job and can possibly uncover any misdeeds.
2. **B.** Rotation of duties enables an organization to have more than one person trained in a position and can uncover fraudulent activities. Separation of duties is put into place to ensure that one entity cannot carry out a critical task alone.
3. **C.** This is just one of several examples of separation of duties. A system must be set up for proper code maintenance to take place when necessary, instead of allowing a programmer to make changes arbitrarily. These types of changes should go through a change control process and should have more entities involved than just one programmer.
4. **C.** Users should be able to access only the resources they need to fulfill the duties of their positions. They also should only have the level of permissions and rights for those resources that are required to carry out the exact operations they need for their jobs, and no more. This second concept is more granular than the first, but they have a symbiotic relationship.
5. **A.** Documentation is a very important part of the change control process. If things are not properly documented, employees will forget what actually took place with each device. If the environment needs to be rebuilt, for example, it may be done incorrectly if the procedure was poorly or improperly documented. When new changes need to be implemented, the current infrastructure may not be totally understood. Continually documenting when virus signatures are updated would be overkill. The other answers contain events that certainly require documentation.
6. **A.** The depth of field refers to the portion of the environment that is in focus when shown on the monitor. The depth of field varies depending upon the size of the lens opening, the distance of the object being focused on, and the focal length of the lens. The depth of field increases as the size of the lens opening decreases, the subject distance increases, or the focal length of the lens decreases. So if you want to cover a large area and not focus on specific items, it is best to use a wide-angle lens and a small lens opening.
7. **A.** Manual iris lenses have a ring around the CCTV lens that can be manually turned and controlled. A lens that has a manual iris would be used in an area that has fixed lighting, since the iris cannot self-adjust to changes of light. An auto iris

lens should be used in environments where the light changes, such as an outdoor setting. As the environment brightens, this is sensed by the iris, which automatically adjusts itself. Security personnel will configure the CCTV to have a specific fixed exposure value, which the iris is responsible for maintaining. The other answers are true statements about CCTV lenses.

8. **A.** A transponder is a type of proximity-based access control device that does not require the user to slide a card through a reader. The reader and card communicate directly. The card and reader have a receiver, transmitter, and battery. The reader sends signals to the card to request information. The card sends the reader an access code.

9. **A.** Although many effective physical security mechanisms are on the market today, none can look at a situation, make a judgment about it, and decide what the next step should be. A security guard is employed when an organization needs to have a countermeasure that can think and make decisions in different scenarios.

10. **B.** An electrostatic IDS creates an electrostatic field, which is just an electric field associated with static electric charges. The IDS creates a balanced electrostatic field between itself and the object being monitored. If an intruder comes within a certain range of the monitored object, there is capacitance change. The IDS can detect this change and sound an alarm.

11. **C.** This type of system is sensitive to sounds and vibrations and detects the changes in the noise level of an area it is placed within. This level of sensitivity can cause many false alarms. These devices do not emit any waves; they only listen for sounds within an area and are considered passive devices.

12. **C.** Every physical security program should have delaying mechanisms, which have the purpose of slowing down an intruder so security personnel can be alerted and arrive at the scene. A warning sign is a deterrence control, not a delaying control.

13. **D.** A user-activated device requires the user to do something: swipe the card through the reader and/or enter a code. A system sensing device recognizes the presence of the card and communicates with it without the user needing to carry out any activity.

14. **B.** Intrusion detection systems are expensive, require someone to respond when they set off an alarm, and, because of their level of sensitivity, can cause several false alarms. Like any other type of technology or device, they have their own vulnerabilities that can be exploited and penetrated.

15. **D.** Cipher locks, also known as programmable locks, use keypads to control access into an area or facility. The lock can require a swipe card and a specific combination that's entered into the keypad.

16. **A.** A security guard would want to be alerted when a door has been open for an extended period. It may be an indication that something is taking place other than a person entering or exiting the door. A security system can have a threshold set so that if the door is open past the defined time period, an alarm sounds.

CHAPTER 21

Security Operations

This chapter presents the following:

- The security operations center (SOC)
- Preventive and detective measures
- Logging and monitoring

There are two types of companies in the world: those that know they've been hacked, and those that don't.

—Misha Glenny

Security operations pertains to everything that takes place to keep networks, computer systems, applications, and environments up and running in a secure and protected manner. But even if you take great care to ensure you are watching your perimeters (both virtual and physical) and ensuring that you provision new services and retire unneeded ones in a secure manner, odds are that some threat source will be able to compromise your information systems. What then? Security operations also involves the detection, containment, eradication, and recovery that is required to ensure the continuity of business operations.

Most of the necessary operational security issues have been addressed in earlier chapters. They were integrated with related topics and not necessarily pointed out as actual operational security issues. So instead of repeating what has already been stated, this chapter reviews and points out the operational security topics that are important for organizations and CISSP candidates.

The Security Operations Center

The security operations center (SOC) is the nerve center of security operations in organizations with a mature information security management system (ISMS). The SOC encompasses the people, processes, and technology that support logging and monitoring of preventive controls, detection of security events, and incident response. By integrating them together in the SOC, an organization streamlines the process of detecting and responding to threats, thereby minimizing organizational losses. In the aftermath of a security incident, lessons learned can be uniformly applied to better mitigate future threats. As defensive processes evolve, they can be rehearsed easily because everyone is on the same team.

Elements of a Mature SOC

Figure 21-1 shows a high-level view of the core elements of a typical mature SOC. More important than the specific components is the fact that they are integrated so that security tasks are performed in a coordinated manner. Still, it's hard to have a SOC that doesn't have at least the three platforms shown in the figure. The *endpoint detection and response (EDR)* tool is deployed on all endpoints and monitors user and process behaviors. Anything like suspicious activities or suspected malware is reported to a central management system, which is typically the *security information and event management (SIEM)* platform. Of course, the EDR can't tell what is going on across the networks, so we need a tool to monitor those for suspicious activity. This is the role of the *network detection and response (NDR)* system, which similarly reports its findings to the SIEM solution. The SIEM solution aggregates these (and many other) data feeds and provides a holistic view into all the security-related information in the organizational environment.

Tier 1 security analysts spend most of their time monitoring security tools and other technology platforms for suspicious activity. For all their sophistication, these tools tend to generate a lot of false positives (that is, false alarms), so we need people to go through and verify the alerts generated by these tools. These analysts are typically the least experienced, so their job is to triage alerts, handling the more mundane and passing on the more complex and dangerous ones to the more experienced staff in the SOC. Tier 2 analysts can dig deeper into the alerts to determine if they constitute security incidents. If they do, these analysts can then coordinate with incident responders and intelligence analysts to further investigate, contain, and eradicate the threats.

The key to a good SOC is to have the policies and procedures in place to ensure the platforms are well tuned, the team is trained and working together, and the context of the organization's business is considered in every action taken. This business context

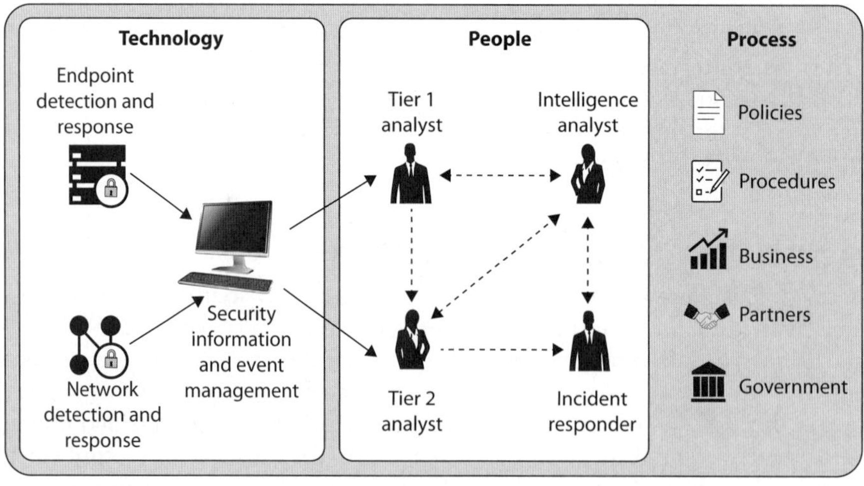

Figure 21-1 Core elements of a mature SOC

includes partners and customers, because the SOC needs to understand the entire ecosystem within which the organization operates. Occasionally, liaising with appropriate government organizations will also be needed, and the SOC must be prepared to do so. Examples of this are scenarios that require reporting cybercrimes and exchanging threat intelligence with the appropriate agencies.

Threat Intelligence

One of the key capabilities of a SOC is to consume (and, ideally, develop) threat intelligence. Gartner defines *threat intelligence* as "evidence-based knowledge…about an existing or emerging menace or hazard to assets. This intelligence can be used to inform decisions regarding the subject's response to that menace or hazard." In other words, threat intelligence is information about our adversaries' past, present, and future actions that allows us to respond or prevent them from being successful. From this definition flow four essential characteristics of good intelligence, known by the acronym CART:

- **Complete** Sufficient to detect or prevent the threat from being realized
- **Accurate** Factual and free from errors
- **Relevant** Useful to detect and prevent the threat from being realized
- **Timely** Received and operationalized fast enough to make an impact

It is important to keep in mind that threat intelligence is meant to help decision-makers choose what to do about a threat. It answers a question that these leaders may have. For example, a C-suite executive may ask a strategic question like, "What cyberthreats will be targeting our industry in the next year?" That person probably doesn't care about (or understand) the technical details of the tools the SOC is using. The SOC director, on the other hand, is interested in tactical issues and may need to know the technical details in order to respond to ongoing threats. The SOC director may ask what command and control infrastructure a particular threat actor is using. So, all good intelligence is, essentially, an answer to a question asked by a decision-maker in the organization. These questions are the requirements that drive the intelligence cycle shown in Figure 21-2.

Figure 21-2 The intelligence cycle

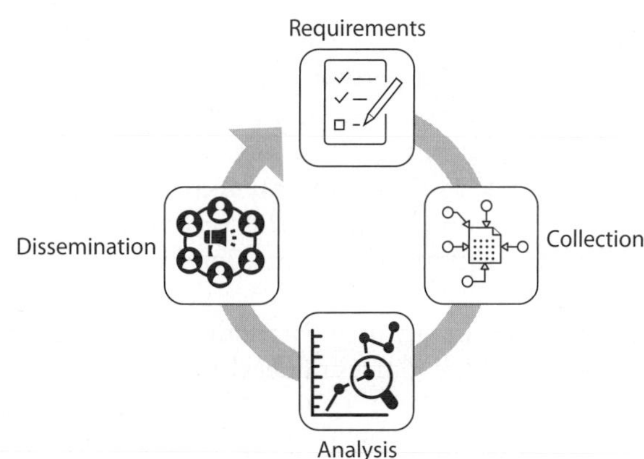

Once the requirements are known and prioritized, the intelligence analyst can get to work collecting data that can help answer those questions. The next section discusses the different data sources that analysts can use, but for now, the important point to consider is that intelligence analysts shouldn't have to start from scratch when it comes to identifying the data sources. A good collection management framework (CMF) allows an organization to determine where data lives that can answer the questions that are being asked by its leaders and identify informational "blind spots" that need to be addressed by developing new data sources.

The data that is collected still needs to be analyzed before it yields intelligence products. The analysis step involves integrating the data and evaluating it. Intelligence analysts may reach out to subject matter experts to ensure specific data items are reliable, valid, and relevant, and to help put them into a broader context. Sometimes the data items will contradict each other, so these conflicts need to be resolved before drawing final conclusions.

The final step in the intelligence cycle is to share the finished intelligence with the appropriate decision-makers. Because the intelligence requirement was meant to answer a question from a given individual (or class of individuals), the analyst already knows how to phrase the report. If the report is going to an executive, it should be written in a nontechnical manner (but, ideally, with a more technical appendix that explains where the conclusions come from). If the report is going to cybersecurity professionals, it requires a lot more technical data.

Typically, one full iteration of the intelligence cycle leads to further questions that must be answered. These questions feed the next cycle by becoming (or contributing to) new intelligence requirements.

Threat Data Sources

Let's get back to the threat data sources that are needed to address intelligence requirements. Numerous third parties offer free or paid threat data feeds. These are subscription services that constantly (or periodically) feed information such as indicators of compromise (IOCs); an IOC is technical data that is characteristic of malicious activity. For example, we may know that a particular domain name is being used to deliver ransomware to compromised targets, so that domain name is an IOC for that particular threat. Unless the question that drove an intelligence requirement was "What is one domain used in ransomware attacks?" this IOC, by itself, would not be an intelligence product. Rather, it is an example of the first of three types of data sources commonly used in cyberthreat intelligence: third-party data feeds.

Another important type of data source is called *open-source intelligence (OSINT)*, which is the name collectively given to any source that is freely available on the Internet. Often, we can get the information we need simply by doing a web search for it. Of course, there are also tools that make this process much easier by integrating queries against multiple open sources. Over time, intelligence analysts assemble lists of URLs that prove useful to their specific intelligence needs.

The third type of commonly used data source, and in many ways the most important, is internal sources. These are sources under the direct control of the organization and that can be tasked to collect data. For example, you may task your DNS server to provide all the domain names for which clients in your organization are requesting resolution. This would likely be a very large list full of repeated entries, particularly for popular domains. From it, however, you could gather data such as newly observed domains (NODs) or domains with a small community of interest (COI) in your organization. Either could be an early indicator of an attack, though it would be fraught with false positives.

Cyberthreat Hunting

If you have a threat intelligence program in your organization, you can use it to stay one step ahead of the adversaries (or at least just one step behind). *Cyberthreat hunting* is the practice of proactively looking for threat actors in your networks. In other words, instead of waiting for an alert from your SIEM system to start investigating an incident, you develop a hypothesis of what an adversary may be up to (informed by threat intelligence, of course) and then set about proving or negating that hypothesis.

For example, suppose that threat intelligence reveals that other organizations in your sector are being targeted by attackers who are enabling the Remote Desktop Protocol (RDP) to move laterally across the environment. RDP is normally disabled in your organization except for on a handful of jump boxes (hardened hosts that act as a secure entry point or gateway into a sensitive part of a network). From these two facts, you develop the hypothesis that an adversary is enabling RDP on regular workstations to move laterally over your organization's networks. Your hunt operation will be centered on proving your hypothesis (by finding evidence that this is going on) or negating it (by finding no workstations with RDP inappropriately enabled). Your hunt would involve checking the registry of every Windows endpoint in your environment, examining the Windows Registry keys that enable Remote Desktop Services (RDS). Hopefully, you would write a script that does this for you automatedly, so you don't have to manually check every endpoint. Suppose you find several endpoints with RDS enabled. You now narrow your hunt to those systems and determine whether they are a) legitimately authorized to use RDS, b) authorized for RDS but didn't follow the configuration management process, or c) evidence of adversarial activities.

This is the crux of threat hunting: you develop a hypothesis of adversarial action based on threat intelligence, and then you prove or negate your hypothesis. Threat hunting is inherently proactive and based on intelligence, whereas incident response is reactive and based on alerts. Because threat hunting requires the skills of intelligence analysts, cybersecurity analysts (typically tier 2), and incident responders, many organizations stand up hunt teams with one or more members from each of these three roles. The team may run a hunt campaign consisting of multiple related hunt operations, and then return to their daily jobs until they're needed for the next campaign.

EXAM TIP Threat hunting involves *proactively* searching for malicious activities that were not detected by other means. If you already know there's been an incident, then you are *reactively* responding to it. This key difference between threat hunting and incident response is important to remember.

Preventive and Detective Measures

As exciting and effective as cyberthreat hunting can be, relatively few organizations have the resources to engage in this effort consistently. Even in organizations that do have the resources, most of the efforts of security operations are focused on preventing and detecting security incidents. A good way to reduce the likelihood of contingencies and disasters is to ensure that your organization's defensive architectures include the right set of tools. These technical controls need to be carefully considered in the context of your organization's own conditions to determine which are useful and which aren't. Regardless of the tools you employ, there is an underlying process that drives their operation in a live environment. The steps of this generalized process are described here:

1. *Understand the risk.* Chapter 2 presented the risk management process that organizations should use. The premise of this process is that you can't ever eliminate all risks and should therefore devote your scarce resources to mitigating the most dangerous risks to a point where their likelihood is acceptable to the senior leaders. If you don't focus on that set of risks, you will likely squander your resources countering threats that are not the ones your CEO is really concerned about.
2. *Use the right controls.* Once you are focused on the right set of risks, you can more easily identify the controls that will appropriately mitigate them. The relationship between risks and controls is many to many, since a given risk can have multiple controls assigned to it and a given control can be used to mitigate multiple risks. In fact, the number of risks mitigated by one control should give you an indicator of the value of that control to the organization. On the other hand, having multiple controls mitigating a risk may be less efficient, but may provide resiliency.
3. *Use the controls correctly.* Selecting the right tools is only part of the battle. You also need to ensure they are emplaced and configured correctly. The network architectures covered in Chapter 7 place some very significant limitations on the effectiveness of tools based on where they are plugged in. If an IDS is deployed on the wrong subnet, it may not be able to monitor all the traffic from the threat sources against which it is supposed to defend. Similarly, that same IDS with the wrong configuration or rule set could well become an expensive ornament on the network.
4. *Manage your configuration.* One of the certainties in life is that, left alone, every configuration is guaranteed to become obsolete at some point in the future. Even if it is not left alone, making unauthorized or undocumented changes will introduce risk at best and at worst quietly render your network vulnerable to an immediate threat. Properly done, configuration management will ensure you have ground truth about your network so that you can better answer the questions that are typically asked when doing security operations.

5. *Assess your operation.* You should constantly (or at least periodically) be looking at your defensive plan, comparing it with your latest threat and risk assessments, and asking yourself, "Are we still properly mitigating the risks?" You should test your controls using cases derived from your risk assessment. This verifies that you are correctly mitigating those risks. However, you should also occasionally test your controls against an unconstrained set of threats in order to validate that you are mitigating the correct risks. A good penetration test (pen test) can both verify and validate the controls.

This process can yield a huge number of possible preventive controls. There are some controls, however, that are so pervasive that every information security professional should be able to incorporate them into a defensive architecture. In the following sections, we describe the most important ones.

Firewalls

Firewalls are used to restrict access to one network from another network. Most organizations use firewalls to restrict access to their networks from the Internet. They may also use firewalls to restrict one internal network segment from accessing another internal segment. For example, if the security administrator wants to make sure unauthorized employees cannot access the research and development network, he would place a firewall between the R&D network and all other networks and configure the firewall to allow only the type of traffic he deems acceptable.

A firewall device supports and enforces the organization's network security policy. An organizational security policy provides high-level directives on acceptable and unacceptable actions as they pertain to protecting critical assets. The firewall has a more defined and granular security policy that dictates what services are allowed to be accessed, what IP addresses and ranges are to be restricted, and what ports can be accessed. The firewall is described as a "choke point" in the network because all communications should flow through it, and this is where traffic is inspected and restricted.

A firewall may be a server running a firewall software product or a specialized hardware appliance. In either case, the firewall monitors packets coming into and out of the network it is protecting. It can discard packets, repackage them, or redirect them, depending upon the firewall configuration. Packets are filtered based on their source and destination addresses, and ports by service, packet type, protocol type, header information, sequence bits, and much more. Many times, organizations set up firewalls to construct a *demilitarized zone (DMZ)*, which is a network segment located between the protected and unprotected networks. The DMZ provides a buffer zone between the dangerous Internet and the goodies within the internal network that the organization is trying to protect. As shown in Figure 21-3, two firewalls are usually installed to form the DMZ. The DMZ usually contains web, mail, and DNS servers, which must be hardened systems because they would be the first in line for attacks. Many DMZs also have an IDS sensor that listens for malicious and suspicious behavior.

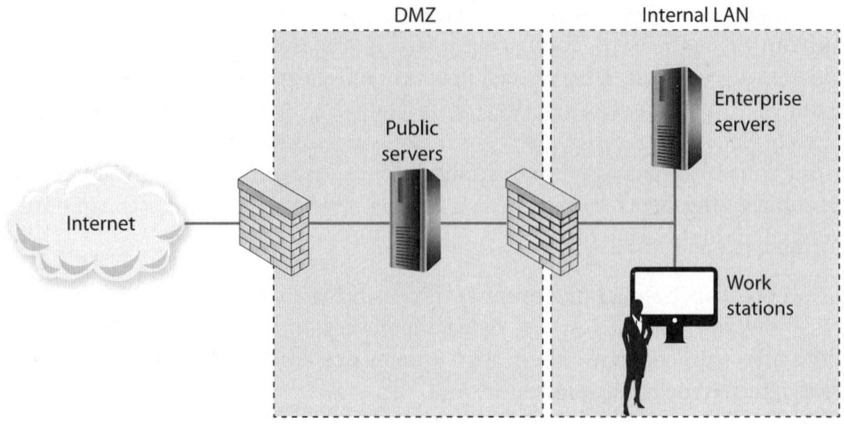

Figure 21-3 At least two firewalls, or firewall interfaces, are generally used to construct a DMZ.

Many different types of firewalls are available, because each environment may have unique requirements and security goals. Firewalls have gone through an evolution of their own and have grown in sophistication and functionality. The following sections describe the various types of firewalls.

The types of firewalls we will review are

- Packet filtering
- Stateful
- Proxy
- Next-generation

We will then dive into the three main firewall architectures, which are

- Screened host
- Multihome
- Screened subnet

NOTE Recall that we discussed another type of firewall, web application firewalls (WAFs), in Chapter 4.

Packet-Filtering Firewalls

Packet filtering is a firewall technology that makes access decisions based upon network-level protocol header values. The device that is carrying out packet-filtering processes is configured with access control lists (ACLs), which dictate the type of traffic that is allowed into and out of specific networks.

Packet filtering was the technology used in the first generation of firewalls, and it is the most rudimentary type of all of the firewall technologies. The filters only have the capability of reviewing protocol header information at the network and transport layers and carrying out permit or deny actions on individual packets. This means the filters can make access decisions based upon the following basic criteria:

- Source and destination IP addresses
- Source and destination port numbers
- Protocol types
- Inbound and outbound traffic direction

Packet filtering is built into a majority of the firewall products today and is a capability that many routers perform. The ACL filtering rules are enforced at the network interface of the device, which is the doorway into or out of a network. As an analogy, you could have a list of items you look for before allowing someone into your office premises through your front door. Your list can indicate that a person must be 18 years or older, have an access badge, and be wearing shoes. When someone knocks on the door, you grab your list, which you will use to decide if this person can or cannot come inside. So your front door is one interface into your office premises. You can also have a list that outlines who can exit your office premises through your back door, which is another interface. As shown in Figure 21-4, a router has individual interfaces with their own unique addresses, which provide doorways into and out of a network. Each interface can have its own ACL values, which indicate what type of traffic is allowed in and out of that specific interface.

Figure 21-4 ACLs are enforced at the network interface level.

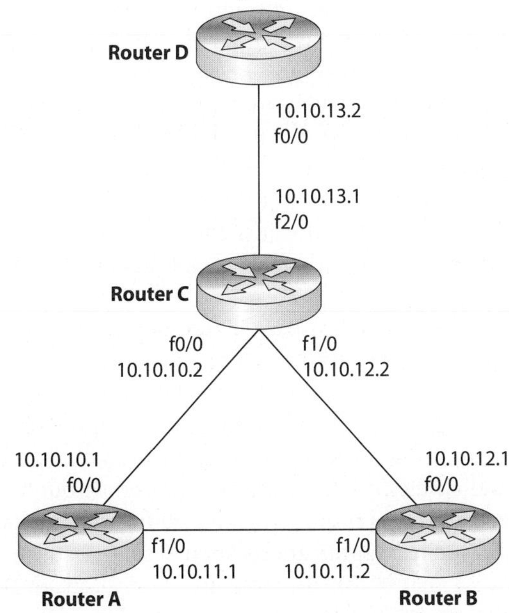

We will cover some basic ACL rules to illustrate how packet filtering is implemented and enforced. The following router configuration allows SMTP traffic to travel from system 10.1.1.2 to system 172.16.1.1:

```
permit tcp host 10.1.1.2 host 172.16.1.1 eq smtp
```

This next rule permits UDP traffic from system 10.1.1.2 to 172.16.1.1:

```
permit udp host 10.1.1.2 host 172.16.1.1
```

If you want to ensure that no ICMP traffic enters through a certain interface, the following ACL can be configured and deployed:

```
deny icmp any any
```

If you want to allow standard web traffic (that is, to a web server listening on port 80) from system 1.1.1.1 to system 5.5.5.5, you can use the following ACL:

```
permit tcp host 1.1.1.1 host 5.5.5.5 eq www
```

NOTE Filtering inbound traffic is known as *ingress filtering*. Outgoing traffic can also be filtered using a process referred to as *egress filtering*.

So when a packet arrives at a packet-filtering device, the device starts at the top of its ACL and compares the packet's characteristics to each rule set. If a successful match (permit or deny) is found, then the remaining rules are not processed. If no matches are found when the device reaches the end of the list, the traffic should be denied, but each product is different. So if you are configuring a packet-filtering device, make sure that if no matches are identified, then the traffic is denied.

Packet filtering is also known as *stateless inspection* because the device does not understand the context that the packets are working within. This means that the device does not have the capability to understand the "full picture" of the communication that is taking place between two systems, but can only focus on individual packet characteristics. As we will see in the next section, stateful firewalls understand and keep track of a full communication session, not just the individual packets that make it up. Stateless firewalls make their decisions for each packet based solely on the data contained in that individual packet.

The lack of sophistication in packet filtering means that an organization should not solely depend upon this type of firewall to protect its infrastructure and assets, but it does not mean that this technology should not be used at all. Packet filtering is commonly carried out at the edge of a network to strip out all of the obvious "junk" traffic. Since the rules are simple and only header information is analyzed, this type of filtering can take place quickly and efficiently. After traffic is passed through a packet-filtering device, it is usually then processed by a more sophisticated firewall, which digs deeper into the packet contents and can identify application-based attacks.

Some of the weaknesses of packet-filtering firewalls are as follows:

- They cannot prevent attacks that employ application-specific vulnerabilities or functions.
- They have limited logging functionality.
- Most packet-filtering firewalls do not support advanced user authentication schemes.
- They may not be able to detect packet fragmentation attacks.

The advantages to using packet-filtering firewalls are that they are scalable, they are not application dependent, and they have high performance because they do not carry out extensive processing on the packets. They are commonly used as the first line of defense to strip out all the network traffic that is obviously malicious or unintended for a specific network. The network traffic usually then has to be processed by more sophisticated firewalls that will identify the not-so-obvious security risks.

Stateful Firewalls

When packet filtering is used, a packet arrives at the firewall, and the firewall runs through its ACLs to determine whether this packet should be allowed or denied. If the packet is allowed, it is passed on to the destination host, or to another network device, and the packet-filtering device forgets about the packet. This is different from stateful inspection, which remembers and keeps track of what packets went where until each particular connection is closed.

A *stateful firewall* is like a nosy neighbor who gets into people's business and conversations. She keeps track of the suspicious cars that come into the neighborhood, who is out of town for the week, and the postman who stays a little too long at the neighbor lady's house. This can be annoying until your house is burglarized. Then you and the police will want to talk to the nosy neighbor, because she knows everything going on in the neighborhood and would be the one most likely to know something unusual happened. A stateful-inspection firewall is nosier than a regular filtering device because it keeps track of what computers say to each other. This requires that the firewall maintain a *state table*, which is like a score sheet of who said what to whom.

Keeping track of the state of a protocol connection requires keeping track of many variables. Most people understand the three-step handshake a TCP connection goes through (SYN, SYN/ACK, ACK), but what does this really mean? If Quincy's system wants to communicate with your system using TCP, it sends your system a packet with the SYN flag value in the TCP header set to 1. This makes this packet a SYN packet. If your system accepts Quincy's system's connection request, it sends back a packet that has both the SYN and ACK flags within the packet header set to 1. This is a SYN/ACK packet. Finally, Quincy's system confirms your system's SYN with its own ACK packet. After this three-way handshake, the TCP connection is established.

While many people know about these three steps of setting up a TCP connection, they are not always familiar with all of the other items that are being negotiated at this time. For example, your system and Quincy's system will agree upon sequence numbers,

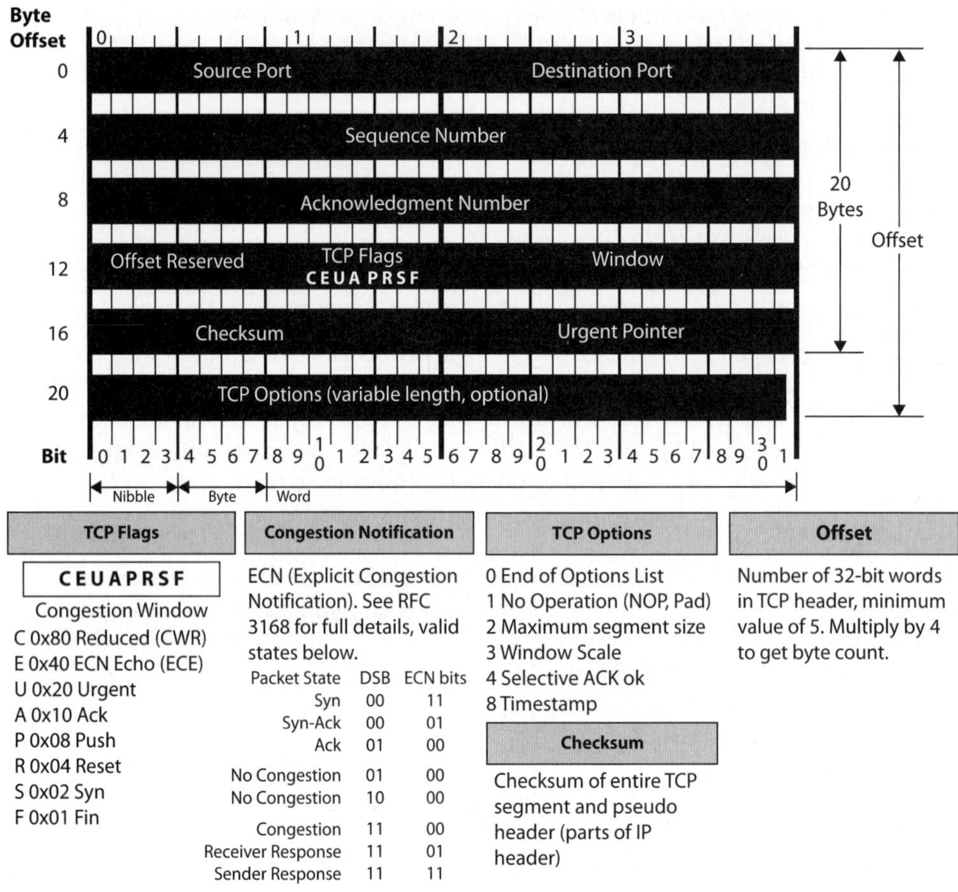

Figure 21-5 TCP header

how much data to send at a time (window size), how potential transmission errors will be identified (CRC values), and so forth. Figure 21-5 shows all of the values that make up a TCP header. So, a lot of information is going back and forth between your systems just in this one protocol—TCP. There are other protocols that are involved with networking that a stateful firewall has to be aware of and keep track of.

So "keeping state of a connection" means to keep a scorecard of all the various protocol header values as packets go back and forth between systems. The values not only have to be correct—they have to happen in the right sequence. For example, if a stateful firewall receives a packet that has all TCP flag values turned to 1, something malicious is taking place. Under no circumstances during a legitimate TCP connection should all of these values be turned on like this. Attackers send packets with all of these values turned to 1 with the hopes that the firewall does not understand or check these values and just forwards the packets onto the target system.

In another situation, if Gwen's system sends your system a SYN/ACK packet and your system did not first send a SYN packet to Gwen's system, this, too, is against the protocol rules. The protocol communication steps have to follow the proper sequence. Attackers send SYN/ACK packets to target systems in an attempt to get the firewall to interpret this as an already established connection and just allow the packets to go to the destination system without inspection. A stateful firewall will not be fooled by such actions because it keeps track of each step of the communication. It knows how protocols are supposed to work, and if something is out of order (incorrect flag values, incorrect sequence, etc.), it does not allow the traffic to pass through.

When a connection begins between two systems, the firewall investigates *all* elements of the packet (all headers, payload, and trailers). All of the necessary information about the specific connection is stored in the state table (source and destination IP addresses, source and destination ports, protocol type, header flags, sequence numbers, timestamps, etc.). Once the initial packets go through this in-depth inspection and everything is deemed safe, the firewall then just reviews the network and transport header portions for the rest of the session. The values of each header for each packet are compared to the values in the current state table, and the table is updated to reflect the progression of the communication process. Scaling down the inspection of the full packet to just the headers for each packet is done to increase performance.

TCP is considered a connection-oriented protocol, and the various steps and states this protocol operates within are very well defined. A connection progresses through a series of states during its lifetime. The states are LISTEN, SYN-SENT, SYN-RECEIVED, ESTABLISHED, FIN-WAIT-1, FIN-WAIT-2, CLOSE-WAIT, CLOSING, LAST-ACK, TIME-WAIT, and the fictional state CLOSED. A stateful firewall keeps track of each of these states for each packet that passes through, along with the corresponding acknowledgment and sequence numbers. If the acknowledgment and/or sequence numbers are out of order, this could imply that a replay attack is underway, and the firewall will protect the internal systems from this activity.

Nothing is ever simple in life, including the standardization of network protocol communication. While the previous statements are true pertaining to the states of a TCP connection, in some situations an application layer protocol has to change these basic steps. For example, FTP uses an unusual communication exchange when initializing its data channel compared to all of the other application layer protocols. FTP basically sets up two sessions just for one communication exchange between two computers. The states of the two individual TCP connections that make up an FTP session can be tracked in the normal fashion, but the state of the FTP connection follows different rules. For a stateful device to be able to properly monitor the traffic of an FTP session, it must be able to take into account the way that FTP uses one outbound connection for the control channel and one inbound connection for the data channel. If you were configuring a stateful firewall, you would need to understand the particulars of some specific protocols to ensure that each is being properly inspected and controlled.

Since TCP is a connection-oriented protocol, it has clearly defined states during the connection establishment, maintenance, and tearing-down stages. UDP is a connectionless protocol, which means that none of these steps take place. UDP holds no state, which makes it harder for a stateful firewall to keep track of. For connectionless protocols,

Stateful-Inspection Firewall Characteristics

The following lists some important characteristics of a stateful-inspection firewall:

- Maintains a state table that tracks each and every communication session
- Provides a high degree of security and does not introduce the performance hit that application proxy firewalls introduce
- Is scalable and transparent to users
- Provides data for tracking connectionless protocols such as UDP and ICMP
- Stores and updates the state and context of the data within the packets

a stateful firewall keeps track of source and destination addresses, UDP header values, and some ACL rules. This connection information is also stored in the state table and tracked. Since the protocol does not have a specific tear-down stage, the firewall will just time out the connection after a period of inactivity and remove the data being kept pertaining to that connection from the state table.

An interesting complexity of stateful firewalls and UDP connections is how ICMP comes into play. Since UDP is connectionless, it does not provide a mechanism to allow the receiving computer to tell the sending computer that data is coming too fast. In TCP, the receiving computer can alter the Window value in its header, which tells the sending computer to reduce the amount of data that is being sent. The message is basically, "You are overwhelming me and I cannot process the amount of data you are sending me. Slow down." UDP does not have a Window value in its header, so instead the receiving computer sends an ICMP packet that provides the same function. But now this means that the stateful firewall must keep track of and allow associated ICMP packets with specific UDP connections. If the firewall does not allow the ICMP packets to get to the sending system, the receiving system could get overwhelmed and crash. This is just one example of the complexity that comes into play when a firewall has to do more than just packet filtering. Although stateful inspection provides an extra step of protection, it also adds more complexity because this device must now keep a dynamic state table and remember connections.

Stateful-inspection firewalls, unfortunately, have been the victims of many types of DoS attacks. Several types of attacks are aimed at flooding the state table with bogus information. The state table is a resource, similar to a system's hard drive space, memory, and CPU. When the state table is stuffed full of bogus information, a poorly designed device may either freeze or reboot.

Proxy Firewalls

A *proxy* is a middleman. It intercepts and inspects messages before delivering them to the intended recipients. Suppose you need to give a box and a message to the president of the United States. You couldn't just walk up to the president and hand over these items.

Instead, you would have to go through a middleman, likely a Secret Service agent, who would accept the box and message and thoroughly inspect the box to ensure nothing dangerous is inside. This is what a proxy firewall does—it accepts messages either entering or leaving a network, inspects them for malicious information, and, when it decides the messages are okay, passes the data on to the destination computer.

A *proxy firewall* stands between a trusted network and an untrusted network and makes the connection, each way, on behalf of the source. What is important is that a proxy firewall breaks the communication channel; there is no *direct* connection between the two communicating devices. Where a packet-filtering device just monitors traffic as it is traversing a network connection, a proxy ends the communication session and restarts it on behalf of the sending system. Figure 21-6 illustrates the steps of a proxy-based firewall. Notice that the firewall does not simply apply ACL rules to the traffic; it stops the user connection at the internal interface of the firewall itself and then starts a new session on behalf of this user on the external interface. When the external web server replies to the request, this reply goes to the external interface of the proxy firewall and ends. The proxy firewall examines the reply information and, if it is deemed safe, starts a new session from itself to the internal system. This is just like our analogy of what the Secret Service agent does between you and the president.

A proxy technology can actually work at different layers of a network stack. A proxy-based firewall that works at the lower layers of the OSI model is referred to as a circuit-level proxy. A proxy-based firewall that works at the application layer is, strangely enough, called an application-level proxy.

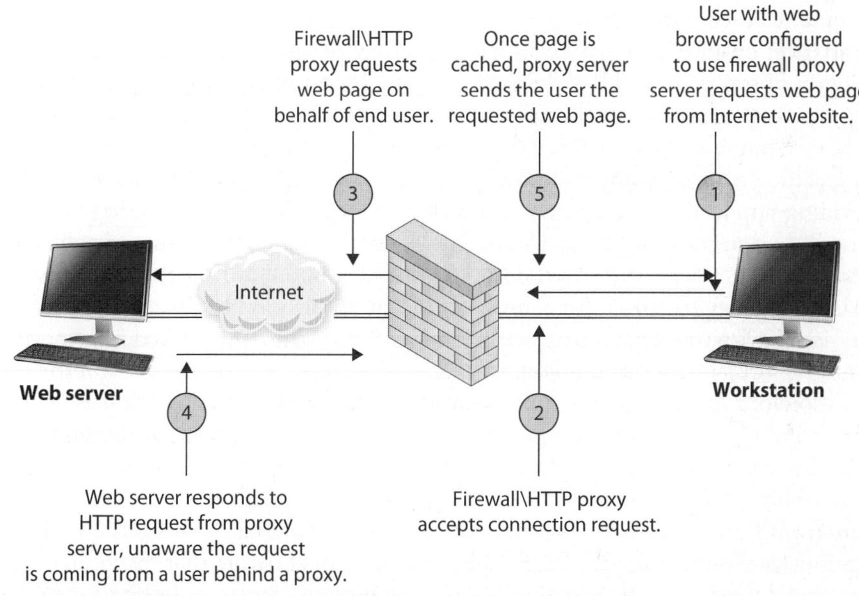

Figure 21-6 Proxy firewall breaks connection

PART VII

A *circuit-level proxy* creates a connection (circuit) between the two communicating systems. It works at the session layer of the OSI model and monitors traffic from a network-based view. This type of proxy cannot "look into" the contents of a packet; thus, it does not carry out deep-packet inspection. It can only make access decisions based upon protocol header and session information that is available to it. While this means that a circuit-level proxy cannot provide as much protection as an application-level proxy, because it does not have to understand application layer protocols, it is considered application independent. So, it cannot provide the detail-oriented protection that a proxy working at a higher level can, but this allows it to provide a broader range of protection where application layer proxies may not be appropriate or available.

NOTE Traffic sent to the receiving computer through a circuit-level proxy appears to have originated from the firewall instead of the sending system. This is useful for hiding information about the internal computers on the network the firewall is protecting.

Application-level proxies inspect the packet up through the application layer. Where a circuit-level proxy only has insight up to the session layer, an application-level proxy understands the packet as a whole and can make access decisions based on the content of the packets. Application-level proxies understand various services and protocols and the commands that are used by them. An application-level proxy can distinguish between an FTP GET command and an FTP PUT command, for example, and make access decisions based on this granular level of information; on the other hand, packet-filtering firewalls and circuit-level proxies can allow or deny FTP requests only as a whole, not by the commands used within FTP.

An application-level proxy firewall has one proxy per protocol. A computer can have many types of protocols (FTP, NTP, SMTP, HTTP, and so on). Thus, one application-level proxy per protocol is required. This does not mean one proxy firewall per service is required, but rather that one portion of the firewall product is dedicated to understanding how a specific protocol works and how to properly filter it for suspicious data.

Providing application-level proxy protection can be a tricky undertaking. The proxy must totally understand how specific protocols work and what commands within that protocol are legitimate. This is a lot to know and look at during the transmission of data. As an analogy, picture a screening station at an airport that is made up of many employees, all with the job of interviewing people before they are allowed into the airport and onto an airplane. These employees have been trained to ask specific questions and detect suspicious answers and activities, and have the skill set and authority to detain suspicious individuals. Now, suppose each of these employees speaks a different language because the people they interview come from different parts of the world. So, one employee who speaks German could not understand and identify suspicious answers of a person from Italy because they do not speak the same language. This is the same for an application-level proxy firewall. Each proxy is a piece of software that has been designed to understand how a specific protocol "talks" and how to identify suspicious data within a transmission using that protocol.

NOTE If the application-level proxy firewall does not understand a certain protocol or service, it cannot protect this type of communication. In this scenario, a circuit-level proxy is useful because it does not deal with such complex issues. An advantage of a circuit-level proxy is that it can handle a wider variety of protocols and services than an application-level proxy can, but the downfall is that the circuit-level proxy cannot provide the degree of granular control that an application-level proxy provides. Life is just full of compromises.

A circuit-level proxy works similarly to a packet filter in that it makes access decisions based on address, port, and protocol type header values. It looks at the data within the packet header rather than the data at the application layer of the packet. It does not know whether the contents within the packet are safe or unsafe; it only understands the traffic from a network-based view.

An application-level proxy, on the other hand, is dedicated to a particular protocol or service. At least one proxy is used per protocol because one proxy could not properly interpret all the commands of all the protocols coming its way. A circuit-level proxy works at a lower layer of the OSI model and does not require one proxy per protocol because it does not look at such detailed information.

Application-Level Proxy Firewalls

Application-level proxy firewalls, like all technologies, have their pros and cons. It is important to fully understand all characteristics of this type of firewall before purchasing and deploying this type of solution.

Characteristics of application-level proxy firewalls:

- They have extensive logging capabilities due to the firewall being able to examine the entire network packet rather than just the network addresses and ports.
- They are capable of authenticating users directly, as opposed to packet-filtering firewalls and stateful-inspection firewalls, which can usually only carry out system authentication.
- Since they are not simply layer 3 devices, they can address spoofing attacks and other sophisticated attacks.

Disadvantages of using application-level proxy firewalls:

- They are not generally well suited to high-bandwidth or real-time applications.
- They tend to be limited in terms of support for new network applications and protocols.
- They create performance issues because of the necessary per-packet processing requirements.

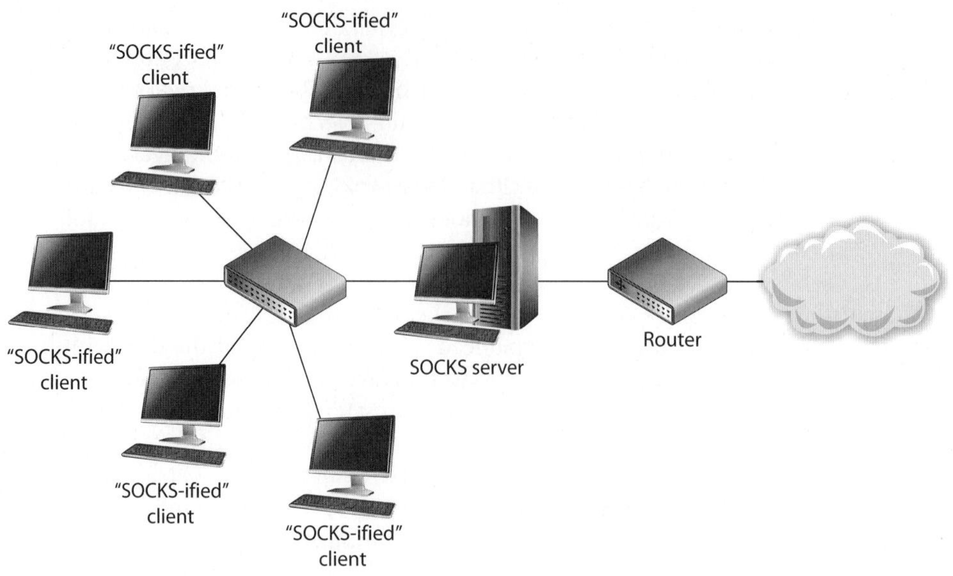

Figure 21-7 Circuit-level proxy firewall

SOCKS is an example of a circuit-level proxy gateway that provides a secure channel between two computers. When a SOCKS-enabled client sends a request to access a computer on the Internet, this request actually goes to the network's SOCKS proxy firewall, as shown in Figure 21-7, which inspects the packets for malicious information and checks its policy rules to see whether this type of connection is allowed. If the packet is acceptable and this type of connection is allowed, the SOCKS firewall sends the message to the destination computer on the Internet. When the computer on the Internet responds, it sends its packets to the SOCKS firewall, which again inspects the data and then passes the packets on to the client computer.

The SOCKS firewall can screen, filter, audit, log, and control data flowing in and out of a protected network. Because of its popularity, many applications and protocols have been configured to work with SOCKS in a manner that takes less configuration on the administrator's part, and various firewall products have integrated SOCKS software to provide circuit-based protection.

NOTE Remember that whether an application- or circuit-level proxy firewall is being used, it is still acting as a proxy. Both types of proxy firewalls deny actual end-to-end connectivity between the source and destination systems. In attempting a remote connection, the client connects to and communicates with the proxy; the proxy, in turn, establishes a connection to the destination system and makes requests to it on the client's behalf. The proxy maintains two independent connections for every one network transmission. It essentially turns a two-party session into a four-party session, with the middle process emulating the two real systems.

Application-Level vs. Circuit-Level Proxy Firewall Characteristics

Characteristics of application-level proxy firewalls:

- Each protocol that is to be monitored must have a unique proxy.
- They provide more protection than circuit-level proxy firewalls.
- They require more processing per packet and thus are slower than circuit-level proxy firewalls.

Characteristics of circuit-level proxy firewalls:

- They do not require a proxy for each and every protocol.
- They do not provide the deep-inspection capabilities of an application-level proxy firewall.
- They provide security for a wider range of protocols.

Next-Generation Firewalls

A *next-generation firewall (NGFW)* combines the best attributes of the previously discussed firewalls, but adds a number of important improvements. Most importantly, it incorporates a signature-based and/or behavioral analysis IPS engine. This means that, in addition to ensuring that the traffic is behaving in accordance with the rules of the applicable protocols, the firewall can look for specific indicators of attack even in otherwise well-behaved traffic. Some of the most advanced NGFWs include features that allow them to share signatures with a cloud-based aggregator so that once a new attack is detected by one firewall, all other firewalls manufactured by that vendor become aware of the attack signature.

Another characteristic of an NGFW is its ability to connect to external data sources such as Active Directory, whitelists, blacklists, and policy servers. This feature allows controls to be defined in one place and pulled by every NGFW on the network, which reduces the chances of inconsistent settings on the various firewalls that typically exist in large networks.

For all their power, NGFWs are not appropriate for every organization. The typical cost of ownership alone tends to make these infeasible for small or even medium-sized networks. Organizations need to ensure that the correct firewall technology is in place to monitor specific network traffic types and protect unique resource types. The firewalls also have to be properly placed; we will cover this topic in the next section.

NOTE Firewall technology has evolved as attack types have evolved. The first-generation firewalls could only monitor network traffic. As attackers moved from just carrying out network-based attacks (DoS, fragmentation, spoofing, etc.) to conducting software-based attacks (buffer overflows, injections, malware, etc.), new generations of firewalls were developed to monitor for these types of attacks.

Firewall Type	OSI Layer	Characteristics
Packet filtering	Network layer	Looks at destination and source addresses, ports, and services requested. Typically routers using ACLs to control and monitor network traffic.
Stateful	Network layer	Looks at the state and context of packets. Keeps track of each conversation using a state table.
Application-level proxy	Application layer	Looks deep into packets and makes granular access control decisions. It requires one proxy per protocol.
Circuit-level proxy	Session layer	Looks only at the header packet information. It protects a wider range of protocols and services than an application-level proxy, but does not provide the detailed level of control available to an application-level proxy.
Next-generation firewall	Multiple layers	Very fast and supportive of high bandwidth. Built-in IPS. Able to connect to external services like Active Directory.

Table 21-1 Comparison of Different Types of Firewalls

Table 21-1 lists the important concepts and characteristics of the firewall types discussed in the preceding sections. Although various firewall products can provide a mix of these services and work at different layers of the OSI model, it is important you understand the basic definitions and functionalities of these firewall types.

Appliances

A firewall may take the form of either software installed on a regular computer using a regular operating system or a dedicated hardware appliance that has its own operating system. The second choice is usually more secure, because the vendor uses a stripped-down version of an operating system (usually Linux or BSD Unix). Operating systems are full of code and functionality that are not necessary for a firewall. This extra complexity opens the doors for vulnerabilities. If a hacker can exploit and bring down a company's firewall, then the company is very exposed and in danger.

In today's jargon, dedicated hardware devices that have stripped-down operating systems and limited and focused software capabilities are called *appliances*. Where an operating system has to provide a vast array of functionality, an appliance provides very focused functionality—as in just being a firewall.

If a software-based firewall is going to run on a regular system, then the unnecessary user accounts should be disabled, unnecessary services deactivated, unused subsystems disabled, unneeded ports closed, and so on. If firewall software is going to run on a regular system and not a dedicated appliance, then the system needs to be fully locked down.

Firewall Architecture

Firewalls can be placed in a number of areas on a network to meet particular needs. They can protect an internal network from an external network and act as a choke point for all traffic. A firewall can be used to segment and partition network sections and enforce access controls between two or more subnets. Firewalls can also be used to provide a DMZ architecture. And as covered in the previous section, the right firewall type needs to be placed in the right location. Organizations have common needs for firewalls; hence, they keep them in similar places on their networks. We will see more on this topic in the following sections.

Dual-Homed Firewall *Dual-homed* refers to a device that has two interfaces: one connected to one network and the other connected to a different network. If firewall software is installed on a dual-homed device—and it usually is—the underlying operating system should have packet forwarding and routing turned off for security reasons. If they are enabled, the computer may not apply the necessary ACLs, rules, or other restrictions required of a firewall. When a packet comes to the external NIC from an untrusted network on a dual-homed firewall and the operating system has forwarding enabled, the operating system forwards the traffic instead of passing it up to the firewall software for inspection.

Many network devices today are *multihomed*, which just means they have several NICs that are used to connect several different networks. Multihomed devices are commonly used to house firewall software, since the job of a firewall is to control the traffic as it goes from one network to another. A common multihomed firewall architecture allows an organization to have several DMZs. One DMZ may hold devices that are shared between organizations in an extranet, another DMZ may house the organization's DNS and mail servers, and yet another DMZ may hold the organization's web servers. Different DMZs are used for two reasons: to control the different traffic types (for example, to ensure HTTP traffic only goes toward the web servers and ensure DNS requests go toward the DNS server), and to ensure that if one system on one DMZ is compromised, the other systems in the rest of the DMZs are not accessible to this attacker.

If a company depends solely upon a multihomed firewall with no redundancy, this system could prove to be a single point of failure. If it goes down, then all traffic flow stops. Some firewall products have embedded redundancy or fault-tolerance capabilities. If a company uses a firewall product that does not have these capabilities, then the network should have redundancy built into it.

Along with potentially being a single point of failure, another security issue that is posed by relying on a single firewall is the lack of defense in depth. If the company depends on just one firewall, no matter what architecture is being used or how many interfaces the device has, there is only one layer of protection. If an attacker can compromise the one firewall, then she can gain direct access to company network resources.

Screened Host A *screened host* is a firewall that communicates directly with a perimeter router and the internal network. Figure 21-8 shows this type of architecture.

Traffic received from the Internet is first filtered via packet filtering on the outer router. The traffic that makes it past this phase is sent to the screened-host firewall, which applies

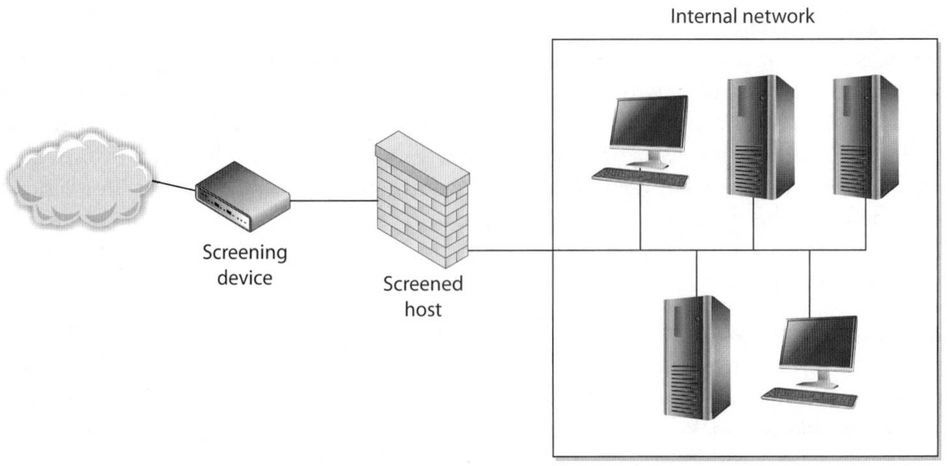

Figure 21-8 A screened host is a firewall that is screened by a router.

more rules to the traffic and drops the denied packets. Then the traffic moves to the internal destination hosts. The screened host (the firewall) is the only device that receives traffic directly from the router. No traffic goes directly from the Internet, through the router, and to the internal network. The screened host is always part of this equation.

If the firewall is an application-based system, protection is provided at the network layer by the router through packet filtering, and at the application layer by the firewall. This arrangement offers a high degree of security, because for an attacker to be successful, she would have to compromise two systems.

What does the word "screening" mean in this context? As shown in Figure 21-8, the router is a screening device and the firewall is the screened host. This just means there is a layer that scans the traffic and gets rid of a lot of the "junk" before the traffic is directed toward the firewall. A screened host is different from a screened subnet, which is described next.

Screened Subnet A *screened-subnet* architecture adds another layer of security to the screened-host architecture. The external firewall screens the traffic entering the DMZ network. However, instead of the firewall then redirecting the traffic to the internal network, an interior firewall also filters the traffic. The use of these two physical firewalls creates a DMZ.

In an environment with only a screened host, if an attacker successfully breaks through the firewall, nothing lies in her way to prevent her from having full access to the internal network. In an environment using a screened subnet, the attacker would have to hack through another firewall to gain access. In this layered approach to security, the more layers provided, the better the protection. Figure 21-9 shows a simple example of a screened subnet.

The examples shown in the figures are simple in nature. Often, more complex networks and DMZs are implemented in real-world systems. Figures 21-10 and 21-11 show some other possible architectures of screened subnets and their configurations.

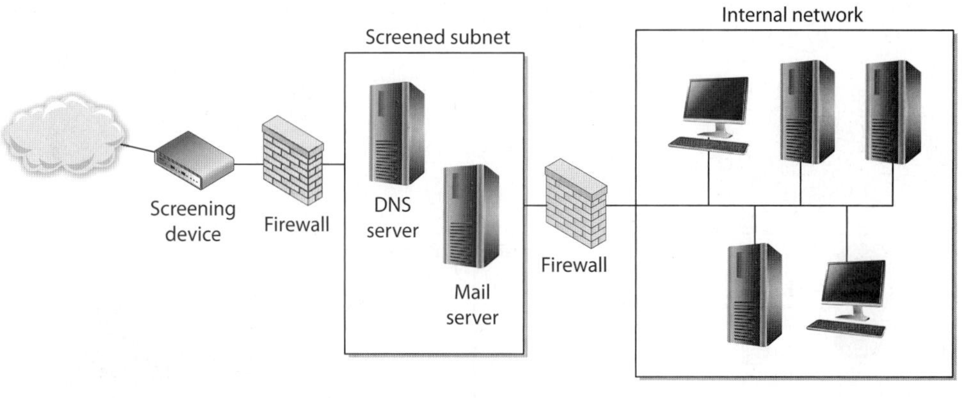

Figure 21-9 With a screened subnet, two firewalls are used to create a DMZ.

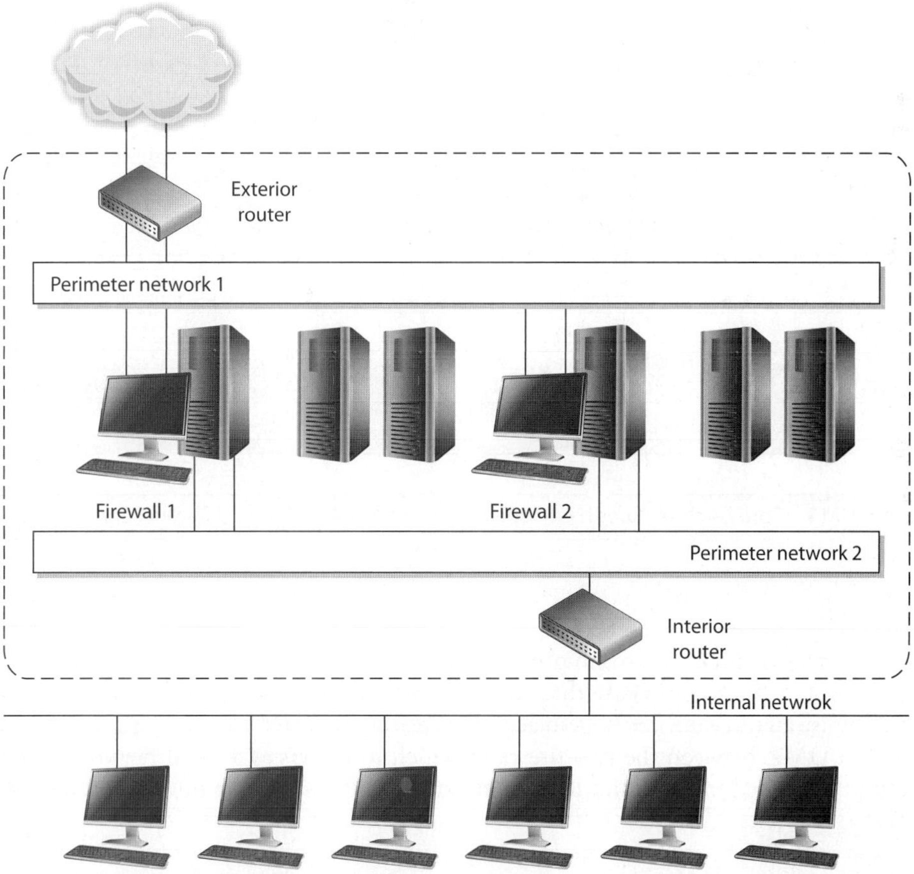

Figure 21-10 A screened subnet can have different networks within it and different firewalls that filter for specific threats.

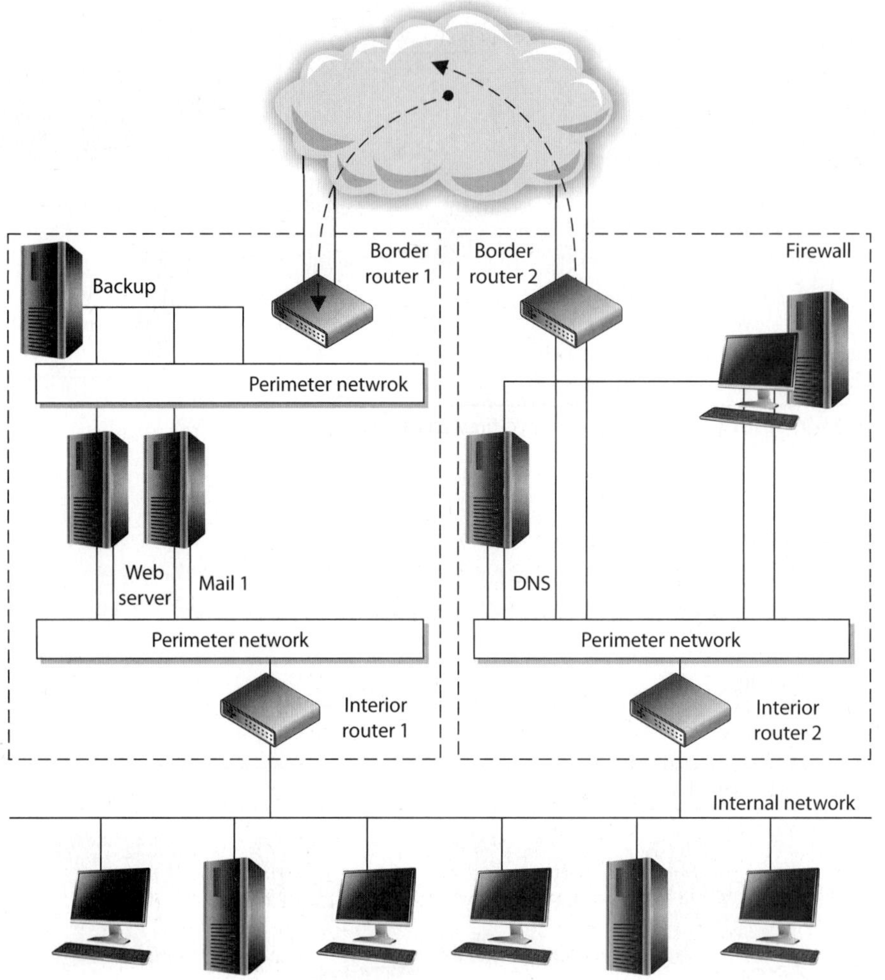

Figure 21-11 Some architectures have separate screened subnets with different server types in each.

The screened-subnet approach provides more protection than a stand-alone firewall or a screened-host firewall because three devices are working together and an attacker must compromise all three devices to gain access to the internal network. This architecture also sets up a DMZ between the two firewalls, which functions as a small network isolated among the trusted internal and untrusted external networks. The internal users usually

Firewall Architecture Characteristics

It is important to understand the following characteristics of these firewall architecture types:

Dual-homed:

- A single computer with separate NICs connected to each network.
- Used to divide an internal trusted network from an external untrusted network.
- Must disable a computer's forwarding and routing functionality so the two networks are truly segregated.

Screened host:

- A router filters (screens) traffic before it is passed to the firewall.

Screened subnet:

- An external router filters (screens) traffic before it enters the subnet. Traffic headed toward the internal network then goes through two firewalls.

have limited access to the servers within this area. Web, e-mail, and other public servers often are placed within the DMZ. Although this solution provides the highest security, it also is the most complex. Configuration and maintenance can prove to be difficult in this setup, and when new services need to be added, three systems may need to be reconfigured instead of just one.

TIP Sometimes a screened-host architecture is referred to as a single-tiered configuration and a screened subnet is referred to as a two-tiered configuration. If three firewalls create two separate DMZs, this may be called a three-tiered configuration.

Organizations used to deploy a piece of hardware for every network function needed (DNS, mail, routers, switches, storage, web), but today many of these items run within virtual machines on a smaller number of hardware machines. This reduces software and hardware costs and allows for more centralized administration, but these components still need to be protected from each other and external malicious entities. As an analogy, let's say that 15 years ago each person lived in their own house and a police officer was placed between each house so that the people in the houses could not attack each other. Then last year, many of these people moved in together so that now at least five people live in the same physical house. These people still need to be protected from each other, so some of the police officers had to be moved inside the houses to enforce the laws and keep the peace. Analogously, virtual firewalls have "moved into" the virtualized environments to provide the necessary protection between virtualized entities.

As illustrated in Figure 21-12, a network can have a traditional physical firewall on the physical network and *virtual firewalls* within the individual virtual environments.

Virtual firewalls can provide bridge-type functionality in which individual traffic links are monitored between virtual machines, or they can be integrated within the hypervisor. The hypervisor is the software component that carries out virtual machine management and oversees guest system software execution. If the firewall is embedded within the hypervisor, then it can "see" and monitor all the activities taking place within the system.

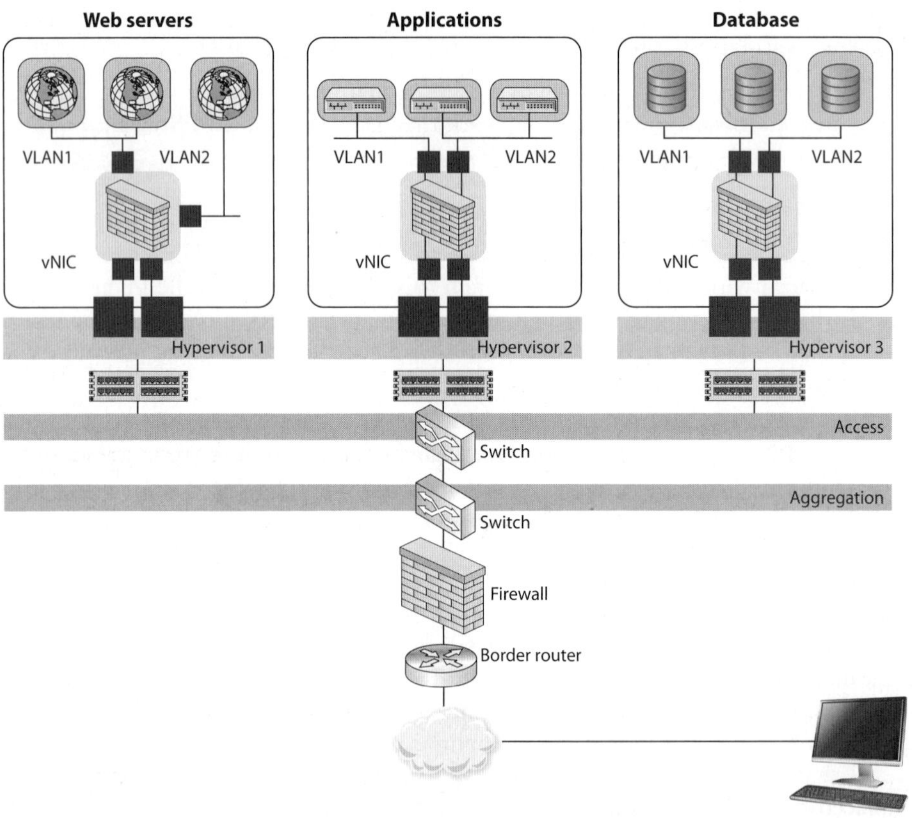

Figure 21-12 Virtual firewalls

Bastion Host

A system is considered a *bastion host* if it is a highly exposed device that is most likely to be targeted by attackers. The closer any system is to an untrusted network, such as the Internet, the more it is considered a target candidate since it has a smaller number of layers of protection guarding it. If a system is on the public side of a DMZ or is directly connected to an untrusted network, it is considered a bastion host; thus, it needs to be extremely locked down.

The system should have all unnecessary services disabled, unnecessary accounts disabled, unneeded ports closed, unused applications removed, unused subsystems and administrative tools removed, and so on. The attack surface of the system needs to be reduced, which means the number of potential vulnerabilities needs to be reduced as much as possible.

A bastion host does not have to be a firewall—the term just relates to the position of the system in relation to an untrusted environment and its threat of attack. Different systems can be considered bastion hosts (mail, web, DNS, etc.) if they are placed on the outer edges of networks.

The "Shoulds" of Firewalls

The default action of any firewall should be to implicitly deny any packets not explicitly allowed. This means that if no rule states that the packet can be accepted, that packet should be denied, no questions asked. Any packet entering the network that has a source address of an internal host should be denied. *Masquerading*, or *spoofing*, is a popular attacking trick in which the attacker modifies a packet header to have the source address of a host inside the network she wants to attack. This packet is spoofed and illegitimate. There is no reason a packet coming from the Internet should have an internal source network address, so the firewall should deny it. The same is true for outbound traffic. No traffic should be allowed to leave a network that does not have an internal source address. If this occurs, it means someone, or some program, on the internal network is spoofing traffic. This is how *zombies* work—the agents used in distributed DoS (DDoS) attacks. If packets are leaving a network with different source addresses, these packets are spoofed and the network is most likely being used as an accomplice in a DDoS attack.

Firewalls should reassemble fragmented packets before sending them on to their destination. In some types of attacks, the hackers alter the packets and make them seem to be something they are not. When a fragmented packet comes to a firewall, the firewall is seeing only part of the picture. It makes its best guess as to whether this piece of a packet is malicious or not. Because these fragments contain only a part of the full packet, the firewall is making a decision without having all the facts. Once all fragments are allowed through to a host computer, they can be reassembled into malicious packages that can cause a lot of damage. A firewall should accept each fragment, assemble the fragments into a complete packet, and then make an access decision based on the whole packet. The drawback to this, however, is that firewalls that do reassemble packet fragments before allowing them to go on to their destination computer cause traffic delay and more overhead. It is up to the organization to decide whether this configuration is necessary and whether the added traffic delay is acceptable.

Many organizations choose to deny network entrance to packets that contain source routing information, which was mentioned earlier. Source routing means that the packet decides how to get to its destination, not the routers in between the source and destination computer. Source routing moves a packet throughout a network on a predetermined path. The sending computer must know about the topology of the network and how to route data properly. This is easier for the routers and connection mechanisms in between, because they do not need to make any decisions on how to route the packet. However, it can also pose a security risk. When a router receives a packet that contains source routing information, the router assumes the packet knows what needs to be done and passes the packet on. In some cases, not all filters may be applied to the packet, and a network administrator may want packets to be routed only through a certain path and not the route a particular packet dictates. To make sure none of this misrouting happens, many firewalls are configured to check for source routing information within the packet and deny it if it is present.

Firewalls are not effective "right out of the box." You really need to understand the type of firewall being implemented and its configuration ramifications. For example, a firewall may have implied rules, which are used before the rules you configure. These implied rules might contradict your rules and override them. In this case, you may think that a certain traffic type is being restricted, but the firewall allows that type of traffic into your network by default.

The following list addresses some of the issues that need you need to understand as they pertain to firewalls:

- Most of the time a distributed approach needs to be used to control all network access points, which cannot happen through the use of just one firewall.
- Firewalls can present a potential bottleneck to the flow of traffic and a single point of failure threat.
- Some firewalls do not provide protection from malware and can be fooled by the more sophisticated attack types.
- Firewalls do not protect against sniffers or rogue wireless access points and provide little protection against insider attacks.

The role of firewalls is becoming more and more complex as they evolve and take on more functionality and responsibility. At times, this complexity works against security professionals because it requires them to understand and properly implement additional functionality. Without an understanding of the different types of firewalls and architectures available, many more security holes can be introduced, which lays out the welcome mat for attackers.

Intrusion Detection and Prevention Systems

The options for intrusion detection and prevention include host-based intrusion detection systems (HIDSs), network-based intrusion detection systems (NIDSs), and wireless intrusion detection systems (WIDSs). Each may operate in detection or prevention mode depending on the specific product and how it is employed. As a refresher, the main difference between an intrusion detection system (IDS) and an intrusion prevention system (IPS) is that an IDS only detects and reports suspected intrusions, while an IPS detects, reports, and stops suspected intrusions. How do they do this? There are two basic approaches: rule-based or anomaly-based.

Rule-Based IDS/IPS

Rule-based intrusion detection and prevention is the simplest and oldest technology. Essentially, we write rules (or subscribe to a service that writes them for us) and load those onto the system. The IDS/IPS monitors the environment in which it is placed, looking for anything that matches a rule. For example, suppose you have a signature for a particular piece of malware. You could create a rule that looks for any data that matches that signature and either raise an alert (IDS) or drop the data and generate the alert (IPS). Rule-based approaches are very effective when we know the telltale signs of an attack. But what if the attacker changes tools or procedures?

The main drawback of rule-based approaches to detecting attacks is that we need to have a rule that accurately captures the attack. This means someone got hacked, investigated the compromise, generated the rule, and shared it with the community. This process takes time and, until the rule is finalized and loaded, the system won't be effective against that specific attack. Of course, there's nothing stopping the adversary from slightly modifying tools or techniques to bypass your new rule either.

Anomaly-Based IDS/IPS

Anomaly-based intrusion detection and prevention uses a variety of approaches to detect things that don't look right. One basic approach is to observe the environment for some time to figure out what "normal" looks like. This is called the *training mode*. Once it has created a baseline of the environment, the IDS/IPS can be switched to *testing mode*, in which it compares observations to the baselines created earlier. Any observation that is significantly different generates an alert. For example, a particular workstation has a pattern of behavior during normal working hours and never sends more than, say, 10MB of data to external hosts during a regular day. One day, however, it sends out 100MB. That is pretty anomalous, so the IDS/IPS raises an alert (or blocks the traffic). But what if that was just the annual report being sent to the regulators?

The main challenge with anomaly-based approaches is that of *false positives*; that is, detecting intrusions when none happened. False positives can lead to fatigue and desensitizing the personnel who need to examine each of these alerts. Conversely, *false negatives* are events that the system incorrectly classifies as benign, delaying the response until the intrusion is detected through some other means. Obviously, both are bad outcomes.

EDR, NDR, and XDR

HIDS and antimalware features are increasingly being bundled into comprehensive *endpoint detection and response (EDR)* platforms. Similarly, NIDSs are evolving into *network detection and response (NDR)* products. These newer solutions do everything that HIDSs and NIDSs do, but also offer a host of other features such as combining rule-based and anomaly detection capabilities. *Extended detection and response (XDR)* platforms take this one step further by correlation of events across multiple sensors, both in the cloud and on premises, to get a more holistic view of what is going on in an environment.

Perhaps the most important step toward reducing errors is to baseline the system. *Baselining* is the process of establishing the normal patterns of behavior for a given network or system. Most of us think of baselining only in terms of anomaly-based IDSs because these typically have to go through a period of learning before they can determine what is anomalous. However, even rule-based IDSs should be configured in accordance with whatever is normal for an organization. There is no such thing as a one-size-fits-all *set* of IDS/IPS rules, though some *individual* rules may very well be applicable to all (e.g., detecting a known specimen of malware).

NOTE The term "perimeter" has lost some of its importance of late. While it remains an important concept in terms of security architecting, it can mislead some into imagining a wall separating us from the bad guys. A best practice is to assume the adversaries are already "inside the wire," which downplays the importance of a perimeter in security operations.

Whitelisting and Blacklisting

One of the most effective ways to tune detection platforms like IDS/IPS is to develop lists of things that are definitely benign and those that are definitely malicious. The platform, then, just has to figure out the stuff that is not on either list. A *whitelist* (more inclusively called an *allow list*) is a set of known-good resources such as IP addresses, domain names, or applications. Conversely, a *blacklist* (also known as a *deny list*) is a set of known-bad resources. In a perfect world, you would only want to use whitelists, because nothing outside of them would ever be allowed in your environment. In reality, we end up using them in specific cases in which we have complete knowledge of the acceptable resources. For example, whitelisting applications that can execute on a computer is an effective control because users shouldn't be installing arbitrary software on their own. Similarly, we can whitelist devices that are allowed to attach to our networks.

Things are different when we can't know ahead of time all the allowable resources. For example, it is a very rare thing for an organization to be able to whitelist websites for every user. Instead, we would rely on blacklists of domain and IP addresses. The problem with blacklists is that the Internet is such a dynamic place that the only thing we can be sure of is that our blacklist will always be incomplete. Still, blacklisting is better than nothing, so we should always try to use whitelists first, and then fall back on blacklists when we have no choice.

Antimalware Software

Traditional antimalware software uses signatures to detect malicious code. Signatures, sometimes referred to as fingerprints, are created by antimalware vendors. A *signature* is a set of code segments that a vendor has extracted from a malware sample. Similar to how our bodies have antibodies that identify and go after specific pathogens by matching segments of their genetic codes, antimalware software has an engine that scans files, e-mail messages, and other data passing through specific protocols and then compares them to its database of signatures. When there is a match, the antimalware software carries out whatever activities it is configured to do, which can be to quarantine the item, attempt to clean it (remove the malware), provide a warning message dialog box to the user, and/or log the event.

Signature-based detection (also called *fingerprint detection*) is a reasonably effective way to detect conventional malware, but it has a delayed response time to new threats. Once malware is detected in the wild, the antimalware vendor must study it, develop and test a new signature, release the signature, and all customers must download it. If the malicious code is just sending out silly pictures to all of your friends, this delay is not so critical. If the malicious software is a new variant of TrickBot (a versatile Trojan behind many ransomware attacks), this amount of delay can be devastating.

Since new malware is released daily, it is hard for the signature-based vendors to keep up. Another technique that almost all antimalware software products use is referred to as *heuristic detection*. This approach analyzes the overall structure of the malicious code, evaluates the coded instructions and logic functions, and looks at the type of data within the virus or worm. So, it collects a bunch of information about this piece of code and assesses the likelihood of it being malicious in nature. It has a type of "suspiciousness counter," which is incremented as the program finds more potentially malicious attributes. Once a predefined threshold is met, the code is officially considered dangerous and the antimalware software jumps into action to protect the system. This allows antimalware software to detect unknown malware, instead of just relying on signatures.

As an analogy, let's say Barney is the town cop who is employed to root out the bad guys and lock them up (quarantine). If Barney uses a signature method, he compares a stack of photographs of bad actors to each person he sees on the street. When he sees a match, he quickly throws the bad guy into his patrol car and drives off. By contrast, if he uses a heuristic method, he watches for suspicious activity. So if someone with a ski mask is standing outside a bank, Barney assesses the likelihood of this being a bank robber against it just being a cold guy in need of some cash.

Some antimalware products create a simulated environment, called a *virtual machine* or *sandbox*, and allow some of the logic within the suspected code to execute in the protected environment. This allows the antimalware software to see the code in question in action, which gives it more information as to whether or not it is malicious.

NOTE The virtual machine or sandbox is also sometimes referred to as an *emulation buffer*. They are all the same thing—a piece of memory that is segmented and protected so that if the code is malicious, the system is protected.

Reviewing information about a piece of code is called *static analysis*, while allowing a portion of the code to run in a virtual machine is called *dynamic analysis*. They are both considered heuristic detection methods.

Now, even though all of these approaches are sophisticated and effective, they are not 100 percent effective because malware writers are crafty. It is a continual cat-and-mouse game that is carried out every day. The antimalware industry comes out with a new way of detecting malware, and the very next week the malware writers have a way to get around this approach. This means that antimalware vendors have to continually increase the intelligence of their products and you have to buy a new version every year.

The next phase in the antimalware software evolution is referred to as behavior blockers. Antimalware software that carries out *behavior blocking* actually allows the suspicious code to execute within the operating system unprotected and watches its interactions with the operating system, looking for suspicious activities. The antimalware software watches for the following types of actions:

- Writing to startup files or the Run keys in the Windows registry
- Opening, deleting, or modifying files
- Scripting e-mail messages to send executable code
- Connecting to network shares or resources
- Modifying an executable logic
- Creating or modifying macros and scripts
- Formatting a hard drive or writing to the boot sector

If the antimalware program detects some of these potentially malicious activities, it can terminate the software and provide a message to the user. The newer-generation behavior blockers actually analyze sequences of these types of operations before determining the system is infected. (The first-generation behavior blockers only looked for individual actions, which resulted in a large number of false positives.) The newer-generation software can intercept a dangerous piece of code and not allow it to interact with other running processes. They can also detect rootkits. In addition, some of these antimalware programs can allow the system to roll back to a state before an infection took place so the damages inflicted can be "erased."

While it sounds like behavior blockers might bring us our well-deserved bliss and utopia, one drawback is that the malicious code must actually execute in real time; otherwise, our systems can be damaged. This type of constant monitoring also requires a high level of system resources. We just can't seem to win.

EXAM TIP Heuristic detection and behavior blocking are considered proactive and can detect new malware, sometimes called "zero-day" attacks. Signature-based detection cannot detect new malware.

Most antimalware vendors use a blend of all of these technologies to provide as much protection as possible. The individual antimalware attack solutions are shown in Figure 21-13.

NOTE Another antimalware technique is referred to as *reputation-based protection*. An antimalware vendor collects data from many (or all) of its customers' systems and mines that data to search for patterns to help identify good and bad files. Each file type is assigned a reputation metric value, indicating the probability of it being "good" or "bad." These values are used by the antimalware software to help it identify "bad" (suspicious) files.

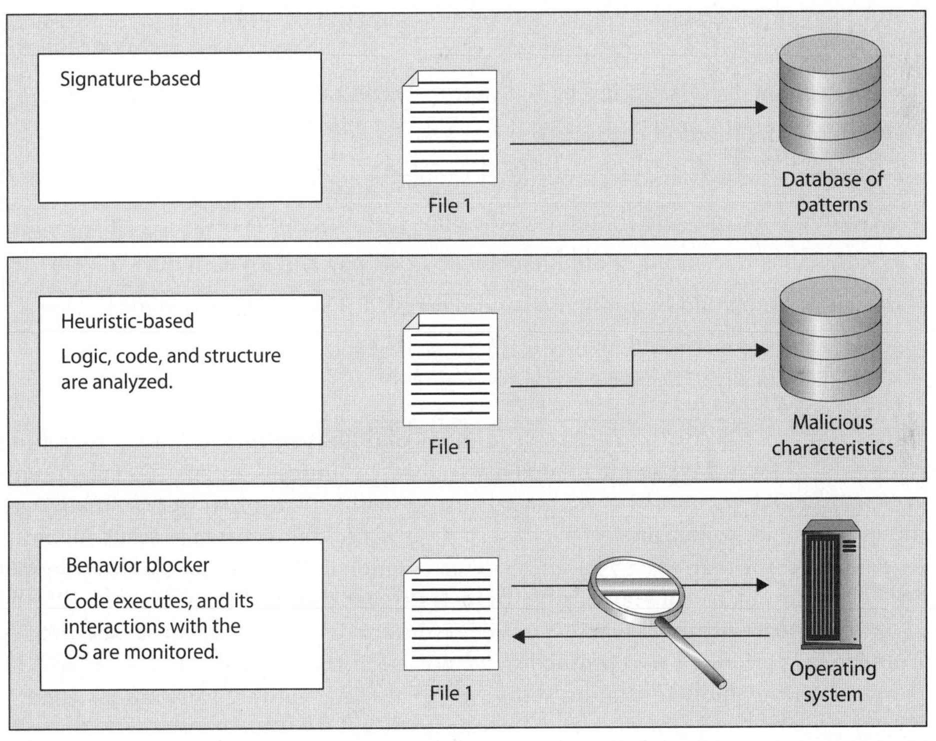

Figure 21-13 Antimalware vendors use various types of malware detection.

Detecting and protecting an enterprise from the long list of malware requires more than just rolling out antimalware software. Just as with other pieces of a security program, certain administrative, physical, and technical controls must be deployed and maintained.

The organization should either have a stand-alone antimalware policy or have one incorporated into an existing security policy. It should include standards outlining what type of antimalware software and antispyware software should be installed and how they should be configured.

Antimalware information and expected user behaviors should be integrated into the security-awareness program, along with who users should contact if they discover a virus. A standard should cover the do's and don'ts when it comes to malware, which are listed next:

- Every workstation, server, and mobile device should have antimalware software installed.
- An automated way of updating malware signatures should be deployed on each device.
- Users should not be able to disable antimalware software.
- A preplanned malware eradication process should be developed and a contact person designated in case of an infection.
- All external disks (USB drives and so on) should be scanned automatically.
- Backup files should be scanned.
- Antimalware policies and procedures should be reviewed annually.
- Antimalware software should provide boot malware protection.
- Antimalware scanning should happen at a gateway and on each device.
- Virus scans should be automated and scheduled. Do not rely on manual scans.
- Critical systems should be physically protected so malicious software cannot be installed locally.

Since malware has cost organizations millions of dollars in operational costs and productivity hits, many have implemented antimalware solutions at network entry points. The scanning software can be integrated into a mail server, proxy server, or firewall. (The solutions are sometimes referred to as *virus walls*.) This software scans incoming traffic, looking for malware so it can be detected and stopped before entering the network. These products can scan Simple Mail Transport Protocol (SMTP), HTTP, FTP, and possibly other protocol types, but what is important to realize is that the product is only looking at one or two protocols and not *all* of the incoming traffic. This is the reason each server and workstation should also have antimalware software installed.

Sandboxing

A *sandbox* is an application execution environment that isolates the executing code from the operating system to prevent security violations. To the code, the sandbox looks just like the environment in which it would expect to run. For instance, when we sandbox an application, it behaves as if it were communicating directly with the OS. In reality, it is interacting with another piece of software whose purpose is to ensure compliance with security policies. Another instance is that of software (such as helper objects) running in a web browser. The software acts as if it were communicating directly with the browser, but those interactions are mediated by a policy enforcer of some sort. The power of sandboxes is that they offer an additional layer of protection when running code that we are not certain is safe to execute.

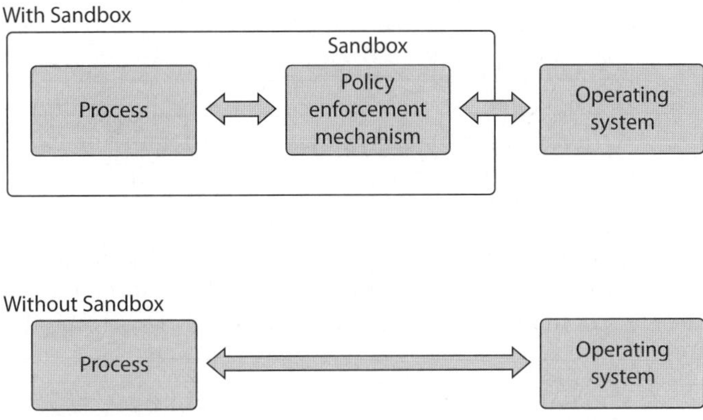

Outsourced Security Services

Nearly all of the preventive and detective measures we've discussed in the preceding subsections can be outsourced to an external service provider. Why would we want to do that? Well, for starters, many small and midsized organizations lack the resources to provide a full team of experienced security professionals. We are experiencing workforce shortages that are not likely to be solved in the near term. This means that hiring, training, and retaining qualified personnel is not feasible in many cases. Instead, many organizations have turned to managed security services providers (MSSPs) for third-party provided security services.

EXAM TIP Outsourced security services are what (ISC)² refers to as *third-party provided security.*

MSSPs typically offer a variety of services ranging from point solutions to taking over the installation, operation, and maintenance of all technical (and some cases physical) security controls. (Sorry, you still have to provide policies and many administrative controls.) Your costs will vary depending on what you need but, in many cases, you'll get more than you could've afforded if you were to provide these services in-house. Still, there are some issues that you should consider before hiring an MSSP:

- **Requirements** Before you start interviewing potential MSSPs, make sure you know your requirements. You can outsource the day-to-day activities, but you can't outsource your responsibility to understand your own security needs.

- **Understanding** Does the MSSP understand your business processes? Are they asking the right questions to get there? If your MSSP doesn't know what it is that your organization does (and how), they will struggle to provide usable security. Likewise, you need to understand their qualifications and processes. Trust is a two-way street grounded on accurate information.
- **Reputation** It is hard to be a subpar service provider and not have customers complain about you. When choosing an MSSP, you need to devote some time to reading online reviews and asking other security professionals about their experiences with specific companies.
- **Costing** You may not be able to afford the deluxe version of the MSSP's services, so you will likely have to compromise and address only a subset of your requirements. When you have trimmed down your requirements, is it still more cost-effective to go with this provider? Should you go with another? Should you just do it yourself?
- **Liability** Any reasonable MSSP will put limits on their liability if your organization is breached. Read the fine print on the contract and consult your attorneys, particularly if you are in an industry that is regulated by the government.

Honeypots and Honeynets

A *honeypot* is a network device that is intended to be exploited by attackers, with the administrator's goal being to gain information on the attackers' tactics, techniques, and procedures (TTPs). Honeypots can work as early detection mechanisms, meaning that the network staff can be alerted that an intruder is attacking a honeypot system, and they can quickly go into action to make sure no production systems are vulnerable to that specific attack type. A honeypot usually sits in the screened subnet, or DMZ, and attempts to lure attackers to it instead of to actual production computers. Think of honeypots as marketing devices; they are designed to attract a segment of the market, get them to buy something, and keep them coming back. Meanwhile, threat analysts are keeping tabs on their adversaries' TTPs.

To make a honeypot system alluring to attackers, administrators may enable services and ports that are popular to exploit. Some honeypot systems *emulate* services, meaning the actual services are not running but software that acts like those services is available. Honeypot systems can get an attacker's attention by advertising themselves as easy targets to compromise. They are configured to look like the organization's regular systems so that attackers will be drawn to them like bears are to honey.

Another key to honeypot success is to provide the right kind of bait. When someone attacks your organization, what is it that they are after? Is it credit card information, patient files, intellectual property? Your honeypots should look like systems that would allow the attacker to access the assets for which they are searching. Once compromised, the directories and files containing this information must appear to be credible. It should also take a long time to extract the information, so that we maximize the contact time with our "guests."

A *honeynet* is an entire network that is meant to be compromised. While it may be tempting to describe honeynets as networks of honeypots, that description might be a bit misleading. Some honeynets are simply two or more honeypots used together. However, others are designed to ascertain a specific attacker's intent and dynamically spawn honeypots that are designed to be appealing to that particular attacker. As you can see, these very sophisticated honeynets are not networks of preexisting honeypots, but rather adaptive networks that interact with the adversaries to keep them engaged (and thus under observation) for as long as possible.

NOTE *Black holes* are sometimes confused with honeynets, when in reality they are almost the opposite of them. Black holes typically are routers with rules that silently drop specific (typically malicious) packets without notifying the source. They normally are used to render botnet and other known-bad traffic useless. Whereas honeypots and honeynets allow us to more closely observe our adversaries, black holes are meant to make them go away for us.

Wrapping up the honey collection, *honeyclients* are synthetic applications meant to allow an attacker to conduct a client-side attack while also allowing the threat analysts an opportunity to observe the TTPs being used by their adversaries. Honeyclients are particularly important in the honey family, because most of the successful attacks happen on the client side, and honeypots are not particularly well suited to track client-side attacks. Suppose you have a suspected phishing or spear phishing attack that you'd like to investigate. You could use a honeyclient to visit the link in the e-mail and pretend it is a real user. Instead of getting infected, however, the honeyclient safely catches all the attacks thrown at it and reports them to you. Since it is not really the web browser it is claiming to be, it is impervious to the attack and provides you with information about the actual tools the attacker is throwing at you. Honeyclients come in different flavors, with some being highly interactive (meaning a human has to operate them), while others involve low interaction (meaning their behavior is mostly or completely automated).

Organizations use these systems to identify, quantify, and qualify specific traffic types to help determine their danger levels. The systems can gather network traffic statistics and return them to a centralized location for better analysis. So as the systems are being attacked, they gather intelligence information that can help the network staff better understand what is taking place within their environment.

It should be clear from the foregoing that honeypots and honeynets are not defensive controls like firewalls and IDSs, but rather help us collect threat intelligence. To be effective, they must be closely monitored by a competent threat analyst. By themselves, honeypots and honeynets do not improve your security posture. However, they can give your threat intelligence team invaluable insights into your adversaries' methods and capabilities.

It is also important to make sure that the honeypot systems are not connected to production systems and do not provide any "jumping off" points for the attacker. There have been instances where companies improperly implemented honeypots and they were exploited by attackers, who were then able to move from those systems to the company's internal systems. The honeypots need to be properly segmented from any other live systems on the network.

On a smaller scale, organizations may choose to implement *tarpits*, which are similar to honeypots in that they appear to be easy targets for exploitation. A tarpit can be configured to appear as a vulnerable service that attackers commonly attempt to exploit. Once the attackers start to send packets to this "service," the connection to the victim system seems to be live and ongoing, but the response from the victim system is slow and the connection may time out. Most attacks and scanning activities take place through automated tools that require quick responses from their victim systems. If the victim systems do not reply or are very slow to reply, the automated tools may not be successful because the protocol connection times out.

NOTE Deploying honeypots and honeynets has potential liability issues. Be sure to consult your legal counsel before starting down this road.

Artificial Intelligence Tools

Artificial intelligence (AI) is a multidisciplinary field primarily associated with computer science, with influences from mathematics, cognitive psychology, philosophy, and linguistics (among others). At a high level, AI can be divided into two different approaches, as shown in Figure 21-14: symbolic and non-symbolic; the key difference is in how each represents knowledge. Both approaches are concerned with how knowledge is organized, how inference proceeds to support decision-making, and how the system learns.

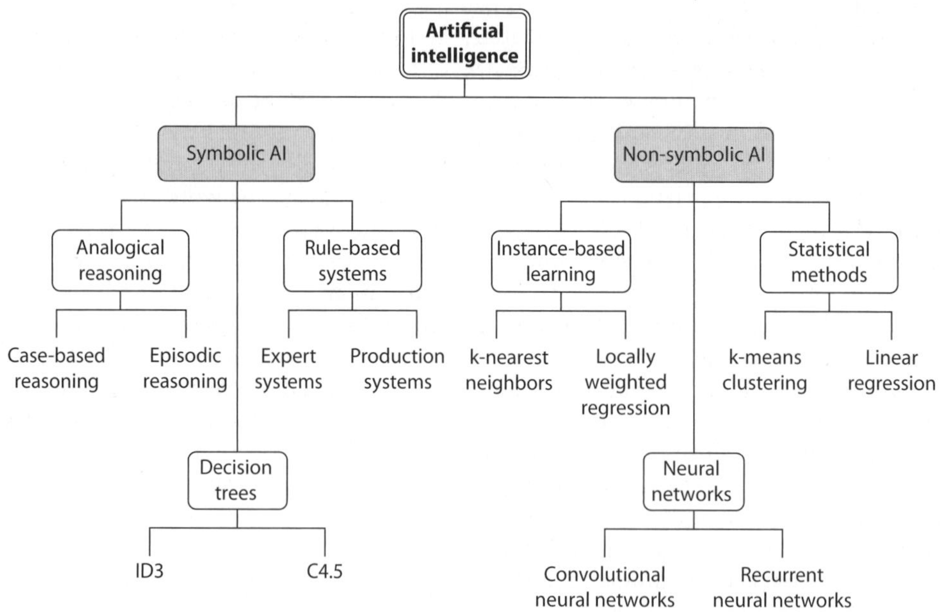

Figure 21-14 A partial taxonomy of artificial intelligence

In symbolic approaches to AI, system developers model real-world concepts, their relationships, and how they interact to solve a set of problems using a set of symbols (e.g., words or tokens). Symbolic AI requires considerable knowledge engineering of both the problem and solution domains, which makes it labor-intensive. However, it yields results that are inherently explainable to humans since the results are derived from human knowledge models in the first place. Symbolic AI systems include the expert systems that became prolific in the 1980s. These relied on extensive interviewing of subject matter experts and time-consuming encoding of their expertise in a series of conditional structures. Unsurprisingly, these early systems were unable to adapt or learn absent human intervention, which is a problem when we consider the number of exceptions that apply to almost all processes.

Another approach to AI departs from the use of symbolic representations of human knowledge and focuses instead on learning patterns in data for classifying objects, predicting future results, or clustering similar sets of data. These non-symbolic AI approaches are where many of the most recent advances have occurred, primarily in classification tasks such as image and voice recognition. In the current vernacular, these non-symbolic approaches are commonly called *machine learning (ML)* even though symbolic systems may also learn. As with symbolic approaches, non-symbolic ML systems also incorporate knowledge representations and reasoning. The knowledge representation is typically quantitative vectors (i.e., non-symbolic) with features from the dataset that describe the input (e.g., pixels from an image, frequencies from an audio file, word vectors, etc.).

Whereas symbolic AI requires considerable knowledge engineering, non-symbolic AI generally requires significant data acquisition and data curating, which can be labor-intensive even for domains where data is readily available. However, rather than having to program the knowledge, as in a symbolic system, the non-symbolic ML system acquires its knowledge in the form of numeric parameters (i.e., weights) through offline training with datasets with millions of examples. As training progresses, the ML model learns the correct parameters that minimize a cost function. That function typically deals with classifying some sample (helpful for finding malware) or making a prediction (allowing us to detect anomalies like spikes in outbound traffic).

Classification determines the class of a new sample based on what is known about previous samples. A common example of this is an algorithm called k-nearest neighbors (KNN), which is a supervised learning technique in which the nearest k neighbors influence the classification of the new point (e.g., if more than half of its k nearest neighbors are in one class, then the new point also belongs in that class). For cybersecurity, this is helpful when trying to determine whether a binary file is malware or detecting whether an e-mail is spam.

Prediction compares previous data samples and determines what the next sample(s) should be. If you have ever taken a statistics class, you may recall a type of analysis called *regression*, in which you try to determine the line (or curve) that most closely approximates a sequence of data points. We use the same approach to prediction in ML by learning from previous observations to determine where the next data point(s) should appear, which is useful for network flow analysis.

On the other hand, there is also unsupervised learning such as clustering, where we do not have a preconception of which classes (or even how many) exist; we determine where the samples naturally clump together. One of the most frequently used clustering algorithms is k-means clustering, in which new data points are added to one of the k clusters based on which one is closest to the new point. Clustering is useful for anomaly detection.

Finally, reinforcement learning tunes decision-making parameters toward choices that lead to positive outcomes in the environment. For example, one might have a security analyst provide feedback to an anomaly detector when it incorrectly classifies a malicious file or event (i.e., a false positive). This feedback adjusts the internal model's weights, so that its anomaly classification improves.

AI has shortcomings that you must consider before employing it. Neither symbolic nor non-symbolic AI approaches cope well with novel situations, and both require a human to re-engineer (symbolic) or retrain (non-symbolic) the algorithms. Symbolic, knowledge-engineered systems may contain underlying biases of the individual(s) who encode the system. Training data sets for non-symbolic approaches may contain biases that are not representative of the operational environment. These biases lead to either false positives or, worse, false negatives when the system is deployed. The best way forward is to combine both approaches, using each other's strengths to offset the other's weaknesses.

Logging and Monitoring

Logging and monitoring are two key activities performed by a SOC using the various tools we just discussed (and probably a few others). These two tasks go hand in hand, since you can't really monitor (at least not very effectively) if you are not logging and, conversely, logging makes little sense if you aren't monitoring. In the sections that follow, we first address how to collect and manage logs, and then discuss the ways in which you should be monitoring those logs (as well as other real-time data feeds).

Log Management

We discussed log reviews and how to prevent log tampering in Chapter 18. To understand how logs support day-to-day security operations, however, we need to take a step back and review why we might be logging system events in the first place. After all, if you don't have clear goals in mind, you will likely collect the wrong events at least some of the time.

Logging Requirements

Earlier in this chapter, we discussed cyberthreat intelligence and, in particular, the collection management framework (CMF). That section on the CMF is a great one to review when you're thinking about what your logging goals should be. After all, logs are data sources that can (and probably should) feed your threat intelligence. Just like intelligence requirements are meant to answer questions from decision-makers, logs should do the same for your SOC analysts. There should be specific questions your security team routinely asks, and those are the questions that should drive what you log and how. For example, you may be concerned about data leaks of your sensitive research projects to overseas threat actors. What events from which system(s) would you need to log in order to monitor data egress? How often will you be checking logs (which determines how long you must retain them)? If you simply go with default logging settings, you may be ill informed when it comes to monitoring.

Log Standards

Another best practice is to standardize the format of your logs. If you are using a security information and event management (SIEM) system (which we'll discuss shortly), then that platform will take care of normalizing any logs you forward to it. Otherwise, you'll have to do it yourself using either the configuration settings on the system that's logging (if it allows multiple formats) or by using a data processing pipeline such as the open-source Logstash.

NOTE It is essential that you standardize the timestamps on all logs across your environment. If your organization is small, you can use local time; otherwise, we recommend you always use Coordinated Universal Time (UTC).

Something else to consider as you standardize your logs is who will be consuming them. Many SOCs leverage tools for automation, such as some of the AI techniques we discussed earlier. These automated systems may have their own set of requirements for formatting, frequency of updates, or log storage. You should ensure that your standards address the needs of all stakeholders (even non-human ones).

Logging Better

Finally, as with anything else you do in cybersecurity, you want to evaluate the effectiveness of your log management efforts and look for ways to sustain what you're doing well and improve the rest. Establishing and periodically evaluating metrics is an excellent approach to objectively determine opportunities for improvement. For example, how often do analysts lack information to classify an event because of incomplete logging? What logs, events, and fields are most commonly used when triaging alerts? Which are never needed? These questions will point to metrics, and the metrics, in turn, will tell you how well your logging supports your goals.

Security Information and Event Management

A *security information and event management (SIEM)* system is a software platform that aggregates security information (like asset inventories) and security events (which could become incidents) and presents them in a single, consistent, and cohesive manner. SIEMs collect data from a variety of sensors, perform pattern matching and correlation of events, generate alerts, and provide dashboards that allow analysts to see the state of the network. One of the best-known commercial solutions is Splunk, while on the open-source side the Elastic Stack (formerly known as the Elasticsearch-Logstash-Kibana, or ELK, stack) is very popular. It is worth noting that, technically, both of these systems are data analytics platforms and not simply SIEMs. Their ability to ingest, index, store, and retrieve large volumes of data applies to a variety of purposes, from network provisioning to marketing to enterprise security.

Among the core characteristics of SIEMs is the ability to amass all relevant security data and present it to the security analyst in a way that makes sense. Before these devices became mainstream, security personnel had to individually monitor a variety of systems and manually piece together what all this information might mean. Most SIEMs now include features that group together information and events that seem to be related to each other (or "correlated" in the language of statistics). This allows the analyst to quickly determine the events that are most important or for which there is the most evidence.

SIEM correlations require a fair amount of fine-tuning. Most platforms, out of the box, come with settings that are probably good enough to get you started. You'll have to let your SIEM tool run for a while (one week or longer) for it to start making sense of your environment and giving you meaningful alerts. Inevitably, you'll find that your analysts are drowning in false positives (sadly, a very common problem with automated platforms) that consume their time and joy. This is where you start tuning your settings using things like whitelists and analyst ratings that will make the platform more accurate. You may also discover blind spots (that is, incidents that your SIEM did not pick up) due to insufficient logging or inadequate sensor placement, so you tune a bit there too.

NOTE SIEM fine-tuning should follow your established configuration management processes.

Security Orchestration, Automation, and Response

A tool that is becoming increasingly popular in SOCs is the security orchestration, automation, and response (SOAR) platform. SOAR is an integrated system that enables more efficient security operations through automation of various workflows. The following are the three key components of a SOAR solution:

- **Orchestration** This refers to the integration and coordination of other security tools such as firewalls, IDS/IPS, and SIEM platforms. Orchestration enables automation.
- **Automation** SOAR platforms excel at automating cybersecurity playbooks and workflows, driving significant efficiency gains where those processes exist (or are created).
- **Response** Incident response workflows can involve dozens (or even hundreds) of distinct tasks. A SOAR platform can automatically handle many of those, freeing up the incident responders to work on what humans do best.

Egress Monitoring

A security practice that is oftentimes overlooked by smaller organizations is *egress monitoring*, which is keeping an eye on (and perhaps restricting) the information that is flowing *out* of our networks. Chapter 6 introduced data loss prevention (DLP), which is a very specific use case of this. Beyond DLP, we should be concerned about ensuring that our platforms are not being used to attack others and that our personnel are not communicating (knowingly or otherwise) with unsavory external parties.

A common approach to egress monitoring is to allow only certain hosts to communicate directly with external destinations. This allows us to focus our attention on a smaller set of computers that presumably would be running some sort of filtering software. A good example of this approach is the use of a web gateway, which effectively implements a man-in-the-middle "attack" on all of our organization's web traffic. It is not uncommon to configure these devices to terminate (and thus decrypt) all HTTPS traffic and to do deep packet inspection (DPI) before allowing information to flow out of the network.

User and Entity Behavior Analytics

While most attacks historically are caused by external threat actors, we must not neglect to monitor the activities of users and entities within our organizations. Even if we never encounter a malicious insider, our users are oftentimes unwitting accomplices when they visit the wrong site, click the wrong link, or open the wrong attachment. *User and entity behavior analytics (UEBA)* is a set of processes that determines normal patterns of behavior so that abnormalities can be detected and investigated. For example, if a user hardly ever sends large amounts of data out to the Internet and then one day starts sending megabytes' worth, that would trigger a UEBA alert. Maybe the transmission was perfectly legitimate, but perhaps it was the early part of a data loss incident.

UEBA can exist as a stand-alone product or as a feature in some other tool, such as an EDR or NDR platform. Either way, UEBA uses machine learning to predict future behaviors based on past observations, and statistical analyses to determine when a deviation from the norm is significant enough to raise an alert. As with any other type of solution that offers behavioral analytics, UEBA solutions are prone to false positives. This means that you would probably need to put some effort into fine-tuning a UEBA solution, even after its training period.

EXAM TIP UEBA is a good choice for detecting both malicious insiders and benign user accounts that have been taken over by a malicious actor.

PART VII

Continuous Monitoring

NIST Special Publication 800-137, *Information Security Continuous Monitoring (ISCM) for Federal Information Systems and Organizations*, defines *information security continuous monitoring* as "maintaining ongoing awareness of information security, vulnerabilities, and threats to support organizational risk management decisions." Think of ISCM as an ongoing and structured verification of security controls. Are the existing controls still the right ones? Are they still effective? If not, why? These are some of the questions to which continuous monitoring provides answers. It is a critical part of the risk management framework we covered in Chapter 2.

There is a distinction here between logging, monitoring, and continuous monitoring. Your logging policies should be pretty expansive. Data storage is cheap and you want to capture as much data as you can in case you ever need it. Monitoring is more limited because it typically requires a human to personally do it, or at least to deal with the reports (such as SIEM alerts) that come out of it. You would, for example, monitor traffic on a certain port when it looks suspicious and then move on to monitoring something else when you determine that traffic is benign. Continuous monitoring is much more prescriptive. It is a deliberate, risk-based process to determine what gets monitored, how it is monitored, and what to do with the information you gather.

In the end, the whole point of continuous monitoring is to determine if the controls remain effective (in the face of changing threat and organizational environments) at reducing risk to acceptable levels. To do this, you need to carefully consider which metrics would allow you to say "yes" or "no" for each control. For example, suppose you are concerned about the risk of malware infections in your organization, so you implement antimalware controls. As part of continuous monitoring for those controls, you could measure the number of infections in some unit of time (day, week, month).

The metrics and measurements provide data that must be analyzed in order to make it actionable. Continuing our malware example, if your controls are effective, you would expect the number of infections to remain steady over time or (ideally) decrease. You would also want to consider other information in the analysis. For example, your malware infections could go up if your organization goes through a growth spurt and hires a bunch of new people, or the infections could go down during the holidays because many employees are taking vacation. The point is that the analysis is not just about understanding what is happening, but also why.

Finally, continuous monitoring involves deciding how to respond to the findings. If your organization's malware infections have increased and you think this is related to the surge in new hires, should you provide additional security awareness training or replace the antimalware solution? Deciding what to do about controls that are no longer sufficiently effective must take into account risk, cost, and a host of other organizational issues.

Continuous monitoring is a deliberate process. You decide what information you need, then collect and analyze it at a set frequency, and then make business decisions with that information. Properly implemented, this process is a powerful tool in your prevention kit.

Chapter Review

Most of the time spent by the typical organization conducting security operations is devoted to emplacing and maintaining the preventive and detective measures, and then using those to log events and monitor the environment. Entire books have been written on these topics, so in this chapter we just covered the essentials. A key takeaway is that tools alone will never be enough to give you the visibility you need to detect attacks; you need the integration of people, processes, and technology. We may have put a bit more focus on technology in this chapter, but we wanted to close it by highlighting the fact that well-trained people, working as a team and following existing processes, are essential components of security operations. This is particularly true when things go wrong and we need to respond to incidents, which we're about to cover in the next chapter.

Quick Review

- The security operations center (SOC) encompasses the people, processes, and technology that allow logging and monitoring of preventive controls, detection of security events, and incident response.
- Tier 1 security analysts spend most of their time monitoring security tools and other technology platforms for suspicious activity.
- Tier 2 security analysts dig deeper into the alerts, declare security incidents, and coordinate with incident responders and intelligence analysts to further investigate, contain, and eradicate the threats.
- Threat intelligence is evidence-based knowledge about an existing or emerging menace or hazard to assets that can be used to inform decisions regarding responses to that menace or hazard.
- Threat intelligence is commonly derived from three types of sources: threat data feeds, open-source intelligence (OSINT), and internal systems.
- Cyberthreat hunting is the practice of proactively looking for threat actors in your networks.
- Firewalls support and enforce the organization's network security policy by restricting access to one network from another network.
- Packet-filtering firewalls make access decisions based upon network-level protocol header values using access control lists (ACLs).
- Stateful firewalls add to the capabilities of packet-filtering firewalls by keeping track of the state of a connection between two endpoints.
- Proxy firewalls intercept and inspect messages before delivering them to the intended recipients.
- A next-generation firewall (NGFW) combines the attributes of the previously discussed firewalls, but adds a signature-based and/or behavioral analysis IPS engine, as well as cloud-based threat data sharing.
- Intrusion detection and prevention systems (IDS/IPS) can be categorized as either host-based (HIDS) or network-based (NIDS) and rule-based or anomaly-based.
- A whitelist is a set of known-good resources such as IP addresses, domain names, or applications. Conversely, a blacklist is a set of known-bad resources.

- Antimalware software is most effective when it is installed in every entry and end point and covered by a policy that delineates user training as well as software configuration and updating.
- A sandbox is an application execution environment that isolates the executing code from the operating system to prevent security violations.
- A honeypot is a network device that is intended to be exploited by attackers, with the administrator's goal being to gain information on the attackers' tactics, techniques, and procedures.
- A honeynet is an entire network that is meant to be compromised.
- Honeyclients are synthetic applications meant to allow an attacker to conduct a client-side attack while also allowing the security analysts an opportunity to observe the techniques being used by their adversaries.
- Machine learning (ML) systems acquire their knowledge in the form of numeric parameters (i.e., weights), through training with datasets consisting of millions of examples. In supervised learning, ML systems are told whether or not they made the right decision. In unsupervised training, they learn by observing an environment. Finally, in reinforcement learning they get feedback on their decisions from the environment.
- Effective logging requires a standard time zone for all timestamps.
- A security information and event management (SIEM) system is a software platform that aggregates security information (like asset inventories) and security events (which could become incidents) and presents them in a single, consistent, and cohesive manner.
- Security orchestration, automation, and response (SOAR) platforms are integrated systems that enable more efficient security operations through automation of various workflows.
- Egress monitoring is the process of scanning (and perhaps restricting) the information that is flowing out of our networks.
- User and entity behavior analytics (UEBA) is a set of processes that determines normal patterns of behavior so that abnormalities can be detected and investigated.
- Continuous monitoring allows organizations to maintain ongoing awareness of information security, vulnerabilities, and threats to support organizational risk management decisions.

Questions

Please remember that these questions are formatted and asked in a certain way for a reason. Keep in mind that the CISSP exam is asking questions at a conceptual level. Questions may not always have the perfect answer, and the candidate is advised against always looking for the perfect answer. Instead, the candidate should look for the best answer in the list.

Use the following scenario to answer Questions 1–3. The startup company at which you are the director of security is going through a huge growth spurt and the CEO has decided it's time to let you build out a security operations center (SOC). You already have two cybersecurity analysts (one is quite experienced), a brand-new security information and event management (SIEM) platform, and pretty good security processes in place.

1. The number of alerts on your SIEM is overwhelming your two analysts and many alerts go uninvestigated each day. How can you correct this?
   A. Hire an intelligence analyst to help you focus your collection efforts.
   B. Tune the SIEM platform to reduce false-positive alerts.
   C. Establish a threat hunting program to find attackers before they trigger alerts.
   D. Establish thresholds below which events will not generate alerts.
2. You hire an intelligence analyst and want her to start addressing intelligence requirements. Which of the following should be her first step?
   A. Finding out what questions decision-makers need answered
   B. Establishing a collection management framework
   C. Identifying data sources
   D. Subscribing to a threat data feed
3. Your SOC is maturing rapidly and you are ready to start a cyberthreat hunting program. Which of the following describes the crux of this effort?
   A. Proving or negating hypotheses of threat actions based on threat intelligence
   B. Neutralizing threat actors before they can breach your organization
   C. Digging deeper into the alerts to determine if they constitute security incidents
   D. Allowing hunters an opportunity to observe techniques used by their adversaries
4. A firewall that can only make decisions based on examining a single network layer header is called a
   A. Stateful firewall
   B. Screened host
   C. Packet filter
   D. Next-generation firewall
5. A firewall that understands the three-step handshake of a TCP connection is called a
   A. Packet filter
   B. Proxy firewall
   C. Transport-layer proxy
   D. Stateful firewall

6. What is the main challenge with anomaly-based approaches to intrusion detection and prevention?
   A. False positives
   B. Needing a rule that accurately captures the attack
   C. Cost
   D. Immaturity of the technology
7. Which of the following is an effective technique for tuning automated detection systems like IDS/IPS and SIEMs?
   A. Access control lists
   B. State tables
   C. Whitelists
   D. Supervised machine learning
8. Which of the following terms would describe a system designed to ascertain a specific attacker's intent and dynamically spawn multiple virtual devices that are designed to be appealing to that particular attacker?
   A. Honeypot
   B. Honeyclient
   C. Honeyseeker
   D. Honeynet
9. Which of the following is *not* a typical application of machine learning?
   A. Classification
   B. Prediction
   C. Clustering
   D. Knowledge engineering
10. Which of the following is *not* true about continuous monitoring?
   A. It involves ad hoc processes that provide agility in responding to novel attacks.
   B. Its main goal is to support organizational risk management.
   C. It helps determine whether security controls remain effective.
   D. It relies on carefully chosen metrics and measurements.

Answers

1. **B.** False positives are a very common problem with automated platforms like SIEMs, but they can be alleviated by fine-tuning the platform. An intelligence analyst could help a little bit but would clearly not be the best answer, while threat hunting would be a distractor for such a young SOC that still needs to get alerts

under control. Ignoring low-scoring alerts as a matter of policy would be a very dangerous move when dealing with stealthy attackers.

2. **A.** Threat intelligence is meant to help decision-makers choose what to do about a threat. It answers a question that these leaders may have. The CMF and data sources are all important, of course, but they are driven by the requirements that come out of leaders' questions. After the requirements are known, the intelligence analyst may (or may not) need to subscribe to a threat data feed.
3. **A.** The crux of threat hunting is to develop a hypothesis of adversarial action based on threat intelligence, and then to prove or negate the hypothesis. Inherent in this description are two factors: a) the adversary is already inside the network, and b) no alerts tipped off the defenders to the adversary's presence. These factors negate answers B and C. Answer D describes the purpose of a honeypot, not threat hunting.
4. **C.** Packet filtering is a firewall technology that makes access decisions based upon network-level protocol header values. The device that is carrying out packet-filtering processes is configured with access control lists (ACLs), which dictate the type of traffic that is allowed into and out of specific networks.
5. **D.** Stateful firewalls keep track of the state of a protocol connection, which means they understand the three-step handshake a TCP connection goes through (SYN, SYN/ACK, ACK).
6. **A.** The main challenge with anomaly-based approaches is that of false positives—detecting intrusions when none happened. These can lead to fatigue and desensitizing the personnel who need to examine each of these alerts. Despite this shortcoming, anomaly-based approaches are mature and cost-effective technologies that are differentiated from rule-based systems by not needing rules that accurately capture attacks.
7. **C.** One of the most effective ways to tune detection platforms like IDS/IPS is to develop lists of things that are definitely benign and those that are definitely malicious. The platform, then, just has to figure out the stuff that is not on either list. A whitelist (more inclusively called an allow list) is a set of known-good resources such as IP addresses, domain names, or applications.
8. **D.** Some honeynets are designed to ascertain a specific attacker's intent and dynamically spawn honeypots that are designed to be appealing to that particular attacker. These very sophisticated honeynets are not networks of preexisting honeypots, but rather adaptive networks that interact with the adversaries to keep them engaged (and thus under observation) for as long as possible.
9. **D.** Machine learning (ML), which is a non-symbolic approach to artificial intelligence (AI), is typically used for classification and prediction (using supervised or semi-supervised learning) as well as clustering (using unsupervised learning). Knowledge engineering is a requirement for symbolic forms for AI, such as expert systems, which are not ML in the common sense of the term.

10. A. Continuous monitoring is a deliberate, data-driven process supporting organizational risk management. One of the key questions it answers is whether controls are still effective at mitigating risks. Continuous monitoring could potentially lead to a decision to implement specific ad hoc processes, but these would not really be part of continuous monitoring.

CHAPTER 22

Security Incidents

This chapter presents the following:

- Incident management
- Incident response planning
- Investigations

It takes 20 years to build a reputation and few minutes of cyber-incident to ruin it.

—Stephane Nappo

No matter how talented your security staff may be, or how well everyone in your organization complies with your excellent security policies and procedures, or what cutting-edge technology you deploy, the sad truth is that the overwhelming odds are that your organization will experience a major compromise (if it hasn't already). What then? Having the means to manage incidents well can be just as important as anything else you do to secure your organization. In this chapter, we will cover incident management in general and then drill down into the details of incident response planning.

Although ISC^2 differentiates incident management and incident investigations, for many organizations, the latter is part of the former. This differentiation is useful to highlight the fact that some investigations involve suspects who may be our own colleagues. While many of us would enjoy the challenge of figuring out how an external threat actor managed to compromise our defenses, there is nothing fun about substantiating allegations that someone we work with did something wrong that caused losses to the organization. Still, as security professionals, we must be ready for whatever threats emerge and deal with the ensuing incidents well and rapidly.

Overview of Incident Management

There are many incident management models, but all share some basic characteristics. They all require that we identify the event, analyze it to determine the appropriate countermeasures, correct the problem(s), and, finally, take measures to keep the event from happening again. (ISC)^2 has broken out these four basic actions and prescribes seven phases in the incident management process: detection, response, mitigation, reporting, recovery, remediation, and lessons learned. Your own organization will have a unique approach, but it is helpful to baseline it off the industry standard.

Although we commonly use the terms "event" and "incident" interchangeably, there are subtle differences between the two. A *security event* is any occurrence that can be observed, verified, and documented. These events are not necessarily harmful. For example, a remote user login, changes to the Windows Registry on a host, and system reboots are all security events that could be benign or malicious depending on the context. A *security incident* is one or more related events that negatively affect the organization and/or impact its security posture. That remote login from our previous example could be a security incident if it was a malicious user logging in. We call reacting to these issues "incident response" (or "incident handling") because something is negatively affecting the organization and causing a security breach.

EXAM TIP A security event is not necessarily a security violation, whereas a security incident is.

Many types of security incidents (malware, insider attacks, terrorist attacks, and so on) exist, and sometimes an incident is just human error. Indeed, many incident response individuals have received a frantic call in the middle of the night because a system is acting "weird." The reasons could be that a deployed patch broke something, someone misconfigured a device, or the administrator just learned a new scripting language and rolled out some code that caused mayhem and confusion.

Many organizations are at a loss as to who to call or what to do right after they have been the victim of a cybercrime. Therefore, all organizations should have an *incident management policy (IMP)*. This document indicates the authorities and responsibilities regarding incident response for everyone in the organization. Though the IMP is frequently drafted by the CISO or someone on that person's team, it is usually signed by whichever executive "owns" organizational policies. This could be the chief information officer (CIO), chief operations officer (COO), or chief human resources officer (CHRO). It is supported by an incident response plan that is documented and tested before an incident takes place. (More on this plan later.) The IMP should be developed with inputs from all stakeholders, not just the security department. Everyone needs to work together to make sure the policy covers all business, legal, regulatory, and security (and any other relevant) issues.

The IMP should be clear and concise. For example, it should indicate whether systems can be taken offline to try to save evidence or must continue functioning at the risk of destroying evidence. Each system and functionality should have a priority assigned to it. For instance, if a file server is infected, it should be removed from the network, but not shut down. However, if the mail server is infected, it should not be removed from the network or shut down, because of the priority the organization attributes to the mail server over the file server. Tradeoffs and decisions such as these have to be made when formulating the IMP, but it is better to think through these issues before the situation occurs, because better logic is usually possible before a crisis, when there's less emotion and chaos.

Incident Management

Incident management includes proactive and reactive processes. Proactive measures need to be put into place so that incidents can be prevented or, failing that, detected quickly. Reactive measures need to be put into place so that detected incidents are dealt with properly.

Most organizations have only reactive management processes, which walk through how an incident should be handled. A more holistic approach is an incident management program that includes both proactive and reactive incident management processes, ensuring that triggers are monitored to make sure all incidents are actually uncovered. This commonly involves log aggregation, a security information and event management (SIEM) system, and user education. Having clear ways of dealing with incidents is not necessarily useful if you don't have a way to find out if incidents are indeed taking place.

All organizations should develop an *incident response team*, as mandated by the incident management policy, to respond to the large array of possible security incidents. The purpose of having an incident response (IR) team is to ensure that the organization has a designated group of people who are properly skilled, who follow a standard set of procedures, and who jump into action when a security incident takes place. The team should have proper reporting procedures established, be prompt in their reaction, work in coordination with law enforcement, and be recognized (and funded) by management as an important element of the overall security program. The team should consist of representatives from various business units, such as the legal department, HR, executive management, the communications department, physical/corporate security, IS security, and information technology.

There are three different types of incident response teams that an organization can choose to put into place. A *virtual* team is made up of experts who have other duties and assignments within the organization. It is called "virtual" because its members are not full-time incident responders but instead are called in as needed and may be physically remote. This type of team introduces a slower response time, and members must neglect their regular duties should an incident occur. However, a *permanent* team of folks who are dedicated strictly to incident response can be cost prohibitive to smaller organizations. The third type is a *hybrid* of the virtual and permanent models. Certain core members are permanently assigned to the team, whereas others are called in as needed.

Regardless of the type, the incident response team should have the following basic items available:

- A list of outside agencies and resources to contact or report to.
- An outline of roles and responsibilities.
- A call tree to contact these roles and outside entities.
- A list of computer or forensic experts to contact.
- A list of steps to take to secure and preserve evidence.

- A list of items that should be included in a report for management and potentially the courts.
- A description of how the different systems should be treated in this type of situation. (For example, remove the systems from both the Internet and the network and power them down.)

When a suspected crime is reported, the incident response team should follow a set of predetermined steps to ensure uniformity in their approach and that no steps are skipped. First, the IR team should investigate the report and determine whether an actual crime has been committed. If the team determines that a crime has been committed, they should inform senior management immediately. If the suspect is an employee, the team should contact a human resources representative right away. The sooner the IR team begins documenting events, the better. If someone is able to document the starting time of the crime, along with the employees and resources involved, that provides a good foundation for evidence. At this point, the organization must decide if it wants to conduct its own forensic investigation or call in experts. If experts are going to be called in, the system that was attacked should be left alone in order to try and preserve as much evidence of the attack as possible. If the organization decides to conduct its own forensic investigation, it must deal with many issues and address tricky elements. (Forensics will be discussed later in this chapter.)

Computer networks and business processes face many types of threats, each requiring a specialized type of recovery. However, an incident response team should draft and enforce a basic outline of how *all* incidents are to be handled. This is a much better approach than the way many organizations deal with these threats, which is usually in an ad hoc, reactive, and confusing manner. A clearly defined incident-handling process is more cost-effective, enables recovery to happen more quickly, and provides a uniform approach with certain expectation of its results.

Incident handling should be closely related to disaster recovery planning (covered in Chapter 23) and should be part of the organization's disaster recovery plan, usually as an appendix. Both are intended to react to some type of incident that requires a quick response so that the organization can return to normal operations. Incident handling is a recovery plan that responds to malicious technical threats. The primary goal of incident handling is to contain and mitigate any damage caused by an incident and to prevent any further damage. This is commonly done by detecting a problem, determining its cause, resolving the problem, and documenting the entire process.

Without an effective incident-handling program, individuals who have the best intentions can sometimes make the situation worse by damaging evidence, damaging systems, or spreading malicious code. Many times, the attacker booby-traps the compromised system to erase specific critical files if a user does something as simple as list the files in a directory. A compromised system can no longer be trusted because the internal commands listed in the path could be altered to perform unexpected activities. The system could now have a back door for the attacker to enter when he wants, or could have a logic bomb silently waiting for a user to start snooping around, only to destroy any and all evidence.

Incident handling should also be closely linked to the organization's security training and awareness program to ensure that these types of mishaps do not take place. Past issues that the incident response team encountered can be used in future training sessions to help others learn what the organization is faced with and how to improve response processes.

Employees need to know how to report an incident. Therefore, the incident management policy should detail an escalation process so that employees understand when evidence of a crime should be reported to higher management, outside agencies, or law enforcement. The process must be centralized, easy to accomplish (or the employees won't bother), convenient, and welcomed. Some employees feel reluctant to report incidents because they are afraid they will get pulled into something they do not want to be involved with or accused of something they did not do. There is nothing like trying to do the right thing and getting hit with a big stick. Employees should feel comfortable about the process, and not feel intimidated by reporting suspicious activities.

The incident management policy should also dictate how employees should interact with external entities, such as the media, government, and law enforcement. This, in particular, is a complicated issue influenced by jurisdiction, the status and nature of the crime, and the nature of the evidence. Jurisdiction alone, for example, depends on the country, state, or federal agency that has control. Given the sensitive nature of public disclosure, communications should be handled by communications, human resources, or other appropriately trained individuals who are authorized to publicly discuss incidents. Public disclosure of a security incident can lead to two possible outcomes. If not handled correctly, it can compound the negative impact of an incident. For example, given today's information-driven society, denial and "no comment" may result in a backlash. On the other hand, if public disclosure is handled well, it can provide the organization with an opportunity to win back public trust. Some countries and jurisdictions either already have or are contemplating breach disclosure laws that require organizations to notify the public if a security breach involving personally identifiable information (PII) is even suspected. So, being open and forthright with third parties about security incidents often is beneficial to organizations.

A sound incident-handling program works with outside agencies and counterparts. The members of the team should be on the mailing list of the Computer Emergency Response Team (CERT) so they can keep up-to-date about new issues and can spot malicious events, hopefully before they get out of hand. CERT is a division of the Software Engineering Institute (SEI) that is responsible for monitoring and advising users and organizations about security preparation and security breaches.

NOTE Resources for CERT can be found at https://www.cert.org/incident-management/.

The Cyber Kill Chain

Even as we think about how best to manage incidents, it is helpful to consider a model that describes the stages attackers must complete to achieve their objectives. In their seminal 2011 white paper titled "Intelligence-Driven Computer Network Defense Informed by Analysis of Adversary Campaigns and Intrusion Kill Chains," Eric Hutchins, Michael Cloppert, and Rohan Amin (employees of Lockheed Martin Corporation, publisher of the white paper) describe a seven-stage intrusion model that has become an industry standard known as the Cyber Kill Chain framework. The seven stages are described here:

1. **Reconnaissance** The adversary has developed an interest in your organization as a target and begins a deliberate information-gathering effort to find vulnerabilities.
2. **Weaponization** Armed with detailed-enough information, the adversary determines the best way into your systems and begins preparing and testing the weapons to be used against you.
3. **Delivery** The cyber weapon is delivered into your system. In over 95 percent of the published cases, this delivery happens via e-mail.
4. **Exploitation** The malicious software is executing on a CPU within your network. This may have launched when the target user clicked a link, opened an attachment, visited a website, or plugged in a USB thumb drive. It could also (in somewhat rare cases) be the result of a remote exploit. One way or another, the attacker's software is now running in your systems.
5. **Installation** Most malicious software is delivered in stages. First, there is the exploit that compromised the system in the prior step. Then, some other software is installed in the target system to ensure persistence, ideally with a good measure of stealth.
6. **Command and Control (C2)** Once the first two stages of the software (exploit and persistence) have been executed, most malware will "phone home" to the attackers to let them know the attack was successful and to request updates and instructions.
7. **Actions on Objectives** Finally, the malware is ready to do whatever it was designed to do. Perhaps the intent is to steal intellectual property and send it to an overseas server. Or perhaps this particular effort is an early phase in a grander attack, so the malware will pivot off the compromised system. Whatever the case, the attacker has won at this point.

As you can probably imagine, the earlier in the kill chain we identify the attack, the greater our odds are of preventing the adversaries from achieving their objectives.

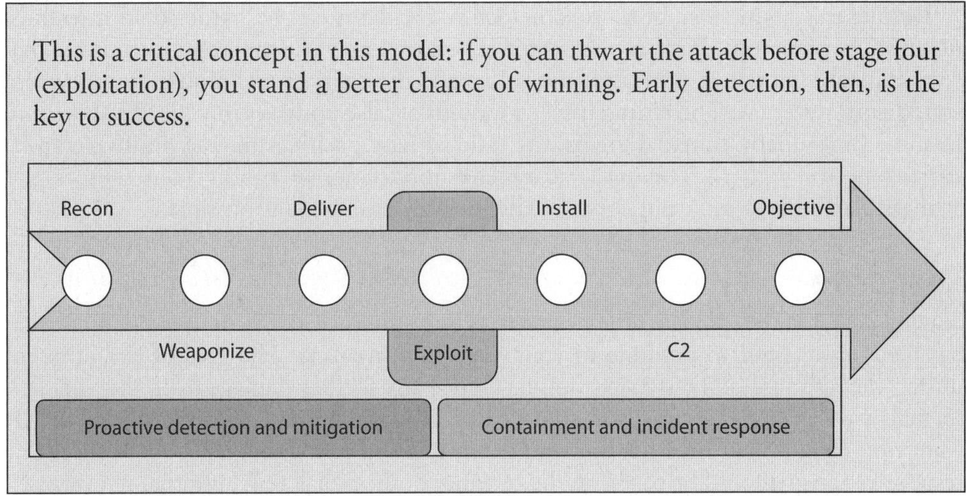
This is a critical concept in this model: if you can thwart the attack before stage four (exploitation), you stand a better chance of winning. Early detection, then, is the key to success.
Recon
Deliver
Install
Objective
Weaponize
Exploit
C2
Proactive detection and mitigation
Containment and incident response

Incident response is the component of incident management that is executed when a security incident takes place. It starts with detecting the incident and eventually leads to the application of lessons learned during the response. Let's take a closer look at each of the steps in the incident response process.

Detection

The first and most important step in responding to an incident is to realize that you have a problem in the first place. The organization's incident response plan should have specific criteria and a process by which the security staff declares that an incident has occurred. The challenge, of course, is to separate the wheat from the chaff and zero in on the alerts or other indicators that truly represent an immediate danger to the organization.

Detection boils down to having a good sensor network implemented throughout your environment. There are three types of sensors: technical, human, and third-party. *Technical sensors* are, perhaps, the type most of us are used to dealing with. They are provided by the previously mentioned SIEM systems and the other types of systems introduced in Chapter 21: detection and response (EDR), network detection and response (NDR), and security orchestration, automation, and response (SOAR). *Human sensors* can be just as valuable if everyone in your organization has the security awareness to notice odd events and promptly report them to the right place. Many organizations use a special e-mail address to which anyone can send an e-mail report. *Third-party sensors* (technical or human) exist in other organizations. For example, maybe you have a really good relationship with your supply chain partners, and they will alert you to incidents in their environments that appear related to you. That third party could also be a government agency letting you know you've been hacked, which is never a good way to start your day, but is better than not knowing.

Despite this abundance of sensors, detecting incidents can be harder than it sounds, for a variety of reasons. First, sophisticated adversaries may use tools and techniques that you are unable to detect (at least at first). Even if the tools or techniques are known to you, they may very well be hiding under a mound of false positives in your SIEM system. In some (improperly tuned) systems, the ratio of false positives to true positives can be ten to one (or higher). This underscores the importance of tuning your sensors and analysis platforms to reduce the rate of false positives as much as possible.

Response

Having detected the incident, the next step is to respond by containing the damage that has been or is about to be done to your most critical assets. The goal of containment during the response phase is to prevent or reduce any further damage from this incident so that you can begin to mitigate and recover. Done properly, mitigation buys the IR team time for a proper investigation and determination of the incident's root cause. The response strategy should be based on the category of the attack (e.g., internal or external), the assets affected by the incident, and the criticality of those assets. So, what kind of mitigation strategy is best? Well, it depends.

When complete isolation or containment is not a viable solution, you may opt to use boundary devices to stop one system from infecting another. This involves temporarily changing firewall/filtering router rule configuration. Access control lists can be applied to minimize exposure. These response strategies indicate to the attacker that his attack has been noticed and countermeasures are being implemented. But what if, in order to perform a root cause analysis, you need to keep the affected system online and not let on that you've noticed the attack? In this situation, you might consider installing a honeynet or honeypot to provide an area that will contain the attacker but pose minimal risk to the organization. This decision should involve legal counsel and upper management because honeynets and honeypots can introduce liability issues, as discussed in Chapter 21. Once the incident has been contained, you need to figure out what just happened by putting the available pieces together.

This is the substage of analysis, where more data is gathered (audit logs, video captures, human accounts of activities, system activities) to try and figure out the root cause of the incident. The goals are to figure out who did this, how they did it, when they did it, and why. Management must be continually kept abreast of these activities because they will be making the big decisions on how this situation is to be handled.

EXAM TIP Watch out for the context in which the term "response" is used. It can refer to the entire seven-phase incident management process or to the second phase of it. In the second usage, you can think of it as *initial* response aimed at containment.

Mitigation

Having "stopped the bleeding" with the initial containment response, the next step is to determine how to properly mitigate the threat. Though the instinctive reaction may be to clean up the infected workstation or add rules to your firewalls and IDS/IPS, this well-intentioned response could lead you on an endless game of whack-a-mole or, worse yet, blind you to the adversary's real objective. What do you know about the adversary? Who is it? What are they after? Is this tool and its use consistent with what you have already seen? Part of the mitigation stage is to figure out what information you need in order to restore security.

Once you have a hypothesis about the adversary's goals and plans, you can test it. If this particular actor is usually interested in PII on your high-net-worth clients but the incident you detected was on a (seemingly unrelated) host in the warehouse, was that an initial entry or pivot point? If so, then you may have caught the attacker before they worked their way further along the kill chain. But what if you got your attribution wrong? How could you test for that? This chain of questions, combined with quantifiable answers from your systems, forms the basis for an effective response. To quote the famous hockey player Wayne Gretzky, we should all "skate to where the puck is going to be, not where it has been."

NOTE It really takes a fairly mature threat intelligence capability to determine who is behind an attack (attribution), what are their typical tactics, techniques, and procedures (TTPs), and what might be their ultimate objective. If you do not have this capability, you may have no choice but to respond only to what you're detecting, without regard for what the adversary may actually be trying to do.

Once you are comfortable with your understanding of the facts of the incident, you move to eradicate the adversary from the affected systems. It is important to gather evidence before you recover systems and information. The reason is that, in many cases, you won't know that you will need legally admissible evidence until days, weeks, or even months after an incident. It pays, then, to treat each incident as if it will eventually end up in a court of justice.

Once all relevant evidence is captured, you can begin to fix all that was broken. The mitigation phase ends when you have affected systems that, while still isolated from the production networks, are free from adversarial control. For hosts that were compromised, the best practice is to simply reinstall the system from a gold master image and then restore data from the most recent backup that occurred prior to the attack. You may also have to roll back transactions and restore databases from backup systems. Once you are done, it is as if the incident never happened. Well, almost.

CAUTION An attacked or infected system should never be trusted, because you do not necessarily know all the changes that have taken place and the true extent of the damage. Some malicious code could still be hiding somewhere. Systems should be rebuilt to ensure that all of the potential bad mojo has been released by carrying out a proper exorcism.

Reporting

Though we discuss reporting at this point in order to remain consistent with the incident response process that (ISC)² identifies, incident reporting and documentation occurs at various stages in the response process. In many cases involving sophisticated attackers, the IR team first learns of the incident because someone else reports it. Whether it is an internal user, an external client or partner, or even a government entity, this initial report becomes the starting point of the entire process. In more mundane cases, we become aware that something is amiss thanks to a vigilant member of the security staff or one of the sensors deployed to detect attacks. However we learn of the incident, this first report starts what should be a continuous process of documentation.

According to NIST Special Publication 800-61, Revision 2, *Computer Security Incident Handling Guide*, the following information should be reported for each incident:

- Summary of the incident
- Indicators
- Related incidents
- Actions taken
- Chain of custody for all evidence (if applicable)
- Impact assessment
- Identity and comments of incident handlers
- Next steps to be taken

Recovery

Once the incident is mitigated, you must turn your attention to the recovery phase, in which the aim is to restore full, trustworthy functionality to the organization. It is one thing to restore an individual affected device, which is what we do in mitigation, and another to restore the functionality of business processes, which is the goal of recovery. For example, suppose you have a web service that provides business-to-business (B2B) logistic processes for your organization and your partner organizations. The incident to which you're responding affected the database and, after several hours of work, you mitigated that system and are ready to put it back online. In this recovery stage, you would certify the system as trustworthy and then integrate it back into the web service, thus restoring the business capability.

It is important to note that the recovery phase is characterized by significant testing to ensure the following:

- The affected system is really trustworthy
- The affected system is properly configured to support whatever business processes it did previously
- No compromises exist in those processes

The third characteristic of this phase is assured by close monitoring of all related systems to ensure that the compromise did not persist. Doing this during off-peak hours helps ensure that, should we discover anything else malicious, the impact to the organization is reduced.

Remediation

It is not enough to put the pieces of Humpty Dumpty back together again. You also need to ensure that the attack is never again successful. In the remediation phase, which can (and should) run concurrently with the other phases, you decide which security controls (e.g., updates, configuration changes, firewall/IDS/IPS rules) need to be put in place or modified. There are two steps to this. First, you may have controls that are hastily put into effect because, even if they cause some other issues, their immediate benefit outweighs the risks. Later on, you should revisit those controls and decide which should be made permanent (i.e., through your change management process) and what others you may want to put in place.

NOTE For best results, the remediation phase should start right after detection and be conducted in parallel with the other phases.

Another aspect of remediation is the identification of indicators of attack (IOAs) that can be used in the future to detect this attack in real time (i.e., as it is happening) as well as indicators of compromise (IOCs), which tell you when an attack has been successful and your security has been compromised. Typical indicators of both attack and compromise include the following:

- Outbound traffic to a particular IP address or domain name
- Abnormal DNS query patterns
- Unusually large HTTP requests and/or responses
- DDoS traffic
- New registry entries (in Windows systems)

At the conclusion of the remediation phase, you have a high degree of confidence that this particular attack will never again be successful against your organization. Ideally, you should incorporate your IOAs and IOCs into the following lessons learned stage and share them with the community so that no other organization can be exploited in this manner. This kind of collaboration with partners (and even competitors) makes the adversary have to work harder.

EXAM TIP Mitigation, recovery, and remediation are conveniently arranged in alphabetical order. First you stop the threat, then you get back to business as usual, and then you ensure the threat is never again able to cause this incident.

Lessons Learned

Closure of an incident is determined by the nature or category of the incident, the desired incident response outcome (for example, business resumption or system restoration), and the team's success in determining the incident's source and root cause. Once you have

PART VII

determined that the incident is closed, it is a good idea to have a team briefing that includes all groups affected by the incident to answer the following questions:

- What happened?
- What did we learn?
- How can we do it better next time?

The team should review the incident and how it was handled and carry out a postmortem analysis. The information that comes out of this meeting should indicate what needs to go into the incident response process and documentation, with the goal of continuous improvement. Instituting a formal process for the briefing provides the team with the ability to start collecting data that can be used to track its performance metrics.

Incident Response Planning

Incident management is implemented through two documents: the incident management policy (IMP) and the incident response plan (IRP). As discussed in the previous section, the IMP establishes authorities and responsibilities across the entire organization. The IMP identifies the IR lead for the organization and describes what every staff member is required to do with regard to incidents. For example, the IMP describes how employees are to report suspected incidents, to whom the report should be directed, and how quickly it should be done.

The IRP gets into the details of what should be done when responding to suspected incidents. The key sections of the IRP cover roles and responsibilities, incident classification, notifications, and operational tasks, all of which are described in the sections that follow. Normally, the IRP does not include detailed procedures for responding to specific incidents (e.g., phishing, data leak, ransomware), but establishes the framework within which all incidents will be addressed. Specific procedures are usually documented in *runbooks*, which are step-by-step scripts developed to deal with incidents that are either common enough or damaging enough to require this level of detailed documentation. Runbooks are described after the IRP sections.

Roles and Responsibilities

The group of individuals who make up the incident response team must have a variety of skills. They must also have a solid understanding of the systems affected by the incident, the system and application vulnerabilities, and the network and system configurations. Although formal education is important, real-world applied experience combined with proper training is key for these folks.

Many organizations divide their IR teams into two sub-teams. The first is the core team of incident responders, who come from the IT and security departments. These individuals are technologists who handle the routine incidents like restoring a workstation whose user inadvertently clicked the wrong link and caused self-infected damage. The second, or extended, team consists of individuals in other departments who are activated for more complex incidents. The extended team includes attorneys, public relations specialists, and human resources staff (to name a few). The exact makeup of this extended team will vary based on the specifics of the incident, but the point is that these are individuals whose day-to-day duties don't involve IT or security, and yet they are essential to a good response. Table 22-1 shows some examples of the roles and responsibilities in these two teams.

Role	Responsibilities
Core IR Team	
Chief information security officer (CISO)	• Develops and maintains the IR plan • Communicates with senior organizational leadership • Directs security controls before and after incidents
Director of security operations	• Directs execution of the IR plan • Communicates with applicable law enforcement agencies • Declares security incidents
IR team lead	• Overall responsibility for the IR plan • Communicates with senior organizational leadership • Maintains repository of incident response lessons learned
Cybersecurity analyst	• Monitors and analyzes security events • Nominates events for escalation to security incidents • Performs additional analyses for IR team lead as required
IT support specialist	• Manages security platforms • Implements mitigation, recovery, and remediation measures as directed by the IR team lead
Threat intelligence analyst	• Provides intelligence products related to incidents • Maintains repository of incident facts to support future intelligence products
Extended IR Team	
Human resources manager	• Provides oversight for incident-related human resource requirements (e.g., employee relations, labor agreements)
Legal counsel	• Provides oversight for incident-related legal requirements (e.g., liability issues, requirement for law enforcement reporting/coordination) • Ensures evidence collected maintains its forensic value in the event the organization chooses to take legal action
Public relations	• Ensures communications during an incident protect the confidentiality of sensitive information • Prepares communications to stockholders and the press
Business unit lead	• Balances IR actions and business requirements • Ensures business unit support to the IR team

Table 22-1 IR Team Roles and Responsibilities

In addition to these two teams, most organizations rely on third parties when the requirements of the incident response exceed the organic capabilities of the organization. Unless you have an exceptionally well-resourced internal IR team, odds are that you'll need help at some point. The best course of action is to enter into an IR services agreement with a reputable provider *before* any incidents happen. By taking care of the contract and nondisclosure agreement (NDA) beforehand, the IR service provider will be able to jump right into action when time is of the essence. Another time-saving measure is to coordinate a familiarization visit with your IR provider. This will allow the folks who may one day come to your aid to become familiar with your organization, infrastructure, policies, and procedures. They will also get a chance to meet your staff, so everyone learns everyone else's capabilities and limitations.

Incident Classification

The IR team should have a way to quickly determine whether the response to an incident requires that everyone be activated 24/7 or the response can take place during regular business hours over the next couple of days. There is, obviously, a lot of middle ground between these two approaches, but the point is that incident classification criteria should be established, understood by the whole team, and periodically reviewed to ensure that it remains relevant and effective.

There is no one-size-fits-all approach to developing an incident classification framework, but regardless of how you go about it, you should consider three incident dimensions:

- **Impact** If you have a risk management program in place, classifying an incident according to impact should be pretty simple since you've already determined the losses as part of your risk calculations. All you have to do is establish the thresholds that differentiate a bad day from a terrible one.
- **Urgency** The urgency dimension speaks to how quickly the incident needs to be mitigated. For example, an ongoing exfiltration of sensitive data needs to be dealt with immediately, whereas a scenario where a user caused self-infected damage with a bitcoin mining browser extension shouldn't require IR team members to get out of bed in the middle of the night.
- **Type** This dimension helps the team identify the resources that need to be notified and mobilized to deal with the incident. The team that handles the data exfiltration incident mentioned earlier is probably going to be different than the one that handles the infected browser.

Not all organizations explicitly call out each of these dimensions (and some organizations have more dimensions), but it is important to at least consider them. The simplest approach to incident classification simply uses severity and assigns various levels to this parameter depending on whether certain conditions are met. Table 22-2 shows a simple classification matrix for a small to medium-sized organization.

Severity	Criteria	Initial Response Time
Severity 1 (critical)	• Confirmed incident compromising mission-critical systems • Active exfiltration, alteration, or destruction of sensitive data • Incident requiring notification to government regulators • Life-threatening ongoing physical situation (e.g., suspicious package on site, unauthorized/hostile person, credible threat)	1 hour
Severity 2 (high)	• Confirmed incident compromising systems that are not mission-critical • Active exfiltration of non-sensitive data • Time-sensitive investigation of employees • Non-life-threatening but serious, ongoing physical situation (e.g., unauthorized person, theft of property)	4 hours
Severity 3 (moderate)	• Possible incident affecting any systems • Security policy violations • Long-term employee investigations requiring extensive collection and analysis • Non-life-threatening past physical situation (e.g., sensitive area left unsecured overnight)	48 hours

Table 22-2 Sample Incident Classification Matrix

The main advantage of formally classifying incidents is that it allows the preauthorized commitment of resources within specific timeframes. For example, if one of your SOC tier 2 analysts declares a severity 1 (critical) incident, she could be authorized to call the external IR service provider, committing the organization to pay the corresponding fees. There would be no need to get a hold of the CISO and get permission.

Notifications

Another benefit of classifying incidents is that it lets the IR team know who they need to inform and how frequently. Obviously, we don't want to call the CISO at home whenever an employee violates a security policy. On the other hand, we really don't want the CEO to find out the organization had an incident from reading the morning news. Keeping the right decision-makers informed at the right cadence enables everyone to do their jobs well, engenders trust, and leads to unified external messaging.

Table 22-3 shows an example notification matrix that builds on the classification shown previously in Table 22-2.

Notifications to external parties such as customers, partners, government regulators, and the press should be handled by communications professionals and not by the cybersecurity staff. The technical members of the IR team provide the facts to these communicators, who then craft messages (in coordination with the legal and marketing teams) that do not make things worse for the organization either legally or reputationally. Properly handled, IR communications can help improve trust and loyalty to the

Stakeholder	Severity Level	Notification
Executive leaders	S1	Immediate via e-mail and phone
	S2	On the next daily operational report
	S3	None
CISO	S1	Immediate via e-mail and phone
	S2	Within 4 hours via e-mail and phone
	S3	On the next daily operational report
Affected business units	S1	Immediate via e-mail and phone
	S2	Within 4 hours via e-mail
	S3	On the next daily operational report
Affected customers/partners	S1	Within 8 hours via e-mail
	S2	Within 72 hours via e-mail
	S3	None

Table 22-3 Sample Incident Notification Matrix

organization. Improperly handled, however, these notifications (or the lack thereof) can ruin (and have ruined) organizations.

Operational Tasks

Keeping stakeholders informed is just one of the many tasks involved in incident response. Just like any other complex endeavor, we should leverage structured approaches to ensure that all required tasks are performed, and that they are done consistently and in the right order. Now, of course, different types of incidents require different procedures. Responding to a ransomware attack requires different procedures than the procedures for responding to a malicious insider trying to steal company secrets. Still, all incidents follow a very similar pattern at a high level. We already saw this in the discussion of the seven phases in the incident management process that you need to know for the CISSP exam, which apply to all incidents.

Many organizations deal with the need for completeness and consistency in IR by spelling out operational tasks in the IRP, sometimes with a field next to each task to indicate when the task was completed. The IR team lead can then just walk down this list to ensure the right things are being done in the right order. Table 22-4 shows a sample operational tasks checklist.

Table 22-4 is not meant to be all-inclusive but it does capture the most common tasks that apply to every IR in most organizations. As mentioned earlier, different types of incidents require different approaches. While the task list should be general enough to accommodate these specialized procedures, we also want to keep it specific enough to serve as an overall execution plan.

Operational Task	Date/Time Completed
Pre-Execution	
Identify assets affected	
Obtain access (physical and logical) to all affected assets	
Determine forensic evidence requirements	
Review compliance requirements (e.g., GDPR, HIPAA, PCI DSS)	
Initiate communications plan	
Response	
Perform immediate actions to mitigate the impact of the incident	
Validate detection mechanisms	
Request relevant intelligence from threat intelligence team	
Gather and preserve incident-related data (e.g., PCAP, log files)	
Develop an initial timeline of incident-related activity	
Develop mitigation plan based on initial assessment	
Mitigation	
Verify availability of backup/redundant system (if mission-critical system was compromised)	
Activate backup/redundant systems for continuity of operations (if mission-critical system was compromised)	
Isolate affected assets	
Collect forensic evidence from compromised systems (if applicable)	
Remove active threat mechanisms to limit further activity	
Initiate focused monitoring of the environment for additional activity	
Recovery	
Restore affected systems' known-good backups or gold masters	
Validate additional controls on restored systems prevent reoccurrence	
Reconnect restored systems to production networks	
Verify no additional threat activity exists on restored systems	
Remediation	
Finalize root cause, threat mechanisms, and incident timeline	
Identify IOCs and IOAs	
Initiate change management processes to prevent reoccurrence	
Implement preventive and detective controls to prevent reoccurrence	

Table 22-4 Sample Operational Tasks List

Runbooks

When we need specialized procedures, particularly when we expect a certain type of incident to happen more than once, we want to document those procedures to ensure we don't keep reinventing the wheel every time a threat actor gets into our systems. A *runbook* is a collection of procedures that the IR team will follow for specific types of incidents. Think of a runbook as a cookbook. If you feel like having a bean casserole for dinner, you open your cookbook and look up that recipe. It'll tell you what ingredients you need and what the step-by-step procedure is to make it. Similarly, a runbook has tabs for the most likely and/or most dangerous incidents you may encounter. Once the incident is declared by the SOC (or whoever is authorized to declare an incident has occurred), the IR team lead opens the runbook and looks up the type of incident that was declared. The runbook specifies what resources are needed (e.g., specific roles and tools) and how to apply them.

When developing runbooks, you have to be careful that the documentation doesn't take more time and resources to develop than you would end up investing in responding to that incident type. As with any other control, the cost of a runbook cannot exceed the cost of doing nothing (and figuring things out on the fly). For that reason, most organizations focus their runbooks on incidents that require complex responses and those that are particularly sensitive. Other incidents can be (and usually are) added to the runbook, but those additions are deliberate decisions of the SOC manager based on the needs of the organization. For example, if an organization experiences high turnover rates, it might be helpful for new staff to have a more comprehensive runbook to which they can turn.

Another aspect to consider is that runbooks are only good if they are correct, complete, and up to date. Even if you do a great job when you first write runbooks, you'll have to invest time periodically in keeping them updated. For best results, incorporate runbooks into your change management program so that, whenever an organizational change is made, the change advisory board (CAB) asks the question: does this require an update to the IR runbooks?

Investigations

Whatever type of security incident we're facing, we should treat the systems and facilities that it affects as potential crime scenes. The reason is that what may at first appear to have been a hardware failure, a software defect, or an accidental fire may have in fact been caused by a malicious actor targeting the organization. Even acts of nature like storms or earthquakes may provide opportunities for adversaries to victimize us. Because we are never (initially) quite sure whether an incident may have a criminal element, we should treat all incidents as if they do (until proven otherwise).

Since computer crimes are only increasing and will never really go away, it is important that all security professionals understand how computer investigations should be carried out. This includes understanding legal requirements for specific situations, the chain of custody for evidence, what type of evidence is admissible in court, incident response procedures, and escalation processes.

Cops or No Cops?

Management needs to make the decision as to whether law enforcement should be called during an incident response. The following are some of the issues to understand if law enforcement is brought in:

- You may not have a choice in certain cases (e.g., cases involving national security, child pornography, etc.).
- Law enforcement agencies bring significant investigative capability.
- The organization may lose control over where the investigation leads once law enforcement is involved.
- Secrecy of compromise is not promised; it could become part of public record.
- Evidence will be collected and may not be available for a long period of time.

Successfully prosecuting a crime requires solid evidence. Computer forensics is the art of retrieving this evidence and preserving it in the proper ways to make it admissible in court. Without proper computer forensics, few computer crimes could ever be properly and successfully presented in court. The most common reasons evidence is deemed inadmissible in court are lack of qualified staff handling it, lack of established procedures, poorly written policy, or a broken chain of custody.

When a potential computer crime takes place, it is critical that the investigation steps are carried out properly to ensure that the evidence will be admissible to the court (if the matter goes that far) and can stand up under the cross-examination and scrutiny that will take place. As a security professional, you should understand that an investigation is not just about potential evidence on a disk drive. The context matters during an investigation, including the people, network, connected internal and external systems, applicable laws and regulations, management's stance on how the investigation is to be carried out, and the skill set of whoever is carrying out the investigation. Messing up just one of these components could make your case inadmissible or at least damage it if it is brought to court.

Motive, Opportunity, and Means

Today's computer criminals are similar to their traditional counterparts. To understand the "why" in crime, it is necessary to understand the motive, opportunity, and means—or MOM. This is the same strategy used to determine the suspects in a traditional, non-computer crime.

Motive is the "who" and "why" of a crime. The motive may be induced by either internal or external conditions. A person may be driven by the excitement, challenge, and adrenaline rush of committing a crime, which would be an internal condition. Examples of external conditions might include financial trouble, a sick family member, or other dire straits. Understanding the motive for a crime is an important piece in figuring out who would engage in such an activity. For example, financially motivated attackers such as those behind ransomware want to get your money. In the case of ransomware purveyors, they realize that if they don't decrypt a victim's data after payment of the ransom, the word will get out and no other victims will pay the ransom. For this reason, most modern ransomware actors reliably turn over decryption keys upon payment. Some ransomware gangs even go the extra mile and set up customer service operations to help victims with payment and decryption issues.

Opportunity is the "where" and "when" of a crime. Opportunities usually arise when certain vulnerabilities or weaknesses are present. If an organization does not regularly patch systems (particularly public-facing ones), attackers have all types of opportunities within that network. If an organization does not perform access control, auditing, and supervision, employees may have many opportunities to embezzle funds and defraud the organization. Once a crime fighter finds out why a person would want to commit a crime (motive), she will look at what could allow the criminal to be successful (opportunity).

Means pertains to the abilities a criminal would need to be successful. Suppose a crime fighter was asked to investigate a case of fraud facilitated by a subtle but complex modification made to a software system within a financial institution. If the suspects were three people and two of them just had general computer knowledge, but the third one was a programmer and system analyst, the crime fighter would realize that this person is much likelier to have the means to commit this crime than the other two individuals.

Computer Criminal Behavior

Like traditional criminals, computer criminals have a specific *modus operandi* (*MO*, pronounced "em-oh"). In other words, each criminal typically uses a distinct method of operation to carry out their crime, and that method can be used to help identify them. The difference with computer crimes is that the investigator, obviously, must have knowledge of technology. For example, the MO of a particular computer criminal may include the use of specific tools or targeting specific systems or networks. The method usually involves repetitive signature behaviors, such as sending e-mail messages or programming syntax. Knowledge of the criminal's MO and signature behaviors can be useful throughout the investigative process. Law enforcement can use the information to identify other offenses by the same criminal, for example. The MO and signature behaviors can also provide information that is useful during interviews (conducted by authorized staff members or law enforcement agencies) and potentially a trial.

Psychological crime scene analysis (profiling) can also be conducted using the criminal's MO and signature behaviors. Profiling provides insight into the thought processes of the attacker and can be used to identify the attacker or, at the very least, the tool he used to conduct the crime.

Evidence Collection and Handling

Good evidence is the bedrock on which any sound investigation is built. When dealing with any incident that might end up in court, digital evidence must be handled in a careful fashion so that it can be admissible no matter what jurisdiction is prosecuting a defendant. Within the United States, the *Scientific Working Group on Digital Evidence (SWGDE)* aims to ensure consistency across the forensic community. The principles developed by SWGDE for the standardized recovery of computer-based evidence are governed by the following attributes:

- Consistency with all legal systems
- Allowance for the use of a common language
- Durability
- Ability to cross international and state boundaries
- Ability to instill confidence in the integrity of evidence
- Applicability to all forensic evidence
- Applicability at every level, including that of individual, agency, and country

The international standard on digital evidence handling is ISO/IEC 27037: *Guidelines for Identification, Collection, Acquisition, and Preservation of Digital Evidence*. This document identifies four phases of digital evidence handling, which are identification, collection, acquisition, and preservation. Let's take a closer look at each.

NOTE You must ensure that you have the legal authority to search for and seize digital evidence before you do so. If in doubt, consult your legal counsel.

Identification

The first phase of digital evidence handling is to identify the digital crime scene. Rarely does only one device comprise the scene of the crime. More often than not, digital evidence exists on a multitude of other devices such as routers, network appliances, cloud services infrastructure, smartphones, and even IoT devices. Whether or not you have to secure a court order to seize evidence, you want to be very deliberate about determining what you think you need to collect and where it might exist.

When you arrive at the crime scene (whether it be physical or virtual), you want to carefully document everything you see and do. If you're dealing with a physical crime scene, photograph it from every possible angle before you touch anything. Label wires and cables and then snap a photo of the labeled system before it is disassembled. Remember that you want to instill confidence in the integrity of evidence and how it was handled from the very onset.

Identifying evidence items at a crime scene may not be straightforward. You could discover wireless networks that would allow someone to remotely tamper with the evidence. This would require you to consider ways to isolate the evidence from radio frequency (RF) signals in order to control the crime scene. There may also be evidence in devices (e.g., thumb drives) that are hidden either deliberately or unintentionally. Law enforcement agents sometimes resort to using specially trained dogs that can sniff out

Controlling the Crime Scene

Whether the crime scene is physical or digital, it is important to control who comes in contact with the evidence of the crime to ensure its integrity. The following are just some of the steps that should take place to protect the crime scene:

- Only allow authorized individuals access to the scene. These individuals should have knowledge of basic crime scene analysis.
- Document who is at the crime scene. In court, the integrity of the evidence may be in question if too many people were milling around the crime scene.
- Document who were the last individuals to interact with the systems.
- If the crime scene does become contaminated, document it. The contamination may not negate the derived evidence, but it will make investigating the crime more challenging.

electronics. Thoroughness in identifying evidence is the most important consideration in this phase, and this may require you to think outside the box to ensure you don't miss or lose a critical evidentiary item.

Collection

Once you've identified the evidence you need, you can begin collecting it. Evidence collection is the process of gaining physical control over items that could potentially have evidentiary value. This is where you walk into someone's office and collect their computer, external hard drives, thumb drives, and so on. It is critical that you have the legal authority to do this and that you document what you take, where you take it from, and what its condition is at the time.

Each piece of evidence should be labeled in some way with the date, time, initials of the collector, and a case number if one has been assigned. The piece of evidence should then be placed in a container, which should be sealed (ideally with evidence tape) so that tampering can be detected. An example of the data that should be collected and displayed on each evidence container is shown in Figure 22-1.

After everything is properly labeled, a chain of custody log should be made for each container and an overall log should be made capturing all events. A *chain of custody* documents each person that has control of the evidence at every point in time. In large investigations, one person may collect evidence, another may transport it, and a third may store it. Keeping track of all these individuals' possession of the evidence is critical to proving in court that the evidence was not tampered with. It is not hard for a good defense attorney to get evidence dismissed from court because of improper handling. For this reason, the chain of custody should follow evidence through its entire life cycle, beginning with identification and ending with its destruction, permanent archiving, or return to owner.

EVIDENCE

Station/Section/Unit/Dept________________
Case number__________ Item#__________
Type of offense________________
Description of evidence________________

Suspect________________
Victim________________
Date and time of recovery________________
Location of recovery________________
Recovered by________________

CHAIN OF CUSTODY

Received from__________ By__________
Date__________ Time__________ A.M./P.M.
Received from__________ By__________
Date__________ Time__________ A.M./P.M.
Received from__________ By__________
Date__________ Time__________ A.M./P.M.
Received from__________ By__________
Date__________ Time__________ A.M./P.M.

WARNING: THIS IS A TAMPER EVIDENT SECURITY PACKAGE. ONCE SEALED, ANY ATTEMPT TO OPEN WILL RESULT IN OBVIOUS SIGNS OF TAMPERING.

Figure 22-1 Evidence container data

Evidence collection activities can get tricky depending on what is being searched for and where. For example, American citizens are protected by the Fourth Amendment against unlawful search and seizure, so law enforcement agencies must have probable cause and request a search warrant from a judge or court before conducting such a search. The actual search can take place only in the areas outlined by the warrant. The Fourth Amendment does not apply to actions by private citizens unless they are acting as police agents. So, for example, if Kristy's boss warned all employees that the management could remove files from their computers at any time, and her boss is not a police officer or acting as a police agent, she could not successfully claim that her Fourth Amendment rights were violated. Kristy's boss may have violated some specific privacy laws, but he did not violate Kristy's Fourth Amendment rights.

In some circumstances, a law enforcement agent is legally permitted to seize evidence that is not included in the search warrant, such as if the suspect tries to destroy the evidence. In other words, if there is an impending possibility that evidence might be destroyed, law enforcement may quickly seize the evidence to prevent its destruction.

This is referred to as *exigent circumstances*, and a judge will later decide whether the seizure was proper and legal before allowing the evidence to be admitted. For example, if a police officer had a search warrant that allowed him to search a suspect's living room but no other rooms and then he saw the suspect putting a removable drive in his pocket while standing in another room, the police officer could seize the drive even though it was outside the area covered under the search warrant.

EXAM TIP Always treat an investigation, regardless of type, as if it would ultimately end up in a courtroom.

Acquisition

In most corporate investigations involving digital evidence, the sort of Crime TV collection we just described will not take place unless law enforcement is involved. Instead, the IR team will probably be able to piece together a timeline of activities from various network resources and you may have to collect only a single laptop. In many cases you can probably acquire the evidence you need remotely without seizing any devices at all. Whatever the case, you ultimately need to get a hold of the data that will confirm or deny the claim that is being investigated, and you must do it in a forensically sound manner.

Acquisition means creating a forensic image of digital data for examination. Generally, speaking, there are two types of acquisition: physical and logical. In *digital acquisition*, the investigator makes a bit-for-bit copy of the contents of a physical storage device, bypassing the operating system. This includes all files, of course, but also free space and previously deleted data. In *logical acquisition*, on the other hand, the forensic image is of the files and folders in a file system, which means we rely on the operating system. This approach is sometimes necessary when dealing with evidence that exists in cloud services, where physical acquisition is normally not possible.

Before creating a forensic image, the investigator must have a medium onto which to copy the data, and ensure this medium has been properly purged, meaning it does not contain any preexisting data. (In some cases, hard drives that were thought to be new and right out of the box contained old data not purged by the vendor.) Two copies are normally created: a *primary image* (a control copy that is stored in a library) and a *working image* (used for analysis and evidence collection). To ensure that the original image is not modified, it is important to compute the cryptographic hashes (e.g., SHA-1) for files and directories before and after the analysis to prove the integrity of the original image.

The investigator works from the duplicate image because it preserves the original evidence, prevents inadvertent alteration of original evidence during examination, and allows re-creation of the duplicate image if necessary.

Acquiring evidence on live systems and those using network storage further complicates matters because you cannot turn off the system to make a copy of the hard drive. Imagine the reaction you'd receive if you were to tell an IT manager that you need to shut down a primary database or e-mail system. It wouldn't be favorable. So these systems and others, such as those using on-the-fly encryption, must be imaged while they are running.

In fact, some evidence is very volatile and can only be collected from a live system. Examples of volatile data that could have evidentiary value include

- Registers and cache
- Process tables and ARP cache
- System memory (RAM)
- Temporary file systems
- Special disk sectors

Preservation

To preserve evidence in a forensically sound manner, you must have established procedures based on legally accepted best practices, and your staff must follow those procedures to the letter. We've already covered two crucial steps in the chain of evidence and the use of hashes to verify that the evidence has not been altered. Another element of preserving digital evidence is ensuring that only a small group of qualified individuals have access to the evidence, and then only to perform specific functions. Again, this access needs to be part of your established procedures. In some cases, organizations implement two-person control of digital evidence to minimize the risk of tampering.

We introduced the topic of evidence storage in Chapter 10, but it bears pointing out that storage of media evidence should be dust-free and kept at room temperature without much humidity, and, of course, the media should not be stored close to any strong magnets or magnetic fields. Even if you don't have a dedicated evidence storage area, you should ensure that whatever space you commandeer is used strictly for this purpose, at least for the life of the investigation.

What Is Admissible in Court?

There are limits to what evidence can be introduced into a legal proceeding. Though the details will be different in each jurisdiction around the world, generally, digital evidence is admissible in court if it meets three criteria:

- **Relevance** Evidence must be relevant to the case, meaning it must help to prove facts being alleged. If a suspect is accused of murder, then a web search history for favorite vacationing spots is probably irrelevant. Judges typically rule on relevance of evidence.
- **Reliability** Evidence must be acquired using a sound forensic methodology that prevents alteration and ensures the evidence remains unaltered during the forensic examination. Multiple high-profile cases in recent years have had evidence rendered inadmissible because the chain of custody was broken.
- **Legality** The persons acquiring and presenting the evidence must have the legal authority to do so. If you have a court-issued search warrant, you must limit collection to whatever is spelled out in it. If you are conducting a workplace investigation, you must limit your collection to organization-owned assets, and only after legal counsel agrees.

The reliability of evidence is most often established by chains of custody and cryptographic hashing. But there is another element to reliability that excludes evidence deemed to be hearsay. *Hearsay evidence* is any statement made outside of the court proceeding that is offered into evidence to prove the truth of the matter asserted in the statement. Suppose that David is accused of fraud and Eliza tells Frank that David told her he was stealing from the company. Eliza's testimony in court would be admissible, but Frank normally wouldn't be allowed to testify about what Eliza claims to have heard because, coming from him, it would be considered hearsay.

Hearsay evidence can also include many computer-generated documents such as log files. In some countries, such as the United States, when computer logs are to be used as evidence in court, they must satisfy a legal exception to the hearsay rule of the Federal Rules of Evidence (FRE) called the business records exception rule or business entry rule. Under this rule, a party could admit any records of a business (1) that were made in the regular course of business; (2) that the business has a regular practice to make such records; (3) that were made at or near the time of the recorded event; and (4) that contain information transmitted by a person with knowledge of the information within the document.

It is important to show that the logs, and all evidence, have not been tampered with in any way, which is the reason for the chain of custody of evidence. Several tools are available that run checksums or hashing functions on the logs, which will allow the team to be alerted if something has been modified.

When evidence is being collected, one issue that can come up is the user's expectation of privacy. If an employee is suspected of, and charged with, a computer crime, he might claim that his files on the computer he uses are personal and not available to law enforcement and the courts. This is why it is important for organizations to conduct security awareness training, have employees sign documentation pertaining to the acceptable use of the organization's computers and equipment, and have legal banners pop up on every employee's computer when they log on. These are key elements in establishing that a user has no right to privacy when he is using organization equipment. The following banner is suggested by CERT Advisory:

> *This system is for the use of authorized users only. Individuals using this computer system without authority, or in excess of their authority, are subject to having all of their activities on this system monitored and recorded by system personnel.*
>
> *In the course of monitoring an individual improperly using this system, or in the course of system maintenance, the activities of authorized users may also be monitored.*
>
> *Anyone using this system expressly consents to such monitoring and is advised that if such monitoring reveals possible evidence of criminal activity, system personnel may provide the evidence of such monitoring to law enforcement officials.*

This explicit warning strengthens a legal case that can be brought against an employee or intruder, because the continued use of the system after viewing this type of warning implies that the person acknowledges the security policy and gives permission to be monitored.

NOTE Don't dismiss the possibility that as an information security professional you will be responsible for entering evidence into court. Most tribunals, commissions, and other quasi-legal proceedings have admissibility requirements. Because these requirements can change between jurisdictions, you should seek legal counsel to better understand the specific rules for your jurisdiction.

Digital Forensics Tools, Tactics, and Procedures

Digital forensics is a science and an art that requires specialized techniques for the recovery, authentication, and analysis of electronic data for the purposes of a digital criminal investigation. It is a fusion of computer science, IT, engineering, and law. When discussing computer forensics with others, you might hear the terms computer forensics, network forensics, electronic data discovery, cyberforensics, and forensic computing.

Forensics Field Kits

When a forensics team is deployed, the forensic investigators should be properly equipped with all the tools and supplies that they'll need to conduct the investigation. The following are some of the common items in forensics field kits:

- **Documentation tools** Tags, labels, forms, and written procedures
- **Disassembly and removal tools** Antistatic bands, pliers, tweezers, screwdrivers, wire cutters, and so on
- **Package and transport supplies** Antistatic bags, evidence bags and tape, cable ties, and others
- **Cables and adapters** Enough to connect to every physical interface you may come across

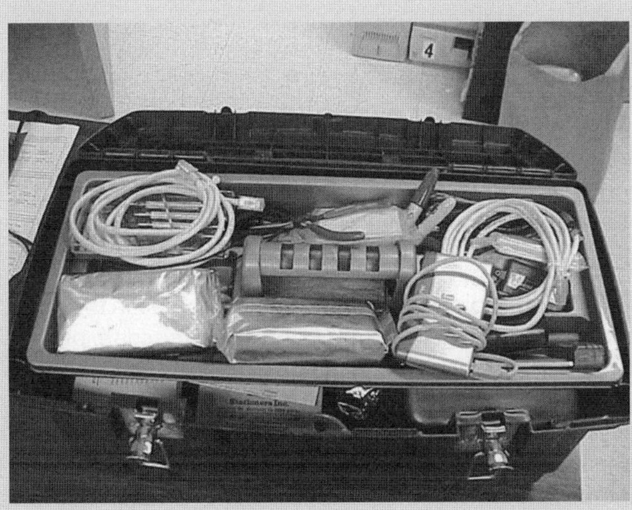

(ISC)^2 uses *digital forensics* as a synonym for all of these other terms, so that's what you'll see on the CISSP exam.

Anyone who conducts a forensic investigation must be properly skilled in this trade and know what to look for. If someone reboots the attacked system or inspects various files, this could corrupt viable evidence, change timestamps on key files, and erase footprints the criminal may have left. Most digital evidence has a short lifespan and must be collected quickly and in the *order of volatility*. In other words, the most volatile or fragile evidence should be collected first. In some situations, it is best to remove the system from the network, dump the contents of the memory, power down the system, and make a sound image of the attacked system and perform forensic analysis on this copy. Working on the copy instead of the original drive ensures that the evidence stays unharmed on the original system in case some steps in the investigation actually corrupt or destroy data. Dumping the memory contents to a file before doing any work on the system or powering it down is a crucial step because of the information that could be stored there. This is another method of capturing fragile information. However, this creates a sticky situation: capturing RAM or conducting live analysis can introduce changes to the crime scene because various state changes and operations take place. Whatever method the forensic investigator chooses to use to collect digital evidence, that method must be documented. This is the most important aspect of evidence handling.

Forensic Investigation Techniques

To ensure that forensic investigations are carried out in a standardized manner and the evidence collected is admissible, it is necessary for the investigative team to follow specific laid-out steps so that nothing is missed. Figure 22-2 illustrates the phases through a common investigation process and lists various techniques that fall under each phase. Each team or organization may come up with its own steps, but all should be essentially accomplishing the same things:

- Identification
- Preservation
- Collection
- Examination
- Analysis
- Presentation
- Decision

NOTE The principles of criminalistics are included in the forensic investigation process. They are identification of the crime scene, protection of the environment against contamination and loss of evidence, identification of evidence and potential sources of evidence, and the collection of evidence. In regard to minimizing the degree of contamination, it is important to understand that it is impossible not to change a crime scene—be it physical or digital. The key is to minimize changes and document what you did and why, and how the crime scene was affected.

Identification	Preservation	Collection	Examination	Analysis	Presentation
Event/crime detection	Case management	Preservation	Preservation	Preservation	Documentation
Resolve signature	Imaging technologies	Approved methods	Traceability	Traceability	Expert testimony
Profile detection	Chain of custody	Approved software	Validation techniques	Statistical	Clarification
Anomalous detection	Time synchronization	Approved hardware	Filtering techniques	Protocols	Mission impact statement
Complaints		Legal authority	Pattern matching	Data mining	Recommended countermeasure
System monitoring		Lossless compression	Hidden data discovery	Timeline	Statistical interpretation
Audit analysis		Sampling	Hidden data extraction	Link	
		Data reduction		Spatial	
		Recovery techniques			

Figure 22-2 Characteristics of the different phases through an investigation process

During the examination and analysis process of a forensic investigation, it is critical that the investigator work from an image that contains *all* of the data from the original disk. It should be a bit-level copy, sector by sector, to capture deleted files, slack spaces, and unallocated clusters. These types of images can be created through the use of a specialized tool such as Forensic Toolkit (FTK), EnCase Forensic, or the dd Unix utility. A file copy tool does not recover all data areas of the device necessary for examination. Figure 22-3 illustrates a commonly used tool in the forensic world for evidence collection.

The next step is the analysis of the evidence. Forensic investigators use a scientific method that involves

- Determining the characteristics of the evidence, such as whether it's admissible as primary or secondary evidence, as well as its source, reliability, and permanence
- Comparing evidence from different sources to determine a chronology of events
- Event reconstruction, including the recovery of deleted files and other activity on the system

This can take place in a controlled lab environment or, thanks to hardware write-blockers and forensic software, in the field. When investigators analyze evidence in a lab, they are dealing with "dead forensics"; that is, they are working only with static data. Live forensics, which takes place in the field, includes volatile data. If evidence is lacking, then an experienced investigator should be called in to help complete the picture.

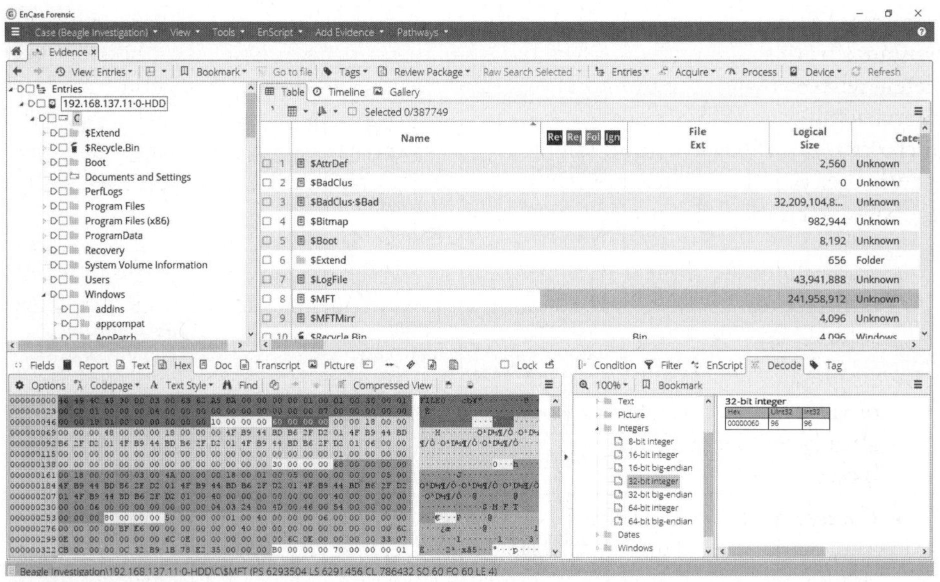

Figure 22-3 EnCase Forensic can be used to collect digital forensic data.

Finally, the interpretation of the analysis should be presented to the appropriate party. This could be a judge, lawyer, CEO, or board of directors. Therefore, it is important to present the findings in a format that will be understood by a nontechnical audience. As a CISSP, you should be able to explain these findings in layperson's terms using metaphors and analogies. Of course, the findings, which are top secret or company confidential, should be disclosed only to authorized parties. This may include the legal department or any outside counsel that assists with the investigation.

Other Investigative Techniques

Unless you work for a law enforcement agency, most of the investigations in which you will be involved are likely to focus on digital forensics investigative techniques. These techniques are applied when a device was compromised, or a malicious insider attempted to steal sensitive files, or something like that. All the evidence you need is probably in a device that you can get your hands on, so you can collect it, acquire it, analyze it, and get to the facts with just digital evidence. However, there may be other situations in which you'll need other types of evidence either in addition to or instead of 1's and 0's copied from some storage device. Interviews, surveillance, and undercover investigative techniques are some of the practices for acquiring evidence that you should be familiar with.

Interviews

Interviews can be effective for ascertaining facts when you have willing interviewees. Interviewing is both an art and a science, and the specific techniques you use will vary from case to case. Typically, interviews are conducted by a business unit manager with assistance from the human resources and legal departments. This doesn't, however, completely relieve you as an information security professional from responsibility during the interviewing process. You may be asked to provide input or observe an interview in order to clarify technical information that comes up in the course of questioning.

Whether you are conducting an interview or your technical assistance is needed for an interview, keep the following best practices in mind:

- *Have a plan.* Without a plan, the interview will be ineffective. Prepare an outline beforehand that focuses on getting the information you need from each interviewee. However, you should remain flexible and not read off a script.
- *Be fair and objective.* If you are conducting an interview, it is to get to the facts of an incident, not necessarily to reinforce whatever conclusions you may have already reached. Keep an open mind, focus on the facts, and try to avoid any biases.
- *Compartmentalize information.* Your interview plan should address what information you share with each interviewee, and what you don't share. You should not tell one interviewee what another said unless it's absolutely essential and legally permissible.
- *One interviewee at a time.* Interviewing multiple individuals together can introduce problematic group dynamics such as peer pressure. It can also lead interviewees to distort or suppress information.
- *Do not record the interview.* Recording devices can have a chilling effect on interviewees. Instead, have at least one notetaker in the room and, after the interview is complete, read back the notes to the interviewee to ensure their accuracy. If you must record the interview, ensure you comply with all applicable legal requirements (e.g., consent of all parties).
- *Keep it confidential.* Do your best to keep every aspect of the investigation under wraps. Even the fact that someone is being interviewed about an incident can have a damaging reputational effect for that person.

The employee interviewer should be in a position that is senior to the employee subject. A vice president is not going to be very intimidated or willing to spill his guts to the mailroom clerk. The interview should be held in a private place, in an environment conducive to making the subject relatively comfortable and at ease. If exhibits are going to be shown to the subject, they should be shown one at a time, and otherwise kept in a folder. It is not necessary to read a person their rights before the interview unless it is performed by law enforcement officers.

Surveillance

Two main types of surveillance are used when it comes to identifying computer crimes: physical surveillance and computer surveillance. *Physical surveillance* pertains to security cameras, security guards, and closed-circuit TV (CCTV), which may capture evidence.

Physical surveillance can also be used by an undercover agent to learn about the suspect's spending activities, family and friends, and personal habits in the hope of gathering more clues for the case.

Computer surveillance pertains to passively monitoring (auditing) events by using network sniffers, keyboard monitors, wiretaps, and line monitoring. In most jurisdictions, active monitoring may require a search warrant. In most workplace environments, to legally monitor an individual, the person must be warned ahead of time that her activities may be subject to this type of monitoring.

Undercover

Undercover investigative techniques are pretty rare in most corporate investigations, but can provide information and evidence that would be difficult to acquire otherwise. The goal of undercover work is to assume an identity that allows the investigator to blend into the suspect's environment to observe, and perhaps record, the suspect's actions.

A thin line exists between enticement and entrapment when it comes to capturing a suspect's actions. *Enticement* is legal and ethical, whereas *entrapment* is neither legal nor ethical. In the world of computer crimes, a honeypot is a good example to explain the difference between enticement and entrapment. Organizations put systems in their screened subnets that either emulate services that attackers usually like to take advantage of or actually have the services enabled. The hope is that if an attacker breaks into the organization's network, she will go right to the honeypot instead of the systems that are actual production machines. The attacker will be *enticed* to go to the honeypot system because it has many open ports and services running and exhibits vulnerabilities that the attacker would want to exploit. The organization can log the attacker's actions and later attempt to prosecute.

The action in the preceding example is legal unless the organization crosses the line to entrapment. For example, suppose a web page has a link that indicates that if an individual clicks it, she could then download thousands of MP3 files for free. However, when she clicks that link, she is taken to the honeypot system instead, and the organization records all of her actions and attempts to prosecute. Entrapment does not prove that the suspect had the intent to commit a crime; it only proves she was successfully tricked.

Forensic Artifacts

One of the grandfathers of forensic science, Dr. Edmond Locard, famously stated that "every contact leaves a trace." This principle, known as Locard's exchange principle, states that criminals always leave something behind at the crime scene. This fragmentary or trace evidence is a *forensic artifact*. A forensic artifact is anything that has evidentiary value. On a typical computer, the following are examples of forensic artifacts:

- Deleted items (in the recycle bin or trash)
- Web browser search history
- Web browser cache files
- E-mail attachments

- Skype history
- Windows event logs
- Prefetch files

Forensic artifacts can also be evidentiary items relating to network traffic. Network forensics is a subdiscipline that is focused on what happened on the network rather than on the endpoints. The tools used in network forensics are unique to that subdiscipline, and so are the artifacts for which the investigator looks. Tools used in network forensics include NDR solutions, SIEM systems, and the log files of any network device or server. They also include network sniffers that can capture full network frames. The following are some of the more useful network artifacts an investigator would be interested in:

- DNS log records
- Web proxy log records
- IDS/IPS alerts
- Packet capture (pcap) files

Finally, with the proliferation of mobile devices such as smartphones, tablets, and smartwatches, we must not overlook forensic artifacts stored on them. Unlike traditional computers, mobile devices are usually carried by their users around the clock. This means mobile devices tend to document multiple aspects of a person's life, some of which can serve as evidence of criminal activity.

Though mobile devices can be a treasure trove of information for the forensic investigator, they are not always easy to acquire and analyze. For starters, there are so many different models that no single tool can acquire all evidence from all devices. Staff expertise is similarly challenged by this diversity, because an investigator who is skilled at iPhone analysis may not be able to operate at the same level given an Android device. Just to make things more interesting, there is also the issue of encryption, which is prevalent in mobile devices these days.

Still, if forensic investigators can overcome these challenges, mobile devices are excellent sources of evidence for a variety of criminal activity. Among the most useful forensic artifacts found in them are

- Call logs
- SMS messages
- E-mail messages
- Web browser history

Reporting and Documenting

We already covered reporting in a fair amount of detail in Chapter 19. When it comes to investigations, however, there are some additional issues to consider. First and foremost, the need to document *everything* you do cannot be overstated. If you cannot account for or explain the why of any activities you undertook, it may render evidence inadmissible in court or even undermine the whole case. For this reason, many organizations assign investigators to work in teams of two, where one person documents while the other conducts the investigation. Most forensic analysis tools have a feature that automatically logs everything an investigator does with the tool.

Another issue that is particularly important in writing investigation reports is the need to remain completely logical and factual. Any conclusions you reach must follow logically from a sequence of facts that you spell out for the reader. For example, suppose that Carlos is one of your staff and is suspected of sending sensitive files to a competitor in hopes of landing a lucrative job with them. Even if you are sure he did it (after examining his computer), you should not just jump out and say so. Instead, you show how the forensic artifacts that you found, when arrayed on a timeline, substantiate the claim that Carlos sent sensitive files to a competitor. You'd start by establishing that he was logged into his computer, and then he logged into his personal e-mail account through a webmail interface, and then an e-mail was sent containing sensitive files x, y, and z, and then the e-mail was deleted from his sent items, and so on. It is ultimately up to the reader (presumably a senior manager or court official) to determine guilt or innocence. Your job is to establish the facts and determine whether or not they are consistent with the allegation.

Chapter Review

Incident management is a critical function for any organization. Odds are that if you are among the lucky few who haven't had a major incident yet, you will be faced with one in the near future. In fact, the IronNet 2021 Cybersecurity Impact Report found that 86 percent of respondents had a cybersecurity incident so severe in the previous year that it required a C-level or board meeting. Even if you've outsourced IR to a third-party service provider, you still need to have an incident management policy and an IR plan to guide the conduct of the entire organization before, during, and after an incident. The policy establishes authorities and responsibilities, while the plan specifies the procedures to be followed.

The other major topic we discussed in this chapter is investigations. Thankfully, the need to conduct investigations is fairly rare in most organizations. But therein lies the problem: if you hardly ever need to recall knowledge or practice skills, you are certain to lose them. This is why having detailed standard procedures for investigative work is absolutely essential. For example, evidence acquisition, as we saw, is a complex process that has very little room for errors, particularly if the evidence will end up in court (and we should always assume it will).

Quick Review

- A security event is any occurrence that can be observed, verified, and documented, whereas a security incident is one or more related events that negatively affect the organization and/or impact its security posture.

- A good incident response team should consist of representatives from various business units, such as the legal department, HR, executive management, the communications department, physical/corporate security, IS security, and information technology.
- Incident management encompasses seven phases according to the CISSP CBK: detection, response, mitigation, reporting, recovery, remediation, and lessons learned.
- The detection phase encompasses the search for indicators that an event has occurred and the formal declaration of the event.
- The response phase entails the initial actions undertaken to contain the damage caused by a security incident.
- The goal of the mitigation phase is to eradicate the threat actor from the affected systems.
- Incident reporting occurs at various phases of incident management.
- The aim of the recovery phase is to restore full, trustworthy functionality to the organization.
- In the remediation phase, the incident response team decides which security controls need to be deployed or changed to prevent the incident from recurring.
- The lessons learned phase is important to determine what needs to go into the incident response process and documentation, with the goal of continuous improvement.
- The incident management policy (IMP) establishes authorities and responsibilities across the entire organization, identifies the incident response (IR) lead for the organization, and describes what every staff member is required to do with regard to incidents.
- The incident response plan (IRP) gets into the details of what should be done when responding to suspected incidents, and includes roles and responsibilities, incident classification, notifications, and operational tasks.
- Incident classification criteria allow the organization to prioritize IR assets and usually consider the impact and type of the incident, and urgency with which the response must be started.
- A runbook is a collection of procedures that the IR team will follow for specific types of incidents.
- The four phases of evidence handling are identification, collection, acquisition, and preservation.
- Evidence collection is the process of gaining physical control over devices that could potentially have evidentiary value.
- A chain of custody documents each person that has control of the evidence at every point in time.
- Acquisition means creating a forensic image of digital data for examination.

- Evidence preservation requires maintaining a chain of custody and cryptographic hashes of all digital evidence, and also controlling access to the evidence.
- To be admissible in court, evidence must be relevant, reliable, and legally obtained.
- To be admissible in court, business records such as computer logs have to be made and collected in the normal course of business, not specially generated for a case in court. Business records can easily be deemed hearsay if there is no firsthand proof of their accuracy and reliability.
- Digital forensics is a science and an art that requires specialized techniques for the recovery, authentication, and analysis of electronic data for the purposes of a digital criminal investigation.
- In addition to forensic techniques, organizations sometimes use interviews, surveillance, and undercover investigation techniques.
- When looking for suspects, it is important to consider the motive, opportunity, and means (MOM).
- A forensic artifact is anything that has evidentiary value.

Questions

Please remember that these questions are formatted and asked in a certain way for a reason. Keep in mind that the CISSP exam is asking questions at a conceptual level. Questions may not always have the perfect answer, and the candidate is advised against always looking for the perfect answer. Instead, the candidate should look for the best answer in the list.

1. What are the phases of incident management?

  A. Identification, collection, acquisition, and preservation

  B. Detection, response, mitigation, reporting, recovery, remediation, and lessons learned

  C. Protection, containment, response, remediation, and reporting

  D. Analysis, classification, incident declaration, containment, eradication, and investigation

2. During which phase of incident management does the IR team contain the damage caused by a security incident?

  A. Preservation

  B. Response

  C. Eradication

  D. Remediation

3. During which phase of incident management are security controls deployed or changed to prevent the incident from recurring?
   A. Preservation
   B. Response
   C. Eradication
   D. Remediation
4. Which document establishes authorities and responsibilities with regard to incidents across the entire organization?
   A. Incident management policy
   B. Incident response plan
   C. Incident response runbook
   D. Incident classification criteria
5. After a computer forensic investigator seizes a computer during a crime investigation, what is the next step?
   A. Label and put it into a container, and then label the container
   B. Dust the evidence for fingerprints
   C. Make an image copy of the disks
   D. Lock the evidence in the safe
6. Which of the following is a necessary characteristic of evidence for it to be admissible?
   A. It must be real.
   B. It must be noteworthy.
   C. It must be reliable.
   D. It must be important.
7. Which of the following is *not* considered a best practice when interviewing willing witnesses?
   A. Compartmentalize information
   B. Interview one interviewee at a time
   C. Be fair and objective
   D. Record the interview

Use the following scenario to answer Questions 8–10. You recently improved your organization's security posture, which now includes a fully staffed security operations center (SOC), network detection and response (NDR) and endpoint detection and response (EDR) systems, centrally managed updates and data backups, and network segmentation using VLANs. It's the end of the workday and just as you are getting ready to go home your SOC detects a ransomware infection affecting at least two workstations in your marketing department. The SOC manager declares an incident and activates the IR team.

8. What should be your IR team's first action?
   A. Determine the scope of the infection across the organization
   B. Isolate the marketing VLAN from the rest of the network
   C. Disconnect the infected computers from the network
   D. Determine why the EDR system failed to protect the workstations
9. Using your NDR system, you determine the external hosts from which the malware was downloaded and with which the infected systems were communicating. As part of the remediation phase, which of the following is the next best action to take with this information?
   A. Determine whether the external hosts you identified are related to the incident
   B. Block traffic to/from the external hosts that you identified
   C. Visit the remote hosts using a forensic workstation to acquire evidence
   D. Share the address of the hosts with your partners as indicators of compromise (IOCs)
10. Luckily, this version of ransomware is buggy, and you find a security researcher's blog with detailed instructions for how to decrypt infected systems. Which of the following approaches will best mitigate the incident and make the affected systems operational again?
   A. Follow the directions to decrypt the systems and remove the malware
   B. Reinstall from a golden master and restore the data from backups
   C. Reinstall from a golden master even though you have no backups
   D. Restore the systems from the last known-good system backup

Answers

1. **B.** Incident management encompasses seven phases according to the CISSP CBK: detection, response, mitigation, reporting, recovery, remediation, and lessons learned.
2. **B.** The goal of containment during the response phase is to prevent or reduce any further damage from this incident so that you can begin to mitigate and recover. Done properly, this buys the IR team time for a proper investigation and determination of the incident's root cause.
3. **D.** In the remediation phase, you decide which control changes (e.g., firewall or IDS/IPS rules) are needed to preclude this incident from happening again. Another aspect of remediation is the identification of indicators of attack (IOAs)

that can be used in the future to detect this attack in real time (i.e., as it is happening) as well as indicators of compromise (IOCs), which tell you when an attack has been successful and your security has been compromised.

4. **A.** The incident management policy (IMP) establishes authorities and responsibilities across the entire organization, identifies the incident response (IR) lead for the organization, and describes what every staff member is required to do with regard to incidents. The incident response plan (IRP) gets into the details of what should be done when responding to suspected incidents, and includes roles and responsibilities, incident classification, notifications, and operational tasks. A runbook is a collection of procedures that the IR team will follow for specific types of incidents.
5. **C.** Several steps need to be followed when gathering and extracting evidence from a scene. Once a computer has been confiscated, the first thing the computer forensics team should do is make an image of the hard drive. The team will work from this image instead of the original hard drive so that the original stays in a pristine state and the evidence on the drive is not accidentally corrupted or modified.
6. **C.** For evidence to be admissible, it must be relevant to the case, reliable, and legally obtained. For evidence to be reliable, it must be consistent with fact and must not be based on opinion or be circumstantial.
7. **D.** Recording devices can have a chilling effect on interviewees. Instead, have at least one notetaker in the room and, after the interview is complete, read back the notes to the interviewee to ensure their accuracy.
8. **B.** Having detected the incident, the next step is to respond by containing the damage that has been or is about to be done to your most critical assets. You could simply disconnect the infected systems from the network, but since there are multiple workstations and they are in the same department, it is probably better to isolate that entire VLAN until you can determine the true scope of the problem. Since this incident happened at the end of the workday, isolating the VLAN should have little or no impact on the marketing department.
9. **B.** In the remediation phase, you decide which security controls need to be put in place to prevent the attack from succeeding again. This includes controls that are hastily put into effect because you have high confidence that they will help in the short term. The situation in the question is a perfect example of when you bypass your change management process and quickly make changes to deal with the incident at hand. You probably want to share the IOCs with your partners (and perhaps your regional CERT), but that happens after you block the traffic.
10. **B.** You have a centralized backup system that was not affected, so you know you should have backups for all the workstations. The problem is that you may not know if any of the full-system backups also include the ransomware, so restoring systems from backups could bring you back to square one. It is best to reinstall the systems from golden masters and then restore only the data files. This process may take a bit longer, but it minimizes the risk of reinfection.

CHAPTER 23

Disasters

This chapter presents the following:

- Recovery strategies
- Disaster recovery processes
- Testing disaster recovery plans
- Business continuity

It wasn't raining when Noah built the ark.

—Howard Ruff

Disasters are just regular features in our collective lives. Odds are that, at some point, we will all have to deal with at least one disaster (if not more), whether it be in our personal world or professional world. And when that disaster hits, figuring out a way to deal with it in real time is probably not going to go all that well for the unprepared. This chapter is all about thinking of all the terrible things that might happen, and then ensuring we have strategies and plans to deal with them. This doesn't just mean recovering from the disaster, but also ensuring that the business continues to operate with as little disruption as possible.

As the old adage goes, no battle plan ever survived first contact with the enemy, which is the reason why we must test and exercise plans until our responses as individuals and organizations are so ingrained in our brains that we no longer need to think about them. As terrible and complex disasters unfold around us, we will do the right things reflexively. Does that sound a bit ambitious? Perhaps. Still, it is our duty as cybersecurity professionals to do what we can to get our organizations as close to that goal as realistically possible. Let's see how we go about doing this.

Recovery Strategies

In the previous chapters in this part of the book, we have discussed preventing and responding to security incidents, including various types of investigations, as part of standard security operations. These are things we do day in and day out. But what happens on those rare occasions when an incident has disastrous effects? That is the realm of disaster recovery and business continuity planning. *Disaster recovery (DR)* is the set of practices that enables an organization to minimize loss of, and restore, mission-critical technology infrastructure after a catastrophic incident. *Business continuity (BC)* is the set of practices that enables an organization to continue performing its critical functions through and after any disruptive event. As you can see, DR is mostly in the purview of safety and contingency operations, while BC is much broader than that. Accordingly, we'll focus on DR for most of this chapter but circle back to our roles in BC as cybersecurity leaders.

EXAM TIP As CISSPs, we are responsible for disaster recovery because it deals mostly with information technology and security. We provide inputs and support for business continuity planning but normally are not the lead for it.

Before we go much further, recall that we discussed the role of *maximum tolerable downtime (MTD)* values in Chapter 2. In reality, basic MTD values are a good start, but are not granular enough for an organization to figure out what it needs to put into place to be able to absorb the impact of a disaster. MTD values are usually "broad strokes" that do not provide the details needed to pinpoint the actual recovery solutions that need to be purchased and implemented. For example, if the business continuity planning (BCP) team determines that the MTD value for the customer service department is 48 hours, this is not enough information to fully understand what redundant solutions or backup technology should be put into place. MTD in this example does provide a basic deadline that means if customer service is not up within 48 hours, the company may not be able to recover and everyone should start looking for new jobs.

As shown in Figure 23-1, more than just MTD metrics are needed to get production back to normal operations after a disruptive event. We will walk through each of these metric types and see how they are best used together.

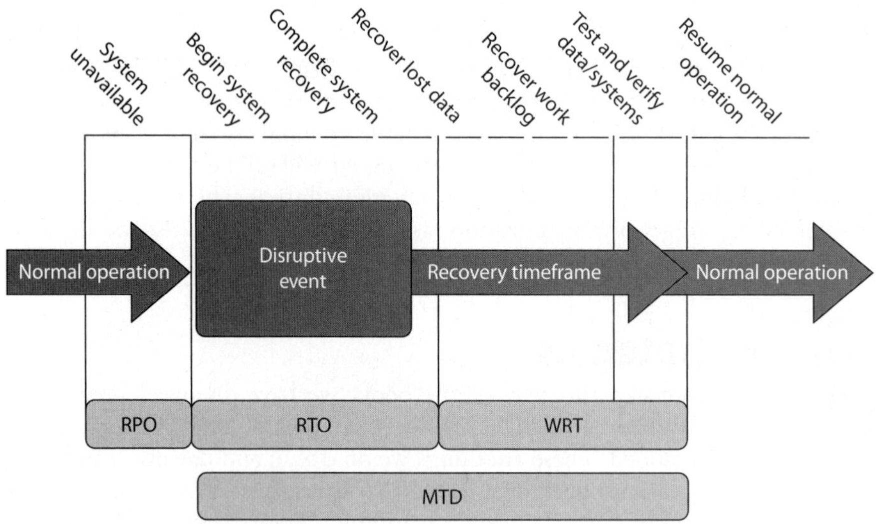

Figure 23-1 Metrics used for disaster recovery

The *recovery time objective (RTO)* is the maximum time period within which a mission-critical system must be restored to a designated service level after a disruption to avoid unacceptable consequences associated with a break in business continuity. The RTO value is smaller than the MTD value, because the MTD value represents the time after which an inability to recover significant operations will mean severe and perhaps irreparable damage to the organization's reputation or bottom line. The RTO assumes that there is a period of acceptable downtime. This means that an organization can be out of production for a certain period of time and still get back on its feet. But if the organization cannot get production up and running within the MTD window, it may be sinking too fast to properly recover.

The *work recovery time (WRT)* is the maximum amount of time available for certifying the functionality and integrity of restored systems and data so they can be put back into production. RTO usually deals with getting the infrastructure and systems back up and running, and WRT deals with ensuring business users can get back to work using them. Another way to think of WRT is as the remainder of the overall MTD value after the RTO has passed.

The *recovery point objective (RPO)* is the acceptable amount of data loss measured in time. This value represents the earliest point in time at which data must be recovered. The higher the value of data, the more funds or other resources that can be put into place to ensure a smaller amount of data is lost in the event of a disaster. Figure 23-2 illustrates the relationship and differences between the use of RPO and RTO values.

The MTD, RTO, RPO, and WRT values are critical to understand because they will be the basic foundational measures used when determining the type of recovery solutions an organization must put into place, so let's dig a bit deeper into them. As an example of RTO, let's say a company has determined that if it is unable to process product order requests for 12 hours, the financial hit will be too large for it to survive. This means that the MTD for order processing is 12 hours. To keep things simple, let's say that RTO and WRT are 6 hours each. Now, suppose that orders are processed using on-premises servers, on a site with no backup power sources, and an ice storm causes a power outage that will take days to restore. Without a plan and supporting infrastructure already in place, it would be close to impossible to migrate the servers and data to a site with power within 6 hours. The RTO (that is, the maximum time to move the servers and data) would not be met (to say nothing of the WRT) and it would likely exceed the MTD, putting the company at serious risk of collapse.

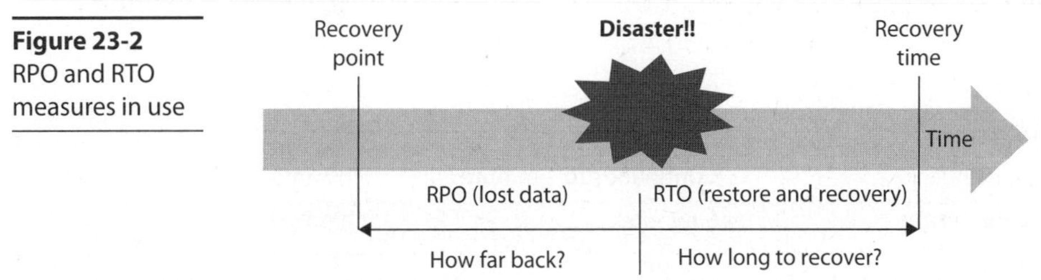

Figure 23-2 RPO and RTO measures in use

Now let's say that the same company did have a recovery site on a different power grid, and it was able to restore the order-processing services within a couple of hours, so it met the RTO requirement. But just because the systems are back online, the company still might have a critical problem. The company has to restore the data it lost during the disaster. Restoring data that is a week old does the company no good. The employees need to have access to the data that was being processed right before the disaster hit. If the company can only restore data that is a week old, then all the orders that were in some stage of being fulfilled over the last seven days could be lost. If the company makes an average of $25,000 per day in orders and all the order data was lost for the last seven days, this can result in a loss of $175,000 and a lot of unhappy customers. So just getting things up and running (meeting the RTO) is just part of the picture. Getting the necessary data in place so that business processes are up to date and relevant (RPO) is just as critical.

To take things one step further, let's say the company stood up the systems at its recovery site in two hours. It also had real-time data backup systems in place, so all of the necessary up-to-date data is restored. But no one actually tested the processes to recover data from backups, everyone is confused, and orders still cannot be processed and revenue cannot be collected. This means the company met its RTO requirement and its RPO requirement, but failed its WRT requirement, and thus failed the MTD requirement. Proper business recovery means *all* of the individual things have to happen correctly for the overall goal to be successful.

EXAM TIP An RTO is the amount of time it takes to recover from a disaster, and an RPO is the acceptable amount of data, measured in time, that can be lost from that same event.

The actual MTD, RTO, and RPO values are derived during the *business impact analysis (BIA)*, the purpose of which is to be able to apply criticality values to specific business functions, resources, and data types. A simplistic example is shown in Table 23-1. The company must have data restoration capabilities in place to ensure that mission-critical data is never older than one minute. The company cannot rely on something as slow as backup tape restoration, but must have a high-availability data replication solution in place. The RTO value for mission-critical data processing is two minutes or less. This means that the technology that carries out the processing functionality for this type of data cannot be down for more than two minutes. The company probably needs failover technology in place that will shift the load once it notices that a server goes offline.

Data Type	RPO	RTO
Mission critical	Continuous to 1 minute	Instantaneous to 2 minutes
Business critical	5 minutes	10 minutes
Business	3 hours	8 hours

Table 23-1 RPO and RTO Value Relationships

> **What Is the Difference Between Preventive Measures and Recovery Strategies?**
>
> Preventive mechanisms are put into place not only to try to reduce the possibility that the organization will experience a disaster, but also, if a disaster does hit, to lessen the amount of damage that will take place. Although the organization cannot stop a tornado from coming, for example, it could choose to move its facility from Tornado Alley to an area less prone to these weather events. As another example, the organization cannot stop a car from plowing into and taking out a transformer that it relies on for power, but it can have a separate power feed from a different transformer in case this happens.
>
> Recovery strategies are processes designed to rescue the company after a disaster takes place. These processes integrate mechanisms such as establishing alternate sites for facilities, implementing emergency response procedures, and possibly activating the preventive mechanisms that have already been implemented.

In this same scenario, data that is classified as "Business" can be up to three hours old when the production environment comes back online, so a less frequent data replication process is acceptable. Because the RTO for business data is eight hours, the company can choose to have hot-swappable hard drives available instead of having to pay for the more complicated and expensive failover technology.

The DR team has to figure out what the company needs to do to actually recover the processes and services it has identified as being so important to the organization overall. In its business continuity and recovery strategy, the team closely examines the critical, agreed-upon business functions, and then evaluates the numerous recovery and backup alternatives that might be used to recover critical business operations. It is important to choose the right tactics and technologies for the recovery of each critical business process and service in order to assure that the set MTD values are met.

So what does the DR team need to accomplish? The team needs to actually define the recovery processes, which are sets of predefined activities that will be implemented and carried out in response to a disaster. More importantly, these processes must be constantly reevaluated and updated as necessary to ensure that the organization meets or exceeds the MTDs. It all starts with understanding the business processes that would have to be recovered in the aftermath of a disaster. Armed with that knowledge, the DR team can make good decisions about data backup, recovery, and processing sites, as well as overall services availability, all of which we explore in the next sections.

Business Process Recovery

A *business process* is a set of interrelated steps linked through specific decision activities to accomplish a specific task. Business processes have starting and ending points and are repeatable. The processes should encapsulate the knowledge about services, resources, and operations provided by an organization. For example, when a customer requests to buy a book via a company's e-commerce site, the company's order fulfillment system must follow a business process such as this:

1. Validate that the book is available.
2. Validate where the book is located and how long it would take to ship it to the destination.
3. Provide the customer with the price and delivery date.
4. Verify the customer's credit card information.
5. Validate and process the credit card order.
6. Send the order to the book inventory location.
7. Send a receipt and tracking number to the customer.
8. Restock inventory.
9. Send the order to accounting.

The DR team needs to understand these different steps of the organization's most critical processes. The data is usually presented as a workflow document that contains the roles and resources needed for each process. The DR team must understand the following about critical business processes:

- Required roles
- Required resources
- Input and output mechanisms
- Workflow steps
- Required time for completion
- Interfaces with other processes

This will allow the team to identify threats and the controls to ensure the least amount of process interruption.

Data Backup

Data has become one of the most critical assets to nearly all organizations. It may include financial spreadsheets, blueprints on new products, customer information, product inventory, trade secrets, and more. In Chapter 2, we stepped through risk analysis procedures and, in Chapter 5, data classification. The DR team should not be responsible for setting up and maintaining the organization's data classification procedures, but the team should recognize that the organization is at risk if it does not have these procedures in place. This should be seen as a vulnerability that is reported to management. Management would need to establish another group of individuals who would identify the organization's data, define a loss criterion, and establish the classification structure and processes.

The DR team's responsibility is to provide solutions to protect this data and identify ways to restore it after a disaster. Data usually changes more often than hardware and software, so these backup or archival procedures must happen on a continual basis. The data backup process must make sense and be reasonable and effective. If data in the files changes several times a day, backup procedures should happen a few times a day or nightly to ensure all the changes are captured and kept. If data is changed once a month, backing up data every night is a waste of time and resources. Backing up a file and its corresponding changes is usually more desirable than having multiple copies of that one file. Online backup technologies usually record the changes to a file in a transaction log, which is separate from the original file.

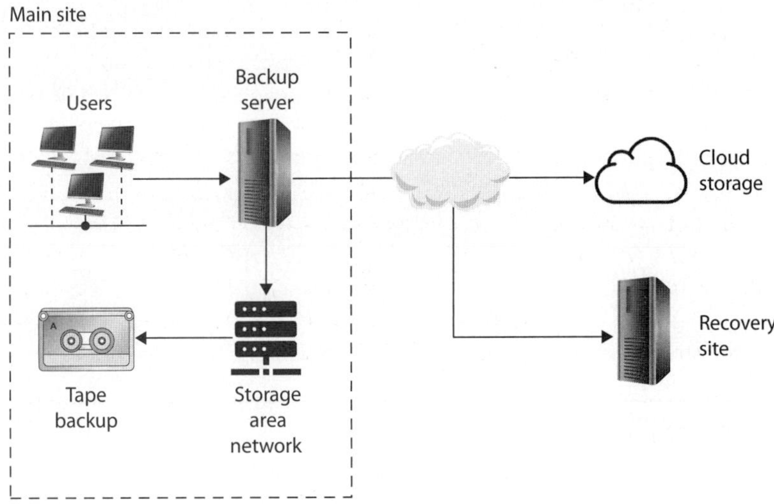

The IT operations team should include a backup administrator, who is responsible for defining which data gets backed up and how often. These backups can be full, differential, or incremental, and are usually used in some type of combination with each other. Most files are not altered every day, so, to save time and resources, it is best to devise a backup plan that does not continually back up data that has not been modified. So, how do we know which data has changed and needs to be backed up without having to look at every file's modification date? This is accomplished by setting an *archive bit* to 1 if a file has been modified. The backup software reviews this bit when making its determination of whether the file gets backed up and, if so, clears the bit when it's done.

The first step is to do a *full backup*, which is just what it sounds like—all data is backed up and saved to some type of storage media. During a full backup, the archive bit is cleared, which means that it is set to 0. An organization can choose to do full backups only, in which case the restoration process is just one step, but the backup and restore processes could take a long time.

Most organizations choose to combine a full backup with a differential or incremental backup. A *differential process* backs up the files that have been modified since the *last full backup*. When the data needs to be restored, the full backup is laid down first, and then

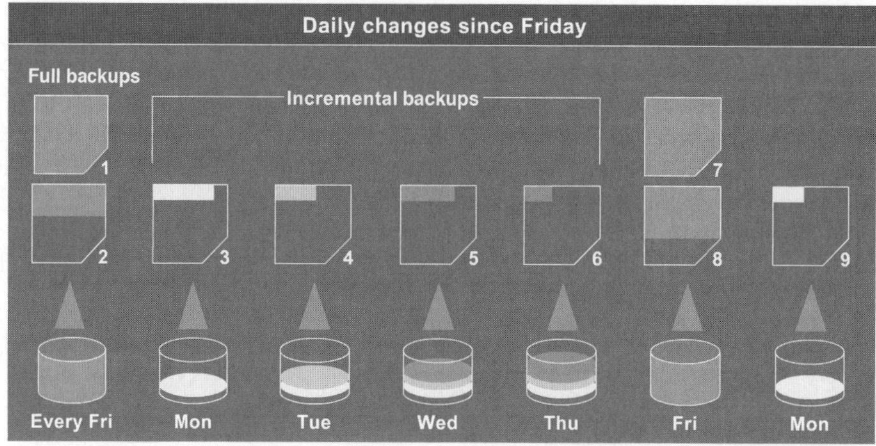

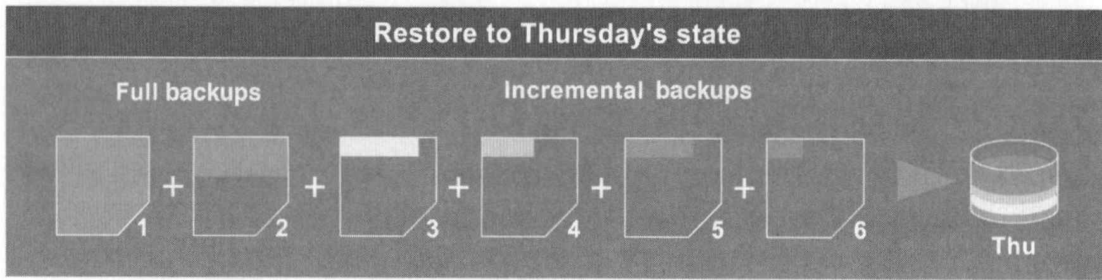

Figure 23-3 Backup software steps

the most recent differential backup is put down on top of it. The differential process does not change the archive bit value.

An *incremental process* backs up all the files that have changed since the *last full or incremental backup* and sets the archive bit to 0. When the data needs to be restored, the full backup data is laid down, and then each incremental backup is laid down on top of it in the proper order (see Figure 23-3). If an organization experienced a disaster and it used the incremental process, it would first need to restore the full backup on its hard drives and lay down every incremental backup that was carried out before the disaster took place (and after the last full backup). So, if the full backup was done six months ago and the operations department carried out an incremental backup each month, the backup administrator would restore the full backup and start with the older incremental backups taken since the full backup and restore each one of them until they were all restored.

Which backup process is best? If an organization wants the backup and restoration processes to be simple, it can carry out just full backups—but this may require a lot of hard drive space and time. Although using differential and incremental backup processes is more complex, it requires fewer resources and less time. A differential backup takes more time in the backing-up phase than an incremental backup, but it also takes less time to restore than an incremental backup because carrying out restoration of a differential backup happens in two steps, whereas in an incremental backup, every incremental backup must be restored in the correct sequence.

Whatever the organization chooses, it is important to not mix differential and incremental backups. This overlap could cause files to be missed, since the incremental backup changes the archive bit and the differential backup does not.

Critical data should be backed up and stored onsite *and* offsite. The onsite backups should be easily accessible for routine uses and should provide a quick restore process so operations can return to normal. However, onsite backups are not enough to provide real protection. The data should also be held in an offsite facility in case of disasters. One decision the CISO needs to make is where the offsite location should be in reference to the main facility. The closer the offsite backup storage site is, the easier it is to access, but this can put the backup copies in danger if a large-scale disaster manages to take out the organization's main facility and the backup facility. It may be wiser to choose a backup facility farther away, which makes accessibility harder but reduces the risk. Some organizations choose to have more than one backup facility: one that is close and one that is farther away.

Backup Storage Strategies

A backup strategy must take into account that failure can take place at any step of the process, so if there is a problem during the backup or restoration process that could corrupt the data, there should be a graceful way of backing out or reconstructing the data

Restoring Data from Backups: A Cautionary Tale

Can we actually restore data from backups? Backing up data is a wonderful thing in life, but making sure it can be properly restored is even better. Many organizations have developed a false sense of security based on the fact that they have a very organized and effective process of backing up their data. That sense of security can disappear in seconds when an organization realizes in a time of crisis that its restore processes do not work. For example, one company had paid an offsite backup facility to use a courier to collect its weekly backup tapes and transport them to the offsite facility for safekeeping. What the company did not realize was that this courier used the subway and many times set the tapes on the ground while waiting for the subway train. A subway has many large engines that create their own magnetic field. This can have the same effect on media as large magnets, meaning that the data can be erased or corrupted. The company never tested its restore processes and eventually experienced a disaster. Much to its surprise, it found out that three years of data were corrupted and unusable.

Many other stories and experiences like this are out there. Don't let your organization end up as an anecdote in someone else's book because it failed to verify that its backups could be restored.

from the beginning. The procedures for backing up and restoring data should be easily accessible and comprehensible even to operators or administrators who are not intimately familiar with a specific system. In an emergency situation, the same person who always does the backing up and restoring may not be around, or outsourced consultants may need to be temporarily hired to meet the restoration time constraints.

There are four commonly used backup strategies that you should be aware of:

- **Direct-attached storage** The backup storage is directly connected to the device being backed up, typically over a USB cable. This is better than nothing, but is not really well suited for centralized management. Worse yet, many ransomware attacks look for these attached storage devices and encrypt them too.
- **Network-attached storage (NAS)** The backup storage is connected to the device over the LAN and is usually a storage area network (SAN) managed by a backup server. This approach is usually centrally managed and allows IT administrators to enforce data backup policies. The main drawback is that, if a disaster takes out the site, the data may be lost or otherwise be rendered inaccessible.
- **Cloud storage** Many organizations use cloud storage as either the primary or secondary repository of backup data. If this is done on a virtual private cloud, it has the advantage of providing offsite storage so that, even if the organization's site is destroyed by a disaster, the data is available for recovery. Obviously, WAN connectivity must be reliable and fast enough to support this strategy if it is to be effective.
- **Offline media** As ransomware becomes more sophisticated, we are seeing more instances of attackers going after NAS and cloud storage. If your data is critical enough that you have to decrease the risk of it being lost as close to zero as you can, you may want to consider offline media such as tape backups, optical discs, or even external drives that are disconnected after each backup (and potentially removed offsite). This is the slowest and most expensive approach, but is also the most resistant to attacks.

Electronic vaulting and remote journaling are other solutions that organizations should be aware of. *Electronic vaulting* makes copies of files as they are modified and periodically transmits them to an offsite backup site. The transmission does not happen in real time, but is carried out in batches. So, an organization can choose to have all files that have been changed sent to the backup facility every hour, day, week, or month. The information can be stored in an offsite facility and retrieved from that facility in a short amount of time.

This form of backup takes place in many financial institutions, so when a bank teller accepts a deposit or withdrawal, the change to the customer's account is made locally to that branch's database and to the remote site that maintains the backup copies of all customer records.

Electronic vaulting is a method of transferring bulk information to offsite facilities for backup purposes. *Remote journaling* is another method of transmitting data offsite, but this usually only includes moving the journal or transaction logs to the offsite facility, not the actual files. These logs contain the deltas (changes) that have taken place to the individual files. Continuing with the bank example, if and when data is corrupted and needs to be restored, the bank can retrieve these logs, which are used to rebuild the lost data. Journaling is efficient for database recovery, where only the reapplication of a series of changes to individual records is required to resynchronize the database.

EXAM TIP Remote journaling takes place in real time and transmits only the file deltas. Electronic vaulting takes place in batches and moves the entire file that has been updated.

An organization may need to keep different versions of software and files, especially in a software development environment. The object and source code should be backed up along with libraries, patches, and fixes. The offsite facility should mirror the onsite facility, meaning it does not make sense to keep all of this data at the onsite facility and only the source code at the offsite facility. Each site should have a full set of the most current and updated information and files.

Another software backup technology is *tape vaulting*. Many organizations back up their data to tapes that are then manually transferred to an offsite facility by a courier or an employee. This manual process can be error-prone, so some organizations use *electronic tape vaulting*, in which the data is sent over a serial line to a backup tape system at the offsite facility. The company that maintains the offsite facility maintains the systems and changes out tapes when necessary. Data can be quickly backed up and retrieved when necessary. This technology improves recovery speed, reduces errors, and allows backups to be run more frequently.

Data repositories commonly have replication capabilities, so that when changes take place to one repository (i.e., database) they are replicated to all the other repositories within the organization. The replication can take place over telecommunication links, which allow offsite repositories to be continuously updated. If the primary repository goes down or is corrupted, the replication flow can be reversed, and the offsite repository updates and restores the primary repository. Replication can be asynchronous or synchronous. *Asynchronous replication* means the primary and secondary data volumes are out of sync. Synchronization may take place in seconds, hours, or days, depending upon the technology in place. With *synchronous replication*, the primary and secondary repositories are always in sync, which provides true real-time duplication. Figure 23-4 shows how offsite replication can take place.

The DR team must balance the cost to recover against the cost of the disruption. The balancing point becomes the recovery time objective. Figure 23-5 illustrates the relationship between the cost of various recovery technologies and the provided recovery times.

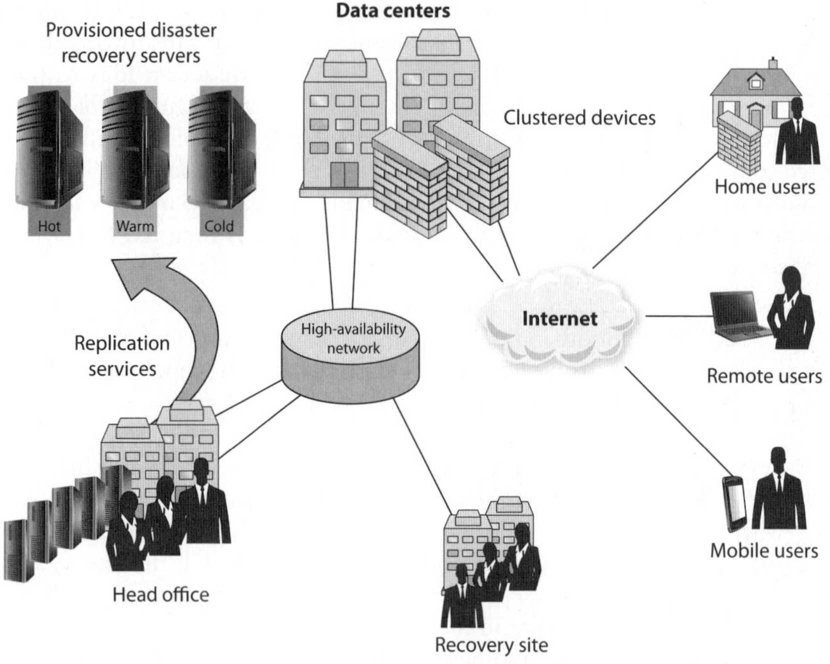

Figure 23-4 Offsite data replication for data recovery purposes

Choosing a Software Backup Facility

An organization needs to address several issues and ask specific questions when it is deciding upon a storage facility for its backup materials. The following list identifies just some of the issues that an organization needs to consider before committing to a specific vendor for this service:

- Can the media be accessed in the necessary timeframe?
- Is the facility closed on weekends and holidays, and does it only operate during specific hours of the day?
- Are the facility's access control mechanisms tied to an alarm and/or the police station?
- Does the facility have the capability to protect the media from a variety of threats?
- What is the availability of a bonded transport service?
- Are there any geographical environmental hazards such as floods, earthquakes, tornadoes, and so on that might affect the facility?
- Does the facility have a fire detection and suppression system?
- Does the facility provide temperature and humidity monitoring and control?
- What type of physical, administrative, and logical access controls are used?

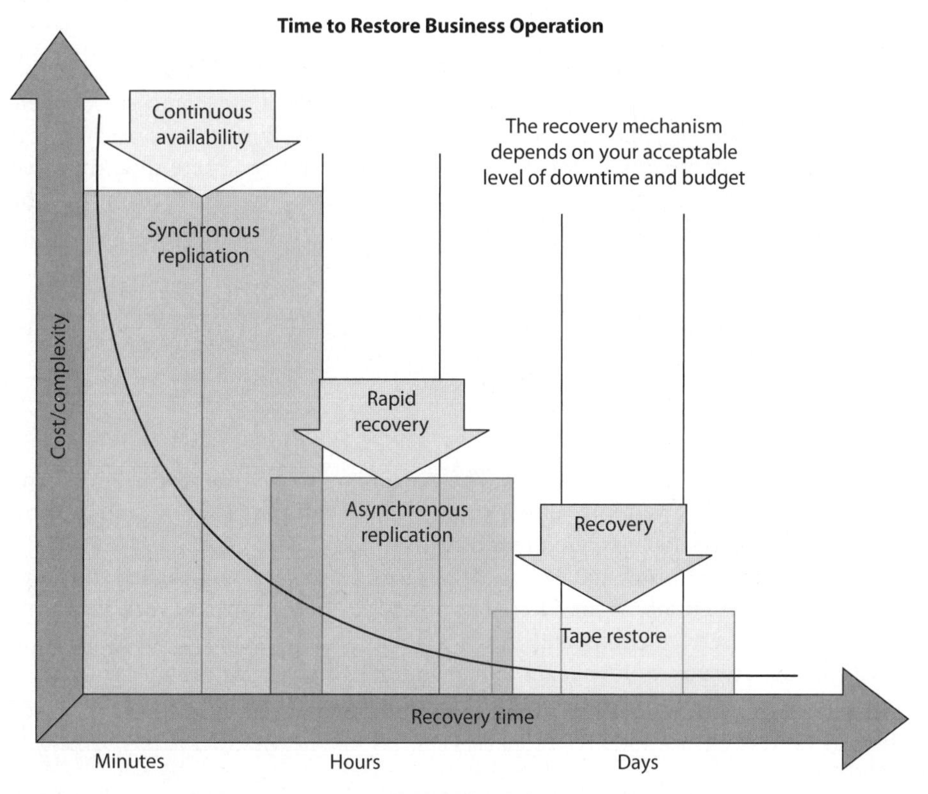

Figure 23-5 The criticality of data recovery will dictate the recovery solution.

The questions and issues that need to be addressed will vary depending on the type of organization, its needs, and the requirements of a backup facility.

Documentation

Documentation seems to be a dreaded task to most people, who will find many other tasks to take on to ensure they are not the ones stuck with documenting processes and procedures. However, without proper documentation, even an organization that does a terrific job of backing up data to an offsite facility will be scrambling to figure which backups it needs when a disaster hits.

Restoration of files can be challenging but restoring a whole environment that was swept away in a flood can be overwhelming, if not impossible. Procedures need to be documented because when they are actually needed, it will most likely be a chaotic and frantic atmosphere with a demanding time schedule. The documentation may need to include information on how to install images, configure operating systems and servers, and properly install utilities and proprietary software. Other documentation could include a calling tree, which outlines who should be contacted, in what order, and

Storing Business Continuity and Disaster Recovery Plans

Once the business continuity and disaster recovery plans are completed, where should they be stored? Should the organization have only one copy and keep it safely in a file cabinet next to Bob so that he feels safe? Nope. There should be two or three copies of these plans. One copy may be at the primary location, but the other copies should be at other locations in case the primary facility is destroyed. This reduces the risk of not having access to the plans when needed.

These plans should not be stored in a file cabinet, but rather in a fire-resistant safe. When they are stored offsite, they need to be stored in a way that provides just as much protection as the primary site would provide.

who is responsible for doing the calling. The documentation must also contain contact information for specific vendors, emergency agencies, offsite facilities, and any other entity that may need to be contacted in a time of need.

Most network environments evolve over time. Software is installed on top of other software, configurations are altered over the years to properly work in a unique environment, and service packs and patches are routinely installed to fix issues and update software. To expect one person or a group of people to go through all these steps during a crisis and end up with an environment that looks and behaves exactly like the original environment and in which all components work together seamlessly may be a lofty dream.

So, the dreaded task of documentation may be the saving grace one day. It is an essential piece of business, and therefore an essential piece in disaster recovery and business continuity. It is, therefore, important to make one or more roles responsible for proper documentation. As with all the items addressed in this chapter, simply saying "All documentation will be kept up to date and properly protected" is the easy part—saying and doing are two different things. Once the DR team identifies tasks that must be done, the tasks must be assigned to individuals, and those individuals have to be accountable. If these steps are not taken, the organization may have wasted a lot of time and resources defining these tasks, and still be in grave danger if a disaster occurs.

Human Resources

One of the resources commonly left out of the DR equation is people. An organization may restore its networks and critical systems and get business functions up and running, only to realize it doesn't know the answer to the question, "Who will take it from here?" The area of human resources is a critical component to any recovery and continuity process, and it needs to be fully thought out and integrated into the plan.

What happens if we have to move to an offsite facility that is 250 miles away? We cannot expect people to drive back and forth from home to work. Should we pay for temporary housing for the necessary employees? Do we have to pay their moving costs? Do we need to hire new employees in the area of the offsite facility? If so, what skill set do we need from them? These are all important questions for the organization's senior leaders to answer.

If a large disaster takes place that affects not only the organization's facility but also surrounding areas, including housing, employees will be more worried about their families than their organization. Some organizations assume that employees will be ready and available to help them get back into production, when in fact they may need to be at home because they have responsibilities to their families.

Regrettably, some employees may be killed or severely injured in the disaster, and the organization should have plans in place to replace employees quickly through a temporary employment agency or a job recruiter. This is an extremely unfortunate scenario to contemplate, but it is part of reality. The team that considers all threats and is responsible for identifying practical solutions needs to think through all of these issues.

Organizations should already have *executive succession planning* in place. This means that if someone in a senior executive position retires, leaves the organization, or is killed, the organization has predetermined steps to carry out to ensure a smooth transition to that executive's replacement. The loss of a senior executive could tear a hole in the organization's fabric, creating a leadership vacuum that must be filled quickly with the right individual. The line-of-succession plan defines who would step in and assume responsibility for this role. Many organizations have "deputy" roles. For example, an organization may have a deputy CIO, deputy CFO, and deputy CEO ready to take over the necessary tasks if the CIO, CFO, or CEO becomes unavailable.

Often, larger organizations also have a policy indicating that two or more of the senior staff cannot be exposed to a particular risk at the same time. For example, the CEO and president cannot travel on the same plane. If the plane were to crash and both individuals were killed, then the company could face a leadership crisis. This is why you don't see the president of the United States and the vice president together too often. It is not because they don't like each other and thus keep their distance from each other. It is because there is a policy indicating that to protect the United States, its top leaders cannot be under the same risk at the same time.

Recovery Site Strategies

Disruptions, in BCP terms, are of three main types: nondisasters, disasters, and catastrophes. A *nondisaster* is a disruption in service that has significant but limited impact on the conduct of business processes at a facility. The solution could include hardware, software, or file restoration. A *disaster* is an event that causes the entire facility to be unusable for a day or longer. This usually requires the use of an alternate processing facility and restoration of software and data from offsite copies. The alternate site must be available to the organization until its main facility is repaired and usable. A *catastrophe* is a major disruption that destroys the facility altogether. This requires both a short-term solution, which would be an offsite facility, and a long-term solution, which may require rebuilding the original facility. Disasters and catastrophes are rare compared to nondisasters, thank goodness.

When dealing with disasters and catastrophes, an organization has three basic options: select a dedicated site that the organization owns and operates itself; lease a commercial facility, such as a "hot site" that contains all the equipment and data needed to quickly restore operations; or enter into a formal agreement with another facility, such as a service bureau, to restore its operations. When choosing the right solution for its needs, the organization evaluates each alternative's ability to support its operations, to do it within an acceptable timeframe, and to have a reasonable cost.

An important consideration with third parties is their reliability, both in normal times and during an emergency. Their reliability can depend on considerations such as their track record, the extent and location of their supply inventory, and their access to supply and communication channels. Organizations should closely query the management of the alternative facility about such things as the following:

- How long will it take to recover from a certain type of incident to a certain level of operations?
- Will it give priority to restoring the operations of one organization over another after a disaster?
- What are its costs for performing various functions?
- What are its specifications for IT and security functions? Is the workspace big enough for the required number of employees?

To recover from a disaster that prevents or degrades use of the primary site temporarily or permanently, an organization must have an offsite backup facility available. Generally, an organization establishes contracts with third-party vendors to provide such services. The client pays a monthly fee to retain the right to use the facility in a time of need, and then incurs an activation fee when the facility actually has to be used. In addition, a daily or hourly fee is imposed for the duration of the stay. This is why service agreements for backup facilities should be considered a short-term solution, not a long-term solution.

It is important to note that most recovery site contracts do not promise to house the organization in need at a specific location, but rather promise to provide what has been contracted for somewhere within the organization's locale. On, and subsequent to, September 11, 2001, many organizations with Manhattan offices were surprised when they were redirected by their backup site vendor not to sites located in New Jersey (which were already full), but rather to sites located in Boston, Chicago, or Atlanta. This adds yet another level of complexity to the recovery process, specifically the logistics of transporting people and equipment to unplanned locations.

An organization can choose from three main types of leased or rented offsite recovery facilities:

- **Hot site** A facility that is fully configured and ready to operate within a few hours. All the necessary equipment is already installed and configured. In many cases, the remote data backup services are included, so the RPO can be down to an hour or even less. These sites are a good choice for an organization with a very small MTD. Of course, the organization should conduct regular tests (annually, at least) to ensure the site is functioning in the necessary state of readiness.

  The hot site is, by far, the most expensive of the three types of offsite facilities. The organization has to pay for redundant hardware and software, in addition to the expenses of the site itself. Organizations that use hot sites as part of their recovery strategy tend to limit them to mission-critical systems only.

- **Warm site** A facility that is usually partially configured with some equipment, such as HVAC, and foundational infrastructure components, but does not include all the hardware needed to restore mission-critical business functions. Staging a facility with duplicate hardware and computers configured for immediate operation is extremely expensive, so a warm site provides a less expensive alternate. These sites typically do not have data replicated to them, so backups would have to be delivered and restored onto the warm site systems after a disaster.

  The warm site is the most widely used model. It is less expensive than a hot site, and can be up and running within a reasonably acceptable time period. It may be a better choice for organizations that depend on proprietary and unusual hardware and software, because they will bring their own hardware and software with them to the site after the disaster hits. Drawbacks, however, are that much of the equipment has to be procured, delivered to, and configured at the warm site after the fact, and testing will be more difficult. Thus, an organization may not be certain that it will in fact be able to return to an operating state within its RTO.
- **Cold site** A facility that supplies the basic environment, electrical wiring, HVAC, plumbing, and flooring but none of the equipment or additional services. A cold site is essentially an empty data center. It may take weeks to get the site activated and ready for work. The cold site could have equipment racks and dark fiber (fiber that does not have the circuit engaged) and maybe even desks. However, it would require the receipt of equipment from the client, since it does not provide any.

  The cold site is the least expensive option, but takes the most time and effort to actually get up and functioning right after a disaster, as the systems and software must be delivered, set up, and configured. Cold sites are often used as backups for call centers, manufacturing plants, and other services that can be moved lock, stock, and barrel in one shot.

After a catastrophic loss of the primary facility, some organizations will start their recovery in a hot or warm site, and transfer some operations over to a cold site after the latter has had time to set up.

It is important to understand that the different site types listed here are provided by service bureaus. A *service bureau* is a company that has additional space and capacity to provide applications and services such as call centers. An organization pays a monthly subscription fee to a service bureau for this space and service. The fee can be paid for contingencies such as disasters and emergencies. You should evaluate the ability of a service bureau to provide services just as you would evaluate divisions within your own organization, particularly on matters such as its ability to alter or scale its software and hardware configurations or to expand its operations to meet the needs of a contingency.

NOTE Related to a service bureau is a *contingency supplier*; its purpose is to supply services and materials temporarily to an organization that is experiencing an emergency. For example, a contingency supplier might provide raw materials such as heating fuel or backup telecommunication services. In considering contingency suppliers, the BCP team should think through considerations such as the level of services and materials a supplier can provide, how quickly a supplier can ramp up to supply them, and whether the supplier shares similar communication paths and supply chains as the affected organization.

Most organizations use warm sites, which have some devices such as networking equipment, some computers and data storage, but very little else. These organizations usually cannot afford a hot site, and the extra downtime would not be considered detrimental. A warm site can provide a longer-term solution than a hot site. Organizations that decide to go with a cold site must be able to be out of operation for a week or two. The cold site usually includes power, raised flooring, climate control, and wiring.

The following provides a quick overview of the differences between offsite facilities.

Hot site advantages:

- Ready within hours or even minutes for operation
- Highly available
- Usually used for short-term solutions, but available for longer stays
- Recovery testing is easy

Hot site disadvantages:

- Very expensive
- Limited systems

Tertiary Sites

An organization may recognize the danger of the primary recovery site not being available when needed. This could be the case if the service provider assumes that not every customer will attempt to occupy the site at the same time, and then a major regional disaster affects more organizations than anticipated. It could also happen if a disaster affects the recovery site itself (e.g., fire, flood). Mitigating this risk could require a *tertiary site*, a backup recovery site just in case the primary is unavailable. The tertiary site is sometimes referred to as a "backup to the backup." This is basically plan B if plan A does not work out. Obviously, this is a very expensive proposition, so its costs should be balanced with the risks it is intended to mitigate.

Warm and cold site advantages:

- Less expensive
- Available for longer timeframes because of the reduced costs
- Practical for proprietary hardware or software use

Warm and cold site disadvantages:

- Limited ability to perform recovery testing
- Resources for operations not immediately available

Reciprocal Agreements

Another approach to alternate offsite facilities is to establish a *reciprocal agreement* with another organization, usually one in a similar field or that has similar technological infrastructure. This means that organization A agrees to allow organization B to use its facilities if organization B is hit by a disaster, and vice versa. This is a cheaper way to go than the other offsite choices, but it is not always the best choice. Most environments are maxed out pertaining to the use of facility space, resources, and computing capability. To allow another organization to come in and work out of the same shop could prove to be detrimental to both organizations. Whether it can assist the other organization while tending effectively to its own business is an open question. The stress of two organizations working in the same environment could cause tremendous levels of tension. If it did work out, it would only provide a short-term solution. Configuration management could be a nightmare. Does the other organization upgrade to new technology and retire old systems and software? If not, one organization's systems may become incompatible with those of the other.

If your organization allows another organization to move into its facility and work from there, you may have a solid feeling about your friend, the CEO, but what about all of her employees, whom you do not know? The mixing of operations could introduce many security issues. Now you have a new subset of people who may need to have privileged and direct access to your resources in the shared environment. Close attention needs to be paid when assigning these other people access rights and permissions to your critical assets and resources, if they need access at all. Careful testing is recommended to see if one organization or the other can handle the extra loads.

Offsite Location

When choosing a backup facility, it should be far enough away from the original site so that one disaster does not take out both locations. In other words, it is not logical to have the backup site only a few miles away if the organization is concerned about tornado damage, because the backup site could also be affected or destroyed. There is a rule of thumb that suggests that alternate facilities should be, at a bare minimum, at least 5 miles away from the primary site, while 15 miles is recommended for most low-to-medium critical environments, and 50 to 200 miles is recommended for critical operations, to give maximum protection in cases of regional disasters.

Reciprocal agreements have been known to work well in specific businesses, such as newspaper printing. These businesses require very specific technology and equipment that is not available through any subscription service. These agreements follow a "you scratch my back and I'll scratch yours" mentality. For most other organizations, reciprocal agreements are generally, at best, a secondary option for disaster protection. The other issue to consider is that these agreements are usually not enforceable because they're not written in legally binding terms. This means that although organization A said organization B could use its facility when needed, when the need arises, organization A may not have a legal obligation to fulfill this promise. However, there are still many organizations who do opt for this solution either because of the appeal of low cost or, as noted earlier, because it may be the only viable solution in some cases.

Organizations that have a reciprocal agreement need to address the following important issues before a disaster hits:

- How long will the facility be available to the organization in need?
- How much assistance will the staff supply in integrating the two environments and ongoing support?
- How quickly can the organization in need move into the facility?
- What are the issues pertaining to interoperability?
- How many of the resources will be available to the organization in need?
- How will differences and conflicts be addressed?
- How does change control and configuration management take place?
- How often can exercising and testing take place?
- How can critical assets of both organizations be properly protected?

A variation on a reciprocal agreement is a consortium, or *mutual aid agreement*. In this case, more than two organizations agree to help one another in case of an emergency. Adding multiple organizations to the mix, as you might imagine, can make things even more complicated. The same concerns that apply with reciprocal agreements apply here, but even more so. Organizations entering into such agreements need to formally and legally document their mutual responsibilities in advance. Interested parties, including the legal and IT departments, should carefully scrutinize such accords before the organization signs onto them.

Redundant Sites

Some organizations choose to have a *redundant site*, or mirrored site, meaning one site is equipped and configured exactly like the primary site, which serves as a redundant environment. The business-processing capabilities between the two sites can be completely synchronized. A redundant site is owned by the organization and mirrors the original production environment. A redundant site has clear advantages: it has full availability, is ready to go at a moment's notice, and is under the organization's complete control. This is, however, one of the most expensive backup facility options, because a full environment must be maintained even though it usually is not used for regular production activities until after a disaster takes place that triggers the relocation of services to the redundant site. But "expensive" is relative here. If a company would lose a million dollars if it were out of business for just a few hours, the loss potential would override the cost of this option. Many organizations are subjected to regulations that dictate they must have redundant sites in place, so expense is not a matter of choice in these situations.

EXAM TIP A *hot* site is a subscription service. A *redundant* site, in contrast, is a site owned and maintained by the organization, meaning the organization does not pay anyone else for the site. A redundant site might be "hot" in nature, meaning it is ready for production quickly. However, the CISSP exam differentiates between a hot site (a subscription service) and a redundant site (owned by the organization).

Another type of facility-backup option is a *rolling hot site*, or mobile hot site, where the back of a large truck or a trailer is turned into a data processing or working area. This is a portable, self-contained data facility. The trailer has the necessary power, telecommunications, and systems to do some or all of the processing right away. The trailer can be brought to the organization's parking lot or another location. Obviously, the trailer has to be driven over to the new site, the data has to be retrieved, and the necessary personnel have to be put into place.

Another, similar solution is a prefabricated building that can be easily and quickly put together. Military organizations and large insurance companies typically have rolling hot sites or trucks preloaded with equipment because they often need the flexibility to quickly relocate some or all of their processing facilities to different locations around the world depending on where the need arises.

It is best if an organization is aware of all available options for hardware and facility backups to ensure it makes the best decision for its specific business and critical needs.

Multiple Processing Sites

Another option for organizations is to have *multiple processing sites*. An organization may have ten different facilities throughout the world, which are connected with specific technologies that could move all data processing from one facility to another in a matter of seconds when an interruption is detected. This technology can be implemented within the organization or from one facility to a third-party facility. Certain service providers provide this type of functionality to their customers. So if an organization's data processing is interrupted, all or some of the processing can be moved to the service provider's servers.

Availability

We close this section on recovery strategies by considering the nondisasters to which we referred earlier. These are the incidents that may not require evacuation of personnel or facility repairs but that can still have a significant detrimental effect on the ability of the organization to execute its mission. We want our systems and services to be available all the time, no matter what. However, we all realize this is just not possible. *Availability* can be defined as the portion of the time that a system is operational and able to fulfill its intended purpose. But how can we ensure the availability of the systems and services on which our organizations depend?

High Availability

High availability (HA) is a combination of technologies and processes that work together to ensure that some specific thing is up and running most of the time. The specific thing can be a database, a network, an application, a power supply, and so on. Service providers have *service level agreements (SLAs)* with their customers that outline the amount of uptime the service providers promise to provide. For example, a hosting company can promise to provide 99 percent uptime for Internet connectivity. This means the company is guaranteeing that at least 99 percent of the time, the Internet connection you purchase from it will be up and running. It also means that you can experience up to 3.65 days a year (or 7.2 hours per month) of downtime and it won't be a violation of the SLA. Increase that to 99.999 percent (referred to as "five nines") uptime and the allowable downtime drops to 5.26 seconds per year, but the price you pay for service goes through the roof.

NOTE HA is in the eye of the beholder. For some organizations or systems, an SLA of 90 percent ("one nine") uptime and its corresponding potential 36+ days of downtime a year is perfectly fine, particularly for organizations that are running on a tight budget. Other organizations require "nine nines" or 99.9999999 percent availability for mission-critical systems. You have to balance the cost of HA with the loss you're trying to mitigate.

Just because a service is available doesn't necessarily mean that it is operating acceptably. Suppose your company's high-speed e-commerce server gets infected with a bitcoin miner that drives CPU utilization close to 100 percent. Technically, the server is available and will probably be able to respond to customer requests. However, response times will likely be so lengthy that many of your customers will simply give up and go shop somewhere else. The service is available, but its quality is unacceptable.

Quality of Service

Quality of service (QoS) defines minimum acceptable performance characteristics of a particular service. For example, for the e-commerce server example, we could define parameters like response time, CPU utilization, or network bandwidth utilization, depending on how the service is being provided. SLAs may include one or more specifications for QoS, which allows service providers to differentiate classes of service that are prioritized for different clients. During a disaster, the available bandwidth on external links may be limited, so the affected organization could specify different QoS for its externally facing systems. For example, the e-commerce company in our example could determine the minimum data rate to keep its web presence available to customers and specify that as the minimum QoS rate at the expense of, say, its e-mail or Voice over Internet Protocol (VoIP) traffic.

To provide HA and meet stringent QoS requirements, the hosting company has to have a long list of technologies and processes that provide redundancy, fault tolerance, and failover capabilities. *Redundancy* is commonly built into the network at a routing protocol level. The routing protocols are configured such that if one link goes down or gets congested, traffic is automatically routed over a different network link. An organization can also ensure that it has redundant hardware available so that if a primary device goes down, the backup component can be swapped out and activated.

If a technology has a *failover* capability, this means that if there is a failure that cannot be handled through normal means, then processing is "switched over" to a working system. For example, two servers can be configured to send each other "heartbeat" signals every 30 seconds. If server A does not receive a heartbeat signal from server B after 40 seconds, then all processes are moved to server A so that there is no lag in operations. Also, when servers are *clustered*, an overarching piece of software monitors each server and carries out load balancing. If one server within the cluster goes down, the clustering software stops sending it data to process so that there are no delays in processing activities.

Fault Tolerance and System Resilience

Fault tolerance is the capability of a technology to continue to operate as expected even if something unexpected takes place (a fault). If a database experiences an unexpected glitch, it can roll back to a known-good state and continue functioning as though nothing bad happened. If a packet gets lost or corrupted during a TCP session, the TCP protocol will resend the packet so that system-to-system communication is not affected. If a disk within a RAID system gets corrupted, the system uses its parity data to rebuild the corrupted data so that operations are not affected.

Although the terms fault tolerance and resilience are often used synonymously, they mean subtly different things. Fault tolerance means that when a fault happens, there's a system in place (a backup or redundant one) to ensure services remain uninterrupted. *System resilience* means that the system continues to function, albeit in a degraded fashion, when a fault is encountered. Think of it as the difference between having a spare tire for your car and having run-flat tires. The spare tire provides fault tolerance in that it enables you to recover (fairly) quickly from a flat tire and be on your way. Run-flat tires allow you to continue to drive your car (albeit slower) if you run over a nail on the road. A resilient system is fault tolerant, but a fault tolerant one may not be resilient.

High Availability in Disaster Recovery

Redundancy, fault tolerance, resilience, and failover capabilities increase the reliability of a system or network, where *reliability* is the probability that a system performs the necessary function for a specified period under defined conditions. High reliability allows for high availability, which is a measure of its readiness. If the probability of a system performing as expected under defined conditions is low, then the availability for this system cannot be high. For a system to have the characteristic of high availability,

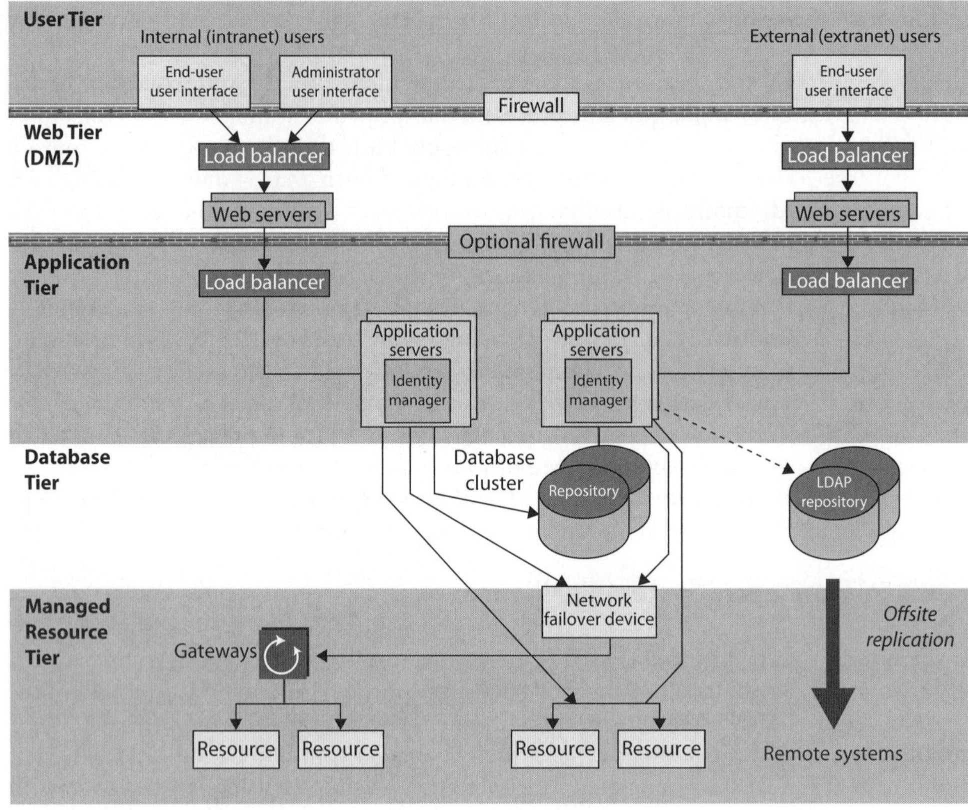

Figure 23-6 High-availability technologies

then high reliability must be in place. Figure 23-6 illustrates where load balancing, clustering, failover devices, and replication commonly take place in a network architecture.

Remember that data restoration (RPO) requirements can be different from processing restoration (RTO) requirements. Data can be restored through backup tapes, electronic vaulting, or synchronous or asynchronous replication. Processing capabilities can be restored through clustering, load balancing, redundancy, and failover technologies. If the results of the BCP team's BIA indicate that the RPO value is two days, then the organization can use tape backups. If the RPO value is one minute, then synchronous replication needs to be in place. If the BIA indicates that the RTO value is three days, then redundant hardware can be used. If the RTO value is one minute, then clustering and load balancing should be used.

HA and disaster recovery are related concepts. HA technologies and processes are commonly put into place so that if a disaster does take place, either the critical functions are likelier to remain available or the delay of getting them back online and running is low.

Many IT and security professionals usually think of HA only in technology terms, but remember that there are many things that an organization needs to have available to keep functioning. Availability of each of the following items must be thought through and planned:

- Facility (cold, warm, hot, redundant, rolling, reciprocal sites)
- Infrastructure (redundancy, fault tolerance)
- Storage (SAN, cloud)
- Server (clustering, load balancing)
- Data (backups, online replication)
- Business processes
- People

NOTE Virtualization and cloud computing are covered in Chapter 7. We will not go over those technologies again in this chapter, but know that the use of these technologies has drastically increased in the realm of business continuity and disaster recovery planning solutions.

Disaster Recovery Processes

Recovering from a disaster begins way before the event occurs. It starts by anticipating threats and developing goals that support the organization's continuity of operations. If you do not have established goals, how do you know when you are done and whether your efforts were actually successful? Goals are established so everyone knows the ultimate objectives. Establishing goals is important for any task, but especially for business continuity and disaster recovery plans. The definition of the goals helps direct the proper allocation of resources and tasks, supports the development of necessary strategies, and assists in financial justification of the plans and program overall. Once the goals are set, they provide a guide to the development of the actual plans themselves. Anyone who has been involved in large projects that entail many small, complex details knows that at times it is easy to get off track and not actually accomplish the major goals of the project. Goals are established to keep everyone on track and to ensure that the efforts pay off in the end.

Great—we have established that goals are important. But the goal could be, "Keep the company in business if an earthquake hits." That's a good goal, but it is not overly useful without more clarity and direction. To be useful, a goal must contain certain key information, such as the following:

- **Responsibility** Each individual involved with recovery and continuity should have their responsibilities spelled out in writing to ensure a clear understanding in a chaotic situation. Each task should be assigned to the individual most logically situated to handle it. These individuals must know what is expected of them, which is done through training, exercises, communication, and documentation. So, for example, instead of just running out of the building screaming, an individual must know that he is responsible for shutting down the servers before he can run out of the building screaming.

- **Authority** In times of crisis, it is important to know who is in charge. Teamwork is important in these situations, and almost every team does much better with an established and trusted leader. Such leaders must know that they are expected to step up to the plate in a time of crisis and understand what type of direction they should provide to the rest of the employees. Everyone else must recognize the authority of these leaders and respond accordingly. Clear-cut authority will aid in reducing confusion and increasing cooperation.
- **Priorities** It is extremely important to know what is critical versus what is merely nice to have. Different departments provide different functionality for an organization. The critical departments must be singled out from the departments that provide functionality that the organization can live without for a week or two. It is necessary to know which department must come online first, which second, and so on. That way, the efforts are made in the most useful, effective, and focused manner. Along with the priorities of departments, the priorities of systems, information, and programs must be established. It may be necessary to ensure that the database is up and running before working to bring the web servers online. The general priorities must be set by management with the help of the different departments and IT staff.
- **Implementation and testing** It is great to write down very profound ideas and develop plans, but unless they are actually carried out and tested, they may not add up to a hill of beans. Once a disaster recovery plan is developed, it actually has to be put into action. It needs to be documented and stored in places that are easily accessible in times of crisis. The people who are assigned specific tasks need to be taught and informed how to fulfill those tasks, and dry runs must be done to walk people through different situations. The exercises should take place at least once a year, and the entire program should be continually updated and improved.

NOTE We address various types of tests, such as walkthrough, tabletop, simulation, parallel, and full interruption, later in this chapter.

According to the U.S. Federal Emergency Management Agency (FEMA), 90 percent of small businesses that experience a disaster and are unable to restore operations within five days will fail within the following year. Not being able to bounce back quickly or effectively by setting up shop somewhere else can make a company lose business and, more importantly, its reputation. In such a competitive world, customers have a lot of options. If one company is not prepared to bounce back after a disruption or disaster, customers may go to another vendor and stay there.

The biggest effect of an incident, especially one that is poorly managed or that was preventable, is on an organization's reputation or brand. This can result in a considerable and even irreparable loss of trust by customers and clients. On the other hand, handling an incident well, or preventing great damage through smart, preemptive measures, can enhance the reputation of, or trust in, an organization.

The *disaster recovery plan (DRP)* should address in detail all of the topics we have covered so far. The actual format of the DRP will depend on the environment, the goals of the plan, priorities, and identified threats. After each of those items is examined and documented, the topics of the plan can be divided into the necessary categories.

Response

The first question the DRP should answer is, "What constitutes a disaster that would trigger this plan?" Every leader within an organization (and, ideally, everyone else too) should know the answer. Otherwise, precious time is lost notifying people who should've self-activated as soon as the incident occurred, a delay that could cost lives or assets. Examples of clear-cut disasters that would trigger a response are loss of power exceeding ten minutes, flooding in the facility, or terrorist attack against or near the site.

Every DRP is different, but most follow a familiar sequence of events:

1. Declaration of disaster
2. Activation of the DR team
3. Internal communications (ongoing from here on out)
4. Protection of human safety (e.g., evacuation)
5. Damage assessment
6. Execution of appropriate system-specific DRPs (each system and network should have its own DRP)
7. Recovery of mission-critical business processes/functions
8. Recovery of all other business processes/functions

Personnel

The DRP needs to define several different teams that should be properly trained and available if a disaster hits. Which types of teams an organization needs depends upon the organization. The following are some examples of teams that an organization may need to construct:

- Damage assessment team
- Recovery team
- Relocation team
- Restoration team
- Salvage team
- Security team

The DR coordinator should have an understanding of the needs of the organization and the types of teams that need to be developed and trained. Employees should be assigned to the specific teams based on their knowledge and skill set. Each team needs to have a designated leader, who will direct the members and their activities. These team leaders will be responsible not only for ensuring that their team's objectives are met but also for communicating with each other to make sure each team is working in parallel phases.

The purpose of the *recovery team* should be to get whatever systems are still operable back up and running as quickly as possible to reduce business disruptions. Think of them as the medics whose job is to stabilize casualties until they can be transported to the hospital. In this case, of course, there is no hospital for information systems, but there may be a recovery site. Getting equipment and people there in an orderly fashion should be the job of the *relocation team*. The *restoration team* should be responsible for getting the alternate site into a working and functioning environment, and the *salvage team* should be responsible for starting the recovery of the original site. Both teams must know how to do many tasks, such as install operating systems, configure workstations and servers, string wire and cabling, set up the network and configure networking services, and install equipment and applications. Both teams must also know how to restore data from backup facilities and how to do so in a secure manner, one that ensures the availability, integrity, and confidentiality of the system and data.

The DRP must outline the specific teams, their responsibilities, and notification procedures. The plan must indicate the methods that should be used to contact team leaders during business hours and after business hours.

Communications

The purpose of the emergency communications plan that is part of the overall DRP is to ensure that everyone knows what to do at all times and that the DR team remains synchronized and coordinated. This all starts with the DR plan itself. As stated previously, copies of the DRP need to be kept in one or more locations other than the primary site, so that if the primary site is destroyed or negatively affected, the plan is still available to the teams. It is also critical that different formats of the plan be available to the teams, including both electronic and paper versions. An electronic version of the plan is not very useful if you don't have any electricity to run a computer.

In addition to having copies of the recovery documents located at their offices and homes, key individuals should have easily accessible versions of critical procedures and call tree information. One simple way to accomplish the latter is to publish a call tree on cards that can be affixed to personnel badges or kept in a wallet. In an emergency situation, valuable minutes are better spent responding to an incident than looking for a document or having to wait for a laptop to power up. Of course, the call tree is only as effective as it is accurate and up to date, so verifying it periodically is imperative.

One limitation of call trees is that they are point to point, which means they're typically good for getting the word out, but not so much for coordinating activities. Group text messages work better, but only in the context of fairly small and static groups. Many organizations have group chat solutions, but if those rely on the organization's servers, they may be unavailable during a disaster. It is a good idea, then, to establish a communications platform that is completely independent of the organizational infrastructure. Solutions like Slack and Mattermost offer a free service that is typically sufficient to keep most organizations connected in emergencies. The catch, of course, is that everyone needs to have the appropriate client installed on their personal devices and know when and how to connect. Training and exercises are the keys to successful execution of any plan, and the communications plan is no exception.

NOTE An organization may need to solidify communications channels and relationships with government officials and emergency response groups. The goal of this activity is to solidify proper protocol in case of a city- or region-wide disaster. During the BIA phase, the DR team should contact local authorities to elicit information about the risks of its geographical location and how to access emergency zones. If the organization has to perform DR, it may need to contact many of these emergency response groups.

PACE Communications Plans

The U.S. armed forces routinely develop Primary, Alternate, Contingency, and Emergency (PACE) communications plans. The PACE plan outlines the different capabilities that exist and aligns them into these four categories based on their ability to meet defined information exchange requirements. Each category is defined here:

- **Primary** The normal or expected capability that is used to achieve the objective.
- **Alternate** A fully satisfactory capability that can be used to achieve the objective with minimal impact to the operation or exercise. This capability is used when the Primary capability is unavailable.
- **Contingency** A workable capability that can be used to achieve the objective. This capability may not be as fast or easy as the Primary or Alternate but is capable of achieving the objective with an acceptable amount of time and effort. This capability is used when the Primary and the Alternate capabilities are unavailable.
- **Emergency** This is the last-resort capability and typically may involve significantly more time and effort than any of the other capabilities. This capability should be used only when the Primary, Alternate, and Contingency capabilities are unavailable.

The PACE plan includes redundant communications capabilities and specifies the order in which the organization will employ the capabilities when communication outages occur.

Assessment

A role, or a team, needs to be created to carry out a *damage assessment* once a disaster has taken place. The assessment procedures should be properly documented in the DRP and include the following steps:

- Determine the cause of the disaster.
- Determine the potential for further damage.
- Identify the affected business functions and areas.
- Identify the level of functionality for the critical resources.
- Identify the resources that must be replaced immediately.
- Estimate how long it will take to bring critical functions back online.

After the damage assessment team collects and assesses this information, the DR coordinator identifies which teams need to be called to action and which system-specific DRPs need to be executed (and in what order). The DRP should specify activation criteria for the different teams and system-specific DRPs. After the damage assessment, if one or more of the situations outlined in the criteria have taken place, then the DR team is moved into restoration mode.

Different organizations have different activation criteria because business drivers and critical functions vary from organization to organization. The criteria may comprise some or all of the following elements:

- Danger to human life
- Danger to state or national security
- Damage to facility
- Damage to critical systems
- Estimated value of downtime that will be experienced

Restoration

Once the damage assessment is completed, various teams are activated, which signals the organization's entry into the *restoration phase*. Each team has its own tasks—for example, the facilities team prepares the offsite facility (if needed), the network team rebuilds the network and systems, and the relocation team starts organizing the staff to move into a new facility.

The restoration process needs to be well organized to get the organization up and running as soon as possible. This is much easier to state in a book than to carry out in reality, which is why written procedures are critical. The critical functions and their resources would already have been identified during the BIA, as discussed earlier in this chapter (with a simplistic example provided in Table 23-1). These are the functions that the teams need to work together on restoring first.

Many organizations create templates during the DR plan development stage. These templates are used by the different teams to step them through the necessary phases and to document their findings. For example, if one step could not be completed until new systems were purchased, this should be indicated on the template. If a step is partially completed, this should be documented so the team does not forget to go back and finish that step when the necessary part arrives. These templates keep the teams on task and also quickly tell the team leaders about the progress, obstacles, and potential recovery time.

NOTE Examples of possible templates can be found in NIST Special Publication 800-34, Revision 1, *Contingency Planning Guide for Federal Information Systems*, which is available online at https://csrc.nist.gov/publications/detail/sp/800-34/rev-1/final.

An organization is not out of an emergency state until it is back in operation at the original primary site or at a new site that was constructed to replace the primary original one, because the organization is always vulnerable while operating in a backup facility. Many logistical issues need to be considered as to when an organization should return from the alternate site to the primary one. The following lists a few of these issues:

- Ensuring the safety of employees
- Ensuring an adequate environment is provided (power, facility infrastructure, water, HVAC)
- Ensuring that the necessary equipment and supplies are present and in working order
- Ensuring proper communications and connectivity methods are working
- Properly testing the new environment

Once the coordinator, management, and salvage team sign off on the readiness of the primary site, the salvage team should carry out the following steps:

- Back up data from the alternate site and restore it within the primary site.
- Carefully terminate contingency operations.
- Securely transport equipment and personnel to the primary site.

The least critical functions should be moved back first, so if there are issues in network configurations or connectivity, or important steps were not carried out, the critical operations of the organization are not negatively affected. Why go through the trouble of moving the most critical systems and operations to a safe and stable alternate site, only to return them to a main site that is untested? Let the less critical departments act as the canary in the coal mine. If they survive, then move the more critical components of the organization to the main site.

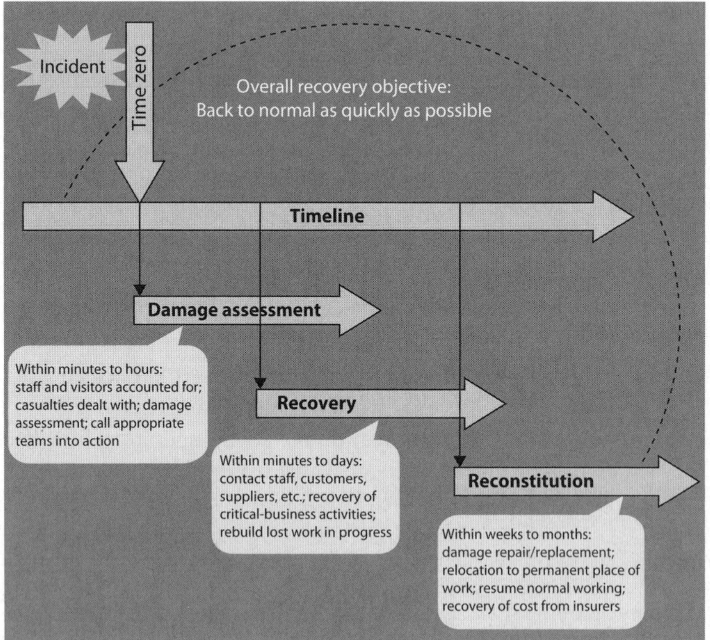

Training and Awareness

Training your DR team on the execution of a DRP is critical for at least three reasons. First, it allows you to validate that the plan will actually work. If your DR team is doing a walkthrough exercise in response to a fictitious scenario, you'll find out very quickly whether the plan would work or not. If it doesn't work in a training event when the stress level and stakes are low, then there is no chance it would work in a real emergency.

Another reason to train is to ensure that everyone knows what they're supposed to do, when, where, and how. Disasters are stressful, messy affairs and key people may not be thinking clearly. It is important for them to have a familiar routine to fall back on. In a perfect world, you would train often enough for your team to develop "muscle memory" that allows them to automatically do the right things without even thinking.

Lastly, training can help establish that you are exercising due care. This could keep you out of legal trouble in the aftermath of a disaster, particularly if people end up getting hurt. A good plan and evidence of a trained workforce can go a long way to reduce liability if regulators or other investigators come knocking. As always, consult your attorneys to ensure you are meeting all applicable legal and regulatory obligations.

When thinking of training and "muscle memory," you should also consider everyone else in the organization that is not part of the DR team. You want all your staff to have an awareness of the major things they need to do to support DR. This is why many of us conduct fire drills in our facilities: to ensure everyone knows how to get out of the building and where to assemble if we ever face this particular kind of disaster. There are many types of DR awareness events you can run, but you should at least consider three types of responses that everyone should be aware of: evacuations (e.g., for fires or explosives), shelter-in-place (e.g., for tornadoes or active shooters), and remain-at-home (e.g., for overnight flooding).

Lessons Learned

As mentioned on the first page of this chapter, no battle plan ever survived first contact with the enemy. When you try to execute your DRP in a real disaster, you will find the need to disregard parts of it, make on-the-fly changes to others, and faithfully execute the rest. This is why you should incorporate lessons learned from any actual disasters and actual responses. The DR team should perform a "postmortem" on the response and ensure that necessary changes are made to plans, contracts, personnel, processes, and procedures.

Military organizations collect lessons learned in two steps. The first steps, called a *hotwash*, is a hasty one that happens right after the event is concluded (i.e., restoration is completed). The term comes from the military practice of dousing rifles with very hot water immediately after an engagement to quickly get the worst grit and debris off their weapons. The reason you want to conduct a hotwash right away is that memories will be freshest right after restoring the systems. The idea is not necessarily to figure out how to fix anything, but rather to quickly list as many things that went well or poorly as possible before participants start to forget them.

The second event at which lessons learned are collected in the military is much more deliberate. An after-action review (AAR) happens several days after completion of the DR and allows participants to think things through and start formulating possible ways to do better in the future. The AAR facilitator, ideally armed with the notes from the hotwash, presents each issue that was recorded (good or bad), a brief discussion of it, and then opens the floor for recommendations. Keep in mind that since you're dealing with things that went well or poorly, sometimes the group recommendation will be to "sustain" the issue or, in other words, keep doing things the same way in the future. More frequently, however, there are at least minor tweaks that can improve future performance.

Testing Disaster Recovery Plans

The disaster recovery plan should be tested regularly because environments continually change. Interestingly, many organizations are moving away from the concept of "testing," because a test naturally leads to a pass or fail score, and in the end, that type of score is not very productive. Instead, many organizations are adopting the concept of "exercises," which appear less stressful, better focused, and ultimately more productive to the participants. Each time the DRP is exercised or tested, improvements and efficiencies are generally uncovered, yielding better and better results over time. The responsibility of establishing periodic exercises and the maintenance of the plan should be assigned to a specific person or persons who will have overall ownership responsibilities for the disaster recovery initiatives within the organization.

The maintenance of the DRP should be incorporated into change management procedures. That way, any changes in the environment are reflected in the plan itself.

Tests and disaster recovery exercises should be performed at least once a year. An organization should have no real confidence in a developed plan until it has actually been tested. Exercises prepare personnel for what they may face and provide a controlled environment to learn the tasks expected of them. These exercises also point out issues to the planning team and management that may not have been previously thought about and addressed as part of the planning process. The exercises, in the end, demonstrate whether an organization can actually recover after a disaster.

The exercise should have a predetermined scenario that the organization may indeed be faced with one day. Specific parameters and a scope of the exercise must be worked out before sounding the alarms. The team of testers must agree upon what exactly is getting tested and how to properly determine success or failure. The team must agree upon the timing and duration of the exercise, who will participate in the exercise, who will receive which assignments, and what steps should be taken. Also, the team needs to determine whether hardware, software, personnel, procedures, and communications lines are going to be tested and whether it is all or a subset of these resources that will be included in the event. If the test will include moving some equipment to an alternate site, then transportation, extra equipment, and alternate site readiness must be addressed and assessed.

Most organizations cannot afford to have these exercises interrupt production or productivity, so the exercises may need to take place in sections or at specific times, which will require logistical planning. Written exercise plans should be developed that will test for specific weaknesses in the overall DRP. The first exercises should not include all employees, but rather a small representative sample of the organization. This allows both the planners and the participants to refine the plan. It also allows each part of the organization to learn its roles and responsibilities. Then, larger exercises can take place so overall operations will not be negatively affected.

The people conducting these exercises should expect to encounter problems and mistakes. After all, identifying potential problems and mistakes is why they are conducting the exercises in the first place. An organization would rather have employees make mistakes during an exercise so they can learn from them and perform their tasks more effectively during a real disaster.

NOTE After a disaster, telephone service may not be available. For communications purposes, alternatives should be in place, such as mobile phones or hand-held radios.

A few different types of exercises and tests can be used, each with its own pros and cons. The following sections explain the different types of assessment events.

Checklist Test

In this type of test, copies of the DRP are distributed to the different departments and functional areas for review. This enables each functional manager to review the plan and indicate if anything has been left out or if some approaches should be modified or deleted. This method ensures that nothing is taken for granted or omitted, as might be the case in a single-department review. Once the departments have reviewed their copies and made suggestions, the planning team then integrates those changes into the master plan.

NOTE The checklist test is also called the desk check test.

Structured Walkthrough Test

In this test, representatives from each department or functional area come together and go over the plan to ensure its accuracy. The group reviews the objectives of the plan; discusses the scope and assumptions of the plan; reviews the organization's reporting structure; and evaluates the testing, maintenance, and training requirements described. This gives the people responsible for making sure a disaster recovery happens effectively and efficiently an opportunity to review what has been decided upon and what is expected of them.

The group walks through different scenarios of the plan from beginning to end to make sure nothing was left out. This also raises the awareness of team members about the recovery procedures.

Tabletop Exercises

Tabletop exercises (TTXs) may or may not happen at a tabletop, but they do not involve a technical control infrastructure. TTXs can happen at an executive level (e.g., C-suite) or at a team level (e.g., SOC), or anywhere in between. The idea is usually to test procedures and ensure they actually do what they're intended to and that everyone knows their role in responding to a disaster. TTXs require relatively few resources apart from deliberate planning by qualified individuals and the undisturbed time and attention of the participants.

After determining the goals of the exercise and vetting them with the senior leadership of the organization, the planning team develops a scenario that touches on the important aspects of the response plan. The idea is normally not to cover every contingency, but to ensure the DR team is able to respond to the likeliest and/or most dangerous scenarios. As they develop the exercise, the planning team considers branches and sequels at every point in the scenario. A *branch* is a point in which the participants may choose one of multiple approaches to respond. If the branches are not carefully managed and controlled, the TTX could wander into uncharted and unproductive directions. Conversely, a *sequel* is a follow-on to a given action in the response. For instance, as part of the response, the strategic communications team may issue statements to the news media. A sequel to that could involve a media outlet challenging the statement, which in turn would require a response by the team. Like branches, sequels must be used carefully to keep the exercise on course. Senior leadership support and good scenario development are critical ingredients to attract and engage the right participants. Like any contest, a TTX is only as good as the folks who show up to play.

EXAM TIP Tabletop exercises are also called read-through exercises.

Simulation Test

This type of test takes a lot more planning and people. In this situation, all employees who participate in operational and support functions, or their representatives, come together to practice executing the disaster recovery plan based on a specific scenario. The scenario is used to test the reaction of each operational and support representative. Again, this is done to ensure specific steps were not left out and that certain threats were not overlooked. It raises the awareness of the people involved.

The exercise includes only those materials that will be available in an actual disaster, to portray a more realistic environment. The simulation test continues up to the point of actual relocation to an offsite facility and actual shipment of replacement equipment.

Parallel Test

In a parallel test, some systems are moved to the alternate site and processing takes place. The results are compared with the regular processing that is done at the original site. This ensures that the specific systems can actually perform adequately at the alternate offsite facility and points out any tweaking or reconfiguring that is necessary.

Full-Interruption Test

This type of test is the most intrusive to regular operations and business productivity. The original site is actually shut down, and processing takes place at the alternate site. The recovery team fulfills its obligations in preparing the systems and environment for the alternate site. All processing is done only on devices at the alternate offsite facility.

This is a full-blown exercise that takes a lot of planning and coordination, but it can reveal many holes in the plan that need to be fixed before an actual disaster hits. Full-interruption tests should be performed only after all other types of tests have been successful. They are the riskiest type and can impact the business in very serious and devastating ways if not managed properly; therefore, senior management approval needs to be obtained prior to performing full-interruption tests.

The type of organization and its goals will dictate what approach to the training exercise is most effective. Each organization may have a different approach and unique aspects. If detailed planning methods and processes are going to be taught, then specific training may be required rather than general training that provides an overview. Higher-quality training will result in an increase in employee interest and commitment.

During and after each type of test, a record of the significant events should be documented and reported to management so it is aware of all outcomes of the test.

Other Types of Training

Other types of training that employees need in addition to disaster recovery training include first aid and cardiac pulmonary resuscitation (CPR), how to properly use a fire extinguisher, evacuation routes and crowd control methods, emergency communications procedures, and how to properly shut down equipment in different types of disasters.

The more technical employees may need training on how to redistribute network resources and how to use different telecommunications lines if the main one goes down. They may need to know about redundant power supplies and be trained and tested on the procedures for moving critical systems from one power supply to the next.

Business Continuity

When a disaster strikes, ensuring that the organization is able to continue its operations requires more than simply restoring data from backups. Also necessary are the detailed procedures that outline the activities to keep the critical systems available and ensure that operations and processing are not interrupted. Business continuity planning defines what should take place during and after an incident. Actions that are required to take place for emergency response, continuity of operations, and dealing with major outages must be documented and readily available to the operations staff. There should be at least two instances of these documents: the original that is kept on-site and a copy that is at an offsite location.

BC plans should not be trusted until they have been tested. Organizations should carry out exercises to ensure that the staff fully understands their responsibilities and how to carry them out. We already covered the various types of exercises that can be used to test plans and staff earlier in this chapter when we discussed DR. Another issue to consider is how to keep these plans up to date. As our dynamic, networked environments change, so must our plans on how to rescue them when necessary.

Although in the security industry "contingency planning" and "business continuity planning (BCP)" are commonly used interchangeably, it is important that you understand the actual difference for the CISSP exam. BCP addresses how to keep the organization in business after a major disruption takes place. It is about the survivability of the organization and making sure that critical functions can still take place even after a disaster. Contingency plans address how to deal with small incidents that do not qualify as disasters, as in power outages, server failures, a down communication link to the Internet, or the corruption of software. Organizations must be ready to deal with both large and small issues that they may encounter.

EXAM TIP BCP is broad in scope and deals with survival of the organization. Contingency plans are narrow in scope and deal with specific issues.

As a security professional you will most likely not be in charge of BCP, but you should most certainly be an active participant in developing the BCP. You will also be involved in BC exercises and may even be a lead in those that focus on information systems. To effectively participate in BC planning and exercises, you should be familiar with the BCP life cycle, how to ensure continuous availability of critical information systems, and the particular requirements of the end-user environments. We look at these in the following sections.

BCP Life Cycle

Remember that most organizations aren't static, but change, often rapidly, as do the conditions under which they must operate. Thus, BCP should be considered a life cycle in order to deal with the constant and inevitable change that will affect it. Understanding and maintaining each step of the BCP life cycle is critical to ensuring that the BC plan remains useful to the organization. The BCP life cycle is outlined in Figure 23-7.

Note that this life cycle has two modes: normal management (shown in the top half of Figure 23-7) and incident management (shown in the bottom half). In the normal mode, the focus of the BC team is on ensuring preparedness. Obviously, we want to start

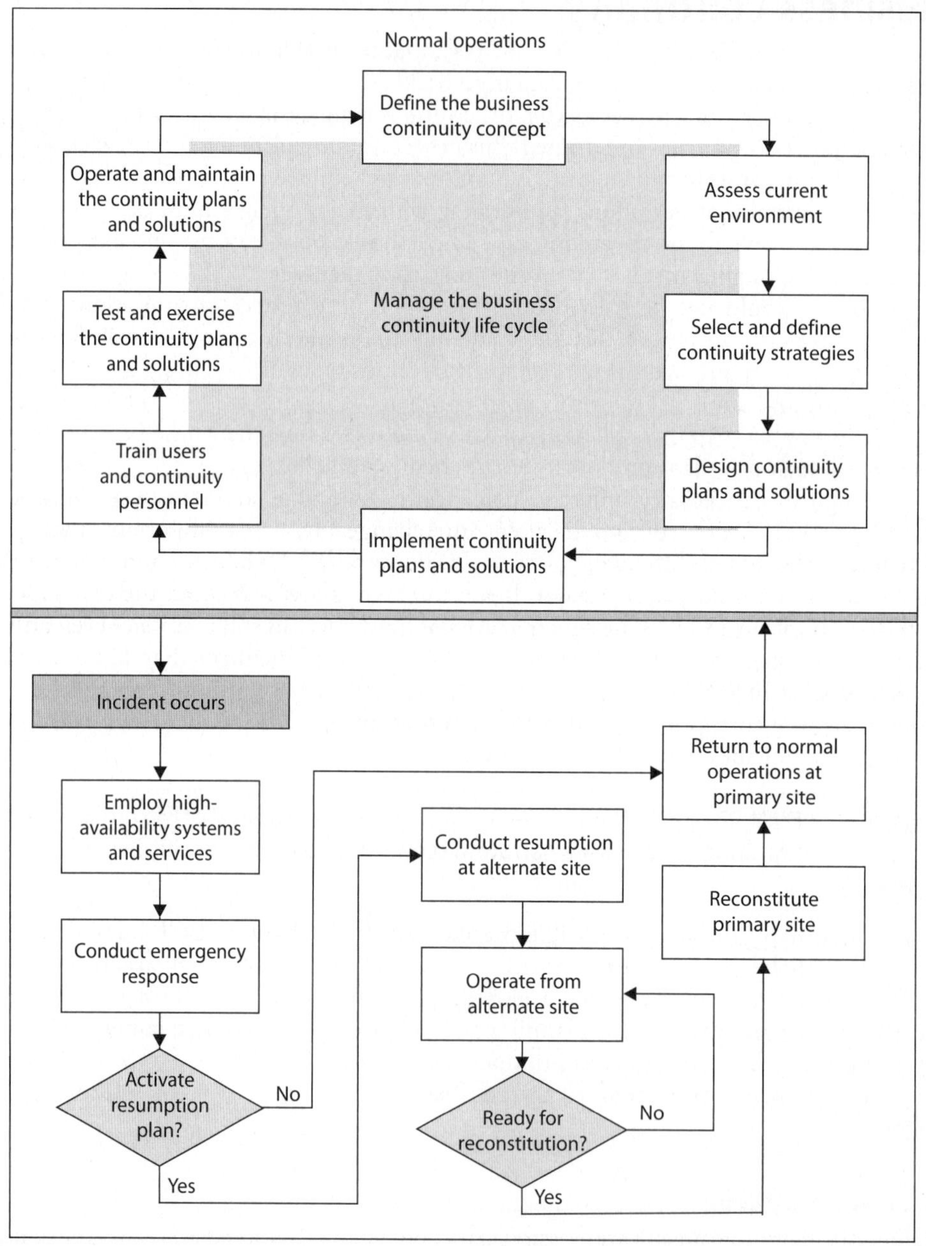

Figure 23-7 BCP life cycle

with a clearly defined concept for what business continuity means for the organization. What are the critical business functions that must continue to operate regardless of what incident happens? What are the minimum levels of performance that are acceptable for these functions?

Once we define the BC concept, we can take a look at the current environment and consider the strategies that would allow continuity of operations under a variety of conditions. It is important to consider that, unlike DR planning, not every type of incident covered in BCP involves loss of IT capabilities. Many organizations suffered tremendously in 2020 because their BCP didn't account for a global pandemic in which many (or even all) staff members would have to work from home for extended periods of time. Information systems are certainly an important part of the continuity strategies, plans, and solutions, but the scope of the BCP is much broader than that of the DRP.

The BC plan is only useful if the organization in general, and the BC team in particular, knows how to execute the plan. This requires periodic training, tests, and exercises to ensure that both the plan and the staff are able to keep the business going no matter what comes their way. As we find gaps and opportunities for improvement, we get to redefine our BCP concept and start another run through the cycle. This continuous improvement is key to being able to switch into incident management mode (at the bottom of Figure 23-7) when needed and execute the BC plan (and, potentially, the DR plan) to keep the business going.

Information Systems Availability

Our main job as CISSPs in the BCP life cycle is to ensure the continuous availability of organizational information systems. To this end, we should ensure the BCP includes backup solutions for the following:

- Network and computer equipment
- Voice and data communications resources
- Human resources
- Transportation of equipment and personnel
- Environment issues (HVAC)
- Data and personnel security issues
- Supplies (paper, forms, cabling, and so on)
- Documentation

The BCP team must understand the organization's current technical environment. This means the planners have to know the intimate details of the network, communications technologies, computers, network equipment, and software requirements that are necessary to get the critical functions up and running. What is surprising to some people is that many organizations do not *totally* understand how their network is configured and how it actually works, because the network may have been established 10 to 15 years ago and has kept growing and changing under different administrators and personnel.

Outsourcing

Part of the planned response to a disaster may be to outsource some of the affected activities to another organization. Organizations do outsource activities—help-desk services, manufacturing, legal advice—all the time, so why not important functions affected by a disaster? Some companies specialize in disaster response and continuity planning and can act as expert consultants.

That is all well and good. However, be aware that your organization is still ultimately responsible for the continuity of a product or service that is outsourced. Clients and customers will expect the organization to ensure continuity of its products and services, either by itself or by having chosen the right outside vendors to provide the products and services. If outside vendors are brought in, the active participation of key in-house managers in their work is still essential. They still need to supervise the work of the outside vendors.

This same concern applies to normal, third-party suppliers of goods and services to the organization. Any BCP should take them into account as well. Note that the process for evaluating an outsourced company for BCP is like that for evaluating the organization itself. The organization must make sure that the outsourced company is financially viable and has its own solid BCP.

The organization can take the following steps to better ensure the continuity of its outsourcing:

- Make the ability of such companies to reliably assure continuity of products and services part of any work proposals.
- Make sure that business continuity planning is included in contracts with such companies, and that their responsibilities and levels of service are clearly spelled out.
- Draw up realistic and reasonable service levels that the outsourced firm will meet during an incident.
- If possible, have the outsourcing companies take part in BCP awareness programs, training, and testing.

The goal is to make the supply of goods and services from outsources as resilient as possible in the wake of a disaster.

New devices are added, new computers are added, new software packages are added, VoIP may have been integrated, and the DMZ may have been split up into three DMZs, with an extranet for the organization's partners. Maybe a company bought and merged with another company and network. Over ten years, a number of technology refreshes most likely have taken place, and the individuals who are maintaining the environment now likely are not the same people who built it ten years ago. Many IT departments experience extensive employee turnover every five years. And most organizational network schematics are notoriously out of date because everyone is busy with their current tasks (or will come up with new tasks just to get out of having to update the schematic).

So the BCP team has to make sure that if the networked environment is partially or totally destroyed, the recovery team has the knowledge and skill to properly rebuild it.

NOTE Many organizations use VoIP, which means that if the network goes down, network and voice capability are unavailable. The BCP team should address the possible need of redundant voice systems.

The BCP team needs to incorporate into the BCP several things that are commonly overlooked, such as hardware replacements, software products, documentation, environmental needs, and human resources.

Hardware Backups

The BCP needs to identify the equipment required to keep the critical functions up and running. This may include servers, user workstations, routers, switches, tape backup devices, and more. The needed inventory may seem simple enough, but as they say, the devil is in the details. If the recovery team is planning to use images to rebuild newly purchased servers and workstations because the original ones were destroyed, for example, will the images work on the new computers? Using images instead of building systems from scratch can be a time-saving task, unless the team finds out that the replacement equipment is a newer version and thus the images cannot be used. The BCP should plan for the recovery team to use the organization's current images, but also have a manual process of how to build each critical system from scratch with the necessary configurations.

The BCP also needs to be based on accurate estimates of how long it will take for new equipment to arrive. For example, if the organization has identified Dell as its equipment replacement supplier, how long will it take this vendor to send 20 servers and 30 workstations to the offsite facility? After a disaster hits, the organization could be in its offsite facility only to find that its equipment will take three weeks to be delivered. So, the SLA for the identified vendors needs to be investigated to make sure the organization is not further damaged by delays. Once the parameters of the SLA are understood, the BCP team must make a decision between depending upon the vendor and purchasing redundant systems and storing them as backups in case the primary equipment is destroyed.

As described earlier, when potential organizational risks are identified, it is better to take preventive steps to reduce the potential damage. After the calculation of the MTD values, the team will know how long the organization can operate without a specific device. This data should be used to make the decision on whether the organization should depend on the vendor's SLA or make readily available a hot-swappable redundant system. If the organization will lose $50,000 per hour if a particular server goes down, then the team should elect to implement redundant systems and technology.

If an organization is using any legacy computers and hardware and a disaster hits tomorrow, where would it find replacements for this legacy equipment? The BCP team should identify legacy devices and understand the risk the organization is facing if replacements are unavailable. This finding has caused many organizations to move from legacy systems to commercial off-the-shelf (COTS) products to ensure that timely replacement is possible.

Software Backups

Most organizations' IT departments have their array of software disks and licensing information here or there—or possibly in one centralized location. If the facility were destroyed and the IT department's current environment had to be rebuilt, how would it gain access to these software packages? The BCP team should make sure to have an inventory of the necessary software required for mission-critical functions and have backup copies at an offsite facility. Hardware is usually not worth much to an organization without the software required to run on it. The software that needs to be backed up can be in the form of applications, utilities, databases, and operating systems. The business continuity plan must have provisions to back up and protect these items along with hardware and data.

It is common for organizations to work with software developers to create customized software programs. For example, in the banking world, individual financial institutions need software that enables their bank tellers to interact with accounts, hold account information in databases and mainframes, provide online banking, carry out data replication, and perform a thousand other types of bank-like functionalities. This specialized type of software is developed and available through a handful of software vendors that specialize in this market. When bank A purchases this type of software for all of its branches, the software has to be specially customized for its environment and needs. Once this banking software is installed, the whole organization depends upon it for its minute-by-minute activities.

When bank A receives the specialized and customized banking software from the software vendor, bank A does not receive the source code. Instead, the software vendor provides bank A with a compiled version. Now, what if this software vendor goes out of business because of a disaster or bankruptcy? Then bank A will require a new vendor to maintain and update this banking software; thus, the new vendor will need access to the source code.

The protection mechanism that bank A should implement is called *software escrow*, in which a third party holds the source code, backups of the compiled code, manuals, and other supporting materials. A contract between the software vendor, customer, and third party outlines who can do what, and when, with the source code. This contract usually states that the customer can have access to the source code only if and when the vendor goes out of business, is unable to carry out stated responsibilities, or is in breach of the original contract. If any of these activities takes place, then the customer is protected because it can still gain access to the source code and other materials through the third-party escrow agent.

Many organizations have been crippled by not implementing software escrow. They paid a software vendor to develop specialized software, and when the software vendor went belly up, the organizations did not have access to the code that their systems ran on.

End-User Environment

Because the end users are usually the worker bees of an organization, they must be provided a functioning environment as soon as possible after a disaster hits. This means that the BCP team must understand the current operational and technical functioning environment and examine critical pieces so they can replicate them.

In most situations, after a disaster, only a skeleton crew is put back to work. The BCP committee has previously identified the most critical functions of the organization during the analysis stage, and the employees who carry out those functions must be put back to work first. So the recovery process for the user environment should be laid out in different stages. The first stage is to get the most critical departments back online, the next stage is to get the second most important back online, and so on.

The BCP team needs to identify user requirements, such as whether users can work on stand-alone PCs or need to be connected in a network to fulfill specific tasks. For example, in a financial institution, users who work on stand-alone PCs might be able to accomplish some small tasks like filling out account forms, word processing, and accounting tasks, but they might need to be connected to a host system to update customer profiles and to interact with the database.

The BCP team also needs to identify how current automated tasks can be carried out manually if that becomes necessary. If the network is going to be down for 12 hours, could the necessary tasks be accomplished through traditional pen-and-paper methods? If the Internet connection is going to be down for five hours, could the necessary communications take place through phone calls? Instead of transmitting data through the internal mail system, could couriers be used to run information back and forth? Today, we are extremely dependent upon technology, but we often take for granted that it will always be there for us to use. It is up to the BCP team to realize that technology may be unavailable for a period of time and to come up with solutions for those situations.

EXAM TIP As a CISSP, your role in business continuity planning is most likely to be that of an active participant, not to lead it. BCP questions in the exam will be written with this in mind.

Chapter Review

There are four key take-aways in this chapter. The first is that you need to be able to identify and implement strategies that will enable your organization to recover from any disaster, supporting your organization's continuity of operations. Leveraging these strategies, you develop a detailed plan that includes the specific processes that the organization (and particularly the IT and security teams) will execute to recover from specific types of disasters. Thirdly, you have to know how to train your DR team to execute the plan flawlessly, even in the chaos of an actual disaster. This includes ensuring that everyone in the organization is aware of their role in the recovery efforts. Finally, the DRP is the cornerstone of the BCP, so you will be called upon to participate in broader business continuity planning and exercises, even if you are not in charge of that effort.

Quick Review

- Disaster recovery (DR) is the set of practices that enables an organization to minimize loss of, and restore, mission-critical technology infrastructure after a catastrophic incident.
- Business continuity (BC) is the set of practices that enables an organization to continue performing its critical functions through and after any disruptive event.
- The recovery time objective (RTO) is the maximum time period within which a mission-critical system must be restored to a designated service level after a disaster to avoid unacceptable consequences associated with a break in business continuity.
- The work recovery time (WRT) is the maximum amount of time available for certifying the functionality and integrity of restored systems and data so they can be put back into production.
- The recovery point objective (RPO) is the acceptable amount of data loss measured in time.
- The four commonly used data backup strategies are direct-attached storage, network-attached storage, cloud storage, and offline media.
- Electronic vaulting makes copies of files as they are modified and periodically transmits them to an offsite backup site.
- Remote journaling moves transaction logs to an offsite facility for database recovery, where only the reapplication of a series of changes to individual records is required to resynchronize the database.
- Offsite backup locations can supply hot, warm, or cold sites.
- A hot site is fully configured with hardware, software, and environmental needs. It can usually be up and running in a matter of hours. It is the most expensive option, but some organizations cannot be out of business longer than a day without very detrimental results.
- A warm site may have some computers, but it does have some peripheral devices, such as disk drives, controllers, and tape drives. This option is less expensive than a hot site, but takes more effort and time to become operational.
- A cold site is just a building with power, raised floors, and utilities. No devices are available. This is the cheapest of the three options, but can take weeks to get up and operational.
- In a reciprocal agreement, one organization agrees to allow another organization to use its facilities in case of a disaster, and vice versa. Reciprocal agreements are very tricky to implement and may be unenforceable. However, they offer a relatively cheap offsite option and are sometimes the only choice.
- A redundant (or mirrored) site is equipped and configured exactly like the primary site and is completely synchronized, ready to become the primary site at a moment's notice.

- High availability (HA) is a combination of technologies and processes that work together to ensure that some specific thing is up and running most of the time.
- Quality of service (QoS) defines minimum acceptable performance characteristics of a particular service, such as response time, CPU utilization, or network bandwidth utilization.
- Fault tolerance is the capability of a technology to continue to operate as expected even if something unexpected takes place (a fault).
- Resilience means that the system continues to function, albeit in a degraded fashion, when a fault is encountered.
- When returning to the original site after a disaster, the least critical organizational units should go back first.
- Disaster recovery plans can be tested through checklist tests, structured walkthroughs, tabletop exercises, simulation tests, parallel tests, or full-interruption tests.
- Business continuity planning addresses how to keep the organization in business after a major disruption takes place, but it is important to note that the scope is much broader than that of disaster recovery.
- The BCP life cycle includes developing the BC concept; assessing the current environment; implementing continuity strategies, plans, and solutions; training the staff; and testing, exercising, and maintaining the plans and solutions.
- An important part of the business continuity plan is to communicate its requirements and procedures to all employees.

Questions

Please remember that these questions are formatted and asked in a certain way for a reason. Keep in mind that the CISSP exam is asking questions at a conceptual level. Questions may not always have the perfect answer, and the candidate is advised against always looking for the perfect answer. Instead, the candidate should look for the best answer in the list.

1. Which best describes a hot-site facility versus a warm- or cold-site facility?
   - **A.** A site that has disk drives, controllers, and tape drives
   - **B.** A site that has all necessary PCs, servers, and telecommunications
   - **C.** A site that has wiring, central air-conditioning, and raised flooring
   - **D.** A mobile site that can be brought to the organization's parking lot
2. Which of the following describes a cold site?
   - **A.** Fully equipped and operational in a few hours
   - **B.** Partially equipped with data processing equipment
   - **C.** Expensive and fully configured
   - **D.** Provides environmental measures but no equipment

3. Which is the best description of remote journaling?
   - A. Backing up bulk data to an offsite facility
   - B. Backing up transaction logs to an offsite facility
   - C. Capturing and saving transactions to two mirrored servers in-house
   - D. Capturing and saving transactions to different media types
4. Which of the following does not describe a reciprocal agreement?
   - A. The agreement is enforceable.
   - B. It is a cheap solution.
   - C. It may be able to be implemented right after a disaster.
   - D. It could overwhelm a current data processing site.
5. If a system is fault tolerant, what would you expect it to do?
   - A. Continue to operate as expected even if something unexpected takes place
   - B. Continue to function in a degraded fashion
   - C. Tolerate outages caused by known faults
   - D. Raise an alarm, but tolerate an outage caused by any fault
6. Which of the following approaches to testing your disaster recovery plan would be least desirable if you had to maintain high availability of over 99.999 percent?
   - A. Checklist test
   - B. Parallel test
   - C. Full-interruption test
   - D. Structured walkthrough test

Use the following scenario to answer Questions 7–10. You are the CISO of a small research and development (R&D) company and realize that you don't have a disaster recovery plan (DRP). The projects your organization handles are extremely sensitive and, despite having a very limited budget, you have to bring the risk of project data being lost as close to zero as you can. Recovery time is not as critical because you bill your work based on monthly deliverables and have some leeway at your disposal. Because of the sensitivity of your work, remote working is frowned upon and you keep your research data on local servers (including Exchange for e-mail, Mattermost for group chat, and Apache for web) at your headquarters (and only) site.

7. Which recovery site strategy would be best for you to consider?
   - A. Reciprocal agreement
   - B. Hot site
   - C. Warm site
   - D. Cold site

8. Which of the following recovery site characteristics would be best for your organization?
   - A. As close to headquarters as possible within budgetary constraints
   - B. 100 miles away from headquarters, on a different power grid
   - C. 15 miles away from headquarters on a different power grid
   - D. As far away from headquarters as possible
9. Which data backup storage strategy would you want to implement?
   - A. Direct-attached storage
   - B. Network-attached storage
   - C. Offline media
   - D. Cloud storage
10. Which of the following would be the best way to communicate with all members of the organization in the event of a disaster that takes out your site?
    - A. Internal Mattermost channel
    - B. External Slack channel
    - C. Exchange e-mail
    - D. Call trees

Answers

1. **B.** A hot site is a facility that is fully equipped and properly configured so that it can be up and running within hours to get an organization back into production. Answer B gives the best definition of a fully functional environment.
2. **D.** A cold site only provides environmental measures—wiring, HVAC, raised floors—basically a shell of a building and no more.
3. **B.** Remote journaling is a technology used to transmit data to an offsite facility, but this usually only includes moving the journal or transaction logs to the offsite facility, not the actual files.
4. **A.** A reciprocal agreement is not enforceable, meaning that the organization that agreed to let the damaged organization work out of its facility can decide not to allow this to take place. A reciprocal agreement is a better secondary backup option if the original plan falls through.
5. **A.** Fault tolerance is the capability of a technology to continue to operate as expected even if something unexpected takes place (a fault), with no degradations or outages.
6. **C.** A full-interruption test is the most intrusive to regular operations and business productivity. The original site is actually shut down, and processing takes place at the alternate site. This is almost guaranteed to exceed your allowed downtime unless everything went extremely well.

7. **D.** Because you are working on a tight budget and have the luxury of recovery time, you want to consider the least expensive option. A reciprocal agreement would be ideal except for the sensitivity of your data, which could not be shared with a similar organization (that could, presumably, be a competitor at some point). The next option (cost-wise) is a cold site, which would work in the given scenario.
8. **C.** An ideal recovery site would be on a different power grid to minimize the risk that power will be out on both sites, but close enough for employees to commute. This second point is important because, due to the sensitivity of your work, your organization has a low tolerance for remote work.
9. **C.** Since your data is critical enough that you have to bring the risk of it being lost as close to zero as you can, you would want to use offline media such as tape backups, optical discs, or even external drives that are disconnected after each backup (and potentially removed offsite). This is the slowest and most expensive approach, but is also the most resistant to attacks.
10. **B.** If your site is taken out, you would lose both Exchange and Mattermost since those servers are hosted locally. Call trees only work well for initial notification, leaving an externally hosted Slack channel as the best option. This would require your staff to be aware of this means of communication and have accounts created before the disaster.

PART VIII

Software Development Security

CHAPTER 24

Software Development

This chapter presents the following:

- Software development life cycle
- Development methodologies
- Operation and maintenance
- Maturity models

Always code as if the guy who ends up maintaining your code will be a violent psychopath who knows where you live.

—John F. Woods

Software is usually developed with a strong focus on functionality, not security. In many cases, security controls are bolted on as an afterthought (if at all). To get the best of both worlds, security and functionality have to be designed and integrated at each phase of the software development life cycle. Security should be interwoven into the core of a software product and provide protection at the necessary layers. This is a better approach than trying to develop a front end or wrapper that may reduce the overall functionality and leave security holes when the software has to be integrated into a production environment.

Before we get too deep into secure software development, however, we have to develop a shared understanding of how code is developed in the first place. In this chapter we will cover the complex world of software development so that we can understand the bad things that can happen when security is not interwoven into products properly (discussed in Chapter 25).

Software Development Life Cycle

The life cycle of software development deals with putting repeatable and predictable processes in place that help ensure functionality, cost, quality, and delivery schedule requirements are met. So instead of winging it and just starting to develop code for a project, how can we make sure we build the best software product possible?

Several *software development life cycle (SDLC)* models have been developed over the years, which we will cover later in this section, but the crux of each model deals with the following phases:

- **Requirements gathering** Determining *why* to create this software, *what* the software will do, and *for whom* the software will be created
- **Design** Encapsulating into a functional design *how* the software will accomplish the requirements
- **Development** Programming software code to meet specifications laid out in the design phase and integrating that code with existing systems and/or libraries
- **Testing** Verifying and validating software to ensure that the software works as planned and that goals are met
- **Operations and maintenance** Deploying the software and then ensuring that it is properly configured, patched, and monitored

EXAM TIP You don't need to memorize the phases of the SDLC. We discuss them here so you understand all the tasks that go into developing software and how to integrate security throughout the whole cycle.

In the following sections we will cover the different phases that make up an SDLC model and some specific items about each phase that are important to understand.

Software Development Roles

The specific roles within a software development team will vary based on the methodology being used, the maturity of the organization, and the size of the project (to name just a few parameters). Typically, however, a team has at least the following roles:

- **Project manager (PM)** This role has overall responsibility for the software development project, particularly with regard to cost, schedule, performance, and risk.
- **Team leads** It is rare for software projects to be tackled by a single team, so we usually divide them up and assign a good developer to lead each part.
- **Architect** Sometimes called a tech lead, this role figures out what technologies to use internally or when interfacing with external systems.
- **Software engineer** The people who actually write the programming code are oftentimes specialists in either frontends (e.g., user interfaces) or various types of backends (e.g., business logic, databases). Engineers that can do all of this are called full-stack developers.
- **Quality assurance (QA)** Whether this is a single person or an entire team, this role implements and runs testing processes that detect software defects as early as possible.

Keep in mind that the discussion that follows covers phases that may happen repeatedly and in limited scope depending on the development methodology being used. Before we get into the phases of the SDLC, let's take a brief look at the glue that holds them together: project management.

Project Management

Many developers know that good project management keeps the project moving in the right direction, allocates the necessary resources, provides the necessary leadership, and hopes for the best but plans for the worst. Project management processes should be put into place to make sure the software development project executes each life-cycle phase properly. Project management is an important part of product development, and security management is an important part of project management.

The project manager draws up a security plan at the beginning of a development project and integrates it into the functional plan to ensure that security is not overlooked. This plan will probably be broad and should refer to documented references for more detailed information. The references could include computer standards (RFCs, IEEE standards, and best practices), documents developed in previous projects, security policies, accreditation statements, incident-handling plans, and national or international guidelines. This helps ensure that the plan stays on target.

The security plan should have a life cycle of its own. It will need to be added to, subtracted from, and explained in more detail as the project continues. Keeping the security plan up to date for future reference is important, because losing track of actions, activities, and decisions is very easy once a large and complex project gets underway.

The security plan and project management activities could be scrutinized later, particularly if a vulnerability causes losses to a third party, so we should document security-related decisions. Being able to demonstrate that security was fully considered in each phase of the SDLC can prove that the team exercised due care and this, in turn, can mitigate future liabilities. To this end, the documentation must accurately reflect how the product was built and how it is supposed to operate once implemented into an environment.

If a software product is being developed for a specific customer, it is common for a *Statement of Work (SOW)* to be developed, which describes the product and customer requirements. A detailed SOW helps to ensure that all stakeholders understand these requirements and don't make any undocumented assumptions.

Sticking to what is outlined in the SOW is important so that *scope creep* does not take place. If the scope of a project continually extends (creeps) in an uncontrollable manner, the project may never end, not meet its goals, run out of funding, or all of the foregoing. If the customer wants to modify its requirements, it is important that the SOW is updated and funding is properly reviewed.

A *work breakdown structure (WBS)* is a project management tool used to define and group a project's individual work elements in an organized manner. It is a deliberate decomposition of the project into tasks and subtasks that result in clearly defined deliverables. The SDLC should be illustrated in a WBS format, so that each phase is properly addressed.

Requirements Gathering Phase

This is the phase in which everyone involved in the software development project attempts to understand why the project is needed and what the scope of the project entails. Typically, either a specific customer needs a new application or a demand for the product exists in the market. During this phase, the software development team examines the software's requirements and proposed functionality, engages in brainstorming sessions, and reviews obvious restrictions.

A conceptual definition of the project should be initiated and developed to ensure everyone is on the right page and that this is a proper product to develop. This phase could include evaluating products currently on the market and identifying any demands not being met by current vendors. This definition could also be a direct request for a specific product from a current or future customer.

Typically, the following tasks should be accomplished in this phase:

- Requirements gathering (including security ones)
- Security risk assessment
- Privacy risk assessment
- Risk-level acceptance

The security requirements of the product should be defined in the categories of availability, integrity, and confidentiality. What type of security is required for the software product and to what degree? Some of these requirements may come from applicable external regulations. For example, if the application will deal with payment cards, PCI DSS will dictate some requirements, such as encryption for card information.

An initial security risk assessment should be carried out to identify the potential threats and their associated consequences. This process usually involves asking many, many questions to elicit and document the laundry list of vulnerabilities and threats, the probability of these vulnerabilities being exploited, and the outcome if one of these threats actually becomes real and a compromise takes place. The questions vary from product to product—such as its intended purpose, the expected environment it will be implemented in, the personnel involved, and the types of businesses that would purchase and use the product.

The sensitivity level of the data that many software products store and process has only increased in importance over the years. After a *privacy risk assessment*, a *privacy impact rating* can be assigned, which indicates the sensitivity level of the data that will be processed or accessible. Some software vendors incorporate the following privacy impact ratings in their software development assessment processes:

- **P1, High Privacy Risk** The feature, product, or service stores or transfers personally identifiable information (PII), monitors the user with an ongoing transfer of anonymous data, changes settings or file type associations, or installs software.
- **P2, Moderate Privacy Risk** The sole behavior that affects privacy in the feature, product, or service is a one-time, user-initiated, anonymous data transfer (e.g., the user clicks a link and is directed to a website).

- **P3, Low Privacy Risk** No behaviors exist within the feature, product, or service that affect privacy. No anonymous or personal data is transferred, no PII is stored on the machine, no settings are changed on the user's behalf, and no software is installed.

The software vendor can develop its own privacy impact ratings and their associated definitions. As of this writing there are several formal approaches to conducting a privacy risk assessment, but none stands out as "the" standardized approach to defining a methodology for an assessment or these rating types, but as privacy increases in importance, we might see more standardization in these ratings and associated metrics.

The team tasked with documenting the requirements must understand the criteria for risk-level acceptance to make sure that mitigation efforts satisfy these criteria. Which risks are acceptable will depend on the results of the security and privacy risk assessments. The evaluated threats and vulnerabilities are used to estimate the cost/benefit ratios of the different security countermeasures. The level of each security attribute should be focused upon so that a clear direction on security controls can begin to take shape and can be integrated into the design and development phases.

The end state of the requirements gathering phase is typically a document called the Software (or System) Requirements Specification (SRS), which describes what the software will do and how it will perform. These two high-level objectives are also known as functional and nonfunctional requirements. A *functional requirement* describes a feature of the software system, such as reporting product inventories or processing customer orders. A *nonfunctional requirement* describes performance standards, such as the minimum number of simultaneous user sessions or the maximum response time for a query. Nonfunctional requirements also include security requirements, such as what data must be encrypted and what the acceptable cryptosystems are. The SRS, in a way, is a checklist that the software development team will use to develop the software and the customer will use to accept it.

The Unified Modeling Language (UML) is a common language used to graphically describe all aspects of software development. We will revisit it throughout the different phases, but in terms of software requirements, it allows us to capture both functional and nonfunctional requirements with use case diagrams (UCDs). We already saw these in Chapter 18 when we discussed testing of technical controls. If you look back to Figure 18-3, each use case (shown as verb phrases inside ovals) represents a high-level functional requirement. The associations can capture nonfunctional requirements through special labels, or these requirements can be spelled out in an accompanying use case description.

Design Phase

Once the requirements are formally documented, the software development team can begin figuring out how they will go about satisfying them. This is the phase that starts to map theory to reality. The theory encompasses all the requirements that were identified in the previous phase, and the design outlines how the product is actually going to accomplish these requirements.

Some organizations skip the design phase, but this can cause major delays and redevelopment efforts down the road because a broad vision of the product needs to be understood before looking strictly at the details. Instead, software development teams should develop written plans for how they will build software that satisfies each requirement. This plan usually comprises three different but interrelated models:

- **Informational model** Dictates the type of information to be processed and how it will move around the software system
- **Functional model** Outlines the tasks and functions the application needs to carry out and how they are sequenced and synchronized
- **Behavioral model** Explains the states the application will be in during and after specific transitions take place

For example, consider an antimalware software application. Its informational model would dictate how it processes information, such as virus signatures, modified system files, checksums on critical files, and virus activity. Its functional model would dictate how it scans a hard drive, checks e-mail for known virus signatures, monitors critical system files, and updates itself. Its behavioral model would indicate that when the system starts up, the antimalware software application will scan the hard drive and memory segments. The computer coming online would be the event that changes the state of the application. If it finds a virus, the application would change state and deal with the virus appropriately. Each state must be accounted for to ensure that the product does not go into an insecure state and act in an unpredictable way.

The data from the informational, functional, and behavioral models is incorporated into the software design document, which includes the data, architectural, and procedural design, as shown in Figure 24-1.

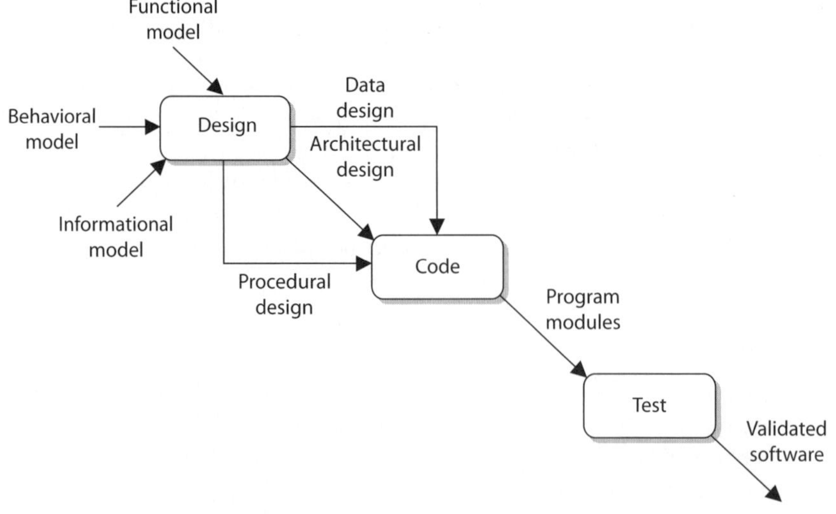

Figure 24-1 Information from three models can go into the design.

From a security point of view, the following items should also be accomplished in the design phase:

- Attack surface analysis
- Threat modeling

An *attack surface* is what is available to be used by an attacker against the product itself. As an analogy, if you were wearing a suit of armor and it covered only half of your body, the other half would be your vulnerable attack surface. Before you went into battle, you would want to reduce this attack surface by covering your body with as much protective armor as possible. The same can be said about software. The software development team should reduce the attack surface as much as possible because the greater the attack surface of software, the more avenues for the attacker; and hence, the greater the likelihood of a successful compromise.

The aim of an *attack surface analysis* is to identify and reduce the amount of code and functionality accessible to untrusted users. The basic strategies of attack surface reduction are to reduce the amount of code running, reduce entry points available to untrusted users, reduce privilege levels as much as possible, and eliminate unnecessary services. Attack surface analysis is generally carried out through specialized tools to enumerate different parts of a product and aggregate their findings into a numeral value. Attack surface analyzers scrutinize files, Registry keys, memory data, session information, processes, and services details. A sample attack surface report is shown in Figure 24-2.

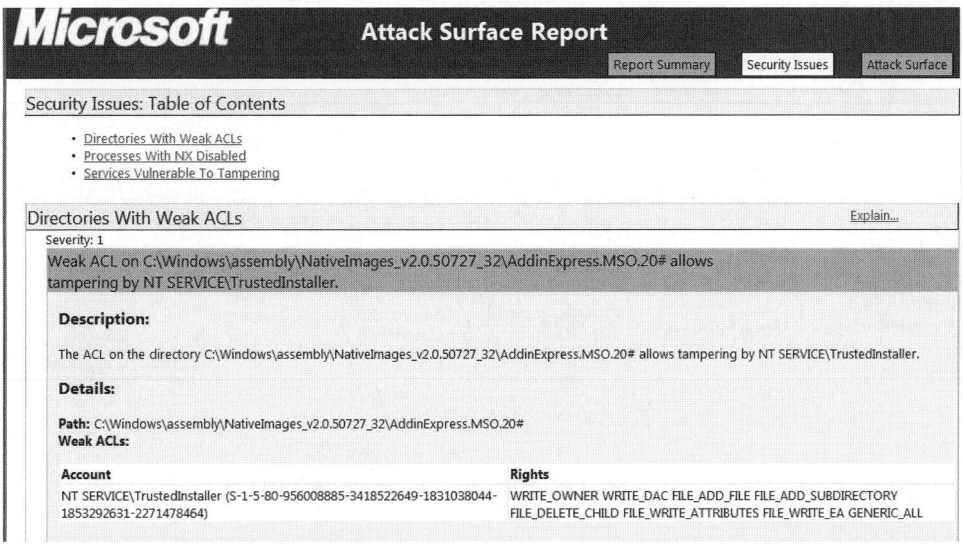

Figure 24-2 Attack surface analysis result

Threat modeling, which we covered in detail in Chapter 9 in the context of risk management, is a systematic approach used to understand how different threats could be realized and how a successful compromise could take place. As a hypothetical example, if you were responsible for ensuring that the government building in which you work is safe from terrorist attacks, you would run through scenarios that terrorists would most likely carry out so that you fully understand how to protect the facility and the people within it. You could think through how someone could bring a bomb into the building, and then you would better understand the screening activities that need to take place at each entry point. A scenario of someone running a car into the building would bring up the idea of implementing bollards around the sensitive portions of the facility. The scenario of terrorists entering sensitive locations in the facility (data center, CEO office) would help illustrate the layers of physical access controls that should be implemented.

These same scenario-based exercises should take place during the design phase of software development. Just as you would think about how potential terrorists could enter and exit a facility, the software development team should think through how potentially malicious activities can happen at different input and output points of the software and the types of compromises that can take place within the guts of the software itself.

It is common for software development teams to develop threat trees, as shown in Figure 24-3. A *threat tree* is a tool that allows the development team to understand all the ways specific threats can be realized; thus, it helps them understand what type of security controls they should implement in the software to mitigate the risks associated with each threat type.

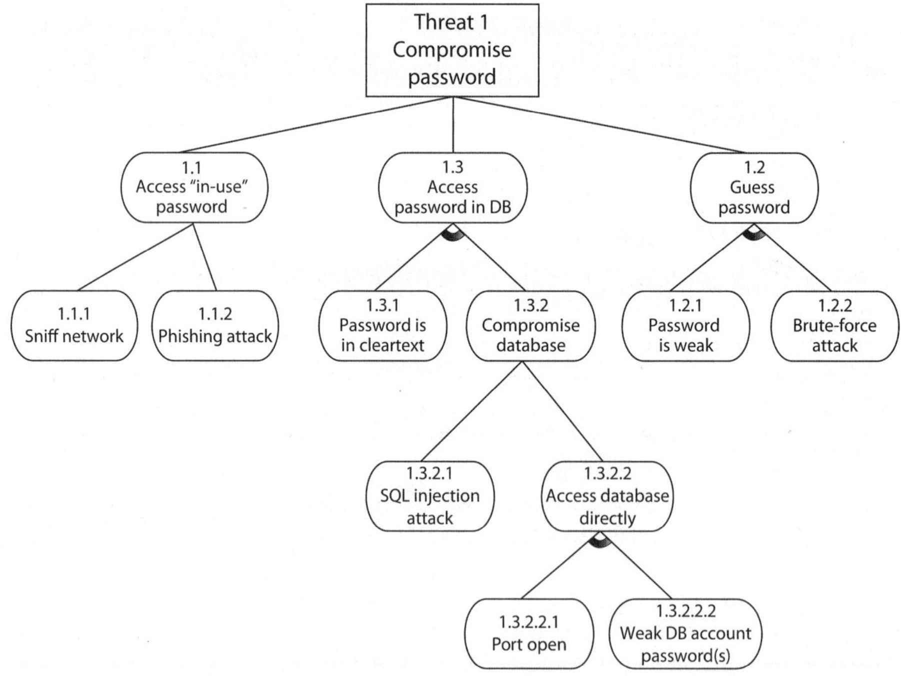

Figure 24-3 Threat tree used in threat modeling

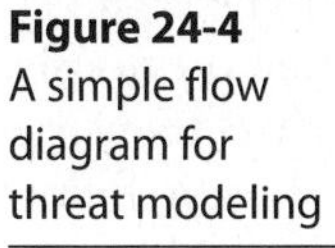

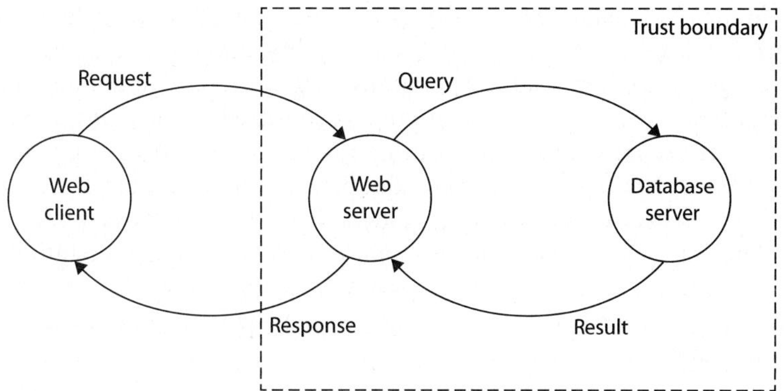

Figure 24-4 A simple flow diagram for threat modeling

There are many automated tools in the industry that software development teams can use to ensure that they address the various threat types during the design stage. One popular open-source solution is the Open Web Application Security Project (OWASP) Threat Dragon. This web-based tool enables the development team to describe threats visually using flow diagrams. Figure 24-4 shows a simple diagram of a three-tier web system showing its trust boundary and the four ways in which the tiers interact. The next step in building the threat model would be to consider how each of these four interactions could be exploited by a threat actor. For example, stolen credentials could allow an adversary to compromise the web server and, from there, issue queries to the database server that could compromise the integrity or availability of records stored there. For each threat identified through this process, the software development team would develop controls to mitigate it.

The decisions made during the design phase are pivotal steps to the development phase. Software design serves as a foundation and greatly affects software quality. If good product design is not put into place in the beginning of the project, the following phases will be much more challenging.

Development Phase

This is the phase where the programmers become deeply involved. The software design that was created in the previous phase is broken down into defined deliverables, and programmers develop code to meet the deliverable requirements.

There are many *computer-aided software engineering (CASE)* tools that programmers can use to generate code, test software, and carry out debugging activities. When these types of activities are carried out through automated tools, development usually takes place more quickly with fewer errors.

CASE refers to any type of software tool that supports automated development of software, which can come in the form of program editors, debuggers, code analyzers, version-control mechanisms, and more. These tools aid in keeping detailed records of requirements, design steps, programming activities, and testing. A CASE tool is designed to support one or more software engineering tasks in the process of developing software. Many vendors can get their products to the market faster because they are "computer aided."

In the next chapter we will delve into the abyss of "secure coding," but let's take a quick peek at it here to illustrate its importance in the development phase. As stated previously, most vulnerabilities that corporations, organizations, and individuals have to worry about reside within the programming code itself. When programmers do not follow strict and secure methods of creating programming code, the effects can be widespread and the results can be devastating. But programming securely is not an easy task. The list of errors that can lead to serious vulnerabilities in software is long.

The MITRE organization's Common Weakness Enumeration (CWE) initiative (https://cwe.mitre.org/top25) describes "a demonstrative list of the most common and impactful issues experienced over the previous two calendar years." Table 24-1 shows the most recent list.

Rank	Name
1	Out-of-bounds Write
2	Improper Neutralization of Input During Web Page Generation ("Cross-site Scripting")
3	Out-of-bounds Read
4	Improper Input Validation
5	Improper Neutralization of Special Elements used in an OS Command ("OS Command Injection")
6	Improper Neutralization of Special Elements used in an SQL Command ("SQL Injection")
7	Use After Free
8	Improper Limitation of a Pathname to a Restricted Directory ("Path Traversal")
9	Cross-Site Request Forgery (CSRF)
10	Unrestricted Upload of File with Dangerous Type
11	Missing Authentication for Critical Function
12	Integer Overflow or Wraparound
13	Deserialization of Untrusted Data
14	Improper Authentication
15	NULL Pointer Dereference
16	Use of Hard-coded Credentials
17	Improper Restriction of Operations within the Bounds of a Memory Buffer
18	Missing Authorization
19	Incorrect Default Permissions
20	Exposure of Sensitive Information to an Unauthorized Actor
21	Insufficiently Protected Credentials
22	Incorrect Permission Assignment for Critical Resource
23	Improper Restriction of XML External Entity Reference
24	Server-Side Request Forgery (SSRF)
25	Improper Neutralization of Special Elements used in a Command ("Command Injection")

Table 24-1 2021 CWE Top 25 Most Dangerous Software Weaknesses List

Many of these software issues are directly related to improper or faulty programming practices. Among other issues to address, the programmers need to check input lengths so buffer overflows cannot take place, inspect code to prevent the presence of covert channels, check for proper data types, make sure checkpoints cannot be bypassed by users, verify syntax, and verify checksums. The software development team should play out different attack scenarios to see how the code could be attacked or modified in an unauthorized fashion. Code reviews and debugging should be carried out by peer developers, and everything should be clearly documented.

A particularly important area of scrutiny is input validation because it can lead to serious vulnerabilities. Essentially, we should treat every single user input as malicious until proven otherwise. For example, if we don't put limits on how many characters users can enter when providing, say, their names on a web form, they could cause a buffer overflow, which is a classic example of a technique used to exploit improper input validation. A *buffer overflow* (which is described in detail in Chapter 18) takes place when too much data is accepted as input to a specific process. The process's memory buffer can be overflowed by shoving arbitrary data into various memory segments and inserting a carefully crafted set of malicious instructions at a specific memory address.

Buffer overflows can also lead to illicit escalation of privileges. *Privilege escalation* is the process of exploiting a process or configuration setting to gain access to resources that would normally not be available to the process or its user. For example, an attacker can compromise a regular user account and escalate its privileges to gain administrator or even system privileges on that computer. This type of attack usually exploits the complex interactions of user processes with device drivers and the underlying operating system. A combination of input validation and configuring the system to run with least privilege can help mitigate the threat of escalation of privileges.

What is important to understand is that secure coding practices need to be integrated into the development phase of the SDLC. Security has to be addressed at each phase of the SDLC, with this phase being one of the most critical.

Testing Phase

Formal and informal testing should begin as soon as possible. *Unit testing* is concerned with ensuring the quality of individual code modules or classes. Mature developers develop the unit tests for their modules before they even start coding, or at least in parallel with the coding. This approach is known as *test-driven development* and tends to result in much higher-quality code with significantly fewer vulnerabilities.

Unit tests are meant to simulate a range of inputs to which the code may be exposed. These inputs range from the mundanely expected, to the accidentally unfortunate, to the intentionally malicious. The idea is to ensure the code always behaves in an expected and secure manner. Once a module and its unit tests are finished, the unit tests are run (usually in an automated framework) on that code. The goal of this type of testing is to isolate each part of the software and show that the individual parts are correct.

Unit testing usually continues throughout the development phase. A totally different group of people should carry out the formal testing. Depending on the methodology and the organization, this could be a QA, testing, audit, or even red team. This is an example

Separation of Duties

Different environmental types (development, testing, and production) should be properly separated, and functionality and operations should not overlap. Developers should not have access to modify code used in production. The code should be tested, submitted to a library, and then sent to the production environment.

of separation of duties. A programmer should not develop, test, and release software. The more eyes that see the code, the greater the chance that flaws will be found before the product is released.

No cookie-cutter recipe exists for security testing because the applications and products can be so diverse in functionality and security objectives. It is important to map security risks to test cases and code. The software development team can take a linear approach by identifying a vulnerability, providing the necessary test scenario, performing the test, and reviewing the code for how it deals with such a vulnerability. At this phase, tests are conducted in an environment that should mirror the production environment to ensure the code does not work only in the labs.

Security attacks and penetration tests usually take place during the testing phase to identify any missed vulnerabilities. Functionality, performance, and penetration resistance are evaluated. All the necessary functionality required of the product should be in a checklist to ensure each function is accounted for.

Security tests should be run to test against the vulnerabilities identified earlier in the project. Buffer overflows should be attempted, interfaces should be hit with unexpected inputs, denial-of-service (DoS) situations should be tested, unusual user activity should take place, and if a system crashes, the product should react by reverting to a secure state. The product should be tested in various environments with different applications, configurations, and hardware platforms. A product may respond fine when installed on a clean Windows 10 installation on a stand-alone PC, but it may throw unexpected errors when installed on a laptop that is remotely connected to a network and has a virtual private network (VPN) client installed.

Verification vs. Validation

Verification determines if the software product accurately represents and meets the specifications. After all, a product can be developed that does not match the original specifications, so this step ensures the specifications are being properly met. It answers the question, "Did we build the product right?"

Validation determines if the software product provides the necessary solution for the intended real-world problem. In large projects, it is easy to lose sight of the overall goal. This exercise ensures that the main goal of the project is met. It answers the question, "Did we build the right product?"

Testing Types

Software testers on the software development team should subject the software to various types of tests to discover the variety of potential flaws. The following are some of the most common testing approaches:

- **Unit testing** Testing individual components in a controlled environment where programmers validate data structure, logic, and boundary conditions
- **Integration testing** Verifying that components work together as outlined in the design specifications
- **Acceptance testing** Ensuring that the code meets customer requirements
- **Regression testing** After a change to a system takes place, retesting to ensure functionality, performance, and protection

A well-rounded security test encompasses both manual tests and automated tests. Automated tests help locate a wide range of flaws generally associated with careless or erroneous code implementations. Some automated testing environments run specific inputs in a scripted and repeatable manner. While these tests are the bread and butter of software testing, we sometimes want to simulate random and unpredictable inputs to supplement the scripted tests.

A manual test is used to analyze aspects of the program that require human intuition and can usually be judged using computing techniques. Testers also try to locate design flaws. These include logical errors, which may enable attackers to manipulate program flow by using shrewdly crafted program sequences to access greater privileges or bypass authentication mechanisms. Manual testing involves code auditing by security-centric programmers who try to modify the logical program structure using rogue inputs and reverse-engineering techniques. Manual tests simulate the live scenarios involved in real-world attacks. Some manual testing also involves the use of social engineering to analyze the human weakness that may lead to system compromise.

At this stage, issues found in testing procedures are relayed to the development team in problem reports. The problems are fixed and programs retested. This is a continual process until everyone is satisfied that the product is ready for production. If there is a specific customer, the customer would run through a range of tests before formally accepting the product; if it is a generic product, beta testing can be carried out by various potential customers and agencies. Then the product is formally released to the market or customer.

NOTE Sometimes developers include lines of code in a product that will allow them to do a few keystrokes and get right into the application. This allows them to bypass any security and access controls so they can quickly access the application's core components. This is referred to as a "back door" or "maintenance hook" and must be removed before the code goes into production.

Operations and Maintenance Phase

Once the software code is developed and properly tested, it is released so that it can be implemented within the intended production environment. The software development team's role is not finished at this point. Newly discovered problems and vulnerabilities are commonly

PART VIII

identified at this phase. For example, if a company developed a customized application for a specific customer, the customer could run into unforeseen issues when rolling out the product within its various networked environments. Interoperability issues might come to the surface, or some configurations may break critical functionality. The developers would need to make the necessary changes to the code, retest the code, and re-release the code.

Almost every software system requires the addition of new features over time. Frequently, these have to do with changing business processes or interoperability with other systems. This highlights the need for the operations and development teams to work particularly closely during the operations and maintenance (O&M) phase. The operations team, which is typically the IT department, is responsible for ensuring the reliable operation of all production systems. The development team is responsible for any changes to the software in development systems up until the time the software goes into production. Together, the operations and development teams address the transition from development to production as well as management of the system's configuration.

Another facet of O&M is driven by the fact that new vulnerabilities are regularly discovered. While the developers may have carried out extensive security testing, it is close to impossible to identify all the security issues at one point and time. Zero-day vulnerabilities may be identified, coding errors may be uncovered, or the integration of the software with another piece of software may uncover security issues that have to be addressed. The development team must develop patches, hotfixes, and new releases to address these items. In all likelihood, this is where you as a CISSP will interact the most with the SDLC.

Change Management

One of the key processes on which to focus for improvement involves how we deal with the inevitable changes. These can cause a lot of havoc if not managed properly and in a deliberate manner. We already discussed change management in general in Chapter 20, but it is particularly important during the lifetime of a software development project.

The need to change software arises for several reasons. During the development phase, a customer may alter requirements and ask that certain functionalities be added, removed, or modified. In production, changes may need to happen because of other changes in the environment, new requirements of a software product or system, or newly released patches or upgrades. These changes should be carefully analyzed, approved, and properly incorporated such that they do not affect any original functionality in an adverse way.

Change management is a systematic approach to deliberately regulating the changing nature of projects, including software development projects. It is a management process that takes into account not just the technical issues but also resources (like people and money), project life cycle, and even organizational climate. Many times, the hardest part of managing change is not the change itself, but the effects it has in the organization. Many of us have been on the receiving end of a late-afternoon phone call in which we're told to change our plans because of a change in a project on which we weren't even working. An important part of change management is controlling change.

Change Control

Change control is the process of controlling the specific changes that take place during the life cycle of a system and documenting the necessary change control activities. Whereas change management is the project manager's responsibility as an overarching process, change control is what developers do to ensure the software doesn't break when they change it.

Change control involves a bunch of things to consider. The change must be approved, documented, and tested. Some tests may need to be rerun to ensure the change does not affect the product's capabilities. When a programmer makes a change to source code, she should do so on the test version of the code. Under no conditions should a programmer change the code that is already in production. After making changes to the code, the programmer should test the code and then deliver the new code to the librarian. Production code should come only from the librarian and not from a programmer or directly from a test environment.

A process for controlling changes needs to be in place at the beginning of a project so that everyone knows how to deal with changes and knows what is expected of each entity when a change request is made. Some projects have been doomed from the start because proper change control was not put into place and enforced. Many times in development, the customer and vendor agree on the design of the product, the requirements, and the specifications. The customer is then required to sign a contract confirming this is the agreement and that if they want any further modifications, they will have to pay the vendor for that extra work. If this agreement is not put into place, then the customer can continually request changes, which requires the software development team to put in the extra hours to provide these changes, the result of which is that the vendor loses money, the product does not meet its completion deadline, and scope creep occurs.

Other reasons exist to have change control in place. These reasons deal with organizational policies, standard procedures, and expected results. If a software product is in the last phase of development and a change request comes in, the development team should know how to deal with it. Usually, the team leader must tell the project manager how much extra time will be required to complete the project if this change is incorporated and what steps need to be taken to ensure this change does not affect other components within the product. If these processes are not controlled, one part of a development team could implement the change without another part of the team being aware of it. This could break some of the other development team's software pieces. When the pieces of the product are integrated and some pieces turn out to be incompatible, some jobs may be in jeopardy, because management never approved the change in the first place.

Change control processes should be evaluated during system audits. It is possible to overlook a problem that a change has caused in testing, so the procedures for how change control is implemented and enforced should be examined during a system audit.

The following are some necessary steps for a change control process:

1. Make a formal request for a change.
2. Analyze the request:
    a. Develop the implementation strategy.
    b. Calculate the costs of this implementation.
    c. Review security implications.
3. Record the change request.
4. Submit the change request for approval.

5. Develop the change:
    a. Recode segments of the product and add or subtract functionality.
    b. Link these changes in the code to the formal change control request.
    c. Submit software for testing and quality control.
    d. Repeat until quality is adequate.
    e. Make version changes.
6. Report results to management.

The changes to systems may require another round of certification and accreditation. If the changes to a system are significant, then the functionality and level of protection

SDLC and Security

The main phases of a software development life cycle are shown here with some specific security tasks.

Requirements gathering:

- Security risk assessment
- Privacy risk assessment
- Risk-level acceptance
- Informational, functional, and behavioral requirements

Design:

- Attack surface analysis
- Threat modeling

Development:

- Automated CASE tools
- Secure coding

Testing:

- Automated testing
- Manual testing
- Unit, integration, acceptance, and regression testing

Operations and maintenance:

- Vulnerability patching
- Change management and control

may need to be reevaluated (certified), and management would have to approve the overall system, including the new changes (accreditation).

Development Methodologies

Several software development methodologies are in common use around the world. While some include security issues in certain phases, these are not considered "security-centric development methodologies." They are simply classical approaches to building and developing software. Let's dive into some of the methodologies that you should know as a CISSP.

EXAM TIP It is exceptionally rare to see a development methodology used in its pure form in the real world. Instead, organizations typically start with a base methodology and modify it to suit their own unique environment. For purposes of the CISSP exam, however, you should focus on what differentiates each development approach.

Waterfall Methodology

The *Waterfall methodology* uses a linear-sequential life-cycle approach, illustrated in Figure 24-5. Each phase must be completed in its entirety before the next phase can begin. At the end of each phase, a review takes place to make sure the project is on the correct path and should continue.

In this methodology all requirements are gathered in the initial phase and there is no formal way to integrate changes as more information becomes available or requirements change. It is hard to know everything at the beginning of a project, so waiting until the whole project is complete to integrate necessary changes can be ineffective and time consuming. As an analogy, let's say that you are planning to landscape your backyard that is one acre in size. In this scenario, you can go to the gardening store only one time to get

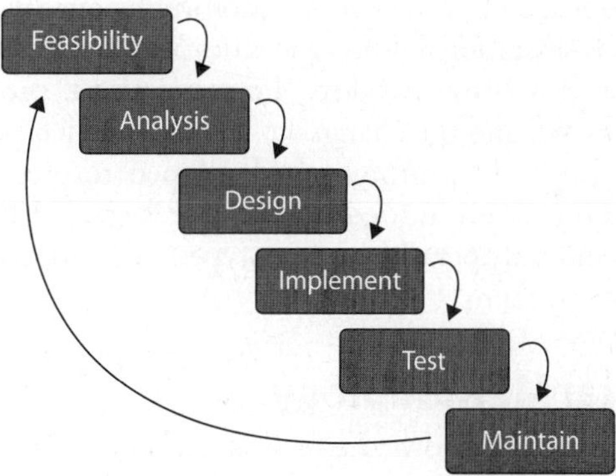

Figure 24-5 Waterfall methodology used for software development

PART VIII

all your supplies. If you identify during the project that you need more topsoil, rocks, or pipe for the sprinkler system, you have to wait and complete the whole yard before you can return to the store for extra or more suitable supplies.

The Waterfall methodology is a very rigid approach that could be useful for smaller projects in which all the requirements are fully understood up front. It may also be a good choice in some large projects for which different organizations will perform the work at each phase. Overall, however, it is not an ideal methodology for most complex projects, which commonly contain many variables that affect the scope as the project continues.

Prototyping

A *prototype* is a sample of software code or a model that can be developed to explore a specific approach to a problem before investing expensive time and resources. A team can identify the usability and design problems while working with a prototype and adjust their approach as necessary. Within the software development industry, three main prototype models have been invented and used. These are the rapid prototype, evolutionary prototype, and operational prototype.

Rapid prototyping is an approach that allows the development team to quickly create a prototype (sample) to test the validity of the current understanding of the project requirements. In a software development project, the team could develop a *rapid prototype* to see if their ideas are feasible and if they should move forward with their current solution. The rapid prototype approach (also called throwaway) is a "quick and dirty" method of creating a piece of code and seeing if everyone is on the right path or if another solution should be developed. The rapid prototype is not developed to be built upon, but to be discarded after serving its purposes.

When *evolutionary prototypes* are developed, they are built with the goal of incremental improvement. Instead of being discarded after being developed, as in the rapid prototype approach, the evolutionary prototype is continually improved upon until it reaches the final product stage. Feedback that is gained through each development phase is used to improve the prototype and get closer to accomplishing the customer's needs.

Operational prototypes are an extension of the evolutionary prototype method. Both models (operational and evolutionary) improve the quality of the prototype as more data is gathered, but the operational prototype is designed to be implemented within a production environment as it is being tweaked. The operational prototype is updated as customer feedback is gathered, and the changes to the software happen within the working site.

In summary, a rapid prototype is developed to give a quick understanding of the suggested solution, an evolutionary prototype is created and improved upon within a lab environment, and an operational prototype is developed and improved upon within a production environment.

Incremental Methodology

If a development team follows the *Incremental methodology*, this allows them to carry out multiple development cycles on a piece of software throughout its development stages. This would be similar to "multi-Waterfall" cycles taking place on one piece of software as

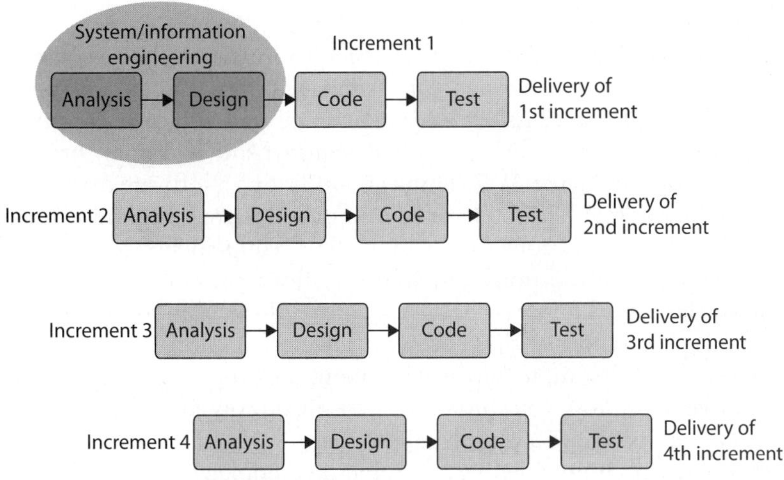

Figure 24-6 Incremental development methodology

it matures through the development stages. A version of the software is created in the first iteration and then it passes through each phase (requirements analysis, design, coding, testing, implementation) of the next iteration process. The software continues through the iteration of phases until a satisfactory product is produced. This methodology is illustrated in Figure 24-6.

When using the Incremental methodology, each incremental phase results in a deliverable that is an operational product. This means that a working version of the software is produced after the first iteration and that version is improved upon in each of the subsequent iterations. Some benefits to this methodology are that a working piece of software is available in early stages of development, the flexibility of the methodology allows for changes to take place, testing uncovers issues more quickly than the Waterfall methodology since testing takes place after each iteration, and each iteration is an easily manageable milestone.

Because each incremental phase delivers an operational product, the customer can respond to each build and help the development team in its improvement processes, and because the initial product is delivered more quickly compared to other methodologies, the initial product delivery costs are lower, the customer gets its functionality earlier, and the risks of critical changes being introduced are lower.

This methodology is best used when issues pertaining to risk, program complexity, funding, and functionality requirements need to be understood early in the product development life cycle. If a vendor needs to get the customer some basic functionality quickly as it works on the development of the product, this can be a good methodology to follow.

Spiral Methodology

The *Spiral methodology* uses an iterative approach to software development and places emphasis on risk analysis. The methodology is made up of four main phases: determine objectives, identify and resolve risks, development and test, and plan the next iteration. The development team starts with the initial requirements and goes through each of these phases, as shown in Figure 24-7. Think about starting a software development project at the center of this graphic. You have your initial understanding and requirements of the project, develop specifications that map to these requirements, identify and resolve risks, build prototype specifications, test your specifications, build a development plan, integrate newly discovered information, use the new information to carry out a new risk analysis, create a prototype, test the prototype, integrate resulting data into the process, and so forth. As you gather more information about the project, you integrate it into the risk analysis process, improve your prototype, test the prototype, and add more granularity to each step until you have a completed product.

The iterative approach provided by the Spiral methodology allows new requirements to be addressed as they are uncovered. Each prototype allows for testing to take place

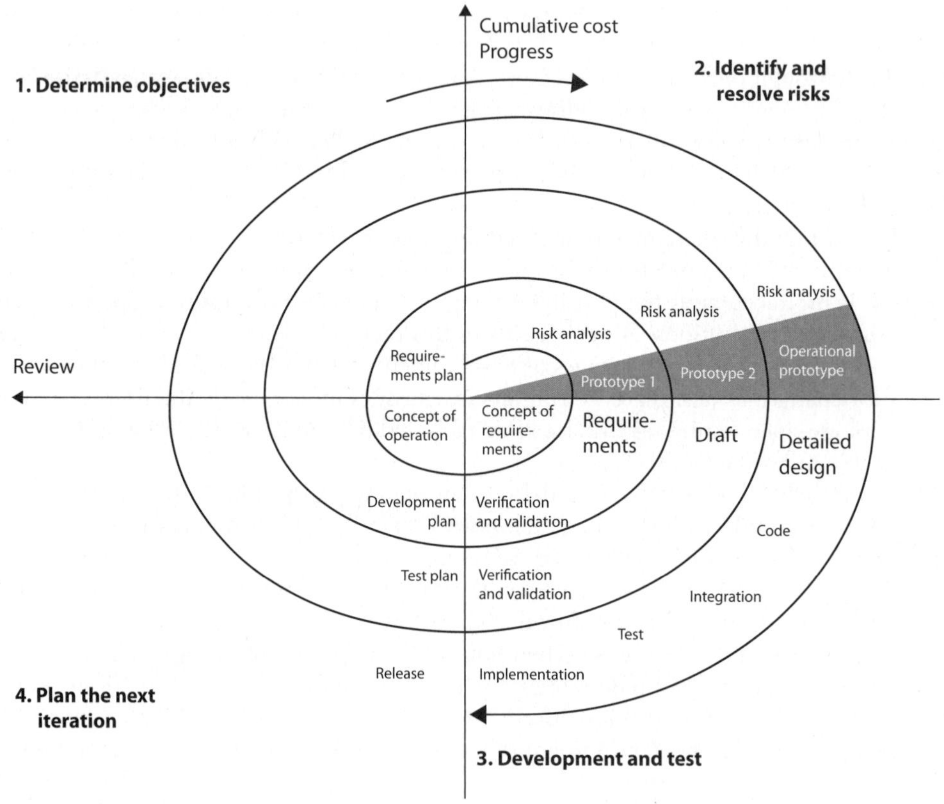

Figure 24-7 Spiral methodology for software development

early in the development project, and feedback based upon these tests is integrated into the following iteration of steps. The risk analysis ensures that all issues are actively reviewed and analyzed so that things do not "slip through the cracks" and the project stays on track.

In the Spiral methodology the last phase allows the customer to evaluate the product in its current state and provide feedback, which is an input value for the next spiral of activity. This is a good methodology for complex projects that have fluid requirements.

NOTE Within this methodology the angular aspect represents progress and the radius of the spirals represents cost.

Rapid Application Development

The *Rapid Application Development (RAD)* methodology relies more on the use of rapid prototyping than on extensive upfront planning. In this methodology, the planning of how to improve the software is interleaved with the processes of developing the software, which allows for software to be developed quickly. The delivery of a workable piece of software can take place in less than half the time compared to the Waterfall methodology. The RAD methodology combines the use of prototyping and iterative development procedures with the goal of accelerating the software development process. The development process begins with creating data models and business process models to help define what the end-result software needs to accomplish. Through the use of prototyping, these data and process models are refined. These models provide input to allow for the improvement of the prototype, and the testing and evaluation of the prototype allow for the improvement of the data and process models. The goal of these steps is to combine business requirements and technical design statements, which provide the direction in the software development project.

Figure 24-8 illustrates the basic differences between traditional software development approaches and RAD. As an analogy, let's say that the development team needs you to tell them what it is you want so that they can build it for you. You tell them that the thing you want has four wheels and an engine. They bring you a two-seat convertible and ask, "Is this what you want?" You say, "No, it must be able to seat four adults." So they leave the prototype with you and go back to work. They build a four-seat convertible and deliver it to you, and you tell them they are getting closer but it still doesn't fit your requirements. They get more information from you, deliver another prototype, get more feedback, and on and on. That back and forth is what is taking place in the circle portion of Figure 24-8.

The main reason that RAD was developed was that by the time software was completely developed following other methodologies, the requirements changed and the developers had to "go back to the drawing board." If a customer needs you to develop a software product and it takes you a year to do so, by the end of that year the customer's needs for the software have probably advanced and changed. The RAD methodology allows for the customer to be involved during the development phases so that the end result maps to their needs in a more realistic manner.

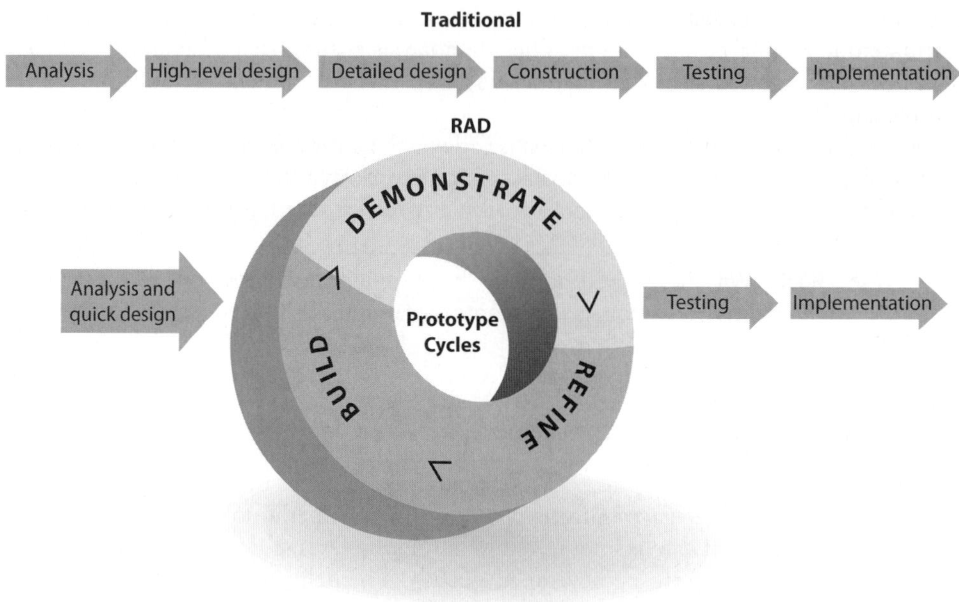

Figure 24-8 Rapid Application Development methodology

Agile Methodologies

The industry seems to be full of software development methodologies, each trying to improve upon the deficiencies of the ones before it. Before the Agile approach to development was created, teams were following rigid process-oriented methodologies. These approaches focused more on following procedures and steps instead of potentially carrying out tasks in a more efficient manner. As an analogy, if you have ever worked within or interacted with a large government agency, you may have come across silly processes that took too long and involved too many steps. If you are a government employee and need to purchase a new chair, you might have to fill out four sets of documents that need to be approved by three other departments. You probably have to identify three different chair vendors, who have to submit a quote, which goes through the contracting office. It might take you a few months to get your new chair. The focus is to follow a protocol and rules instead of efficiency.

Many of the classical software development approaches, as in Waterfall, provide rigid processes to follow that do not allow for much flexibility and adaptability. Commonly, the software development projects that follow these approaches end up failing by not meeting schedule time release, running over budget, and/or not meeting the needs of the customer. Sometimes you need the freedom to modify steps to best meet the situation's needs.

Agile methodology is an umbrella term for several development methodologies. The overarching methodology focuses not on rigid, linear, stepwise processes, but instead on incremental and iterative development methods that promote cross-functional teamwork and continuous feedback mechanisms. This methodology is considered "lightweight" compared to the traditional methodologies that are "heavyweight," which just means this methodology is not confined to a tunnel-visioned and overly structured approach. It is nimble and flexible enough to adapt to each project's needs. The industry found out that even an exhaustive library of defined processes cannot handle every situation that could arise during a development project. So instead of investing time and resources into deep upfront design analysis, the Agile methodology focuses on small increments of functional code that are created based on business need.

The various methodologies under the Agile umbrella focus on individual interaction instead of processes and tools. They emphasize developing the right software product over comprehensive and laborious documentation. They promote customer collaboration instead of contract negotiation, and emphasize abilities to respond to change instead of strictly following a plan.

A notable element of many Agile methodologies is their focus on user stories. A *user story* is a sentence that describes what a user wants to do and why. For instance, a user story could be "As a customer, I want to search for products so that I can buy some." Notice the structure of the story is "As a <user role>, I want to <accomplish some goal> so that <reason for accomplishing the goal>." For example, "As a network analyst, I want to record pcap (packet capture) files so that I can analyze downloaded malware." This method of documenting user requirements is very familiar to the customers and enables their close collaboration with the development team. Furthermore, by keeping this user focus, validation of the features is simpler because the "right system" is described up front by the users in their own words.

EXAM TIP The Agile methodologies do not use prototypes to represent the full product, but break the product down into individual features that are continuously being delivered.

Another important characteristic of the Agile methodologies is that the development team can take pieces and parts of all of the available SDLC methodologies and combine them in a manner that best meets the specific project needs. These various combinations have resulted in many methodologies that fall under the Agile umbrella.

Scrum

Scrum is one of the most widely adopted Agile methodologies in use today. It lends itself to projects of any size and complexity and is very lean and customer focused. Scrum is a methodology that acknowledges the fact that customer needs cannot be completely understood and will change over time. It focuses on team collaboration, customer involvement, and continuous delivery.

The term *scrum* originates from the sport of rugby. Whenever something interrupts play (e.g., a penalty or the ball goes out of bounds) and the game needs to be restarted, all players come together in a tight formation. The ball is then thrown into the middle and the players struggle with each other until one team or the other gains possession of the ball, allowing the game to continue. Extending this analogy, the Scrum methodology allows the project to be reset by allowing product features to be added, changed, or removed at clearly defined points. Since the customer is intimately involved in the development process, there should be no surprises, cost overruns, or schedule delays. This allows a product to be iteratively developed and changed even as it is being built.

The change points happen at the conclusion of each *sprint*, a fixed-duration development interval that is usually (but not always) two weeks in length and promises delivery of a very specific set of features. These features are chosen by the team, but with a lot of input from the customer. There is a process for adding features at any time by inserting them in the feature backlog. However, these features can be considered for actual work only at the beginning of a new sprint. This shields the development team from changes during a sprint, but allows for changes in between sprints.

Extreme Programming

If you take away the regularity of Scrum's sprints and backlogs and add a lot of code reviewing, you get our next Agile methodology. Extreme Programming (XP) is a development methodology that takes code reviews (discussed in Chapter 18) to the extreme (hence the name) by having them take place continuously. These continuous reviews are accomplished using an approach called *pair programming*, in which one programmer dictates the code to her partner, who then types it. While this may seem inefficient, it allows two pairs of eyes to constantly examine the code as it is being typed. It turns out that this approach significantly reduces the incidence of errors and improves the overall quality of the code.

Another characteristic of XP is its reliance on test-driven development, in which the unit tests are written before the code. The programmer first writes a new unit test case, which of course fails because there is no code to satisfy it. The next step is to add just enough code to get the test to pass. Once this is done, the next test is written, which fails, and so on. The consequence is that only the minimal amount of code needed to pass the tests is developed. This extremely minimal approach reduces the incidence of errors because it weeds out complexity.

Kanban

Kanban is a production scheduling system developed by Toyota to more efficiently support just-in-time delivery. Over time, Kanban was adopted by IT and software systems developers. In this context, the *Kanban* development methodology is one that stresses visual tracking of all tasks so that the team knows what to prioritize at what point in time in order to deliver the right features right on time. Kanban projects used to be very noticeable because entire walls in conference rooms would be covered in sticky notes representing the various tasks that the team was tracking. Nowadays, many Kanban teams opt for virtual walls on online systems.

The Kanban wall is usually divided vertically by production phase. Typical columns are labeled Planned, In Progress, and Done. Each sticky note can represent a user story as it moves through the development process, but more importantly, the sticky note can also be some other work that needs to be accomplished. For instance, suppose that one of the user stories is the search feature described earlier in this section. While it is being developed, the team realizes that the searches are very slow. This could result in a task being added to change the underlying data or network architecture or to upgrade hardware. This sticky note then gets added to the Planned column and starts being prioritized and tracked together with the rest of the remaining tasks. This process highlights how Kanban allows the project team to react to changing or unknown requirements, which is a common feature among all Agile methodologies.

DevOps

Traditionally, the software development team and the IT team are two separate (and sometimes antagonistic) groups within an organization. Many problems stem from poor collaboration between these two teams during the development process. It is not rare to have the IT team berating the developers because a feature push causes the IT team to have to stay late or work on a weekend or simply drop everything they were doing in order to "fix" something that the developers "broke." This friction makes a lot of sense when you consider that each team is incentivized by different outcomes. Developers want to push out finished code, usually under strict schedules. The IT staff, on the other hand, wants to keep the IT infrastructure operating effectively. Many project managers who have managed software development efforts will attest to having received complaints from developers that the IT team was being unreasonable and uncooperative, while the IT team was simultaneously complaining about buggy code being tossed over the fence at them at the worst possible times and causing problems on the rest of the network.

A good way to solve this friction is to have both developers and members of the operations staff (hence the term DevOps) on the software development team. *DevOps* is the practice of incorporating development, IT, and quality assurance (QA) staff into software development projects to align their incentives and enable frequent, efficient, and reliable releases of software products. This relationship is illustrated in Figure 24-9.

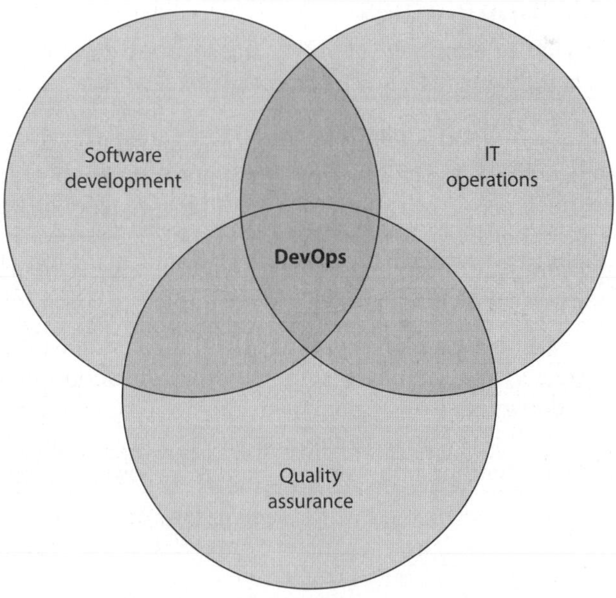

Figure 24-9 DevOps exists at the intersection of software development, IT, and QA.

Ultimately, DevOps is about changing the culture of an organization. It has a huge positive impact on security, because in addition to QA, the IT teammates will be involved at every step of the process. Multifunctional integration allows the team to identify potential defects, vulnerabilities, and friction points early enough to resolve them proactively. This is one of the biggest selling points for DevOps. According to multiple surveys, there are a few other, perhaps more powerful benefits: DevOps increases trust within an organization and increases job satisfaction among developers, IT staff, and QA personnel. Unsurprisingly, it also improves the morale of project managers.

DevSecOps

It is not all that common for the security team to be involved in software development efforts, but it makes a lot of sense for them to be. Their job is to find vulnerabilities before the threat actors can and then do something about it. As a result, most security professionals develop an "adversarial mindset" that allows them to think like attackers in order to better defend against them. Imagine being a software developer and having someone next to you telling you all the ways they could subvert your code to do bad things. It'd be kind of like having a spell-checker but for vulnerabilities instead of spelling!

DevSecOps is the integration of development, security, and operations professionals into a software development team. It's just like DevOps but with security added in. One of the main advantages of DevSecOps is that it bakes security right into the development process, rather than bolting it on at the end of it. Rather than implementing controls to mitigate vulnerabilities, the vulnerabilities are prevented from being implemented in the first place.

Other Methodologies

There seems to be no shortage of SDLC and software development methodologies in the industry. The following is a quick summary of a few others that can also be used:

- **Exploratory methodology** A methodology that is used in instances where clearly defined project objectives have not been presented. Instead of focusing on explicit tasks, the exploratory methodology relies on covering a set of specifications likely to affect the final product's functionality. Testing is an important part of exploratory development, as it ascertains that the current phase of the project is compliant with likely implementation scenarios.
- **Joint Application Development (JAD)** A methodology that uses a team approach in application development in a workshop-oriented environment. This methodology is distinguished by its inclusion of members other than coders in the team. It is common to find executive sponsors, subject matter experts, and end users spending hours or days in collaborative development workshops.

Integrated Product Team

An *integrated product team (IPT)* is a multidisciplinary development team with representatives from many or all the stakeholder populations. The idea makes a lot of sense when you think about it. Why should programmers learn or guess the manner in which the accounting folks handle accounts payable? Why should testers and quality control personnel wait until a product is finished before examining it? Why should the marketing team wait until the project (or at least the prototype) is finished before determining how best to sell it? A comprehensive IPT includes business executives and end users and everyone in between.

The Joint Application Development methodology, in which users join developers during extensive workshops, works well with the IPT approach. IPTs extend this concept by ensuring that the right stakeholders are represented in every phase of the development as formal team members. In addition, whereas JAD is focused on involving the user community, an IPT is typically more inward facing and focuses on bringing in the business stakeholders.

An IPT is not a development methodology. Instead, it is a management technique. When project managers decide to use IPTs, they still have to select a methodology. These days, IPTs are often associated with Agile methodologies.

- **Reuse methodology** A methodology that approaches software development by using progressively developed code. Reusable programs are evolved by gradually modifying preexisting prototypes to customer specifications. Since the reuse methodology does not require programs to be built from scratch, it drastically reduces both development cost and time.
- **Cleanroom** An approach that attempts to prevent errors or mistakes by following structured and formal methods of developing and testing. This approach is used for high-quality and mission-critical applications that will be put through a strict certification process.

We covered only the most commonly used methodologies in this section, but there are many more that exist. New methodologies have evolved as technology and research have advanced and various weaknesses of older approaches have been addressed. Most of the methodologies exist to meet a specific software development need, and choosing the wrong approach for a certain project could be devastating to its overall success.

EXAM TIP While all the methodologies we covered are used in many organizations around the world, you should focus on Agile, Waterfall, DevOps, and DevSecOps for the CISSP exam.

Review of Development Methodologies

A quick review of the various methodologies we have covered up to this point is provided here:

- **Waterfall** Very rigid, sequential approach that requires each phase to complete before the next one can begin. Difficult to integrate changes. Inflexible methodology.
- **Prototyping** Creating a sample or model of the code for proof-of-concept purposes.
- **Incremental** Multiple development cycles are carried out on a piece of software throughout its development stages. Each phase provides a usable version of software.
- **Spiral** Iterative approach that emphasizes risk analysis per iteration. Allows for customer feedback to be integrated through a flexible evolutionary approach.
- **Rapid Application Development** Combines prototyping and iterative development procedures with the goal of accelerating the software development process.
- **Agile** Iterative and incremental development processes that encourage team-based collaboration. Flexibility and adaptability are used instead of a strict process structure.
- **DevOps** The software development and IT operations teams work together at all stages of the project to ensure a smooth transition from development to production environments.
- **DevSecOps** Just like DevOps, but also integrates the security team into every stage of the project.

Maturity Models

Regardless of which software development methodology an organization adopts, it is helpful to have a framework for determining how well-defined and effective its development activities are. Maturity models identify the important components of software development processes and then organize them in an evolutionary scale that proceeds from ad hoc to mature. Each maturity level comprises a set of goals that, when they are met, stabilize one or more of those components. As an organization moves up this maturity scale, the effectiveness, repeatability, and predictability of its software development processes increase, leading to higher-quality code. Higher-quality code, in turn, means fewer vulnerabilities, which is why we care so deeply about this topic as cybersecurity leaders. Let's take a look at the two most popular models: the Capability Maturity Model Integration (CMMI) and the Software Assurance Maturity Model (SAMM).

Capability Maturity Model Integration

Capability Maturity Model Integration (CMMI) is a comprehensive set of models for developing software. It addresses the different phases of a software development life cycle, including concept definition, requirements analysis, design, development, integration, installation, operations, and maintenance, and what should happen in each phase. It can be used to evaluate security engineering practices and identify ways to improve them. It can also be used by customers in the evaluation process of a software vendor. Ideally, software vendors would use the model to help improve their processes, and customers would use the model to assess the vendors' practices.

EXAM TIP For exam purposes, the terms CMM and CMMI are equivalent.

CMMI describes procedures, principles, and practices that underlie software development process maturity. This model was developed to help software vendors improve their development processes by providing an evolutionary path from an ad hoc "fly by the seat of your pants" approach to a more disciplined and repeatable method that improves software quality, reduces the life cycle of development, provides better project management capabilities, allows for milestones to be created and met in a timely manner, and takes a more proactive approach than the less effective reactive approach. It provides best practices to allow an organization to develop a standardized approach to software development that can be used across many different groups. The goal is to continue to review and improve upon the processes to optimize output, increase capabilities, and provide higher-quality software at a lower cost through the implementation of continuous improvement steps.

If the company Stuff-R-Us wants a software development company, Software-R-Us, to develop an application for it, it can choose to buy into the sales hype about how wonderful Software-R-Us is, or it can ask Software-R-Us whether it has been evaluated against CMMI. Third-party companies evaluate software development companies to certify their product development processes. Many software companies have this evaluation done so they can use this as a selling point to attract new customers and provide confidence for their current customers.

The five maturity levels of CMMI are shown in Figure 24-10 and described here:

- **Level 0: Incomplete** Development process is ad hoc or even chaotic. Tasks are not always completed at all, so projects are regularly cancelled or abandoned.
- **Level 1: Initial** The organization does not use effective management procedures and plans. There is no assurance of consistency, and quality is unpredictable. Success is usually the result of individual heroics.
- **Level 2: Managed** A formal management structure, change control, and quality assurance are in place for individual projects. The organization can properly repeat processes throughout each project.

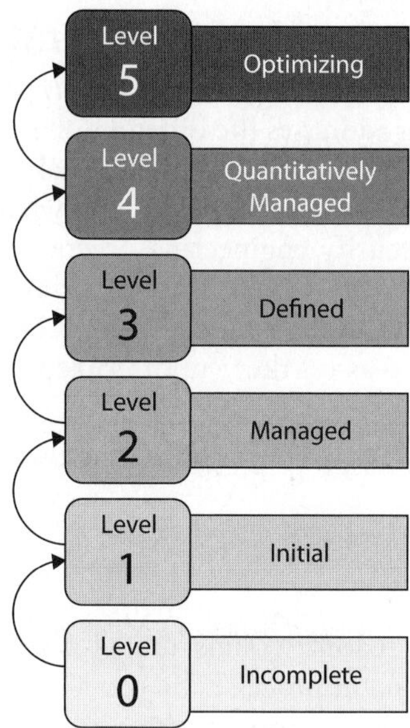

Figure 24-10 CMMI staged maturity levels

- **Level 3: Defined** Formal procedures are in place that outline and define processes carried out in all projects across the organization. This allows the organization to be proactive rather than reactive.
- **Level 4: Quantitatively Managed** The organization has formal processes in place to collect and analyze quantitative data, and metrics are defined and fed into the process-improvement program.
- **Level 5: Optimizing** The organization has budgeted and integrated plans for continuous process improvement, which allow it to quickly respond to opportunities and changes.

Each level builds upon the previous one. For example, a company that accomplishes a Level 5 CMMI rating must meet all the requirements outlined in Levels 1–4 along with the requirements of Level 5.

If a software development vendor is using the Prototyping methodology that was discussed earlier in this chapter, the vendor would most likely only achieve a CMMI Level 1, particularly if its practices are ad hoc, not consistent, and the level of the quality that its software products contain is questionable. If this company practiced a strict Agile SDLC methodology consistently and carried out development, testing, and documentation precisely, it would have a higher chance of obtaining a higher CMMI level.

Capability maturity models (CMMs) are used for many different purposes, software development processes being one of them. They are general models that allow for maturity-level identification and maturity improvement steps. We showed how a CMM can be used for organizational security program improvement processes in Chapter 4.

The software industry ended up with several different CMMs, which led to confusion. CMMI was developed to bring many of these different maturity models together and allow them to be used in one framework. CMMI was developed by industry experts, government entities, and the Software Engineering Institute at Carnegie Mellon University. So CMMI has replaced CMM in the software engineering world, but you may still see CMM referred to within the industry and on the CISSP exam. Their ultimate goals are the same, which is process improvement.

NOTE CMMI is continually being updated and improved upon. You can view the latest documents on it at https://cmmiinstitute.com/learning/appraisals/levels.

Software Assurance Maturity Model

The OWASP *Software Assurance Maturity Model (SAMM)* is specifically focused on secure software development and allows organizations of any size to decide their target maturity levels within each of the five critical business functions: Governance, Design, Implementation, Verification, and Operations, as shown in Figure 24-11. One of the premises on which SAMM is built is that any organization that is involved in software development must perform these five functions.

Each business function, in turn, is divided into three security practices, which are sets of security-related activities that provide assurance for the function. For example, if you want to ensure that your Design business function is done right, you need to perform activities related to threat assessment, identification of security requirements, and securely architecting the software. Each of these 15 practices can be independently

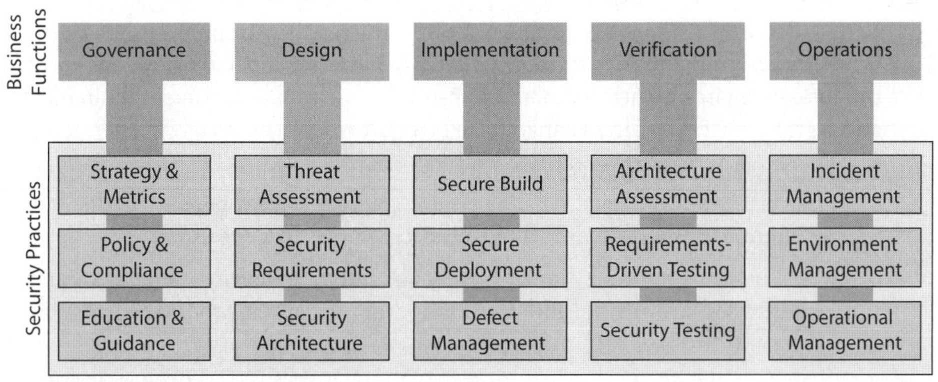

Figure 24-11 Software Assurance Maturity Model

assessed and matured, which allows the organization to decide what maturity level makes sense for each practice.

NOTE You can find more information on SAMM at https://owaspsamm.org/model/.

Chapter Review

While there is no expectation that you, as a CISSP, will necessarily be involved in software development, you will almost certainly lead organizations that either produce software or consume it. Therefore, it is important that you understand how secure software is developed. Knowing this enables you to see what an organization is doing, software development-wise, and quickly get a sense of the maturity of its processes. If processes are ad hoc, this chapter should have given you some pointers on how to formalize the processes. After all, without formal processes and trained programmers in place, you have almost no hope of producing software that is not immediately vulnerable as soon as it is put into production. On the other hand, if the organization seems more mature, you can delve deeper into the specifics of building security into the software, which is the topic of the next chapter.

Quick Review

- The software development life cycle (SDLC) comprises five phases: requirements gathering, design, development, testing, and operations and maintenance (O&M).
- Computer-aided software engineering (CASE) refers to any type of software that allows for the automated development of software, which can come in the form of program editors, debuggers, code analyzers, version-control mechanisms, and more. The goals are to increase development speed and productivity and reduce errors.
- Various levels of testing should be carried out during development: unit (testing individual components), integration (verifying components work together in the production environment), acceptance (ensuring code meets customer requirements), and regression (testing after changes take place).
- Change management is a systematic approach to deliberately regulating the changing nature of projects. Change control, which is a subpart of change management, deals with controlling specific changes to a system.
- Security should be addressed in each phase of software development. It should not be addressed only at the end of development because of the added cost, time, and effort and the lack of functionality.

- The attack surface is the collection of possible entry points for an attacker. The reduction of this surface reduces the possible ways that an attacker can exploit a system.
- Threat modeling is a systematic approach used to understand how different threats could be realized and how a successful compromise could take place.
- The waterfall software development methodology follows a sequential approach that requires each phase to complete before the next one can begin.
- The prototyping methodology involves creating a sample of the code for proof-of-concept purposes.
- Incremental software development entails multiple development cycles that are carried out on a piece of software throughout its development stages.
- The spiral methodology is an iterative approach that emphasizes risk analysis per iteration.
- Rapid Application Development (RAD) combines prototyping and iterative development procedures with the goal of accelerating the software development process.
- Agile methodologies are characterized by iterative and incremental development processes that encourage team-based collaboration, where flexibility and adaptability are used instead of a strict process structure.
- Some organizations improve internal coordination and reduce friction by integrating the development and operations (DevOps) teams or the development, operations, and security (DevSecOps) teams when developing software.
- An integrated product team (IPT) is a multidisciplinary development team with representatives from many or all the stakeholder populations.
- Capability Maturity Model Integration (CMMI) is a process improvement approach that provides organizations with the essential elements of effective processes, which will improve their performance.
- The CMMI model uses six maturity levels designated by the numbers 0 through 5. Each level represents the maturity level of the process quality and optimization. The levels are organized as follows: 0 = Incomplete, 1 = Initial, 2 = Managed, 3 = Defined, 4 = Quantitatively Managed, 5 = Optimizing.
- The OWASP Software Assurance Maturity Model (SAMM) is specifically focused on secure software development and allows organizations to decide their target maturity levels within each of five critical business functions: Governance, Design, Implementation, Verification, and Operations.

Questions

Please remember that these questions are formatted and asked in a certain way for a reason. Keep in mind that the CISSP exam is asking questions at a conceptual level. Questions may not always have the perfect answer, and the candidate is advised against always looking for the perfect answer. Instead, the candidate should look for the best answer in the list.

1. The software development life cycle has several phases. Which of the following lists these phases in the correct order?
   - **A.** Requirements gathering, design, development, maintenance, testing, release
   - **B.** Requirements gathering, design, development, testing, operations and maintenance
   - **C.** Prototyping, build and fix, increment, test, maintenance
   - **D.** Prototyping, testing, requirements gathering, integration, testing
2. John is a manager of the application development department within his company. He needs to make sure his team is carrying out all of the correct testing types and at the right times of the development stages. Which of the following accurately describe types of software testing that should be carried out?
   - **i. Unit testing** Testing individual components in a controlled environment where programmers validate data structure, logic, and boundary conditions
   - **ii. Integration testing** Verifying that components work together as outlined in design specifications
   - **iii. Acceptance testing** Ensuring that the code meets customer requirements
   - **iv. Regression testing** After a change to a system takes place, retesting to ensure functionality, performance, and protection
   - **A.** i, ii
   - **B.** ii, iii
   - **C.** i, ii, iv
   - **D.** i, ii, iii, iv
3. Marge has to choose a software development methodology that her team should follow. The application that her team is responsible for developing is a critical application that can have few to no errors. Which of the following best describes the type of methodology her team should follow?
   - **A.** Cleanroom
   - **B.** Joint Application Development (JAD)
   - **C.** Rapid Application Development (RAD)
   - **D.** Reuse methodology

4. Which level of Capability Maturity Model Integration allows organizations to manage all projects across the organization and be proactive?
   - **A.** Defined
   - **B.** Incomplete
   - **C.** Managed
   - **D.** Optimizing
5. Mohammed is in charge of a large software development project with rigid requirements and phases that will probably be completed by different contractors. Which methodology would be best?
   - **A.** Waterfall
   - **B.** Spiral
   - **C.** Prototyping
   - **D.** Agile

Use the following scenario to answer Questions 6–9. You're in charge of IT and security at a midsize organization going through a growth stage. You decided to stand up your own software development team and are about to start your first project: a knowledge base for your customers. You think it can eventually grow to become the focal point of interaction with your customers, offering a multitude of features. You've heard a lot about the Scrum methodology and decide to try it for this project.

6. How would you go about documenting the requirements for this software system?
   - **A.** User stories
   - **B.** Use cases
   - **C.** System Requirements Specification (SRS)
   - **D.** Informally, since it's your first project
7. You are halfway through your first Scrum sprint and get a call from a senior vice president insisting that you add a new feature immediately. How do you handle this request?
   - **A.** Add the feature to the next sprint
   - **B.** Change the current sprint to include the feature
   - **C.** Reset the project to the requirements gathering phase
   - **D.** Delay the new feature until the end of the project

8. Your software development team, being new to the organization, is struggling to work smoothly with other teams within the organization as needed to get the software into production securely. Which approach can help mitigate this internal friction?

   A. DevSecOps

   B. DevOps

   C. Integrated Product Teams (IPT)

   D. Joint Analysis Design (JAD) sessions

9. What would be the best approach to selectively mature your software development practices with a view to improving cybersecurity?

   A. Software Assurance Maturity Model (SAMM)

   B. Capability Maturity Model Integration (CMMI)

   C. Kanban

   D. Integrated product teams (IPTs)

Answers

1. **B.** The following outlines the common phases of the software development life cycle:

   i. Requirements gathering

   ii. Design

   iii. Development

   iv. Testing

   v. Operations and maintenance

2. **D.** There are different types of tests the software should go through because there are different potential flaws to look for. The following are some of the most common testing approaches:

   - **Unit testing** Testing individual components in a controlled environment where programmers validate data structure, logic, and boundary conditions
   - **Integration testing** Verifying that components work together as outlined in design specifications
   - **Acceptance testing** Ensuring that the code meets customer requirements
   - **Regression testing** After a change to a system takes place, retesting to ensure functionality, performance, and protection

3. **A.** The listed software development methodologies and their definitions are as follows:

   - **Joint Application Development (JAD)** A methodology that uses a team approach in application development in a workshop-oriented environment.

- **Rapid Application Development (RAD)** A methodology that combines the use of prototyping and iterative development procedures with the goal of accelerating the software development process.
- **Reuse methodology** A methodology that approaches software development by using progressively developed code. Reusable programs are evolved by gradually modifying preexisting prototypes to customer specifications. Since the reuse methodology does not require programs to be built from scratch, it drastically reduces both development cost and time.
- **Cleanroom** An approach that attempts to prevent errors or mistakes by following structured and formal methods of developing and testing. This approach is used for high-quality and critical applications that will be put through a strict certification process.

4. A. The six levels of Capability Maturity Integration Model are

- **Incomplete** Development process is ad hoc or even chaotic. Tasks are not always completed at all, so projects are regularly cancelled or abandoned.
- **Initial** The organization does not use effective management procedures and plans. There is no assurance of consistency, and quality is unpredictable. Success is usually the result of individual heroics.
- **Managed** A formal management structure, change control, and quality assurance are in place for individual projects. The organization can properly repeat processes throughout each project.
- **Defined** Formal procedures are in place that outline and define processes carried out in all projects across the organization. This allows the organization to be proactive rather than reactive.
- **Quantitatively Managed** The organization has formal processes in place to collect and analyze quantitative data, and metrics are defined and fed into the process-improvement program.
- **Optimizing** The organization has budgeted and integrated plans for continuous process improvement, which allow it to quickly respond to opportunities and changes.

5. A. The Waterfall methodology is a very rigid approach that could be useful for projects in which all the requirements are fully understood up front or projects for which different organizations will perform the work at each phase. The Spiral, prototyping, and Agile methodologies are well suited for situations in which the requirements are not well understood, and don't lend themselves well to switching contractors midstream.

6. A. Any answer except "informally" would be a reasonable one, but since you are using an Agile methodology (Scrum), user stories is the best answer. The important point is that you document the requirements formally, so you can design a solution that meets all your users' needs.

7. **A.** The Scrum methodology allows the project to be reset by allowing product features to be added, changed, or removed at clearly defined points that typically happen at the conclusion of each sprint.
8. **A.** DevSecOps is the integration of development, security, and operations professionals into a software development team. This is a good way to solve the friction between developers and members of the security and operations staff.
9. **A.** CMMI and SAMM are the only maturity models among the possible answers. SAMM is the best answer because it allows for more granular maturity goals than CMMI does, and it is focused on security.

CHAPTER 25

Secure Software

This chapter presents the following:

- Programming languages
- Secure coding
- Security controls for software development
- Software security assessments
- Assessing the security of acquired software

A good programmer is someone who always looks both ways before crossing a one-way street.

—Doug Linder

Quality can be defined as fitness for purpose. In other words, quality refers to how good or bad something is for its intended purpose. A high-quality car is good for transportation. We don't have to worry about it breaking down, failing to protect its occupants in a crash, or being easy for a thief to steal. When we need to go somewhere, we can count on a high-quality car to get us to wherever we need to go. Similarly, we don't have to worry about high-quality software crashing, corrupting our data under unforeseen circumstances, or being easy for someone to subvert. Sadly, many developers still think of functionality first (or only) when thinking about quality. When we look at it holistically, we see that quality is the most important concept in developing secure software.

Every successful compromise of a software system relies on the exploitation of one or more vulnerabilities in it. Software vulnerabilities, in turn, are caused by defects in the design or implementation of code. The goal, then, is to develop software that is as free from defects or, in other words, as high quality as we can make it. In this chapter, we will discuss how secure software is quality software. We can't have one without the other. By applying the right processes, controls, and assessments, the outcome will be software that is more reliable and more difficult to exploit or subvert. Of course, these principles apply equally to software we develop in our own organizations and software that is developed for us by others.

Programming Languages and Concepts

All software is written in some type of programming language. Programming languages have gone through several generations over time, each generation building on the next, providing richer functionality and giving programmers more powerful tools as they evolve.

The main categories of languages are machine, assembly, high-level, very high-level, and natural languages. *Machine language* is in a format that the computer's processor can understand and work with directly. Every processor family has its own machine code instruction set, which is represented in a binary format (1 and 0) and is the most fundamental form of programming language. Since this was pretty much the only way to program the very first computers in the early 1950s, machine languages are the first generation of programming languages. Early computers used only basic binary instructions because compilers and interpreters were nonexistent at the time. Programmers had to manually calculate and allot memory addresses and sequentially feed instructions, as there was no concept of abstraction. Not only was programming in binary extremely time consuming, it was also highly prone to errors. (If you think about writing out thousands of 1's and 0's to represent what you want a computer to do, this puts this approach into perspective.) This forced programmers to keep a tight rein on their program lengths, resulting in programs that were very rudimentary.

An *assembly language* is considered a low-level programming language and is the symbolic representation of machine-level instructions. It is "one step above" machine language. It uses symbols (called mnemonics) to represent complicated binary codes. Programmers using assembly language could use commands like ADD, PUSH, POP, etc., instead of the binary codes (1001011010, etc.). Assembly languages use programs called *assemblers*, which automatically convert these assembly codes into the necessary machine-compatible binary language. To their credit, assembly languages drastically reduced programming and debugging times, introduced the concept of variables, and freed programmers from manually calculating memory addresses. But like machine code, programming in an assembly language requires extensive knowledge of a computer's architecture. It is easier than programming in binary format, but more challenging compared to the high-level languages most programmers use today.

Programs written in assembly language are also hardware specific, so a program written for an ARM-based processor would be incompatible with Intel-based systems; thus, these types of languages are not portable. Once the program is written, it is fed to an assembler, which translates the assembly language into machine language. The assembler also replaces variable names in the assembly language program with actual addresses at which their values will be stored in memory.

NOTE Assembly language allows for direct control of very basic activities within a computer system, as in pushing data on a memory stack and popping data off a stack. Attackers commonly use assembly language to tightly control how malicious instructions are carried out on victim systems.

The third generation of programming languages started to emerge in the early 1960s. They are known as *high-level languages* because of their refined programming structures.

High-level languages use abstract statements. Abstraction naturalizes multiple assembly language instructions into a single high-level statement, such as IF – THEN – ELSE. This allows programmers to leave low-level (system architecture) intricacies to the programming language and focus on their programming objectives. In addition, high-level languages are easier to work with compared to machine and assembly languages, as their syntax is similar to human languages. The use of mathematical operators also simplifies arithmetic and logical operations. This drastically reduces program development time and allows for more simplified debugging. This means the programs are easier to write and mistakes (bugs) are easier to identify. High-level languages are processor independent. Code written in a high-level language can be converted to machine language for different processor architectures using compilers and interpreters. When code is independent of a specific processor type, the programs are portable and can be used on many different system types.

Fourth-generation languages *(very high-level languages)* were designed to further enhance the natural language approach instigated within the third-generation languages. They focus on highly abstract algorithms that allow straightforward programming implementation in specific environments. The most remarkable aspect of fourth-generation languages is that the amount of manual coding required to perform a specific task may be ten times less than for the same task on a third-generation language. This is an especially important feature because these languages have been developed to be used by inexpert users and not just professional programmers.

As an analogy, let's say that you need to pass a calculus exam. You need to be very focused on memorizing the necessary formulas and applying the formulas to the correct word problems on the test. Your focus is on how calculus works, not on how the calculator you use as a tool works. If you had to understand how your calculator is moving data from one transistor to the other, how the circuitry works, and how the calculator stores and carries out its processing activities just to use it for your test, this would be overwhelming. The same is true for computer programmers. If they had to worry about how the operating system carries out memory management functions, input/output activities, and how processor-based registers are being used, it would be difficult for them to also focus on real-world problems they are trying to solve with their software. Very high-level languages hide all of this background complexity and take care of it for the programmer.

The early 1990s saw the conception of the fifth generation of programming languages *(natural languages)*. These languages approach programming from a completely different perspective. Program creation does not happen through defining algorithms and function statements, but rather by defining the constraints for achieving a specified result. The goal is to create software that can solve problems by itself instead of a programmer having to develop code to deal with individual and specific problems. The applications work more like a black box—a problem goes in and a solution comes out. Just as the introduction of assembly language eliminated the need for binary-based programming, the full impact of fifth-generation programming techniques may bring to an end the traditional programming approach. The ultimate target of fifth-generation languages is to eliminate the need for programming expertise and instead use advanced knowledge-based processing and artificial intelligence.

Language Levels

The "higher" the language, the more abstraction that is involved, which means the language hides details of how it performs its tasks from the software developer. A programming language that provides a high level of abstraction frees the programmer from the need to worry about the intricate details of the computer system itself, as in registers, memory addresses, complex Boolean expressions, thread management, and so forth. The programmer can use simple statements such as "print" and does not need to worry about how the computer will actually get the data over to the printer. Instead, the programmer can focus on the core functionality that the application is supposed to provide and not be bothered with the complex things taking place in the belly of the operating system and motherboard components.

As an analogy, you do not need to understand how your engine or brakes work in your car—there is a level of abstraction. You just turn the steering wheel and step on the pedal when necessary, and you can focus on getting to your destination.

There are so many different programming languages today, it is hard to fit them neatly in the five generations described in this chapter. These generations are the classical way of describing the differences in software programming approaches and what you will see on the CISSP exam.

The industry has not been able to fully achieve all the goals set out for these fifth-generation languages. The human insight of programmers is still necessary to figure out the problems that need to be solved, and the restrictions of the structure of a current computer system do not allow software to "think for itself" yet. We are getting closer to achieving artificial intelligence within our software, but we still have a long way to go.

The following lists the basic software programming language generations:

- **Generation one** Machine language
- **Generation two** Assembly language
- **Generation three** High-level language
- **Generation four** Very high-level language
- **Generation five** Natural language

Assemblers, Compilers, Interpreters

No matter what type or generation of programming language is used, all of the instructions and data have to end up in a binary format for the processor to understand and work with. Just like our food has to be broken down into specific kinds of molecules for our body to be able to use it, all code must end up in a format that is consumable by specific systems. Each programming language type goes through this transformation through the use of assemblers, compilers, or interpreters.

Assemblers are tools that convert assembly language source code into machine language code. Assembly language consists of mnemonics, which are incomprehensible to processors and therefore need to be translated into operation instructions.

Compilers are tools that convert high-level language statements into the necessary machine-level format (.exe, .dll, etc.) for specific processors to understand. The compiler transforms instructions from a source language (high-level) to a target language (machine), sometimes using an external assembler along the way. This transformation allows the code to be executable. A programmer may develop an application in the C language, but when you purchase this application, you do not receive the source code; instead, you receive the executable code that runs on your type of computer. The source code was put through a compiler, which resulted in an executable file that can run on your specific processor type.

Compilers allow developers to create software code that can be developed once in a high-level language and compiled for various platforms. So, you could develop one piece of software, which is then compiled by five different compilers to allow it to be able to run on five different systems.

Figure 25-1 shows the process by which a high-level language is gradually transformed into machine language, which is the only language a processor can understand natively. In this example, we have a statement that assigns the value 42 to the variable *x*. Once we feed the program containing this statement to a compiler, we end up with assembly language, which is shown in the middle of the figure. The way to set the value of a variable in assembly language is to literally move that value into wherever the variable is being stored. In this example, we are moving the hexadecimal value for 42 (which is 2a in hexadecimal, or 2ah) into the ax register in the processor. In order for the processor to execute this command, however, we still have to convert it into machine language, which is the job of the assembler. Note that it is way easier for a human coder to write *x* = 42 than it is to represent the same operation in either assembly or (worse yet) machine language.

If a programming language is considered "interpreted," then a tool called an *interpreter* takes care of transforming high-level code to machine-level code. For example, applications that are developed in JavaScript, Python, or Perl can be run directly by an interpreter, without having to be compiled. The goal is to improve portability. The greatest advantage of executing a program in an interpreted environment is that the platform independence and memory management functions are part of an interpreter. The major disadvantage

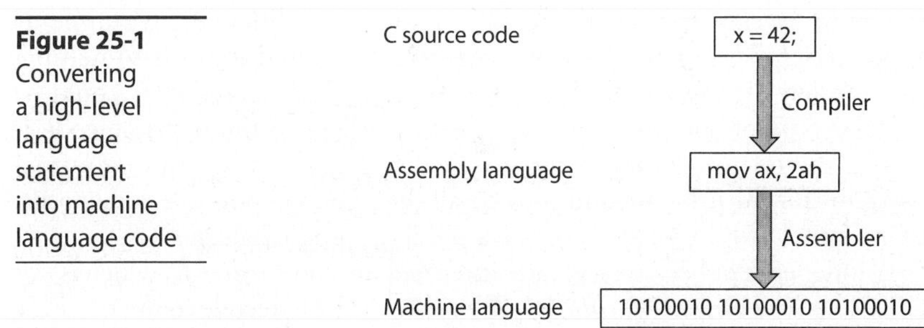

Figure 25-1 Converting a high-level language statement into machine language code

PART VIII

with this approach is that the program cannot run as a stand-alone application, requiring the interpreter to be installed on the local machine.

NOTE Some languages, such as Java and Python, blur the lines between interpreted and compiled languages by supporting both approaches. We'll talk more about how Java does this in the next section.

From a security point of view, it is important to understand vulnerabilities that are inherent in specific programming languages. For example, programs written in the C language could be vulnerable to buffer overrun and format string errors. The issue is that some of the C standard software libraries do not check the length of the strings of data they manipulate by default. Consequently, if a string is obtained from an untrusted source (i.e., the Internet) and is passed to one of these library routines, parts of memory may be unintentionally overwritten with untrustworthy data—this vulnerability can potentially be used to execute arbitrary and malicious software. Some programming languages, such as Java, perform automatic memory allocation as more space is needed; others, such as C, require the developer to do this manually, thus leaving opportunities for error.

Garbage collection is an automated way for software to carry out part of its memory management tasks. A *garbage collector* identifies blocks of memory that were once allocated but are no longer in use and deallocates the blocks and marks them as free. It also gathers scattered blocks of free memory and combines them into larger blocks. It helps provide a more stable environment and does not waste precious memory. If garbage collection does not take place properly, not only can memory be used in an inefficient manner, an attacker could carry out a denial-of-service attack specifically to artificially commit all of a system's memory, rendering the system unable to function.

Nothing in technology seems to be getting any simpler, which makes learning this stuff much harder as the years go by. Ten years ago assembly, compiled, and interpreted languages were more clear-cut and their definitions straightforward. For the most part, only scripting languages required interpreters, but as languages have evolved they have become extremely flexible to allow for greater functionality, efficiency, and portability. Many languages can have their source code compiled or interpreted depending upon the environment and user requirements.

Runtime Environments

What if you wanted to develop software that could run on many different environments without having to recompile it? This is known as *portable code* and it needs something that can sort of "translate" it to each different environment. That "translator" could be tuned to a particular type of computer but be able to run any of the portable code it understands. This is the role of *runtime environments (RTEs)*, which function as miniature operating systems for the program and provide all the resources portable code needs. One of the best examples of RTE usage is the Java programming language.

Java is platform independent because it creates intermediate code, *bytecode*, which is not processor-specific. The *Java Virtual Machine (JVM)* converts the bytecode to the machine

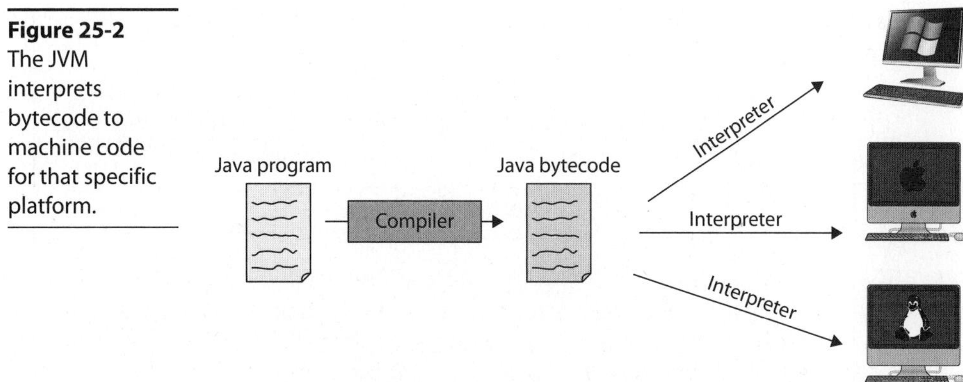

Figure 25-2 The JVM interprets bytecode to machine code for that specific platform.

code that the processor on that particular system can understand (see Figure 25-2). Despite its name, the JVM is not a full-fledged VM (as defined in Chapter 7). Instead, it is a component of the Java RTE, together with a bunch of supporting files like class libraries.

Let's quickly walk through these steps:

1. A programmer creates a Java applet and runs it through a compiler.
2. The Java compiler converts the source code into bytecode (not processor-specific).
3. The user downloads the Java applet.
4. The JVM converts the bytecode into machine-level code (processor-specific).
5. The applet runs when called upon.

When an applet is executed, the JVM creates a unique RTE for it called a *sandbox*. This sandbox is an enclosed environment in which the applet carries out its activities. Applets are commonly sent over within a requested web page, which means the applet executes as soon as it arrives. It can carry out malicious activity on purpose or accidentally if the developer of the applet did not do his part correctly. So the sandbox strictly limits the applet's access to any system resources. The JVM mediates access to system resources to ensure the applet code behaves and stays within its own sandbox. These components are illustrated in Figure 25-3.

NOTE The Java language itself provides protection mechanisms, such as garbage collection, memory management, validating address usage, and a component that verifies adherence to predetermined rules.

However, as with many other things in the computing world, the bad guys have figured out how to escape the confines and restrictions of the sandbox. Programmers have figured out how to write applets that enable the code to access hard drives and

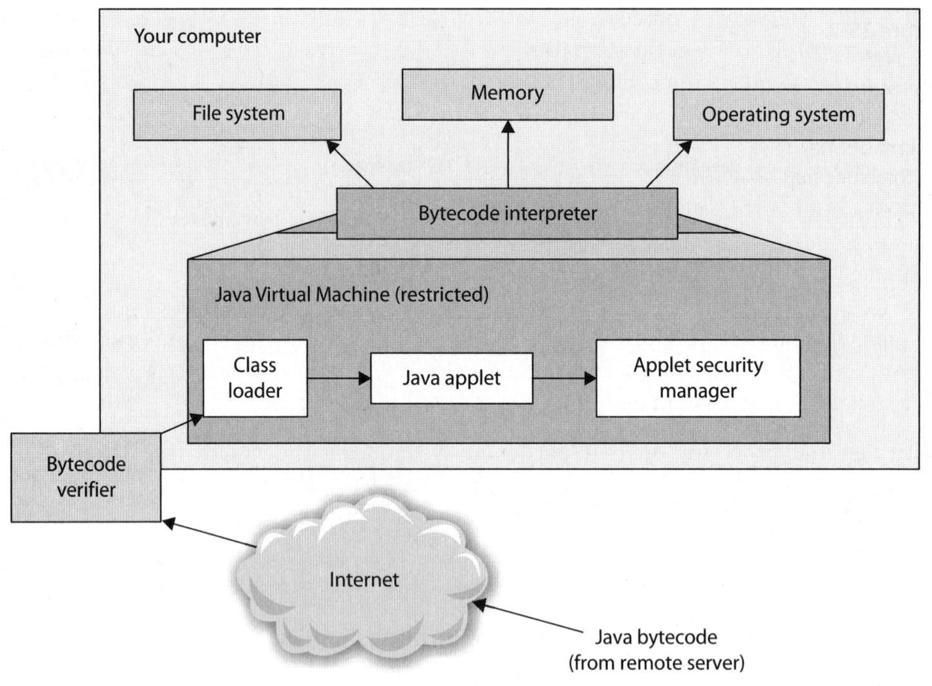

Figure 25-3 Java's security model

resources that are supposed to be protected by the Java security scheme. This code can be malicious in nature and cause destruction and mayhem to the user and her system.

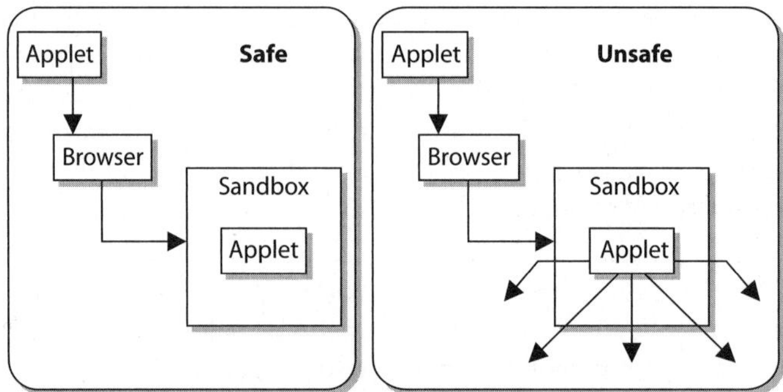

Object-Oriented Programming Concepts

Software development used to be done by classic input–processing–output methods. This development used an information flow model from hierarchical information structures. Data was input into a program, and the program passed the data from the beginning to end, performed logical procedures, and returned a result. *Object-oriented programming (OOP)* methods perform the same functionality, but with different techniques that work in a more efficient manner. First, you need to understand the basic concepts of OOP.

OOP works with classes and objects. A real-world object, such as a table, is a member (or an instance) of a larger class of objects called "furniture." The furniture class has a set of attributes associated with it, and when an object is generated, it inherits these attributes. The attributes may be color, dimensions, weight, style, and cost. These attributes apply if a chair, table, or loveseat object is generated, also referred to as *instantiated*. Because the table is a member of the class furniture, the table inherits all attributes defined for the class (see Figure 25-4).

The programmer develops the class and all of its characteristics and attributes. The programmer does not develop each and every object, which is the beauty of this approach. As an analogy, let's say you developed an advanced coffee maker with the goal of putting Starbucks out of business. A customer punches the available buttons on your coffee maker interface, ordering a large latte, with skim milk, vanilla and raspberry flavoring, and an extra shot of espresso, where the coffee is served at 250 degrees. Your coffee maker does all of this through automation and provides the customer with a lovely cup of coffee exactly to her liking. The next customer wants a mocha Frothy Frappé, with whole milk and extra foam. So the goal is to make something once (coffee maker, class), allow it to accept requests through an interface, and create various results (cups of coffee, objects) depending upon the requests submitted.

But how does the class create objects based on requests? A piece of software that is written in OOP will have a request sent to it, usually from another object. The requesting object wants a new object to carry out some type of functionality. Let's say that object A wants object B to carry out subtraction on the numbers sent from A to B. When this request comes in, an object is built (instantiated) with all of the necessary programming code. Object B carries out the subtraction task and sends the result back to object A.

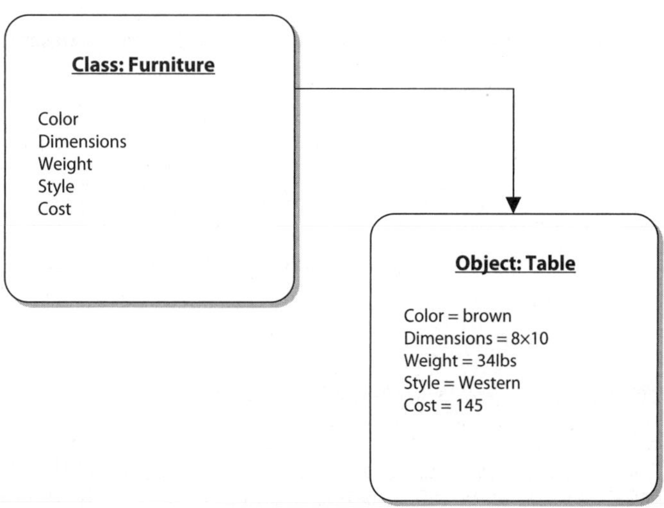

Figure 25-4 In object-oriented inheritance, each object belongs to a class and takes on the attributes of that class

It does not matter what programming language the two objects are written in; what matters is if they know how to communicate with each other. One object can communicate with another object if it knows the application programming interface (API) communication requirements. An API is the mechanism that allows objects to talk to each other (as described in depth in the forthcoming section "Application Programming Interfaces"). Let's say you want to talk to Jorge, but can only do so by speaking French and can only use three phrases or less, because that is all Jorge understands. As long as you follow these rules, you can talk to Jorge. If you don't follow these rules, you can't talk to Jorge.

TIP An object is an instance of a class.

What's so great about OOP? Figure 25-5 shows the difference between OOP and procedural programming, which is a non-OOP technique. Procedural programming is built on the concept of dividing a task into procedures that, when executed, accomplish the task. This means that large applications can quickly become one big pile of code (sometimes called *spaghetti code*). If you want to change something in this pile, you have to go through all the program's procedures to figure out what your one change is going to break. If the program contains hundreds or thousands of lines of code, this is not an easy or enjoyable task. Now, if you choose to write your program in an object-oriented

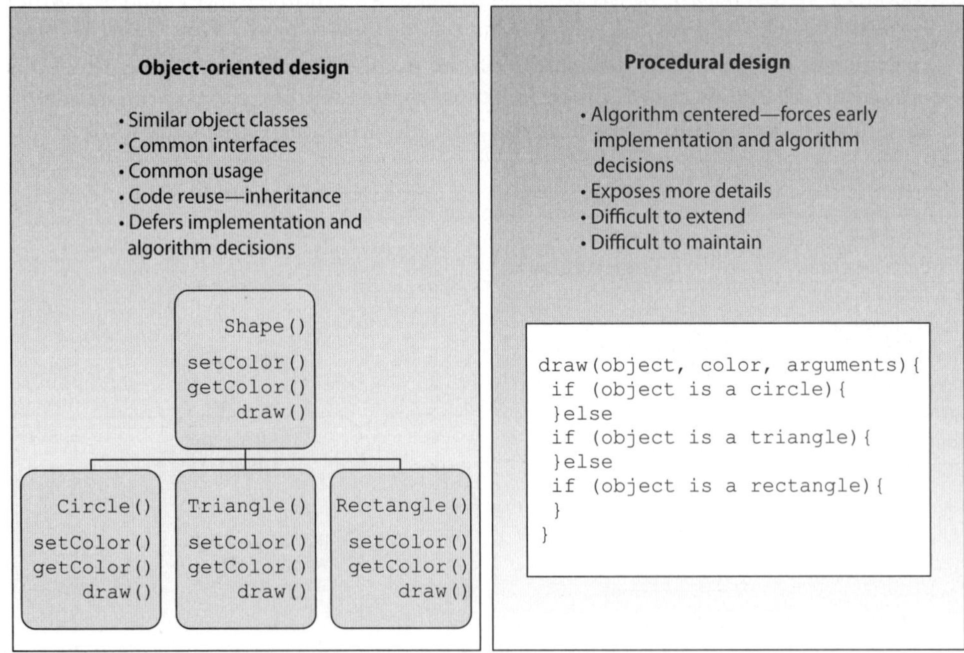

Figure 25-5 Procedural vs. object-oriented programming

language, you don't have one monolithic application, but an application that is made up of smaller components (objects). If you need to make changes or updates to some functionality in your application, you can just change the code within the class that creates the object carrying out that functionality, and you don't have to worry about everything else the program actually carries out. The following breaks down the benefits of OOP:

- **Modularity** The building blocks of software are autonomous objects, cooperating through the exchange of messages.
- **Deferred commitment** The internal components of an object can be redefined without changing other parts of the system.
- **Reusability** Classes are reused by other programs, though they may be refined through inheritance.
- **Naturalness** Object-oriented analysis, design, and modeling map to business needs and solutions.

Most applications have some type of functionality in common. Instead of developing the same code to carry out the same functionality for ten different applications, using OOP allows you to create the object only once and reuse it in other applications. This reduces development time and saves money.

Now that we've covered the concepts of OOP, let's clarify the terminology. A *method* is the functionality or procedure an object can carry out. An object may be constructed to accept data from a user and to reformat the request so a back-end server can understand and process it. Another object may perform a method that extracts data from a database and populates a web page with this information. Or an object may carry out a withdrawal procedure to allow the user of an ATM to extract money from her account.

The objects *encapsulate* the attribute values, which means this information is packaged under one name and can be reused as one entity by other objects. Objects need to be able to communicate with each other, and this happens by using *messages* that are sent to the receiving object's API. If object A needs to tell object B that a user's checking account must be reduced by $40, it sends object B a message. The message is made up of the destination, the method that needs to be performed, and the corresponding arguments. Figure 25-6 shows this example.

Messaging can happen in several ways. A given object can have a single connection (one-to-one) or multiple connections (one-to-many). It is important to map these communication paths to identify if information can flow in a way that is not intended. This helps to ensure that sensitive data cannot be passed to objects of a lower security level.

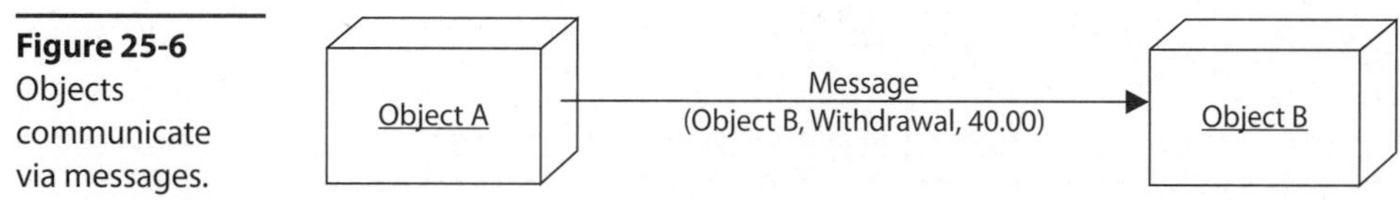

Figure 25-6 Objects communicate via messages.

An object can have a shared portion and a private portion. The *shared* portion is the interface (API) that enables it to interact with other components. Messages enter through the interface to specify the requested operation, or method, to be performed. The *private* portion of an object is how it actually works and performs the requested operations. Other components need not know how each object works internally—only that it does the job requested of it. This is how *data hiding* is possible. The details of the processing are hidden from all other program elements outside the object. Objects communicate through well-defined interfaces; therefore, they do not need to know how each other works internally.

NOTE Data hiding is provided by encapsulation, which protects an object's private data from outside access. No object should be allowed to, or have the need to, access another object's internal data or processes.

These objects can grow to great numbers, so the complexity of understanding, tracking, and analyzing can get a bit overwhelming. Many times, the objects are shown in connection to a reference or pointer in documentation. Figure 25-7 shows how related objects are represented as a specific piece, or reference, in a bank ATM system. This enables analysts and developers to look at a higher level of operation and procedures without having to view each individual object and its code. Thus, this modularity provides for a more easily understood model.

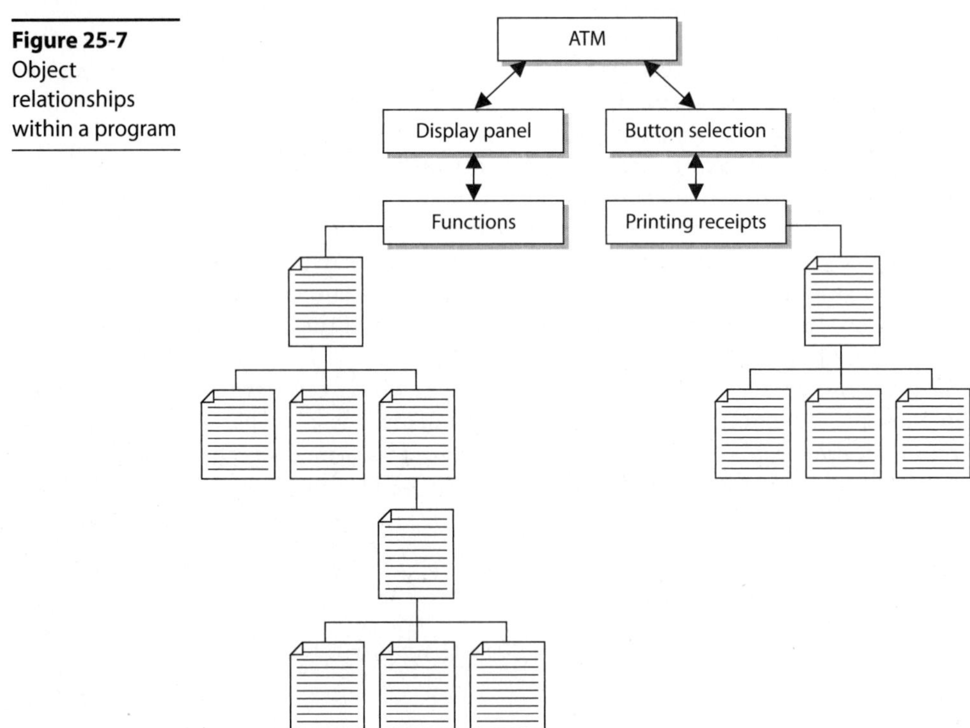

Figure 25-7 Object relationships within a program

Abstraction, as discussed earlier, is the capability to suppress unnecessary details so the important, inherent properties can be examined and reviewed. It enables the separation of conceptual aspects of a system. For example, if a software architect needs to understand how data flows through the program, she would want to understand the big pieces of the program and trace the steps the data takes from first being input into the program all the way until it exits the program as output. It would be difficult to understand this concept if the small details of every piece of the program were presented. Instead, through abstraction, all the details are suppressed so the software architect can understand a crucial part of the product. It is like being able to see a forest without having to look at each and every tree.

Each object should have specifications it adheres to. This discipline provides cleaner programming and reduces programming errors and omissions. The following list is an example of what should be developed for each object:

- Object name
- Attribute descriptions
- Attribute name
- Attribute content
- Attribute data type
- External input to object
- External output from object
- Operation descriptions
- Operation name
- Operation interface description
- Operation processing description
- Performance issues
- Restrictions and limitations
- Instance connections
- Message connections

The developer creates a class that outlines these specifications. When objects are instantiated, they inherit these attributes.

Each object can be reused as stated previously, which is the beauty of OOP. This enables a more efficient use of resources and the programmer's time. Different applications can use the same objects, which reduces redundant work, and as an application grows in functionality, objects can be easily added and integrated into the original structure.

The objects can be catalogued in a library, which provides an economical way for more than one application to call upon the objects (see Figure 25-8). The library provides an index and pointers to where the objects actually live within the system or on another system.

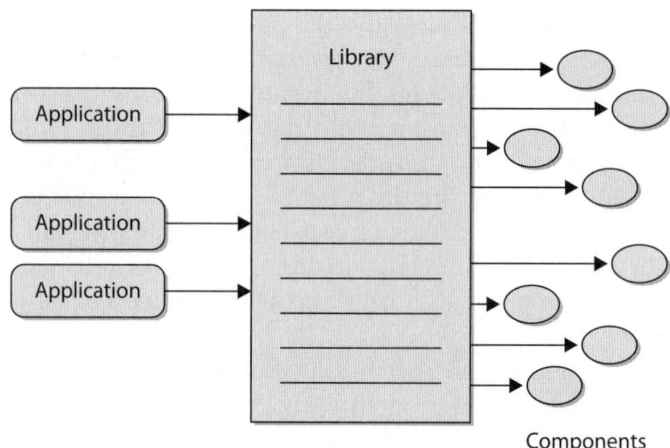

Figure 25-8 Applications locate the necessary objects through a library index.

When applications are developed in a modular approach, like object-oriented methods, components can be reused, complexity is reduced, and parallel development can be done. These characteristics allow for fewer mistakes, easier modification, resource efficiency, and more timely coding than the classic programming languages. OOP also provides functional independence, which means each module addresses a specific subfunction of requirements and has an interface that is easily understood by other parts of the application.

An object is *encapsulated*, meaning the data structure (the operation's functionality) and the acceptable ways of accessing it are grouped into one entity. Other objects, subjects, and applications can use this object and its functionality by accessing it through controlled and standardized interfaces and sending it messages (see Figure 25-9).

Cohesion and Coupling

Cohesion reflects how many different types of tasks a module can carry out. If a module carries out only one task (i.e., subtraction) or tasks that are very similar (i.e., subtract, add, multiply), it is described as having high cohesion, which is a good thing. The higher the cohesion, the easier it is to update or modify the module and not affect other modules that interact with it. This also means the module is easier to reuse and maintain because it is more straightforward when compared to a module with low cohesion. An object with low cohesion carries out multiple *different* tasks and increases the complexity of the module, which makes it harder to maintain and reuse. So, you want your objects to be focused, manageable, and understandable. Each object should carry out a single function or similar functions. One object should not carry out mathematical operations, graphic rendering, and cryptographic functions—these are separate functionality types, and keeping track of this level of complexity would be confusing. If you are attempting to create complex multifunction objects, you are trying to shove too much into one object. Objects should carry out modular, simplistic functions—that is the whole point of OOP.

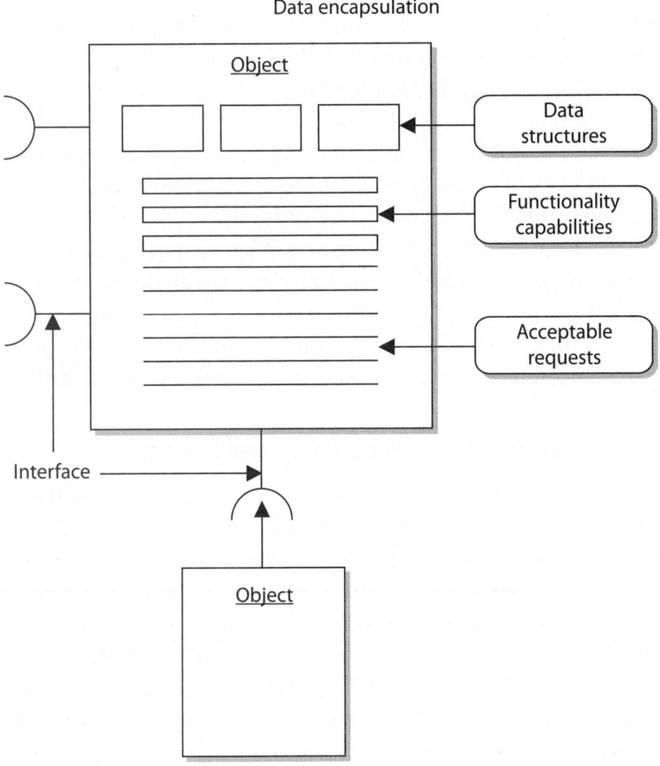

Figure 25-9 The different components of an object and the way it works are hidden from other objects.

Coupling is a measurement that indicates how much interaction one module requires to carry out its tasks. If a module has low (loose) coupling, this means the module does not need to communicate with many other modules to carry out its job. High (tight) coupling means a module depends upon many other modules to carry out its tasks. Low coupling is more desirable because the module is easier to understand and easier to reuse, and it can be changed without affecting many modules around it. Low coupling indicates that the programmer created a well-structured module. As an analogy, a company would want its employees to be able to carry out their individual jobs with the least amount of dependencies on other workers. If Joe has to talk with five other people just to get one task done, too much complexity exists, the task is too time-consuming, and the potential for errors increases with every interaction.

If modules are tightly coupled, the ripple effect of changing just one module can drastically affect the other modules. If they are loosely coupled, this level of complexity decreases.

An example of *low coupling* would be one module passing a variable value to another module. As an example of *high coupling*, Module A would pass a value to Module B, another value to Module C, and yet another value to Module D. Module A could not complete its tasks until Modules B, C, and D completed their tasks and returned results to Module A.

EXAM TIP Objects should be self-contained and perform a single logical function, which is high cohesion. Objects should not drastically affect each other, which is low coupling.

The level of complexity involved with coupling and cohesion can directly impact the security level of a program. The more complex something is, the harder it is to secure. Developing "tight code" not only allows for efficiencies and effectiveness but also reduces the software's attack surface. Decreasing complexity where possible reduces the number of potential holes a bad guy can sneak through. As an analogy, if you were responsible for protecting a facility, your job would be easier if the facility had a small number of doors, windows, and people coming in and out of it. The smaller number of variables and moving pieces would help you keep track of things and secure them.

Application Programming Interfaces

When we discussed some of the attributes of object-oriented development, we spent a bit of time on the concept of abstraction. Essentially, abstraction is all about defining *what* a class or object does and ignoring *how* it accomplishes it internally. An *application programming interface (API)* specifies the manner in which a software component interacts with other software components. We already saw in Chapter 9 how this can come in handy in the context of Trusted Platform Modules (TPMs) and how they constrain communications with untrusted modules. APIs create checkpoints where security controls can be easily implemented. Furthermore, they encourage software reuse and also make the software more maintainable by localizing the changes that need to be made while eliminating (or at least reducing) cascading effects of fixes or changes.

Besides the advantages of reduced effort and improved maintainability, APIs often are required to employ the underlying operating system's functionality. Apple macOS and iOS, Google Android, and Microsoft Windows all require developers to use standard APIs for access to operating system functionality such as opening and closing files and network connections, among many others. All these major vendors restrict the way in which their APIs are used, most notably by ensuring that any parameter that is provided to them is first checked to ensure it is not malformed, invalid, or malicious, which is something we should all do when we are dealing with APIs.

Parameter validation refers to confirming that the parameter values being received by an application are within defined limits before they are processed by the system. In a client/server architecture, validation controls may be placed on the client side prior to submitting requests to the server. Even when these controls are employed, the server should perform parallel validation of inputs prior to processing them because a client has fewer controls than a server and may have been compromised or bypassed.

Software Libraries

APIs are perhaps most familiar to us in the context of software libraries. A *software library* is a collection of components that do specific tasks that are useful to many other components. For example, there are software libraries for various encryption algorithms, managing network connections, and displaying graphics. Libraries allow software developers to work on whatever makes their program unique, while leveraging known-good code for the tasks that similar programs routinely do. The programmer simply needs to understand the API for the libraries she intends to use. This reduces the amount of new code that the programmer needs to develop, which in turn makes the code easier to secure and maintain.

Using software libraries has potential risks, and these risks must be mitigated as part of secure software development practices. The main risk is that, because the libraries are reused across multiple projects in multiple organizations, any defect in these libraries propagates through every program that uses them. In fact, according to Veracode's 2020 report "State of Software Security: Open Source Edition," seven in ten applications use at least one open-source library with a security flaw, which makes those applications vulnerable. Keep in mind that these are open-source libraries, which (as we will discuss later in this chapter) are subject to examination by any number of security researchers looking for bugs. If you use proprietary libraries (including your own), it may be much harder to find these vulnerabilities before the threat actors do.

Secure Software Development

So far in this chapter (and the previous one), we've discussed software development in general terms, pointing out potential security pitfalls along the way. We now turn our attention to how we can bake security into our software from the ground up. To do so, however, we have to come from the top down, meaning we need an organizational policy document that clearly identifies the strategic goals, responsibilities, and authorities for mitigating risks associated with building or acquiring software. If the executive leadership doesn't push this, it just won't happen, and the policy document puts everyone on notice that secure coding is an organizational priority.

Secure coding is a set of practices that reduces (to acceptable levels) the risk of vulnerabilities in our software. No software will ever be 100 percent secure, but we can sure make it hard for threat actors to find and exploit any remaining vulnerabilities if we apply secure coding guidelines and standards to our projects.

Source Code Vulnerabilities

A *source code vulnerability* is a defect in code that provides a threat actor an opportunity to compromise the security of a software system. All code has defects (or bugs), but a vulnerability is a particularly dangerous one. Source code vulnerabilities are typically caused by two types of flaws: design and implementation. A *design flaw* is one that, even if the programmer did everything perfectly right, would still cause the vulnerability. An *implementation flaw* is one that stems from a programmer who incorrectly implemented a part of a good design. For example, suppose you are building an e-commerce application that collects payment card information from your customers and stores it for their future purchases. If you design the system to store the card numbers unencrypted, that would be a design flaw. If, on the other hand, you design the system to encrypt the data as soon as it is captured but a programmer incorrectly calls the encryption function, resulting in the card number being stored in plaintext, that would be an implementation vulnerability.

Source code vulnerabilities are particularly problematic when they exist in externally facing systems such as web applications. These accounted for 39 percent of the external attacks carried out, according to Forrester's report "The State of Application Security, 2021." Web applications deserve particular attention because of their exposure.

The *Open Web Application Security Project (OWASP)* is an organization that deals specifically with web security issues. OWASP offers numerous tools, articles, and resources that developers can utilize to create secure software, and it also has individual member meetings (chapters) throughout the world. OWASP provides development guidelines, testing procedures, and code review steps, but is probably best known for its OWASP Top 10 list of web application security risks. The following is the most recent Top 10 list as of this writing, from 2017 (the 2021 version should be published by the time you're reading this):

- Injection
- Broken Authentication
- Sensitive Data Exposure
- XML External Entities (XEE)
- Broken Access Control
- Security Misconfiguration
- Cross-Site Scripting (XSS)
- Insecure Deserialization
- Using Components with Known Vulnerabilities
- Insufficient Logging & Monitoring

This list represents the most common vulnerabilities that reside in web-based software and are exploited most often. You can find out more information pertaining to these vulnerabilities at https://owasp.org/www-project-top-ten/.

Secure Coding Practices

So, we've talked about secure coding practices, but what exactly are they? Although the specific practices vary from one organization to the next, generally, they break down into two categories: standards and guidelines. Recall from Chapter 1 that *standards* are mandatory activities, actions, or rules, whereas *guidelines* are recommended actions and operational guides that provide the necessary flexibility for unforeseen circumstances. By enforcing secure coding standards and maintaining coding guidelines that reflect best practices, software development organizations dramatically reduce their source code vulnerabilities. Let's see how this works.

Coding Standards

Standards are the strongest form of secure coding practices because, to be considered a standard, a practice must meet the following requirements:

- Demonstrably reduce the risk of a particular type of vulnerability
- Be enforceable across the breadth of an organization's software development efforts
- Be verifiable in its implementation

EXAM TIP The rigorous application of secure coding standards is the best way to reduce source code vulnerabilities.

A very good reference for developing coding standards is the OWASP Top 10 list referenced in the previous section. Though it's focused on web applications, most of the vulnerabilities apply to any kind of software. Another good source of information is the organization's own past experience in developing code with vulnerabilities that later had to be patched.

Once the vulnerabilities are identified, even if at a fairly high level, coding standards can be developed to reduce the risk of building code that contains them. This is where things get a bit sticky, because the standards vary from one programming language to the next. If your organization develops web applications in Ruby (a common language for web apps), the way in which you reduce the risk of, say, broken authentication will be different than if you use PHP (another popular web app language). Still, there are plenty of opportunities to build standards that apply to all languages when we take a step back and consider the processes by which we develop, operationalize, and maintain that code. We'll cover this in more detail when we discuss security controls for software development later in this chapter.

Finally, a standard is only good if we can verify that we are complying with it. (Otherwise, why bother?) So, for instance, if we have a standard that reduces the risk of injection by validating inputs and parameters, then we should have a way to verify that none of our code fails to validate them. An excellent way to verify compliance with secure coding standards is the practice of code reviews, as discussed in Chapter 18. Ideally, though, we can verify at least some of our standards automatedly.

Coding standards enable secure coding by ensuring programmers always do certain things and never do others. For example, a standard could require use of a particular library for encryption functions because it's been analyzed and determined to be sound and free from vulnerabilities. Another example of a standard could be forbidding programmers from using specific unsafe functions, such as the notorious `strcpy()` function in the C programming language. This function copies a string from one memory location to another, but doesn't check the length of the string being copied compared to the destination. If the string is longer than the destination, it will overwrite other areas of memory, which can result in a buffer overflow condition.

Software-Defined Security

A promising new area of security builds on the idea of software-defined networking (SDN), which we covered in Chapter 13. Recall that, in SDN, the control plane (i.e., the routing and switching decisions) is separate from the data plane (i.e., the packets and frames moving around). This allows centralized control of the network, which in turn improves performance, flexibility, and security. SDN also enables the separation of security functions from more traditional network appliance approaches. *Software-defined security (SDS or SDSec)* is a security model in which security functions such as firewalling, intrusion detection and prevention (IDS/IPS), and network segmentation are implemented in software within an SDN environment. One of the advantages of this approach is that sensors (for functions like IDS/IPS) can be dynamically repositioned depending on the threat environment.

SDS is a new technology but promises significant security advantages. Because of its dependence on SDN, SDS is best used in cloud and virtualized network environments.

NOTE Coding standards are required in certain regulated sectors such as automobile and railroad control software, among others.

Coding Guidelines

Secure coding guidelines are recommended practices that tend to be less specific than standards. For example, coding guidelines might encourage programmers to use variable names that are self-explanatory and not reused anywhere else in the program because this makes the code easier to understand. Applied to secure coding, these standards can help by ensuring code is consistently formatted and commented, which makes the code easier to read during code reviews. Guidelines may also recommend that coders keep functions short (without specifying how short) because this reduces the chance of errors. These practices may not sound like much, but they make it easier to spot errors early in the development process, thus improving quality, while decreasing vulnerabilities and costs.

Security Controls for Software Development

We tend to think of security controls as something to be added to an environment in order to reduce risks to it. While this is certainly true of software development environments, secure coding adds another layer, which consists of the security controls we build into the code itself. Regardless of whether we are protecting the development subnetwork or the software that is produced therein, we should implement security controls only after conducting deliberate threat modeling tied to a risk analysis process.

Keep in mind, however, that the threat models for an internal subnet are different from the threat models for software you're deploying throughout your organization or even selling to your customers. Either way, the goals are to reduce vulnerabilities and the possibility of system compromise, but the manner in which we do so will be very different.

Let's zoom in on just software you're developing. Which specific software controls you should use depends on the software itself, its objectives, the security goals of its associated security policy, the type of data it will process, the functionality it is to carry out, and the environment in which it will be placed. If an application is purely proprietary and will run only in closed, trusted environments, it may need fewer security controls than those required for applications that will connect businesses over the Internet and provide financial transactions. The trick is to understand the security needs of a piece of software, implement the right controls and mechanisms, thoroughly test the mechanisms and how they integrate into the application, follow structured development methodologies, and provide secure and reliable distribution methods.

In the sections that follow, we'll identify and describe the application of security controls for the major aspects of software development. These include aspects of the software itself, of course, but also the tools used to develop it, the manner in which we test it, and even how to integrate the software development environment into the broader security architecture.

Development Platforms

Software is normally developed by a team of software engineers who may or may not use the same tools. The most important tool in their tool set is an *integrated development environment (IDE)*, which enables each engineer to pull code from a repository (more on that later), edit it, test it, and then push it into the repository so the rest of the team can build on it. Depending on the programming language, target environments, and a host of other considerations, your developers may use Eclipse, Microsoft Visual Studio, Xcode, or various other applications. The software they develop will likely be tested (formally or otherwise) using development clients and servers that are supposed to represent the production platforms on which the finished software product will run. When we talk about security of the development platforms, therefore, we mean both the development endpoints and the "fake" clients and servers on which the software gets tested.

It may seem obvious, but the first step in ensuring the security of development platforms is to secure the devices on which our software engineers practice their craft. The challenge that many organizations face is that their engineers tend to be more sophisticated than the average user and will make changes to their computers that may or may not be authorized. Their principal incentive, after all, is to develop code quickly and correctly. If the configuration of their workstation gets in the way, it may find itself being modified. To avoid this, you should resist the temptation of giving your software engineers unfettered privileged access to their own devices. Enforcing good change management practices is critical to securing these development endpoints.

Even harder than ensuring change controls on your developers' workstations is securely provisioning the development clients and servers that they will need for testing.

Many organizations allow their developers to stand up and maintain their own development environment, which may be fine provided that these devices are isolated from the production environments. It may sound like common sense, but the problem is that some organizations don't do a good enough job of isolating development and production systems. In principle, doing so simply requires putting the development nodes in an isolated VLAN. In practice, the demarcation is not that cut and dry. This gets even more challenging when the team is distributed, which requires your developers (or perhaps their external collaborators) to remotely access the development hosts.

The best solution is to require use of a VPN to connect to the isolated development network. This may create a bit of work for the operations staff but is the only way to ensure that development and production code remains separate. Another good approach is to create firewall rules that prevent any unauthorized external connections (and even then only the bare minimum) to or from development servers. It should be clear by now that the provisioning of hosts on the development network should not be left to the software development team.

Tool Sets

As the old saying goes, you can't make everyone happy. Your IDE may be awesome, but invariably your software developers will need (or just want) additional tool sets. This is particularly true for developers that have a favorite tool that they've grown used to over the years, or if there is new work to be done for which the existing tools are not ideal. There are two approaches we've seen adopted by many organizations, and neither is ultimately good. The first is to force strict compliance with the approved tool sets that the organization provides. On the surface, this makes sense from a security and operations perspective. Having fewer tools means more standardization, allows for more thorough security assessments, and streamlines provisioning. However, it can also lead to a loss in productivity and typically leads the best coders to give up and move on to another organization where they're allowed more freedom.

The other (not good) approach is to let the developers run amuck in their own playground. The thinking goes something like this: we let them use whatever tools they feel are good, we set up and maintain whatever infrastructure they need, and we just fence the whole thing off from the outside so nothing bad can get in. The end of that sentence should make you shake your head in disagreement because keeping all the bad stuff out obviously is not possible, as you've learned throughout this book. Still, this is the approach of many small and mid-sized development shops.

A better approach is to treat the software development department the same way we treat any other. If they need a new tool, they simply put in a request that goes through the change management process, discussed in Chapter 20. The change advisory board (CAB) validates the requirement, assesses the risk, reviews the implementation plan, and so on. Assuming everything checks out and the CAB approves, the IT operations team integrates the tool into the inventory, updating and provisioning processes; the security team implements and monitors the appropriate controls, and the developers get the new tool they need.

Application Security Testing

Despite our best efforts, we (and all our programmers) are human and will make mistakes. Some of those mistakes will end up being source code vulnerabilities. Wouldn't it be nice to find them before our adversaries do? That's the role of application security testing, which comes in three flavors that you should know for the CISSP exam: static analysis, dynamic analysis, and fuzzing.

Static Application Security Testing

Static application security testing (SAST), also called *static analysis*, is a technique meant to help identify software defects or security policy violations and is carried out by examining the code without executing the program, and therefore is carried out before the program is compiled. The term SAST is generally reserved for automated tools that assist analysts and developers, whereas manual inspection by humans is generally referred to as *code review* (covered in Chapter 18).

SAST allows developers to quickly scavenge their source code for programming flaws and vulnerabilities. Additionally, this testing provides a scalable method of security code review and ensures that developers are following secure coding policies. There are numerous manifestations of SAST tools, ranging from tools that simply consider the behavior of single statements to tools that analyze the entire source code at once. However, you must remember that static code analysis can never reveal logical errors and design flaws, and therefore must be used in conjunction with manual code review to ensure thorough evaluation.

Dynamic Application Security Testing

Dynamic application security testing (DAST), also known as *dynamic analysis*, refers to the evaluation of a program in real time, while it is running. DAST is commonly carried out once a program has cleared the SAST stage and basic programming flaws have been rectified offline. DAST enables developers to trace subtle logical errors in the software that are likely to cause security mayhem later on. The primary advantage of this technique is that it eliminates the need to create artificial error-inducing scenarios. Dynamic analysis is also effective for compatibility testing, detecting memory leakages, identifying dependencies, and analyzing software without having to access the software's actual source code.

EXAM TIP Remember that SAST requires access to the source code, which is not executed during the tests, while DAST requires that you actually run the code but does not require access to the source code.

Fuzzing

Fuzzing is a technique used to discover flaws and vulnerabilities in software by sending large amounts of malformed, unexpected, or random data to the target program in order to trigger failures. Attackers can then manipulate these errors and flaws to inject their own code into the system and compromise its security and stability. Fuzzing tools, aka fuzzers, use complex inputs to attempt to impair program execution. Fuzzing tools

Manual Penetration Testing

Application security testing tools, together with good old-fashioned code reviews, are very good at unearthing most of the vulnerabilities that would otherwise go unnoticed by the software development team. As good as these tools are, however, they lack the creativity and resourcefulness of a determined threat actor. For this reason, many organizations also rely on *manual penetration testing (MPT)* as the final check before code is released into production environments. In this approach, an experienced red team examines the software system in its intended environment and looks for ways to compromise it. It is very common for this testing to uncover additional vulnerabilities that cannot be detected by automated tools.

are commonly successful at identifying buffer overflows, DoS vulnerabilities, injection weaknesses, validation flaws, and other activities that can cause software to freeze, crash, or throw unexpected errors.

Continuous Integration and Delivery

With the advent of Agile methodologies, discussed in Chapter 24, it has become possible to dramatically accelerate the time it takes to develop and release code. This has been taken to an extreme by many of the best software development organizations through processes of continuous integration and continuous delivery.

Continuous integration (CI) means that all new code is integrated into the rest of the system as soon as the developer writes it. For example, suppose Diana is a software engineer working on the user interface of a network detection and response (NDR) system. In traditional development approaches, she would spend a couple of weeks working on UI features, pretty much in isolation from the rest of the development team. There would then be a period of integration in which her code (and that of everyone else who's ready to deliver) gets integrated and tested. Then, Diana (and everyone else) goes back to working alone on her next set of features. The problem with this approach is that Diana gets to find out whether her code integrates properly only every two weeks. Wouldn't it be nice if she could find out instantly (or at least daily) whether any of her work has integration issues?

With continuous integration, Diana works on her code for a few hours and then merges it into a shared repository. This merge triggers a batch of unit tests. If her code fails those tests, the merge is rejected. Otherwise, her code is merged with everyone else's in the repository and a new version of the entire software system is built. If there are any errors in the build, she knows her code was the cause, and she can get to work fixing them right away. If the build goes well, it is immediately subjected to automated integration tests. If anything goes wrong, Diana knows she has to immediately get back to work fixing her code because she "broke the build," meaning nobody else can commit code until she fixes it or reverses her code merge.

Continuous integration dramatically improves software development efficiency by identifying errors early and often. CI also allows the practice of *continuous delivery (CD)*, which is incrementally building a software product that can be released at any time. Because all processes and tests are automated, you could choose to release code to production daily or even hourly. Most organizations that practice CI/CD, however, don't release code that frequently. But they could if they wanted to.

CI/CD sounds wonderful, so what are the security risks we need to mitigate? Because CI/CD relies heavily on automation, most organizations that practice it use commercial or open-source testing platforms. One of those platforms is Codecov, which was compromised in early 2021, allowing the threat actor to modify its bash uploader script. This is the script that would take Diana's code in our earlier example and upload it for testing and integration. As an aside, because the tests are automated and don't involve actual users, developers typically have to provide access credentials, tokens, or keys to enable testing. The threat actor behind the Codecov breach modified the bash uploader so that it would exfiltrate this access data, potentially providing covert access to any of the millions of products worldwide that use Codecov for CI/CD.

The Codecov breach was detected about three months later by an alert customer who noticed unusual behavior in the uploader, investigated it, and alerted the vendor to the problem. Would you be able to tell that one of the components in your CI/CD toolset was leaking sensitive data? You could if you practice the secure design principles we've been highlighting throughout the book, especially threat modeling, least privilege, defense in depth, and zero trust.

Security Orchestration, Automation, and Response

The Codecov breach mentioned in the previous section also highlights the role that a security orchestration, automation, and response (SOAR) platform can play in securing your software development practices. Chapter 21 introduced SOAR in the context of the role of a security information and event management (SIEM) platform in your security operations. Both SOAR and SIEM platforms can help detect and, in the case of SOAR, respond to threats against your software development efforts. If you have sensors in your development subnet (you did segment your network, right?) and a well-tuned SOAR platform, you can detect new traffic flowing from that subnet (which shouldn't be talking much to the outside world) to a new external endpoint. If the traffic is unencrypted (or you use a TLS decryption proxy to do deep packet inspection), you'd notice access tokens and keys flowing out to a new destination. Based on this observation, you could declare an incident and activate the playbook for data breaches in your SOAR platform. Just like that, you would've stopped the bleeding, buying you time to figure out what went wrong and how to fix it for the long term.

One of the challenges with the scenario just described is that many security teams treat their organization's development environment as a bit of a necessary chaos that must be tolerated. Software developers are typically rewarded (or punished) according to their ability to produce quality code quickly. They can be resistant (or even rebel against) anything that gets in the way of their efficiency, and, as we well know, security tends to do just that. This is where DevSecOps (discussed in Chapter 24) can help build the right culture and balance the needs of all teammates. It can also help the security team identify and implement controls that mitigate risks such as data breaches, while minimally affecting productivity. One such control is the placement of sensors such as IDS/IPS, NDR, and data loss prevention (DLP) within the development subnets. These systems, in turn, would report to the SOAR platform, which could detect and contain active threats against the organization.

Software Configuration Management

Not every threat, of course, is external. There are plenty of things our own teammates can do deliberately or otherwise that cause problems for the organization. As we'll see later in this chapter when we discuss cloud services, improper configurations consistently rank among the worst threats to many organizations. This threat, however, is a solved problem in organizations that practice proper configuration management, as we covered in Chapter 20.

Anticipating the inevitable changes that will take place to a software product during its development life cycle, a configuration management system should be put into place that allows for change control processes to take place through automation. Since deploying an insecure configuration to an otherwise secure software product makes the whole thing insecure, these settings are a critical component of securing the software development environment. A product that provides *software configuration management (SCM)* identifies the attributes of software at various points in time and performs a methodical control of changes for the purpose of maintaining software integrity and traceability throughout the software development life cycle. It tracks changes to configurations and provides the ability to verify that the final delivered software has all of the approved changes that are supposed to be included in the release.

During a software development project, the centralized code repositories are often kept in systems that can carry out SCM functionality. These SCM systems manage and track revisions made by multiple people against a single master set and provide concurrency management, versioning, and synchronization. *Concurrency management* deals with the issues that arise when multiple people extract the same file from a central repository and make their own individual changes. If they were permitted to submit their updated files in an uncontrolled manner, the files would just write over each other and changes would be lost. Many SCM systems use algorithms to version, fork, and merge the changes as files are checked back into the repository.

Versioning deals with keeping track of file revisions, which makes it possible to "roll back" to a previous version of the file. An archive copy of every file can be made when it is checked into the repository, or every change made to a file can be saved to a transaction log. Versioning systems should also create log reports of who made changes, when they were made, and what the changes were.

Some SCM systems allow individuals to check out complete or partial copies of the repositories and work on the files as needed. They can then commit their changes back to the master repository as needed and update their own personal copies to stay up to date with changes other people have made. This process is called *synchronization*.

Code Repositories

A *code repository*, which is typically a version control system, is the vault containing the crown jewels of any organization involved in software development. If we put on our adversarial hats for a few minutes, we could come up with all kinds of nefarious scenarios involving these repositories. Perhaps the simplest is that someone could steal our source code, which embodies not only many staff hours of work but, more significantly, our intellectual property. An adversary could also use our source code to look for vulnerabilities to exploit later, once the code is in production. Finally, adversaries could deliberately insert vulnerabilities into our software, perhaps after it has undergone all testing and is trusted, so that they can exploit it later at a time of their choosing. Clearly, securing our source code repositories is critical.

Perhaps the most secure way of managing security for your code repositories is to implement them on an isolated (or "air-gapped") network that includes the development, test, and QA environments. The development team would have to be on this network to do their work, and the code, once verified, could be exported to the production servers using removable storage media. We already presented this best

Software Escrow

If a company pays another company to develop software for it, it should have some type of *software escrow* in place for protection. We covered this topic in Chapter 23 from a business continuity perspective, but since it directly deals with software development, we will mention it here also.

In a software escrow framework, a third party keeps a copy of the source code, and possibly other materials, which it will release to the customer only if specific circumstances arise, mainly if the vendor who developed the code goes out of business or for some reason is not meeting its obligations and responsibilities. This procedure protects the customer, because the customer pays the vendor to develop software code for it, and if the vendor goes out of business, the customer otherwise would no longer have access to the actual code. This means the customer code could never be updated or maintained properly.

A logical question would be, "Why doesn't the vendor just hand over the source code to the customer, since the customer paid for it to be developed in the first place?" It does not always work that way. The code may be the vendor's intellectual property. The vendor employs and pays people with the necessary skills to develop that code, and if the vendor were to just hand it over to the customer, it could be giving away its intellectual property, its secrets. The customer oftentimes gets compiled code instead of source code. *Compiled code* is code that has been put through a compiler and is unreadable to humans. Most software profits are based on licensing, which outlines what customers can do with the compiled code. For an added fee, of course, most custom software developers will also provide the source, which could be useful in sensitive applications.

practice in the preceding section. The challenge with this approach is that it severely limits the manner in which the development team can connect to the code. It also makes it difficult to collaborate with external parties and for developers to work from remote or mobile locations.

A pretty good alternative would be to host the repository on the intranet, which would require developers to either be on the local network or connect to it using a VPN connection. As an added layer of security, the repositories can be configured to require the use of Secure Shell (SSH), which would ensure all traffic is encrypted, even inside the intranet, to mitigate the risk of sniffing. Finally, SSH can be configured to use public key infrastructure (PKI), which allows us to implement not only confidentiality and integrity but also nonrepudiation. If you have to allow remote access to your repository, this would be a good way to go about it.

Finally, if you are operating on a limited budget or have limited security expertise in this area, you can choose one of the many web-based repository service providers and let them take care of the security for you. While this may mitigate the basic risks for small organizations, it is probably not an acceptable course of action for projects with significant investments of intellectual property.

Software Security Assessments

We already discussed the various types of security assessments in Chapter 18, but let's circle back here and see how these apply specifically to software security. Recall from previous sections in this chapter that secure software development practices originate in an organizational policy that is grounded in risk management. That policy is implemented through secure coding standards, guidelines, and procedures that should result in secure software products. We verify this is so through the various testing methods discussed in this chapter (e.g., SAST and DAST) and Chapter 24 (e.g., unit, integration, etc.). The purpose of a software security assessment, then, is to verify that this entire chain, from policy to product, is working as it should.

When conducting an assessment, it is imperative that the team review all applicable documents and develop a plan for how to verify each requirement from the applicable policies and standards. Two areas that merit additional attention are the manner in which the organization manages risks associated with software development and how it audits and logs software changes.

Risk Analysis and Mitigation

Risk management is at the heart of secure software development, particularly the mapping between risks we've identified and the controls we implement to mitigate them. This is probably one of the trickiest challenges in secure software development in general, and in auditing it in particular. When organizations do map risks to controls in software development, they tend to do so in a generic way. For example, the OWASP Top 10 list is a great starting point for analyzing and mitigating vulnerabilities, but how are we doing against specific (and potentially unique) threats faced by our organization?

Threat modeling is an important activity for any development team, and particularly in DevSecOps. Sadly, however, most organizations don't conduct threat modeling for their software development projects. If they're defending against generic threats, that's good, but sooner or later we all face unique threats that, if we haven't analyzed and mitigated them, have a high probability of ruining our weekend.

Another area of interest for assessors are the linkages between the software development and risk management programs. If software projects are not tracked in the organization's risk matrix, then the development team will probably be working in isolation, disconnected from the broader risk management efforts.

Change Management

Another area in which integration with broader organizational efforts is critical to secure software development is change management. Changes to a software project that may appear inconsequential when considered in isolation could actually pose threats when analyzed within the broader context of the organization. If software development is not integrated into the organization's change management program, auditing changes to software products may be difficult, even if the changes are being logged by the development team. Be that as it may, software changes should not be siloed from overall organizational change management because doing so will likely lead to interoperability or (worse yet) security problems.

Assessing the Security of Acquired Software

Most organizations do not have the in-house capability to develop their own software systems. Their only feasible options are either to acquire standard software or to have a vendor build or customize a software system to their particular environment. In either case, software from an external source will be allowed to execute in a trusted environment. Depending on how trustworthy the source and the code are, this could have some profound implications to the security posture of the organization's systems. As always, we need to ground our response on our risk management process.

In terms of managing the risk associated with acquired software, the essential question to ask is, "How is the organization affected if this software behaves improperly?" Improper behavior could be the consequence of either defects or misconfiguration. The defects can manifest themselves as computing errors (e.g., wrong results) or vulnerability to intentional attack. A related question is, "What is it that we are protecting and this software could compromise?" Is it personally identifiable information (PII), intellectual property, or national security information? The answers to these and other questions will dictate the required thoroughness of our approach.

In many cases, our approach to mitigating the risks of acquired software will begin with an assessment of the software developer. Characteristics that correlate to a lower software risk include the good reputation of the developer and the regularity of its patch pushes. Conversely, developers may be riskier if they have a bad reputation, are small or new organizations, if they have immature or undocumented development processes, or if their products have broad marketplace presence (meaning they are more lucrative targets to exploit developers).

A key element in assessing the security of acquired software is, rather obviously, its performance in an internal assessment. Ideally, we are able to obtain the source code from the vendor so that we can do our own code reviews, vulnerability assessments, and penetration tests. In many cases, however, this will not be possible. Our only possible assessment may be a penetration test. The catch is that we may not have the in-house capability to perform such a test. In such cases, and depending on the potential risk posed by this software, we may be well advised to hire an external party to perform an independent penetration test for us. This is likely a costly affair that would only be justifiable in cases where a successful attack against the software system would likely lead to significant losses for the organization.

Even in the most constrained case, we are still able to mitigate the risk of acquisition. If we don't have the means to do code reviews, vulnerability assessments, or penetration tests, we can still mitigate the risk by deploying the software only in specific subnetworks, with hardened configurations, and with restrictive IDS/IPS rules monitoring its behavior. Though this approach may initially lead to constrained functionality and excessive false positives generated by our IDS/IPS, we can always gradually loosen the controls as we gain assurances that the software is trustworthy.

Commercial Software

It is exceptionally rare for an organization to gain access to the source code of a commercial-off-the-shelf (COTS) product to conduct a security assessment of it. However, depending on the product, we may not have to. The most widely used commercial software products have been around for years and have had their share of security researchers (both benign and malicious) poking at them the whole time. We can simply research what vulnerabilities and exploits have been discovered by others and decide for ourselves whether or not the vendor uses effective secure coding practices.

If the software is not as popular, or serves a small niche community, the risk of undiscovered vulnerabilities is probably higher. In these cases, it pays to look into the certifications of the vendor. A good certification for a software developer is ISO/IEC 27034 Application Security. Unfortunately, you won't find a lot of vendors certified in it. There are also certifications that are very specific to a sector (e.g., ISO 26262 for automotive safety) or a programming language (e.g., ISO/IEC TS 17961:2013 for coding in C) and are a bit less rare to find. Ultimately, however, the security of a vendor's software products is tied to how seriously it takes security in the first place. Absent a secure coding certification, you can look for overall information security management system (ISMS) certifications like ISO/IEC 27001 and FedRAMP, which are difficult to obtain and show that security is taken seriously in an organization.

Open-Source Software

Open-source software is released with a license agreement that allows the user to examine its source code, modify it at will, and even redistribute the modified software (which, per the license, usually requires acknowledgment of the original source and a description of modifications). This may seem perfect, but there are some caveats to keep in mind. First, the software is released as-is, typically without any service or support agreements (though these can be purchased through third parties). This means that your staff may have to figure out how to install, configure, and maintain the software on their own, unless you contract with someone else to do this for you.

Second, part of the allure of open-source software is that we get access to the source code. This means we can apply all the security tests and assessments we covered earlier. Of course, this only helps if we have the in-house capabilities to examine the source code effectively. Even if we don't, however, we can rely on countless developers and researchers around the world who do examine it (at least for the more popular software). The flip side of that coin, however, is that the adversaries also get to examine the code to either identify vulnerabilities quicker than the defenders or gain insights into how they might more effectively attack organizations that use specific software.

Perhaps the greatest risk in using open-source software is relying on outdated versions of it. Many of us are used to having software that automatically checks for updates and applies them automatically (either with or without our explicit permission). This is not all that common in open-source software, however, especially libraries. This means we need to develop processes to ensure that all open-source software is periodically updated, possibly in a way that differs from the way in which COTS software is updated.

Third-Party Software

Third-party software, also known as *outsourced software*, is software made specifically for an organization by a third party. Since the software is custom (or at least customized), it is not considered COTS. Third-party software may rely partly (or even completely) on open-source software, but, having been customized, it may introduce new vulnerabilities. So, we need a way to verify the security of these products that is probably different from how we would do so with COTS or open-source software.

EXAM TIP Third-party software is custom (or at least customized) to an organization and is not considered commercial off-the-shelf (COTS).

The best (and, sadly, most expensive) way to assess the security of third-party software is to leverage the external or third-party audits discussed in Chapter 18. The way this typically works is that we write into the contract a provision for an external auditor to inspect the software (and possibly the practices through which it was developed), and then issue a report, attesting to the security of the product. Passing this audit can be a condition of finalizing the purchase. Obviously, a sticking point in this negotiation can be who pays for this audit.

Another assessment approach is to arrange for a time-limited trial of the third-party software (perhaps at a nominal cost to the organization), and then have a red team perform an assessment. If you don't have a red team, you can probably hire one for less money than a formal application security audit would cost. Still, the cost will be considerable, typically (at least) in the low tens of thousands of dollars. As with any other security control, you'd have to balance the cost of the assessment and the loss you would incur from insecure software.

Managed Services

As our organizations continue to migrate to cloud services (IaaS, PaaS, and SaaS, discussed in depth in Chapter 7), we should also assess the security impact of those services. This is highlighted by a 2020 study by global intelligence firm IDC, which found that nearly 80 percent of the companies surveyed had experienced at least one cloud data breach in the past 18 months. The top three reasons were misconfigurations, lack of visibility into access settings and activities, and improper access control. The major cloud services provide tools to help you avoid these pitfalls, but the bottom line is that, if you don't have the in-house expertise to secure and assess your cloud services, you really should consider contracting an expert to help you out.

Chapter Review

Building secure code requires commitment from many parts of the organization, not just the development and security teams. It starts at the very top with a policy document that is implemented through standards, procedures, and guidelines. A key part of these is the inclusion of the various types of tests that must be run regularly (even continuously) on the software as it is being written, integrated, and prepared for delivery. Software development environments are complex and could require different approaches from those you'd take in a normal network environment. For this reason, teamwork among all stakeholders is absolutely critical. A really good way to facilitate this collaboration is by using the DevSecOps approach introduced in Chapter 24 and highlighted in this one.

Even if your organization doesn't develop software, it most certainly uses applications and services developed by others. That's why the concepts discussed in this chapter are universally applicable to any cybersecurity leader. You must understand how secure code is built, so that you can determine whether the software you're getting from others presents any undue risks to your organization's cybersecurity.

Quick Review

- Machine language, which consists of 1's and 0's, is the only format that a computer's processor can understand directly and is considered a first-generation language.
- Assembly language is considered a second-generation programming language and uses symbols (called mnemonics) to represent complicated binary codes.
- Third-generation programming languages, such as C/C++, Java, and Python, are known as high-level languages due to their refined programming structures, which allow programmers to leave low-level (system architecture) intricacies to the programming language and focus on their programming objectives.
- Fourth-generation languages (aka very high-level languages) use natural language processing to allow inexpert programmers to develop code in less time than it would take an experienced software engineer to do so using a third-generation language.

- Fifth-generation programming languages (aka natural languages) approach programming by defining the constraints for achieving a specified result and allowing the development environment to solve problems by itself instead of a programmer having to develop code to deal with individual and specific problems.
- Assemblers are tools that convert assembly language source code into machine code.
- Compilers transform instructions from a source language (high-level) to a target language (machine), sometimes using an external assembler along the way.
- A garbage collector identifies blocks of memory that were once allocated but are no longer in use and deallocates the blocks and marks them as free.
- A runtime environment (RTE) functions as a miniature operating system for the program and provides all the resources portable code needs.
- In object-oriented programming (OOP), related functions and data are encapsulated together in classes, which may then be instantiated as objects.
- Objects in OOP communicate with each other by using messages that conform to the receiving object's application programming interface (API) definition.
- Cohesion reflects how many different types of tasks a module can carry out, with the goal being to perform only one task (high cohesion), which makes modules easier to maintain.
- Coupling is a measure of how much a module depends on others; the more dependencies it has, the more complex and difficult the module is to maintain, so we want low (or loose) coupling.
- An API specifies the manner in which a software component interacts with other software components.
- Parameter validation refers to confirming that the parameter values being received by an application are within defined limits before they are processed by the system.
- A software library is a collection of components that do specific tasks that are useful to many other components.
- Secure coding is a set of practices that reduce (to acceptable levels) the risk of vulnerabilities in our software.
- A source code vulnerability is a defect in code that provides a threat actor an opportunity to compromise the security of a software system.
- Secure coding standards are verifiable, mandatory practices that reduce the risk of particular types of vulnerabilities in the source code.
- Secure coding guidelines are recommended practices that tend to be less specific than standards.

- Software-defined security (SDS or SDSec) is a security model in which security functions such as firewalling, IDS/IPS, and network segmentation are implemented in software within an SDN environment.
- Software development tools should be authorized, implemented, and maintained just like any other software product through the organization's change management process; developers should not be allowed to install and use arbitrary tools.
- Static application security testing (SAST) is a technique meant to help identify software defects or security policy violations and is carried out by examining the source code without executing the program.
- Dynamic application security testing (DAST) refers to the evaluation of a program in real time, while it is running.
- Fuzzing is a technique used to discover flaws and vulnerabilities in software by sending large amounts of malformed, unexpected, or random data to the target program in order to trigger failures.
- Continuous integration means that all new code is integrated into the rest of the system as soon as the developer writes it.
- Continuous delivery is incrementally building a software product that can be released at any time and requires continuous integration.
- A software configuration management (SCM) platform identifies the attributes of software at various points in time and performs a methodical control of changes for the purpose of maintaining software integrity and traceability throughout the SDLC.
- The purpose of a software security assessment is to verify that this entire development process, from organizational policy to delivered product, is working as it should.
- Security assessments of acquired software are essential to mitigate the risk they could pose to the organization that acquired it.
- The most practical way to assess the security of commercial software is to research what vulnerabilities and exploits have been discovered by others and decide for ourselves whether or not the vendor uses effective secure coding practices.
- The greatest risk in using open-source software is relying on outdated versions of it.
- The best way to assess the security of third-party (i.e., custom or customized) software is to perform external or third-party audits.

Questions

Please remember that these questions are formatted and asked in a certain way for a reason. Keep in mind that the CISSP exam is asking questions at a conceptual level. Questions may not always have the perfect answer, and the candidate is advised against always looking for the perfect answer. Instead, the candidate should look for the best answer in the list.

1. What language is the only one that a computer processor can natively understand and execute?
   A. Machine language
   B. Register language
   C. Assembly language
   D. High-level language
2. To which generation do programming languages such as such as C/C++, Java, and Python belong?
   A. Second generation
   B. Third generation
   C. Fourth generation
   D. Fifth generation
3. Which type of tool is specifically designed to convert assembly language into machine language?
   A. Compiler
   B. Integrated development environment (IDE)
   C. Assembler
   D. Fuzzer
4. Which of the following is not very useful in assessing the security of acquired software?
   A. The reliability and maturity of the vendor
   B. The vendor's software escrow framework
   C. Third-party vulnerability assessments
   D. In-house code reviews if source code is available
5. Cohesion and coupling are characteristics of quality code. Which of the following describes the goals for these two characteristics?
   A. Low cohesion, low coupling
   B. Low cohesion, high coupling
   C. High cohesion, low coupling
   D. High cohesion, high coupling

6. Yichen is a new software engineer at Acme Software, Inc. During his first code review, he is told by his boss that he should use descriptive names for variables in his code. What is this observation an example of?
   A. Secure coding guidelines
   B. Secure coding standards
   C. Secure software development policy
   D. Use of fifth-generation language
7. On what other technology does software-defined security depend?
   A. Software-defined storage (SDS)
   B. Software-defined networking (SDN)
   C. Security orchestration, automation, and response (SOAR)
   D. Continuous integration (CI)
8. If you wanted to test source code for vulnerabilities without running it, which approach would be best?
   A. Static application security testing (SAST)
   B. Fuzzing
   C. Dynamic application security testing (DAST)
   D. Manual penetration testing
9. If you wanted to test software for vulnerabilities by executing it and then exposing it to large amounts of random inputs, which testing technique would you use?
   A. Static application security testing (SAST)
   B. Fuzzing
   C. Dynamic application security testing (DAST)
   D. Manual penetration testing
10. Which of the following is not a common reason for data breaches in managed cloud services?
    A. Misconfigurations
    B. Lack of visibility into access settings and activities
    C. Hardware failures
    D. Improper access control

Answers

1. **A.** Machine language, which consists of 1's and 0's, is the only format that a computer's processor can understand directly and is considered a first-generation language.

2. **B.** Third-generation programming languages, such as C/C++, Java, and Python, are known as high-level languages due to their refined programming structures, which allow programmers to leave low-level (system architecture) intricacies to the programming language and focus on their programming objectives.
3. **C.** Assemblers are tools that convert assembly language source code into machine code. Compilers also generate machine language, but do so by transforming high-level language code, not assembly language.
4. **B.** In a software escrow framework, a third party keeps a copy of the source code, and possibly other materials, which it will release to the customer in specific circumstances such as the developer going out of business. While software escrow is a good business continuity practice, it wouldn't normally tell us anything about the security of the software itself. All three other answers are part of a rigorous assessment of the security of acquired software.
5. **C.** Cohesion reflects how many different types of tasks a module can carry out, with the goal being to perform only one task (high cohesion), which makes modules easier to maintain. Coupling is a measure of how much a module depends on others; the more dependencies it has, the more complex and difficult the module is to maintain, so we want low (or loose) coupling.
6. **A.** Secure coding guidelines are recommended practices that tend to be less specific than standards. They might encourage programmers to use variable names that are self-explanatory and to keep functions short (without specifying how short). Secure coding standards, on the other hand, are verifiable, mandatory practices that reduce the risk of particular types of vulnerabilities in the source code.
7. **B.** Software-defined security (SDS or SDSec) is a security model in which security functions such as firewalling, IDS/IPS, and network segmentation are implemented in software within an SDN environment.
8. **A.** Static application security testing (SAST) is a technique meant to help identify software defects or security policy violations and is carried out by examining the source code without executing the program. All the other answers require that the code be executed.
9. **B.** Fuzzing is a technique used to discover flaws and vulnerabilities in software by sending large amounts of malformed, unexpected, or random data to the target program in order to trigger failures.
10. **C.** The top three reasons for data breaches in cloud services are misconfigurations, lack of visibility into access settings and activities, and improper access control.

APPENDIX

Comprehensive Questions

Use the following scenario to answer Questions 1–3. Josh has discovered that an organized hacking ring in China has been targeting his company's research and development department. If these hackers have been able to uncover his company's research findings, this means they probably have access to his company's intellectual property. Josh thinks that an e-mail server in his company's DMZ may have been successfully compromised and a rootkit loaded.

1. Based upon this scenario, what is most likely the biggest risk Josh's company needs to be concerned with?

A. Market share drop if the attackers are able to bring the specific product to market more quickly than Josh's company.

B. Confidentiality of e-mail messages. Attackers may post all captured e-mail messages to the Internet.

C. Impact on reputation if the customer base finds out about the attack.

D. Depth of infiltration of attackers. If attackers have compromised other systems, more confidential data could be at risk.

2. The attackers in this situation would be seen as which of the following?

A. Vulnerability

B. Threat

C. Risk

D. Threat agent

3. If Josh is correct in his assumptions, which of the following best describes the vulnerability, threat, and exposure, respectively?

A. E-mail server is hardened, an entity could exploit programming code flaw, server is compromised and leaking data.

B. E-mail server is not patched, an entity could exploit a vulnerability, server is hardened.

C. E-mail server misconfiguration, an entity could exploit misconfiguration, server is compromised and leaking data.

D. DMZ firewall misconfiguration, an entity could exploit misconfiguration, internal e-mail server is compromised.

4. Aaron is a security manager who needs to develop a solution to allow his company's mobile devices to be authenticated in a standardized and centralized manner using digital certificates. The applications these mobile clients use require a TCP connection. Which of the following is the best solution for Aaron to implement?
   - **A.** TACACS+
   - **B.** RADIUS
   - **C.** Diameter
   - **D.** Mobile IP
5. Terry is a security manager for a credit card processing company. His company uses internal DNS servers, which are placed within the LAN, and external DNS servers, which are placed in the DMZ. The company also relies on DNS servers provided by its service provider. Terry has found out that attackers have been able to manipulate several DNS server caches to point employee traffic to malicious websites. Which of the following best describes the solution this company should implement?
   - **A.** IPSec
   - **B.** PKI
   - **C.** DNSSEC
   - **D.** MAC-based security
6. Which of the following is not a key provision of the GDPR?
   - **A.** Requirement for consent from data subjects
   - **B.** Right to be informed
   - **C.** Exclusion for temporary workers
   - **D.** Right to be forgotten
7. Jane is suspicious that an employee is sending sensitive data to one of the company's competitors but is unable to confirm this. The employee has to use this data for daily activities, thus it is difficult to properly restrict the employee's access rights. In this scenario, which best describes the company's vulnerability, threat, risk, and necessary control?
   - **A.** Vulnerability is employee access rights, threat is internal entities misusing privileged access, risk is the business impact of data loss, and the necessary control is detailed network traffic monitoring.
   - **B.** Vulnerability is lack of user monitoring, threat is internal entities misusing privileged access, risk is the business impact of data loss, and the necessary control is detailed user activity logs.
   - **C.** Vulnerability is employee access rights, threat is internal employees misusing privileged access, risk is the business impact of confidentiality, and the necessary control is multifactor authentication.
   - **D.** Vulnerability is employee access rights, threat is internal users misusing privileged access, risk is the business impact of confidentiality, and the necessary control is CCTV.

8. Which of the following best describes what role-based access control offers organizations in reducing administrative burdens?
   A. It allows entities closer to the resources to make decisions about who can and cannot access resources.
   B. It provides a centralized approach for access control, which frees up department managers.
   C. User membership in roles can be easily revoked and new ones established as job assignments dictate.
   D. It enforces an enterprise-wide security policy, standards, and guidelines.
9. Mark works for a large corporation operating in multiple countries worldwide. He is reviewing his company's policies and procedures dealing with data breaches. Which of the following is an issue that he must take into consideration?
   A. Each country may or may not have unique notification requirements.
   B. All breaches must be announced to affected parties within 24 hours.
   C. Breach notification is a "best effort" process and not a guaranteed process.
   D. Breach notifications are avoidable if all PII is removed from data stores.
10. A software development company released a product that committed several errors that were not expected once deployed in their customers' environments. All of the software code went through a long list of tests before being released. The team manager found out that after a small change was made to the code, the program was not tested before it was released. Which of the following tests was most likely not conducted?
   A. Unit
   B. Compiled
   C. Integration
   D. Regression
11. Which of the following should not be considered as part of the supply chain risk management process for a smartphone manufacturer?
   A. Hardware Trojans inserted by downstream partners
   B. ISO/IEC 27001
   C. Hardware Trojans inserted by upstream partners
   D. NIST Special Publication 800-161
12. Data sovereignty is increasingly becoming an issue that most of us in cybersecurity should address within our organizations. What does the term data sovereignty mean?
   A. Certain types of data concerning a country's citizens must be stored and processed in that country.
   B. Data on a country's citizens must be stored and processed according to that country's laws, regardless of where the storing/processing takes place.

C. Certain types of data concerning a country's citizens are the sovereign property of that data subject.

D. Data on a country's citizens must never cross the sovereign borders of another country.

Use the following scenario to answer Questions 13–15. Jack has just been hired as the security officer for a large hospital system. The organization develops some of its own proprietary applications. The organization does not have as many layers of controls when it comes to the data processed by these applications, since it is assumed that external entities will not understand the internal logic of the applications. One of the first things that Jack wants to carry out is a risk assessment to determine the organization's current risk profile. He also tells his boss that the hospital should become ISO certified to bolster its customers' and partners' confidence in its risk management processes.

13. Which of the following approaches has been implemented in this scenario?

- **A.** Defense-in-depth
- **B.** Security through obscurity
- **C.** Information security management system
- **D.** ISO/IEC 27001

14. Which ISO/IEC standard would be best for Jack to follow to meet his goals?

- **A.** ISO/IEC 27001
- **B.** ISO/IEC 27004
- **C.** ISO/IEC 27005
- **D.** ISO/IEC 27006

15. Which standard should Jack suggest to his boss for compliance with best practices regarding storing and processing sensitive medical information?

- **A.** ISO/IEC 27004
- **B.** ISO/IEC 27001
- **C.** ISO/IEC 27799
- **D.** ISO/IEC 27006

16. You just received an e-mail from one of your hardware manufacturers notifying you that it will no longer manufacture a certain product and, after the end of the year, you won't be able to send it in for repairs, buy spare parts, or get technical assistance from that manufacturer. What term describes this?

- **A.** End-of-support (EOS)
- **B.** End-of-service-life (EOSL)
- **C.** Deprecation
- **D.** End-of-life (EOL)

17. The confidentiality of sensitive data is protected in different ways depending on the state of the data. Which of the following is the best approach to protecting data in transit?
    - **A.** SSL
    - **B.** VPN
    - **C.** IEEE 802.1X
    - **D.** Whole-disk encryption
18. Your boss asks you to put together a report describing probable adverse effects on your assets caused by specific threat sources. What term describes this?
    - **A.** Risk analysis
    - **B.** Threat modeling
    - **C.** Attack trees
    - **D.** MITRE ATT&CK
19. A(n) __________ is the graphical representation of data commonly used on websites. It is a skewed representation of characteristics a person must enter to prove that the subject is a human and not an automated tool, as in a software robot.
    - **A.** anti-spoofing symbol
    - **B.** CAPTCHA
    - **C.** spam anti-spoofing symbol
    - **D.** CAPCHAT
20. Mark has been asked to interview individuals to fulfill a new position in his company, chief privacy officer (CPO). What is the function of this type of position?
    - **A.** Ensuring that company financial information is correct and secure
    - **B.** Ensuring that customer, company, and employee data is protected
    - **C.** Ensuring that security policies are defined and enforced
    - **D.** Ensuring that partner information is kept safe
21. A risk management program must be developed properly and in the right sequence. Which of the following provides the correct sequence for the steps listed?
    - **i.** Develop a risk management team.
    - **ii.** Calculate the value of each asset.
    - **iii.** Identify the vulnerabilities and threats that can affect the identified assets.
    - **iv.** Identify company assets to be assessed.
    - **A.** i, iii, ii, iv
    - **B.** ii, i, iv, iii
    - **C.** iii, i, iv, ii
    - **D.** i, iv, ii, iii

22. Juan needs to assess the performance of a critical web application that his company recently upgraded. Some of the new features are very profitable, but not frequently used. He wants to ensure that the user experience is positive, but doesn't want to wait for the users to report problems. Which of the following techniques should Juan use?

    A. Real user monitoring

    B. Synthetic transactions

    C. Log reviews

    D. Management review

23. Which of the following best describes a technical control for dealing with the risks presented by data remanence?

    A. Encryption

    B. Data retention policies

    C. File deletion

    D. Using solid-state drives (SSDs)

24. George is the security manager of a large bank, which provides online banking and other online services to its customers. George has recently found out that some of the bank's customers have complained about changes to their bank accounts that they did not make. George worked with the security team and found out that all changes took place after proper authentication steps were completed. Which of the following describes what most likely took place in this situation?

    A. Web servers were compromised through cross-scripting attacks.

    B. TLS connections were decrypted through a man-in-the-middle attack.

    C. Personal computers were compromised with malware that installed keyloggers.

    D. Web servers were compromised and masquerading attacks were carried out.

25. Internet Protocol Security (IPSec) is actually a suite of protocols. Each protocol within the suite provides different functionality. Which of the following is not a function or characteristic of IPSec?

    A. Encryption

    B. Link layer protection

    C. Authentication

    D. Protection of packet payloads and the headers

26. In what order would a typical PKI perform the following transactions?
    - i. Receiver decrypts and obtains session key.
    - ii. Public key is verified.
    - iii. Public key is sent from a public directory.
    - iv. Sender sends a session key encrypted with receiver's public key.
    - A. iv, iii, ii, i
    - B. ii, i, iii, iv
    - C. iii, ii, iv, i
    - D. ii, iv, iii, i

Use the following scenario to answer Questions 27–28. Tim is the CISO for a large distributed financial investment organization. The company's network is made up of different network devices and software applications, which generate their own proprietary logs and audit data. Tim and his security team have become overwhelmed with trying to review all of the log files when attempting to identify if anything suspicious is taking place within the network. Another issue Tim's team needs to deal with is that many of the network devices have automated IPv6-to-IPv4 tunneling enabled by default, which is not what the organization needs.

27. Which of the following is the best solution to Tim's difficulties handling the quantity and diversity of logs and audit data?
    - A. Event correlation tools
    - B. Intrusion detection systems
    - C. Security information and event management
    - D. Hire more analysts
28. How could Tim best address the IP version issue described in the scenario?
    - A. Change management
    - B. Zero trust
    - C. Converged protocols
    - D. Configuration management
29. Which of the following is not a concern of a security professional considering adoption of Internet of Things (IoT) devices?
    - A. Weak or nonexistent authentication mechanisms
    - B. Vulnerability of data at rest and data in motion
    - C. Difficulty of deploying patches and updates
    - D. High costs associated with connectivity

30. What is an advantage of microservices compared to traditional server-based architectures?
    A. Web services support
    B. Security
    C. Scalability
    D. Database connectivity
31. __________, a declarative access control policy language implemented in XML and a processing model, describes how to interpret security policies. __________ is an XML-based language that allows for the exchange of provisioning data between applications, which could reside in one organization or many.
    A. Service Provisioning Markup Language (SPML), Extensible Access Control Markup Language (XACML)
    B. Extensible Access Control Markup Language (XACML), Service Provisioning Markup Language (SPML)
    C. Extensible Access Control Markup Language (XACML), Security Assertion Markup Language (SAML)
    D. Security Assertion Markup Language (SAML), Service Provisioning Markup Language (SPML)
32. Doors configured in fail-safe mode assume what position in the event of a power failure?
    A. Open and locked
    B. Closed and locked
    C. Closed and unlocked
    D. Open
33. Next-generation firewalls combine the best attributes of other types of firewalls. Which of the following is not a common characteristic of these firewall types?
    A. Integrated intrusion prevention system
    B. Sharing signatures with cloud-based aggregators
    C. Automated incident response
    D. High cost
34. The purpose of security awareness training is to expose personnel to security issues so that they may be able to recognize them and better respond to them. Which of the following is not normally a topic covered in security awareness training?
    A. Social engineering
    B. Phishing
    C. Whaling
    D. Trolling

Use the following scenario to answer Questions 35–36. Zack is a security consultant who has been hired to help an accounting company improve some of its current e-mail security practices. The company wants to ensure that when its clients send the company accounting files and data, the clients cannot later deny sending these messages. The company also wants to integrate a more granular and secure authentication method for its current mail server and clients.

35. Which of the following best describes how client messages can be dealt with and addresses the first issue outlined in the scenario?

A. The company needs to integrate a public key infrastructure and the Diameter protocol.

B. The company needs to require that clients encrypt messages with their public key before sending them to the company.

C. The company needs to have all clients sign a formal document outlining nonrepudiation requirements.

D. The company needs to require that clients digitally sign messages that contain financial information.

36. Which of the following would be the best solution to integrate to meet the authentication requirements outlined in the scenario?

A. TLS

B. IPSec

C. 802.1X

D. SASL

37. Which of the following is not considered a secure coding practice?

A. Validate user inputs

B. Default deny

C. Defense in depth

D. High (tight) coupling

38. A __________ is the amount of time it should take to recover from a disaster, and a __________ is the amount of data, measured in time, that can be lost and be tolerable from that same event.

A. recovery time objective, recovery point objective

B. recovery point objective, recovery time objective

C. maximum tolerable downtime, work recovery time

D. work recovery time, maximum tolerable downtime

39. Mary is doing online research about prospective employers and discovers a way to compromise a small company's personnel files. She decides to take a look around, but does not steal any information. Is she still committing a crime even if she does not steal any of the information?

    A. No, since she does not steal any information, she is not committing a crime.

    B. Probably, because she has gained unauthorized access.

    C. Not if she discloses the vulnerability she exploited to the company.

    D. Yes, she could jeopardize the system without knowing it.

40. In the structure of Extensible Access Control Markup Language (XACML), a Subject element is the __________, a Resource element is the __________, and an Action element is the __________.

    A. requesting entity, requested entity, types of access

    B. requested entity, requesting entity, types of access

    C. requesting entity, requested entity, access control

    D. requested entity, requesting entity, access control

41. The Mobile IP protocol allows location-independent routing of IP datagrams on the Internet. Each mobile node is identified by its __________, disregarding its current location in the Internet. While away from its home network, a mobile node is associated with a __________.

    A. prime address, care-of address

    B. home address, care-of address

    C. home address, secondary address

    D. prime address, secondary address

42. Because she has many different types of security products and solutions, Joan wants to purchase a product that integrates her many technologies into one user interface. She would like her staff to analyze all security alerts from the same application environment. Which of the following would best fit Joan's needs?

    A. Dedicated appliance

    B. Data analytics platform

    C. Hybrid IDS\IPS integration

    D. Security information and event management (SIEM)

43. When classifying an information asset, which of the following is true concerning its sensitivity?

    A. It is commensurate with how its loss would impact the fundamental business processes of the organization.

    B. It is determined by its replacement cost.

C. It is determined by the product of its replacement cost and the probability of its compromise.

D. It is commensurate with the losses to an organization if it were revealed to unauthorized individuals.

44. Which of the following is an international organization that helps different governments come together and tackle the economic, social, and governance challenges of a globalized economy and provides guidelines on the protection of privacy and transborder flows of personal data rules?

A. Council of Global Convention on Cybercrime

B. Council of Europe Convention on Cybercrime

C. Organisation for Economic Co-operation and Development

D. Organisation for Cybercrime Co-operation and Development

45. System ports allow different computers to communicate with each other's services and protocols. The Internet Assigned Numbers Authority (IANA) has assigned registered ports to be __________ and dynamic ports to be __________.

A. 0–1024, 49152–65535

B. 1024–49151, 49152–65535

C. 1024–49152, 49153–65535

D. 0–1024, 1025–49151

46. When conducting a quantitative risk analysis, items are gathered and assigned numeric values so that cost/benefit analysis can be carried out. Which of the following formulas could be used to understand the value of a safeguard?

A. (ALE before implementing safeguard) – (ALE after implementing safeguard) – (annual cost of safeguard) = value of safeguard to the organization

B. (ALE before implementing safeguard) – (ALE during implementing safeguard) – (annual cost of safeguard) = value of safeguard to the organization

C. (ALE before implementing safeguard) – (ALE while implementing safeguard) – (annual cost of safeguard) = value of safeguard to the organization

D. (ALE before implementing safeguard) – (ALE after implementing safeguard) – (annual cost of asset) = value of safeguard to the organization

47. Patty is giving a presentation next week to the executive staff of her company. She wants to illustrate the benefits of the company using specific cloud computing solutions. Which of the following does not properly describe one of these benefits or advantages?

A. Organizations have more flexibility and agility in IT growth and functionality.

B. Cost of computing can be increased since it is a shared delivery model.

C. Location independence can be achieved because the computing is not centralized and tied to a physical data center.

D. Scalability and elasticity of resources can be accomplished in near real-time through automation.

Use the following scenario to answer Questions 48–49. Francisca is the new manager of the in-house software designers and programmers. She has been telling her team that before design and programming on a new product begins, a formal architecture needs to be developed. She also needs this team to understand security issues as they pertain to software design. Francisca has shown the team how to follow a systematic approach that allows them to understand different ways in which the software products they develop could be compromised by specific threat actors.

48. Which of the following best describes what an architecture is in the context of this scenario?

A. Tool used to conceptually understand the structure and behavior of a complex entity through different views

B. Formal description and representation of a system and the components that make it up

C. Framework used to create individual architectures with specific views

D. Framework that is necessary to identify needs and meet all of the stakeholder requirements

49. Which of the following best describes the approach Francisca has shown her team as outlined in the scenario?

A. Attack surface analysis

B. Threat modeling

C. Penetration testing

D. Double-blind penetration testing

50. Barry was told that the IDS product that is being used on the network has heuristic capabilities. Which of the following best describes this functionality?

A. Gathers packets and reassembles the fragments before assigning anomaly values

B. Gathers data and assesses the likelihood of it being malicious in nature

C. Gathers packets and compares their payload values to a signature engine

D. Gathers packet headers to determine if something suspicious is taking place within the network traffic

51. Bringing in third-party auditors has advantages over using an internal team. Which of the following is not true about using external auditors?
    A. They are required by certain governmental regulations.
    B. They bring experience gained by working in many other organizations.
    C. They know the organization's processes and technology better than anyone else.
    D. They are less influenced by internal culture and politics.
52. Don is a senior manager of an architectural firm. He has just found out that a key contract was renewed, allowing the company to continue developing an operating system that was idle for several months. Excited to get started, Don begins work on the operating system privately, but cannot tell his staff until the news is announced publicly in a few days. However, as Don begins making changes in the software, various staff members notice changes in their connected systems, even though they have a lower security level than Don. What kind of model could be used to ensure this does not happen?
    A. Biba
    B. Bell-LaPadula
    C. Noninterference
    D. Clark-Wilson
53. Betty has received several e-mail messages from unknown sources that try and entice her to click a specific link using a "Click Here" approach. Which of the following best describes what is most likely taking place in this situation?
    A. DNS pharming attack
    B. Embedded hyperlink is obfuscated
    C. Malware back-door installation
    D. Bidirectional injection attack
54. Rebecca is an internal auditor for a large retail company. The company has a number of web applications that run critical business processes with customers and partners around the world. Her company would like to ensure the security of technical controls on these processes. Which of the following would not be a good approach to auditing these technical controls?
    A. Log reviews
    B. Code reviews
    C. Personnel background checks
    D. Misuse case testing

55. Which of the following multiplexing technologies analyzes statistics related to the typical workload of each input device and makes real-time decisions on how much time each device should be allocated for data transmission?

    A. Time-division multiplexing

    B. Wave-division multiplexing

    C. Frequency-division multiplexing

    D. Statistical time-division multiplexing

56. In a VoIP environment, the Real-time Transport Protocol (RTP) and RTP Control Protocol (RTCP) are commonly used. Which of the following best describes the difference between these two protocols?

    A. RTCP provides a standardized packet format for delivering audio and video over IP networks. RTP provides out-of-band statistics and control information to provide feedback on QoS levels.

    B. RTP provides a standardized packet format for delivering data over IP networks. RTCP provides control information to provide feedback on QoS levels.

    C. RTP provides a standardized packet format for delivering audio and video over MPLS networks. RTCP provides control information to provide feedback on QoS levels.

    D. RTP provides a standardized packet format for delivering audio and video over IP networks. RTCP provides out-of-band statistics and control information to provide feedback on QoS levels.

57. Which of the following is not descriptive of an edge computing architecture?

    A. It eliminates the need for cloud infrastructure.

    B. Processing and storage assets are close to where they're needed.

    C. It reduces latency and network traffic.

    D. It typically has three layers.

58. Which cryptanalytic attack method is characterized by the identification of statistically significant patterns in the ciphertext generated by a cryptosystem?

    A. Differential attack

    B. Implementation attack

    C. Frequency analysis

    D. Side-channel attack

59. IPSec's main protocols are AH and ESP. Which of the following services does AH provide?

    A. Confidentiality and authentication

    B. Confidentiality and availability

    C. Integrity and accessibility

    D. Integrity and authentication

60. When multiple databases exchange transactions, each database is updated. This can happen many times and in many different ways. To protect the integrity of the data, databases should incorporate a concept known as an ACID test. What does this acronym stand for?
    A. Availability, confidentiality, integrity, durability
    B. Availability, consistency, integrity, durability
    C. Atomicity, confidentiality, isolation, durability
    D. Atomicity, consistency, isolation, durability

Use the following scenario to answer Questions 61–63. Jim works for a large energy company. His senior management just conducted a meeting with Jim's team with the purpose of reducing IT costs without degrading their security posture. The senior management decided to move all administrative systems to a cloud provider. These systems are proprietary applications currently running on Linux servers.

61. Which of the following services would allow Jim to transition all administrative custom applications to the cloud while leveraging the service provider for security and patching of the cloud platforms?
    A. IaaS
    B. PaaS
    C. SaaS
    D. IDaaS
62. Which of the following would *not* be an issue that Jim would have to consider in transitioning administrative services to the cloud?
    A. Privacy and data breach laws in the country where the cloud servers are located
    B. Loss of efficiencies, performance, reliability, scalability, and security
    C. Security provisions in the terms of service
    D. Total cost of ownership compared to the current systems
63. Which of the following secure design principles would be most important to consider as Jim plans the transition to the cloud?
    A. Defense in depth
    B. Secure defaults
    C. Shared responsibility
    D. Zero trust

64. A group of software designers are at a stage in their software development project where they need to reduce the amount of code running, reduce entry points available to untrusted users, reduce privilege levels as much as possible, and eliminate unnecessary services. Which of the following best describes the first step the team needs to carry out to accomplish these tasks?

  A. Attack surface analysis

  B. Software development life cycle

  C. Risk assessment

  D. Unit testing

65. Jenny needs to engage a new software development company to create her company's internal banking software. The software needs to be created specifically for her company's environment, so it must be proprietary in nature. Which of the following would be useful for Jenny to use as a gauge to determine how advanced the various software development companies are in their processes?

  A. Waterfall methodology

  B. Capability Maturity Model Integration level

  C. Auditing results

  D. Key performance metrics

66. Which type of organization would be likeliest to implement Virtual eXtensible Local Area Network (VxLAN) technology?

  A. Organizations that need to support more than 2,048 VLANs

  B. Small and medium businesses

  C. Organizations with hosts in close proximity to each other

  D. Cloud service providers with hundreds of customers

67. Kerberos is a commonly used access control and authentication technology. It is important to understand what the technology can and cannot do and its potential downfalls. Which of the following is not a potential security issue that must be addressed when using Kerberos?

  i. The KDC can be a single point of failure.

  ii. The KDC must be scalable.

  iii. Secret keys are temporarily stored on the users' workstations.

  iv. Kerberos is vulnerable to password guessing.

  A. i, iv

  B. iii

  C. All of them

  D. None of them

68. If the annualized loss expectancy (ALE) for a specific asset is $100,000, and after implementation of a control to safeguard the asset the new ALE is $45,000 and the annual cost of the control is $30,000, should the company implement this control?

    A. Yes

    B. No

    C. Not enough information

    D. Depends on the annualized rate of occurrence (ARO)

69. ISO/IEC 27000 is a growing family of ISO/IEC information security management system (ISMS) standards. Which of the following provides an incorrect mapping of the individual standard number to its description?

    A. ISO/IEC 27002: Code of practice for information security controls

    B. ISO/IEC 27003: ISMS implementation guidance

    C. ISO/IEC 27004: ISMS monitoring, measurement, analysis, and evaluation

    D. ISO/IEC 27005: ISMS auditing guidelines

70. Yazan leads the IT help desk at a large manufacturing company. He is concerned about the amount of time his team spends resetting passwords for the various accounts that each of his organizational users has. All of the following would be good approaches to alleviating this help desk load *except* which one?

    A. Single sign-on (SSO)

    B. Just-in-time (JIT) access

    C. Password managers

    D. Self-service password reset

71. Encryption and decryption can take place at different layers of an operating system, application, and network stack. End-to-end encryption happens within the __________. IPSec encryption takes place at the __________ layer. PPTP encryption takes place at the __________ layer. Link encryption takes place at the __________ and __________ layers.

    A. applications, transport, data link, data link, physical

    B. applications, transport, network, data link, physical

    C. applications, network, data link, data link, physical

    D. network, transport, data link, data link, physical

72. Which of the following best describes the difference between hierarchical storage management (HSM) and storage area network (SAN) technologies?

    A. HSM uses optical or tape jukeboxes, and SAN is a network of connected storage systems.

    B. SAN uses optical or tape jukeboxes, and HSM is a network of connected storage systems.

C. HSM and SAN are one and the same. The difference is in the implementation.

D. HSM uses optical or tape jukeboxes, and SAN is a standard of how to develop and implement this technology.

73. Which legal system is characterized by its reliance on previous interpretations of the law?

A. Tort

B. Customary

C. Common

D. Civil (code)

74. In order to be admissible in court, evidence should normally be which of the following?

A. Subpoenaed

B. Relevant

C. Motioned

D. Adjudicated

75. Which type of authorization mechanism can incorporate historical data into its access control decision-making in real time?

A. Rule-based access control

B. Risk-based access control

C. Attribute-based access control

D. Discretionary access control

76. Which of the following is an XML-based protocol that defines the schema of how web service communication takes place over HTTP transmissions?

A. Service-Oriented Protocol

B. Active X Protocol

C. SOAP

D. Web Ontology Language

77. Which of the following has an incorrect definition mapping?

i. Operationally Critical Threat, Asset, and Vulnerability Evaluation (OCTAVE) Team-oriented approach that assesses organizational and IT risks through facilitated workshops

ii. Facilitated Risk Analysis Process (FRAP) Stresses prescreening activities so that the risk assessment steps are only carried out on the item(s) that need(s) it the most

iii. ISO/IEC 27005 International standard for the implementation of a risk management program that integrates into an information security management system (ISMS)

iv. Failure Modes and Effect Analysis (FMEA) Approach that dissects a component into its basic functions to identify flaws and those flaws' effects

v. Fault tree analysis Approach to map specific flaws to root causes in complex systems

A. None of them

B. ii

C. iii, iv

D. v

78. For an enterprise security architecture to be successful in its development and implementation, which of the following items must be understood and followed?

i. Strategic alignment

ii. Process enhancement

iii. Business enablement

iv. Security effectiveness

A. i, ii

B. ii, iii

C. i, ii, iii, iv

D. iii, iv

79. Which of the following best describes the purpose of the Organisation for Economic Co-operation and Development (OECD)?

A. An international organization where member countries come together and tackle the economic, social, and governance challenges of a globalized economy

B. A national organization that helps different governments come together and tackle the economic, social, and governance challenges of a globalized economy

C. A United Nations body that regulates economic, social, and governance issues of a globalized economy

D. A national organization that helps different organizations come together and tackle the economic, social, and governance challenges of a globalized economy

80. Many enterprise architecture models have been developed over the years for specific purposes. Some of them can be used to provide structure for information security processes and technology to be integrated throughout an organization. Which of the following provides an incorrect mapping between the architecture type and the associated definition?

A. **Zachman Framework** Model and methodology for the development of information security enterprise architectures

B. **TOGAF** Model and methodology for the development of enterprise architectures developed by The Open Group

C. **DoDAF** U.S. Department of Defense architecture framework that ensures interoperability of systems to meet military mission goals

D. **SABSA** Framework and methodology for enterprise security architecture and service management

81. Which of the following best describes the difference between the role of the ISO/IEC 27000 series and COBIT?

A. COBIT provides a high-level overview of security program requirements, while the ISO/IEC 27000 series provides the objectives of the individual security controls.

B. The ISO/IEC 27000 series provides a high-level overview of security program requirements, while COBIT maps IT goals to enterprise goals to stakeholder needs.

C. COBIT is process oriented, and the ISO/IEC 27000 series is solution oriented.

D. The ISO/IEC 27000 series is process oriented, and COBIT is solution oriented.

82. The Capability Maturity Model Integration (CMMI) approach is being used more frequently in security program and enterprise development. Which of the following provides an incorrect characteristic of this model?

A. It provides a pathway for how incremental improvement can take place.

B. It provides structured steps that can be followed so an organization can evolve from one level to the next and constantly improve its processes.

C. It was created for process improvement and developed by Carnegie Mellon.

D. It was built upon the SABSA model.

83. If Jose wanted to use a risk assessment methodology across the entire organization and allow the various business owners to identify risks and know how to deal with them, what methodology would he use?

A. Qualitative

B. COBIT

C. FRAP

D. OCTAVE

84. Information security is a field that is maturing and becoming more organized and standardized. Organizational security models should be based on an enterprise architecture framework. Which of the following best describes what an enterprise architecture framework is and why it would be used?

A. Mathematical model that defines the secure states that various software components can enter and still provide the necessary protection

B. Conceptual model that is organized into multiple views addressing each of the stakeholder's concerns

C. Business enterprise framework that is broken down into six conceptual levels to ensure security is deployed and managed in a controllable manner

D. Enterprise framework that allows for proper security governance

85. Which of the following provides a true characteristic of a fault tree analysis?

A. Fault trees are assigned qualitative values to faults that can take place over a series of business processes.

B. Fault trees are assigned failure mode values.

C. Fault trees are labeled with actual numbers pertaining to failure probabilities.

D. Fault trees are used in a stepwise approach to software debugging.

86. It is important that organizations ensure that their security efforts are effective and measurable. Which of the following is not a common method used to track the effectiveness of security efforts?

A. Service level agreement

B. Return on investment

C. Balanced scorecard system

D. Provisioning system

87. Capability Maturity Model Integration (CMMI) is a process improvement approach that is used to help organizations improve their performance. The CMMI model may also be used as a framework for appraising the process maturity of the organization. Which of the following is an incorrect mapping of the levels that may be assigned to an organization based upon this model?

i. Maturity Level 2 – Managed or Repeatable

ii. Maturity Level 3 – Defined

iii. Maturity Level 4 – Quantitatively Managed

iv. Maturity Level 5 – Optimizing

A. i

B. i, ii

C. All of them

D. None of them

88. An organization's information systems risk management (ISRM) policy should address many items to provide clear direction and structure. Which of the following is not a core item that should be covered in this type of policy?

i. The objectives of the ISRM team

ii. The level of risk the organization will accept and what is considered an acceptable level of risk

iii. Formal processes of risk identification

iv. The connection between the ISRM policy and the organization's strategic planning processes

v. Responsibilities that fall under ISRM and the roles to fulfill them

vi. The mapping of risk to specific physical controls

vii. The approach toward changing staff behaviors and resource allocation in response to risk analysis

viii. The mapping of risks to performance targets and budgets

ix. Key metrics and performance indicators to monitor the effectiveness of controls

A. ii, v, ix

B. vi

C. v

D. vii, ix

89. More organizations are outsourcing supporting functions to allow them to focus on their core business functions. Organizations use hosting companies to maintain websites and e-mail servers, service providers for various telecommunication connections, disaster recovery companies for co-location capabilities, cloud computing providers for infrastructure or application services, developers for software creation, and security companies to carry out vulnerability management. Which of the following items should be included during the analysis of an outsourced partner or vendor?

i. Conduct onsite inspection and interviews

ii. Review contracts to ensure security and protection levels are agreed upon

iii. Ensure service level agreements are in place

iv. Review internal and external audit reports and third-party reviews

v. Review references and communicate with former and existing customers

A. ii, iii, iv

B. iv, v

C. All of them

D. i, ii, iii

90. Which of the following is normally not an element of e-discovery?

A. Identification

B. Preservation

C. Production

D. Remanence

91. A financial institution has developed its internal security program based upon the ISO/IEC 27000 series. The security officer has been told that metrics need to be developed and integrated into this program so that effectiveness can be gauged. Which of the following standards should be followed to provide this type of guidance and functionality?
    A. ISO/IEC 27002
    B. ISO/IEC 27003
    C. ISO/IEC 27004
    D. ISO/IEC 27005
92. Which of the following is not an advantage of using content distribution networks?
    A. Improved responsiveness to regional users
    B. Resistance to ARP spoofing attacks
    C. Customization of content for regional users
    D. Resistance to DDoS attacks
93. Sana has been asked to install a cloud access security broker (CASB) product for her company's environment. What is the best description for what CASBs are commonly used for?
    A. Monitor end-user behavior and enforce policies across cloud services
    B. Provision secure cloud services
    C. Enforce access controls to cloud services through X.500 databases
    D. Protect cloud services from certain types of attacks
94. Which of the following allows a user to be authenticated across multiple IT systems and enterprises?
    A. Single sign-on (SSO)
    B. Session management
    C. Federated identity
    D. Role-based access control (RBAC)
95. Which of the following is a true statement pertaining to markup languages?
    A. Hypertext Markup Language (HTML) came from Generalized Markup Language (GML), which came from Standard Generalized Markup Language (SGML).
    B. Hypertext Markup Language (HTML) came from Standard Generalized Markup Language (SGML), which came from Generalized Markup Language (GML).

C. Standard Generalized Markup Language (SGML) came from Hypertext Markup Language (HTML), which came from Generalized Markup Language (GML).

D. Standard Generalized Markup Language (SGML) came from Generalized Markup Language (GML), which came from Hypertext Markup Language (HTML).

96. What is Extensible Markup Language (XML) and why was it created?

A. A specification that provides a structure for creating other markup languages and still allow for interoperability

B. A specification that is used to create static and dynamic websites

C. A specification that outlines a detailed markup language dictating all formats of all companies that use it

D. A specification that does not allow for interoperability for the sake of security

97. Which access control policy is based on the necessary operations and tasks users need to fulfill their responsibilities within an organization and allows for implicit permission inheritance using a nondiscretionary model?

A. Rule-based

B. Role-based

C. Identity-based

D. Mandatory

98. Which of the following centralized access control protocols would a security professional choose if her network consisted of multiple protocols, including Mobile IP, and had users connecting via wireless and wired transmissions?

A. RADIUS

B. TACACS+

C. Diameter

D. Kerberos

99. Javad is the security administrator at a credit card processing company. The company has many identity stores, which are not properly synchronized. Javad is going to oversee the process of centralizing and synchronizing the identity data within the company. He has determined that the data in the HR database will be considered the most up-to-date data, which cannot be overwritten by the software in other identity stores during their synchronization processes. Which of the following best describes the role of this database in the identity management structure of the company?

A. Authoritative system of record

B. Infrastructure source server

C. Primary identity store

D. Hierarchical database primary

100. Proper access control requires a structured user provisioning process. Which of the following best describes user provisioning?

A. The creation, maintenance, and deactivation of user objects and attributes as they exist in one or more systems, directories, or applications, in response to business processes

B. The creation, maintenance, activation, and delegation of user objects and attributes as they exist in one or more systems, directories, or applications, in response to compliance processes

C. The maintenance of user objects and attributes as they exist in one or more systems, directories, or applications, in response to business processes

D. The creation and deactivation of user objects and attributes as they exist in one or more systems, directories, or applications, in response to business processes

101. Which of the following protocols would an Identity as a Service (IDaaS) provider use to authenticate you to a third party?

A. Diameter

B. OAuth

C. Kerberos

D. OpenID Connect

102. Johana needs to ensure that her company's application can accept provisioning data from the company's partner's application in a standardized method. Which of the following best describes the technology that Johana should implement?

A. Service Provisioning Markup Language

B. Extensible Provisioning Markup Language

C. Security Assertion Markup Language

D. Security Provisioning Markup Language

103. Lynn logs into a website and purchases an airline ticket for her upcoming trip. The website also offers her pricing and package deals for hotel rooms and rental cars while she is completing her purchase. The airline, hotel, and rental companies are all separate and individual companies. Lynn decides to purchase her hotel room through the same website at the same time. The website is using Security Assertion Markup Language to allow for this type of federated identity management functionality. In this example which entity is the principal, which entity is the identity provider, and which entity is the service provider, respectively?

A. Portal, Lynn, hotel company

B. Lynn, airline company, hotel company

C. Lynn, hotel company, airline company

D. Portal, Lynn, airline company

104. John is the new director of software development within his company. Several proprietary applications offer individual services to the employees, but the employees have to log into each and every application independently to gain access to these discrete services. John would like to provide a way that allows each of the services provided by the various applications to be centrally accessed and controlled. Which of the following best describes the architecture that John should deploy?

   A. Service-oriented architecture

   B. Web services architecture

   C. Single sign-on architecture

   D. Hierarchical service architecture

105. Which security model is defined by three main rules: simple security, star property, and strong star property?

   A. Biba

   B. Bell-LaPadula

   C. Brewer-Nash

   D. Noninterference

106. Khadijah is leading a software development team for her company. She knows the importance of conducting an attack surface analysis and developing a threat model. During which phase of the software development life cycle should she perform these actions?

   A. Requirements gathering

   B. Testing and validation

   C. Release and maintenance

   D. Design

107. Bartosz is developing a new web application for his marketing department. One of the requirements for the software is that it allows users to post specific content to LinkedIn and Twitter directly from the web app. Which technology would allow him to do this?

   A. OpenID Connect

   B. OAuth

   C. SSO

   D. Federated Identity Management

108. Applications may not work on systems with specific processors. Which of the following best describes why an application may work on an Intel processor but not on an AMD processor?

   A. The application was not compiled to machine language that is compatible with the AMD architecture.

   B. It is not possible for the same application to run on both Intel and AMD processors.

C. The application was not compiled to machine language that is compatible with the Windows architecture.

D. Only applications written in high-level languages will work on different processor architectures.

109. Which of the following is *not* true about software libraries?

A. They make software development more efficient through code reuse.

B. They are typically accessed through an application programming interface (API).

C. They almost never introduce vulnerabilities into programs that use them.

D. They are used in most major software development projects.

110. Kim is tasked with testing the security of an application but has no access to its source code. Which of the following tests could she use in this scenario?

A. Dynamic application security testing

B. Static application security testing

C. Regression testing

D. Code review

111. Hanna is a security manager of a company that relies heavily on one specific operating system. The operating system is used in the employee workstations and is embedded within devices that support the automated production line software. She has uncovered a vulnerability in the operating system that could allow an attacker to force applications to not release memory segments after execution. Which of the following best describes the type of threat this vulnerability introduces?

A. Injection attacks

B. Memory corruption

C. Denial of service

D. Software locking

112. Which of the following access control mechanisms gives you the most granularity in defining access control policies?

A. Attribute-based access control (ABAC)

B. Role-based access control (RBAC)

C. Mandatory access control (MAC)

D. Discretionary access control (DAC)

113. All of the following are weaknesses of Kerberos *except* which one?

A. Principals don't trust each other.

B. Only the KDC can vouch for individuals' identities and entitlements.

C. Secret keys are stored on the users' workstations temporarily.

D. Susceptibility to password guessing and brute-force attacks.

114. A company needs to implement a CCTV system that will monitor a large area of the facility. Which of the following is the correct lens combination for this?

A. A wide-angle lens and a small lens opening

B. A wide-angle lens and a large lens opening

C. A wide-angle lens and a large lens opening with a small focal length

D. A wide-angle lens and a large lens opening with a large focal length

115. What is the name of a water sprinkler system that keeps pipes empty and doesn't release water until a certain temperature is met and a "delay mechanism" is instituted?

A. Wet

B. Preaction

C. Delayed

D. Dry

116. There are different types of fire suppression systems. Which of the following answers best describes the difference between a deluge system and a preaction system?

A. A deluge system provides a delaying mechanism that allows someone to deactivate the system in case of a false alarm or if the fire can be extinguished by other means. A preaction system provides similar functionality but has wide open sprinkler heads that allow a lot of water to be dispersed quickly.

B. A preaction system provides a delaying mechanism that allows someone to deactivate the system in case of a false alarm or if the fire can be extinguished by other means. A deluge system has wide open sprinkler heads that allow a lot of water to be dispersed quickly.

C. A dry pipe system provides a delaying mechanism that allows someone to deactivate the system in case of a false alarm or if the fire can be extinguished by other means. A deluge system has wide open sprinkler heads that allow a lot of water to be dispersed quickly.

D. A preaction system provides a delaying mechanism that allows someone to deactivate the system in case of a false alarm or if the fire can be extinguished by other means. A deluge system provides similar functionality but has wide open sprinkler heads that allow a lot of water to be dispersed quickly.

117. Which of the following best describes why Crime Prevention Through Environmental Design (CPTED) would integrate benches, walkways, and bike paths into a site?

A. These features are designed to provide natural access control.

B. These features are designed to emphasize or extend the organization's physical sphere of influence so legitimate users feel a sense of ownership of that space.

C. These features are designed to make criminals think that those in the site are more attentive, well resourced, and possibly alert.

D. These features are designed to make criminals feel uncomfortable by providing many ways observers could potentially see them.

118. Which of the following frameworks is a two-dimensional model that uses six basic communication interrogatives intersecting with different viewpoints to give a holistic understanding of the enterprise?

A. SABSA

B. TOGAF

C. CMMI

D. Zachman

119. Not every data transmission incorporates the session layer. Which of the following best describes the functionality of the session layer?

A. End-to-end data transmission

B. Application client/server communication mechanism in a distributed environment

C. Application-to-computer physical communication

D. Provides application with the proper syntax for transmission

120. What is the purpose of the Logical Link Control (LLC) layer in the OSI model?

A. Provides a standard interface for the network layer protocol

B. Provides the framing functionality of the data link layer

C. Provides addressing of the packet during encapsulation

D. Provides the functionality of converting bits into electrical signals

121. Which of the following best describes why classless interdomain routing (CIDR) was created?

A. To allow IPv6 traffic to tunnel through IPv4 networks

B. To allow IPSec to be integrated into IPv4 traffic

C. To allow an address class size to meet an organization's need

D. To allow IPv6 to tunnel IPSec traffic

122. Johnetta is a security engineer at a company that develops highly confidential products for various government agencies. Her company has VPNs set up to protect traffic that travels over the Internet and other nontrusted networks, but she knows that internal traffic should also be protected. Which of the following is the best type of approach Johnetta's company should take?

A. Implement a data link technology that provides 802.1AE security functionality.

B. Implement a network-level technology that provides 802.1AE security functionality.

C. Implement TLS over L2TP.

D. Implement IPSec over L2TP.

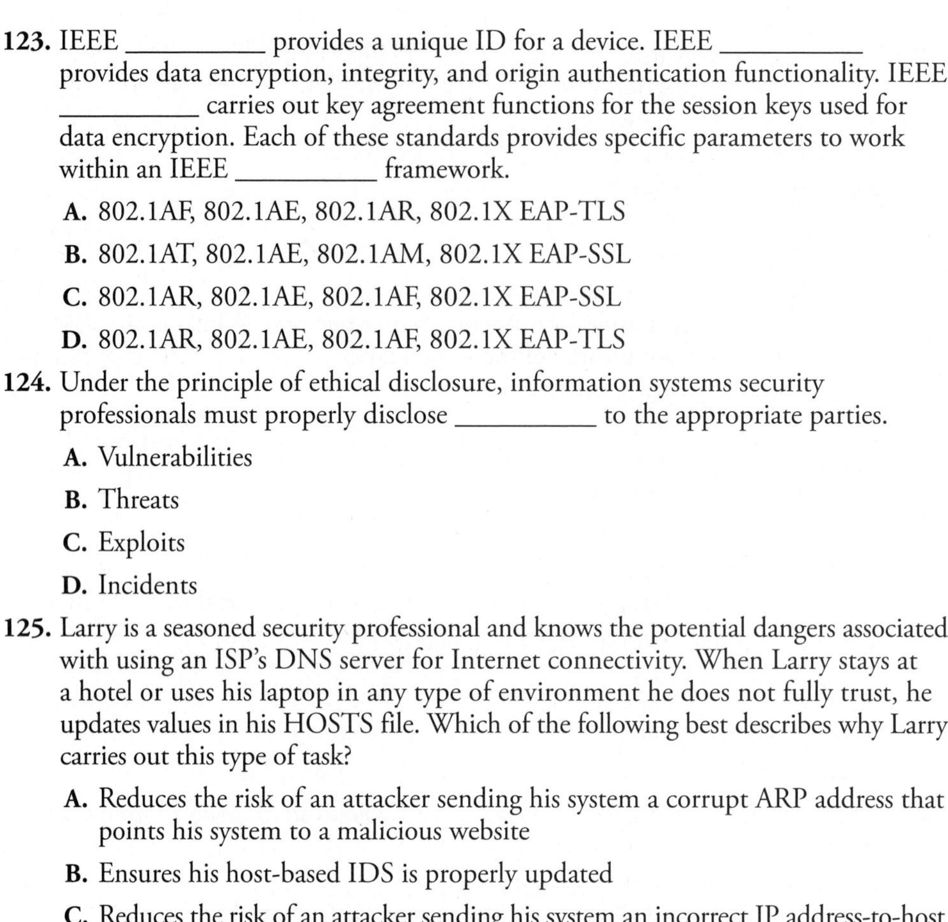

123. IEEE __________ provides a unique ID for a device. IEEE __________ provides data encryption, integrity, and origin authentication functionality. IEEE __________ carries out key agreement functions for the session keys used for data encryption. Each of these standards provides specific parameters to work within an IEEE __________ framework.

A. 802.1AF, 802.1AE, 802.1AR, 802.1X EAP-TLS

B. 802.1AT, 802.1AE, 802.1AM, 802.1X EAP-SSL

C. 802.1AR, 802.1AE, 802.1AF, 802.1X EAP-SSL

D. 802.1AR, 802.1AE, 802.1AF, 802.1X EAP-TLS

124. Under the principle of ethical disclosure, information systems security professionals must properly disclose __________ to the appropriate parties.

A. Vulnerabilities

B. Threats

C. Exploits

D. Incidents

125. Larry is a seasoned security professional and knows the potential dangers associated with using an ISP's DNS server for Internet connectivity. When Larry stays at a hotel or uses his laptop in any type of environment he does not fully trust, he updates values in his HOSTS file. Which of the following best describes why Larry carries out this type of task?

A. Reduces the risk of an attacker sending his system a corrupt ARP address that points his system to a malicious website

B. Ensures his host-based IDS is properly updated

C. Reduces the risk of an attacker sending his system an incorrect IP address-to-host mapping that points his system to a malicious website

D. Ensures his network-based IDS is properly synchronized with his host-based IDS

126. John has uncovered a rogue system on the company network that emulates a switch. The software on this system is being used by an attacker to modify frame tag values. Which of the following best describes the type of attack that has most likely been taking place?

A. DHCP snooping

B. VLAN hopping

C. Network traffic shaping

D. Network traffic hopping

127. Frank is a new security manager for a large financial institution. He has been told that the organization needs to reduce the total cost of ownership for many components of the network and infrastructure. The organization currently maintains many distributed networks, software packages, and applications. Which of the following best describes the cloud service models that Frank could leverage to obtain cloud services to replace on-premises network and infrastructure components

   A. Infrastructure as a Service provides an environment similar to an operating system, Platform as a Service provides operating systems and other major processing platforms, and Software as a Service provides specific application-based functionality.

   B. Infrastructure as a Service provides an environment similar to a data center, Platform as a Service provides operating systems and other major processing platforms, and Software as a Service provides specific application-based functionality.

   C. Infrastructure as a Service provides an environment similar to a data center, Platform as a Service provides application-based functionality, and Software as a Service provides specific operating system functionality.

   D. Infrastructure as a Service provides an environment similar to a database, Platform as a Service provides operating systems and other major processing platforms, and Software as a Service provides specific application-based functionality.

128. Terry works in a training services provider where the network topology and access controls change very frequently. His boss tells him that he needs to implement a network infrastructure that enables changes to be made quickly and securely with minimal effort. What does Terry need to roll out?

   A. Wi-Fi

   B. Infrastructure as a Service

   C. Software-defined networking

   D. Software-defined wide area networking

129. On a Tuesday morning, Jami is summoned to the office of the security director, where she finds six of her peers from other departments. The security director gives them instructions about an event that will be taking place in two weeks. Each of the individuals will be responsible for removing specific systems from the facility, bringing them to the offsite facility, and implementing them. Each individual will need to test the installed systems and ensure the configurations are correct for production activities. What event is Jami about to take part in?

   A. Parallel test

   B. Full-interruption test

   C. Simulation test

   D. Structured walk-through test

130. While disaster recovery planning (DRP) and business continuity planning (BCP) are directed at the development of "plans," __________ is the holistic management process that should cover both of them. It provides a framework for integrating resilience with the capability for effective responses that protects the interests of the organization's key stakeholders.

A. continuity of operations

B. business continuity management

C. risk management

D. enterprise management architecture

131. Your company enters into a contract with another company as part of which your company requires the other company to abide by specific security practices. Six months into the effort, you decide to verify that the other company is satisfying these security requirements. Which of the following would you conduct?

A. Third-party audit

B. External (second-party) audit

C. Structured walk-through test

D. Full-interruption test

132. Which of the following statements is true about employee duress?

A. Its risks can be mitigated by installing panic buttons.

B. Its risks can be mitigated by installing panic rooms.

C. Its risks can be mitigated by enforcing forced vacations.

D. It can more easily be detected using the right clipping levels.

133. The main goal of the Wassenaar Arrangement is to prevent the buildup of military capabilities that could threaten regional and international security and stability. How does this relate to technology?

A. Cryptography is a dual-use tool.

B. Technology is used in weaponry systems.

C. Military actions directly relate to critical infrastructure systems.

D. Critical infrastructure systems can be at risk under this agreement.

134. Which world legal system is used in continental European countries, such as France and Spain, and is rule-based law, not precedent-based?

A. Civil (code) law system

B. Common law system

C. Customary law system

D. Mixed law system

135. Which of the following is not a correct characteristic of the Failure Modes and Effect Analysis (FMEA) method?

A. Determining functions and identifying functional failures

B. Assessing the causes of failure and their failure effects through a structured process

C. Structured process carried out by an identified team to address high-level security compromises

D. Identifying where something is most likely going to break and either fixing the flaws that could cause this issue or implementing controls to reduce the impact of the break

136. A risk analysis can be carried out through qualitative or quantitative means. It is important to choose the right approach to meet the organization's goals. In a quantitative analysis, which of the following items would not be assigned a numeric value?

i. Asset value

ii. Threat frequency

iii. Severity of vulnerability

iv. Impact damage

v. Safeguard costs

vi. Safeguard effectiveness

vii. Probability

A. All of them

B. None of them

C. ii

D. vii

137. Uncovering restricted information by using permissible data is referred to as ___________.

A. inference

B. data mining

C. perturbation

D. cell suppression

138. Meeta recently started working at an organization with no defined security processes. One of the areas she'd like to improve is software patching. Consistent with the organizational culture, she is considering a decentralized or unmanaged model for patching. Which of the following is not one of the risks her organization would face with such a model?

A. This model typically requires users to have admin credentials, which violates the principle of least privilege.

B. It will be easier to ensure that all software products are updated, since they will be configured to do so automatically.

C. It may be difficult (or impossible) to attest to the status of every application in the organization.

D. Having each application or service independently download the patches will lead to network congestion.

139. Clustering is an unsupervised machine learning approach that determines where data samples naturally clump together. It does this by calculating the distance between a new data point and the existing clusters and assigning the point to the closest cluster if, indeed, it is close to any of them. What is this approach typically used for in cybersecurity?

A. Spam filtering

B. Anomaly detection

C. Network flow analysis

D. Signature matching

140. Sam wants to test the ability of her technical security controls to stop realistic attacks. Her organization is going through significant growth, which is also increasing the complexity of the networks and systems. To ensure she stays ahead of the adversaries, Sam wants to run these tests frequently. Which approach should she use?

A. Breach and attack simulations

B. Tabletop exercises

C. Red teaming

D. Synthetic transactions

Use the following scenario to answer Questions 141–142. Ron is in charge of updating his company's business continuity and disaster recovery plans and processes. After conducting a business impact analysis, his team has told him that if the company's e-commerce payment gateway was unable to process payments for 24 hours or more, this could drastically affect the survivability of the company. The analysis indicates that after an outage, the payment gateway and payment processing should be restored within 13 hours. Ron's team needs to integrate solutions that provide redundancy, fault tolerance, and failover capability.

141. In the scenario, what does the 24-hour time period represent and what does the 13-hour time period represent, respectively?

A. Maximum tolerable downtime, recovery time objective

B. Recovery time objective, maximum tolerable downtime

C. Maximum tolerable downtime, recovery data period

D. Recovery time objective, data recovery period

142. Which of the following best describes the type of solution Ron's team needs to implement?

A. RAID and clustering

B. Storage area networks

C. High availability

D. Grid computing and clustering

Answers

1. **D.** While they are all issues to be concerned with, risk is a combination of probability and business impact. The largest business impact out of this list and in this situation is the fact that intellectual property for product development has been lost. If a competitor can produce the product and bring it to market quickly, this can have a long-lasting financial impact on the company.
2. **D.** The attackers are the entities that have exploited a vulnerability; thus, they are the threat agent.
3. **C.** In this situation the e-mail server most likely is misconfigured or has a programming flaw that can be exploited. Either of these would be considered a vulnerability. The threat is that someone would find out about this vulnerability and exploit it. The exposure is allowing sensitive data to be accessed in an unauthorized manner.
4. **C.** Diameter is a protocol that has been developed to build upon the functionality of RADIUS and TACACS+ while overcoming some of their limitations, particularly with regard to mobile clients. RADIUS uses UDP and cannot effectively deal well with remote access, IP mobility, and policy control. Mobile IP is not an authentication and authorization protocol, but rather a technology that allows users to move from one network to another and still use the same IP address.

5. **C.** DNS Security Extensions (DNSSEC, which is part of the many current implementations of DNS server software) works within a PKI and uses digital signatures, which allows DNS servers to validate the origin of a message to ensure that it is not spoofed and potentially malicious. Suppose DNSSEC were enabled on server A, and a client sends it a DNS request for a resource that is not cached locally. Server A would relay the request to one or more external DNS servers and, upon receiving a response, validate the digital signature on the message before accepting the information to make sure that it is from an authorized DNS server. So even if an attacker sent a message to a DNS server, the DNS server would discard it because the message would not contain a valid digital signature. DNSSEC allows DNS servers to send and receive only authenticated and authorized messages between themselves and thwarts the attacker's goal of poisoning a DNS cache table.
6. **C.** The General Data Protection Regulation (GDPR) impacts every organization that holds or uses European personal data both inside and outside of Europe. In other words, if your company is a U.S.-based company that has never done business with the EU but it has an EU citizen working even as temporary staff (e.g., a summer intern), it probably has to comply with the GDPR or risk facing stiff penalties. There is no exclusion based on the nature of the relations between the data subjects and the data controllers and processors.
7. **B.** A vulnerability is a lack or weakness of a control. The vulnerability is that the user, who must be given access to the sensitive data, is not properly monitored to deter and detect a willful breach of security. The threat is that any internal entity might misuse given access. The risk is the business impact of losing sensitive data. One control that could be put into place is monitoring so that access activities can be closely watched.
8. **C.** A role-based access control (RBAC) model uses a centrally administrated set of controls to determine how subjects and objects interact. An administrator does not need to revoke and reassign permissions to individual users as they change jobs. Instead, the administrator assigns permissions and rights to a role, and users are plugged into those roles.
9. **A.** Many (but not all) countries have data breach notification requirements, and these vary greatly in their specifics. While some countries have very strict requirements, others have laxer requirement, or lack them altogether. This requires the security professional to ensure compliance in the appropriate territory. Applying the most stringent rules universally (e.g., 24-hour notification) is usually not a good idea from a business perspective. The term "best effort" is not acceptable in countries with strict rules, nor is the notion that personally identifiable information (PII) is the only type of data that would trigger a mandatory notification.
10. **D.** Regression testing should take place after a change to a system takes place, retesting to ensure functionality, performance, and protection.

11. **B.** ISO/IEC 27001 is a standard covering information security management systems (ISMSs), which is a much broader topic than supply chain risk management. The other three options are better answers because they are directly tied to this process: NIST Special Publication 800-161, *Supply Chain Risk Management Practices for Federal Information Systems and Organizations*, directly addresses supply chain risk, and the insertion of hardware Trojans could happen at any point in the chain, upstream or downstream.
12. **B.** Various countries have data sovereignty laws that stipulate that anyone who stores or processes certain types of data (typically personal data on their citizens), whether or not they do so locally, must comply with those countries' laws. Data localization laws, on the other hand, require certain types of data to be stored and processed in that country (examples include laws in China and Russia).
13. **B.** Security through obscurity depends upon complexity or secrecy as a protection method. Some organizations feel that since their proprietary code is not standards based, outsiders will not know how to compromise its components. This is an insecure approach. Defense-in-depth is a better approach, with the assumption that anyone can figure out how something works.
14. **C.** ISO/IEC 27005 is the international standard for risk assessments and analysis.
15. **C.** ISO/IEC 27799 is a guideline for information security management in health organizations. It deals with how organizations that store and process sensitive medical information should protect it.
16. **D.** End-of-life (EOL) for an asset is that point in time when its manufacturer is neither manufacturing nor sustaining it. In other words, you can't send it in for repairs, buy spare parts, or get technical assistance from the manufacturer. The related term, end-of-support (EOS), which is sometimes also called end-of-service-life (EOSL), means that the manufacturer is no longer patching bugs or vulnerabilities on the product.
17. **B.** A virtual private network (VPN) provides confidentiality for data being exchanged between two endpoints. While the use of VPNs may not be sufficient in every case, it is the only answer among those provided that addresses the question. The use of Secure Sockets Layer (SSL) is not considered secure. IEEE 802.1X is an authentication protocol that does not protect data in transit. Finally, whole-disk encryption may be a good approach to protecting sensitive data, but only while it is at rest.
18. **B.** Threat modeling is the process of describing probable adverse effects on an organization's assets caused by specific threat sources. This modeling can use a variety of approaches, including attack trees and the MITRE ATT&CK framework. However, since the question refers to a report and neither of those approaches specifically points to a report, the more general answer of threat modeling is the best one.
19. **B.** A CAPTCHA is a skewed representation of characteristics a person must enter to prove that the subject is a human and not an automated tool, as in a software robot. It is the graphical representation of data.

20. **B.** The CPO position was created mainly because of the increasing demands on organizations to protect a long laundry list of different types of data. This role is responsible for ensuring that customer, organizational, and employee data is secure and kept secret, which keeps the organization out of criminal and civil courts and hopefully out of the headlines.

21. **D.** The correct sequence for the steps listed in the question is as follows:

    i. Develop a risk management team.

    ii. Identify company assets to be assessed.

    iii. Calculate the value of each asset.

    iv. Identify the vulnerabilities and threats that can affect the identified assets.

22. **B.** Synthetic transactions are scripted events that mimic the behaviors of real users and allow security professionals to systematically test the performance of critical services. They are the best approach, because they can detect problems before users notice them. Real user monitoring (RUM) would rely on users encountering the problem, whereupon the system would automatically report it.

23. **A.** Data remanence refers to the persistence of data on storage media after it has been deleted. Encrypting this data is the best of the listed choices because the recoverable data will be meaningless to an adversary without the decryption key. Retention policies are important, but are considered administrative controls that don't deal with remanence directly. Simply deleting the file will not normally render the data unrecoverable, nor will the use of SSDs even though these devices will sometimes (though not always) make it difficult to recover the deleted data.

24. **C.** While all of these situations could have taken place, the most likely attack type in this scenario is the use of a keylogger. Attackers commonly compromise personal computers by tricking the users into installing Trojan horses that have the capability to install keystroke loggers. The keystroke logger can capture authentication data that the attacker can use to authenticate as a legitimate user and carry out malicious activities.

25. **B.** IPSec is a suite of protocols used to provide VPNs that use strong encryption and authentication functionality. It can work in two different modes: tunnel mode (payload and headers are protected) or transport mode (payload protection only). IPSec works at the network layer, not the data link layer.

26. **C.** In a typical public key infrastructure, the sender first needs to obtain the receiver's public key, which could be from the receiver or a public directory, and then verify it. The sender needs to protect the symmetric session key as it is being sent, so the sender encrypts it with the receiver's public key. The receiver decrypts the session key with the receiver's private key.

27. **C.** Today, more organizations are implementing security information and event management (SIEM) systems. These products gather logs from various devices (servers, firewalls, routers, etc.) and attempt to correlate the log data and provide analysis capabilities. Organizations also have different types of systems on a network (routers, firewalls, IDS, IPS, servers, gateways, proxies) collecting logs in various proprietary formats, which requires centralization, standardization, and normalization. Log formats are different per product type and vendor.

28. **D.** Configuration management is a process aimed at ensuring that systems and controls are configured correctly and are responsive to the current threat and operational environments. Since the IPv6-to-IPv4 tunneling is not desirable, ensuring all devices are properly configured is the best approach of those listed. Change management is a broader term that includes configuration management but is not the best answer listed because it is more general.

29. **D.** IoT devices run the gamut of cost, from the very cheap to the very expensive. Cost, among the listed options, is the least likely to be a direct concern for a security professional. Lack of authentication, encryption, and update mechanisms are much more likely to be significant issues in any IoT adoption plan.

30. **C.** Each microservice lives in its own container and gets called as needed. If, for example, you see a spike in orders, you can automatically deploy a new container (in seconds), perhaps in a different host, and destroy it when you no longer need it. This contrasts with traditional servers that have fixed resources available and don't scale as well. Both approaches deal equally well with both web and database services and (properly deployed) have comparable security.

31. **B.** Extensible Access Control Markup Language (XACML), a declarative access control policy language implemented in XML and a processing model, describes how to interpret security policies. Service Provisioning Markup Language (SPML) is an XML-based language that allows for the exchange of provisioning data between applications, which could reside in one organization or many; allows for the automation of user management (account creation, amendments, revocation) and access entitlement configuration related to electronically published services across multiple provisioning systems; and allows for the integration and interoperation of service provisioning requests across various platforms. Security Assertion Markup Language (SAML) is an XML-based language that allows for the exchange of provisioning data between applications, which could reside in one organization or many.

32. **C.** A company must decide how to handle physical access control in the event of a power failure. In fail-safe mode, doorways are automatically unlocked. This is usually dictated by fire codes to ensure that people do not get stuck inside of a burning building. Fail-secure means that the door will default to lock.

33. **C.** Incident response typically requires humans in the loop. Next-generation firewalls (NGFWs) do not completely automate the process of responding to security incidents. NGFWs typically involve integrated IPS and signature sharing capabilities with cloud-based aggregators, but are also significantly more expensive than other firewall types.
34. **D.** Trolling is the term used to describe people who sow discord on various social platforms on the Internet by starting arguments or making inflammatory statements aimed at upsetting others. This is not a topic normally covered in security awareness training. Social engineering, phishing, and whaling are important topics to include in any security awareness program.
35. **D.** When clients digitally sign messages, this ensures nonrepudiation. Since the client should be the only person who has the client's private key, and only the client's public key can decrypt it, the e-mail must have been sent from the client. Digital signatures provide nonrepudiation protection, which is what this company needs.
36. **D.** Simple Authentication and Security Layer (SASL) is a protocol-independent authentication framework for authentication and data security in Internet protocols. It decouples authentication mechanisms from application protocols, with the goal of allowing any authentication mechanism supported by SASL to be used in any application protocol that uses SASL. SASL's design is intended to allow new protocols to reuse existing mechanisms without requiring redesign of the mechanisms, and allows existing protocols to make use of new mechanisms without redesign of protocols.
37. **D.** Coupling is not considered a secure coding practice, though it does affect the quality (and hence the security) of software. It is a measurement that indicates how much interaction one module requires to carry out its tasks. High (tight) coupling means a module depends upon many other modules to carry out its tasks. Low (loose) coupling means a module does not need to communicate with many other modules to carry out its job, which is better because the module is easier to understand and easier to reuse, and changes can take place to one module and not affect many modules around it.
38. **A.** A recovery time objective (RTO) is the amount of time it takes to recover from a disaster, and a recovery point objective (RPO) is the amount of data, measured in time, that can be lost and be tolerable from that same event. The RPO is the acceptable amount of data loss measured in time. This value represents the earliest point in time by which data must be recovered. The higher the value of data, the more funds or other resources that can be put into place to ensure a smaller amount of data is lost in the event of a disaster. RTO is the maximum time period within which a business process must be restored to a designated service level after a disaster to avoid unacceptable consequences associated with a break in business continuity.
39. **B.** Though laws vary around the world, many countries criminalize unauthorized access, even if it lacked malicious intent.

40. **A.** XACML uses a Subject element (requesting entity), a Resource element (requested entity), and an Action element (types of access). XACML defines a declarative access control policy language implemented in XML.

41. **B.** The Mobile IP protocol allows location-independent routing of IP packets on web-based environments. Each mobile device is identified by its home address. While away from its home network, a mobile node is associated with a care-of address, which identifies its current location, and its home address is associated with the local endpoint of a tunnel to its home agent. Mobile IP specifies how a mobile device registers with its home agent and how the home agent routes packets to the mobile device.

42. **D.** A SIEM solution is a software platform that aggregates security information and security events and presents them in a single, consistent, and cohesive manner.

43. **D.** The sensitivity of information is commensurate with the losses to an organization if that information were revealed to unauthorized individuals. Its criticality, on the other hand, is an indicator of how the loss of the information would impact the fundamental business processes of the organization. While replacement costs could factor into a determination of criticality, they almost never do when it comes to sensitivity.

44. **C.** Global organizations that move data across other country boundaries must be aware of and follow the Organisation for Economic Co-operation and Development (OECD) *Guidelines on the Protection of Privacy and Transborder Flows of Personal Data*. Since most countries have a different set of laws pertaining to the definition of private data and how it should be protected, international trade and business get more convoluted and can negatively affect the economy of nations. The OECD is an international organization that helps different governments come together and tackle the economic, social, and governance challenges of a globalized economy. Because of this, the OECD came up with guidelines for the various countries to follow so that data is properly protected and everyone follows the same type of rules.

45. **B.** Registered ports are 1024–49151, which can be registered with the Internet Assigned Numbers Authority (IANA) for a particular use. Vendors register specific ports to map to their proprietary software. Dynamic ports are 49152–65535 and are available to be used by any application on an "as needed" basis. Port numbers from 0 to 1023 are well-known ports.

46. **A.** The correct answer for cost/benefit analysis is the formula: (ALE before implementing safeguard) – (ALE after implementing safeguard) – (annual cost of safeguard) = value of safeguard to the organization.

47. **B.** Each of the listed items are correct benefits or characteristics of cloud computing except "Cost of computing can be increased since it is a shared delivery model." The correct answer would be "Cost of computing can be *decreased* since it is a shared delivery model."

48. **A.** An architecture is a tool used to conceptually understand the structure and behavior of a complex entity through different views. An architecture provides different views of the system, based upon the needs of the stakeholders of that system.

49. **B.** Threat modeling is a systematic approach used to understand how different threats could be realized and how a successful compromise could take place. A threat model is a description of a set of security aspects that can help define a threat and a set of possible attacks to consider. It may be useful to define different threat models for one software product. Each model defines a narrow set of possible attacks to focus on. A threat model can help to assess the probability, the potential harm, and the priority of attacks, and thus help to minimize or eradicate the threats.

50. **B.** Many IDSs have "heuristic" capabilities, which means that the system gathers different "clues" from the network or system and calculates the probability an attack is taking place. If the probability hits a set threshold, then the alarm sounds.

51. **C.** External auditors have certain advantages over in-house teams, but they will almost certainly not be as knowledgeable of internal processes and technology as the folks who deal with them on a daily basis.

52. **C.** In this example, staffers with lower security clearance than Don has could have deduced that the contract had been renewed by paying attention to the changes in their systems. The noninterference model addresses this specifically by dictating that no action or state in higher levels can impact or be visible to lower levels. In this example, the staff could learn something indirectly or infer something that they do not have a right to know yet.

53. **B.** HTML documents and e-mails allow users to attach or embed hyperlinks in any given text, such as the "Click Here" links you commonly see in e-mail messages or web pages. Attackers misuse hyperlinks to deceive unsuspecting users into clicking rogue links. The most common approach is known as URL hiding.

54. **C.** Personnel background checks are a common administrative (not technical) control. This type of audit would have nothing to do with the web applications themselves. The other three options (log reviews, code reviews, misuse case testing) are typical ways to verify the effectiveness of technical controls.

55. **D.** Statistical time-division multiplexing (STDM) transmits several types of data simultaneously across a single transmission line. STDM technologies analyze statistics related to the typical workload of each input device and make real-time decisions on how much time each device should be allocated for data transmission.

56. **D.** The actual voice stream is carried on media protocols such as RTP. RTP provides a standardized packet format for delivering audio and video over IP networks. RTP is a session layer protocol that carries data in media stream format, as in audio

and video, and is used extensively in VoIP, telephony, video conferencing, and other multimedia streaming technologies. It provides end-to-end delivery services and is commonly run over the transport layer protocol UDP. RTCP is used in conjunction with RTP and is also considered a session layer protocol. It provides out-of-band statistics and control information to provide feedback on QoS levels of individual streaming multimedia sessions.

57. **A.** Edge computing is a distributed system in which some computational and data storage assets are deployed close to where they are needed in order to reduce latency and network traffic. An edge computing architecture typically has three layers: end devices, edge devices, and cloud infrastructure.

58. **C.** A frequency analysis, also known as a statistical attack, identifies statistically significant patterns in the ciphertext generated by a cryptosystem. For example, the number of zeroes may be significantly higher than the number of ones. This could show that the pseudorandom number generator (PRNG) in use may be biased.

59. **D.** IPSec is made up of two main protocols, Authentication Header (AH) and Encapsulating Security Payload (ESP). AH provides system authentication and integrity, but not confidentiality or availability. ESP provides system authentication, integrity, and confidentiality, but not availability. Nothing within IPSec can ensure the availability of the system it is residing on.

60. **D.** The ACID test concept should be incorporated into the software of a database. ACID stands for:
    - **Atomicity** Either the entire transaction succeeds or the database rolls it back to its previous state.
    - **Consistency** A transaction strictly follows all applicable rules on all data affected.
    - **Isolation** If transactions are allowed to happen in parallel (which most of them are), then they will be isolated from each other so that the effects of one don't corrupt another. In other words, isolated transactions have the same effect whether they happen in parallel or one after the other.
    - **Durability** Ensures that a completed transaction is permanently stored (for instance, in nonvolatile memory) so that it cannot be wiped by a power outage or other such failure.

61. **B.** In a Platform as a Service (PaaS) contract, the service provider normally takes care of all configuration, patches, and updates for the virtual platform. Jim would only have to worry about porting the applications and running them.

62. **B.** The biggest advantages of cloud computing are enhanced efficiency, performance, reliability, scalability, and security. Still, cloud computing is not a panacea. An organization must still carefully consider legal, contractual, and cost issues since they could potentially place the organization in a difficult position.

63. **C.** Shared responsibility addresses situations in which a cloud service provider is responsible for certain security controls, while the customer is responsible for others. It will be critical for Jim to delineate where these responsibilities lie. The other principles listed would presumably be equally important before and after the transition.

64. **A.** The aim of an attack surface analysis is to identify and reduce the amount of code accessible to untrusted users. The basic strategies of attack surface reduction are to reduce the amount of code running, reduce entry points available to untrusted users, reduce privilege levels as much as possible, and eliminate unnecessary services. Attack surface analysis is generally carried out through specialized tools to enumerate different parts of a product and aggregate their findings into a numerical value. Attack surface analyzers scrutinize files, registry keys, memory data, session information, processes, and services details.

65. **B.** The Capability Maturity Model Integration (CMMI) model outlines the necessary characteristics of an organization's security engineering process. It addresses the different phases of a secure software development life cycle, including concept definition, requirements analysis, design, development, integration, installation, operations, and maintenance, and what should happen in each phase. It can be used to evaluate security engineering practices and identify ways to improve them. It can also be used by customers in the evaluation process of a software vendor. Ideally, software vendors would use the model to help improve their processes, and customers would use the model to assess the vendor's practices.

66. **D.** VxLANs are designed to overcome two limitations of traditional VLANs: the limit of no more than 4,096 VLANs imposed by the 12-bit VLAN ID (VID) field, and the need for VLANs to be connected to the same router port. Accordingly, VxLANs are mostly used by cloud service providers with hundreds of customers and by large organizations with a global presence.

67. **D.** These are all issues that are directly related to Kerberos. These items are as follows:

    - The Key Distribution Center (KDC) can be a single point of failure. If the KDC goes down, no one can access needed resources. Redundancy is necessary for the KDC.
    - The KDC must be scalable to handle the number of requests it receives in a timely manner.
    - Secret keys are temporarily stored on the users' workstations, which means it is possible for an intruder to obtain these cryptographic keys.
    - Session keys are decrypted and reside on the users' workstations, either in a cache or in a key table. Again, an intruder can capture these keys.
    - Kerberos is vulnerable to password guessing. The KDC does not know if a dictionary attack is taking place.

68. A. Yes, the company should implement the control, as the value would be $25,000. The cost/benefit calculation is (ALE before implementing safeguard) – (ALE after implementing safeguard) – (annual cost of safeguard) = value of safeguard to the organization, which in this case is $100,000 – $45,000 – $30,000 = $25,000.

69. D. The correct mappings for the individual standards are as follows:

- ISO/IEC 27002: Code of practice for information security controls
- ISO/IEC 27003: ISMS implementation guidance
- ISO/IEC 27004: ISMS monitoring, measurement, analysis, and evaluation
- ISO/IEC 27005: Information security risk management
- ISO/IEC 27007: ISMS auditing guidelines

70. B. Just-in-time (JIT) access temporarily elevates users to the necessary privileged access to perform a specific task, on a specific asset, for a short time. This approach mitigates the risk of privileged account abuse by reducing the time a threat actor has to gain access to a privileged account. While this could reduce some of the workload on the IT staff, it would have no impact on the time needed to reset a multitude of passwords.

71. C. End-to-end encryption happens within the applications. IPSec encryption takes place at the network layer. PPTP encryption takes place at the data link layer. Link encryption takes place at the data link and physical layers.

72. A. Hierarchical storage management (HSM) provides continuous online backup functionality. It combines hard disk technology with the cheaper and slower optical or tape jukeboxes. Storage area network (SAN) is made up of several storage systems that are connected together to form a single backup network.

73. C. The common law system is the only one that is based on previous interpretations of the law. This means that the system consists of both laws and court decisions in specific cases. Torts can be (and usually are) part of a common law system, but that would be an incomplete answer to this question.

74. B. It is important that evidence be relevant, complete, sufficient, and reliable to the case at hand. These four characteristics of evidence provide a foundation for a case and help ensure that the evidence is legally permissible.

75. B. Risk-based access control estimates the risk associated with a particular request in real time and, if it doesn't exceed a given threshold, grants the subject access to the requested resource. This estimate can be based on multiple factors, including the risk history of similar requests. It is possible to improve a rule-based access control mechanism over time (based on historical data), but that would have to be a manual process and wouldn't happen in real time.

76. C. SOAP enables programs running on different operating systems and written in different programming languages to communicate over web-based communication methods. SOAP is an XML-based protocol that encodes messages in a web service environment. SOAP actually defines an XML schema or a structure of how communication is going to take place. The SOAP XML schema defines how objects communicate directly.

77. **A.** Each answer lists the correct definition mapping.

78. **C.** For an enterprise security architecture to be successful in its development and implementation, the following items must be understood and followed: strategic alignment, process enhancement, business enablement, and security effectiveness.

79. **A.** The OECD is an international organization where member countries come together to address economic, social, and governance challenges of a globalized economy. Thus, the OECD came up with guidelines for the various countries to follow so data is properly protected and everyone follows the same type of rules.

80. **A.** The Zachman Framework is for business enterprise architectures, not security enterprises. The proper definition mappings are as follows:
    - **Zachman Framework** Model for the development of enterprise architectures developed by John Zachman
    - **TOGAF** Model and methodology for the development of enterprise architectures developed by The Open Group
    - **DoDAF** U.S. Department of Defense architecture framework that ensures interoperability of systems to meet military mission goals
    - **SABSA** Model and methodology for the development of information security enterprise architectures

81. **B.** The ISO/IEC 27000 series provides a high-level overview of security program requirements, while COBIT maps IT goals to enterprise goals to stakeholder needs through a series of transforms called cascading goals. COBIT specifies 13 enterprise and 13 alignment goals that take the guesswork out of ensuring we consider all dimensions in our decision-making processes.

82. **D.** This model was not built upon the SABSA model. All other characteristics are true.

83. **D.** The Operationally Critical Threat, Asset, and Vulnerability Evaluation (OCTAVE) relies on the idea that the people working in a given environment best understand what is needed and what kind of risks they are facing. This places the people who work inside the organization in the power positions of being able to make the decisions regarding what is the best approach for evaluating the security of their organization.

84. **B.** An enterprise architecture framework is a conceptual model in which an architecture description is organized into multiple architecture views, where each view addresses specific concerns originating with the specific stakeholders. Individual stakeholders have a variety of system concerns, which the architecture must address. To express these concerns, each view applies the conventions of its architecture viewpoint.

85. **C.** Fault tree analysis follows this general process. First, an undesired effect is taken as the root, or top, event of a tree of logic. Then, each situation that has the potential to cause that effect is added to the tree as a series of logic expressions. Fault trees are then labeled with actual numbers pertaining to failure probabilities.

86. **D.** Security effectiveness deals with metrics, meeting service level agreement (SLA) requirements, achieving return on investment (ROI), meeting set baselines, and providing management with a dashboard or balanced scorecard system. These are ways to determine how useful the current security solutions and architecture as a whole are performing.

87. **D.** Each answer provides the correct definition of the four levels that can be assigned to an organization during its evaluation against the CMMI model. This model can be used to determine how well the organization's processes compare to CMMI best practices and to identify areas where improvement can be made. Maturity Level 1 is Initial.

88. **B.** The ISRM policy should address all of the items listed except specific physical controls. Policies should not specify any type of controls, whether they are administrative, physical, or technical.

89. **C.** Each of these items should be considered before committing to an outsource partner or vendor.

90. **D.** The steps normally involved in the discovery of electronically stored information, or e-discovery, are identifying, preserving, collecting, processing, reviewing, analyzing, and producing the data in compliance with the court order. Data remanence is not part of e-discovery, though it could influence the process.

91. **C.** ISO/IEC 27004:2016, which is used to assess the effectiveness of an ISMS and the controls that make up the security program as outlined in ISO/IEC 27001. ISO/IEC 27004 provides guidance for ISMS monitoring, measurement, analysis, and evaluation.

92. **B.** Content distribution networks (CDNs) work by replicating content across geographically dispersed nodes. This means that regional users (those closest to a given node) will see improved responsiveness and could have tailored content delivered to them. It also means that mounting a successful DDoS attack is much more difficult. An ARP spoofing attack, however, takes place on the local area network and is therefore unrelated to the advantages of CDNs.

93. **A.** A CASB is a system that provides visibility and security controls for cloud services. A CASB monitors what users do in the cloud and applies whatever policies and controls are applicable to that activity.

94. **C.** A federated identity is a portable identity, and its associated entitlements, that can be used across business boundaries. It allows a user to be authenticated across multiple IT systems and enterprises. Single sign-on (SSO) allows users to enter credentials one time and be able to access all resources in primary and secondary network domains, but is not the best answer because it doesn't specifically address the capability to provide authentication across enterprises. A federated identity is a kind of SSO, but not every SSO implementation is federated.

95. B. HTML came from SGML, which came from GML. A markup language is a way to structure text and data sets, and it dictates how these will be viewed and used. When developing a web page, a markup language enables you to control how the text looks and some of the actual functionality the page provides.

96. A. XML is a universal and foundational standard that provides a structure for other independent markup languages to be built from and still allow for interoperability. Markup languages with various functionalities were built from XML, and while each language provides its own individual functionality, if they all follow the core rules of XML, then they are interoperable and can be used across different web-based applications and platforms.

97. B. A role-based access control (RBAC) model is based on the necessary operations and tasks a user needs to carry out to fulfill her responsibilities within an organization. This type of model lets access to resources be based on the user's roles. In hierarchical RBAC, role hierarchies define an inheritance relation among roles.

98. C. Diameter is a more diverse centralized access control administration technique than RADIUS and TACACS+ because it supports a wide range of protocols that often accompany wireless technologies. RADIUS supports PPP, SLIP, and traditional network connections. TACACS+ is a RADIUS-like protocol that is Cisco-proprietary. Kerberos is a single sign-on technology, not a centralized access control administration protocol that supports all stated technologies.

99. A. An authoritative system of record (ASOR) is a hierarchical tree-like structure system that tracks subjects and their authorization chains. The authoritative source is the "system of record," or the location where identity information originates and is maintained. It should have the most up-to-date and reliable identity information.

100. A. User provisioning refers to the creation, maintenance, and deactivation of user objects and attributes as they exist in one or more systems, directories, or applications, in response to business processes.

101. D. OpenID Connect (OIDC) is a simple authentication layer built on top of the OAuth 2.0 protocol. It allows transparent authentication and authorization of client resource requests. Though it is possible to use OAuth, which is an authorization standard, for authentication, you would do so by leveraging its OpenID Connect layer. Diameter and Kerberos are not well-suited for IDaaS.

102. A. The Service Provisioning Markup Language (SPML) allows for the exchange of provisioning data between applications, which could reside in one organization or many. SPML allows for the automation of user management (account creation, amendments, revocation) and access entitlement configuration related to electronically published services across multiple provisioning systems. SPML also allows for the integration and interoperation of service provisioning requests across various platforms.

103. B. In this scenario, Lynn is considered the principal, the airline company is considered the identity provider, and the hotel company that receives the user's authentication information from the airline company web server is considered the service provider. Security Assertion Markup Language (SAML) provides the authentication pieces to federated identity management systems to allow business-to-business (B2B) and business-to-consumer (B2C) transactions.

104. A. A service-oriented architecture (SOA) is way to provide independent services residing on different systems in different business domains in one consistent manner. This architecture is a set of principles and methodologies for designing and developing software in the form of interoperable services.

105. B. The Bell-LaPadula model enforces the confidentiality aspects of access control and consists of three main rules. The simple security rule states that a subject at a given security level cannot read data that resides at a higher security level. The *-property rule (star property rule) states that a subject in a given security level cannot write information to a lower security level. Finally, the strong star property rule states that a subject who has read and write capabilities can only perform both of those functions at the same security level; nothing higher and nothing lower.

106. D. In the system design phase, the software development team gathers system requirement specifications and determines how the system will accomplish design goals, such as required functionality, compatibility, fault tolerance, extensibility, security, usability, and maintainability. The attack surface analysis, together with the threat model, inform the developers' decisions because they can look at proposed architectures and competing designs from the perspective of an attacker. This allows them to develop a more defensible system. Though it is possible to start the threat model during the earlier phase of requirements gathering, this modeling effort is normally not done that early. Furthermore, the attack surface cannot be properly studied until there is a proposed architecture to analyze. Performing this activity later in the SDLC is less effective and usually results in security being "bolted on" instead of "baked in."

107. B. OAuth is an open standard for authorization to third parties. It lets you authorize a web application to use something that you control at a different website. For instance, if users wanted to share an article in the web app directly to their LinkedIn account, the system would ask them for access to their accounts in LinkedIn. If they agree, they'd see a pop-up from LinkedIn asking whether they want to authorize the web app to share a post. If they agree to this, the web app gains access to all their contacts until they rescind this authorization.

108. A. Each CPU type has a specific architecture and set of instructions that it can carry out. The application must be developed to work within this CPU architecture and compiled into machine code that can run on it. This is why one application may work on an Intel processor but not on an AMD processor. There are portable applications that can work on multiple architectures and operating systems, but these rely on a runtime environment.

109. **C.** According to Veracode, seven in ten applications use at least one open-source software library with a security flaw, which makes those applications vulnerable. This estimate doesn't include proprietary libraries, which are probably even more insecure because they haven't been subjected to the same amount of scrutiny as open-source ones. This is the main risk in using software libraries.

110. **A.** Dynamic application security testing (DAST), which is also known as dynamic analysis, refers to the evaluation of a program in real time, while it is running. It is the only one of the answers that is effective for analyzing software without having access to the actual source code.

111. **C.** Attackers have identified programming errors in operating systems that allow them to "starve" the system of its own memory. This means the attackers exploit a software vulnerability that ensures that processes do not properly release their memory resources. Memory is continually committed and not released, and the system is depleted of this resource until it can no longer function. This is an example of a denial-of-service attack.

112. **A.** Attribute-based access control (ABAC) is based on attributes of any component of the system. It is the most granular of the access control models.

113. **A.** The primary reason to use Kerberos is that the principals do not trust each other enough to communicate directly; they only trust the Key Distribution Center (KDC). This is a strength, not a weakness, of the system, but it does point to the fact that if only the KDC can vouch for identities, this creates a single point of failure. The fact that secret keys are stored on users' workstations, albeit temporarily, presents an attack opportunity for threat actors, who can also perform password attacks on the system.

114. **A.** The depth of field refers to the portion of the environment that is in focus when shown on the monitor. The depth of field varies, depending upon the size of the lens opening, the distance of the object being focused on, and the focal length of the lens. The depth of field increases as the size of the lens opening decreases, the subject distance increases, or the focal length of the lens decreases. So if you want to cover a large area and not focus on specific items, it is best to use a wide-angle lens and a small lens opening.

115. **B.** In a preaction system, a link must melt before the water will pass through the sprinkler heads, which creates the delay in water release. This type of suppression system is best in data-processing environments because it allows time to deactivate the system if there is a false alarm.

116. **B.** A preaction system has a link that must melt before water is released. This is the mechanism that provides the delay in water release. A deluge system has wide open sprinkler heads that allow a lot of water to be released quickly. It does not have a delaying component.

117. **D.** CPTED encourages natural surveillance, the goal of which is to make criminals feel uncomfortable by providing many ways observers could potentially see them and to make all other people feel safe and comfortable by providing an open and well-designed environment. The other answers refer to the other three CPTED strategies, which are natural access control, territorial reinforcement, and maintenance, respectively.

118. **D.** The Zachman Framework is a two-dimensional model that uses six basic communication interrogatives (What, How, Where, Who, When, and Why) intersecting with different viewpoints (Executives, Business Managers, System Architects, Engineers, Technicians, and Enterprise-wide) to give a holistic understanding of the enterprise. This framework was developed in the 1980s and is based on the principles of classical business architecture that contain rules that govern an ordered set of relationships.

119. **B.** The communication between two pieces of the same software product that reside on different computers needs to be controlled, which is why session layer protocols even exist. Session layer protocols take on the functionality of middleware, enabling software on two different computers to communicate.

120. **A.** The data link layer has two sublayers: the Logical Link Control (LLC) and Media Access Control (MAC) layers. The LLC sublayer provides a standard interface for whatever network protocol is being used. This provides an abstraction layer so that the network protocol does not need to be programmed to communicate with all of the possible MAC-level protocols (Ethernet, WLAN, frame relay, etc.).

121. **C.** A Class B address range is usually too large for most companies, and a Class C address range is too small, so CIDR provides the flexibility to increase or decrease the class sizes as necessary. CIDR is the method to specify more flexible IP address classes.

122. **A.** 802.1AE is the IEEE MAC Security (MACSec) standard, which defines a security infrastructure to provide data confidentiality, data integrity, and data origin authentication. Where a VPN connection provides protection at the higher networking layers, MACSec provides hop-by-hop protection at layer 2.

123. **D.** 802.1AR provides a unique ID for a device. 802.1AE provides data encryption, integrity, and origin authentication functionality. 802.1AF carries out key agreement functions for the session keys used for data encryption. Each of these standards provides specific parameters to work within an 802.1X EAP-TLS framework.

124. **A.** As information systems security professionals, if we discover a vulnerability, we have an ethical obligation to properly disclose it to the appropriate parties. If the vulnerability is in our own product, we need to notify our customers and partners as soon as possible. If it is in someone else's product, we need to notify the vendor or manufacturer immediately so they can fix it. The goal of ethical disclosure is to inform anyone who might be affected as soon as feasible, so a patch can be developed before any threat actors become aware of the vulnerability.

125. **C.** The HOSTS file resides on the local computer and can contain static hostname-to-IP mapping information. If you do not want your system to query a DNS server, you can add the necessary data in the HOSTS file, and your system will first check its contents before reaching out to a DNS server. Some people use these files to reduce the risk of an attacker sending their system a bogus IP address that points them to a malicious website.

126. **B.** VLAN hopping attacks allow attackers to gain access to traffic in various VLAN segments. An attacker can have a system act as though it is a switch. The system understands the tagging values being used in the network and the trunking protocols, and can insert itself between other VLAN devices and gain access to the traffic going back and forth. Attackers can also insert tagging values to manipulate the control of traffic at the data link layer.

127. **B.** The most common cloud service models are

    - **Infrastructure as a Service (IaaS)** Cloud service providers offer the infrastructure environment of a traditional data center in an on-demand delivery method.
    - **Platform as a Service (PaaS)** Cloud service providers deliver a computing platform, which can include an operating system, database, and web server as a holistic execution environment.
    - **Software as a Service (SaaS)** Cloud service providers give users access to specific application software (e.g., CRM, e-mail, and games).

128. **C.** Software-defined networking (SDN) is an approach to networking that relies on distributed software to provide unprecedented agility and efficiency. Using SDN, it becomes much easier to dynamically route traffic to and from newly provisioned services and platforms. It also means that a service or platform can be quickly moved from one location to another and the SDN will just as quickly update traffic-flow rules in response to this change.

129. **A.** Parallel tests are similar to simulation tests, except that parallel tests include moving some of the systems to the offsite facility. Simulation tests stop just short of the move. Parallel tests are effective because they ensure that specific systems work at the new location, but the test itself does not interfere with business operations at the main facility.

130. **B.** While DRP and BCP are directed at the development of plans, business continuity management (BCM) is the holistic management process that should cover both of them. BCM provides a framework for integrating resilience with the capability for effective responses in a manner that protects the interests of the organization's key stakeholders. The main objective of BCM is to allow the organization to continue to perform business operations under various conditions. BCM is the overarching approach to managing all aspects of BCP and DRP.

131. **B.** An external audit (sometimes called a second-party audit) is one conducted by (or on behalf of) a business partner to verify contractual obligations. Though this audit could be conducted by a third party (e.g., an auditing firm hired by either party), it is still considered an external audit because it is being done to satisfy an external entity.

132. **A.** Duress is the use of threats or violence against someone in order to force them to do something they don't want to do. A popular example of a countermeasure for duress is the use of panic buttons by bank tellers. A panic room could conceivably be another solution, but it would only work if employees are able to get in and lock the door before an assailant can stop them, which makes it a generally poor approach.

133. **A.** The Wassenaar Arrangement implements export controls for "Conventional Arms and Dual-Use Goods and Technologies." The main goal of this arrangement is to prevent the buildup of military capabilities that could threaten regional and international security and stability. So, everyone is keeping an eye on each other to make sure no one country's weapons can take everyone else out. One item the agreement deals with is cryptography, which is considered a dual-use good because it can be used for both military and civilian purposes. The agreement recognizes the danger of exporting products with cryptographic functionality to countries that are in the "offensive" column, meaning that they are thought to have friendly ties with terrorist organizations and/or want to take over the world through the use of weapons of mass destruction.

134. **A.** The civil (code) law system is used in continental European countries such as France and Spain. It is a different legal system from the common law system used in the United Kingdom and United States. A civil law system is rule-based law, not precedent-based. For the most part, a civil law system is focused on codified law—or written laws.

135. **C.** FMEA is a method for determining functions, identifying functional failures, and assessing the causes of failure and their failure effects through a structured process. It is commonly used in product development and operational environments. The goal is to identify where something is most likely going to break and either fix the flaws that could cause this issue or implement controls to reduce the impact of the break.

136. **B.** Each of these items would be assigned a numeric value in a quantitative risk analysis. Each element is quantified and entered into equations to determine total and residual risks. Quantitative risk analysis is more of a scientific or mathematical approach to risk analysis compared to qualitative.

137. **A.** Aggregation and inference go hand in hand. For example, a user who uses data from a public database to figure out classified information is exercising aggregation (the collection of data) and can then infer the relationship between that data and the data the user does not have access to. This is called an inference attack.

138. B. This option is not a risk, but a (probably unrealistic) benefit, so it cannot be the right answer. The other three options are all risks associated with an unmanaged patching model.

139. B. Clustering algorithms are frequently used for anomaly detection. Classifiers are helpful when trying to determine whether a binary file is malware or detect whether an e-mail is spam. Predictive machine learning models can be applied wherever historical numerical data is available and work by estimating what the value of the next data point should be, which makes them very useful for network flow analysis (e.g., when someone is exfiltrating large amounts of data from the network).

140. A. Breach and attack simulations (BAS) are automated systems that launch simulated attacks against a target environment and then generate reports on their findings. They are meant to be run regularly (even frequently) and be realistic, but not to cause any adverse effect to the target systems. They are usually a much more affordable approach than red teaming, even if you use an internal team.

141. A. Maximum tolerable downtime (MTD) is the outage time that can be endured by an organization, and the recovery time objective (RTO) is an allowable amount of downtime. The RTO value (13 hours) is smaller than the MTD value (24 hours) because the MTD value represents the time after which an inability to recover significant operations will mean severe and perhaps irreparable damage to the organization's reputation or bottom line. The RTO assumes that there is a period of acceptable downtime. This means that a company can be out of production for a certain period of time (RTO) and still get back on its feet. But if the company cannot get production up and running within the MTD window, the company is sinking too fast to properly recover.

142. C. High availability (HA) is a combination of technologies and processes that work together to ensure that critical functions are always up and running at the necessary level. To provide this level of high availability, a company has to have a long list of technologies and processes that provide redundancy, fault tolerance, and failover capabilities.

APPENDIX

Objective Map

Domain	Objective	All-in-One Coverage Ch #	Heading
Domain 1: Security and Risk Management			
1.1	**Understand, adhere to, and promote professional ethics**	1	Professional Ethics
1.1.1	(ISC)² Code of Professional Ethics	1	(ISC)² Code of Professional Ethics
1.1.2	Organizational code of ethics	1	Organizational Code of Ethics
1.2	**Understand and apply security concepts (confidentiality, integrity, and availability, authenticity and nonrepudiation)**	1	Fundamental Cybersecurity Concepts and Terms
1.3	**Evaluate and apply security governance principles**	1	Security Governance Principles
1.3.1	Alignment of the security function to business strategy, goals, mission, and objectives	1	Aligning Security to Business Strategy
1.3.2	Organizational processes (e.g., acquisitions, divestitures, governance committees)	1	Organizational Processes
1.3.3	Organizational roles and responsibilities	1	Organizational Roles and Responsibilities
1.3.4	Security control frameworks	4	Security Control Frameworks
1.3.5	Due care/due diligence	3	Due Care vs. Due Diligence
1.4	**Determine compliance and other requirements**	3	Compliance Requirements
1.4.1	Contractual, legal, industry standards, and regulatory requirements	3	Contractual, Legal, Industry Standards, and Regulatory Requirements
1.4.2	Privacy requirements	3	Privacy Requirements
1.5	**Understand legal and regulatory issues that pertain to information security in a holistic context**	3	Laws and Regulations

Domain	Objective	All-in-One Coverage Ch #	Heading
Domain 1: Security and Risk Management			
1.5.1	Cybercrimes and data breaches	3	Cybercrimes and Data Breaches
1.5.2	Licensing and Intellectual Property (IP) requirements	3	Licensing and Intellectual Property Requirements
1.5.3	Import/export controls	3	Import/Export Controls
1.5.4	Transborder data flow	3	Transborder Data Flow
1.5.5	Privacy	3	Privacy
1.6	**Understand requirements for investigation types (i.e., administrative, criminal, civil, regulatory, industry standards)**	3	Requirements for Investigations
1.7	**Develop, document, and implement security policy, standards, procedures, and guidelines**	1	Security Policies, Standards, Procedures, and Guidelines
1.8	**Identify, analyze, and prioritize Business Continuity (BC) requirements**	2	Business Continuity
1.8.1	Business Impact Analysis (BIA)	2	Business Impact Analysis
1.8.2	Develop and document the scope and the plan	2	Business Continuity
1.9	**Contribute to and enforce personnel security policies and procedures**	1	Personnel Security
1.9.1	Candidate screening and hiring	1	Candidate Screening and Hiring
1.9.2	Employment agreements and policies	1	Employment Agreements and Policies
1.9.3	Onboarding, transfers, and termination processes	1	Onboarding, Transfers and Termination Processes
1.9.4	Vendor, consultant, and contractor agreements and controls	1	Vendors, Consultants, and Contractors
1.9.5	Compliance policy requirements	1	Compliance Policies
1.9.6	Privacy policy requirements	1	Privacy Policies
1.10	**Understand and apply risk management concepts**	2	Risk Management Concepts
1.10.1	Identify threats and vulnerabilities	2	Identifying Threats and Vulnerabilities
1.10.2	Risk assessment/analysis	2	Assessing Risks
1.10.3	Risk response	2	Responding to Risks
1.10.4	Countermeasure selection and implementation	2	Countermeasure Selection and Implementation

Domain	Objective	All-in-One Coverage Ch #	Heading
Domain 1: Security and Risk Management			
1.10.5	Applicable types of controls (e.g., preventive, detective, corrective)	2	Types of Controls
1.10.6	Control assessments (security and privacy)	2	Control Assessments
1.10.7	Monitoring and measurement	2	Monitoring Risks
1.10.8	Reporting	2	Risk Reporting
1.10.9	Continuous improvement (e.g., Risk maturity modeling)	2	Continuous Improvement
1.10.10	Risk frameworks	4	Risk Frameworks
1.11	**Understand and apply threat modeling concepts and methodologies**	9	Threat Modeling
1.12	**Apply Supply Chain Risk Management (SCRM) concepts**	2	Supply Chain Risk Management
1.12.1	Risks associated with hardware, software, and services	2	Risks Associated with Hardware, Software, and Services
1.12.2	Third-party assessment and monitoring	2	Other Third-Party Risks
1.12.3	Minimum security requirements	2	Minimum Security Requirements
1.12.4	Service level requirements	2	Service Level Agreements
1.13	**Establish and maintain a security awareness, education, and training program**	1	Security Awareness, Education, and Training Programs
1.13.1	Methods and techniques to present awareness and training (e.g., social engineering, phishing, security champions, gamification)	1	Methods and Techniques to Present Awareness and Training
1.13.2	Periodic content reviews	1	Periodic Content Reviews
1.13.3	Program effectiveness evaluation	1	Program Effectiveness Evaluation
Domain 2: Asset Security			
2.1	**Identify and classify information and assets**	5	Information and Assets
2.1.1	Data classification	5	Data Classification
2.1.2	Asset classification	5	Asset Classification
2.2	**Establish information and asset handling requirements**	5	Classification
2.3	**Provision resources securely**	5	Secure Provisioning
2.3.1	Information and asset ownership	5	Ownership

Domain	Objective	All-in-One Coverage Ch #	Heading
Domain 2: Asset Security			
2.3.2	Asset inventory (e.g., tangible, intangible)	5	Inventories
2.3.3	Asset management	5	Managing the Life Cycle of Assets
2.4	**Manage data lifecycle**	5	Data Life Cycle
2.4.1	Data roles (i.e., owners, controllers, custodians, processors, users/subjects)	5	Data Roles
2.4.2	Data collection	5	Data Collection
2.4.3	Data location	5	Where in the World Is My Data?
2.4.4	Data maintenance	5	Data Maintenance
2.4.5	Data retention	5	Data Retention
2.4.6	Data remanence	5	Data Remanence
2.4.7	Data destruction	5	Data Destruction
2.5	**Ensure appropriate asset retention (e.g., End-of-Life (EOL), End-of-Support (EOS))**	5	Asset Retention
2.6	**Determine data security controls and compliance requirements**	6	Data Security Controls
2.6.1	Data states (e.g., in use, in transit, at rest)	6	Data States
2.6.2	Scoping and tailoring	6	Scoping and Tailoring
2.6.3	Standards selection	6	Standards
2.6.4	Data protection methods (e.g., Digital Rights Management (DRM), Data Loss Prevention (DLP), Cloud Access Security Broker (CASB))	6	Data Protection Methods
Domain 3: Security Architecture and Engineering			
3.1	**Research, implement and manage engineering processes using secure design principles**	9	Secure Design Principles
3.1.1	Threat modeling	9	Threat Modeling
3.1.2	Least privilege	9	Least Privilege
3.1.3	Defense in depth	9	Defense in Depth
3.1.4	Secure defaults	9	Secure Defaults
3.1.5	Fail securely	9	Fail Securely
3.1.6	Separation of Duties (SoD)	9	Separation of Duties
3.1.7	Keep it simple	9	Keep It Simple
3.1.8	Zero Trust	9	Zero Trust
3.1.9	Privacy by design	9	Privacy by Design

		All-in-One Coverage	
Domain	**Objective**	**Ch #**	**Heading**
Domain 3: Security Architecture and Engineering			
3.1.10	Trust but verify	9	Trust But Verify
3.1.11	Shared responsibility	9	Shared Responsibility
3.2	**Understand the fundamental concepts of security models (e.g., Biba, Star Model, Bell-LaPadula)**	9	Security Models
3.3	**Select controls based upon systems security requirements**	9	Security Requirements
3.4	**Understand security capabilities of Information Systems (IS) (e.g., memory protection, Trusted Platform Module (TPM), encryption/decryption)**	9	Security Capabilities of Information Systems
3.5	**Assess and mitigate the vulnerabilities of security architectures, designs, and solution elements**	7	General System Architectures
3.5.1	Client-based systems	7	Client-Based Systems
3.5.2	Server-based systems	7	Server-Based Systems
3.5.3	Database systems	7	Database Systems
3.5.4	Cryptographic systems	8	Cryptosystems
3.5.5	Industrial Control Systems (ICS)	7	Industrial Control Systems
3.5.6	Cloud-based systems (e.g., Software as a Service (SaaS), Infrastructure as a Service (IaaS), Platform as a Service (PaaS))	7	Cloud-Based Systems
3.5.7	Distributed systems	7	Distributed Systems
3.5.8	Internet of Things (IoT)	7	Internet of Things
3.5.9	Microservices	7	Microservices
3.5.10	Containerization	7	Containerization
3.5.11	Serverless	7	Serverless
3.5.12	Embedded systems	7	Embedded Systems
3.5.13	High-Performance Computing (HPC) systems	7	High-Performance Computing Systems
3.5.14	Edge computing systems	7	Edge Computing Systems
3.5.15	Virtualized systems	7	Virtualized Systems
3.6	**Select and determine cryptographic solutions**	8	Cryptography Definitions and Concepts
3.6.1	Cryptographic life cycle (e.g., keys, algorithm selection)	8	Cryptographic Life Cycle

Domain	Objective	All-in-One Coverage Ch #	Heading
Domain 3: Security Architecture and Engineering			
3.6.2	Cryptographic methods (e.g., symmetric, asymmetric, elliptic curves, quantum)	8	Cryptographic Methods
3.6.3	Public Key Infrastructure (PKI)	8	Public Key Infrastructure
3.6.4	Key management practices	8	Key Management
3.6.5	Digital signatures and digital certificates	8	Digital Signatures Digital Certificates
3.6.6	Non-repudiation	8	Cryptosystems
3.6.7	Integrity (e.g., hashing)	8	Cryptosystems
3.7	**Understand methods of cryptanalytic attacks**	8	Integrity
3.7.1	Brute force	8	Brute Force
3.7.2	Ciphertext only	8	Ciphertext-Only Attacks
3.7.3	Known plaintext	8	Known-Plaintext Attacks
3.7.4	Frequency analysis	8	Frequency Analysis
3.7.5	Chosen ciphertext	8	Chosen-Ciphertext Attacks
3.7.6	Implementation attacks	8	Implementation Attacks
3.7.7	Side-channel	8	Side-Channel Attacks
3.7.8	Fault injection	8	Fault Injection
3.7.9	Timing	8	Side-Channel Attacks
3.7.10	Man-in-the-Middle (MITM)	8	Man-in-the-Middle
3.7.11	Pass the hash	8	Replay Attacks
3.7.12	Kerberos exploitation	17	Weaknesses of Kerberos
3.7.13	Ransomware	8	Ransomware
3.8	**Apply security principles to site and facility design**	10	Security Principles
3.9	**Design site and facility security controls**	10	Site and Facility Controls
3.9.1	Wiring closets/intermediate distribution facilities	10	Distribution Facilities
3.9.2	Server rooms/data centers	10	Data Processing Facilities
3.9.3	Media storage facilities	10	Media Storage
3.9.4	Evidence storage	10	Evidence Storage
3.9.5	Restricted and work area security	10	Restricted Areas

		All-in-One Coverage	
Domain	**Objective**	**Ch #**	**Heading**
Domain 3: Security Architecture and Engineering			
3.9.6	Utilities and Heating, Ventilation, and Air Conditioning (HVAC)	10	Utilities
3.9.7	Environmental issues	10	Environmental Issues
3.9.8	Fire prevention, detection, and suppression	10	Fire Safety
3.9.9	Power (e.g., redundant, backup)	10	Electric Power
Domain 4: Communication and Network Security			
4.1	**Assess and implement secure design principles in network architectures**	13	Applying Secure Design Principles to Network Architectures
4.1.1	Open System Interconnection (OSI) and Transmission Control Protocol/Internet Protocol (TCP/IP) models	11	Network Reference Models
4.1.2	Internet Protocol (IP) networking (e.g., Internet Protocol Security (IPSec), Internet Protocol (IP) v4/6)	11	Internet Protocol Networking
4.1.3	Secure protocols	13	Secure Protocols
4.1.4	Implications of multilayer protocols	13	Multilayer Protocols
4.1.5	Converged protocols (e.g., Fiber Channel Over Ethernet (FCoE), Internet Small Computer Systems Interface (iSCSI), Voice over Internet Protocol (VoIP))	13	Converged Protocols
4.1.6	Micro-segmentation (e.g., Software Defined Networks (SDN), Virtual eXtensible Local Area Network (VXLAN), Encapsulation, Software-Defined Wide Area Network (SD-WAN))	13	Network Segmentation
4.1.7	Wireless networks (e.g., Li-Fi, Wi-Fi, Zigbee, satellite)	12	Wireless Networking Fundamentals
4.1.8	Cellular networks (e.g., 4G, 5G)	12	Mobile Wireless Communication
4.1.9	Content Distribution Networks (CDN)	14	Content Distribution Networks
4.2	**Secure network components**	14	Network Devices
4.2.1	Operation of hardware (e.g., redundant power, warranty, support)	14	Operation of Hardware
4.2.2	Transmission media	14	Transmission Media
4.2.3	Network Access Control (NAC) devices	14	Network Access Control Devices
4.2.4	Endpoint security	14	Endpoint Security

		All-in-One Coverage	
Domain	**Objective**	**Ch #**	**Heading**
Domain 4: Communication and Network Security			
4.3	**Implement secure communication channels according to design**	15	All of Chapter 15
4.3.1	Voice	15	Voice Communications
4.3.2	Multimedia collaboration	15	Multimedia Collaboration
4.3.3	Remote access	15	Remote Access
4.3.4	Data communications	11	Data Communications Foundations
4.3.5	Virtualized networks	15	Virtualized Networks
4.3.6	Third-party connectivity	15	Third-Party Connectivity
Domain 5: Identity and Access Management (IAM)			
5.1	**Control physical and logical access to assets**	17	Controlling Physical and Logical Access
5.1.1	Information	17	Information Access Control
5.1.2	Systems	17	System and Application Access Control
5.1.3	Devices	17	Access Control to Devices
5.1.4	Facilities	17	Facilities Access Control
5.1.5	Applications	17	System and Application Access Control
5.2	**Manage identification and authentication of people, devices, and services**	16	Identification, Authentication, Authorization, and Accountability
5.2.1	Identity Management (IdM) implementation	16	Identity Management
5.2.2	Single/Multi-Factor Authentication (MFA)	16	Identification and Authentication
5.2.3	Accountability	16	Accountability
5.2.4	Session management	16	Session Management
5.2.5	Registration, proofing, and establishment of identity	16	Registration and Proofing of Identity
5.2.6	Federated Identity Management (FIM)	16	Federated Identity Management
5.2.7	Credential management systems	16	Credential Management
5.2.8	Single Sign On (SSO)	16	Single Sign-On
5.2.9	Just-In-Time (JIT)	16	Just-in-Time Access
5.3	**Federated identity with a third-party service**	16	Federated Identity with a Third-Party Service
5.3.1	On-premise	16	On-Premise

Domain	Objective	All-in-One Coverage Ch #	Heading
Domain 5: Identity and Access Management (IAM)			
5.3.2	Cloud	16	Cloud
5.3.3	Hybrid	16	Hybrid
5.4	**Implement and manage authorization mechanisms**	17	Authorization Mechanisms
5.4.1	Role Based Access Control (RBAC)	17	Role-Based Access Control
5.4.2	Rule based access control	17	Rule-Based Access Control
5.4.3	Mandatory Access Control (MAC)	17	Mandatory Access Control
5.4.4	Discretionary Access Control (DAC)	17	Discretionary Access Control
5.4.5	Attribute Based Access Control (ABAC)	17	Attribute-Based Access Control
5.4.6	Risk based access control	17	Risk-Based Access Control
5.5	**Manage the identity and access provisioning lifecycle**	17	Managing the Identity and Access Provisioning Life Cycle
5.5.1	Account access review (e.g., user, system, service)	17	System Account Access Review
5.5.2	Provisioning and deprovisioning (e.g., on /off boarding and transfers)	17	Provisioning Deprovisioning
5.5.3	Role definition (e.g., people assigned to new roles)	17	Role Definitions
5.5.4	Privilege escalation (e.g., managed service accounts, use of sudo, minimizing its use)	17	Privilege Escalation Managed Service Accounts
5.6	**Implement authentication systems**	17	Implementing Authentication and Authorization Systems
5.6.1	OpenID Connect (OIDC)/Open Authorization (Oauth)	17	OpenID Connect Oauth
5.6.2	Security Assertion Markup Language (SAML)	17	Access Control and Markup Languages
5.6.3	Kerberos	17	Kerberos
5.6.4	Remote Authentication Dial-In User Service (RADIUS)/Terminal Access Controller Access Control System Plus (TACACS+)	17	Remote Access Control Technologies

Domain	Objective	All-in-One Coverage Ch #	Heading
Domain 6: Security Assessment and Testing			
6.1	**Design and validate assessment, test, and audit strategies**	18	Test, Assessment, and Audit Strategies
6.1.1	Internal	18	Internal Audits
6.1.2	External	18	External Audits
6.1.3	Third-party	18	Third-Party Audits
6.2	**Conduct security control testing**	18	Testing Technical Controls
6.2.1	Vulnerability assessment	18	Vulnerability Testing
6.2.2	Penetration testing	18	Penetration Testing
6.2.3	Log reviews	18	Log Reviews
6.2.4	Synthetic transactions	18	Synthetic Transactions
6.2.5	Code review and testing	18	Code Reviews
6.2.6	Misuse case testing	18	Misuse Case Testing
6.2.7	Test coverage analysis	18	Test Coverage
6.2.8	Interface testing	18	Interface Testing
6.2.9	Breach attack simulations	18	Breach Attack Simulations
6.2.10	Compliance checks	18	Compliance Checks
6.3	**Collect security process data (e.g., technical and administrative)**	19	Security Process Data
6.3.1	Account management	19	Account Management
6.3.2	Management review and approval	19	Management Review and Approval
6.3.3	Key performance and risk indicators	19	Key Performance and Risk Indicators
6.3.4	Backup verification data	19	Backup Verification
6.3.5	Training and awareness	19	Security Training and Security Awareness Training
6.3.6	Disaster Recovery (DR) and Business Continuity (BC)	19	Disaster Recovery and Business Continuity
6.4	**Analyze test output and generate report**	19	Reporting
6.4.1	Remediation	19	Remediation
6.4.2	Exception handling	19	Exception Handling
6.4.3	Ethical disclosure	19	Ethical Disclosure

Domain	Objective	All-in-One Coverage Ch #	Heading
Domain 6: Security Assessment and Testing			
6.5	**Conduct or facilitate security audits**	18	Conducting Security Audits
6.5.1	Internal	18	Conducting Internal Audits
6.5.2	External	18	Conducting and Facilitating External Audits
6.5.3	Third-party	18	Facilitating Third-Party Audits
Domain 7: Security Operations			
7.1	**Understand and comply with investigations**	22	Investigations
7.1.1	Evidence collection and handling	22	Evidence Collection and Handling
7.1.2	Reporting and documentation	22	Reporting and Documenting
7.1.3	Investigative techniques	22	Other Investigative Techniques
7.1.4	Digital forensics tools, tactics, and procedures	22	Digital Forensics Tools, Tactics, and Procedures
7.1.5	Artifacts (e.g., computer, network, mobile device)	22	Forensic Artifacts
7.2	**Conduct logging and monitoring activities**	21	Logging and Monitoring
7.2.1	Intrusion detection and prevention	21	Intrusion Detection and Prevention Systems
7.2.2	Security Information and Event Management (SIEM)	21	Security Information and Event Management
7.2.3	Continuous monitoring	21	Continuous Monitoring
7.2.4	Egress monitoring	21	Egress Monitoring
7.2.5	Log management	21	Log Management
7.2.6	Threat intelligence (e.g., threat feeds, threat hunting)	21	Threat Intelligence
7.2.7	User and Entity Behavior Analytics (UEBA)	21	User and Entity Behavior Analytics
7.3	**Perform Configuration Management (CM) (e.g., provisioning, baselining, automation)**	20	Configuration Management

Domain	Objective	All-in-One Coverage	
		Ch #	**Heading**
Domain 7: Security Operations			
7.4	**Apply foundational security operations concepts**	20	Foundational Security Operations Concepts
7.4.1	Need-to-know/least privilege	20	Need-to-Know/Least Privilege
7.4.2	Separation of Duties (SoD) and responsibilities	20	Separation of Duties and Responsibilities
7.4.3	Privileged account management	20	Privileged Account Management
7.4.4	Job rotation	20	Job Rotation
7.4.5	Service Level Agreements (SLAs)	20	Service Level Agreements
7.5	**Apply resource protection**	20	Resource Protection
7.5.1	Media management	20	Hierarchical Storage Management
7.5.2	Media protection techniques	20	Resource Protection
7.6	**Conduct incident management**	22	Overview of Incident Management
7.6.1	Detection	22	Detection
7.6.2	Response	22	Response
7.6.3	Mitigation	22	Mitigation
7.6.4	Reporting	22	Reporting
7.6.5	Recovery	22	Recovery
7.6.6	Remediation	22	Remediation
7.6.7	Lessons learned	22	Lessons Learned
7.7	**Operate and maintain detective and preventative measures**	21	Preventive and Detective Measures
7.7.1	Firewalls (e.g., next generation, web application, network)	21	Firewalls
7.7.2	Intrusion Detection Systems (IDS) and Intrusion Prevention Systems (IPS)	21	Intrusion Detection and Prevention Systems
7.7.3	Whitelisting/blacklisting	21	Whitelisting and Blacklisting
7.7.4	Third-party provided security services	21	Outsourced Security Services
7.7.5	Sandboxing	21	Sandboxing
7.7.6	Honeypots/honeynets	21	Honeypots and Honeynets

Domain	Objective	All-in-One Coverage Ch #	Heading
Domain 7: Security Operations			
7.7.7	Anti-malware	21	Antimalware Software
7.7.8	Machine learning and Artificial Intelligence (AI) based tools	21	Artificial Intelligence Tools
7.8	**Implement and support patch and vulnerability management**	20	Vulnerability and Patch Management
7.9	**Understand and participate in change management processes**	20	Change Management
7.10	**Implement recovery strategies**	23	Recovery Strategies
7.10.1	Backup storage strategies	23	Data Backup
7.10.2	Recovery site strategies	23	Recovery Site Strategies
7.10.3	Multiple processing sites	23	Multiple Processing Sites
7.10.4	System resilience, High Availability (HA), Quality of Service (QoS), and fault tolerance	23	Availability
7.11	**Implement Disaster Recovery (DR) processes**	23	Disaster Recovery Processes
7.11.1	Response	23	Response
7.11.2	Personnel	23	Personnel
7.11.3	Communications	23	Communications
7.11.4	Assessment	23	Assessment
7.11.5	Restoration	23	Restoration
7.11.6	Training and awareness	23	Training and Awareness
7.11.7	Lessons learned	23	Lessons Learned
7.12	**Test Disaster Recovery Plans (DRP)**	23	Testing Disaster Recovery Plans
7.12.1	Read-through/tabletop	23	Checklist Test Tabletop Exercises
7.12.2	Walkthrough	23	Structured Walkthrough Test
7.12.3	Simulation	23	Simulation Test
7.12.4	Parallel	23	Parallel Test
7.12.5	Full interruption	23	Full-Interruption Test
7.13	**Participate in Business Continuity (BC) planning and exercises**	23	Business Continuity
7.14	**Implement and manage physical security**	20	Physical Security
7.14.1	Perimeter security controls	20	External Perimeter Security Controls
7.14.2	Internal security controls	20	Internal Security Controls

Domain	Objective	All-in-One Coverage Ch #	Heading
Domain 7: Security Operations			
7.15	**Address personnel safety and security concerns**	20	Personnel Safety and Security
7.15.1	Travel	20	Travel
7.15.2	Security training and awareness	20	Security Training and Awareness
7.15.3	Emergency management	20	Emergency Management
7.15.4	Duress	20	Duress
Domain 8: Software Development Security			
8.1	**Understand and integrate security in the Software Development Life Cycle (SDLC)**	24	Software Development Life Cycle
8.1.1	Development methodologies (e.g., Agile, Waterfall, DevOps, DevSecOps)	24	Development Methodologies
8.1.2	Maturity models (e.g., Capability Maturity Model (CMM), Software Assurance Maturity Model (SAMM))	24	Maturity Models
8.1.3	Operation and maintenance	24	Operations and Maintenance Phase
8.1.4	Change management	24	Change Management
8.1.5	Integrated Product Team (IPT)	24	Integrated Product Team
8.2	**Identify and apply security controls in software development ecosystems**	25	Security Controls for Software Development
8.2.1	Programming languages	25	Programming Languages and Concepts
8.2.2	Libraries	25	Software Libraries
8.2.3	Tool sets	25	Tool Sets
8.2.4	Integrated Development Environment (IDE)	25	Development Platforms
8.2.5	Runtime	25	Runtime Environments
8.2.6	Continuous Integration and Continuous Delivery (CI/CD)	25	Continuous Integration and Delivery
8.2.7	Security Orchestration, Automation, and Response (SOAR)	25	Security Orchestration, Automation, and Response
8.2.8	Software Configuration Management (SCM)	25	Software Configuration Management
8.2.9	Code repositories	25	Code Repositories
8.2.10	Application security testing (e.g., Static Application Security Testing (SAST), Dynamic Application Security Testing (DAST))	25	Application Security Testing

Domain	Objective	All-in-One Coverage Ch #	Heading
Domain 8: Software Development Security			
8.3	**Assess the effectiveness of software security**	25	Software Security Assessments
8.3.1	Auditing and logging of changes	25	Change Management
8.3.2	Risk analysis and mitigation	25	Risk Analysis and Mitigation
8.4	**Assess security impact of acquired software**	25	Assessing the Security of Acquired Software
8.4.1	Commercial-off-the-shelf (COTS)	25	Commercial Software
8.4.2	Open source	25	Open-Source Software
8.4.3	Third-party	25	Third-Party Software
8.4.4	Managed services (e.g., Software as a Service (SaaS), Infrastructure as a Service (IaaS), Platform as a Service (PaaS))	25	Managed Services
8.5	**Define and apply secure coding guidelines and standards**	25	Secure Software Development
8.5.1	Security weaknesses and vulnerabilities at the source-code level	25	Source Code Vulnerabilities
8.5.2	Security of Application Programming Interfaces (APIs)	25	Application Programming Interfaces
8.5.3	Secure coding practices	25	Secure Coding Practices
8.5.4	Software-defined security	25	Software-Defined Security

APPENDIX C

About the Online Content

This book comes complete with TotalTester Online customizable practice exam software with more than 1,400 practice exam questions, separate graphical questions, and access to online CISSP flash cards.

System Requirements

The current and previous major versions of the following desktop browsers are recommended and supported: Chrome, Microsoft Edge, Firefox, and Safari. These browsers update frequently, and sometimes an update may cause compatibility issues with the TotalTester Online or other content hosted on the Training Hub. If you run into a problem using one of these browsers, please try using another until the problem is resolved.

Your Total Seminars Training Hub Account

To get access to the online content you will need to create an account on the Total Seminars Training Hub. Registration is free, and you will be able to track all your online content using your account. You may also opt in if you wish to receive marketing information from McGraw Hill or Total Seminars, but this is not required for you to gain access to the online content.

Privacy Notice

McGraw Hill values your privacy. Please be sure to read the Privacy Notice available during registration to see how the information you have provided will be used. You may view our Corporate Customer Privacy Policy by visiting the McGraw Hill Privacy Center. Visit the **mheducation.com** site and click **Privacy** at the bottom of the page.

Single User License Terms and Conditions

Online access to the digital content included with this book is governed by the McGraw Hill License Agreement outlined next. By using this digital content you agree to the terms of that license.

Access To register and activate your Total Seminars Training Hub account, simply follow these easy steps.

1. Go to this URL: **hub.totalsem.com/mheclaim**
2. To register and create a new Training Hub account, enter your e-mail address, name, and password on the **Register** tab. No further personal information (such as credit card number) is required to create an account.

   If you already have a Total Seminars Training Hub account, enter your e-mail address and password on the **Log in** tab.
3. Enter your Product Key: `khth-vc35-9bqs`
4. Click to accept the user license terms.
5. For new users, click the **Register and Claim** button to create your account. For existing users, click the **Log in and Claim** button.

   You will be taken to the Training Hub and have access to the content for this book.

Duration of License Access to your online content through the Total Seminars Training Hub will expire one year from the date the publisher declares the book out of print.

Your purchase of this McGraw Hill product, including its access code, through a retail store is subject to the refund policy of that store.

The Content is a copyrighted work of McGraw Hill, and McGraw Hill reserves all rights in and to the Content. The Work is © 2022 by McGraw Hill.

Restrictions on Transfer The user is receiving only a limited right to use the Content for the user's own internal and personal use, dependent on purchase and continued ownership of this book. The user may not reproduce, forward, modify, create derivative works based upon, transmit, distribute, disseminate, sell, publish, or sublicense the Content or in any way commingle the Content with other third-party content without McGraw Hill's consent.

Limited Warranty The McGraw Hill Content is provided on an "as is" basis. Neither McGraw Hill nor its licensors make any guarantees or warranties of any kind, either express or implied, including, but not limited to, implied warranties of merchantability or fitness for a particular purpose or use as to any McGraw Hill Content or the information therein or any warranties as to the accuracy, completeness, correctness, or results to be obtained from, accessing or using the McGraw Hill Content, or any material referenced in such Content or any information entered into licensee's product by users or other persons and/or any material available on or that can be accessed through the licensee's product (including via any hyperlink or otherwise) or as to non-infringement of third-party rights. Any warranties of any kind, whether express or implied, are disclaimed. Any material or data obtained through use of the McGraw Hill Content is at your own discretion and risk and user understands that it will be solely responsible for any resulting damage to its computer system or loss of data.

Neither McGraw Hill nor its licensors shall be liable to any subscriber or to any user or anyone else for any inaccuracy, delay, interruption in service, error or omission, regardless of cause, or for any damage resulting therefrom.

In no event will McGraw Hill or its licensors be liable for any indirect, special or consequential damages, including but not limited to, lost time, lost money, lost profits or good will, whether in contract, tort, strict liability or otherwise, and whether or not such damages are foreseen or unforeseen with respect to any use of the McGraw Hill Content.

TotalTester Online

TotalTester Online provides you with a simulation of the CISSP exam. Exams can be taken in Practice Mode or Exam Mode. Practice Mode provides an assistance window with hints, references to the book, explanations of the correct and incorrect answers, and the option to check your answer as you take the test. Exam Mode provides a simulation of the actual exam. The number of questions, the types of questions, and the time allowed are intended to be an accurate representation of the exam environment. The option to customize your quiz allows you to create custom exams from selected domains or chapters, and you can further customize the number of questions and time allowed.

To take a test, follow the instructions provided in the previous section to register and activate your Total Seminars Training Hub account. When you register you will be taken to the Total Seminars Training Hub. From the Training Hub Home page, select your certification from the Study drop-down menu at the top of the page to drill down to the TotalTester for your book. You can also scroll to it from the list of Your Topics on the Home page and then click the TotalTester link to launch the TotalTester. Once you've launched your TotalTester, you can select the option to customize your quiz and begin testing yourself in Practice Mode or Exam Mode. All exams provide an overall grade and a grade broken down by domain.

Graphical Questions

In addition to multiple-choice questions, the CISSP exam includes graphical questions. You can access the practice questions included with this book by navigating to the Resources tab and selecting Graphical Questions Quizzes. After you have selected the quizzes, they will appear in your browser, organized by domain.

Hotspot questions are graphical in nature and require the test taker to understand the concepts of the question from a practical and graphical aspect. You will have to point to the correct component within the graphic to properly answer the exam question. For example, you might be required to point to a specific area in a network diagram, point to a location in a network stack graphic, or choose the right location of a component within a graphic illustrating e-commerce–based authentication. It is not as easy to memorize answers for these types of questions, and they in turn make passing the exam more difficult.

The drag-and-drop questions are not as drastically different in format as compared to the hotspot questions. These questions just require the test taker to choose the correct answer or answers and drag them to the right location.

Online Flash Cards

Access to *Shon Harris' Online CISSP Flash Cards* from CISSP learning products company Human Element, LLC is also provided. These flash cards are another great way to study for the CISSP exam.

Privacy Notice Human Element, LLC values your privacy. Please be sure to read the Privacy Notice available during registration to see how the information you have provided will be used. You may view Human Element's Privacy Policy by visiting https://www.humanelementsecurity.com/content/Privacy-Policy.aspx.

To access the flash cards:

1. Go to www.humanelementsecurity.com and navigate to the CISSP Flash Cards page.
2. Choose the desired product and click the Add to Cart button.
3. Enter all required information (name and e-mail address) to set up your free online account.
4. On the payment method page enter the following code: 7YKL3

After following these instructions, you will have access to the CISSP Flash Cards. The Flash Card application is compatible with all Microsoft, Apple, and Android operating systems and browsers.

Single User License Terms and Conditions

Online access to the flash cards included with this book is governed by the McGraw Hill License Agreement outlined next. By using this digital content you agree to the terms of that license.

Duration of License Access to your online content through the Human Element website will expire one year from the date the publisher declares the book out of print.

Your purchase of this McGraw Hill product, including its access code, through a retail store is subject to the refund policy of that store.

Restrictions on Transfer The user is receiving only a limited right to use the Content for user's own internal and personal use, dependent on purchase and continued ownership of this book. The user may not reproduce, forward, modify, create derivative works based upon, transmit, distribute, disseminate, sell, publish, or sublicense the Content or in any way commingle the Content with other third-party content, without Human Element's consent. The Content is a copyrighted work of Human Element, LLC and Human Element reserves all rights in and to the Content.

Limited Warranty The Content is provided on an "as is" basis. Neither McGraw Hill, Human Element nor their licensors make any guarantees or warranties of any kind, either express or implied, including, but not limited to, implied warranties of merchantability or fitness for a particular purpose or use as to any Content or the information therein or any warranties as to the accuracy, completeness, correctness, or results to be obtained from, accessing or using the Content, or any material referenced in such Content or any information entered into licensee's product by users or other persons and/or any material available on or that can be accessed through the licensee's product (including via any hyperlink or otherwise) or as to non-infringement of thirdparty rights. Any warranties of any kind, whether express or implied, are disclaimed. Any material or data obtained through use of the Content is at your own discretion and risk and user understands that it will be solely responsible for any resulting damage to its computer system or loss of data.

Neither McGraw Hill nor its licensors shall be liable to any subscriber or to any user or anyone else for any inaccuracy, delay, interruption in service, error or omission, regardless of cause, or for any damage resulting therefrom.

In no event will McGraw Hill, Human Element or their licensors be liable for any indirect, special or consequential damages, including but not limited to, lost time, lost money, lost profits or good will, whether in contract, tort, strict liability or otherwise, and whether or not such damages are foreseen or unforeseen with respect to any use of the Content.

Technical Support

- For questions regarding the TotalTester or operation of the Training Hub, visit **www.totalsem.com** or e-mail **support@totalsem.com**.
- For questions regarding the flash cards, e-mail **info@humanelementsecurity.com**.
- For questions regarding book content, visit **www.mheducation.com/customerservice**.

access A subject's ability to view, modify, or communicate with an object. Access enables the flow of information between the subject and the object.

access control Mechanisms, controls, and methods of limiting access to resources to authorized subjects only.

access control list (ACL) A list of subjects that are authorized to access a particular object. Typically, the types of access are read, write, execute, append, modify, delete, and create.

access control mechanism Administrative, physical, or technical control that is designed to detect and prevent unauthorized access to a resource or environment.

accountability A security principle indicating that individuals must be identifiable and must be held responsible for their actions.

accredited A computer system or network that has received official authorization and approval to process sensitive data in a specific operational environment. There must be a security evaluation of the system's hardware, software, configurations, and controls by technical personnel.

acquisition The act of acquiring an asset. In organizational processes, this can mean either acquiring infrastructure (e.g., hardware, software, services) or another organization.

administrative controls Security mechanisms that are management's responsibility and referred to as "soft" controls. These controls include the development and publication of policies, standards, procedures, and guidelines; the screening of personnel; security-awareness training; the monitoring of system activity; and change control procedures.

aggregation The act of combining information from separate sources of a lower classification level that results in the creation of information of a higher classification level that the subject does not have the necessary rights to access.

Agile development An umbrella term for several development methodologies that focus on incremental and iterative development methods and promote cross-functional teamwork and continuous feedback mechanisms.

annualized loss expectancy (ALE) A dollar amount that estimates the loss potential from a risk in a span of a year.

single loss expectancy (SLE) × annualized rate of occurrence (ARO) = ALE

annualized rate of occurrence (ARO) The value that represents the estimated possibility of a specific threat taking place within a one-year timeframe.

antimalware Software whose principal functions include the identification and mitigation of malware; also known as antivirus, although this term could be specific to only one type of malware.

artificial intelligence (AI) A multidisciplinary field concerned with how knowledge is organized, how inference proceeds to support decision-making, and how systems learn.

asset Anything that is useful or valuable to an organization.

assurance A measurement of confidence in the level of protection that a specific security control delivers and the degree to which it enforces the security policy.

asymmetric key cryptography A cryptographic method that uses two different, or asymmetric, keys (also called public and private keys).

attribute-based access control (ABAC) An access control model in which access decisions are based on attributes of any component of or action on the system.

audit A systematic assessment of significant importance to the organization that determines whether the system or process being audited satisfies some external standards.

audit trail A chronological set of logs and records used to provide evidence of a system's performance or activity that took place on the system. These logs and records can be used to attempt to reconstruct past events and track the activities that took place, and possibly detect and identify intruders.

authentication Verification of the identity of a subject requesting the use of a system and/or access to network resources. The steps to giving a subject access to an object should be identification, authentication, and authorization.

authorization Granting a subject access to an object after the subject has been properly identified and authenticated.

availability The reliability and accessibility of data and resources to authorized individuals in a timely manner.

back door An undocumented way of gaining access to a computer system. After a system is compromised, an attacker may load a program that listens on a port (back door) so that the attacker can enter the system at any time. A back door is also referred to as a maintenance hook.

back up Copy and move data to a medium so that it may be restored if the original data is corrupted or destroyed. A full backup copies all the data from the system to the backup medium. An incremental backup copies only the files that have been modified since the previous backup. A differential backup backs up all files since the last full backup.

baseline The minimum level of security necessary to support and enforce a security policy.

Bell-LaPadula model A formal security model for access control that enforces the confidentiality of data (but not its integrity) using three rules: simple security, star property (*-property), and strong star property.

Biba model A formal security model for access control that enforces data integrity (but not confidentiality) using three rules: the *-integrity axiom (referred to as "no write up"), the simple integrity axiom (referred to as "no read down"), and the invocation property.

biometrics When used within computer security, identifies individuals by physiological characteristics, such as a fingerprint, hand geometry, or pattern in the iris.

blacklist (or deny list) A set of known-bad resources such as IP addresses, domain names, or applications.

breach attack simulation An automated system that launches simulated attacks against a target environment and then generates reports on its findings.

brute-force attack An attack that continually tries different inputs to achieve a predefined goal, which can be used to obtain credentials for unauthorized access.

business continuity (BC) Practices intended to keep the organization in business after a major disruption takes place.

business impact analysis (BIA) A functional analysis in which a team collects data through interviews and documentary sources; documents business functions, activities, and transactions; develops a hierarchy of business functions; and applies a classification scheme to indicate each individual function's criticality level.

Capability Maturity Model Integration (CMMI) A process model that captures the organization's maturity and fosters continuous improvement.

certificate authority (CA) A trusted third party that vouches for the identity of a subject, issues a certificate to that subject, and then digitally signs the certificate to assure its integrity.

certification The technical evaluation of the security components and their compliance for the purpose of accreditation. A certification process can use safeguard evaluation, risk analysis, verification, testing, and auditing techniques to assess the appropriateness of a specific system processing a certain level of information within a particular environment. The certification is the testing of the security component or system, and the accreditation is the approval from management of the security component or system.

challenge/response method A method used to verify the identity of a subject by sending the subject an unpredictable or random value. If the subject responds with the expected value in return, the subject is authenticated.

change management A business process aimed at deliberately regulating the changing nature of business activities such as projects.

chosen-ciphertext attack A cryptanalysis technique in which the attacker can choose the ciphertext to be decrypted and has access to the resulting decrypted plaintext, with the goal of determining the key that was used for decryption.

chosen-plaintext attack A cryptanalysis technique in which the attacker has the plaintext and ciphertext, but can choose the plaintext that gets encrypted to see the corresponding ciphertext in an effort to determine the key being used.

CIA triad The three primary security principles: confidentiality, integrity, and availability. Sometimes also presented as AIC: availability, integrity, and confidentiality.

ciphertext Data that has been encrypted and is unreadable until it has been converted into plaintext.

ciphertext-only attack A cryptanalysis technique in which the attacker has the ciphertext of one or more messages, each of which has been encrypted using the same encryption algorithm and key, and attempts to discover the key used in the encryption process.

Clark-Wilson model An integrity model that addresses all three integrity goals: prevent unauthorized users from making modifications, prevent authorized users from making improper modifications, and maintain internal and external consistency through auditing. A distinctive feature of this model is that it focuses on well-formed transactions and separation of duties.

classification A systematic arrangement of objects into groups or categories according to a set of established criteria. Data and resources can be assigned a level of sensitivity as they are being created, amended, enhanced, stored, or transmitted. The classification level then determines the extent to which the resource needs to be controlled and secured and is indicative of its value in terms of information assets.

cleartext In data communications, describes the form of a message or data that is transferred or stored without cryptographic protection.

cloud access security broker (CASB) A system that provides visibility and security controls for cloud services, monitors user activity in the cloud, and enforces policies and controls that are applicable to that activity.

cloud computing The use of shared, remote computing devices for the purpose of providing improved efficiencies, performance, reliability, scalability, and security.

code review A systematic examination of the instructions that comprise a piece of software, performed by someone other than the author of that code.

collusion Two or more people working together to carry out a fraudulent activity. More than one person would need to work together to cause some type of destruction or fraud; this drastically reduces its probability.

compensating controls Alternative controls that provide similar protection as the original controls but have to be used because they are more affordable or allow specifically required business functionality.

compliance Verifiable adherence to applicable laws, regulations, policies, and standards. The term is typically used to refer to compliance with governmental regulations.

compromise A violation of the security policy of a system or an organization such that unauthorized disclosure or modification of sensitive information occurs.

confidentiality A security principle that works to ensure that information is not disclosed to unauthorized subjects.

configuration management An operational process aimed at ensuring that systems and controls are configured correctly and are responsive to the current threat and operational environments.

containerization A type of virtualization in which individual applications run in their own isolated user space (called a container), which allows for more efficient use of computing resources.

content distribution network Multiple servers distributed across a large region, each of which provides content that is optimized for users closest to it. These networks are used not only to improve the user experience but also to mitigate the risk of denial-of-service attacks.

continuous improvement The practice of constantly measuring, analyzing, and improving processes.

continuous integration and continuous delivery (CI/CD) Processes and technologies that allow source code to be integrated, tested, and prepared for delivery to production environments as soon as a change to the code is submitted.

continuous monitoring Maintaining ongoing awareness of information security, vulnerabilities, and threats to support organizational risk management decisions.

control A policy, method, technique, or procedure that is put into place to reduce the risk that a threat agent exploits a vulnerability. Also called a countermeasure or safeguard.

control zone The space within a facility that is used to protect sensitive processing equipment. Controls are in place to protect equipment from physical or technical unauthorized entry or compromise. The zone can also be used to prevent electrical waves carrying sensitive data from leaving the area.

converged protocols Protocols that started off independent and distinct from one another but over time converged to become one.

copyright A legal right that protects the expression of ideas.

corrective controls Controls that fix components or systems after an incident has occurred.

cost/benefit analysis An assessment that is performed to ensure that the cost of a safeguard does not outweigh the benefit of the safeguard. Spending more to protect an asset than the asset is actually worth does not make good business sense. All possible safeguards must be evaluated to ensure that the most security-effective and cost-effective choice is made.

countermeasure A policy, method, technique, or procedure that is put into place to reduce the risk that a threat agent exploits a vulnerability. Also called a safeguard or control.

covert channel A communications path that enables a process to transmit information in a way that violates the system's security policy.

covert storage channel A covert channel that involves writing to a storage location by one process and the direct or indirect reading of the storage location by another process. Covert storage channels typically involve a resource (for example, sectors on a disk) that is shared by two subjects at different security levels.

covert timing channel A covert channel in which one process modulates its system resource (for example, CPU cycles), which is interpreted by a second process as some type of communication.

cryptanalysis The practice of breaking cryptosystems and algorithms used in encryption and decryption processes.

cryptography The science of secret writing that enables storage and transmission of data in a form that is available only to the intended individuals.

cryptology The study of cryptography and cryptanalysis.

cryptosystem The hardware or software implementation of cryptography.

data at rest Data that resides in external or auxiliary storage devices such as hard disk drives, solid-state drives, or optical discs.

data classification Assignments to data that indicate the level of availability, integrity, and confidentiality that is required for each type of information.

data controller A senior leader that sets policies with regard to the management of the data life cycle, particularly with regard to sensitive data such as personal data.

data custodian An individual who is responsible for the maintenance and protection of the data. This role is usually filled by the IT department (usually the network administrator). The duties include performing regular backups of the data; implementing and maintaining security controls; periodically validating the integrity of the data; restoring data from backup media; retaining records of activity; and fulfilling the requirements specified in the organization's security policy, standards, and guidelines that pertain to information security and data protection.

data in transit (or data in motion) Data that is moving between computing nodes over a data network such as the Internet.

data in use Data that temporarily resides in primary storage such as registers, caches, or RAM while the CPU is using it.

data loss (or leak) prevention (DLP) The actions that organizations take to prevent unauthorized external parties from gaining access to sensitive data.

data mining The analysis of the data held in data warehouses in order to produce new and useful information.

data owner The person who has final responsibility of data protection and would be the one held liable for any negligence when it comes to protecting the organization's information assets. The person who holds this role—usually a senior executive within the management group—is responsible for assigning a classification to the information and dictating how the information should be protected.

data processor Any person who carries out operations (e.g., querying, modifying, analyzing) on data under the authority of the data controller.

data remanence A measure of the magnetic flux density remaining after removal of the applied magnetic force, which is used to erase data. Refers to any data remaining on magnetic storage media.

data subject The person about whom the data is concerned.

data warehousing The process of combining data from multiple databases or data sources into a large data store for the purpose of providing more extensive information retrieval and data analysis.

declassification An administrative decision or procedure to remove or reduce the security classification of information.

defense in depth A secure design principle that entails the coordinated use of multiple security controls in a layered approach.

degauss Process that demagnetizes magnetic media so that a very low residue of magnetic induction is left on the media. Used to effectively erase data from media.

Delphi technique A group decision method used to ensure that each member of a group gives an honest and anonymous opinion pertaining to what the result of a particular threat will be.

denial of service (DoS) Any action, or series of actions, that prevents a system, or its resources, from functioning in accordance with its intended purpose.

detective controls Controls that help identify an incident's activities and potentially an intruder.

DevOps The practice of incorporating development, IT, and quality assurance (QA) staff into software development projects to align their incentives and enable frequent, efficient, and reliable releases of software products.

DevSecOps The integration of development, security, and operations professionals into a software development team. It's DevOps with the security team added in.

dial-up The service whereby a computer terminal can use telephone lines, usually via a modem, to initiate and continue communication with another computer system.

dictionary attack A form of attack in which an attacker uses a large set of likely combinations to guess a secret, usually a password.

digital certificate A mechanism used to associate a public key with a collection of components in a manner that is sufficient to uniquely identify the claimed owner. The most commonly used standard for digital certificates is the International Telecommunications Union's X.509.

Digital Rights Management (DRM) A set of technologies that is applied to controlling access to copyrighted data.

digital signature A hash value that has been encrypted with the sender's private key.

disaster recovery (DR) The set of practices that enables an organization to minimize loss of, and restore, mission-critical technology infrastructure after a catastrophic incident.

disaster recovery plan (DRP) A plan developed to help an organization recover from a disaster. It provides procedures for emergency response, extended backup operations, and post-disaster recovery when an organization suffers a loss of computer processing capability or resources and physical facilities.

discretionary access control (DAC) An access control model and policy that restricts access to objects based on the identity of the subjects and the groups to which those subjects belong. The data owner has the discretion of allowing or denying others access to the resources it owns.

Distributed Network Protocol 3 (DNP3) A communications protocol designed for use in SCADA systems, particularly those within the power sector, that does not include routing functionality.

domain The set of objects that a subject is allowed to access. Within this domain, all subjects and objects share a common security policy, procedures, and rules, and they are managed by the same management system.

due care The precautions that a reasonable and competent person would take in a given situation.

due diligence The process of systematically evaluating information to identify vulnerabilities, threats, and issues relating to an organization's overall risk.

duress The use of threats or violence against someone in order to force them to do something they don't want to do.

dynamic application security testing (DAST) Also known as dynamic analysis, the evaluation of a program in real time, while it is running.

edge computing A distributed system in which some computational and data storage assets are deployed close to where they are needed in order to reduce latency and network traffic.

egress monitoring Maintaining awareness of the information that is flowing out of a network, whether it appears to be malicious or not.

electronic discovery (e-discovery) The process of producing for a court or external attorney all electronically stored information pertinent to a legal proceeding.

electronic vaulting The transfer of backup data to an offsite location. This process is primarily a batch process of transmitting data through communications lines to a server at an alternative location.

elliptic curve cryptography A cryptographic method that uses complex mathematical equations (plotted as elliptic curves) that are more efficient than traditional asymmetric key cryptography but also much more difficult to cryptanalyze.

emanations Electrical and electromagnetic signals emitted from electrical equipment that can transmit through the airwaves. These signals carry information that can be captured and deciphered, which can cause a security breach. These are also called *emissions*.

embedded system A self-contained, typically ruggedized, computer system with its own processor, memory, and input/output devices that is designed for a very specific purpose.

encryption The transformation of plaintext into unreadable ciphertext.

end-of-life (EOL) The point in time when a manufacturer ceases to manufacture or sustain a product.

end-of-support (EOS) The point in time when a manufacturer is no longer patching bugs or vulnerabilities on a product, which is typically a few years after EOL.

endpoint A networked computing device that initiates or responds to network communications.

endpoint detection and response (EDR) An integrated security system that continuously monitors endpoints for security violations and uses rules-based automated response and analysis capabilities.

end-to-end encryption A technology that encrypts the data payload of a packet.

ethical disclosure The practice of informing anyone who might be affected by a discovered vulnerability as soon as feasible, so a patch can be developed before any threat actors become aware of the vulnerability.

exposure An instance of being exposed to losses from a threat. A weakness or vulnerability can cause an organization to be exposed to possible damages.

exposure factor The percentage of loss a realized threat could have on a certain asset.

failover A backup operation that automatically switches to a standby system if the primary system fails or is taken offline. It is an important fault-tolerant function that provides system availability.

fail-safe A functionality that ensures that when software or a system fails for any reason, it does not compromise anyone's safety. After a failure, a fail-safe electronic lock might default to an unlocked state, which would prevent it from interfering with anyone trying to escape in an emergency.

fail-secure A functionality that ensures that when software or a system fails for any reason, it does not end up in a vulnerable state. After a failure, a fail-secure lock might default to a locked state, which would ensure the security of whatever it is protecting.

federated identity management (FIM) The management of portable identities, and their associated entitlements, that can be used across business boundaries.

Fibre Channel over Ethernet (FCoE) A converged protocol that allows Fibre Channel frames to ride over Ethernet networks.

firmware Software instructions that have been written into read-only memory (ROM) or a programmable ROM (PROM) chip.

forensic artifact Anything that has evidentiary value.

formal verification Validating and testing of highly trusted systems. The tests are designed to show design verification, consistency between the formal specifications and the formal security policy model, implementation verification, consistency between the formal specifications, and the actual implementation of the product.

full-interruption test A type of security test in which a live system or facility is shut down, forcing the recovery team to switch processing to an alternate system or facility.

gamification The application of elements of game play to other activities such as security awareness training.

gateway A system or device that connects two unlike environments or systems. The gateway is usually required to translate between different types of applications or protocols.

guidelines Recommended actions and operational guides for users, IT staff, operations staff, and others when a specific standard does not apply.

handshaking procedure A dialog between two entities for the purpose of identifying and authenticating the entities to one another. The dialog can take place between two computers or two applications residing on different computers. It is an activity that usually takes place within a protocol.

high-performance computing (HPC) The aggregation of computing power in ways that exceed the capabilities of general-purpose computers for the specific purpose of solving large problems.

honeynet A network of honeypots designed to keep adversaries engaged (and thus under observation) for longer than would be possible with a single honeypot.

honeypot A network device that is intended to be exploited by attackers, with the administrator's goal being to gain information on the attackers' tactics, techniques, and procedures (TTPs).

identification A subject provides some type of data to an authentication service. Identification is the first step in the authentication process.

Identity as a Service (IDaaS) A type of Software as a Service (SaaS) offering that normally provides single sign-on (SSO), federated identity management (IdM), and password management services.

identity management (IdM) A broad term that encompasses the use of different products to identify, authenticate, and authorize users through automated means. It usually includes user account management, access control, credential management, single sign-on (SSO) functionality, managing rights and permissions for user accounts, and auditing and monitoring all of these items.

industrial control system (ICS) Information technology that is specifically designed to control physical devices in industrial processes. The two main types of ICS are distributed control systems (DCSs) and supervisory control and data acquisition (SCADA) systems. The main difference between them is that a DCS controls local processes while SCADA is used to control things remotely.

inference The ability to derive information not explicitly available.

Infrastructure as a Service (IaaS) A cloud computing model that provides users unfettered access to a cloud device, such as an instance of a server, which includes both the operating system and the virtual machine on which it runs.

Integrated Product Team (IPT) A multidisciplinary software development team with representatives from many or all the stakeholder populations.

integrity A security principle that makes sure that information and systems are not modified maliciously or accidentally.

Internet of Things (IoT) The global network of connected, uniquely addressable, embedded systems.

Internet Small Computer System Interface (iSCSI) A converged protocol that encapsulates SCSI data in TCP segments in order to allow peripherals to be connected to computers across networks.

intrusion detection system (IDS) Software employed to monitor and detect possible attacks and behaviors that vary from the normal and expected activity. The IDS can be network based, which monitors network traffic, or host based, which monitors activities of a specific system and protects system files and control mechanisms.

intrusion prevention system (IPS) An intrusion detection system (IDS) that is also able to take actions to stop a detected intrusion.

IP Security (IPSec) A suite of protocols that was developed to specifically protect IP traffic. It includes the Authentication Header (AH), Encapsulating Security Payload (ESP), Internet Security Association and Key Management Protocol (ISAKMP), and Internet Key Exchange (IKE) protocols.

isolation The containment of processes in a system in such a way that they are separated from one another to ensure integrity and confidentiality.

job rotation The practice of ensuring that, over time, more than one person fulfills the tasks of one position within the organization. This enables the organization to have staff backup and redundancy, and helps detect fraudulent activities.

just in time (JIT) access A provisioning methodology that elevates users to the necessary privileged access to perform a specific task.

Kerberos A client/server authentication protocol based on symmetric key cryptography that is the default authentication mechanism in Microsoft Active Directory environments.

kernel The core of an operating system, manages the machine's hardware resources (including the processor and the memory) and provides and controls the way any other software component accesses these resources.

key A discrete data set that controls the operation of a cryptography algorithm. In encryption, a key specifies the particular transformation of plaintext into ciphertext, or vice versa, during decryption. Keys are also used in other cryptographic algorithms, such as digital signature schemes and keyed-hash functions (also known as HMACs), which are often used for authentication and integrity.

keystroke monitoring A type of auditing that can review or record keystrokes entered by a user during an active session.

known-plaintext attack A cryptanalysis technique in which the attacker has the plaintext and corresponding ciphertext of one or more messages and wants to discover the key used to encrypt the message(s).

least privilege The secure design principle that requires each subject to be granted the most restrictive set of privileges needed for the performance of authorized tasks. The application of this principle limits the damage that can result from accident, error, or unauthorized use.

Li-Fi A wireless networking technology that uses light rather than radio waves to transmit and receive data.

Lightweight Directory Access Protocol (LDAP) A directory service based on a subset of the X.500 standard that allows users and applications to interact with a directory.

link encryption A type of encryption technology that encrypts packets' headers, trailers, and the data payload. Each network communications node, or hop, must decrypt the packets to read their addresses and routing information and then re-encrypt the packets. This is different from end-to-end encryption.

machine learning (ML) Systems that acquire their knowledge, in the form of numeric parameters (i.e., weights), through training with data sets consisting of millions of examples. In supervised learning, ML systems are told whether or not they made the right decision. In unsupervised training they learn by observing an environment. Finally, in reinforcement learning they get feedback on their decisions from the environment.

maintenance hook Instructions within a program's code that enable the developer or maintainer to enter the program without having to go through the usual access control and authentication processes. Maintenance hooks should be removed from the code before it is released to production; otherwise, they can cause serious security risks. Also called a back door.

malware Malicious software. Code written to perform activities that circumvent the security policy of a system. Examples are viruses, malicious applets, Trojan horses, logic bombs, and worms.

mandatory access control (MAC) An access policy that restricts subjects' access to objects based on the security clearance of the subject and the classification of the object. The system enforces the security policy, and users cannot share their files with other users.

message authentication code (MAC) In cryptography, a generated value used to authenticate a message. A MAC can be generated by HMAC or CBC-MAC methods. The MAC protects both a message's integrity (by ensuring that a different MAC will be produced if the message has changed) and its authenticity, because only someone who knows the secret key could have modified the message.

microsegmentation The practice of isolating individual assets (e.g., data servers) in their own protected network environment.

microservice An architectural style that consists of small, decentralized, loosely coupled, individually deployable services built around business capabilities.

multifactor authentication (MFA) Authentication mechanisms that employ more than one factor. Factors are something a person knows (e.g., password), something a person has (e.g., a hardware token), and something a person is (e.g., biometrics).

multilayer protocol A protocol that works across multiple layers of the OSI model.

multilevel security A class of systems containing information with different classifications. Access decisions are based on the subject's security clearances, need to know, and formal approval.

Multiprotocol Label Switching (MPLS) A converged data communications protocol designed to improve the routing speed of high-performance networks.

need to know A security principle stating that users should have access only to the information and resources necessary to complete their tasks that fulfill their roles within an organization. Need to know is commonly used in access control criteria by operating systems and applications.

network detection and response (NDR) Systems that monitor network traffic for malicious actors and suspicious behavior, and react and respond to the detection of cyberthreats to the network.

nonrepudiation A service that ensures the sender cannot later falsely deny sending a message or taking an action.

OAuth An open standard for authorization (not authentication) to third parties that lets users authorize a web system to use something that they control at a different website.

object A passive entity that contains or receives information. Access to an object potentially implies access to the information that it contains. Examples of objects include records, pages, memory segments, files, directories, directory trees, and programs.

onboarding The process of turning a candidate into a trusted employee who is able to perform all assigned duties.

one-time pad A method of encryption in which the plaintext is combined with a random "pad," which should be the same length as the plaintext. This encryption process uses a nonrepeating set of random bits that are combined bitwise (XOR) with the message to produce ciphertext. A one-time pad is a perfect encryption scheme because it is unbreakable and each pad is used exactly once, but it is impractical because of all of the required overhead.

Open System Interconnection (OSI) model A conceptual framework used to describe the functions of a networking system along seven layers in which each layer relies on services provided by the layer below it and provides services to the layer above it.

OpenID Connect A simple authentication layer built on top of the OAuth 2.0 protocol that allows transparent authentication and authorization of client resource requests.

password A sequence of characters used to prove one's identity. It is used during a logon process and should be highly protected.

patent A grant of legal ownership given to an individual or organization to exclude others from using or copying the invention covered by the patent.

Payment Card Industry Data Security Standard (PCI DSS) An information security standard for organizations that are involved in payment card transactions.

penetration testing A method of evaluating the security of a computer system or network by simulating an attack that a malicious hacker would carry out. Pen testing is performed to uncover vulnerabilities and weaknesses.

personnel security The procedures that are established to ensure that all personnel who have access to sensitive information have the required authority as well as appropriate clearances. Procedures confirm a person's background and provide assurance of necessary trustworthiness.

physical controls Controls that pertain to controlling individual access into the facility and different departments, locking systems and removing unnecessary USB and optical drives, protecting the perimeter of the facility, monitoring for intrusion, and checking environmental controls.

physical security Controls and procedures put into place to prevent intruders from physically accessing a system or facility. The controls enforce access control and authorized access.

piggyback Unauthorized access to a facility or area by using another user's legitimate credentials or access rights.

plaintext In cryptography, the original readable text before it is encrypted.

Platform as a Service (PaaS) A cloud computing model that provides users access to a computing platform but not to the operating system or to the virtual machine on which it runs.

preventive controls Controls that are intended to keep an incident from occurring.

privacy A security principle that protects an individual's information and employs controls to ensure that this information is not disseminated or accessed in an unauthorized manner.

privacy by design A secure design principle that ensures privacy of user data is an integral part of the design of an information system, not an afterthought or later-stage feature.

procedure Detailed step-by-step instructions to achieve a certain task, which are used by users, IT staff, operations staff, security members, and others.

protocol A set of rules and formats that enables the standardized exchange of information between different systems.

public key encryption A type of encryption that uses two mathematically related keys to encrypt and decrypt messages. The private key is known only to the owner, and the public key is available to anyone.

public key infrastructure (PKI) A framework of programs, procedures, communication protocols, and public key cryptography that enables a diverse group of individuals to communicate securely.

qualitative risk analysis A risk analysis method that uses opinion and experience to judge an organization's exposure to risks. It uses scenarios and ratings systems. Compare to quantitative risk analysis.

quantitative risk analysis A risk analysis method that attempts to use percentages in damage estimations and assigns real numbers to the costs of countermeasures for particular risks and the amount of damage that could result from the risk. Compare to qualitative risk analysis.

quantum key distribution (QKD) A system that generates and securely distributes encryption keys of any length between two parties.

RADIUS (Remote Authentication Dial-In User Service) A security service that authenticates and authorizes dial-up users and is a centralized access control mechanism.

recovery point objective (RPO) The acceptable amount of data loss measured in time.

recovery time objective (RTO) The maximum time period within which a mission-critical system must be restored to a designated service level after a disaster to avoid unacceptable consequences associated with a break in business continuity.

reference monitor concept An abstract machine that mediates all access subjects have to objects, both to ensure that the subjects have the necessary access rights and to protect the objects from unauthorized access and destructive modification.

registration authority (RA) A trusted entity that establishes and confirms the identity of an individual, initiates the certification process with a CA on behalf of an end user, and performs certificate life-cycle management functions.

reliability The assurance of a given system, or individual component, performing its mission adequately for a specified period of time under the expected operating conditions.

remote journaling A method of transmitting changes to data to an offsite facility. This takes place as parallel processing of transactions, meaning that changes to the data are saved locally and to an offsite facility. These activities take place in real time and provide redundancy and fault tolerance.

repudiation When the sender of a message denies sending the message. The countermeasure to this is to implement digital signatures.

residual risk The remaining risk after the security controls have been applied. The conceptual formulas that explain the difference between total risk and residual risk are

threats × vulnerability × asset value = total risk

(threats × vulnerability × asset value) × controls gap = residual risk

risk The likelihood of a threat agent taking advantage of a vulnerability and the resulting business impact. A risk is the loss potential, or probability, that a threat will exploit a vulnerability.

risk analysis A detailed examination of the components of risk that is used to ensure that security is cost-effective, relevant, timely, and responsive to threats.

risk assessment A method of identifying vulnerabilities and threats and assessing the possible impacts to determine where to implement security controls.

risk management The process of identifying and assessing risk, reducing it to an acceptable level, and implementing the right mechanisms to maintain that level of risk.

risk-based access control An authorization mechanism that estimates the risk associated with a particular request in real time and, if it doesn't exceed a given threshold, grants the subject access to the requested resource.

role-based access control (RBAC) Type of access control model that provides access to resources based on the role the user holds within the organization or the tasks that the user has been assigned.

rule-based access control (RB-RBAC) Type of access control model that uses specific rules that indicate what can and cannot happen between a subject and an object; built on top of traditional RBAC and is thus commonly called RB-RBAC to disambiguate the otherwise overloaded RBAC acronym.

safeguard A policy, method, technique, or procedure that is put into place to reduce the risk that a threat agent exploits a vulnerability. Also called a countermeasure or control.

sandboxing A type of control that isolates processes from the operating system to prevent security violations.

scoping The process of taking a broader standard and trimming out the irrelevant or otherwise unwanted parts.

secure defaults A secure design principle that entails having every system start off in a state where security trumps user friendliness and functionality, and then has controls deliberately relaxed to enable additional features and generally make the system more user friendly.

Security Assertion Markup Language (SAML) An XML standard that allows the exchange of authentication and authorization data to be shared between security domains.

security awareness The knowledge and attitude of an individual concerning likely threats.

security control Any measure taken by an organization to mitigate information security risks.

security evaluation Assesses the degree of trust and assurance that can be placed in systems for the secure handling of sensitive information.

security information and event management (SIEM) A software platform that aggregates security information and security events and presents them in a single, consistent, and cohesive manner.

security label An identifier that represents the security level of an object.

security orchestration, automation, and response (SOAR) Integrated systems that enable more efficient security operations through automation of various workflows.

security testing Testing all security mechanisms and features within a system to determine the level of protection they provide. Security testing can include penetration testing, formal design and implementation verification, and functional testing.

sensitive information Information that would cause a negative effect on the organization if it were lost or compromised.

sensitivity label A piece of information that represents the security level of an object. Sensitivity labels are used as the basis for mandatory access control (MAC) decisions.

separation of duties A secure design principle that splits up a critical task among two or more individuals to ensure that one person cannot complete a risky task by himself.

serverless architecture A computing architecture in which the services offered to end users, such as compute, storage, or messaging, along with their required configuration and management, can be performed without a requirement from the user to set up any server infrastructure.

service level agreement (SLA) A contract between a service provider and a service user that specifies the minimum acceptable parameters of the services being provided.

shared responsibility A secure design principle that addresses situations in which a service provider is responsible for certain security controls, while the customer is responsible for others.

shoulder surfing When a person looks over another person's shoulder and watches keystrokes or watches data as it appears on the screen in order to uncover information in an unauthorized manner.

simple security property A Bell-LaPadula security model rule that stipulates that a subject cannot read data at a higher security level.

single loss expectancy (SLE) A monetary value that is assigned to a single event that represents the organization's potential loss amount if a specific threat were to take place.

asset value × exposure factor = SLE

single sign-on (SSO) A technology that allows a user to authenticate one time and then access resources in the environment without needing to reauthenticate.

social engineering The act of tricking another person into providing confidential information by posing as an individual who is authorized to receive that information.

Software as a Service (SaaS) A cloud computing model that provides users access to a specific application that executes in the service provider's environment.

Software Assurance Maturity Model (SAMM) A maturity model that is specifically focused on secure software development and allows organizations of any size to decide their target maturity levels within each of five critical business functions.

software-defined networking (SDN) An approach to networking that relies on distributed software to provide improved agility and efficiency by centralizing the configuration and control of networking devices.

software-defined security (SDS or SDsec) A security model in which security functions such as firewalling, IDS/IPS, and network segmentation are implemented in software within an SDN environment.

spoofing Presenting false information, usually within packets, to trick other systems and hide the origin of the message. This is usually done by hackers so that their identity cannot be successfully uncovered.

standards Rules indicating how hardware and software should be implemented, used, and maintained. Standards provide a means to ensure that specific technologies, applications, parameters, and procedures are carried out in a uniform way across the organization. They are compulsory.

star property (*-property) A Bell-LaPadula security model rule that stipulates that a subject cannot write data to an object at a lower security level.

static application security testing (SAST) A technique, also called static analysis, that identifies certain software defects or security policy violations by examining the source code without executing the program.

subject An active entity, generally in the form of a person, process, or device, that causes information to flow among objects or that changes the system state.

supervisory control and data acquisition (SCADA) A system for remotely monitoring and controlling physical systems such as power and manufacturing plants.

supply chain An interconnected network of interdependent suppliers and consumers involved in delivering some product or service.

symmetric key cryptography A cryptographic method that uses instances of the same key (called the secret key) for encryption and decryption.

synthetic transaction A transaction that is executed in real time by a software agent to test or monitor the performance of a distributed system.

tabletop exercise (TTX) A type of exercise in which participants respond to notional events to test out procedures and ensure they actually do what they're intended to and that everyone knows their role in responding to the events.

TACACS (Terminal Access Controller Access Control System) A client/server authentication protocol that provides the same type of functionality as RADIUS and is used as a central access control mechanism mainly for remote users.

tailoring The practice of making changes to specific provisions of a standard so they better address organizational requirements.

technical controls Controls that work in software to provide availability, integrity, or confidentiality protection; also called logical access control mechanisms. Some examples are passwords, identification and authentication methods, security devices, auditing, and the configuration of the network.

test coverage A measure of how much of a system is examined by a specific test (or group of tests), which is typically expressed as a percentage.

threat A potential cause of an unwanted incident, which can result in harm to a system or organization.

threat intelligence Evidence-based knowledge about an existing or emerging menace or hazard to assets that can be used to inform decisions regarding responses to that menace or hazard.

threat modeling The process of describing probable adverse effects on an organization's assets caused by specific threat sources.

top-down approach An approach in which the initiation, support, and direction for a project come from top management and work their way down through middle management and then to staff members.

topology The physical construction of how nodes are connected to form a network.

total risk The risk an organization faces if it chooses not to implement any type of safeguard.

trade secret Something that is proprietary to a company and important for its survival and profitability.

trademark A legal right that protects a word, name, product shape, symbol, color, or a combination of these used to identify a product or an organization.

transborder data flow (TDF) The movement of machine-readable data across a political boundary such as a country's border.

Trojan horse A computer program that has an apparently or actually useful function, but that also contains hidden malicious capabilities to exploit a vulnerability and/or provide unauthorized access into a system.

trust but verify A secure design principle that requires that even when an entity and its behaviors are trusted, they should be monitored and verified.

user A person or process that is accessing a computer system.

user and entity behavior analytics (UEBA) Processes that determine normal patterns of behavior so that abnormalities can be detected and investigated.

user ID A unique set of characters or code that is used to identify a specific user to a system.

validation The act of performing tests and evaluations to test a system's security level to see if it complies with security specifications and requirements.

Virtual eXtensible Local Area Network (VxLAN) A network virtualization technology that encapsulates layer 2 frames onto UDP (layer 4) datagrams for distribution anywhere in the world.

virtualization The practice of running a virtual computing system in an environment that is abstracted from the actual hardware.

virus A small application, or string of code, that infects applications. The main function of a virus is to reproduce, and it requires a host application to do this. It can damage data directly or degrade system performance.

vulnerability A weakness in a system that allows a threat source to compromise its security. It can be a software, hardware, procedural, or human weakness that can be exploited.

Waterfall methodology A software development methodology that uses a strictly linear, sequential life-cycle approach in which each phase must be completed in its entirety before the next phase can begin.

whitelist (or allow list) A set of known-good resources such as IP addresses, domain names, or applications.

work factor The estimated time and effort required for an attacker to overcome a security control.

worm An independent program that can reproduce by copying itself from one system to another. It may damage data directly or degrade system performance by tying up resources.

zero trust A secure design principle that assumes that every entity is hostile until proven otherwise.

INDEX

B

C

D

E

F

G

H

I

J

M

N

O

P

Q

R

U

V

W

X

Y

Z